ENCYCLOPEDIA OF WORLD DRESS AND FASHION

Volume 7

Australia, New Zealand,
and the Pacific Islands

ENCYCLOPEDIA WORLD

OF
DRESS
AND FASHION

Volume 7

Australia, New Zealand, and the Pacific Islands

Edited by Margaret Maynard

OXFORD

UNIVERSITY PRESS

2010

OXFORD
UNIVERSITY PRESS

Oxford University Press, Inc., publishes works that further
Oxford University's objective of excellence
in research, scholarship, and education.

Oxford   New York
Auckland   Cape Town   Dar es Salaam   Hong Kong   Karachi
Kuala Lumpur   Madrid   Melbourne   Mexico City   Nairobi
New Delhi   Shanghai   Taipei   Toronto

With offices in
Argentina   Austria   Brazil   Chile   Czech Republic   France   Greece
Guatemala   Hungary   Italy   Japan   Poland   Portugal   Singapore
South Korea   Switzerland   Thailand   Turkey   Ukraine   Vietnam

Published by Oxford University Press, Inc.
198 Madison Avenue, New York, NY 10016
http://www.oup.com/us/

The Library of Congress Cataloging-in-Publication Data

Encyclopedia of world dress and fashion.
v. cm.

"Published simultaneously outside North America by Berg Publishers"–V. 1, t.p. verso.

"Available online as part of the Berg Fashion Library"–V. 1, t.p. verso.

Includes bibliographical references.

Contents: v. 1. Africa / editors, Joanne B. Eicher, Doran H. Ross – v. 2. Latin America and the Caribbean /
editor, Margot Blum Schevill ; consulting editor, Blenda Femenías – v. 3. The United States and Canada /
editor, Phyllis Tortora ; consultant, Joseph D. Horse Capture – v. 4. South Asia and Southeast Asia /
editor, Jasleen Dhamija – v. 5. Central and Southwest Asia / editor, Gillian Vogelsang-Eastwood –
v. 6. East Asia / editor, John Vollmer – v. 7. Australia, New Zealand, and the Pacific Islands /
editor, Margaret Maynard – v. 8. West Europe / editor, Lise Skov ; consulting editor, Valerie Cumming –
v. 9. East Europe, Russia, and the Caucasus / editor, Djurdja Bartlett ; assistant editor, Pamela Smith –
v. 10. Global perspectives / editor, Joanne B. Eicher ; assistant editor, Phyllis Tortora.

ISBN 978-0-19-537733-0 (hbk.)

1. Clothing and dress–Encyclopedias.   I. Eicher, Joanne Bubolz.   II. Oxford University Press.

GT507.E54   2010
391.003—dc22   2010008843

ISBN 978-0-19-975728-2 (vol. 1)
ISBN 978-0-19-975729-9 (vol. 2)
ISBN 978-0-19-975730-5 (vol. 3)
ISBN 978-0-19-975731-2 (vol. 4)
ISBN 978-0-19-975732-9 (vol. 5)
ISBN 978-0-19-975733-6 (vol. 6)
ISBN 978-0-19-975734-3 (vol. 7)
ISBN 978-0-19-975735-0 (vol. 8)
ISBN 978-0-19-975736-7 (vol. 9)
ISBN 978-0-19-975737-4 (vol. 10)

1   3   5   7   9   8   6   4   2

This Encyclopedia is available online as part of the Berg Fashion Library.
For further information see www.bergfashionlibrary.com.

Typeset by Apex CoVantage, Madison, WI.
Printed in the USA by Courier Companies Inc., Westford, MA.

Editor-in-Chief

Joanne B. Eicher, University of Minnesota

Volume 1: Africa

Editors: *Joanne B. Eicher, University of Minnesota*

Doran H. Ross, Fowler Museum, University of California, Los Angeles

Volume 2: Latin America and the Caribbean

Editor: *Margot Blum Schevill, Textiles and Folk Art Consultant*

Consulting Editor: *Blenda Femenías, George Washington University*

Volume 3: The United States and Canada

Editor: *Phyllis G. Tortora, Queens College, City University of New York*

Consultant: *Joseph D. Horse Capture, Minneapolis Institute of Arts*

Volume 4: South Asia and Southeast Asia

Editor: *Jasleen Dhamija, Independent Scholar, India
and University of Minnesota*

Volume 5: Central and Southwest Asia

Editor: *Gillian Vogelsang-Eastwood, Textile Research Centre
and the National Museum of Ethnology, Leiden*

Volume 6: East Asia

Editor: *John E. Vollmer, Vollmer Cultural Consultants Inc.*

**Volume 7: Australia, New Zealand,
and the Pacific Islands**

Editor: *Margaret Maynard, University of Queensland*

Volume 8: West Europe

Editor: *Lise Skov, Copenhagen Business School*

Consulting Editor: *Valerie Cumming, Dress Historian,
Costume Society and formerly Museum of London*

Volume 9: East Europe, Russia, and the Caucasus

Editor: *Djurdja Bartlett, London College of Fashion,
University of the Arts London*

Assistant Editor: *Pamela Smith, Independent Writer
and Speaker on Russian and East European Arts*

Volume 10: Global Perspectives

Editor: *Joanne B. Eicher, University of Minnesota*

Assistant Editor: *Phyllis G. Tortora, Queens College,
City University of New York*

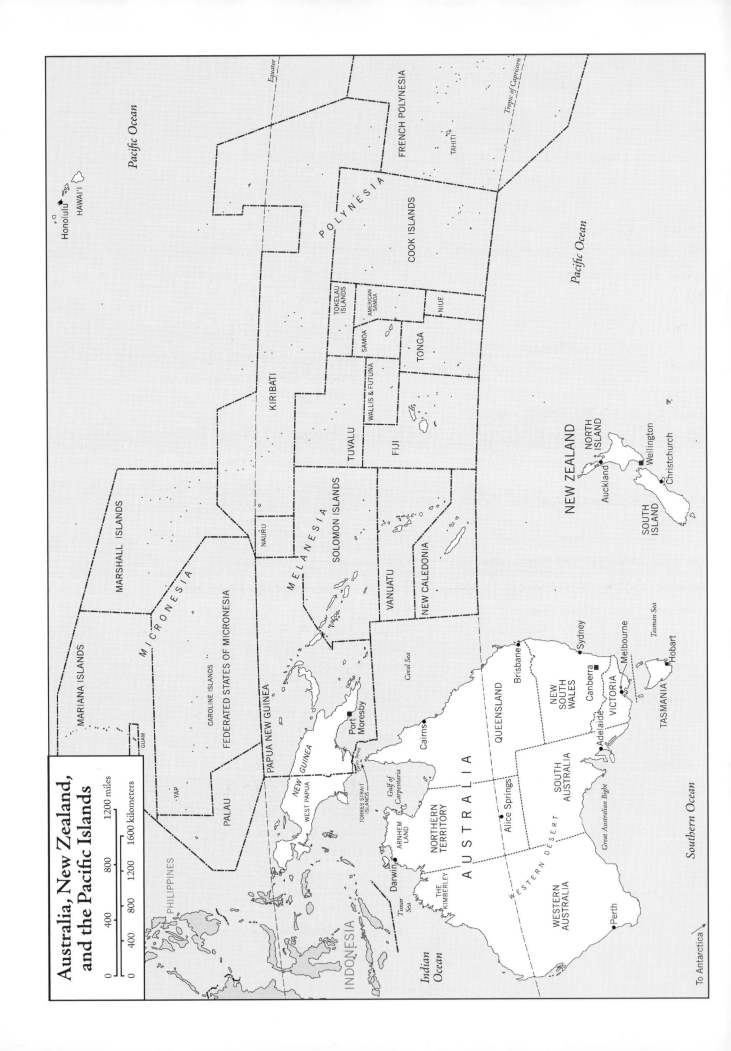

Australia, New Zealand, and the Pacific Islands

	miles
0 400 800 1200	
0 400 800 1200 1600 kilometers	

Pacific Ocean

Equator

Tropic of Capricorn

HAWAI'I

Honolulu

POLYNESIA

FRENCH POLYNESIA

TAHITI

COOK ISLANDS

TOKELAU ISLANDS

AMERICAN SAMOA

SAMOA

NIUE

TONGA

KIRIBATI

WALLIS & FUTUNA

FIJI

TUVALU

MARSHALL ISLANDS

MICRONESIA

NAURU

MELANESIA

SOLOMON ISLANDS

VANUATU

NEW CALEDONIA

MARIANA ISLANDS

GUAM

FEDERATED STATES OF MICRONESIA

CAROLINE ISLANDS

YAP

PALAU

PHILIPPINES

PAPUA NEW GUINEA

NEW GUINEA

WEST PAPUA

TORRES STRAIT ISLANDS

Port Moresby

Coral Sea

Pacific Ocean

NEW ZEALAND

NORTH ISLAND

Auckland

Wellington

Christchurch

SOUTH ISLAND

Tasman Sea

INDONESIA

Timor Sea

Darwin

THE KIMBERLEY

ARNHEM LAND

Gulf of Carpentaria

NORTHERN TERRITORY

Cairns

QUEENSLAND

Brisbane

Sydney

NEW SOUTH WALES

Canberra

Melbourne

VICTORIA

Hobart

TASMANIA

Adelaide

SOUTH AUSTRALIA

Alice Springs

WESTERN DESERT

A U S T R A L I A

WESTERN AUSTRALIA

Perth

Great Australian Bight

Indian Ocean

Southern Ocean

To Antarctica

Contents

Publishing, Editorial and Production Staff

Project Manager
Sarah Waldram

Head of Production
Ken Bruce

Publishing Assistants
Louise Butler
Helen Caunce
Augusta Dörr

E-content and Systems Managers
Helen Toone
Fanny Thépot

Production Editor
Jonathan Mazliah

Editorial Manager
Janet Phillips

Editorial Administrators
Angela Greenwell
Amy Laurens

Editorial Assistant
Jessica Hobbs

Freelance Editors
Andrea Belloli
Fiona Corbridge
Catherine Foley
Julene Knox
Fintan Power

Picture Researcher
Sophie Basilevitch

Picture Assistants
Aisling Hanrahan
Simon Reid

Interns
Cecilia Bertilsson
Lacey Decker
Sian Jones
Kimberly Manning
Maria Sarnowska
Nina Schipper
Cathryn Steele

Maps
Martin Lubikowski, ML Design

Project Managers, Apex CoVantage
Emily Johnston
Julia Rosen

Freelance Proofreading Manager
Timothy DeWerff

Managing Director
Kathryn Earle

Consultant
Sylvia K. Miller

Head of Sales and Marketing
Jennifer Howell

Contributors

Prue Ahrens, *University of Queensland, Australia*

Kim Akerman, *Independent Scholar and Anthropological Consultant, Australia*

Kalissa Alexeyeff, *The University of Melbourne, Australia*

Frédéric Angleviel, *Université de la Nouvelle-Calédonie, New Caledonia*

Petra M. Autio, *University of Helsinki, Finland*

Michelle Bakar, *Independent Scholar, Australia*

Prudence Black, *University of Technology, Sydney, Australia*

Fabri Blacklock, *Powerhouse Museum, Australia*

Lissant Bolton, *British Museum, United Kingdom*

Linda Boynton Arthur, *Washington State University, United States*

Ben Burt, *British Museum, United Kingdom*

Natalie Cadenhead, *Canterbury Museum, New Zealand*

Julia Clark, *Port Arthur Historic Site, Australia*

Linda Clark, *Queen Victoria Museum and Art Gallery, Australia*

Jennifer Craik, *University of Canberra, Australia and RMIT University, Australia*

Jo Diamond, *University of Canterbury, New Zealand*

Anna Edmundson, *National Museum of Australia, Australia*

Damayanthie Eluwawalage, *State University of New York at Oneonta, United States*

Anna Epstein, *Jewish National Museum of Australia, Australia*

Roderick Ewins, *University of Tasmania, Australia*

Anne Farren, *Curtin University of Technology, Australia*

Judith S. Flores, *University of Guam, United States*

Alison Goodrum, *Nottingham Trent University, United Kingdom*

Sally Gray, *College of Fine Arts, University of New South Wales, Australia*

Louise Hamby, *Australian National University, Australia*

Robyn Healy, *RMIT University, Australia*

Sandra Heffernan, *Massey University, New Zealand*

Lynne Hume, *University of Queensland, Australia*

Laura Jocic, *National Gallery of Victoria, Australia*

Glynis Jones, *Powerhouse Museum, Australia*

Philip Jones, *South Australian Museum, Australia*

Adrienne L. Kaeppler, *Smithsonian Institution, Washington D.C., United States*

Vicki Karaminas, *University of Technology, Sydney, Australia*

Kate Khan, *Australian Museum, Australia*

Sylvia Kleinert, *Australian National University, Australia*

Susanne Küchler, *University College London, United Kingdom*

Makiko Kuwahara, *Kinjo Gakuin University, Japan*

Bronwyn Labrum, *Massey University, New Zealand*

Raechel Margaret Laing, *University of Otago, New Zealand*

Angela Lassig, *Museum of New Zealand Te Papa Tongarewa, New Zealand*

Roger Leong, *National Gallery of Victoria, Australia*

Jacquelyn A. Lewis-Harris, *University of Missouri–St Louis, United States*

Billie Lythberg, *Independent Consultant, New Zealand*

Sean Mallon, *Museum of New Zealand Te Papa Tongarewa, New Zealand*

Margaret Maynard, *University of Queensland, Australia*

Peter McNeil, *University of Technology, Sydney, Australia*

Naomi M. McPherson, *University of British Columbia Okanagan, Canada*

Michael A. Mel, *University of Goroka, Papua New Guinea*

Andrea Mitchell, *University of Queensland, Australia*

Jane Freeman Moulin, *University of Hawai'i at Mānoa, United States*

Linda Waimarie Nikora, *University of Waikato, New Zealand*

Daniel Palmer, *Monash University, Australia*

Juliette Peers, *RMIT University, Australia*

Giles Peterson, *Whitecliffe College of Art and Design, New Zealand*

Carmen C. H. Petrosian-Husa, *Independent Scholar, Austria*

Nancy J. Pollock, *Victoria University, New Zealand (retired)*

Max Quanchi, *Queensland University of Technology, Australia*

Jennifer Quérée, *Canterbury Museum, New Zealand*

Catherine Reade, *Formerly of the Powerhouse Museum, Sydney*

Kate Rhodes, *RMIT University, Australia*

Margot Riley, *State Library of New South Wales, Australia*

Mohi Robert Rua, *University of Waikato, New Zealand*

Sue Ryan, *RMIT University, Australia*

Christine Schmidt, *Queensland University of Technology, Australia*

Kim Simpson, *Heritage Tasmania, Tasmania*

Natalie Smith, *University of Otago, New Zealand*

Karen Stevenson, *University of Canterbury, New Zealand*

Jinna Tay, *University of Queensland, Australia*

Ngahuia Te Awekotuku, *University of Waikato, New Zealand*

Ian Terry, *Tasmanian Museum and Art Gallery, Australia*

Hilke Thode-Arora, *Independent Scholar, Germany*

Petronella J. M. van de Wijdeven, *Manukau Institute of Technology, New Zealand*

Paulina van der Zee, *University of Ghent, Belgium*

Feeonaa Wall, *Independent Scholar, New Zealand*

Patricia Te Arapo Wallace, *University of Canterbury, New Zealand*

Lindie Ward, *Powerhouse Museum, Australia*

Elaine Webster, *University of Otago, New Zealand*

Sally Weller, *University of Melbourne, Australia*

Graeme Were, *University College London, United Kingdom*

Danielle Whitfield, *National Gallery of Victoria, Australia*

Craig Wilcox, *Independent Scholar*

Cheryl Anne Wilson, *University of Otago, New Zealand*

Elspeth Wishart, *Tasmanian Museum and Art Gallery, Australia*

Fanny Wonu Veys, *Cambridge University, United Kingdom; Musée du quai Branly, France*

Diana Young, *University of Brisbane, Australia*

Encyclopedia Preface

The *Encyclopedia of World Dress and Fashion* covers a fundamental and universal human activity relating to personal and social identity—the vast topic of how more than six billion people dress across the globe. To accomplish this, the first nine volumes are organized geographically, and the tenth addresses global issues. The approach throughout is both cross-cultural and multidisciplinary and allows readers to appreciate the richness and complexity of dress in all its manifestations. However, even a ten-volume encyclopedia must limit itself in either time or geography in order to provide in-depth scholarship. The focus is therefore on the nineteenth to the early twenty-first centuries, although overview materials covering the long history of dress have been included to provide essential context, as is appropriate in so ambitious a scholarly undertaking.

Many disciplines have developed an interest in dress studies, underscoring the need for a major reference work with a broad scope. The range of interpretations will help readers develop a critical understanding of cultural practices. The intended audience for the *Encyclopedia* is broad and encompasses general and curious readers as well as students and teachers in the humanities and social sciences, in short, anyone interested in the full spectrum of issues relating to dress in a given time and place. More specialized researchers in anthropology, apparel design, art and cultural history, cinema, cultural studies, dance and drama, fashion, folklore, history, and sociology will also find the *Encyclopedia* an invaluable reference.

Dress, costume, and *fashion* are often used interchangeably in common parlance, but this work makes crucial distinctions between them because terminology is important. The aim of this preface is to clarify for readers the distinctions that have been drawn throughout this particular project by the editors and contributors, in order to achieve scholarly consistency across the work. Contributors were asked to define *dress* as any supplement or modification to the body, the purpose of which is either to cover or to adorn. Dress is a broad category that includes costume and fashion, with the term *costume* defined as a specific type of dress that is worn for theatrical, dance, or masquerade performances. *Costume* is frequently used by many distinguished museum curators and scholars in connection with both the historical study and the display of clothing in a general way. In contrast to dress, which ordinarily expresses a wearer's identity, costume hides or conceals it in various degrees. *Fashion* is defined as changes relating to body modifications and supplements, usually easily perceived and tracked, often within short periods of time.

While fashions may have permanent consequences with respect to an individual (as in the case of tattooing, for example), most are characterized by impermanence within the larger socioeconomic or fashion system (a complex process by which changing fashions in dress spread through formal and/or informal channels of design, manufacture, merchandising, and communication).

Supplements to the body include conventional attire such as clothing, jewelry, and items typically called *accessories*, such as hats, shoes, handbags, and canes. Modifications include cosmetics, hair care (cutting, combing, and styling), scarification, tattooing, tooth filing, piercings, and gentle molding of the human skull or binding of feet (the latter two usually done during infancy). Thus, in many cultures where people display these modifications alone, a person can be unclothed but still dressed. In addition to visually oriented practices, the definition of *dress* acknowledges that all senses may be incorporated, not just the visual. Therefore, sound (for example, rustling or jingling), odor (perfumes or incense), touch (such as tight or loose, silky or rough), and even taste when applicable (some cosmetics, breath fresheners, and tobacco products) frequently feature in discussions.

Being dressed is a normative act because human beings are taught what is right and wrong in concealing and revealing the body and keeping it clean and attractive. Contributors to this encyclopedia primarily describe dress and explain how it is worn within specific cultural contexts, although, where it is likely to be helpful, they have been encouraged to embrace and explain theoretical approaches to the interpretation of dress (for example, postmodernism, psychoanalytic theory, semiotics, and queer theory). The geographic organization provides overviews by country. An attempt has been made to focus on all countries, but in some cases, qualified authors could not be found and an entry was regretfully omitted. Readers may, however, find references to a country in the volume and section introductions and in the index. Supplementing country essays are articles on types or categories of dress along with select articles on influential or particularly well-known ethnic groups. Shorter "snapshots" on specific topics serve as sidebars to longer articles. Volume 10 addresses issues of global interest relating to the first nine volumes and is divided into five main sections: Overview of Global Perspectives; Forms of Dress Worldwide; Dress and the Arts Worldwide; Fashion Worldwide; and Dress and Fashion Resources Worldwide. Inclusion of a timeline on the development of dress and related technologies is a special feature.

At the end of each article, a list of references and suggestions for further reading has been included. Where possible, cross-references to other relevant articles in the *Encyclopedia* have also been inserted. Each volume has its own index, and readers will find a cumulative index to the entire set in volume 10. Volumes 1 to 9 also each feature a regional map.

While it is tempting when writing on the body and dress to focus on the most spectacular or visually engaging examples of dress from a given culture, authors have been asked to balance their discussions between the ordinary dress of daily life and the extraordinary dress of special occasions. In both instances this includes protective clothing of various sorts as well as general distinctions between genders, among age groups and various vocations, and within other realms of social status, as defined by religion, wealth, and political position. Along with prehistoric and historical traditions of dress, authors have been charged with addressing contemporary fashions in their own areas of interest, as well as traditional dress forms. An important aim of the *Encyclopedia* is to show the full range and transformative power of dress in cultural exchanges that occur all over the world, of which the influence of Western fashion on other parts of the world is only one example.

The editor in chief recruited scholars with particular expertise in dress, textiles, and fashion in their geographic areas and a scholarly network to edit specific volumes, develop tables of contents, draft a descriptive scope for articles requested, and contact and commission contributors. (Some experts were not available to participate in contributing articles.) The ten volumes include 854 articles written by 585 authors residing in over 60 different countries. Authors had freedom to develop their articles but always with a general reader in mind. Scholarship around the world and in different disciplines has many approaches; this presents daunting challenges for authors, who were asked to employ a relatively broad but consistent definition of dress. As a result of a rigorous review and revision process, their work has resulted in a comprehensive compilation of material not found before in a reference work of this type. Their efforts allow readers to find the excitement, variety, sensuality, and complexity of dress presented in clear descriptions, reinforced by historical and cultural context. As much as possible, entries have been written by experts from within the culture being discussed. Each was assigned a certain number of words, determined by the volume editor and editor in chief in the context of the desired depth and balance of the *Encyclopedia* as a whole, and each followed instructions and guidelines developed by the editorial board and publisher. The structure of each volume also varies according to the editor's perspective, the constraints of the historical, political, and social configuration of the geographic area, and the research known to be available.

A variety of images have been included, from museum photographs that show detail, to anthropological photographs that show dress in action and context, to fashion and artistic images that help to convey attitudes and ideals. Many of these have come from the contributors' own fieldwork. The goal is that the variety of approaches and interpretations presented within the *Encyclopedia*'s architecture combine to create a worldwide presentation of dress that is more varied, less biased, and more complete than any heretofore published. Articles are extensively illustrated with 2,300 images—many seen here for the first time.

The process of conceiving of and completing the *Encyclopedia* took place over a number of years and involved much scholarly consultation among editors, contributors, and staff. The common goal demanded a flexible approach within a set framework, and such a balancing act presented a range of challenges. Doubtless some decisions could be argued at further length, but hopefully readers will find most were sensible, bearing in mind the daunting ambitions of the work. Specific terms for items of dress vary throughout the world, and such variation often also reflects regional differences in the item of dress itself. Where possible, the editors have worked with contributors and translators to preserve the closest regional spelling of the indigenous term for the area under discussion, bearing in mind also the necessity to translate or transliterate such terms into English, the language of publication. While the *Encyclopedia* cannot be perfectly complete and consistent, the goal has been to produce a landmark achievement for its scholarly standards and impressive scope. The editorial team has endeavored to present authoritative treatments of the subject, with the particular hope that readers will find in the *Encyclopedia*'s pages a measure of the excitement, fun, and fascination that characterize dress across time and cultures. Browsing or reading in depth, volume to volume, will provide readers with many examples of what people wear, whether mundane or marvelous, uniform or unique, commonplace or rare. The encyclopedia will continue to grow as articles on recent developments, new information, and research add to knowledge on dress and fashion in the online Berg Fashion Library.

The volume editors and contributors are gratefully acknowledged and thanked for their enthusiasm for and dedication to the enormous task that has culminated in this encyclopedia. Many thanks also go to the publisher and project management team, who have valiantly seen the project to its successful completion.

Joanne B. Eicher

Preface to Australia, New Zealand, and the Pacific Islands

This volume offers an account of the clothing, body modifications, supplements and attachments, cloth, and handheld objects worn and used in Australia and a widely representative number of its Pacific Island neighbors from the past up to the early twenty-first century. It includes the islands of New Zealand, consisting of the large North and South Islands (Te Ika a Maui and Te Wai Pounamu, respectively), and other smaller islands, which together make up the region otherwise known as Aotearoa.

The Pacific Islands section has been divided into three parts: Polynesia in the east, Melanesia in the west, and Micronesia and the Federated States of Micronesia to the northwest. It must be emphasized that this is for organizational purposes only. This historical, early-nineteenth-century tripartite division is rather arbitrary, for it gives insufficient recognition to the numerous ethnic groupings, physical differences, and migratory and diasporic patterns of settlement in the Pacific region, a complexity that inevitably flows through to dress, both ordinary and extraordinary, and techniques of clothing production.

Social anthropologists, historians, archaeologists, and linguists have argued that a clear-cut division between Polynesia and Melanesia fails to account for archaeological and linguistic continuities between parts of Melanesia and western Polynesia. It also distracts from the significant social and cultural differences that exist between western and eastern Polynesia. Some islands fit more easily into this "triangle" than do others. Fiji is an example of the difficulty, for it sits geographically at the junction of all three. Thus, the tripartite terminology is used in full knowledge that some scholars regard the Pacific Islands as a cartographic description and prefer the term *Oceania* (which may include the Malay Archipelago outside the present frame of reference), as more indicative of the intimate connections between places in the region.

Clearly, there are complexities of terms and shifting meanings given to peoples, ethnicities, places, and, of course, all forms of dress and body modification. Aboriginal and Torres Strait Islander people encompass the indigenous inhabitants of Australia. All mainland Aboriginal groups share the same "ethnicity," while Torres Strait Islanders are Melanesian in origin. Yet to think that the former peoples, with numerous moiety, clan, and language differences, including local customs of wearing, exhibit a cohesive "ethnic" group is to misrepresent the nature of their attire.

In Australia, the term *ethnic* is used to describe migrants including Greeks and Italians, who for the most part wear European-style clothing. The word *Māori* refers to descendants of the original Polynesian immigrants to New Zealand and distinguishes those who are different from *Pākehā*, a term that from the nineteenth century usually meant Europeans or, more recently, peoples of non-Māori or non-Polynesian origin. The term *Pākehā* is used sparingly, as its meaning and use are debated.

The vast geographic region covered by this volume is comprised of widely differing social groupings and ethnicities, many of whom have experienced unstable governance. The legacies of colonial rule, and mismatches between ethnic and political boundaries, are still prevalent and inflect dress practices. These differences remain contentious in some areas, and geographic terminology may be artificial or arbitrary. The decision to include New Zealand in the title was made after deliberation, as the country is essentially comprised of a number of Pacific Islands. Justification for its separation in the volume's title and structure is based on the country's stable political circumstances, its geography, its climate (which is not tropical like the others but ranges from temperate to sub-Antarctic in the southernmost parts), its industrialized economy, its vibrant designer-fashion industry, and its long history of wool production. All these factors have impacted clothes and their making. Hawai'i with its complex dress history proved another difficult decision regarding inclusion, as it is a Pacific island but has been part of the United States of America since the late nineteenth century. Thus, the dress of Hawai'i is discussed only prior to U.S. annexation in 1898. (Readers requiring information on dress of the island after this date should refer to volume 3 of this *Encyclopedia*.) For ease of use, the indigenous peoples of Australia are divided into six geographic regions, but this grossly oversimplifies the dress of multifarious groups of people that have occupied and continue to live in Australia and the Torres Strait. No hierarchy or priority should be assumed by the order in which peoples and their attire are discussed.

Studies of European dress in Australia and New Zealand have been rather patchy in the past, although less sparse perhaps than research into the clothing of indigenous Australian, Māori, and Pacific peoples. Increasingly, and sometimes in a profound way, recognition is being given to the significance of attire and cloth as they relate to the ways indigenous cultures have been embedded in their environments, accommodated newcomers, communicated and sustained their identity, and lived out their lives. This current enterprise is a demonstrable example. In Australia, specialists have tended to focus on fashion as an aspect of cultural studies, rather than to study dress historically or as an aspect of material culture, economics, retailing, or manufacturing. This situation is changing. In Australia and New Zealand, research into the historical aspects of fashion and modern designer style is growing, and public interest in exhibitions of dress and fashion is high. Historians across the region have begun to analyze clothing at moments of encounter between indigenous groups and Europeans, and anthropologists, including museum curators, are undertaking important studies of indigenous Australian, Māori, and other Pacific Islander dress. Since the later twentieth century, significant analyses of body modification, aesthetics, and the ways Pacific Islanders have creatively adapted European attire and cloth have been published, but there is no previous comparable attempt, as here, to unite all these approaches in one volume and across such a broad area.

The present aim is to give an overview of the dress of the original peoples that inhabited the region through to the twenty-first century, with an emphasis on attire from the nineteenth century on, and to identify resources by means of which it may be studied. Central to the present approach is concern with links between dress, culture, and the environment, as well as the impact of global markets on customary clothing and its technologies. The volume does not focus on fashion, although fashion and special-occasion attire, conventional and unconventional, is necessarily a part of the overall picture of dress, as well as modifications to the body including oils, paints, tattoos, and perfumes. Small cultural and subcultural groups considered significant in Australia and New Zealand are included, but it was impossible to give a similar breakdown for the entire Pacific. In a number of instances, one essay covers the entire dress history of a geographic area or, alternatively, focuses on aspects of attire deemed crucial to the overall project. Where traditional dress is discussed, it is done so in the understanding that no attire is fully static and that customs of wearing and making clothing are dynamic and change over time. No preference is accorded to Western or modern systems of dress as being of higher value than any other.

The intended audience for this volume is broad and includes the scholarly community but also students and the public with interest in the subject. For this reason essays are accessibly written. Libraries will find the *Encyclopedia* an indispensable resource. Indigenous terms for dress are used with English translations, as these original terms often resonate quite differently from their translations and, importantly, convey a sense of clothing as worn in a particular culture. There is also acceptance that some terms cannot be fully translated. It should be noted that across the Pacific, spelling conventions for some indigenous words are debated. While respecting scholarly views that different conventions pertain to various geographic areas, a decision was taken to standardize consonants as opposed to following particular authors' preferences.

The volume comprises 78 contributors, 360,000 words, 80 articles, and 217 illustrations. Essays vary in length due to the nature and complexity of the topics and/or the necessity to cover historically broad quantities of material. Cross-references occur at the end of articles, and an analytical index, along with a cumulative index of all the volumes, can be found in volume 10. A map is included as a basic reference to the region.

In conclusion, acknowledgment is given to the generosity of many contributors and specialist scholars who guided the understanding of New Zealand and Pacific topics and made suggestions in relation to the attire of less-familiar indigenous Australians. Without this assistance, subtleties of wearing, language, and culture might easily have been missed. The names of some who gave particularly sustained help follow, but there are others whose names may have been omitted: Ping-Ann Addo, Prudence Ahrens, Kim Akerman, Linda Boynton Arthur, Prudence Black, Valerie Carson, Susan Cochrane, Anna Edmundson, Roderick Ewins, Anne Farren, Alison Goodrum, Louise Hamby, Laura Jocic, Glynis Jones, Philip Jones, Adrienne L. Kaeppler, Sylvia Kleinert, Susanne Küchler, Bronwyn Labrum, Angela Lassig, Sean Mallon, Peter McNeil, Michael Mel, Louise Mitchell, Mike O'Hanlon, Andrew Pawley, Juliette Peers, Giles Peterson, Max Quanchi, Jennifer Quérée, Margot Riley, Leonn Satterthwait, Christine Schmidt, Natalie Smith, Nicholas Thomas, Feeonaa Wall, Patricia Wallace, Lindie Ward, Sally Weller, Danielle Whitfield, and Craig Wilcox. Special thanks to Joanne B. Eicher and the entire publishing team for their assistance and encouragement during the course of this extensive project.

Margaret Maynard

PART 1

Overview of Dress and Fashion in Australia, New Zealand, and the Pacific Islands

Geographical and Geopolitical Introduction

- Demographics: Migrations and Patterns of Settlement
- Climate and Materials
- Regionalism

The Pacific region covers a vast geographic area. From the continent of Australia it reaches its southernmost point at Antarctica, while to the north it extends to the shores of Asia, and to the west, the Americas. It includes all the island groups of Micronesia, Polynesia, and Melanesia. The first inhabitants arrived between forty thousand and sixty thousand years ago and populated Australia and New Guinea with successive waves of Austronesians, settling island after island. The Māori were among the last, arriving in New Zealand about twelve hundred years ago. First nation peoples of the Pacific, including Australian Aboriginals with their ethnolinguistic differences, have inhabited a great diversity of climatic environments from extensive deserts in Australia to high volcanic islands and fragile atolls. Throughout the Pacific, communities made use of local resources for clothing and established trading links with neighbors. A variety of organic materials was used for dress and self-decoration. These included elaborate ornaments of shells and plumes for rituals and ceremonies, with many prestigious objects part of ceremonial exchange cycles. The arrival of Europeans and Asians profoundly affected island peoples, introducing manufactured fabrics, different types of clothing, and adornment expressive of their own cultures.

Patterns of settlement and migrations of peoples, including inter-Pacific ones, have been and still are instrumental in shaping relativities of dress over this extensive area. Each group demonstrates its own specific characteristics and intricacies of clothing, body patterning and modification, hairstyling, and ideals of embodiment. These can be found in customary dress, adaptations to it over time, modern reclamations of past traditions, or, in the case of settlers, styles brought from home. The latter dress was in many cases adopted and modified by indigenous inhabitants. Gender, status and age differences, religious beliefs, and ceremonies including rites of passage have all contributed to types of clothes, body attachments, headwear, and hand-held objects. The social practices of each group have affected how, why, and by whom dress is made.

Precontact and later generations of indigenous peoples in temperate areas, deserts, and rain forests wore little substantive clothing apart from barkcloth wraps, aprons of natural fibers, grass skirts, necklaces, waist and armbands, and wigs. People in cooler climates made fur or feather cloaks. In Aboriginal and Melanesian cultures men and women modified and marked their bodies with ocher, clay, and charcoal, especially for ceremonial occasions. Some practiced scarification and tooth evulsions. In the Pacific body paint and scented oils had qualities of sheen, smell, even mythical aural qualities. Indigenous cultures everywhere had particular spiritual connections to the environment that were incorporated into meanings of dress. Asmat people in West Papua, for instance, believed in deep analogies between appearance and local plants, particularly trees, extending sensitivities to the sounds of dried sago palm leaves in dancing skirts.

Colonialism, and missionary influence, especially in the nineteenth century, introduced Western concepts of dress and fashion, tailoring, alien notions of morality, techniques of needlework, and modern ways of producing cloth. Shifts in economic and political circumstances, ever-increasing industrialization, urbanization, greater affluence for some, and the influx of tourists had further profound effects. The imprecise array of transformations in business and trade networks since the 1970s produced all manner of shifts and accommodations in attire across the region. These include products of newly emerging fashion industries, rapid access to global clothing styles, greater reliance on imports, and, in some instances, breakdown in customary practices.

Writing concerned specifically with the history and sociology of clothing and body modifications across the region has emerged slowly, deriving chiefly from a Western perspective. Rock art from twenty thousand years ago is a source for studying attire in the Kimberley region of Australia, as are archaeological finds in New Zealand. Oral traditions and songs can be used in understanding dress across preliterate societies. But after first contact with Europeans primary dress information arises from accounts by navigators, explorers, travelers, and settlers, including missionaries. These all betray interests and biases of class, race, and gender. Supplementing written records are early ethnographic engravings, sketches, and idealized paintings. From the nineteenth century amateur and professional photography also provides further evidence. In the case of photography it was often the case that photographers artificially posed their subjects to fit with preconceived notions of what indigenous life and social customs might be. Newspapers and magazines as well as film and television are added repositories of information, but all sources have strengths and weaknesses that need to be gauged. The prior tendency for anthropologists to focus on typology or to relegate the study of cloth and clothing to the periphery of their interests has seen a dramatic reversal. Clothing is now a leading concern. Twentieth-century texts relating to Pacific cultures and dress, as well as that of Aboriginal and Torres Strait Islander people (with notable exceptions), have tended to stress artifacts as part of the "decorative arts." Some of these studies have been published by museums keen to explore the meanings of their own collections, which in turn arose largely out of "curiosity" collecting in the nineteenth century. In general, increasingly insightful dress and fashion histories of the region since European contact are being written, shedding new light on the complexities and investment cultures have in clothing.

Geopolitically, the region is complex. In the nineteenth century the colonial powers of Great Britain, Germany, France, and the United States competed for Pacific territories, many of which changed hands after the two world wars. The legacies of colonial rule, and mismatches between ethnicity and political boundaries, are endemic. This makes discussion of dress complicated and generalizations impossible. For instance, the nation of Papua New Guinea, granted independence in 1975, makes up only half of the island of New Guinea; the western half, previously a Dutch colony, is now the Indonesian province of West Papua. The inhabitants of New Guinea and its adjacent archipelagoes are estimated to have over eight hundred languages, with stark differences in build and dress between highland, coastal, and island peoples. Each cultural group and each clan (subgroup) had its own particularities of dress. The problems of politics, ethnicity, mixed heritages, increasing adoption of Western clothing, and the tourist market complicate definitions of what makes dress local. In Hawai'i, for instance, people who consider themselves local claim multiple ethnicities due to waves of immigration of Chinese, Japanese, Caucasian, Portuguese, Korean, and Filipino peoples.

The incompatibility between ethnicity and polity is apparent in Australia. Indigenous people on the mainland were nomadic hunter-gatherers whose idea of country is still central to traditional belief systems. Identity was associated with constellations of sites and territories reinforced by totemic links to prior activities of ancestors. This was reiterated via ceremony, song, and ritualized body decoration. More broadly, language groups were aligned with ecological zones, which in turn resulted in patterns of material culture, including dress and adornment. However, both indigenous and European concepts of mapping shared concerns with features of topography, such as water sources, and the idea of boundaries as declared by colonial settlers was not entirely alien to Aborigines. In some senses ideas about country overlapped.

Colonial settlement occurred at different periods across the region, impacting on indigenous cultures unevenly and in unexpected ways. How each culture perceived the dress and indeed the sexuality of others at the time of first encounter is complex. European responses to the dress of Polynesians were different from that to, for example, Australian Aborigines, and vice versa, though it is impossible to fully comprehend what European dress meant to indigenous people. Western clothing became more widespread as British, as well as German and French, immigrants brought with them clothing habits, and dressmaking and tailoring skills from their countries of origin. Chinese traders established in every port town in the Pacific had a large share of the market for imported fabrics, clothing, and accessories. To these factors, we must acknowledge the major impact of the different denominations of missionaries, whose ideas about clothing were selectively accepted by indigenous peoples across the region.

Self-government for the Pacific islands had profound flow-on effects. Although decolonization was inevitable, colonialism was replaced in the twentieth century by a much less coherent array of divisions and political governance. In some cases, as in Samoa and Tonga, this resulted in relatively stable governments; in others, like Fiji, less so. In the post-Colonial era populations have continued to be further altered by intermarriage. In Australia, for instance, since the 1950s migrants from Italy, Greece, and Asia and latterly African refugees such as the Sudanese have augmented the population. In the case of some Asians and Africans their dress and headwear can be in some contrast to the clothes of other Australians in both garment type and patterning. Muslim women's hijabs (head scarves) and colorful Indian saris have provided further variety.

A renaissance of cultural identity, one result of political self-determination, has encouraged indigenous peoples to reclaim or modify inherited customs, including dress, such as the reinstatement of Māori ceremonial cloaks. Thus, in the twenty-first century symbols of ethnicity embodied by clothing have been retained, reconceived, or resurrected, especially as national attire and souvenirs. Tourism also demands ethnic-style clothing to satisfy an appetite for "authentic" events and experiences. Aboriginal and Torres Strait Islander peoples of Australia, positioned ambiguously in relation to the nation-state, continue to paint their bodies in traditional patterns, or versions of them, on modern festive or ceremonial occasions. They also do this commercially for tourists and other entertainment. Conversely, the Pacific tourist T-shirt industry has itself been indigenized by a new generation of local designers. So tourism has, to a degree, produced an artificial commodity culture, which has in part helped to construct national dress identities rather than the other way around.

Tattoos, the term derived from the Polynesian term *tatau*, were common in Polynesia (and parts of Melanesia) as marks of rank and achievement, their often dense designs integrated into ritual, and differing according to gender. The patterns bear similarities with traditional carved incisions on paddles and shields, which have symbolic links to Polynesian ancestry. In the twenty-first century some Samoans regard age-old customs such as tatau as a way of vigorously signaling their identity in countries far from home. With no traditional restrictions Samoan-type *taulima* (armband tattoos) are among the most popular and, while island-specific tattoos have been collaged into worldwide styles, accessed across gender and class. Even so, the use of Māori tattoos by non-Māori remains particularly controversial. There is no doubt that new meanings for body wear are constantly being forged.

DEMOGRAPHICS: MIGRATIONS AND PATTERNS OF SETTLEMENT

Colonial settlement occurred at different times across Australia, New Zealand, and the Pacific Islands. Population differences are extreme if we compare Australia, with a total population of twenty-one million (Census 2006), and the island of Niue with a population under two thousand (Census 2001). Aborigines make up only 2.3 percent of Australia's population, outnumbered by migrants from Asia, Central Europe, the United States, and New Zealand, an impact that has inevitably diversified the nature of dress. Other nations, such as Fiji, have several large ethnic groups; as well as indigenous Fijians, there are significant sections of the population descended from Chinese merchants and Indian plantation workers, giving the island a complex mix of attire.

New Zealand, originally settled by Central Polynesians, has a population of just over four million people (Census 2006). People of European extraction are the largest group, followed by Māori and then by Asians, Pacific Islanders, and other ethnic groups. After waves of first settlement a distinct culture developed, though in the twenty-first century the definition of Māori (as indeed Aborigine) is not necessarily one of pure blood. The Treaty of Waitangi in 1840, made between most of the chiefs and the British Crown, encouraged settlers to come to New Zealand in considerable numbers, along with their alien habits of dress and behavior. The treaty encouraged a strongly coherent sense of political and cultural identity among Māori people, in turn reflected in a distinctive sense of dressing. Striking ceremonial clothes and artifacts are evidence of this cohesiveness; splendid *kākahu* (Māori feather cloaks), *pounamou* (green stone ornaments), and *moko* (facial and body tattoos) are worn with pride, the latter two forms of embellishment also appropriated by Pākehā men and women. Complex patterns of settlement are nowhere more

A group of senior Māori weavers leading the way into their National Hui (formal gathering) in 2003. They wear traditional-style cloaks as a demonstration of their support for the art. Photograph by Patricia Wallace.

evident than in Auckland, the most diverse city in New Zealand, with more Pacific Islanders (particularly Samoans, but also Tongans and Niueans) than Māori. Here reside vibrant Pacific youth cultures that devise new fashions and streetwear inspired by concerns with indigenous identity and transnational networks of style.

In the twenty-first century more than half of all indigenous people of Australia live in New South Wales and Queensland, three-quarters in urban rather than rural regions. Aborigines in remote centers are the least advantaged economically, socially, and educationally. The use of basic, often worn-out clothing in settlements reflects their poverty, compared with a small minority of more affluent Aborigines, usually urban-based. Most Europeans in cities are able to obtain clothes from high-end or middle-market stores, or on travels abroad, but there are pockets of disadvantage as well. For Māori, signs of disadvantage in dress may be less evident compared to Australia's indigenous people. The islands of the Torres Strait, annexed by Queensland in 1879, lie between the tip of Cape York and Papua New Guinea. The people are ethnically and culturally distinct from mainland Aborigines. Their traditional dress is noticeably more elaborate and colorful. Yet in the twenty-first century more live in North Queensland than on the islands, and their everyday wear is little different from that of the general European population.

CLIMATE AND MATERIALS

Clothing in pre-European contact societies related significantly to prevailing climates and available source materials, although being naked or seminaked was common across the entire region. Lack of cumbersome dress suited the daily lifestyle of hunter-gatherers in hot desert and rain forest areas but contrasted with elaborate forms of self-adornment practiced on ceremonial occasions. As well, climatic conditions varied. Australia is the world's driest continent, with a number of desert areas. It is also temperate to very cold around the southern coastline in the winter, especially

in Tasmania. It has noticeably tropical rain forest regions to the north. There are very similar, if not more intensely hot, humid conditions verging on monsoonal across the Pacific and its coral atolls. New Zealand has a very cool to subalpine climate in the extreme south requiring specialized clothes for harsh weather, including Antarctic conditions. Like many islands, it has mountainous and volcanic areas. Its climatic and geographical conditions gave rise to fauna and flora used as resources for making indigenous attire, as well as allowing introduced species (sheep) to flourish. The introduction of sheep has produced Western-style cloth and knitted garments up to the twenty-first century.

Each ethnic group, be they Māori, Pacific, or Aboriginal and Torres Strait Islanders, has variously used local feathers, tree sap, plant dyes, scented and other flowers, seeds, pods, shells, marine mammal teeth, boar's tusks, quills, bamboo, coconut, reeds, bark, fur, animal grease, and leaves to make body coverings and modifications. Native Hawaiians made elaborate feathered cloaks from two species of indigenous birds. Tahitians treated their bodies with scented oils, and New Guinea highlanders painted them with clay and plant-derived pigments. The use of material types, the fabrication of body coverings, and restrictions regarding who might wear different types of dress, body modification, and accessories was gender-specific in traditional societies.

Throughout the Pacific patterned barkcloth made from the inner bark of the paper mulberry tree has been a common method of body wrapping, from simple loincloths to the multilayered wrappings worn by Fijian chiefs. In the twenty-first century making and decorating barkcloth is still common in Tonga, Fiji, and Samoa, where it is a necessary part of birth, death, and marriage presentations and chiefly investitures. Barkcloth for ceremonial costumes and structures worn on the head is also common in some areas of New Guinea. It is worked in various island-specific ways and has names specific to place of origin—*masi* in Fiji, *hiapo* in Niue, *siapo* in Samoa, and *ngatu* in Tonga. Nineteenth-century Samoan men wrapped siapo around their heads or waists (*malo*, a term used throughout Polynesia for loincloths). The sound of

Fort Street schoolboys being shown rabbit-fur felt-hat making at the Akubra stand of the Australian Manufacturers' Exhibition in 1927. Akubra hats were to become one of Australia's best-known quasi-national symbols. Photograph by Sam Hood. State Library of New South Wales.

barkcloth being beaten can still be heard in western Polynesia, evoking the idea of tattooing that taps design into the skin. The Māori, on the other hand, used weft-twining to make capes and loincloths from New Zealand flax (*Phormium tenax*). The paper mulberry they brought with them did not grow well, and the cold climate required other forms of clothing like rain capes and feather, bird-skin, or dog-skin *kahu* (Māori cloaks). In Australia's cold southern areas like Tasmania kangaroo and opossum skins were made into cloaks, while covering bark mats derived from fig trees were used for warmth in rain forests.

Colonial settlers in Australia discouraged craft skills among indigenous peoples, urging European techniques of needlework and dressmaking. The disappearance of hand skills was responsible for a decline in traditional making and wearing of attire, in turn causing health problems related to exposure. On pastoral stations, and in controlled communities, possum-skin cloaks were replaced by hard-wearing government blankets (primarily as a reward for good behavior) requiring no effort to make. Imported clothing and fabrics were rapidly intermingled everywhere with traditional dress. Polynesians seized with alacrity vivid imported floral trade cloths. They integrated it into preexisting views of the life-giving spirituality of barkcloth and fiber, its believed animacy leading to activities that could harness its *mana* (power), such as cutting or shredding, or regard for its high value by storing or exchange rather than wear. Urbanization, rural development, and deforestation caused indigenous peoples to further forsake traditional dress and to accommodate to modern living and occupations. However, in Australia, New Zealand, and the Pacific Islands traditional skills are being revived or reframed. Making *rito* hats (woven from coconut shoots or pandanus leaf) continues in Samoa, but woven

raffia, recycled plastic bags, and packaging tape are also popular materials. Māori are making contemporary versions of traditional clothing such as cloaks, and Pacific Islanders in New Zealand specialize in using modern materials including packing materials and even candy wrappers to create hats and baskets.

Indigenous peoples of necessity formed their dress from local materials and were subject to vagaries of climate, but colonial newcomers across the Pacific challenged weather conditions, often with unsuitable clothing. Middle-class proprieties insisted men wear hats and black suits and women corsets and cumbersome clothing for public occasions, although beyond the gaze of others, and of course on the land, clothing formalities for some activities were abandoned. Ever-increasing urbanization, the use of air-conditioned homes and offices for the affluent, and convenience has furthered this indifference to climatic influences, apart from wear for rugged outdoor and specialized sporting activities.

Even so, from colonial times Australia and New Zealand built their economies on agricultural success, especially in the use of wool. In Australia, from the time of first European settlement, unsuccessful attempts were made to grow flax. Some locally produced wool was also woven, but its coarse quality suited only work wear. In time pastoral industries like wool growing in Australia and New Zealand sustained the export economies of both countries, perhaps more so in raw rather than processed forms. Wool fabrics are unsuited to the warmer climates of much of Australia, yet new wool blends are being marketed, especially lightweight and soft products such as "cool wool," in an attempt to create climatically appropriate and more attractive fabrics. In Australia wool and cotton production, though notoriously vulnerable to market fluctuation, is still crucial to the economy.

Use of local materials and cross-cultural trading patterns, and also imported clothes and textiles, across Australia, New Zealand, and the Pacific Islands are germane to understanding dress in the region. Trading materials for body modification began in precontact times. Australian Aborigines traded precious forms of ocher, pearlshell, and also pelts across vast distances of the continent. Precious strands of finely ground shell beads, armbands, and dolphin teeth were traded along extensive networks linking island and coastal Melanesian communities; gold-lipped pearlshell was coveted in the New Guinea Highlands. Contact with European traders, whalers, and seamen introduced new types of beads. West Solomon people wore patterned armbands made in Bougainville.

From the late nineteenth century on, Europeans in Australia and New Zealand relied on cloth, leather, and clothing imports from the United States, Europe, and increasingly from Asia. Modern synthetic fibers like nylon, Lycra, terylene, and spandex augmented, and to a large extent replaced, the use of natural materials for most clothes by the twentieth century, with cosmetics, perfumes, and hair products also being derived from overseas supplies. High-end fashion and fabrics as well as everyday clothing has always been imported into Australia and New Zealand. France was the desired model for fashionable dressing from colonial times on but now is superseded by many other sources, including products of local fashion design industries. In addition, imported textiles, garments, and accessories, as well as cosmetics and perfumes purchased on European travels, have become important status symbols. In the early twenty-first century, however, most imports of mid-range quality as well as mass-produced clothing comes from China and to some extent India.

Specialized beach- and leisure wear has been a noticeable strength of Australian and New Zealand design. Extreme sportswear and surfwear have become national commercial strengths, reaching into worldwide markets. In many, but not all, cases these are dependent on imported textiles, increasingly produced by offshore workers in Asia. Globalization and the demolition of trade barriers have meant that the former textile, clothing, and footwear industries in Australia and New Zealand have practically disappeared.

REGIONALISM

Geographical isolation among islands of the Pacific has meant that in the pre-European period communities developed quite different body modifications and dress practices, as well as island-specific techniques and terminology. Solomon Islands people from Santa Cruz dressed differently from those of Makira or Malaita. Every Pacific nation has its own version of the Aloha or loose-fitting shirt. Each Melanesian and Polynesian country has its characteristic style of "mission dress." At the same time there have been some commonalities of wrapping style and fabric types. A woman's *liku* (grass skirt) in Fiji is a good example. This is a unique word and garment, but it has affinities with other grass skirts in the Pacific.

For early Aborigines in Australia regionalism pertained to the complexity of their clans and moieties, with specificities of ceremonial body markings and attire, the striking dress adopted by the northerly Torres Strait Islanders being substantially different from other indigenous Australians. Yet in the twenty-first century, women on remote settlements now commonly wear a form of loose-fitted dress related to the pan-Pacific "mother hubbard"

dress, probably a derivative of missionary styles, one scarcely found in urban areas.

The dress of Europeans in colonial Australia was itself marked by provincial relativities linked to climate and differences between urban and rural clothing. Even in the country the moneyed "squattocracy" dressed in ways that distinguished them from laboring men. In Australia's rural areas men's dress for stock raising and agricultural work and on the goldfields consisted of cabbage palm or slouch felt hats and hard-wearing moleskin trousers and boots. This style pertains to some degree even in the twenty-first century, though branded versions of Australian rural male clothing are sold worldwide, both as practical work wear and as souvenirs, and for both sexes. In New Zealand's heartland there is also a divide, in this case between rough outdoor styles and a form of gentrified country attire. These clothes differ from urban clothing, the latter most often ready-made but occasionally tailored.

Since the late nineteenth century in Australia, Sydney dress tended to be close to American, with Melbourne more British and conservative. Inhabitants of subtropical cities like Perth, Darwin, and Brisbane favored brighter, casual clothing, affected by the warm prevailing climate. This form of regionalism is less evident in New Zealand, though in both nations there has been a small fashion-conscious elite plus something of a casual attitude to dress, especially for leisure activities. Yet a popular horse-racing event such as the Melbourne Cup, held in November each year, is an occasion for Australian women to indulge in a particularly excessive taste for festooned hats and colorful outfits, while men adopt unusually formal wear, in contrast to everyday dress.

Europeans and increasing numbers of indigenous peoples and ethnic groups in Australia and New Zealand are fixated on outdoor activities and sport of all kinds. These have attendant particularities of clothing according to state or club membership and sponsorship logos. Similarly, in some Pacific islands, uniforms are well-liked and may represent specific clan, village, or island identity. These are not only school uniforms but ones for sport, women's associations, island magistrates, and performance groups. Globalized trade, which accelerated in the late twentieth century, has not rendered dress in the vast region homogeneous. Rather, generic clothes have been variously adopted for specific reasons and occasions. Evidence exists that acceptance of Western dress such as jeans and sneakers among North Mekeo people of Papua New Guinea embodies meanings continuous with preexisting local dress practices, especially those associated with *bakai* (ceremonial courting). Fashion-conscious Solomon Islands youth wear global clothes and hairstyles but often combined with local money-bead necklaces signaling specificity of identity. Globally sourced body wear (clothes imported as new or as bales of secondhand clothing in poorer nations) may be worn, or it can be hybridized with that of local manufacture. In the Solomon Islands, where missionary influence has enforced outside values of modesty, women wear Western bras with calico or fiber skirts as dance costumes. Tongans use body wraps made from worked bark or leaves layered on top of Western-style dress, while Samoans and Cook Islands people have occasionally mimicked European dress using local barkcloth.

Clearly, geography, climate, and regionalism have had profound effects on the nature of clothing and accessories, and the impact of European culture has been crucial to body modification. Yet the degree to which indigenous peoples and others have accommodated and transformed introduced cloth and garments for their own purposes, despite the significant influences of global trade, is remarkable.

References and Further Reading

Colchester, Chloë, ed. *Clothing the Pacific*. Oxford: Berg, 2003.

Küchler, Susanne, and Graeme Were. *The Art of Clothing: A Pacific Experience*. London: University College, 2005.

Küchler, Susanne, and Graeme Were. *Pacific Pattern*. London: Thames & Hudson, 2005.

Labrum, Bronwyn, Fiona McKergow, and Stephanie Gibson, eds. *Looking Flash: Clothing Aotearoa New Zealand*. Auckland, NZ: Auckland University Press, 2007.

Mallon, Sean. *Samoan Art and Artists = O Measina a Samoa*. Honolulu: University of Hawai'i Press, 2002.

Maynard, Margaret. *Fashioned from Penury: Dress as Cultural Practice in Colonial Australia*. Cambridge: Cambridge University Press, 1994.

Maynard, Margaret. "Blankets: The Visible Politics of Indigenous Dress." In *Fashioning the Body Politic*, edited by Wendy Parkins, 189–204. Oxford: Berg, 2002.

Pendergrast, Mick. *Kakahu: Maori Cloaks*. Auckland: David Bateman in association with the Auckland Museum, 1997.

Sturma, Michael. "Dressing, Undressing, and Early European Contact in Australia and Tahiti." *Pacific Studies* 21, no. 3 (1998): 87–104.

Wolfe, Richard. *The Way We Wore: The Clothes New Zealanders Have Loved*. London: Penguin, 2001.

Margaret Maynard

See also Dressing the Body in the Western Desert, Australia; Introduction to Maori Dress; The Social World of Cloth in the Pacific Islands; Fijian Dress and Body Modifications.

Economies and Cultures of Dress

- Economies
- Cultures and Status
- Body, Gender, and Behavior
- Cultural Exchanges and Identity

The economic and cultural history of dress in Australia, New Zealand, and the Pacific is extraordinarily complex and varied. The region spans highly industrialized nations, communities based on subsistence living, and intermediary economies. Shifts in cultural attitudes toward dress and the body and alteration to economies over time have been accentuated by trade with Europe, the United States, and Asia. Clothing demarcating gender and age differences must be acknowledged, as well as cross-cultural influences and consciousness of national identity. The issue of prestige and status is pertinent across the region, though expressed in vastly different ways. Indigenous peoples customarily fabricated body wear and painted and incised their skins with materials from plants and animals, mostly but not entirely from their own locality. Contact with colonial cultures began the process of introducing European textiles, clothing, and associated behaviors, many class-based. The interplay that subsequently occurred between daily and ceremonial clothing made from local materials and traded or imported goods is significant and ongoing. Generic imported dress in some places intermingles with customary clothing on a daily basis. In all forms of everyday and indeed celebratory attire, there appears to be a continuing but altered link with the past.

The rise of China in the twentieth century as a modern engine of clothing and textile production, plus low costs of making garments in India and Vietnam, means the global economy has strongly impacted on the textile, clothing, and footwear industries of Australia and New Zealand. Australia's policy of multicultural tolerance changed focus early in the twenty-first century. While economic globalization increased cosmopolitanism, it also encouraged more divisive attitudes toward minority ethnicities. For Australians of European origin and many who wish to blend in with the culture, the overarching style of clothing is Western, with dress and hairstyling characterized by informality and ease of wear. Urban business attire is an exception. Nevertheless, the dressed visibility of Muslims, and occasionally Africans and Indians, is still evident.

Localized dress is found throughout the region. In places like Fiji many ethnic groups wear Western dress (primarily locally made), but differences persist even in towns, though these differences are most obvious in rural areas, particularly among women. Yet some urban Fijian men prefer the cloth kilt (*sulu vakataga*) with shirt, jacket, and tie for formal wear, Indian women wear saris for social events, and urban Fijian women may wear the Chinese-like *cheongsam*, a dress with diagonal front closing, stand-up collar, and side slits. This ethnic mix occurs elsewhere. Pacific Islanders who have moved to Auckland, New Zealand's largest city, may mark out their street identity with T-shirts declaring their island of origin, frequently with political messages, or to satirize well-known brands in island terms. Elsewhere, specialties for tourists like colorful, even glittery, island-designed Hawaiian T-shirts with local imagery, T-shirts and scarves printed with Aboriginal designs, and in New Zealand paua shell jewelry are niche market products and valued as souvenirs. In the twenty-first century Western dress, ethnic specificities, tourist products, localized groups, and subculture clothing, sometimes reclaiming or rewriting the past, provide a dynamic picture of dress.

ECONOMIES

If we look across Australia, New Zealand, and the Pacific Islands, we find vast differentials of economic prosperity. Whereas Australia ranked 11th in the World Bank's scale of gross national

Fijian High Chief Rātū Mitieli Narukutabua, his wife, Lavenia Lave, and young son Rātū Meli, on their way to church in 1993. The men wear modern formal Fijian dress kilts with white shirts, which do not indicate their status. Rātū Meli wears typical men's leather sandals, but his waistcoat is unusual. Lavenia's clothing is a typical formal ladies' layered dress, a short-sleeved frock with an underskirt or long half-slip made of shiny material. Photograph courtesy of Roderick Ewins.

income per capita in 2003, Vanuatu came in at 103. Some smaller islands do not even make the list, relying on subsistence gardening and foreign aid. Life in remote Australian Aboriginal communities dependent on welfare seems little better than that of poorer Pacific Islanders. In the twenty-first century those living in conspicuously wealthy areas, who travel extensively and have high per capita income, can afford high-end branded clothing, expensive footwear, accessories, and cosmetics. These are sold in grandiose shopping precincts and designer boutiques, airport malls, and even over the Internet. Others, at the base of the social scale, including the elderly, rely on discount chain stores or clothing from secondhand charity shops. People who live away from urban environments, or who are extremely isolated, like the Asmat (West Papua), have a further materially deprived existence. They may rely on secondhand goods from Europe, the United States, and Australia. On occasion those who have acquired secondhand clothes have customized them to suit their own tastes.

After European settlement Australia and New Zealand gradually became industrialized economies, commencing a long history of woolen textile, footwear, and clothing manufacturing. Although always dependent on imported attire and fabrics, especially high-grade goods, local industries were set up in eastern Australia and in New Zealand during the nineteenth century. In Australia wool was being milled at least by the 1820s; cotton textile mills making yarns for garments commenced later, during the 1920s. New Zealand had woolen mills by 1873, which became a well-established clothing industry before World War I. World War II stimulated the Australian woolen textile industry and clothing production. Manufacture of mid-range dress and footwear from local and imported materials flourished mid-century.

From the 1960s on, Australia's textile and clothing industries started to lose what market share they had. Chronic lack of capital, a relatively small population, little ability to market high-volume goods, and the lifting of tariffs beginning in the mid-1970s made Australia's garment industries less and less competitive with imports. By the 1980s China had become Australia's chief source of clothing. In the long term neither Australia nor New Zealand could compete with cheaper, volume goods from abroad. Male and female underwear products, made in Australia and formerly New Zealand, are standout exceptions. Others are innovative designer garments and textiles. Despite strong efforts in both countries to encourage a high-quality export fashion industry in the late twentieth century, success has been sporadic and limited (if seen from a worldwide perspective), and overseas acceptance has been sporadic.

Australia and New Zealand, with their cultural emphasis on sport, are, not surprisingly, most successful in design of leisure and beachwear. The major ingredient in the pervasive view of Australia as an outdoor nation is a glowing tanned body, enhanced by attractive swimwear. The local label Speedo was created in 1928, becoming one of the most successful brands of Australian swimwear. Many mainstream designers have become household names. Perhaps more significantly, innovative youth-oriented and surfwear brands with bright, fun-loving designs, such as Billabong, Rip Curl, and Mambo, represent Australia most successfully as they integrate into the international market. New Zealand, known for extreme sports clothing, exports Icebreaker merino wool outdoor wear and undergarments, and they sell other leisure brands including Exposay and Moontide swimwear. Globalization, offshore takeovers, and shifts of manufacturing plants to Asia have transformed dress production but have certainly not meant total capitulation to homogenization. National pride and identity is still evident, especially in celebratory dress within the Pacific area, less evident in mainstream Australia and New Zealand.

CULTURES AND STATUS

Dress conveys information about social or religious position, prosperity, occupation, gender, occasion, rites of passage, age, and race and is inevitably subject to stylistic changes over time. Modern imported clothing still signals high value and importance. Yet indigenous peoples have had their own indicators of status, mostly linked to religious ritual, governance, and myths. Ceremonial body modification made with traded feathers and shells in Pacific cultures offered powerful statements about social value and relationships. Some Solomon Islanders regarded gleaming accessories, rings, necklaces, and armbands of shells, beads, and teeth as having high value in customary exchange cycles. In the Western Highlands of Papua New Guinea decisions about male prestige are decided via *moka* (competitive exchanges), where wealth displayed in the number of *kina* (gold-lipped pearlshell necklaces) worn by women and neckpieces of bamboo (pig tallies) worn by men are statements of clan success. Spectacular plumed headdresses made from feathers of different species are constructed for performances that signal the beginning, climax, or end of moka ceremonies.

Samoans considered status to reside in highly recognizable *tuiga* (feather, shell, and dyed hair headdresses). In Tahiti tall *fau* (headwear of cane and feathers) worn by priests and warriors signaled grandeur, prowess, and links to the gods. Fiber products such as fine mats worn around the waist by Tongans were linked to prestige; silky pandanus mats were worn by the elite, while those of barkcloth signified slightly lesser significance. In Polynesia, red feathers were generally regarded as sacred; the spectacular red and yellow feather cloaks of Hawaiian high chiefs linked the wearer not only with the gods but with previous rulers. For Māori, visual display of power and affluence was important too; *kākahu kura* (rare red feathered cloaks) were highly esteemed, as were other richly adorned cloaks (*kahu waero*), densely covered with white *awe* clusters (dog hair tassels).

Yet information conveyed by dress may be misread. Australian colonial history is rich in accounts of misunderstandings between indigenous and settler culture. Colonial society had as its basis class differentiation, and clothing hierarchies existed even among convicts, but there were many cases of mistaken social identity among Europeans. Social differences were less secure than in Britain. Problems of decoding signs of class were often due to supposed incompatibilities between social position and displays of new-found wealth. The sudden swing in fortunes acquired on the goldfields meant women and men bedecked themselves with gold ornaments and showed tastes for what seemed unorthodox color preferences and styles, and supposed lack of social etiquette.

What were divisions of class in colonial times (admittedly not always that clear-cut) have given way to separations between the very well-off, various categories of middle classes, and under classes, with the gap between rich and poor widening. For people of European descent in Australia, New Zealand, and in the Pacific, expensive clothes, jewelry, and other accessories are the means to display power, hierarchy, and prestige. Certain occupations of importance or authority, such as judges, clerics, and law enforcement agents, as well as corporations and sporting clubs have their own uniforms and vestments, setting them apart.

It is ironic that Australia, with problems decoding social status, regarded itself as an egalitarian and fair-minded society beginning in the late nineteenth century, with "mateship" a common ethos among men. Supposed egalitarianism, less evident in the twentieth century, manifested itself in rough, rural dress and broad-brimmed hats, such as the Akubra, worn by European landowners as well as Aboriginal stockmen (the latter garment having acquired status as a quasi-national symbol). Some of the supposed lack of class differences were related to informality in social interactivities and the dominance of the open-air lifestyle, though in colonial times bourgeois women still endeavored to keep up appearances. In both New Zealand and Australia rural clothing is different from city dress, and for men to wear suits in the bush is deemed untrustworthy. Yet Australia has also had an intense awareness of the minutiae of social position, to the point of over-investment in elaborate dress and fetishization of high office. Classlessness is essentially a myth, one, incidentally, that largely excludes women.

BODY, GENDER, AND BEHAVIOR

Attitudes toward and beliefs about the male and female body, as well as differentials of age, have deeply affected both dress and attitudes toward indigenous ritual, morality, and daily life. Across the Pacific the word commonly used for the body is *skin*, conveying the idea of a form of envelope. Self-presentation is central to social design of the body and linked to transformations of the body over its life journey. The body itself is not regarded as something independent or individualistic as in European cultures. Rather a person is a divisible, unstable, and transformable entity from birth to death. In Polynesia, for example, this supposed instability and potential for dissipation appears to have been partially redressed by use of tattoos and layers of fiber and fabric. Bodies are hardened with paint when maintaining distance is required, as in mourning rituals, or greased and perfumed with oil for joyous ceremonies like marriages.

Racial categorizing was most evident in nineteenth-century European observations of indigenous cultures across Australia, New Zealand, and the Pacific. These determinations were based on comparative physical indicators such as physique and height, body color (lighter-skinned Polynesians, as opposed to the darker appearance of Melanesians), hair length and quality (woolly or coarse), beards, temperament, social position of women, degree of body covering, and state of technological development. Polynesians with light skins were rated higher than Aboriginal peoples, who were thought to occupy the base of the hierarchy in terms of social Darwinism. Appearances of Aboriginal peoples from historic photographs and topographical illustrations reflect the prejudices of Europeans who saw these people mostly as curiosities.

Pacific Islanders have customarily oiled and perfumed the skin for celebrations like marriage. In the twenty-first century modern women, and now more frequently men, are consumers of cosmetics and skin products of all kinds, and both genders are concerned with hair styling as indicators of attractiveness.

A group of Samoan schoolgirls, ca. 1900. The young girls wear a variety of different types of "mother hubbard" dress in a range of fabrics. Their European teacher is glimpsed in the back row in Western dress. Photograph by Thomas Andrew. Museum of New Zealand Te Papa Tongarewa C.001463.

Hair is a particularly potent sign of fashionable taste and subcultural affiliation, but styles also have particular links with age. For indigenous cultures across the Pacific, hair too has meaning. Among some the ritual cutting of men's hair may signal the end of mourning or the onset of maturity. For Cook Islanders a child's first haircutting, sometime after the infant turns three, is cause for a family celebration as the dangers of infant mortality have passed. In Australia's Kimberley region male Aborigines could wear their hair tied in a conical bun after completion of the initiation cycle, a practice that no longer occurs.

Gender is crucial to understanding dress among all peoples of the region. It is pertinent to those who made and make garments and cloth, and of course the ways bodies are modified by garments. Issues of gender in Aboriginal Australia, for instance, are complex. To be a man or a woman is less biological than to have moved through different phases of life such as initiation of men, or in the case of women to have been drawn into a web of physical and body expressions around the idea of gender. In traditional societies a sign of this might be circumcision, scarification, or tooth extraction. Yet garments and accessories can be ambiguously gendered. Asmat *ésé* (bags with one carrying strap) are plaited by women. Used by men to carry personal items, they signaled prestige. This was especially so in precontact times, particularly if decorated with white cockatoo feathers, the sign of a good headhunter. Wives of successful headhunters also used them at initiations, but today they have become more widely used. Gender was also pertinent to dress in the Solomon Islands, where the use of prestigious shell ring ornaments was reserved for men except when a girl married; then she was allowed to wear them.

In the twenty-first century gender continues to inflect dress, hairstyles, and most articles associated with the body across the region. Although clothes for men, women, and children are customarily different, some Westernized everyday women's dress from the 1970s grew stylistically close to that of men. There are also gender complications related to subsets of gay and lesbian people who have their own preferences of attire and body modification and interests in body maintenance. However, some garments, like track suits, sandals such as the Australian slip-on open-toed thong (New Zealand *jandal*), and certain leisure-wear hats, seem to ignore gender entirely as part of a widespread informality of everyday wear.

CULTURAL EXCHANGES AND IDENTITY

Over the years and in different ways indigenous peoples variously accepted, transformed, or disavowed Western clothing and traded both with Europeans and their neighbors. Dress and body modification showing community affiliations, ritual adornment, and specific practices linked to local customary behavior was interrupted or reshaped by sustained contact with Europeans. Accommodations occurred, some of great ingenuity. Women in Solomon Islands might wear Western bras with calico or fiber skirts as dance costumes. In Torres Strait Island culture subtle changes began with the incorporation of European calico in dress, and dance masks fashioned from modern materials. Dyed chicken feathers can be a substitute for heron feathers; plastics and commercial paint for ochers and shells; and heavy cardboard, plywood, and tin for turtle shell. Papua New Guinean *bilum* (net bags), originally of fiber, may now have plastic wrappers from chewing gum, trimmed plastic, and Christmas tinsel inserted into the twisted twine, and the technique can extend to the making of stylish dresses and tops.

Indigenous people are recorded as regarding clothing of incomers with a range of emotions: fear, curiosity, mockery, even eager acquisitiveness. But cultural exchanges have not always been benign, and misunderstandings about dress, or its absence, occurred between local people and European explorers and settlers. Unclothed indigenous bodies were of moral concern to settlers and missionaries during the nineteenth century, and they urged the use of coverings. However, the issue is not straightforward. Early Protestant missionaries to the Pacific keenly sought adoption of European dress and manners. Yet when modernization was felt to have corrupted indigenous people, greater sensitivity to local culture was observed. In turn, some Pacific people found possibilities in European clothes, willingly modifying them as a new medium of ritual efficacy. Garments were selectively adopted, with stitching unpicked, or transformed into new, island-specific styles, or worn within a traditional performance framework.

Missionary insistence on covering the body had its greatest impact on indigenous women. The generic, loose-fitting pan-Pacific "mother hubbard" dress (with island variations) continues to be worn, its association with a child's outfit desexualizing women's bodies. This "island dress," fully integrated culturally, was officially nominated as national attire for Vanuatu women after independence in 1980. Especially for central Vanuatu women, it is integral to their *kastom* (identity). Since the independence movement of the 1980s, Kanak women in New Caledonia have kept their local style of "la robe mission" but integrated it further into their culture, creating matching garments for their cricket teams, choirs, and other social groups. The Papua New Guinea *meriblaus* (a woman's short overdress), the long-sleeved floor-length Hawaiian garment, the *holokū* (generally worn by Kama'aina women to signal local identity), the *mu'umu'u* (the loose-fitting female dress that can be worn by anyone), and the Tahitian *tiputa* (barkcloth poncho) can all be traced back to missionary or settler influences. So powerful was the impact of Christianity in the region that its symbolism continues to be interwoven into dress for celebrations of nationhood.

Many indigenous peoples are reclaiming with pride versions of lost practices of attire, reviving traditional textile production for sale to tourists, and using tattoos to assert identity; the latter is increasingly and sometimes controversially appropriated by others as a style statement. Older forms of dress are being reframed and modified for celebratory occasions. With self-determination in many areas more emphasis has been placed on dress as a sign of national and political identity. Australian indigenous people, for instance, wear printed red, yellow, and black logo T-shirts (the colors of the Aboriginal flag), well-known activists wear black Akubra hats, and performers at celebratory events often wear red headbands. Otherwise they conform to a large degree with European-style everyday clothing. Clearly it is impossible to generalize about dress throughout Australia, New Zealand, and the Pacific, due to vast cultural differences. These cut across highly industrial modern societies, small ethnic minorities, and indigenous groups, as well as urban and rural areas. Global trading has undoubtedly had significant impact. At the same time, across the region people continue to communicate their ethnicities, nationalities, religious preferences, statuses, genders, and memberships in social or official groups via particularities of clothing, hairstyling, and body modification.

References and Further Reading

Colchester, Chloë, ed. *Clothing the Pacific*. Oxford: Berg, 2003.

Dalley, Bronwyn. "Appearances: Hair and Clothing." In *Living in the Twentieth Century: New Zealand History in Photographs 1900–1980*, 172–211. Wellington, NZ: Bridget Williams Books/Craig Potton Publishing in association with the Ministry for Culture and Heritage, 2000.

Goodrum, Alison, Wendy Larner, and Maureen Molloy. "Wear in the World? Fashioning Auckland as a Globalising City." In *Almighty Auckland?*, edited by Ian Carter, David Craig, and Steve Matthewman, 257–274. Palmerston North, NZ: Dunmore Press, 2004.

Küchler, Susanne, and Graeme Were. *The Art of Clothing: A Pacific Experience*. London: University College, 2005.

Küchler, Susanne, and Graeme Were. *Pacific Pattern*. London: Thames & Hudson, 2005.

Mallon, Sean. *Samoan Art and Artists = O Measina a Samoa*. Honolulu: University of Hawai'i Press, 2002.

Maynard, Margaret. *Fashioned from Penury: Dress as Cultural Practice in Colonial Australia*. Cambridge: Cambridge University Press, 1994.

Maynard, Margaret. *Dress and Globalisation*. Manchester, UK: Manchester University Press, 2004.

Mead, Sidney M. *Traditional Maori Clothing: A Study of Technological and Functional Change*. Wellington, NZ: A. H. & A. W. Reed, 1969.

Sturma, Michael. "Dressing, Undressing, and Early European Contact in Australia and Tahiti." *Pacific Studies* 21, no. 3 (1998): 87–104.

Margaret Maynard

See also The Wool Industry in Australia; Rural Dress in Australia; Hawaiian Dress Prior to 1898; Bilas: Dressing the Body in Papua New Guinea; Asmat Dress.

PART 2

First Nation Peoples of Australia

Aboriginal Dress in Australia: Evidence and Resources

- Clothing in "Naked Times"
- Clothing Before European Contact
- Body Modifications
- "Mine Tink It, They Fit!"
- Sources: Museum Collections and Published Records
- Sources: Visual Records

A
s Bernard Smith, eminent historian of the art of colonial encounter, has demonstrated so clearly, Australian Aboriginal people have often been portrayed in terms of "hard primitivism." Their minimalist suite of material possessions, their enforced nomadism and capacity to survive the harshest conditions, has been readily juxtaposed with the "soft primitivism" of hierarchically organized and sedentary Pacific peoples. This tendency can be traced from the earliest descriptions made by Dutch seafarers during the seventeenth century through the early twenty-first century. But whether couched in harsh or romantic terms, early characterizations of Aboriginal people usually hinged on perceptions of their appearance. Clothing, or its lack, was a major influence on those perceptions.

On western Cape York in 1623 the Dutch explorer Cartensz wrote that "these natives are coal-black, with lean bodies and stark-naked." His remarks, and similar observations made by another Dutchman, Willem De Vlamingh, in 1696 and by French explorers Marc-Joseph Marion Dufresne and Jean-Louis Féron in Tasmania during 1772 and 1793, were not necessarily pejorative, although they reinforced European stereotypes equating "otherness" with nakedness and an accompanying lack of shame. No such ambiguity accompanied the remarks of the British seafarer William Dampier, following his encounter with Aboriginal people of northwestern Australia during 1688. His conclusion that they were the "miserablest People in the world" was founded upon their perceived lack of housing, domesticated animals, and clothing. With "no Houses and skin Garments, Sheep, Poultry and Fruits of the Earth," Dampier wrote, "and setting aside their Humane shape, they differ but little from the Brutes" (quoted in Smith 1984, p. 169).

Dampier's inability to see that a minimal material culture reflected a particular adaptive relationship between Aboriginal people and their environment was hardly unusual for his time. More surprising is that barely a century later, Captain James Cook, whose ship the *Endeavour* was the first European vessel to encounter the east coast of Australia, was able to mark his shift in attitude from that of Dampier, applying principles of cultural relativism. Cook wrote of the "natives of New Holland" that

> they may appear to some to be the most wretched people upon Earth, but in reality they are far more happier than we Europeans; being wholly unacquainted not only with

the superfluous but the necessary Conveniences so much sought after in Europe, they are happy in not knowing the use of them…they live in a warm and fine Climate and enjoy a very wholesome Air, so that they have very little need of Clothing and this they seem to be fully sensible of, for many to whom we gave Cloth etc to, left it carelessly upon the Sea beach and in the woods as a thing they had no manner of use for. (Quoted in Smith 1984, p. 169)

Reflecting Enlightenment attitudes, Cook's opinion is close enough to modern assessments, such as the framing statement by historians of clothing, Mary Ellen Roach and Joanne B. Eicher (quoted in Cordwell and Schwarz 1979, p. 1): "Personal adornment is characteristic of all societies, whereas coverings that protect are not."

CLOTHING IN "NAKED TIMES"

Cook shared an impression that Aboriginal people effectively wore no clothing at all and exhibited no shame as to their nakedness. As Joseph Banks, naturalist on Cook's first voyage, put it: "Of Cloths they had not the least part but naked as ever our general father was before his fall," and "they seem'd no more conscious of their nakedness than if they had not been the children of Parents who eat the fruit of the tree of knowledge" (quoted in Dyer 2005, p. 24). Yet it is clear, both from Cook's own accounts and from those of other observers, that Aboriginal people they encountered during these voyages were all dressed in some way with necklaces or nosebones, or with belts, aprons, or skin cloaks.

As European accounts of Aboriginal society became more focused and detailed during the nineteenth century, these items of material culture were recorded either in general descriptions or in vocabulary lists. The apparent contradiction became difficult to ignore. In 1896 the German founder of anthropogeography, Friedrich Ratzel, offered one resolution: "Even the poorest and most wretched do not forget to paint their bodies…what they wear is ornament, rather than clothing" (Ratzel 1896, vol. 1, p. 350). An earlier, even more perceptive remark was made by the explorer Edward John Eyre. His western traverse from Adelaide across the Nullarbor Plain to Perth brought him into contact with Aboriginal people wearing skin cloaks as well as minimal desert attire. He observed them to be "very vain" about their "rude decorations," which in his view were all worn for "*effect*" (Eyre 1845, vol. 2, p. 209).

Perhaps the key question bearing on dress in the various regions of Aboriginal Australia is the nature of this *effect*. If Aboriginal embellishment, decoration, or clothing was worn primarily for effect on those observing it (within the proximate social group), then we might well consider the underlying dynamic to be similar to Western concepts of fashion, subject to the ebb and flow of taste and opinion. Eyre may have had this in mind, but, if so, he was wrong. For it is clear that while concepts of personal vanity and comfort undoubtedly played a role in Aboriginal clothing and body modifications, if any general effect was

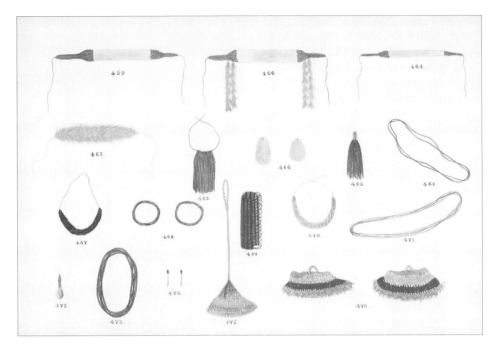

Body ornaments and ceremonial accoutrements worn by Aboriginal people of the Cooper Creek region, northeastern South Australia. The objects include men's ceremonial forehead bands (nos. 459–462, 467, 470), a woman's fur-string pendant (no. 463), a man's beard ornament (no. 465), men's armbands (no. 468), bone discs worn as pendants by male initiates (no. 464), and *kurdaitcha* slippers of emu feathers and human-hair string, worn during revenge expeditions (no. 476). Watercolor illustration by Henry Hiller, 1904. South Australian Museum Archives.

intended, this was to emulate a shared ideal of the *proper* way to be clothed. This ideal, held in common by all members of the group, was prescribed through unvarying custom and tradition, established unambiguously in the "Dreaming"—a mythical time both long ago and proximate, when the landscape and the social world were formed and peopled by totemic ancestors. This was a self-evident truth.

The closer lens applied to Aboriginal societies by twentieth-century anthropologists gave the lie to the idea that clothing somehow exerted a moral transformation on otherwise "naked savages." Early European descriptions of frontier encounters often carried the judgment that unclothed Aborigines were without shame. This conclusion was developed further when Aboriginal people began to frequent settlements and towns, exposing European women to the sight of their unclothed bodies. As the French observer Jacques Arago put it in 1819, "These unfortunate people…come as far as Port Jackson, audacious and naked, thus seeming to mock the civilisation which surrounds them without seducing them" (quoted in Dyer 2005, p. 24). In reminiscences and oral history accounts, elderly Aboriginal people who have experienced the transition from precontact society to mission or settlement life often refer to "*nikiti* time" (naked time) in self-deprecatory terms, as a time of immodest, even wanton, nakedness. Anthropological accounts suggest otherwise, that even in nikiti time Aboriginal people deployed clothing as one element, among several, in mediating their social selves. The ethnographer Anthony Piele has documented the Kukatja people of Balgo's use of the term *kurnta* as "an emotion…experienced when breaches of modesty occur in the wearing of clothes" (Piele 1997, p. 122). In his study of Arnhem Land erotic behavior and beliefs, the anthropologist Ronald Berndt noted that "nudity or near-nudity was normal for people of both sexes and all ages, and

did not in itself arouse sexual feeling" (Berndt 1976, pp. 4–5). The linguist T.G.H. Strehlow reinforced this point:

> It was regarded as rude to stare openly at a person of the opposite sex. In the normal attitudes of sitting, men and women, particularly the latter, took care not to display their more intimate parts too blatantly. (Strehlow 1971, p. 473)

Aboriginal women of Groote Eylandt and other Arnhem Land coastal and island communities held bark screens or woven mats in front of their bodies when confronted with strangers. But these screens protected them from the gaze of outsiders—particularly Macassan trepang fishermen—rather than from men from their own social groups (Tindale 1925, p. 101). Similarly, the tiny string aprons woven from vegetable fiber or animal or human hair, worn by Aboriginal men and women in the Australian deserts, served in the sparest and most efficient manner to avert or deflect a gaze, rather than to block it altogether. For adult women of the central western desert, who did not wear even a string apron, their pubic hair served as an adequate screen against their unclothed bodies. In the central deserts string aprons were worn only by younger, prepubescent girls to cover themselves, and were discarded upon puberty as unnecessary. With such insights into Aboriginal codes of etiquette the opinion expressed by geologist and explorer Charles Chewings that the Arrernte people of the late nineteenth and early twentieth centuries were perhaps "guilty of immodesty, but I would not call them immoral" (Chewings 1936, p. 117) seems a reasonable assessment for its time.

CLOTHING BEFORE EUROPEAN CONTACT

The form and style of pre-European Aboriginal attire was influenced not by shifting tenets of fashion but by long-held custom rooted in belief. The most articulate exposition of this fundamental verity was advanced by T.G.H. Strehlow in reference to the Arrernte of Central Australia. He made two fundamental points in passing, which may be applied in turn to Aboriginal clothing across the continent. The first was that custom and belief enhanced Aboriginal clothing's aesthetic effect. Strehlow's *Songs of Central Australia* (1971) makes it clear that both mundane and sacred paraphernalia worn by men or women originated from Dreaming Ancestors whose exploits resonated in song and ceremony with a powerful aesthetic charge. Strehlow quoted verses from the Hale River, relating to male novices "proudly wearing the armbands, neckbands and headbands given to them by their sire [ritual leader] Therambalkaka" following their initiation. His translation reads:

> Let us put on our armbands!
> Let us put on our neckbands!
> Let us put on our necklaces!
> Let us put on our neckbands!
> The embracing armbands,
> Let the armbands send out their slender roots!
> The closely-stranded armbands,
> Let the armbands send out their slender roots!
> The headband encircles tightly,
> The headband covered with white down.
> (Strehlow 1971, p. 467)

As for the diminutive string aprons worn by men of the Arrernte and other desert groups, Strehlow recorded two short verses commemorating the gift of these, as new garments, to young initiates:

> Matati matima banba
> The pubic tassel glistens and gleams
> Matati marima banba
> The pubic tassel is altogether beautiful
> (Strehlow 1971, p. 407)

For Strehlow, the clothing worn by Arrernte men and women could hold aesthetic power and an appeal as potent as the raiment of Greek or Norse heroes. This power derived from a sacred context, ensuring that the elements of Aboriginal clothing would not vary under ordinary circumstances. Even if headbands, necklaces, aprons, and other items were worn as ordinary attire, their form and origins were linked to the Dreaming Ancestors who first devised and wore them. Few Australian ethnographers gained this insight, being content with the standard rationale provided by Aboriginal people for all their cultural practices— that the "old people" did things that way. Strehlow and his Lutheran missionary father, Carl Strehlow, provide exceptions. So also did Carl Strehlow's brother missionary, J. G. Reuther, who documented the beliefs and material culture of the Diyari and other eastern Lake Eyre peoples (Reuther 1981). Reuther traced the origins of a diverse repertoire of ceremonial costume, as well as secular dress such as waistbands, aprons, necklets, and nosebones, to particular named ancestors. Like the Strehlows, Reuther also observed that mythological accounts of landscape features carried references to these sacred accoutrements, further reinforcing their unchanging status in the imagination and perceptions of Aboriginal people.

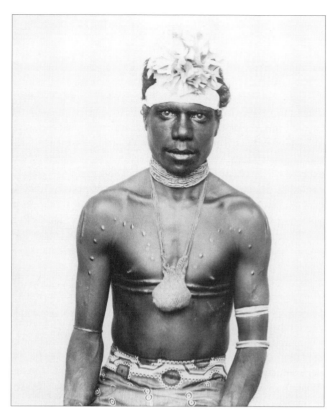

A man of the Mary River, Darwin, 1880s. He wears a headband coated with white pipe-clay, a feather head ornament, grass necklace, cane armbands, and a netted bag (probably containing personal items) around his neck. The photographer (policeman and ethnographer Paul Foelsche) may have provided the cloth sarong as payment to the sitter; such clothing was a desirable trade item at the time. The man's torso is also decorated with cicatrices, signifying his initiated status. Photograph by Paul Foelsche. South Australian Museum Archives.

T.G.H. Strehlow's second, related point was that Arrernte men acquired the main elements of their wardrobe as a direct consequence of initiation ceremonies. The pride with which an Arrernte youth wore his hair belt and its pubic tassel reflected his acquisition of an object of status; the right to wear such belts was won through a testing mental and physical ordeal. Varying in content and intensity, and whether involving circumcision or not, this ordeal characterized the initiation process for youths across Aboriginal Australia. In every region the completion of the ordeal and the transformation of novice into man was symbolized by the initiate donning the hair-string belt or its equivalent. Most importantly, in most regions these belts were made from hair spun by the initiate's womenfolk. There can be no clearer example of Aboriginal clothing's symbolic role, both in evoking the mythological past and the contemporary associations of close kin, a constant reminder of the initiate's responsibilities in both domains.

Barbara Glowczewski (1983) and Fred Myers (1986) have each written about the circulation of hair string by means of intimate trading relationships across regions of the Western Desert. The phenomenon provides a further illustration of the way in which personal trajectories and associations mirror those of Dreaming Ancestors, more familiarly recorded since the 1970s in the corpus of Western Desert paintings. The closely regulated traffic in hair string was, as Myers puts it, governed by a system of "relatedness" whose constant imbalance supplied the dynamic force that kept objects and obligations circulating. Clothing was part of this dynamic system in pre-European times and continued to fulfill that role as hair-string belts were joined by cloth and blankets, shirts, trousers, and skirts in the period following first European contact. The anthropologist Donald Thomson (1949) documented the role of European clothing in Arnhem Land ceremonial exchange, as Mervyn Meggitt (1962) did for the Warlpiri of northern Central Australia. But, for reasons outlined above, hair-string belts occupied a particular place in this system and could never be regarded as secular trade objects. This explains the great difficulty experienced by the museum ethnographer Edward Stirling in obtaining hair-string belts through trade during the 1894 Horn Scientific Expedition to the MacDonnell Ranges in Central Australia. Fashioned with the hair of their female kin, these belts carried their owners' essential identity and could not be traded away as readily as a boomerang or a wooden dish.

It is ironic that in comparison to hair-string belts, more spectacular accoutrements and headdresses associated with elaborate ceremonies were often obtained by European collectors with relative ease. The reason lies in the fact that these items of ceremonial clothing were essentially costumes to be made and worn for the performance and were rarely intended to be retained afterwards. Those Europeans, such as the anthropologists Spencer and Gillen, who won the trust of the Arrernte or Warramungu groups sufficient to witness and record their ceremonies, found it relatively straightforward to acquire the headdresses. These objects carried little sacred charge once they were dissociated from the performers who had taken on the persona of Dreaming Ancestors during the ceremony itself. In this sense Spencer and Gillen's photographs of the performers in action carry greater sacred weight (Spencer and Gillen 1899).

The ceremonial paraphernalia consists of elaborate headdresses consisting of ochered down-feather designs applied to cruciform structures of hair string and wood. Worn bound to the back of the performer's head and neck, each headdress symbolizes a moment in an ancestor's heroic trajectory, in three dimensions, just as a Western Desert painting captures the same mythic episode on canvas. Spencer and Gillen's collection of headdresses, armbands, belts, and pendants, held mainly in the South Australian Museum and Museum Victoria, constitutes one of the great treasures of Aboriginal sacred adornment. Another collection, mentioned previously, is the J. G. Reuther collection of eastern Lake Eyre sacred headdresses and accessories, also held at the South Australian Museum. Less well known are collections of ceremonial accoutrements from Arnhem Land, gathered by twentieth-century collectors such as Donald Thomson, Harold Shepherdson, and Ronald Berndt, relating to particular ceremonial cycles (held respectively in the collections of Museum Victoria, South Australian Museum, and the Berndt Museum of Anthropology, Western Australia). Shepherdson's collection of tasseled lorikeet-feather armlets and chest harnesses are among the most striking and vivid examples of Aboriginal clothing, but they were seen only in performative, ceremonial contexts.

The decorated skin cloaks of southeastern Australia were also deployed in ceremony. Worn with the fur facing in, their stitched panels of intricate, incised designs extended across the cloak's surface. Here it seems that an item of clothing, probably developed as a necessary protection against harsh southern winters, had

shifted in purpose to become a complex graphic depiction of the owner's totemic affiliations to country and kin.

BODY MODIFICATIONS

For men and women initiation and other rites of passage resulted in a series of modifications or alterations to their bodies. Taken together, these interventions may be regarded as amounting to dress or embellishment; they were certainly regarded as aesthetic improvements, combining with clothing such as headbands, armbands, and belts to produce an overall, ideal effect. They included the application of ochers or charcoal, cicatrices (scars), nosebones, tooth avulsion, and decorating or dressing hair. While each of these modifications can be linked to rites of passage, it is also true that personal taste and self-definition played a role. In traditional Aboriginal society, characterized so often as one in which the individual's tastes and desires were often sublimated to the welfare of the group, these aspects are noteworthy.

It is certainly true that individuals dressed themselves purely for personal taste or whim. Tasmanian Aboriginal women, as well as mainland women and children, were observed with flowers in their hair in casual situations, for example. Discussing the use of nosebones or pegs among the Larrakia and related groups in the Port Darwin region, the photographer and ethnographer Paul Foelsche recorded that the practice occurred in childhood and was intended, in their own words, "to make young girls and boys look nice" (Foelsche 1895, p. 194). The sources indicate that nosebones or wooden nose-pegs were more often worn by men, but not exclusively, and that their use was more widespread in northern and central regions. The bones or pegs were generally undecorated, except in Central Australia, where nosebones made from kangaroo fibulae were often incised transversely, and hollow bird bones might have the ends plugged with plant resin, sometimes decorated with orange tail feathers of the black cockatoo. The primary context for these items seems to have been occasions requiring a degree of formality, when one's appearance might be scrutinized, such as the arrival of visitors or ceremonial events.

Foelsche and another Port Darwin ethnographer, Thomas A. Parkhouse, observed that both men and women added cicatrices to their torsos, shoulders, backs, or thighs to mark the deaths of close kin, or "merely for ornament" (Parkhouse 1896, p. 8). The anthropologist Phyllis Kaberry lent weight to this interpretation, suggesting that cicatrices applied by women of the eastern Kimberley "had no totemic significance and were said to be decorative." She concluded wryly that "clothing now offers a less painful means of making oneself attractive" (Kaberry 1939, p. 77). Elsewhere in Australia commentators noted that women sometimes applied cicatrices to mark the birth of children. Tasmanian Aboriginal women were apparently unique in applying cicatrices to their buttocks and lower legs (Plomley, 1966, p. 143). A degree of informality seems more pronounced in northern and southern Australia than in the central desert regions, where these practices align more closely with rites of passage. On reaching marriageable age Arrernte girls underwent nose-boring and cicatrisation, as well as tooth avulsion.

There is more unanimity among ethnographers as to the role of male cicatrisation. T.G.H. Strehlow, for example, recorded that male initiates earned the right to pierce the nasal septum to take the ornamental nosebone, *lalkara*, and were permitted to cut cicatrices on their torsos and upper arms. These were cut with sharp stone

Aboriginal family returning to the desert after visiting Warburton Mission, Western Australia, ca. 1958. The man retains his mission loincloth and the child wears a ragged shirt. Photograph by H. E. Green. South Australian Museum Archives.

or shell tools, and ash or sand was rubbed into the wounds to produce a raised scar. Personal taste also played a role. This much can be seen from the series of 250 close portraits taken by Paul Foelsche, which reveal a varying incidence of cicatrisation among the Larrakia and nearby groups. These portraits (preserved in the South Australian Museum) confirm the general pattern: Women's cicatrices in this region were generally applied as horizontal scoring between the breasts, and as vertical lines on the upper arms. Male cicatrices were also vertical on the upper arms and horizontal on the chest, extending as low as the stomach area. In southeastern and southwestern Australia early accounts, photographs, and the ethnographic watercolors of George French Angas, for example, confirm that cicatrisation was also common among men and women. In these areas women's cicatrices tended to take the form of single, rounded scars, rather than continuous scored lines.

While the West has become used to regarding the body as either unclothed or clothed, it seems that Aboriginal people perceived an intermediate range in which the unclothed body was nevertheless embellished, covered, or modified in various ways. Across Australia, red ocher, usually applied with animal fat (emu or goanna by preference), provided a standard coating. In ordinary circumstances ocher was regarded as both protective and beneficial, connoting vigor, life, and renewal. In ceremonial contexts the symbolic significance of particular red ocher sources as representing sacred, mythological blood of Dreaming Ancestors came to the fore. Charcoal was also applied to the body for aesthetic reasons in parts of Australia. The government-appointed "protector," George Augustus Robinson, observed this among

Tasmanian Aborigines. They also applied red ocher and grease or fat to the face and hair during mourning and before fighting or ceremony. Unlike the Tasmanians, mainland Aborigines used white pipe-clay or gypsum as the single color of mourning. White pipe-clay was also applied with red and yellow ochers, black manganese, or charcoal to create a range of body decorations for ceremony.

Across Aboriginal Australia, ensembles of finely made girdles or aprons (or skin cloaks in the case of the southeastern and southwestern regions), accessories, and cicatrices, together with correctly dressed hair and red ocher applied to the skin with animal fat, would signify fully initiated men in the prime of life. A complementary combination of women's clothing and other items, comprising cloaks or aprons, chest harnesses, necklaces, armbands, nosebones, and headbands, functioned similarly, in combination with cicatrices, hair, and ocher. The combination of characteristic elements defined individual men and women within particular cultural regions as distinctly as their physique, language, and accent.

"MINE TINK IT, THEY FIT!"

Anthropologists and other observers have sought to account for the readiness with which Aboriginal people adopted European clothing—in some cases shifting almost overnight from an unclothed state to wearing several layers of garments. In his classic anthropological study of the people of northeast Arnhem Land, Lloyd Warner suggested that this was "not so much an adoption by [Aboriginal man] of an element of white civilization to meet his needs, as a more or less complete abandonment of his own material culture and his adoption of…the white men's culture as his own" (Warner 1958, p. 475). For Warner, the decision to adopt European clothing was particularly disastrous for Aboriginal people in northern Australia, placing them at a disadvantage in their own accustomed environment. Certainly, by adopting clothing, Aboriginal people entered the European domain and increasingly came to rely upon it. But the evidence also suggests that in different parts of the country Aboriginal people exerted considerable agency in selecting and adapting European clothing to their needs.

Nothing quite like woven cloth existed in Aboriginal Australia, and it quickly became one of the most favored trade goods on the frontiers of contact. Calico and red turkey-twill cloth feature in many explorers' journals and early ethnographies. Along the coast of northern Australia, where Arnhem Land communities and people of the Tiwi Islands and Groote Eylandt had experienced extended contact with Macassan trepang fishermen on their annual visits, demand for cloth was already high by the time the British established their first settlements during the 1820s. Surviving museum artifacts reveal that the preferred red cloth was incorporated into armbands and twined baskets, rather than used as clothing in its own right.

None of the early accounts of contact between the British and Aboriginal people along the northern coast indicate that forms of the loincloth or the sarong had been adopted as a result of Macassan contact. The sarong took hold in the Darwin area briefly during the 1870s and 1880s and is evident in a number of Paul Foelsche's portrait photographs, being worn by both women and men. The garment is still worn today among Wik people of western Cape York.

By the late nineteenth and early twentieth centuries, though, the loincloth or *naga*, as it became known in several Aboriginal languages from the Kimberley coast to the Gulf of Carpentaria, was a common article of dress among Aboriginal men and women. It has been paid little attention either by historians or museum curators, and most references to it are found in popular accounts of the frontier, ranging from Ernestine Hill to Vic Hall. The naga, or "cock-rag" as it was known colloquially by Aboriginal people and white stockmen alike, was clearly an introduced item, yet it soon became a marker of authentic Aboriginality. As late as the 1950s, Aboriginal workers at Mataranka Station near Katherine were encouraged to wear the naga when tourists arrived, to create the required "native" ambience. Accompanying the garment itself, the term naga may have arrived in Australia from northern British India.

Until at least the 1960s the naga was preferred as a garment worn by northern Australian Aboriginal men in ceremonies performed with a European audience. An alternative was a *lap lap*, a length of cloth folded over a string belt, taking the place of a string apron. It is unclear as to whether this article arose as an indigenous adaptation of the customary apron, or whether it was introduced by Europeans, perhaps missionaries with experience among Pacific Islander communities. Since the 1960s the most commonly worn garment in performances of Aboriginal dance, and seen by larger European audiences than any traditional garment, is anything but indicative of precontact clothing. Usually made of red cloth, the garment is not tied in loincloth fashion but is fixed with safety pins, resembling more than anything a baby's diaper.

Lloyd Warner's antipathy toward Aboriginal people's apparently indiscriminate adoption of discarded European clothing stemmed partly from the way in which it cast them as marginal fringe-dwellers, reinforcing European stereotypes. In eastern, southern, and southwestern Australia, these stereotypes quickly became fixed in the decades following first contact. In colonial Sydney the quaint preference of the precocious Broken Bay man, "King Bungaree," for European uniforms, including brocaded jackets and admirals' hats, strengthened the parodic image of the "comic savage" in the European imagination. Each colonial capital had its equivalent figures, usually characterized ironically as a "king" or a "queen", with an accompanying engraved breastplate.

Perhaps as a reaction to these stereotypes, by the late nineteenth century, Aboriginal people who could afford it were commissioning their own photographic portraits from traveling photographers such as Henry King in New South Wales or Samuel Sweet in South Australia. In these portraits Aboriginal people are wearing their Sunday best clothes, generally indistinguishable from those of working-class Europeans. The adoption of a cloth head scarf by Aboriginal women, noticeable in southeastern Australia from the 1840s, provided one point of difference. Aboriginal women in towns, settlements, and missions continued to wear the head scarf until the last decades of the twentieth century.

The adoption of conventional European clothing in southeastern Australia was confirmed with Charles Walter's series of photographic portraits of more than one hundred inhabitants of Corranderrk Mission in Victoria, commissioned for the 1867 Melbourne Intercolonial Exhibition. But the emergence of literate, well-dressed Aboriginal families in southeastern Australia during the 1890s, coming mainly from Christian mission stations such as Corranderrk, Ramahyuck, and Point MacLeay, for example, could do little to overturn the dominant stereotype of indigent fringe-dwellers. It was this racist stereotype of the incongruously garbed "savage" that would later provide the leverage for the highly successful 1920s advertising campaign for Pelaco white business shirts, with the byline, "Mine tink it, they fit!"

It is worth contemplating that beneath their garments (whether cast-off or not) at least a few of these Aboriginal individuals bore the cicatrices of their youth, a reminder of the collision between two worlds in colonial Australia. Other examples abound. On cattle stations in central and northern Australia, Aboriginal housemaids wore European clothing during working hours but took it off after completing the day's work, storing it in a hollow tree for the next day, as they made their way back to camp, naked. During the 1950s the northern Australian policeman Vic Hall observed one of his Aboriginal trackers removing his uniform as he readied himself to engage in a revenge killing, replacing it with a hair-string girdle into which he thrust his weapons.

The artist and ethnographer George French Angas described this woven seaweed cloak, worn by a Milmendura man of South Australia's Coorong during 1844, as "the most complete and perfect garment to be met with." He noted that this was rarely seen, being made only "during an inclement season, to protect the individual from the weather on those exposed shores." Drawing by George French Angas. South Australian Museum Archives.

As mentioned previously, European clothing became incorporated into trading relationships in Aboriginal Australia, and these practices continue into the present day. Particular ethnographers have provided insights. Kaberry's study of Kimberley women and Mervyn Meggitt's study of the Warlpiri, undertaken during the 1930s and 1950s, document the way in which European clothing had become incorporated into bride payments in these communities, alongside hair-string belts, headbands, and weapons. The anthropologist Charles Mountford's record of his involvement in the 1948 American-Australian Expedition to Arnhem Land includes descriptions of mnemonic symbols carved onto message sticks, which he carried back to Darwin on behalf of Aboriginal men and women. The symbols amounted to reminders for promised European commodities—a hair comb and hair oil, two skirts, a looking glass, two small belts, a singlet, two khaki shirts, two long white trousers, and a hat, for example. Mountford's documentation provides a remarkable insight into Aboriginal preferences and desires for particular forms of European clothing by Aboriginal men and women, who were to emerge as the exemplars and custodians of their ancient, unchanging art traditions.

SOURCES: MUSEUM COLLECTIONS AND PUBLISHED RECORDS

A great breadth of published and unpublished sources inform our understanding of Aboriginal dress. These sources range from the earliest explorers' journals to recent fashion magazines. Museum collections are the richest source, and they remain largely untapped and unanalyzed for this purpose. Australian museums are only gradually publishing their collections, and it is likely that in most cases, brief online catalogs will become available in the first instance, usually without vital contextual information relating to circumstances of collection. Often it will be a single artifact that will direct a researcher to an obscure published or manuscript source, possibly opening a new line of inquiry. For example, the South Australian Museum collection contains half a dozen nose-pegs made of softly furred banksia stems, otherwise undocumented in the ethnographic record. These were collected by Paul Foelsche during the 1880s.

It is important when considering museum collections of Aboriginal clothing to consider the "distributed collection," which lies not only in the main metropolitan Australian museums, but in smaller provincial museums, university museums, and, most importantly, international museums. It is the case, for example, that the largest and most representative series of early-nineteenth-century Aboriginal clothing from southeastern and southwestern Australia is to be found in European museums. Extremely rare skin cloaks are located in the Pigorini National Museum of Prehistory and Ethnography in Rome and in the Berlin Ethnographic Museum, for example. Several delicate emu-feather aprons, similar to examples depicted in Robert Brough Smyth's *The Aborigines of Victoria* (1878), are held in the Royal Scottish Museum in Edinburgh and the Ethnographic Museum in Dresden.

Museum collections provide undeniable evidence that categories of Aboriginal clothing exist, even if these categories have been poorly discussed or described in the ethnographic literature. An example is the string "harness" worn by women and girls of the Darwin area, Arnhem Land, and north Queensland. The garment is composed of a continuous strand of between twelve and eighteen strings of extremely thin two-ply vegetable fiber, configured into two large loops, which cross below the breast, with a joined section falling down the middle of the back. Partly because these objects are difficult to describe and may not have been observed in use by many male anthropologists or observers, they have a low profile in the ethnographic literature and are only visible in a few ethnographic photographs, such as Paul Foelsche's northern Australian portraits.

Aboriginal women of northern Australia no longer make or wear these articles. Several dozen of the harnesses exist in museum collections though, even if they are rarely described accurately in museum registers. We can be grateful then, for Lloyd Warner's published description and his observation that women and small children wore this "curious body ornament [which] looks, when worn, much like a harness used for hitching horses to a carriage" (Warner 1958, p. 479). Warner's assertion that the string harness was worn in ceremonies applied to painted examples described by him, but museum collections suggest a wider and more secular distribution. Paul Foelsche's portraits support that interpretation, as does the observation made by the nineteenth-century Swedish traveler Carl Lumholtz, who had "even seen civilised blacks wearing these bands under their clothes" (Lumholtz 1980, p. 358).

A performer in the Pedlku dance, of the Rankpareidkee clan or local group, near Lake Bonney in South Australia, 1844. He is decorated with stripes of red ocher as well as overlaying lines of cicatrices, and he wears an apron (possibly of feathered tassels), a folded bark pendant, and a feather headdress. Watercolor drawing by George French Angas. South Australian Museum Archives.

The string harness provides a good example of a little-discussed article of Aboriginal dress, which is best illuminated by drawing upon diverse sources, including museum collections.

Published and manuscript records of Aboriginal dress and decoration occasionally reveal items that have not been preserved in museum collections. George Augustus Robinson's journal of his travels among Aboriginal people in western Victoria during 1841, edited by G. Presland (1977), provides several examples. In July of that year he described and sketched the *pundarerer*, a form of bonnet or headdress made of rushes, worn by Aboriginal people of the Hopkins River. A few weeks earlier, Robinson had noted two other items of clothing, otherwise uncollected and unrecorded: coiled rush mats worn as hats by women and women's hair decorations made by drawing their hair through hollow pieces of reed.

Robinson's journal also provides a rich insight into the way Aboriginal people first encountered and received European clothing. Like other early commentators, Robinson was amused by initial Aboriginal mistakes with clothing, as men attempted to wear dresses, or stepped into trousers the wrong way around. Such accounts are common enough in the literature of frontier contact. Robinson was an acute observer though, and as he traveled with Aboriginal people to whom he had given clothing, he was able to see how they behaved on meeting newcomers who had not yet encountered it. He noted that it was standard practice for the clothing he had given to be passed on or exchanged on these occasions, and that this practice was embedded in customary protocol. At Wannon Marsh in June 1841, for example, Robinson observed an encounter between Mar. ke, an Aboriginal man, and one of his own "native attendants." Recognizing the woman, Mar. ke "took the kangaroo teeth ornaments that adorned his hair and reed necklace that adorned his neck and decorated her child therewith." "This," Robinson wrote, "was the custom of the natives when meeting with friends" (Presland 1977, p. 49). Such insights are unique to the frontier literature of early contact and illuminate our understanding of Aboriginal clothing and its social function.

SOURCES: VISUAL RECORDS

Visual records provide another rich source of data about Aboriginal clothing. These range from rock art to European sketches and photographs. Surprisingly, given the prominence now enjoyed by Aboriginal art, it took Europeans some time to appreciate rock art as an expressive art form. For several decades the most widely known Aboriginal rock art was that discovered in the Kimberley in 1838 by the explorer George Grey, depicting what are now understood to be full-length Wandjina figures, ancestral Dreaming figures associated with rain ceremonies. Following Grey's lead, but relying on inaccurately drawn copies of the images, commentators considered that the figures were clothed in robes and must therefore represent a separate, non-Aboriginal race, which had visited Australia and left rock paintings as evidence (Worsnop 1897, pp. 18–26). With the prevailing image of Aborigines defined by their lack of clothing, this interpretation seemed logical enough. It is ironic that the Kimberley has subsequently yielded hundreds of rock art galleries, many containing delicate images of men and women wearing headdresses, tasseled armbands, and aprons. Together with rock art recorded in Arnhem Land depicting similarly clad people, these "Bradshaw" figures, named after their discoverer, Joseph Bradshaw, who first noticed them in 1891, provide rich insights into the sophistication of ancient Aboriginal clothing.

Depictions of Aboriginal clothing in art have added greatly to our knowledge of types and styles of garments and decorative elements. In general, artists working in the European tradition of the picturesque have delivered less useful information than artists trained in the tradition of natural illustration. Thus the watercolor illustrations of Tasmanian Aborigines made by the French artists Lesueur and Petit during the 1801–1802 Baudin expedition have immense value for their accurate depictions of the kangaroo skin cloaks, shell necklaces, and ochered and dressed hair worn by men and women. By contrast, the drawings made by the naval artist accompanying Matthew Flinders's expedition, which crossed paths with Nicolas Baudin on several occasions, convey very little ethnographic information (Jones 2002).

Aged just twenty-three during his first Australian sojourn of 1844–1845, George French Angas made a comprehensive visual record of clothing and decorations worn by Aboriginal men, women, and children of southeastern South Australia. He had trained as a natural history artist in London. Many of the original watercolors for his lithographs, published as *South Australia Illustrated* in 1847, provide meticulously delineated illustrations of articles that are rare or unknown in museum collections. The most notable of these is the plaited seaweed cloak worn by Aboriginal men and women of the Coorong peninsula and lagoon, adjacent to the Southern Ocean. Angas's painting is complemented by his published descriptions of this garment, and of many of the other items of clothing depicted in his work.

The growing demand for ethnographic images of Australian Aborigines was fueled by the late-nineteenth-century vogue for photography in international exhibitions. Several photographers began catering to this new demand, and an unsophisticated international audience began consuming studio images of Aboriginal people dressed in photographers' props, such as skin cloaks, garlands of leaves, or feather headdresses. J. W. Lindt and Henry King were two photographers whose manipulations in this respect matched their technical skills. Other photographers were prepared to represent Aboriginal people as they found them. Charles Walter's 1866 photographs of Ramahyuck Mission Aborigines in Victoria, attired in European clothing of the period, provides one example (Lyndon 2005). Another was the remarkable series of more than two hundred and fifty seated portraits of men, women, and children of the Larrakiah, Wulna, and other groups in the region of Port Darwin, photographed by Paul Foelsche during the 1870s and 1880s. At first sight the photographs document a full inventory of customary Aboriginal clothing and accoutrements, including bark and string belts, grass necklaces, woven armbands, tasseled headbands, and nose-pegs. The photographs also show many of the women, and some of the men, wearing brightly patterned sarongs, possibly supplied by the photographer or worn within the town of Port Darwin. Almost all the men and women are decorated with cicatrices, on their arms and chests.

A closer examination of the Foelsche photographs reveals yet another clothing element. Several of the men and women wear leather strapping, either as armbands or as belts, often in combination with traditional clothing. Foelsche's photographs are a vivid reminder of the way in which Aboriginal people chose and

a generation, the unchanging realm of Aboriginal clothing had begun responding to and reacting with a shifting world of external influences.

Aboriginal stockmen and a woman playing cards on a cattle station near Oodnadatta, ca. 1910. Their clothing, including typical stockmen garb and the woman's head scarf, would all have been obtained from the station store (together with their pipe tobacco), probably in lieu of wages. Photographer unknown. South Australian Museum Archives.

adapted particular elements of European clothing for their own purposes. As more photographs of the frontier period are examined, further evidence of this active engagement with clothing as a new resource will emerge.

Photography was a key tool for analyzing Aboriginal clothing during the twentieth century, as the old descriptive ethnographies became rarer and other visual records diminished. These more modern images provide clear evidence of the rise of women's head-scarf use and the naga loincloth, particularly in central and northern Australia, and document the increasing popularity of the stockman style favored by Aboriginal men (and women, to some extent) in Central Australia. City-based retailers responded to this new trend and catered to it. For many Aboriginal people the style signaled the shift from mission-based dependency (often with a mission-influenced wardrobe of homemade clothes) and the ration era, when shirts, trousers and dresses were distributed with monthly rations at government depots.

During the mid-twentieth century the emergence of an Aboriginal stockman look became an ideal for young men and a source of pride for older stockmen and their womenfolk. Both men and women emulated the style, and young women approved and encouraged men in wearing it. The phenomenon, which still persists in Central Australia in the twenty-first century, provides one of the first clear reminders of the way in which unvarying Aboriginal custom rooted in the Dreaming had become supplanted by a new paradigm. The key clothing reference for aspirant Aboriginal stockmen of Oodnadatta during the 1950s, for example, was the cowboy films shown in the town's open-air cinema on Saturday nights. With remarkable rapidity, in the span of

References and Further Reading

Angas, George French. *South Australia Illustrated*. London: Thomas Mc-Lean, 1847.

Berndt, Ronald M. *Love Songs of Arnhem Land*. Melbourne, Australia: Thomas Nelson, 1976.

Chewings, Charles. *Back in the Stone Age: The Natives of Central Australia*. Sydney: Angus and Robertson, 1936.

Cordwell, Justine, and Ronald Schwarz, eds. *The Fabrics of Culture: The Anthropology of Clothing and Adornment*. The Hague, Paris, and New York: Mouton, 1979.

Dyer, Colin. *The French Explorers and the Aboriginal Australians, 1722–1839*. St Lucia, Australia: University of Queensland Press, 2005.

Eyre, Edward. *Journals of Expeditions of Discovery into Central Australia*. 2 vols. London: T. and W. Boone, 1845.

Foelsche, Paul. "On the Manners, Customs, Religion, Superstitions of the Tribes in the Neighbourhood of Port Darwin and West Coast of the Gulf of Carpentaria." *Journal of the Royal Anthropological Institute* 24 (1895): 190–198.

Glowczewski, Barbara. "Death, Women and 'Value Production': The Circulation of Hair Strings among the Warlpiri of the Central Australian Desert." *Ethnology* 22 (1983): 225–239.

Hall, Vic. *Dreamtime Justice*. London: Angus and Robertson, 1962.

Hill, Ernestine. *The Territory*. London: Angus and Robertson, 1951.

Jones, Philip. "In the Mirror of Contact: Art of the French Encounters." In *The Encounter, 2002: Art of the Flinders and Baudin Voyages*, edited by Sarah Thomas, 164–175. Adelaide, Australia: Art Gallery of South Australia, 2002.

Kaberry, Phyllis. *Aboriginal Woman: Sacred and Profane*. London: George Routledge, 1939.

Lumholtz, Carl. *Among Cannibals: Account of Four Years Travels in Australia, and of Camp Life with the Aborigines of Queensland*. Canberra, Australia: Australian National University Press, 1980.

Lyndon, Jane. *Eye Contact: Photographing Indigenous Australians*. Durham, NC: Duke University Press, 2005.

Meggitt, Mervyn. *Desert People: A Study of the Warlbiri Aborigines of Central Australia*. Sydney: Angus and Robertson, 1962.

Mountford, C. P. *Records of the American-Australian Expedition to Arnhem Land*. Vol. 1, *Art, Myth and Symbolism*. Melbourne, Australia: Melbourne University Press, 1956.

Myers, Fred. *Pintupi Country, Pintupi Self: Sentiment, Place and Politics among Western Desert Aborigines*. Canberra, Australia: AIATSIS, 1986.

Parkhouse, Thomas A. "Native Tribes of Port Darwin and its Neighbourhood." *Australasian Association for the Advancement of Science—Report* 6 (1896): 638–647.

Piele, Anthony. *Body and Soul: An Aboriginal View*. Perth, Australia: Hesperian Press, 1997.

Plomley, N.J.B., ed. *Friendly Mission: The Tasmanian Journals and Papers of George Augustus Robinson 1829–1834*. Hobart, Australia: Tasmanian Historical Research Association, 1966.

Presland, G., ed. *Journals of George Augustus Robinson, March–May 1841*. Melbourne, Australia: Records of Victorian Archaeological Survey, no. 6, 1977.

Ratzel, Friedrich. *The History of Mankind*. 3 vols. London: Macmillan, 1896.

Reuther, J. G. *The Diary*. Vols. 1–13. *AIAS microfiche no. 2*. Canberra, Australia: Australian Institute of Aboriginal Studies, 1981.

Smith, Bernard. *European Vision and the South Pacific*. Sydney: Harper and Row, 1984.

Smyth, R. Brough. *The Aborigines of Victoria*. 2 vols. London: John Ferres, 1878.

Spencer, W. B., and F. J. Gillen. *Native Tribes of Central Australia*. London: Macmillan, 1899.

Strehlow, T.G.H. *Songs of Central Australia*. Sydney: Angus and Robertson, 1971.

Thomson, Donald. *Economic Structure and the Ceremonial Exchange Cycle in Arnhem Land*. Melbourne, Australia: Macmillan, 1949.

Tindale, N. B. "Natives of Groote Eylandt and of the West Coast of the Gulf of Carpentaria." *Records of the South Australian Museum 3*, no. 1 (1925): 61–102.

Warner, Lloyd. *A Black Civilization: A Social Study of an Australian Tribe*. New York: Harper & Brothers, 1958.

Worsnop, Thomas. *The Prehistoric Arts, Manufactures, Works, Weapons etc of the Aborigines of Australia*. Adelaide, Australia: Govt. Printer, 1897.

Philip Jones

See also Aboriginal Dress in Southeast Australia; Snapshot: Aboriginal Skin Cloaks; Dressing the Body in the Western Desert, Australia; Aboriginal Dress in Arnhem Land; Aboriginal Dress in North Queensland, Australia; Aboriginal Dress in the Kimberley, Western Australia.

Aboriginal Dress in Southeast Australia

- Indigenous Dress
- Cross-Cultural Exchange
- Assertions of Identity from the 1970s onward

Dress embodies a complex system of meanings in Aboriginal society. On the one hand, dress is seen to be pivotal to the formation of individual and group identity, articulating relationships between private and public. On the other hand, dress expands our understanding of the way in which Aboriginal people have engaged in cross-cultural relations with a colonial regime. Prior to European contact, the dressed body and its embellishment with artifacts encoded multiple meanings as a marker of individual identity and social affiliations in relation to wider territorial connections. With the dramatic intervention of colonizers, dress came to assume more ambiguous meanings, open to a range of interpretative possibilities across competing local, cultural, and political agendas. For an ethnic minority, entangled within the complicated and contested cross-cultural relations of a settler society, clothing is crucial to understanding the politics of Aboriginal identity within the wider framework of the nation-state.

Aborigines in southeastern Australia occupied an environment that ranged from the semitropical north in what is now Queensland and New South Wales to the cool temperate region of Tasmania. Such a diverse geography and climate provided an array of plant- and animal-based fibers that could be exploited by the productive activity of Aboriginal people for their attire. As the first to experience colonization, Aboriginal people in southeastern Australia came under considerable duress, affected by disease and violence, dispossession, and forced removal to remote missions and reserves. Yet they forged a dynamic and resilient culture. As in other parts of Australia, the people have implemented conscious adjustments and adaptations, maintained or revived past practices, and engaged in political struggles for equality and recognition.

INDIGENOUS DRESS

Prior to British colonization in 1788, dress was crucial to survival both in spiritual and material terms. In this context dress, body modifications, and the artifacts worn on the body as part of everyday life carried a nuanced range of meanings connecting ancestral law, relations between people and place, utilitarian needs, and aesthetic sensibilities.

In a hunter-gatherer mode of production, the environment provided the resources for a range of functional items that supported life. Drawing upon their intimate knowledge of the environment, Aboriginal people used fiber and grease from animals and plants to create items of clothing that protected the body from the extremes of rain, wind, and cold. They also produced a wide range of functional items that enabled them to pursue daily activities. According to Aboriginal custom, dress was very minimal. Perhaps the single most important item was the possum-skin belt worn by men, which enabled them to carry personal weapons such as the boomerang while leaving their arms free. Another essential item of dress was the kangaroo-skin bag, in which men carried weapons and implements such as teeth, mussels, and shells. Marking gender differences in lifestyle, women wore netted string bags supported from string handles around the forehead or the neck, which were used for carrying food, nuts, berries, and small mammals. In harsh terrains a form of shoe or sandal was worn, made of seaweed and kangaroo skin, to protect the feet. As another use of fauna, women in Tasmania covered themselves in animal grease as a protection from the cold when diving for crustaceans and shellfish.

Both men and women wore cloaks, although style and form varied in accordance with local and regional differences. In the drier, more arid climate of South Australia, Ngarrindjeri from the Coorong region used coiled circular mats for carrying food, tools, and personal possessions, and the mats also served as a means of carrying babies when strapped to women's backs. In cooler regions and at periods of inclement weather, men and women wore kangaroo-skin rugs for shelter and warmth. With the fur inside, the cloaks provided warmth, and with the fur outside, the cloak offered protection against the rain. In Tasmania these rugs took the form of a single kangaroo skin tied over the shoulder with a string across the chest and abdomen, which enabled women to carry a child on their backs. While possum-skin cloaks were worn in both southeastern Australia and Queensland, the rare and quite magnificent variety of possum-skin cloaks, made from a number of skins sewn together and engraved with complex designs colored with ocher, are distinctive to the southeast.

In many cases items of dress encoded complex meanings as markers of individual identity in relation to social hierarchies, age, and gender. For example, the possum-skin belt worn by all adult men was awarded at puberty as a badge of manhood—equivalent to the string belt of human hair worn across much of northern Australia. As a mark of their social status, young women wore an apron of emu feathers prior to the birth of their first child and in dances. As in other parts of Australia, people placed great value on mortuary ceremonies to ensure that the spirit of the deceased returned to the ancestral realm. In the southeast the body may have been wrapped in the individual's clothing—possibly a possum-skin cloak, a circular coiled mat, or a netted bag—together with their personal weapons and portions of food. In burial sites at the world heritage site of Lake Mungo in far western New South Wales, dated to forty thousand years ago, the presence of ashes and artifacts stained with red ocher—an indication of complex mortuary ceremonies—point to the ancient origins of these spiritual beliefs. Other nearby sites reveal pendants and necklaces for personal adornment made from animal teeth, stone, and pearlshell. That the ocher and pearlshell found at these sites has been sourced from elsewhere is an indication of well-established traditions of cultural exchange.

Thus the symbolic meanings encoded in dress, body modifications, and artifacts provided a direct line of connection between each individual, the ancestral realm, and the wider community. In the visual system of the southeast, the figurative and geometric

designs used on possum-skin cloaks and engraved wooden artifacts such as boomerangs were the same as those found on
dendroglyphs (the carved trees associated with burial sites) and
cicatrices (body scars) performed at initiation. These designs denoted individual and group identity, social affiliations, and connections between people and place. In Tasmania research has
revealed that the designs used in cicatrices (crescents, circles with
radiating lines, and parallel lines) are similar to those used on
bark panels found in graves on Maria Island on the east coast
and in rock engravings at Mt. Cameron and Sundown Point in
the northwest. This evidence mirrors northern Australia, where
designs inherited by individuals and painted on the body at puberty are the same as those used in mortuary ceremonies and on
hollow log coffins.

Because Aboriginal culture places great value on aesthetics,
much creative effort was expended on the embellishment of the
body. Hairstyles varied. Among Tasmanian Aborigines hair was
worn in two distinctive styles: trimmed into one or two circlets of
longer hair, or worn in thick ringlets almost covering the eyes
and dressed with red ocher and fat. A much-prized item of dress
worn by men and women was the intricate forehead band made of
tightly woven string with open net-work at either end and pairs of
kangaroo or dingo teeth attached so as to fall to either side at the
temple. Reed necklaces were particularly prized by young women,
although few have been preserved. One example, in the collection of Museum Victoria, is made of 478 almost exactly uniform
reed pieces. Another prominent item of adornment for men and
women in Tasmania was the elegant shell necklace unique to the
region. Early portraits by Nicolas Baudin in 1800–1804 depict
men wearing short necklaces made of possum-fur string with
several large shells separated by knots. Women favored longer
necklaces falling in deep folds around the neck. Many varieties of

Aborigines of Australia, corrobori [sic] or native festival: one of twenty-nine engravings of a projected two hundred in the zoologist William Blandowski's unpublished
work, *Australia terra cognita,* ca. 1855. The engraving shows ceremonial embellishment of the body, with the dancers most likely daubed in ocher, pipe-clay, or
charcoal. Engraved by J. Redaway & Sons. National Library of Australia.

shell suitable for necklaces occur in the waters of Tasmania, and the production of shell necklaces continues today.

Ceremonies were and are an integral part of Aboriginal culture, serving both ritual and public purposes. Such complex performances create a powerful spectacle, bringing together a combination of elements including dance, song, and music. During ceremonies performers become the living form of ancestors, their bodies transformed by glistening red and yellow ocher, white pipe-clay and charcoal, elaborate headdresses, and ceremonial regalia. Drawings by the nineteenth-century Wurundjeri artist William Barak (ca. 1824–1903) depict men dancing in possum-skin cloaks worn like protective mantles. Accompanying the performance are clap sticks and drums, provided by the women, seated with possum-skin cloaks rolled tightly across their knees. European observers also commented on the branches of eucalyptus tied at the knee and ankle and the strange rustling sound they produced as the dancers moved from side to side. With ensuing colonization many ceremonies waned or were held in secret as a means of protecting restricted knowledge. Others assumed new forms, thus providing continuity between past and present.

CROSS-CULTURAL EXCHANGE

In the first decades following the arrival of Europeans in 1788, differences in dress created confusion and misunderstanding on both sides. Informed by the ideal of the "noble savage," Europeans found the apparent nakedness of Aborigines at once curious and unsettling. And Aborigines were initially perplexed because European clothing seemed to disguise gender and the separation between clothing and flesh. In keeping with their own well-established exchange relations, the Eora, who lived in the vicinity of Port Jackson, readily engaged in trade with visiting sailors, bartering artifacts such as boomerangs (much sought after by Europeans) for objects they greatly desired like the knitted woolen cap or beanie—now a standard item of dress for Aboriginal men and women, particularly in Central Australia.

But there were many variables at work in the indigenous incorporation of European clothing. In some instances individual items, such as an English penny or metal buttons from a military uniform, presented as gifts, might be casually included in everyday dress as part of a necklace or belt. But equally, Aborigines might display utter disregard for European clothing. Frequently European apparel was temporarily tolerated and then discarded at will. At other times individual items such as shirts or crinolines were worn with aplomb with utter disregard for European conventions. For example, Ku-ring-gai man Bungaree (?–1830), from Sydney's north, gained renown for wearing full-dress military uniform, including a cocked hat, presented to him by naval officers. Dressed in this fashion, Bungaree made a habit of welcoming every arriving ship, demanding payment in return. At the time his attempts to emulate colonial codes allowed Bungaree to be cast as a figure of ridicule, but today Bungaree's strategic and intelligent response is seen in more complex ways as a valid means of negotiating a colonial situation on his own terms. There are many instances when Aborigines combined ceremonial attire with European clothing or men's body paint was streaked over shorts, as at Taroom in southwestern Queensland in the 1920s. Such an eclectic response suggests that the Aboriginal understanding of the language of dress was very much more sophisticated than Europeans allowed.

British explorers and government officials increasingly played an interventionist role by dispensing blankets and clothes. Governor Arthur Philip, for example, ordered a supply of dresses, jackets, and blankets from England, hoping to create a physical dependence on warmth and inculcate the idea of modesty. In 1816 Governor Lachlan Macquarie initiated the first official issue of government slops (ready-made clothing), thinking that in so doing he would keep Aboriginal people away from towns. Building on this precedent, blanket distribution extended throughout the southeast and continued until well into the twentieth century. Highly desired by Aborigines, when animal skins were no longer available, the blanket distribution became a symbol of colonial generosity and a means for the Aborigines of bargaining with government authorities. However, the blankets also contributed to ill health, because they did not have the same waterproof qualities as a kangaroo- or possum-skin cloak, and they may have contributed to the spread of disease. Most particularly, by masking gender distinctions so crucial to indigenous society, the distribution of blankets revealed Europeans' lack of understanding and respect for the fundamental values of indigenous culture.

Breastplates, or king plates, were also initiated by Governor Macquarie, the first of which was presented in 1815 to Bungaree. Based on the symbolic metal gorgets worn around the neck as a military badge of office, crescent-shaped breastplates were awarded to Aboriginal leaders as a symbol of authority, as recognition for their service or bravery, and for their assistance to pastoralists. Initially the polished bronze breastplates, engraved with the name of the recipient, were appreciated for the status they conferred and the protection they provided against discrimination and prejudice, although sometimes there was an element of mockery in these gifts. Over time attitudes have changed. While contemporary Aborigines acknowledge the importance of the breastplates as a means of tracing family and clan affiliations, today such honorifics are seen as a form of coercion intended to incorporate Aboriginal people as allies of the colonial regime.

A lack of clothing became a mark of difference. Increasingly the nudity of Aborigines came to be seen as a threat to European morality and sensibility and incompatible with a civilized way of life. In the late 1820s government policies in Tasmania sought to introduce religious instruction, the adoption of village life, and the use of European clothes. At Oyster Cove, Tasmania, where remnants of the Flinders Island community were relocated in 1847 in pitiful conditions, further attempts were made to encourage Aboriginal people to adopt European peasant-like garments. Photographs by J. W. Beattie in 1860 show the women in folksy hand-knitted polka jackets with decorative trims and the men in tam o'shanters and braces. But in reality these attempts yielded little success. All the evidence points to both Aborigines' resistance to control and the true poverty of their existence. Elsewhere the issuing of clothing and blankets through governors, protectorates, and missions regularized Aboriginal lifestyles and imposed Western values on those who intended to work as pastoral laborers and domestic servants. Attendance at school required the adoption of European clothing, and it was compulsory for Aborigines traveling into towns. Failure to heed these regulations could result in imprisonment.

Aborigines were not, however, the so-called primitive savages of European stereotypes but sophisticated and determined people willing to participate in a European world if they saw opportunities to their own advantage. For instance, young Aboriginal

A portrait of Bungaree, a native of New South Wales, with Fort Macquarie, Sydney Harbor, in the background, ca. 1826. Bungaree was well known for wearing full military uniform as he welcomed ships into the harbor, and for expecting payment in return. Oil on canvas painting by Augustus Earle. National Library of Australia.

men enlisted eagerly in the Native Police Corp established in 1837 in the Port Philip Protectorate (Victoria). In many ways the discipline and obedience demanded by the Native Police Corp offered a parallel to the strict training and order of indigenous society. Moreover, troopers gained access to guns and cutlasses and they were provided with a horse—a prestigious item giving them equivalent status to European gentleman and merchants. They also wore the uniform of the Native Police Corp, complete with a cap and gold braid, polished leather boots, and a belt, and they were allowed a pair of blankets and ample food in addition to a small wage. Dressed and accoutered thus, young Aboriginal men gained status, recognition, and prestige both from their own community and colonial society.

Sport represented another arena in which it was possible for Aborigines to excel and gain recognition from colonial society—although not without exploitation and racism. Cricket was the universal sport, encouraged by missions as a recreational pursuit that accorded with the tenets of civilized life; it was widely played on pastoral "runs." In 1864 the first all-Aboriginal cricket team was formed, and they played a match with the Melbourne Cricket Club before touring England in 1868. As they were not regarded as much of a challenge to the English team, the result of playing forty-seven matches with nineteen draws, fourteen wins, and fourteen losses was considered remarkable. Throughout the tour the thirteen players wore a uniform of white trousers, a red shirt, and a peaked cap with individual colored sashes. And at Lords the team provided enthusiastic supporters with a display of their own indigenous sport of boomerang throwing!

Christian missions established beginning in the 1860s were also agents of change. While the protective and pastoral role missionaries performed involved civilizing and conversion, missions also provided the education and training that allowed Aborigines to promote their cause. These advantages allowed the Kulin living at Coranderrk Mission near Melbourne to achieve a considerable degree of economic independence: While women sold possum-skin rugs, baskets, and embroidery, men earned cash wages working in the nearby district. Coranderrk residents also took great pride in their homes and dressed with great elegance. In keeping with members of the European working class, on Sundays the residents put aside their despised government clothing and wore their best clothes. And the Kulin well understood how to manipulate political opinion. In 1863, soon after the establishment of Coranderrk, a deputation attended Governor Henry Barkly's Levee in Melbourne. For this occasion they wore European clothes, and they were wrapped in possum-skin cloaks and carried spears. In keeping with cultural protocols, the Kulin and nearby Jajowrong presented gifts. These included wooden weapons for the Prince of Wales and rugs and a basket for Queen Victoria, plus a lace collar crocheted by a young girl, Ellen. Thus, through the judicious incorporation of European dress within their own indigenous knowledge system, the Kulin astutely drew clothing into a wider political domain, and they took a self-reflexive pleasure in their own appearance as the very means by which they had achieved their status.

While missionaries placed great emphasis upon weddings as a sign of conversion, over time they became an important means for Aboriginal women to gain status and respect in wider society. Aboriginal women assumed a leading role in the care of children, gaining equality in new ceremonies and in the Christian community. In material terms the weddings on Christian missions

and government reserves were very elaborate. Every aspect of the ceremony conformed to European conventions: the wedding dress and hat, handmade shoes, and a specialty iced cake. It seems that young Aboriginal women appreciated the opportunity to wear fashionable items and were very adept at dressmaking. Very quickly a photographic record of the event became an essential part of the ceremony, a souvenir that would in time encapsulate both memory and history, and a document that offered proof of respectability within the constraints imposed by colonial society.

Away from government reserves many Aborigines found work in the pastoral industry. Young Aboriginal men enjoyed the outdoor life, and the seasonal work provided the opportunity for increased mobility. Indeed, participation in the pastoral industry materially contributed toward retaining connections to country and customary life. In the process of moving the cattle from one waterhole to another, Aboriginal drovers were "singing the land," following the *muras* (pathways) of the ancestral heroes. Aboriginal stockmen and drovers were proud of their status as "flash" or "smart" men, and they adopted the distinctive clothing worn by Europeans: high-heeled boots, long-necked spurs, and a cabbage-tree hat. Aboriginal drovers, like their European counterparts, took pride in making plaited stock whips and riding stocks decorated and personalized with carving and pokerwork (designs burned into wood). These customs continued until the 1920s, when changing patterns of land use and mechanization gradually diminished the need for Aboriginal labor in the pastoral industry.

In the early twentieth century clothing continued to reflect the political struggles of Aboriginal people. Discriminatory legislation implemented in the late nineteenth century imposed new restrictions on Aboriginal people, including the separation of families and the forcible removal of children. Girls sent into domestic service, for example, were expected to wear the dress of a servant class. In this context, a very real need existed for women to use dress as means of asserting their social status and success in the eyes of the European community. As a sign of respectability, dress offered some degree of protection against the restrictions imposed by discriminatory legislation. With little access to stores, women living in rural areas and on reserves gained access to sewing machines, and they demonstrated great skill and ingenuity in recycling clothing, creating outfits that suited their own self-image. These skills made it possible for young women living on the Cummeragunga reserve, situated on the New South Wales side of the Murray River opposite the township of Barmah in Victoria, to form a concert party and perform in modern fashionable dress. Initially formed in the 1920s to entertain the local community, the concert party subsequently developed into a traveling troupe who performed locally and in Melbourne. Aboriginal leaders, who formed the first political organizations to fight for equal rights and citizenship, also demonstrated their pride and self-esteem through their choice of dress. In 1907, when the Coloured Progressive Association of New South Wales threw a farewell affair for the visiting American boxer Jack Johnson in Sydney, Aboriginal women danced in elegant low-cut evening dresses while the men wore dinner suits.

During both World Wars I and II Aboriginal men served with pride in the Australian infantry forces despite the fact they were denied full citizenship in their own country. In the postwar era, with increasing migration into the capital cities, Koories, as many Aboriginal people in southeast Australia prefer to be called,

An Aboriginal wedding at Coranderrk (Willie Russell and Julie Sherwin), ca. 1910. Aboriginal people often commissioned photographs for European-style weddings around this time. Note the use of European-style dress, including a veil for the bride, in the ceremony. Photograph by Ernest Fysh. LaTrobe Picture Collection, State Library of Victoria.

organized clubs and dances to raise funds and gain respect and dignity for their people. During the 1960s and 1970s debutante balls were a feature of life in urban and rural centers. For white Australians the debutante balls were intended to build connections with the wider community; for Aboriginal people they served a broader purpose as a means of promoting social solidarity and a public affirmation of pan-Aboriginality. In the process, mainstream rituals were transformed to meet indigenous needs. For instance, at the 1973 National Aboriginal Day Ball at Moree, New South Wales, the debutantes, according to convention, wore full-length white gowns. Notable guests of honor included Sir Doug and Lady Nicholls, leading figures in the Aboriginal community, and Wanduk Marika, a founding member of the Aboriginal Arts Board. Entertainment was provided by the renowned dancer David Gulpilil—accompanied on the didgeridoo—and Sydney's National Black Theatre.

ASSERTIONS OF IDENTITY FROM THE 1970s ONWARD

The 1970s and 1980s ushered in a new era for indigenous Australians, with the land rights movement supported by policies of self-determination. As the performative dress for subcultures and political protest worldwide, the T-shirt provided a ready-made form of dress for the public display of solidarity and a symbol of resistance. Whether an expression of pride, anger, or sorrow, the T-shirt could be appropriated as a form of clothing in the public display of Aboriginality at events such as the Black Protest Committee against the Commonwealth Games in Brisbane in 1982, the celebration of the Uluru handover in 1985, Invasion Day 1988 in Sydney (a protest against the official bicentenary celebrations), and as an expression of mourning for Aboriginal Deaths in Custody—the focus of a Royal Commission in 2000. As a functional role marker of group identity, the T-shirt was transformed

through the use of the symbolic yellow, red, and black of the Aboriginal flag designed in 1971 by Luritja artist Harold Thomas. Frequently the T-shirt was coupled with a red bandana and (for a brief period) worn with a black "afro" hairstyle—emulating leaders of the American black power movement.

Yet such overt displays of Aboriginality have the potential to provoke a public crisis. In the 1994 Commonwealth Games in Victoria, Canada, Aboriginal athlete Cathy Freeman completed a victory lap with the Aboriginal flag around her shoulders like a winner's cloak. Freeman's action was hailed by the majority of the public and the media, but not by the head of the Australian team. The subsequent public controversy highlighted the tension between Freeman's celebrity status as a role model for indigenous people and their symbolic place as an ethnic minority within the nation-state. The previous year there had been another controversy when racial vilification occurred during a football match in Melbourne between rivals St. Kilda and Collingwood. In response to catcalls from the crowd, Aboriginal footballer Nicky Winmar pulled up his jersey and pointed with pride to his black chest. Two separate incidents—one, involving a clothed body, the other an exposed body—point to the tensions implicit in public and private representations of Aboriginality.

Increasingly the public performance of Aboriginality takes place in conjunction with festivals, exhibitions, and cultural events such as the Olympic Games in Sydney in 2000. Engaged in an extraordinary process of cultural revival, these performances create a cultural continuum linking individual lives with the broader stream of colonial history. Necessarily such performances involve a degree of improvisation. Costumes typically involve a hybrid mix of old and new: body painting, T-shirts, dance, and didgeridoo make implicit the intersection between ancient and modern. For example, the costume devised by Tasmanian women Nikki Smith and Leah Brown for their contemporary dance group, Yula Kawara Paya (two mutton-bird feathers), draws upon a story told by an Aboriginal elder to refer directly to the social and symbolic significance of mutton-birds in the survival of Tasmanian Aboriginal people.

In a remarkable demonstration of cultural survival Tasmanian women have never ceased to make the shell necklaces unique to their region. Since the 1830s the production of shell necklaces has represented an important means of economic survival; today the necklaces are considered prestigious items, commissioned by private collectors and collected by museums. Knowledge about the production of the shell necklaces is restricted to a few families. Each family has its own distinctive style of threading, passed down from mother to daughter. Using long strands up to almost two meters (approximately six and a half feet) in length, the necklaces incorporate various types of shells collected from different sites. Contemporary shell necklaces fulfill multiple roles: an expression of personal and communal identity worn on special occasions, treasured family heirlooms, gifts presented to important visitors, and an integral part of community workshops and festivals. First cleaned and smoked, then rubbed by hand and polished with oil from penguins or mutton-birds, the shells reveal a mother of pearl luster whose shimmer and brilliance connect the shell necklaces with Aboriginal culture to the north.

The production of possum-skin cloaks has similarly undergone a process of cultural revival. Because of their ephemeral nature and their use in mortuary ceremonies, there are very few remaining cloaks in collections. However, in 1999, in a spirit of cultural renewal, a group of four artists, Treanha Hamm, Lee Darroch, Vicki Couzens, and Debra Couzens, embarked upon a project to revitalize the production of possum-skin cloaks, drawing inspiration from two remaining cloaks in the Museum Victoria collection. In 2004 a group of Victorian artists and elders working with Regional Arts Victoria created thirty-seven cloaks (now housed in the Melbourne Museum and the National Museum of Australia)—one from each of the cultural language groups in the state. Contemporary possum-skin cloaks play a crucial role in the cultural revival of ceremonies concerned with naming and welcoming to country, in research on family history, and in the transmission of cultural knowledge. For instance, when Ngambri elder Matilda House Williams performed the first "Welcome to Country" as part of the historic ceremony

Christian Bumbarra Thomson's hand-knitted jumper for the 2002 Blaks Palace series, with impossibly long sleeves and improbable color combinations, addresses the way in which colonial representations are played out against the wider framework of nationalism and the uneven power relations of a settler society. Gallery Gabrielle Pizzi. National Gallery of Australia.

marking the forty-second opening of the Australian Parliament in Canberra in February 2008, she wore a magnificent possum-skin cloak made by Yorta Yorta artist Treahna Hamm.

Indigenous design occupies another entirely different economic, social, and political register through its connections with the fashion industry. The 1970s and 1980s witnessed a growing interest in a distinctive indigenous fashion style, albeit mediated through different agendas and practices. In association with the general promotion of Aboriginal design as a unique symbol of Australian identity, designers Jenny Kee and Linda Jackson produced fashions, printed fabrics, and knitwear for their boutique Flamingo Park in Sydney. In addition to their own designs, Kee and Jackson collaborated with Yolngu artist Banduk Marika and with indigenous women engaged in batik production and silk-screen printing in communities such as Utopia, Santa Teresa, Tiwi Islands, Maningrida, and Yuendumu. Importantly, Kee and Jackson also employed indigenous designers Laurence Leslie and Euphemia Bostock.

In 1985 Bandjalang artist Bronwyn Bancroft founded Designer Aboriginals in Rozelle, Sydney—the first indigenous design company. Bancroft produced fabrics, fashion, and jewelry, and she employed young Aboriginal women in design, production, and retailing. With the support of the Aboriginal Medical Service, Bancroft staged a fashion parade at Printemps department store in Paris in 1987, working with Bostock and Mimi Heath. Bancroft's use of young Aboriginal models made a further political statement. Since the 1990s a number of indigenous fabric design firms have been established: Yurundiali Aboriginal Corporation and Spirit Lines at Moree, New South Wales; Tobwabba Arts at Forster on the central New South Wales coast; and Jumbana in Sydney, the company formed by John and Ros Moriarty using indigenous and nonindigenous designers to produce a range of indigenous-inspired textiles and fashions.

Black is possibly the preferred color option for urban Aborigines. While teenagers may opt for the ubiquitous hooded parka, professional men and women working as lawyers, filmmakers, or academics may choose to incorporate dramatic and distinctive items such as an evocative string necklace, a head scarf by an Aboriginal artist, and an Akubra, the distinctive bush hat still favored by Aboriginal stockmen, usually worn with a hatband in the colors of the Aboriginal flag: red, yellow, and black. Equally they may eschew any overt expression of Aboriginality, opting instead for an elegant tailored suit from a designer outlet or retail store. The point is that today, the complex cross-cultural entanglements of a globalized world allow for such a complex and eclectic range of individual choices and preferences.

Dress has meanwhile become a focus of interest for contemporary artists. Engaged in the effort to give voice to their place within the broader framework of colonial history, some artists have chosen to transform tradition. Building on an earlier use of kelp as a water carrier, Tasmanian artist Vicki West has created a sewn vest (National Museum of Australia) like the armor of a cultural warrior. Wiradjuri artist Lorraine Connelly-Northey recreates the string bags and possum-skin cloaks of an earlier era using recycled wire mesh and rusted metal. Her work is represented in the National Gallery of Victoria, the Art Gallery of South Australia, and the Flinders University Art Museum in Adelaide. Other artists seek to draw attention to the unequal power relations of a settler society. Blankets feature in several of the installations by Julie Gough, a Trawlwoolway artist from northeast Tasmania, and Badtjala artist Fiona Foley. For Foley, blankets reference both gender relations between white and black and the items exchanged in return for traditional land under the terms of the infamous 1835 Batman Treaty made between senior Kulin men and John Batman's Port Phillip Association (later rejected by imperial and colonial governments). The knitted sweaters created by Bidjarra artist Christian Bumbarra Thomson for the 2002 Blaks Palace series (National Gallery of Australia and the National Gallery of Victoria) refer directly to designer clothing of the 1980s. Using strange proportions and confusing color combinations together with kitsch symbols of Australia like the boomerang and kangaroo, Thomson addresses the way in which colonial representations are played out against the wider framework of nationalism and the uneven power relations of a settler society. Whether modeled by indigenous friends or rehoused in display cases like museum exhibits, Thomson's knitwear challenges existing ideas of Aboriginality. These wide-ranging critiques of dress and its role in the broader framework of race relations unsettle the carapace of colonization. Such twenty-first-century initiatives are a sign that dress continues to evolve as a diverse expression of identity and difference.

References and Further Reading

Aird, M. *Portraits of Our Elders*. Brisbane, Australia: The Queensland Museum, 1993.

Bonnemains, Jacqueline, Elliott Forsyth, and Bernard Smith. *Baudin in Australian Waters: The Artwork of the French Voyage of Discovery to the Southern Lands 1800–1804*. Melbourne, Australia: Oxford University Press, 1988.

Cooper, C. "Art of Temperate South-East Australia." In *Aboriginal Australia*. Sydney: Australian Gallery Directors Council, 1981.

Maynard, M. *Fashioned from Penury Dress as Cultural Practice in Colonial Australia*. Cambridge: Cambridge University Press, 1994.

Maynard, M. "Indigenous Dress." In *The Oxford Companion to Aboriginal Art and Culture*, edited by Sylvia Kleinert and Margo Neale, 384–390. Melbourne, Australia: Oxford University Press, 2000.

Maynard, M. *Dress and Globalisation*. Manchester, UK: Manchester University Press, 2004.

Reynolds, Amanda J., ed. *Keeping Culture: Aboriginal Tasmania*. Canberra: National Museum of Australia, 2006.

Smyth, R. Brough. *The Aborigines of Victoria*. 2 vols. Melbourne, Australia: John Currey O'Neil, 1972. (Originally published in 1876.)

Sylvia Kleinert

See also Dressing the Body in the Western Desert; Aboriginal Dress in Arnhem Land; Aboriginal Dress in the Kimberley, Western Australia; The Australiana Phenomenon in Australia.

Snapshot: Aboriginal Skin Cloaks

In customary societies Aboriginal people were minimally clothed until contact with Europeans began to alter their habits. One exception was the skin cloaks widely worn by men and women throughout temperate zones of southeastern and western Australia. Cloaks were their main article of dress, important as rugs for warmth, but also for ceremonial use, trade, and as burial shrouds. Indigenous peoples made a variety of cloaks from different types of skin: possums, kangaroos, wallabies, and other fur-bearing animals. These were specific to locations where they were trapped and were decorated in ochers with clan-specific motifs. Very few cloaks have survived. It is interesting that the practice of cloak making has begun to be revived in the twenty-first century.

A skin cloak was worn by placing it over one shoulder and under the other, fastened at the neck using a small piece of bone or wood. Wearing the cloak this way allowed for unrestricted movement of both arms, and daily activities could be carried out with ease. Some almost reached the ground; others were shorter, at knee level. The cloaks were worn either with the fur on the outside or on the inside, depending on the weather. If it was raining, the fur would be worn on the outside, providing the same waterproof qualities as it did to the animal. The cloaks were also used as rugs to sleep on. Many women wore cloaks that had a special pouch at the back in which they could easily carry a small child.

The many processes involved in the making of these cloaks were complex and time-consuming. Men trapped the animals, and women incised the designs and sewed the skins together. Some cloaks used up to seventy skins, taking over a year to collect before beginning the process of making them. Once the skins were taken from the animals, women removed the flesh using a sharp stone implement or mussel shell. The skins were then stretched over bark and hung out to dry, often near a fire. This would slightly tan them and protect them from insect attack. After the skins dried they were rubbed with fat, ochers, and even ashes to keep them supple. The cloaks were sewn together using sinew, which was taken from the tails of kangaroos. Holes were pierced through the skins using a sharp pointed stick or a pointed bone needle. The sinew was then threaded through the premade holes to form the cloak.

There appears to have been some difference in the manufacture of cloaks across Australia. In New South Wales, Victoria, and South Australia the skins were shaped into square pelts and then sewn together. The cloaks from western Australia are called *buka* or *boka* and are mainly of whole kangaroo skins sewn together, leaving the tails to hang at the bottom of the cloak.

Designs incised into the leathery side of the skin were important to both wearer and the clan group. The combination of patterns helped identify the wearer and what group he or she came from. The motifs often found on the cloaks from southeastern Australia include naturalistic figures, cross-hatching, wavy lines, diamonds, geometric designs, lozenges, and zigzag patterns. When wearing the fur on the inside the spectacular designs incised into the skins could be clearly seen.

Anthropologist John Fraser, in his book *The Aborigines of New South Wales* (1892), discussed the meaning of the patterns found on the cloaks. He suggested that each family had

Australian Aboriginal artists Lee Darroch and Vicki Couzens have recently begun reviving the tradition of skin cloak making. This cloak is titled "Thanampool Kooramook, Gunya-Winyarr," meaning "women's possum cloak" in Couzens's Keeray Wurrong language and Darroch's Yorta Yorta language. Cloak made for Yinalung Yenu: Women's Journey exhibition. Powerhouse Museum.

their own design, or what Aboriginal people called a *mombar-rai*, incised onto the cloak, which helped identify the owner. He said that a friend had told him that he had an opossum cloak that a man of the Kamalarai tribe made for him a long time ago, who had marked it with his own mombarrai. When the cloak was later shown to another Aboriginal, he remarked, "I know who made this; here is his 'mombarrai'" (p. 198).

Anthropologist Alfred Howitt noted in his book *The Native Tribes of South-East Australia* (1904) the importance of patterns on cloaks and how these were a way of identifying wearers. He said that each man's rug was marked with distinctive signs of ownership, and designs from his possum-skin rug could also be inscribed on trees around his burial site. Other commentators noted that individual designs on each pelt could represent rivers, camps, grubs, snakes, lizards, and plants.

There are many reasons why the majority of skin cloaks have not survived. One is because when a person died all their belongings were disposed of, and some people were wrapped in their skin cloaks after death. During early colonial days institutions were not capable of adequately preserving these cloaks, especially as they were highly susceptible to insect attacks. But a major reason was the introduction of European-style clothing. This was easy to obtain and discouraged Aborigines from making cloaks. With the annual issuing of blankets by the Crown (from 1816 in New South Wales), the manufacture and use of skin cloaks began to cease.

There are only fifteen skin cloaks located in museums within Australia and overseas. In Australia these are held in the Western Australian Museum; Gloucester Lodge Museum, Yanchep, Western Australia; the South Australian Museum; and the Museum of Victoria. Overseas there are cloaks in the Smithsonian Institution, Washington, D.C.; the British Museum, London; the Museum of Ethnology, Berlin, Germany; and the Luigi Pigorini National Museum of Prehistory and Ethnography in Rome, Italy. European anthropologists collected most of the cloaks found in overseas museums during field trips to Australia in the late 1800s and early 1900s.

The most spectacular Australian possum cloak is the Lake Condah cloak, collected in 1872 and now held by Museum Victoria. The designs on this cloak feature square and diamond-shaped lozenges, wavy lines, circles, and naturalistic figures. Some of the pelts on this cloak have decorated ocher patterns. Diamond and square shapes were commonly used on cloaks, partly because they made the skin more pliable. In 1928 Herbert Hale and Norman Tindale from the South Australian Museum interviewed Ivaritji, a Kaurna woman from the Adelaide area. She specifically requested to be photographed in her skin cloak, as it was typical of the clothing she remembered wearing as a child. Her cloak is part of the collection of the South Australian Museum.

In the twenty-first century many Aboriginal people have begun to make these skin garments again. They are used in performances or often, as was customary, for nice warm rugs or cloaks. There has been a particular revival by a group of Victorian artists, the Gunditjmara sisters Vicki and Debra Couzens and Yorta Yorta women Lee Darroch and Treahna Hamm. After viewing the Lake Condah cloak they decided to make a commitment to ensuring that the tradition of making possum-skin cloaks was not lost, and to continue this practice for future generations. Lee and Treahna began making a reproduction of the Echuca cloak (collected in 1853, also in Museum Victoria), and Vicki and Debra began reproducing the Lake Condah cloak. They called this project Tooloyn Koortakay, which translates as "squaring skins for rugs." Ngambri elder Matilda House Williams wore a striking possum-skin cloak made by Yorta Yorta artist Treahna Hamm when she performed a "Welcome to Country" for the opening of the Australian Parliament in 2008.

The women continue to make cloaks for communities and museums, and Vicki Couzens and Lee Darroch made a cloak for Yinalung Yenu: Women's Journey, an exhibition held at the Powerhouse Museum, Sydney, in 2008. The cloak titled "Thanampool Kooramook, Gunya-Winyarr" means "women's possum cloak" in their respective languages. The spiral is the universal symbol of birth, life, death, and rebirth. The arms that come from the spiral represent bloodlines. Other markings, like the *coolamon* (a collecting bowl), represent gathering food.

REFERENCES AND FURTHER READING

Chisholm, M. *The Use, Manufacture and Decoration of Possum Skin Cloaks in Nineteenth Century Victoria.* Canberra, Australia: AIATSIS, 1990.

Fraser, J. *The Aborigines of New South Wales.* Sydney: Charles Potter, Government Printer, 1892.

Howitt, A. *The Native Tribes of South-East Australia.* London: Macmillan, 1904.

Mountford, C. "Decorated Aboriginal Skin Rugs." In *Records of the South Australian Museum,* vol. 13, 504–509. Adelaide, Australia: South Australian Museum, 1960.

Mountford, C. "Australian Aboriginal Skin Rugs." In *Records of the South Australian Museum*, vol. 14, 525–543. Adelaide, Australia: South Australian Museum, 1963.

Fabri Blacklock

See also Aboriginal Dress in Southeast Australia.

Dressing the Body in the Western Desert, Australia

The accounts of Aboriginal people themselves and other historical documentation suggest that from the time indigenous people came into contact with European clothes and other textiles such as blankets and woolen yarns, they were highly desirous of them. That period of contact was later in Central Australia than elsewhere (except perhaps eastern Arnhem Land). In the Western Desert, the area south and west of what came to be called Alice Springs on Arrernte country, it was as late as the 1950s and 1960s for some. The change from unclothed to clothed, naked being how Aboriginal people refer to their past selves, is within living memory. Prior to contact with the colonizing culture, Western Desert people employed no weaving or clothing made from skins. They did, though, spin human hair and the fur of various animals, and this formed the basis of their attire.

The construction of a postcontact social world via novel goods, a construction achieved through consumption, has been rather neglected in accounts of Australia. There is thus little written about the distinctive and creative uses of clothing by indigenous people, who, by their own account and actions, found clothing to enhance their humanity rather than to detract from it. Clothes work on so many levels. It is what clothes do, what they are able to embody and perform, their transformative potential, and what they communicate that is central to their desirability. There is also an ambiguity between the desire of Aboriginal people to emulate the look of "whitefellas" (a word indigenous people use to describe Europeans), in certain contexts, and clothing as embodying a resistance to colonialism. Historian Tim Rowse has suggested that both Aboriginal and non-Aboriginal stockmen working together on Central Australian cattle stations prior to the 1960s were vying for the attention of the same Aboriginal women. By donning what they felt were seductive, "flash," and prestigious cowboy clothes, the men were expressing a kind of locker room camaraderie in their competition for the attention of women. There is also the wearing of clothing to reinforce ties to country and kin. This is a mode of dressing that might have appeared as mimetic of white people but did, and frequently still does, embody distinctly different values.

The memories of older Aboriginal people and the written accounts of the settlers, along with their photographs and films, provide glimpses sufficient to piece together an idea of the clothing styles worn by the first Australians after contact. For the settler society, clothed Aboriginal people were a sign of assimilation, of loss of indigenous culture, and thus, more than any other imported material thing that Aboriginal people came to possess, regarded by many Europeans with ambivalence. This was especially so in the center of the continent. Aboriginal people were clothed, but mostly they did not have access to enough clothes, or the right clothes, or means of washing either clothes or themselves. (Dr. Charles Duguid, who was instrumental in founding a mission at Ernabella in South Australia, was unusual in wishing Aboriginal people, or at least children, to remain naked in order to reduce the possibility of the acquisition and spread of disease.) Particularly during the 1920s, 1930s, and 1940s, Aboriginal modes of dressing in Central Australia were thus most often seen by settlers as an outward sign that confirmed their inner degradation, pauperization, and loss of culture. By this time many Aboriginal people were gravitating toward the new rail depots, ration stations, and missions in search of food, clothes, and other commodities.

Written accounts of the dress of Central Desert indigenous peoples are found in the reports of various colonial officials—mounted police constables or mission staff for example—and these often contain judgment rather than just observation. Such accounts mention "rags" and "dirtiness," and perhaps, if the writer was an anthropologist or enlightened missionary, a yearning for the unclothed splendor of the native might be added. These are often in unpublished work, as in the journals of C. P. Mountford, who carried out anthropological fieldwork in the area. On the one hand, transitional clothing such as old army jackets, dresses made from sugar bags, and ragged garments evinced for such colonists a corruption of the authenticity of the noble naked hunter-gatherer, proof of the fragility of his or her humanity in succumbing to a craving for clothes. On the other hand, there was the imperative for moral or Christian decency in the clothing of the native body. It is apparent from the way that clothing traveled ahead of the settler via exchange among Aboriginal people, that cloth was highly valued and was kept and worn even when it had become shredded. Settlers and indigenous people were, in short, seeing and experiencing cloth and clothing in different ways.

There are many local histories of how and when Central Australian Aboriginal peoples obtained clothing, although it is not possible to detail them here. Central Australia is a vast area with many indigenous groups comprising different language groups and cultures. It is therefore only possible to sketch some generalizations in an account such as this. It is important to concentrate on what is and was worn on the body, and what it does. What follows is an account of the "stringiness" of precontact attire, the transition that people made to clothing, and, last, the development of a Western Desert clothing style or styles and the connections and disconnections that stringiness has with the latter.

THE IMPORTANCE OF STRING

The desire for clothing did not obliterate what Brigitta Hauser-Schaublin has called the "thrill of the line" for indigenous people in Central Australia. In the twenty-first century people use both strings and clothing to emphasize parts of their bodies and the dynamic state of relations with others. Striped clothing echoes the binding qualities of string. Although there were plenty of animals whose skins could have been used as clothing, such as kangaroo, dingo, possum, or wallaby, none were used in this way as they were in more eastern areas, except for men's wallets or bags. This is despite the fact that the climate in the huge central area of Australia is very hot in summer but can fall to freezing during the cold months. Western Desert people employed, and continue to employ, fires to keep warm, sleeping between them. Instead of clothes, the hair of humans and the fur of animals was spun into strings that were used to create attachments between people. Different animal furs yielded various textures and colors of string. String could be colored using ochers or white pipe-clay mixed with fat.

Anthropologist Barbara Glowsceski has argued that for the Warlpiri people both cloth and hair string are analogous to the bond between mother and child during pregnancy. At birth the child is detached from its mother, and then once again a boy is detached from her at his initiation. She suggests that clothing is a symbol both of the alliance between men and their need for physical autonomy. Glowsceski also records cloth being used as payment in ritual.

If string was a means of attaching and detaching, of binding various body areas, ochers mixed with fat resurfaces the skin, effecting a means of creating startling and immediately visible imagery but also making apparent a shift in an individual's emotional and social status. In the 1890s Spencer and Gillen recorded Arrernte widows as being smeared—hair, faces, and breasts—with white clay during the mourning period. Ochers of reds and yellows, white pipe-clay, and ashes and black charcoal were, and indeed are, used mixed with grease to paint designs on skin for ceremony. There appears to remain a differentiation between body painting and clothes, between the agency of skin and cloth in ceremonies that access the Dreaming Ancestors. (*Dreaming* is an English term for the period and events that created the world through the actions of Aboriginal ancestral beings who take many forms: animal, bird, plant, human. Each language group has their own term for this.) Aboriginal people in Central Australia seem to have valued cloth for its ability to perform a transformation of body surfaces. Clothing can replace, augment, or expand the role of ochers in recoloring the skin, but in secret sacred religious contexts, designs painted onto the bodies of dancers and, for men, sometimes augmented with down, is not replaceable with cloth. The clothing that people choose for everyday wear does not mimic in its iconography secret ceremonial designs, but in its color contrasts or texture it might allude to this. Cloth has thus come largely to serve the purposes of both string and ocher, except in rituals concerning the Ancestral Dreamings.

Returning to string wear, Aboriginal people spun animal fur and human hair into two-ply string and from this made garments for the body that were meant less to conceal than to draw attention to certain topographical features. These included the neck, upper arms, waist, pubic area, and head, especially forehead and nose. Pubic tassels for men, for example, were made to decorate rather than conceal: Europeans reported in the first half of the twentieth century that for older men they were made of dark fur and human hair string, then colored with red ocher, while younger men wore tassels of white rabbit fur. Color was used to differentiate the rank of a man. The decorative tufts of the fur string worn by Musgrave men were attached to the pubic hairs. The headband that initiated men wore and still wear was of red ochered string. During contemporary ritual men and women frequently substitute red cloth for red string.

Pubic "aprons," that is, string belts with a section of fringe, were also worn by both sexes. However, the length of the fringe and the context of wear and gender of the wearer varied. As a patrol officer for the Presbyterian Mission Board, J.R.B. Love recorded a frontal apron of kangaroo fur string worn by a man in the Macdonnell Ranges, near Alice Springs. Spencer and Gillen recorded that women north of the Ranges wore small aprons formed of strands of fur. String aprons were also worn by girls before puberty, but less often (if at all) by boys.

Men's use of articles of string around the waist seems also to have been common across the region. Ian Dunlop's films, made with a Martu family group who had just "come in" from the desert in the early 1960s, takes them back to the place they had just left and shows them customarily attired, that is, more or less unclothed. The father, Minma, wears a hair string belt and through this hitches the heads of all he catches, mostly lizards and a rabbit, so that their bodies and tails dangle around his body. Such belts were also used to carry boomerangs.

A shaped bone was a common nasal decoration throughout the region, passed through a piercing in the nasal septum. These bones were often embellished with transverse incisions or by the addition of feathers. The last generation of people who were born in the bush are those who still wear these during ceremony. Bones, feathers, teeth, seeds, and the tail tips of dingo and bandicoots were all used to elaborate string wear. For example, according to Spencer and Gillen, animal teeth or bones embedded in spinifex grass resin were used as forehead pendants, suspended from red ochered string. These would have thus been of contrasting colors—the dark resin against white bones or teeth.

Arrernte women wore a necklet of fur string, bound around with more string and red ochered, and a similar headband. Women also wore strings of seeds, bright red and shiny, of the bean tree (*Erythrina verspertilio*), either as long strings redoubled, or hitched under each armpit. Upper armbands, attire for men, could be, like headbands, elaborated with feathers, white or pink cockatoo for example, or emu or owl feathers. Hairstyles also indicated status for men. Emu feathers, which are long, narrow, and pliable, were used as wrapping for precious items and also to form the padding for the initiated man's chignon, which was bound with hair and attached low at the back of his head. Women and young girls wore gum nuts that were threaded onto the base of locks of hair around the face area. These were excellent, women said, for keeping the persistent and small bush flies out of the wearers' eyes. The hairstyle that covers a woman's forehead, in which she loops longer hair over it, is one worn by women about to symbolically lose their sons or grandsons at the time of initiation.

Aboriginal people did use shoes, perhaps in times of great heat or cold, to protect their soles. Richard Gould, for example, recorded a Ngaanyatjara woman making sandals from bark during his travels with her family in the 1960s. *Kurdaitcha* shoes (assassin's shoes) were, and possibly still are, made to obscure an assassin's footmarks using string and emu feather matted together to form a sandal in such a way as to leave no traces of his passage.

Since the demand for string was considerable, both for clothing the body and for less quotidian uses, indigenous people rapidly saw the potential for ready-made string, one of the novel goods the settler culture offered. The Ernabella Mission in South Australia ran sheep from its inception in 1937 to provide employment for the Pitjantjatjara and Yankunytjatjara people who came in from the bush. The mission began an employment initiative for women in the Ernabella craft room based on the wool grown locally. Women learned to adjust their spinning tension to wool. The brightly colored sweaters that the young women craft workers knitted for themselves at Ernabella in 1951 were unraveled by their male kin to use in ritual objects and headbands. Yet despite being taught knitting in the craft room, it is crochet that has become an embedded practice of women across the Western Desert.

Ooldea, situated further south in South Australia, is an important indigenous ritual site with its permanent waterhole, a place that became a stop on the railway line. It attracted many Western Desert people in the early decades of the twentieth century. Here spinning native string was a universal occupation for indigenous people, including children. But the settlers' industrially produced wool yarn was also greatly in demand, and old socks and other articles were always being unthreaded for their wool. It was at Ooldea that Daisy Bates, who lived there for many years championing the cause of Aboriginal people in pragmatic ways and collecting much ethnographic data, met new arrivals from the desert ranges and gave them clothes. She records in her letters their delight with the clothing that they received. By 1941, when Ronald and Catherine Berndt were fieldworkers in Ooldea, they noted that any money people received was spent on clothing, knives, axes, and colored wool.

More textile-like sheets were created by the Arrernte by knotting string in rows, to arrive at strips or panels. They also flattened out skeins of possum string for men's headbands. The panels were plastered with kaolin and might be left white or embellished with red or yellow ocher designs, depending on requirements. The resemblance to industrially produced printed scarves used today as headbands is resonant. Much clothing with stripes that run around the body is popular now. The first sweaters mentioned above, knitted by the Ernabella girls, were of stripes that encircled the torso. Beanies (woolen hats), almost always of a design of concentric stripes, are ubiquitous Western Desert wear during winter for men and women. They are the topological concentric circles that Nancy Munn has pointed out in her Walpiri iconography as multivalent—breasts or hills for example—when viewed from above, or as successive layers of becoming through each colored stripe. The hats are also reminiscent of the doughnut-shaped headrest made from hair string bound around grass that women used to carry wooden dishes full of water as they walked through the country in the past. The carefully arranged parallel strings of headbands are like Western Desert art, in which no line must cross another. Aboriginal people consider that string keeps what it binds safe.

THE ADVENT OF CLOTHING

Items of settler material culture, such as ration-issue blankets and sugar and flour bags, often traveled ahead of actual contact with non-Aboriginal people. These items were exchanged among indigenous people themselves, although clothes were part of direct exchange with the settlers. This occurred at first randomly through doggers (men who lived off the government bounty offered on dingo skins—native dogs—to prevent their damage to the pastoral industry), then as part of rations and through the sexual relationships of Aboriginal women with non-Aboriginal men. The women who spun the Ernabella wool were paid in rations and dresses as an incentive for them to stay on the mission. The clothes that young women especially wanted were bright, printed dresses. Women often obtained dresses from white men as a result of sexual liaisons. Anthropologist Annette Hamilton recorded that many of her informants at Mimili in 1970–1971

recalled actively seeking such liaisons as young women and were appreciative of the material rewards, especially of clothing. Nganyintja, a Pitjantjatjara woman, remembered this too. By the 1950s clothing (and flour) had become a part of marriage payment.

The nature of Aboriginal clothing during the early years of contact varied considerably with age, gender, and location. The missionary J.R.B. Love visited Finke Well, where he noted, in his unpublished "Journal of an Expedition from Leigh's Creek," a large number of blacks gathered. The women, he considered, were rather better dressed than the men. Their clothing was a single garment that covered them and reached to about the knees, mostly dirty and ragged. The young men were dressed in shirts, trousers, boots, and hats like Europeans. But the old men had only a short and rather inadequate shirt. From the point of view of the old indigenous men, the powerful players in this scene, they were probably indifferent to, or perhaps actively against, covering their genitals. Covering has of course now become an established part of what clothes do, but it took some years, perhaps decades, before this was an essential aspect for Aboriginal people, and it also seems to have varied with age, gender, and context.

Secondhand clothing has continued to be much sought after by Aboriginal people living in remote areas. Of course one reason is that it is inexpensive, sometimes free. But because clothing has become valuable and is used as payment in ritual, the acquisition of secondhand clothing is an acquisition of capital. The fact that the clothing has already been socialized seems to be an important factor too. The ability to rapidly change one's body color, one's "skin," is an embodiment of ritual power linked to the Dreaming Ancestors, and clothing can achieve this instantly. Certain set combinations of colors in clothes make visible and embody an individual's social circumstances of the moment. During ritual this may change rapidly over hours. To reiterate, the transformative potential of clothing was evidently a connection that Aboriginal people quickly made.

In the twenty-first century Pitjantjatjara and Yankunytjatjara people wear black and white clothing when one of their relations dies. As long as the clothing is black and white, the pattern of its distribution across the garment does not seem to matter. For women, wearing a black dress with white dots often fulfills this. For men, white shirts and black trousers are a common option. This is a style that is reminiscent of the Sunday best, inculcated by the mission, but Aboriginal people have come to reinvent it in their own way for their own creative purposes.

WOMEN'S AND MEN'S CLOTHING IN THE EARLY TWENTY-FIRST CENTURY

In bush settlement life women do not wear trousers, only dresses and skirts, although young girls, that is, teenagers, do wear loose tracksuit pants. Indigenous fashions followed fashion in the rest of Australia so that during the 1960s, film and photographs show women in much shorter skirts, during the early 1970s in maxiskirts, and so on. The knee length or longer dresses and skirts women wear now are combinations of bright prints, bright plain colors, stripes, and animal skin prints. But the colors or fabric patterns of clothes are, for much of the time, governed by the wearer's relationship and response to deaths, initiations, religious ceremonies, changes in the land, and other events. Mature women, who were Christian girls in the 1940s and early 1950s, favor the respectable dresses that are an updated version of the 1950s frocks with set-in (short) sleeves that they might have worn as girls on the mission. Out of the bush, in Alice Springs or Adelaide, women favor this sort of dress, often worn with white ankle socks and black canvas shoes. The contrasting socks are important as an element of style and marking out feet and ankles.

Younger women also cultivate an aesthetic of contrasting skirts and tops in highly saturated colors. Pink/orange, dark red/orange, pink/purple, and green/blue are common pairings of colors, of skirt with top. These color combinations are mimetic of sunsets or the seasonal colors of vegetation, such as new green growth or blooming mats of flowers. Wearing tops with sleeves in contrasting colors to the body of the shirt is another variation. Sports shirts provide this, often offering shine too, like the black glossy Adidas shirt with blue sleeves trimmed with black stripes. For ritual, women all over the Western Desert wear a uniform of a black skirt, and it is their breasts and arms that are painted with designs. The explanation for the black fabric given by Pitjantjatjara and Yankunytjatjara colleagues was that it was like skin and does not show the dirt.

Men's fashion has changed more slowly than that of women, as it has generally in Western fashion. Older men favor trousers and shirts of browns and beiges, which are already, or become, dust colored and are camouflage against the red dirt of the country. At night this renders them almost invisible. This camouflage indicates their ritual power and influence. Like the drabber women's outfits, all black for example, it is an outfit that men top off with a multicolored beanie, the concentric ringed hat. Men often wear their red headbands made from string or fabric, underneath their hats, showing that they are fully initiated.

The clothing that is seemingly the opposite of this style of elusive blending into the land is the flamboyant dandyish stockman, which most men, young and middle-aged, seem to adopt at some time. Many mature men were stockmen in their youth. The stockman shirt has a yoke in a color or print that contrasts with the main body fabric, which Pitjantjatjara speakers call *rikina* or "flash." A checked shirt, often with the sleeves cut off, is a more casual version of the stockman style. With this are donned blue jeans or jean-type trousers, preferably with a belt decorated with silver studding and a brilliant buckle. Pointed-toed, Cuban-heeled cowboy boots are also crucial to the style. To really look "flash" and attract women the stockman needs a wide-brimmed hat. The conventional stockman's hat is an Australian brand called Akubra, made of rabbit felt. Men also wear more striking hats with tall crowns that complete what has become a characteristic style of dressing. There is a strong element of sexual availability in this ensemble, of being on the lookout for a woman. It is a style that has persisted despite the demise of the stockman's work. Men's ritual wear is for public ceremony, shorts or trousers leaving chest and perhaps thighs bare for body painting.

CLOTHING AS SOLIDARITY

Sportswear worn widely across the region consists of fabrics that gleam like well-oiled skin, but it also alludes to a wider black identity, a global identity as a black person in a black culture. Jogging pants are highly desirable wear for children and teenagers. The black shiny fabric with fluorescent stripes up the outside of the leg, originally designed by Adidas (with three stripes) is much copied by other clothing manufacturers but with two or four stripes, preventing copyright infringements. For both young men and women, sportswear is fashionable. Boys and young men wear singlets (sleeveless vests) with the team numbers of black American basketball players on the backs. These vests are in basketball team stripes, such as those for the Los Angeles Lakers, orange or yellow singlets with black and white trim and numbers. Chicago Bulls shirts are also a favorite: red with white numbers. Girls wear these shirts too, but with short sleeves. At Ernabella in 1999 there were new versions of the basketball shirts with the player's photographic portrait printed on the backs of the garments instead of his number. The Ernabella store had a large number of Manchester United soccer shirts printed with the image of an iconic white British player (David Beckham), and these of course did not sell. Black teenagers did not want a "whitefella" emblazoned on their back when they could have a powerful black basketball player there. Similarly, Rastafarian clothing featuring the face and lyrics of Bob Marley is widely purchased by Aboriginal people. This solidarity with black people is enhanced by the fact that Rasta colors—red, yellow, green, and black—are a series or sequence of colors that are of great salience across all central desert cultures. Clothes printed with the red, yellow, and black Aboriginal flag are also best-sellers.

Another sports-generated style, worn particularly by young people of both genders and by adult men, is for football (which in Australia means soccer, various rugby codes, and the Australian football league [AFL]). These clothes are mostly a local identification with AFL teams, whose stripes are always of two or three contrasting colors. Each remote settlement identifies with a team geographically near to it. The two Adelaide AFL teams, the Adelaide Crows and the Port Power, are the sides supported by Ernabella people, and everyone wears beanies in their colors and sometimes jackets and socks.

The continuity between string wear and ochered skin and clothed bodies is, at first, far from evident, but many of the choices that Aboriginal people make do follow precontact concepts, most notably in the evocation of string in cloth patterns. The shiny synthetic fabrics of contemporary sportswear imitate shiny fat and ocher-covered skin even if the labels that kids desire are, like those desired by kids in London or New York, Nike and Adidas. These clothes of man-made fiber fabrics are not really practical for the Central Desert climate, but that is overridden by the look, the "flashness."

Donning Western clothing was not and is not a performance of Western or settler identity by Aboriginal people, who choose to remain living on remote settlements in Central Australia. Clothing is a performance of something else far more complex and in certain contexts far more ambiguous.

References and Further Reading

Berndt, R., and C. Berndt. *A Preliminary Report of Fieldwork in the Ooldea Region, Western South Australia*. Sydney: Australian Medical Publishing, 1945.

Bolam, A.G. *The Trans-Australian Wonderland*. Melbourne, Australia: McCubbin-James Press, 1923.

Comaroff, J. "The Empire's Old Clothes: Fashioning the Colonial Subject." In *Cross Cultural Consumption: Global Markets Local Realities*, edited by David Howes, 19–38. London and New York: Routledge, 1996.

Dunlop, Ian, director. *A Family Moves Camp and Gathers Food.* Film documentary. Part 4 of *People of the Australian Western Desert.* Australian Commonwealth Film Unit, 1966.

Elkin, A.P. "Reaction and Interaction: A Food Gathering People and European Settlement in Australia." *American Anthropologist* 53, no. 2 (1951): 164–186.

Gibson, J. "Digging Deep: Aboriginal Women in the Oodnadatta Region of South Australia in the 1980s." In *Women's Rites and Sites: Aboriginal Women's Cultural Knowledge,* edited by P. Brock, 60–75. St. Leonards, Australia: Allen and Unwin, 1989.

Gould, Richard A. *Yiwara: Foragers of the Australian Desert.* New York: Scribner, 1969.

Hamby, L., and D. Young. *Art on a String: Threaded Objects from the Western Desert and Arnhem Land.* Canberra, Australia: Object Gallery, Australian Centre for Craft and Design and Centre for Cross Cultural Research, 2001.

Hauser-Schaublin, Brigitta. "The Thrill of the Line and the String or Why the Abelam Are a Non Cloth Culture." *Oceania* 67, no. 2 (1996): 81–106.

Hilliard, W. *The People in Between: The Pitjantjatjara People of Ernabella.* London: Hodder and Stoughton, 1968.

Miller, Daniel. "Consumption." In *The Handbook of Material Culture,* edited by C. Tilley, W. Keane, S. Küchler, M. Rowlands, and P. Spyer, 341–354. London, Thousand Oaks, CA, and New Delhi: Sage, 2006.

Munn, Nancy. *The Warlpiri Iconography.* Chicago: University of Chicago Press, 1973.

Myers, Fred. *Pintupi Country, Pintupi Self: Sentiment, Place and Politics among Western Desert Aborigines.* Berkeley: University of California Press, 1988.

Rowse, Tim. *White Flour, White Power: From Rations to Citizenship in Central Australia.* Cambridge: Cambridge University Press, 1998.

Spencer, B., and F.J. Gillen. *The Arunta: A Study of a Stone Age People.* Vols. 1 and 2. London: Macmillan and Co. 1927.

Diana Young

See also Aboriginal Dress in Australia: Evidence and Resources; Sportswear in Australia.

Aboriginal Dress in Arnhem Land

- Rock Art History and Early Anthropological Collections
- Types of Bodywear
- Mission Times
- Post-Mission Times

The items that Aboriginal people wore on their bodies in Arnhem Land, an Aboriginal reserve in the top portion of the Northern Territory, before contact with outsiders from Macassar and the rest of Australia, were influenced by environmental, cultural, and social factors. The landscape varies from the coast; Arnhem Land changes from escarpment to open woodlands. It has a monsoonal climate with hot to warm temperatures in both the wet and the dry seasons. Bodily items were not worn for warmth, protection, or modesty, but primarily for cultural purposes. In 2006 Louise Hamby first employed the term *bodywear* to refer to items that may be called body adornment in the Australian context. It is an inclusive term, as it refers to all items worn on the body or even carried, not just those used for embellishment. Precontact items were made with natural materials. The advent of missionaries, pastoralists, and anthropologists changed the resources used in their construction to include European manufactured materials. The presence of mission settlements, after 1923 in some places, imposed requirements for changes of dress for the Aboriginal people who chose to live there. Pubic covers and breast harnesses were replaced with trousers and dresses of rather plain fabrics. As time passed, floral patterns and bright colors started appearing in the clothes. Today's dress in Arnhem Land is reflective of a dynamic culture. Community members now wear Hawaiian print shirts, Indonesian sarongs, skirts, baggy football shorts, and guernseys (sleeveless shirts or jumpers). However, a ceremonial event will bring out customary items, which are often worn with everyday wear.

ROCK ART HISTORY AND EARLY ANTHROPOLOGICAL COLLECTIONS

It is difficult to ascertain exactly what Aboriginal people in Arnhem Land wore before contact with outsiders, but easier in Arnhem Land than elsewhere because of the remarkable visual records found in rock art. Among the types of rock art, painted ochered images are the ones that depict items worn on the body. George Chaloupka's study of rock art in Arnhem Land, *Journey in Time*, indicates that some of the earliest ochered images (fifty thousand years ago) are imprints of items of dress formed by those objects dipped in paint and thrown against the wall, most of which appear to be pieces of string and possibly some belts made from similar material. Depictions of material culture first appear in Chaloupka's Pre-Estuarine period of rock art, ranging from 9,000 to 20,000 B.C.E. One phase of this chronological period is characterized by human figures in motion, known

as dynamic figures. The majority of the small figures, less than fifty centimeters (about twenty inches) in size, are male, generally depicted with long headdresses and often carrying spears, boomerangs and sometimes axes. The males wear hair belts, aprons, or bustles and wear armbands, some with pendants. Often the women are depicted carrying bags and digging sticks. Later images from Chaloupka's Contact period (three hundred years ago) depict some objects of material culture in more detail and often include European items such as guns and clothing.

There are depictions of fiber objects in rock art across this so-called Top End of Australia, extending to the fringes of the stone country south of Maningrida. Murray Garde's Bawinanga Rock Art Recording Project of 1994 documented an excellent example of a dynamic figure near the Mann River. This figure is rare in that less than 10 percent of documented dynamic figures are female. She is running, wearing a hair belt, and carrying a digging stick in her right hand, held above her head. Streaming out behind her is a rounded triangular-shaped basket. It was not unusual for dynamic figures to be depicted with headdresses, armbands, and belts. Some of the types of bodywear were still in evidence, if not the exact form depicted in the rock art, by the late 1890s when missionaries, explorers, and others arrived in Arnhem Land.

The establishment of a more complete picture of what people were wearing in the early part of the twentieth century is made through the early known anthropological collections and photographs from Arnhem Land. The major anthropologists working in Arnhem Land were Sir Baldwin Spencer (1860–1929), William Lloyd Warner (1898–1970), and Donald Thomson (1901–1970). Others who were involved in collecting in this early time period included the missionaries T. T. Webb and Harold Shepherdson. It is from the collections of items now held in museums that the following information is drawn.

Baldwin Spencer, as the director of Museum Victoria (then known as the National Museum of Victoria) and an anthropologist, was responsible for a well-known collection. His position as Special Commissioner for Aboriginals and Chief Protector of the Northern Territory facilitated his work in the Northern Territory in 1912. It was at this time he made one of the earliest collections from western Arnhem Land (Kakadu and Alligator Rivers area), now held in Museum Victoria. He documented some items people were wearing in his landmark book of 1914, *Native Tribes of the Northern Territory* of Australia. From his 1912 field trip, approximately 30 percent of the items he collected were worn on the body.

William Lloyd Warner was an American social anthropologist who worked at Milingimbi from 1927 to 1929. Although his main concern was not material culture, he collected a representative sample of works including bodywear. Included in the original 1937 edition of his ethnography, *A Black Civilization*, is an appendix, "Murngin Artifacts," which includes some items of bodywear. Murngin was Warner's term for the Aboriginal people of northeast Arnhem Land; they are now known as Yolngu. Louise Hamby has researched his collection and has found approximately four hundred objects; items worn on the body comprise 20 percent of the total. In Australia Warner's collection is spread between the National Museum of Australia, the Macleay Museum, the Berndt Museum, and the Archives of Sydney University. In

America the major holdings are at the Peabody Museum at Harvard University and the Phoebe Apperson Hearst Museum of Anthropology at Berkeley.

Donald Thomson's Arnhem Land collection in Museum Victoria of over 4,500 objects and 2,500 photographs provides us with a snapshot of the time in which he lived in Arnhem Land, from 1935 to 1937, and again during World War II from 1942 to 1943. Thomson worked with people from over fifty language groups, including Djambarrpuyngu, Djinang, Djinba, Ritharrngu, Burarra, Liyagalawumirr, Gupapuyngu, Djapu, Mara, Wulaki, and Wangurri. One-fourth of Thomson's collection consists of items worn on the body. Within the broad category of ornament used by Museum Victoria in the twenty-first century, the body parts on which the objects are worn identify the categories employed in the collection, such as arm ornaments and head ornaments. So bodywear includes armbands, necklaces, chest ornaments, pubic covers, and others. Armbands comprise 63 percent of all bodywear. The next highest percentage of objects are headdresses, encompassing 15 percent of the grouping, and necklaces make up approximately 10 percent.

When these collections were made in the early days of exploration and settlement, clothing was thought of in terms of Western-style garments such as shirts, trousers, and dresses. Therefore, many outsiders did not really consider the items that Aboriginal people wore as clothing. Aboriginal people were not concerned by the fact they were not wearing "clothing," because they were wearing items made by themselves on their bodies and in their hair and had no need or desire for Western apparel. Everyone wore these items, from babies to very old people, and sometimes dogs wore items made for them. Donald Thomson wrote in his field notes on 5 July 1935:

> Have seen no naked women or children and only one naked old man here…although in many cases the fringe dress, etc, is quite inadequate. This old man never wears any covering.…A large number of ornaments, some worn over head and standing up in front, others hanging down, are worn, by younger men especially. (Thomson 1937, p. 1221)

At that point in history Aboriginal people were "clothed" in appropriate items and saw no need to adopt the cultural customs of the intruders in their country. The objects that collectively made up bodywear were complex, with variations dependent on gender, stage of life, health, and identity and were worn every day and for ceremonial events. As seen by the relatively high proportion of these items in collections, from 20 to 30 percent of the total, they were a significant part of the culture.

TYPES OF BODYWEAR

In Arnhem Land people divide themselves into two main groups or moieties: Dhuwa and Yirritja. There are many clan groups of each moiety. People of both moieties from eastern Arnhem Land refer to themselves as Yolngu, and their collective spoken languages are referred to as Yolngu Matha. Most of the early collections of bodywear are Yolngu, with the exception of the Spencer material. Everything belongs to a moiety, including the plants and animals from which items of bodywear are made, which makes those items moiety-specific as well. A general term for items worn on the body given by some Yolngu is *girringgirring'*, which can also refer to necklaces or to the type of grass used in

the making of some necklaces. One of the meanings for the word *girri'* is "clothes and parts of the body," aligning body adornment with the European practice of wearing clothes.

There are two or three ways of organizing all the items (such as by function, body parts, and perhaps by material), but the body parts where the articles were worn are adopted as general categories. First, head- and neckwear are considered The head and hair of Arnhem Landers was the site for many types of bodywear. Some items, mainly feathered ones, were designed to be either attached directly to hair or to be stuck in by means of a long pin. Pendants of feathers held together with beeswax with hair string extending from the end of the pendant were waxed or tied straight into the hair. Several of these are found in Spencer's collection. Hairpins are perhaps the most common hair ornament. Feathers bound together and held by beeswax in a triangular form have a pin made from bone or wood extending from the wax. The feathers used most often were cockatoo, brolga, and emu. Hairpins were mainly worn by men for ceremonial activities.

Forehead bands were of three basic types: flat bands, loose string, and pendants. String bands twined together, approximately the width of the forehead of the male wearer, were ochered either in designs or plain white pipe-clay. The ends of the strings were looped so that strings could be attached to tie around the back of the head. Loops of string bound at one point simply fit around the forehead. An alternative method of wearing the loops of string was to attach short pendants of wax and feathers to either end of the loops. These would be worn so they fell behind the ears.

Pendants were a subset of forehead attire. These were either composed of several small items, such as teeth set in beeswax, or a single item, such as a crocodile tooth. Of the multiple types, many were made from the teeth of kangaroos, crocodiles, or dogs inserted in wax or resin in a flattened form worn next to the skin. The waxed surface was sometimes ochered but generally was left plain. The wax forms varied from rectangular to semicircular, with the teeth extending outward. Larger items, such as the beak of a spoonbill or a single shell, were used for the single-item pendants. These could be worn by men or women, as was the case with nose ornaments. Another style of pendant, attached to a loop of string, is one in which multiple pendants made from string are looped over the circle of string. Joined to these strings are animal teeth or sometimes items like the claws from emus. Another variation was to attach a long pendant of strings bound in places by wax, and feathered pendants worn down the back of the head.

Customarily a sharpened kangaroo bone, bird bone, pieces of wood, and flower stems of the Banksia plant or other natural material were also used in the pierced nasal septum. This bone often performed double duty for women. In times of mourning it was used to cut the head in remorse. Although these are rarely worn today, many older men and women have pierced septums.

Necklaces in a general sense are known as girringgirring' or *manimani* in eastern Arnhem Land. The latter term makes reference to the neck, which is *mani*. Threaded items on some type of hand-spun string comprised the majority of necklaces. Shark vertebrae, either plain or ochered red, are specific to the Dhuwa moiety, as shark are "owned" by clans in that moiety. Rose Mamuniny, a senior fiber artist from Elcho Island, revealed this in an interview with Louise Hamby at Galiwin'ku in May 2001. "It is indeed special. For Djambarrpuyngu—Guyula and other Djambarrpuyngu groups—for Djapu, and for others D̲äti'wuy,

Ngaymil Gälpu. We sing this one, this one is ours." Shark neck-laces in collections are usually one strand, single threading that ties at the back of the neck. Sometimes there will be two strands joined together. This same style is seen in necklaces made from tusk shells, *Dentalium* sp., collected by Warner and Thomson. In both collections the dominant necklace form is a choker type with threaded grass stems, known as *nanarr'*. A continuous threading of grass stems is looped into a circle, and a tie is attached on both sides of the loops in order for the wearer to secure the piece tightly around the neck. There was immense variation in the material for the ties, with both ties usually being made of the same material but not always. Plain bark fiber string, hair string, feathered string, or pendants of fur or feathers could be attached.

In terms of chestwear there is a small group of items, known as ties by Warner and bibs by Thomson, that were worn only by men in ceremony. These were flat rectangular twined items, roughly twenty by forty centimeters (approximately eight by six-teen inches), made from string with string ties. Heavily ochered men would wear these over their chests for ceremonies and often grasp the far edge of the piece in their teeth. The bibs are now restricted to ceremonial usage and only for men who have passed through different stages of initiation.

Items known as *matjka* were chest harnesses or breast girdles commonly worn by women. They consisted of two equal loops of string approximately twelve to fourteen inches (roughly thirty to thirty-five centimeters) in diameter, bound together by wrap-ping in a section about six inches (fifteen centimeters) long. The wrapped section, often ochered with simple designs, was worn at the back, with the arms going through the loops such that the strings crossed over the breasts. From Thomson's field notes, a comment from one of his informants describes one matjka on 2 September 1935: "make himself look nice, that girl." Young men sometimes wore the matjka during one stage of their ini-tiation ceremony, reversing the roles of the boys with women. Thomson noted in 1935 that a Wagilag matjka was worn by a young man to "make himself flash."

Armbands, a further category of bodywear, worn on the upper arm by most individuals, made up a large proportion of items worn on the body. For example, in Warner's material they com-prise 25 percent of items of bodywear, and in Thomson's material 70 percent. Four categories of armbands have been delineated based on their means of construction: cut, wrapped, interlaced, and attached pendants. There is an additional type, tied, which is known only from photographic and oral evidence. This armband would be made from a piece of string, either tied once or wrapped around the arm and then tied. These were not collected.

Various types of animal skin are the material of armbands made by cutting. In the collections discussed, all of these come from Trial and Caledon Bay on the coast of eastern Arnhem Land. They are formed from a single piece of skin that is removed from the tail or leg of an animal. If it is the tail of a kangaroo, two or three armbands can be made. In most cases the fur is still attached to the skin. Bands made using a slit and knot combina-tion were made from the leg of emus. There is one of these in the Thomson Collection from a known maker, Matjirri the son of Wonggo, a local leader, in the 1930s. Generally men wear the skin armbands for ceremonial purposes.

A larger group are interlaced armbands. They vary in diameter and width, from those made for babies to those made for adult men and women. Murabuda Wurramarrba, from Groote Eylandt,

explained in a May 2006 interview with Lindy Allen and Louise Hamby that people wore them partly because they liked them, using the analogy of western jewelry, "just like Australian white—they love to wear!" Sedge grass (*Cyperus javanicus*) or lawyer vine (*Flagellaria indica*) are the materials used in their construction. Sedge grass, it seems, was used for armbands when finer widths of material were required. Lawyer vine would be split and shaved into fine strips in preparation for interlacing. The majority of interlaced armbands have a plain surface, but some are ochered either in one color or more complicated designs. Interlacing of an armband was completed on the arm of the wearer by the man himself or by another person if worn on the wrist. Beeswax was rubbed on the surface to facilitate manipulating the strips.

The majority of armbands in the collections were constructed with the wrapping technique. Within this category are three groups: plain, feathers, and combinations of materials. The core material of these armbands is normally a thin strip of cane (*Flagellaria indica*) wrapped around itself a couple of times to the appro-priate diameter, and then wrapped with a base of vegetable fiber string made from the bark of the Kurrajong tree (*Brachychiton megaphylus*) or Banyan tree (*Ficus virens*). The string was some-times wound on a shuttle to make the wrapping easier. Occasion-ally the surface of the plain string armbands would be painted in simple strokes with ochers by men.

The armbands made with a combination of materials still had a base of bark fiber string. Possum fur, a Yirritja moiety item, was sometimes wrapped with the string or spun into the string. There are two types of feather-wrapped armbands: those made with *raman* or down and those made with small bird feathers, often from the breast of lorikeets. The raman ones are plain string, with the down either spun into the string or wrapped with the string around the cane. The down is distributed on all surfaces of the armband, not just the outside surface. The other feathered type of band contains whole mature feathers. The lorikeet feath-ers are wrapped onto the outside surface of the armband. The red breast-feathers belong to the Dhuwa moiety. Plain wrapped string armbands would be worn underneath the feathered ones.

Armbands made with the coiling technique are found in the material acquired by Baldwin Spencer from western Arnhem Land. The base or core material for the armbands is a strip of cane, probably *Flagellaria indica*. Coiled around the strip of cane was bark fiber, not spun string. These bands were connected with a coiling stitch not dissimilar to the coiling technique used by Arnhem Land women today for making baskets.

Armbands with attached pendants were primarily used for ceremonies like a boy's initiation. The main portion would be constructed by wrapping. Attached to this base would be two to three pendants. They were made from fur, feathers, or combina-tions of these items, often with beeswax nodules.

Belts are a further category of bodywear considered. Belts or materials that go around the waist have been worn by people of Arnhem Land on their own, or in combination with a pubic tas-sel of some description. When the two items are together they are thought of as a pubic cover. Belts could be a simple piece of bark fiber string or lengths of string tied around the waist. Wide bark belts painted in clan designs were also worn by men. A more complex belt generally worn on its own was made of human hair string. A length of hair string would be laid out in a loop in the same manner as making a choker necklace. At several places along the length of the belt, other string would be twined, keeping the strands separate. The entire structure would have ties attached from the loops. The belt would be placed lower on the hips, with the twined structure remaining flat. Hair belts were worn for ceremonial occasions and were sometimes made from the hair of a deceased male.

Items that Thomson classified as garments included mats and skirts, which had multiple purposes. A primary one was to cover parts of the body or, in the case of the conical mat, entire bodies. Groote Eylandt women held a rectangular-shaped piece of bark known as *yinukwamba* in front of their bodies. Women were usually hidden from outsiders, and when they did make an appearance, they held the bark for modesty. This style of skirt was made by sewing together broad-leaved paperbark sheets with strips of cane. Conical mats made of pandanus, called *nganmarra*, could be large enough to cover several young men. There was only one ceremonial use for this style of mat. It could also be used to cover the body while folded in half, or used as a working mat. A triangular flat mat made from pandanus is sometimes called a skirt and was worn primarily for ceremony. These were sometimes painted with ochers. They were tied around the body by strings attached to the edges of the skirt.

Pubic covers, sometimes known as *dhirrithirri*, could be worn by everyone in Arnhem Land but were not worn all the time. They were mainly differentiated by the materials from which they were made. Sometimes the cover could be as simple as a piece of string tied around the waist with the ends hanging in the front. More often the string around the waist served as a holder for a more substantial pubic cover. The simplest cover was made from a sheet of paperbark folded over the string. Bark from the Kurrajong tree (*Brachychiton megaphylus*) was the source of the fiber used to make several styles of covers, called *ballara*. Some were bundled together and the string was passed through a loop. Another method was to fold the fiber over the string and twine the top edges together. Feathers were also used as covers by tying them together and attaching them to the string. Possum fur was spun into string and attached to waist strings made of human hair, Kurrajong string, or fur string. The fur pubic covers were known as *bulnyin*. Men wore ones that were longer and narrow. Women wore those that were shorter and wider.

MISSION TIMES

By the 1930s in Arnhem Land several missions had been established at Oenpelli (now known as Gunbalanya), Goulburn Island, Milingimbi, and Yirrkala. The type of items that Aboriginal people wore changed dramatically from that point, not only for those who lived at the missions but for those who were on the fringe, living in the bush. For those who chose to live at the missions there were many rules to follow, including rules about dress. For the Christian missionaries modesty was seen as a virtue, and Aboriginal people had to be clothed in a manner that was acceptable for them, which meant European-style dresses, shirts, and trousers. Wearing clothing was most important to the missionaries, but this form of dress caused a decline in customary methods of making bodily attire.

In 1937 Lloyd Warner, who worked at Milingimbi in northeastern Arnhem Land, commented that the wearing of Western-style clothing by Aboriginal people in Arnhem Land had done more damage than any other aspect of Western culture. Aboriginal people became sick from wearing damp clothes, particularly

Layered colorful skirts worn by women in Arnhem Land in 2006. Much of this clothing is imported from Asia but is later made into skirts and dresses locally. Photograph by Louise Hamby.

during the wet season. Some caught diseases from the outsiders, and resulting infections often caused death. Warner felt the missionaries' desire to clothe people was deleterious to their health. However, the idea that they were not clothed was an opinion voiced from a European perspective, as Aboriginal people were wearing items of bodywear. In his book Warner made the statement, "The women's food bags (like the men's baskets) are so much a part of their ordinary equipment that the writer has placed them in the category of things worn. The natives think of them as such" (Warner 1937, p. 478). At that time it would be difficult to find individuals who did not wear something on their bodies, whether bag or armband. It is probable that Warner would have agreed with Donald Thomson and acknowledged the role played by items worn on the body. They were part of the cultural and social practices of the time.

For those living in the bush there were other changes as well. Even before missionaries arrived in their country, visitors were introducing items of material culture that were readily adapted or adopted into the repertoire of bodywear of Aboriginal people. The items most closely related to items worn include cloth, wool, and other yarns, leather, and beads. Generally speaking outsider materials are classed as belonging to the Yirritja moiety. Manufactured cloth was an important item starting with the coming of Macassans fishing for trepang along the coast. Cloth was known by the terms *djalinda* and *djärritjarri*. Other words for cloth, *manydjarrka*, *maradhakal*, and *barrambarra*, have extended meanings, also referring to clothing or dress materials. Cloth was originally traded and was a valuable item. It later became more readily available, particularly in the forms of rags and pieces of old clothing. These strips of cloth are the ones that start appearing in articles of bodywear. Pieces, known as djarritjarri, were used to bind feathers in hairpins, served as ties for necklaces, and were wrapped around armbands. In larger pieces cloth was used as pubic covers, draped over pieces of strings around the

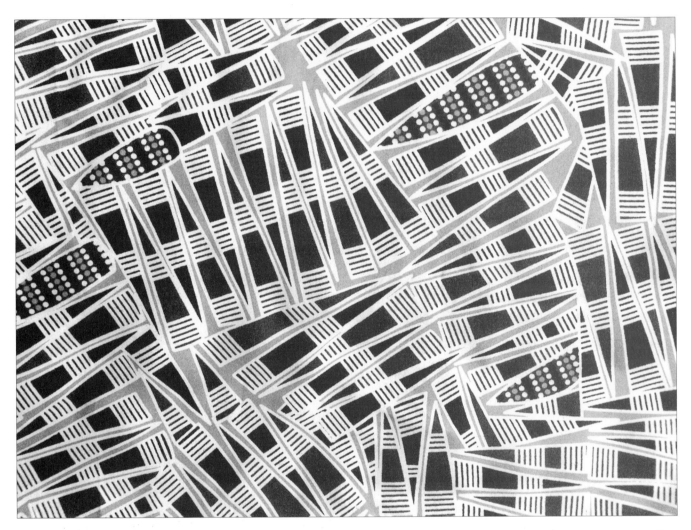

Detail of fabric reproduced from one of Wudalpa Ashley's paintings of stone spear points from Ngilipidji, the famous stone quarry in Arnhem Land, Australia, 2006. This fabric has been made into clothing and housewares. Photograph by Leise Knowles.

waist, or strips were ochered and used as headbands. An early example of a headband is one collected by Lloyd Warner that is now in the Phoebe A. Hearst Museum of Anthropology at the University of California, Berkeley. This one is made from a checked cloth that Warner bought in Darwin to use for trade with Aboriginal people. It came full circle when he then collected the piece of cloth transformed into a headband. Pubic covers of cloth have not been found in collections, most likely because they had not received additional treatment, such as the application of ocher.

Wool and other yarns were popular with Aboriginal people for several reasons. The color range was appealing, and its physical structure was such that it could be spun into other fibers, or respun into string they might wish to use. Wool and other outsider materials were generally used by members of the Yirritja moiety. The dominant use of wool was in items normally made with string, like bags, but other items of bodywear were also popular. A most dramatic example is a group of armbands in the Thomson Collection. These are wrapped with plain string in which brightly colored wool yarn has been imbricated into the outside surface of the armbands. They are most unusual for 1935. Through recent research, it is accepted that these pieces are probably from Nunggubuyu people from Numbulwar, located in eastern Arnhem Land in the Gulf of Carpentaria.

In addition to modified items like cloth headbands, Aboriginal people were wearing European items with their own bodywear. Leather belts were popular and are seen in both the photographs of Warner and Thomson. They were either worn as a waist garment alone or were worn in combination with attached pubic covers or tassels. The belts were also manipulated and made into necklaces and an occasional armband. Pieces of leather belts have been found inside string bags, along with other materials in the Thomson Collection.

Hats, especially caps and Akubra-style cowboy hats (broad brimmed felt hats often worn in the outback), are very popular. However, the idea of wearing hats is an old one. European-style hats made by Aboriginal people are found in early collections, for example the pandanus hat from the 1891 collection of Harry Stockdale from the Alligator Rivers area in western Arnhem Land. This hat is in the collection of the Australian Museum in Sydney. There was an early mission in the Kapalga area near Alligator River in the 1880s, and perhaps the European hats worn there could account for the influence seen on this hat. However, from Donald Thomson's field notes comes the statement from one of his informants: "We get from Macassar," referring to hats. Even in Thomson's time an old word for hat was *bathapu'*, which was really a basket worn on the head of a bald man. *Bathi* is the generic word for basket. Thomson also notes that a Wangurri man who was bald was literally called "head with basket on." In Gapuwiyak in eastern Arnhem Land, an old Ritharrangu woman, Minawala Bidingal, continues to make hats from pandanus, which she and others refer to as *djonggu'*.

POST-MISSION TIMES

As Aboriginal people became more closely associated with settlements of white people, whether they were missionaries or buffalo shooters, they adopted more articles of Western dress. As this clothing became accepted, words for these items also became part of the language. Customary items were sometimes still worn in combination with the Western garments, particularly when the Aboriginal person only had one article, for example, a shirt, *djät*, or a pair of trousers, *duratjitj*. The style of clothing worn depended on where the individual spent his or her time. Those working in the cattle or buffalo industry tended to wear the same things as their Western counterparts. On the missions it was the clothes of the women that changed the most dramatically. It was from mission times that a Western concern for modesty insisted that women cover the body. Early on, Aboriginal women were taught to sew so they could also make their own clothes, mainly dresses (*duratj*), skirts (*get*), and petticoats (*batigut*). One woman from Groote Eylandt remembered that they used to make dresses from the bags that flour came in. Women have adopted the wearing of clothes for at least sixty years and now have a style that is very much one determined by their own interest in color, style, and modesty. Sophie Creighton in 1996 examined the zipper-dress (*djaypa-duratj*) in detail since its introduction in the 1960s. This one-piece dress with a zipper down the front and two big pockets is also known as the mission dress, since its construction was taught as a means of earning income and covering the body. She proposes that this dress has become a "symbol of femininity," particularly for mature women.

In 2007 in Arnhem Land the zipper-dress was still around but had perhaps been surpassed in popularity by colorful skirts and tops imported from Indonesia. They do serve the function of modesty to cover the knees and breasts but perhaps work better than the zipper-dress, in that the skirts are very full, giving the wearer greater movement. Petticoats have been replaced by the wearing of more than one skirt or dress. It is not uncommon to see a zipper-dress with a skirt underneath. Of interest in 2007 was the manufacturing of Aboriginal-style clothing in the Northern Territory using Aboriginal artists' designs. One such example was cloth reproduced from the painting of Wuḏalpa Ashley of stone spear points from the famous stone quarry, Ngilipidji. The fabric was not sold but made into a range of dresses and skirts. However, with the design come obligations and rules of conduct. The family, Wagilag clan, own the design, so they are not allowed to wear the clothes; only the caretakers entrusted with their respectful and proper use can wear this clothing. It is a complex way in which Aboriginal customs have become entwined with Western clothing in Arnhem Land.

References and Further Reading

Chaloupka, George. *Journey in Time: The World's Longest Continuing Art Tradition.* Chatswood, Australia: Reed, 1993.

Creighton, Sophie. *The Zipper-Dress: Gender, Contemporary Dress and Identity—Yirrkala, NT.* Canberra, Australia: Australian National University, 1996.

Garde, Murray. *Mann River Region Rock Art Recording Project.* Maningrida, Australia: Maningrida Arts and Culture/Bawinanga Aboriginal Corporation, 1994.

Hamby, Louise. "Sighting Body Adornment: Insights from the Donald Thomson Collection." In *On Location Making Stories: Siting, Citing, Sighting*, edited by Karin Findeis, 23–34. Sydney: Jewellers and Metalsmiths Group of Australia (JMGA NSW Inc.), 2007.

Hamby, Louise. "Thomson Time and Ten Canoes." *Studies in Australasian Cinema* 1, no. 2 (2007): 127–146.

Hamby, Louise. "Wrapt with String." *Textile: The Journal of Cloth and Culture* 5, no. 2 (2007): 206–229 .

Hamby, Louise. "Lloyd Warner: The Reluctant Collector." In *The Makers and Making of Indigenous Australian Museum Collections*, edited by Nicolas Peterson, Lindy Allen, and Louise Hamby, 359–391. Melbourne, Australia: Melbourne University Press, 2008.

Spencer, Baldwin. *Native Tribes of the Northern Territory of Australia*. London: Macmillan and Co., 1914.

Thomson, Donald. *Unpublished Fieldnotes of Donald Fergusson Thomson on Arnhem Land, 1935–1937*. Melbourne, Australia: Museum Victoria, 1937.

Warner, William. Lloyd. *A Black Civilization: A Social Study of an Australian Tribe*. New York: Harper and Brothers, 1937.

Louise Hamby

See also Aboriginal Dress in the Kimberley, Western Australia.

Aboriginal Dress in North Queensland, Australia

- Climate and Dress at the Time of European Contact
- Everyday Dress
- Ceremonial Dress
- The Inevitability of Change: "Borrowed" Clothing

Although there had been occasional contact between Europeans and Aboriginal people in north Queensland since 1606, by the 1860s the increasing influx of Europeans and Chinese occupying Aboriginal lands made conflict inevitable. Until the 1870s tribal groups living in the rain forest region of Cape York Peninsula, north Queensland, escaped the upheavals of foreign contact and continued to lead the life of successful hunter-gatherers in this rich natural environment. Many items were unique to the region, such as bark blankets, crescent-shaped baskets, and heavy single-handed swords used only with ornate kidney-shaped shields.

Daily dress for men and women was minimal except for headbands, baskets, necklaces, nose pins, and sometimes skirts. But when ceremonies and fighting were involved, male dress and body painting was ornate and complex. Clothing did not denote power and status but lay rather in secret ritual knowledge.

Cultural life of the rain forest people of north Queensland from the late nineteenth century to the first decade of the twentieth century is known through only a few sources. These include oral histories handed down by Aboriginal people, and writings of early explorers such as Carl Lumholtz, a Norwegian zoologist who was in north Queensland from 1882 to 1883, and Eric Mjoberg, a Swedish entomologist who led a scientific expedition to Queensland from 1912 to 1913. Perhaps the best source concerning nineteenth-century dress and material culture in north Queensland is the work of the first Protector of Aboriginals for North Queensland, Dr. Walter Edmund Roth (1898–1905). Roth's collection is one of the best documented and diverse collections of Aboriginal artifacts ever gathered together by one person. Much of it is now held at the Australian Museum, Sydney. Even so, it should be remembered that the scant knowledge we have today of rain forest dress in the nineteenth and early twentieth centuries relies heavily on the personal interests of the collectors/observers, who were all males.

Roth's 1894–1905 collections (some made before he became Protector of Aboriginals) and descriptions of Aboriginal dress were made against a background of turmoil exacerbated by settlement of peoples from many different countries, in particular Europe and China. In 1865 the first property sales depriving Aboriginal people of their lands were recorded at Cardwell. In 1869 gold was discovered in the Palmer River area inland from Cooktown, and at Mulgrave nearby. Suddenly some thirty-five thousand Europeans and Chinese rushed to the goldfields and spread their tents onto land belonging to local Aboriginal people. Rain forest people were denied access to their lands to hunt and forage and were unable to wander across land to keep up trading links, which often provided access to exotic local materials. Shells, for example, to make necklaces and headdresses were traded by coastal dwellers for possum fur and ochers from inland peoples. Aboriginal people lost their land and livelihood and were decimated by diseases such as measles and influenza. They fought back but were outnumbered. But the rain forest people were never entirely wiped out.

However, the new settlers did not have it all their own way. The original track to the goldfields from Cooktown was called Battle Camp, because Aboriginal people came down from the hills to challenge the right of strangers to travel through their country without permission. There were many reports in local newspapers about Aboriginal communities fighting back.

The collection of material cultural items held at the Australian Museum and Queensland Museum gives a glimpse of a rich cultural life at a point of sudden alien contact.

CLIMATE AND DRESS AT THE TIME OF EUROPEAN CONTACT

The mountainous tropical rain forest region stretched along the east coast from Cairns to Townsville and inland to Mt. Bartle Frere and Bellenden Ker. It has the highest rainfall average in Australia. The dense canopy of heavy-foliaged trees entwined with prickly climbers and thick, claustrophobic undergrowth made movement through the forest almost impossible. Aboriginal communities living in the rain forest had little use for clothing except for ceremonial occasions and fighting battles. It was uncomfortable to wear clothes in such a wet and humid environment.

In the wet season, from about December to March, the rain forest people led a fairly settled life, sheltering from torrential rains in domed huts that were up to 140 centimeters (about 56 inches) in height and heavily thatched with leaves. Fires were always burning in the huts, and Aboriginal people wrapped themselves in bark blankets to keep warm. These bark blankets were made from the pounded inner bark of the fig tree and could only be made in the wet when the bark was pliable and soft. The blankets were not decorated. Roth saw one being made at Atherton; it took five to six hours of work to produce the soft sheet of bark, which could be folded into a package about 30 centimeters (about 12 inches) square. This was a good size to fit into a woven bag or basket. These blankets were also used as mats on the floor of a hut. There is some suggestion that bark blankets show a Papua New Guinea influence, together with grass skirts and headdresses worn further north.

The main tribal groups living here were the Djabugandjdji, whose homeland stretched from Trinity Bay to near Cairns; the Yidinjdji, who moved between the Atherton Tableland and Cairns and Innisfail on the coast; and the Mbabaram, who lived in the Atherton Tablelands. The largest group, the Djirbalngan, occupied land from Innisfail to Central Rockingham Bay. The Wargamaygan lived around the Herbert River region and went as far south as Hinchinbrook Island, and the Ngawaygi homeland was around Halifax Bay. Difference in clothing was minimal. The total population in the 1800s was thought to be about five thousand to five thousand five hundred people.

Aboriginal settlements tended to be small, compact, and fairly stable due to a permanent supply of water, a rich and varied plant life, and a careful use of available resources. These rain forest hunter-gatherers had a social structure based on kin, clan, and tribe. Status was not reflected in dress. Even ceremonial dress among the rain forest people did not especially distinguish the status of people. Together with maturity, it was the inner, secret ritual knowledge of a certain individual that was gained at different stages that allowed a man to marry and to be held in respect by his community. It was this knowledge together with age, rather than the outward show, that mattered. Not that this was understood by the early explorers, who talked about meeting Aboriginal kings or chiefs, neither positions existing in Aboriginal society. King-plates, engraved metal plates with a chain to hang around the neck, were given to what Europeans considered leaders of Aboriginal communities.

The rain forest people had a range of raw material at their disposal and showed great skill in all they made. Feathers, fur, bone, shell, wood, human hair, and rain forest vegetation provided their clothing, which kept them warm in the wet season and dressed their bodies for ceremonies and battles in the dry. Trading occurred between communities, but even so the environment still provided all the raw materials for making domestic objects, tools, and weapons. But by the end of the nineteenth century, European materials were increasingly being added to customary clothing and domestic objects. Aboriginal women at Atherton used to unpick the blue and yellow stripes down the center and sides of government blankets and weave the threads into their bags and baskets. Ends of necklaces and headbands were often bound over with strips of fabric and/or wool. Aboriginal people in contact with Europeans often adopted a variety of Western clothing and objects. Shirts, felt hats, and clay pipes were highly prized.

EVERYDAY DRESS

European descriptions of Aboriginal people invariably recorded them as being "stark naked." However, it is probable that male observers missed the occasional personal adornments being worn by both men and women. Women also would have been wary of strangers and would have kept their distance.

Most accounts were biased toward the more exotic ceremonial dress, and there are few detailed descriptions of everyday wear. Although everyday dress was sparse, from the partial accounts we do have there is evidence that there was versatility in the way some body decorations were worn and at times color was used to individualize items commonly worn. There were inter-regional variations depending on gender, availability of scarce resources, and some seasonality to the manufacture of specific items.

Roth wrote about the difficulties involved in describing local dress:

> A necklet may be worn as a waist-belt:…an ornament worn throughout one district with a special significance attached to it may have no meaning whatsoever in another; certain ornaments according to their materials of construction are found only in certain areas;…an article of dress essential in early life may be discarded with adolescence; and often nothing may be worn. (Roth 1910, Bulletin 15, p. 21)

One item of everyday dress noticed by all the male observers was the grass reed necklace. These necklaces were made from hundreds of small lengths of grass reeds cut to size with the sharp edge of a mussel shell or a stone knife. They were then threaded on a twine. The necklace could be from 360 to 408 centimeters (roughly 144 to 163 inches) long, with each grass reed segment measuring about one and a quarter centimeters (half an inch). These long necklaces could be worn wound round and round the neck, or else rolled into a thick loop and worn with their ends tied with bark fiber twine. Sometimes grass reeds were threaded on a number of shorter hand-spun bark fiber strings, and a tying string was attached at either end so it could be worn as a short multiple string necklace. They were made and worn by women, but in the Tully River region both men and women wore them.

There was a profusion of forehead bands and necklaces. At Cape Grafton, Cairns, Atherton, and around the Tully River region, Roth saw small oval-cut pieces of pearlshell fixed with beeswax to the beard and forelock of men. Rectangular-shaped pieces of nautilus shell were strung together on hand-spun bark fiber twine to make delicate forehead bands for men and necklaces for women. These little rectangular pieces of shell, usually about one centimeter (less than half an inch) long and just over half a centimeter (one-fifth of an inch) wide, each had a small hole drilled through the center using a shell drill. The shell drill was made of a sharply pointed piece of broken shell or kangaroo tooth, fixed with hand-spun bark fiber twine and adhesive into the split end of a small, straight wooden stick. When holes had been drilled in each shell, a double strand of hand-spun bark fiber twine, woven into a fine chain twist, was threaded through the holes to link all the pieces of shell together so they overlapped. The twine was made from the inner bark or sometimes the roots of a tree, the most common being the tea-tree, a species of Melaleuca. Most head and neck bands had from forty-three to about fifty-nine pieces of rectangular shell making up the head and neck band. Occasionally oval-shaped shell pieces were used, but Roth thought they had been traded in from the Gulf of Carpentaria. Sometimes a single pearlshell, nautilus shell, or piece of baler or melon shell was suspended on bark fiber twine and hung down the back of a man, or between the breasts of a woman (milbar or kwi-anchal). After contact, shells sometimes were suspended on strips of European fabric rather than hand-spun bark fiber twine.

Another form of headband was made from two eel cheekbones, held together opposite each other with a blob of beeswax. Several such units were then attached to a length of bark-fiber twine that was tied at the back of the head so that the bones were held across the forehead. They could also be worn as necklaces.

Women sometimes wore hand-spun bark fiber twine skirts made by forming loops over the top string to form tassels about seven to ten centimeters (about three to four inches) long. Roth said that at Princess Charlotte Bay he occasionally saw these skirts being worn around the necks of women. Women living around the Bloomfield River wore similar skirts, but Roth reports an early settler said this was a fairly recent occurrence, dating from 1898. Older women living around the Bloomfield River sometimes wore a circlet of hand-spun human hair string around the waist. An example of individualization was in the way red color was often woven into this human hair string.

Nose pins, worn by both men and women through the nasal septum, were common all over north Queensland. They were made of bamboo, wood, shell, reed, or bone. In the rain forest there seemed to be no significance attached to the wearing of nose pins, but in some regions it was connected with initiation ceremonies.

Lumholtz said that on the Herbert River older women occasionally covered themselves with a blanket from the inner bark of the tea-tree, worn over the shoulders, just covering the shoulder blades. On the Lower Tully River, during initiation ceremonies, young boys wore a bark blanket around them for concealment. By the late 1800s customary possum-skin cloaks and kangaroo-skin rugs were no longer being made, possibly due to restricted access to hunting grounds. Bark blankets also were fast disappearing as government issue blankets were given out.

One of the essential and unique accessories of rain forest life, for both men and women, was the possession of an elegantly constructed, crescent-shaped woven basket (*jawun*). Women used these baskets to gather and leach foods, especially the Moreton Bay chestnut, a year-round staple. Part of the process of rendering this toxic nut edible was to put sliced nuts in these baskets and place them overnight in a stream of running water, which leached out the bitter taste. In flood times women caught large quantities of small fish with these baskets.

The perfect time to make these baskets was in the wet season, as the lawyer cane was more pliable. These beautifully crafted baskets were made from lengths of split lawyer cane, a prolific climbing plant of tropical and subtropical rain forests. Strips of cane, with the prickles skillfully removed, were brought back to camp and woven into baskets. Lawyer cane was not collected until needed, because after five days, it could no longer be made pliable by soaking.

The distinctive crescent shape of the base of the basket was formed by stringing the ends of a length of split lawyer cane like a bow and attaching it by top-stitching to the inner surface. While women used these baskets for domestic purposes, men used smaller baskets to carry ritual objects, for trade or as a gift to a friend. Sometimes men painted the outer surface of a basket with customary designs using locally obtained red and yellow ochers, charcoal, and white clay mixed with blood to form an adhesive.

CEREMONIAL DRESS

The late wet/early dry season from May to September was a time of social and ceremonial life, supported by a plentiful supply of food. Among the plants were staples such as the black bean, zamia nuts, yams, ginger, and quandong fruits. Fish, eels, snakes, scrub hen eggs, sand goannas, scrub turkeys, tree kangaroos, and edible grubs supplemented the diet.

Large gatherings called *pruns* were held for dancing, socializing, trading, arranging marriages, and settling disputes by carefully orchestrated fighting matches. These gatherings, only held when food was plentiful in the hottest months, helped maintain relationships between people. Lumholtz talked of four such gatherings held at the Herbert River when he was there in the early 1880s, in November, December, January, and February.

Preparation for dancing took several days. Afternoons were spent in painting up, women to a lesser degree than men. Although body designs differed between men and women, the only colors used were charcoal, red, and yellow ocher and white clay. Dancing carried on into the evening, with performers silhouetted against the campfires.

Trade was wide ranging. In the Bloomfield River region, for example, dilly bags, spears, spear throwers, shields, swords, and red ocher were traded with their neighbors for stingray spears, shell necklaces, and forehead bands. Cape Bedford people exported iron tomahawks, nautilus-shell necklaces, and pearlshell ornaments up the northern coastline in return for forehead bands and kangaroo bones for awls. The Cairns and Cape Grafton people traded crescent-shaped baskets and grass-reed necklaces up the coast to the Mulgrave and Russell River people; from Port Douglas they got nautilus-shell necklaces and cockatoo-feather top-knot headdresses.

This was also a time to settle long-running disputes. Lumholtz watched preparations near the Herbert River in the early 1880s for what he referred to as duels between two men. On the morning the men covered their bodies with red and yellow ocher, and sometimes with a mixture of crushed charcoal and animal fat. Red and yellow ocher and white clay mixed with water were painted on the upper body in horizontal stripes to the waist, and vertical stripes down the legs. This was a fairly universal design. Males had their hair filled with beeswax so it stood out in large tufts, into which feathers were often stuck. The waxed hair shone and glistened in the sun.

Around Cardwell men smeared their bodies with a sticky milky sap from a tree, the white cheesewood, and then covered themselves entirely in white cockatoo-feather down. It was a most striking total body decoration from the top of the head to the feet. It was believed that the more complex the body decoration, the greater success in a forthcoming fight. Two men in fighting dress would finally stand facing each other. They each carried a highly decorated large rectangular or kidney-shaped shield in one hand and a flat single-handed heavy ironwood sword in the other. One sword from the Bloomfield River was 128 centimeters by 14 centimeters (approximately 51 inches by 5.5 inches) and weighed 1,643.9 grams (3.6 pounds). The small handgrip on the sword was bound with hand-spun bark fiber twine and adhesive to afford a firmer grip. Both objects were made only in the rain forests of north Queensland and were only used together. The large softwood shields were cut from the natural buttresses of giant fig trees. Designs belonging to the owner's clan were painted with lawyer cane brushes on the outer surfaces in earth pigments. The flat heavy sword was always used with one hand stretched over the shoulder so that the sword hung behind the man's back. The light shield was held to parry the blows. A fight to the death was not envisaged. After European settlement men started to use discarded chain saw blades, but these proved lethal, and this way of settling disputes disappeared in the early 1900s.

For neighborhood fights men also were highly decorated. They wore sulfur-crested cockatoo-feather headdresses, mounted on pliable beeswax. These headdresses were found all over north Queensland but were particularly common in the east coast of Cape York Peninsula. They came in many shapes and sizes and were worn only by men. One variety had the yellow sulfur-crested cockatoo topknot feathers bound together at the quills with red ochered hand-spun bark fiber twine and held together with beeswax. Circular cockatoo feather headdresses were made from the white wing feathers. They were tied to a wooden handle with hand-spun bark fiber twine and beeswax and pushed into the hair on the back of the head. Cockatoo feather tufts made from a bird's topknot stuck into a large knob of beeswax and fixed to the back of a man's head made him look as if he had a yellow halo. The whole effect was to impress and overwhelm the opposition.

Beeswax used in these headdresses was prepared by roasting over a fire. Once warmed, it was squeezed a few times in the hands and hammered until soft enough to use. When cold, it made a hard fixative. To stop the melted gum from sticking to the stones or hands, both were rubbed with animal fat. Feather tufts consisting of bird feathers tied to a small twig, or even single feathers, could be stuck indiscriminately in the hair. These feathers came from emus, white and other colored cockatoos, eagle hawks, pelicans, and bush turkeys.

In Cardwell and the Tully River areas a particular type of headdress was made. The man's head was covered with blobs of beeswax and feathers were stuck into the sticky mass. To remove the cap, it was cut from the wearer's head, including the hair.

Hair was usually kept short. Aboriginal men living in the Bloomfield River region usually cut their hair with a sharpened quartz stone, until these objects were replaced with glass. If in mourning, a person's hair was allowed to grow and was finally spun into human hair string using a twig as a spindle.

Part of male ceremonial dress common all over Cape York Peninsula was a pandanus armband (*mong-gan*). The leaf of the pandanus was first dried in the sun or over a fire for a few minutes. It was then cut straight at one end and angled at the other. The angled end was split into six strips and passed through holes in the straight end. These strips were knotted with a granny knot or just tied. They were about nine or ten centimeters (roughly four inches) in diameter and could be from three to six centimeters (one and a half to two and a half inches) wide. The outer surface carried a burned decoration. Men and women living in the Tully River region wore plaited lawyer cane armlets (*raingkan*). Will Mjoberg also described these body decorations, including the feather headdresses, kangaroo teeth, and pearlshell forehead bands, so some ceremonies were still being held during his stay in 1912–1914, even though European and missionary influence was all-pervasive.

Roth was privileged to see an initiation ceremony on the McIvor River, in June 1899, which lasted for six weeks. Initiation ceremonies were very private affairs meant only for men, initiated and those to be initiated. About one hundred and fifty men from Cape Bedford and the Endeavour, McIvor, and Starcke Rivers were involved. He said no special decoration was worn to signify successful participation in this ritual apart from body scars.

Burial ceremonies marked the end of a life. Roth recorded a detailed account of a burial ceremony at Cape Bedford on the east coast. When in mourning, men and women slept at and cried over the grave. Men wore mourning belts, and women wore mourning strings and covered themselves with white clay. The mourning belts, made of possum fur or human hair string, were worn around the waist. Mourning-string chains were made of bark fiber twine. These string chains could be several meters (yards) long, each link in the chain being about two centimeters (just under an inch) long. They were worn either over one shoulder, across to and under the opposite armpit, or else around the neck. One person could wear three different sets at a time. Lumholtz saw possum-fur string worn under European clothes as a cross-shoulder decoration suggestive of a possible mourning symbol.

THE INEVITABILITY OF CHANGE: "BORROWED" CLOTHING

In the 1900s the impact of European settlement changed everything. Dress was now recorded on film, and staged studio photographs were taken of Aboriginal men in ceremonial dress, posed with their painted shields and swords, as well as men, women, and children in European dress on mission stations or working as servants in European homes. Rain forest Aboriginal people living on the fringes of European society now dressed in cast-off clothing, skirts, sweaters, shirts, trousers, and hats. Communities in close contact with European settlers had been incorporating bits and pieces of European dress since the 1800s.

Linguist R.M.W. Dixon, writing about the Djirbalngan people in 1972, said:

> The original way of life has gradually broken down…. The last initiated man, with a full set of tribal scars, is now about 50. The last fighting corroboree was held in the mid-fifties: it was broken up by the police on the third day. Singing corroborees were still held from time to time in the sixties, with the approval and attendance of the white settlers. (Dixon 1972, p. 36)

The dramatic ceremonial body decoration in all its richness and color was no more. Ceremonies are now held as public events organized for tourists. The relatively unclothed bodies of the rain forest people are now fully clothed.

References and Further Reading

Cosgrove, R. "Origin and Development of Australian Aboriginal Tropical Rainforest Culture: A Reconsideration." *Antiquity* 70 (1996): 900–912.

Dixon, R.M.W. *The Dyirbal Language of North Queensland. Cambridge Studies in Linguistics 9.* Cambridge: Cambridge University Press, 1972.

Harris, D. "Adaptation to a Tropical Rainforest Environment: Aboriginal Subsistence in Northeastern Queensland." In *Human Behaviour and Adaptation*, edited by N. Blurton-Jones and V. Reynolds, 113–134. *Symposium for the Society for the Study of Human Biology*, vol. 18. London: Halstead Press, 1978.

Khan, K. "Adornment and Design in North Queensland: A View from the Nineteenth Century." In *The Oxford Companion to Aboriginal Art and Culture*, edited by S. Kleinert and M. Neale, 180–184. Melbourne, Australia: Oxford University Press, 2000.

Khan, K. *Catalogue of the Roth Collection of Aboriginal Artefacts from North Queensland*. 4 vols. *Technical Reports of the Australia Museum*, vols. 10, 12, 17, 18. Sydney: Roden Press, 1993, 1996, 2003; Sydney: Albion Place Group, 2004.

Loos, N. *Invasion and Resistance: Aboriginal-European Relations on the North Queensland Frontier, 1861–1897*. Canberra: Australian National University Press, 1982.

Lumholtz, C. *Among Cannibals: An Account of Four Years' Travels in Australia and of Camp Life with the Aborigines of Queensland*. London: John Murray, 1890.

Mjoberg, E. *Among Stone Age Men of the Queensland Wilderness*. Translated by S. M. Fryer. Stockholm: Albert Bonniers Forlag, 1918.

Roth, W. E. *North Queensland Ethnography*. Bulletins 1–8, Brisbane: Department of Home Secretary, 1901–1905; Bulletins 9–18, Sydney: Records of the Australian Museum, 1907–1910.

Thomson, J., ed. *Reaching Back: Queensland Aboriginal People Recall Early Days at Yarrabah*. Canberra, Australia: Aboriginal Studies Press, 1989.

Kate Khan

See also Torres Strait Islander Dress, Australia.

Aboriginal Dress in the Kimberley, Western Australia

A s in most other areas of Australia, the Aboriginals of the Kimberley were traditionally unclothed. For them, dress consisted of headbands and hair belts. Pubic tassels (made by tying multiple strands of spun fur or hair string into a mop, suspended over the genital area) were worn occasionally. Other elements of dress consisted of ornaments made from feathers, fibers, animal teeth, or shell, the use of which was often dictated by the ceremonial and social status of the wearer. More complex ornamentation was often worn within secret-sacred ceremonial contexts. In providing an overview of Aboriginal dress in the Kimberley, the evidence of ancient rock art and historical records for the past three hundred years have been considered along with changes caused by contact with Europeans.

THE KIMBERLEY

To understand the complexities of the dress of the region, we need to understand something of the geographical, environmental, and social conditions. Located in the northwest corner of the Australian continent, the Kimberley Region covers an area of some 345,350 square kilometers (133,340 square miles). It is bordered on the west and north by the Indian Ocean and the Timor Sea. The Great Sandy Desert lies to the south, and to the east is the Northern Territory. The central and northern Kimberley is a rugged sandstone plateau bordered and dissected by a number of large river systems. The vegetation is of open sclerophyll woodland type with patches of vine thicket and jungle, especially in the north.

Indigenous peoples across the region recognize at least six seasons, marked by subtle changes in the habits of flora and fauna and the climate. Nonindigenous people recognize two seasons—the summer monsoonal wet and the cooler dry period in the middle of the year. Because of the generally hot climate, clothing is not required to protect the body from the elements. The relatively high humidity, coupled with the presence of a wide variety of insects that scavenge on organic materials, makes it difficult for a mobile population to maintain or store articles of dress made from fragile fibers, hair, or feathers.

There has been an Aboriginal presence in the Kimberley for at least forty thousand years, the major time periods being the

A "Tassel Bradshaw" rock art figure, Wungkulin, the north Kimberley, Western Australia, photographed in 1990. The beardless figure wears its hair drawn back, tightly bound and tipped with an apical ornament. Tasseled armbands and bracelets are indicated. Around the waist is a tasseled girdle, with each tassel further divided and ornamented. The figure carries either a bag with a string handle or perhaps a feather fan in its right hand. Some rock art in this area is over twenty thousand years old. Photograph by Kim Akerman.

Prehistoric period, which covers the last forty thousand years until 1644 C.E., when Abel Tasman touched on the shores of the Dampierland Peninsula. The Proto-Historic period lasted from 1644 until the early nineteenth century, in which visits to the region by Europeans were infrequent and fleeting and there was increasing contact with Indonesian fishermen. The Historic period is considered to have begun with the detailed exploration of the coast and the interior, which commenced in about 1819 and continues until the present time.

The Historic period may be divided into four phases: The first three were the Exploration phase; the Settlement phase, which saw the establishment of a number of small towns across the region; and the Pastoral phase, which saw the pastoral industry develop as a major industry across much of the region. More recently the Contemporary phase has seen a decline in pastoralism, and employment is focused on pearling, agriculture, mining, and tourism. The Pastoral phase may be considered as commencing in the 1880s and lasting until about 1970, when the Contemporary phase commenced.

The region is linguistically complex. In the nineteenth century there were some thirty-one different Aboriginal languages, belonging to five distinct language groups. Five major cultural blocs, differentiated primarily on the basis of social and ceremonial organization, have been identified within the region, although it must be recognized that social interaction occurs between them. These blocs lie within the following areas: the Dampierland Peninsula, an area of land north of Broome; the central Kimberley plateau, which lies to the north of the Fitzroy River; the Ord River Basin in the east; the southeast Kimberley; and the arid Kimberley, which lies to the south of the Fitzroy River.

ABORIGINAL DRESS IN KIMBERLEY PREHISTORY

Some Kimberley rock art is more than twenty thousand years old. Much of the early rock art depicts humans interacting with one another or carrying out day-to-day activities. In the central Kimberley the most important early rock art style has been called the Bradshaw style, after the explorer who initially discovered it in 1891. More recently it has been referred to as Gwion-Gwion art—a name derived from the bird that some Aboriginal groups believe created the paintings. Bradshaw art provides graphic evidence of the complexity of ancient material culture made of organic materials otherwise unavailable in the archaeological record.

With few exceptions the earliest archaeological evidence shows that the stone tools are of the simplest forms imaginable, cores and the small flakes that have been struck from them. These simple relics are offset by the presence of ocher (pigments used in making dye) in many ancient sites and, in the south Kimberley, thirty-thousand-year-old scaphopod (tusk shell) beads. These shell bugles are not only evidence of ancient ornaments, but also of long-distance trade with the coast, at least three hundred kilometers (186 miles) to the west. Today similar shell beads are worn as multistrand necklaces.

The presence of the shells and ocher attest to more complex notions of dress and ornament than is otherwise indicated by the general archaeology. It is here that the importance of the evidence provided by the Bradshaw art becomes apparent. The art itself consists of a series of identified phases in which humans and many aspects of their material culture are depicted. The elegant figures, often less than three hundred millimeters (twelve inches) in length, have been painted with consummate skill. Unlike more recent rock art, there appears to be a complex preparation of paints that rendered them more stable, lasting long enough to become laminated within the cortical surface of the rocks on which they were applied.

The various phases of Bradshaw art style depict a vast suite of material culture elements that include weapons, receptacles, ornaments, hairstyles, and dress. They provide a clear indication of the complexity of dress, hairstyles, and ornaments more than sixteen thousand years ago. Equally important, they record changes in the form of these elements over time.

ABORIGINAL DRESS IN THE HISTORICAL PERIOD

William Dampier provided the first written records of Aboriginal life in the Kimberley. His brief and unflattering description gave no hint of the richness and complexity of the more esoteric aspects of Aboriginal existence. In 1688 while beached near Karrakatta Bay on the Dampierland Peninsula, Dampier noted that the adult Aboriginals he encountered had their central upper incisors removed and that the men were clean-shaven. He noted that the only article of dress he saw was a bark belt, in which tufts of grass or leafy twigs were inserted to cover the genitals.

Later accounts made by nineteenth-century explorers confirmed that the Kimberley Aboriginals generally went unclothed in their day-to-day activities. However, variations in dress, hairstyle, and body modification practices are found within the region. "Dressing" was not concerned with covering the genitals but provided clues to ritual and social status of individuals, as did ornamentation and manipulation of the body, including piercing of the nasal septum and cicatricization. Apart from those ornaments of shell, animal teeth, or bone, most other artifacts are of fragile organic materials, hair or fur, feathers and plant leaves, and fibers—materials that have rarely survived.

In 1865 the explorer James Martin noted that a group of unclothed men that had attacked his party had their foreheads and temples painted with a white crescent-shaped motif. It is possible that Martin was describing pipe-clay, possum, or wallaby fur-string headbands, worn on the forehead and tied at the back of the head.

In the southwest Kimberley, Martin noted that the hair of both sexes was allowed to grow long and was worn gathered back and tied in a knot about the size of a cricket ball. At Roebuck Bay men wore both beard and moustache. Martin also drew attention to ornaments worn, including pearlshell pendants worn on hairstring cords, and necklaces of other shells, probably scaphopod shells, and he noted a fondness for wearing painted body designs. (Pearlshell is a nacreous shell usually obtained in the Kimberley from the pearl oyster *Pinctada maxima*.)

Ada Peggs, living in Broome, made the first detailed descriptions of indigenous dress in the Kimberley in a series of letters written between 1898 and 1901. Peggs noted that mourning women rubbed their hair with ocher and fat to form thrums, and that kangaroo teeth were also attached to the hair to hang over the face. Peggs also recorded tribal marks, painted designs worn by individual Aboriginals when dressed for ceremonies, and the use of red ocher and small engraved wooden boards, worn by men across the back of the head to denote initiation stages. Ornaments of wood shavings worn on the head and in armbands of string wound around the upper arm during ceremonies are also described by Peggs, as are pearlshell ornaments—large "chastity" emblems and smaller pearlshells attached to hair string that were carried by messengers. Amulets to ward off sickness, made from small pearlshell blades or kangaroo teeth, fixed to hair string, were worn as necklaces by women. Single women seeking a husband were said to have worn necklaces of scaphopod shells. Nosebones worn through the septum are described, as are plumes made by binding the split feathers of cockatoos to bone points. Peggs also noted the use of masks in initiation ceremonies and footwear, the latter said to be worn by sorcerers.

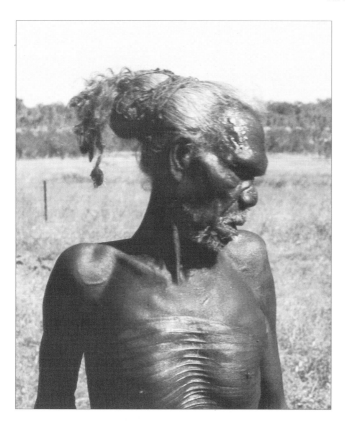

An elderly man from Kalumburu, the north Kimberley, Western Australia, 1975. He bears a dense pattern of cicatrices across his chest, and his hair is tied back in the *yakara* style once common to the region. Photograph by Kim Akerman.

Although living in a settlement, Peggs noted that when the Aboriginal men and women employed by the settlers finished work, they removed their vests and trousers, or sarongs, and resumed a more customary dress of string or hair belt with a piece of cloth or a pearlshell suspended from it. (Hair belts were made by creating a large skein of string spun from human hair or wallaby fur and were fastened around the waist with a simple tie. Some were wrapped to form a flexible cylinder.) Children wore no clothes. However, Peggs clarified that men and children generally went nude, but the women, however little covering they wore elsewhere, always covered their breasts—possibly with a piece of cloth.

MODIFICATION OF THE BODY

A brief survey of indigenous body modification, including painting, hairstyle, dress, and ornamentation in the Historic period must now be considered. Body modifications practiced in the Kimberley include hair styling, body painting, tooth avulsion (removal), piercing of the nasal septum, and scarification. As in many other areas of the continent, men generally wore their hair long while women wore theirs short. Women usually had their hair shorn at the death of near kin and contributed hair to the manufacture of hair-belts.

At the completion of the initiation cycle males would on formal occasions wear their hair clubbed back and tied in a conical bun. The bun could be fashioned around a core of bark or feathers or reinforced externally by strips of bark bound around

with string. When traveling or hunting, a man would use the hair bun as a wallet to carry spare spearheads or sinew lashings, small things that might be needed on the trip.

In the central Kimberley beards and mustaches were often shaped with the use of beeswax and tufts of feathers secured to them with the same material. In other areas facial hair was removed by singeing or plucking. At death a person's hair was plucked and either used directly or spun into a special cord used for divination purposes. In some areas the cord was subsequently used in the manufacture of ritual objects or hair belts.

From the descriptions provided by early explorers and settlers, and from photographic evidence, it is apparent that complex forms of body painting were found across the Kimberley—until World War II. At Broome, Peggs recorded that men were painted with elegant bilaterally symmetrical designs, reminiscent of the artwork found on engraved pearlshells from the region. On the Dampierland Peninsula broad bands of white pigment were applied horizontally across the legs, while one or more lines of white were drawn in an arc from the point of the shoulder to the mid-chest region and down to the abdomen. The white paint was sometimes of mineral origin but also often derived by chewing the inner bark of the caustic tree (*Grevillea pyrimidalis*).

In the early half of the twentieth century in the central Kimberley, body painting included naturalistic figures of goannas, fish, and possibly either yams or beehives, in manner similar to the more recent rock art of the region. In the same area the colors red and white are each identified with and used to represent a specific moiety. Red ocher reflects the crest of the brolga crane (*Grus rubicundus*), a major totemic figure associated with one moiety, while white pigment is associated with the silvery nuptial feathers that grow on the neck of the male bustard (*Ardeotis australis*), a major totemic species of the opposite moiety. Other colors used in body painting, but without the same significance as red or white, were yellow, usually produced from the mineral limonite, and black, derived from charcoal.

From about the 1920s new ceremonies that came into the Kimberley from both from the east and the southwest introduced a new style of body painting to the region. The novel mode of embellishment clearly reflected a desert origin. As well as painting with ochers, bird and vegetal down, often colored with ocher, was fixed to the body with blood, honey, or mucilaginous tree sap. More recently, in the mid-twentieth century body painting became very simple. Red or white ocher, mixed with water, is usually rubbed or slapped onto the body without any attempt at design. The exceptions again seem to be in those areas where there has been an influence from migrant desert dwellers.

Tooth avulsion occurred primarily in coastal areas in the southwest Kimberley and along the Fitzroy River Valley. Men and women had one or two teeth removed as part of their rites of induction into adulthood. On the Dampierland Peninsula the two upper central incisors were removed at, or just before, puberty but before, in the case of males, they were circumcised. The desert-oriented tribes of the south Kimberley removed only a single upper incisor. Tooth avulsion was not practiced in the north, central, and eastern Kimberley. The piercing of the nasal septum and the subsequent enlarging of the hole to take a pin of wood or bone was also an initiation ritual shared by both males and females in some areas of the Kimberley. It was not universally practiced, generally being restricted to those areas where tooth avulsion occurred.

During the early to mid-twentieth century Walmajarri and other arid-zone dwellers migrated north into the south Kimberley from the Great Sandy Desert area. Culturally more conservative, these immigrants continued both tooth avulsion and nasal piercing for a time, long after the resident Aborigines had abandoned the practices.

The cutting of cicatrices (decorative scarring) on the chest and abdomen of both men and women was practiced throughout the Kimberley. In some areas the scars were seen as marks of beauty, or insignia that bespoke the close relationship between the operator and the scarred person. In other areas they were made as part of the initiation sequence. Wounds cut to form decorative scars were either left to heal normally or were irritated by the inclusion of ash or ocher into the wound to promote the growth of scar tissue.

The Worora, Wunambal, and Ngarinyin peoples of the north and central Kimberley had some of the most complex and dense patterns of scars recorded in Australia. As well as long transversal sets of cicatrices across the chest and abdomen, one or more rows of short, vertical, and also horizontal scars were cut on the upper arms. A row of short vertical scars was often cut on the forearm below the elbow. Long scars were cut both horizontally and in vertical rows on the back. Across the loins a long row of short vertical scars ran almost around the body above the hips. Long vertical rows and horizontal bands of scars were cut on the thighs, while below the knees a vertical row of long scars was often cut into the skin of the calf. The scars were cut over a period of several years, and a young man was required to have a complete set of cicatrices before being admitted to the highest ranks of religious status. In other areas of the Kimberley the body was not so densely decorated, with scarring restricted to the abdomen, chest, and shoulders.

DRESS AND ORNAMENTS

Headbands were worn throughout the Kimberley. In most areas men wore a flat headband as a formal mark of maturity and status. The bands were made from small skeins of fur string that had been flattened and fixed with tree resin then painted with white pipe-clay or the mineral huntite. Short lengths of string at each end were tied off behind the head. Women wore plain string loops around their head but would don male headbands in some ritual situations.

In the south Kimberley headdresses consisting of a bound string loop that had ten or so pendant pairs of wallaby incisors, each pair fixed with resin to a length of hair string attached to it, were worn by women during some ceremonies. The pendants hung over and veiled the face of the dancer. In some examples large seeds of *Erythrina vespertilio* were substituted for the teeth.

Belts of animal fur or human hair were also worn by both sexes. While worn on occasion as general dress in which weapons or small game could be carried, they were more usually only donned during formal situations such as ceremonies. In the past both sexes donned hair-string girdles as part of their initiation regalia.

Belts were made from a two-ply string spun from either human hair or winter fur taken from female possums or from the belly of female wallabies and other small macropods. The string was spun using cross-shaped spindles with one or two arms that caught up and twisted the developing yarn. Both sexes could make hair string, although women were generally more adept at the task.

Three sorts of hair belts were made and worn in the Kimberley region. The first type of belt consisted of a single length of yarn that was wound into a many-stranded skein about six hundred millimeters (about two feet) long. A short length of hair string

A woman breaks scaphopod shells into bugles that will be strung on twine to form multistrand necklaces, Mowanjum, the Kimberley, Western Australia, 1974. She has received the raw shell as a gift from a friend, with whom she has a ceremonial-exchange relationship and who resides in another community. Photograph by Kim Akerman.

was then attached at one or both ends of the skein and used as a tie when wearing the belt. The belt could be shortened if necessary by twisting the skein before tying it off. The second form, restricted to the northern areas of the Kimberley, consisted of a core of either fibrous bark or hair string, which was then closely bound with string to form a relatively rigid girdle. A third form of hair belt was imported into the Kimberley from the adjacent Northern Territory. This belt consisted of a loose skein of hair string that is flattened by weaving in one or more panels with a weft of hair string or, today, commercial wool. Dangling tassels of natural or commercial fibers occasionally decorated with tufts of feathers are often attached to these belts, which are worn by men when dancing.

Belts were an important article of the ceremonial gift exchange cycle that underpinned social relationships between individuals and groups in the region. A man also gave hair belts as gifts to his affinal kin, and hair-belts incorporating the hair of the dead were important *memento mori* (reminders of death). The general use of bark belts, first noted by William Dampier, has changed since 1688. Since the twentieth century or so they have only been made and worn in secret-sacred rituals restricted to males in some areas of Dampierland.

Short, mop-like pubic tassels made of hair or fur string were attached, either directly to the pubic hair or to hair belts. There is very little information about the significance of pubic tassels, although they were first placed on a youth as a mark of approaching maturity and they appear to have been worn only on more formal ceremonial occasions.

Spectacular ornaments worn attached to belts were made from carefully shaped and engraved valves of pearlshell. One or more pearlshells were worn attached to the belt, fore and aft. In the past males, young and old, wore pearlshell pubic ornaments, although certain types of these were symbols of ceremonial status and could only be worn with general approval. Originating in the Kimberley, pearlshells were traded extensively beyond the region. On the Dampierland Peninsula hair belts were occasionally strung with clusters of abalone shell that acted as rattles or tinklers when dancing.

A wide variety of necklaces were made and worn in the region. The simplest were long loops of twine, heavily ochered and anointed with fat. They could be worn around the neck, crossed around the neck and under the arms like bandoliers, or, when further looped into a smaller diameter, worn on the head. Individuals of both sexes wore cord necklaces. Other necklaces were made by cutting lengths of grass into bugles and stringing them on cord to create multistrand necklaces.

Necklaces of scaphopod-shell bugles were made on the Dampierland Peninsula and traded across the Kimberley, east into the adjacent Northern Territory and south into the desert. The discovery of thirty-thousand-year-old scaphopod-shell bugles at Mimbi Caves, ninety kilometers (about fifty-six miles) southeast of Fitzroy Crossing in the south Kimberley, in 1999 attest to one of the world's longest continuous traditions of use of any species of shell.

Small pieces of pearlshell were either pierced or fixed with resin or wax to cords and worn as pendants. The shell was positioned to lie between the shoulder blades rather than on the chest, or could be lifted and placed within the strands of the headband over the forehead. Pendants were also made in the north Kimberley, from the tail skin of a dingo.

In historic times armbands were simply made by winding cords around the upper arm. In some areas these cords were tied extremely tightly and left on for a period of time as part of male initiation ordeals. Ties were also placed above the calf to support bunches of leaves in some costumes worn for public and secret-sacred dances. Woven armbands and bracelets appear not to have been made in the Kimberley Region.

Bird feathers were worn in a number of ways, usually during ceremonies or intergroup meetings. Small feathers such as the filmy throat feathers of bustards or long, twin-shafted emu feathers were simply tied together and worn tucked into belts, armbands, and headbands. Feathers were also tied to bone or wood pins that were then skewered into the hair or dress. Other feathers, such as those taken from the wings and tails of cockatoos and raptors, were prepared by stripping the vanes from the quills and tying them together or to pins.

Occasionally simple feathers were worn in the headband over the forehead. In the comparatively recent Wandjina rock art style, unique to the region, Wandjina beings are sometimes depicted wearing the gaudy tail feathers of the red-tailed black cockatoo in their hair. Bunches of plumes may also be carried by dancers and used as whisks or batons to emphasize the tempo of the music or singing.

In the southern Kimberley bunches of long, fine shavings of wood were worn in the hair or tucked into armbands by dancers during some types of performances. In some dance performances shaved sticks, pins of wood scraped so that the fine shavings remain attached at one end, are also worn in headbands, and dancers may carry longer wands with multiple bunches of shavings attached.

Nosebones are usually made from the ulnas of larger flying birds such as eagles or bustards, with the condyles removed. Beeswax or resin may be used to plug the medullary cavity at one

A sandal woven from crotalaria bark and used in the hottest months of the year in the desert areas of the south Kimberley, Western Australia, late twentieth century. Photograph by Kim Akerman.

or both ends of the bone. They are worn usually only on formal occasions. Sections of a large grass-stem were worn as a bone substitute. A person suffering from a cold or blocked nose might wear a tuft of leaves from an aromatic shrub in the septum to clear the sinuses.

The use of footwear was relatively widespread in the south Kimberley and adjacent arid areas. Sandals woven from the bark of either acacia or crotalaria bushes were worn when traversing sandy areas during the hotter times of the year. In the south Kimberley assassins wore shoes, made from felted emu feathers, often with woven or knitted uppers of hair string. The use of these shoes concealed the identity, not the tracks, of the wearer by concealing any characteristics of foot size, gait, and so on.

Face masks were first recorded in the Kimberley in the latter part of the nineteenth century and continue to be used in the early twenty-first century. Masks are used far more widely than appreciated in Aboriginal Australia, and their occurrence in the Kimberley is widespread. Masks in the Kimberley vary greatly. The simplest involve the covering of the face and body with bird or vegetable down, or binding the face with cords to distort the features. Full-face masks of bark, wood, tin, or cardboard that represent the character depicted are more common in the north and east Kimberley. False beards and wigs made from fur, cow or horse tails and manes have been regularly used in many dance forms from the late nineteenth century into the present day.

ABORIGINAL DRESS SINCE THE SETTLEMENT PERIOD

As noted earlier, after contact Aboriginal dress was predicated by the immediate situation—when in the presence of non-Aboriginals, Western dress was adopted and shed only when returning to the Aboriginal milieu. This situation prevailed in many areas of the Kimberley into the 1950s, with older and more conservative people preferring not to adopt Western clothing unless absolutely necessary.

Lengths of cloth tied diaper-like at the hips were used by men, while women wore sarong-like cloths around their bodies. Red diapers were often worn when dancing, and bolts of cloth became important trade items. Strips of cloth or lengths of commercial yarn replaced the fur-string headband. Broad leather belts, worn by stockmen in day-to-day work, were also worn by dancers. Colorful handkerchiefs were important items of dress on formal occasions, worn by both sexes around the head or the neck. Dresses and handkerchiefs were important elements of the customary gift exchange ceremonies in this period. The use of hair belts became limited to ceremonial occasions.

At ceremonies attended by people of both sexes, women usually wore skirts and went bare-breasted. Today only more conservative women are prepared to dance publicly in this fashion, and most wear a brassiere. When performing female-specific ceremonies away from male eyes, women usually dance without clothes or at least topless.

Contrary to general belief in many of the early pastoral and town situations on the frontier, many Aboriginal men and women of the workforce wore very much the same clothes as non-Aboriginal workers. Early photos show women wearing blouses and long skirts, rather than the shapeless "mother hubbard" that became more dominant between the wars. Women also worked sheep and cattle wearing male attire: shirts, trousers, hats, and belts. Men and women who were not directly involved in the workforce wore dress of lesser quality, often sourced from charities. Footwear was rarely worn in the early pastoral days. From the earliest mission days in the nineteenth century, Christian converts were invariably married wearing Western clothes, the bride in white and with a veil or lace head covering, the groom in a suit with shirt, tie, and shoes. Since about the 1950s, when clothing hire businesses began to appear in the major towns in the region, formalwear is also commonly worn by men, at funerals of particularly close kin, or by other community leaders.

There have been many changes since the 1970s in the attire worn by Aboriginals in the Kimberley. These can be attributed in part to the decline of the pastoral industry and the gradual movement of many Aboriginals to an urban environment. Scarification and nose piercing generally declined after World War II; however, since the late 1970s a number of men have undergone the former ordeal, both as an expression of their commitment to traditional customs, and also as a symbol of wider political and ethnic identity. The use of customary hairstyles has similarly declined. Some hunters in remote areas, however, after stripping to a pair of shorts when hunting, carry their pocket knives by closing the folding blade on a lock of hair, rather than trust it to a pocket.

There has been a rise, among many mature men, in the custom of growing flowing beards. Beards, in the twenty-first century, have become for many men an emblem of Aboriginal elder. From the Kimberley perspective at least, the custom seems to have been influenced by elders living in the East Arnhem Land Region of the Northern Territory, who have cultivated the beard as a symbol of rank and seniority for many generations.

Apart from the use of casual daubing of white paint over the body found in the north and central Kimberley, the most elaborate style of body painting, involving the patterned application of red, yellow, or white down (or commonly cotton wool), is still found among the people of the south and southeast Kimberley. Body painting is usually only worn during ceremonies or at more open cultural events. Contemporary head- and armbands, usually worn only during ceremonies or more public events such as cultural festivals, consist of small skeins of commercial wool, or strips of cloth, rather than the homespun animal fur used in the past. Hair-string girdles are now rarely made and are primarily worn by participants of male initiation ceremonies.

Women at a number of centers in the Kimberley still produce scaphopod-shell necklaces, a number of which continue to enter the indigenous economic systems that mesh the continent. Men of the Dampierland Peninsula wear pearlshells attached to wool or cord belts at public performances and cultural festivals and during initiation ceremonies. Use of pearlshell in other areas of the Kimberley is more restrained than in the past.

Since the late 1970s there has been a marked upsurge in certain elements of customary religious and ceremonial life that has been further encouraged by the general acceptance of things ethnic in the wider community. As wider Australia discovers the rich heritage that underpinned the lives of so many Aboriginal people, so have Aboriginals themselves become more open in sharing many aspects of cultural life that were for a long time maintained away from alien eyes.

In the early twenty-first century, Aboriginal people of the Kimberley wear Western clothing, adopting indigenous dress only on ceremonial occasions or when celebrating their cultural

Masked dancers, Turkey Creek, 1979. They enact a dream sequence in the *Kurirr Kurirr*, a popular dance cycle from the east Kimberley, Western Australia. Photograph by Kim Akerman.

affiliations within the wider community. Since the 1980s a number of Aboriginal artists, such as the late Jimmy Pike, have been creating designs for the fashion market or producing their own high-quality fabrics commercially. In addition, a wide range of lifestyles is encountered—from the meanest fringe-dwelling situations, to the modern pastoral life, focusing on motor vehicle and helicopter as much as horse and rider, and the full cosmopolitan experience of actors, playwrights, singers, and artists. Mining and cultural tourism have greatly expanded the economic base for many Aboriginal people of the region, and contemporary fashion is both admired and catered to.

References and Further Reading

Akerman, K. "Shoes of Invisibility and Invisible Shoes: Australian Hunters and Gatherers and Ideas on the Origins of Footwear. *Australian Aboriginal Studies 2005* 2 (2006): 55–64.

Akerman, K., with J. Stanton. *Riji and Jakuli: Kimberley Pearl Shell in Aboriginal Australia.* Darwin, Australia: Northern Territory Museum of Arts and Sciences, 1994.

Balme, J. "Excavations Revealing 40,000 Years of Occupation at Mimbi Caves, South Central Kimberley, Western Australia." *Australian Archaeology* 51 (2000): 1–5.

Crawford, I. *The Art of the Wandjina.* Oxford: Oxford University Press, 1968.

Dampier, W. *A New Voyage around the World.* London: The Argonaut Press, 1927.

Grey, G. *Journals of Two Expeditions of Discovery in North-West and Western Australia, during the Years 1837–38 and 39.* Vol. 1. London: Boone, 1841.

Martin, J. "Explorations in North-West Australia." *Journal of the Royal Geographic Society* 35 (1865): 237–289.

Peggs, A. J. "Notes on the Aborigines of Roebuck Bay, Western Australia." *Folklore* 14, no. 4 (1903): 324–367.

Walsh, G. *Bradshaws: Ancient Rock Paintings of North-West Australia.* Geneva, Switzerland: Edition Limitée, 1994.

Walsh, G. *Bradshaw Art of the Kimberleys.* Toowoomba, Australia: Takarakka Nowan Kas Publications, 2000.

Kim Akerman

See also Aboriginal Dress in Australia: Evidence and Resources; Aboriginal Dress in Southeast Australia; Dressing the Body in the Western Desert, Australia; Aboriginal Dress in Arnhem Land; Aboriginal Dress in North Queensland, Australia.

Torres Strait Islander Dress, Australia

- Torres Strait Islander Dress: Pre-1870s
- Change and Continuity: Post-1870s
- Twentieth- and Twenty-first-Century Dance Attire

The Torres Strait is a narrow underwater shelf connecting the northernmost tip of mainland Australia to the Gulf of Papua New Guinea. Torres Strait Islanders are the indigenous people of the region, which forms part of the Australian state of Queensland. The term *ailan kastom* (island custom) is used to denote those products and practices that are unique to the Torres Strait Islands, including dress.

Torres Strait Islander dress is Melanesian in origin. However, Islander attire also reflects long-standing cultural links forged over thousands of years with Australian Aboriginal people. More recent historical changes have resulted in the addition of elements of European, Samoan, New Caledonian, Rotuman, Malay, Japanese, and Filipino dress to Torres Strait Islander attire.

Some of the most significant transformations in Islander fashion occurred during the mid- to late nineteenth century with the arrival of capitalism, Christianity, and colonial rule in rapid succession. The reformist attitudes of church and state led to a period of decline in ailan kastom. However, despite ensuing changes, Islander people have worked hard to keep their ailan kastom alive.

Although many Torres Strait Islanders now live on the mainland, they continue to maintain strong connections with their islands of origin. While Western-style clothing is generally preferred as everyday wear, both on the mainland and in the islands, there remains a high social value in wearing customary dress for important cultural events. The continuing popularity of dance has been a particularly strong force in both the preservation of older styles of customary dress as well the invention of new forms. Customary dress serves as an important symbol of cultural cohesion and identity for all Torres Strait Islander people. At the same time it is something that is constantly evolving as each generation adds its own interpretation of ongoing cultural traditions.

TORRES STRAIT ISLANDER DRESS: PRE-1870s

In order to understand current modes of Torres Strait Islander dress, it is necessary to know something of its origins. The ancestors of today's Torres Strait Islander communities migrated from the Papuan Gulf around twenty-five hundred years ago. Over the millennia five main cultural areas emerged in the Torres Strait, corresponding with five geographically distinct island groups: the Top Western Islands (Boigu, Dauan, and Saibai); the Western Islands (Badu, Mabuaig, and Moa); the Lower Western Islands (Kiriri, Muralug, Ngurupai, and Waiben); the Central Islands (Iama, Masig, Poruma, and Warraber); and the Eastern Islands (Mer, Ugar, and Erub).

Prior to annexation by the Queensland government in 1879, the different island groups did not form a unified political unit.

Women dancers performing at the opening of the Gab Titui Cultural Centre on Waiben (Thursday) Island, in the Torres Strait, 2004. They wear typical dance costumes consisting of "grass" skirts (made from fresh green leaves suspended from a belt) and flowers in their hair. Photograph by George Serras. National Museum of Australia.

Rather, each area had its own distinct way of life and set of beliefs and customs, influenced by the different physical geographies of the islands. For example, the attire of the Top Western Islands was closely affiliated with their Papuan Gulf neighbors, while the dress of the Lower Western Islands reflected long-standing social networks (including intermarriage) with the Aboriginal people of the Cape York Peninsula. These differing cultural networks combined with regional variations in the natural resources of the islands led to a rich and diverse material culture base across the Torres Strait.

All of the precolonial Islander societies followed a Melanesian pattern of social organization. Leadership was not hereditary but achieved by the ability to marshal the labor and resources of others through personal influence. The manufacture, use, and appearance of ceremonial attire tended to closely follow clan rules, reflecting dominant religious and social ideologies. Social organization was patriarchal and patrilineal, and throughout the Strait, men's cults or grade societies formed the focus of much ritual and political activity and provided an important forum for artistic production. Bodies were embellished for warfare, to indicate clan affiliation, status, and gender, and for rituals and ceremonies used to mark different stages of life such as birth, initiation into adulthood, marriage, and death.

The ethnographer Alfred Cort Haddon was the first person to attempt a thorough report on the material culture and customs of the different communities of the Torres Strait. In 1898 he led the Cambridge Expedition to the Torres Strait, which eventuated in six volumes of reports on Torres Strait life and environment.

Although Haddon's research was conducted at a time when substantial changes were affecting the region, his work allows for a relatively detailed reconstruction of Islander dress prior to the nineteenth century.

According to Haddon, across the Strait certain qualities such as dark skin, a high forehead, elongated ears, and long thick hair for men were associated with beauty. Various forms of body modification occurred before or around puberty to improve upon the natural body. Mothers massaged their baby's foreheads, pressing backwards and upwards to encourage a high forehead, and rubbed their baby's skin with charcoal to make it dark and shiny.

Children had their nasal septums pierced at an early age, and in some areas the tip of the nose was also pierced. Nose sticks (*gub* or *kirkub*) in the shape of cylinders or crescents were ground from clam shell and worn by both sexes. Green leaves, bamboo segments, or other natural elements were also used to decorate the nose. Children's ears were pierced prior to puberty, and arc-shaped ear weights (*ubar* or *laip tut*) of polished wood were worn to elongate the holes. The rim of the ear was occasionally subject to multiple piercings, and blades of grass or leaves were inserted to form a line of small tufts along the outside of the ear. Earlobes were sometimes split as part of the mourning process. When the mourning period ended, delicate ear pendants of nautilus nacre (*godegode* or *laip*) could be worn, tied to the split lobes.

Around puberty young people underwent a process of scarification. Incisions were made on the shoulders, chest, and thighs with a sharp bamboo or shell knife. These incisions were rubbed with various substances to form a raised welt. This painful process produced beautiful permanent patterns on the skin in simple curvilinear designs.

The period of active body modification ended after puberty. Individuals, having been transformed through initiation, were ready to assume the roles and responsibilities of adulthood. Where the child body was transformed through physical modifications, the adult body was transformed through dress. The tropical climate of the region favored minimal clothing for everyday wear. Before puberty, children went naked. However, upon reaching puberty women were expected to wear a grass skirt (*zazi* or *nesur*) when in the village or the gardens. These skirts were made of sago, coconut, or banana leaves, or of beaten ficus bark knotted onto a woven belt, and there was also a fuller, more decorative version worn for ceremonies and dancing. Men wore little clothing for everyday activities such as gardening, sailing, or harvesting marine resources, other than personal jewelry and a belt (*wakau* or *wak*) plaited from palm leaves and decorated in hibiscus fiber or ocher designs. During ceremonial occasions or warfare, however, initiated men were expected to wear a range of socially prescribed clothing, including a grass skirt (*tu zazi* or *su nesur*) or bailer-shell groin covering and a warrior's headdress.

Ceremonial occasions, such as weddings, initiation ceremonies, or intercommunity dances, provided an opportunity for men and women to dress up to display their wealth and good looks. Dressing the hair in elaborate styles and wearing wigs was an important part of self-adornment in Melanesian societies. Thick long hair was associated with male virility in the Papuan Gulf, and this was likely the case in the Torres Strait as well. Men's hair was worn at shoulder length, dressed in tight ringlets held in place with a little ocher or clay as a fixative. For important events, such as mourning, men cropped their hair short and wore elaborate wigs (*adazi ial* or *kerem mus*) of human hair decorated with ocher and parrot

A warrior's dance costume featuring a *dhari* headdress, *kadig* armband, grass skirt over a red *lavalava*, and fresh croton leaves, Torres Strait, 2004. Photograph by George Serras. National Museum of Australia.

feathers. Wigs were worn by some older men to hide gray or receding hair and also appear on masks associated with men's cults. Women wore their hair short, although sometimes a tuft of hair was left long for decoration. Both sexes wore simple decorative combs (*ial sak* or *kerem seker*) of wood or turtle shell.

In the premonetary economy, shell valuables were an important form of collectable wealth. The most valuable of these were conus shell pendants (*dibidibi*), conus shell armbands (*waiwi* or *wauri*), olive shell necklaces (*waraz*), and pearlshell breastplates (*mai*). These formed a central currency among the Torres Strait Islands and along Coastal New Guinea. Over the course of a lifetime an individual would acquire shell valuables both as part of the prescribed life-cycle and through individual effort. For example, a woman would receive her first quality items at puberty. When she married, she received further shell jewelry from her mother and brothers and as a portion of her bridewealth. After the birth of each child, her in-laws were expected to give food and shell valuables to mark the occasion. Throughout her life she would add to her personal wealth of jewelry through her own trading activities or in payment for her labor.

Many items of jewelry were worn by both sexes. For example, at a wedding feast a man and woman's basic attire might include

A man from Mabuaig Island performing the Aeroplane Dance, Torres Strait, 2004. Photograph by George Serras. National Museum of Australia.

several shared elements: a skirt of sago or coconut leaves, woven anklets (*makamak*), woven armbands (*musur* or *put*), wooden ear weights or nautilus nacre ear pendants, clam-shell nose sticks, and an array of shell valuables. Men and women further embellished their bodies from a shared palette of foliage and plumes, including hibiscus flowers, croton, and dracaena leaves, as well as cassowary, bird-of-paradise, Torres Strait pigeon, parakeet, and cockatoo feathers.

Other items were not shared but restricted according to gender or religious status. For example, only married women were allowed to wear dog's teeth necklaces (*umai-dangal* or *sesirig*) imported from New Guinea or triangular conus-shell pendants (*wauri o*). Only initiated men wore crescent-shaped breastplates made from pearlshell, known as mai, certain accoutrements of war such as the *dhari* headdress, or special turtle-shell masks associated with male ancestor-heroes.

There was a sharp distinction between making secular dance masks, a festive activity performed by all members of the community, and the making of sacred masks. Sacred masks such as those associated with men's cults were reserved for men's initiation and secret ritual practices. There were grave restrictions on who could make, own, use, and see them. These restrictions were so strong that a woman or uninitiated boy could be killed for seeing a sacred mask. In the pre-Colonial era masks were used in a wide range of rituals—for spiritual power and protection, success in trading and warfare, to ensure the abundance of crops and animals, and in mortuary rituals, rain-making magic, initiation ceremonies, sorcery, and hero cults.

Historically, masks were divided into two main types—wood and turtle shell. Before Christianity wooden masks known as *mawa* were used in annual harvest festivals in the Top Western Islands. Unembellished wooden masks carved from a single piece of hardwood were imported from New Guinea. The mask was then finished locally in the Torres Strait through adding ocher face paint designs, human hair, feathers, fibers, and seeds. In the ritual act of decorating, the masks' spiritual power would be activated. Old mawa masks are easily recognizable by their characteristic elongated faces, ears with stretched lobes, and long thin triangular-shaped noses rendered in dark wood. Although the general outline of wooden masks is of Papuan Gulf style, their finishes make them distinct to the Torres Strait Islands.

Wood suitable for large carvings was scarce in the islands, whereas turtle shell was abundant. Turtle-shell carving in the Torres Strait reached a level of aesthetic excellence unparalleled anywhere else in the world. Elaborate turtle-shell masks were made in almost all areas of the Strait. Made from the shell of the hawksbill turtle, they are known as *krar* in the Western Islands and *op le* (face of man) in the Eastern Islands. Turtle-shell masks come in many different shapes and sizes, from simple representations of the human face to complex sculptural pieces in which human faces morph into totemic animal designs.

The mask-making traditions of the Torres Strait were not static. When the ethnographer Alfred Cort Haddon visited the Strait in 1888, and again in 1898, which resulted in his published reports, he noted the opportunistic use of new materials. Wooden crates, kerosene tins, calico, and cardboard were reworked to create masks of beauty and power. New ideas, materials, and manufacturing techniques have always been a part of Torres Strait customary dress. Changes have arisen through local invention and long-term cross-cultural exchanges, as well as more dramatic historical events.

CHANGE AND CONTINUITY: POST-1870s

The nineteenth century was a period of intense change in the Torres Strait. In the 1840s the first European *bêche de mer* (sea cucumber) harvesting station was built. The first pearling station was established in 1868, and the pearlshell industry rapidly expanded. Pearling luggers were usually owned and captained by Europeans but were worked by Asian and South Sea Islander crews, who brought a wide range of new cultural influences to the Strait. "Blackbirding" (the capture of Islanders for forced labor) became rife. The suppression of blackbirding was one of the major reasons forwarded for the annexation of the Torres Strait by the colony of Queensland, which occurred in a series of acts between 1872 and 1879. All these events brought manifold changes to Torres Strait Islander dress.

The increasing European presence and work for wages made a number of new materials available for fashioning clothing and ceremonial wear. Short strings of red, blue, and white ceramic trade beads appear on masks and items of jewelry from the mid-nineteenth century. Strips of red calico were attached as ribbon or cut into decorative tufts. Wood from packing crates and tin sheets from kerosene containers were also popular sources of raw material.

The arrival of Christianity in the 1870s marked perhaps the most significant changes to Torres Strait Islander dress. On 1 July 1871 Reverend Samuel MacFarlane, Reverend A. W. Murray, and eight Melanesian converts from the London Missionary Society (LMS) arrived on Erub in the Eastern Islands. Their timing was good. Many Torres Strait Islanders were weary of blackbirding, the violence brought by sailing crews, and interisland warfare, and they looked to the missions to end the exploitation and bring stability and peace to the region. Another reason for the success of the LMS foray was their policy of recruiting Melanesian and Polynesian converts as assistants, teachers, and lay preachers. The LMS brought to the Strait an influx of teachers from other areas of the Pacific, particularly the Loyalty Islands and Samoa. From this early platform Christianity rapidly spread and took permanent hold. The arrival of Christianity continues to be celebrated in the twenty-first century in the annual "Coming of the Light" festival.

The LMS teachers had very clear ideas on what constituted proper dress. Men were instructed to wear knee-length cloths, called *lavalava*, which wrapped around the waist and were tied or held in place by a belt. In the beginning they were made from flour bags for daily wear and calico for more formal events. In some areas the term *calico* is still used as an alternative to lavalava. Women were instructed to replace their grass skirts with long cotton dresses known as "mother hubbards." These dresses, featuring high-yoked necks and leg-o-mutton sleeves, first appeared in Hawaii in the 1820s and accompanied the spread of Christianity across the Pacific. Today almost every Pacific Island nation has a regional variation of the dress. Known in the Torres Strait as an *augemwali*, the garment remains an important item of women's traditional dress, worn as formalwear and for dancing. Many women on the islands wear them as part of casual dress. For men's formalwear the calico has been replaced by a short-sleeved cotton shirt in a floral design, known colloquially across the Pacific as an aloha shirt.

Although the adoption of Christianity led to significant changes to customary dress, the continued performance of "old style" dances has been instrumental in preserving many elements of the precolonial styles. While many cultural practices were discouraged by the missions, some dances were deliberately maintained as part of secular celebrations.

A young dancer wearing a *terig* shark-totem mask, Torres Strait, 2004. Photograph by George Serras. National Museum of Australia.

TWENTIETH- AND TWENTY-FIRST-CENTURY DANCE ATTIRE

Dance is a cornerstone of Torres Strait Islander culture. Most special occasions are marked by dancing, including cultural festivals, art openings, weddings, and tombstone unveilings. Each island group is characterized by a distinct set of dance attire, and at large interisland festivals the origins of each dance group can be discerned from what they are wearing. Dances are generally segregated along gender lines. Men and women from each community coordinate their dress and ornamentation to ensure that they appear as a cohesive unit during extended dance performances. Nondancing members of the audience celebrate their Islander identity through wearing floral-patterned augemwali dresses and/or aloha shirts.

Women's dance attire reflects more strongly the innovations introduced by Christianity. South Sea Islander converts discouraged the local songs and dances, replacing them with dances from their own cultures. As a result, many are influenced by elements of music and dance originating from the Loyalty Islands, Cook Islands, Samoa, Nuie, and Rotuma. From these influences developed a genre of song and dance called *ailan dans*. These reflect some older elements of Torres Strait dance, combined with newer styles and costumes introduced from South Sea Islander sources. Some elements of Asian dance were also adopted as a result of Japanese, Malay, and Filipino migrants who relocated to the Torres Strait as part of the pearling industry.

In the twenty-first century women's dance attire is representative of a Pan-Pacific Islander style, reflecting a long history of innovation in secular dance. A woman's basic dance costume usually begins with an augemwali dress. Over the dress is tied a "grass" skirt made of fresh green leaves suspended from a cotton belt. The skirt may be further embellished with fresh or artificial flowers and contrasting colored foliage, such as the yellow and purple leaves of the croton plant. "Grass skirts" of synthetic fiber, dyed raffia, or white chicken feathers are also worn. A woman usually wears at least one flower behind her ear or in her hair. Hats and headbands woven from pandanus palm leaves, decorated with fresh or synthetic flowers, are also popular. The shell valuables that used to be such an important part of bridewealth are represented today by pearlshell pendants that are made locally, and shell jewelry imported from Papua New Guinea and the Philippines. White feather bracelets, skirts, and leis (garlands) are also popular.

Both men and women commonly wear white anklebands and wristbands, which allow the audience to trace the dancers' movements and to see how closely they are synchronized. A range of hand-held dance artifacts such as dance staffs, "dance machines," bow and arrows, or fans edged in white feathers are also used to punctuate the movements of the dance. Koa seed rattles known as *kulap* are also important dance items, adding drama to the performances. Dancers coordinate their movements in time with the rattle, which is shaken or slapped on the thighs.

Men's dance attire more closely resembles the pre-1870s styles than women's, as it reflects a conscious preservation of ceremonial regalia derived from the early men's cults. A male dancer usually begins with red shorts and a white singlet. A lavalava that falls to around thigh level covers the shorts. The color of the lavalava depends on the dancer's island of origin. A grass skirt or kilt made from pandanus fiber is worn over the top. To these are added white ankle- and wristbands. A man's dance costume is usually finished with a spectacular mask or headdress.

The most famous type of headdress throughout the Torres Strait is the dhari, originally worn by warriors in battle. The widespread distribution of this headdress is reflected in the fact that different groups have their own spellings for the headdress—*deri/dari* in the Eastern Islands, dhari in the Western Islands, and *dhoeri* in the Top Western Islands. Dhari and other customary masks and headdresses are designed to be shown at dusk, by firelight in the evenings, or in the dim light of a forest clearing. Particular dance movements enhance this aspect, with dancers shaking their heads so the feathers vibrate or shimmer. Another move, consisting of a sudden turn of the head, makes the headdress seem to temporarily disappear. Most dharis feature an arc of white feathers made from the reef heron or Torres Strait Island pigeon, attached to a woven cane frame. Cassowary feather headdresses and headbands known as *dagui* or *samu* were once a common form of masculine ceremonial attire in both New Guinea and the Strait. Nowadays they are referred to by the more general name, dhari.

Beizam (shark) dance machine featuring triple hammerhead sharks, made by the artist Ken Thaiday Senior from Erub (Darnley) Island, Torres Strait, ca. 2000. The machine is worn on the dancer's head and its parts can be moved by the dancer by manipulating a series of strings. National Museum of Australia.

Cassowary feathers are still sourced from Papua, but other customary trade items such as bird-of-paradise feathers are no longer available. However, new materials are regularly being introduced. The age-old resources of sea and shore have been supplemented by eBay and the local hardware store. Horsehair is sometimes substituted for cassowary plumes, dyed chicken for heron feathers, plastics, enamel, and acrylic paint for ochers and shells, heavy cardboard, plywood, and tin for turtle shell, and so forth.

The artist Sipau Audi Gibuma, for example, specializes in making customary headdresses, known as a *mayngu* or *moelpalau dhoeri*, that combine a mix of old and new elements. These feature in a warrior's dance from Boigu in the Top Western Islands known as *meripal kulkan patan* (blood covering the moon), customarily associated with the lunar eclipse. The headdress is made from wood, tinplate, enamel paint, pearlshell, cotton, nails, and cassowary feathers and features a wooden eight-pointed morning star (an important symbol in the Strait), mounted on two gold-lip pearlshells.

Since World War II a number of new dances have become widely popular, accompanied by new forms of dance attire. For example, James Eseli, from the island of Mabuiag, is known for designing distinctive headdresses for the Aeroplane Dance, choreographed to commemorate the experiences of Torres Strait Islanders during World War II. The unusual headdresses made by James Eseli, in the shape of a model World War II plane, are now widely collected by art institutions.

While innovation and an easy embrace of new ideas marked secular dance, those dances associated with men's ceremonial cults were deliberately held static and were subject to strong cultural taboos. Dances that derive from before missionary contact, such as men's secret ceremonies, are known as "old-fashioned dance." Though men's cults had virtually ceased by the end of the nineteenth century, a revival occurred on Mer, in the Eastern Islands, in the 1920s when a local Anglican priest encouraged the reintroduction of pre-Christian dances, particularly the sacred dances of the Malo-Bomai religion. The revival of these older dances has, over time, contributed to a renaissance in Torres Strait Islander mask making throughout the region.

A number of main artists can be accredited with the resurrection of mask and headdress making in the mid- to late twentieth century, and their inclusion into the world of contemporary art. These include Ken Thaiday, Vic McGrath, Audi Gibuma, Allson Edrick Tabuai, and James Eseli. A number of younger artists are also following this tradition, including Patrick Thaiday and George Nona. Such artists tend to specialize in one or two types of mask. For example, Patrick Thaiday and Vic McGrath are known for producing works based on the *op le* (face of man) masks of the Eastern Torres Strait, whereas Allson Edrick Tabuai is famous for making large, striking masks based on the mawa ritual masks of the Top Western Islands.

One of the most important innovations in mask making has been the creation and evolution of the "dance machine," associated with the artist Ken Thaiday Senior. Thaiday began to design dance regalia in the late 1980s for the Darnley Island Dance Troupe. His dance masks, originally made for customary dance performances,

evolved over time into elaborate articulated dance machines that are now highly prized by collectors. Thaiday's dance machines are worn on a dancer's head, with a number of articulated parts moved by the dancer through a series of strings. His most popular form features the shark totem (*beizam*, pronounced "bi zam"), associated with the ancestor-hero Malo, and symbolizing law and order. These masks have evolved from some of the earliest known examples of Torres Strait masks, including late-nineteenth-century masks collected by Haddon.

Information about both mask-making techniques and the oral histories that accompany them continue to be passed along the male line, and even young mask makers are mindful of the spiritual power of masks when making or "dancing" them. Art galleries and museums across Australia and the Pacific now collect masks and headdresses originally developed for dance performances. Many Torres Strait Islander artists represent masks and headdresses in their paintings, textiles, and print work as key symbols of Torres Strait Islander cultural identity. If the end of the nineteenth century was marked by a period of upheaval and decline in the customary dress of the Torres Strait, the end of the twentieth century has seen a marked renaissance in the form of spectacular dance costumes and artful masks, which embody and enrich the unique *ailan kastom* (island customs) of Torres Strait Islander people.

References and Further Reading

Beckett, Jeremy. *Torres Strait Islanders: Custom and Colonialism.* Cambridge: Cambridge University Press, 1987.

Fraser, Douglas. *Torres Strait Sculpture.* New York & London: Garland Publishing, 1978.

Haddon, Alfred C. *Reports of the Cambridge Anthropological Expedition to Torres Straits.* Vols. 1–6. New York: Johnson Reprint Corp., 1971. Reprint of the Cambridge University Press edition: Cambridge, 1901–1935.

Herle, Anita, and Sandra Rouse, eds. *Cambridge and the Torres Strait: Centenary Essays on the 1898 Anthropological Expedition.* Cambridge: Cambridge University Press, 1998.

Kleinert, Sylvia, and Margo Neale, eds. *The Oxford Companion to Aboriginal Art and Culture.* Oxford: Oxford University Press, 2000.

Moore, David R. *The Torres Strait Collections of A. C. Haddon.* London: British Museum Publications, 1984.

Moore, David R. *Arts and Crafts of Torres Strait.* Aylesbury, UK: Shire Press, 1989.

Mosby, Tom, and Brian Robinson. *Ilan Pasin: This Is Our Way.* Cairns, Australia: Cairns Regional Gallery, 1999.

Philp, Jude. *Past Time: Torres Strait Islander Material from the Haddon Collection, 1888–1905.* Canberra: National Museum of Australia, 2000.

Wilson, Lindsay. *Kerkar Lu: Contemporary Artefacts of the Torres Strait Islanders.* Brisbane, Australia: Department of Education, 1993.

Wilson, Lindsay. *Thatigaw Emeret Lu: A Handbook of Traditional Torres Strait Islands Material Culture.* Brisbane, Australia: Department of Education, 1998.

Anna Edmundson

PART 3

European Dress in Australia

Images as a Resource for the Study of Australian Dress

- Painted and Drawn Images of Dress
- Dress in Photographs and Motion Pictures
- Printed Images of Dress
- Images of Dress in Women's Magazines

Paintings, drawings, photographs, prints, illustrated newspapers, magazines, and newsreels provide vital sources of information about appearance, upper-class fashions, and the broader social picture of dress in Australia. Through such representations, the overall look and detail of attire survives long after original garments have disappeared. In the emerging penal society of colonial Australia, from the late eighteenth century, it was important for the well-to-do to cultivate the appearance of respectability and substance, and dress offered a visible measure of prosperity, if not a reliable indicator of class. However, portrait images (or indeed any image) should not be regarded as accurate reference material without testing the authenticity of the clothes depicted by cross-examination against contemporary descriptive texts and surviving garments.

Naval and military personnel and convicts recorded the first views of the post–European contact era, providing the British government with detailed evidence of the progress of settlement. These images included vignettes of people set as figures in the landscape, giving some idea of how the first settlers were clothed but without much useful detail. Colonial Australians were enthusiastic patrons of portrait painters. Most early portraits depict wealthy individuals, painted by artists trained in European academic traditions, who were themselves recent immigrants or ex-convicts. Drawings, sketches, and engravings provide further dress information, often revealing cut, drape, and body movement with greater effectiveness than more formal portrait studies. Painted portraits diminish as a useful resource during the twentieth century, as photographs, illustrated newspapers, fashion magazines, and motion pictures become of greater primary use.

PAINTED AND DRAWN IMAGES OF DRESS

Most of the painted portraits from the nineteenth century derive from the colonies of New South Wales (from 1788), Van Diemen's Land (subsequently called Tasmania, 1803), Victoria (1835), and South Australia (1836), with fewer from Western Australia and Queensland due to later settlement. Portraiture was the primary economic mainstay for many early colonial artists, with itinerant artists traveling into the interior to produce portraits of people in newly settled outposts. As family ties stretched around the globe, it became important to have permanent images of loved ones, and these provide useful records of attire. An increased demand for portraiture in Sydney, New South Wales (NSW), from the 1830s is an indicator that, under the influence of free immigration, the

penal settlement was developing into a town capable of supplying many of the finer things of life. Silhouettes, watercolor portraits, pencil drawings, crayon drawings, wax portrait medallions, prints, and oil portraits were all advertised for sale.

The rationale for a portrait painting, photograph, or any other representation of a person is to record the likeness, personality, or demeanor of the sitter, as well as to signify importance in society. Portraits usually depict people who are seemingly well off, in the prime of their lives, and at the height of their attractiveness. The extremes of fashion are rarely seen, lest a painting later appear outdated or ridiculous. Curiously, evidence that an accurate likeness took precedence over rendition of dress in colonial portraiture, particularly those by less sophisticated artists, may be indicated by the number of extant portraits showing sitters in indistinct clothing.

Portraiture was an important status symbol in early colonial society. For pioneer settler families, portraits were commissioned to begin the process of gentrification, to make new money respectable, or to legitimize questionable social position. Clothing is a portable, visual form of collateral. By recording success in pictures of themselves, their attire, and their possessions, colonial clients sought a reflection of their own civilized values and self-esteem.

The first portraits to reveal detailed evidence of how early settlers were dressed are a pair of wash drawings made within five years of colonization, during the visit to Sydney in 1793 of the Spanish Scientific Expedition (1789–1794). Attributed to Juan de Ravenet, one of the expedition artists, these sketches are believed to have been created on the spot at Parramatta, near Sydney, providing proof of local interest in contemporary fashion. They depict an officer (a single epaulette denotes his rank) and a convict, with their respective consorts. Both men are shown dressed in trousers, the habitual wear of soldiers, sailors, and workmen, later appropriated as an acceptable daytime alternative to breeches for men of fashion. The women wear high-crowned hats and "round" gowns of soft, light materials, their shoulders tightly swathed in buffoon fichus, fashionable in Europe in the 1790s.

Full-length images rendered in a standing pose are rare in Australian art but more beneficial for the study of dress than faces or seated portraits. Most surviving early colonial portraits are miniatures and generally show only the subject's head and upper torso. Miniatures were probably the first European artworks imported into the country, transported in the baggage of settlers. Portrait miniatures are most useful for the detail they show of military uniforms, regalia, hairstyles, bodice designs, and jewelry. Richard Read Sr., a convict artist and miniaturist and the colony's first specialist portrait painter, arrived in 1813, followed in 1819 by his son, Richard Read Jr. Along with fellow watercolorists William Griffiths and William Nicholas, the half- and three-quarter-length seated portraits produced by these artists show skillful rendering of the quiet, decorous fashions of the first half of the nineteenth century, with fine attention to details of cut, color, and construction. Exquisitely painted in the English style, when identified, signed, and dated, these colonial portraits can provide excellent references for local fashions.

The first oil portraits in Sydney were produced by Augustus Earle (1793–1838), a traveling artist and lithographer, who arrived in 1825. He spent several years painting landscapes and portraits, including some full-length commissions of government officials, the social elite, and nouveaux riches such as Captain John Piper, with its companion group portrait of Mrs. Piper and her children set inside the Piper family home (ca. 1826). While companion portraits of husband and wife (or mother with child) and other family members are common in colonial art, group portraits of any kind are an exception. Family portraits, usually modeled on the so-called conversation style of paintings of eighteenth-century English artists, provide a rare opportunity to study the range of clothing of men, women, and children within the same social context. Displaying generations of family portraits created a sense of dynastic significance, underpinning the idea that such families belonged to a colonial lineage of some standing.

Having a portrait painted was a sociable affair, in which friends often made comments and suggestions. Such was the case when the newly married, wealthy Sydney merchant Alexander Brodie Spark engaged Dr. Maurice Felton (1803–1842) to paint a portrait of his "bonny Bride" Maria. Felton, an artist and surgeon, had arrived in Sydney in 1839 and quickly established his reputation as Sydney's finest portraitist. This portrait, painted between May and August 1840, is one of the grandest to survive, and its significance is heightened by Spark's minute documentation of the commissioning process in his diary. Mrs. Spark is portrayed in lustrous evening wear, possibly her wedding gown, worn with an alternate, low-cut, blonde lace-trimmed bodice, likely to have been part of her trousseau and probably of colonial manufacture. Her swansdown-trimmed gloves are an expensive, imported luxury item, as is the parure of seed pearl jewelry (a *parure* is a suite of coordinated jewelry)—while European in origin, it was purchased in Sydney as a wedding gift from her best friend.

Learning to paint and draw was part of a well-rounded education for both men and women in the eighteenth and nineteenth centuries. The compilation of drawing-room albums and sketchbooks gave amateur colonial artists the opportunity to practice their skills while entertaining friends with their artwork and recording details of their social milieu. Unpracticed in the traditions and conventions of portraiture and view painting, the work of amateur artists can provide interesting source material for the study of dress. Lady painters such as the professionally trained Martha Berkley (1813–1899) also brought the added advantage of aesthetic and technical knowledge of fashionable textiles, cut, and construction detail to the rendering of apparel.

Not all portraits were for the elite. Capitalizing on the difficulty country people experienced in accessing a portrait painter, itinerant journeyman painters like ex-convict Joseph Backler (ca. 1813–1895) secured clients from the rising ranks of emancipists, bakers, publicans, builders, and the merchant classes. These works show a different caste of clothing to that worn by the colonial establishment; in such "coat and waistcoat" paintings, details of the sitter's apparel are of primary importance, with crochet work and jewelry carefully rendered in a somewhat literal style. In Backler's likenesses the plain remain plain, wrinkled or weathered faces are faithfully recorded, and if teeth are missing they are left out. His numerous commissions were probably due to his accessibility and affordability.

Beyond portraits, a broad spectrum of colonial Australian dress is recorded in other art works. Well-observed figures populate

"Ingleses enla Nueva Olanda" (English in New Holland), wash drawing by Juan de Ravenet. One of several drawings made on the Spanish Scientific Expedition to Australia and the Pacific in the ships *Descubierta* and *Atrevida* under the command of Alessandro Malaspina, 1789–1794, and collected by Felipe Bauza. State Library of New South Wales.

picnic scenes, bustling metropolitan streetscapes thronged with pedestrians, crowds of spectators attending sporting fixtures like the Anniversary Day regatta, test cricket matches, and the races, or can be seen in paintings that document historic events like John Rae's epic watercolor, *The Turning of the Turf of the First Railway in the Australasian Colonies at Redfern, Sydney, NSW 3 July 1850*. Care needs to be taken when viewing nostalgic depictions of discovery and exploration in commemorative history paintings produced long after the event. For example, *The Founding of Australia by Capt. Arthur Phillip R. N., Sydney Cove, Jan 26th 1788*, by Algernon Talmage (1871–1939), was commissioned to mark the 150th anniversary of white settlement in 1938 and should not be mistaken for an eyewitness document.

Painter William Strutt (1825–1915) made many preliminary sketches, in preparation for his large-scale commissions, showing the clothing of ordinary people among his now iconic images of life on the diggings, bushrangers, Aboriginal policemen, and the Afghan cameleers who participated in the Burke and Wills expedition of 1860. Strutt's detailed diaries of the time he spent in Australia provide important contextual information about the people he encountered and the scenes he chose to record. Samuel Thomas Gill (1818–1880) also captured life on the diggings, and the effects of mass immigration on street life in the city, which he published in his popular series of views and character sketches and work for the illustrated press. Gill may also be responsible for the first Australian fashion plates, which seem not to have been published. Though the drawings survive in the collections of the State Library of New South Wales, they remain without valuable contextual details.

DRESS IN PHOTOGRAPHS AND MOTION PICTURES

Between 1860 and 1900 photography was the most popular method of portraiture for conventional middle-class families in Australia. By the 1840s unique positive photographic images, first daguerreotypes (1836) and later ambrotypes (1854), were faithfully depicting the appearance of colonists. As the century progressed, further developments in photography put the price of portraiture within the reach of most levels of society, and these images continue to provide a remarkable record of how Australians dressed. But even after the improvements in quality of the 1880s, a photographic portrait could not boast the prestige of a painted portrait. It was only after World War I that portrait photographs began to attain a status comparable with that of painted portraits, and only after World War II that photographic portraiture finally overtook the role of paintings.

The first photographer to set up business in Australia was George Goodman in 1842. On 13 December, in the *Sydney Morning Herald*, Goodman advertised himself ready to produce likenesses that were "indeed exact and the sitter is only kept in suspense about half a minute…the charge is extremely moderate—a portrait frame, frame, and case being less that the cost of a new hat, or a box at the theatre."

Douglas T. Kilburn (1811–1871) opened Melbourne's first commercial studio in 1847. As a promotional exercise and speculative venture aimed at international sales, Kilburn took about ten daguerreotypes of Port Phillip indigenous people, which are believed to be among the earliest photographs of Aboriginal people. One group portrait shows three individuals wearing an unusual array of embellishments and clothing, including cloaks and a blanket almost certainly supplied by the photographer as, by then, urban Aborigines no longer lived or dressed in customary ways. These photographs were copied by at least two local artists and later formed the basis of wood engravings published in the *Illustrated London News*. Although Kilburn intended his images as ethnographic studies rather than individual portraits, suspected manipulation of so-called traditional clothing must always be taken into account when viewing such images.

Development of the collodion (1851) wet plate process produced negative images on glass plates, which could be mass printed onto paper (1854). In 1855 Eugène Disdéri perfected the small photographic visiting card, or *carte de visite*. This format was introduced into Australia by William Blackwood in 1859, and by the mid-1860s cameras with multiple lenses were taking many images on a single plate, making portraits even cheaper. The carte format remained the dominant form of portraiture for the next twenty years. Their convenient size and weight made these photographs ideal for sending to far-flung family and friends. The affordability of cartes provided the first opportunity for people from all social classes to own images of themselves and loved ones. It was now possible for ordinary Australians to obtain their likeness, affecting the way individuals thought about themselves and their clothing forevermore.

There was a proliferation of photographic studio portraits, modeled on the grand portrait paintings of the upper classes. Formal dress was the order of the day, with sitters depicted in the act of receiving visitors or making a social call. Photographers often loaned garments or accessories and provided advice about clothing choices. Clients were encouraged to wear garments that draped nicely and to avoid light colors, shiny fabrics, bold patterns, and fussy trims or too many accessories. The subjects were often presented in full figure, so their complete attire was recorded. Accessories such as a book, fan, or top hat were used to suggest an air of culture and high social standing. Painted screens, backdrops, carpets, and studio furniture—including curtains, columns, urns, posing chairs, and papier maché doorways or balustrades—were incorporated to create the illusion that the sitter was positioned in an upper-middle-class drawing room. As props were reused and regularly updated, these can appear in many photographs and may be useful aids in dating or identifying studios.

Thomas Bock (1790–1855) used the same repertoire of stylistic devices in his paintings as in his daguerreotypes—a medium capable of producing many portrait images a day compared with the several months required for a painted portrait. Elaborately hand-colored photographs increasingly offered an affordable alternative to painted portraits. Photographs also became an invaluable tool in an artist's work, for documentary purposes and as aide-mémoires to recording likenesses.

The gold rushes provided a major impetus to the expansion of photography from the 1850s to the 1870s. The sudden increase in population accelerated the demand for portraiture. Photographic operations such as Beaufoy Merlin's American & Australasian Photographic Company (A&APC) took their apparatus on the road. One aspect of this company's work was the introduction of figures into their streetscapes. While recording the progress of towns in Victoria and central-western New South Wales, the photographers also captured portraits of people standing outside buildings. These images provide a detailed survey of the clothing worn in newly expanding rural communities, some, like the Chinese, documenting their ethnic dress, others recording serviceable utilitarian clothing. Many immigrants sent these images back home, and, as exchanging photographs became the rage, photograph albums were developed to store pictures of loved ones placed alongside collections of celebrity images.

The State Library of New South Wales holds 3,500 A&APC glass-plate negatives as well as more than 100,000 negatives and a selection of sitters' books from the Sydney-based Freeman Studio (begun in 1875), a collection of 300,000 negatives from the New South Wales Government Printing Office (1869–1989), and pioneer news photographer Sam Hood's archive of about 33,000 negatives (1925–1950) accompanied by his diaries and catalogs. These collections are extremely well documented, some with names and negative numbers from which a date may be ascertained. For many of the Hood negatives, additional contextual information can be gleaned from the news stories published alongside the images.

In 1880 the introduction of dry-plate negatives for paper-based photographs brought more changes to the business of portraiture. Photographers were freed from the need to sensitize their own plates or develop them immediately after exposure, enabling greater flexibility for working outside. Group portraits of sporting teams, social clubs, or work colleagues were posed in open-air settings. Thus, photographic portraiture could not only represent the character of its subject but also a sense of place. Reduced exposure time (from approximately five seconds to one second) resulted in the growth of child portraiture, with larger cabinet cards and postcards superseding the carte de visite.

Most photography illustrates dress in some way; however, the term *fashion photography* usually refers to a genre—the purpose of which is to *sell* clothing. This definition becomes more complex when we consider that a photograph can be *used* as a fashion photograph even though it may originally have been taken for another purpose, such as celebrity portraiture.

By the 1860s photographs of fashionable women had provided models of bourgeois dress for the viewer. Carte de visite portraits and postcards of theatrical performers and other celebrities were broadly distributed and inspired widespread sartorial imitation. At a time when the theater functioned as a key medium for the proliferation of clothing trends, portraits of Australian theatrical celebrities constitute an important archive of protofashion photography that is often difficult to distinguish from portraiture. The early history of Australian fashion photography emerged in the 1900s and can be linked to social and glamour portraiture. Photographic portraits of wealthy socialites and theatrical celebrities are primarily about the individual but also reveal their clothing, and, in the mutual quest for publicity, actresses often posed in designer gowns, which the public rushed to copy.

In 1888 Eastman Kodak pioneered the manufacture of do-it-yourself photography, thus actively encouraging all aspects of everyday life as worthy subject matter for snapshots. Street photography emerged in the late nineteenth century with the development of small and easily concealed cameras, offering the operator the opportunity to catch subjects in informal, impromptu, and even intimate moments.

A series of street scenes photographed in Sydney by Arthur K. Syer, ca. 1885–1890, show barrow-shoppers and hawkers, children playing, queues at Circular Quay, shipping, street cleaning, scenes at horse races, and a fairground, all invaluable in revealing everyday clothing. These images were commissioned by artist Phil May to assist him in lampooning Sydney types in his cartoons for the *Bulletin*. The viewpoint of these images indicates they were probably taken with a hidden camera, enabling the photographer to capture the subjects without their knowledge and showing rare details, including back views.

The worldwide depression of the 1930s saw the proliferation of street photographers. Using small-format cameras, snapping passersby, these commercial street photographers worked without the overhead costs of studios, thus cutting prices. Such images provide some of the most important documents of how people actually dressed going about their everyday business. Capturing clothing in action, they record unsuspecting subjects in street wear rather than dressed for the camera. Unfortunately, public repositories are poor sources of street photography as few, if any, negative archives have been collected. The isolated examples that do exist are scattered across individual collections, stored in family albums, or filed within personal papers.

As photography became reasonably fast and inexpensive, the pleasure of personally recording a person, place, or event soon ensured that many took up the hobby. In just two months in 1896,

"Young Girls," an albumen print taken with a hidden camera, ca. 1885. The photographer's many shots of this kind are useful documents of everyday dress around 1880s Sydney. Photograph by Arthur K. Syer. Mitchell Library, State Library of New South Wales.

three thousand Pocket Kodak cameras were sold in Australia. Libraries, museums, and families must own many millions of examples of private snapshots, and these images are another source of clothing information. Although snapshots have been little used by dress historians, when housed within original albums and annotated with dates, places, family names, and images of the family home, candid photographs and home movies can provide an invaluable resource for the study of Australian dress.

The Australian film industry was one of the earliest in the world. For over four decades most cinema programs comprised two features with one or two trailers, a cartoon, and a couple of newsreels, most containing dependable dress information. One of the newsreels would be either the locally produced *Cinesound Review* or *Australian Movietone News*, and the other an international edition of an American or British newsreel. Like newspapers, the format of newsreels was similar the world over. There were the obligatory sporting and fashion segments, and novelty items helped when hard news was lacking. The Australian newsreels were issued weekly and usually reached the cinema a week or so after an event. By 1956 television had arrived, and the age of the newsreel in Australia came to an end with the last issue of *Australian Movie Magazine* on 27 November 1975.

Although only a fraction of the pre-1930 newsreel output survives in archives, some date back to 1896. The surviving footage provides a record of how people looked, behaved, and amused themselves, as well as a rich resource for the study of dress; and, from the commentaries that accompany them, newsreels also tell us something of the attitudes of the times. In 1988 the National Film and Sound Archive (NFSA) launched Operation Newsreel, designed to collect and preserve surviving *Cinesound* and *Movietone* newsreel footage. The NFSA currently has twenty thousand newsreel stories in its collection, recording most major events in Australian history, entertainment, and sport from 1929 to 1975. Compilations of newsreel footage, copied to VHS videotape format, are now available for sale from the NFSA, covering a range of topics including Australia lifestyle, fashion, sport, and war service.

PRINTED IMAGES OF DRESS

Although a printing press had been included in the cargo of the First Fleet, printing did not begin in the colony until the late 1790s. In 1803 the government established a newspaper and John Lewin produced Australia's first engraved and printed images. In 1812–1814 entrepreneurial emancipist Absalom West published the first printed views of New South Wales produced for the local market, engraved by convicts assigned to him. The printed image was not inexpensive, but it was more accessible and covered a much wider range of subject matter than paintings—architectural prints with distinctively dressed figures to indicate lifestyle and scale, contemporary events from the popular to the historic, portraits, fashion plates, and occupational scenes, many containing details of people and their clothes.

Augustus Earle published Australia's first pictorial lithograph, a portrait of *Bungaree, a Native of New South Wales*, produced in Sydney in 1826. Once back in England, Earle quickly made further use of this image in his *Views of New South Wales and Van Diemens Land*, published in 1830, along with others executed during his time in the colony, including *A Government Jail Gang* with its rare depiction of convict workers and their garb.

In 1834 convict artist Charles Rodius produced his two set series of twelve portraits of chiefs of various New South Wales tribes and their wives. Rodius also contributed at least one portrait (*The Orator—Robert Lowe*) to *Heads of the People: An Illustrated Journal of Literature, Whims, and Oddities*, appearing weekly during 1847–1848. Published by William Baker and running through two volumes and fifty issues, each issue included a pen-portrait lithograph of a well-known colonial identity principally drawn by William Nicholas. The three-quarter-length studies of each "type" supply more than serviceable likeness, as they are accompanied by tongue-in-cheek commentaries laced with local intelligence. *Heads of the People* included an unprecedented range of colonists in its series of portraits, the only exclusion being the indigenous population. Rather than picking out the wealthiest citizens, or those who loomed largest in public life, Baker sought to document contemporary Sydney society through "types," using living examples as representative of each class, such as the Schoolmaster, Actor, Draper, and Undertaker. These images provide rare documentation of occupational dress accompanied by contextual information to create an overall portrait of metropolitan Sydney in the 1840s.

The illustrated press played a key role in the "frenzy of the visible" during the nineteenth century. The image-making technology used to create most images appearing in the mass illustrated press was made possible by wood engraving. Developed in the late eighteenth century, wood engraving rose to prominence in colonial Australia during the 1840s and lasted for fifty years before the emergence of the photographic half-tone process. The target audience of the illustrated papers was the urban, middle-class family keen to see their belief in the progress of the colony confirmed by visual representation of the Australian way of life.

The *Illustrated Sydney News* (ISN) was launched in October 1853. While it lacked the backing of a parent daily paper, like the *Illustrated Australian News* (1862–1896), which was published by the Melbourne *Age* (beginning in 1854), the *ISN* was much better served in its production, as Walter Mason, one of the original partners and the principal engraver, had previously worked on both the *Illustrated London News* and *Punch*. The *ISN* was the colonial paper most closely modeled on the *Illustrated London News* and, under Mason's guidance, was much more astute in its choice of images, subject matter, and production quality than other colonial publications.

By the middle of the nineteenth century every large Australian town had its own version of London's *Punch*, the world's leading illustrated comic journal. *Melbourne Punch* (1855–1925), *Sydney Punch* (1864–1888), *Tasmanian Punch* (1866–1878), *Hobart Town Punch* (1867–1868), *Adelaide Punch* (1864–1884), and *Queensland Punch* (1878–1913) were all modeled on their English namesake, which, from its start in 1841, had filled its pages with witty sketches parodying the dress of both sexes and all ages and classes. The State Library of New South Wales acquired a large archive of original cartoons from the *Bulletin* (1880–2008) in the 1960s, and several Australian cultural institutions have been systematically collecting cartoons since the 1980s.

In August 1888 the *ISN* became the first Australian newspaper to produce a photograph using the photomechanical half-tone process, by which the even gray tones of photographs could be reproduced, and two weeks later the *Sydney Mail* became the first weekly paper to use the same process. With the ongoing refinement of the half-tone process, photographs of society weddings began to appear, as well as other photographic features, typically photogrids of fashionable men and women attending important social functions, or scenes from sporting events.

Detailed local fashion information can be gleaned from contemporary Australian illustrated newspapers and magazines, such as the *Australasian Town and Country Journal* (1870–1931) and the *Sydney Mail* (1860–1938), both printing a fashion column and plate in each issue. Mail-order catalogs, trade publications, and other advertising ephemera all provide valuable imagery for the study of dress. The fashion plates included in Australian illustrated newspapers and magazines are likely to have been redrawn directly from imported ones, especially those found inside high-end women's magazines, or from plates reproduced in illustrated newspapers published overseas—an important consideration when determining the usefulness or appropriateness of a fashion plate as a reliable source of dress information.

IMAGES OF DRESS IN WOMEN'S MAGAZINES

From the eighteenth century consumers could subscribe to lifestyle magazines and periodicals containing small black-and-white prints depicting court occasions, famous people, and new styles of dress with detailed descriptions of fashions, fabrics, accessories, and jewelry. Copies of these journals, such as *Ackermann's Repository* (1809–1829), are known to have been available in the colony, along with other magazines for women.

In the second half of the nineteenth century imported women's magazines proliferated, providing a mixture of content including housekeeping tips, instructions for fancy work, hints on etiquette, and news of the latest fashions, as well as paper dressmaking patterns. No Australian artist was routinely engaged in producing practical fashion plates until the advent of Madame Weigel. Establishing a dress pattern publishing service in 1879 and a fashion magazine in 1880, *Weigel's Journal of Fashion* would have found its way into many Australian households. The use of photography in fashion magazines emerged slowly and did not immediately follow the development of the half-tone process in 1881. When advertisements for clothing and department stores did appear in print they remained hand-drawn rather than photographic until at least the 1920s.

Beginning in the late 1920s the range of fashion publications and women's magazines widened to attract a far broader social readership. Although the more up-market international periodicals, like *Vogue*, *Harper's Bazaar*, and the locally produced *The Home* (1920–1942), continued to offer fashion drawings and photographs, cheaper magazines like the *Australian Women's Weekly* (beginning in 1933), *Women's Budget* (1906–1934), and *New Idea* (beginning in 1928) showed more down-to-earth, though still idealized, images of young working girls and married women.

By the 1930s magazine editors became aware that their younger readers were more attuned to Hollywood than the high fashions of Paris. The *Australian Women's Weekly* published a regular *Movie World* supplement in the 1930s and 1940s devoted to screen stars, their clothes, and their lifestyles, fully illustrated with photographs supplied by the studio publicity departments. As for its fashion pages, *The Weekly* aimed for a sense of chic without showing clothes that were beyond the reach of its middle-class readership. Fashion advice and advertisements recognized the mass ready-to-wear market, and its pattern service was an ongoing success with the home consumer.

"The Undertaker" (Mr. Richard Hayes), 1847, from *Heads of the People: An Illustrated Journal of Literature, Whims, and Oddities*, published weekly by William Baker during 1847 and 1848, and always featuring one such study of a different Sydney "type." Lithograph by William Nicholas. Mitchell Library, State Library of New South Wales.

In the 1950s and 1960s *The Weekly* continued to present the best of world fashion and document the development of Australian style in its "Fashion in the Shops" feature. From the mid-1950s *The Weekly* also targeted the next new market of fashion consumers, teenage girls, and a monthly teenage supplement was introduced in 1954. From the 1960s color photography took over from sketches as the primary mode of fashion reporting as *The Weekly* continued its quest to offer, across the broad spectrum of its readership, something for everyone. *Pix* (1938–1972), one of the most recognizable Australian magazines of the twentieth century, provides another rich source of local imagery with its mix of fashion, culture, politics, entertainment, and scandal.

To accurately explain dress in any image so that it may be viewed correctly, one must attempt to recreate its social context. This is not difficult in magazines and newspapers. We can speculate most confidently about a portrait image when we know the name of the creator, the identity and social class of the sitter, and the date of production. But faced with an image that has lost its history, how can one reconstruct the circumstances of its production? When nothing is known about the subject, the place, or the creator, the one identifiable element common to all portraits is the clothing; even in nude studies, the hairstyles, accessories, and studio props can usually provide sufficient detail to suggest a fairly accurate date.

What people choose to wear to have their portrait taken can be influenced by many factors. The age and social position of the sitter and circumstances or the event for which it was commissioned can all provide valuable details of context. People tend not to record the more mundane moments in their lives. Tradition dictates specific attire for rites of passage and professional milestones, which are often marked by ceremonial occasions in which dress plays an important part.

Documentary images usually found in library and archival collections more often meet the needs of the dress researcher than those collected by art galleries. As the primary purpose of documentary images is the provision of an objective visual record that illustrates social anthropology rather than artistic idealism, their information content may exceed their artistic merit. However, a picture is more than just an image, and placing any image in an archival repository takes it out of its social context.

Keeping the image in an original frame or album or within a collection of papers or ephemera will retain something of its past, and knowing who created it and where it came from will secure some of its life. With the image as the starting point, it is important to seek out a range of artworks and objects to compare the different ways in which dress is depicted in different media, each making its own contribution to the study of Australian dress.

References and Further Reading

Butler, Roger. *Printed Images in Colonial Australia 1801–1901.* Canberra: National Gallery of Australia, 2007.

Cumming, Valerie. "Dress in Art and Dress as Art." In *Understanding Fashion History*, edited by Valerie Cumming, 82–98. Hollywood, CA: Costume and Fashion Press, 2004.

Davies, Alan, and Peter Stanbury. *The Mechanical Eye in Australia: Photography 1841–1900.* Melbourne, Australia: Oxford University Press, 1985.

Dowling, Peter. "Destined Not to Survive: The Illustrated Newspapers of Colonial Australia." In *Studies in Newspaper and Periodical History*, edited by M. Harris and T. O'Malley, 85–98. Westport, CT: Greenwood Press, 1995.

Frost, Lenore. *Dating Family Photographs.* Essendon, Australia: Lenore Frost, 1991.

Kerr, Joan, ed. *The Dictionary of Australian Artists: Painters, Sketchers, Photographers and Engravers to 1870.* Melbourne, Australia: Oxford University Press, 1992.

McDonald, Patricia, and Barry Pearce. *The Artist and the Patron: Aspects of Colonial Art in New South Wales.* Sydney: Art Gallery of NSW, 1988.

Messenger, Jane. "Identity: Photographic Portraiture in the 19th Century." In *A Century in Focus: South Australian Photography, 1840s–1940s*, edited by Julie Robinson, 22–27. Adelaide: Art Gallery of South Australia, 2007.

Neville, Richard. *Faces of Australia: Image Reality and the Portrait.* Sydney: State Library of NSW, 1992.

Palmer, Daniel. "Tracing the Origins of Australian Fashion Photography." *The La Trobe Journal* 76 (Spring 2005): 87–105.

Severa, Joan. *Dressed for the Photographer: Ordinary Americans and Fashion 1840–1900.* Kent, OH: Kent State University Press, 1995.

Taylor, Lou. *The Study of Dress History.* Manchester, UK: Manchester University Press, 2002.

Margot Riley

See also Resources: Collections of Colonial Dress and Fashion in Australia; Fashion Photography in Australia.

Resources: Collections of Colonial Dress and Fashion in Australia

- Early Settler Dress
- Specialized and Occupational Dress
- Regional, Trust, and Special Interest Collections
- City Fashions
- Resources and Heritage Collection Management

The Colonial period in Australia began with the establishment of the penal colony of New South Wales in 1788 and ended with the federation of Australia's six colonies in 1901. By this time the Australian population reached just over 3.7 million, although immigration and birth rates were in decline. During this period Australia attained many hallmarks of a modern society, including urban and regional centers with good shopping facilities, cultural and educational institutions, clothing manufacturers, and a wide variety of other business and industrial activities. Despite their distance from Europe, the harsh climate, and initial lack of resources, many Australians developed a keen interest in dress and sometimes over-invested in elaborate attire. Clothing and dress from the Colonial period reflected the social, cultural, economic, and physical environments that distinguished Australia at the time.

Surviving examples of Australian colonial dress are dispersed across most states in a network of significant government institutions, most notably the Powerhouse Museum in Sydney and the National Gallery of Victoria in Melbourne. There are collections also in many regional museums, National Trust branches, house museums, and historical societies. Except for the Sydney organization, Cavalcade, none of these focuses exclusively on clothing but instead acquires material relating broadly to social history or the decorative arts. This situation is different from that in countries like France, England, and the United States, which support national dress collections. In comparison to these countries, however, Australia had only a small population in the late eighteenth and nineteenth centuries, creating an equally small pool of clothing to survive the decades. Until fairly recently, collecting fashion, dress, and accessories has not been a priority area for museums. By the early twenty-first century, Australian collections contain more examples of women's clothing, followed by lesser numbers of children's clothing and rare though exceptional examples of male dress.

Australia's largest collections of colonial dress were established between the 1950s and 1970s, when high-quality garments were favored over the mass-produced and homemade. As a result, wedding dresses, mourning dresses, ball gowns, baptism gowns, and other specialty pieces were acquired in substantial quantities for their aesthetic and sentimental appeal. Because it was comparatively plain and ubiquitous, major institutions overlooked everyday clothing, and, unfortunately, those examples that do survive are often unprovenanced. Policies in the twenty-first century have changed, and this rare material has become much sought-after.

A significant example is the large and well-documented collection of late-nineteenth-century clothing and undergarments, acquired by the Powerhouse Museum, that belonged to the Sydney working-class Flavelle family. This collection includes handmade and machine-made items for day-to-day wear. The National Trust of Victoria is also collecting everyday wear while improving records of its existing items.

Working Australians were highly resourceful in their use of fabric, adopting numerous measures to extend the lifespan of their wardrobes. Everyday items were mended, altered, and reworked into new garments or passed on to other family members. In contrast, special items of clothing were worn sparingly to survive several years and sometimes several decades. The legacy of this behavior is that few examples of everyday colonial clothing exist today. It is interesting that a fair number of male convict garments, including headwear, survives, primarily in collections in Tasmania and at the National Museum of Australia in Canberra.

EARLY SETTLER DRESS

Given the scarcity of everyday clothing, it is ironic that one of Australia's oldest garments is a simple infant's dress, homemade from recycled fabric in Parramatta, New South Wales, in about 1803. The item was probably made by Elizabeth Marsden, wife of Reverend Samuel Marsden, for their two-year-old son, William. It is unlikely that this humble garment would have survived had William not been wearing it when he fell into a pot of boiling water in the kitchen and died. His mother kept the dress in remembrance. The incident highlights the sense of isolation that must have overcome many settlers in times of illness or tragedy. The dress is held by the Powerhouse Museum along with several other articles that belonged to the Marsden family.

Samuel Marsden migrated to Australia in 1794 and became the assistant to the chaplain of New South Wales. In 1795 he moved to the colonial settlement of Parramatta, where he established a large farm and raised a family. Gradually, he reached the positions of resident chaplain and magistrate and became well known for his brutal punishment of the convict population. The piety of the Marsden family is reflected in a simple muslin gown and silk petticoat that the eldest daughter, Ann Marsden, wore to a Government House ball in 1822. This would have been a lavish affair for the Sydney elite, particularly women, who followed French and English fashions. Made from fine tambour-embroidered muslin with a high waist, long lace-cuffed sleeves, and a high round collar, this pretty dress probably seemed rather plain in comparison to those worn by the more stylish guests. It was nonetheless a practical item for a woman whose family refrained from fashionable society. Today it is also an example of the prevalence of imported muslin.

Throughout the early 1800s Chinese and Indian muslin were popular materials in colonial wardrobes and homes. The New South Wales branch of the National Trust of Australia has an embroidered muslin gown that was made in around 1805 for the wife of the third governor of New South Wales, Mrs. Philip Gidley King. Some historians suggest that its simple construction, of an adjoining bodice and skirt, indicates that its maker may have been a Sydney seamstress. The fabric itself is elegantly embroidered in silver thread in a pattern of floral sprigs.

Silk was also favored by the colonial elite and was imported extensively from India, China, and England. The Historic Houses Trust of New South Wales, in Sydney, has the silk ensemble that Anna Elizabeth Blaxland wore to her wedding to Thomas Walker, the assistant commissary general, in January 1823. The outfit consists of a striped silk gown, silk veil, kid gloves, cotton stockings, silk slippers, and a silk shawl that is possibly of Chinese origin. The gown has a high waist and bodice and trimmings of laced cord and tassels, demonstrating the military styling that remained in fashion after the Napoleonic wars. Such an elaborate outfit was appropriate for the daughter of a wealthy landowner and merchant like John Blaxland.

By the 1820s the number of Sydney dressmakers had increased in tandem with the population of freed convicts seeking an income. Colonial-made clothing improved significantly in quality, gradually shedding its reputation for being inferior to imported articles. Anna Blaxland may well have taken advantage of these developments by employing a local seamstress to make her dress from imported silk.

Life in the colonies captivated the imagination of people in far-off Britain. The Tasmanian writer Louisa Anne Meredith gained great fame in England for her candid accounts of Australian society. She was also a painter, naturalist, and early champion for the conservation of Tasmania's wilderness. The Narryna Heritage Museum in Hobart has a printed cotton day dress with a full-tiered skirt and matching shawl that Meredith wore in about 1853. The garment was made either in England or India and is printed with borders of blue boteh (a paisley motif). Printed cotton was a popular material in Australia because it was decorative, cool, and easy to clean. However, frequent usage meant that it deteriorated faster than printed silk, which was reserved for special occasions. Today there are few examples of printed cotton gowns in Australian collections, although silk varieties are common.

SPECIALIZED AND OCCUPATIONAL DRESS

Practical and sturdy work-wear was an important component of the Australian colonial wardrobe. It was a necessity in remote and rural areas, where time and money could not always be spent on fluctuating fashions. Nonetheless, written records do indicate that many country people were remarkably fashion-conscious. The Powerhouse Museum has one of the earliest examples of ready-made moleskin trousers that date to about 1830. Paintings and photographs show that these hard-wearing items remained part of the bushman's attire for many decades. The Powerhouse Museum also has two examples of waterproof waistcoats, ready-made in the late nineteenth century from animal hide lined with kangaroo fur and checked flannel. Both examples fasten across the chest with leather straps and buckles. These thick and sturdy items probably belonged to men working in Australia's colder climates, perhaps as timber cutters in the alpine regions or as stockmen on the open tablelands.

Work-wear was not always plain and practical, however, and it sometimes displayed fine craftsmanship and a high degree of detail. The Tasmanian Museum and Art Gallery has an example

of an English shepherd's smock that belonged to John Allen, who migrated to Bicheno, on the east coast of Tasmania, in about 1833. Made from natural linen, it is embroidered with floral motifs, chains, and diamond shapes that are traditional to the region of Somersetshire where Allen was born. These types of smocks were undoubtedly worn by some of the English shepherds who continued their professions on Australian soil. Other examples are held by Museum Victoria, the Devonport Gallery and Arts Centre, the Powerhouse Museum, and the Western Australian Museum.

Also from Tasmania is an interesting and well-provenanced collection of clothing that belonged to Sarah Benson Walker, a member of the Quaker movement, which gained great momentum in the colony. Established in Hobart in 1832, the Quaker community was dedicated to improving conditions for the local indigenous people, destitute women, and convicts. One of its founding members, George Washington Walker, married Sarah Benson Walker in 1840 and established a drapery business and savings bank. He also promoted temperance, education, and penal reform. The Society of Friends Meeting House in Hobart

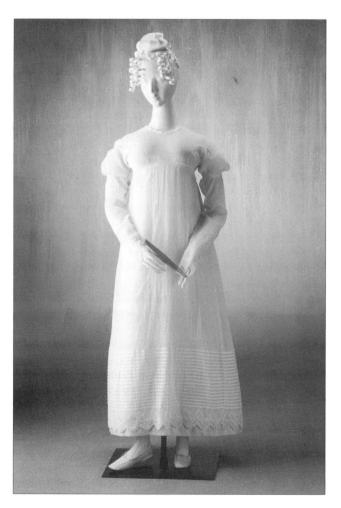

A muslin dress worn by Ann Marsden to a Government House ball, Sydney, 1822. Ann was the daughter of Reverend Samuel Marsden, who became resident chaplain and magistrate of Parramatta. The high-collared, long-sleeved dress reflects the piety of the Marsden family and would have been plain compared to the more stylish guests at the ball. Photograph by Penelope Clay. Powerhouse Museum.

now has Sarah's hand-sewn, smocked black dress, black cape, black bonnet, and shawl. The Queensland Museum also has one of her gray Quaker dresses, along with petticoats and bonnets.

Throughout the eighteenth and nineteenth centuries, hats and sunbonnets were customary components of the European female wardrobe. In Australia, however, they were far more than fashion accessories, providing necessary protection from the harsh sun. Colonial headwear is held in collections around Australia, often stained and sun-bleached or crudely constructed for simple necessity. Indeed, signs of production and wear reveal a great deal about the history of these items, despite the fact that they are frequently unprovenanced.

Sun helmets or pith hats were popular in the late nineteenth century, especially in the tropical regions of northern Australia. An example at the Powerhouse Museum was made in India in about 1880 for the Sydney department store Anthony Hordern & Sons Ltd. It retailed under the brand name Solar. The museum also has a puggaree, or neck shade, made in India in about 1850 from lightweight, honeycombed cotton. Popular in Australia's warmer climates, these accessories were secured around a hat or helmet with a portion draping down the neck to provide shade.

The Castlemaine Art Gallery and Historical Museum has a cabbage tree hat (a hat made from the leaves of the cabbage palm tree) that was made for the 1880 Melbourne International Exhibition as an example of colonial industry. Plaited from the straw of the native cabbage palm, the cabbage tree hat was practical, cool, and common in both the bush and town. It was a distinctive item of colonial dress, worn by men of different professions and economic positions and made in Australia from local materials. By the late nineteenth century, production had evolved into a form of cottage industry, so that many surviving examples show a high level of craftsmanship. Another cabbage tree hat, held by the Illawarra Historical Society, comes from the Illawarra area of southern New South Wales, where stands of cabbage palm were abundant. The cabbage tree hat appears frequently in the work of S. T. Gill and other colonial artists who depicted diggers on the Australian goldfields.

A ready-made sailor suit that Albert and Harriet Glük bought for their nine-year-old son, Leopold, in England, in 1889 is now in the Western Australian Museum. The Austrian-Jewish family migrated to Australia in 1890, living in the Victorian gold-mining town of Nhil before spending several years in a tent camp on the Western Australian goldfields. In about 1900 the family of seven settled in Perth and opened a fruit shop. The outbreak of World War I brought new hardships for the family, which changed its name to Glik to conceal its Austrian heritage. Leopold, by this time a qualified tailor's cutter, enlisted with the Australian forces and went to Gallipoli. He was wounded on the second day of the campaign and died one week later, on 2 May 1915. His sailor suit is thus a significant record of one of the state's migrant families and of someone who eventually fought for his new country.

REGIONAL, TRUST, AND SPECIAL INTEREST COLLECTIONS

Australia's first inland town, Bathurst, was established in 1815 along the Macquarie River in central-eastern New South Wales. Its colonial population consisted of military personnel, convicts, and some pastoralists who farmed the surrounding tablelands. The Bathurst District Historical Society and Regional Museum

holds an important collection of colonial dress, including an elegant gown of embroidered Indian muslin. Records show that this petite piece was worn to a wedding in Bristol in 1795. One of these early settlers may well have brought the gown to the Bathurst area. The historical society also holds colonial christening gowns, evening gowns, and a mantle that belonged to Sarah Piper, a former convict and the wife of Captain John Piper, who owned a large property in the region.

Australia's regional museums and historical societies hold many significant examples of colonial dress that reflect the individuals who contributed to a district's development. The township of Tongarra was settled on the south coast of New South Wales in 1843 under a scheme that encouraged immigrants to escape Sydney's high unemployment. The area would soon prosper from dairy farming, timber cutting, and shipping. The Tongarra Museum now has an important collection of clothing provenanced to the English immigrant Sarah Thomas, including the silk tartan skirt she made aboard the *City of Westminster*, the ship that brought her to Australia in 1838. The brightly colored skirt was probably worn with its now-missing bodice on special occasions.

From 1820 the rate of free immigration to Australia began to exceed the level of convict transportation. This commenced a new and expansive phase in the history of Australian settlement. While the majority of migrants came from Britain and Ireland, other nationalities would arrive in significant numbers at particular times. German migration, for example, escalated in 1838 following the persecution of Old Lutherans in their Prussian homeland. From the late 1840s until the early twentieth century, the Barossa Valley in South Australia would be a major center of German settlement.

The Migration Museum in Adelaide, South Australia, has the brown dress that Martha Hulda Kutzer wore for her traditional Lutheran wedding to Carl Christian Gehrike in 1900. The Prussian-born couple raised a family and ran a butcher shop in the South Australian township of Salem. The wedding was an important religious occasion within the Lutheran faith and a sacred rite of passage. Customarily, the wedding dress was made in black silk taffeta, though it sometimes came in brown, gray, dark blue, or dark green. This example is trimmed with lace, which was a popular and modest form of adornment. The Migration Museum also has the silk handkerchief that Martha probably carried with her on her wedding day.

Discovered in Bathurst in 1851, gold brought great changes to the Australian colonies, including a huge influx of hopeful migrants. In Victoria prospecting centered on the inland townships of Ballarat and Bendigo, although the ensuing wealth also transformed the city of Melbourne. The Gold Museum in Ballarat holds a brown day dress worn on the Victorian goldfields by English immigrant Eliza Perrin.

Married in West Yorkshire in 1851, John and Eliza Perrin were together for only a few months before John left for the Victorian goldfields. Eliza followed her husband to Australia in the following year and arrived in Ballarat with their newborn daughter. In this unconventional environment, women like Eliza were free to make independent and valuable contributions to the family income. Within a short period of time, she had established a successful store and refreshment house, before she and her husband opened a butcher shop in a nearby town. The Gold Museum has a photograph of Eliza wearing the day dress in a Ballarat studio with her three young children.

The Victorian Branch of the National Trust of Australia has a pair of children's leather boots that were handmade in the 1850s on the Ballarat goldfields. They feature engraved buckles and toe caps and iron reinforcements on their hand-carved heels and soles. Today the boots are an example of colonial resourcefulness and a reminder that children also experienced the often harsh conditions of the diggings.

Gradually, the goldfields developed a community atmosphere, visible in the establishment of schools, churches, hospitals, theaters, and sporting clubs. The Bradman Museum in Bowral, New South Wales, has a collection of cast brass buckles that diggers wore when playing cricket around the Ballarat goldfields. Although these items are crudely made, their cast and painted cricket scenes must have added a festive flair to the traditional cream uniforms. This particular set was discovered by modern-day fossickers using metal detectors. Another excellent set is held by the Melbourne Cricket Club.

The discovery of gold also brought a sharp increase in bushranging activities, particularly on roads between the diggings and major cities or towns. The Historic Houses Trust of New South Wales has part of the uniform and kit issued to Edward Montague Battye, Sub-Inspector of the New South Wales Mounted Police Patrol from 1851 to 1861. Established in 1850, the patrol escorted gold deliveries along the dangerous roads between Bathurst and Sydney. The Trust has Battye's pillbox style cap, black woolen tunic, leather belt, and riding boots.

CITY FASHIONS

As the nineteenth century progressed, an air of sophistication could be seen in Australian cities and larger towns. Palatial shops and department stores were established, servicing not only city folk but also rural customers via mail order catalogs. In Victoria high import tariffs and developments in textile manufacturing led to a strong clothing industry. The Victorian branch of the National Trust of Australia has an impressive collection of late-nineteenth-century clothing made by Melbourne tailors and department stores, including Bright and Hitchcock, Foy & Gibson, Madame Eels, Myer, and Robertson & Moffatt.

In 1883 the British journalist Richard Twopeny remarked that Melbourne was the most fashionable of Australian cities and that Sydney was comparatively provincial in its style of wardrobe. The National Gallery of Victoria has a collection of late-nineteenth-century garments that belonged to the fashionable Sprigg family of Melbourne. Some of the locally made items include a twill wool equestrienne outfit of 1880, a white satin wedding dress of 1885, and another wedding dress made by Robertson & Moffatt in 1892. Until the 1890s, however, many Melbourne dressmakers did not label their garments, so that precise identifications are difficult today. Both the National Gallery of Victoria and the National Trust of Victoria are currently researching the anonymous pieces in their collections.

Sydney also supported large department stores that included Farmers, David Jones, and Anthony Hodern's & Sons Ltd. In 1872 English immigrant Rachel Henning wrote to her sister, Etta, about a successful shopping trip to Farmer's for clothing. In her letter she described the store as an immense establishment where a customer could choose a dress and have the material sent to the dressmaking department, where it was made "in the best fashion." She found its range to be among the finest in Sydney and its departments to be a "wonderful save of time and trouble."

The Powerhouse Museum has a beaded and sequined silk brocade dress, bought ready-made from David Jones in Sydney in about 1890. Its cut, fabric, and finish demonstrate that ready-made garments did not necessarily lack the quality and sophistication of the tailor-made. Still in operation today, David Jones has an extensive archive of historic catalogs, while the Historic Houses Trust of New South Wales has a collection of mail order catalogs from Anthony Hodern's & Sons Ltd. This printed material now provides a typical impression of late-nineteenth-century middle-class Australian clothing.

The Queensland Museum has a small collection of late-nineteenth-century ready-made items that include a bodice from the Brisbane department store Allen and Stark and a cotton bustle dress from Stuarts of Rockhampton. It also has a collection of garments by Janet Walker, a Scottish migrant and one of the most successful dressmakers in colonial Queensland. Walker established a dressmaking business in Brisbane in 1882 and opened a Ladies Emporium with her new partner, Margaret Caldwell, in the following decade. By 1898 the pair employed 120 staff and ran a large atelier that produced made-to-measure and ready-made items. The business served "most of the well-known society ladies of the time" as well as rural clientele who purchased items through mail-order catalogs. Walker's gowns were worn at several official Federation celebrations in 1901. The Brisbane Museum has an important collection of Walker garments, including a short-sleeved, silk brocade ball gown that is believed to have been worn by Barbara Jane Drury, wife of the manager of the Queensland National Bank, to a vice-regal ball at Government House in Brisbane in 1892. The Powerhouse Museum also has a taffeta and silk brocade dressing jacket, made by Walker in Brisbane in about 1885.

RESOURCES AND HERITAGE COLLECTION MANAGEMENT

Many regional museums and historical societies in Australia are now seeking advice on ways to manage their heritage collections. Through its Regional Services Program, the Powerhouse Museum is assisting organizations like the Bathurst District Historical Society, which hold important examples of colonial clothing. The program was established to connect museum staff with regional communities that need advice on the development, research, and care of their collections. Although the program relates to a range of heritage material, its influence on costume and dress has been significant. Indeed, it was through this service that the 1795 muslin gown at Bathurst was dated to the Regency period, and not classified as a twentieth-century replica as initially believed.

In 2001 the government-funded body the Collections Council of Australia published *Significance: A Guide to Assessing the Significance of Cultural Heritage Objects and Collections*. This was the first publication in Australia to provide a single framework for assessing the provenance, rarity, condition, and interpretative value of heritage items. Since its publication, it has informed organizations that range from major museums and galleries to regional museums and historical societies. Although its content exceeds costume and dress, its influence on this field has been particularly significant.

The Powerhouse Museum is also developing an online register of Australian dress. Drawing together documentation, photographs, and published articles, it will reflect the range of clothing styles held in major and regional institutions. Through the site, the museum hopes to discover rare or important pieces while improving general understandings of bush dress, occupational dress, and other everyday clothing.

All this is indicative of a new approach to collecting and managing surviving dress. Since the beginning of the twenty-first century, Australian institutions have begun to reassess collections of colonial dress, particularly items that lack context and provenance. However, poor record-keeping of previous decades means that physical attributes are sometimes the only clues to an item's origins. Fortunately, paintings, journals, pattern books, and mail-order catalogs provide an insight into colonial clothing, including the style and setting in which it was worn. Introduced to Australia in the early 1940s, the camera provided another important source of pictorial information.

State libraries hold vast collections of studio photographs and *cartes de visites* that show Australians in their finest clothing. Offering a more candid view of the Australian population is the Holtermann Collection, held by the State Library of New South Wales. It consists of over thirty-five hundred glass plate negatives of the buildings and residents of the New South Wales gold-mining towns Gulgong and Hill End. Taken between 1870 and 1872 by Henry Beaufoy Merlin and Charles Bayliss, these images were part of an epic project to record every premises in Melbourne, Sydney, and several towns. The photographs show men, women, and children in everyday clothing outside their homes or places of business. The photographs of Nicholas Caire, George Bell, Charles Kerry, and Henry King also offer naturalistic views of the colonial population.

For historical societies and regional museums problems with identification and documentation often merge into broader issues of collections management. For this reason the Collections Council of Australia offers practical advice to organizations that frequently suffer from limited resources and funding. It provides information on common types of damage to textiles and describes the best methods of handling, storage, and preventative conservation. Where once there was little interest in collecting and preserving historical garments of all kinds in Australia, there are signs of a growing desire to document and preserve clothing as an important part of the heritage of this country.

References and Further Reading

Adams, David, ed. *The Letters of Rachel Henning*. Sydney: The Bulletin Newspaper Co., 1952.

Broadbent, James, and Joy Hughes, eds. *The Age of Macquarie*. Melbourne, Australia: Melbourne University Press, 1992.

Broadbent, James, Suzanne Rickard, and Margaret Steven. *India, China, Australia: Trade and Society 1788–1850*. Sydney: Historic Houses Trust of New South Wales, 2003.

Davies, Alan, and Peter Stanbury. *The Mechanical Eye in Australia: Photography 1841–1900*. Melbourne, Australia: Oxford University Press, 1985.

Fletcher, Marion. *Costume in Australia: 1788–1901*. Melbourne, Australia: Oxford University Press, 1984.

Flower, Cedric. *Cabbage Tree: A Pictorial History of Clothes in Australia 1788–1914*. Sydney: Angus and Robertson, 1968.

Heritage Collections Council. *Significance: A Guide to Assessing the Significance of Cultural Heritage Objects and Collections*. Canberra: Collections Council of Australia, 2001.

Ioannou, Noris. *The Barossa Folk: Germanic Furniture and Craft Traditions in Australia*. Sydney: Craftsman House, 1995.

Jackson, Robert. *The Population History of Australia*. Melbourne, Australia: McPhee Gribble Publishers, 1988.

Maynard, Margaret. "Terrace Gowns and Shearer's Boots: Rethinking Dress and Public Collections." *Culture and Policy* 3, no. 2 (1992): 77–84.

Maynard, Margaret. *Fashioned from Penury: Dress as Cultural Practice in Colonial Australia*. Cambridge: Cambridge University Press, 1994.

Twopeny, Richard. *Town Life in Australia*. Harmondsworth, UK: Penguin, 1973 (reprint).

Catherine Reade

See also Images as a Resource for the Study of Australian Dress; Resources for the Study of European Dress and Fashion in New Zealand; Settler Dress in Australia; Rural Dress in Australia; Urban Fashion Culture in Australia; Footwear in Australia.

Settler Dress in Australia

- Dress and Colonial Settlement
- Class, Gender, and Identity
- Clothing Production and Supplies

Clothing was a problematic aspect of the social and cultural life of colonial Australia from the time of first settlement in 1788. Apart from military officers and civil officials, much everyday clothing was working-class wear. Yet fashionable dress was soon to become a key aspect of cultural practice, emphasizing the social status and power of the elite and aspirational elite, as well as being a symbolic indicator of class. Status signals were important in this fledgling society made up of disparate kinds of people. Declaration of status was a complex mix of quite subtle elements and associated behaviors that sometimes challenged accepted European understandings of class. Differences between masculine and feminine dress reinforced separate gender roles, but adhering to bourgeois mores was not always possible in rural areas. Here life was dominated by men, and except for the "squatocracy" (the class of wealthy, influential landowners in Australia), fashionable dress was often given a low priority. Problems of supply of cloth and clothing were endemic, especially in the early years. The effects of geography and a variable climate across the continent also played a part, as did the harsh life experienced on the land and the goldfields. There was a regional component to clothes in Australia almost from the earliest years of settlement, gradually cohering into a distinctive metropolitan and rural divide. Settlers in colonial Australia dressed in ways that reflected their British and European heritage, but unique colonial social, cultural, and geographical circumstances often resulted in distinctive dress codes and demeanor.

DRESS AND COLONIAL SETTLEMENT

Australia was first settled by the British in the late eighteenth century, primarily to house convicted felons, following the country's defeat in the American and French wars. Emigration and transportation to the colonies provided a solution to British social and economic problems such as unemployment, overcrowded prisons, and destitution. Convict transportation to Australia took place in the colony of New South Wales between 1788 and 1840, with convict settlements initiated at various times in Van Diemen's Land (Tasmania), Moreton Bay (Brisbane), and the Port Phillip District (Victoria). Convicts were sent to Western Australia much later, between 1850 and 1868. South Australia was never a penal colony. This convict presence had a major impact on settlers, who felt the need to distinguish themselves via their attire, yet the lack of convicts in South Australia made society there less abrasive and social customs more conservative. Colonial history is indeed rich in accounts of dress occasioning mistaken social identity. Some class tension arose from problems strangers had in decoding signs of social position. At the same time there was an intense awareness of social position characteristic of a small population.

Australia has a wide-ranging climate and geographical regions that vary from the tropical north to the temperate southeast that spans South Australia to New South Wales, producing warm summers and mild winters. The climate inevitably impacted on colonial dress, though British customs of dressing remained strong. In the north very hot humid conditions meant male and female settlers of the middle class chose to wear tropical white, as did colonialists in India. Pioneers also experienced harsh conditions on land that often had scanty and unreliable rainfall, and in the vast semiarid central desert areas that covered more than one-third of the continent. This unforgiving environment and necessary pastoral work, as well as farming, required stout clothing, hats, and shoes.

During the early nineteenth century Australia was transformed by the growth of the pastoral industry and by rapid expansion of settlement in eastern Australia and Tasmania between 1821 and 1850. The internal exploration of the country proceeded swiftly after the crossing of the Blue Mountains of New South Wales in 1813. The discovery of copper in 1842 and of gold deposits near Bathurst, New South Wales, in 1851 spurred the colonial gold rush in the mid-nineteenth century, causing a huge influx of population to every Australian colony. The newfound wealth of the gold rushes created a tendency to dress in gaudy fashions with considerable amounts of jewelry and accessories.

Australia was an urbanized society fairly soon after settlement. Sydney and Hobart were already flourishing towns by the 1830s, and Melbourne was settled in 1836. During the 1840s 40 percent of the population of Australia lived in towns, by the 1860s one-quarter lived in capital cities, and by the 1890s almost two-thirds lived in cities and towns. The middle classes became increasing prosperous, and a widening population had a significant effect on social patterns. Bourgeois women in the colony endeavored to keep up the social standards they had been accustomed to in Britain. The need to dress appropriately, especially in towns, created many personal wants for women of this class in the way of decoration and fine accessories, and shops began to cater to the needs of stylish settlers.

Immigrants of different nationalities were attracted to the colonies, and they brought their traditional habits of dress with them. As a result, during the 1840s towns like Adelaide gained a colorful and cosmopolitan appearance due to their Irish, Scottish, German, French, and Chinese inhabitants. Even boat crews from China, Tahiti, and other South Sea Islands were seen in what seemed like fantastic costume in Sydney in the 1820s. Towns embraced a market economy, and as a consequence of social mobility, dress styles became accessible to a range of social groups. By the 1860s much colonial urban dress closely emulated European styles. Some of this was due to the major development in the structure of the dress retail trade, persuasive advertising, transport and distribution, availability of supplies, and affordability. The numbers of available sewing machines, the emergence of mail-order catalogs selling patterns, and self-tuition and dressmaking instructions provided by journals and newspapers in the 1860s inspired the imitation of European trends. Much fashionable dress was imported or made up in accordance with European patterns. Gowns for special occasions could also be made locally, closely following the latest styles of London and Paris.

In the early years of urban settlement, especially prior to the 1840s, one of the distinguishing features of dress for men and women was the use of lightweight tropical materials. Gradually, though, urban men's day-wear in Australia began to follow the European model of homogeneously dark clothing, often ready-made. Frock coats, trousers, waistcoats, and top hats became generally accepted by the mid-1840s. Nonetheless, the specific demographic, economic, and class patterns in the colonies, and the disproportionate ratio of men to women still evident after mid-century in the emerging suburbs and fringes of metropolitan areas, shaped the overall practices of Australian clothing in distinctive ways. In particular, there were acknowledged regional differences among Australia's urban centers. Melbourne was the most fashionable of the eastern colonial cities, while men in smaller, more conservative cities like Brisbane reacted more slowly to European urban dress conventions than in the south. As colonial traveler Richard Twopeny observed in the 1880s, Melbourne styles most closely resembled the latest European styles and were therefore distinguishable from those of Sydney and other towns. There were also small groups of working men in Melbourne who dressed in exaggerated styles of jackets, trousers, and hats. They were called *larrikins*, a term that is used even in the twenty-first century to describe unconventional Australian youth.

Rural dress, a vestige of working-class dress of the early settlement years, was sometimes worn alongside urban clothing in colonial towns in the 1830s and 1840s. The occasional appearance of bush clothing in towns had much to do with the seasonal mobility of labor. The dress of experienced rural old hands consisted of rough attire quite different from conventional urban clothing. It included cabbage tree (palm leaf) hats or slouch felt hats, smock frocks, checked shirts, hard-wearing moleskin trousers, and boots. This clothing came to signify a form of egalitarianism in Australia, a mythic concept and one that did not include women. Women in rural areas felt a compulsion to keep up acceptable standards of dress and behavior. Rachel Henning, in North Queensland in the 1860s, regarded certain styles of garments as "too good" for the bush. However, all classes of women, and indeed some Aborigines in rural areas or settlements, wore stays and the cage crinoline that was fashionable in the 1850s and 1860s. Women generally continued to wear restrictive clothing of one sort or another until the 1890s.

The difficulties of generalizing about the appearance of rural women are highlighted by accounts of dress on the goldfields. Working women in these areas were often dressed shabbily for their class. Their often careless and rather masculine appearance and demeanor, as well as tattered gowns, thrown bonnets (bonnets worn well to the back of the head), and thick working shoes constantly aroused comment. On the other hand, travelers reported high fashion seen on goldfield ladies, and in 1853 William Howitt found the women at Bendigo, Victoria, more neatly dressed than one would expect in Europe. In 1880 traveler May Vivienne was surprised to observe women sumptuously dressed on the Western Australian goldfields.

The pastoral gentry, mercantile capitalists, and emancipists (freed convicts) regarded fashion as a significant way to signal their social standing as Australia's settlements slowly progressed from being penal establishments. The bourgeoisie made concerted

THE LARRIKIN.

"The Larrikin": an 1885 lithograph by Nelson P. Whitelocke, from his collection *A walk in Sydney streets on the shady side*. In Australia larrikins were young working-class men sometimes associated with criminal or loutish behavior and identified by wearing exaggerated versions of the male suit with tight trousers (or bell-shaped from the knee) and high-heeled, pointed-toed boots. National Gallery of Australia.

efforts to introduce and maintain dress codes practiced in Britain, and the rituals of social life were rigorously preserved where possible. Urban living and its affiliated activities had a significant effect on colonial bourgeois women's appearance, as female attire was considered essential to the formation of their genteel social role. Similar to European conventions, colonial fashions varied stylistically as skirts expanded and deflated, waistlines rose and fell, and sleeves enlarged and compressed. Nevertheless, certain features remained constant throughout the era. Skirts for bourgeois women, for instance, never elevated above the ankle, and sleeves of daytime dresses were long at all times. Dress for middle-class women moved stylistically from leg-of-mutton sleeves, full sweeping skirts, and flowered and feathered hats in the 1830s, to crinoline dresses in the 1850s, bustle dresses in the 1870s, and the tailor-mades (practical gowns with a tailored bodice, suited to more active women) in the 1890s. Fashionable finery for societal gatherings such as balls, promenading, and leisure closely followed styles in Europe, though visitors commented that women's dress had some regional differences.

Undoubtedly the exertion of British influence was a crucial leverage for colonial Australian dress, and the European influence on fashion continued throughout the nineteenth century. The significant influence of French styles also emerged in the 1820s and continued to play an important role throughout the nineteenth century. French fabrics, jewelry, haberdashery, and accessories were readily available in Hobart and Sydney in the 1820s and in Western Australia from 1835. During the 1870s and 1880s French fashions, accessories, and novelties continued to exert a strong impression. Bon Marché—the famous French department store—had an agent in Western Australia in the 1880s.

CLASS, GENDER, AND IDENTITY

Dress and etiquette were gendered cultural practices that determined social position in the nineteenth century. As a society dissimilar to Britain, with elites who were attempting to perpetuate the privileges and standards of behavior associated with the British upper and upper-middle classes and at the same time incorporate the newfound wealth of the gold rush, it was often difficult to identify class in Australia, especially through dress codes. Visitor Clara Aspinall observed colonial class discrepancy in the 1850s, expressing her disgust to see ordinary people in very glossy coats and distinguished-looking men who were not gentlemen. The difficulty in distinguishing social distinction through dress was recorded by colonial traveler Richard Twopeny when he advised that one must beware of judging a man's position by his coat, as the older the coat and the dirtier the shirt, the more likely he was wealthy. The problems of identifying class do not seem to measure up entirely with surviving garments. It is likely that what survives is better dress, probably kept as mementoes of special occasions. It is worth noting that most surviving dress is that of bourgeois women, and little if any male and working-class dress can be found in collections.

The gold rushes contributed to the complex nature of class difference and its dress signifiers from mid-century onward. By 1850 negotiating social status through clothing was a necessity as a result of the intrusion of emancipists and newly rich into the social hierarchy. The immoderate dressing of the newcomers meant that one of the visual means of defining class became even more unreliable. In return, the upper social classes attempted to distance themselves from ostentatious dressing by a reserved manner and appearance. Yet toward the end of the century newcomers continued to be baffled by the difficulties of assessing the social place of urban men by clothing. Identifying that of women was less difficult.

Power relations, whether of class, race, age, or sex, are constantly being negotiated through the practice of dress and its corollary, fashion. Dress in patriarchal early colonial society was considered a social control mechanism. The styles of dress were sexually differentiated in that bourgeois men wore trousers, shirts, jackets, and boots, and the women gowns, aprons, bonnets, and shawls. Factors governing relationships of class and economics, along with regional demographic patterns and the climate, affected local taste and dress practice. As in Europe, in contrast to the relatively static and austere dress of men, in Australia women's dress exhibited stylistic mobility. Splendor of dress signified the social status of their families, especially on public occasions such as visiting, balls, entertainment, shopping, and promenading, although their domestic garb displayed more simplicity. The clothing of this class of women was considered to be essential to the formation of their role as genteel and pleasing adjuncts to men. Repressed by clothing and deportment mores, they were coerced into believing that their femininity was somewhat defined by fashion and etiquette.

In rural areas where women had to contend with insufficient supplies, lack of communication and transport, and deprivation and scarcity of servants, contradictions abound. For some women femininity of dress was observed. The practice of fine dressing was observed in bush tents in Western Australia in 1830, as traveler Jane Roberts commented on taking tea with a nicely dressed and hatted hostess. In rural Queensland settler Katie Hume in 1867 displayed her stylish dressing by wearing dinner dress in the bush. Even so, young women who were formulated into a type, such as the so-called Australian Girl, did let their hair down in rural areas by neglecting their appearance, riding astride, and flouting some bourgeois conventions.

The belief in the existence of a distinctly Australian national type of man, derived from the supposed egalitarian life in the bush, originated during the 1840s and was consolidated during the later nineteenth century. Defined in part by physique and attire, it came to be believed the real Australian was a man of the outdoors. This was someone who wore leather boots, knee breeches or moleskin trousers, open-necked flannel shirts with rolled-up sleeves, and cabbage tree hats (hats made of the leaves of the cabbage tree palm). Australian culture has been shaped by admiration for the physical prowess required to contend with unforgiving conditions on the land, exploration, pastoral laboring, boundary riding, and sheep washing and shearing, as well as pastoralism and later the mateship of diggers. Practical, durable, and coarse bush dress, which had evolved from the late 1830s and derived from European working-class clothing, was well suited to colonial conditions. As traveler Twopeny described in the 1880s, slop clothes (coarse, loose-fitting ready-made clothes for men) became rather picturesque from the cavalier fashion in which they were worn by bush men. Despite some minor regional differences, this bush dress became a signifier of ideals shared by hard-working men in harsh living conditions, who by necessity had to endure physical hardship rather than concern themselves with social position. Bush man outfits are still being marketed as genuine Australian attire by the firm of R. M. Williams.

CLOTHING PRODUCTION AND SUPPLIES

Dressing in the early penal settlement was difficult due to extraordinary social, economic, and environmental circumstances. For a short time after the arrival of the First Fleet in 1788, there was no network of supplies, shops, or marketing facilities; all supplies and equipment were issued from government stores. The Navy Board was responsible for the clothing of convicts on the First and Second Fleets; then, after 1825, supplies were administered by the Board of Ordnance. Once settlers arrived, all classes endured shortages and inadequacies of dress. These problems were the combined result of an uncertain economy, the ignorance or parsimony of the British government, irregularity of shipments, speculative trading, and the lack of encouragement to local industries. Also fabric, apparel, haberdashery, and footwear arriving on supply vessels were often saturated with water, of inappropriate sizes, or crudely constructed.

Detail from a photograph of pioneer settler Lucy Sawtell, in front of a wood and corrugated-iron cottage with her children, near Dorrigo, New South Wales, Australia, 1895. They wear European-style clothing in common with the majority of settlers. Photograph probably by George Bell for Kerry & Co. Powerhouse Museum.

In 1789 the captain of the *Justinian* set up the first shop on board his ship, selling goods he had brought with him. Most of the early commercial advertising was for auction sales. Bartering was a standard method for acquiring clothing in the early years. As the century progressed, personal bartering extended to commercial bartering. Despite the operation of the public store and a gradually increasing number of private shops, public auctions were a popular method of retailing clothing in Sydney until the 1840s, but even by the 1820s observers recorded the existence of elegant retail shops and specialized garment businesses in Sydney.

Beginning in the 1790s some civilian clothing and footwear was imported into New South Wales, mostly from Britain. It comprised ready-made items, fabric, and sewing accessories. Some supply ships came from India as a result of the robust trade with the subcontinent. There were several ways of bringing clothing and textiles into the colony: direct imports, the personal requests of colonists or gifts from immigrants' relatives and friends, trade carried out by whalers, and the personal effects of immigrants. One could also obtain clothing from stores and later larger shops, local clothing manufacturers, convict and free dressmakers and tailors, and women who made everyday clothes for themselves and their families. Secondhand or recycled dress was available, and toward the end of the nineteenth century mail-order and made-to-measure clothes could be obtained from department stores.

The inadequacy of clothing in the early years ignited the interest in establishing local cloth manufacturing. In the early 1800s the government established a wool and linen factory at Parramatta, producing coarse fabrics from poor-quality colonial products. In 1821 the foundation of the Female Factory in Parramatta with three hundred female employees increased local cloth production, and by 1828 thirty thousand yards of cloth were produced annually.

Local manufacture of clothing and footwear was initiated as an alternative to sometimes ill-fitting ready-made imports. As a solution, convict and free tailors, dressmakers, and shoemakers of both sexes began making clothing and footwear beginning in the early years of the settlement. Throughout the transportation period, unskilled convict women were required to make clothes for occupation and for the sake of economizing.

The colony's first private enterprise, by Simeon Lord, began producing expensive better-quality fabrics in 1813, and by 1830 there were eleven privately owned cloth mills in New South Wales. The scarcity of experienced labor was one of the major problems associated with the cloth manufacturing industry in the colony. By 1820 some small-scale private clothing businesses were established in New South Wales, and along with private cloth manufacturing, they sold ready-made shirts, stockings, hats, trousers, and shoes. Simeon Lord operated two millinery workshops producing cheap, coarse hats.

From 1840 to 1852 South Australian shoemakers were able to provide much of the footwear for the local market, as Adelaide had four tanneries in full production in 1843. Wages for bootmakers in New South Wales doubled between the 1840s and the 1860s due to the gold rush. Footwear supplies remained restricted due to the scarcity of tradespeople in the colony and resulted in continued importation of boots and shoes. Nonetheless, after the 1840s the local trade continuously improved, and by 1870 productivity had increased.

The nature of shopping in Australia changed radically after 1830. Clothing that had been sold by drapers, hawkers, dressmakers, tailoring establishments, warehouses, and auctions was increasingly distributed by department stores. David Jones and Co., one of Sydney's earliest department stores, was opened in 1838 as a drapery business. Farmer's began in 1839 as Caroline Farmer's dressmaking and millinery shop and later a drapery. All the Hordern stores of the late nineteenth century were descended from a stay-making business established in 1825 by Ann Hordern. Edward Arnold's haberdashery was established in Oxford Street, Sydney, in 1858. In Melbourne by the mid-century ladies could walk along Collins Street and find many varieties of finery. Melbourne's Belmore Markets operated from 1869, selling goods including clothing, and the Queen Victoria Market was established in 1878. Hobart had clothing and haberdashery shops from 1829, and by 1848 ranges of fine shops could supply every want for fashionable settlers. In Western Australia, merely six months after settlement in 1830, the first general store selling clothing was established in Guildford in 1830. Perth and Fremantle were the main centers for clothing shops, but dedicated clothing stores existed in Guildford and York by 1840, in Geraldton, Greenough, and Beverley by 1880, and in Albany by the 1890s, reflecting the settlement pattern of the colony. By 1870 Sydney, Melbourne, Brisbane, and Perth had a number of large stores with goods displayed on several floors. Stores like David Jones, G.C. Tuting, and Farmer's in Sydney, Foy and Gibson in Melbourne, and J.G.C. Carr in Perth all had agents overseas, which meant that their establishments had direct control over design, orders, and retailing of the imported goods. From the 1870s convincing advertising in newspapers, trade catalogs and circulars, sales notices, and posters exhorted customers into the stores where they could browse through fixed-price merchandise elegantly displayed in showrooms.

During the 1800s ready-made clothing was brought on speculative consignment or retailed through the government stores. Tailors in Hobart in 1834 were reported to be out of work because local garments were undercut by cheap imported clothes, verifying the popularity of the imported clothing trade in the colonies. The problems faced by the local clothing industry, in regard to competition from imported ready-made clothing, intensified during the gold rush years. In New South Wales the total amount of imported British-made clothing more than quadrupled between 1848 and 1853. In Australia, as in Britain and America, development of the women's ready-made industry occurred more slowly than the comparable industry for men. By the 1850s the variety of imported ready-made garments and accessories for ladies had increased. There is no evidence that women's or children's ready-to-wear clothing was manufactured locally until the late 1870s.

A vast private economy of home dressmaking and tailoring provided a further dimension to the Australian clothing market. Colonial stores catered to women's dressmaking requirements from the early years of settlement, but after 1850 additional services such as sewing instructions, mail-order patterns, self-tuition, and dressmaking lessons were provided. Specific dressmaking rooms and fabric showrooms appeared in large stores by the 1860s. For example, Farmer's Great Drapery Emporium in 1869 had a section of the store devoted to the display of French and British silks for dressmaking. The introduction of graded, mass-produced dress patterns pioneered by Butterick and later the firms of Worth and Madame Weigel gave women ready access to fashionable international styles in the second half of the century. Sewing machines

in Australia cost approximately ten pounds each during the 1860s, and brands such as Singer, Wertheim, and Grover and Baker were frequently advertised. By the 1870s local newspapers and magazines supplied fashion information ranging from fashion illustrations to dressmaking, clothing suggestions, and general advice on women's dress interests. The *Town and Country Journal* had a weekly "Ladies Column" that included fashion illustrations beginning in the mid-1870s. *Weigel's Journal of Fashions*—the first dedicated Australian women's fashion magazine—was circulated beginning in the 1880s. *The Western Australian* newspaper during the 1870s published a "Ladies Column" with fashion information, and from the 1890s fashion description with illustrations. Similar press coverage occurred in other large towns.

A great deal of dressmaking, tailoring, and leatherwork was undertaken by women. Women in Australian towns and country areas made clothes for themselves and their families as well as repairing and altering garments. Those in rural areas—where there were few professional dressmakers—had to make their own clothes. Men's ready-made clothing was not always of good quality and at times necessitated further domestic stitching. Women in both towns and country areas mended boots and shoes, and even sewed slippers. Rachel Henning of rural Queensland repaired her boots with bits of leather every day in 1863.

Throughout the colonial years, in spite of their close connection to Britain, early Australian settlers clothed themselves and behaved in unique ways. The differences were caused by the elements that were unique to the locality: social and environmental conditions, economic structure, and demographic patterns. Despite many acknowledgments of the differences observed in colonial and British classes, throughout the Colonial era, upper-class social customs and etiquette were generally regarded as aspirational markers of class and status. Women's dress of all classes was conducted by different factors and practices from that of men. Unlike British society, during Australia's Colonial era, appearance did not define social class with clear-cut precision. Throughout the century, dress was entangled in the ways whereby diversified social structures were empowered, to command the etiquette and behavior of early Australians.

References and Further Reading

Fletcher, Marion. *Costume in Australia 1788–1901.* Melbourne, Australia: Oxford University Press, 1984.

Joel, Alexandra. *Best Dressed: Two Hundred Years of Fashion in Australia.* Sydney: William Collins Press, 1984.

Kingston, Beverley. *Basket, Bag and Trolley: A History of Shopping in Australia.* London: Oxford University Press, 1994.

Maynard, Margaret. *Fashioned from Penury: Dress as Cultural Practice in Colonial Australia.* Cambridge: Cambridge University Press, 1994.

Twopeny, Richard. *Town Life in Australia.* Melbourne, Australia: Penguin Books, 1976.

Damayanthie Eluwawalage

See also Images as a Resource for the Study of Australian Dress; Resources: Collections of Colonial Dress and Fashion in Australia; Rural Dress in Australia.

Retailing, Clothing, and Textiles Production in Australia

Although the Australian textiles and clothing manufacturing industries have been contracting steadily since the early 1970s, the range of activities involved in bringing clothing and related products to the market remain a major component of the national economy and an important source of employment, especially in urban areas. The people engaged in bringing clothing and clothing-related textiles to Australia's consumer markets work in a variety of industries including retailing, importing, wholesaling, garment production, and garment-related textiles production. In addition, there are the numerous intermediaries who link these functions together and ensure that the garments reaching consumer markets accord with local tastes.

The organizational configuration of the clothing and related industries in Australia differs from those in Europe and the United States for four principal reasons. First, the unique spatial configuration of the Australian economy constitutes a major barrier to firm growth. The vast distances between urban centers and the sparse population densities within cities make it difficult for firms to develop national markets. Consequently, in most industries one or two large firms specializing in high-volume products dominate at the national scale, while large numbers of smaller firms operate in local, citywide, or state territories. This geography encourages firms to serve specialized niche markets and to create multiple quasi-monopolistic market spaces. In the clothing and related industries, these circumstances are intensified by Australia's informal lifestyle and moderate climate, which depresses per-head expenditures on clothing and encourages national firms to concentrate their activities in sportswear and casual-wear markets.

Second, Australia's southern hemisphere location means that its seasonal rhythms are the reverse of those in Europe, an accident of geography that effectively puts Australia six months behind the leading edge of fashion trends (Weller 2007). As a result, the rapid stylistic innovation cycles characteristic of European fast fashion are less pronounced in the Australian context. At the same time Australia's location close to Asia has enabled large firms with high-volume orders to cost-effectively access China's massive production capacity.

Third, Australia's policy attitude to the clothing and textiles industries is unique among Western economies. Australia liberalized its trade policies and opened its markets to imported clothing in the late 1980s and early 1990s, well ahead of the trade liberalization schedules of the World Trade Organization's Agreement on Textiles and Clothing (which have guided the pace of liberalization elsewhere). Nevertheless, and in contrast to the United States and Europe, Australian policies have not enabled firms to develop effective and sustainable off-shore assembly structures in nearby countries such as Fiji or Indonesia.

As a result of these conditions, a high and increasing proportion of garments sold in the Australian market now originate in China. However, the structures through which these imports enter Australia—and therefore the distribution of profit along garment supply chains—continue to evolve with changing relative prices of labor and materials, trade policy reforms, and the shifting geography of expertise in Australia, Hong Kong, and China.

It is important to consider how the sector's development over the last twenty years has shaped its contemporary form. In the twenty years from 1987 to 2007 trade and industry policy reforms, the internationalization of the supply structures, and the consequent rationalization of domestic production have transformed the consumer market and garment retailing, clothing importing and wholesaling, and domestic clothing and textile manufacturing in ways that have altered the relationships between subsectors, often blurring the divisions between them as firms' activities extend to span multiple stages of the commodity production sequence.

AUSTRALIA'S TEXTILES AND CLOTHING INDUSTRIES

Throughout the early years of Australia's development, when (Keynesian) national policies promoted nation building, employment creation, and industrialization, successive governments set trade policies to protect local clothing and textiles (C&T) manufacturing industries from competing imports. As intended, the C&T industries became a major source of low-skilled employment, especially for women and migrants. Industrial protection created a "branch plant" economy in which overseas firms wishing to access the domestic market were impelled to establish production facilities in Australia, literally inside the tariff wall. But parent firms tended not to locate specialized production or research and development functions in Australia. High-value commodities were imported, generally from the United Kingdom.

As the worldwide economic crises of the 1970s made it increasingly difficult for the national government to maintain demand management policy settings, market-oriented economic theories gained ascendancy. In the context of increasing concern that Australia was falling behind in the race for economic growth, industry protection came to be viewed not only as inefficient and impractical, but as impeding Australia's prosperity. The policy community became convinced that Australia should internationalize its economy and integrate its industries into global trade flows. There was, however, considerable disagreement about how this reorientation should be achieved. Some argued that policies should promote industries in which Australia already held a natural comparative advantage (for example, in agricultural production), while others sought to support emerging industries in which Australia could develop a competitive advantage (for example, knowledge-intensive industries and the production of elaborately transformed manufactures). Both visions saw the clothing and related manufacturing industries as low-skill and low-productivity sectors that were better suited to the economies of developing nations with abundant less-skilled labor.

After the election of the Hawke (Labor) government in 1983, Australia began implementing a new strategic vision in which revitalized high-technology industries would lead Australia's repositioning in the global economy. Four compelling arguments recommended dismantling the trade barriers that protected Australian clothing and textiles manufacturers from overseas competition. First, given Australia's relatively high wages, clothing and textiles producers were inefficient by world standards. Government support was therefore inhibiting the flow of capital to more efficient activities in which Australia could potentially develop internationally competitive export industries. In addition, it was apparent that the structure of Australia's quota-based system of protection had distorted local industry structures in ways that encouraged anticompetitive practices. Because quotas had been allocated to importing firms rather than to exporting nations, they had empowered large firms and encouraged hostile takeover activity. Second, allowing overseas-made commodities into the local market would increase consumer choices. Third, opening the Australian market to imported garments would reduce clothing prices and enable households to redirect their expenditures to more technologically advanced products and services. Again, this would promote the economy's reorientation to more advanced industries. Fourth, and perhaps most importantly, demonstrating to Australia's trading partners that Australia was serious about its commitment to trade barrier liberalization would help unlock market access for Australia's efficiently produced agricultural commodities and minerals exports.

In 1988, after a major inquiry into the future of the clothing and textiles sector (IAC 1986), the government embarked on a structural adjustment program comprising: first, liberalization of the tariff, quota, and bounty provisions that had protected the C&T sector from competition; second, the introduction of incentives for the industries to restructure for internationally competitive operation; and third, a labor adjustment scheme to assist workers who would be displaced in the ensuing rationalization process. These reforms were vigorously resisted by textiles and clothing firms and workers but were supported by retailers, who were keen to secure greater access to imported garments.

The statutory body set up to promote the reform process, the Textiles Clothing and Footwear Development Authority (TCFDA), directed its energies to modernizing the textiles sector, which, given its capital-intensive nature and the obvious opportunities for downstream processing (processing that occurs close to or in the direction of the end use) of Australia's wool and cotton production, was adjudged to be potentially competitive in an open economy. The TCFDA directed less attention to the clothing production industry, which was deemed unlikely to prosper without trade protection. In March 1991, in response to the perception that C&T firms were not restructuring quickly enough, the government unexpectedly accelerated the pace of trade barrier liberalization.

But the restructuring process did not play out in the manner anticipated by policy makers. As Webber and Weller (2001) explain, policy settings wrongly assumed that firms operated independently in competitive markets; they did not consider how interventions would impact on the relationships between textiles production, clothing manufacture, and retailing; how they would change the power relations between small and large firms in complex interdependent supply structures; or how reduced duty rates would impact on firm profitability in a finite market.

As these policy settings came into effect in the recession years of 1991 to 1993, large numbers of clothing and textiles firms closed down or significantly restructured their operations. Retailers and wholesalers increased their direct importing, buying at prices well below local production costs. Some clothing manufacturing firms went out of business as their orders evaporated or as their suppliers of essential inputs closed down. Others—predominantly larger firms with knowledge of the policy direction and its implications—closed local factories and shifted the labor-intensive aspects of their production overseas. They retained core planning, design, research, and merchandising functions in Australia but either opened subsidiaries in China or Fiji or shifted to a (vertically disintegrated) subcontracting model using cut-make-trim (CMT) contractors. Many local textiles producers, including some of the most technologically advanced firms, failed, as their clothing industry customers exited local production.

As the old industry restructured, a new generation of firms—often established by displaced former production managers—entered the market to create new industry structures. These importers, merchandisers, quality control specialists, logistics consultants, and the like became intermediaries in the transformation of the relationship between retailing and production. As the recession ended after 1993, they were joined by new locally based CMT production subcontractors that organized their production around a home-based workforce. In the second half of the 1990s, the intense competition generated by rapid trade liberalization tested the efficiency of competing models of industrial organization.

In 1992 and 1994 the government introduced new policies intended to encourage internationalization, to support technologically advanced textiles production and to sustain local clothing brands. These initiatives encouraged the offshore assembly of garments and provided incentives for export market development. However, by 1997, when the government again reviewed the textiles and clothing reform process (IC 1997), these industry incentives had been outlawed by the World Trade Organization (WTO). They were replaced in 2000 by a WTO-admissible incentive scheme promoting innovation and structural reform to assist firms to further consolidate their activities and adjust their labor requirements. The government also resolved in 1997 to slow the rate of industrial change by pausing tariff reductions in the years 2000–2005.

In January 2005 the liberalization process recommenced. Import duty rates on clothing fell to 17.5 percent. They will fall incrementally, to 10 percent in 2010 and then to the same rate as other manufactured goods—5 percent—in 2015. However, these duty rates do not apply universally: imports from developing countries attract a 5 percent concession; imports originating in New Zealand (with which Australia shares a common market) are free of duties; and production inputs are duty-free when there is no competing local production. As tariff barriers fall, garment-related importing and exporting is governed increasingly by fluctuations in the Australian dollar's exchange rate. The main beneficiaries of higher exchange rates are clothing importers that can buy more with each Australia dollar, and the main losers are Australia's handful of garment exporters (La Frenz 2007). Counterintuitively, however, the strong Australian dollar in 2006–2007 appeared to promote local production by reducing the costs of (imported) fabrics.

In 2007 the local garment and garment-related textiles production industries were still declining, with production falling by 8 percent between 2001–2002 and 2004–2005. Nonetheless, the sector still accounted for $5 billion in Australian dollars (AUD) of Gross Domestic Product (GDP) in 2004–2005, contributed over $1.5 billion of added value to the economy, and represented about 1.6 percent of total manufacturing industry value added. Employment numbers also continued to decline; by June 2005 the sectors employed 29,748 people, a fall of almost 25 percent since June 2002 (ABS 2006a). Full-time employment in the broader classification, Textiles Clothing Footwear and Leather Industries (TCF&L), fell by 60 percent in the twenty years from 1985 to 2005, from 104,800 to 42,800 workers (ABS 2007). The jobs that were eliminated in the restructuring process were mainly less-skilled jobs, especially clothing machinist jobs (which in Australia are gender-typed as women's work). Accordingly, the job losses have affected women's jobs (43,400 jobs, or 64 percent of the 1985 workforce) more than men's jobs (19,400 jobs, or 53 percent of the 1985 workforce). In aggregate, some of the decline in manufacturing employment has been offset by increased employment in clothing importing, wholesaling, retailing, and various associated services. The next sections describe in turn how these overall changes have altered the clothing and fashion industries.

CLOTHING MARKETS

It is not possible to understand the structure of Australia's clothing industry without first understanding the characteristics of its clothing markets. Like other Western markets, the Australian one is highly segmented or fragmented, not only into income-related strata, but also into segments defined by combinations of gender, age, body type (size), and aesthetic preferences. These break the market up into multiple small national markets defined by lifestyle preferences.

Australia's casual lifestyle and moderate climate leads Australians to spend less on clothing than people in otherwise comparable Western economies. In 2005–2006 retail turnover in clothing retail stores was estimated at AUD $10.1 billion, suggesting that after the addition of clothing sales in department stores, about AUD $14 billion is spent on clothing each year. To put these figures in an international perspective, Australia's population is about one-third the population of the United Kingdom (twenty million compared to sixty million), but its clothing market is only one-seventh the size (roughly, AUD $14 billion compared to AUD $100 billion). Moreover, the Australian market is spread across a land area about thirty times larger than the United Kingdom. By international standards, then, the Australian market is thin indeed. This context militates against the development of strong national markets in any but the most popular lifestyle segments.

As an outcome of Australia's geography, Australians spend relatively high proportions of their household incomes on housing,

transportion, and communications equipment. Household expenditure data reveal that the three lowest income quintiles spend respectively AUD $12.75, $19.50, and $30.68 per week on clothing, while the upper two quintiles spend AUD $46.40 and $67.07 per week. Only in the highest income quintile does weekly household expenditure on clothing exceed expenditures on alcohol and cigarettes. Clothing's share of household expenditure has fallen over the last ten years, partly as a result of real price reductions associated with trade liberalization, but also because other products (such as mobile phones and iPods) have captured consumer interest.

In addition to changes in trade and industry policy, other regulatory changes have contributed to the restructuring of retail markets. Most Australian states deregulated trading hours during the 1990s, thereafter allowing stores to remain open for long hours, including Saturdays and Sundays. Subsequently, a high proportion of the retail sector workforce has been employed on a part-time and casual basis as retailers tailor their staffing to the daily, weekly, and annual rhythms of demand. For many people, shopping—or perhaps window-shopping—has become an important recreational pastime. The introduction of the Goods and Services Tax in 2000 (and the simultaneous abolition of sales tax) had complex impacts on relative prices but on balance was favorable to clothing sales.

The increasing workforce participation of Australian women, the ready availability of credit (cards), new mass communications technologies, and the changing strategies of retail firms have altered local buying patterns. The media, now extended to include the Internet, cable TV, and e-mail, have been influential in altering the character of consumer preferences, most recently by encouraging fashion-savvy consumers to eclectically select items from across a range of price and brand categories (Tungate 2005). The fashion event industry now also plays a powerful role in shaping consumer tastes in the fashion-oriented parts of the market. Importantly, as these activities insert a new tier of specialized intermediaries—stylists, event-staging specialists, fashion journalists, and a range of marketing roles—between clothing retailers and consumers, they tend to blur the boundaries between the clothing industries and other fashion-related consumer products sectors. Finally, as firms across the sector have focused on their core activities, a new business services sector has developed to assist retailers, wholesalers, and manufacturers with market and consumer research services, business planning, benchmarking, design services, computing, pressing services, logistics, and a range of advanced retail and stock control technologies. Although many of these associated businesses work exclusively for garment industry clients, they appear in aggregate data in business service industry categories. In other words, if these new specialized businesses were considered a part of the clothing sector, the local industry's contraction would not be as severe as the official data suggests.

CLOTHING RETAILERS

In June 2001 Australia's 10,673 clothing retailing establishments were distributed across the nation in rough proportion to population densities—that is, concentrated in the key cities of Sydney, Melbourne, Brisbane, and Perth (ABS 2006b). The structure of the Australian garment retail sector reflects its historical development. Under industry protection before 1990, clothing retail markets were dominated by the firms that controlled access to import quotas and therefore the supply of imported garments. When quotas were abolished in 1993, retailers quickly reorganized their supply chains, jettisoning relationships with local manufacturers and shifting to direct or subcontracted importing. Consistent with overseas trends in retail management, retailers also increased their investments in brand identity and customer loyalty. Often they became more involved in micromanaging subcontracted production to ensure that garments reflected (or, more exactly, became a material form of) retail brand identities. Changes to the scope of retail operations were facilitated by technological advances that have enabled retailers to accurately track sales, more actively manage their supply and distribution chains, reduce inventories, and limit (end-of-season) stock markdowns (Greig 1990). These innovations have also enabled multistore retailers (a retail business with more than one store, such as department stores and fashion chains, as well as many smaller boutique businesses) to consolidate and centralize their warehousing functions.

Overall, since the early 1990s many firms that were formerly "pure" retailers have either incorporated their wholesaling functions or formed close alliances with quasi-independent wholesalers. Although subcontracting has been the dominant sourcing model, albeit with varying degrees of retailer control, some smaller-volume specialized retailers have established their own vertically integrated production facilities. These trends have in part produced and in part reflected the shifting competitiveness of different forms of retailing. In Australia, clothing retailing takes four main forms: department stores, specialty retail chains, boutiques, and other retailers. Since liberalization, the configuration and market shares of different forms of clothing retailing have altered with the changing competitiveness of different garment-sourcing strategies. In 1998–1999, the last year for which detailed data are

available, dedicated clothing stores (that is, specialty chains and boutiques) held a 40 percent share and department stores held a 34 percent share of Australia's clothing market. The remainder comprises sales in supermarkets, lifestyle stores, and other outlets. It is likely that the department store share has increased in recent times.

In department stores clothing represents a significant proportion of total sales. Australia's highly concentrated department store sector is dominated by two national firms operating in mainstream markets and two national firms competing in the discount sector. At the high end of the market David Jones and Myer stores have competed for supremacy in fashion-oriented clothing markets. Both have sought to attract local fashion designers to exclusive "store within a store" concessions, but David Jones's pioneering decision to favor "edgy" Australian and New Zealand designers in 2007 positioned it as the clear leader. In addition to stocking elite designer garments, both stores offer a range of less expensive clothes at multiple price points, including designer "diffusion" labels and each store's own-brand versions. An innovation in 2007 was the introduction of cheaper diffusion versions of Australian designs. It appears that in the department store environment, local designers have been able to compete successfully against high-profile imported designer brands. In addition, the competition among high-end department stores has generated positive spin-offs across the industry through increased interest in fashion. It also appears to have improved the position of department stores relative to specialty retailers, in terms of both sales and fashion status.

The discount department store sector is also concentrated. It is dominated by two multistore brands, Target and Kmart. Both operate within the Coles group of companies. Throughout the 1990s Target Stores operated in what is known locally as the

Derelict machinery at a former knitting mill in Maryborough, Victoria, Australia. The recession of the early 1990s led to the restructuring and closure of many firms. Later, displaced workers and cheap, unused equipment began to regenerate the industry as "outwork" production flourished. Photograph by Sally Weller.

"Marks & Spencer" organizational model. It stocked quality, reasonably priced Target-brand garments made by preferred suppliers in accordance with Target's own standards and specifications. Kmart's Now brand clothing, on the other hand, targets a more budget-oriented market, and its stock is predominantly imported from China. In both Target and Kmart stores, significant proportions of stock are Australian icon brands, sourced from local wholesale firms but manufactured in China. The imported proportion of discount store stock has increased recently with firm-level policy changes and with the escalating value of the Australian dollar. In 2006 Target Stores embarked on a "fast fashion" strategy, engaging well-known fashion designers (Stella McCartney, then Josh Goot) to produce one-off budget-priced ranges. This "massification" of design is a strategy borrowed from European retailers. Its appeal is the momentary illusion of scarcity created by combining limited availability with concentrated marketing. This represents a significant shift in the structure of the fashion system in Australia and may pose a threat to the market position of midrange (that is, specialty) fashion firms.

The specialty clothing retail sector includes national chain stores, smaller regional chains, and highly specialized niche chains. Six national clothing chain retail groups—the Just Group, Retail Holdings, Specialty Fashion Group, Colorado Group, Country Road, and Noni B—are included among Australia's top twenty retailers and together account for a large proportion of the total specialty store sales. These firms typically control a stable of multistore retailer brands, each targeting a different segment of the market—a strategy that moderates the risks associated with fashion unpredictability. National brands are represented in most of the nation's shopping malls and main shopping precincts and have in the range of 180 to 300 stores each. As in other parts of the world, the garments, store designs, and staff profiles within each brand aim to present a coherent image targeted to a specific lifestyle demographic. By emphasizing product differentiation and customer loyalty within niche markets, brand strategies aim to build quasi-monopolistic control over a (small) market. Most clothing chain stores have expanded their product ranges to include complementary footwear and accessories. Growth in the specialty sector is driven by new store openings and acquisitions. New stores generally open in parallel to new shopping center developments. In fact, it could be argued that the specialty clothing sector relies on the property development sector for knowledge of demographic trends and shifting regional fortunes. However, firms use acquisitions—either of competitors or of complementary brands—to increase their market share and profitability. Over the last ten years this has resulted in a dramatic increase in ownership concentration. By 2007 the major players were:

- The Just Group, which had become one of Australia's largest specialty retailers with about a 5.8 percent share of the local market. It originally specialized in denim streetwear but by 2007 held multiple brands: Just Jeans (285 stores in 2006), Jay Jays (227 stores), Portmans (116 stores), Jacqui-E (97 stores), Peter Alexander (9 stores), and Dotti (48 stores).
- Retail Holdings Pty Ltd., which was formed after Sussan Corporation purchased the ailing younger fashion chain, Sportsgirl, in 1999. (A *fashion chain* is a multistore fashion retail business that controls its supply chain through a combination of commissioned subcontracted manufacture, purchasing, and sometimes direct manufacture. Fashion chain retailers have centralized distribution structures, uniform store formats, and national pricing policies.) In 2007 it owned women's fashion brands Sussan, Sportsgirl, and Suzanne Grae stores and was the only one of the sector's large firms to have remained in private ownership.
- Specialty Fashion Group, which was created after budget Miller's Fashion Club purchased the Katies chain in 2001. It had also acquired Crossroads (150 stores), Autograph (100 stores), and Big City Chic (25 stores). It purchased its largest supplier, Look Sharp Concepts Pty Ltd., in January 2002.
- Up-market brand Country Road which, in addition to its independent brand stores, operated concessions in major department stores. In 2004–2005 it also supplied wholesale garments to Myer department stores.
- The Noni B group, comprising the Noni B, Liz Jordan, and La Voca brands, which operated over 200 stores, many of them in regional areas.
- ARH Investments (Australia) Pty Ltd., which purchased the Colorado Group (105 stores) in September 2006. The group acquired the Palmer Corporation in 2001 to gain control of the up-market Jag label (35 stores).
- Pretty Girl Fashion Group, owned by Consolidated Press Holdings. In 2007 it operated 300 Rockmans Stores, 15 Hiltons stores, and 22 BeMe boutiques. It purchased Table Eight corporate wear in 2004.

Other important groups include: the up-market Witchery chain, which in 2007 had more than 70 stores in Australia and operated concessions within David Jones department stores; Jeans West, which had grown to 150 stores; Cue fashion stores; the teen label Supré; Lowes-Manhattan, which operated 110 Lowes menswear stores; and the Esprit clothing group. M. Webster Holdings Pty Ltd., the holding company for the Jigsaw and David Laurence brands, was developing a high-fashion niche after purchasing the Marcs and Morrissey businesses in 2006.

The specialty retail sector is predominantly locally owned, but many firms have been listed on the stock exchange in the last ten years. For example, Noni B was listed in 2000 and the Just Group in 2004. Listing helps firms raise capital, but the discipline of the share price may discourage the risk taking characteristic of fashion leaders. Private capital is increasingly influential: Private equity firm Gresham purchased Witchery, and a private group (including Texas Pacific and Myer family interests) purchased Myer Stores in 2006. Colorado's owner, ARH Investments, is owned by Hong Kong's Affinity Equity Partners and in 2007 was moving to return the firm to private control. In 2007 Specialty Fashion Group and Just Group were also offering investors share buy-back schemes. Influential private investors (such as former Myer director Solomon Lew) play important strategic roles in the configuration of capital across the Australian fashion retail subsector.

In the late 1990s European designer brands aggressively moved into the Australian market, but few prospered beyond the tourist precincts of capital cities (primarily due to their uncompetitive prices). Although Australia has permitted "parallel importing" since 1998, garments imported by that means are mainly sold in discount stores. A handful of overseas brands have consolidated their position in the market through exclusive licensing arrangements. The publicly listed Oroton Group Limited, for example, holds the license for the Oroton and Polo Ralph Lauren brands in Australia. In addition to operating its own stores, Oroton supplies Myer and David Jones stores. More often, overseas interests access the Australian market via the acquisition of local brands. Country Road, for example, is owned by the South African Woolworths group, and Jeans West by Hong Kong's Glorious Sun Enterprises. Overseas brands (for example Jigsaw, Laura Ashley, FCUK, and Giordano) are represented only in major cities. The largest global players (Gap and Zara, for example) have not entered the Australian market.

During the 1990s, when the federal government was promoting export market development and offering assistance to exporters, a number of larger Australian fashion chains attempted to enter the United States and other export markets. These ventures generally failed. However, Australian surfwear firms—principally Billabong and Rip Curl—have become influential transnational companies since 2005. More than half of Billabong's revenue derives from overseas sales. In addition, numerous Australian fashion designers market their products through specialist retailers (such as Antipodium in London), major department stores in high-income countries, and online. Since the establishment of a common market between Australia and New Zealand, Australia's more up-market chains—Country Road, Witchery, and Sportsgirl—have increased their presence in New Zealand, while a handful of New Zealand retailers, such as Zambesi, have expanded into Australia.

Australia has a large number of small businesses involved in clothing retail. Boutique clothing stores are generally independent businesses, with one or two shops located in adjacent suburbs. They typically employ fewer than six people. High-fashion boutiques frequently stock garments brought to them by local designers and sometimes retail on a commission or on a sale-or-return basis. In major cities specialist directional boutique retailers, such as Alice Euphemia in Melbourne, act as intermediaries linking emerging young designers with mainstream markets.

A considerable proportion of clothing in Australia is sold in lifestyle stores that combine clothing with adventure or sporting product sales. These stores are popular with less fashion-aware consumers and include retailers such as Rebel Sports, Ray's Outdoors, Kathmandu, and Mountain Designs. Shopping for bargains is a popular pastime for some Australians. Bargain clothing can be found in street markets, factory outlets, and discount or liquidation stores. Property developer Austexx has created numerous DFO (Designer Fashion Outlet) discount fashion complexes in recent years. These stores attract factory shop tour groups from regional areas. In 2007 Internet-based clothing retailing had not yet captured the imagination of Australian consumers despite high rates of Internet use.

SOURCING AND IMPORTING

All imports to the Australian market arrive as the result of purposeful sourcing activities by firms in different parts of the clothing production system. Retailers, agents, and wholesalers draw on similar sourcing strategies, and most use a combination of strategies, sourcing garments locally and from overseas depending on the fabrics, labor content, and fashion orientation of particular styles in the context of cost, quality, and time comparisons. Strategies—and therefore the ratio of locally made to imported products in the market—may shift from season to season or stock turn to stock turn, depending on the fashion mood, the exchange rate, and the availability of manufacturing capacity.

Before trade barrier liberalization garment importing had been governed and constrained by the quota system. But after liberalization, larger manufacturers "hollowed out" their operations, retaining management, design, and logistics functions in Australia while shifting their manufacturing activities to low-wage countries, principally to China. In effect, they became importers. Australia's largest clothing manufacturer, Pacific Dunlop, for example, initially closed down local production (with the loss of some ten thousand jobs) and opened its own factories in China. But these factories were later sold, and Pacific Dunlop became a sourcing wholesaler, Pacific Brands.

A second sourcing strategy for former manufacturing firms has been to opt for managed cut-make-trim production in Fiji, where local economic development and trade incentives have facilitated the creation of a competitive production structure. This form of offshore production created a new group of intermediaries specialized in the technicalities of trade and customs rules. For a variety of reasons, however, these schemes have not produced the robust transnational assembly structures achieved in the United States and Europe (Weller 2000). The strategy became less attractive when policy incentives were discontinued in 2000, and the production model declined rapidly after Fiji's 2000 political coup d'état (Weller 2006). Nonetheless, Fiji's isolation makes it a valuable production site for Australian clothing firms with a genuine design edge, such as surfwear firms, because in Fiji original designs are less susceptible to counterfeiting.

Larger retailers tend to work directly with agents in Hong Kong or China, often reducing their decision set by using the same agent as an overseas brand targeted to a similar demographic profile. Firms can choose whether to have garments made to their own specifications, to have generic designs modified to better accord with their brand image or with local aesthetic preferences, or to simply buy a design from a catalog. Increasingly, brand owners (which include retailers and former manufacturers) buy fully designed garments from OEM (original equipment manufacture) firms, following the European trend to fast fashion (the "Zara" model), although Australia's off-season location blunts the fashion edge of this strategy. Basic staple garments (a black shirt, for example) can be purchased in "spot" markets in Hong Kong or China.

After liberalization, fewer resource-rich manufacturing firms adopted a vertically disintegrated subcontracting model, either forming direct relationships with factories in China or securing the services of agents in Hong Kong to arrange manufacture in China on their behalf. However, these firms often underestimated the hidden costs of overseas production or misjudged the challenges of quality control. In addition, their small orders put them at a bargaining disadvantage in Hong Kong's global markets. Some firms returned to local manufacturing, while others transformed again to become importers of overseas-designed garments.

The sourcing strategies of boutiques and other small retailers vary with firm size, fashion orientation, and brand identity. Small retailers in regional Australia often purchase stock through buying groups that operate in a similar way to retail chains. Smaller retailers also purchase independent brand garments from agents who act on behalf of manufacturers (in Australia or China), or from wholesalers that purchase stock overseas and on-sell it to local retailers. However, retailers operating in high-fashion markets will source small volumes directly from overseas designers.

As a result of these reconfigurations, the import share of domestic demand for clothing and knitting mill products has increased steadily from 18.5 percent in 1990–1991 to 51.8 percent in 2000–2001 (TFIA 2006). The import share varies from product to product but had reached 60 percent or more in most outerwear subsegments by 2001–2002. The largest percentage increases since 2000 have been in the women's- and girls'-wear segment, a part of the industry that was previously assumed to enjoy protection derived from local fashion preferences. The annualized rate of growth of imported women's and girls' clothing was 10 percent in 2000–2001 to 2005–2006, compared to 3.3 percent in men's and boys' clothing (TFIA 2006). For men's and boys' clothing, the rate of import penetration has slowed compared to the mid-1990s. These trends reflect the different rates at which the production of different commodities has moved offshore. These changes also reflect China's expanding capacity, which by 2006 accounted for over 70 percent of all garment imports (TFIA 2006), as well as improved transnational transportion and logistics services and the growth in fashion imports from New Zealand.

WHOLESALING

Wholesalers have facilitated much of the growth in Australia's clothing imports. Since trade barriers were liberalized, the clothing wholesale sector has grown significantly. Between 1986 and 1996, the clothing wholesaling workforce grew by 31.1 percent, from 12,801 to 16,785 (Webber and Weller 2001). In recent years new entrants to this sector have included firms established by recently arrived immigrants with links to China (especially people emigrating from Hong Kong after 1997). These intermediaries have a dual role: They link retailers to manufacturers and at the same time manage the relationship between importing and local production.

Since Australian retail markets are fragmented and include large numbers of small firms, Australia's specialized sourcing and wholesaling sector plays a powerful role in garment supply chains. The upshot is that the Australian clothing supply industry does not always accord with the retailer-led supply chain structure characteristic of globalized firms. Rather, Australian supply structures are shaped by the uneasy power relationship between major retailers and the brand-owning wholesalers that control large segments of garment import trade. Although the wholesale sector includes large numbers of very small firms, the national scene is dominated by two key players: Pacific Brands and Gazal Corporation.

Before trade liberalization Pacific Brands had been Australia's largest clothing manufacturer. In the early 1990s it restructured, closed down most of its clothing production facilities, and recreated itself as a brand manager, wholesaler, and distributor, specializing in basic necessities such as underwear and commodity outerwear. It employs approximately nine thousand people, making it one of Australia's largest employers. Each year, it manufactures or

sources in excess of 160,000 products and sells over 250 million units. Pacific Brands is a leading supplier to the four main department store retailers. Its products are sold by independent retailers (44.6%), discount department stores (28.9%), department stores (15.2%), and supermarkets (5.5%). The remainder is exported, mainly to New Zealand. In 2007 Pacific Brands controlled many of Australia's "icon" clothing brands: in underwear (Jockey, Rio, Bonds, AntzPantz, and Underdak), socks (Holeproof and Explorer), intimate apparel (Berlei, Hestia, Playtex, and LoveKylie), hosiery (Kayser, Kolotex, Razzamatazz, and Voodoo), work-wear (King Gee, Stubbies, Yakka, Hard Yakka, and Can't Tear 'Em), and sportswear (Dunlop, Everlast, Slazenger, and Hang Ten). Its underwear and hosiery division accounts for almost 40 percent of total sales. Throughout its history, Pacific Brands has grown through acquisitions. The King Gee and Stubbies labels were acquired in 2001 after it purchased Sara Lee Apparel. In 2006 it added Peri bed linen and the DKNY license, and later that year it acquired the Globe streetwear brands (Mossimo, Stuzzy, Mooks, Paul Frank, Freshjive, Independent, and M-ONE-11). In 2007 it purchased the Australian icon work-wear firm Yakka and its brands Yakka, Hard Yakka, and Can't Tear 'Em.

Much of the contracted production of Pacific Brands (a former Pacific Dunlop division) is carried out in China, where the group has more than a thousand employees (based in either China or Hong Kong). In 2006 it entered a joint venture with Asian conglomerate Li & Fung to develop a technologically advanced warehouse complex in Shanghai that will reduce lead times, improve inventory control, and enable stock to be delivered directly to customers without warehousing in Australia. The scale of Pacific Dunlop's operations, and its volume-leveraged price advantage, place it in a formidable position in the Australian market. In recent years it has begun to manage the supply chain for other brands; in 2005, for example, it agreed to supply footwear and bed linen for the Esprit chain.

The second major player in the wholesale market, Gazal Corporation, also restructured in the early 1990s, shifting from direct production to supply chain management. It specializes in business, corporate, and school wear though its brands Van Heusen, Midford, Bisley, Paramount, and Bracks. It also has multiple youth wear interests including the Nautica, Maui & Sons, Mambo, Mambo Goddess, and SMP brands. Its intimate apparel business specializes in licensing arrangements with fashion brands (Trent Nathan, Calvin Klein, Lovable, Oroton, Crystelle, Kookai, Playboy, Morrissey, Davenport, and Body). In 2005 Gazal acquired Bracks Apparel, the uniforms division of Australian Defence Apparel and Ultimate Factory Outlets. In 2006 it added Coronet Corporate, a corporate uniform business.

Three remaining firms that hold substantial positions in the wholesale market are the Austin Group, Voyager Distributing Company, and the Discovery Group. The Austin Group is a publicly listed specialist importer that sells its brands through independent retailers and selected department stores. Its brands span women's wear (Rochford, Purr, Contempo, Playboy, Voodoo Dolls, French Kitty, Ivory, Who's Billy, and Itsu), men's wear (Roar, Globalocal, Blueprint, Hope & Glory, Town & Country, and Crusty Demons), and children's wear (Billiecart, Purr Girls, Roar, SP Girl, Nuggets, Milly, NG Surf, Spud, Jimmy Jams, Precious Pumpkins, and Baby Gund). Although the Voyager Distributing Company is primarily a wholesaler, it combines importing with factory-based local production.

LOCAL CLOTHING AND TEXTILE PRODUCTION

As Australia climbed out of recession in the mid-1990s, the clothing production system generated new firms, new organizational configurations, and a new workforce. Despite the pessimistic outlook in 1986, the clothing production sector continued to supply a significant share of local consumption. Although the income generated in the local garment-related production sector fell between 2001–2002 and 2004–2005, it still exceeded AUD $5 billion dollars per annum in 2004–2005 (ABS 2006a). The volume of clothing manufactured in Australia fell from 28.8 to 22.8 thousand items between 2001–2002 and 2004–2005, a fall of a little less than 20 percent (TFIA 2006). In recent years, profit margins have been modest relative to the manufacturing industry average. These figures suggest that the restructuring process has not yet reached a point of equilibrium.

The clothing production sector is characterized by a large number of very small firms. In fact, one-quarter of all employees (including working proprietors) work in firms with fewer than five workers. The handful of workplaces with one hundred or more employees employs a quarter of the workforce. In the financial years 2001–2002 to 2004–2005, firms employing between ten and fifty people grew in relative terms, increasing their share of employment by 7.1 percent. Australia's clothing production capacity is concentrated in the southern state of Victoria, where 44 percent of the industry's sales and service income and 45 percent of its industry value added (IVA) is produced (ABS 2006a). Export activity has declined with the withdrawal of export incentive schemes—in the three years 2001–2002 to 2004–2005, exports by textiles, clothing, footwear, and leather firms fell by 43 percent. In 2004–2005, 56.9 percent of firms in the TCF&L industries did not export any of their output. As might be expected, small firms are much less likely to be exporters.

After the crisis of the early 1990s, the clothing production industry regenerated as a production system based on home-based labor, known in Australia as clothing outwork. It mushroomed in the mid-1990s with the fortuitous intersection of buoyant demand, large numbers of skilled clothing workers who had been displaced when factories closed down, and large amounts of unused equipment (which could be bought cheaply at liquidation auctions). By 1995 the Textiles, Clothing and Footwear Union of Australia confidently asserted that domestic production was based on the outwork model (TCFUA 1995). Since 1995 clothing unions have spearheaded campaigns to improve the regulation of labor standards in the outwork sector. Although outwork is regulated under Australia's Award framework, many firms have flouted the law, underpaying workers, ignoring occupational health and safety rules, and avoiding taxation obligations. Because outworker-based production quickly adjusts to shifts in demand and brings garment production closer to the market, it outperforms imports in fashion-oriented segments of the industry (principally because it enables retailers to buy small volumes on demand, keep inventories low, and avoid end-of-season markdowns).

After community concern about the plight of outworkers, activist campaigns in the late 1990s managed to recruit firms into a voluntary Outwork Code of Practice. Subsequently, state governments in New South Wales (2001) and Victoria (2003) have legislated to protect outworkers by tightening responsibilities in the supply chain and introducing laws that make an "apparent" employer higher in the production hierarchy responsible to unpaid wages. In 2006 both states were in the process of introducing mandatory codes of practice.

In 2007 Australia's remaining garment manufacturing sector operated at world-standard productivity levels as lead firms' sourcing flexibility thrust local manufacturers into direct competition with products manufactured in low-wage countries. Because the fragmented local market is too small to generate economies of scale, this context encourages small firms to maximize efficiency and minimize costs—that is, to take the "low road" to international competitiveness. The strong Australian dollar since 2005 has reduced the cost of inputs and improved the competitiveness of local sourcing.

In 2007 the critical issue for clothing manufacturers was Australia's plans to enter free trade agreements with Malaysia, the United Arab Emirates, and, most importantly, China. Although these agreements are likely to preserve existing tariff reduction schedules, industry concerns center on nontariff barriers, rules of origin, and intellectual property issues. Local firms opposed changes to rules of origin for Australia–New Zealand garment trade, for example, arguing that the shift from a 50 percent regional value added to a "change in tariff classification" (CTC) criterion would enable more transshipment of otherwise dutiable commodities via New Zealand (PC 2004).

Different issues shape the fortunes of the high-technology textiles production industry. Policy changes have not been kind to garment-related textiles production, and it accounts for a diminishing proportion of the Australian textiles production industry. In its early years Australia's garment-related textiles industry had focused on the downstream processing of Australia's wool production. Many production plants were then owned by British textile interests. Until the late 1970s garment-related textiles production was supported by a structure of yarn bounties, import quotas, and tariffs that prevented cheaper overseas-made fabrics from entering Australia. The government's Tariff Board had micromanaged protection levels with a view to maintaining employment, especially for workers in regional areas. As Australia prepared to liberalize its markets, British capital exited the local textiles sector. Local entrepreneur Abe Goldberg purchased multiple plants, but his empire failed in 1989, marking the beginning of a new era for the local textiles industries. Many less efficient garment-related textiles firms exited the industry in the early 1990s as clothing production moved offshore.

Employment in garment-related textiles fell throughout the 1990s. The position of local textiles firms stabilized briefly in the mid-1990s, as government incentives encouraged the use of Australian fabric in offshore processing firms in Fiji and China. Offshore processing stimulated a new generation of textiles finishing firms specializing in importing basic cloth from Asia, dyeing and finishing it in Australia, and then exporting to Fiji for use in garment manufacture. Finished garments were then reimported to Australia. When the Fiji production system became uncompetitive after 2000, the fortunes of garment-related textiles firms declined, and a number of larger firms that had struggled to compete in the 1990s finally went out of business. In 2007 surviving textiles production firms were opposing a Fijian proposal to further alter the structure of the South Pacific Regional Trade and Economic Cooperative Agreement (SPARTECA) trade arrangements to enable Fijian clothing manufacturers to source fabrics from a wider range of origin countries. The disappearance of Fiji's preference for Australian fabric would displace much of Australia's remaining textile production (TFIA 2007).

The garment-related textiles production sector continues to decline. Yarn production fell by more than 60 percent between 2001 and 2005 (from 58.6 to 21.6 thousand tons), as did broad-woven fabric production (from 131.6 thousand tons to 46.7 thousand tons). Only the high-technology knitting mill sector remains competitive under Australia's current (2005–2010) industry policy framework. The hosiery sector, which is controlled by Pacific Brands, experienced the smallest decline. Since 1997, with employment falling only 5.7 percent from 1997–1998 to 2002–2003 (from 2,259 to 2,130), Pacific Brands upgraded its textiles production capacity significantly with the support of government subsidies and incentives. The fabric it produces is exported for use in the firms' branded clothing.

There are some positive developments in textiles production. An increasing proportion of local garment-related textiles activity is in textile finishing—technologically advanced processes that add value to basic cloth. Innovations include the application of nano-technologies and the use of polymers and polyurethanes to produce odor-resistant and light-sensitive fabrics, fabrics that offer ultraviolet (UV) protection, fabrics with advanced flexibility and breathability, and synthetic fabrics that mimic the properties of natural fibers. Global garment firms Levi Strauss, Kathmandu, and Champion have incorporated Australian nano-technologies into their products. Government-funded research centers have played a leading role in these developments.

CONCLUSION

The Australia clothing and textiles industries have been the first among Western economies to face the realities of open trading arrangements and internationalized markets. The effects were devastating for most of the 1985 workforce (Weller and Webber 1999). However, after twenty years of reform, some parts of the industry have established a place in the new economy.

This positioning exemplifies the contradictions of market economies. On the one hand, the sector is no longer viewed as backward and low skilled, but is now understood as an essential component of creative advanced capitalist economies and as a sector integral to regional development. As the new industry orients to design and fashion, it is forging new associations with consumer goods sectors and creating new market partitions based on lifestyle branding. On the other hand, the Dickensian conditions of the unregulated parts of the outwork production sector epitomize the dark side of deregulation and the perils of a trade-exposed and market-led economy.

The history of the Australian clothing production industries over the last twenty years demonstrates that no matter how inhospitable the policy settings, the clothing production industries do not disappear from high-wage economies. It seems clear from this story that because people want to work in the fashion and clothing industries, neither labor nor capital will ever entirely shift to the more "efficient" uses predicted by economic theory. However, when these highly mobile industries are exposed to global competition, the price of labor is inevitably pushed downward, creating segments of the Australian workforce—outworkers and young clothing designers working at the edge of unemployment—living at standards well below the national average.

References and Further Reading

Australian Bureau of Statistics (ABS). "Manufacturing Industry, Australia, 2004–05." ABS Cat. No. 8221.0. Australian Bureau of Statistics. Ausstats, 2006a.

Australian Bureau of Statistics (ABS). "Retail Trade, Australia." ABS Cat. No. 8501.01. Australian Bureau of Statistics. Ausstats, 2006b.

Australian Bureau of Statistics (ABS). "Labour Force, Australia." ABS Cat. No. 6291.0.55.003. Detailed Quarterly Estimates, Australian Bureau of Statistics. Ausstats, 2007.

Greig, A. W. "Technological Change and Innovation in the Clothing Industry: The Role of Retailing." *Labour and Industry* 2, no. 3 (1990): 330–353.

Industries Assistance Commission. *The Textiles Clothing and Footwear Industries.* Vol. 1 (Chapters). Industries Assistance Commission Report No. 386. Canberra: Australian Government Publishing Service, 1986.

Industry Commission. *The Textiles, Clothing and Footwear Industries.* Vol. 1 (Report). Industry Commission Report No. 59. Canberra: Australian Government Publishing Service, 1997.

La Frenz, C. "$A Rise Boosts Key Brands." *The Herald-Sun* (Melbourne), 11 March 2007: 17.

Meagher, D. "Designers Take a Slow Coat to China." *The Australian* (Canberra), 18 May 2007: 18.

Productivity Commission. *Rules of Origin under the Australia–New Zealand Closer Economic Relations Trade Agreement: Research Report.* Canberra, Australia: Productivity Commission, 2004.

Safe, G. "Flying under the Radar." *The Australian* (Canberra), 18 July 2007: 17.

Textile, Clothing, and Footwear Union of Australia. *The Hidden Cost of Fashion: Report on the National Outwork Information Campaign.* Sydney: Textiles Clothing and Footwear Union of Australia, 1995.

TFIA. *The Australian TCF Industry—A Profile.* Mimeo. Melbourne, Australia: TFIA Business Services, 2006.

TFIA. *TFIA Newsletter.* Melbourne: Textiles and Fashion Industries of Australia, May 2007.

Tungate, M. *Fashion Brands: Branding Styles from Armani to Zara.* London: Kogan Page, 2005.

Webber, M., and S. Weller. *Re-Fashioning the Rag Trade: The Internationalisation of the TCF Industries in Australia.* Sydney: University of New South Wales Press, 2001.

Weller, S. A. "International Competitiveness and Export Performance: The Case of Clothing and Textiles." *Journal of Australian Political Economy* 46 (December 2000): 71–102.

Weller, S. A. "Networks, Commodity Chains and Crisis: The Impact of Fiji's Coup on Garment Production Networks." *Environment & Planning A* 38, no. 7 (2006): 1249–1267.

Weller, S. A. "Fashion as Viscous Knowledge: Fashion's Role in Shaping Trans-National Garment Production." *Journal of Economic Geography* 7, no. 1 (2007): 39–66. http://joeg. oxfordjournals. org/cgi/content/abstract/7/1/39 (accessed March 2008).

Weller, S., and M. Webber. "Re-Employment after Retrenchment: Evidence from the TCF Industry Study." *Australian Economic Review* 32, no. 2 (1999): 105–129.

Sally Weller

See also Jews in the Melbourne Garment Trade; The Wool Industry in Australia; Making and Retailing Exclusive Dress in Australia—1940s to 1960s; New Zealand Textiles and Apparel Sectors.

Jews in the Melbourne Garment Trade

For a large part of the twentieth century the garment trade was an important industry in the southern Australian state of Victoria. Since clothing was a big part of the country's manufacturing, the Jews of the garment trade made a large contribution to Australia's economy. This multifaceted industry had its own economic and social history, gorgeous products, and camaraderie and color at its heart, Flinders Lane. It gave rise to the individualism, flair, entrepreneurial spirit, and sheer fun that characterized the *schmatte* (rag in Yiddish, pronounced shmutta) business.

THE BEGINNING

The discovery of gold in Victoria in 1850 gave the state the impetus for historic growth, but even before the gold rush, Jews were involved in the local clothing trade. In 1845, of forty-seven clothing shops in Victoria, twenty-five were owned by Jews. Since then, in tandem with the rest of the Australian manufacturing industry, the garment industry has witnessed a cycle in which at first almost all attire was imported; increasingly from the later nineteenth century clothing was manufactured locally; but from the 1980s onward imports again dominated.

In the 1880s big soft goods–importing warehouses established Flinders Lane in the central business district of the Victorian capital, Melbourne, as the heart of the trade, because of the Lane's proximity to wharves and railway stations and its centrality to Melbourne's population. These warehouses, which dominated the Flinders Lane trade for the first two decades of the twentieth century, were not Jewish. A notable exception was the underclothing business of Lazar Slutzkin, probably the first Jewish clothing manufacturer in Melbourne.

Lazar Slutzkin arrived in 1893 from Russia, and, it is said, he virtually founded the Australian garment industry. About the turn of the century, he opened a warehouse making and selling ladies' white underwear. No ready-to-wear garments had been locally produced in real quantity before this. Lazar's brother Sholem joined him in the business and eventually took it over when Lazar retired. Both brothers were very religious; twice daily the business came to a standstill when they and their staff, consisting of fellow Jewish migrants, stopped for morning and afternoon prayers. "Makers-up" (or "maker-uppers"—the meaning is obvious) were not given material on Fridays lest they work on Shabbat (the Sabbath). A set percentage of the company's net profit was donated

annually to charities. Much of the early Jewishness of Flinders Lane was due to Sholem Slutzkin, who employed so many Jewish newcomers to Melbourne and generously offered advice when they wanted to set up their own businesses.

The migration to Australia of nearly nine thousand Jews in a general population of about seven million between 1920 and 1939 coincided with the development of the fashion industry. Previously, the wealthy had bought clothes in retail shops, however as fashion found a mass market, clothes became self-expression rather than just necessity. Melbourne's rapid population growth fed the new outerwear industry, while the entrepreneurial energy and business acumen of Sidney Myer (of the Slutzkin family) led the innovations in retailing. Government assisted with tariff protection; the aim was to reduce the dependence on British goods.

World War II and its aftermath gave a further tremendous boost to Australia's manufacturing industry. From 1945 to 1950 the postwar baby boom and a massive immigration program produced a fast-growing and increasingly cosmopolitan population with a heightened sense of fashion. Postwar Victoria blossomed economically, and the manufacturing industry produced good profits and full employment. After the austerity of the war years, an emphasis on luxury, femininity, and glamour meant that fashion was very big business. The stimulation of working amid such thriving businesses is what gave the industry its excitement, as Victoria, and particularly Flinders Lane, led the Australian fashion industry.

In 1956, 40 percent of Melbourne's Jews were in the rag trade (a colloquial term for the garment industry) and the majority of clothing businesses belonged to Jews. The annual cycle of Jewish festivals and holidays dictated the rhythm of the business. The onus was on the non-Jewish garment traders to fit in with their Jewish workmates: to acquire some fluency in Yiddish, which was spoken in the Lane as a matter of course, or at least an acquaintance with Jewish humor.

Why was it such a Jewish trade? Many Jews traditionally had mercantile, entrepreneurial, or tailoring skills, or European clothing trade experience. However, this was by no means always the case for those who went into schmattes. What they appeared to have in common was a desire, because of trauma in their pasts, for early material security, and to build on this foundation a strong family life. They worked for others for as short a time as possible, then went into their own businesses.

> Most post-war Jewish refugees were in either milk bars (neighbourhood general stores) or schmattes. Young survivors had had their education interrupted by the war, so they arrived here without trade, profession, education, money, or in most cases, language. They had to go into something that required none of these. (Rachel Silverman, owner-manufacturer)

Most involved in the industry came from Germany and eastern and central Europe. In Melbourne the majority came from Poland, but also Russia (the boundaries between Poland and Russia shifted many times in the twentieth century). In fact, all the refugees required were a couple of sewing machines and some fabric on credit.

It's easy to start—two sewing machines in the bedroom, cut on the dining-room table, make-up samples, and go get orders. The easiest thing to get into—and it was really alive. (Diana Kahn, owner-manufacturer)

The extent of the business was remarkably broad. As well as all men's and women's outerwear and underwear, swimwear, footwear, and millinery, there were accessories such as fasteners, buttons, sliders, buckles, studs, zippers, hooks—the endless large and small necessities of the trade, along with artificial flowers and trimmings. Furs were imported, dressed, dyed, and manufactured; there was hosiery—socks, stockings (including stockings for nuns), and pantyhose. Several schmatte businesses began in the markets, most notably Spotlight, which grew from a single stall in the Victoria Market to one of Australia's largest names in fabrics and home interiors, across to Singapore and New Zealand. In addition, rags were lucrative in an international trade of new waste off-cuts and old rags to make yarn.

Several Jewish names were and still are among the well-known retailers. "Travelers" visited them all. Playing a major part in the schmatte business, these manufacturers' representatives traveled many miles, taking samples into shops in the city and country.

Uniforms—all kinds from shop salespersons' and Olympic blazers to police and local council workers'—were important money makers. During World War II a firm would win a tender to make army uniforms; the contract would be secured and the government would deliver the cloth made in Australian woolen mills—there were 350 in Victoria until the 1970s, many in country areas, and over three thousand knitwear manufacturers. In 2001 there were two or three mills remaining.

For the makers-up a bonus opportunity existed if, for example, the wholesaler ordered a hundred garments each using 1.5 meters (4.9 feet) of fabric and the makers-up managed to do it with less. They could sell garments, called "cabbage," made from the leftover material, as long as they were not the same as the garments that had originally been ordered. The profit for the maker-up depended on her skill. The small manufacturers tolerated it; even the tax department turned a blind eye. Cabbage could bring in more than the maker-uppers' legitimate income. Was it stealing? Some scrupulous makers-up thought so. It was a matter of interpretation. Many makers-up, feeling squeezed by the manufacturer, thought it was only fair to make money from cabbage when they could.

From the industry's vibrancy emerged several innovations that the manufacturers believed were world firsts. Among these were sparkling Lurex evening pants for women, which in 1964 caused the models, with their delighted manufacturer Simon Shinberg, in a clever publicity stunt, to be evicted from a Sydney nightclub for noncompliance with dress regulations.

Innovative money-spinners seen as a boon for the busy modern woman with limited time for housework were Crimplene fabric; stretch, printed wool; no-iron shirts; and permanent pleating. Glo-Weave had their own miracle material produced on new flat machines to make the Four Seasons range of men's shirts, knitting over nine million yards of the fabric over a ten-year period. Every traveling Australian wore Four Seasons shirts because they were "wash 'n' wear." New fire-retardant jacquard fabrics were woven by Classweave for Qantas aircraft seats. The first stretch fabric made of nylon and viscose was developed by Bruck Mills around 1960. With that and stretch wool, Aywon

was producing thirty thousand pairs of stretch pants per week at that time.

In a marketing innovation entrepreneurial manufacturers saw the potential of television for sales. Television advertising in the 1950s, when TV came to Melbourne, lent these novel fabrics glamour and status because it was new, modern, and symbolized affluence.

In the 1960s and especially the 1970s, designed to maintain standardization in a mass-manufacturing environment, new operations evolved out of the piecework system, dividing the making of every garment into sectional tasks carried out by individual machinists. Companies that wanted to retain a competitive edge adopted the new methods of mass production. Commercial viability was the top priority.

WOMEN IN THE JEWISH RAG TRADE

Females dominated the workforce of the schmatte business. Women were designers and sample hands. All the buyers, so powerful they were called prima donnas, were women. Above all, the seamstresses were women. For many of them it was a stimulating world, although they were often underpaid, working in archaic conditions in a paternalistic environment. Especially during the euphoric 1950s, they shared the sense of postwar prosperity and of glamour. For the skilled dressmakers it was a fulfilling profession. They were proud of the fine dresses they made and saw worn by prominent people and displayed in expensive stores. They developed marketable skills that they could use for the rest of their lives.

Recent arrivals struggling to build their lives, the owners' wives often worked and contributed as much as the men. Few of the owner-manufacturers were women, partly because they could not get bank loans. However, there was a raft of notable exceptions,

Buyers in the showroom of Haskin & Company, Flinders Lane, Melbourne, ca. 1958. Gift of Henry Haskin's family for the 2001 exhibition Schmatte Business—Jews in the Garment Trade. Jewish Museum of Australia.

usually women who had to take over because of the death or illness of their husbands. In the circumstances they seemed to enjoy the challenge. Although it was tough being a woman and a migrant in a man's world, some women were clearly in their element, enjoying fashion as an addiction—the excitement of seeing what had been created by the brilliance of the designers. It is of some interest that Orthodox Jews in Melbourne are a small minority, and neither male nor female workers in the garment business appear to have exhibited any particular dress codes specific to their culture, as is apparently the case in New York in the twenty-first century.

> I had the best job in Australia. Exciting times, the 60s and 70s, because we were developing new things. It was a good time for women. You could get real jobs. There were big parades, variety in the work, travel, social activity—a function every night—we lived the work from dawn to midnight. (Moira Wallis, fashion administrator in Flinders Lane)

FLINDERS LANE

For over a hundred years "The Lane" was an Australian institution. Famous fashion houses flourished and fell, characters larger than life wheeled and dealed on this little street that was the home and heart of Australian fashion. Labels were given French, English, or American names including Henry Haskin, Charlotte of Fifth Avenue, Cherry Lane, Saba of California, Leroy, Park Avenue Gowns, Hartnell, Samos, French Modes, Margeaux Hayes, and Champs Elysées.

Large and small factories, Jewish retailers, and especially woolen mills certainly existed outside Flinders Lane and indeed all around the country in Victoria. In the 1940s the government encouraged decentralization, and in the boom years between 1945 and 1960, when migrants created such a huge demand, it was easier to get staff in the country plants, which trained completely inexperienced country workers. These people were not Jews. Very few Jews left the city for the country, and these workers were simply people who happened to be living in the country towns.

But undoubtedly Flinders Lane had many advantages. It was close to shops, department stores, transportation terminals, and financial institutions, and to suppliers and manufacturers, the labor pool, and the potential market. Buyers could come from the country and "do" the Lane in one session; comparison buying was important: They needed to survey the scene and then backtrack to place orders. For the manufacturers there was easy communication with rival firms. They could keep up with market trends and sometimes help with urgent orders—in this there was a reciprocity of favors. And importantly, the ancillary services were within walking distance: pressers, machine importers, embroiderers, button coverers, and so on.

With modern fabrics and modern manufacturing processes, it was a glamorous industry, but over the years the Lane hardly changed physically, and the conditions were far from glamorous. The decrepit buildings housed rats that ate the sequins off luxury garments. The vermin came from the wharves, and fox terriers were used to hunt them between floors. With no air-conditioning there was heat in summer and, in winter, cold, relieved by open radiators, which could combine with the new, flammable materials to cause fires. (No one is willing to say to what degree fires and financial trouble went together. What they will say is that the manufacturer was always undercapitalized and taking big risks, so that in the 1950s, 1960s, and 1970s, there were plenty of bankruptcies, and many fires started at night or on weekends.)

These old buildings were worse than the average workplace at the time, yet they were accepted as part of the experience. With hindsight they could be seen as an area with built-in inconveniences—except the togetherness and mutual support, which produced the magic of creativity, innovation, and success. Schmattes was not just business, it was a lifestyle. Flinders Lane was like a big, extended family. Jews liked it because it was reminiscent of the ghetto, but still it was a glamorous industry with glamorous women.

Traveling overseas, often several times a year, was a necessary part of the schmatte business, and there was excitement in it, meeting people internationally at all levels, working at a furious pace, visiting mills and factories to learn new methods and to exchange ideas, seeing their fabrics, their sources, and what was being displayed by couturiers.

> I used to go to the *prêt-a-porter* shows in Paris twice a year; I would go from one tiny little boutique or factory to another, in St Tropez for example, or buy a fantastic design in Copenhagen and have it made in India. T-shirts were designed from ideas gleaned on the French and Italian Riviera, and manufactured in Hong Kong, where I set up an agent and an office. In China I had to carry Mao's Little Red Book to demonstrate pro-Communist credentials! (Diana Kahn, owner-manufacturer)

In 1939 the number of clothing firms in the Lane reached 610, and this level of activity was maintained until the early 1960s. Flinders Lane itself is a mile long, mostly of four- to five-story buildings. Just about half of it was given over to the schmatte business. In the 1960s and 1970s these businesses began to leave, or they closed. With changing requirements for space and labor, rising rents, and traffic congestion, many relocated to the suburbs.

The first cohorts of the clothing trade had aged. These entrepreneurs had high aspirations for their children, who mainly went into the professions—for men medicine and law and for women the same but less so, and often teaching. Dependent on the personality and acumen of the owners, the businesses were not saleable when the owners were ready to retire. Closing was simple: no more orders, the "girls" were paid off, the machines sold, and the premises vacated.

Despite a reduction in the number of businesses, Flinders Lane remained the center of fashion innovation throughout the 1970s, the marketing center from which designs were contracted out to makers-up in the suburbs. The new entrepreneurs began with the 1960s "rat pack"—Norma Tullo, Geoff Bade, Prue Acton, Kenneth Pirrie, and Thomas Wardle—all in their twenties, the first generation of important non-Jewish designers in the rag trade.

UNIONS AND EMPLOYER–WORKER RELATIONS

In the boom times, the 1950s and 1960s, everyone benefited from the heady economic climate and full employment. Skilled staff were not easy to find; they set their own terms or moved, so they were treated well. Workers were not attracted to the confrontational union model of employer-worker relations. From all accounts they preferred the shared understanding and the paternalism in a workplace with a family atmosphere. The boss cared for his workers; they respected him. "Poppa" was treated with awe. Women were more interested in glamour than in women's rights. Skilled people earned good wages and were in great demand.

> Our staff was like a United Nations. We looked after them and they were very loyal. Because their parents worked so hard for us, I took their children, at least once a year, to an art gallery or a concert or a museum. (Marysia Kohn, owner-manufacturer)

"Sweating"—working for low wages—and piecework were issues that concerned the unions, and over which there were disputes. Unions directed blame at the large number of Jewish refugees in the industry after the war and their "will to sweat." These issues were never definitively resolved, as fewer than half the garment trade employees were union members. As the manufacturing industry declined, employers believed that unions compounded the problems in some cases, causing the collapse of companies by making demands that excessively sapped company resources.

MANUFACTURING IN AUSTRALIA AFTER THE BOOM

> Business changed overnight with Whitlam. You couldn't compete with cheap imports. We went to Asia to see what NOT to make in Australia—we made large sizes, found specialties for which we could charge higher prices—like pleated skirts. It took two seasons *to reconstruct ourselves*. (Abrasha Feigin, owner-manufacturer)

Gough Whitlam was the new Australian prime minister elected in 1972, and his government lowered the tariff barrier that had until then protected Australian manufacturing. Imported goods quickly began to appear on the market. The shock of imports and the trade's inability to apprehend its full potential can be gauged by this conclusion to an article in *The Bulletin* (Sydney) in April 1972:

> Despite the wrangling over imports, Ray Aitchison (Executive Director, Australian Confederation of Apparel Manufacturers) is quietly confident that the clothing industry's campaign for protection will be successful….Australian manufacturers have generally reached a point where their quality and advanced fashion will make them impregnable in a market which is constantly changing.

He was sadly mistaken. Australian manufacturers were stunned to find that imports could be sold for less than their own cost to produce the same items. Despite mass production, they could not compete with cheap labor in Asia. But some manufacturers—worldly, well-traveled, politically and economically astute—found the means to survive, finding niches, using innovative design and economy of scale—either very big, or very small with no overheads.

Often for those who have stayed in the business, a dynasty has been in evidence. In many cases children of the second, the third,

or sometimes the fourth generation in the trade, many tertiary-educated, carried on ever more sophisticated enterprises. These enterprises were defined by the move to a greater degree of mass production with the use of computer-aided design, cutting, and finishing and a greater specialization of skills. The factories in the twenty-first century look more like production lines, with each machinist doing, for example, only the sleeves, or the buttons, whereas in the old days most of any one garment was produced by one person. Alternatively, there are manufacturers who produce tiny lines for a niche market.

IMPORTING

Some manufacturers dealt with the new environment by becoming importers or undertaking offshore manufacturing. One group bought a warehouse in Flinders Lane in 1961—Dick Harbig, who previously had a business manufacturing artificial flowers, joined Walter Rothfield and Norman Rockman to buy Brooks McGlashan. They imported knitwear, blouses, swimwear, and children's wear from Asia, mainly Taiwan. During the late 1970s they began importing menswear. Later, Rothfield and Rockman were bought out and the business owned by Harbig imported women's wear and menswear. At this time they were operating within import quota limits. This was a limit designated for a company by the Australian government, something that businesses were permitted to buy and sell. In 1985 Dick Harbig sold his import quota for millions of dollars. In 1970, at the beginning of offshore manufacture, an Australian, Diana Kahn of Cherry Lane, established a cottage industry in Delhi making embroidered cheese-cloth blouses.

As early as the late 1940s, a successful textile manufacturer, Alan Selwyn of Selwyn Fabric Imports, saw that there was money to be made selling fancy imported textiles in Melbourne to better-class manufacturers and retail stores—bridal goods, evening wear, brocades, satins, chiffons, georgettes. Speaking several European languages, the firm's principal traveled and bought in Switzerland, France, and Italy, brought paintings and sketches of fabrics, and in 1953 began to have them produced in Japan at half-price. The prejudice at that time against dealing with Japan, so soon after Australia's wartime experiences in the Pacific, provided an opening for those who dared. Between 1985 and 1993 the production was moved to Korea where it was cheaper.

A famous Australian knitwear importer, Mary Lipshut of Meredith Imports, began by importing embroidered knitwear from Hong Kong. The business grew into a two-sided operation of European imports, with clothes designed in Australia and made in Hong Kong. In the early 1990s shirt manufacturer Glo-Weave employed 496 machinists. Only ten years later, 95 percent of their shirts were made in Indonesia and only the samples were made in Melbourne.

CONCLUSION

The most interesting years of the Australian fashion industry saw the androgynous, austere style prevalent during the war years move into the glamorous style of the 1950s, which celebrated femininity and fertility with volumes of fabric. However, following the hippie revolution, the youth cult of the 1970s seemed to signify the end of high fashion. Although some observers persisted in forecasting a return to glamour, in general people stopped wanting to dress up, and women were happy in denim and pants when they were not working.

Cars changed fashion. There's no room in a car for beautiful dresses or high hats. Artificial flowers and hats used to be a big industry, with fifty or sixty hat factories in Melbourne. (Dick Harbig, owner-manufacturer)

We used to have so many different categories for clothes, like mother-of-the-bride. But who now wants to look like the mother-of-the-bride? (Leon Haskin, owner-manufacturer)

I hate fashion today, which is designed by accountants and greedy businessmen. With worldwide take-overs of once creative businesses, fashion is now run by computers that calculate what is selling best. There is no spontaneity and no surprise. The body is now the fashion, not the dress upon it. (Miriam Kuna, Melbourne School of Fashion)

Opinions differ as to when the good times ended. The process was gradual and not total—there are still Jews doing well in the schmatte business. The decline reflected events in the Australian manufacturing industry generally. The credit squeeze in 1961 was followed by the growth in cheap imports, the effects of which were exacerbated by the tariff cuts and the more stringent labor laws of the early 1970s, both instituted by the Labour government of the time.

For the Jews, as with other ethnic groups who followed them, schmattes was a migrant industry with which to establish their families in Australia. Their carefully educated children went into the professions, and the parents went into property, continuing in a new variety of careers to make a valuable contribution to the Australian economy.

They shared traditional values, and many saved others financially when the bad times arrived in the cycle of business. Most were generous supporters of community needs and causes, and it was these benefactors who created opportunities for employment and growth in the community through their creativity. Their generosity and the high priority that they gave to family and community created a framework for the community to grow and prosper for many years. (Joe Lederman, owner-manufacturer)

Acknowledgment

This essay is based on unique primary research undertaken for an exhibition at the Jewish Museum of Australia entitled Schmatte Business—Jews in the Garment Trade in 2001. Almost all of the material comes from a series of about eighty interviews with people who had worked in the Victorian garment trade in various capacities. Quotes are excerpts from these interviews and reprinted here by kind permission of the Jewish Museum of Australia, Melbourne.

References and Further Reading

Ashton, Kaye, and Susan Ryan, eds. *Gloweave*. Melbourne, Australia: Frances Burke Textile Research Centre, School of Fashion and Textiles, RMIT University, 2000.

Cohen, Susan E. "Flinders Lane 1899–1975: An Historical Geography of Melbourne's Clothing District." Honours thesis, Department of Geography, University of Melbourne, 1975.

Marshall, Julie. "Work and Community: The Jews of Flinders Lane." Honours thesis, Department of History, University of Melbourne, 1990.

Marshall, Roslyn. "The Heyday of the Flinders Lane Rag Trade." Honours thesis, University of Melbourne, 1997.

Rosenthal, Lesley. *Schmattes: Stories of Fabulous Frocks, Funky Fashion and Flinders Lane*. Published by the author, 2005.

Anna Epstein

See also Making and Retailing Exclusive Dress in Australia—1940s to 1960s.

The Wool Industry in Australia

- The Development of the Wool Industry in Australia
- Marketing Australian Wool and Its Clothing Products
- The Role of Wool Innovation in the Australian Fashion Industry
- Long-Term Challenges

That the wealth of Australia rode "on the sheep's back" is a well-known expression. In particular, it has been Merino wool (a thick fine fleece suited to weaving into quality fabric) for the international and increasingly global clothing market that has been Australia's most significant product. The Merino sheep has been selectively bred for over two hundred years and is recognized worldwide for its uniformly fine and soft fibers. While Australia is home to only a small proportion of the world's sheep, it produces almost two-thirds of the world's Merino wool and around 95 percent of its fine and superfine apparel wool. Australian Merino wool is 100 percent natural fiber, which is renewable, biodegradable, and flame-resistant.

Australian processed wool has had great successes over the years but faces continual issues of sustainability and long-term challenges. Producers, manufacturers, designers, and researchers in the twenty-first century are responding to this and focused on improvements in industry performance. But in the final analysis it is the usefulness and aesthetics of fabric that determine a designer's choice of cloth. One of the difficulties for the wool industry is that despite the merits of its natural properties, wool fiber quality is not necessarily an important consideration for purchasers. Style, color, and brand factor sit above fiber in selection criteria.

Over the years the Australian wool industry has diversified and developed into a number of independent businesses, which produce many different types of wool from Australian Merino and crossbred sheep. Coarse-fiber "woolens" are used to make

A promotional picture for Simplicity Patterns taken at Werribee Station, Victoria. It was published in *Vanity Fair* in August 1968. The models are surrounded by Merino sheep, which are recognized for their uniformly fine wool. Australia produces most of the world's Merino wool, despite having a small fraction of the world's sheep. Photograph by Henry Talbot. Powerhouse Museum.

carpets, bedding, and upholstery, and the longer, worsted super-fine wools (twisted yarns made from long-staple wool) are used for lightweight woven and knitted fabrics in the world of fashion. Fiber diameter is the single most important factor affecting wool price and also one of the most heritable traits of the Merino. A low fiber diameter combined with high staple (strength) is a key element in the production of lightweight and comfortable wool products for the clothing and textile market.

THE DEVELOPMENT OF THE WOOL INDUSTRY IN AUSTRALIA

In 1770 Captain James Cook claimed eastern Australia for the British Crown. The First Fleet arrived in 1788 and, with disregard to the sovereignty of the Aboriginal people, populated New South Wales with convicts, some settlers, and civil and military officials. The first sheep, Cape Fat Tails, from the Cape of Good Hope, that came out with the Fleet in 1788 were suitable for meat but not for wool production. It was not until 1797 with the arrival of the Spanish Merino, also from the Cape of Good Hope, that the wool industry in Australia began. Some of the early clothing worn by convicts was made from a coarse, felted wool manufactured in Sydney, and by the end of the 1820s a reasonably viable government industry was in place. Government-run woolen mills set up in prisons provided coarse materials for clothing for the mentally ill, prisoners, and needy Aboriginal people. In Victoria woolen fabric manufactured at the penal establishment Pentridge was known as Pentridge Tweed.

The longer, softer fibers, for which Australia was to become famous, came later when the Spanish Merino was cross-bred with long-wooled sheep from England, the Cape, and Bengal. Over time other breeds of Merino such as the Saxon (German), Rambouillet (French), and later the Peppin, from the Riverina in New South Wales, were bred in the quest to produce the finest-quality fleece.

Reverend Samuel Marsden, a wool-grower from Sydney, pioneered this selective breeding in Australia in 1798. Samples of wool were sent to England in 1804, but it was not until 1807 that the first bale of wool was exported from Australia to London. Marsden carried the wool to England, and while he was there some of it was woven into cloth at William Thompson's Yorkshire mill. It was then tailored into a suit and Marsden wore it to meet King George III, probably as a form of promotion for colonial products.

Woven wools, unless they were imported into Australia, were scarce, as the technology available to comb, spin, and weave was designed for shorter cotton strands, not wool. There was also a shortage of skilled labor, and it was not until 1812 with the arrival of more technically proficient weavers that the local textile industry could be expanded. Three years later the first substantial, privately run wool mill was established at Botany Bay, employing convicts to manufacture cloth for the government. Simeon Lord, an ex-convict, set up the mill, and by the 1820s the quality of his fabrics was being compared to that of English cloth.

There was early recognition that Australia could not be just a primary producing nation, and other manufacturing companies, such as the Waverly Woollen Mills, were set up in Launceston, Tasmania, in 1874. This company was to have a long history of manufacturing blankets, rugs, and knitting wools. Up to this time most wool produced was for the woolen industry, whose fabrics

were suitable only for making blankets, rugs, flannels, and rough tweeds. But as a result of successful breeding programs, the quality of the wool improved. By the late 1880s the majority of wool produced was lighter and could be used in the woven worsted, knitting, and apparel industries.

The 1870s and 1880s were known as the golden age of the wool industry, when wool received high prices. The Suez Canal had opened in 1869, and this meant the time taken to transport wool from Australia to England was considerably reduced. During this period the British colonies in Australia were being encouraged to "Buy British," which meant that wool grown in Australia was sent to Britain, where it was processed and then returned as manufactured cloth or ready-made clothing.

By the 1890s Australia was in a depression, and the country was severely affected by drought. Sheep numbers fell by almost 50 percent and would not recover until the 1920s. Around the time of Federation (1901), the slogan "Australian goods for Australian people" was devised to promote the expansion of the local textile industry. The introduction of a uniform customs tariff throughout the Commonwealth encouraged the establishment of companies such as the WA Woollen Mills in Western Australia, Australian Woollen Mills in New South Wales, Onkaparinga Woollen Company in South Australia, and Australian Knitting Mills in Victoria.

By 1913 the textile and clothing industry was the largest employer in Australia with eighty-four thousand workers, and wool was the major fiber used in the industry. Despite the local industry, cottons, blends, and finer woolen textiles were still largely imported until the 1920s, when increasingly refined production processes enabled fashionable, finer qualities of yarn and cloth to be made locally. Yarra Falls in Victoria, for instance, became well known for its fine wool crepe well into the twentieth century. All states apart from the Northern Territory and the Federal Capital Territory (from 1938 the Australian Capital Territory) had mills, with the concentration in Victoria and New South Wales.

World War I boosted the textile industry and the expansion of textile and garment factories peaked afterwards in an attempt to dispose of vast stockpiles of unsold Australian wool. Almost two million bales (the entire wool clip) was purchased by Britain at a fixed price at the onset of the war but had remained in stockpiles in Australia. After the war the British Australian Wool Realization Association (BAWRA) was established to sell the surplus, with some of the profit going to the Australian wool-growers.

Until World War I there had been little government regulation of the wool industry. After the war the United Kingdom was buying about 44 percent of Australia's wool export. Japan and the United States were strong markets, and the French and even the Germans were interested buyers. Britain, looking after its own interests, tried to block Japan and the United States out of the trade. It was they who in turn developed man-made fibers, which had a dramatic effect on wool sales. As early as 1922, Australian wool was being used and developed by overseas companies such as Dormeuil (France), which created Sportex, a wool sports cloth that had durable qualities and was utilized in both business and leisure clothing. But it was the competition from synthetics and man-made fibers that led to innovations such as permanent pleats and shrink-proof wool.

The Wall Street crash in 1929 had an impact across the world, and in Australia wool prices bottomed. By 1932–1933 there was an oversupply of wool. "Wool Weeks" were promotional events

The Print on the Sheep's Back, a touring exhibition, was shown in venues throughout Australia between 1994 and 1996 with the support of Art on the Move. Photograph by Ashley de Prazer.

held in many cities and major country towns to create awareness of and encourage the sales of woolen products. Following recommendations from the Australia Wool-Growers' Council and the Graziers' Federal Council, the Australian Wool Board was set up in 1936 under the Wool Publicity and Research Act. The aim was to improve the production of wool in Australia and extend its use throughout the world. It was also established to finance publicity and research with funds levied from wool-growers.

As a result of discussions at the January 1937 Empire Wool Conference in Melbourne, representatives of Australia, New Zealand, and South African wool-growers decided to establish a jointly funded International Wool Secretariat (IWS) in London. Established in August 1937, its purpose was to promote the use and export of Australian wool, working with textile companies, designers, and retailers. The International Wool Secretariat soon began special export promotions to the United States and South Africa, and during the 1940s and 1950s offices were established in Belgium, France, Italy, Canada, Holland, Sweden, Switzerland, Germany, and Japan.

During World War II Britain once again purchased the entire Australian wool clip. Research designed to improve the qualities of wool continued throughout the war, resulting in outcomes such as the development of the thermal insulating properties of wool, wool-resistant acid dyes, and chemical methods to help prevent moth grubs. Synthetic fibers continued to create a particular challenge for wool during the war years, as they were in higher supply and had a much lower coupon value than wool (clothing coupons were issued during the war to ration the amount of clothing a person could purchase).

MARKETING AUSTRALIAN WOOL AND ITS CLOTHING PRODUCTS

In 1945 the Wool Use Promotion Act reconstituted the Australian Wool Board, and their efforts to promote wool, along with the rapid postwar recovery of the textile industries in Europe, resulted in a better-than-expected disposal of Australian wool in the period 1945–1946. In 1945, in an attempt to increase the market for wool in India, some superfine scoured Merino wool was sent to Mahatma Ghandi to be woven into a shawl. (Interestingly, at this same period Ghandi himself was encouraging

villagers in India to weave hand-spun cloth, or *khādī*.) After the war and throughout the 1950s advertising campaigns to promote Australian woolen fashion intensified, accompanied with slogans such as "There is no substitute for wool."

In 1946 Claudio Alcorso of Silk and Textiles Printers Ltd. developed and promoted the "Modernage" range of fabrics using the designs of thirty-three Australian artists. He hoped that the designs printed on lightweight wools and other fabrics would inspire other Australian manufacturing industries to work with artists in the same way. The fabrics were a critical success, with displays shown in exhibitions in Sydney and Melbourne and in the shop windows of the David Jones department store in Sydney.

Other promotional activities at this time included Wool Fashion Parades held at Royal Agricultural Shows and an exhibition, Wool on Wheels, which traveled the country, stopping at small towns and showing wool fashions and products. Organizations such as the Country Women's Association, and national women's magazines such as the *Australian Women's Weekly*, provided important support in promoting wool throughout regional and urban Australia. A film unit was set up in 1945 and films like *Shearing Time at Billabong*, about sheep growing and shearing, and *Men in Wool* received wide screenings. Nationwide knitting competitions were held, and knitting books, project sheets, and other materials were supplied to teachers and schoolchildren. The *Australia and Wool* radio show, starting in April 1956, was broadcast to over fifty radio stations all over Australia and ran for a number of years.

In general though, during the twentieth century the long-term trend for the wool industry was downward, apart from the impact of the Korean War, which in 1951 created a demand for wool that outstripped world output by 20 percent. This anomaly created concern that the boom and subsequent inflated prices would create consumer resistance to woolen products. Much of the wool went to provide uniforms worn during the Korean War. The heavy, thick, and scratchy cloth used actually damaged wool's reputation for garments, because it accentuated perceptions of the prickle sensation of the fiber.

In 1955 the Australian Wool Bureau (1953–1963), the new name for the Australian Wool Board, started its annual fashion awards to stimulate the use of wool in the fashion trade and to increase public interest in Australian fashions. Clothes from the awards were sold in department stores such as David Jones in Sydney and Myers Emporium in Melbourne. Promotional activities continued throughout the 1960s. The Bureau started a Colour Sponsorship program that resulted in the establishment of the Australian Wool Colour Council in 1961 to standardize colors across the manufacturing and retail industries. The first color theme launched occurred in 1963 and was called "Wild Colonial Colours," with a theatrical fashion parade, coordinated with the press, TV, and radio advertising the following day. With a return to the name Australian Wool Board in 1963, further promotional activities occurred. In 1965 French model Christine Borge appeared at the Melbourne Spring Race Week carnival in European wool couture garments (this was the same occasion that British fashion model Jean "The Shrimp" Shrimpton created a stir in her dress by Du Pont, a company using synthetics).

One of the most important technical developments occurred in 1960 when Si-Ro-Set, a permanent creasing process developed in Australia in 1957, became available for licensing to firms across the world. This washable, lightweight, minimum-iron wool was made into tennis frocks for the Australian women's team for Wimbledon, but it was more commonly used for men's trousers, women's slacks, and school uniforms.

By the 1960s Japan and other European countries were challenging Britain's dominance in the purchase of Australian wool. The nature of the wool industry had shifted, and in 1962 the IWS introduced the Woolmark label to promote a new international identity for wool. The Woolmark symbol guarantees 100 percent pure new wool, and its label, designed by Italian graphic designer Francesco Saroglia, has become one of the most recognized logos in the world. In 1967 French couturier Pierre Cardin visited Australia (arranged through the IWS Paris Fashion Offices) with his spring/summer collection made almost exclusively from wool. The purpose was to create prestige publicity for Woolmark.

The 1970s were a challenging period for the wool industry, with low wool prices combined with record wool clips. In 1971 the Woolmark brand was extended to include the Woolmark Blend, a wool fabric that contains a minimum of 50 percent wool. Sub-branding also became important, as the pure new Woolmark label did not reflect the innovation and diversity of Australian wool types.

The 1980s were a high point in the promotion of Australian wools. In 1982 a photograph of Diana, Princess of Wales, made world news when she wore a hand-knitted "Blinky Bill" sweater by Sydney designer Jenny Kee, whose label Flamingo Park was renowned for its hand-knits using Australiana motifs. In 1988, as part of the Australian Bicentennial celebrations, Diana attended the Australian Bicentennial Wool Collection at the Sydney Opera House. World-famous designers such as Gianni Versace, Claude Montana, Kenzo Takada, and Jean Muir, along with Australian designers such as George Gross, Stuart Membery, and Adele Palmer, designed outfits from Australian Merino. One of Australia's most famous models, Elle Macpherson, modeled clothing for the parade.

One of the strongest overseas marketers among Australian clothing companies in the 1990s was the Melbourne knitwear company Coogi Australia. Established in Melbourne in 1969, at one stage 90 percent of their market was in the United States. In particular, their three-dimensional multicolored sweaters were popular with young black Americans. The Cooper-Hewitt, National Design Museum has a collection of Coogi garments in their textile collection as an example of the creative integration of computer technology with traditional knitting techniques.

In the late twentieth century promoting local wool fashions was somewhat sporadic, and design elements often originated overseas. Paul Keating, the prime minister of Australia from 1991 to 1996, was constantly derided because his favored brand of suit was made by the Italian company Ermenegildo Zegna. What the media failed to acknowledge was that these suits were made from Merino wool, which the Zegna company had been importing from Australia for decades. Zegna in turn has supported technological advances in the Australian wool industry with their widespread use of Cashwool (a 100 percent extra fine Australian Merino wool yarn made in Italy by Zegna Baruffa).

Yet the 1990s did see a number of local initiatives for the use of wool. The Print on the Sheep's Back was a project and exhibition developed by designer Jemma Dacre in the early part of the 1990s. Dacre commissioned eleven Australian artists and textile designers to develop designs that were printed onto locally produced fine wool fabric, creating a range of shawls shown in an exhibition that toured Australia between 1994 and 1996. The Moora Wool awards project (1992–1996) was also an initiative that aimed to highlight the importance of design to the wool industry and demonstrate the quality of Western Australian wool by providing fashion designers and textile artists from around Australia with local wool fabrics as inspiration for their work. Another interesting initiative during the 1990s was the knitting book designs made by Aboriginal artists Jimmy Pike (of the Walmajjari people) and Doris Gingingara from Maningrida.

Australia, a keen sporting nation, has dressed its Olympic teams in wool for over fifty years. Prue Acton, who was a recipient

This shawl print, "The Neighbourhood," was designed by Western Australian artist Theo Koning in 1994 as part of The Print on the Sheep's Back project managed by Textiles for Nomads. Eleven artists and designers based in Western Australia were commissioned to create designs for printing onto wool shawls, woven from locally produced fiber. Photograph by Ashley de Prazer.

of five Wool Fashion Awards, used wool in many of the garments she designed for Olympic athletes. As part of the Woolmark Company's association with the Sydney 2000 Olympics, Australian wool products were used by all thirty thousand visiting athletes and by the international media. In 2004 new wool technologies such as Sportwool, a bilayer fabric made from wool and polyester, were used in clothing for the Australian Olympic athletes in Athens.

In 2003 Australian fashion designer Peter Morrissey designed new Qantas uniforms using Australian Merino wool. These uniforms were given the Aboriginal name Wirriyarra because of the use of an indigenous textile design by Balarinji Design Studio. The Qantas uniform became part of a long history in which wool has been worn in Australian work-wear, from the use of wool in shearers' singlets (sleeveless under-vests), to heavyweight wool police uniforms dating back to the 1800s, through to flame-retardant wool coats used by firefighters.

THE ROLE OF WOOL INNOVATION IN THE AUSTRALIAN FASHION INDUSTRY

The new millennium has heralded new strategies in product development and promotion of Australian wool within the local fashion industry. Organizations such as Australian Wool Innovation (AWI), The Woolmark Company (TWC), Commonwealth Scientific and Industrial Research Organisation (CSIRO), and the Department of Agriculture and Food Western Australia (DAFWA) have been actively involved in the development of strategies focused on meeting the demands of the local fashion industry. Research and developments into wool fiber, fiber blending, new knit technology, knitwear production, and finishing are generating new interest in wool for fashion.

AWI implemented promotional strategies that involved working with Australian designers, such as Linda Grant, Josephine Nathan (woolliwoolli), Akira Isogawa, Josh Goot, Jayson Brunsdon, Lydia Pearson and Pamela Easton (Easton Pearson), Peter Morrissey, and Tina Kalivas. These designers have been assisted with sourcing and the development of wool fabrics suitable for their labels and also in the presentation of their designs to new national and international markets.

To help build demand for Australian Merino wool in international markets, AWI developed the first machine-washable suit. The new suit, developed with Berkley Apparel of Australia in 2003, was made from 60 percent wool and 40 percent polyester. In 2005 the suits were manufactured by Heilan, China's largest manufacturer of wool textiles and menswear. Other countries introduced modifications. Marks & Spencer of the United Kingdom in 2006 made their own version of the wash-and-wear suit, in which a small amount of Lycra was added to the wool/polyester mix.

Preconceptions about the limiting qualities of wool in the Australian fashion market have been a factor influencing its use. Many Australian designers have shied away from wool because of the associations with it being a winter fabric and potentially prickly. Comfort is of great importance to consumers, and the perception of wool as uncomfortable has negatively influenced some Australian designers' use of the fabric and its consumption by wearers.

Many local consumers make do through winter, layering up their lighter-weight garments to deal with the short winter period, and are not looking to invest seriously in a winter wardrobe. Based on this consumer attitude, many Australian designers focus more on the presentation of summer and trans-seasonal collections, while at the same time creating an awareness that wool has the potential to be cool and comfortable.

Garment comfort is a complex experience involving psychological, physiological, and tactile sensations. It is an area of research DAFWA and the Fashion Department of Royal Melbourne Institute of Technology (RMIT). DAFWA's reverse engineering and fabric appraisal research has shown that the consumer responds to the combined effects of wool fiber, yarn, and fabric structure. DAFWA research reveals that comfort is not achieved unless all three of these factors are correct.

In 2005 staff from the Department of Design at Curtin University's Faculty of Built Environment, Art and Design (BEAD) partnered with the DAFWA Wool Desk to extend the scope of its comfort-related research, resulting in The Design for Comfort Project. This project brought contemporary designers into the research process. Five Western Australian fashion designers, Aurelio Costarella, Rebecca Paterson, Megan Salmon, Louise Snook, and Melissa Yap, were invited to work on the project. Each of these designers had an affinity for wool and, based on consultation, researchers developed customized knit fabrics. As part of the exercise, Megan Salmon, who had copyright use of the designs of the Walmajarri artist Jimmy Pike, had one of his designs scanned and translated into a knit fabric that was produced using the Shima Seiki Wholegarment (technology that produces one entire piece, three-dimensionally, directly on the knitting machine) knitting system.

DAFWA is also utilizing new knit technology in seamless garment production, as part of their investigations into wool garment comfort. Seamless garments are emerging as a major new production technology. The development of systems integrating new digital and knit technology is providing the opportunity for the Australian fashion industry to investigate new design possibilities in knitted wool garments. CSIRO is also providing the local fashion industry with support to access the latest technology in this area.

Akira Isagowa, an internationally recognized Australian designer, has applied his unique design interpretations to Australian Merino wool, showcasing them worldwide via trade and industry events. Isagowa is one of the first designers to be involved with AWI on the development of customized fine Merino fabrics. In 2005 another designer, Josh Goot, partnered with AWI and DPK (Design Performance Knit, a knit fabric and garment manufacturer based in Sydney, Australia) to develop wool fabrics for his collection. Prior to this, Goot had primarily worked with cotton jersey for its natural stretch, drape, durability, and versatility, which suited the requirements of his signature look. The fabric for his 2007 Target collection was a blend of Australian Merino wool, tactel, and elastene. This fabric also features a special finish, a dense silver resin coating that gave garments a unique "Goot" finish.

Other Australian designers such as Josephine Nathan and Lorinda Grant have built their labels on an exploration of the beauty and unique capabilities of Australian Merino wool. Woolliwoolli (Josephine Nathan) creates hand-knitted fabric that is crafted into comfortable relaxed garment shapes by working with the natural drape of the cloth. Lorinda Grant's work also reflects qualities often associated with Australian design, a strong connection to the land, and the innovation that emerges from the challenges of isolation. She is a designer who retains close links with local farmers to understand the fleeces and consults directly with processing mills, local knitters, and CSIRO about new techniques.

As Australian designers move into international markets, the potential for the use of wool has increased as collections are developed with cooler climates in mind. If there was an Australian label that might have resisted using wool in its collections, it could have been the Easton Pearson label based in subtropical Brisbane. However, with the development of their international markets and a new spring/summer (northern hemisphere) collection showcased at Paris Fashion Week in 2007, Easton Pearson turned to a new Australian Merino wool jersey, an innovative lightweight fabric composed of 50 percent Australian Merino wool, 20 percent cashmere, and 30 percent silk, sourced with the help of AWI. While the focus of their use of wool remains northern hemisphere international markets, indications are that this design team represents another convert to the properties and value of wool.

While there may still be a need to sell the value of wool to new and emerging Australian designers, there are those who have for many years been committed to its use. One Australian designer who stands out in this regard is Liz Davenport. She supported the establishment of "Wear Wool Wednesday," initiated in 1998 by Wool Industry Promotions in Queensland, and has for many years been a strong advocate for the benefits of wool in fashion.

LONG-TERM CHALLENGES

The long-term challenges for the Australian wool industry still exist. They are linked to shifts in retail consumption patterns in which the amount spent on clothing has decreased in comparison to higher expenditure on computers, mobile phones, and overseas holidays; a progressive improvement in the quality and price reduction of artificial fibers such as polyester, nylon, and acrylic compared to the high cost of wool; and, most significantly, the development of microfibers and problems with the quality and reliability of supplies of raw wool.

Problems were identified as early as the 1970s. In response to the falling demand for wool created by competitive and alternative fabrics, the Australian Wool Corporation was established in 1973 (replacing the Australian Wool Board and Australian Wool Commission). This body was set up to facilitate research, promotion, and marketing operations. As a result of their promotional activity, China increased its presence in the Australian wool market, and by the early part of the twenty-first century, it had become the largest processor of Australian wool, despite having the world's largest sheep population.

Various organizational changes occurred, signs of an industry concerned with its future. In 1994 the activities of the International Wool Secretariat were merged with those of the Australian Wool Research and Promotion Organisation (AWRAP), and they operated as one organization under the control of AWRAP. In 1997 the International Wool Secretariat became The Woolmark Company, specializing in textile innovation and technical research. The London office was closed and Woolmark moved its operations and headquarters to Melbourne, Australia.

The release of the 1999–2000 McLachlan Report on the Australian wool industry meant that in 2001 AWRAP was replaced with Australian Wool Services (AWS). Initially the AWS was divided into two subsidiary companies: The Woolmark Company, which dealt with the commercial development of the Woolmark labels and intellectual property matters, while the other subsidiary, Australian Wool Innovation Limited, managed the proceeds from the wool levy and outsourced research and development and intellectual property management. In an attempt to reinvigorate the Woolmark brand, Australian Wool Innovation (AWI) took management control of AWS assets, thus acquiring The Woolmark Company in October 2007. Projects by AWI resulted in the development of textiles in the areas of medical, disposable, smart, electronic, sports, surf, and aged-care wear.

Other challenges exist. Environmental factors have affected the use of wool in clothing, with better heating and air-conditioning in all environments such as work, public transportation, cars, and homes. These environments have created a new demand for lightweight clothes, replacing the traditional use of wool for overcoats, heavy sweaters, and formal men's suits. And in Australia as with other developed nations, there has been a shift in the workplace to more casual clothing rather than tailored wool. This has been fostered by activities such as the casual Fridays that emerged in the 1990s, which encourage the wearing of informal

A garment produced by Australian fashion designer Arelio Costarella for the Design for Comfort Project (2006), using fabrics designed and knitted from specially selected Merinotech fiber. Photograph by Ashley de Prazer.

A garment produced by Australian fashion designer Louise Snook for the Design for Comfort Project (2006), using fabrics designed and knitted from specially selected Merinotech fiber. Photograph by Ashley de Prazer.

clothes such as jeans. While there have been significant reductions in the overall production levels of Australian wool, quality has improved with 80 percent in the twenty-first century used to create fine apparel. Although the rest of the world appreciates the quality and properties of fine Merino, there remains a lag in the appreciation of wool among consumers and indeed application of wool fabrics within the local fashion industry, though the move of Australian designers into international markets has broadened the possibilities for its use.

Developments in man-made and synthetic fibers and nano finishes combined with the relative high production costs for wool have resulted in the need to position wool for both high-end fashion and specialist applications. Research continues at all stages of wool production and use, resulting in discoveries about its properties and potential.

Whole garment technologies present researchers with new capabilities for manipulating garment structure. This technology produces an entire piece, three-dimensionally and directly, on the knitting machine. The advantage of whole garment, seamless knitwear is that it provides the wearer with superior fit and comfort, freer movement and stretch, enhanced drape and flow of fabric, and improved structural integrity. What research is making possible is the integration of three-dimensional digital imaging systems into wool garment production. This digital research is also considering the thermophysiological factors of clothing, for example, insulation, moisture and vapor transfer, heat exchange, and air penetration, all of which impact on comfort. Wool is proving to be a fiber that can improve these properties in a garment.

Despite the historical challenges of the industry, wool is a natural fiber suited to the development of so-called smart clothing, with the potential to adapt, integrate, and support new technologies, for everyday garment use, medical applications, protective clothing, and for fashion into the future.

References and Further Reading

Australian Wool Innovation (AWI). http://www.wool.com.au.2008 (accessed 25 August 2007).

Commonwealth Scientific and Industrial Research Organisation (CSIRO). http://www.csiro.au/. 2008 (accessed 10 August 2007).

Design for Comfort Project. http://www.designforcomfort.com.au .2008 (accessed 10 October 2007).

Farren, Anne, Emma Kopke, and John Stanton, eds. A Touch of Wool. Perth: Department of Agriculture and Food Western Australia, 2006.

Massy, Charles. The Australian Merino: The Story of a Nation. Sydney: Random House Australia, 2007. (Originally published in 1990.)

Maynard, Margaret. Out of Line: Australian Women and Style. Sydney: University of New South Wales Press, 2001.

McLachlan, Hon Ian, Chairman. Diversity and Innovation for Australian Wool: Report of the Wool Industry Future Directions Task Force. Canberra: Commonwealth of Australia, 1999.

Neller, Shelly, ed. Wool in the Australian Imagination. Sydney: Historic Houses Trust of NSW, 1994.

Taylor, D. S. "Australian Innovation in Textile Technology." In Technology in Australia 1788–1988. http://www.austehc.unimelb.edu.au/tia/263 .html. 2000 (accessed 22 January 2009).

Tsokhas, Kosmas. Markets, Money and Empire: Political Economy of the Australian Wool Industry. Melbourne, Australia: Melbourne University Press, 1990.

Webber, Michael, and Sally Weller. Refashioning the Rag Trade: Internationalising Australia's Textiles, Clothing and Footwear Industries. Sydney: University of New South Wales Press, 2001.

Prudence Black and Anne Farren

See also The Australiana Phenomenon in Australia; Military and Civil Uniforms in Australia.

Rural Dress in Australia

A distinctive Australian sense of dress for Europeans is often considered to be bush wear, that is, clothes that have become synonymous with rural life and the outback. The typical elements of this rural dress include moleskin trousers, elastic-sided boots, cotton or wool shirt, bush jacket (in denim, wool, or leather) or waterproof oilskin coat, and a wide-brimmed felt hat. These garments are typically worn by men, so particular traits of masculinity are woven into the image of Australian bush wear. Yet, Australia is the most urbanized country in the world, and a great many Australians have never ventured into rural Australia and especially not the remote outback. So, how has it come about that a form of clothing worn by a minority of (primarily male) Australians now epitomizes the national dress of Australia? The answer lies in the way that rural Australia—or the bush—has figured in the history of Australia and has shaped the development of a sense of national culture—of which dress is a part.

THE CLOTHING HABITS OF RURAL AUSTRALIA

Despite the common perception that dress has not been a preoccupation of Australians, who prefer practical and comfortable clothes, in fact, the history of Australia reveals a strong preoccupation with clothing from the outset. Established as a penal colony by England, the early settlers were far from home with few material comforts or familiar accoutrements of everyday life. The climate, landscape, vegetation, fauna, and flora were exotic, harsh, and alien. Immediate priorities were establishing supplies of food and creating habitable shelter—clothing the prisoners and settlers ran a close third.

As well as dependence on unreliable supplies arriving from Europe and other colonies such as India, the new arrivals also had to learn how to farm this inhospitable land, build up herds of animals, and process raw materials thus produced. Imported clothing and footwear were copied and to a degree manufactured locally, so early settlers wore a mixture of imports and domestically produced forms of dress. In this mix, styles, materials, and finishings often varied according to taste, climate, and available supplies. So, while dress habits of the urban bourgeoisie and the elite were largely modeled on English and French fashions, there was to a large degree a distinctly colonial inflection. In the early 1800s Alexander Harris, a visitor to Sydney, was surprised to find that the colonists had assumed their own identity in matters of dress.

Early bourgeois settlers were supremely preoccupied with their clothed appearances. They wrote home about it, they recorded dress in art, poetry, and literature, and they organized dances, balls, dinner parties, picnics, and shopping expeditions as occasions to dress up. But it was the ordinary settler, the emancipated convict, and the bush man who created what has come to be regarded an identifiable dress for white settlers. Not only were there different degrees of fashionability among these people, there were also distinct differences between urban and rural or country dress. Differences in the dress of settlers in particular regions could also be discerned (for example, in seperate colonies—later states—and climatic regions). These diverse dress conventions are at odds with the belief that the casual, adaptable bush wear of men was the only distinctive form of Australian dress. It also makes discussion of the characteristics of rural dress more complex. But it is rural clothing, especially but not entirely worn by men, that has come to stand for the distinctiveness of Australian dress. As early as the 1840s, observers such as printmakers were depicting settlers in their distinctive bush clothes as typifying Australian life. This mode of dress was regarded as being as particular to Australia as was the landscape and its flora and fauna. It was already a kind of national costume, even though it was not celebrated as such until the 1890s.

Close analysis of literary records and images such as cartoons, prints, and paintings show that male rural dress was quite variable. There are practically no surviving examples of rural dress in museum collections. Some outfits were derived from slops (hard-wearing trousers—sometimes called duck trousers—made of strong untwilled cotton or jersey), worn with a loose shirt and belt, that were typical of working men and the quasi-uniform of sailors. Other outfits had their origins in suits with better-cut (usually dark-colored) trousers, collarless shirts, neckties, optional waistcoats or vests, and various kinds of jackets. Smocks were also sometimes worn—and often another was kept for Sunday best. Boots were the common footwear, though these were usually lace-up and ankle length. Hats were common, but more often the cabbage tree hat was worn rather than the broad-brimmed felt hat that came to be called an Akubra (it seems the trade name Akubra was registered in 1912 but there is no proof the term was used until the 1920s). The latter headwear was later to acquire specific iconic status. Cabbage tree hats were finely woven from strips of the fronds of the cabbage palm tree and featured a flat crown and wide brim, something like a modern straw boater. Although expensive, these hats proved perfect for the climate and were quickly popularized, spawning a profitable manufacturing cottage industry.

Much of the clothing of rural women remains unrecorded, for there is virtually no information on the rural dress (or lives) of working-class women. Outside urban environments there was a minority of women who spurned conventional behavior and clothing, such as women who worked as timber cutters and goldfields women, some in shirts, trousers, and boots like the men. While station stores and small settlement drapery shops stocked ready-made clothing and boots for men, there was hardly anything available for women apart from fabrics, plus some hats and shoes. Women were obliged to make their own attire and that of men, as well as modifying and mending clothes, shoes, and accessories extensively, to make them last. As many of these women had never learned needlework, this was a particular challenge, and they relied on advice from magazines, women's groups,

Bush Travellers, Queensland. Oil on canvas by Richard Daintree, ca. 1865. Their casual bush attire, including hats woven of cabbage tree palm, came to be regarded as a particularly Australian mode of dress, increasingly depicted in paintings, prints, poetry, and literature in the late nineteenth century. National Library of Australia.

and neighbors. So, although Europe remained the inspiration for fashion and style, the adaptations and influences, allied to domestic craft and women's networks in rural areas, shaped the emergence of a distinctive mode of colonial dress.

Everyday rural dress was noncontrived, given the demands of rural life—mustering, shearing, fencing, sowing and harvesting, and so on. For women, the relentless demands of running the homestead and bringing up children militated against a constant obsession with looking fashionable. But most extant accounts of women's rural dress refer to a special occasion dress, including consternation about being presentable for the arrival of visitors, for outings, or for going to the cities. Of course, most of these accounts are about middle-class women who had more disposable income to spend on dress and more time to take an interest in fashion trends. For the majority, dressing for practicality and comfort was the primary concern. Women did, however, put on their special outfits and dressy aprons for afternoon tea parties that were common in the outback. In some cases these were hand-sewn using any materials on hand, remodeled and embellished with embroidery, patches of colorful fabric scraps, and pleating.

The complete lack of shopping facilities in remote places and limited options even in some sizable regional towns prior to the 1850s at least meant that most purchases of clothing were confined to visits from peddlers, parcels from abroad, rare trips to the city, and, later, mail-order catalogs. This meant that there was a lag between the fashions of cities and those of towns and rural areas as well as regional differences between dress codes, especially between different urban centers, colonies, and districts.

CLIMATE

Many rural areas in Australia experience climatic extremes that oscillate from harsh and dry to hot and humid to bitter cold and windy. Cycles of drought and flood punctuate this pattern. These factors inevitably affected (and continue to affect) what working people wore and wear. During the nineteenth century when people lived in rough, drafty, uninsulated homesteads, dressing for the climate was an important factor. Clothes also varied between seasons and were modified for subtropical and tropical areas such as Queensland. Here middle-class women favored bright, cool, and casual dresses made from Indian muslins, Ceylon skirtings,

Liberty cretonnes, zephyrs, and embroidered silks. Lighter underwear and corsetry was also adopted. Sunhats in straw or cotton as well as broad-brimmed felt hats were obligatory to ward off the sun and shade the complexion. In the bush, women wore lightweight muslins or print gowns and ginghams, which were just as cool but more durable than muslin. Crinolines were also popular from the late 1850s, both in the town and the bush, since they had the advantage of lightening the weight of clothing and keeping petticoats away from the legs. Generally, the dress of hotter regions was more colorful than in the south, where duller colors prevailed, a trend that has persisted into the twenty-first century. In the tropics, bush wear for men made concessions to the climate, including lightweight trousers or moleskins (trousers of soft, twilled cotton) with either a short-sleeved, open-necked shirt or a colored flannel waistcoat. Many lighter fabrics came from India and China, sparking a valuable trade with these regions.

THE MYTHOLOGY OF BUSH WEAR

The most common myth about Australian rural dress concerns the primacy of rugged masculinity as the sole preserve of the bush and the ways in which this is linked with bush wear. As countless examples of traditional and contemporary folklore and cultural representations attest, rural Australia was an inhospitable place where inhabitants survived by hard work, continual hardship, making do (improvisation), isolation, and an unshakable belief that one is right. These hardships were offset by a strong camaraderie among one's fellow workers. So-called mateship or male bonding was common. Neither the bush nor the outback was said to be an appropriate place for a woman. Even so, despite mateship (a defining concept in Australia), men depended a good deal on women for assistance on the land and continue to do so.

Women who did find themselves on some isolated station had few opportunities for female camaraderie, especially with their own race. Few women who left the city for the bush to follow their husbands—let alone those who emigrated from England—had any idea what lay ahead. As letters home and autobiographies—such as those of Rachel Henning and Katie Hume—recollected, life in the bush was a constant struggle and challenge to overcome remoteness; lack of food, raw materials, consumer goods, and services or facilities; isolation; and occasional threats from Aboriginals and passing rogues, as well as the rigors of giving birth, treating illnesses and accidents, and dealing with fatalities. Above all, the outback was a vast space that was sparsely populated. Pioneer women faced insurmountable isolation and deprivation. Their nearest neighbors could be a hundred miles away and only visited on special occasions. Probably most women stayed because they simply had no choice. Yet their contribution to the development of the outback was crucial and until recently largely unheralded.

The image of the outback and the bush has revolved around the idea of male camaraderie and men's egalitarian ways of dressing, a notion that began around the 1840s and 1850s and set in motion what was to become a nationalistic myth that coalesced in the 1890s. Reflecting this, the majority of bush poems paint romantic images of male heroism and the spirit of the outback as bush men: shearing sheep, mustering cattle, droving, camping under the stars, and enduring heat, cold, drought, bushfires, and flood. Visual images also embodied these themes, depicting

A portrait of the Lynch sisters, early timber cutters from the Kingaroy district, Queensland, Australia, posing in front of a large pine tree with a saw. They wear long skirts, long-sleeved blouses, and hats with brims. In early colonial times clothing for rural women carrying out such work adapted quite slowly to the demands of such activities. Photographer unknown. John Oxley Library, State Library of Queensland 64649.

battlers against the odds, be they pioneer selectors and squatters, shearers, farm hands, miners and prospectors, or bushrangers. The height of nationalistic ethos occurred during the 1890s with writings in the *Bulletin* magazine and artworks by the Heidelberg School (including artists like Frederick McCubbin, Tom Roberts, Arthur Streeton, Roland Wakelin, and Elioth Gruner) and their efforts to develop a distinctive aesthetic to depict the Australian landscape in contrast to European landscape tradition.

In real life there was a clear difference between what the workers and itinerants (including shearers and indigenous stockmen) wore and the dress of the squatters and station owners. The dress of the latter derived from town wear (essentially modifications of suits), apart from the clothes worn for horse riding. It is possible that it was a cross between the modified slops of the working class and modified riding gear of the upper class that evolved into the iconic version of bush wear that we now imagine. In fact, this notion that emerges in the 1890s reflects a period redolent with strident nationalism and the forging of a distinctive idea of national identity. Whether this clothing really signaled the egalitarianism that contemporary commentators applauded or was simply a fusion of different dress codes in an environment shaped by practicality and necessity rather than an abstract commitment to fashion is debatable. Nonetheless, rural dress increasingly symbolized the political quest for independence. Bush clothes became symbols of political independence and rejection of authority and convention, the qualities that were synonymous with the push for nation status. Images of male bush men and pioneer settlers captured these qualities. Even bushrangers were depicted in bush clothes (red blouse over a blue shirt, loose trousers, and cabbage tree hat)—such as William Strutt's *Study for Bushrangers on St Kilda Road*, painted in 1886–1887 but set in 1852.

Interestingly, however, there are also a few close-up paintings of single female bush figures, such as Julian Ashton's 1888 *A Solitary Ramble*, George Lambert's 1923–1924 *The Squatter's Daughter*, and Hilda Rix-Nicholas's 1935 *The Fair Musterer*. While Ashton's painting shows a woman fashionably dressed in kimono-style over a simple black dress with sunhat and parasol, the Lambert and Rix-Nicholas paintings each show a young girl in bush wear, namely, broad-brimmed hat, loose white shirt, camel-colored jodhpurs, and knee-length boots. These clothes had their origin as much in equestrienne wear as in male rural dress, though the cross-dressing implications linger in these depictions of two women alone in an environment not normally associated with the fair sex and undertaking traditional men's work.

This overview of rural dress in Australia suggests that a distinctive kind of male bush wear is to a degree fabricated and had more diverse and complex origins than has been assumed. In fact, its iconization as distinctly Australian was more an urban phenomenon than an outback consciousness, and the timing of its appearance coincided with political events surrounding the emergence of a sense of national identity and character.

MAJOR PROVIDERS OF RURAL DRESS OR BUSH WEAR

By the mid-nineteenth century the supply of clothing became more plentiful, and local suppliers were specifically advertising bush clothing as well as hats (in rabbit, possum, beaver, silk, and wool) and imported and local footwear. Many contemporary writings record the goods available in country stores as well as city emporia, thus providing a much greater range of dress choices for settlers. By the 1860s and 1870s an increasing percentage of available clothing and accessories was locally manufactured.

Companies began to specialize in bush wear, such as Baxters' boot company (established in Goulburn in 1850) and Blundstone footwear (established in Hobart in the 1870s). Blundstone designed an elastic-sided boot using thick leather and double-locked stitching on the uppers and a thick rubber tread sole that could withstand the rigors of the goldfields and bush conditions. These tough boots gained a strong reputation, and during World War I Blundstone was contracted by the Australian army to supply the troops. In a parallel development the firm Dunkerley Hat Mills began a hat-making business in 1874 and developed a mechanical method of making felted rabbit-fur hats. Moving to Sydney in the late 1880s, their hat business became profitable and they became known for selling the Akubra hat. That the term Akubra derives from an Aboriginal word meaning head covering is apocryphal,

although *gabarra* is the Dharuk (Sydney region) word for head, and variants of this word, *cobbra* (head) and *gabara*, *kubbura*, or *kubera*, have been recorded. Like Blundstone, Dunkerley's breakthrough came with a World War I contract to supply the Australian Defence Forces with broad-brimmed slouch hats (a colloquial term for an item of military headwear with one side turned up), which themselves came to be imbued with symbolic national meaning (especially for men) and regarded as iconic. But the Akubra is not just a man's hat. Women working the land in rural areas commonly wear them as well. In the twenty-first century the Akubra is considered the most representative item of all Australian clothing.

The hat has played a significant part in the legends of Australian dress, while at the same time the company has employed canny marketing techniques. In 1986 Greg Norman (an expatriate golfer) initiated a five-year agreement to exclusively wear these hats on the greens. He also has a style named after him. Using Norman, the company was able to extend association with the Australian bush myth to include links with Australian sporting prowess. Other formal sporting ambassadors have included Australian surfer Pam Burridge, world motorcycle champion Wayne Gardiner, and motorcar racer Allan Grice. Politicians like former deputy prime minister and National Party leader Tim Fischer have acted as ambassadors for this headwear on overseas trade missions. City politicians (male and female) also wear the Akubra during trips to rural areas as a calculated way to indicate their supposed sympathies for regional dwellers. All these factors have aided in the marketing success of this brand.

Perhaps the best-known rural dress company, however, is R.M. Williams (known as RMW), which was set up in 1932. Other well-known providers of rural dress and working wear include brands such as King Gee, Stubbies (slang for shorts), Hard Yakka (slang for hard work), and Redback (a footwear brand, named after the poisonous redback spider).

In the twentieth century rural dress or bush wear came to epitomize the distinctiveness of Australian clothing style. Thus it was used as an example of the legacy of British colonial dress in New York columnist Alison Lurie's populist book, *The Language of Clothes*. In a much quoted characterization Lurie depicted male (and female) Australians as dressed in khaki shirts and jackets, sheepskin vests, leather boots, and bush hats. She elided this choice of dress with the Australian penchant for outback life.

Despite how quaint this characterization of Australian rural dress might seem, it has been picked up by the clothing industry. This notion of what real Australians wear was given further impetus during the bicentennial celebrations of 1988 and associated promotional material. Interestingly, in 1983 a company called the Outback Trading Company (subtitled The Original Bush Outfitters) was established to exploit the rugged bush clothes of the film *The Man from Snowy River* (1982), such as oilskin coats, wide-brimmed hats, boots, and leather belts, which are characterized as genuine drover gear. Based in Australia, the aim was to sell Australian bush wear to Americans, especially oilskin dusters, hats, parka-style jackets, and diverse sorts of outdoor clothing. The company is now based in Pennsylvania and sells throughout the United States, Canada, and New Zealand. While the names of products reference Australian bush clothes and rural life, and the legend of the oilskin dusters worn by pioneer Australian stockmen in the rugged outback structures their marketing, the pitch is perhaps as much to overseas clients as domestic ones.

A film still from a 2007 advertising campaign by Akubra Hats. The successful Akubra brand is over a century old, and its iconic national status persists because it strongly identifies itself with rural Australia. Courtesy of Akubra Hats. www.akubra.com.au.

The company is also seeking an urban market to complement the existing one for working gear and rural (or bush) wear, in other words, transforming nonurban Americans into up-market "Aussie" drovers.

This marketing shift has occurred in most of the bush-wear companies. For example, according to Hamish Turner, the CEO of R. M. Williams, in 2007, although the primary market remains traditional customers from the bush, the company also sells its sturdy work-wear for men on the land to urban men who are part of the casual luxury market. These are men who cross the divide between city and country dressing by combining contemporary fashion with bush-wear classics.

The challenge for RMW has been to maintain the balance between contemporary relevance and reputation for quality. To celebrate their seventy-fifth anniversary in 2007, R. M. Williams produced a catalog that reworked classics from previous catalogs into contemporary fashion bush wear, as well as establishing lines for women, young people (under the Longhorn label), boys (under the Colts label), and girls (under the Fillies label). With over a thousand outlets worldwide in the early twenty-first century, and lucrative mail-order and online marketing arms, RMW epitomizes the transition from rural dress to high fashion and the dominant role of smart casual dress in Australian style. Increasingly, the main market for bush wear is now in urban centers, and, where bush wear is worn in rural settings, it is often for special occasions as well as everyday wear.

While RMW may be the best-known bush-wear brand, other brands have modernized in different ways. For example, Blundstone boots became fashionable in the 1980s when they were taken up by punks (as a cheaper alternative to Doc Martens boots) and then appropriated by youth culture celebrities such as former Democrats leader Natasha Stott Despoja. Their success as popular culture icons was confirmed by a national competition to paint a Blundstone boot (won by an indigenous artist), and their adoption by the cast of the internationally successful *Tap Dogs* male musical. Due to the pressures of global marketing, in 2007 the company was forced to move its operations offshore.

Akubra hats have become international symbols of Australianness, due to their use in a number of movies, including the Hollywood film *Crocodile Dundee* (1986), in which the actor Paul Hogan wore one with a crocodile-skin headband. Akubra hats are commonly given as gifts to visiting celebrities, confirming their international diffusion. But it should not be forgotten that indigenous activists have also appropriated the black Akubra as their own particular symbol of nation. Driza-Bone and other long oilskin coats have also reached international attention through films, visual art, marketing, and export. At the 2007 Asia-Pacific Economic Cooperation (APEC) forum for world leaders, hosted in Sydney, delegates were formally photographed wearing a Driza-Bone coat given to them as an example of Australia's "national dress," as well as receiving the gift of an Akubra hat.

Many versions of bush wear have been used as national attire at sporting events (e.g., the Olympic Games and Commonwealth Games) and for modeling and beauty competitions (e.g., Miss World, Miss Universe), and they have been worn by Australian groups and teams on international tours. In the lead-up to the Sydney Olympic Games in 2000, RMW used an image of a square-jawed Australian male in a Driza-Bone, moleskins, elastic-sided boots, Akubra hat, and stockwhip as the centerpiece of its nationalist advertising campaign with the slogan, "If We had a National Costume, This Would Be It."

The globalization of Australian rural dress is taking place at the same time as it migrates from the bush to the city—not only in Australia but throughout the world and across genders, ages, and ethnicities.

References and Further Reading

Craik, Jennifer. "Is Australian Fashion Distinctively Australian?" *Fashion Theory* 13, no. 4 (2009): 409–442.

Elliot, Jane. "The Politics of Antipodean Dress." *Journal of Australian Studies* 52 (1997): 20–33.

Fletcher, Marion. *Costume in Australia 1778–1901.* Melbourne, Australia: Oxford University Press, 1984.

Flower, Cedric. *Duck and Cabbage Tree: A Pictorial History of Clothes in Australia 1788–1914.* Sydney: Angus and Robertson, 1968.

Lurie, Alison. *The Language of Clothes.* London: Bloomsbury, 1992.

Maynard, Margaret. *Fashioned from Penury: Dress as Cultural Practice in Colonial Australia.* Cambridge, New York, and Melbourne, Australia: Cambridge University Press, 1994.

Maynard, Margaret. "A Good Deal Too Good for the Bush: Women and the Experience of Dress in Queensland." In *On the Edge: Women's Experiences of Queensland,* edited by Gail Reekie, 51–65. St. Lucia, Australia: Queensland University Press, 1994.

McGregor, Ken. "New Adventures in Bush Market." *Australian Business Monthly* (October 1986): 9.

"RM Williams." *Qantas* (September 2007): 189.

Williams, R. M. "R. M. Williams: 75 Years in the Making." *Spring/ Summer 2008 Catalogue.* Adelaide, Australia: R. M. Williams, 2007.

Jennifer Craik

See also Images as a Resource for the Study of Australian Dress; Settler Dress in Australia.

Swimwear, Surfwear, and the Bronzed Body in Australia

- Moral Debates about Swimwear in Colonial Australia
- Twentieth-Century Developments
- The Rise of Beach Culture
- The Bikini Revolution
- The Global Reach of Australian Surfwear

For many people, Australia is synonymous with the dream of sun, surf, and sand. Australia is perceived as a land of leisure and lounging around—preferably by the water. In order to do this, Australians dress in a casual way in swimsuits, surfwear, or leisure wear such as tank tops (sleeveless, low-necked tops) or T-shirts, shorts, and thongs (rubber sandals). Sunhats are, of course, obligatory in the Australian climate if skin cancer is to be avoided. Accordingly, popular representations of this country depict the outdoor life and the temperate climate, with swimming and associated activities such as surfing and sunbathing as epitomizing the "Australian way of life." The figure of the bronzed "Aussie" and the centrality of the sun, sunbathing, and sun protection have a long history. So, although Australians have often followed swimwear fashions from elsewhere, they have made significant contributions to the development of swimming as a sport and the design of swimwear and, more recently, of surfwear. Moreover, swimwear—and the debates surrounding it—has played a central role in the evolving articulation of national culture and a distinctive sense of Australian style.

MORAL DEBATES ABOUT SWIMWEAR IN COLONIAL AUSTRALIA

While the beach and surfing connote freedom, active sports, and outdoor leisure, the history of swimwear and surfwear in Australia is one of successive attempts to regulate swim and surf behavior and sanction appropriate modes of dress. In short, swimwear ignited cyclical battles between modesty and immodesty. The legacy of Victorian morality was intense concern about the naked body, and bathing costumes inevitably created a play between revelation and concealment. While the swimmer might revel in being seen in her/his athletic glory, the spectator also revels in watching the spectacle of the swimmer. In years past, brazen young men known as "Kodak fiends" were accused of loitering by the shore or pool to catch apparitions of "Venuses" rising from the sea. In essence, swimwear and spectatorship are intertwined.

When Australia was first settled by Europeans in 1788, the sea was undoubtedly a source of fear and awe, but brave men (soldiers and later free settlers) ventured into the surf to bathe and swim. Like certain indigenous people who already populated these shores, early European swimmers wore no clothes, and the issue of suitable attire for the ocean was only raised after mixed bathing became accepted in the early 1800s. The colony passed an Act

for the Reform and Regulation of Female Apparel, which was designed to ensure that female bathers were appropriately covered. Bathing in the nude or even in undergarments was banned. But as the popularity of bathing and swimming in the sea soared, so too did concerns about moral rectitude, and in 1833 (strengthened in 1838 due to transgressions), the Government of the Colony of New South Wales legislated to prohibit daylight bathing between 6 A.M. and 6 P.M. Victoria followed suit in 1841. Promenading, picnicking, and paddling were, however, permitted, and the beach became an even more popular recreational pastime.

While the intention of the law was to preserve modesty and decorum, eager bathers and recreationists enjoyed evening outings to the beach, and soon there was a perceived problem of disorder caused by so-called gypsy tea parties and moonlight swims. Drunken women were also reckoned to be a problem. Further issues were created by the zoning of beaches into segregated

Australian company MacRae Knitting Mills branded their bathing suits with the now-familiar Speedo name in 1928. In this promotional photograph, Arne Borg, described as "holder of all World's records from 300 yards to 1 mile," wears a Speedo one-piece tank-style swimsuit, and two cameo photographs show the back view, focusing on the "racer-back" design. The caption claims that he achieved all of his records while wearing Speedo. Photograph by Sidney Riley.

areas for men and women, as prohibition only fanned the desire to mingle and was difficult to monitor.

Beachgoers wore street clothes, wide-brimmed sunhats, and canvas shoes and carried parasols as they learned to relax on the white, fine sandy beaches of the Australian colonies. Reflecting this trend, the beach became a popular subject for contemporary artists who portrayed the particularities of the beach landscape as well as the figures populating the beach. These paintings combined a moral discourse about the emerging beach culture with the documentation of a nascent distinctive "Australian way of life." Coinciding with the nationalist movements of the 1890s, paintings such as Rupert Bunny's *Tritons* (ca. 1890, Art Gallery of New South Wales), Arthur Streeton's *Beach Scene* (1890, Art Gallery of New South Wales), and Girolamo Nerli's *Beach Scene, Sandringham* (ca. 1900, Art Gallery of New South Wales) captured impressionistic, picturesque, and mythical qualities of Australians by the sea.

Although daylight bathing was prohibited, beachgoers and swimmers in the late nineteenth century flouted the law. They readily adopted the swimwear of the day—neck-to-knee tops and pants for men and voluminous tunics over pants for women. While these were mostly made to measure, patterns for the home sewer were available by the 1880s. Bathing machines (that were wheeled down to the water) and beach huts (erected near the sand dunes) enabled the modest bather to preserve her/his dignity on the beach. By 1919 oriental kimonos had replaced these devices.

As more people took up swimming, they were faced by the danger of drowning in the strong surf (especially at night when bathing was legal). Shark attacks, as well as jellyfish, blue bottle, and stinger lesions, were also a palpable threat. For women, these physical threats were enhanced by the weight of their cumbersome costumes, especially if they were not strong swimmers.

TWENTIETH-CENTURY DEVELOPMENTS

By 1900, however, daytime swimming was so common that, despite continuing moral concerns, in 1903 surf bathing in daylight was legalized in New South Wales, and in 1906 the first surf life-saving club (at Bondi Beach in Sydney) was formed. Body surfing became immensely popular, and lifesaving clubs proliferated, including all-female teams (although women were not allowed to compete in lifesaving competitions until 1980). Percy Spence's painting *Women Lifesavers, Manly Beach* (1910, Art Gallery of New South Wales) shows fiercely determined young women in relatively brief neck-to-thigh tunics over thigh shorts reeling out a line to a surfer in trouble. Photographs from the period show a diversity of bathing wear, from nude children, to various swimming costumes, to women in day dresses and wide-brimmed hats pulling up their skirts to paddle at the water's edge. Bathing costumes—whether male or female—were adorned with ribbons, bows, buckles, and belts, apparently in an effort to make them seem more like streetwear.

Swimwear was soon modified to better suit the exigencies of the surf and, within a decade, had become a sleeveless guernsey that was a figure-hugging tunic usually made of wool and worn over thigh-length knickers, called the Canadian costume. The New South Wales government's Sun-bathing Parliamentary Committee advocated the Canadian costume as compulsory wear in 1912, declaring that "no person over ten years of age shall bathe from any beach within the shire, unless dressed in a Canadian bathing costume" (one effectively covering the body from neck to knee). Furthermore, no one was allowed to sit, lie, run, or loiter on a beach in a bathing costume. Many local municipalities imposed regulations about suitable bathing dress on its beaches and at swimming pools. At Manly Beach in Sydney, regulations decreed that men must be covered in a garment concealing the body from neck to knees, while fines were imposed for day bathing and improper attire and mixed bathing was prohibited irrespective of matrimonial status. It was a losing battle, as beachgoers and sun-worshippers continually ignored such edicts. As the costumes became briefer (sleeveless, body-hugging tops with shorter skirts and leggings), the bathers became more adventurous, venturing deeper into the water and learning to body surf the waves.

In 1905 an Australian champion swimmer, Annette Kellerman, turned aquatic entertainer as the "Australian mermaid." The film star first wore her trademark longline unitard costume (a man's knitted one-piece suit with tights attached) for an aquatic performance in the United Kingdom. Later she scandalized American audiences in the outfit, making international news, and was allegedly arrested in Boston for indecent exposure in 1907. But, undaunted, Kellerman popularized her outfit and collaborated with Asbury Mills, a New York knitting company, to design a range of functional Kellerman swimwear. Another Australian champion swimmer, Beatrice Kerr, also stunned audiences of her diving routines with a fashionable black-and-silver spangled bathing dress. Competitive swimmers followed suit, and Australian Fanny Durack won gold medals at the 1912 Olympics in a sleeveless, mid-thigh, form-fitting, one-piece knitted costume. This style dominated competitive swimming until the new millennium, though getting briefer and tighter over the decades. Wool was replaced by elasticized (shirred) cotton, which in turn was substituted by new artificial stretch fabrics such as Lastex, rayon, nylon, Lycra, neoprene, spandex, and microfiber.

By the end of World War I swimwear was becoming not only an acceptable form of attire, but a coveted one. The Australian Girl, generally defined as an active, athletic type late in the previous century, had swimming added to her repertoire during the 1910s. She was healthy, golden-skinned, blonde-haired and usually depicted in a swimsuit—a perfect foil to the 1890s icon of the bush man. Her image symbolized the convergence of eugenics and national myth-making. In an effort to raise wartime morale, a department store in Sydney held a fashion parade featuring swimsuits in 1918, the first time such scanty garments had been publicly displayed. Not only was the design of swimwear changing, but so too were the physical activities associated with swimming. In 1902 Richard Cavill introduced the Australian crawl, an overarm stroke that was more efficient and faster than the breast stroke. Swimming and diving were introduced to the Olympics in 1912. In 1915 visiting Hawaiian Olympics swimming champion Duke Kahanamoku introduced surfing with a long board into Australia. Isobel Letham accompanied him into the surf and thus became—amazingly, given the restrictions on women—the first Australian to ride a surfboard. Water-based recreation became immensely popular, whether in a swimming pool, in rivers, on lakes, or at the ocean beach.

THE RISE OF BEACH CULTURE

In Australia the beach dominated popular representations of swimming. Beach culture took a number of forms, the best known of which were surf culture and lifesaving, since the freedom and hedonism of the beach were matched by the danger of the waves (especially dumpers), cross-currents (rips), and tides. Surf life-savers, members of voluntary organizations established at almost all popular beaches, became a symbol of national culture not only for their vigilance and bravery, but for their spectacular surf carnivals, which became major recreational attractions (feature events in royal tours and a constant subject of early Australian newsreels from the 1930s to the 1970s). Between the 1920s and 1950s the surf lifesaver joined the bush man and the digger as a national icon. Although this period was the heyday of Australian beach culture, its popularity of the beach has never waned. By 2006 an estimated eighty million visits to Australia's eleven thousand beaches were made annually by Australians, 85 percent of whom live within a two-hour drive of a beach. One in four Australians visits the beach during the summer holidays.

The lure of the beach grew still further in the 1920s and 1930s due to a number of converging factors: an interest in healthy recreation, the promotion of holidays and tourism, the appearance of beach fashions and accessories, the popularity of suntanning, and the development of a new sense of nationalism based on strength and physical fitness. Photographs such as Harold Cazneaux's "Sun Bathers" (1929, Art Gallery of New South Wales) and Max Dupain's "The Sunbaker" (1937, National Gallery of Australia) and "Form at Bondi" (1939, Art Gallery of New South Wales) captured the image of the bronzed "Aussie," the sun-worshipping physical figure who colonized and transformed the space of the beach. Travel posters, such as Percy Trompf's much reproduced "Australia" (1932, Art Gallery of New South Wales), which depicted a Riviera-styled Bondi Beach, extolled the virtues of perfect Australian beach culture, climate, and the latest swim and après-swim beach fashions.

Images of bronzed figures in swimwear and leisure wear have continued to dominate the visual arts and popular culture in Australia, including Charles Merewether's painting "Australian Beach Pattern" (1940, Art Gallery of New South Wales), or Anne Zahalka's 1989 photographic satire of the latter, "The Bathers" (Art Gallery of New South Wales), in which she challenged the mythology of the Australian beach and the bronzed "Aussie." She did this by substituting swarthy migrant beachgoers and women as the heroic figures, thus replacing the bronzed blonde, blue-eyed male icon.

Swimming costumes (one- and two-piece) were complemented by coordinated outfits of hats, kimonos, robes, overskirts, towels, sandals, shorts, parasols, belts, and swimming caps. Manufacturers of swimsuits chiseled away at the male swim top, replacing sleeves with straps and cutting away the back. Women's suits were also gradually modified. To complement swimwear, leisure wear became a stylish new genre of clothing. Beach bags, deck chairs, picnic baskets, picnic sets, and picnic blankets became essential accoutrements for the fashionable beachgoer. Companies such as the U.S. firm Jantzen (which set up a bathing suit factory in Sydney), Cole of California, and MacRae Knitting Mills, who named their brand Speedo in 1928, soon dominated the mass marketing of swimwear, the latter becoming a major competitive global brand. In Australia beach worshippers became a feted national stereotype, while the beach became the epitome of public hedonism.

Leisure wear—and swimwear in particular—was to become the centerpiece of Australian fashion design. When Vogue published its first Australian supplement in 1955, it proclaimed: "To think in terms of Australian Fashion is to bring beachwear immediately to mind." Not only did Australian designers and clothing companies concentrate on leisure wear as a jewel in the crown of local production, but they recognized its distinctiveness in stylistic terms. Leisure wear—and informal clothing more generally—has become the trademark of Australian style, reflected in what people wear, apparel production, and consumer behavior. It has also dominated images of Australian national culture, both within Australia and in international perceptions of Australia and its way of life. Inevitably, then, swimwear is woven into the fabric of national identity. The debates and conflicts surrounding it (around modesty, respectability, nudity, shifting erogenous zones, sexual impropriety, male voyeurism and sexism, and antisocial behavior) have become embedded in the national consciousness.

In the 1930s bosoms and bare backs were the focus of swimwear, and both men's and women's swimsuits were streamlined. The adoption of Lastex enabled body-hugging designs to dominate the market. In 1934 Jantzen developed the Topper model for men, which had a zippered top that could be removed. The battle to enforce swim tops for men lost out, and after 1935 men wore trunks only, although these retained their modesty skirt until the 1950s. Elizabeth Arden began marketing tinted skin protection cream in the 1930s, spearheading what was to become a multimillion-dollar industry of sun-related skin-care products. Images of people at the beach dominated visual culture, featuring prominently in domestic photography and the growing demand for professional photography. Ray Leighton and Fred Lang were two of the first photographers to specialize in beach and swimsuit studies and were hired by guest houses and resorts to photograph the tourists. Swimsuit parades and dressing-up competitions became part of the holiday frivolities.

THE BIKINI REVOLUTION

Australian swimwear of the 1940s reflected both European fashions and postwar leisure trends that were also increasingly influenced by American popular culture. The Americanization of Australian culture had begun during World War II when American servicemen were stationed in Queensland. This led to a culture war between conservative and older Anglophiles and young women intrigued by the brash, informal, commodity-oriented mass culture that the GIs represented. Fights broke out on Brisbane streets between Australian men and American soldiers, while media campaigns warned innocent Queenslanders against being seduced by the preferences of American servicemen for girls in short skirts. It was a losing battle. In the aftermath of the war, many aspects of Australian culture became infused with American values: movies, music, stars, architecture, town planning, shopping, lifestyles, and—of course—fashions. Swimwear, too, reflected this.

The most significant item of swimwear of the period was the bikini, sometimes called a French bathing suit. Dates for its first appearance vary between 1945 and 1946. Its brevity far exceeded that of the Hubba-Hubba, a wrapped nappy-style two-piece banned by beach inspectors (as recorded in a newsreel around 1945, Hubba-Hubba Fashion Swimsuit). The bikini was immediately adopted in Australia by adventurous girls, especially on the Gold Coast in Queensland. Here leisure-wear designer Paula Stafford cornered the bikini market and pressured the beach

"Surf Sirens." From a series of photographs taken at Manly Beach, New South Wales, Australia, from 1938 to 1946. Australian beachwear of the 1940s reflects the strong American cultural influence introduced during World War II. Photograph by Ray Leighton.

inspectors to legalize the bikini on its beaches. Two famous Australian newsreels of the time recorded the bikini controversy—*Oo La La: French Swimsuit Girl Ordered off Beach* (1948) and *Beach Inspectors Battle of the Bikini* (1955).

In 1952, at Surfers Paradise (the central locality of the Gold Coast, Queensland), a beach inspector, Johnny Moffat, ordered Sydney model Ann Ferguson off the beach because of her bikini, so the next day she returned with five friends in identical bikinis—made overnight by Stafford—who invited councilors, clergy, and the media to judge whether these outfits were decent. Amid the publicity, the ban on bikinis was waived, and by 1958 Surfers Paradise had become the bikini capital of Australia. Meanwhile, the Gold Coast City Council introduced an innovative promotional campaign centering on meter maids, dressed in gold bikinis covered with gold coins topping up parking meters in the resort city. By the 1960s the bikini was synonymous with Surfers Paradise in Australia and with youth popular culture in America. *Vogue Australia* declared that 1959 was "the bikiniest summer. The startled phase of the bikini is over; it has become almost a classic, the best undressed look on the beach." This became the mantra of Australian beach culture. In 1961 bikinis were finally permitted on Bondi Beach. Television programs like *Gidget* fanned the popularity of the bikini, which was also celebrated in the international hit song "Itsy-Bitsy Teenie Weenie, Yellow Polka-Dot Bikini" (1960).

Swimwear became increasingly less structured as well as briefer, inevitably resulting in the topless "monokini" (consisting of the bottom of a bikini only, leaving the breasts bare) invented by U.S. designer Rudi Gernreich in 1964. Mainstream youth and subculture groups were heavily involved with surfing, swimming, and thus leisure wear, with the beach at the center of their activities. Swimming costumes acquired slang names that varied across states, for example, "bathers," "cossies," "swimmers," and "togs." Men's basic nylon swimming briefs were called "scungies," "dick togs," and "budgie [budgerigar] smugglers."

California was the model for beach and surf culture, while swinging London became the model for youth music and street fashion. The apparel industry in Australia accelerated production of its own swimwear, with independent manufacturing labels springing up, including Brian Rochford, Watersun, Sunseeker Swimwear, and Sea Folly. Using the basic elements of the bikini, designers experimented with variations such as crochet bikinis, string bikinis, ever briefer side seams (even hoops to join front and back), g-strings or thong bikinis, and triangular cut pieces (with the potential to reveal pubic hair above the "bikini line"). Independent small-scale swimwear manufacturers proliferated in the 1970s, offering consumers unparalleled choice.

By the 1980s swimwear had become so brief that nudity was inevitable, and Maslin's Beach in South Australia became the first to legalize nudity in 1975. The skimpy designs of Brazilian swimwear had a major impact on local design, and a new generation of swimwear designers emerged, including Done Art (Ken and Judy Done), Balarinji, Linda Jackson, Cheetah, and Exposay. Swimwear was also changing due to the convergence with gym wear and exercise apparel, using new fabrics (such as Lycra, neoprene, and spandex) and fluorescent dyes to produce cross-garments such as bodysuits, bikini gym wear, and body-hugging sportswear. The revival of nationalism in Australia resulted in fabrics that embodied the flora, fauna, icons, and lifestyle of the continent, as well as brash colorful garments that reflected the sun,

sea, and distinctive light of the landscape and climate. There was a new confidence in Australian style.

At the point when it seemed that Australian fashion design had come into its own, the 1980s witnessed major restructuring of manufacturing industries due to deregulatory policies such as the scaling back of industry protection measures like tariffs, and deunionization of the workforce. This had a significant impact on Australian fiber, fabric, and apparel manufacturing capacity due to the threat from imports and offshore production. A shake-out of the apparel sector followed, and many companies and designers disappeared. The longer-term effects have had numerous dimensions. The largest and best-organized companies have retained their share through increasingly designing locally and producing offshore. Small and independent companies have either folded or, like Tiger Lily, been bought out (sometimes under licensing agreements) by the larger apparel companies such as Gazal Corporation (one of Australia's largest apparel groups). Other companies have focused on niche and/or celebrity collections and markets. A further challenge to Australian design has come from the growing number of global fashion labels now marketed in Australia. As a consequence, since the 1990s, Australian high-profile swimwear brands like Nicole Zimmermann, Tiger Lily, Jets, Aqua Blu, Lisa Ho, Kookai Swim, Wahine, Azzolini, Bond-eye, aussieBum, and 2 Chillies have looked to export markets.

The range of types of swimwear has also proliferated. The concern about modesty and immodesty seemed to have abated as bodies and clothing became coextensive, and body-hugging garments became the basis of many forms of dress—swimwear, underwear, sportswear, gym wear, leisure wear, evening wear, even nightclub wear. Topless and nude bathing no longer creates the same moral panic, and the pressure to "cover up" has dissipated (other than for skin cancer protection). Bikinis come in many forms, including bandeaus (wraparound tops), the string (g-string style or triangles with tie sides and shoulder/center front ties), the underwire bikini (for fuller figures), "retro" bikinis (also known as "bombshell bikinis," with high waists, belts, and boy legs), and "tankinis" (half bikini, half one-piece with cut-off singlet tops over bikini bottoms, designed by Anne Cole in 1997 as a more modest swimsuit).

Bikinis are increasingly sold as separate tops and bottoms, thus addressing variable body sizes. One-piece swimwear comes in many styles (e.g., halter necks, peek-a-boo fronts, cut-away fronts, low-cut legs, string straps) often almost as brief as a bikini. Swimwear is also marketed and promoted by magazines such as *Marie Claire* for different body shapes: the column (straight up and down), the apple (rounded stomach), the rod (stick thin), the bell (bottom heavy), or the wineglass (large bust, narrow hips). As swimwear becomes almost indistinguishable from leisure wear, the outfits found on beaches and at pools vary enormously.

Yet, covering up has not entirely gone away. Since the 2000 Sydney Olympics, competitive swimmers have worn neoprene extremely tight-fitting "fastsuits," designed to cut down water resistance and streamline the body. These come in various types: from long-sleeved neck-to-ankle suits, or bottom-only pants, to sleeveless mid-thigh suits. More recently, there have been disputes about modest beach clothing where Muslim migrants have settled in traditional beach suburbs such as Cronulla to Sydney's south. After violent racially motivated clashes in 2005, a long-sleeved, hooded tunic over full-length leggings known as the "burquini" (swimwear that combines pants, a long-sleeved tunic, and a head covering) was designed for female Muslims in 2007 by Australian retailer Aheda Zanetti. A burquini uniform for Muslim female lifesavers (yellow tunic over red leggings) was also adopted in an effort to make beach culture more appealing to other cultures. The burquini is now marketed worldwide in slim, modest, and active cuts to meet the demand of Muslim women involved in swimming, sport, and leisure.

While the burquini is still controversial among mainstream Australian communities, ironically, concern about the effects of the sun on pale Anglo-Saxon skins has grown since the 1970s. Australia's soaring incidence of skin cancer prompted health authorities to pressure governments to fund campaigns to "slip [on a shirt], slop [on suncream], slap [on a hat]." To meet the demand, the skin-care industry has developed UV ratings for its sun-care products and generated a huge number of products offering sun protection and fake tans. While health-conscious fashion advocates extol the virtues of pale skin as a fashionable look, the proliferation of tanning salons simultaneously promotes bronzed skin as celebrity fashion (and has been implicated in the deaths of young women from skin cancer). Hats, rash shirts (with short or long sleeves, worn to stop sunburn), and swimwear made from fabrics with high UV protection are now compulsory in Australian schoolyards and at swimming events. As a result, many Australian children—and an increasing number of adults—wear UV protection rash shirts, French legionnaire-style hats, and shorts or leggings at the beach, although they are still a minority of all beachgoers. It seems that the days of "neck-to-knee" have partially returned.

THE GLOBAL REACH OF AUSTRALIAN SURFWEAR

Australian design has had a major impact on the evolution of specialized surfwear. Board surfing originated in Hawai'i in pre-European contact days, later being emulated on the West Coast of the U.S. mainland, especially California. Surfers tended to wear some form of swimming costume or shorts or cut-off jeans ("baggies"). It was not until the surf culture of the 1960s and 1970s that surfing moved from being a minority sport for fanatics to becoming a youth subculture. The advent of the balsa-wood or fiberglass short board ("Malibu") in 1967, which was lighter, cheaper, and more compact, made surfing accessible to a wider group of amateurs and holiday makers. Surf culture spawned not just a craze for the sport of surfing but surf music, surf films, and surf fashion. The surfer look was lean and tanned, with long blonde hair. Songs such as Little Pattie's hit "He's My Blonde-Headed Stompie-Wompie Real Gone Surfer Boy" (1963) reinforced the fact that surfing was a key element of youth culture.

The keenest surfers became itinerant travelers, piling their belongings into a Kombi VW van and heading up and down the coast chasing the best waves. Driven by this quest, the evolution

Women and men sunbathing on the Gold Coast, Queensland, 1963. In the 1960s, the bikini was particularly popular in Surfers Paradise, the central locality of the Gold Coast. Swimwear in general became briefer and increasingly less structured during the following two decades. Photograph by Jeff Carter.

of surfwear came out of dissatisfaction with swimming trunks (the inner thighs chafed due to sitting on the waxed surfboards, and the back seam got caught in the bottom—a "wedgie"), cut-off jeans (studs, seams, zippers, pockets, and buttons were uncomfortable to lie on while waiting for waves), and T-shirts to protect from the sun or cold (they became wet and clammy). Surfers began to experiment with modifications to their gear, starting with wetsuits borrowed from diving. These enabled surfers to keep surfing in the colder months, while the body-hugging design enhanced the ability to surf. In summer surfers gravitated to long board shorts (shorts with a wide cut that reach the knees, originally worn by board riders), often made from fabric with Hawaiian or Polynesian floral prints (okanuis). In 1965 surfer Dick Ash made his first cotton canvas board shorts using a mailbag. Soon his shorts were being printed with monochrome Hibiscus designs. These became the basis of Okanui Classics, a brand that is still a niche player in Australian surfwear.

The first Australian company to get into surf gear was Rip Curl (established in 1969), producing surfboards for the local market and adapting the technology of wetsuits to make them more suitable for surfing. Other companies followed, including Quiksilver (in 1970) and Billabong (in 1973). Fiberglass made it possible to make surfboards in the garage, and board manufacture proliferated up and down Australia's coastline, although over time the more business-savvy companies consolidated their market share with more professional finishes, innovative products, and the cachet of a known surf label.

Quiksilver also turned its attention to surf clothing, discarded the parts of traditional surf "trunks" that did not work, and developed the "board shorts" ("boardies"), a garment made from lightweight, durable, fast-drying fabric (adapted from yachting). Gone was the inner leg seam, replaced by short scalloped legs that did not bunch up—rather like knee-length jodhpurs. The shorts were plain with a wide waistband, a pocket for wax, and a flat Velcro front closure. The advantages of the new design were immediate and adopted by competition surfers with alacrity. Other brands copied the new design. Overseas interests followed, and an agreement to distribute Quiksilver board shorts in the United States was signed in 1976.

Other kinds of surf clothing followed, including surf shoes, T-shirts, rash shirts, shorts, wrist straps, caps, sunglasses, towels, and jackets. The surfwear industry has been quick to adopt new fibers, materials, and manufacturing technologies and adapt them to product innovation and new product development. In 1991 Quiksilver launched the Roxy label for women and has been a major sponsor of women's surf tournaments. It has also expanded into children's wear (Roxy Teenie Weenie and Raisins) and swimwear (Leilani). Quiksilver moved its headquarters to Huntington Beach in California and has become the largest surfwear company in the world, producing a wide range of surfing, sporting, and leisure apparel with annual global sales in 2007 of over US$1.5 billion compared with Rip Curl's US$300 million.

Rip Curl and Billabong have similar histories, branching out into apparel, extreme sportswear, mountain wear, and accessories while remaining leading players in developing new surfing products in the global market. Surf brands can be seen on T-shirts, cargo shorts, sunglasses, bags and hold-alls, caps, watches, hoodies (lightweight jackets with pull-up hoods), flannel shirts, snowboard jackets, sunhats, thongs (footwear), towels, and wallets. This ensures global exposure but runs the risk of losing focus and diluting a loyal consumer base. This was the experience of Rusty, a surfboard brand that originated in California and made a licensing agreement with Western Australian surfboard company Santosha to use the Rusty logo in 1984. The arrangement flourished, boosted by the success of the surfing apparel rather than the boards, and Rusty gained a reputation for being more adventurous than competitors Billabong, Rip Curl, and Quiksilver. However, the company floundered after the U.S. parent brought in C&C, a major apparel manufacturer, to run this side of the business, because C&C failed to appreciate the significance of surf culture to branding and market positioning. In 2006 Rusty Australia was offered a controlling share in the company and directorship of the apparel side of the business due to their success in knowing the surf scene and designing for fellow surfers. In 2007 the turnover of Rusty Australia (over US$45 million) was more than double that of the U.S. part of the company.

The success of designing apparel to complement the surfwear has also worked for Mambo, established in 1984. Mambo designed shorts and shirts emblazoned with colorful and satirical graphics lampooning Australian suburban and subterranean culture. Their products were embraced by surf culture and shocked the mainstream. Mambo developed a reputation for mixing irreverent humor with a commitment to political, indigenous, and environmental causes. Its product lines diversified into leisure wear and accessories (for wider markets) although its core business of shirts, shorts, board shorts, and swimwear remains. In 2000 Mambo was bought by Gazal Corporation to produce Mambo under license and market globally.

Surf culture has a double-faced nature. While media and public attention focus on the glamour of the professional circuits and celebrity endorsements, surfing has had a traditionally masculine image, multiple subcultures (for example, surfboard riders, surf lifesavers, clubbies, and surfies who engage in varying degrees of hostility), and a dominant culture of misogyny and racial intolerance. From the 1960s women were generally only tolerated as spectators on the shore watching their bronzed "Aussie" heroes maneuver across the waves—and as entertainment and company après surfing. Surf clubs have a heroic image associated with competitive surfing and surf lifesaving, but also a darker history of excessive behavior including rape, drug taking, and violence. A sense of the currents underpinning surf culture infuses surf magazines like *Tracks*, *Surfing World*, *Australia's Surfing World*, and *Deep*, as well as online surf forum sites.

From the outset of surfing becoming a major subculture, Australian surfwear brands have had an international impact. As well as Quiksilver, Rip Curl, and Billabong, other brands include Brother Nielsen, Oakley, Hot Tuna, and Hot Buttered. Although a number of these companies are now global concerns, their products and mode of operation indicate their Australian origins, with products characterized by their colorful, irreverent, humorous, and laid-back styling. These global surf brands also sponsor the major surfing tournaments and star professional surfers and skateboarders.

As swimwear and surfwear converge with sportswear, extreme sports, and leisure wear, these brands can be found far from the beaches where they began, also shaping global streetwear fashion trends. Australian beach culture continues to be promoted, exploited, and exported in its swimwear and surfwear, arguably constituting the most significant Australian contribution to world dress in the twentieth century.

References and Further Reading

Art Gallery of New South Wales. *On the Beach*. Sydney: Art Gallery of New South Wales, 1982.

Cushing, Nancy. "Ocean Baths and Arc Lights: Newcastle City Council and Control on the Beach." In *Forging Identities: Bodies, Gender and Feminist History*, edited by J. Long, J. Gothard, and H. Brash, 88–110. Nedlands: University of Western Australia Press, 1997.

Fletcher, Marion. *Costume in Australia 1788–1901*. Melbourne, Australia: Oxford University Press, 1984.

Hall, Marion, with Marjorie Carne and Sylvia Sheppard. *California Fashion: From the Old West to New Hollywood*. New York: Harry N. Abrams, 2002.

Joel, Alexandra. *Parade: The Story of Fashion in Australia*. Sydney: HarperCollins, 1998.

Kidwell, Claudia Brush, and Valerie Steele, eds. *Men and Women: Dressing the Part*. Washington, DC: Smithsonian Institution Press, 1989.

Martyn, Norma. *The Look: Australian Women in Their Fashion*. Stanmore: Cassell Australia, 1976.

Maynard, Margaret. *Out of Line: Australian Women and Style*. Sydney: University of New South Wales Press, 2001.

National Film and Sound Archive Australia. *Sun, Surf and Sand: Australia's Newsreels*. Video. Canberra, Australia: National Film and Sound Archive, 1995.

National Museum of Australia. *Between the Flags: Years of Surf Lifesaving*. Canberra: National Museum of Australia Press, 2006.

O'Neill, Helen. "Mambo King." *The Australian* (27 February 1996): 13.

Pawle, Fred. "Board Meetings." *Wish Magazine (The Australian)* (November 2007): 28–30.

Pearson, Kent. *Surfing Subcultures of Australia and New Zealand*. St. Lucia, Australia: University of Queensland Press, 1979.

Robinson, Felicity. *Fashion*. Sydney: Murdoch Books, 2005.

Safe, Mike. "Revenge of the Longboarders." *The Bulletin* (21–22 October 1995): 30–34.

Stedman, Leanne. "From Gidget to Gonad Man: Surfers, Feminists and Postmodernization." *Australia and New Zealand Journal of Sociology* 33, no. 1 (1997): 75–90.

Stewart, Cameron. "Surf City Inc." *The Weekend Australian Magazine* (17–18 August 2002): 16–20.

Thoms, Albie, director. "From Neck to Knee to Nude." Television documentary. Sydney: Albie Thoms Productions, 1985.

Jennifer Craik

See also Cosmetics and Beauty Culture in Australia; The Australiana Phenomenon in Australia.

PART 4

Fashion in Australia

Urban Fashion Culture in Australia

Australian fashions for men and women between 1870 and 1945 were rich, complex, and volatile. Clothing and textiles were a central pivot of settler society from the social life of the small wealthy elite, both in town and country, to the daily grind of thousands of factory hands in large cities like Melbourne and Sydney. The making, promotion, selling, and wearing of stylish dress existed in a continuum that stretched from modern integrated capitalist conglomerates controlling supply, ranging from raw material to end product and publicity, through to glittering ultramodern central-city emporiums and thence to petit bourgeois households. Despite the strong gender divide in Australia, fashionable dressing was not simply a female pursuit; the production of male clothing found a place in this continuum of dress from ordinary to couture. From early in the nineteenth century Australians manifested a demonstrable enthusiasm for fashion and the status it conferred, belying the country's self-created reputation for egalitarianism. This fascination continued and even increased with the passage of time. The actual formats of fashion and associated etiquette followed norms established as middle-class and upper-class styling (especially derived from France, Britain, and the United States), with some regional dress influences from the wide range of migrants, mostly working-class, who came to Australia prior to the notorious White Australia policy set up after Federation in 1901. Not surprisingly, World War I and particularly World War II had significant impacts on the nature of stylish dressing, affecting the availability of both imports and local production of high-end clothing.

To be truly fashionable involved a high degree of consciousness of what were believed to be practices and behaviors derived from the northern hemisphere. Styling developments in gowns, hairstyles, millinery, ladies shoes, men's suits, boots, and headwear were adopted as available technologies of dissemination and manufacture evolved. Time lapses for stylistic ideas shortened during the early twentieth century with unfolding technologies such as telegraphic communication. The emergence of new media formats, such as gravure reproduction of photographs and the cinema, offered new sites for spreading information on fashion. Concurrently, these, as well as imported fashion magazines, confirmed the extreme vigilance and curiosity displayed by Australians around overseas fashion.

Studies of Australian fashion, whether academic or museum-based, have been limited in their concerns to the late nineteenth and the twentieth centuries. While relatively invisible until recent years in the history of Australian culture, fashion ironically stands at the metaphorical center of the chimerical—even anxious—qualities that drove and still drive the Australian sense of stylish identity. This sense of identity is one that demands to be hailed for regional specificity and individualism, yet simultaneously dreaming of the only recognition that seems to count, that of the cultural Meccas of the "old" world. Surviving dress examples and images in paintings and popular prints as well as photographs document that fashion garments, both imported and locally produced, were technically and aesthetically of high quality. Museum holdings in institutions such as the Powerhouse in Sydney and the National Gallery of Victoria show that locally worn garments match styles of those surviving in public collections of Europe, England, and the United States. The elaborately cut, sumptuously trimmed, and embroidered silk gowns of women during the later nineteenth century are well represented, as is the smart and sophisticated dress of the 1920s and 1930s. Fewer men's clothes have been collected, and they can be hard to identify as made in Australia unless specifically labeled or provenanced.

URBAN LIFE

Australian urban life is a key to this fluent and confident, multilayered culture of fashion and dress. Despite popular stereotypes of the continent as a land of natural wonders, strange creatures, a living indigenous culture, and a vast empty land, Australia—especially on the eastern seaboard—is one of the most heavily urbanized countries in the world per capita. The reality of this was already established by the late nineteenth century with cities like Melbourne, Sydney, and even Brisbane being major sites of fashionable dressing. This set up the cultural pattern of east coast dominance that has persisted in Australian public life to the twenty-first century. Certain rivalries did creep in between Melbourne and Sydney, and prior to World War II the latter was considered to be most influenced by American styles of clothing.

Fashion knowledge, forecasting, and actual product was disseminated particularly from these dominant cities, not only to the hinterland and the regions where, especially in Queensland and New South Wales, there were considerably sized regional cities with many facilities, but also to those seen as slightly lower in the ranking of commerce: Adelaide, Hobart, and Perth. It should be noted that Australia had a rural elite who were networked into various urban centers, and men, women, and children were often supplied by mail-order services, supplementing shopping trips to town.

In each city fashion matched the visual direction offered by its sophisticated and inspirational urban setting, which, like stylish dress, was never solely Anglocentric. The origins of the federated Australian states as independent colonies created a tendency to look toward the particular capital city of a given region for signs of sophistication and social guidance. This political and economic structure certainly promoted the duplication of many fashion design and retailing businesses across Australia to serve each capital city's claim to social status.

There is nothing surprising in the fact that metropolitan life was seen as the crucible of fashion in Australia, as it was in Europe. Here were concentrations of people, urban activity, modern restlessness, and abundant new opportunities for display and style. Melbourne was initially the major city that became a credible site for sustaining a sense of the fashionable. It had the grandeur and amenities of comparable European cities, from noble architectural perspectives to lively social life, with multiple opportunities for fashionable display from grand civic balls, to race meetings, to upper-class weddings where admiring spectators blocked major city intersections to watch the guests. The fashions worn by elite men and women at these events were usually sourced from local designers and makers and styled locally from expensive fabrics and trims (although many everyday men's textiles were increasingly produced in Australia as the 1870–1945 period evolved). This attire provided lengthy copy for the press, which further disseminated a sense of fashionable participation and knowledge. The vice-regal households stood in for the royal courts as social leaders. Elite dressmakers in the late nineteenth century noted in their advertising that they were under vice-regal patronage as a quasi-royal warrant.

Fashion practices in urban Australia were informed and modified by social developments that frequently mirrored Anglo-American paradigms, although sources do suggest that Australian dressing often had its own resonances. An example of the changes would be the expansion of women's social and professional lives, particularly toward the end of the period. These new roles affected dress and other elements of fashionable appearance. Those

that impacted on dress, especially after World War I, include the wearing of makeup in public, as an expected norm for respectable women, the shortening of skirts (by 1925 to knee length), the bobbed hairstyles of the 1920s, and the development of lighter corsetry. The new acceptability of sport for women by the late nineteenth century led to the development of many novel types of clothing, including cycling dress and swimwear, the latter a strong point of Australian fashion ever since. The vagaries of fashion held less sway over men's dress, which has had a long-standing reputation for conservatism.

Changes in household practices in the 1920s and 1930s, especially the shifting of responsibility for routine domestic work from paid servants to middle-class wives, simplified the design of fabrics, the styling, and also the rituals of construction, maintenance, and cleaning of dress. With the middle-class wife no longer a "lady," but a productive, reliable operative within the home unit, home dressmaking for self and family in the interwar period was of major significance. The Australian fashion industry included a number of local pattern services. One of these was Madame Weigel's mail-order service, which became a dominant fashion influence for women in the Australasian region extending to New Zealand and the Pacific and even to Southeast Asia. Her service offered patterns for both domestic clothing (including children's wear) and highly fashionable garments, emphasizing the sense of

In the late nineteenth century central Melbourne was a busy environment where a range of classes mingled, both workers and the well-to-do. The latter paid little heed to the Australian climate when dressing for public appearances. Even in summer formal clothing closely followed European styles. Great Bourke Street, Melbourne, 1872. Getty Images.

continuum between high and low fashions in Australia, as well as—by the 1930s—striking patterns for novelty fancywork, craft, crochet, and knitting.

Large Australian department stores' contribution to promoting style and chic from the second quarter of the nineteenth century onwards cannot be underestimated. Given the vitality of Australia's urban identity, there was an almost perfect marriage between the city, fashion, and the department store, positioned as aristocratic and exclusive, as well as directed to the middle and lower sections of the market. Department stores were found in all Australian capitals and in larger provincial cities. Gradually throughout the early twentieth century these businesses were taken over by others to form networks of linked stores, with the last independent business, Ahearns of Perth, only absorbed by David Jones in the late 1990s. David Jones (originally set up in Sydney in 1838), believed to be the oldest department store in the world continually trading under its original name, was, with Myers, one of the two most important Australian department stores during the period.

Australian industrial production of fashion and textiles was closely tied to large retail concerns such as these, which from the late nineteenth century owned large-scale factories. The manufacturing wing of the Myer stores was, for instance, established about 1911 and expanded from apparel construction to weaving and textile production by about 1918. Particularly notable was the Foy and Gibson complex of factories and warehouses, developed from about 1897 onwards and covering several complete blocks in Collingwood. Foy and Gibson claimed to have converted raw materials into exclusive consumer goods under their own roof. The factory areas covered more land than the retail buildings, but the latter boasted the novelty of an underground tunnel between either side of Smith Street so that shoppers could move throughout the showrooms without getting wet or being held up by traffic, trams, or horse-drawn and motorized vehicles.

There was a widespread pattern of Australian businesses at all levels of the fashion and dress industry being embedded in family networks and inherited experience. English families, for instance, extended existing familial interests in retail, manufacturing, and wholesaling dress, accessories, and textiles successfully in Australia. In some cases people who only worked as employees in Britain used their experience to establish themselves as business owners, entrepreneurs, and managers in the new country, such as the Grace family and their Sydney-based Grace Brothers network of stores and manufacturing. In other cases there was a more symbiotic, colonial pattern of control, with the Australian concern being a branch office of established British firms. Part of the ongoing volatility of the garment industries was the tensions throughout this period between British manufacturers and designers who wanted to export product to a passive and receptive Australia, and local enterprises who claimed authority to design and produce within Australia. These tensions arose especially in the area of cloth production, finishing, and value adding. They informed tariff debates in Federal Parliament from as early as 1906–1907 and still influence debate in a globalized era. These tensions can be tracked in the histories of individual companies, and also at the level of official trade promotions; the tensions extended into the post–World War II era, especially as Britain tried to counter its slipping position in the world economy against the United States.

LIMITED REGIONALISM IN AUSTRALIAN FASHION

The existence of an urban-based and bourgeois fashion culture may be highly surprising in view of widely held stereotypes of Australia. Moreover, the climate seems to have had little influence on dress, to judge from surviving examples and pictorial records, including early film. However, this apparent lack of visible adaptation to climate may indicate that any sign of laxness, relaxation, or concession to the weather was carefully avoided in self-presentation for the camera, particularly in the nineteenth century.

In a country as large as Australia there are several climate zones, which run from a genial European-like four seasons, generally without extended extremes of cold, to the harsh dryness of Central Australia, to a wet tropical north, with multiple variants in between. For some urban areas climatic adaptations of dress were not particularly relevant or necessary unless for seasonal wear. While there are written descriptions of mid-nineteenth-century Australian women and their servants—when not seen by outsiders or when menfolk and servants were engaged outside the house in daily work—going about in chemises and petticoats, by the late nineteenth century there is far less evidence, written or visual, of such undress.

The lack of adaptation to the climate during the period is seen particularly in men's dress. Woolen suiting was the fabric of first preference from the working classes to the elite, from schoolboy to senior politician, and provided a solid market for local manufacture. Paintings such as the celebrated images of workers by the iconic painter Tom Roberts during the 1880s and 1890s, although rural scenes, show that the removal of jackets and rolling up of shirtsleeves was the main response to hot weather, even during heavy laboring.

Despite the dominance of keeping up standards against the climate, artist William Dobell in his late 1930s and early 1940s images of working men shows that the modern practices of urban construction workers wearing only shorts and brief singlets—teamed with protective footwear—was established by this date. Women were never offered this option of visible undress, at least not in the public eye, not until swimming was a commonplace activity. By the 1920s, rather than being an oppressive nuisance, the sun was associated with glamour and elegance but also healthy living. Many wealthy families, in Sydney for example, boasted private swimming and sailing facilities on their large waterfront estates around the harbor. Swimwear and leisure clothes were certainly an adaptation to climatic conditions and, associated with pleasure and the good life, they have remained a major site of settler Australian identification with the geography of the country.

One climate-based adaptation, associated with Queensland in particular, was the "tropical suit" in light white materials, including silk. Sometimes the silks were obtained from the East, especially with the development in the 1920s and 1930s of tourism north of Australia. Having dresses and suits made by professional tailors and dressmakers in Singapore, Bangkok, Kuala Lumpur, or Hong Kong became a styling option as Australians traveled more frequently for pleasure in the region. This practice grew further in popularity with the advent of post–World War II air travel to become an important alternative source of finely made garments in Australia. The white suit was a fashion statement and not so clearly associated with the white hierarchy, the "boss," the local politician, as it was in the southern United States. On the other hand, white suits could be a sign of dandy-like fastidiousness. Worn—as by the artist John Longstaff with a crimson cummerbund—it had an attention-seeking quality. William Longstaff, an Australian artist, used it during the 1880s and 1890s as a social passport to elite Melbourne functions as an exotic bachelor—while keeping his cockney-voiced wife at home—and to mask the fact that he did not own a proper gentleman's evening suit.

The country-based elites leading a de facto urban life tended to wear finer versions of clothes worn by rural workers, for instance, well-tailored riding gear. What workers bought ready-made, the family at the big house had made by specialist outfitters and by department stores in the capital cities. By the 1920s jodhpurs, puttees, and equestrienne outfits were acceptable wear for wealthy young women, becoming a demonstration of class and status and thus refuting the potent legend of Australian egalitarianism and defying the notion of regionalism in dress.

ETHNIC DIVERSITY AND FASHION VITALITY

No specific "ethnic" dress exclusively symbolized white settler culture in Australia between 1870 and 1945 (although male rural wear has come to stand for a recognizable sense of Australianness). At

Reg Waugh in a light tropical suit on the couch lawn of 12 Alexandra Road, Elsternwick, Victoria, Australia, early twentieth century. White silk or cotton suits for men were most prevalent in the early nineteenth century in Australia, but they continued to be worn occasionally in summer for informal occasions, mostly by the well-to-do, until the 1940s. Photographer unknown. State Library of Victoria.

the same time a certain cultural diversity informed fashion and its sources for some of this period, even if not remembered as symbolic of the country. Australian cities grew larger at a time when mass-produced printed fabrics, the expansion of fashion journalism and mass literacy, the development of mass retailing, and the spread of sewing machines and printed dress patterns had destroyed much ethnic difference, especially among the middle and upper working classes across those areas in Britain and Europe from where migrants came. Concurrently in the United States, at the turn of the twentieth century, European regional dress was retained to some degree in cities with large ethnic neighborhoods (at least directly after arrival in the new country), as photographs and films suggest. Curiously, this adherence to dress formats from rural Europe rarely appears in Australian visual imagery after the diversity of dress during the 1850s gold rush. European ethnic dress was a mere fantasy for costume balls, ballets, and operettas. It gained a profile during World War I, making tangible links of loyalty and solidarity to other Allied countries whose political and humanitarian interests were often physically and conceptually far removed from everyday life and people in wartime Australia. French, Belgian, Russian, Rumanian, Serbian, and Italian styles were frequently seen at carnivals, street parades, and other such activities, not stigmatized as foreign and inferior, but associated with the interests of Imperial Britain. For instance, members of the Rumanian, Russian, and Serbian royal families had British links during the 1910s and 1920s.

Contradicting the invisibility of European regional dress, prior to World War I Australian men and women did wear Asian dress. Chinese miners, market gardeners, city traders of produce and groceries, Japanese pearl divers, Indian and Middle Eastern peddlers, camel drivers, and other working-class men all brought non-European dress formats into daily life. Dragon robes and official garments of late Imperial China were worn by Chinese community leaders at civic functions around the turn of the century in both Melbourne and Sydney, offering a more aesthetically sumptuous vision of non-European dress. Japanese prostitutes, who formed a significant expatriate community in Western Australia in the 1890s and early 1900s, had themselves photographed by local studios in their meticulously styled kimonos, documenting one of the few visible "ethnic" modifications for female styling in Australia. Some regional textiles especially made in China and Japan for Western markets, such as embroidered blouses or Japanese kimonos, were exported to Australia in large quantities. Kimonos were popular as summer dressing gowns in the interwar period. Chinese and Japanese migrants established successful wholesale houses in Australia by the last quarter of the nineteenth century and included textiles and garments among their ranges. These businesses continued to supply fine apparel and accessories made in Asia throughout the twentieth century.

Although it is assumed that Australia was solely under British influence and thus a monocultural society between 1870 and 1945, the consolidation of British influence did not really occur until after federation of the individual colonies in 1901 and was greatly strengthened during World War I. The war alienated Australia from its cultural fascination with Europe (both allied and enemy countries). White Australia began to see itself as pristine and superior to the polluted, overdeveloped, over-urbanized—and, in some cases, physically devastated—nations of the northern hemisphere. The myth of rural, classical, clean, white Australia as opposed to the flawed urbanism of Europe has always stood in contradiction to the Eurocentricity of Australian fashion, from where ironically not only products themselves but forecasting and product information as well as technological expertise was sourced. So, fashion in Australia was informed by a degree of ethnic and cultural diversity in the nineteenth century and retained this vitality against the grain of increasing homogenization of public culture in the first four decades of the next.

Undoubtedly the liveliness of the local fashion scene by the 1880s and 1890s reflected the many national backgrounds in Australia. Production and retailing of fashion was facilitated by familial networks and preestablished experts from home countries. Most particularly celebrated is the influence of European Jewish families on the Flinders Lane fashion precinct in Melbourne, and within major retail dynasties such as the Myer and Bardas families, both of whose businesses were established in the first two decades of the twentieth century. While persecution of Jews during the 1930s and World War II brought many refugees to Australia, especially Melbourne, central and eastern European migration had already enriched Australian fashion culture throughout the previous century via such personalities as Melbourne's Madame Johanna Weigel of Posnan/Posen and Sidney Myer of Krichev, Byelorussia.

Weigel, a German dress designer who had worked for McCall's in New York, established a dress pattern publishing service in 1879 and a fashion magazine in 1880, supposedly after many requests as to where she obtained her beautiful clothes. She claimed to make regular overseas trips to gather firsthand information and to keep in touch with Berlin, London, and Paris for her fashion forecasting on behalf of Australian women. She named the bringing of first-rate fashion to all Australian women, whatever their class or geographic location, as her major achievement. By 1916 one million patterns were sold annually throughout Australia, New Zealand, the Pacific, including New Guinea, and Southeast Asia (core customers). Catalogs were also sent to individuals in many other countries. The Weigel business continued to publish patterns after Johanna withdrew from its day-to-day management in the 1920s. Although the final years of the company in the 1960s showed the Australian product as less polished than patterns from the large international firms, as well as Madame's own earlier publications, Weigel productions of the late 1940s offered surprisingly credible reiterations of French haute couture.

The eastern European immigrant Jewish origins of the Myer chain, embedded in familial experience in retail, manufacturing, and even door-to-door sales, had links to patterns of retail expansion in the United States. Sidney Myer was the most charismatic of the European migrants who shaped the fashion and textiles industry in Australia. He arrived on the Melbourne docks from Byelorussia in 1899 with little English. Through his instinctive and mercurial, psychologically astute salesmanship and his striving to deploy modernizing techniques of both marketing and production, he captured public attention and constantly reconfigured the parameters of expectations in which his competitors were forced to work. He traveled to North America to research modern retailing practices before World War I and continued to do so until his sudden death in the 1930s.

The Myer business was a highly individual fusion that could serve as a metaphor for the often highly distinctive Australian permutations of seemingly familiar structures and practices. His closest partner was a drapery businessman named Edwin Neil, from a conservative Protestant family. Their talents and backgrounds were entirely different but in tandem were extremely effective. Myer was alert to newness and sudden shifts in consumer behavior and expectations, and Neil could organize and manage corporate structures. Together they oversaw an unparalleled expansion of the store, unique in corporate Australian history to that date, catering to all levels of trade from the cut-price to the highest quality. Myer firstly consolidated the mass retail trade in Bourke Street in central Melbourne by the 1930s, leading to the permanent decline of the retail concentrations in Prahran and Collingwood at the city's edge. In the twenty-first century they face only one last competitor, the David Jones network, which has always emphasized its refined, exclusive identity, against the more raucous, multistranded Myer chain.

FRENCH COUTURE INFLUENCE

During the interwar years French immigrants or Europeans who could boast of French connections also successfully transplanted their fashion technical and marketing skills to replicate a haute couture culture for women customers in Australia. A typical example of these labels with French connections was the couturier Madame Paulette Pellier. She was active by the 1920s, already charging fashionable Sydney women one hundred pounds for a blouse, a premium above ready-to-wear prices. By this time the house employed a large staff of seamstresses and four vendeuses (saleswomen). Germaine Rocher, née Vera Fels, a Russian, and Henriette Lamotte, a Parisian milliner, also established substantial businesses in Sydney. With Thomas Harrison in Melbourne, Lamotte represented the elite of Australian milliners, and the surviving work of both houses again testifies to the impeccable standards of design and production expected and achieved in Australian couture prior to 1945. Rocher and Lamotte are more associated with the postwar era but started their businesses in the 1930s. At an early date they had already set the course of high prices combined with retail and manufacturing practices that replicated Parisian and London norms. The Melbourne-based labels G. V. Thomas and Lucy Secor also consciously promoted themselves as couture houses. Secor of Collins Street, with a Sydney branch office as well as her Melbourne headquarters, claimed to outdo Paris in her advertising copy, stating that Australian woman had no need to look to Paris when she supplied their clothes. Like Worth and Vionnet, her logo was her signature.

To serve this trade, Australian apprentices were taught haute couture style construction and decorative techniques by European immigrants to safeguard a pool of workers with the necessary skill bases. Australian commercially made garments from the 1870s onward are of superlative quality. With labels such as Farmers, Bright and Hitchcock, and Robertson and Moffat, they demonstrate the presence in urban centers of makers capable of the highest grade of handwork, no different from European or British production of the same date. One of the first Australian-based designers to not only claim a skill base that matched Paris, but also the imaginative creativity to match overseas designs, was Janet Walker of Brisbane (flourishing between the 1880s and 1930s). Walker's pneumatic dress form, a blow-up adjustable dressmakers' stand invented in Brisbane to deal with repeat business from distant clients from across the Australian continent, was actually patented and sold at the turn of the century to major international ateliers (couture houses) such as Worth and Redfern.

Clara Butt, a singer, with her husband, Kennerly Rumford, ca. 1905. Beginning in the late nineteenth century singers, musicians, and actors were seen as trendsetters in Australia, and their widely publicized photographs were influential for followers of fashion. Library of Congress, Prints and Photographs Division, LC-DIG-ggbain-50097.

Expertise in dress construction and design was not only imported, but also increasingly refined and nurtured by Australians themselves. In the late 1930s the working-class teenager Beril Jents bluffed her way into an elite dressmaking studio claiming to be able to cut without paper patterns. Clearly this skill was expected at the top end of Australian fashion industries during the interwar period, and press photographs show that Vionnet-style dress designing direct onto small model figures was part of the Melbourne Workingman's College (later RMIT) curriculum in the late 1930s. The complexity of the Australian fashion trade and its aspirational, always polished, and refined outlook can be exemplified by the curriculum of the Perth Technical College. By World War I fashion illustration was taught alongside more practical subjects, suggesting that there was a market for promotion and public relations–based skills as well, even in the most isolated of all Australia's capitals.

Beginning in the 1880s Paris was a constant referent on dress production, as it had been aspirationally in earlier newspaper columns, women's diaries, and letters. The Empress Eugenie's wardrobe choices were a matter of almost constant discussion in the Australian press, at least in Melbourne, as also were visits to the ateliers of Worth and other designers, as well as to London cosmetician Madame Rachel. At first, columns were copied from overseas publications, especially the *Englishwoman's Domestic Magazine*, but by the 1880s Australian papers were paying women to provide fashion and social news of royalty, aristocrats, and stage and musical celebrities. By the 1920s and 1930s these correspondents reporting Parisian and European trends were expatriate Australians addressing their co-nationals rather than British or American women syndicating their columns. At least two of these women, Betty Dyson and Kate O'Connor, had close contacts to circles of Australian expatriate artists in Europe. These columns appeared in publications across Australia, including in Perth, demonstrating the widespread circulation of information about international sophistication.

Technology facilitated the spread of more detailed information about French couture. By about 1910 quality gravure magazines of social and artistic news printed large-scale photographic plates sent from Paris couturiers. The promotion of new fashions by Parisian studios, through documentary short films distributed internationally, had emerged by the same time and was copied by Australian stores. Brief fragments of Australian footage survive, advertising novelties and new styles in dresses and furs; they were undoubtedly shot in Melbourne, not France, and are certainly datable to the period about 1910–1914. A film from about 1918 includes the unmistakable Sydney Harbour as backdrop to fashionable dresses, proving its Australian origins. The Berlei Company, in their elaborate multimedia productions of live models and cinematic features promoting their corsetry in the 1920s, appeared to splice Australian footage with French footage. They advertised that French models of day and evening wear by named designers, including Jacques Heim, were available for personal inspection at their headquarters, as were Parisian corsets they purchased to set off their locally made garments.

There was considerable interest in actual couture garments in Australia. International houses such as Redfern of London and Paris advertised their ateliers in the Melbourne press by the late 1880s, in expectation of serving traveling Australians. Aspiring diva Nellie Melba (Helen Mitchell of Melbourne) was getting clothes made at Worth by the late 1880s and moved freely among European and American elites by 1889. By this time also individual dressmakers and milliners in Australia were importing model garments from Paris in particular, exhibiting them by invitation to favored clients and reproducing them for the local market, as their advertisements attest. Later, by the interwar years, if not earlier, model gowns from known couturiers including Molyneux and Schiaparelli were purchased and reproduced by Australian companies such as David Jones. A number of key Victorian theatrical luminaries, such as Illma Da Murska, Sarah Bernhardt, Cora Brown Potter, and Titell Brune, visited Australia, with sumptuous on-stage and off-stage wardrobes, thus demonstrating a key conduit of communication about fashion in the late nineteenth century. Even classical musicians, hardly regarded as trend setters in the twenty-first century, such as Lady Hallé, Emma Albani, and Dame Clara Butt, were widely photographed and their images used as fashion copy. Classical musicians' wardrobe choices were a point of education and display throughout the 1890s and up to World War I.

THE COUNTER-AUTHORITY OF AUSTRALIAN FASHION DESIGN

The Myer department store conversely took a different approach to their long-term traditional rival David Jones. In their advertisement for elegant evening gowns of the 1930s, they captioned them "Paris? No Melbourne!" and promoted Australian designs at special parades. This cheeky counter-move against the Eurocentric inspiration of Australian dress did not always indicate a nationalist view. The ability to "pass" as authentic European styling was cherished as much as the expression of Australian identity. Possibly the practice (even among the socially prominent) of commissioning local makers to copy illustrations of French garments, claiming them as originals, dated back to the circulation of photographic images of French garments, or perhaps even earlier.

While surviving garments and the social pages in the press indicate that Australians saw nothing second rate in sourcing elegant fashion from Australian makers from the late 1870s onward, the values and style of the extremely wealthy and chic in Australia became an inescapable backdrop and inspirational guide to the less privileged as the twentieth century drew onward. The centrality of elite social life as styling authority came to the fore particularly during the 1920s. There was a strong local nationalist inflection to this celebration of the life and image of the rich. New technologies—particularly in the print media and fashion journalism, promoted by publisher Sydney Ure Smith and Australian Consolidated Press—ensured that images of the ideal fashionable life were circulated more widely than ever before. Ure Smith's flagship *Home* journal, first issued in 1920, and influenced by classy magazines like Condé Nast's *Vogue* and the British upper-class press such as the *Tatler* and the *Queen*, circulated images of the wealthy, their homes, their social events, and their fashions, but for the benefit of a readership that also extended beyond the upper classes. The *Home* featured the talents of Australian artists, couturiers, and fashion photographers and further imbricated the imprimatur of high style with the locally made.

For some, this glamorous lifestyle was only a distant fantasy to be savored from afar, read about in magazines, or seen in newsreels (which included Australian fashion stories from about 1910 onward) when the 1930s economic depression impacted on ordinary women's choices in making and wearing dresses. Frugal housewives kept themselves and their family clothed by sheer ingenuity. Adaptive garments of scrounged fabric survive in museum collections, such as underwear cut from bleached and laundered flour sacks or patchwork made from sales samples of men's suitings. The *Sun* newspaper in Melbourne hosted a competition for cheap chic and renovated garments to respond to economic downturns in the mid-1930s and then during World War II ran a very similar competition following government's "Make Do and Mend" campaigns—suggesting that for some, wartime restrictions were a continuum of ongoing restraint upon their consumption. Clothes rationing was introduced in Australia in 1942, and there are documented evidences of enterprising responses to enforced shortages, such as a wedding dress loaned to several high-society brides in Melbourne during the early 1940s.

The war disrupted not only shipment of textiles and apparel from Britain and France, but also the Axis countries such as Japan and Germany, which were major producers of mass market fabrics. Japanese fabrics were available until Pearl Harbor. During World War II the fad of "harlequin set" bridesmaids dressed in different shades but in the same style of dresses emerged, as it was impossible to find enough cloth of the same shade to clothe the whole wedding party. This fashion outlasted rationing into the early 1950s. Conversely, World War II also extended Australian's choice in fashion. There were a number of artisanal start-up businesses

A painted plastic mannequin torso of the Australian company Bonds's advertising character, Chesty Bond, wearing the Bonds white-cotton, hip-length, sleeveless singlet, ca. 1950. Beginning in the 1930s the Chesty Bond motif was positioned to represent the typical Australian male. By this time singlets had long been associated with the nation's manual workers. Made by Bonds Industries Limited. Powerhouse Museum.

that prospered in the light of widespread shortages of imports—that is, when they could locate raw supplies or devise means of readily adapting available materials—such as the Melbourne Eclarté weavers, who wove fine suitings by hand from about 1940 onwards. Many skilled beaders, embroiderers, and accessory manufacturers who arrived from central Europe as refugees also began to start manufacturing again almost on a craft basis, expanding their businesses to commercial scale in the postwar era. Occasionally labels in surviving dresses suggest that the extremely wealthy and enterprising imported their own fashionable garments from South America, which remained unaffected by the war. Women joined the armed forces in unprecedented numbers, and there was much popular fascination in the press with the image of the well-turned-out, well-groomed young woman in a tailored uniform, suggesting that the war opened out as well as foreclosed upon fashion options. Cosmetics, hairdressing, and personal styling became a site of close attention, too, and offered a point of agency and self-expression in the wake of ongoing shortages.

BEHIND THE FASHION CULTURE: MANUFACTURING

Although the ongoing presence of haute couture ateliers and up-to-date high fashion knowledge for women has been noted, enterprise and vitality were demonstrated at a more functional level of the marketplace in the mass production of textiles and garments. This mass industry was one of the most important for settler Australia from the early 1900s to the 1970s and provided a backbone to the manufacturing economy for nearly a century. It took place in most major capital cities, and in Victoria and New South Wales it spread into regional centers as well. In these establishments there existed totally integrated Australian-based production from raw material to finished garment, in the case of menswear serving a solid clientele that stretched from the working to the upper classes. Many iconic surviving Australian labels—Blundstone and Rossi bootmakers, Driza-Bone, Akubra hatters, R. M. Williams, and Christy's—all date from this period and originally specialized as male outfitters. By the 1930s Fletcher Jones, a wholesale tailor with a vast distribution network based in Warnambool, Victoria, was synonymous with reliability in male outfitting, not to mention liberation from the extremes of fashion. These long-term survivors of the Australian garment trade—if not the fashion industry—originally supplied men and only later on catered to women.

World War I expanded both infrastructure and output in clothing and textile manufacture. The Commonwealth Weaving Mills, in Geelong, were set up in 1911 to ensure that Australia could clothe its cadets and soldiers without relying either upon private companies or on imports, a potential problem during international conflict. Geelong had been a noted center of wool finishing and weaving since the 1880s, and elements of the industry have continued, but apparel products are no longer the main focus.

Despite the early 1890s depression, one mill alone, the Excelsior Mill, employed one hundred people by 1895, and by the end of World War I this number was trebled, due to contracts for army uniforms. Establishing state-run enterprises in dress and textiles reflected the radical left-wing outlook of Andrew Fisher's prime ministership. Governmental participation in the dress, apparel, and textile industries is also demonstrated by the Commonwealth Clothing Factory in Clifton Hill, Melbourne. Established by the Fisher government alongside the textile mills, as an obviously modern integration of the supply chain, in 1912 there were three hundred employees, mostly women. It became an industrial and economic success. It ran for over a half century, through different Australian political regimes, mostly producing uniforms, not only for the military, but also for police and justice divisions, post offices, and tramways. Although uniforms are not fashion per se, they were the everyday and workday dress of many urban Australians, men and women, and their production provided hundreds of jobs.

Australian suitings and locally produced fabrics were not shoddy (inferior woolen cloth made from reprocessed yarn). Retailers enthusiastically advertised their qualities of reliability and serviceability that merited customers' attention. Moreover, it was claimed in Federal Parliament during the 1920s that profit-hungry wholesalers and retailers would fraudulently label Australian fabrics as British and extract a higher markup from the unsuspecting customer. The interesting aspect of this assertion is that the Australian product was of a quality to plausibly sustain the scam. One of the last of the surviving clothing mills, the Yarra Falls, certainly offered woolen fabrics of the finest quality, including pure wool crepes that were treasured by home dressmakers. Production of fabrics such as wool crepe suggests that by the 1930s and 1940s there was also some consideration of a female customer base.

Another similarly functional aspect of dress that became a major player in the national economy was the knitting industry, which produced underwear, sleepwear, swimwear, and hosiery, again often intended for male customers, who were a more stable client base with relatively standardized expectations. Wool was readily available, there were local facilities to process it into yarn, and the importation of knitting machines from Britain and Europe made it easy to set up small manufacturing units that flourished in inner suburban Melbourne and Sydney. Women's fashion impacted upon the hosiery industry. With short skirts in the 1920s and increased visibility of hosiery, local companies expanded rapidly during the 1920s and played an important part in the Australian textile industry. Prestige Knitting Mills products first entered the market in 1922 and included fine quality silk stockings, which sold as well as any imports. The advertising and packaging emphasized fashionability and cosmopolitan glamour, and the founders of the company, the Foletta family, held out against advice from bankers and investors during the 1920s to concentrate on lower-quality items.

Changing mores and increased social freedoms also made swimwear a profitable sector for commercial knitters. The linkage, which remains strong in the twenty-first century, between a widely accepted image of the supposedly relaxed Australian lifestyle and leisure wear became explicit during this period. One iconic company distributing such knitwear was Bonds, founded in 1915 and manufacturing its own product from 1917 onward. A gift to Australian folklore and its vision of masculinity was the 1938 Bonds advertising character Chesty Bond, who in his singlet supposedly represented the average Australian male. Speedo was another manufacturer of knitted garments whose products, especially male swimming trunks, have become a potent sign for Australian identity. Speedo started off as the MacRae Knitting Mills in 1914, producing women's hosiery, and became the swimwear firm Speedo in 1928. Effective design was a foundation block of the company, catering to competitive and amateur swimmers with products like the Racer-Back. The use of the world champion Swedish swimmer Arne Borg (who set records in Australia wearing Speedos, which was also the name of a brand of swimsuit that was manufactured by the company beginning in 1928) was an early form of celebrity product endorsement. The firm's relatively creative ads from 1929 to 1935 focused on comfort and functionality and were an indication that even at this more workaday level the Australian apparel industry was enterprising and certainly not without flair. Victory in races was assured by purchase of Speedos—or so advertising slogans proclaimed.

Industrial production of dress accessories developed from pre-Federation Australia. The shoe industry was mostly concentrated in the inner Melbourne suburbs of Collingwood and Clifton Hill. It was established in the last quarter of the nineteenth century, and, like the processing and spinning of wool, the shoe trade was partly a natural outgrowth of the vast monied interests in Australian rural production, with the cattle industry providing a reliable source of leather. While there was a downturn with the land crash in 1891 to 1892, by the late 1930s the shoe industry was considered to be one of the most important manufacturing industries in Australia. It served the local market and also exported. Commercial hatters became significant as well. Again, they were mostly established in the 1870–1900 period of expansion of colonial manufacturing. The size and complexities of these enterprises should not be underestimated. The Denton hat mills in 1887 boasted 208 employees and a turnover of over thirty thousand (presumably Colonial) pounds per annum at the time. Among the managers of the mill in the 1880s was the son of a Lancashire hatter, again indicating the strong influence that British and European familial traditions played in establishing an effective and sophisticated industrial structure around apparel in Australia. Denton's supported a city retail outlet and also imported supplies for the hat-making industry. While the footwear and hat industries first supplied male customers, increasingly in the early twentieth century, items for a more fashion-conscious female customer were made. Certainly by the end of the first decade of the twentieth century, advertisements for Australian shoes were depicting elegant women in high fashion.

As early as 1910, fashion was posited as a point of distinction about Australia, as much as its democracy, its trade union tradition, its masculine bravery, or its unique flora and fauna. *Grace Brothers Review* stated: "We are among the most becomingly dressed people in the world and are so because our clothes show more individuality and personality than those of any other nation." In 1945, heralding the imminent rebirth of the French fashion industry, *Madame Weigel's Journal of Fashion* (which claimed to be the first Australian-produced and -owned fashion magazine, founded in the 1880s) naturally praised Parisians as embodying a special degree of chic. But she noted that the Australian woman could manage self-presentation with as much aplomb as the fabled Parisienne, even down to the arcane skill of wearing the "little black dress."

References and Further Reading

Amos, Douglas James. *The Story of the Commonwealth Woollen Mills.* Adelaide, Australia: E. J. McAlister & Co., 1934.

Callaway, Anita. "A Right Royal Masquerade: Costume Balls in Nineteenth Century Australia." *Art and Australia* 27, no. 1 (1989): 74–80.

Callaway, Anita. *Visual Ephemera: Theatrical Art in Nineteenth-Century Australia.* Sydney: University of New South Wales Press, 2000.

Clark, Rowena. *Hatches, Matches and Dispatches: Christening, Bridal and Mourning Fashions.* Melbourne, Australia: National Gallery of Victoria, 1987.

Fletcher, Marion. *Costume in Australia, 1788–1901.* Melbourne, Australia: Oxford University Press, 1984.

Holden, Robert. *Cover Up: The Art of Magazine Covers in Australia.* Sydney: Hodder & Stoughton, 1995.

Joel, Alexandra. *Best Dressed: 200 Years of Fashion in Australia.* Sydney: Collins, 1984.

Joel, Alexandra. *Parade: The Story of Fashion in Australia.* Pymble, Australia: Harper Collins, 1998.

Kingston, Beverley. *Basket, Bag and Trolley: A History of Shopping in Australia.* Melbourne, Australia: Oxford University Press, 1994.

Martyn, Norma. *The Look: Australian Women in Their Fashion.* Stanmore: Cassell Australia, 1976.

Maynard, Margaret. *Fashioned from Penury: Dress as Cultural Practice in Colonial Australia.* Melbourne, Australia: Cambridge University Press, 1994.

Maynard, Margaret. *Out of Line: Australian Women and Style.* Sydney: University of New South Wales Press, 2000.

Peers, Juliette. "The Practice of Australian Art: Tom Roberts' Trousers, Dress in Historic Australian Art." *In/Stead* 1 (2005): n.p.

Peers, Juliette. "Paris or Melbourne? Garments as Ambassadors for Australasian Fashion Cultures." In *Generation Mode: Expedition zu den Modeschulen der Welt,* edited by Susanne Anna and Eva Gronbach, 32–153. Ostfildern-Ruit, Germany: Hatje Cantz, 2006.

Webber, Michael John, and Sally Weller. *Refashioning the Rag Trade: Internationalising Australia's Textiles, Clothing and Footwear Industries.* Sydney: University of New South Wales Press, 2001.

Zierer, Clifford M. "Melbourne as a Functional Center." *Annals of the Association of American Geographers* 31, no. 4 (1941): 251–288.

Juliette Peers

See also Resources: Collections of Colonial Dress and Fashion in Australia; Jews in the Melbourne Garment Trade; Fashion Photography in Australia.

Making and Retailing Exclusive Dress in Australia—1940s to 1960s

- The Dressmakers and Milliners: Sydney
- The Dressmakers and Milliners: Melbourne
- Promoting Couture
- Changes in the 1960s

From the 1940s through to the 1960s a handful of Australian society dressmakers, milliners, and quality stores made and sold couture-quality fashion. These key purveyors of exclusive and custom-made dress were found mainly in Sydney and Melbourne. They catered to an elite group of women, regarded as the leaders of fashionable society, whose demands for exclusive styles grew considerably after World War II. In the same period a small number of media organizations and department stores joined forces to present international couture as an entertaining spectacle. A series of dazzling parades toured the major capital cities, thus making high-end fashion more accessible. The growth of ready-to-wear clothing in the late 1950s, with better quality control and sizing, and the more formal licensing of couture designs to manufacturers in Australia also changed the way couture filtered through to the broader market. While this practice had been apparent during the 1920s and 1930s, the marketing of reproduction couture models took a different path in the postwar era when the ready-to-wear market began to make inroads.

The most loyal patrons of exclusive fashion were the women who formed the backbone of Sydney and Melbourne society. Known as the elegant set, they numbered only in the hundreds, and their social activities were frequently reported in newspapers and magazines. This galvanized their status as icons of style. In the postwar era there seemed to be a never-ending stream of glamorous events—fashion parades, luncheons, cocktail parties, receptions, and balls, as well as the coronation of Queen Elizabeth II in 1953 and the Royal Tour of 1954. These events contributed to a resurgence of formality in women's fashion and boosted the market for afternoon, cocktail, and evening wear.

At the very top of the market was a widespread belief that the best fashion came from overseas, above all from Paris. The hegemony of Paris was temporarily challenged during the Nazi occupation, when London, New York, and Beverly Hills acquired a certain cachet, but French haute couture was firmly reinstated after the success of Christian Dior's famous New Look in 1947. Parisian styles, however, were sometimes considered too extreme for the Australian lifestyle, and these trends were often filtered through the designs of British and American fashion houses. The suppliers of exclusive fashion in Australia nevertheless built their reputations around the prestige of the imported model, a finished hat or garment from a highly regarded couture house or milliner, the most newsworthy almost always French.

The couture original formed the basis for further reproductions that were custom-made to clients' orders, but it also served a broader function as a beacon of new trends and standards for the best in design and fabrication. The marketing of reproduction model outfits had been an established part of department and specialty store culture since the 1920s. By the 1940s both appear to have targeted couture models more specifically toward the upper end of the market. Shops like Incley's, Rue de la Paix, and Suzanne et Cie in Melbourne and Curzons and Jean Ducet in Sydney stocked Parisian couture imports while selling copies made in their own workrooms. Department stores such as Myers and Georges in Melbourne and David Jones and Mark Foys in Sydney opened discrete salons, within the stores themselves, where couture models or couture patterns were sold and reproduced. These exclusive zones, such as the French Room at David Jones and the Myers Model Salon and Chandelier Room, were especially popular with country squatters' wives and wealthy city women, as much as Curzons's Salon was with the leaders of Sydney society.

There was an exception to this fascination with Paris. In the late 1930s Georges in Melbourne's Collins Street had repositioned itself as an arbiter of high fashion. Under the direction of Rita Findlay (1893–1954) the store concentrated on retailing the work of leading European and American designers. But from the late 1940s into the 1950s the store appears to have become a significant bastion of English style, with heavy promotion of couturiers such as Peter Russell, Norman Hartnell, and Hardy Amies. Even when Georges stocked Christian Dior, they chose to buy boutique-style garments from the London rather than the Paris branch.

THE DRESSMAKERS AND MILLINERS: SYDNEY

The role of exclusive couture-quality trade within large department stores appears to have varied considerably throughout the postwar years. The few mid-size specialty stores that traded successfully in the 1940s, like Incley's, were less evident in the following decade. For the most part, then, the market for select, custom-made clothing became the province of a small but growing number of discrete society dressmakers and milliners. These businesses offered their clients made-to-measure clothes of the latest European styles, in an exclusive setting somewhere between the atmosphere of a private club and a Parisian couture house. The service and the workmanship of these dressmakers aspired to the heights of a European couture house, and, thus, in the Australian context they were regarded as couturiers.

The wealthy and fashion-conscious women of New South Wales embraced the virtues of European-born talents to the extent that the Sydney dressmaking scene from the 1940s and into the 1960s was largely dominated by a handful of émigrés and their imported skills. Locally born dressmakers and milliners, however, did establish successful businesses despite the fact that Sydney media remained somewhat besotted with the continental style and the charm of the Europeans.

Betty Rose Stormon in the extravagant cream-colored wedding gown that she wore for her marriage to Dr. Bob McInerney in Sydney in May 1952. Consisting of a long, pencil-line silk satin dress with a voluminous overskirt trimmed with silk satin roses, it was the most complicated gown that Beril Jents ever made. Photograph by John Hearder. Gift of Dr. and Mrs. Bob McInerney. Powerhouse Museum.

Madame Paulette Pellier (in business from the 1920s to the 1940s) presided over Sydney's elite dressmaking scene during the 1930s and 1940s. When she returned to France, the mantle passed to Germaine Rocher (working from 1935 until 1971), who rapidly became the city's most celebrated couturier until the 1960s. Russian-born Rocher came to Australia in 1934, having lived in Paris. She quickly earned a reputation for simple yet elegant clothes in haute couture models or her own interpretations. One of her earliest designs was a striking, chevron-striped organdy evening ensemble, published in the *Home* on 1 August 1935. Rocher's clothes maintained a strict demeanor and were rarely overstated. Considered by admirers to be the country's leader of French couture standards, her biannual parades at her King Street salon were popular social events attended by crowds of over two hundred women. Rocher traveled to Paris twice a year to buy models, toiles, fabrics, buttons, and trims.

Escaping Rumania and then Austria, Zita Waine and her family arrived in Australia in 1949 after having worked in Paris for haute couturier Jacques Fath. In 1951 she opened Zita Couture in Double Bay, where she offered compelling interpretations of the latest Parisian trends. The streamlined aesthetic of the salon, designed by the fashionable decorator Marion Hall Best, reflected Waine's own take on fashion: purity of line, flawless tailoring, and impeccable finishing.

Beril Jents (1918–) and Frank Mitchell (1920–1999) were locally born and self-taught dressmakers who did not import models, nor did they offer line-for-line copies. Jents established her business in 1944, perfecting a style, suited to the city's sunny climate, that was bright in tone, palette, and embellishment and exuberant in character. She adopted Christian Dior's New Look as well as his strategy of introducing novel lines each year with themes such as the swan, vamp, and penguin. Her parades had a theatrical character, often drawing on the romance of Hollywood film and appealing to a broad clientele, including the racing fraternity and the society establishment, as well as new moneyed Europeans. Despite the hard-edged glamour of his designs, from the 1950s Mitchell ran a modest trade in Queen Street, Woollahra, that had a small but loyal following among Sydney's well-dressed eastern suburbs women.

Sydney boasted a number of successful milliners in the 1940s and 1950s, such as the Viennese-born Stella Frankel, as well as Maggy Hutchinson, Miss Rawson, Mim Hunter-Kerr, and Madge Wainwright, and also Margot McRae, whose hats drew the praise of Queen Elizabeth II. Few had the prominence and commercial success of Henriette Lamotte (in business from 1938 to 1974), who was dubbed Sydney's most exclusive milliner. Lamotte learned her craft in Paris and arrived in Sydney in 1938 with her husband, the Count d'Espinay, a title that enhanced her appeal. She opened her first shop in 1946, in Darlinghurst. A sense of Parisian frivolity prevailed in Lamotte's work, manifest partly by the whimsical adornments that she used. On her regular trips to Paris she bought model hats by the best French designers, including Jean Barthet, Christian Dior, and the Legroux Soeurs. These models would serve as inspiration for her own designs, often preferred by her customers over the originals. She designed hats to accompany Germaine Rocher's parades, while her own showings and charity parades, held at fashionable lunch and nightspots, were considered "quite the thing to do" among the social set in Sydney.

THE DRESSMAKERS AND MILLINERS: MELBOURNE

At the beginning of the 1940s the center of Melbourne boasted select dressmakers such as Madame Louis Peltier and exclusive dress and millinery salons like Rue de la Paix, Suzanne et Cie, and Incley's, which sold couture models as well as their own workroom reproductions. After World War II the number of society dressmakers increased substantially. They were chiefly located in and around the "Paris end" of Collins Street, as it was affectionately known.

Dominating the custom-made scene in Melbourne were Le Louvre, Hall Ludlow, La Petite, Magg, and Elvie Hill, alongside milliners such as Thomas Harrison. Mostly self-taught, these dressmakers and milliners offered a taste of Paris to the women of Melbourne. They imported couture models for sale and for adaptation, they interpreted Parisian trends with panache, and some created their own designs using luxurious European fabrics and trims.

With its evocatively decorated salon, Le Louvre, which was founded in 1929 by Lillian Wightman (1903–1992), was Melbourne's premier couture dressmaking establishment. Avoiding English clothes because she considered them too rigid, Wightman's success lay in her self-assured blend of establishment conservatism and self-taught Parisian flamboyance. She promoted the work of new French couture houses such as Chanel and Balenciaga, and the store's best-selling dress has been a Molyneux design from the 1930s, which remains popular into the twenty-first century. Alongside the imported offerings, Le Louvre developed its own signature pieces, especially ocelot-print dresses, coats, handbags, and scarves, which became a familiar trait of Melbourne society gatherings.

Pat Rodgers named her Collins Street salon La Petite (in business from 1940 to 1986) in reference to her own tiny stature. Rodgers's aesthetic in the 1950s closely followed the work of Dior, Balenciaga, and Balmain, where she purchased models. La Petite specialized in occasion gowns decorated with intricate hand-worked embroidery, beading, appliqué, and lace. A late 1950s evening dress of velvet and tulle lavishly encrusted with beads and sequins, reproduced in Rodgers's workrooms after a Dior, betrays the faithfulness that can only be achieved by working directly from a model gown.

A number of designers and dressmakers, particularly after World War II, established prestigious salons without the use of imported models and chose instead to create their own designs based on international trends. Hall Ludlow (1919–2003) came to Australia from New Zealand in 1947 and quickly established a clientele, opening a salon decorated like a grand Parisian apartment. His distinctive style combined dramatic silhouettes, full-bodied fabrics, and finely wrought finishes, such as multiple rows of perfect topstitching. Inspired particularly by Balenciaga, Ludlow's skillful approach to design and making earned him numerous accolades as Australia's only true couturier.

Zara Holt (1904–1989) and Betty Grounds (1909–2007), reopened their Magg boutique (1920–1925, 1949–1977) in the wealthy suburb of Toorak. Magg was no less exclusive than its peers but it was considerably less formal. Holt, the label's designer, did not rely on overseas models and was known for her use of strong color and luxurious imported materials. Married to a federal government minister (later the prime minister), Holt understood the desires of wealthy women who attended official functions and galas.

As prominent as the society dressmakers were in Melbourne, their creations were not complete without the custom-made services of numerous milliners in the city. The three most prestigious millinery salons were Ann Austin, William Beale, and Thomas Harrison. Ann Austin opened around 1949. From the salon in the highly fashionable Block Arcade, off Collins Street, they offered the latest international styles, either purchased overseas or reproduced in their workrooms. William Beale, whose salon was at the top end of Collins Street, was known for his theatrical concoctions, for whimsical details and unique materials, an approach much influenced by Schiaparelli's surrealist hat designs.

Melbourne's best-known milliner was Thomas Harrison (1897–1981), who ran a custom millinery from 1929 until 1975. His hats were coveted by women from all over Australia and recognizable for their exceptional finish, inventive forms, and drama. Harrison's handiwork included one-off pieces for individual clients, ranges accompanying the collections of local dressmakers, particularly Le Louvre, and whimsical showpieces. From 1931 until 1968 Harrison's salon in Collins Street was a grand space opulently furnished in the Louis XV style. Harrison was a major importer of model hats by London milliners like Aage Thaarup, Otto Lucas, and Rudolf and Parisians such as Jean Barthet, which he sold and adapted for his clients.

PROMOTING COUTURE

After the war the European fashion industry wasted little time in promoting its image abroad. In Australia the battle lines were

An evening dress (based on a design by Christian Dior), 1956, by Pat Rodgers, La Petite, Melbourne. La Petite specialized in occasion gowns decorated with intricate hand-worked embroidery, beading, appliqué, and lace. Courtesy of the National Gallery of Victoria, Melbourne.

sharpest between the French and British couture industries, which were vying with each other to redress the rapid growth of American imports from the preceding decade. In 1945 a collection of lavish gowns, created for the export trade under the auspices of the Guild of British Creative Designers, was sold to an Australian retailer, and in 1946 David Jones, the Sydney department store, flew five embroidered evening gowns by Norman Hartnell to Sydney to promote British couture and to raise the standards of the local industry. However, within a season of introducing his controversial New Look in 1947, Christian Dior had triumphantly reestablished Paris haute couture as the leading force in high fashion, and for the next decade Australian women once again dreamed of wearing a Paris couture gown.

A number of media organizations and major department stores joined forces to exploit the lofty appeal of haute couture. They shipped collections of high fashion to Australia on special promotional tours that culminated in a series of spectacular parades. These promotions showcased the latest and, sometimes, more extreme fashion trends, especially haute couture from Paris but also high-quality ready-to-wear from London and other European and North American fashion capitals.

The parades were organized by popular women's magazines, particularly *The Australian Women's Weekly*, as well as *Woman's Day* and metropolitan newspapers such as the *Daily Telegraph* and *Sunday Telegraph*, in conjunction with the larger, more prestigious department stores such as Myers, Mark Foys, and David Jones. Staged in Melbourne, Sydney, Brisbane, and Adelaide, they were integrated into the social season of the city's elites. The parades were highly publicized events intended primarily as public relations vehicles for the organizers, the media companies, and the department stores, as well as the participating couture houses. At the time parading of couture was also characteristic of certain Canadian department stores and to an extent some in New Zealand as well. In Australia, as in America, department stores leveraged the prestige of imported and often unattainable couture to gain the cultural capital that affirmed their status as style leaders.

The Australian Women's Weekly's French Fashion Parades were the most spectacular fashion events of the 1940s. Organization of these parades fell to the Weekly's fashion reporter Mary Hordern, who developed the project with Madame Chambrelent, directrice at the House of Worth in Paris. There were four tours starting in 1946 until 1949, selected from the most fashionable Parisian haute couture houses, milliners, and shoe designers. As Margaret Maynard has shown, these parades, which had precedents in popular theatrical fashion events in Australia, marked a dramatic change in the nature of fashion shows and the roles accorded to the mannequins. A contingent of several top French mannequins traveled from Paris especially for the tour and subsequently became celebrities in their own right. The organizers sought to recreate all the glitter and excitement of Paris couture week, with the addition of theatrical settings inspired by iconic monuments such as the Paris Opéra and Dior's couture house on the Avenue Montaigne.

There was a gala premiere in each city, a charitable fundraising event, attended by hundreds of society leaders. Each occasion generated substantial news coverage in print and film newsreel, and later television. Programs of twice-daily parades were staged, including a special parade for business girls on a Saturday morning. This formula became the successful template for subsequent parades of international fashion in Australia up till the 1960s.

In general, the outfits in the Women's Weekly's parades were not intended for sale. Rather, as Louise Mitchell and Danielle Whitfield have shown, the broader ambition of the undertakings was that they would act as a stimulus to the emerging fashion industry in Australia. They gave the average woman a taste of the luxury and quality of French haute couture, hoping that this exposure would raise the standards of the local industry. The imported models also provided the opportunity for the participating department stores and some manufacturers to make accurate copies and credible adaptations affordable to everyday Australian women. As the promoters stressed, these reproductions by local manufacturers, including Adelyn, Leroy, Stell-Ricks, House of Youth, and others, were retailed throughout the country at a wide range of prices to suit all income groups.

The Weekly claimed that their inaugural parade of 1946 featured over 120 garments borrowed from the most important Parisian houses, including Worth, Fath, Lelong, Patou, Molyneux, Carven, and Balmain, and was the first to be shown outside Paris after the war. The second parade premiered in August 1947 at Mark Foys in Sydney, showing ninety-five outfits, which drew from an even broader range of the most up-to-date Paris couture houses and included notable examples, such as Christian Dior's famous Bar suit as well as shoes by Andre Perugia and hats by Maud et Nano. It is recorded that the Weekly purchased the ensembles for the 1947 parades for a sum of £6,000.

In a spirit of mounting rivalry the department stores independently organized high-profile parades in the same vein.

David Jones launched a Paris Fashion for All policy with a parade in 1947 of original models and reproductions made in the store's workrooms, the latter for sale at affordable prices. Within months Myers held their French Reproduction Parade, also aimed at the middle market. In September the same year David Jones achieved a coup by securing the exclusive visit of Paris haute couturier Pierre Balmain to Sydney for a parade of his Round the Clock Fashions. In 1948 David Jones achieved another triumph by bringing Dior's 1948 autumn-winter collection to Sydney, allowing Australians to see at first hand the most exaggerated and thus most definitive examples of the New Look.

The intense focus on French haute couture in the late 1940s gave way, in the 1950s, to a more comprehensive approach, with parades of couture and exclusive ready-to-wear from France, but also from Britain, Ireland, the United States, Germany, Italy, Switzerland, and other European countries. In 1950 the Daily Telegraph, Sunday Telegraph, and Myers brought the Neiman Marcus collection of American Couturier Fashions to Melbourne and then to David Jones in Sydney. The parade showcased the work of fifty American designers, including McCardell, Adrian, Irene, Cashin, and Trigere. Comparisons were made between the similarly relaxed lifestyles of Americans and Australians. One of the best-received designers in Australia during the 1950s was the Irish-based designer Sybil Connolly, who came with a collection of her designs in 1954 and again in 1957 as part of the Irish Fashion Parades organized by The Australian Women's Weekly.

The powerful allure of Parisian haute couture nevertheless reasserted its might in the latter half of the 1950s. In 1956 David Jones collaborated with the Chambre Syndicale de la Couture Parisienne to bring a modest sixty ensembles by thirty-four Parisian designers for their Fashions from the Paris Haute Couture parade. One of the most publicized parades was The Australian Women's Weekly's Christian Dior Autumn Collection, which arrived in November 1957, within weeks of Dior's sudden and unexpected death. Seven of the house's most famous mannequins traveled to Australia along with eighty-three models representing over half of Dior's entire and final collection. Dior had created a number of special models for the tour, with titles such as Australie, Canberra, Melbourne, Sydney, and Wattle. The frenzy surrounding the tour appears to have been due to the immediate novelty of the fashions as much as to Dior's passing. As the program notes declared, "Never before has any country outside France itself been privileged to see so many of Dior's top models nor so large a part of his current collection, within so short a time of the Paris Premiere."

Toward the end of the decade, department stores began to introduce showings of local Australian fashions, a practice that became more common in following decades with the developing profile of Australian designers. The reputation of local designers had earlier received a boost in prestige through the establishment of the Australian Wool Bureau Fashion Awards in 1954 and the Gown of the Year competition, inaugurated in 1953. French fashion parades nevertheless continued to feature prominently, although with less frequency than before. In 1959 The Australian Women's Weekly's Paris Parades introduced the work of younger French haute couturiers such as Cardin, Saint Laurent, and Ricci. A novel aspect of these promotions was the Anyone Can Win competition, for which the prize was an original Paris model for six successful readers.

French fashion models on a French Fashion Parades tour at Geiger's Handbag Shop in Collins Street, Melbourne, 1946. Organized by reporter Mary Hordern (*The Australian Women's Weekly*) and Madame Chambrelent, directrice at the House of Worth in Paris, the tours of the most fashionable couture shops sought to recreate all the glitter and excitement of Paris couture week and act as a stimulus to the emerging Australian fashion industry. Photograph by Wolfgang Sievers. State Library of Victoria.

CHANGES IN THE 1960s

Rapid development and changing demographics leading up to the 1960s encouraged Melbourne's dressmakers and milliners to move closer to their wealthy clients, many of whom lived in the leafy environs of Toorak and South Yarra. Elvie Pelman opened Elvie Hill in Collins Street, where she offered custom-made clothes between 1956 and 1991 and marketed ready-to-wear throughout the country. The Parisian-trained Leonard Legge (1917–1998) established Raoul Couture in Toorak (ca. 1958 and continuing until 1964), where he maintained a strictly couture-style approach. Robert Fritzlaff (1931–) benefited from formal couture studies in Paris and returned to Melbourne to establish a custom-made salon in Toorak in 1961. Erna Vilks and Arija Austin opened Tu boutique in South Yarra in 1963, specializing in custom-made clothes.

At this time the practice of importing and reproducing couture models began to wane, although this did not cease altogether until the early 1970s. A new youth market was opening up that was to spell change for the future. A small number of couture-minded dressmakers did open businesses, seemingly against the tide, some even sustaining their practices well into the 1980s,

albeit for an increasingly conservative clientele. But handmade fashions now had to compete with the ever-more-popular market for ready-to-wear clothes. After financial difficulties Ludlow relocated his business to Sydney in 1960 and, after three years, to Hong Kong, where he designed custom-made and ready-to-wear collections for export to the United States. When Wightman's daughter Georgina Weir entered the business in the 1960s, Le Louvre embraced more youthful, ready-to-wear labels.

The 1960s was a decade of change, in which custom-made clothing was dealt a severe blow by a ready-to-wear industry of well-made clothes in Australia, which had been growing during the 1950s. A number of Australian dress companies, such as Lucas and Leroy, obtained the rights to copy and mass-produce couture originals. The period saw a growing interest in local talent and a declining concern for postwar formality, which contributed to a decrease in the frequency of the large international parades. In their stead was a succession of promotions and parades featuring Australian ready-to-wear fashion, which, in general, was aimed at the middle market. In 1960 David Jones staged its first Australian Show. In 1962 *The Australian Women's Weekly* organized the First All-Australian Fashion Parades, and department stores including David Jones–produced shows with titles such as Wool's Wild

Colonial Colours (1963) and Welcome Winter in the Luxury of (True Blue) Wool (1965). Beginning in 1965 the Australian Wool Board organized a series of high-profile awards and parades that raised the profile of local designers.

By the late 1960s international couture no longer mesmerized the Australian market and, indeed, seemed irrelevant in a fast-changing world. The notion of exclusivity was in itself becoming outdated as more egalitarian impulses filtered through to the world of fashion. Custom-made clothing was associated with an older generation, and consumers were demonstrating a strong interest in local talent, design, and manufacture. The virtues of elite fashion may have been overlooked during the next few decades; however, the work of several generations of high-quality couture dressmakers, retailers, and promoters left an indelible legacy of craftsmanship, sophistication, and style.

References and Further Reading

Healy, Robyn. *Dressed to the Eyes: The Fashions of Hall Ludlow.* Melbourne, Australia: RMIT Gallery, 2005.

Jents, Beryl. *Little Ol Beryl from Bondi.* Sydney: Pan Macmillan, 1993.

Joel, Alexandra. *Parade: The Story of Fashion in Australia.* Sydney: Harper Collins Publishers, 1998.

Leong, Roger. "Sydney's Most Fashionable Europeans." In *The Europeans: Emigré Artists in Australia, 1930–1960,* edited by Roger Butler, 209–210. Canberra: National Gallery of Australia, 1997.

Loxley, Anne. *Belles of the Ball: 60 Years of the Black and White Committee.* Sydney: State Library of New South Wales, 1997.

Maynard, Margaret. *Out of Line: Australian Women and Style.* Sydney: University of New South Wales Press, 2001.

Mitchell, Louise. *Christian Dior: The Magic of Fashion.* Sydney: Powerhouse Museum, 1994.

Somerville, Katie, and Danielle Whitfield. *Thomas Harrison: Milliner.* Melbourne, Australia: National Gallery of Victoria, 2006.

Whitfield, Danielle. "La Mode Française Australian Style." In *The Paris End: Photography, Fashion and Glamour,* edited by Susan van Wyk, 105–113. Melbourne, Australia: National Gallery of Victoria, 2006.

Winkworth, Kylie. "Dress in the Fifties." In *The Australian Dream: Design of the Fifties,* edited by Judith O'Callaghan, 59–73. Sydney: Powerhouse Museum, 1993.

Roger Leong

See also Urban Fashion Culture in Australia.

The Melbourne Cup and Racewear in Australia

- Fashions for the Track
- The Melbourne Cup
- Further Changes to Fashion and Racing Culture

Racewear is a highly visible (and commercially lucrative) sub-genre of apparel in Australia. The genre is broadly characterized by persistent trans-seasonal traits of formality and a visible degree of conscious nostalgia or conservative styling, most notably the persistence of hats throughout the last quarter of the twentieth century when they had generally disappeared from fashionable female day-wear. There is also a wider range of colors worn than the generally strictly regulated forecast color palettes of commercial fashion, and a stronger emphasis on print and patterning detail. Although male racewear is perhaps not so high in profile, it similarly emphasizes a formality of components often absent from everyday dress of the time, for example, in the twenty-first century, insistence upon a tie. Norms of racewear are promulgated by strict dress codes stipulated by many racetracks in Australian state capital cities. Such dress codes are explicitly detailed in promotional pre-event coverage of racing events by the press and also on racing clubs' Web sites. Remarkably these laws are not seen as restrictive but are promoted adroitly by the racing clubs as demonstrating the racing experience's special and singular glamour, and marking racing's difference from cricket or football (including rugby and soccer) spectatorship, not to mention other racing codes from cars to greyhounds. Many forms of popular everyday garments for both genders are often forbidden in the members' reserves of Australian racetracks, including windbreakers, hoodies (jackets with hoods), knitted cardigans, jeans, sports shoes, thongs (sandals), tracksuits, and shorts.

Racewear also encompasses a contradictory genre to these conservative directives. This contradiction features eye-catching and startling styling, including millinery, that crosses over into costuming. The flat green picture hat upon whose brim plastic horses are set out in race formation is a perennial cliché. Such attention-seeking dress has flourished and expanded in the wake of the widespread post–World War II coverage of trackside dress at premium celebrity meets in both the print and electronic media, although press descriptions suggest there were incipient forms of extroverted display visible even among otherwise respectable matrons in the nineteenth century. Unusual and novelty outfits at important events also blend with a more rowdy and vernacular parody of formal dress among less wealthy race patrons, especially males. Parody dressing has in the last three decades captured press attention, as much as more formal outfits. The elaborate sculptural headwear constructed from empty beer cans at outback race meetings such as the Birdsville Races (Queensland) also directly references, as well as mocks, the importance of millinery to female fashion at city-based meets. Millinery made of beer cans, sometimes combined with crochet, was a popular Australian vernacular craft in the 1970s especially but remains visible at more informal race meetings.

Like formal racewear, parody dressing demonstrates the manner in which fashion and dress as a hyperbolic, competitive, and hedonistic theater of display and observation have become, in the last half century, the quintessential touchstone of the Australian experience of professional thoroughbred racing. Fashion has greatly sustained and supported the Australian racing industry in economic earnings and media visibility during the last three decades. There is also a highly reflexive social and cultural relationship between the formal and the disorderly, the aspirational and the satiric that speaks specifically of Australian practices and offers a different inflection to press coverage of racewear outside Australia. Despite the clear angling for press attention and short-term celebrity via showy hats at Royal Ascot, for example, Australian dress stratagems are equally directed to peers and fellow race goers as to roaming television cameras. Racewear also indicates how high fashion has always been a vernacular participator's sport as much as an authoritative forecasting edict in settler Australia.

FASHIONS FOR THE TRACK

Fashion's relationship to the Australian racing industry has undergone complex changes in the past two centuries. High society always played a part in racing. The earliest race meetings were organized by officers of the British 73rd regiment, the first in Sydney in 1810, and an extension of the expected gentlemanly country pursuits characteristic of British aristocratic lifestyle. Good breeding in racehorses was believed to uphold the quality of cavalry and military horse stock, and horsemanship was essential to officer training and demeanor. Thus, racing was linked to the efficient governance and power hierarchies of the Australian colonies. As one of the trophies was presented in person by Elizabeth Macquarie, the governor's wife, on behalf of the "ladies of the colonies," it is clear that elite women were also expected to show an interest in racing and would have attended in their best outfits. An observer noted that the first race meeting held in Australia was graced by "all the Beauty and Fashion" that the city of Sydney then offered. In the Eurocentric social life of nineteenth-century Australia, racing became closely linked to the social calendar. Governors attended with state ceremony, often being drawn down the straight in an open landau, with military escort, or, for more dash, driving themselves and their associates in a four-in-hand or a six-in-hand vehicle. In presenting awards and gracing official podia, boxes, and stands, governors and their extended family and connections replicated the expected symbolic display function of royalty—the showing of the "king's body" of the northern hemisphere—for the colonies. Of course, women in the party were the focus of all eyes.

Dress is an essential aspect of making an impact within this volatile arena. The presence of highly elaborate fashionable wear at major Australia race meetings is documented immediately after the emergence of the illustrated papers in the 1870s and remains a key to the visual setting of premier Australian racing up to the twenty-first century. Conversely, bookmakers and their staff have consciously styled themselves with loud vaudevillian dressing, emphatically patterned suits, showy hats, badges, and

Women wearing fashionable dress accessorized with hats, gloves, and bags at the Centenary Melbourne Cup, 1960. In the early 1960s the Fashions on the Field competition was established, which encouraged a more feminine tone at the races. Photograph by Cliff Bottomley. National Archives of Australia: A1200, L36676.

rosettes to distinguish themselves from the mass of their clients, especially in the early and mid-nineteenth century when they had no fixed platforms but constantly roamed among their potential clients. Legendary early-twentieth-century Melbourne book-maker Sol Green, for example, challenged the dubious social status of both Jews and bookmakers by styling himself as a dandy in high-quality tailored garments and accessories and concentrating vulgar display on his Rolls Royce, generally rumored by an adoring public to have twenty-four-karat gold fittings. Later in the twentieth century male trackside officials' and bookmakers' dress became more sober, possibly due to the strongly conservative nature of men's clothing in Australia at this period. However, by the 1970s the conservative styling of males at the racetrack, possibly consciously referencing international trends of nostalgia for 1920s and 1930s gangster and pimp styling in menswear, also recalled the heyday of Australian racing in the interwar period. Trackside male dress acquired a distinctly performative (rather then simply default) nostalgia, and the fedora hat is often seen as the key symbol of the "racing man" as much as the expensive and old-fashioned binoculars.

Australian racewear has changed over the years, but the racetrack was, and remains, a forum for the elites to be seen on display. Moreover, it is not another example of the invented, nonseasonal, so-called traditions of ritualized apparel that have mushroomed throughout the twentieth century in Western (and non-Western) cultures, including debutante dresses, cotillion parties, bridal gowns, wedding guest fashions, child beauty pageant dressing, ballroom dancing outfits, and dressage wear, to name some examples. The complexity of the genre expresses the central, contradictory, and multistranded positioning of the racing industry in settler Australian social life. At the start it was royalty, aristocracy, and vice-regal households (and their associated visiting relatives from England and employees such as aides de camp and diplomatic attachés) who were the center of the spectacle. In the twenty-first century this role is performed more frequently by media and entertainment celebrities, including paid/sponsored guests of honor from overseas, sometimes actual stars or supermodels, sometimes faux celebrities of more obscure reputation. Simultaneously, racing has always been a locus of all types of disreputable—even criminal—behaviors, from race

The formality of this typical 1960 Melbourne Cup race outfit, accessorized with hat and gloves, was to be challenged by U.K. model Jean Shrimpton when she attended the Derby at Flemington a few years later with a skirt that ended four inches (about ten centimeters) above the knee, hatless, gloveless, and wearing no stockings. Photograph by Cliff Bottomley. National Archives of Australia: A1200, L36675.

fixing to money laundering. In the nineteenth and early twentieth centuries racing was an avenue of social advancement in Australia, offering to the underclasses the elusive hope of spectacular economic return, as punter, trainer, jockey, owner, or bookmaker. Racing culture was a fulcrum of social mix and blur, and a point of meeting of diverse strands in settler society.

THE MELBOURNE CUP

The Melbourne Cup, founded in 1861 and run on the first Tuesday in November at Flemington Race Course every year, rapidly established itself as both the highest professional challenge of horseracing and the most desirable social event on the Australian continent. By the 1880s and 1890s elites from across the country, including colonial governors, met to socialize at the Melbourne Cup. Around the Cup itself clustered ancillary race fixtures on other days before and after the great event, and many social functions: balls, garden parties, and dinners. The social photographer Walter Barnett produced the first formally organized extended film sequence taken in Australia around the Melbourne Cup of 1896. This significant choice of subject indicates how the Cup was the popular and symbolic center of white experience in Australia. The film provides a continual parade of elaborate and formal fashion for both men and women, as it was mostly shot in the members' reserve, for indeed the horses were more difficult to capture on early movie cameras than were the spectators. The Oaks Day race meeting became known as Ladies Day and was equally renowned for fashionable wear as Cup day itself.

Melbourne Cup festivities were the colonial version of the London "season," at least up to World War II. Pages were devoted

in the press to describing the dress of the women in attendance at both day and evening functions. By the 1880s social commentators were tartly noting how prudent and parsimonious Melbourne beauties gave their Cup day dresses a second airing, without any attempt at renovating or remaking, for the summer race fixtures that started as early as Boxing Day and New Year's Day. Industrial reformers documented that conditions in dressmakers' workrooms were appalling during the lead-up to the Melbourne Cup festivities, with many new hands being taken on for short periods with no job security and seamstresses forced to work late into the night or even twenty-four hours nonstop to meet orders. In the interwar period racing assumed enormous popularity, with the emergence of mass entertainment and more working-class leisure opportunities that arose in tandem with the expansion of the manufacturing base in urban Australia, but also greater workplace and union regulation. New stands and expanded public amenities such as on-course betting and eating facilities were built to accommodate huge crowds, including women who were expected to be well dressed and presented. Racing was still a driver of the fashion industry in Australia, with the traditional racing carnival periods of spring, summer, and Easter catalyzing high-volume retail turnover.

Since World War II the popularity and the high reputation of racing have diminished. Audiences at the track dwindled particularly with the rise of electronic media and with the disappearance of horses from everyday urban life. At the same time fashion, once an inevitable but incidental expression of the role of racing in serving elite interests, has become an important medium for selling and making over the potential appeal of racing to an urban population that have neither moneyed connections to pastoral wealth nor direct workplace contact to horses. The first move toward this changed relationship came not solely from the racing industry but was a corollary of the expanded modalities of fashion marketing and promotion in postwar Australia, particularly at an industry and national trade level. Jean Shrimpton's iconic visit, in a sleeveless above-the-knee synthetic shift dress without hat, gloves, or pantyhose, to Derby Day Melbourne, 30 October 1965 (not as generally assumed even by fashion historians the Melbourne Cup a few days later, where she actually wore a more conservative suit), is usually regarded as marking the advent of "youthquake" fashion in Australia. Her Australian tour was sponsored by the makers of the synthetic fabric Orlon (DuPont) as well as by the Victorian Racing Club. Shrimpton's visit to the spring racing carnival has even been credited anecdotally with establishing the popularity of British mod fashion outside Britain. Promoting fashion at the races was related to highly publicized parades and trade displays in department stores and public spaces during the 1950s, backed up by detailed advertorial coverage in the media.

Important to renewing the appeal of racing was the Fashions on the Field competition established at the Melbourne Cup in 1962 (although smaller experiments with fashion promotion had been toyed with by the Victorian Racing Club since the very late 1950s). The aim was to encourage a better tone, and more feminine culture, on the racetrack, which was increasingly perceived as more masculinist and raffish than ever before. Although monied interests still bought and raced horses, it was feared that thoroughbred racing was increasingly out of step with social mores in wider Australian society and potentially losing relevance to many people. Fashions on the Field was a successful attempt to market

Deborah Thomas at the Melbourne Cup, 1977, in a breast-shaped hat. This photograph was used on the cover of the October 1978 *Bulletin* alongside the headline "Melbourne Madness." There was a growing trend toward the rowdy vernacular in Cup fashions during the 1970s. Photograph by Rennie Ellis. © Rennie Ellis Photographic Archive.

the racetrack as a place of glamour, encourage a more woman-friendly, female-centered social ambience, and ensure that thoroughbred racing would not be dismissed as a gritty subcultural pastime, like greyhound racing and certain vehicle racing codes. Concurrently, Fashions on the Field offered new marketing opportunities and facilitated a raft of product placements for the nascent publicity and marketing sectors in Australia at that period, including prizes supplied by the fashion, cosmetic, and travel industries. Links to the beauty pageant, also a popular feature of public life at this era, were obvious. At the same time Fashions on the Field expressed typical mid-century anxiety about visible female self-management and took care not to overtly promote frivolous extravagance or uncontained narcissism. In the early years prizes included categories for small-budget and homemade outfits. Contestants were expected to swear on a Bible as to the cost of their outfit or that they had sewed it themselves and were even photographed for the press taking this oath, as demonstration of refined female behavior in public.

FURTHER CHANGES TO FASHION AND RACING CULTURE

In 1971 the Fashions on the Field competition, as a formal entity on Melbourne Cup day, lapsed, but there remained a vestigial structure of competitions and prizes for well-dressed race goers throughout the decade. While the rules and management of fashion competitions at Flemington Race Course varied from year to year, the general concept never was fully abolished. During the 1970s a rowdy vernacular culture of satiric dressing for the Cup emerged, with favorite classics immediately being established, including the dinner jacket teamed with underpants, the T-shirt printed with the outlines of a tuxedo with floral buttonhole, the scuba diving gear with flippers on dry land, the sleepwear as day-wear, males in tutus or fairy dress, nun's habits, the hired historical dress from ancient Rome to the 1920s, superhero, cosplay-type (Japanese animé-styled whole-body outfits, often in molded plastics), and animal outfits. The latter includes (of course) pantomime horse suits or sometimes horses' heads worn with otherwise conventional racewear. From the 1970s onward outfits, straight or bent, were, and still are, coordinated by groups as well as individuals for extra visual effect.

In 1981 Fashions on the Field was revived. The Myer department store became principal sponsor in 1983 and has been closely associated with the event ever since. Fortuitously, the competition resonated with the 1980s materialistic ethos of display and flourished as never before. Two and a half decades later Fashions on the Field was still a core feature of the Melbourne Cup, with a number of specialized competition categories such as Millinery awards, and from 2001 a competition for Men's Classic Racewear. Competition has become codified at a national level, with regional finalists from different race meets competing for an overall grand prize during the spring racing carnival in Melbourne. Since the 1980s the Fashions on the Field concept has been extended to many provincial meetings across the nation to attract a young and more style-driven clientele and also to rescue economically precarious racing clubs.

Not only are garments per se promoted through this linkage between racing and fashion marketing, major cosmetic companies are setting up shop on the courses. "Pamper tents," with professional makeup artists and stylists in attendance, are an important point of sale for new products. The more exclusive "corporate marquees" offer similar services for free, but for invited guests only. Slow food, gourmet specialties, fine wines, and local produce are other typical promotional crossovers in trackside festivities across Australia. These promotional stratagems are increasingly overlapping with the typical activities seen around fashion festivals and fashion weeks in Australia, especially the high level of novelty in-servicing and free gifts to VIPs and the paid importation of international celebrities from the fashion and entertainment industries. Other major racing fixtures, such as the Sydney-based Easter racing carnival, are also formalizing the links between fashion, leisure, lifestyle promotion, and a glamourous trackside ambience pioneered by the Melbourne Cup and its host body, the Victorian Racing Club, since the 1960s.

Ironically, as the fashion at the racetracks grows ever more elaborate and costly for even the ordinary punter, a heavy drinking culture has developed, particularly outside the highly regulated members' enclosure, that stands at odds with the consciously red-carpet or princess styling that race goers aspire to. However, this juxtaposition continues the tradition of contrary or mixed messages that cluster around Australian racing culture, which are so clearly mirrored in racing fashions. Despite, or because of, the drinking culture, the Melbourne Cup, particularly since the late twentieth century, has attracted a large component of adolescent schoolgirls. Although Cup Day itself is a public holiday, girls skip classes on other days throughout the spring racing carnival to attend race meetings in highly formal and expensive outfits, often of much beauty and displaying intense skill and application in personal styling. Since about 2003 embrace of racewear culture has been expanding rather than diminishing, as new groups join in the self-conscious display. Remarkably, adolescent males have also enthusiastically taken up the formal aesthetic of racewear in very recent years, willingly wearing suits, ties, and even nostalgic-styled hats, when they usually would actively resist such signs of regularized, conservatively inflected dressing practices and formats.

Orthodox racewear is now as popular as satiric dressing among young males. Visiting Asian university students are another highly visible social group who since the early twenty-first century have been flocking to the Melbourne Cup and associated race fixtures while again conforming faithfully to highly ritualized dress codes that clearly cross age, class, and cultural divisions. Racewear is also worn to off-course social events during the spring racing carnival around Australia, such as racing-themed parties and interstate live video hook-ups of racing events, and even to workplace events, denoting an increasingly widespread and popular participation in the spirit and ethos of the Melbourne Cup and the spring racing carnival.

References and Further Reading

Cavanough, Maurice. *The Melbourne Cup, 1861–1982*. Melbourne, Australia: Currey O'Neil, 1983.

Fletcher, Marion. *Costume in Australia, 1788–1901*. Melbourne, Australia: Oxford University Press, 1984.

Goldsworthy, Shirley, and Annette Shiell. *A Passion for Fashion: A History of the Fashions on the Field Competition*. Caulfield: Australian Racing Museum, 1999.

Hayes, Mike. *The Track: The Story of Good Breeding and Bad Behaviour.* Sydney: ABC Books for the Australian Broadcasting Corporation, 2000.

Joel, Alexandra. *Best Dressed: 200 Years of Fashion in Australia.* Sydney: Collins, 1984.

Lemon, Andrew. *The History of Australian Thoroughbred Racing.* 2 vols. Melbourne, Australia: Classic Reproductions, 1987–1990.

Pollard, Jack. *The Pictorial History of Australian Horse Racing.* Sydney: Hodder & Stoughton, 1989.

Juliette Peers

See also Urban Fashion Culture in Australia; Global Positioning of Australian Fashion.

Cosmetics and Beauty Culture in Australia

Cosmetics and beauty culture are forms of body modification that have a place in the language of all cultures of fashion and dress. Australia has both indigenous and European traditions of body modification and aesthetics. In precontact times indigenous traditions were centrally connected with ritualistic practices, but they were also about making the body attractive. After European settlement colonists largely followed the cosmetic practices and beauty cultures of Europe and America. Among European settlers these became symbols of racial superiority and civility, and early Australians developed a passion for keeping up with the latest products and beauty practices, both using homemade products and importing European ones. A contributing factor was the effect of the harsh climate (hot, humid, dry) on sensitive Anglo-Saxon skin. While men by and large endured these effects and were celebrated as "bronzed Aussie battlers," colonial women tried to protect their skin and look as best they could using soap, rudimentary skin lotions, and hair oil. Women's magazines, newspaper features (on the "women's" pages), etiquette manuals, and visual culture reflected this passion for cosmetics and obsession with beauty culture as an integral part of building the new colony and civilizing its customs.

So the history of commodity beauty culture in Australia mirrors the emergence of a distinctive sense of Australian femininity and successive models of ideal Australian womanhood. Accordingly, concerns about cosmetics and beauty culture have shaped a national sense of dress style and cultural identity. While body building was an important activity for men from early in the twentieth century, and of course the role of a man's barber cannot be underestimated, since the 1980s men have also become keen consumers of cosmetics, skin care products, hair gels, and associated routines. Children as well have become a significant market for specially formulated skin-care and sun-block products—and even makeup and perfume. As migrant groups with different skin types and customs have altered the population demographics, products for Mediterranean, Asian, and other skin types have also proliferated. Although multinational brands dominate contemporary beauty culture, niche Australian brands offer locally made products and services that use local ingredients.

BODY MODIFICATION AND BEAUTIFICATION IN COLONIAL AUSTRALIA

The story of modern cosmetics and beauty routines in Australia runs parallel to the story of the development of modern femininity. However, treatments for the skin and body (cleansing lotions, oils, and balms) have existed in all cultures and at all times, and the use of enhancements for the skin (coloring, manipulation, tonics, and medicinal products) has a long history. Indigenous Australians modified their bodies by embellishing the surface for over forty thousand years as part of ancient traditions. Practices included body painting, hair styling, tooth avulsion, nasal piercing, and scarification. Permanent body alterations such as scarification often coincided with rites of passage. Early explorers and anthropologists were impressed by the complexity and variability of Aboriginal forms of body modification, but it was little if ever seen by Europeans in major urban areas.

The cultivation of European beauty accompanied the emergence of civility (especially during the eighteenth century), when makeup (white face and red cheeks) was a key part of self-presentation for royalty and the elite, although copied by aspiring classes. However, the idea of beauty products and treatments fell out of favor in the Victorian era during the nineteenth century, when they became imbued with moral approbation as visible signs of sin and sex, largely relegated to the theater and prostitution. Beauty products were still regarded with suspicion in the early 1900s, and women chose products that were barely visible to the observer. Cold creams, rice powder for the face, and toilet water were permitted, but rouge on the cheeks and coloring of the lips or eyelids were deemed excessive. The beauty products that existed were mostly homemade, using recipes handed down and around (just as recipes for food are today). They used locally available ingredients like flowers, herbs, and plants that contained natural oils, moisture, scents, and therapeutic and medicinal properties. Folklore and alchemy were an integral part of early beauty cultures.

When Australia was settled by Europeans in 1788, it is unlikely that the supply of beauty products was a priority for the colonists, and certainly not for the convicts, although undoubtedly recipes for skin treatments, cosmetics, and medicines arrived as oral traditions and possibly in women's luggage. It seems likely, however, that beauty culture remained based on English and European traditions rather than adopting Australian indigenous customs—although it is possible (and has been argued in the case of Helena Rubinstein) that some eastern practices were learned during stopovers on the long sea journey to the colony. Generally, however, we must assume that Australian women "made do" with creams, soap, and hair oil that were homemade and increasingly used local alternatives to replace scarce imported ingredients up until the beauty culture revolution of the 1910s.

Why this revolution occurred has been the subject of some speculation, due to the radical turnaround from condemning to embracing beauty culture and cosmetics in just a few years. It seems to have been the conjunction of several factors: new roles for women; the popularity of eugenics and the physical culture movement (which extolled the benefits of regimented exercise and dance as the key to achieving the body beautiful); new ideals of femininity; the proliferation of consumer culture; the birth of modern advertising; the rise of the Hollywood film industry and growth of the star system; and the growing importance of American approaches to business culture that globally transformed patterns of import and export. In the case of Australia no one epitomizes these factors better than Helena Rubinstein.

HELENA RUBENSTEIN AS BEAUTY ENTREPRENEUR

Australia's greatest claim to fame regarding the development of modern cosmetics and beauty culture is arguably the period spent by Helena Rubinstein in Australia. Rubinstein (1870–1965) was Polish (born in Krakow) and came to Australia seeking escape from homeland poverty (and an arranged marriage) in 1896. En route, she spent a few years in Vienna—then the center of dermatological knowledge—and may have acquired her fascination with cosmetic potions there. Pale skin was the ideal, and early products sought to enhance and maintain whiteness and softness. Rubinstein was very striking, with beautiful skin, something apocryphally attributed to her eastern European heritage and the custom of skin care maintained by women living there to deal with the effect on the skin of harsh winters and dry summers. Homemade skin-care products based on recipes handed down through generations aimed to moisturize and protect the skin by forming a barrier (hence the term *barrier cream*). Rubinstein purportedly brought jars of her family's skin-care potion with her (supposedly made by a chemist friend of her mother's, Jacob Lykusky, although this cannot be verified).

Staying with an uncle at Coleraine, a small town set among sheep farms in western Victoria, she did not fit in. The locals regarded her as "haughty and difficult," and she hated what she called "that awful place." She was also shocked by the red, cracked, and raw skin of Australian women due to the extreme climatic conditions, who reportedly admired her complexion and sought her secret. Rubinstein hated the sun and the heat, a lifelong passion that drove her to develop one of the first sun-block creams. After three "miserable years," she left. But she had found the miracle ingredient that was to become the secret of her cosmetic empire—lanolin, or natural sheep oil—which was a cheap, plentiful, and effective softener to use in creating moisturizing and protecting skin-care cosmetics.

What happened then is a matter of dispute, as Rubinstein was adept at reinventing the past. After moving to Melbourne, she began making potions and learning the basics of cosmetic manufacture—after a stint in Queensland where she possibly gained some familiarity with indigenous therapeutic and medicinal uses of native plants (especially water lilies), trees (tea tree and eucalyptus), and bark (from hoop, bunya, cyprus, and kauri pines). She enjoyed experimenting with potions and creams in what she called her "kitchen" and continued to play a hands-on role in her laboratories for the rest of her life. She called herself a "beauty scientist" and dressed her assistants in red laboratory uniforms to emphasize the scientific theme. After securing financial backing and technical expertise provided by Victoria's leading pharmaceutical company, Rubinstein was ready to launch her first commercial cosmetic product.

In 1903 she opened a beauty salon at 138 Elizabeth Street, Melbourne, and began selling Crème Valaze, marketed as a combined cold cream and barrier cream (with even the ability to remove freckles). Although she claimed that the cream was imported from Europe (made from "rare herbs" found only in the "Carpathian Mountains"), the cream was manufactured and packaged in her kitchen (and later factory) by herself and assistants. Instead of rare herbs, the cream was based on locally sourced lanolin and paraffin scented with rose, pine bark, and water lilies. But Rubinstein quickly realized the value of exoticism to market her cream and adopted an advertising formula based on offering women a miracle cream with transformative powers all the way from cosmopolitan Europe.

Later endorsed by the famous Australian actress Nellie Stewart (1858–1931), who was renowned for her beautiful complexion and attention to skin care, Rubinstein was soon expanding production to meet demand for her cream. She offered women not just something practical but a magical potion to redress skin damage. More importantly, she advocated a daily regime of skin care that used perfumed products, identified different skin types (dry, normal, and oily), and offered a range of treatments for diverse skin conditions. The "need" for diverse products to address particular "problems" drove product development and diversification. Rubinstein also distributed a pamphlet, "Guide to Beauty," which instructed women on self-help beauty tips and made use of fear as a factor, through copy that first criticized a woman's appearance before offering the solution. This genre of beauty advice became the model for the industry. Rubinstein had captured a lucrative clientele desperate for reassurance and transformation. For women who lived in the bush, mail-order catalogs were an essential lifeline to the city. Recognizing this, Rubinstein established a mail-order service for her products as well as stocking them in "good chemists" throughout Australia, thus guaranteeing access to her brand throughout the vast continent.

Such was the margin between the cost of production (10 pence) and sale price (6 shillings) that Rubinstein made enough money (£12,000) in just two years to expand her operation to Sydney and New Zealand, where she opened salons. However, bigger markets beckoned, and she left for Europe in 1905. After familiarizing herself with continental trends in beauty culture, she opened salons in London (1908) and Paris (1909). But she realized that America offered even better opportunities. Her first salon opened in New York in 1916. Inspired by the range of beauty treatments and spas available in Europe, Rubinstein expanded her products and services accordingly. Although she realized that Europe and America were better places to consolidate her business, she retained her Australian (and later New Zealand) salons under the care of her sisters until the 1940s, when she began to concentrate on wholesale. The Helena Rubinstein name persisted as a cornerstone of Australian beauty culture in dedicated Helena Rubinstein counters and window displays in department and fashion stores and chemists (pharmacies), Helena Rubinstein Beauty Schools, and extensive media advertising.

For practical reasons Rubinstein took Australian citizenship in 1907, but she never identified with Australia, although she made periodic visits to Australia when she played the celebrity expatriate star for a salivating media and public. She charmed interviewers and sealed her popularity by presenting them with samples of her products. So Australia's involvement with the birth of modern cosmetics is a somewhat ambiguous one. Nonetheless, Rubinstein epitomized the first generation of cosmetic brands, in that she was a formidable, energetic, marketing-conscious, and innovative female entrepreneur at a time when few women were in the paid workforce, let alone running international businesses. Others included her great rival, Elizabeth Arden, and, later, another self-made entrepreneur, Estée Lauder. Male competitors included Max Factor (who developed cosmetics for film and created the "looks" of much-imitated Hollywood stars) and Charles Revson (founder of Revlon, who made his fortune selling nail polish).

The entertainer Jenny Howard using Helena Rubinstein cosmetics, 1957. Rubinstein was a self-made entrepreneur and was one of the first to use lanolin, or natural sheep oil, as an ingredient in her cosmetics. State Library of New South Wales.

THE COMMERCIALIZATION OF AUSTRALIAN BEAUTY CULTURE

Rubinstein was not the only Melbournian offering beauty services in the early 1900s. Her competitors included Miss Stone (who offered "electric" removal of hairs and moles), Miss Chant (who offered hairdressing, manicures, and "face brushing"), Madame Bosseree (who promoted Royal Hair Tonic and Reval Skin Food), the Oriental Massage Company (offering "scalp massage, singeing and manicures"), and Madame Fokjar (offering "Danish" face treatments and hair removal). These were specialist services, while other skin-care, cosmetic, and beauty products were manufactured by pharmaceutical companies such as Felton, Grimwade (Rubinstein's backer), and, later, Potter and Moore, Proctor and Gamble, Australian Cosmetic Company, and (Colgate) Palmolive.

The example of Helena Rubinstein reflected the secret of early cosmetic entrepreneurs in providing a combination of attractive products, personal attention to customers, and seductive advertising. She took beautification out of the home and into salons, where women felt comfortable and cosseted. This was part of the revolution in ideas of femininity and consumerism that was central to the emergence of modern beauty culture. Rubinstein paid considerable attention to the furnishing of her salons by combining a laboratory-like professionalism with elaborate décor, genuine objets d'art (from her own collection), yet a layout that reflected the comforts of home. In other words, she co-opted the fashion for modernism into the business of beauty culture in a way that appealed to female customers and spurred their love affair with consumer culture. It also created new ideas of taste and fashionable femininity that embraced active engagement by women in public life.

A column by Mere Man in *The Magnet*, department store Mark Foy's magazine, observed in 1910 that there was a new ideal Australian woman: a "cream-complexioned girl" in preference to the "leather-skinned and brick-dust-hued child of Nature." But it was the significance of both world wars that cannot be underestimated, as these proved to be the real turning points in the public perception of women's appearances, as much as they did in providing new opportunities for work. The period between the wars saw a massive expansion of the manufacture and consumption of consumer goods, the sophistication of advertising, and use of the mass media, as well as new consumer-based leisure opportunities for the independent, beauty-conscious New Woman. An unquenchable thirst for cosmetics accompanied these trends. Face powder was worn by 90 percent of American women by the late 1920s, talc by 83 percent, toilet water by 73 percent, perfume by 71 percent, and rouge by 55 percent. While Australian women may have been more conservative, contemporary records suggest similar patterns of uptake of cosmetics. Books on beauty proliferated from the 1930s, including Helena Rubinstein's *The Art of Feminine Beauty* (1930), *This Way for Beauty* (1936), and *Food for Beauty* (1938).

Between the 1920s and the 1950s there was a massive growth in the development and marketing of beauty products associated with skin care, exposure to the sun (from tanning to sunblock and sunburn), makeup, and perfume. Types of cosmetics proliferated to meet the hunger of women for the new beauty culture: dental products such as toothpaste and mouthwash from 1911; feminine hygiene products, hair preparation products, and rouge in the 1920s; soaps and shaving products from the mid-1910s; makeup products (pancake, mascara, lipstick, eye shadow) in the 1920s with new skin-care products competing on an already crowded market; and sun-care products in the 1930s reflecting new leisure habits and the desire for tanned skin. Rouge and lipstick were transformed from being sinful to symbols of ultra-fashion and progressive femininity. Indicative of this turnaround, in the decade up until 1925, the use of perfume went from being a minority habit of the wealthy and aristocratic to being used by 71 percent of American women. Daring Australian women followed suit, although older matrons stuck to toilet water. Output of beauty products trebled between 1919 and 1929, while advertising expenditure multiplied tenfold in the same period. By 1927 seven thousand cosmetic products were sold in America, and Australians kept pace with this level of spending. Demand was not just stimulated but created, and modern beauty habits were actively formed. For example, it was mandatory for working women to acquire hairbrush, comb, toilet soap, talcum powder, Vaseline, face cream, and face powder in order to enhance their beauty and healthiness—and remain employed.

By the late 1920s department stores, clothiers, and pharmacies all stocked plentiful ranges of cosmetics (lipstick, powder compacts, rouge, liquid face powder, vanishing cream, eyebrow pencils, and astringents). A number of stores ran competitions to find the Most Beautiful or Most Charming Girl. As well as cosmetic counters, stores added beauty salons and parlors, hairdressers, and lingerie departments along with barbers and manicure parlors for men. Magazines (such as *The Australian Women's Weekly*, *Home*, *Australasian Post*, and *The Australian Home Beautiful*) and newspapers carried features promoting the latest products, routines, and regimes of celebrities. Australian commercial radio (and later television) programs were sponsored by a number of the cosmetic companies. Although "wowsers" (Puritanical enthusiasts or fanatics) still derided the morals of "painted ladies," the demand for commodity beauty culture continued unabated.

By World War II the cosmetic and beauty industry was substantial, but it was given a further fillip by deliberate campaigns to enlist the moral support of women for the war effort by using cosmetics and by marketing new products (sometimes with patriotic names) to them. While women could not buy new outfits (due to rationing), they could afford a new lipstick or face powder compact. Disposable consumerism and brand loyalty were here to stay. New products, beauty salons and parlors, cosmetic counters and makeup rooms, mass advertising, new media (films and magazines), and beauty competitions were all part of the machinery of the modern beauty culture.

Increasingly, however, the market was dominated by international cosmetic brands such as Innoxa, Cyclax, Elizabeth Arden, Yardley, Ponds, Max Factor, and Avon. In 1930 Elizabeth Arden's counter in David Jones, Sydney, made a 42.3 percent gross profit in its first year of operation. The grandeur of earlier product promotion was displaced by explicit advertising campaigns featuring before-and-after scenarios or ugly duckling transformations. Romance and seduction were underlying themes. In the postwar period advertisements became even more sexually explicit, epitomized by the now famous promotion of Revlon's 1952 "Fire and Ice" lipstick and nail polish using a provocatively dressed siren in a seductive red evening dress with the slogan, "for you who love to flirt with fire…who dare to skate on thin ice."

Although imported products limited the availability of major cosmetic brands in Australia, there was intense interest in new products and promotion. To some extent, the gap was filled by the local production of cosmetics by Australian companies (or under license). Companies such as Potter and Moore, Colgate-Palmolive, Olay, and Ponds manufactured, distributed, and exported cosmetics into the 1970s, but the deregulation of the industry gradually squeezed out much of the industry, and imports became the norm, especially for the luxury end of the beauty product market. Beauty salons remained a feature of beauty culture until the 1950s, when a new phase of consumerism ushered in a self-help approach to beauty by consumers who relied on fashion and beauty magazines, advertising, mass media, and department store assistants for beauty advice rather than the ministrations of specialist beauty technicians. Nevertheless, the culture of the beauty salon has been revived in a substantial way, and the day spa of the twenty-first century is a place where women, and increasingly men, can supposedly receive total beautification and bodily well-being.

THE QUESTS FOR BEAUTY

The notion of beauty and bodily appearance dominated popular culture from the late nineteenth century as it does in the twenty-first century. Beauty pageants and competitions legitimated the quest for beauty and display of (scantily) dressed girls in public and became the stock of newsreels and film scripts. The first Miss America competition was run in 1921. The first Miss Australia competition was even earlier, staged in 1908 as a photographic competition (and won by Alice Buckridge). It was subsequently reinvigorated as the first Miss Australia Quest in 1926 (won by Beryl Mills). It was then held spasmodically until 1953 (won by Maxine Morgan) and thereafter annually until 2000 (the last Miss Australia being Sheree Primmer). Organized initially by the nationalist *Lone Hand* magazine to promote an Australian sense of female beauty and ideals, the quest later gained major sponsors but in particular the lingerie company Hickory and (perhaps ironically) spastic, that is cerebral palsy, organizations in each state. Miss Australias were national icons and attracted immense publicity during their reign and sometimes long after.

The Miss Australia Quest was a distinctly Anglo-Saxon affair until 1961 when Russian immigrant Tania Verstak won and went on to take the Miss World crown. Finally, Australia was on the verge of recognizing its multicultural makeup. Although indigenous entrants had entered the quest (such as Marguerite Tatipata in 1961, Dulcie Carlton in 1967, and Annabella Charles in 1973), it was not until 1999 that Kathryn Hay, an indigenous teacher, became Miss Australia. By this time the quest had been under fire for a number of years, accused of being out of touch with contemporary ideas of femininity and women's roles, of being racist and contributing to the negatives of beauty culture (such as anorexia). The quest was also accused of being sexist by not allowing male entrants, and in 1996 the board changed the name to Quest Australia to accommodate male entrants (such as Brad Rodgers, who won the 1997 National Fundraiser title). The quest was losing its raison d'être (and sponsorship backing) and ended in 2000. Looking back, public fascination with the winners and the immense media coverage of the event and year-long activities of each Miss Australia provide a rich cultural history of the changing parameters of Australian ideals of femininity and beauty culture in the twentieth century.

New role models of Australian femininity from the late 1990s, such as sportswomen (Cathy Freeman, Lauren Jackson), models (Elle Macpherson, Megan Gale), entertainers (Kylie Minogue,

Natalie Imbruglia), fashion designers (Jenny Kee, Colette Din-negan), politicians (Pauline Hansen, Julia Gillard), and actors (Nicole Kidman, Cate Blanchett), have become the templates of Australian womanhood. Just as indigenous motifs have peri-odically featured in Australian fashion design (most notably in the work of Bronwyn Bancroft, Balarinji, Desert Designs, Jenny Kee, and Linda Jackson), so too indigenous models (some profes-sional, like Lois Briggs in the 1970s, and many amateur) have been used by designers and photographers in annual events such as National Aborigines and Islanders Day Observance Committee (NAIDOC) weeks, which celebrate indigenous culture.

Offering further models of attractive women, department stores in Australia such as Farmers, David Jones, Anthony Hordens, Mark Foy's, Myers, Aherns (in Perth), John Martin's (in Adelaide), and Briggs, Finney Isles and Eatons (both in Brisbane) have all hosted immensely popular fashion events that attracted huge media coverage. Stores were keen advocates of beauty cul-ture, stocking local and imported products, staging competitions, and training beauty consultants to serve female customers. Of particular interest were the lingerie company Berlei's musical corset reviews from 1924 to 1940, which attracted large, unruly crowds—often men as well as women. What was unique about beauty culture in Australia was that it was not confined to the elite or to the cities. Fashion parades occurred in towns all over the country, sometimes in traveling shows and sometimes locally

organized. Air travel enhanced the ability to visit far-flung places and was seized upon by entrepreneurs. Although there was an in-satiable hunger for fashion parades, the events themselves seemed more important to Australian audiences than being introduced to new fashions, and retailers and promoters lamented that Austra-lian women "stubbornly refuse to accept any judgment but their own." From the 1970s fashion parades shifted in focus, possibly due to new ways of promoting fashion, such as television adver-tising, popular music shows, and videos, as well as youth-oriented fashion magazines. The new shows included Jenny Kee and Linda Jackson's funky Flamingo Park parades, upbeat shows of seasonal collections by stores like Myer and David Jones, industry-based parades such as the Fashion Industry Association events in the 1980s, the Australian Fashion Week from 1996, festivities such as the Melbourne Fashion Festival from 1997, and events sponsored by the Australian Wool Corporation (now Australian Wool In-novation) until the 1990s.

Australia in fact contributed to the burgeoning modeling industry from the 1920s, both in Australia and abroad. Austra-lian models were deemed to be tall, slim, fit, and healthy—with just the right balance of grace and languidness. During the 1920s Dorothy Woolley became the highest-paid model in the world, promoting not just fashion but artistry of presentation and an obsession with good health and weight loss, a theme that re-emerged throughout the century. Modeling was only just gaining

Beryl Mills, the winner of the inaugural Miss Australia Quest in 1926, was deemed the ideal Australian girl, judged by criteria including sporting ability, poise, and education. The competition was closely associated with fashionable attire, as well as attractiveness. Standing next to her new Studebaker President Sedan in 1927, Mills wears a low-waisted outfit and cloche hat with turned-up brim that were the height of mid-1920s style. Miss Australias were national icons and attracted immense publicity during their reign. Photograph by Ted Hood. State Library of New South Wales.

legitimacy as a respectable occupation for women, so the gestures and routines of aspiring models were carefully orchestrated, while makeup was restrained to avoid sending the wrong message.

Conventions of modeling generally followed overseas ideals of femininity, and sometimes models for fashion shows were imported until the 1960s. Nonetheless, Australian models were successful overseas, including Judy Barraclough (1940s) and June Dally-Watkins and Pat Woodley (models who later established modeling agencies in the 1950s). A new confidence in the 1960s saw models like Maggie Tabberer, Maggie Eckhardt (who also established a successful modeling agency), and Pat Firman become household names. From the 1980s supermodels like Elle Macpherson, Megan Gale, Gemma Ward, Catherine McNeil, and Kristy Hinze ensured Australia's place in the pantheon of fashion modeling.

Equally, Australia has produced a number of eminent fashion photographers who seemed to provide a counterpoint to the conventions of leading European and American photographers—perhaps shaped by the strong light, bright colors, striking landscape, and informal lifestyle of Australia. Successful photographers include Harold Cazneaux, Max Dupain, Helmut Newton, Athol Shmith, Henry Talbot, Laurie Le Guay, David Mist, Patrick Russell, and Grant Matthews. Best known internationally perhaps was Helmut Newton (although not Australian by birth and living in Australia only for a short period), whose work from the 1970s explicitly strove to create fashion images that conveyed brutal and erotic realism as well as unrestrained overt sexuality.

BEAUTY CULTURE, YOUTH, AND THE NEW MILLENNIUM

As popular culture became more youth-oriented in the 1950s and 1960s, new products and brands (such as Mary Quant's bold cosmetics to match her clothes in mod-themed daisy packaging in England, and Prue Acton's and Australis cosmetics in Australia) captured teenage markets that wanted new-age products that reflected their teenage preoccupations and lifestyles. The established cosmetic leaders faced the challenge of continuing to cater to an older generation or revamping their product lines to appeal to younger markets. In the 1970s and 1980s beauty products experimented with a pitch for "natural" ingredients versus "scientific" breakthroughs to reestablish their preeminence. During this period a men's market for cosmetics began to emerge, much to the delight of cosmetic brands that had appealed unsuccessfully for decades to this demographic. Perhaps driven by male role models who embraced cosmetics, makeup, and costumes, men began to add new products to the staple of shaving creams, aftershave lotion, toilet water, and hair cream. Moisturizers, deodorants, perfumes, sports sunblock, depilatory creams, and other products began to be marketed especially for men. Marketers used masculine names for their product lines (Old Spice, Polo, Boss) to convince men that these products would enhance their manhood, and gradually a sizable market share was achieved. Men also began exercising in gyms (rather than sporting venues such as boxing or body-building clubs) and began using a plethora of beauty treatments and regimes. This change signaled shifting ideas about gender types and roles, often called the rise of the New Man, although the acceptance of gay and queer culture also contributed to this expansion of male-oriented beauty culture.

From the 1970s the beauty culture industry has been subject to takeovers, with established brands being successively bought by large multinational companies that have engaged in cartel manipulation of prices and markets. As competition for the female market has become ever fiercer, brands have looked to new markets such as skin care and cosmetics for men—as well as products for people of color, Latinos, Asians, and South Americans. These have become the new growth niche markets. Australia has inevitably been caught up in this global activity.

In the 1980s and 1990s consumers became skeptical of glossy consumer products and associated advertising, turning to "natural" products and later "organic" ones that (ostensibly) used only real ingredients (instead of synthetic substitutes) and were not tested on animals. This trend in beauty culture was accompanied by a renewed interest in traditional forms of beauty and health treatment, such as naturopathy, homeopathy, aromatherapy, acupuncture, herbalism, tai chi, yoga, mud baths, milk baths, colonic irrigation, and health farms. A number of Australian companies, such as Jurlique, Redwin, Aesop, Cedel, Australian All Natural (ANN), G&M Australian Cosmetics, and Miessence, marketed products using ingredients such as tea tree oil, eucalyptus oil, camphor, emu oil, aloe vera, avocado, and native flowers. Australia is also the largest provider of echinacea in the southern hemisphere. The irony is that the modern beauty industry has developed out of the clinics and spas of the earlier times when many of these "modern" treatments were first tried and tested.

In the early 2000s cosmetic companies went high tech, investing in research and development at unprecedented rates, and were extolling a new generation of products based on scientific research into antioxidents, cell biology, and mitochondrial DNA to develop products. In part this occurred due to the greater scientific literacy of consumers, as well as the globalization of the beauty industry and absorption of cosmetic companies into a handful of conglomerates such as L'Oréal (also owners of Garnier, Maybelline, Kérastase, Redken, Lancôme, Biotherm, Giorgio Armani, Ralph Lauren, Cacharel, and Viktor & Rolf), Proctor and Gamble (Olay, Noxema, Braun, Gillette, Aussie, Head and Shoulders, Herbal Essences, and Pantene), and Beiersdorf (Nivea, La Prairie, and Juvena). Australia's cosmetics industry is dominated by subsidiaries of Colgate-Palmolive, L'Oréal, Proctor and Gamble, and Unilever, though a number of Australian-owned companies have a small market share, including Creative Brands, Jurlique, Private Formula International (formerly Dr. Lewins), Pro-Ma Systems, and Redwin Industries. In 2005–2006 Australia's cosmetics industry was worth $700 million and employed 3,300 people, with exports increasing from $23 million in 1986 to $269 million in 2005–2006. The major export markets are New Zealand (44%), the United States (11%), the United Kingdom (8%), Hong Kong (6%), and Singapore (5%). Exports to China and Europe are also growing as organically conscious consumers look for new types of products. Industry reports anticipate further expansion of the Australian cosmetic and beauty industry well into the 2000s.

Australia's rapidly aging population in the twenty-first century has fueled a demand for "health"-oriented cosmetics and beauty treatments that promise youth, sun care, and hygiene. There has been a significant increase also in sales of baby products, as well as sun-care, body wash/shower gel, deodorant spray, and men's skin-care products. As incomes have risen, cosmetic sales have soared, and department stores, chemists, and supermarkets have revamped their beauty halls and upgraded their beauty services.

Simultaneously, discount cosmetic stores and online sales have made major inroads into the market share of major global brands.

Where potions fail, consumers have eagerly embraced cosmetic surgery, a practice Helena Rubinstein long advocated, and the effects of which caused the septicemia that led to the death of her fan Nellie Stewart. Since the 1990s cosmetic surgery procedures have grown exponentially to 214 per 100,000 clients in Switzerland in 2002—the highest rate worldwide. Australia recorded 66 per 100,000 (7th) compared with 30 per 100,000 in the United States (19th) and 7 per 100,000 in the United Kingdom (28th). Of surgical procedures, the most common for women were liposuction, breast augmentation, eyelid surgery, tummy tucks, and face lifts; for men, liposuction, eyelid surgery, rhinoplasty, breast reduction, and hair transplantation. Men accounted for 8 percent of all surgical procedures. The most common nonsurgical procedures were botox injections, laser hair removal, and chemical peels. Despite the popularity of cosmetic surgery, it still carried risks, with 40 percent of breast implants in Australian women each year being surgically removed or replaced. This underscores the point that the achievement of beauty comes at a cost.

Once again, women have been promised "weapons" to protect skin from aging by using procedures and ingredients that "pause" the aging process. It seems that "hope in a jar" continues to fuel the expansion of the beauty industry. Australian beauty products in the twenty-first century are well integrated into the global marketplace. Climate and the outdoor lifestyle have had a significant influence on shaping the priorities of Australians in delineating a distinctive approach to skin care, cosmetics, and beauty routines. Fortunately, these have also been exported to international markets keen to address the consequences of exposure to the elements (sun, sea, wind, temperature, and snow), so that Australian beauty culture in the new millennium thrives locally as well as globally.

References and Further Reading

Brain, Robert. *The Decorated Body.* 1st ed. New York: Harper and Row, 1979.

Clifford, Marie. "Helena Rubinstein's Beauty Salons, Fashion, and Modernist Display." *Winterthur Portfolio* 38 (2003): 83–108.

Conor, Liz. *The Spectacular Modern Woman: Feminine Visibility in the 1920s.* Bloomington: Indiana University Press, 2004.

Isaacs, Jennifer. "The Body as Living Art." In *Australia's Living Heritage: Arts of the Dreaming,* 52–103. Sydney: Ure Smith Press, 1990 (reprinted in 1992).

Joel, Alexandra. *Parade: The Story of Fashion in Australia.* Sydney: HarperCollins, 1998.

King, Elisabeth. "Tech It to the Limit." *The Sunday Telegraph Magazine* (25 November 2007): 48–49.

Maynard, Margaret. *Out of Line: Australian Women and Style.* Sydney: University of New South Wales Press, 2001.

O'Brien, Denis. *The Weekly.* Ringwood, Australia: Penguin, 1982.

Peiss, Kathy. *Hope in a Jar: The Making of America's Beauty Culture.* New York: Henry Holt and Company, 1999.

Reekie, Gail. *Temptations: Sex, Selling and the Department Store.* Sydney: Allen and Unwin, 1993.

Robinson, Felicity. *Fashion: Australian Memories in Black and White.* Sydney and London: Murdoch Books, 2000.

Saunders, Kay, and Juliet Ustinoff. *A Crowning Achievement: A Study in Australian Beauty, Business and Charitable Enterprise.* Canberra: National Museum of Australia Press, 2005.

Sheridan, Susan. *Who Was That Woman? "The Australian Women's Weekly" in Postwar Years.* Sydney: University of New South Wales Press, 2001.

Vinikas, Vincent. *Soft Soap, Hard Sell: American Hygiene in an Age of Advertisement.* Ames: Iowa State University Press, 1992.

Woodhead, Lindy. *War Paint: Madame Helena Rubinstein and Miss Elizabeth Arden.* London: Virago, 2003.

Jennifer Craik

See also Swimwear, Surfwear, and the Bronzed Body in Australia; Fashion Photography in Australia.

The Australiana Phenomenon in Australia

- Early Australiana Motifs and Adornment
- Twentieth-Century Modernism and Australiana
- The Australiana Phenomenon: 1970s and 1980s
- Humor, Irony, and Exotic Appeal in Australiana
- Australiana and Mass Production
- Trade, Exhibitions, and Cultural Promotion

The 1970s and 1980s saw a trend in Australian fashion design, fashionable consumption, fashion writing, and exhibitions toward the celebration of local landscape, color, flora and fauna, urban vernacular themes, Aboriginal art motifs, and the idea of a national "personality" in dress. While the use of native flora and fauna and other local motifs in adornment was not unique to these decades, it was associated at this time with a great range of wearable items, leading designers and curators, and key dates in Australian cultural history—including the Bicentenary of European settlement in 1988, which engendered public support for cultural nationalism.

Fashion has not been exempt from Australia's relentless search for identity. This search, historian Richard White has suggested, amounts to a national obsession. Australia has long supported a range of activities that aim to catch the essence of "Australianness" and give the continent and its people an individual personality. When Moreen Clark entitled her 1989 hand-knit suit, skillfully embroidered with native flora, "Taking the Bush to London," she was expressing a widely held interest in representing Australia through its landscape. Clark's outfit was included in the 1989 exhibition Australian Fashion, shown in London, in which many of the exhibits expressed Australiana themes.

The idea of genius loci—creative spirit of place, which had always been strong in Australian art and culture—was resurrected, in a period that opened in the cultural climate of the Whitlam Labor government (1972–1975) and concluded with the celebratory environment of the Bicentenary. Through these two decades the idea became almost a fixation. Fashion magazines gave both implicit and explicit coverage to issues of national identity and to fashion designers who used visual conventions located both in the land and in notions of light, color, and ironic humor—designated as "Australian."

EARLY AUSTRALIANA MOTIFS AND ADORNMENT

Twentieth-century codes of representation of national identity revisited visual motifs believed to represent Australia for more than a century. While colonial elites and subsequent wealthy and privileged Australians adopted Eurocentric taste in dress, a locally inflected identity had provided a counterpoint to this. From the early Colonial period the specificity of Australian flora and fauna were regarded as unique markers of place, with artists, colonists, and natural history collectors being fascinated by Australian difference. An 1860 sketch for a fancy-dress costume design by colonial artist Nicholas Chevalier, for Lady Barkly,

featured lyre-bird feather and fern motifs and was inscribed by the artist: "Fancy Costume Emblematic of Australia or of this Colony." However, these motifs rarely had application in clothing worn in everyday life or for formal occasions other than fancy dress.

Design historian Michael Bogle has noted that patriots encouraged the use of Australian flora in design. One such was the women's group called the Wattle Blossom League, which was formed as part of the Adelaide chapter of the Australian Natives Association, a patriotic settler group, in 1889. Flora and fauna motifs appeared on many examples of colonial and post-Federation design—furniture, poster and advertising graphics, book design, pottery, glass and porcelain tableware, carpets, ceramic tiles, and architectural detail. However, their use in dress and adornment was largely confined to jewelry and other accessories, such as the (ca. 1860) brooch, attributed to Hogarth and Erichsen jewelers of Sydney, in the collection of the Powerhouse Museum. Made in stippled gold with a nugget of local gold-bearing milky quartz, it featured a cluster of indigenous pear, tree fern, and Banksia (an indigenous plant often used for design motifs). The late-nineteenth-century advocate of Australiana motifs in design, French émigré Lucien Henry, made pencil, watercolor, and gouache designs for jewelry using motifs such as waratah, lyre-bird, fire-wheel blossom, kangaroos, maps of Australia, and the Southern Cross constellation. As an artist and teacher, Henry had promoted the idea of finding inspiration in Australian nature and made a significant contribution to the adoption of decorative designs based on Australiana motifs.

Maude Wadsworth Smith designed a range of Coo-ee jewelry, named after the Aboriginal call *coo-ee*, when she was resident on the Western Australian goldfields at the turn of the twentieth century, in the context of the movement toward Federation and nationhood in 1901. Smith's brooches, pins, and pendants featured kangaroos, emus, koalas, Western Australian black swans, boomerangs, and maps of the Australian continent. Her designs were made up by the Melbourne firm of Johnson and Simonsen and were exhibited at the Perth Exhibition Buildings in 1907. Other items of personal adornment include Margaret Hope's watercolor fans of the 1880s and 1890s, painted with Tasmanian wildflowers. Rare curiosities include the (ca. 1880) fan of black cockatoo feathers and ivory made in Darwin by Chinese settlers, and the woman's face-screen made of a stuffed kookaburra, by taxidermist Eliza Catherine Wintle, possibly from the early 1890s. Dress accessories such as lace collars could also include flora and fauna designs. Mary Dufour has noted that of 500 lace exhibits at a September 1910 Hobart exhibition of local lace work, no less than 109 employed Australian flora and fauna motifs. One prize-winning example, a machine-made lace collar made about 1910 by Miss Patty Mault, employed a design of two kangaroos encircled by a branch of an apple tree, the fruit of which was becoming a Tasmanian export staple.

TWENTIETH-CENTURY MODERNISM AND AUSTRALIANA

Australian modernist artist Margaret Preston's 1930 *Self Portrait* in the collection of the Art Gallery of New South Wales shows the artist adorned in a plain black dress and jacket with an emblematic pot of native Christmas lilies behind her. Preston had promoted the idea that the adoption of local, especially Aboriginal, motifs in art and design was a precondition for arrival at a mature Australian cultural identity. Preston's visual concerns, expressed in her 1925 essay, "The Indigenous Art of Australia," were revived by Australiana enthusiasts later in the twentieth century, including fashion designers Jenny Kee and Linda Jackson and fabric print designer Bruce Goold. Preston's designer contemporaries had created wearable items using the local motifs she advocated. Olive Nock's 1928 scarf with a fluid design of gum leaves and blossoms was one of several of her modernist designs using Australian flora printed onto silk fabric and scarves by Liberty of London. Lucie Dalgarno used Australian flora in her designs such as her painted silk scarf from about 1930 with gum blossoms and leaves. Appropriated motifs from indigenous culture were added to local urban themes and flora and fauna by Australian modernists as markers of a national design sensibility. Textile designers Frances Burke and Alexandra Nan Mackenzie were among those who used Aboriginal shields, boomerangs, and Aboriginal art conventions such as cross-hatching, concentric circles, and dots. Douglas Annand created Australiana print designs for Claudio Alcorso's Modernage fabric range, such as his Sydneyside fabric featuring the Harbour Bridge, ferries and beaches, historical buildings, and landmarks. He also designed, from the 1950s to the early 1970s, fashionable scarves featuring kangaroos and other local motifs, including a 1970 Qantas commission for a Captain Cook scarf to

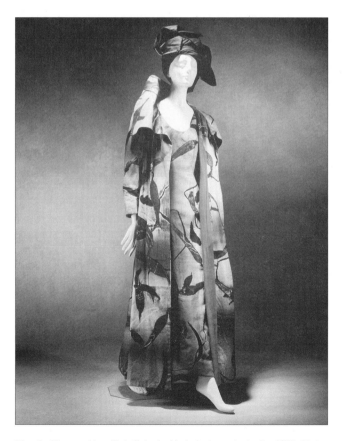

"Gumleaf" ensemble, silk taffeta, by Linda Jackson, Australia, 1985. Photograph by Sue Stafford. Powerhouse Museum.

commemorate the bicentenary of Cook's voyage to the east coast of Australia. These form a link between mid-century modernist design and the later, more eclectic and flamboyant practices of the young designers of the 1970s and 1980s.

THE AUSTRALIANA PHENOMENON: 1970s AND 1980s

From the early 1970s a distinct fashionable trend toward use of national symbols, including flora and fauna, permeated Australian dress at all levels from high fashion to sports clothing. This trend formed part of a renewed search for a national symbolic identity, which included the enlistment by government and media of creative individuals and groups in the framing of this endeavor. By the late 1980s the trend had become what design scholar Anne-Marie Willis referred to as a form of hypernationalism, with an excessive emphasis on local flora and fauna, and the repositioning of utilitarian outback clothing such as Akubra hats and Driza-Bone raincoats as fashionable urban dress. (Akubra is a brand name for a broad-brimmed hat worn by and emblematic of male workers on the land, later also worn by women, and the Dryza-Bone, a brand of oilskin coat worn originally on pastoral runs.) A number of themes marked a uniquely Australian identity in fashion. Beyond the employment of flora and fauna, appropriated Aboriginal motifs, and an ironic play with urban vernacular icons, these included an emphasis on the creative effects of bright light and intense color, bush aesthetics, and iconoclastic humor. A "larrikin personality" in design—larrikin in this context being a colloquial term meaning rebellious and individualistic—was seen as an essential element of Australian cultural identity, an expression of both bush and urban sensibility.

Jenny Kee and Linda Jackson were leading creative forces and emblematic figures of the Australiana phenomenon. Starting in the early 1970s, when they settled in Sydney after extended overseas travel, the pair became a force for a stylish and highly original reinstatement of pride in the Australian environment, natural and cultural. On their return to Australia, Jackson and Kee brought with them significant exposure to a broad fashion world. Kee had experienced the best in fashion history through her work in vintage clothing at the Chelsea Antique Market, London, with Vern Lambert between 1969 and 1972. Jackson settled in Sydney in 1973 after traveling in Asia, the Pacific, and Europe since 1969. She had worked in Paris, making clothes for the designers Mia and Vicki, and had made a study of the work of couturiers Madeleine Vionnet and Charles James, which would influence her later work. Jackson and Kee met in Sydney when Jackson was showing her clothes at Paul Craft's Paraphernalia stand at the Bonython Winter Fair in Sydney in June 1973, just before Kee opened her highly influential boutique Flamingo Park in Sydney's Strand Arcade later that year. The Flamingo Park label would be carried by the garments of both of these designers until Jackson started her Bush Couture label in 1982. The first of their Flamingo Follies fashion parades, held at the Hingara restaurant in Sydney's Chinatown in 1974, was a youthful and glamorous moment in a new mood of confidence and daring in Australian fashionable dress. The first garment to appear on the catwalk was Jackson's "Opera House" dress, with white Opera House roof segment motifs appliquéd on blue. The parade attracted an enthusiastic following of young Australians, some of whom were recently returned expatriates particularly receptive to these confident Australian-inflected voices in fashion and style.

Together Jackson and Kee gave Australiana in fashion a creative momentum, a coherent visual, and verbal language. Jane de Teliga, fashion writer and curator of several seminal Australian fashion exhibitions in the 1980s, claimed in *Vogue Australia* in 1989 that while Australians might be blasé about Australiana in dress, Jenny Kee and Linda Jackson were the stylists who elevated Australian motifs, previously the preserve of kitsch tourist souvenirs, to the realm of fashion. As design practitioners, stylists of their own self-presentation, and public voices, they were advocates for the Australiana trend and galvanized a wide interest in the adoption of vernacular cultural symbols. They were accompanied by a range of other designers. These included milliners, shoemakers, fiber and fabric artists, and jewelers who shared their interest in Australiana themes. Jackson's garments, as well as carrying her own innovative prints—some made by using actual gum leaves with their distinct "eaten" edges as screen-printing stencils—were enhanced by collaborators. These included artist David McDiarmid, who hand-painted gum leaves and blossoms, scribbly-bark patterns, and other native flora motifs on silk and wool, and Debra Leser, who used Japanese silk-painting techniques to paint waratahs, Sturt desert peas, and gum blossoms on fabrics used in Linda Jackson garments. Bruce Goold (better known for his printed fabrics and scarves with Australian motifs) had also hand-painted silk chiffon with barrier reef motifs for Linda Jackson's 1979 collection. Kee's confident graphic motifs for her Blinky, Koala, Kooka, and Kanga knitwear from 1974 were interpreted by pattern-drafter and hand-knitter Jan Ayres.

Jackson and Kee's impulse toward a creative artistic life, rather than an industry career in fashion, and their independent studio and boutique approach to the making, selling, and wearing of clothing were part of the freshness of their vision and had an impact on the "art clothes" and "wearable art" trend that was also associated with Australiana. Jackson and Kee's approach saw clothing and style as an art form, and a 1985 exhibition at the Australian National Gallery curated by John McPhee and Robyn Healy, entitled Linda Jackson and Jenny Kee: Flamingo Park and Bush Couture, placed the work of these two designers in the context of art museum collecting. In 1977 they won the newly inaugurated Lyrebird Fashion Industry Award for Innovation in recognition of their unique contribution to the Australian fashion scene. Jackson's atelier in Bondi Road resembled an artist's studio or a small couture house and bore no resemblance to the factory-based clothing industry of the big names in Australian fashion. Jane de Teliga wrote ten years later in *Vogue Australia* that Jackson and Kee's 1979 Flamingo Follies parade was one of the catalysts leading to the concept for her Art Clothes exhibition at the Art Gallery of New South Wales in 1980. For Kee and Jackson the gestation of ideas for clothing was intrinsically linked to the making of an Australian creative life and a response to the local landscape. Both had chosen to settle in Sydney, overlooking the Pacific Ocean to the south of iconic Bondi Beach, and their ideas were impacted by daily exposure to this environment. Both later moved to the mountains west of Sydney, Kee to form a permanent home and Jackson to create a bush retreat from the city. When Jackson severed her business association with Flamingo Park and founded her Bush Couture label in 1982, she continued to work with Australiana themes that emphasized the Central Desert, Uluru, Kata Tjuta, and the Australian gemstone, the opal. She designed a range of free-form opal jewelry in 1983 and a perfume, Opalessence.

HUMOR, IRONY, AND EXOTIC APPEAL IN AUSTRALIANA

Melbourne jeweler Kate Durham noted in *Vogue Australia* in June 1981 the Australian tendency toward national pride mixed with self-deprecatory larrikin humor. Durham's jewelry, using local beer labels and bottle tops among other urban detritus, embodied this ironic larrikin tone. The humor that was played out in the Australiana trend was the contemporary manifestation of a rebellious antiauthoritarian heritage. The camp reappropriation of tourist and urban kitsch, characteristic of this trend, was part of a rebellious insistence on low-brow taste, thumbing the nose at Eurocentric notions of good taste.

Influential cultural activist Peter Tully created jewelry, making satiric comment on urban Australian vernacular themes. His Harbour Bridges, Opera Houses, and Vegemite jars carry a larrikin camp inflection. Tully's hand-painted, laser-cut, black-and-white plastic necklace of 1979, "Black and White Oz," piled it on with abandon. Individually crafted, hand-painted, and laser-cut, objects hanging from a plastic chain included: emu, gum leaves, surfboards, gum-nuts, appropriated Aboriginal Mimi figures, kookaburra, koala, Sydney Harbour Bridge, outline map of Australia with capital cities, Sydney Opera House, kangaroo, Vegemite label, beer mug, meat pie, and boomerang. This flamboyant object of adornment is the embodiment of larrikin humor, with its reference to "ocker" culture (an Australian term for vulgar masculinist aspects of Australian culture) and "surfie" culture (meat pie, beer, and surfboards), flora and fauna, and Aboriginal motifs. Its cheap production methods and materials and shameless appropriation of kitsch tourist themes are in turn a snubbing of elite notions of cultural quality. Jenny Bannister's white leather "Opera House" mini-dress of 1979, in the collection of the National Gallery of Victoria, with its architectural profile of Sydney Opera House perched on one shoulder, employs the ironic reappropriation of tourist kitsch also associated with Tully. Katie Pye's "Emoh Ruo" outfit of 1980, based on a deconstructed map of Australia, lampooned the Australian suburban vernacular of labeling "Our Home." Mambo's inventive, irreverent print graphics on T-shirts and shirts expressed similar larrikin themes of urban banality.

Tully, like his friends Jackson and Kee, had returned to Australia after extensive travel—in Tully's case in Africa, Europe, and Asia. In 1969 he had spent time with Linda Jackson and photographer Fran Moore in New Guinea. Like Jackson and Moore, he chose to settle in Sydney rather than return to Melbourne. It was in Sydney that the Australiana trend in fashion and adornment had its strongest flowering, although the Adelaide crafts community was vigorously exploring Australian flora and fauna in crafted garments, especially knits. For many of the adherents of this playful cultural nationalism, time spent away from Australia had engendered an awareness of a rebellious, ironically self-conscious, and iconoclastic idea of what it meant to be Australian. Jenny Kee had returned to Sydney in December 1972, just ten days after the election of the Whitlam government, into the youthful cultural ferment abounding at that time, and recalled how Sydney seemed brash, bright, relaxed, informal, and optimistic. Richard Neville's *Oz* magazine in London

Australian fashion designer Jenny Kee wearing her own "Wattle" design, 1977. The calf-length, loose-fitting dress features a wattle motif worked in yellow, green, brown, and gray on a blue ground and is made from wool and mohair. Powerhouse Museum.

had established the nexus between larrikinism, iconoclasm, and youthful self-confidence as hallmarks of Australianness. It was this externally fermented idea of being Australian that came to Sydney with the returning expatriates, which would inflect the predominantly Sydney-based Australiana phenomenon in fashion. Kee's response to *Vogue Australia*'s rhetorical question, for the end-of-year edition, asking what she wanted for Christmas in 1978, was: "No Pucci, no Gucci, no bushfires, no blowies." In this utterance the designer encapsulated all of the Australiana themes. Her humorous riposte simultaneously displaced the importance of Eurocentric style (no Pucci, no Gucci), affirmed the primacy of untamed nature embodied in the bush (no bushfires), and adopted a larrikin tone by using Australian slang for the unmentionable blowfly (no blowies). The popular 1965 publication *Let's Talk Strine* (a popular satire on the Australian accent written by Afferbeck Lauder, which was the pseudonym used by Alastair Ardoch Morrison), along with Barry Humphries's created character Barry McKenzie, who shocked Londoners with his rough vernacular—both in Humphries's *Private Eye* cartoon strip and the later 1972 Bruce Beresford film—had instated Australian slang as an ironic and original form of the English language. Witty use of Australiana forms continued into the 1980s in many dress-related manifestations. Jonathan Sceats used a "coat

of arms" with camp kangaroos and a holographic skull to launch an eyewear range in 1988, and a Sydney Gay and Lesbian Mardi Gras parade costume group in 1985 consisted of brightly colored moveable rosella parrots.

Jackson and Kee responded in their work both to an emerging Australian consciousness and to an interest in the antipodean "exotic" from metropolitan centers of Europe and America. As early as 1977, Jackson and Kee had shown their collections in "trunk shows" (private showings of designer clothes to an invited audience, presented from a suitcase (trunk) in a hotel room) in Milan, Paris, and New York, to an admiring audience. Kee's knits, along with Jackson's opulent silk taffeta outfit emulating the shape and color of native gum trees, appeared in *Vogue Italia* in December 1977. Heading text by Anna Piaggi announced that "the fashion from another hemisphere" bore witness to the appeal this witty Australiana held for the European predilection for the exotic. Kee's elegant oversized wool and cotton knits, bearing confidently drawn wattle, koalas, waratahs, and other Australiana emblems, were made internationally famous by the widely disseminated photograph of a pregnant Princess of Wales wearing a Flamingo Park koala sweater at an English polo match in 1983. By October 1982 Kee's silk Opal prints had been chosen by Karl Lagerfeld for Chanel's 1983 spring–summer prêt-à-porter collection. Fashion illustrator Antonio Lopez had drawn Kee, wearing a scarf of Opal print, in 1982 for the Italian magazine *Vanity*. In the same year Kee had been commissioned to design a large silk scarf bearing Australiana motifs to celebrate the launch of the new Australian National Gallery in Canberra, another occasion for the celebratory 1980s impulse in Australian cultural branding. Kee's public image and her creative output had become emblematic of being Australian, as further evidenced by her series of television and print ads for the wool-washing product Softly—bringing together wool, Australiana, and the idea of stylish celebrity. In October 1986 Kee and Jackson chose an Australiana focus for the presentation of their collections at Nieman Marcus in Dallas, Texas, part of an Australian fashion promotion. Kee and Jackson's designs were also stocked in the Koala Blue shop of singer Olivia Newton John in Los Angeles, with its logo designed by artist and designer of Australiana prints Ken Done. Ken Done had also developed a major following in Australia and internationally, especially in Japan, with a range of beach and resort wear bearing prints based on his paintings of Sydney Harbour, beach scenes, Sydney Opera House, Harbour Bridge, and other colorful Australiana motifs. Australia, to fashion consumers from Tokyo to Los Angeles, London to Milan, was at this time represented by Australiana.

AUSTRALIANA AND MASS PRODUCTION

While *Vogue Australia* claimed in September 1983 that Kee took the kitsch out of the koala and the kangaroo and created a lasting trend, it could be said that the kitsch was put back into the koala by the end of the 1980s. This occurred with a motley variety of Australiana motifs evident in mass-produced garments that were of varying design quality and originality. The pages of fashion magazines were full of advertisements for products such as Kangarucci's garments, subtitled "the Australian way to dress." Outback Emu and Man from Snowy River were advertised knitwear lines from Me Designs. Mainstream labels such as Rae Ganim, Prue Acton, and Weiss were using kangaroos and koalas, while a company called The Proud Australian was advertising in *Vogue Australia* its range of mass-produced garments for all ages, such as their "G'day mate" T-shirts, garments with koalas, kangaroos, Opera Houses, and Harbour Bridges, with "bicentenary souvenirs a specialty." In 1985 the Sydney hair salon Get Smart redecorated with appropriated Aboriginal motifs. Australiana had also become controversial. Prue Acton's "Wattle yellow" and white dress design, which won the award for best ceremonial women's outfit at the 1984 Los Angeles Olympic Games, generated negative comment from the fashion magazine *Mode*, which had claimed the designs looked like tea towels. The garments in question showcased graphic designs by artist Betty Greenhatch, featuring koalas, kangaroos, emus, and kookaburras, accessorized with gum-leaf necklaces and belts.

TRADE, EXHIBITIONS, AND CULTURAL PROMOTION

Government enlistment of art and culture in the promotion of Australian trade interests did not exclude fashion, and the Australiana phenomenon gave a literal coherence to these endeavors. The Weiss Art fashion collection shown at the Australian embassy in Tokyo in 1987 included T-shirts printed with the word *Australia* and images of kangaroos, koalas, and the Sydney Harbour Bridge. For the 1988 Bicentennial Wool Collection, which brought together a range of local and international designers, artist Brett Whiteley was commissioned by *Vogue Australia* to create a painting in which he incorporated what *Vogue* called the "hearts of Australia, a sheep, the Sydney Opera House and Harbour Bridge and Ayers Rock."

Exhibitions played an important role in highlighting Australian contemporary fashion design as an art form and simultaneously gave momentum to the Australiana phenomenon in dress. Jane de Teliga curated the most influential of the exhibitions for Sydney art and design museums. Her 1980–1981 exhibition Art Clothes and the 1988 Art Knits, both at the Art Gallery of New South Wales, included many of the creators whose work was associated with aspects of Australiana, such as Bruce Goold, whose Australian bird and wildflower designs appeared on fabrics, T-shirts, and other garments, David McDiarmid, Jenny Bannister, Katie Pye, and jewelers Peter Tully, Kate Durham, and Robyn Gordon. The Art Knits show supported by the New South Wales Bicentennial Council opened at the Art Gallery of New South Wales in May 1988 and toured to regional galleries in New South Wales and Victoria until January 1989. Some whose work was shown in the Art Knits exhibition, such as Kee and Jackson, had appeared in Art Clothes and would be represented in an exhibition the following year curated by de Teliga. This was the 1989–1990 exhibition Australian Fashion: A Contemporary Art, curated for the Powerhouse Museum, Sydney, with support from the Australia Council for the Arts, which was shown at the Victoria and Albert Museum from June to August 1989 and at the Powerhouse from October 1989 to February 1990. It was claimed by its institutional supporters to represent "the spirit of Australian design and designers," including a "pioneering spirit tempered by a certain larrikin quality," part of "our dry humour," and to reflect Australian "light, colour, energy and wit." The more than fifty Australian designers represented had created work especially for the exhibition. De Teliga stated that the exhibits had been chosen for their "independent spirit" and originality. Nonmainstream one-off production was the focus. While there was no requirement to use Australiana imagery, many chose to use some form of vernacular approach.

Kate Durham's "Silly European Jewellery Improved by Fosterisation" used, among other "found" urban detritus, beer bottle caps and remnants of aluminum beer cans bearing the iconic logotypes for Fosters and Carlton United Breweries. Ian McMaugh's "Ned Kelly Suit" used the motif of the outlaw Kelly's steel mask replicated in metal buttons and shoe caps. Marcus Davidson and Maree Menzel's "Snakeproof" outfit irreverently commented on Australian urban dwellers' fear of snakes. Robyn Gordon's "Time and Tide Remnants" necklace and earrings referenced the east coast of Australia. Kate McPherson's "Bottle Brush Shoes" employed the crimson color of the native *Callistemon citrinus*. Robyn Russell's shoes featured Australian flora, fauna, and birds. Dinosaur Designs chose sea and sun as the themes for their Paco Rabanne–derived dress. Paul Worstead's "Ayres Rock Aspirin," based on Aboriginal medicinal and food plants, encompassed both the larrikin irreverence and the flora motifs, which characterized the interpretation of a national style, adopted by many of the creative practitioners represented in this exhibition.

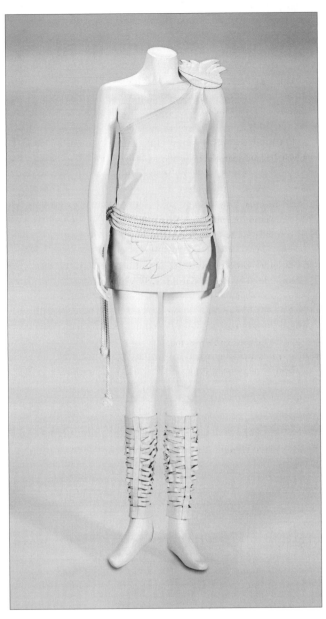

"Opera House" dress, 1979, by Australian designer Jenny Bannister. This white leather dress has the profile of the Sydney Opera House suspended on one shoulder and is made to be worn with leggings. A dress with a design inspired by the Sydney Opera House was also made by designer Linda Jackson for the first Flamingo Follies fashion parade in Sydney, 1974. National Gallery of Victoria.

Linda Jackson, describing her inspiration for her "Rainbow Opal" outfit in the exhibition, said that it referred unambiguously to the Australian bush, the green and yellow scrubby desert, and patterns of wildflowers. It also referenced the intense blue of the sky, the rich reds of the earth, the bold flashing colors of Australia's national stone (the opal), and the beautiful pure grays, whites, and sliver green of the gum tree. Rosella Paletti (Sally Owen), whose adopted name itself implied an embrace of Australiana—an implicit claim to a color palette inspired by the Rosella, a multi-colored indigenous parrot—had a colorful knitted frock coat in the show. She had also been represented in Art Knits and a smaller

scale exhibition, Fabulous Frocks and Fancy Follies, with Wendy Walker and Susan Moore at the Adelaide Festival Centre in 1981. This exhibition, which included Australiana themes, toured to the Art Gallery of Western Australia, Perth, in 1982.

Bronwyn Bancroft's printed silk fabric "Campfire Calling" was included in de Teliga's 1989 exhibition and was part of the range of fabric designs and garments sold through Bancroft's Sydney shop, Designer Aboriginals, established in 1985. Bancroft was one of several Aboriginal designers working within this period whose work was associated with the renewed interest in Australian identity, although it must be said that the priorities of post-settlement Australians and Australians of indigenous descent were inevitably dissimilar. Indigenous Australians, differently placed in relation to the question of what it means to be Australian, were alert to sensitive issues of cultural ownership of visual iconography. Many of the non-Aboriginal Australians involved in the Australiana trend had appropriated Aboriginal cultural motifs in their designs. This was later rightly understood as a breach of both copyright and cultural protocol. Artists Vincent Tipiloura and Connie Puautjimi from the indigenous print workshop Tiwi Designs were included in the 1989 exhibition, represented by batik on silk scarves bearing designs of native plants. Two local artists who had an interest in wood-block printing—Bede Tungatulum and Giovanni Tipungwuti—had initiated the Tiwi workshop in 1969 on Bathurst Island north of Darwin. Tiwi Designs had a fashionable following in Sydney in the 1980s through Coo-ee boutique in Paddington. Aboriginal women from Utopia station in the Northern Territory, who had worked in this medium since the late 1970s, also created batik printing on silk. Fabric designs from Utopia, partly based on traditional indigenous forms, were also included in Australian Fashion: The Contemporary Art. Other Aboriginal designers whose work made an impact in this period include Jimmy Pike from Western Australia, whose bold graphic forms in bright colors were printed on scarves, ties, T-shirts, and shirts for the Desert Designs label. Adelaide-based Balarinji designs, started in 1983, produced swimwear, children's wear, and leisure wear bearing motifs, often in subdued ocher and blue tones, inspired by the saltwater country Northern Territory near Barroloola, where designer John Kundereri Moriarty was born.

The 1989 exhibition, supported by the Australia Council and nurtured in the atmosphere of the Bicentenary, may be seen as the celebratory concluding emblem of the Australiana trend in Australian fashion. Australiana motifs and some aspects of larrikin humor did endure in aspects of garment design, for example, in Ken Done and Mambo leisure wear. Overall, however, there was less interest in these themes by the end of the 1980s. Aboriginal design continued to be used emblematically to represent Australia, for example in Balarinji's print design for Qantas airline uniforms in the early twenty-first century. But by the 1980s the widespread preoccupation with vernacular nationalist themes had been displaced by a renewed interest in global metropolitan fashion. The enthusiastic cultural nationalism, which characterized the Australiana tendency in fashion, had been replaced by a critical awareness of the limitations of nationally inflected creative concerns. As the patriotic impetus of the Bicentenary, which had been an overwhelmingly Sydney-centered phenomenon, came and went, fashion consumers, designers, design students, and fashion writers were less concerned with local identity issues and sought other inspirations.

References and Further Reading

Betteridge, Margaret. "Olive Nock." In *Heritage: The National Women's Art Book*, edited by Joan Kerr, 414–416. Sydney: G and B Arts International, 1995.

Bogle, Michael. *Design in Australia 1880–1970*. Sydney: Craftsman House, 1998.

Cawthorne, Zelda. *Australia in Fashion: Six Great Designers*. Melbourne: Australia Post Corporation, 2005.

de Teliga, Jane. *Australian Fashion: The Contemporary Art*. Sydney: Powerhouse Museum of Applied Arts and Sciences, The Australia Council, and Bernard Leser Publications, 1989.

Dufour, Mary. "M. E. (Patty) Mault and Ada Grey Wilson." In *Heritage: The National Women's Art Book*, edited by Joan Kerr, 278–279. Sydney: G and B Arts International, 1995.

Erickson, Dorothy, and Joan Kerr. "Maude Wordsworth James." In *Heritage: The National Women's Art Book*, edited by Joan Kerr, 276. Sydney: G and B Arts International, 1995.

Fletcher, Marion. *Costume in Australia 1788–1901*. Melbourne, Australia: Oxford University Press, 1984.

Kee, Jenny. *A Big Life: Jenny Kee*. Melbourne, Australia: Penguin Books, 2006.

Kerr, Joan, ed. *Heritage: The National Women's Art Book*. Sydney: G and B Arts International, 1995.

Maynard, Margaret. *Out of Line: Australian Women and Style*. Sydney: University of New South Wales Press, 2001.

McDonald, Anne. *Douglas Annand: The Art of Life*. Canberra: National Gallery of Australia, 2001.

McPhee, John. *Linda Jackson and Jenny Kee: Flamingo Park and Bush Couture*. Canberra: Australian National Gallery, 1985.

Mitchell, Louise. "Lucie Dalgarno." In *Heritage: The National Women's Art Book*, edited by Joan Kerr, 339. Sydney: G and B Arts International, 1995.

Peers, Juliette. "Paris or Melbourne? Garments as Ambassadors for Australian Fashion Cultures." In *Generation Mode: The Fashion Generation*, edited by Susanne Anna and Eva Gronbach, 133–151. Düsseldorf, Germany: Stadtmuseum der Landeshauptstadt Düsseldorf and Hatje Cantz Publishers, 2006.

Sear, Martha, and Joan Kerr. "Eliza Catherine Wintle." In *Heritage: The National Women's Art Book*, edited by Joan Kerr, 173. Sydney: G and B Arts International, 1995.

Stephens, Ann, ed. *Visions of a Republic: The Work of Lucien Henry*. Sydney: Powerhouse Publishing, 2001.

Vogue Australia (June 1981, August 1982, April 1985, September 1987, October 1989).

Webb, Belinda. "Brooch circa 1860." In *A Companion to The Mint Collections*, edited by Robert Barton. Sydney: Museum of Applied Arts and Sciences, 1982.

White, Richard. "Inventing Australia." In *Images of Australia*, edited by Gillian Whitlock and David Carter, 23–53. Brisbane, Australia: University of Queensland Press, 1992.

Willis, Anne-Marie. *Illusions of Identity: The Art of Nation*. Sydney: Hale and Iremonger, 1993.

Sally Gray

See also Independent Australian Fashion; Queer Dress in Australia.

Urban Menswear in Australia

- Men's Dress Prior to World War I
- The Two World Wars and After
- Individuality and Style
- The 1990s Onward

Australia was relatively sparsely populated with Europeans until the discovery of gold in 1851. Immigration, together with increased urbanization and industrialization, led to growing prosperity for its colonies. A new class of professional city men, civil servants and entrepreneurs, emerged. While the governing class had always looked to Britain for their styles of fashionable dress, men abandoned the diversity of everyday town dress in the early colonies and began to conform to European standards of urban style and manners. By the late nineteenth century Australia had two main cities, Sydney and Melbourne, with smaller towns of Brisbane and Darwin in the north, Perth in the west, and Hobart and Adelaide in southern parts. From this period until the later decades of the twentieth century, men in urban areas have generally been rather conservative dressers. The climatic and social features of each have affected types of dress worn. In the second half of the nineteenth century, some lightweight, white tropical clothing, including headwear (popular in early colonial days especially in the north), was still worn in a number of towns. Elsewhere, darker colors and heavier fabrics, similar to European city wear, were increasingly the norm for formal and business occasions. Much fabric was imported, although first rough tweeds and later on in the twentieth century finer suiting fabrics were locally produced.

The Australian demographic was not divided by a specific class system as in Britain, and servants were used by few of the populace, but wealth and family did mark differentials in class. At the end of the nineteenth century and into the early part of the next, observers noted the common use of rather ill-fitted, ready-made wear in towns and, perhaps for this reason, reported that class differences were hard to detect. Men's appearances were said to deteriorate in the colonies. But the perception that Australia is an egalitarian society is, to a large degree, erroneous. Occupation, the occasion, and the different social milieu affected men's attire in urban areas. Professionals dressed differently than workers, evident in the fabric of their clothes, their cut, fit, and price, and they appeared more fashionable for special social events. The well-to-do did not live only in towns and cities, and the wealthy in regional areas did have access to department store mail-order catalogs, and individualized garments based on personal measurements could be ordered. The method of sending in measurements without first trying on a garment was a convenience of catalog purchases for men, providing a functional method of acquiring clothes, particularly for those living away from urban areas. Indeed, tailors' and store catalogs are a significant, if somewhat limited, resource for the study of men's attire and more informal dress, along with photographs, paintings, and, later on toward the end of the twentieth century, fashion magazines. Few surviving examples of men's everyday dress exist.

MEN'S DRESS PRIOR TO WORLD WAR I

Sydney and Brisbane men, living in a subtropical climate, have tended to dress in more relaxed and casual styles than those in Adelaide and Melbourne. The capital city of Canberra was an artificially built city of the twentieth century, and as Melbourne and Canberra are both renowned for their cold weather in the winter months, men there use heavier clothing. For the well off, the double-breasted frock coat, with its fitted waist in black vicuna or worsteds, was widely available, remaining so until late in the nineteenth century. Worn with a top hat, it was the most formal style, together with a morning coat. Because of the high population of European immigrants in Victoria and specifically Melbourne, the dress there was arguably the most European in style, with darker fabrics used for suits. Yet even in the warmer climate of Brisbane, professional men had converted to drab, dark-colored attire by the end of the nineteenth century. In Sydney, where the demographic has come to include a high gay population, and where there is a relaxed and distinct beach culture, some men have tended to follow a more personal aesthetic, especially by the late twentieth century, less formal though still stylish. This studied informality

A portrait of a seated man in a three-piece suit wearing a broad-brimmed hat, Australia, ca. 1900. At this time professional men in Australia continued to wear English styles despite the hot climate. Photograph possibly by Arthur Phillips. Gift of the Estate of Raymond W. Phillips, 2008. Powerhouse Museum.

has spread, and in the twenty-first century professional men in all Australia's major cities tend to wear formal suits with no ties, suggesting a loosening of strict dress codes.

With growth in city densities, increased population, and merchant expansion came new urban developments, emporia, and department stores. The latter provided ready-to-wear clothing as well as custom-made services. Importing, retailing, and manufacturing took place under one roof using store-owned workrooms and later factories. David Jones and Co., a major Sydney department store, had its own men's clothing line, Orient, and offered ready-made imported garments as well as made-to-measure fashions. With mechanization in factories came faster production and subsequent mass output. Men's dress, as with other clothing, could be made from cheaper fabrics in styles with little need for durability. The services of the custom tailor gradually became less common, used only by the wealthiest of patrons or for special occasions.

Toward the end of the nineteenth century the catalogs of David Jones and Anthony Hordern and Sons, the latter store also located in Sydney, advertised the loose sac suit, which was gradually to replace the frock coat, becoming rapidly fashionable for urban men. While being the forerunner of the lounge suit of the twenty-first century, the sac suit was smart but somewhat informal when first introduced, despite its allusion to English styling. It was slightly rounded in front, single breasted as opposed to the double-breasted frock coat, and buttoned high toward the neck, allowing for a high-collared shirt and cravat or thin tie to peek above a high-necked waistcoat. The most fashionable of men could use a walking stick or cane as an accessory. Trousers contained either plain or raised seams with side or cross pockets and were cut close to the ankle. The made-to-measure tailored suit came in a choice of imported fabrics, such as English tweed, flannel, and worsted serge in gray, navy, or brown, checks or stripes. At this time catalogs also offered other suit styles: lounging suit, dress suit—with silk facings—and walking coat suits, which, if bought via catalog, were "carriage free" with "all materials thoroughly shrunk" to enhance quality.

Top coats were rarely needed in Australia; nevertheless, overcoats were advertised in catalogs in a variety of colors and styles. The lightweight Chesterfield was a popular knee-length coat with silk facings and braid trimmings. It was made from black, brown, or blue worsted or cheviot (a woolen fabric with a coarse twill weave, a crisp texture similar to serge). And there was the top frock coat, preferred for morning wear, being heavier and looser in cut. The Inverness and loose Ulster coats had capes attached at the neck. The Gladstone coat was a short, double-breasted overcoat with a shoulder cape, sometimes trimmed with fur. The Albert was an overcoat with a half-circle cape.

In the period up to World War I men's shirts had a variety of names and styles, as shown in store catalogs. Tunic shirts were a popular item, with fast colors, including blue, black, and heliotrope, and also brown stripes on white backgrounds. These shirts had a soft centered pleat, stiff round cuffs, and a stiff neckband and came in subcategory styles like the York and the Captain. Coat shirts and working shirts were also available. A wide range of headwear was available, ranging from top hats and bowlers to a variety of caps, as well as straw hats for their lightweight and sun-protective qualities. For evening wear fashionable professional men could knot a silk cravat into a thick bow and wear a Paris silk top hat.

Australia is a country that favors casual clothing. Outdoor recreation activities such as picnics, bathing, and tennis were very popular from colonial times, the former two pastimes enjoyed across the classes. Cricketing, golf, and bicycle riding became common, with styles specifically made to provide freedom of movement. When the bulk of trousers was gathered into a band, they were termed "plus fours" and became popular particularly for golf. In the nineteenth century the Ceylon golf and tennis shirt of cashmere or cream flannel was designed for sporting wear. Riding pants were made of buck cord or whipcord tweed. Norfolk jackets and knickerbockers were worn for shooting or golfing, and versions of tropical trousers and shirts were used when boating, and for tennis, picnics, and beach holidays. Lightweight checked suits, white caps, and cabbage tree hats (plaited from the cabbage tree palm) were common, and even sun helmets were worn with continued popularity at least until the end of the nineteenth century.

Cycling was an activity popular for men of all classes. For the well off, cycling dress consisted of a tight military-style jacket worn with breeches, puffed and tight around the knees, often worn with a pillbox cap. The rider also carried a bugle to warn pedestrians of his approach. In the twenty-first century tight, functional cycling styles are still prevalent, as the popularity of riding in the city increases. Modern shirts and shorts, though, are made from Lycra and more breathable fabrics to accommodate the modern speed-conscious bicycle rider. Bugles are not used.

Apart from the range of professional and semiprofessional men who lived and worked in urban environments, workingmen wore rough, ready-made trousers and shirts, and, for the poor, secondhand clothing was available. An important exception to the general conservatism in Australia were homosexual dressers, who from the nineteenth century were said to show affectation in attire and contrived mannerisms (a topic about which little is known). Another significant exception was the so-called larrikin subculture. These young men (and women) were first noted in Melbourne at the end of the nineteenth century, the men known for wearing exaggerated suits with tight waists, velvet collars, bell-bottomed trousers, loud ties, perhaps a black slouch hat, and shoes with relatively high heels. They had an almost Spanish appearance. This term *larrikin* has entered into popular parlance in Australia and continues to be commonly used to describe a youth or man who has independent, wayward tendencies.

THE TWO WORLD WARS AND AFTER

Australians went to war from 1914 to 1918. After the war preexisting styles for men in urban occupations continued. However, the Depression of the late 1920s greatly affected Australian spending. English suits and Scottish tweeds became scarce because of tariffs and the devaluation of the currency. The fashionable city man then owned a respectable plain or tweed suit, and a sports jacket, perhaps a pullover, and casual woolen trousers for weekends. Some fashion-conscious men in the 1920s responded to what was an increasingly consumerist society, particularly evident in leisure wear. At this period the Oxford bag was worn—deep brown or fawn-colored trousers with very wide-cut baggy legs, first made popular by students at Oxford University, where it is said they were inspired by the toweling trousers of rowing crews. The first male photographic and catwalk models are documented during the 1930s (despite the Depression), suggesting that a new era was emerging in the advertising of fashionable dress. The war interrupted this situation.

During World War II Australian mills such as Sydney Felt and Textiles of Australia Limited, which had operated since

1921, were mobilized, along with most tailors and clothing mak-ers, to contribute to the war effort by producing khaki uniforms, blankets, flannel linters for gun cotton, and other items. Clothes rationing was introduced in 1942. According to the Australian Bu-reau of Statistics, the primary reasons for clothes rationing were a fall in imports, increased armed services demands, and reduced labor for local production of textiles and garment making. Retail-ing of men's apparel was restricted to slightly more than half of the average prewar use. Everyone was encouraged to demonstrate the utmost frugality. Choice was reduced, outerwear was chiefly army regulation, and there were fewer available colors, leaving, for instance, a meager selection of long-sleeved pullovers and cardi-gans. Issues of clothing coupons expired in November 1945, but rationing for other commodities continued.

An interesting example of an enterprising Australian man's outfitter was the company of Fletcher Jones. David Fletcher Jones, starting as a traveling salesman with a hawker's wagon in 1918 selling Manchester goods, later settled in Warnambool, Vic-toria, setting up a tailoring business. By 1939 his tailor's room was one of the largest in Australia, soon selling in all states. In 1941 he restricted his production to trousers. He prospered during the war, supplying ready-made clothing and filling army uniform supply contracts as well as producing rough Coverdine trousers. In 1946 he set up The Mans Shop of Fletcher Jones Trousers Pty Ltd. in Collins Street, Melbourne. At the end of the 1940s he was mass-producing men's trousers in a purpose-built factory in War-nambool. Fletcher Jones became one of Australia's best-known outfitters. His firm is still in business in the twenty-first century. Jones's interest was in quality and exceptional fit. He would even-tually boast fractional fittings in seventy-two scientific sizes with the motto that "No man is hard to fit." One of his most well-known lines of ready-to-wear trousers was called Plus 8s.

Fletcher Jones adopted the Japanese Kagawa business model of factory cooperation, a pioneering move in Australia. By 1947 the company was called Fletcher Jones and Staff Pty Ltd., each employee having shares in the company and organized in coop-erative groups, a model highly successful for the firm. At first his factory workers were mostly locals, but later he sought out immi-grants. With Prime Minister John Curtin's "Populate or Perish" campaign to attract immigrants in the 1940s, many skilled tailors from Italy and other nationalities brought their own brands of male style to urban Australia. Merchants like Fletcher Jones had men stationed on the docks to head-hunt men and women for factory work. The immigrants brought their own distinct influ-ences, such as "Continental" suits, spats, and wide lapels reminis-cent of Hollywood glamour.

As ready-to-wear clothing boomed after the war, and tailors opened up stores across the country, new forms of synthetic cloth-ing materials like nylon, acrylic, polyester, and vinyl were intro-duced for menswear. These fabrics were especially appealing to wives because they were easy to wash, dried quickly, and did not crease or require ironing. Adult men's fashion in the 1950s was largely quiet and conservative, mostly featuring suits of plain fab-rics in dark, muted shades like blue, brown, and gray. In town, men wore hats as a formality, something that increasingly died out in later decades. These conservative clothes somewhat widened the generation gap between older men and the sometimes more dar-ingly dressed younger generation interested in rock and roll music, who tried to emulate the subcultural styles of Britain and America. Indeed, the 1950s witnessed moral panic at what was regarded as

An example of men's clothing worn in Australia during the Great Depression. This three-piece gray pinstriped wool suit was made by Farmers and worn by Dr. C. A. Monticone, Sydney, in the 1930s. Gift of Sunny Hastings (nee Monti-cone), Rey Monticone, and Lea Monticone, 2007. Powerhouse Museum.

extreme hooliganism and petty crime of teenage gang activities of the so-called bodgies (young men wearing American drape suits, pegged trousers, and moccasins) and widgies (their female com-panions). Hanging around street corners like the larrikins, they first attracted attention in Sydney, but later in other cities.

Urban men continued to wear suits, shorts, casual trousers, shirts, and jeans in the 1960s. Casual shirts were sometimes plaid and buttoned down the front, although a conservative "college look" of shirt and woolen or cotton vest was favored by others. The younger age group was aware of the variety of fashionable styles originating in Europe and America, increased by the intro-duction of television. The influence of the teenage "rebel" divided young from older men as it did in Britain and America. Youthful styles with crew cuts were common. Some young people modeled their appearance on musical idols like the Beatles and Elvis in both hairstyles—using hair products—and clothing. By the mid-1960s men's hair tended to be longer than previously, along with the growing popularity of beards and mustaches on younger men.

INDIVIDUALITY AND STYLE

Although Australian men continued overall to remain conservative dressers in the later years of the twentieth century, some ventured into less staid clothing. Dress style for men began to include brighter colors, double-breasted sports jackets, polyester pants suits with Nehru jackets, and turtlenecks. Some experimented with very thin ties and with wider ones that were patterned even when worn with pinstripe suits and safari suits. Unisex dressing appeared, featuring long straight hair or frizzed afros for men, bell-bottomed jeans, love beads, and embellished T-shirts in paisley, flower, or broad patterns. Clothing was as likely to be purchased at surplus stores as specialized outlets, and the concept of hand-me-downs and secondhand items was as acceptable among the youth as the tailored styles of the 1930s were for their fathers. All of this was part of greater access to the media, including magazines, cinema, and British and American television. Interestingly, while an increasing sense of national pride and self-expression in the early 1970s was exploited in women's fashion design, men's attire did not follow their degree of color and experimentation. A large number of men stuck with their conservative suits and the beige shorts, long cotton socks, and brown shoes common thirty years before.

What was evident was an exploration of self-expression by adoption of garments derived from the burgeoning import industry. A number of types of attire could coexist, expressing the wearer's personal feelings and beliefs. There were those who wore suits, those who chose jeans and casual wear, and those who chose even smart casual styles of shirt and trousers. Punk dress centered on the music scene in London; British designer Vivienne Westwood and Malcolm McLaren, a boutique owner before he became the manager of the punk group The Sex Pistols, publicized their ideas through their joint design ventures. Their boutique Sex, which was renamed Seditionaries, produced famous clothes including the "God Save the Queen" and "Destroy" shirts. Such garments informed punk style and were imported into Australia via magazines and music video clips. Some of this streetwear became threatening and politically defiant in higher-density city areas such as Sydney, Melbourne, and eventually Brisbane. Plaid kilts, ripped tights, pins, studs on leather collars, self-fashioned accessories, and mohawk hair were adopted. Their use was not as extreme as in London, but punk styles have enjoyed extreme longevity in Australia, worn even in the twenty-first century.

New romantic styles with frilled shirts derived from British clothes of the 1980s were exported to Australia. Popular music video artists such as Wham!, Duran Duran, Boy George, and Elton John influenced androgynous styles, including stark white T-shirts emblazoned with captions and video clips depicting highly sexualized men and women. Fluorescent colors reminiscent of the aerobics and gym-goers in Olivia Newton John's "Let's Get Physical" video were a staple of the 1980s and were adopted by both men and women for their sportswear. Australia's well-known stubbie shorts (extremely short, sometimes with frayed leg ends) worn at this time were a sign of the diversity of dress, popularized by young men often as a sign of overt masculinity (a stubbie is also a colloquial term for a beer). On the other hand,

from America, musicians such as Michael Jackson and Prince created a style of elegance, which would transform and carry on into the 1990s, while the music movement of rapping and break dancing saw the emergence of "ghetto" aesthetic styles such as tracksuits, expensive customized sneakers, and gold chains.

At the same time as popular culture from Europe, Britain, and America influenced Australian youth, the country's own rock scene emerged, with bands such as INXS, Cold Chisel, and Midnight Oil, expressing nationalistic sentiment. These bands encouraged the wearing of styles that emphasized dark jeans, low-maintenance, no-product hair, and casual leather jackets with T-shirts or singlets, epitomizing the working-class man, idealized as a "true" Australian. Sleeveless singlets, originally blue, worn by sheep shearers for comfort and freedom of movement, have continued to be renowned as one of Australia's iconic clothing items, even in the twenty-first century. The Bonds underwear company (registered in 1920 followed by the Chesty Bond advertising campaign of 1938) brought them to the attention of urban wearers. Bonds singlets and T-shirts are staple items of men's attire, both as underwear and as outerwear worn with jeans, other casual trousers, or shorts. A tight-fitted white Bonds T-shirt has also come to identify homosexual streetwear.

A man's suit designed for Waltons Limited, Australia, in the early 1960s, made of a blue-gray wool blend. The single-breasted jacket has narrow lapels and flap pockets. The trousers are designed in the "stove-pipe" style: straight-cut and narrow at the ankles. Gift of Terry Mooney, 2008. Powerhouse Museum.

THE 1990s ONWARD

While Australian men have continued to favor casual styles except for corporate wear, there has been a clear increase in fashion consciousness among the young and more affluent since the 1990s. Advertising culture has responded to the so-called metrosexual, a term coined by British journalist and writer Mark Simpson in 1994 to describe the deliberate sense of style, even vanity, driven by English soccer player David Beckham. Beckham has worn diamond earrings and cares for his body with regular massages and manicures, as well as having a special skin-care regime that includes wearing nail polish. Some Australian men responded by adopting carefully styled hair and neat, coordinated clothing, including caps and sunglasses or branded shirts with cuff links under waistcoats, with brown leather saddlebags or satchels as accessories. Whatever they wore, the metrosexual sent deliberate messages of style quite different from the stereotype of the conservative Australian man. It was to spark controversy about the crisis of masculinity and was counterstyled by men who stayed loyal to the Australian distinct look of relaxed elegance, including GStar jeans, logo T-shirts, and casual cotton shirts that could take a man from the business day into evening events.

While Australian women's wear fashion designers found a place on the international stage from the mid-1990s, it has been a slow but deliberate process to see men's fashion designers highlighted as prominently. One example is Joseph Saba, a shirt maker from Melbourne's Flinders Lane since 1965, whose sharkskin weave suits for men grew the brand until its takeover by The Apparel Group in 2003. Arthur Galan, who, like Saba, started in Melbourne in 1998 under the label AG, also took to a reinstated trend of classic men's tailoring with a modern, sharp, and sexy twist. He opened a store in Chapel Street and in 2001 a "men's boudoir" store at Sydney's Bondi Beach. Other trends in menswear are labels such as Mooks, Tsubi (now Ksubi), and General Pants, offering casual cargo pants, motif jeans, T-shirts, thongs (rubber sandals), and sneakers, which capture the skaterboy and urban junkie look. Shirt and suit makers such as AG, Saba, MARCS, and Morrissey cater to the sophisticated yet casual executive, and innovative pajama designers such as Peter Alexander dress men in the bedroom with bright, brushed cotton drawstring pants and one-size-fits-all pajama tops.

Due to a reduction in import taxes and the rise in offshore enterprise, the Australian men's clothing industry since the late twentieth century has become global, purchasing lower-cost labor in countries like China, India, Indonesia, and Bali. With a rise in embellishments, mostly in casual wear for younger men, including appliquéd patches, logos, and detailed stitching, or unique features such as patterned lining and opposing colored stitching on suiting, it is more cost-effective for high-end designers to create their ranges overseas and bring them into Australia.

The twenty-first century has witnessed a brief rebirth of the dandy, with layers of coordinated textures and colors, cravats, and designer wear. With overlarge sunglasses making a brief appearance, men have adopted a level of consciousness that has included the return to three-piece suits in wool, velvet, or linen, occasional cummerbunds and matching cravats, slicked center- or side-parted haircuts, designer rings and watches, and matching shoes and bags. Led by fashion designers such as Tom Ford from the United States, men can be as immaculately fashioned as they like, or can afford.

With globalization it is difficult to find identifiable Australian male styles in urban areas. Men's dress conforms to attire worn worldwide. Melbourne, Sydney, Brisbane, Adelaide, and Perth have similar trends and even work-wear is similar. However, ethnographically, its European population influences Melbourne's fashion culture in suburban pockets like South Melbourne, and Sydney has subcultural styles in its gay precincts of East Sydney. Yet in Australia climate continues to ensure certain differences in everyday street styles. While professional workers still stick to corporate suits and shirts, the warmer climate of Sydney and Perth lends itself to casual styles, and in seaside suburbs surfwear, jeans, board shorts, singlets, and T-shirts are worn with rubber sandals called thongs. In Melbourne, perhaps Hobart, and Adelaide there is a stronger leaning toward clothing more suitable to the colder weather experienced there. Darwin is the warmest of Australia's cities, and the dress there is correspondingly casual.

The overall impression of urban fashion in Australia in the twenty-first century is one of casualness, although for those with disposable incomes there are many high-end labels and local designers that cater to their tastes. Nighttime events and clubs would be places to see this clothing, as well as the classy areas of Melbourne and Sydney. There is a blurring of casual and formal attire, and it is now as common for a man to wear a suit to an event at the Sydney Opera House as it is for another to wear denim jeans, a liberty-printed cotton shirt with open neck, and sneakers. Suits are found in air-conditioned offices and in central city streets, but jeans, trousers, and shorts worn with T-shirts or open-neck shirts are ubiquitous, in shopping malls, at sporting events, and in the suburbs. Nevertheless, men's designer fashion continues to thrive and transform as modern trends change the landscape of Australian fashion.

References and Further Reading

Cannon, Michael. *Life in the Cities: Australia in the Victorian Age.* Melbourne, Australia: Penguin, 1988

David Jones and Company Catalogue. Spring and Summer Fashions. 1895–1896. Sydney, Australia.

David Jones and Company Catalogue. Spring and Summer Fashions. 1913, 1914, and 1915. Sydney, Australia.

David Jones and Company Catalogue. Autumn–Winter 1919. Sydney, Australia.

David Jones and Company Orient Clothing Catalogue. Autumn–Winter 1885. Sydney, Australia.

Flower, Cedric. *Clothes in Australia: A Pictorial History 1788–1980s.* Kenthurst, Australia: Kangaroo Press, 1984.

Joel, Alexandra. *Best Dressed: 200 Years of Fashion in Australia.* Sydney: Collins, 1984.

Maynard, Margaret. *Fashioned from Penury: Dress as Cultural Practice in Colonial Australia.* Cambridge: Cambridge University Press, 1994.

McDowell, Colin. *The Man of Fashion: Peacock Males and Perfect Gentlemen.* London: Thames and Hudson, 1997.

Vicki Karaminas

See also Images as a Resource for the Study of Australian Dress; Settler Dress in Australia; Retailing, Clothing, and Textiles Production in Australia; Jews in the Melbourne Garment Trade; Subcultural and Alternative Dress in Australia; Queer Dress in Australia; Popular Music and Dress in Australia.

Fashion Photography in Australia

Australian fashion photography has a relatively short history, starting with the earliest examples of fashion advertisements from the beginning of the twentieth century through to the popularization of the genre in Australia via the work of modernist photographers such as Max Dupain and the postwar heyday of Helmut Newton and others. An exploration of the strong voice of independent publishers who have helped to market Australian fashion and style is noted and includes the internationally recognized fashion imagery produced by photographers working today in a globalized industry. With a very small magazine publishing industry in the early years, to a considerable degree Australian fashion photography has followed in the footsteps of British and U.S. image making. The late twentieth and early twenty-first centuries brought new energy to Australian fashion publishing, in particular more experimental publications such as the highly successful magazine *doingbird*.

ORIGINS OF AUSTRALIAN FASHION PHOTOGRAPHY

Fashion photography in Australia, as elsewhere, grew out of society and glamour portraiture, which in turn descended from *carte de visite* (a small photograph the size of a visiting card) portraits of theatrical performers and other celebrities, widely distributed from the 1860s. International histories of photography tend to mark the beginning of fashion photography as a distinct genre in the late nineteenth century. The early history of Australian fashion photography is still a largely unknown and under-researched area. In Australia some fashion photography, like the innovative modernist work of Athol Shmith, produced in the 1950s, is well represented in art museum collections and published histories. However, obscurity still surrounds Australian fashion photography's broader history.

The search for the origin of fashion photography in Australia prompts the question: What is fashion photography? The most frequently offered answer is that fashion photography is photography that illustrates fashion. Victorian and Edwardian portraits of theatrical performers and other celebrities, together with postcards, inspired widespread sartorial imitation. However, the term *fashion photography* is usually reserved for a genre of photography whose primary purpose is to sell clothing—either itemized and listed as available for sale (editorial) or presented as part of a promotion for a fashion house or label (advertising). Hence its intimate link with the mass print media of newspapers and magazines.

The question of definition becomes more complex when we consider that a photograph can be used as a fashion photograph even though it was originally taken for another purpose, such as celebrity portraiture. Since early fashion photography is often indistinguishable from portraiture, named images of Australian theatrical celebrities from the late nineteenth and early twentieth centuries constitute an important archive of "proto-fashion photography." In Australia the publication of photographs in this regard follows similar patterns to those that developed in France, Britain, and the United States.

The use of photography in fashion journalism occasionally appears in the late nineteenth century in colonial society newspapers such as *Table Talk* (1885–1939). There is an isolated instance of commercial fashion photography dated 1889 in the Brisbane magazine *The Princess: A Lady's Newspaper* by photographer Paul Poulson. But for the most part, enhanced by the refinement of the half-tone process, we find in the early twentieth century it is photographs of society weddings and fashionable celebrities that are the most frequently reproduced in newspapers. Extended features such as "Seen in Melbourne Streets," typically photo-grids of fashionable men and women, or scenes from Melbourne's famous Flemington races, were also common. With isolated exceptions, print advertisements for clothing and department stores in Australia remained hand-drawn rather than photographic until at least the second decade of the twentieth century.

The years between Australian Federation (1901) and the outbreak of World War I were marked by social progress and an economic boom. Australia had recovered from the depression of the 1890s, and women, in particular, were given more democratic rights, including the vote. In the major cities of Melbourne and Sydney, this period coincided with significant growth in the retail industry. Department stores led the way in all aspects of retailing, including advertising, which created and stimulated the wants of the growing middle-class population. As in other industrialized nations, advertising and the novel leisure activity of shopping belonged to a new culture of mass production and its consumption. By the 1890s consumerism reached an unprecedented level, along with the creation of a range of new service positions for women, such as shop assistants. Women, as managers of the domestic budget, also became the main targets of advertisers.

The development of Australian advertising photographs unfolded on the pages of popular magazines such as *The Lone Hand*, an elaborate and influential monthly cultural magazine. The first fashion advertisement in *The Lone Hand* that used photography, rather than line drawing, appeared in the September 1907 issue, entitled "Portfolio of Spring and Summer Millinery Fashions," for the department store Anthony Hordern and Sons. This color insert into the normally black-and-white publication featured eight pages of multiple, hand-colored, head-and-shoulder photographs. Hats were an enormously important fashion accessory for the entire first decade of the twentieth century, and for women a particular indicator of their femininity. Other sites for fashion advertising included mail-order catalogs. For women who lived outside the cities, mail-order fashion was important in a country as large as Australia. Established department stores such as David Jones produced lavishly illustrated books twice a year. For the most part, however, the clothes in these publications were illustrated rather than photographed, until at least the mid-1920s.

The Lone Hand offers many examples of the struggle between drawing and photography for dominance in the representation of male, but particularly female, fashions. One of the most instructive examples is a Robert Hurst Shoes advertisement from May 1910. The advertisement features a formally innovative and humorous montage of multiple photographs combined with hand drawing to create the striking effect of a giant-sized woman resting her foot on top of a shoe factory, demanding her shoes. While advertisements for dresses and corsets continued to utilize the idealizing mode of fashion illustration, one advertisement for Gowing Bros. suits from 1910 illustrates the evidential role of photography at the time. It shows a hand-colored photograph of a man in a suit, with the text: "The suit here actually photographed shows how Gowings 'cut.'" This is one of the first examples of Australian fashion advertising photography.

In the first two decades of the twentieth century, the relationship between the fashion and theater worlds was one of crucial interdependence, mediated by photography. The pages of *The Lone Hand* in the 1910s reveal an extraordinary hunger for detailed descriptions of clothing, as fashion photography was so limited. Theatrical reviews and written accounts of stage celebrities' wardrobes describe their garments in close detail. The success of New Zealand–born, Australian-based sisters May and Mina Moore, who produced stylish portraits with chiaroscuro lighting of theatrical personalities, can be seen as the visual element of this interest. It was somewhat later in the 1920s that true fashion photography responded to, and fueled, a desire to know more about the clothes of influential women, which came predominately from overseas (Paris in particular) and offered details about where customers could obtain them or their replicas. There is almost no fashion photography of men's dress at this time.

MODERN AUSTRALIAN FASHION PHOTOGRAPHY

Histories of Australian photography that deal with fashion imagery usually mark its origins in the pages of the high-quality Sydney journal *The Home* in the 1920s. *The Home* was a tastemaking magazine in the international style of American and British *Vogue*, *Harper's Bazaar*, and the *Tatler*. It published images and essays on modern, applied, and decorative arts alongside fashion, and it patronized local art photographers. The involvement of art photographers, both as "amateur" pictorialists and as commercial illustrators, was crucial to the development of Australian fashion photography. Pictorialist photography consisted of mostly black-and-white or sepia-colored photographs that emulated painting.

Along with a new nationalist taste in graphic design, interior design, and fashion itself, *The Home* reveals a fluidity of photographic styles revolving around an imported modernist photographic aesthetic found in the early work of Max Dupain and Russell Roberts in the mid-1930s. Credited photographic fashion work, in which a photographer is privileged as a creative figure, appears from the first issue in 1920, in which the editorial promoted its "special photographic service to record the latest and best achievements in dress that commerce has been able to make available for Australian wardrobes."

The Home's first official photographer was Harold Cazneaux (1878–1953), a personal friend of the publisher, Sydney Ure Smith, and a well-known Sydney-based pictorialist. The pictorialist

A cropped version of this photograph of Doris Zinkeisen appeared as Australian style magazine *The Home*'s first photographic cover in February 1931. Photograph by Harold Cazneaux. National Gallery of Victoria.

photographers—notably John Kauffmann and Walter Barnett (before he left for England)—had helped legitimate the expressive potentials of artistic photography. Ure Smith understood the potential of photography as a modern medium, and the possibility that a photographer might adopt a unique style was increasingly being recognized. It is in this context that Cazneaux's elevation as the magazine's chief Australian fashion photographer of the 1920s is noted. Like Cazneaux, Monte Luke (1885–1962) regularly contributed to *The Home* in the 1920s, his style influenced by his earlier glamour work in the theater and practice as an exhibiting art photographer.

Various women portrait photographers regularly provided images for *The Home* at this time—including Ruth Hollick and Pegg Clarke in Melbourne and Bernice Agar and Judith Fletcher in Sydney. But although women photographers were often applauded for sensitivity toward their subjects, the status of professional artist usually eluded them—especially after the consolidation of the pictorialist aesthetic and the professionalization of fashion photography following the return of men from the Great War (World War I). The contribution of women photographers to the early history of Australian fashion photography is less recognized. Ruth Hollick (1883–1977), for example, was the most successful of the group but is better known for her portraits of children, while her professional fashion work has been neglected until relatively recently. The photographs of Cazneaux and Hollick dominated early issues of *The Home* in the 1920s and included pictorialist-influenced portraits of society women in the most glamorous attire of the day. Of these, the rare images whose primary purpose shifted away from portraiture to the display of itemized clothes for sale effectively serve as the first credited Australian fashion photographs.

Despite the Depression, the 1930s saw a rapid growth in commercial photographic studios. While women had featured prominently as glamour portraitists, men soon dominated the emerging profession of fashion photographer. In the 1930s Russell Roberts (1904–1999), Max Dupain (1911–1992), and Athol Shmith (1914–1990) all frequently worked on fashion commissions for *The Home* as well as other magazines. As exponents of the so-called New Photography, which reached Australia via European publications, their work was of particular interest to advertising clients, who quickly realized that bold compositions, sharp and often unusual angles, and dramatic lighting would make for innovative product presentations. This fact, combined with innovations in printing technologies and artificial studio lighting, as well as the rise in local magazine publishing, meant that fashion photography in the 1930s was a viable profession in Australia.

Russell Roberts is known for advocating progressive photo-illustration techniques in fashion and portraiture and is credited with establishing the largest studio of its kind in Australia at that time. With a sharp eye and astute business sense, Roberts effectively created a new style for Australian fashion photography. His studio seems to have pioneered the use of color film for fashion photographs in the early 1930s. Along with traditional studio glamour work, Roberts's Sydney-based studio brought a modern and more naturalistic approach, inspired by location shots from Europe. Roberts's successful studio played a vital role early in the careers of many of Australia's most influential photographers, including Max Dupain.

By 1935 Dupain was cast as the leader of avant-garde photography when a portfolio of his modernist still lifes and radical nudes and figure studies was published in *Art in Australia*. Some of these images had surrealist overtones, expressing Dupain's enthusiasm for the work of the Paris-based American artist Man Ray. Soon Dupain's fashion images, inspired by the work of leading international figures, began appearing in the up-market lifestyle magazine *The Home*. An apprentice of Cecil Bostock (1884–1939)—well known for his fashion work for David Jones—Dupain deployed both the dramatic lighting and geometry of modernist advertising and some of the contorted spaces and odd conjunctions of surrealism. Most of Dupain's known fashion work, however, is relatively somber: static, studio-based tableaux of women and clothes. Dupain left fashion entirely after the 1940s in favor of architectural and documentary photography.

It is important to note that while the strict separation of commercial and artistic photography is of recent invention, commercial photographers did not think of themselves as artists. In many cases fashion photography was only one of the genres these photographers worked in. Practitioners like Dupain and Laurence Le Guay (1917–1990) are better remembered for their documentary work, while Hans Hasenpflug (1907–1977), Roberts, Janice

Wakely (1935–), and Henry Talbot (1920–1999) are today less well known.

Hans Hasenpflug was largely self-taught, and his work represents an interest in the visual vocabulary of New Photography and capturing action. His most famous images produce a tonal rhythm across the surface of the print, a formal tension in content and composition typical of New Photography as it sought to embrace fresh ways of seeing the modern world. Hasenpflug worked for the influential advertising studio of Russell Roberts in the mid-1930s, after his arrival in Australia from Germany in 1927. After 1937 Hasenpflug worked for Athol Shmith's studio in Melbourne.

Athol Shmith is today recognized as the greatest pioneer of modern Australian fashion photography. He began to take fashion photographs in Melbourne in the 1930s at a time when the profession of fashion modeling was still in its infancy. By the 1940s Shmith had established a reputation for elegant fashion photography that incorporated the conventions of modernist photographic practice and seductive Hollywood glamour portraiture. His was an elegance of simple postures, elegant backdrops, and often dramatic close-ups. Shmith continued to be a leader in fashion photography through to the 1960s, when his style began to seem dated.

POST–WORLD WAR II PHOTOGRAPHY

In 1946 Laurence Le Guay established a magazine called *Contemporary Photography*, which focused on documentary photography's role in exposing and redressing the social ills besetting postwar Australia. *Contemporary Photography* also published fashion photographs and works of commercial photo-illustration from the burgeoning class of professional photographers. In 1947 Le Guay entered into a partnership with John Nisbett in a studio that specialized in fashion and commercial illustration. Later, his work occasionally took on space age themes. Other important figures of the 1940s, 1950s, and 1960s include Ray Leighton, Geoffrey Lee, Rob Hillier, Geoffrey Powell, John Nisbett, and Norman Ikin.

By the 1950s—a time of affluence following the constraints of the war years—fashion advertising and illustration work had become a major specialist industry for photographers and their growing teams of collaborators. Fashion photographic modeling was becoming a career in its own right, and increasingly standard rates for sessions were being set. A professional training course for such models was started in Sydney in 1947, supervised by the fashion photographer Robert Hillier. *Vogue*'s Australian edition was established in 1959. This was the era of grand Collins Street studios in Melbourne and major clients such as Myers, as chain department stores benefited from the upsurge in production of consumer goods following World War II. But as curator Gael Newton has observed, agencies tended to be in awe of overseas trends in fashion photography and wanted locals simply to copy such models. The individual photographer's control over design and approach was increasingly subject to direction from specialized advertising departments.

Helmut Neustadter (1920–2004) (who changed his name to Newton in 1946) arrived in Australia in 1940, after fleeing Nazi Germany via Singapore. In Australia, he was interned at the Tatura detention camp. After a stint in the Australian army, Newton began working as a photographer in Melbourne, taking

The Australian model Patricia "Bambi" Tuckwell in a Dior dress, 1949, as photographed by Athol Shmith. The work of his 1950s heyday was characterized by his use of elegant modernist compositions with dramatic lighting. He is recognized as the greatest pioneer of modern Australian fashion photography. Courtesy of the National Gallery of Victoria, Melbourne.

up the profession from his earlier training in a fashionable Berlin salon in the 1930s known as Yva's. By the mid-1950s Newton was established as one of Australia's leading fashion photographers, his work regularly appearing in the newly independent *Vogue Australia* beginning in 1959. In Newton's Australian work there is already a characteristic technical precision and a breezy appreciation of coolly beautiful women (such as the celebrity model and personality Maggie Tabberer), yet there is no hint of the dark erotic mood, the "porno-chic" that was to become Newton's distinctive contribution to photography. His Australian fashion images make maximum use of bright outdoor settings—the beach, lush gardens, or picturesque ghost towns such as Walhalla. He used urban environments imaginatively—road signs appear often, adding a lighthearted, optimistic view of the city and geometric drama. In 1961 Newton left Australia, believing that it was possible to build a career in fashion photography only in Paris or New York. Indeed, he became one of the most significant international names in fashion photography of the 1960s and 1970s.

Responding to the altered social, political, and economic conditions of the 1950s, Bruno Benini (1925–2001) created a style of photography that conveyed an image of opulence and sophistication. Along with Melbourne's other leading fashion photographers

of the time, Athol Shmith and Helmut Newton, Benini positioned his models as glamour icons and created a new ideal of femininity responsive to the evolving fashion industry of the 1950s. In many respects the brilliance and intrigue of Benini's photography during the 1950s lay within his use of unexpected locations to create a deliberate ambiguity. For example, he shot one of his most famous photographs outside a dingy soup kitchen as a means of augmenting the impression of sensuous luxury through stark contrasts.

In a decade when it was rare for women to work professionally as photographers, Janice Wakely established the Penthouse Model Agency and Photographic Studio (1963–1965) with co-model Helen Homewood. Wakely and Homewood's enterprise functioned both as modeling agency and photographic studio—probably the first of its kind in Australia. Wakely produced photographs for Australian fashion houses, designers, and companies like Sportscraft and Watersun swimwear.

Like Newton, Henry Talbot was an émigré artist who brought an invigorating internationalism to Australian photography. Talbot arrived in Australia in 1940 aboard the infamous *Dunera*—an overcrowded ship of European "enemy aliens." Initially he worked in some of the leading photographic studios of the day and quickly established a significant reputation, and in 1956 he was invited to go into partnership with Newton (with whom he formed a friendship during the war). The Melbourne studio of Helmut Newton and Henry Talbot was a great success, securing a vast number of clients, including Sportscraft and the Australian Wool Board. The fresh modern look of his work—linking contemporary fashion and popular culture—reflected the emerging youth culture and widespread social changes that characterized the 1960s. In these years the exoticism of an overseas shoot became more common, as Australian fashion was gaining international credibility and overseas air travel was more prevalent.

In the late 1960s fashion photography in Australia gained a new confidence. With an increased reliance on higher-quality color processing, the exuberant fashion photography of this period was best exemplified by the images found in *POL* magazine (1968–1985), later revived as *Pol Oxygen*. *POL* gave unprecedented freedom to individual innovators such as Wesley Stacey and Grant Mudford (both better known for their conceptual documentary work), as well as Brett Hilder, Dieter Muller, Rennie Ellis, and John Lethbridge. Most were art or documentary photographers who made crossovers into fashion or social commentary. Part of the first wave of desktop publishing, *POL* reflected a changing Australia that was being radicalized by the 1960s. It featured high production values, a quirky sense of humor, and a liberated sense of sexuality. In the 1970s, in tune with a new cultural nationalism in Australia, Uluru (Ayres Rock) and Alice Springs also became fashionable backdrops. From this period onward Australian fashion photography exhibits a general obsession with nature. Unsurprisingly, given the country's coast-hugging population, the beach has become a key backdrop for Australian fashion photography.

AFTER THE 1970s

A new wave of magazines followed in the 1970s and 1980s. *Rag Times*, produced in a newspaper format, was a short-lived magazine that ran beginning in 1977. It was informal, offbeat, streetwise, and guided by a romantic manifesto based around personal freedom. The best-known magazine of the 1980s was *Follow Me*, which catered to a more commercialized market, as well as new wave crossovers between art, music, and fashion. Grant Matthews's vibrant and often Australiana-style images were typical. Along with Matthews, Monty Coles and Peter McLean's work was featured in the first exhibition of contemporary Australian fashion photography shown in an art context. It took place at the Australian Centre for Photography and was entitled Image Perfect: Australian Fashion Photography in the 80s, curated by Sandy Edwards in 1987.

Since the early to mid-1990s a number of independent, street-style/fashion/lifestyle magazines have come onto the Australian market, and many are now established names, such as *Black and White, Cream, Oyster, Yen,* and *Russh*. The Australian market consumes more magazines per capita than any other country in the Organisation for Economic Co-operation and Development. Most fashion magazines continue to be published in Sydney, as has been the case historically. More magazines, each with their own house style and design formats for specialized readerships, have meant more places for publication and more varied assignments for photographers. Independent magazines are also an area where fashion photographs frequently cross into an art and popular culture mix. While magazines like *Vogue Australia* tend to employ only a small number of regular photographers (Richard Bailey, Troyt Coburn, and Justin Smith are some of the key names in the first decade of the twenty-first century), faster turnaround times, lower budgets, and fewer advertising constraints also mean independent magazines are the chief publishing avenues for aspiring fashion photographers. Some are short-lived, such as Pierre Touissant's *Processed*, which had only two issues in the early 2000s, which is typical of start-up magazines designed as quick promotional tools for those involved.

Increasingly, fashion photographers do not limit themselves to working for Australian magazines. As well as assignments in Europe and the United States, Australian fashion photographers are now regularly working in Asia. Likewise, Australian magazines more frequently publish the work of international photographers. One of the most original of the new independent magazines is the biannual art-fashion publication for men and women *doingbird*, edited by Max Doyle and Malcolm Watt. It features only a handful of Australian photographers in preference for international photographers, models, writers, and illustrators. Indeed, *doingbird* has a higher international than local circulation, countering the general flow of imported magazines. Contemporary Australian fashion photographers who regularly work overseas include Lyn Balzer and Tony Perkins, Harold David, Liz Ham, Derek Henderson, Ingvar Kenne, Tim Richardson, and Justin Smith. All exhibit their work in galleries or are involved with self-publishing and collaborations with artists and fashion designers. Some of these photographers, notably Richardson and Smith, are also experimenting with digital imaging in distinctive ways.

Because the market for fashion and fashion photography in Australia is small, conservatism still rules in the glossy magazines; only very few photographers manage to go beyond conventional formulas and create their own style. There appears to be a continued obsession with the landscape—both the bush and the beach—that is common to all forms of artistic expression in white settler Australia, from film to literature. This often ironic exploration of the Australian environment may be ascribed to an uneasy relationship with a largely uninhabitable environment, now figured as the background for cutting-edge urban fashion imagery.

References and Further Reading

Crombie, Isobel. *Athol Shmith Photographer*. Melbourne, Australia: Schwartz Publishing, 1989.

Hall, Barbara, and Jenni Mather. *Australian Women Photographers 1840–1960*. Melbourne, Australia: Greenhouse Publications, 1986.

Maynard, Margaret. *Out of Line: Women and Style in Australia*. Sydney: University of New South Wales Press, 2001.

Maynard, Margaret. "Where Do Flappers Fit In? The Photography of Modern Fashion in Australia." *Cultural History* 25 (2006): 273–290.

Newton, Gael. *Shades of Light: Photography and Australia, 1839–1988*. Canberra: Australian National Gallery, 1988.

Palmer, Daniel. "Tracing the Origins of Australian Fashion Photography." *The La Trobe Journal* 76 (Spring 2005): 87–103.

Palmer, Daniel, and Kate Rhodes, eds. *Photofile* 71 (Winter 2004).

Sayers, Andrew, ed. *POL: Portrait of a Generation*. Canberra, Australia: National Portrait Gallery, 2003.

Van Wyk, Susan. *The Paris End: Photography, Fashion and Glamour*. Melbourne, Australia: National Gallery of Victoria, 2006.

Willis, Anne-Marie. *Picturing Australia: A History of Photography*. North Ryde, Australia: Angus & Robertson, 1988.

Daniel Palmer and Kate Rhodes

See also Making and Retailing Exclusive Dress in Australia—1940s to 1960s; The Australiana Phenomenon in Australia.

Independent Australian Fashion

- Fashion as Art
- The Fashion Design Council
- New Models of Design, Retail, and Production
- MaterialByProduct (MBP) and the Twenty-first Century

Straddling the boundaries between art, craft, and fashion, independent fashion design first emerged as a defiant new aesthetic and mode of cultural production in Australia during the mid-1970s. An energetic current that introduced new visual and conceptual models to Australian fashion, independent fashion culture quickly became the radical alternative to existing mainstream and commercial, or traditional (European) fashion systems. Fundamental to the movement was the endeavor to situate contemporary Australian fashion design within a much broader discourse, one that allowed for an exploration of the relationship between fashion and art, product and concept. Since then, independent design has remained an influential and vital element within the Australian fashion landscape, its presence resulting in unique, provocative, disruptive, and experimental methods of production and retail.

FASHION AS ART

For the majority of Australians the existence of an alternative fashion culture was first revealed by Jane de Teliga's influential Art Clothes exhibition at the Art Gallery of New South Wales in 1980. Featuring eight young designers, David McDiarmid, Peter Tully, Jenny Bannister, Kate Durham, Mark Arbuz, Katie Pye, Jenny Kee, and Linda Jackson, the exhibition validated the dynamism of Australian avant-garde artists who were challenging the conventional limits of fashionable dress. An exhibition about departures from the norm, Art Clothes radically positioned contemporary clothing and accessories as wearable art objects, exceeding accepted clothing categories.

In part, de Teliga's exhibition signaled an early attempt at redefining the terms of Australian fashion through an expanded vocabulary of references, be they national, pop-cultural, or anti-fashion. All of the works on display were characterized by innovative construction techniques, the use of eclectic materials and imagery, multidisciplinary practice, and, more fundamentally, adherence to the aesthetic concerns of art. Designer Katie Pye, who had five works in the exhibition, expressed this new vision best when interviewed for a nationwide television report. She stated, "what you call fashion, I call a product, what I call fashion is art."

Pye was typical of the first wave of young designers who sought to challenge the commercial constraints of the mainstream Australian fashion world. For them, fashion was a forum for ideas. Pye herself had first enrolled in a Diploma of Art (Painting) at East Sydney Technical College, but she soon began painting fabrics and making clothes for friends and fellow students. By 1976 she had opened a concept clothing store called Duzzn't Madder and was producing clothing "statements": theatrical and original garments that often incorporated some level of social commentary. Pye regarded clothing as a three-dimensional canvas and a kind of personal performance, not unlike fellow Australian Leigh Bowery, who later pushed this idea into much more radical territory.

Establishing the Katie Pye Studio with her partner Georg Nezovic in 1979, Pye began selling her limited edition clothing from a stall at Sydney's Paddington Market (a secondhand and crafts market). Their label, Clothes for Modern Lovers, took inspiration from what was happening in other art forms such as film and music. Although not directly influenced by U.S. and British punk (an anarchic style of music and dress that began in the 1970s), Pye was working in an environment that had benefited from punk's liberation of nonconformity. Her work during this period had a "new wave" aesthetic, and her collections possessed a strong visual literacy.

In approach, Pye shared the sensibility of her independent peers, who were looking inward for inspiration, and whose work remained closely linked to their own lifestyles. Pye's futuristic and androgynous "Spinnaker Jacket" from 1978 (National Gallery of Victoria) was made at the time of her involvement with the local rock scene. Through Nezovic, Pye had started styling up-and-coming Australian bands for performances and video clips. Drawing upon graphic traditions of abstract color, geometric shape, and strong oppositional elements, the patchwork composition of "Spinnaker Jacket" was Pye's attempt to create her own material handwriting through use of unique splicing and piecing arrangements.

Broadcasting new fashion ideas, however, was not so straightforward. Independent designers frequently had to look beyond traditional publishing platforms to garner coverage for their ideas. During the 1970s Jenny Kee and Linda Jackson self-staged the extravagant Flamingo Follies parades. Likewise during the 1980s Katie Pye devised "pop-art presentations" and employed highly stylized video recordings and art photography in order to convey the concepts and moods of her collections to clients.

Indeed, very few of Pye's or her peers' garments were featured in mainstream fashion publications like *Vogue Australia*. Rather, it was alternative magazines such as *POL* and its subsidiary, fashion bimonthly *Rag Times* (established in 1977), that proved to be vital and sympathetic voices for independent culture. Combining edgy photography, credible writing, and street-style currency, *POL* and *Rag Times* proved seminal for young designers by bringing them into contact with like-minded people who could inform and support their practice.

In response to the increasing interest in alternative fashion culture, small, designer-run boutiques soon surfaced in inner-city locations across the country. These also formed a vital component of the independent Australian fashion landscape. Arguably the most influential store was Flamingo Park (1973–1995), run initially by Jenny Kee and Linda Jackson (Jackson set up her own label in 1982). The boutique stocked their original and innovative designs, which incorporated Australian imagery and motifs—Kee's knitwear and Jackson's signature taffeta evening wear—as well as jewelry by Peter Tully. Further south, Melbourne's equivalent was Clarence Chai's Chai, Clothes and Accessories, established in

1974. Trained as a graphic designer, Chai had first established an antique and vintage clothing store called Paraphernalia with Paul Craft, before branching out on his own. A local institution, Chai, Clothes and Accessories sold Chai's own innovative ranges, knitwear from London, and, exclusively, a limited range by emerging designer Jenny Bannister.

As well as designer-run stores, Sydney boutiques such as Stephanie Meares's Black Vanity and Susan Bowden's Little Pink played an important part in educating consumers about the merits of local style by retailing a combination of secondhand or vintage clothing, small in-house-designed ranges, and the work of up-and-coming local designers. Appropriately, a counterculture clientele of artists, musicians, and hairdressers formed the biggest audience for these new avant-garde labels.

Melbourne designer Jenny Bannister was another exponent of "art-fashion." After completing a three-year Fashion Design and Production Diploma in 1974 at the Emily McPherson College in Melbourne, Bannister first began working for a suburban boutique in Chapel Street. Here she created outfits from recycled denim and army surplus before moving on to make her own small range of garments from "tat" (pre-worn 1950s fabrics). These she sold through the Vanilla boutique in Chapel Street and Chai's in the city, before finally establishing her own label in 1977.

Bannister shared the concerns of fellow artists and designers, who were highly critical of a tendency within the mainstream Australian fashion industry to copy overseas trends. Like her peers, she expressed a post-punk, anarchic sensibility in her approach to fashion. Bannister's aesthetic embraced shock value and the "transgressive power of style" as she experimented with unconventional materials and construction methods.

Early works, such as the "Punk Tea Towel Dress" from 1977 (National Gallery of Victoria), visibly cited subcultural influences. Combining a do-it-yourself approach to the making and reworking of cheap materials, Bannister incorporated black fishnet, tea towels, plastic, and found objects. Designing for people like her, who desired to wear something different, Bannister's work found an appreciative audience among the underground music scene that was burgeoning in St. Kilda, Melbourne, by way of proto-punk bands such as Nick Cave's Birthday Party. Theme parties, gigs, and events were often the catalysts for some of her more outlandish creations.

Bannister's "Dress 1980" (National Gallery of Victoria), from the Medieval Stud collection, was part of an outfit that belonged to Amanda King, who worked at Melbourne's Inflation disco in 1980. It was worn with a wide leather belt with chains, fishnet stockings, and a pair of Vivienne Westwood spiked Court shoes (1976). Of a different temperament to British punk, the outfit is pieced together from uncut pelts of black leather and joined with heavy, metal, pyramid studs. Bannister regarded her labor-intensive work as "body sculpture," a style of urban tribal wear created at the boundaries of art, craft, and fashion.

THE FASHION DESIGN COUNCIL

Throughout the 1980s Bannister was one of several key participants in the innovative Fashion Design Council parades (FDC, 1983–1993), which aimed to change ideas about Australian fashion. In 1983 artists Jillian Purvis, Julie Burt, and Robert Pearce staged Fashion '83 at the Seaview Ballroom, an infamous underground club. The seminal event presaged the creation of

the FDC. Featuring twenty local artists, designers, and fashion "experimentalists," the event questioned "who is brave enough to determine where fashionable ends and where fashion becomes art."

To this end, Fashion '83 flew in the face of Australian fashion conventions. At the time these consisted of imports, established, conservative designers, and a growing number of mass-market chain stores dependent on offshore manufacturing. Audacious and innovative, the two-day event seemed to unite all of Melbourne's disparate avant-garde and underground fashion elements into a coherent statement. Incorporating fashion, new music, film, video, acrobatics, and over a hundred models, significant designers who participated included Clarence Chai, Despina Collins, Inars Lacis, Jenny Bannister, jeweler Kate Durham, and knitwear specialist Maureen Fitzgerald. In particular, Fitzgerald's three-dimensional knitwear typified the kind of break-away designs that were launched at Fashion '83. Her architecturally conceived outfits, mixed with fur or leather, displayed the kind of in-your-face visual excitement lacking in mainstream clothing.

By 1984 the original underground movement had consolidated into a professional organization known as the Fashion Design Council (FDC), receiving annual financial support from the Victorian Ministry for the Arts. Cofounded by Kate Durham, Robert Buckingham, and Robert Pearce, the FDC assumed

"Dress 1980" by Australian designer Jenny Bannister. The dress was part of the Medieval Stud collection and features a wide leather belt with studs and chains. National Gallery of Victoria.

responsibility for supporting, nurturing, and advocating for independent Australian design.

Throughout its lifetime the FDC acted as a vibrant nerve center, providing a public voice and profile for independent fashion designers. Their mandate stated a commitment to the art of fashion design: to the individualistic, idiosyncratic, experimental, new, and provocative in its wearable and unwearable form, or, as cofounder Robert Pearce put it, to high-risk dressing. In this sense the FDC's philosophical roots were seen to lie in the style cults and subcultures of English street fashion: post-punk new wave and the neo-romantic movements. With reform strategies that included adventurous parades, exhibitions, publications, and a boutique (1989–1992), the FDC created an artistic and intellectual platform—positioned within contemporary street culture—from which to engage with fashion's more radical edge.

Two other notable designers to emerge from under the Fashion Design Council auspices were fashion graduate Sara Thorn and her partner, fine art (printmaking and painting) graduate Bruce Slorach. Launching in 1983, the pair established the Sara Thorn label (later renamed Shrubbery, Abyss and Galaxy) as a vehicle for exploring innovative textile ideas. Pushing the boundaries of printed fabric, the pair began by hand screen-printing their designs from a small studio located in the heart of Melbourne. They then developed these prints into street-savvy collections of men's and women's wear.

Thorn and Slorach saw their clothing as a way of "commenting on and creating culture." Their free-form print designs comprised complex visual narratives, which cited references as diverse as science fiction, cartoons, art, technology, and history. "Cartoon Print Tracksuit" from 1983 (Powerhouse Museum Collection), worn with silver chains, studded metal belts, and combat boots, exemplifies Slorach's vibrant graphic style, which was influenced by the work of New York graffiti artists such as Keith Haring. Haring later visited Melbourne in 1984. Many of the pair's designs did not follow conventional methods of textile production. Instead of creating repeats, fabric was often treated like a huge canvas, with the designers completing graffiti-inspired, ink-filled screens measuring up to ten meters by one meter (32.8 by 3.28 feet) across.

By establishing their own fabric-printing studio and then retail shop, Galaxy Emporium, Thorn and Slorach had full control over the development of their trademark style. Their ideas found expression in inspired combinations of clashing patterns and fabrics, visual puns, and idiosyncratic imagery. Their design ethos was to make clothing for the urban environment. Deciding to produce in Melbourne and to use local manufacturers also enabled them to maintain a minimal turnaround time of two weeks, a factor that allowed them to keep pace with what was happening on the street.

The approach taken by Thorn and Slorach was also emulated by the Printintin print studio, cofounded in 1986 by textile artists Douglas McManus, Matthew Flinn, and Andrea McNamara. Flinn, who had studied textile design at Melbourne's Royal Institute of Technology (RMIT), had already begun designing fabric for garments and exhibiting them at the FDC parades. He remarked: "I couldn't just show rolls of fabric on stage. I was forced to do something with them."

Contemporary street culture was vital to the success of the FDC's aim to broaden people's understanding of Australian fashion. Recognizing fashion to be a means of expressing identity and an instrument for communicating larger ideas, the FDC staged many of their events at underground clubs. By creating opportunities for people to dress up, perform, participate, and party, they exploited the relationship between clothing and lifestyle. The FDC saw fashion as a relevant part of popular culture, in the same manner as music, art, theater, or dance.

The cumulative effect of FDC-organized events created new audiences and awareness of Australian fashion that sat outside of the mainstream. Feeding into a new optimism, the FDC encouraged a greater proportion of the general public to seek out underground designers and to consider the merits of locally designed product. Inversely, it also forced many of the designers involved to expand and to become more professional.

In 1985 Thorn and Slorach took their Moderno tourist collection to Japan as part of an Australian Fashion Show. They paraded twelve outfits, including several prints and a series of Bomb jacquard knits. By 1990 Thorn and Slorach's unique designs were featured in English style bibles *The Face* and *i-D*. "Men's Jacket and Kilt," from 1985 (National Gallery of Victoria), illustrates the type of inventive design work that was gaining the pair international recognition. Marrying Scottish tailoring with a contemporary urban edge, the black cotton canvas outfit is decorated with a complex hand silk-screen print comprising a vernacular Greek frieze, Napoleonic bees, winged boots, and robot faces.

Martin Grant, who has been based in Paris since 1992, was another young designer to benefit from his association with the Fashion Design Council during its early years. Informally taught dressmaking by his grandmother, Grant had left school and home at sixteen, moving into Melbourne's inner city. Hanging out in galleries, warehouse studios, and clubs, Grant met fashion designer Despina Collins, who fostered his childhood interest in fashion. Collins encouraged Grant to assist her in the creation of dramatic one-off evening and bridal gowns for her own label and invited him to share her studio space in Stalbridge Chambers.

At 443 Little Collins Street, Stalbridge Chambers was the informal epicenter of Melbourne's independent fashion movement. As Flinders Lane had been the locus for the rag trade in the early part of the century, Stalbridge Chambers was home to the studios of local fashion designers Fiona Scanlan, Gavin Brown, and Tony Syme, milliner Tamasine Dale, and jeweler Jane Burke, as well as the offices of *Crowd* and *Collections* magazines, a modeling agency, and the newly formed FDC.

Among a concentration of fashion talent, lured in by the low-rent studios, Grant soon began producing made-to-measure garments, club wear, and evening gowns. Establishing his own studio space in the building, Grant produced twice yearly, ready-to-wear collections for men and women as well as special orders for private clients under his own label. His aesthetic was a fusion of femininity, modernity, and exact tailoring.

Throughout the early 1980s Grant was an active participant in the FDC's parades and exhibition program, along with fellow Stalbridge residents Fiona Scanlan and Tamasine Dale. His work was also sold at Empire, a studio, workroom, and retail outlet run by fashion designer Brighid Lehmann and her sister. Opening in 1984, Empire also carried other new young designers such as Christopher Graf and Kara Baker, who had immigrated to Melbourne from New Zealand in 1981. Unlike many of the home-grown designers, Baker was technically trained and had spent a number of years working in the New Zealand fashion industry. Her work was primarily silhouette driven, influenced by the

Parisian-style, tailored designs of Claude Montana and Thierry Mugler, who were advocating a new version of 1940s hardened glamour. Baker formed her own label, Sirens, in 1981, and her collections were presented at all of the FDC parades throughout the mid- to late 1980s.

Grant's public profile as the self-taught boy wonder grew beyond the independent fashion scene. By 1985 his simple, structured garments, which cleverly reworked classic forms, appeared in nearly every major Australian fashion magazine from *Vogue Australia* to *Stiletto*. Grant's "Slash Back Coat Dress 1986" (National Gallery of Victoria) is a typical early design. Classic in outlook, the linen coat-dress balances flat color with soft feminine tailoring to play upon the romantic revivalism of the mid-1980s. Conservative from the front, the back yoke reveals Grant's then-trademark signature of slashed or split seams. Single horizontal or vertical slashes had characterized the previous few collections, playfully allowing suggestive glimpses of flesh above the nipple or across the back. The accompanying "Hat 1986" was made by Tamasine Dale, with whom Grant had formed a creative partnership. An innovative milliner, Dale's adventurous, quirky headpieces were partially inspired by the hat revival in London by leading milliners such as Stephen Jones.

By 1987 Grant had received national attention, winning the inaugural Ice Breakers innovative young designer award, organized by *Follow Me* magazine. The award aimed to credit the place that emerging designers occupied within the Australian fashion industry. Moreover, it acknowledged the viability of independent design within the mainstream marketplace. Grant's success proved that an independent design practice could exist autonomously with fashion industry convention. Ironically, that same year Grant pulled back from fashion, citing exhaustion after five years of designing developing, producing, and promoting his label.

By the time the last major Fashion Design Council parade was held in 1988, the organization represented more than two hundred emerging designers and makers. Perhaps recognizing the contribution that young contemporary designers working in the realm of limited production and one-off garments were making to the Australian fashion industry, Jane de Teliga curated her second exhibition, Australian Fashion: The Contemporary Art in 1989. Different than Art Clothes, the exhibition now understood independent fashion design as an important aspect of Australian cultural practice. Staged at the Powerhouse Museum, Sydney, and the Victoria and Albert Museum, London, the exhibition showcased the work of fifty fashion designers, jewelers, milliners, shoemakers, and textile artists.

NEW MODELS OF DESIGN, RETAIL, AND PRODUCTION

By the end of the 1980s, however, the cultural climate within which the Australian fashion industry operated had changed significantly. In broad terms the economy was in recession. Many large and mainstream fashion businesses had fallen victim to hard times, while financial troubles had forced both the closure of the FDC store and the organization in 1992. In its absence many questioned the viability of independent Australian fashion.

The independent designers who emerged during the 1980s had been interested in creating alternative fashion for people like themselves, rather than the mass market. With the downturned economy the ethos of autonomy that defined independent practice now clashed with the commercial realities of the marketplace. To survive, many of the independents were forced to restrain their creativity and become more business-oriented, producing larger quantities on a commercial scale. In the process independent fashion shifted from a form of wearable art to wearable contemporary design. At the same time mainstream labels also responded to the recession by embracing the quirks that were once the trademarks of the independents. Thus, the early 1990s saw greater flexibility and movement between the main and alternative fashion sectors.

The loss of the FDC as the public face and support network for independent designers left emerging designers with limited avenues of exposure. At the start of the decade the few directional boutiques in Australia continued to cater to the very high end of the market, stocking well-admired international fashion labels. Yet, by the mid-1990s attempts to reinvigorate the Australian fashion industry started to happen concurrently on three levels.

The most high profile was the part corporate-, part government-financed Australian Fashion Week (AFW). First held in Sydney in 1996, AFW was established by Simon Lock and Australian Fashion Innovators Pty Ltd. with the aim of raising the international profile of the Australian fashion industry. The intention was to insert the Australian spring/summer collections into the international fashion week calendar. It was hoped that this would engender opportunities for emerging and established designers as they presented to the fashion media, buyers, and possible new markets. AFW also aimed to be a critical platform from which to assess the merits of Australian fashion before an international audience. The most well-known Australian designers to benefit from this exposure were Collette Dinnigan and Akira Isogawa, both of whom participated in the inaugural event.

In 1997, a year after AFW began, the Victorian government also supported the establishment of the Melbourne Fashion Festival (MFF). The intention was to create a local and public platform for profiling design, processing, manufacturing, and retail. Consumer-focused and managed by a board and creative director in consultation with the fashion industry, the MFF possessed a clear commitment to advocating emerging young designers as well as independent design. Similar to the activities of the FDC, the early Melbourne Fashion Festivals oversaw an eclectic program of exhibitions, parades, lectures, and forums that promoted an exchange of ideas around fashion. With events such as Independent runway, the Innovators parade, and a sponsor-backed Young Designer Award with substantial prize money, MFF gave support to those designers operating at very small levels of retail and production.

Johanna Preston was a young designer whose work was presented in a number of MFF parades and exhibitions throughout the late 1990s. Professionally trained as a custom shoemaker, Preston established her own client-based practice in 1993. By 1996 she had set up a small studio in inner-city Collingwood, from which to develop contemporary footwear. Forming the Preston Zly label in partnership with Petr Zly, the pair has since consolidated a signature style that combines traditional design methods—hand welting, sole stitching, hand blocking, and wooden last making—with a clever reinterpretation of historical shoe forms. Preston Zly's aesthetic oscillates between structural and sculptural components, visible in their exaggerated shoe forms, use of bold, contrasting color, decorative leather work, broguing (small punched holes), top-stitching, and piping.

The renewed effort to promote original Australian design was also mirrored in the growing number of small retail boutiques in Melbourne's inner city that professed a mandate to support, nurture, and cultivate local designers. Among the most influential were Alice Euphemia, Robe Collective, and Fat 52. Alice Euphemia was established in 1996 by Fine Arts graduates Caroline Price and Karen Rieschieck. With a philosophy to retail only locally designed and ethically produced fashion, the store supported independent design over trend-driven mass manufacturing. As a model, Alice Euphemia showed that the marketplace could accommodate the presence of forward-thinking labels. Over its lifetime the store has proved pivotal in identifying, supporting, and nurturing Australian and New Zealand designers at the beginning of their careers. Several of the young designers stocked, such as Toni Maticevski and Karen Walker, have since gone on to high-profile international acclaim.

Throughout the 1990s greater public interest in independent design grew as a result of radical fashion's infiltration of the global fashion system via the work of designers such as the late Alexander McQueen and Rei Kawakubo. This presence opened up critical space for local designers to question and experiment within the safety of a commercially successful context. Responding to these changes, Australian designers began to search for and adopt new models of practice. Again, the vision proved to be part fashion, part art. In the same manner as the Japanese or Belgian avant-garde designers who pioneered new postmodern frameworks for fashion, a handful of local designers sought to apply similar conceptual rigor to their creative practices.

In Melbourne the S!X design cooperative was established in 1994 by RMIT fashion graduates Denise Sprynskyj, Peter Boyd, and Melina Raft. Greatly influenced by designers such as Maison Martin Margiela, Rei Kawakubo, and Junya Watanabe, S!X endeavored to interrogate the fashion system through an examination of the fundamentals of design. Producing small ranges of men's and women's wear, S!X employed demi-couture (a step down from haute couture) techniques in their collections. (The term haute couture describes made-to-measure, very high-quality and labor-intensive fashion.) They cited an academic interest in the process of garment construction, or what they termed "reconstruction." Following this, their clothing analyzed tailoring techniques, investigating and transposing the placement and function of traditional components such as collars, lapels, pockets, sleeves, and linings.

S!X aspired to question the machinery of fashion by thinking about it as an art form with ideas, skills, and a vigorous tradition. Their philosophy of reconstruction placed emphasis on recycling and exhibited concern for the ecological effects of textile manufacturing. Reversing the traditional design process, in which a sketch is converted into a toile and then made up in a selected fabric, S!X began with found clothing or secondhand garments, which they then took apart to rework in a number of ways. Keeping particular elements of the original garment, S!X also added or treated fabrics as required to create new one-off pieces. In doing so, they advocated the value of the hand-worked over the mass-produced.

The work "The 3R's—Recycle, Reconstruct, Ready to Wear," 1996 (National Gallery of Victoria), illustrates the complexity of this design process. Comprising a suit, shirt, bag, and pair of shoes, the outfit has been executed much like a collage. Beginning with a number of vintage men's suits, which the designers then deconstructed, select pattern pieces were administered with a range of experimental surface treatments, namely, immersion, stone washing, printing, and weathering. These were then reconstructed into a new outfit in combination with sections of calico and voile.

Material and visual references overlap in "The 3R's—Recycle, Reconstruct, Ready to Wear" with Victoriana decoupage, vintage fabrics, and original nineteenth-century patterns forming the postmodern framework for construction. Yet the outfit is also typical of S!X's interest in clothing demarcation and the transposition of gender. In this case the metamorphosis from masculine to feminine is achieved through the careful displacement of seams, pockets, waistbands, cuffs, collars, and zippers.

Alongside academically trained designers, by the end of the 1990s street labels also comprised a vital part of the Australian independent fashion scene. Sought-after cult labels such as Perks and Mini (PAM), and initially Tsubi, evinced the same sort of philosophical approach as earlier designers like Thorn and Slorach. Established in 2000 by graffiti artist Mischa Hollenbach (Perks) and fashion design graduate Shaune Tooney (Mini), PAM began as a graphics-led label, known for their irreverent T-shirts and limited-production womens wear. Appropriating the language and symbols of pop culture and employing artistic tropes, Perks and Mini injected art and graphics into fashion. The visual social commentary resident within their practice suggested fashion to be a means of creating and interrogating culture. The view was supported by their exploitation of the relationship between fashion, art, and product via accessories, books, magazines, films, toys, installations, artistic collaborations, and their gallery/shop Someday.

Similarly, Sydney-based design duo Romance was Born (RWB) has infused Australian fashion with a sense of theatrics that has echoes of wearable art practice. The label, started in 2004 by East Sydney Technical College fashion graduate Anna Plunkett and her partner Luke Sales, is not dissimilar in approach to that of Katie Pye. The pair's "transeasonal stagewear for the street" combines elements of fashion, art, and handicraft, and they produce one-off pieces that sit alongside their ready-to-wear ranges. For their tongue-in-cheek Regional Australia and the follow-up Weird Science collections, RWB worked with acclaimed Australian artist Del Kathryn Barton to produce a series of original fabric prints.

MATERIALBYPRODUCT (MBP) AND THE TWENTY-FIRST CENTURY

By contrast, academic foundations inform the practice of Melbourne-based label MaterialByProduct (MBP). Founded in 2002 by RMIT graduates Susan Dimasi and Chantal McDonald, the studio functions as a conceptual design practice. In this, the designers aim to explore the fundamental processes that cloth undergoes in order to become a garment, and to invent new ways for cutting, joining, marking, draping, and tailoring. Working outside of trend-driven seasons, the studio develops collections as part of the by-product of a system embedded within theoretical and intellectual concerns. Philosophically, MBP's intent is to create new design and business models over products. As an aesthetic, this translates to luxury avant-garde in which artisanal process and new manufacturing methods sit in dialogue with each other.

By 2007 the studio had produced six trans-seasonal collections as well as the innovative Mark#1 and Mark#2 projects. Their Soft Hard (spring/summer 2006) collection was the first to fully articulate the relationship between "soft" couture, handmade or artisanal modes of production, and "hard" prêt-à-porter (ready-to-wear clothing), machine-made modes of production through the effect of marking. In the latter the design system or approach is recorded on the material surface of the garment, simultaneously evidential, decorative, metaphorical, and functional.

For example, "Dress Prototype 1/1"—a hard piece—is constructed from georgette that has been marked through a sports mesh (synthetic open-weave fabric used in athletic outfits) template in the manner of traditional lace making. The blotting informs the cutting, joining, and pleating of fabric to determine shape and size. The accompanying "Tattoo Leather Sleeves" (National Gallery Victoria) and custom-made "Shoes," made by Preston Zly Design, are examples of the soft process, in which the hand of the custom maker or artist is clearly visible. To create the sleeves, MaterialByProduct worked with local tattoo artist Benjamin Ross to develop the designs that decorate the raw kangaroo hide.

The Mark project (#1 and #2), on the other hand, proposes a way of working that addresses the issues of sustainability and waste that lie at the heart of the fashion system. Radically, MBP recalls the leftover stock at the end of each season in order to produce a new body of work from it, often refining through time-consuming embellishments or decorative details. As a strategy, Mark inverts the framework of the fashion system by adding value to their unsold garments. As there is no limit to the number of times a garment can go through the Mark process, fashion is created with an infinite life, built on what Liliana Pomazan has described as "use, reuse and chance." The act of recycling importantly allows MaterialByProduct to be self-reflective, revising and evaluating the success of their original design ideas.

Independent fashion design occupies an important place in the history of Australian fashion. As a cultural practice that has explored both the art of fashion and the expression of art in fashion, independent design has contributed both vision and intellect. Since the late 1970s independent fashion has shifted from the hybrid realm of wearable "art clothes," to an underground movement of fashion "experimentalists," to cult labels, to conceptual design practices that interrogate the fundamentals of design as well as the fashion system itself. At each evolution designers have sought to personalize, question, and critically evaluate contemporary models of practice, provoking, challenging, disrupting, or modifying the status quo of the mainstream. The result has been the injection of new and often ingenious ways of thinking and making into contemporary Australian fashion traditions.

References and Further Reading

Bagnall, Diana. "A Fashionable Hothouse." *Vogue Australia*, March 1987, 200–205.

de Teliga, Jane. *Art Clothes—Project 33*. Exhibition catalog. Sydney: Trustees of Art Gallery of New South Wales, 1980.

de Teliga, Jane. *Australian Fashion: The Contemporary Art*. Exhibition catalog. Sydney: Trustees of the Museum of Applied Arts and Sciences, 1989.

Dimasi, S., and C. McDonald. "MaterialByProduct artist statement." http://www. agenturv. de/page/material-by-product.html (accessed 28 August 2007).

Healy, Robyn. *Couture to Chaos, Fashion from the 1960s to Now, from the Collection of the National Gallery of Victoria*. Exhibition catalog. Melbourne, Australia: Council of Trustees of the NGV, 1996.

Jelly, N. "Idealistic." *Australian Style* no. 6 (April 2000): 114.

Jillian, Burt, and J. Purvis. "Party Architecture Program." 17 May 1983. Located in the Fashion Design Council of Australia Collection, Design Archives relating to Australian fashion, Frances Burke Centre, RMIT University, Melbourne.

Maynard, Margaret. *Out of Line: Australian Women and Style*. Sydney: University of New South Wales Press, 2001.

Pearce, R. "Innocent and Vain: The Rise of Independent Fashion." Manuscript of speech, 1986. Located in the Fashion Design Council of Australia Collection, Design Archives relating to Australian fashion, Frances Burke Centre, RMIT University, Melbourne.

Pomazan, Liliana. *Defining Punch Out in MaterialByProduct, Punch Out 2005*. Melbourne, Australia: 3 Deep Publishing, 2005.

Somerville, Katie. *Martin Grant: Paris*. Exhibition catalog. Melbourne, Australia: Council of Trustees of the NGV, 2005.

Whitfield, Danielle. *Katie Pye, Clothes for Modern Lovers*. Exhibition catalog. Melbourne, Australia: Council of Trustees of the NGV, 2007.

Wood, C. "The Fashion Design Council of Australia." *Design World* 10 (1986): 18–21.

Danielle Whitfield

See also Jews in the Melbourne Garment Trade; The Australiana Phenomenon in Australia; Global Positioning of Australian Fashion; Footwear in Australia.

Global Positioning of Australian Fashion

Over the years Australia has found it difficult to establish a presence in the fashion centers of Europe and the United States. Yet when Sydney fashion designer Collette Dinnigan staged a full-scale parade in the 1995 official Paris ready-to-wear calendar, it changed forever the perception of Australian fashion as being somewhat out of touch. This defining moment sparked debate and extensive media coverage about a new wave of emerging designers and was crucial in the development of the local industry. Dinnigan's accreditation in Paris by the French Chambre Syndicale du prêt-à-porter des Couturiers et des Createurs de la Mode presents an opportunity to rethink the image of Australian fashion, one now linked with the global market but also with local design and small-scale production qualities.

From the 1990s developments in the world economy, including improved communications, new trade policies, and increasing globalization, transformed the marketing of local fashion. Removal of protective domestic clothing quotas in 1991 meant retailers sought out imported items instead of Australian-made clothing. According to Webber and Weller, competition and volatile pricing during the decade made imported commodities seem more affordable, but it turned out this was due to competition, not quotas. Nor did consumers really reap any benefits. Significant restructuring of the industry took place, and within this relatively new market format, government incentives encouraged major clothing producers to process offshore. Consequently, attention moved away from production to design practice, with government and industry bodies keen to investigate ways to support creativity and innovation. Global ideas were encouraged in this environment, as well as opportunities to develop Australian fashion's collective profile, increase its visibility and diversity, and position itself more prominently in domestic and international markets.

During the 1990s, despite a weak local economy, an official system of regular Australian fashion events, backed by organizations, was activated to promote industry, profile designers, critique design, and assist commercial viability. Through a network of trade shows, consumer retail events, and professional awards, it was hoped Australian fashion would be branded and traded. This ambitious program was assisted by generous financial incentives established with federal, state, and local government grant and subsidy schemes. The media played and continues to play a crucial role in the success and dispersal of such events through critical reporting and increased exposure, generating further recognition for Australian design.

IMAGE PROBLEMS

Australia's geographical isolation from the world's major fashion centers is one that has conventionally supported an image of a fashion wasteland. The perception of a "tyranny of distance" is a factor placing Australia outside other well-known destinations frequented by "cool" style hunters, or international retail buyers, thereby reinforcing the impression that it lacks design talent. This image, further complicated by seasonal differences, is brought about through the predominance of a world fashion calendar traditionally determined by the northern hemisphere seasons, which allegedly disadvantages the market. An unfortunate trade agenda exists in which design, production, and buying cycles in the southern hemisphere imply that the Australian industry is always behind. Obviously, collections shown six months in advance of the European retail season translate into twelve months' difference before designs reach the Australian market. This situation contributes to copycat designs and routine accusations targeting designers for shadowing major European trends rather than creating distinctive signatures. Adding to seasonal differences, of course, is the stereotypical image of Australian dress, which is not a fashionable one. Tourism promotions picture a majestic landscape of great beauty, humor, and friendliness. Indicative of this was the use of extroverted Paul Hogan (star of the immensely popular film *Crocodile Dundee*) in a well-known 1980s tourist advertisement intended to tempt international travelers to enjoy the lifestyle of the "land down under."

Yet one could argue that Australia's laid-back, casual style of living, one uninhibited by clothing protocols, mixed with an inherent larrikinism, offers exciting design possibilities. Indeed, Australian dress culture harbors a boutique fashion industry nurturing design specializations in surf-, swim-, and streetwear, cultivating less structured tailoring systems, trans-seasonal collections, and an environment encouraging the proliferation of characteristically modest, independent custom-making practices.

However, it has been crucial, within a global marketplace, for the continual growth and sustainability of Australian design to build up a marketing system embracing diverse practices, sensitive to small-scale enterprises and conscious of financial restraints and low production capacity. The advantages produced by official networks within the local industry, acting collectively to develop promotional strategies and establish a critical platform to showcase Australian design to the world, are essential for supporting small- to medium-scale enterprises. Sophisticated global communications through Internet and digital interfaces have quickly changed the perception of isolation. Flexible trading, climate change that has altered weather patterns, and frequent world travel have all contributed to a shift in marketing and encouraged resort and trans-seasonal collections as a way to disseminate an image of Australian design as fashionable. Trade opportunities are further supported by achievements of Australian film and music exports.

Not surprisingly, Australia places importance on capturing the illusive international market, gaining a reputation and as a result winning buyer confidence at home. Historically there has been an admiration of Parisian garments (the city being the center of the European fashion system), and participating in the official

Paris calendar is an aspirational goal for talented and original designers. It is, however, an elusive one given the selection process and overall market scale. Yet the trend for designers, including Australians, to increasingly show outside their country of origin is a form of strategic positioning enabling them to pitch their collections in an appropriate place to achieve optimum critical exposure and commercial prospect. Since the Japanese label Comme des Garçons 1981 launch in Paris and the Antwerp Six (Dries Von Noten, Ann Demeulemeester, Dirk Bikkembergs, Marina Yee, Dirk Van Saene, and Walter Van Beirendonck) showed as a sensational collective at London Fashion week in 1987, the exciting potential of a world market has grown outside established canons. In the wake of the Japanese and Belgian initiatives, and a new fashion environment, an opportunity for Australian design to extend traditional markets was a strong possibility. Yet given the nature of the Australian industry, this might have seemed either overly ambitious or naïve.

Within a scenario fraught with complex issues concerning financial viability and sustainable production levels, the question was raised: Did Australia have the design acumen and talent to initiate an international fashion week?

COLLETTE DINNIGAN

The role of Collette Dinnigan in the new positioning of Australian fashion is crucial. Her label offered a pioneering and very different reading of Australian fashion by establishing an international profile through deluxe garment designs and clothing grounded in a sound knowledge of historical costume and technical detail. Her approach has redefined boundaries for Australian designers playing with classic notions of boudoir attire, merging with current street styles.

Originally specializing in lingerie, Dinnigan formed her distinctive eponymous label in 1990, designs originally coveted as intimate wear. Even so, her pajamas, slip dresses, corsets, and camisoles are regularly worn as outerwear, delivering an ultra-feminine yet contemporary look. Delicate clothing items crafted from shimmering silks, antique fabrics, and lace trims combine a subtle fusion of old and the latest textile technologies, offering a refreshing contrast to often poorly manufactured, disposable fashion, which has dominated the local market. Ironically, after opening a shop in Melbourne, Dinnigan faced difficulties with low retail sales, although the label had secured major contracts with prestigious stores such as Barneys and Henri Bendel in New York.

Preparing to develop the international market further, Dinnigan applied to become an official part of the Paris fashion calendar in 1994 and participate in the prominent ready-to-wear collections. In the Rue de Rivoli at the famous Angelina tearooms, "l'australienne" received a warm reception for her first Paris collection. Subsequently Dinnigan's designs were featured on the August 1996 cover of *Women's Wear Daily*, the leading fashion forecaster in the United States. Dinnigan's achievement was complemented by the blossoming career of Martin Grant, an Australian living in Paris. By 1996 Grant's boutique and atelier in the Marais district was gaining notoriety with demi-couture clothing (a hybrid system between haute couture and ready-to-wear offering a partial degree of customization and limited production). At first running outside the official catwalk showings, Grant crafted small collections based upon intimate experiences, describing the close relationship between designer and client. Collections were paraded in the shop window and drew the attention and delight of passersby. This discrete spectacle secured Grant distinguished clients from Naomi Campbell and Lee Radziwill to Cate Blanchett.

AUSTRALIAN FASHION WEEK AND ITS SUCCESSES

Undoubtedly Dinnigan and Grant added momentum to the idea of an Australian Fashion week, a concept supported by increasing circulation of designer labels abroad, and escalating discussion at home about prospects for Australian fashion. Similarly, the Morrissey Edmiston label of design partners Peter Morrissey and Leona Edmiston made inroads into the United States, with garments stocked in Henri Bendel, Bloomingdales, and Fred Segal stores. Their clothing gained extensive publicity through the antics of their celebrity clientele, including pop star Kylie Minogue, INXS front man Michael Hutchence, and actors Nicole Kidman and Tom Cruise. Recognition was highlighted in 1995 when the partners were listed in U.S. *Harper's Bazaar*'s twenty-one hottest up-and-coming designers.

In the 1990s, riding on a wave of international media coverage, a timely chance came to showcase local design. A fashion week proposal was canvassed by the company Australian Fashion Innovators Pty Ltd, headed by Simon Lock, intending to place Australia into the world fashion calendar, joining centers like Paris, Milan, London, and New York. First held in 1996, this significant event aimed to create new trade opportunities through a regular critical platform, covering a region that included New Zealand and Asia. It supported designers by providing infrastructure to reinforce the standing of labels and helped to form relationships between international and Australian buyers. The goal to create strong designer profiles for the region was paramount.

Australian Fashion Week (AFW) continues to be marketed as a major vehicle for promotion, trade, tourism, and reputation. As a result it seeks and attracts major funding from government and business. With funding initiated in 1995 from a New South Wales state government grant, a New South Wales regional development grant, and Mercedes Benz corporate sponsorship for naming rights, the Mercedes Australian Fashion Week was launched in May 1996, with Simon Lock appointed director. Originally AFW was an annual event, suggesting an alternate format to conventional twice-yearly seasonal showings.

The first AFW was staged at the Sydney showgrounds, and it was an important milestone, but there were many anxious industry observers doubting the caliber of the event and contemplating the possibility of failure. This ambitious program comprised seventeen shows and captured thirty-one invited designer labels. The selection was drawn from the ranks of established, emerging, and relatively unknown designers, participants including Collette Dinnigan, Robert Burton, Saba, Scanlan & Theodore, Jodie Bofa, Nicole Zimmermann, and Akira Isogawa. The catwalks starred Australian models Sarah O'Hare, Emma Balfour, and Anneliese Seubert, who came home especially from the world circuit to participate.

A small contingent of international buyers and journalists attended this exciting new venture, but surprisingly there were no American retailers. Making the journey to Australia were representatives from Harvey Nichols, Liberty of London, Hong Kong's

Lane Crawford, and CK Tangs from Singapore. The extensive media coverage documented various responses to the inaugural program. Overseas buyers were impressed with swimwear collections. The Zimmermann label achieved particularly favorable editorial coverage and lucrative orders. Nicole Zimmermann acknowledged in *The Age* newspaper the high cost of participating in AFW, with a $10,000 catwalk fee for an experience that lasted twenty-nine minutes; however, she considered this a worthwhile investment, because orders would sustain business for the rest of the year and possibly set up key buyer relationships for the future.

The highlight for many attendees, however, came at the end of the program, the New Generation parade. The parade, representing emerging designers, included work by relatively unknown designer Akira Isogawa, whose garments aptly illustrated the eclecticism and "cultural craftsmanship" of Australian design. Japanese-born Isogawa studied fashion at East Sydney Technical College and has continued to inspire a creative way of dressing, translated through elaborately constructed garments, using fabrics sourced from antique Japanese kimonos (originally from his family's wardrobes), generous sizing, and multiple layering.

Of course, AFW drew criticism. In particular, certain industry sectors questioned the principal focus on exports. They suggested that perhaps government support funds were more effectively spent by reinforcing designers in the local market, considering that many on the show had neither the production infrastructure nor financial backing to fill large international orders. Marion Hume, writing for the London *Financial Times*, added weight to this view, advising Australian designers not to ignore the domestic market by simply focusing on exports, stressing that local market recognition and business experience should come first.

One question asked was whether the emphasis on high fashion was misplaced. Were broader views of the leisure market, including lower-priced brands and Australia's most successful leisurewear exports, like Ken Done or R. M. Williams, more profitable as models? The selection process for designers was also disputed, and the fee structure was found too expensive for emerging designers without assistance.

Timing was a crucial issue, especially synchronizing with buying cycles, for European buyers had already spent their budgets and were therefore not interested in ordering summer clothes for winter. Fortunately, a drop in world tariff barriers made the pricing of Australian exports far more attractive. Expatriate Lee Tulloch, fashion correspondent for *Elle International*, acknowledged the industry's cynical forecast "that Australian fashion would look shocking but it hasn't. It's looked brilliant." Tulloch's comment draws attention to a certain lack of confidence by industry to place local design into a critical arena of commercial, professional, and public assessment. It seems in a small industry the concern was mainly about how to gauge the success of this event and its consequences.

AFW not only provided a short-term forum for potential export orders, but it set up long-term contacts for designers to build upon. Designers were also given a major break by participating in a vibrant promotional medium. Suggestions identified by international buyers and journalists were to offer essential professional development for participants, including editing ranges, and to strengthen potential niche markets like swimwear. However, AFW's significance has not been about individual success stories, but about representing the collective of Australian high-fashion labels.

The 1996 AFW was perhaps the most important fashion trade event ever staged in Australia, in its attempts to capture the breadth of design and optimize commercial opportunities en masse. This event inevitably changed the way the Australian fashion industry did business. The following year, Simon Lock noted that AFW was trying to sell something more than clothes—rather the idea of Australia as a design destination.

The second AFW in 1997 attracted a larger international contingent of registered buyers, media, and other fashion industry representatives, including Joan Burstein from London's Browns fashion store and Anna Piaggi from *Italian Vogue*. Akira Isogawa's individual parade was a standout, impressing key commentators. Joan Burstein enthused in the Melbourne *Age* newspaper about Isogawa, claiming he was the only designer who presented something she had not seen previously, alluding to the derivative nature of other designers. Burstein's comments were deemed particularly powerful by AFW organizers, as her reputation as a talent spotter was legendary, from John Galliano's graduation collection to recognition of Hussein Chalayan. Anna Piaggi was also overwhelmed by Isogawa's work, noting a potent mix of the exotic combined with "great modernity."

MEDIA COVERAGE AND ITS EFFECTS

Rising media coverage boosted the scope of journalistic reports via critical analytical reviews. Fashion claimed large editorial space in national newspapers and magazines, in the lead-up to and in the post-AFW period. Critical appraisals entitled "The Verdict" or "Fashion Weak" sought to balance out excess promotional praise. Cable television and later a Web site broadcasted AFW to an extensive audience. Significantly, at this time the well-known British journalist Marion Hume was appointed editor of *Vogue Australia* magazine, replacing Nancy Pilcher. Hume aspired to reposition the magazine through more extensive coverage of high fashion and international news in order to address *Vogue Australia*'s decreased sales. Hume's contribution to Australian fashion criticism is substantial, although not popular. Dedicating pages of *Vogue Australia* to analytical observations about Australian Fashion Week, she included few rave reviews. For her first cover Hume picked a gown by Isogawa.

Her commentary for the second AFW focused on the overall lack of ideas or technical prowess, and there were rip-off allegations. The popular Morrissey Edmiston garments, Hume suggested (quoting other media opinion), "looked as if they were cut from Simplicity patterns, coded easy to Sew," an allegation that affronted the design credibility and production qualities of Australian design. The impact of such commentaries, from an experienced and well-respected journalist like Hume, was formidable and polarized the fashion industry. Yet this influential coverage probably made it more difficult for designers to blatantly appropriate others, as it acted to set high professional standards. Ironically, Hume has been criticized for lowering the Australian content of *Vogue Australia* by placing too much importance on international content, including international writers, locations, and clothing.

Isogawa's triumph in the New Generation parade made this event the most significant for discovering new talent. Representation at AFW extended beyond Australia in the 1998 New Generation show. Here New Zealand designer Karen Walker premiered her controversial "Live Wire" collection, models trailing power cords referencing a power strike in her native Auckland. Other New Zealanders participated in AFW, including Zambesi, World, Nom D, and Trelise Cooper, until the establishment of New Zealand fashion week in 2001. Asian designers joined the AFW repertoire, offering an engaging contrast to homegrown designers. In 1999 six Hong Kong designers made their debut at AFW under the auspices of the Hong Kong Trade Development Council. Designers including Barney Cheng, Pacino Wan, William Chan, and Joseph Li paraded their spring/summer 2000 collections.

Increasing opportunities for young emerging designers was also an important initiative. The Mercedes-Benz Start-up scheme, running from 2001 to 2007, was a mentoring program with a statewide competition focusing on business development and industry advice. This innovative and exciting national small business scheme was specifically intended to seek excellence in design innovation and enhance the future of the next generation of fashion designers. Winners, who received a financial prize plus support, were mentored within the industry and offered a place in AFW's New Generation parade. In 2004 the first individual AFW menswear collection, the highly theatrical costuming label from Western Australian, ericaamerica, tantalized audiences with the futuristic inspired suiting of their Victoriana collection and was the inaugural Start-up winner.

Improvements to infrastructure ensured AFW's place in the fashion industry's calendar. In 2002 an advisory committee was established, made up of leading retailers, media, and designers, to review all designers and ensure the finest representation of Australian and Asia Pacific fashion. Expanding the program to include a September week, a second AFW was held in Melbourne between the years 2002 and 2006, placing the event across two major cities. This caused overlap with other major fashion events in Melbourne, in particular the Melbourne Fashion Festival and the Spring Fashion Festival. It also increased competition for sponsorship, media, and designer participation, and confused international branding.

MELBOURNE FASHION FESTIVAL

In the early 1990s the idea of creating a major Melbourne fashion event was discussed, funded with monies from the Victorian state government and in response to changes in the marketplace. Instigated by the premier of Victoria, Jeff Kennett, the Melbourne Fashion Festival (MFF) was an annual event first staged on 17–23 February 1997. It was organized by a committee chaired by Craig Kimberley, the director and founder of the Just Jeans company, the board consisting of representatives from industry, manufacturing, education, and tourism. Robert Buckingham was appointed the inaugural director (1997–2004), bringing a strong background in the visual arts and management of the multidisciplinary agency the Fashion Design Council of Australia (FDC). The event was concerned to address the increasing decline in clothing sales in the retail sector, promoting Australian fashion directly to consumers rather than being aimed at the media and trade sectors. Buckingham through FDC organized exhibitions, seminars, and fashion parades in Melbourne and Sydney, showcasing independent design talent in a mix of high art, popular culture, and commerce. His ability to expand fashion's perspective was key to the success of this event. Quoted in the *Sydney Morning Herald* newspaper in 2004, he discussed Melbourne's art-designer culture, showing that strong connections existed between various creative communities

such as fashion, art, film, music, theater, and architecture. This connectivity positioned Melbourne differently from cities like Los Angeles and Sydney and enabled Buckingham to place the fashion industry in a transdisciplinary context.

MFF's mission to boost a flagging local industry saw the event supported by retail competitors, bringing together department stores Myers, David Jones, and Daimaru. Major Australian edition magazines such as *Vogue, Marie Claire, Elle*, and *Mode* participated in the festival and provided sponsorship for the main events. The first MFF took fashion to the streets, engaging local retailers, department stores, magazines, and cultural institutions, crafting a mass spectacle to open a broad range of experiences for community interaction with the fashion industry. Ready-to-wear parades showcased designs that were immediately available for purchase or viewing in the shops.

An essential part of the professional development agenda was an annual professional development and business seminar for local retailers and manufacturers, conducted by local and international design and business experts. The program concentrated on stimulating innovation and creativity, with participants like Martin Raymond and Christopher Sanders (Future Laboratory and *Viewpoint* magazine, UK), Lil Edelkoort (Studio Edelkoort, Paris), Jane Shepherdson (Topshop), Richard Florida (*The Rise of the Creative Class*), and Charles Leadbeater (*Living on Thin Air*). A "ways of doing" business seminar addressed key issues in the design, retail, and manufacturing sectors, from trend forecasting, retail design, and patterns of consumer spending to design profiles.

In the first year, 1997, Greville Street Prahran, an edgy streetscape of clubs, boutiques, and secondhand stores, was closed to create an urban space to position smaller independent designers away from the main venues of the more established designers. The area was transformed to stage a major outdoor free event, with a catwalk running through an adjoining park, a venue attracting a younger audience enthusiastic to view relatively unknown designers in the highly anticipated New Designer parade. The inaugural winner S!X, the design partnership between Denise Sprynskyj and Peter Boyd, followed the practice of recycling found garments and experimenting with structure and decorative elements in their collection. They were rewarded with a cash prize, business support, and substantial media coverage. An impressive list of past winners includes Toni Maticevski, Mad Cortes, and Claude Maus.

Complementing the catwalk spectacle, fashion was viewed through installations, surveys, group exhibitions, and debate. MFF's vibrant public arts program of exhibitions, lectures, and performances articulated cross-disciplinary perspectives and forged cultural partnerships between art institutions and commercial galleries. Local talent was highlighted in exhibitions: Leigh Bowery: Look at Me, RMIT Gallery (Melbourne, 1999), and Martin Grant, Paris at the Ian Potter Centre, National Gallery of Victoria (Melbourne, 2006). International designers visiting the festival included Richard Tyler, Dirk Bikkembergs, Walter Van Beirendonck, Philippe Starke, Bernhard Willhelm, John Fluevog, Joe Core, and Philip Treacy, who commented on their experiences but also had the opportunity to become familiar with Australian design.

FACILITATING AND GLOBALLY POSITIONING AUSTRALIAN FASHION

The establishment of the AFW was a key marketing tool for the local industry and the Asian region. However, the impact of globalization quickly increased connections between Australia and the world. Rapid communication systems, speedy distribution of information, and reduction of world trade barriers all facilitated for the local industry opportunities to access diverse international markets.

Yet many established Australian designers chose not to participate in AFW at all, increasingly showing their work across the "global landscape," sometimes using less expensive or unconventional tactics. Akira Isogawa and Easton Pearson have presented unofficially off the main ready-to-wear Paris calendar, and others show from suitcases in hotel rooms. London Fashion Week is open to the less established designers and the more quirky styles. However, New York Fashion Week has emerged as a vital conduit for Australian design, a platform for less formal and youthful clothing lines. Surf culture has inspired some of Australia's most successful clothing and lifestyle companies, such as RipCurl, Billabong, and Quiksilver. An established tradition born of surf, conveying the essence of informality, nurtures a range of small exclusive streetwear labels, filling the gap between large surfwear enterprises and the high-fashion market. The rise of demi-couture denim and T-shirts recognizes a major luxurious streetwear niche, notably through the work of Sass & Bide, and Ksubi (formally known as Tsubi), who discovered a core market at New York's Fashion Week.

Coming from a surf and music background, Ksubi's founders Dan Single, Gareth Moody, and George Gorrow formed the Skull Club design studio in 2000 at Manly Beach, Sydney. Debuting at AFW in 2001, Ksubi's renegade approach surprised the audience with live rats released onto the stage. Creating an unconventional palette for the leisure activities of imaginative urbanites, Ksubi's distressed jeans, violated by graffiti-paint, embroidery, or badges, and his graphic T-shirts are signature items. With raucous party launches, live music performances, and publicity pranks, Ksubi boasts an impressive following from the music industry, with clients including the Yeah, Yeah, Yeahs, The Avalanches, Scissor Sisters, and Gwen Stefani. Premiering at London Fashion Week in 2002, off-schedule, the Ksubi team curated artistic clothing installations in the abandoned Aldwych tube station. Collaborating with U.S. designer Jeremy Scott ("Jeremy loves Ksubi"), they premiered at the 2006 New York Fashion Week, and the pair continue to position their work through the United States.

Self-trained designers Sarah-Jane Clarke and Heidi Middleton of Sass & Bide (established in 1999) are known for low-slung denim jeans fastened with a characteristic two-inch zipper. They gained notoriety in 2001 through celebrity endorsement, when Sarah Jessica Parker, dressed in Sass & Bide, appeared on the highly popular *Sex and the City* U.S. television show. Sass & Bide made their international debut at London Fashion Week in 2003, but by 2004 they were showing at New York Fashion Week and continued to do so in 2007.

New York fashion supports the participation of emerging world designers through a program that has assisted a number of Australian designers. In 2006 Toni Maticevski was selected as one of ten emerging designers, part of the New York UPS company's "Delivering Fashion's Future" initiative. Debunking suggestions that Australia has developed a "deluxe" streetwear reputation, Maticevski courts sophisticated silhouettes, beautiful organza confections, and clothing crafted with rigorous technical detail through draping, shredding, pin-tucking, and intricate cut, playing cheeky homage to Australia with models in high heels trimmed with kangaroo fur. He describes his collection as

an emotional expression: "Fresh, sheer, like a splash of water on your face." Interviewed in New York after his well-received first showing, Maticevski argued that his collection challenged the perception that Australian fashion was simply about denim and swimwear, his feminine, finely crafted ensembles opening up alternative dialogues about the nature of Australian design.

AFW initially offered a trade model specifically targeting high-end design and consumption. However, there was scope to develop a more diverse dialogue about fashion and related creative industries, one that could further embrace the public and underground scene. Although Sydney became the official location for AFW, Melbourne contributed and in 2007 continued to do so through festivals engaging the broader community, suggesting that there is more to fashion than just selling clothes. True to historical rivalries, Melbourne and Sydney compete for the elusive claim to be Australia's fashion capital, but this healthy competition has resulted in increased consolidation of quality Australian design.

In the 2000s AFW became involved in a variety of controversial global issues relating to fashion's pervading influence on young people's health and body image. The Smoke Free Fashion initiative, supported by the federal government to address this major health issue, was launched at the AFW 2003 spring/summer collection, aiming to tackle the glamorous portrayal of cigarettes and smoking in the fashion industry. AFW became the first smoke-free fashion event in Australia (New Zealand had a Smoke Free Fashion Award event in 1996), encouraging participants to pledge not to have their photo taken by the media when smoking. Although not entirely successful, it was a brave campaign to highlight the mortality rate caused by this habit.

In 2005 Simon Lock and his company, Australian Fashion Innovators, sold AFW to the New York–based International Management Group (IMG), a major sports, entertainment, and media enterprise. Lock was also appointed CEO of IMG Fashion Asia Pacific. This new ownership aligned AFW to an international fashion circuit and an extensive global network. IMG was responsible for a number of key fashion events, including fashion weeks in New York, Milan, Moscow, and Berlin and the Singapore Fashion Festival. This relationship in particular extended media coverage of AFW, increasing the production of film and video content through the media division of IMG, which distributed footage through cable television, free to air television, the Internet, downloads into iPods, and the webzine *The Daily Fashion Week Insider*. During AFW 2006 spring/summer collection, IMG media facilitated viewing the program online via MSN video, escalating marketing opportunities and the scale of its potential audience.

Further changes to AFW occurred in 2006, with their major naming-rights sponsorship deal with the luxury car manufacturer Mercedes Benz ending an eleven-year association from 1995 to 2006. Subsequently a five-year sponsorship deal was signed with the Foster's group, owners of Rosemount Estate winery, rebranding the event Rosemount Australian Fashion Week until 2011. In this image-conscious market, many commentators believe the new sponsorship arrangement has altered the style of the event from a prestige one to one based in the mass market.

AUSTRADE

The federal government facilitates independent exporting outside the fashion week structure through Austrade (Australian Trade

Commission). Providing essential advice and financial assistance, this agency supports businesses with global positioning through promotion. In particular, Export Market Development grants (EMDG) help small to medium businesses develop their markets. EMDG is a very valuable tool for nonmainstream labels, investigating outlets beyond conventional retail. PAM (Perks and Mini), designed by Mischa Hollenbach and Shauna Toohey, creates fashion collections, books, films, toys, and curated exhibitions. International recognition was assisted by six export grants, placing their label in the United Kingdom, United States, and Japan. PAM opened their first international boutique within the department store Parco in Tokyo's Shibuya district.

One of the first retail outlets to stock PAM was the Paris boutique Colette, opened in 1997, which has a reputation for selecting innovative approaches to design, curating an eclectic array of design, art, and publications, frequently changing the style and contents of its retail mix. Colette has also stocked Beci Orphin of Princess Tina and *Sneaker Freaker Magazine* from Melbourne, to name a few.

Alternate venues for independent design are supported at home through an eclectic retail scene. The Melbourne store Alice Euphemia shows only local independent design, integrating retail with an exhibition program and limited edition product. Fat stores follow a similar network: "We don't care about Europe," says Kim Purtell, part owner of the Fat boutiques. "Our designers aren't interested in getting that big. You've got to stay small to stay cool." This statement is indicative of alternative retail approaches, in this case one supporting local identity, smaller niche markets, sustainability of limited production, and artisanal design.

Creative industries have assumed increasing importance in Australia in order to realize economic success and international competitiveness. Major fashion events, with funding from government and private agencies, focus upon developing professionalism, promotion, and export trade. This in turn has enriched the understanding of local design, developed creative business practices, and supported small-scale industry. Australian consumers are drawn to buy local brands, not through patriotism but through relevant issues of sustainability and a high level of original design ideas and production values.

References and Further Reading

Australian Fashion Week clippings file, Melbourne Fashion Festival clippings file. Located in the Design Archives relating to Australian fashion, RMIT Design Archives, Melbourne. www.rmit.edu.au/ad/designarchives (accessed 14 December 2008).

Cawthorne, Zelda. *Australia in Fashion: Six Great Designers*. Melbourne: Australia Post, 2005.

Healy, Robyn. *Couture to Chaos: Fashion from 1960s to Now*. Melbourne, Australia: National Gallery of Victoria, 1996.

Joel, Alexandra. *Parade: The Story of Fashion in Australia*. Sydney: HarpersCollins, 1998.

Maynard, Margaret. *Out of Line: Australian Women and Style*. Sydney: University of New South Wales Press, 2001.

Maynard, Margaret. *Dress and Globalisation*. Manchester, UK: Manchester University Press, 2004.

Parkes, Brian, ed. *Freestyle New Australian Design for Living*. Sydney, Melbourne: Object: Australian Center for Craft and Design, 2006.

Powerhouse Museum, Sydney. "Australian Fashion Week archive." http://www.powerhousemuseum.com/collection/database (accessed 14 December 2008).

Somerville, Katie. *Martin Grant, Paris*. Melbourne, Australia: National Gallery of Victoria, 2005.

Van Schaik, Leon. *Design City Melbourne*. Chichester, UK: Wiley-Academy, 2006.

Webber, M., and S. Weller. *Re-Fashioning the Rag Trade: The Internationalisation of the TCF Industries in Australia*. Sydney: University of New South Wales Press, 2001.

Robyn Healy

See also Retailing, Clothing, and Textiles Production in Australia; Fashion Photography in Australia; Independent Australian Fashion; Popular Music and Dress in Australia.

PART 5

Types of Dress in Australia

Footwear in Australia

Warm to hot summers, preferences for the outdoor life, and liking for sport and leisure have created a unique environment for the evolution of specific footwear made and used in Australia. Although shoes of felted emu feathers are known to have been worn by early Aborigines in the south Kimberley region, for example, wearing nothing on the feet has been common at times for all Australians, a practice diminishing in the twenty-first century. Since shoes last longer in a dry climate, and when people go barefoot at home and to the beach they need fewer shoes, this factor has had some influence in Australia. From soon after first settlement there was a significant demand for shoes for convicts and free settlers, men, women, and children. Local tradespeople could not keep up with demand. As more settlers of means arrived, imports of high-end shoes were constant, and ever since, Australia has been an importer of shoes from Britain and the United States. A manufacturing industry did commence early after settlement in New South Wales, spreading to other colonies, and by the nineteenth century Australia gained a reputation for its locally made, strong, hard-wearing boots and shoes, one reason being that those working the land needed a reliable supply of sturdy, comfortable, and unpretentious footwear to protect their feet. Choice, however, was limited.

As towns and cities developed, it became clear that Australians had a preference for casual wear, which influenced footwear and its use. Even in urban areas, the population of all classes gravitated to the beach in their leisure time. A large market for sports shoes and casual summer styles using leather but also rubber, canvas, and other materials was developed. For a range of economic reasons, prevailing circumstances no longer support local large-scale shoe manufacture (even hard-wearing boots and shoes are mostly produced offshore), but a healthy market for small-production, niche designer-made products emerged beginning in the 1990s. Despite this, 90 percent of everyday shoes bought in Australia in the twenty-first century come from China and Brazil.

HISTORY

In the early years of New South Wales shoes were in short supply. Footwear issued to convicts was of inferior quality, and many poorer residents went barefoot due to scarcity. From the 1790s convict shoemakers were producing a considerable amount of footwear for local use, using imported leather, but maintaining sufficient supplies was a continuing problem. Tanning leather was a major difficulty, and local tanned leather remained of poor quality. Most often footwear had to be imported.

Although the government requisitioned shoes from Britain for both convicts and its employees, elite members of society also placed orders annually for finer-quality shoes even in the 1830s. One of the problems in the early years, though, was that when shipments did arrive, the shoes were often badly mildewed from the journey. In 1797 the ship *Sydney Cove* sank off Tasmania, with bundles of Indian goatskin shoes, indicating that supplies came not only from Britain but from wider afield. As life improved for some and a small affluent society grew in the colony, social functions were held requiring stylish dressing. In 1826 the *Sydney Gazette* noted that "tailors and tailoresses, shoemakers and shopmen were in great requisition for the King's Birthday Ball"—an annual society event.

An example of a local tradesperson was third-generation shoemaker James Thearle, who began producing quality work in Sydney in 1838. He made a miniature kangaroo-skin boot to advertise his skills when he first arrived in Australia. He later placed it in Abbeys shop window, challenging that if anyone matched the forty-two stitches to the inch he would pay them £50. This indicated that local manufacturing was improving, and not only in Sydney, for by the 1840s Adelaide, South Australia, was almost self-sufficient in colony-made footwear.

Australian manufacturing industries were slow to mechanize prior to the 1850s. Lockstitch sewing machines, imported from Britain and America, transformed the production of better-class clothing and footwear and facilitated more stylish products, sometimes to the point of extravagance, usually following European styles. The 1851 gold rush in New South Wales, Victoria, and elsewhere brought large numbers of foreigners seeking their fortunes. Money flowed freely, and this inevitably created desires

Boot by R. M. Williams, 2008. R. M. Williams is one of Australia's most recognizable and reputable brands, and their boots are an iconic example of Australian hard-wearing footwear. Courtesy of R. M. Williams Pty Ltd.

for dress commodities, including shoes. But colonial-made boots and shoes were expensive in comparison to imports, thus reducing their competitiveness. In fact, wages for boot makers in New South Wales doubled between the 1840s and the 1860s. The pressure came from British imports, and between 1851 and 1853 these increased tenfold. On the other hand, productivity improved, and boot and shoe making came to be one of the most successful of the garment trades toward the late nineteenth century, especially middle-priced items.

As more colonies were established and towns grew, the demand for locally made saddlery, boots, and shoes dictated the need for leather workshops and tanneries. The environment itself supplied raw materials that played an important role in the initial development of the industry. Once the process of tanning improved, many animal skins such as emu, crocodile, seal, horse, goat, sheep, and snake were used, but kangaroo and wallaby hides were soon prized for their fineness and strength and were exported in quantity from the colony. The 1.2-millimeter (0.047-inch) thickness, very large-sized skins, and the excellent blocking properties of the hide have made kangaroo leather widely accepted as one of the strongest lightweight leathers available. When split to 20 percent of its original thickness, it maintains 30 to 60 percent of its original strength compared

with only 1 to 4 percent for cowhide. Boots, fashion shoes, and, more recently, sports shoes have been made from kangaroo hide around the world, although tanning is not necessarily done in Australia. In fact, from the 1990s Australia has had its kangaroo hides tanned in Japan. In the early twenty-first century there are estimated to be some fifty-five species of kangaroos and wallabies, numbering fifty million animals in Australia, making them a rich resource.

Other raw materials available during the nineteenth century included black wattle tree bark, used for tanning. The Tasmanian myrtle tree proved an excellent supply of wood for shoe lasts (wooden blocks shaped like a foot, used to create three-dimensional foot shapes for leather shoes). Metal tacks, stiffeners, and linen threads were all locally made.

After 1901, when Australia became a Federation of six previously separate British colonies, federal tariff legislation provided protection for Australian manufacturers. Until then American and British shoes (particularly from Northampton) had been imported in large numbers. This supply fed into the mail-order business and department stores. Mail order facilitated purchases for those Australians in rural areas, who would have been lucky to visit a city once a year, the distances being so great and transportation slow. However, under protection from imports, the footwear industry became very profitable and quality improved. Although Federation engendered a new pride in the nation, there was still a tendency to sell products with "American styling" or "British comfort," since the buying public were not confident in the local product.

Operating from 1908 to 1996, the Melbourne company Public Benefit Bootery sold well-made fashion shoes at good prices for city workers. By the 1930s this family-run business had three stores in Sydney. They filled an important niche in the market for quite fashionable, yet inexpensive shoes. The company had a very democratic pricing policy. Initially all shoes sold at the one price of ten shillings.

In Australia shoe production has been most evident in New South Wales and Victoria. Trade schools were established, including the Technical Boot Making School (subsequently TAFE) in 1906 in Erskineville (a suburb of Sydney), home to some 350 shoe and boot factories in the first half of the twentieth century. Never a very prestigious vocation, and usually carried out under poor conditions, during the Depression (1929–1931) the shoe trade became an especially desperate occupation. Fourteen-year-old girls could be condemned to a life of industrial noise and oppression in shoe factories. During that time wholesale prices dropped by a third, and unscrupulous sales methods were adopted. Salesgirls in Melbourne would receive a bonus for selling imperfect shoes. A sliver of red flannel under a seam might deceive the buyer into thinking the shoe was expensively lined!

World Wars I and II restricted shoe making to sturdy practical everyday footwear for both sexes. But after World War II Australia became a burgeoning garment-manufacturing nation, and this flowed through to quality shoe production, with fine Australian leather released from war production. During the 1950s and 1960s women's fashion shoes reached their highest standards of design and manufacture, although styling and ideas for both men's and women's shoes were often borrowed from overseas. Selby, the exclusive brand of David Jones department store, Westbrook and Mason, Goldberg International, and Parker Shoes contributed to the thirty-five million pairs of shoes a year then being manufactured in Australia. At that time the

A certificate awarded in 1905 by the Australian Natives Association of New South Wales to Enoch Taylor & Co. for boot manufacture. The company carried out detailed research on the size of Australian feet to create suitable wooden lasts that guaranteed their footwear was comfortable and hard-wearing. Photograph courtesy of Alistair Lee.

manufactures 80 percent of its production offshore but also supports local niche designer brands whose runs are often too small to be viably manufactured overseas. Robins produces them with a five-day lead time from the order being placed.

In 1973 a downward trend in productivity began with a federal government reduction of tariffs by 25 percent in the textile, clothing, and footwear industries. Although this was intended to make manufacturing more competitive, the footwear industry suffered badly from the influx of low-cost imports. Thirty companies closed in 1974, and by 1979 New South Wales alone had lost half its shoe-making factories.

RURAL LIFE: BOOTS AND SHOES

Australia has a reputation for producing hard-wearing boots and shoes. Many items were designed as practical work-wear for the relentless dry heat, dusty harsh conditions of inland farming, and cattle droving. This footwear now has a global reputation not necessarily restricted to farm or stockmen clients. Some of the most enduring and profitable footwear manufacturers in Australia have, since the later part of the twentieth century, used what is a somewhat romantic image of the stockman to sell these sturdy boots and shoes. Supported by a guaranteed clientele of blue-collar workers, pastoralists, and stockmen, production of boots and hard-wearing shoes continued through two world wars, when sales of fancy fashion footwear ground to a halt. The minimal change in style from year to year has meant costs could be reduced and has sustained the quality of the product. This reputation for quality has serviced an extensive rural and industrial sector throughout Australia, at the same time being the most successful Australian footwear sold globally.

Prior to motor vehicles, fine leather skills were essential for stockmen and pastoralists using tack and harnesses for horse-drawn transportation. In the 1930s Reginald Murray Williams, a South Australian drover, well digger, and miner, gained a knowledge of bush saddlery from an itinerant saddler, and the company he started soon after became a global success. R.M. Williams boots are probably the most iconic example of Australian hard-wearing footwear—built to last, they continue to be made in Australia from local materials, catering to a distinctly male ethos (although also worn by women and children). The use of the popular Australian bush heritage theme has been a highly successful marketing tool for the company and has fitted well with one of Australia's formative legends—that a "real" Australian is a man of the bush. Extremely long-lasting, R.M. Williams boots can be worn for up to fifteen years and come in different styles for different occasions. Their elastic-sided boots are made from one piece of hide with a welted sole (a sole in which a piece of leather is stitched to the upper and insole together and then the outer sole is attached to the welt with invisible stitching, rendering it extremely hard-wearing), so they are waterproof and keep their shape. As a work boot and a riding boot, the smooth leather sole does not stick in the stirrup. In the event of a fall, first the boot comes out of the stirrup, then the foot comes out of the boot. In contrast, the ridged sole of an ordinary work boot can get dangerously caught in stirrups. R.M. Williams has steadily increased production with new machinery, though methods remain basically the same.

Other famous elastic-sided work boots, Blundstones, are available on the Internet, as are R.M. Williams, and Blundstones are probably the most well-known Australian brand overseas. John

Doran Mcquire wearing "herringbone"-soled Dunlop Volleys, Sydney, 2007. The special sole gives a good grip, and they are Australia's best-selling sports shoe. Photograph by Jessica Matino.

Sydney department store David Jones advertised: "Our newest fashion flats—we had them copied from selected styles acclaimed as New York's favourites."

Australian designers of leather shoes have frequently employed immigrant European shoemakers, many from strife-torn countries. A good number came from several generations of skilled craftspeople with proud traditions of design and manufacture. These shoemakers were familiar with the entire process, unlike their Australian counterparts, who had only completed one part of it in a mass production line. Their skills were consciously marketed with labels such as Athenian Shoes and Caesar Shoes, which reflected the Italian, Greek, Croatian, or Rumanian origins of these small businesses.

Adam and Morris Perkale, Austrian shoemakers working in Sydney since the late 1950s, delighted in using the finest Australian leathers for their custom-made shoes (including polo boots for the former media magnate Kerry Packer), while conscious of the deterioration in the Australian leather industry. J. Robins and Sons is a large Sydney company that has been manufacturing women's leather shoes in Australia since 1873. In the twenty-first century they produce the Sandler, Easy Step, and Widestep brands. Their loyal migrant workforce produces several thousand pairs of shoes a week. Robins introduced the just-in-time process, which relies on low stock and organizes people in small groups, each worker completing an entire pair of shoes. This process leads to a more satisfied team. In the twenty-first century Robins

A thong stranded on Whitehaven Beach, Whitsunday Island, Queensland, 1987. Thongs are a very common shoe style in Australia and have become part of beach culture. Photograph by Bill and Sue Mansill.

Blundstone, first an importer of footwear, started his own manufacturing firm in Hobart, Tasmania, in 1878 and was joined by his son in 1883 to become J. Blundstone and Son. In 2007 the company, then producing 1.4 million pairs of boots a year, announced it was moving production to India and Thailand. Workingmen who had stood by their steel-toed "Blunnies" for decades threatened to change their allegiance after the move. Another Australian boot maker, Enoch Taylor & Co. Pty Ltd., moved production to Fiji in 2004. Established in 1851, the company carried out systematic research into the size of Australian feet to create suitable wooden lasts that guaranteed their footwear was comfortable and hard-wearing. They manufacture a range of lace-up and elastic-sided boots and shoes, and their well-known T-boots.

One firm continuing to manufacture sturdy footwear in Australia is Baxter Boots and Shoes of Goulburn, about 200 kilometers southwest of Sydney. This labor-intensive company was founded in the 1850s by Henry Baxter (its sole owner in 1885) and has remained in the family up until 2008. In 2007 the Baxters found production was increasingly threatened by a lack of component suppliers, machinery parts, skilled technicians, and tanneries, forcing them to import materials. Such established companies have taken pride in the notion of family enterprise but have had finally to transfer offshore. Nevertheless, this sector looks likely to thrive, and, with online retailing, Australian boots will continue to be purchased and appreciated for their high quality and even by some for a romanticized dream of the bush.

SPORT AND LEISURE

Australia is essentially an urban culture despite its reputation as a nation of beach and sport lovers, and the pastoral imagery it cultivates in some advertising. Even so, Australia has a strong interest in the leisure and sports market, where there has been mass-marketing success. Dunlop Australia has been manufacturing

rubber shoes, soles, and heels since the 1920s, relying on large-volume production, with branches in all Australian states. Jim Merser joined the firm in 1951 and was involved in the design and production of the famous Dunlop Volleys. In 1939 Australian Davis Cup winner Adrian Quist had bought a pair of American canvas deck shoes from a ship's chandlery. In his next match he was the only player not slipping on the wet grass. He attributed this success to the deck shoes. Quist encouraged Dunlop to duplicate the herringbone-patterned sole and improve the arch support and the canvas upper. They were named the Volley OC (Orthopaedically Correct) and sold for $2.50. Bushwalkers and mountaineers would leave the distinctive tread marks throughout Australia's national parks. Up to the twenty-first century, twenty-six million pairs have been sold, being Australia's biggest-selling sports shoe. Volleys typify an easy, healthy lifestyle. They have entered the realm of casual urban footwear, with their price and comfort suiting most feet.

The beach is central to Australian life. Since the majority of the population lives along the coastline, they have year-round access to beautiful sandy beaches, swimming, surfing, and diving. Australian feet are on average about three millimeters (⅛ inch) wider than American feet. It is thought that the warm climate and long summer months of going bare foot and wearing open sandals cause the feet to spread. This has led to problems with the fit of imported shoes. Thought to be originally a Japanese design, thongs (the simplest form of rubber- or plastic-soled sandal, held by a three-point strap secured between the big toe and second toe and at each side of the sole, known variously as jandles in New Zealand and flip flops in the United Kingdom) were enthusiastically adopted as a symbol of the fun-loving beach culture.

Rubber thongs were first seen in Australia just after the 1956 Olympics, where they were slipped on and off at the poolside by triumphant Japanese swimmers. A footwear buyer for the Sydney department store David Jones saw an opportunity for promotion

Amelie Peep Mule (with peep disk pushed aside) by Australian shoemaker Donna May Bolinger, 2006. Bolinger has been designing fashionable footwear since 2002, and the printed leather surfaces often include art references. Photograph by Sotha Bourn. Powerhouse Museum.

At the other end of the scale a Sydney designer, Marc Newson (now based in London), created the Zvezdochka sports shoe for international sports company Nike in 2004. Specially styled on the footwear of Russian cosmonauts, they were named after the fifth Russian dog in space. Newson employed his broad range of design skills to create an innovative double-skinned shoe using new materials. The shoe has a sock-like, rubber-soled inner shoe and plastic outer layer. Initially a limited edition of 140 pairs was launched at a prestigious event at the Moss design store in New York.

HIGH FASHION: NICHE MARKETS

The size of Australia's major cities (Sydney, 4.3 million, and Melbourne, 3.8 million, in 2007) and increasing affluence mean that a lucrative market for boutique designers is emerging, as the mass market loses place. Australians do not readily conform to fashion edicts, and with a range of lifestyles and climates to be enjoyed, they like possibility of choice. Where a designer has a carefully identified clientele, this has led to very successful businesses. Many designers produce niche-couture shoes concerned with sustainable in-house production, responding to the demand by affluent consumers for customized fashion.

A surprising number of women shoemaker-designers are currently running successful businesses in Australia employing fewer than fifty people. They satisfy high-end fashion, custom-made footwear, and theatrical markets. Melbourne shoe innovators Petri Zly and Johanna Preston design quirky, colorful, beautifully made shoes for a selected client base. There are ten niche Preston Zly outlets in Australia, selling six to seven hundred pairs a year overseas. Since 1996 they have operated from their studio in Fitzroy, Melbourne, teaming up with Melbourne and Sydney fashion designers. They tailor their designs to clients whose tastes they know well.

Provocative stiletto sandals are the specialty of Dahto Shoes in Sydney. Mario Dahto learned his trade in Calabria, Italy. The

and had ten thousand pairs of thongs flown in, which sold so quickly that they placed an ongoing order for many thousands at a time. Dunlop Australia recognized their potential and began to manufacture rubber thongs. Jim Merser, who was responsible for thong design and production at Dunlop Australia, reports that some years they sold over a million pairs. Merser was charged with solving the problem of thong plugs, which had a tendency to pull through the hole in the sole. He realized the solution was to make the plug spread when it was pulled upwards. He cupped the disc so that it was like a saucer instead of just being flat across the top, and the spindle went into the center of this cup. When pulled up, the cup spreads. The company patented Merser's design as a "device by which central forces are diverted externally."

Rubber thongs came to be a recognized antiestablishment symbol in 1960s Australia. Known as bangers and double pluggers, they epitomized an unpretentious and egalitarian society and reached iconic status. Some men wore thongs all the time, but thongs are still banned from many clubs and restaurants. Provocative fashion statements soften with time though, and thong sandals have now evolved into a benign, unthreatening style of footwear, the most popular shoe style in Australia.

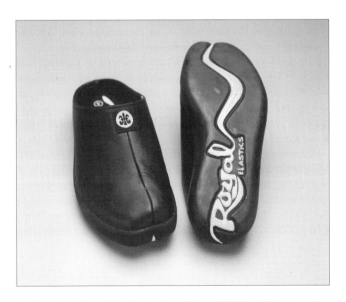

A splice clog by Royal Elastics, Australia/China, 1999. Royal Elastics makes fashionable shoes that are easy to wear and nongender specific. Photograph by Sue Stafford. Powerhouse Museum.

heels of their handmade sandals sometimes rise to fifteen centimeters (six inches). Dahto sandals, styled by Janice Puddephatt, appear in catwalk parades and are frequently worn by elegant actresses and media personalities. Another high-end fashion shoe designer is Donna May Bolinger, who has been designing fashion footwear since 1992, including time working with Sergio Rossi in Milan. Her work is notable for its intriguing printed leather surfaces, sometimes cheeky, often featuring historical and art references. The process of cutting, blocking, machining, and finishing her one-off shoes for clients requires several highly skilled craftspeople. Bolinger admires the Australian lifestyle but regrets that the same casual lifestyle makes it difficult to make a profitable business from high-end fashion shoes. Bolinger's couture shoes are entirely made in Australia, but recently she has streamlined a less expensive range. Offshore machinists and craftspeople carry out piecework that is then made up in her workshop in Sydney. She makes shoes for Australian designers Ginger & Smart, who supply many fashion outlets in Europe and Australia.

Jodie Morrison's Sydney company, Steppin' out, creates shoes for theater and film productions. Morrison has been making theatrical shoes since the 1980s. She has the advantage of diverse historical references from film and theater work for inspiration. Her sound practical knowledge, born out of working with dancers and performers, enhances her teaching at the Sydney Institute of TAFE (Technical and Further Education). Her colleague Andrew McDonald has worked with Australian designers Akira Isogawa and Nicole Zimmermann, and his shoes are frequently seen on catwalks.

Brisbane designer Christopher McCullom markets traditional design methods with "drawings with graphite on paper" in creating Veinwear and Oken men's shoes. With many manufacturers using CAD (computer-aided design) and not employing designers, McCullom is keen to emphasize the originality of his designs, "drawn by hand, made by hand." His Oken range was created for export using a unique range of skins—emu, kangaroo, and crocodile—with leather soles and linings. The adventurous male is their marketing target.

While Australia shares with many Western countries a sharp decline in domestic shoe manufacturing, sneakers manufactured in Asia and South America have taken a lion's share of the market. Fascinated with the design of sneakers, Australian Simon Wood set up a Web site, *Sneaker Freaker*, in 2003. Based in a Melbourne design studio, he has intensified a global fascination for sneaker design and gained an international following, who wait eagerly for each new development in materials and styling. Pandering to this market, manufacturers are issuing limited-edition sneakers, and the instant feedback on Web blogs leads to knowledge of just what their clients want.

As an example of the strength of niche marketing, Australian skateboarders Tull Price and Rodney Adler set out to make nongender-specific laceless footwear with their brand, Royal Elastics. Shoes need to be easy to put on and take off, so they researched global fastening systems. Royal Elastics are inspired by sport and leisure, but their designs emphasize fashion, rather than sporting performance. Marketing was ingenious, with a rave culture launch in Britain—Australians and Britons flocked to buy them. The company was bought in 2001 by K-Swiss for US$3 million. Price and Adler have now launched beautifully styled and finely crafted leather shoes under the label FEIT, selling both online and from an inner-city Darlinghurst boutique in Sydney.

Australia's domestic production of shoes has continued to contract from the twenty-three million manufactured in 1990, despite a significant growth in population (estimated at 20,434,176 in July 2007). With declining numbers of important businesses manufacturing footwear (reduced to less than ten in 2005), it is evident that most everyday footwear manufacturing is done overseas, a trend affecting many countries in the Organisation for Economic Co-operation and Development.

On a more positive note, Australian designers in the twenty-first century are moving into a new era of global marketing, Web shopping, and "e-tailing," putting their marketing and technical ideas to work. Free trade agreements offer opportunities to join with other nations in the manufacturing industries. Whether the office is in a beachside Sydney suburb, a rural Australian town, or downtown Shanghai, business is global and sophisticated. New shoe designers have emerged in the twenty-first century with quite a different style of manufacturing, marketing, and selling from the past, with niche companies functioning successfully alongside global giants.

References and Further Reading

Australian Leather Trades Review (June 1903, March 1934, August 1935, July 1961, March 1962).

Butler, Roger, ed. *The Europeans: Emigré Artists in Australia 1930–1960.* Canberra: National Gallery of Australia, 1997.

Delaney, William J. *Erskineville to Ultimo: A History of the NSW School of Footwear 1906–1996.* Sydney: School of Footwear, Department of Technical and Further Education, 1996.

English, Bonnie. *A Cultural History of Fashion in the 20th Century: From the Catwalk to the Sidewalk.* Oxford: Berg, 2007.

Marshall, Alan. *In Mine Own Heart.* Melbourne, Australia: F. W. Cheshire, 1963.

Maynard, Margaret. *Fashioned from Penury: Dress as Cultural Practice in Colonial Australia.* Cambridge: Cambridge University Press, 1994.

Mitchell, Louise, and Lindie Ward. *Stepping Out: Three Centuries of Shoes.* Sydney: Powerhouse Museum, 1997.

Riello, Giorgio, and Peter McNeil. *Shoes: A History from Sandals to Sneakers.* Oxford and New York: Berg, 2006.

Lindie Ward

See also Rural Dress in Australia; Independent Australian Fashion; Settler Dress in Australia.

Ceremonial and Religious Dress in Australia

While indigenous Australians have occupied the continent of Australia for over forty thousand years, the British, including convicts, only began arriving in 1788 on the First Fleet, and Christian clergy arrived with them. Religion, customs, and dress of Europeans in those early years of colonization were based on the motherland of Great Britain, the settlers being largely monocultural. Since then Australian ceremonial and religious dress has been characterized by considerable diversity, and in the twenty-first century the country is fully multicultural. The early British population has been augmented by waves of immigrants from all over the world, especially after World War II, bringing with them their own cultures, religious beliefs and affiliations, approaches to life, and ways of religious dressing. Much European ceremonial dress has its basis in British colonial history, but peculiarly local slants on some clothing have been introduced over time, to the extent that it is identifiable as Australian.

All the major world religions are present in Australia, as well as numerous alternative ones, but Christianity in all its forms is still dominant, therefore influential in Australian ceremonial life. The Church of England (Anglican Church), Methodist, Presbyterian, Roman Catholic, Congregationalist, and Baptist churches exist in Australia, and there is a wide range of beliefs, organizational structures, and dress among all the Christian groups, from the hierarchical displays of rank and authority exhibited in Roman Catholicism, to Pentecostal ministerial clothing that is indistinguishable from that of lay people. Many other Australians belong to one of several Christian Orthodox faiths, such as the Greek Orthodox Church and the Macedonian, Serbian, and Russian Orthodox churches.

Buddhism has a large following, and its numbers increase each year. Chinese miners were probably the first Buddhists to arrive in Australia in the mid-nineteenth century, and Hinduism was introduced when Asian people arrived as crews on trading ships or as laborers in the same century. Afghan and Indian migrants were the first Islamic adherents. There were some Jewish convicts on the First Fleet in 1788, and a synagogue was established in Sydney in the 1820s. There are also small communities of Sikhs in Australia, some of whom are descendants of people who came into Australia in the 1890s to work on the sugarcane fields in Queensland.

The religions considered here are by no means the only ones present in Australia. World faiths such as the Bahai and a significant number of alternative and New Age beliefs exist, as well as mystery schools (such as the Rosicrucians), each with its own form of ceremonial dress, from extremely simple to highly elaborate. But we should not forget that many Australians profess to have no religious affiliation.

The practices associated with all these religions and communal ideas are often visibly demonstrated by unique forms of dress. So while some of this clothing is universal and has undergone little or no change on being imported to Australia, other forms of dress show slight alterations or have been somewhat modified. Some attire has been creatively invented for functional purposes due to the Australian climate and ethos, and the tendency to enjoy relaxed lifestyles. Dress worn by lay members of Christian congregations has grown more informal. In the first half of the twentieth century "Sunday best" clothing was worn to church, including hats, gloves, and stockings for women, but this has changed. Hats and gloves are no longer worn except sometimes at weddings, and dress can be as informal as blue jeans.

Rites of passage are those events that mark an individual's four major stages of life: birth, puberty, marriage, and death. In Australia they are celebrated according to the particular traditions of each religion. Although puberty is not religiously celebrated by many groups, except for the Jewish ritual of bar mitzvah (for boys) and bat mitzvah (for girls), both weddings and funerals are important events in most, if not all, religions. In Australia mourning rituals such as the custom, common in the nineteenth century, of wearing all-black clothing to funerals have markedly decreased, except among the older generation.

A wedding is the rite of passage par excellence that colorfully and explicitly distinguishes ethnic and/or religious background. The most universally worn wedding dress in Australia is the traditional white wedding dress for the bride and a formal suit for the groom. The "white" wedding is a lavish and growing phenomenon. Many Asians visit Australia to be married and photographed in a demonstrably Australian landscape such as Uluru (formerly known as Ayers Rock) in central Australia or one of the many beaches. In fact, wedding tourism has become an important part of the tourist industry, with brides donning Western-style white wedding dresses and grooms sporting formal suits to accompany them.

RELIGIOUS DRESS: CHRISTIANS AND JEWS

Of the 20.1 million people living in Australia (2006 census), 70 percent profess to be Christian. Of these, the largest numbers are Roman Catholics (26.8%) and Anglicans (21.8%). The liturgical dress of the Roman Catholic Church is hierarchical, especially evident in the specified use of colors and lavish, rich fabrics. In spite of the egalitarian nature of the Australian way of life, Roman Catholic vestments worn in Australia do not differ from their counterparts in Rome. In general, the use of color to denote rank is: black for seminarians, deacons, priests, and chaplains; violet for bishops, prelates, and proto-notaries; scarlet for cardinals; and white for the supreme representative and head of the Roman Catholic Church, the pope, who resides in Rome.

The central vestment of the Church is the cassock (a long, close-fitting black vestment), which is also worn by other Christian denominations, such as the Anglicans. The simar (or zimarra) resembles the cassock and has an additional shoulder-cape of the same fabric and color. The fascia is the sash around the waist, which functions as a belt. Again, colors are: white for the pope, scarlet for a cardinal, violet for a bishop, and black for others. The chasuble is the major liturgical vestment of a priest or bishop and resembles a long, sleeveless poncho-like cloak. It matches the liturgical colors and is worn over the alb (a long white vestment, tied at the waist with a cincture or girdle).

The hierarchical nature of the Roman Catholic Church is also reflected in headdresses. The zucchetto, a silk skullcap, originated in the very early Church as the covering of the clerical tonsure (shaved crown of the head). The miter, which is usually made of layered white damask silk, is a tall headdress worn at liturgical functions by bishops and cardinals. A hat that evolved from the soft square academic hat of the high Middle Ages is the biretta, a square-shaped hat with silk trim and tuft, and three raised wings (called horns). A scarlet biretta is for cardinals (of which there are only a few in Australia), violet for bishops, and black for priests, deacons, and seminarians.

The dress of women religious (nuns) in the Roman Catholic Church (approximately thirty different orders in Australia) has lacked the elaborate richness accorded to the male hierarchy. It has been much less ostentatious, almost always black or black and white, demonstrating the lowly status of women religious compared to the men and their deep commitment to holy and modest clothing. The nun's habit was a plain wide-sleeved tunic, veil, belt, scapular, cloak, and simple footwear, which varied little until the church reforms of the 1960s. The tunic's T shape was reminiscent of the Cross of Calvary; to wear it was to clothe oneself in the mystery of the Passion. In stark black-and-white habits, with starched white linen headbands, wimples (a cloth around the head that leaves the face open), and long heavy woolen dresses with flowing black veils, the nuns were noticeably set apart from their secular sisters. What demarcated specific orders of nuns was principally the distinctive headgear of each.

The twentieth century was one of great change in the clothing of women religious. Pope John XXIII announced in 1959 at the Second Vatican Council that the habit needed to be replaced by more contemporary clothing. For some Australian nuns the changes were very painful, as the habit was an important part of their identity. The stark habit was replaced by modern, sometimes colorful, clothing, and nuns had to become reacquainted with the idea of selecting other modes of dress, as well as jewelry. Religious women moved from full habit to modified habit with shorter dress lengths and short veils, to clothes that do not distinguish them from other Australian women, virtually making them disappear from view as nuns.

The population of the Anglican Church (Church of England) in Australia (2006 census) is 21.8 percent and diminishing. Within the Anglican Church we find a wide variety of clerical vestments. The white gown worn by the priest is called the surplice, worn over the cassock. A tippet is a black scarf, with ends that hang down, that can be worn at daily prayers. Some Anglican clergy wear this instead of a stole. The miter is the bishop's hat, and the crosier, which resembles a shepherd's crook, is carried by the bishop to symbolize that he is the chief shepherd of Christ's flock in his region.

The most common article of clothing is the clerical collar, worn by ministers principally when leading services or conducting other official duties. Colors of vestments, altar cloths, and other church decorations change according to the religious calendar as with Catholics; for example, for Christmas and Epiphany the main color is white or gold, which symbolizes joy and purity;

for Lent the color is purple to symbolize mourning and penitence. Ministers use white for weddings and funerals. Women were not ordained as deacons in the Anglican Church of Australia until 1986 and as priests until 1992, only after much debate and controversy. Their vestments mirror those for men clergy. The first Anglican female bishop was ordained in 2008.

Several generations of Aborigines became Christians from the late nineteenth century onward, due to missionary zeal. In the early days missionaries insisted that Aborigines wear so-called civilized Western-style dress to conserve modesty, although this clothing was not always worn. In the late twentieth century some Aborigines became Anglican ministers, and one, Arthur Malcolm, in the North Queensland Diocese reached the status of bishop in 2001. His consecration was accompanied by didjeridoo and clapsticks, and his choice of motif for his cope was distinctly Aboriginal. A cope is a very long mantle or cloak, open in front and fastened with a clasp. It is worn over a cassock and may be worn by any rank of clergy. The cope is individualistic to the degree that the design on each cope is selected by the particular priest to convey something that has personal meaning.

Arthur Malcolm selected a design that reflected both his Aboriginality and the purpose of his ministry: to act as a bridge between the Aboriginal and white communities. His cope is embossed with a Christian cross, flames emerging from the cross, and a pair of upturned hands (one white, one black); underneath all this is a boomerang (a curved Aboriginal wooden weapon) with three crosses inside, reflecting the Christian themes of crucifixion and the Holy Spirit, and symbols of Aboriginality and his hope for the future. As a design, it was intended to depict the partnership of the two races, which, as he stated, are "one in Christ." Some Christian youth began wearing sweatshirts with a similar theme: a pair of hands, one black, one white, representing the hands of God reaching out to all people, visibly expressing the hope for unity and equality among all Australians.

Several other Anglican clergy in the same Diocese of North Queensland marked their distinctiveness from European clergy by selecting Aboriginal symbols on their copes. One priest chose warrior motifs: spears, spear-throwers, and boomerangs, because he wanted to emphasize fighting for the faith. Another chose "benign" symbols such as a fish, a turtle, and a lizard, in traditional ocher colors. Yet another selected four boomerangs laid out in the shape of a cross, with an emu and a kangaroo above the cross and a crocodile below the cross. A further priest selected designs from a collection of Aboriginal shields to convey "defending the faith." The use of customary motifs on religious vestments and other clothing such as sweatshirts also illustrates the hope for a pan-Aboriginal Christianity.

Followers of Judaism in Australia are extremely few (only 0.4 percent of the total population). Jewish law requires Jewish people to honor their bodies and to dress modestly. Although the everyday dress of most is the same as other Australians, Orthodox Jews retain the custom of wearing white clothing on Yom Kippur (Day of Atonement), and some Jewish men have beards and wear a yarmulke or *kippah* (skullcap) or hat at all times. Some married Orthodox Jewish women cover their hair with a sheitel (a wig), a hat, or a scarf, and they do not wear trousers, preferring to wear dresses to below the knees and blouses that cover the elbows.

The basic male garment for special ritual occasions is a kittel, a white robe worn over other clothing that signifies purity, holiness,

Muslim lifesavers at Sydney's Cronulla Beach in February 2007. Mecca Laa Laa (center) is wearing the full-body covering known as the *burquini*, as designed by Lebanese Australian Aheda Zanetti. The garment allows Muslims in Australia to observe their Islamic dress code while participating in Australian beach culture. Anoek De Groot/AFP/Getty Images.

and humility. It is a custom that the first time a man wears a kittel is on his wedding day, then subsequently for Rosh Hashanah, Yom Kippur, and Passover, and finally it forms his burial shroud. The kittel serves to remind Jews of their own mortality and the need to follow Jewish teachings. Both single and married men wear a kippah, which can vary from classic black velvet to a variety of styles and fabrics.

During morning prayer Orthodox Jewish men bind one arm and their head with the *tefillin*, a set of black leather straps and boxes containing scrolls of passages from the Torah. Jewish males from thirteen years of age are expected to wear tefillin. Women are not obliged to do so; indeed, they are generally discouraged from doing this. When not worn, the tefillin are rolled up carefully and placed in a special silk or velvet bag.

The bride's white wedding dress signifies purity and her new beginning as a married woman. Both men and women must cover their heads in the synagogue and when in prayer. Married (and formerly married) women are required to cover their hair entirely; the head scarf used by women to cover their heads is called a *tichl*. Single women and girls may leave their hair uncovered.

A prayer shawl (tallis/tallit/talit) is a large wraparound garment, which is traditionally woven of white wool or silk, with black or blue stripes at the ends. The tallis has bound tassels (tzitzis) on all four corners, and each tassel has four strings (at least 1.5 inches,

or 3.8 centimeters, long); each corner has ten knots, which serve as reminders to the wearer to keep the Commandments.

RELIGIOUS DRESS: ASIAN

Buddhism is arguably the fastest growing religion in Australia, though in 2006 Buddhists were still only 2.1 percent of the total population. Indian in origin, Buddhism was introduced to Australia by Chinese immigrants in the mid-nineteenth century. The major Buddhist traditions are Theravada, Mahayana, and Vajrayana, each having robes that distinguish them from one another, principally by color. The historical Buddha is said to have worn a humble monk's robe made from pieces of donated patched cloth. While Buddhist monastic robes vary, they all reflect the basic Buddhist ideology of humility, simplicity, and detachment from the physical world. The Sanskrit and Pali word for monastic robes is *civara*, which consists of three parts: an inner garment, from the waist to the knee; an upper robe, around the torso and shoulders; and an outer robe used as an overgarment. In addition to these three items worn by men, a Buddhist nun also wears a vest or bodice.

Shaving the head also denotes the renunciation of worldly things and the overcoming of vanity to embrace the monastic life. Lay Buddhist clothing is indistinguishable from the dress of other people in any community. Modest dress and behavior is expected, and shoes are removed at the entrance of Buddhist temples.

The Islamic faith in Australia makes up 1.7 percent of the population. Since its entry into the country in the nineteenth century, via Afghan camel drivers, numbers have been steadily increasing. The Islamic texts, the Qu'ran and Hadith, call on Muslim women and men to be modest. The specific passages that relate to veiling call on women only to "draw their veils over their bosoms" when in public and "not display their beauty" except in the presence of their husbands and certain relatives.

The strictness of dress codes differs quite remarkably from one culture to another. In Australia some women wear veils, and some do not. Some wear a simple scarf over the head, while some cultures insist on the most concealing garment of all, the chador, which is head-to-toe veiling, with only a latticed opening for the eyes. The latter is rarely seen in Australia. The most common covering for Muslim women living in Australia is the *hijab* (literally curtain), or head scarf. Muslim women who voluntarily wear the hijab report that they do not feel it oppressive; on the contrary, they feel liberated, as they are not slaves to fashion and are treated more respectfully.

Young Muslims living in Australia and wanting to adhere to Muslim dress codes, yet participate in beach culture and water sports, are faced with a dilemma: being at the beach dressed in minimal coverage, as do most Australians, or adhering to the Islamic code of covering the body. This dilemma, however, has been resolved with the introduction of a unique mode of dress: the burquini, which offers an acceptable compromise to all concerned.

The *burquini* (a conflation of *burqa* and *bikini*) is a top-to-toe, two-piece Lycra swimsuit with hijab attached, designed by a Lebanese Australian, Aheda Zanetti. It is comfortable and light enough to enable swimming. The head, neck, and arms are completely covered by a thigh-length, long-sleeved dress, which is worn over loose pants with straight legs. The only parts of the body revealed are the face, hands, and feet. Printed motifs over the chest area provide extra modesty to that area of the body.

Burquini-garbed women have even joined Surf Life Saving teams, whose bronzed, blonde-haired men and women are as quintessentially an Australian icon as that of the ANZAC (Australian and New Zealand Army Corps) "digger" with his slouched hat. While not a ceremonial dress in itself, the burquini reflects Islamic mores with regard to acceptable Islamic dress in a way that demonstrates the adaptability and innovativeness of a religion that has found its way to a country that has quite different attitudes and beliefs about the clothed and unclothed body, both secular and sacred.

Hindus form a relatively small part of Australia's population (0.7%). Hindu dress is based on that worn all over India, the *sari* for women and the cotton dhoti for men. The man's traditional *dhoti* is a long draped garment worn in place of pants, topped by a long, loose Indian shirt, slit at both sides with a long one-sided cape tied at the right shoulder, and draped to the knees. The sari consists of several meters of fabric, pleated and tucked into a slip. It also covers the head. Under the sari a modest, short-sleeved short top (*coli/choli*) is worn. Pants are usually only worn by men, never by women, except for the *punjabi*, which consists of loose pants over which is worn a long tunic, slit on both sides. Many male and female Hindus living in Australia choose to wear either Western-style clothing, their customary clothing, or a modified

version of the sari and dhoti. Elaborate Hindu dress is usually reserved for special events like weddings.

The International Society for Krishna Consciousness (ISK-CON), popularly known as the Hare Krishnas, was established in Australia in 1970, during the hippie era. In Australian cities their flowing saffron robes, hairstyles, public chanting, and dancing to the accompaniment of finger cymbals, and their Eastern beliefs, mark them as different from other Australians. Because of the multicultural nature of Australia and the general acceptance of difference, together with their familiarity on the Australian religious scene, the Hare Krishnas now form just another religious group among numerous others.

Male Hare Krishna devotees in Australia wear the traditional dhoti, while women wear the sari. Each person wears *japa beads* (prayer beads, usually carried in a small cloth bag) and a few items of jewelry such as necklaces, earrings, bracelets, nose studs, or rings. The male devotee shaves his head except for the *sikha*, a lock of hair that demonstrates his surrender to a life of Krishna-consciousness. *Tilaka* (clay markings) are worn on the body to mark it as a temple, the most prominent mark worn on the forehead, from the hairline to a point on the nose.

Another religion that emanated from India is Sikhism, and there are some small communities in Australia. They first came sometime after the 1830s to work as shepherds, laborers, and camel drivers in the interior of Australia. Sikh men and women wear distinctive turbans (*dastaar*) with their everyday clothing in order to show their commitment to their faith. Their long hair is carefully hidden underneath, tied into a topknot (*joora*) before the turban is wound around the head. Young men and less traditional adult Sikhs may wear a *patka*, a simple cloth head covering in the place of a turban. The men do not shave. Sikhs also have items of wearing apparel that include a small wooden comb (*kangha*), a symbol of cleanliness; a short sword (*kirpan*), representing their duty to fight evil; and a plain steel bangle (*kara*), symbolizing one God and one truth, without beginning or end. Women might wear a scarf instead of a turban, or a less elaborately tied turban.

PAGANISM

A distinctively different religion from those mentioned is Paganism. In its contemporary form it entered Australia around the mid-twentieth century. Paganism is polytheistic and animistic, and Western Paganism has been called a nature religion with mystical elements. The number of Australian Pagans is difficult to ascertain, though they would form one part of the 3 percent of the population that are listed under "Other" in the Australian Census and Statistics on religion. Pagans are dispersed throughout the continent and regularly gather for religious festivals, the location changing from one year to the next.

Clothing, or lack of clothing, is closely linked to Pagan cosmology. Ritual nudity, "going skyclad," is regarded by some as a natural state of being, which allows freedom from inhibitions. The skyclad body also indicates the casting aside of social masks and roles, honoring the sacredness of each and every body, and placing all on an equal footing regardless of the size, shape, and flaws of the individual body. Although the majority of people remain robed at Pagan religious festivals that celebrate the changing of the seasons, some dance skyclad around the sacred circle during a ritual.

The most basic item of dress common to the various subgroups of Paganism is the black hooded robe. In its most simple

This woman is dressed in a hooded, floor-length robe for a pagan spring ritual in Queensland, Australia, September 2008. Photograph by Paul Frost.

form the shape of the robe resembles an ankh, the ancient symbol of life, with the flared sleeves forming the horizontal bar of a T shape and the hood the rounded loop of the cross. The robe is a floor-length cape with either flared long sleeves, or no sleeves but with two slits so that the arms may go through to enable movement. The hood is usually large, so that it drapes slightly onto the neck, giving it a medieval appearance. The cingulum, a long cord or cords generally associated with initiations, is worn around the waist over the robe. Pagans place importance on being connected with the energy of the earth, so the feet are usually bare.

Jewelry includes necklaces, earrings, rings, bracelets, toe rings, headbands, amulets, or talismans. The pentacle (five-pointed star within a circle), as well as Celtic designs on dress and jewelry, is favored by Australian Pagans, and these designs may also be tattooed on the body.

SECULAR CEREMONIAL DRESS

Australians wear comparatively little secular ceremonial dress. There are several exceptions, though. One of these is the quasi-religious status accorded to returned soldiers or "diggers" and their attire, embedded in the concept of mateship. This concept can be traced back to early settlers who closely relied on each other for help and companionship in sometimes very harsh conditions. A mate implies a sense of shared experience, mutual respect, unconditional assistance, and egalitarianism, something reinforced during wartime. *Digger* was a slang term for Australian and New Zealand soldiers first used during World War I. It has possible associations with goldfields diggers of the 1850s, but the link is

unproven. When Australian and New Zealand soldiers fought side by side in World War I, the term *ANZAC* (Australian and New Zealand Army Corps) merged with the term *digger*. The felt digger hat or slouch hat, colloquial terms for the formal military hat with one side turned up, was caught up with the ANZAC ethos and became an emblem of courage and a national symbol. Although the slouch hat has undergone slight modifications over the years, the hat worn by the Australian military in the twenty-first century is a khaki felt hat with leather chin straps, its brim turned up and flattened on the left-hand side, fastened with a "rising sun" badge.

Australians celebrate, as one of their official holidays, ANZAC Day, which falls on 25 April. This day has become a quasi-religious event that features a parade of returned soldiers and their descendants marching through cities and small towns across the country wearing their uniforms, medals of honor, and the emblematic slouch hat. Many people then spend time in the Returned Soldiers' League clubs, where there is a one-minute silence to mark respect for those who have died in battle. The hat is a reminder to those living of all the Australians who died for their country. It has become an Australian icon.

A more codified form of secular ceremonial dress is worn by the legal profession. It is derived, again, from Britain. Apart from slight variations from one state to another, judges wear black gowns with a black trim for normal court occasions, and red gowns with a white trim for special ceremonial events and for criminal cases. While the full-bottomed wig was worn more frequently in past times, in the twenty-first century Australian judges wear this wig only on ceremonial occasions.

Barristers wear black robes. Senior barristers are distinguished from junior barristers by the design, cut, and fabric of their gowns and the style of the wig. Judges, as well as senior and junior barristers, all wear a jabot, which consists of two rectangles of stiff, white linen worn around the neck over a collarless shirt. In some states the senior barrister's gown incorporates a square piece of black silk, decorated with one bow on each corner.

Junior barristers wear a black wool gown, whereas the Queen's Counsel and Senior Counsel robes are of silk, hence the expression "taking silk" when moving from junior to senior level. The junior barrister's gown also carries a feature known as the "money bag," a thin strip of material trailing down the front of the gown. It is not obligatory for a barrister to wear a wig and gown, except when appearing before a judge.

When women first entered the legal profession, there was some debate about dress and whether or not they should be allowed to wear wigs. It was decided they should and that dresses worn under the gowns would be of dark color. Dresses and blouses had to be long-sleeved and high-necked. Both men's shirts and women's blouses were to be predominantly white and their shoes black. No conspicuous jewelry was to be worn by either men or women. The practice of wearing wigs and gowns remains a matter of continuing debate in Australia. Many have questioned the practicalities of wearing heavy garb in such a hot climate.

Another secular occasion when ceremonial dress is worn is during academic graduation ceremonies. These are formal occasions that explicitly demonstrate the vertical nature of status within academia. Established conventions for academic dress in Australian universities are prescribed, from chancellor down to newly graduated bachelor degree students, and regulations for wear are to be found in each university's set of rules and guidelines for academic dress. The historical links between Britain and Australia are again evident, as all gowns use either the Oxford University or Cambridge University pattern.

The knee-length (or longer) black gown is the basic item of dress. Each academic discipline is singled out by the colors of hoods on gowns and the front panels worn over the gowns. The names of the colors generally follow the *British Color Council Dictionary of Standard Colors*, but exceptions, such as specific colors that reflect Australian flora (wattle and waratah), are included as color terms for some hoods.

In general, a black mortarboard, a relic of the square academic hat worn in the high Middle Ages, is worn by students receiving bachelors and masters degrees, and a black soft bonnet by those being awarded a doctoral degree. The biretta is the ancestor of the modern academic mortarboard. The mortarboard is still worn by students and faculty at university graduation ceremonies in Australia, an anachronism for Australians, who pride themselves on egalitarianism and a general antipathy toward pomp and ceremony.

Religious and ceremonial dress instills in the wearer a sense of the sacred and a demarcation between the sacred and the secular, as well as establishing certain codes of behavior and mores. Dress gives a public face to personal religious beliefs, making strong statements about ideology, identity, and community, which sometimes cause friction and tension within the larger community.

When religious beliefs are transplanted from one country to another, they undergo change for a number of reasons: the geography, climate, flora and fauna (especially with regard to naturistic religions), ideas and rules that may conflict with those of the host country (particularly regarding freedom of dress and bodily exposure), the clash between hierarchical systems and egalitarianism, and evolving value systems.

References and Further Reading

Daner, Francine Jean. *The American Children of Krsna: A Study of the Hare Krsna Movement*. New York: Holt, Rinehart and Winston, 1974.

Hume, Lynne. *Witchcraft and Paganism in Australia*. Carlton, Australia: Melbourne University Press, 1997.

Kuhns, Elizabeth. *The Habit: A History of the Clothing of Catholic Nuns*. New York: Doubleday, 2003.

Muir, Claire. *Wigs and Gowns: A Lasting Tradition*. 1st ed. Melbourne, Australia: Victoria Law Foundation, 2005.

Lynne Hume

See also Military and Civil Uniforms in Australia; Liturgical Robes in New Zealand.

Military and Civil Uniforms in Australia

Lacking the powerful and intimidating presence exerted in authoritarian and militaristic societies, uniforms have nonetheless been ubiquitous in Australia for the past two hundred years. A large minority of men have worn them since the 1860s, if only for a few hours a week as citizen soldiers or volunteer firefighters. In the 1940s a significant minority of women and the majority of children began to wear uniforms too, the former in the military or at work, the latter in school. The first uniforms in Australia were British. Subsequent uniforms have remained Western if not outright British in their fabrics, styles, and messages, though modified to suit a sometimes hot climate and inclined to proclaim national and institutional identities. That inclination has contributed to the national iconography. Both the slouch hat (a broad-brimmed felt hat turned up on one side) worn by soldiers and the patrol cap of surf lifesavers have become visual shorthand for Australia.

CONTEXTS AND COMMON TRENDS

Aborigines were the dominant peoples of Australia for at least forty thousand years. They did not wear uniforms, which migrated to the continent only from 1788 with the first British settlers and their military and naval guardians. The red coat worn by most British soldiers on garrison duty was the first iconic uniform in Australia, representing both colonial authority and the society from which the new arrivals had come. Aborigines snatched up red coats whenever soldiers cast them aside for new ones. Aboriginal men whom the settlers acknowledged as chiefs were given full sets of naval or military officers' uniforms, with metal gorgets (crescent-shaped regalia worn on a chain around the neck as a badge of rank) spelling out, sometimes with irony, a semiofficial status.

Military cut and color was also adopted by early settlers, from former soldiers who continued to wear parts of their old uniforms to women of the gentry whose dresses were sometimes decorated with military braiding in the popular hussar style. In the 1860s better-off boys began to be dressed as sailors or zouaves, the last being outlandishly clothed soldiers from French North Africa. The zouave suit soon disappeared, but the sailor suit endured for a century. Eventually it would be worn by girls too, with a pleated skirt instead of trousers.

White men in Australia began to wear real uniforms in large numbers in the 1860s as a consequence of a surge in community activity around the English-speaking world, which, over the next fifty years, built clubs and civic institutions, from local sporting teams to national armies. Australian participants in the surge chose similar uniforms to those worn elsewhere in the British Empire, from the white flannel trousers and cotton shirts of local cricket teams to the loose gray wool coats of local companies of citizen soldiers. They disdained the extravagant styles popular in the United States, a country whose uniforms would not influence Australian ones until the 1940s.

Australian governments began to copy British uniforms at the same time. During the final third of the nineteenth century the blue, brightly buttoned, semimilitary uniforms worn in Britain by police, mail carriers, ambulance crews, and other officials were imported to Australia. The intention was to invite trust but also advertise authority. Local modifications such as pith helmets (light sun helmets made from the dried pith of the sola plant) were allowed where permitted by the British. As in Britain, numbers or letters, usually in the form of a metal badge, allowed individual wearers to be identified by the public and held accountable. In a small way these badges supported the civic rights that ordinary English-speaking people were proud to possess.

In 1901, when the Australian colonies federated, most uniforms of the infant nation followed British styles, often with pith helmets added, sometimes in the same drab hues, and slouch hats (elsewhere known as bush hats), which were then seen on other British imperial frontiers in Asia and Africa. The new style was widely thought to have been developed in Australia, a misunderstanding that gave it a nationalistic appeal. Its popularity became universal during World War I after slouch hats became a symbol of Australian soldiers, and by implication of Australia. Their drabness was also in tune with a public preference for economy and equality. The slouch hat was discontinued only in the 1950s when it made Australian soldiers seem provincial beside Allied troops.

When large numbers of women and children began to follow men into uniform during the 1940s, the styles and fabrics chosen closely followed British models. Soon American models would be just as important. Modifications of uniforms to suit Australia's generally warm and sometimes hot climate had so far been few or, where they involved changing into an informal dress such as the shirtsleeves and straw hats of some mounted police, were temporary and kept from public view where possible. This changed in the mid-twentieth century with the wider Western sartorial retreat from heavy wool, heraldic colors, and martial stiffness, following the American preference for casual smartness. Polyester was added to wool and cotton. Coats were increasingly left aside in winter for woolen pullovers or cardigans, in summer for shirts that bore the necessary insignia on shoulder straps or breast pockets. Peaked caps replaced pith helmets, which now seemed quaint. Shorts and long socks proved acceptable for transportation workers, ambulance crews, bank clerks, and mail carriers, though not for police.

In the 1970s women's uniforms, even in the armed forces, became physically flattering, reflecting a brief congruity between
sexual appeal and gender liberation. Large employers paid designers to clothe women in something modern enough to appeal
to wearers. Yet such uniforms diverted women from the equality
many sought in the workplace. From the 1980s, as in Britain and
the United States, Australian women's uniforms began to resemble men's.

That decade also saw a growing use of protective clothing,
another international trend, but a perplexing one given the de-
creasing dangers facing Australians in uniform, whether in the
factory or on the battlefield. Safety helmets, sun hats, and fluorescent reflective vests in lime or orange became common for
mail carriers, road workers, traffic officers, ambulance workers,
and police, as did gas- and flame-proof clothing for police and
firefighters and torso-covering body armor for soldiers.

Despite an unmilitary mood, from the 1950s on, many young
Australians wore pieces of uniform as everyday dress. As with
army and navy greatcoats, this sometimes reflected the low

prices and high quality found in ubiquitous army surplus stores.
At other times the impulse was to find a new and interesting
look or, particularly when wearing black leather jackets originally derived from the German army, to claim attention or express discontent. These last motives explained the formal, almost
obsolete school uniforms worn on stage by two Australian pop
singers, Angus Young of the band AC/DC (1973–) and Chris-
tina Amphlett of the Divynls (1980–1997).

Australian uniforms have continued moving toward informality, protection from sun and injury, and similarity in cut for men
and women when physical activity is required. They are also increasingly likely to point to a national or corporate identity and,
outside the armed forces, to include eye-catching reflective items.

POLICE UNIFORMS

The first mounted police raised to keep order on the early colonies' expanding frontiers were seconded from British soldiers on
garrison duty. They inclined to a sleek blue British cavalry jacket
with light trousers and cloth caps (1820s–1840s). When trousers
gave way to cord riding breeches in the 1860s and caps to pith helmets in the 1870s, the result was the first distinctively Australian
uniform. What seemed smart to settlers longing for order and
pageantry seemed affected to bushrangers (rural criminals) and
their many sympathizers, a view eventually presented to a global
audience through Sidney Nolan's paintings (1946–1947) of the
bushranger Ned Kelly and the police who hunted him down in
1880. By the time Nolan was painting, mounted police uniform
had diverged into a military-style working dress, which reminded
observers of the force's martial origins and culture, and a blue-
and-white ceremonial dress, which allowed state governments to
inject a military air into official parades.

Some of the small native police units raised from Aboriginal
recruits from the 1830s to the early twentieth century were also
dressed for ceremony. In Victoria they appeared as light cavalry (1842–1853), in the same sleek green uniform trimmed with
scarlet that their white officers were wearing. Queensland's native police received a special uniform in 1868 to better impress
the visiting Duke of Edinburgh. Such smartness came at a cost.
New South Wales politicians were told in 1856 that tight woolen
uniforms were shortening their wearers' lives. But fine outfits fell
victim to the apparently more compelling argument that they
were not helping to discipline the Aborigines who wore them and
nor helping make black Australians more like white ones. Some
native police were already wearing standard mounted police uniform by the 1860s; gradually all of them were issued with cheaper,
shabbier versions of it. In the hot and remote Northern Territory
they made do with cheap, sack-like coats or even civilian clothes.

Early nonmounted town police in Australia wore the clumsy
coats and top hats of their English counterparts. Urban police forces created around the 1860s adopted the blue, heavily
buttoned uniforms modeled on London's metropolitan police.
Badges in the form of numbers told observers the identity of the
officer addressing them in the name of the law. Victoria's police
adopted a unique and practical headdress, a leather shako (a hat
with an all-round brim covered with white cloth in summer). Pith
helmets and white trousers became more common concessions
to the climate. Commissioners and bandsmen often wore heavily
braided hussar tunics and caps on official occasions, providing a
chance to outshine the army at public festivals.

Studio portrait from the last quarter of the nineteenth century of a young
bandsman wearing a braided uniform based on that worn by citizen soldiers
in his town of Ballarat in Victoria, Australia. Photograph by George Willetts.
John Etkins Collection, State Library of Victoria.

The collars of police coats were turned down and their lapels turned back after World War II, when visible pockets in military style also appeared. By the 1970s synthetic material and shirt-sleeves in summer were common, and a new British import, the blue-and-white checkered hat band of London's metropolitan police, was beginning to identify Australian police too. A further break with tradition came with the issue of body armor, helmets, and shields to police on riot duty and eventually to special squads trained to break up protests and shoot down armed criminals. Black as well as bulky, and giving personal anonymity to a force hitherto identifiable to the public gaze, the outfit was designed to intimidate observers as well as protect wearers.

After World War II women in calf-length skirts, thick stockings, and peaked caps or brimmed hats were sharing police work. Their uniform reflected their largely unphysical role. But within twenty years it was transformed to allow active work, for example, by the culottes (full-cut trousers that resemble skirts) issued to New South Wales policewomen in 1982. Women's hats and neckties are now among the few distinctive marks of their sex, and even these are replaced by men's uniform items when serving on motorbike, on horseback, or in rescue and forensic work.

MALE MILITARY UNIFORMS

The first military forces raised in Australia in the mid-nineteenth century were citizen rather than professional ones. Their members, not any government, chose their uniforms, and they looked to what their cousins in Britain's Volunteer Force were wearing and what their own girlfriends and wives found attractive.

Australian citizen soldiers flirted at first with the red shirts made famous by the followers of Garibaldi, the Italian revolutionary nationalist, thus signaling romantic and democratic martial beliefs. But Garibaldi shirts were edged aside by a loose woolen uniform, usually gray, which pointed to a more practical military vision of acting as the British army's skirmishers. Climate, cost, and sensibility inclined citizen soldiers against traditional and extravagant dress. Hussar tunics were tolerable if their wearers proclaimed themselves to be modern mounted riflemen rather than old-fashioned cavalry, but the hussar's furred busby was rare in Australia. Spurned were the square-topped lancer's cap and the baggy trousers of the zouave, however popular these were with children and with citizen soldiers in the United States.

The fading in the 1870s of a unique martial vision among citizen soldiers, along with increasing admiration for the British army, was marked by a turn to red coats and, in the 1880s and 1890s, adoption of what was called "national" dress by regiments organized along ethnic lines. Those who proclaimed themselves Irish wore dark green; if Scots, they chose red doublets, tartan kilts, and white pith helmets. Two regiments calling themselves Australian chose green, red, or blue uniforms (1897) before being forced, like many other citizen soldiers, into khaki and slouch hats.

The gradual imposition of this uniform reflected both military fashion and the declining autonomy of citizen soldiers. The combination of khaki woolen tunics, cord riding breeches, and felt hats whose broad brims turned up on one side, giving them the name of slouch hats, was first seen in India before being introduced to Australian soldiers around 1885. In standing out from red coats, in further diminishing the modest braid that proclaimed officers to be superior men, and in mimicking the drab hues worn by bush workers and the sleek cut of mounted police

dress, the new uniform was soon regarded as an embodiment of Australianness. Indeed, it was increasingly assumed to have been invented locally. In 1889 a visiting British general, Bevan Edwards, urged that all Australian soldiers wear what he called this "distinctive national dress."

Governments tried to comply. Most urban citizen soldiers preferred red coats, though, and clung tenaciously to them on parade. Federation and the approach of World War I ended their resistance. Political leaders and staff officers now favored simple, modern uniforms, and they got their way when a militia was created from citizen soldiers in 1912 and its members were squeezed into the cheapest possible khaki uniform. Staff officers escaped the drabness they endorsed for others, usually wearing the same blue dress favored by off-duty British officers. The style would be taken up by the cadets at Australia's military college at Duntroon.

Khaki and slouch hats were worn in Europe and the Middle East during World War I by an Australian Imperial Force raised beside the homebound militia to fight overseas. Though other armies had worn this combination, and a few continued to do so, none shaped their hat peaks or turned up their hat brims quite like the Australians did. The slouch hat thus became a national symbol and was worn by Australia's prime minister, W.M. Hughes, when visiting the troops overseas and in Australia during the 1919 election campaign. Almost as distinctive were the bright cloth "colour patches" worn on soldiers' upper sleeves to identify their unit. But most soldiers were more likely to think about the quality of their boots and underwear, politicians about how to provide uniforms at all. Government clothing factories built during the previous few decades to manufacture uniforms and give work to Australian men could no longer meet demand. Private companies such as Bidencope's in Hobart met some of the shortfall. Most was met by British industry.

Uniforms kept after the war were sometimes worn by the New Guard, a secret Sydney-centered group of war veterans active in the early 1930s. The group considered adopting blue shirts, the color indicating a militant conservatism remote from true Nazism. The Guard's only notable achievement came when a member wearing a British khaki uniform disrupted the opening of the Sydney Harbour Bridge in 1932 by infiltrating the official party. His choice of dress placed him above suspicion in what was still a devoted province of the British Empire.

In 1922 the infant Royal Australian Air Force adopted the same uniform as its British counterpart, but in a color that would become almost as much a shorthand for Australia as the slouch hat. The air force's choice of indigo rather than the pale blues being considered by Britain's air force reflected rising Australian pride within the empire. It was also a successful maneuver to raise the air force's profile and ward off a mooted merger into the militia and navy. Thousands of indigo-clad airmen served in Europe during World War II. Otherwise interchangeable cogs within Britain's air force, they could immediately be distinguished by their unique uniform color. Back home, where they were better paid and better educated than Australian soldiers, indigo marked them out for admiration and envy, flattery or ridicule. Soldiers sarcastically dubbed them "blue orchids" after the title of a 1933 *Biggles* story.

Before World War II the militia had added colored collars and regimental badges to its uniforms and allowed its artillerymen and engineers to swap khaki for blue. It retained its signature slouch hats, even though these were beginning to seem quaint. It also refused to follow the British army into battle dress, a radical, almost unmilitary suit derived from sporting and factory wear. If the refusal indicated a provincial mindset, it pointed also to a prudent reluctance to abandon proven imagery.

World War II eventually imposed new clothing on Australian soldiers. At first a new Australian Imperial Force dressed much like its famous predecessor (sometimes even in its predecessor's mothballed tunics), with a proud new series of color patches. But the uniform was obsolete. Fighting in hot climates, Australian soldiers required cool cotton uniforms more often than woolen ones, and in the jungle campaigns of 1942–1945 they needed loose green rather than khaki, neat berets more than hot, unwieldy slouch hats. With Australian clothing manufacturers once again overwhelmed, the government turned to British and American suppliers. By 1945 it was hard to tell an Australian soldier from a British one who had raided an American depot.

Heavy borrowing continued for another thirty years among Australian soldiers fighting in Korea, Malaya, and Vietnam. Traditional dress was also cast aside at home. A new professional army, which in 1948 replaced both the militia and Australian Imperial Force, abandoned color patches and slouch hats for regimental badges and berets like those worn by the British army. In 1972 the air force abandoned its indigo for the pale blue of British and American airmen. Australian sailors remained in the dark blue, white, or khaki British naval uniforms worn since 1911 but joined in a growing informality seen off the parade ground. In 1982, for example, naval officers were permitted to wear the same shapeless wool pullovers as their men.

In 1987 the army relegated khaki to full dress and jungle green to the history books and adopted disruptive pattern camouflage to make its soldiers harder to detect at a distance. With camouflage came American combat helmets of Kevlar, a strong but light synthetic fiber, and later body armor, again of such bulk as to have a psychological as well as protective purpose. At the same time the armed forces led a nationalist, backward-looking trend in Australian uniforms. In 1987 the army began to wear color patches again and in 1993 returned to slouch hats for routine though not combat wear. The navy and air force also adopted slouch hats, in doing so surrendering institutional identities for a national one. The air force restored some of its independence when it returned to indigo in 2001.

FEMALE MILITARY UNIFORMS

The first military uniforms worn by Australian women were the long gray serge dresses, shoulder-length red capes, and white aprons and bonnets that militia nurses began to copy from their British army counterparts in 1899. The uniform seemed practical, efficient, apparently sexless and divorced from fashion, and appropriately identical with British army styles. By the end of World War I, though, the red capes were as distinctively Australian as slouch hats. In the British army these capes were confined to a handful of professional army nurses and were thus rare in hospital wards except on the shoulders of matrons. By wearing the same vivid emblem as their British superiors, Australian army nurses seemed to be claiming equality with them. Some British nurses disliked what seemed colonial presumption. But the red capes endured, admired in any case by soldiers who saw them as a relief from the prevailing drab khaki.

They were finally put aside in World War II. Army nurses had to fight simply to keep their gray dresses when military authorities wanted them, like everyone else, in khaki or jungle green. In any case, capes were too hot for tropical climates. They disappeared for good when nurses went into the jackets, skirts, and ties worn by women's armed services.

These services were formed during World War II to relieve men from noncombat duties. They assumed the businesslike tunics, dowdy knee-length skirts, modest gloves and stockings, and sometimes pert hats of their British counterparts. The uniform discouraged men from seeing its wearers as amateurs or as sexual partners and yet, adjusted suitably, could still draw a male gaze. More eye-catching, though, were the bright sky-blue overalls and summer dresses of volunteer nursing assistants early in World War II. When these disappeared in 1942 it was the end of bright color in Australian military uniforms, apart from heritage costumes worn occasionally for public relations purposes.

After 1945 the female services retained uniforms of British inspiration. The Women's Royal Australian Army Corps, for example, adopted the same deep green as their British counterparts, judged more feminine and more flattering than khaki. Their choice reflected an expectation that women would never serve in combat, as well as a need to appeal to as many potential recruits as possible. Both reasons, along with a brief congruity between sexual appeal and gender liberation, put the Corps in 1978 into a dark green and ice green suit with a black handbag as an accessory. Intended to be flexible and fashionable, the uniform was unpopular with most wearers, who judged it suitable for cafeteria staff but not for soldiers. It disappeared by 1992, when separate army units for women were disbanded and female and male soldiers began to wear the same dress.

SCHOOL UNIFORMS

Australian school uniform settled early in the twentieth century on the English model. Poorer children wore what their parents could afford, which rarely extended to shoes but increasingly to pale cotton shirts or blouses. Better-off boys were put into caps and blazers in school colors, their sisters into pleated tunics along with hats, stockings, and gloves, which advertised modesty and gentility. Little concession was made to hot weather beyond the Edwardian straw boaters, which were already obsolete outside the schoolyard and which boys at some elite schools still wear today.

Teachers valued uniform for the discipline of wearing it and, within their school, for reducing evidence of social differences. Children often challenged the first virtue, while their parents' incomes eroded the second: shoes were uncommon for many children until the 1950s. Uniforms nonetheless gave a sense of security and belonging to many who wore them.

School uniform changed little until the 1970s, when social trends toward informality and against authority began to shape it. Caps, blazers, and gloves were largely cast aside by 1980, and sometimes neckties and leather shoes as well. By 2001 uniforms often consisted of the polo shirts, tracksuit components, and pullovers once seen only on sports days, with the heads of smaller children protected from the sun by "foreign legion caps," which, though called Havelocks after a British general (Havelock being the light cloth falling over the back of the neck to protect from the sun), had last been worn 140 years earlier by citizen soldiers and police. Still, the English practice of making

Boys in the gray coats, blue trousers, and slouch hats that for more than a century have constituted the uniform worn at the elite King's School in Sydney, Australia, ca. 1931. Photographer unknown. John Oxley Library, State Library of Queensland 196172.

children wear uniforms at all was retained rather than embracing the American one of a simple dress code. Meanwhile elite schools, which saw value in maintaining seemingly strict standards, clung to what now seemed formal school dress, increasing their appeal among parents.

One elite school's uniform stood out from all the others. When British private schools began to impose uniforms on their boys, the headmaster of King's School at Parramatta did the same but, unusually, took what citizen soldiers were wearing as his model. In 1874 the uniform settled on a gray military coat and blue trousers, both trimmed with scarlet. In the 1880s the headdress became the newly fashionable slouch hat. The tunic was updated early in the twentieth century with the addition of the patch pockets, turned-down collars, and turned-back lapels, which now signaled an army officer. By the 1930s younger boys were wearing shorts, but the uniform changed little after this. Already an oddity for its martial style, it seemed even odder by the 1970s. In 2005 even the headmaster acknowledged it as extraordinary if not bizarre. Still, it marked his boys out as products of some of the wealthiest families in the country. Its survival suggested that tradition and authority still carried weight in Australia.

CORPORATE UNIFORMS

During the latter part of the twentieth century large Australian companies followed the Western trend toward corporatization of their employees' dress. Staff uniforms often carefully balanced an air of efficiency with a touch of informality designed to appeal to the public. The Australian company that devoted the most attention to its uniforms was the aircraft operator Qantas, largely because national carriers have been seen as emissaries of their country. Qantas flying officers followed British and American cues, from 1947 wearing double-breasted blue uniforms with brass buttons, evoking both the navy and the air force. At the end of the 1940s female stewards went into naval style, with brass buttons and forage caps pulled toward one eye. The uniform defied the prevalent postwar casualness, and it was accordingly subverted. Many stewards wore sheer stockings and high heels instead of the regulation heavy stockings and low heels.

These unofficial modifications launched fifty years of official fashion-chasing for Qantas crews. In 1959 blue gave way to green, skirts slimmed down, and coats grew shorter and lost some of their buttons. Five years later came a self-consciously modern aqua uniform with handbag and gloves like the one that would soon be seen on the children's television series *Thunderbirds*. It was replaced in 1969 by pink miniskirts and berets, which themselves gave way in 1974 to the first Qantas uniform designed by an international designer, the Italian Emilio Pucci, known for his bright colors and bold patterns and the notoriously avant-garde outfit he had created for an American airline.

Pucci's uniform for Qantas was relatively conservative, its mix-and-match components centering on a green jacket and floral-print dress. Popular with wearers and with the public, it endured for a decade. Since 1986, though, Qantas uniforms have defied the trend toward informality, growing sober in cut and color to reflect increasing respect for women at work and increasing concern about security. The trend toward proclaiming national identity was embraced in 2003 with a uniform conceived by Australian designer Peter Morrissey. Black and charcoal was enlivened for stewards by an Aboriginal "dot" motif fabric for neckties, scarves, and dresses, commissioned from Balarinji Aboriginal Designs.

Since the 1970s corporate uniforms have come to include those worn by professional sports teams, increasingly crowded with the emblems of their sponsors. These emblems have changed as sponsors waxed and waned in their support. During a single decade (1984–1995) the jerseys of one rugby league team, South Sydney, advertised a whiskey, a golf ball, a snack food, a computer company, and a home printer company.

Lifesaver in a patrol cap as depicted in a 1950s advertisement made for the wall of an Australian hotel. Artist unknown. Coleman Signs for Tooth & Company Limited. Powerhouse Museum.

SURF LIFESAVERS AND OLYMPIC GAMES VOLUNTEERS

By 1908 the first surf lifesavers to patrol Australian beaches were wearing the standard men's racing swimsuit and patrol cap in club colors that, little modified, their successors would cling to for sixty years. The public admired the uniform as much as wearers did for the way it seemed to blend discipline with leisure and evoke a new, distinctive beach culture. That sense of discipline prompted lifesavers to keep their chests covered when other male swimmers were beginning to bare them. At the same time, around 1935, they began to wear patrol caps in red and yellow rather than club colors when on duty, presumably inspired by the maritime signal

flag indicating "man overboard." Whatever the inspiration, these colors became standard in the 1940s.

By the 1970s lifesavers' racing swimsuits shrank to the briefs worn by other male swimmers. The red and yellow patrol cap remained, though, having become a visual shorthand for Australian beach life. In 2003 it was joined by protective shirts in the same colors provided by a sponsor, the German-owned courier company DHL, whose livery was likewise red and yellow. Protection went further four years later when a *burquini* was introduced to clothe young Muslim women lifesavers from head to ankle as their faith dictated, and thus attract them to a well-loved Australian institution and in doing so promote ethnic harmony.

A uniform that summed up trends toward informality and gender equality, and advertising national and corporate identities, was issued to fifty thousand voluntary staff during the Olympic Games held in Sydney in 2000. It consisted of a multicolored polo shirt bearing the games logo, a white sun hat, beige trousers, socks, a water bottle, and a blue raincoat in the shape of a Driza-Bone (a full-length oilskin coat that is an Australian variant of the mackintosh); shoes would have been included had their sponsor not withdrawn. Garish and folksy, the uniform was undeniably practical too, being comfortable and highly visible. The organizing committee that commissioned the uniform described it as "casual, sport-loving, bright, open, welcoming and essentially Australian."

Some performers at the opening ceremony to the Sydney Olympics wore what is becoming the newest Australian uniform—the *naga*, or red ceremonial loincloth, originally worn from the Kimberley to the Gulf of Carpentaria. It may, like their didgeridoos, become a shorthand for all Aborigines.

ATTITUDES AND ICONS

Australians in uniform have regarded their clothes with the mixtures of respect and subversion and of pride and embarrassment common among English-speaking people. Respect and pride were strongest in the nineteenth century, as was desire for admiration from women. A striving for formality was almost as strong in the twentieth century as a retreat into sloppiness. Embarrassment at being clad in what army conscript (later comedian) Barry Humphreys called the drab, ill-fitting uniform of a private increased after 1945, though it was balanced by pride at wearing something similar to what Australians had fought in during the world wars.

Preferences for economy and equality, perhaps also puritanism and philistinism, were at work from the start in the minds of many Australians who observed the uniforms around them. In 1864 a citizen soldier's wife complained that her husband was "cased in a tight tunic when a loose jumper would answer all the purposes." Yet complaints have met uniforms that seemed too informal as well as too fancy. Comment was sharp when the slouch hat was introduced after 1885, some journalists judging it sloppy, brutal, or foreign. Uniforms that seemed to get the balance right were remembered with affection, especially Pucci's uniform for Qantas.

Among the most treasured items of Australian uniform has been the color patch. Mothers of soldiers away in World War I had lapel pins made whose design was the color patch their son was wearing, while families bought wall charts showing the color patch worn by every unit in the Australian Imperial Force. Another treasured item was the army nurses' red cape. The figure of a nurse in one was included (1950) in the stained glass windows of the Hall of Memory, the sacred heart of the Australian War Memorial in Canberra. Later, the red cape worn by Sister Vivien Bullwinkel, survivor of murderous Japanese captivity during World War II, came to be seen as a sacred relic.

In the 1990s, a decade of officially sanctioned nationalism, some items of uniform were widely promoted as iconically Australian. The slouch hat, the red and yellow patrol cap, and the red cape were among them, the hat's status reinforced by being manufactured by Akubra, a much-loved and long-lived Australian maker of bush hats as well as military ones. The slouch hat was now an item of folk dress, whether worn ironically, as in the 1972 Bruce Beresford film *The Adventures of Barry McKenzie*, or with special reverence, notably by young men and women visiting Gallipoli to see where the first large numbers of Australian soldiers had fought and died. The red and yellow patrol cap of surf lifesavers may follow the same path, as suggested by its use by Australia's entrant in the 2007 Miss Universe competition. A more lighthearted affection exists for costume now seen as amusingly provincial, from the shorts and long socks of bus drivers and mail carriers to the gold bikinis of young women promoting tourism to the Gold Coast.

Sometimes indifferent to this sartorial nationalism are Australian participants in the pastime of historical reenactment. Some wear the khaki, slouch hats, and spurs of Australian mounted troops from the Boer war and World War I. Many more retreat with their British and American counterparts into the colorful dress of eighteenth- and nineteenth-century European armies.

COLLECTIONS AND COLLECTORS

Sydney's Powerhouse Museum is one of several state museums that, modeled on London's Victoria and Albert Museum, began to collect designed or manufactured objects that included uniforms, typically police, postal, and sporting ones. It is, however, the Australian War Memorial in Canberra that holds the greatest single collection of Australian military dress. Other military uniforms are kept in army, navy, and air force museums around the country, though nineteenth-century ones are sometimes reconstructions.

There have been a handful of significant uniform collectors in Australia. One was Eric Baume (1900–1967), a journalist, soldier, and New Guard supporter who sometimes wore a slouch hat on the streets. Another was Edwin Dollery (1897–1973), a staff officer whose uniform collection passed to the Tasmanian Museum and Art Gallery on his death.

Australia has likewise produced uniform illustrators, though few of them and rarely of the caliber of their best overseas counterparts. The most culturally important was Carl Jess (1884–1948), another staff officer, whose watercolors of early Australian military uniforms shrouded them in a Germanic smartness they conspicuously lacked.

References and Further Reading

Burness, Peter. "The Australian Army Uniform of 1914–18." *Sabretache* 18, no. 2 (April 1977): 73–83.

Cashman, Richard, with Peter Sharpham. "Symbols, Emblems, Colours and Names." In *Sport in the National Imagination: Australian Sport in the Federation Decades*, edited by Richard Cashman, 58–102. Sydney: Walla Walla, 2002.

Connolly, Ellen. "Burquini Hits the Beach." *Sydney Daily Telegraph*, 4 February 2007.

Craik, Jennifer. *Uniforms Exposed: From Conformity to Transgression*. Oxford and New York: Berg, 2005.

Holden, Steve. "The Uniform Question." *Teacher* (August 2005): 15–17.

Maynard, Margaret. *Fashioned from Penury: Dress as Cultural Practice in Colonial Australia*. Melbourne, Australia: Cambridge University Press, 1994.

Ollif, Lorna. "Army Fashions Down the Years." In *Colonel Best and Her Soldiers*, 21–37. Sydney: Author, 1985.

Stanley, Peter. *The Remote Garrison: The British Army in Australia 1788–1870*. Sydney: Kangaroo, 1986.

Stell, Marion K. "Sportswear." In *Half the Race: A History of Australian Women in Sport*, 155–169. Sydney: Allen and Unwin, 1991.

Wedd, Monty. *Australian Military Uniforms 1800–1982*. Sydney: Kangaroo, 1982.

Craig Wilcox

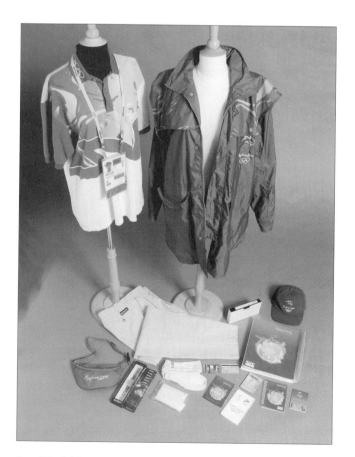

One of the bright, loose-fitting uniforms worn by tens of thousands of volunteer staff during the Olympic Games held in 2000 in Sydney, Australia. Powerhouse Museum.

See also Aboriginal Dress in Australia: Evidence and Resources; Settler Dress in Australia.

Sportswear in Australia

- Cricket
- Football
- Athletic Uniforms and Technological Developments

Australia prides itself on being a sporting nation, and sport is an integral part of the nation's identity. Some say that it verges on being a religion, helping to build healthy Australian men, women, and young aspirants, and to spread the fame of Australians overseas. The combined effects of a temperate climate and rugged landscape have produced a national psyche that privileges the strong, outdoor-oriented, sports-loving body—yet a body clothed in sportswear for the most part similar to that worn for sport all over the world. The hot "Aussie" sun, the world-famous surf beaches, and emphasis on open-air pursuits all help produce the situation revealed by the 2006 census figures, which indicate that a third of Australians play sports or exercise twice a week or more. These activities range from the individualized sports of golf and surfing to team sports like rugby, soccer, lawn bowls, and netball. Surprisingly, serious research into sportswear in Australia has been uneven, and little has been written about its social, political, and cultural dimensions. Archival photographs and other images, although an incomplete record, are thus one of the most significant resources available.

As elsewhere in the world, Australian sports enthusiasts look to the uniforms of their sporting heroes and teams to provide an immediate point of recognition for national status, state, position, or sports genre: The colors, logos, and shapes incorporated into clothing of athletes invite fans to register loyal support or orchestrate disdain. Yet, despite the fact that golf, tennis, cricket, and many other sports have a long history in Australia, there are not many types of sporting wear that are singularly Australian. An example of an identifiable garment worn by an Australian athlete would be the internationally recognizable wide-brimmed hat of golfer Greg Norman, a product of the New South Wales Akubra company, and his wide straw hat with its shark logo.

For Australia the question of which colors were appropriate for national sporting teams was part of an ongoing debate prior to Federation in 1901. Eventually the matter was resolved in 1984, in an official proclamation by the governor general of the day, Sir Ninian Stephen. The colors green and gold were declared the nation's colors, inspired by the national flower of Australia, the golden wattle. The green and gold are worn by a range of international sports teams, including the Australian Cricket Team (one-day matches), the Kangaroos (rugby league), and the Matildas (women's football team). However, prior to official proclamation, the use of the two designated colors unofficially influenced many national sporting uniforms, producing iconic sports memorabilia such as the "baggy green" cap of Sir Donald Bradman, Australia's most renowned cricketer (now held in the National Sports Museum, Melbourne, which opened in 2008).

Australia participates strongly in annual ritualistic sporting events such as those that start on Boxing Day (26 December).

These are the Sydney-to-Hobart yacht race and the five-day Boxing-Day Cricket Test. In fact, cricket pervades each Australian summer, marking holidays as intensely as soccer signifies winter in western Europe, every state having its own colored shirts and trousers for one-day matches. International one-day cricket tests draw large crowds of fans, as do the annual State of Origin Rugby League series (the New South Wales team wearing blue versus the Queensland team in maroon), the Australian Rules final football matches (AFL), and netball (similar to basketball) contests with New Zealanders. Soccer (the Socceroos being the men's international team and the Matildas being the women's team) is gaining popularity, and each new contest brings forth novel designs for uniforms and new sponsor logos on clothing, as it does anywhere professional sport is played. Big sporting spectacles attract audiences in the stadium and on television, and sporting uniforms plus associated merchandising play an important part in the promotion of these events. The race that "stops the nation," the Melbourne Cup horse race, not only brings in vast numbers of punters, it draws attention to the brilliance of owners' racing colors, and, as one of the social events of the year, attracts large crowds of fashionable dressers.

Historically, sporting wear, particularly that of men, facilitated the athlete's ability to excel, or at least make it easier than performing in everyday clothing. Much has changed over the years. New developments in high-performance fabrics like Speedo's Fastskin are good examples of the ways in which technology has entered the realm of competitive sports. Sportswear has also reflected social norms about class and gender roles and their shifts over time. For example, like their sisters in England and North America, early Australian netballers used to play in long restrictive skirts, and rules did not permit players to run the full length of the court, given prevailing mores about women's physical frailty. All this has changed, and netballers now wear extremely brief garments.

Uniforms for team sports such as cricket and football have deviated minimally from their original forms, although they are ruled by utilitarianism. Perhaps to facilitate movement and enhance competitiveness but also to attract increased media coverage, and thus gain financial sponsorship and heighten the visual appeal for spectators, sports administrators have increasingly encouraged uniforms that reveal much of athletes' bodies. One example is the skimpy outfits used for Olympic beach volleyball competitions, or the shortening not just of netball players' skirts, but also rugby shorts, and a return to closer-fitting jerseys in many codes. As with all sports, the commodification and sexualization of athletes' bodies (both male and female) starts on the field with their physical agility and seeps into the wider promotional sphere, with athletic celebrities used for direct product advertising. The styling of sportswear tends to be international, with national teams using unique combinations of color and pattern to distinguish players in the global arena. The same thing also happens at the local level.

CRICKET

Cricket was played very early in the settlement of New South Wales and has grown to assume unofficial status as *the* national

Dianne Alagich of Australia signs autographs after a match between the Australian Matildas and the New Zealand Football Ferns at North Sydney Oval on 12 July 2008. The colors of the Matildas' kit, green and gold, were declared to be Australia's colors in 1984, inspired by the national flower of Australia, the golden wattle. Photograph by Brendon Thorne/Getty Images.

sport of Australia, monopolizing the weeks of summer holiday entertainment (Boxing Day to New Year's Day). By 1803 the *Sydney Gazette* carried reports of cricket matches being played by civilians and officers from the ship *Calcutta* at what has become Hyde Park. Opposing teams tied colored sashes or ribbons around their necks or bodies, a practice that has long since died out. The Australian cricket balls were made by local shoemakers out of leather stitched around cork (or other stuffing), and their bats were of ironbark, cedar, or local timbers much harder than the woods used in England.

In England the game moved from its early origins, played on English village greens or open areas, with a cric or curved staff, to the major ground of Lords in London. In Australia it moved from similar origins to the Melbourne Cricket Club ground (MCG). There appears to have been some rivalry between native-born white Australians and English-born immigrants, and clubs catered to both, for example, the Military Cricket Club and the Australian Cricket Club, both in existence by 1826. At one match in 1830 the military wore tall black hats while the locals wore cabbage tree hats (made of cabbage tree palm). Players wore male attire of that era: tailored trousers and shirts buttoned down the front, with the sash or ribbon on their necks or bodies, without

pads or gloves—any protection was seen as unmanly. Soldiers sometimes wore their boots. It was only after the introduction of round-arm bowling, which increased the speed of the balls, that players were persuaded to take on protective equipment. After the 1930s helmets became available, but even in the twenty-first century they are not compulsory.

Cricket came to be played across classes, and players could come from a variety of backgrounds, something that appealed to Australians and contributed to the game's popularity. Interestingly, Tom Wills, the state of Victoria's fastest round-arm bowler between 1857 and 1860, who had a rather dubious social background, suggested the playing of football during the winter months to keep cricketers fit, kick-starting the development of Australian Rules Football (Australian Football League or AFL). An important instance in Australian cricket history is that the first Australian team to tour England was an Aboriginal one, in 1868 (they were the most competent cricketers at the time), captained by Charles Lawrence. Managed and coached by Wills, they toured England for a year, and before each game the Aborigines dressed up in "native" wear—possum fur on loins and head—to perform spearing and boomerang activities. But in their proper cricket uniforms they were no less impressive in red Garibaldi shirts (named after the Italian military leader Giuseppe Garibaldi), white linen collars, white flannel trousers, blue belts and neckties, a blue-and-white diagonally striped flannel sash, and merino undershirts for warmth. They were very well received.

Unlike the dress of the Aboriginal team, cricketers in Sydney in 1864 were still playing in everyday clothes, with shoes and socks often taken off if they were uncomfortable. Tailored flannel trousers represented a level of professionalism that did not exist at the time. However, by the late 1870s photographs represent players with pads on, and shortly after, it seems gloves and pads had been widely adopted. What differed between teams was the color of shirts and caps.

By 1900 several changes had occurred. One was the official adoption of white uniforms for test matches; white polo shirts, stretch trousers, sports shoes, pads, and gloves are still the basis of test cricket in the twenty-first century. Since the late twentieth century the prominent emblem of the game sponsors appears on the front and sleeves of the white polo shirt. The other significant change was the adoption of the baggy green cap, worn by no other cricket team, which has become the national icon of Australian cricket. While a protective helmet is worn in the actual game, the baggy green cap awarded to test cricketers has become a much-loved item, partly due to its association with Sir Donald Bradman. Modern captains since the 1990s, Steve Waugh, Mark Taylor, and Ricky Ponting, have helped grow its stature, and some players refuse to replace worn caps, thus adding to their memorializing value. The "baggy green" is also worn for the first innings

of a test match (international five-day matches) as a means of reinforcing the symbolism of the cap.

Sponsorship and profit-sharing were arguably part of the history of cricket even one hundred years before Kerry Packer stepped in to create World Series Cricket (WSC) in 1977. But for better or worse, it made more money available for the game, enhanced professionalism, and created opportunities for its players, although the format was taken from one-day matches, which had existed as early as the 1960s in England. This format was ideal for television as well. By taking on many of the attributes set in place by previous One Day Internationals (ODI), World Series Cricket also created a permanent code of play, such as the white ball for night play, what seemed to spectators radical colored shirts and trousers (often termed "the pyjamas"), and dark sight screens. The Australian team first wore a national green and gold uniform against the West Indians at the MCG on 17 January 1971. The ODI allowed teams to carry two sets of uniforms, one for home games and the other for away matches. The uniforms are often emblazoned with huge logos on the sleeves or across the chest, such as KFC or Travelex. Where one-day uniforms have a more informal (and chaotic) look, test match white uniforms have fewer sponsorship signs. Many still regard test matches and their dress as being classic, "first-class cricket."

By contrast, the Australian national women's cricket team does not receive as much media coverage or sponsorship as the men, even though they are widely recognized as the best women's team in the world. Their first recorded test match was in 1934, although women were playing as early as the 1870s. In the twenty-first century, even though they compete as regularly as the men do, spectator numbers are low, and until early 2000 players have had to pay for the privilege of playing cricket. The women's national team wears trousers rather than skirts, as they did when they first started. The national colors of green and gold are inscribed on their ODI uniform, except it is predominantly green with gold trimmings.

FOOTBALL

Football (soccer and rugby) was played in Australia from colonial times, and during the mid-to-late 1800s it formed an image of community—players and spectators celebrating a society where for many, leisure and life as free men and women was a new experience. In more recent times Australians play three main codes of football: Rugby Union (ARU), Rugby League (NRL), and Australian Rules (AFL, a conjoining of state teams). Australian football, or soccer, as it is more commonly known, was played beginning in the 1880s and, although less popular than the other codes, gained a stronger foothold from the 1950s and 1960s with the arrival of large numbers of immigrants from Britain and southern Europe. AFL, originating in Melbourne in the state of Victoria, is unique to Australia, is not played internationally, and has its own particular form of dress. The Union and League codes were imported from England and are predominantly played in Sydney and Brisbane, while in Melbourne, Australian Rules was a homegrown form of football. It was possibly influenced by Gaelic football (where players use hands and feet) and an ancient ball game called Gunditjmara, played by Aboriginals. Union and League were loosely defined by religion and class—Union being regarded a higher class of game, plucking amateur players from the Anglican private school system. It was in 1995 the last code

Don (Donald George) Bradman, cricketer, ca. 1935. He is wearing the "baggy green," a cap strongly associated with his test career, and the icon of Australian cricket. Popperfoto/Getty Images.

to professionalize, leading to significant changes in its uniforms. League, on the other hand, built its professional teams (from 1908) primarily from Roman Catholic, working-class footballers. Australian Rules players were from less clearly defined social groups. Barbara Schreier suggests that the playing field is a "men-only club," a chance for men to validate their masculinity. But Australian women also play all three codes of football, although often in a modified form, and wear a similar style of uniform: jersey, shorts, long socks, and football boots.

The dress of footballers has evolved over the last century. Early footballers wore long white trousers, possibly their summer cricket whites, a long-sleeved jersey, and a colored cap (often red or blue), used to identify their team. There were early associations between cricket and AFL, with cricket clubs allowing AFL to be played on their grounds in winter, after an initial resistance for fear of surface damage to the pitch. The authority figures and nonplayers on the field, the umpires for cricket and goal umpires for AFT, wore, until recently, a distinct mid-thigh-length white lab coat of rather unusual styling with no clear sportswear links. AFL goal umpires have changed to wearing long trousers, long-sleeved shirts, and often baseball caps. The former white coat did, however, ensure particular visibility, and in cricket it marked umpires as those who made sure the game was played according to the rules.

As with many sporting garments, football team clothing was a result of participants requiring functional clothes that allowed freedom of movement. By the 1880s individual football clubs developed distinctly patterned jerseys, many striped, with a more noticeable fashion for bare arms exposed in either short or three-quarter-length sleeve style. But it is the AFL uniform that has uniquely Australian characteristics, for players wear tight sleeveless shirts with very abbreviated shorts, socks, and boots, in part to stop opposition players pulling them down in play. The original shirts or upper body coverings in the late 1800s and early 1900s (which came to be called guernseys or jerseys) featured a center-front lace-up detail. This may have been the only method of creating a firm fit. They were worn with three-quarter-length knickerbockers, giving players a rather rakish, pirate-like appearance. Colors and club emblems individualize teams, and the designs emblazoned on the jerseys or guernseys are reminiscent of heraldic tunics worn by medieval knights, with dramatic geometric patterns, predominantly stripes, and combinations of strong primary and secondary colors that create a sense of pageantry and heroism.

Male clubs have nicknames such as the Demons (AFL), Tigers (NRL), Dragons (NRL), and Vikings (ARU)—consolidating the idea that footballers are a modern variation of medieval combatants garnering spectator support through their recognizable team logos and colors. As well, both jersey and shorts function as moving billboards onto which sponsors place their corporate branding. For instance, Rugby League club St George, Illawarra, wear jerseys that display the club colors of red and white with a distinctive red V on the center front neckline. The Dragons' major sponsor, St. George Bank, has a convenient association with the club logo, which sports the gallant St. George on rearing steed slaying a decoratively rendered dragon encased in a heraldic shield. However, for most clubs a number of sponsors' logos on the jerseys of a team jostle for attention, producing a clashing pattern of companies and products.

Australian Mark Gasnier, photographed in 2008 at the Sydney Football Stadium when he played for the Dragons (Rugby League). His jersey and shorts feature many club sponsors, including adidas and St. George Bank, whose heroic logo has a fortunate association with the club name. Modern players operate as both moving billboards, covered in advertising, and recognizably colorful heroes for their fans to cheer on. Photograph by Mark Nolan/Getty Images.

Union and League, when played by men, are not codes for the faint-hearted; at times they are brutal, gladiatorial blood sports where players must display strength, courage, and stamina. Australian Rules is a strenuous and at times violent contact sport, but it relies mostly on agility, with a focus on high leaping, as opposed to scrummaging and mauling. Footballers exemplify a type of male body muscled and honed through rigorous training. From the game's inception the uniforms have morphed to reveal more of these elite athletes' physiques, with bodies packaged in tight-fitting jerseys and shorts, creating a heightened form of bodily spectacle. Since the 1980s clubs and sponsors realized that their players, especially those who were deemed handsome, were an exploitable asset; that sex sells. AFL player Warrick Capper, with his long blonde hair, rippling muscles, and super-short tight shorts, led the way. He earned large sums from advertisements, eventually transcending the sporting arena by posing with his wife for *Playboy* magazine and appearing in the Australian version of *Big Brother*. Football may be "blokey" (an Australian colloquial term implying a rather tough form of masculinity and often said about groups of men), but in the twenty-first century players have had a makeover, moving into a larger cultural arena, where sports heroes can also be fashion and beauty icons.

In Australia, as elsewhere, modern emphasis on the sculpted body and the celebrity status of elite sportspersons draws fashion even closer to the arena of sports. Here everything from the sporting jersey to sweat suits and running shoes is transformed into a twin site of performance and promotion, companies targeting specific demographic markets by associating uniforms with sports heroes. A trend emerged in the 1980s for supporters to purchase their own version of the team kit to wear to games, or as casual wear, creating an additional market for football jerseys and other team items. Australian wearers, like other fans worldwide, see these as fashion as well as sporting gear, blurring the boundaries between the sports field and everyday life.

ATHLETIC UNIFORMS AND TECHNOLOGICAL DEVELOPMENTS

Australian track and field athletes have not had sustained international success or prominence on the world stage when compared, for example, to Australian swimmers or cricket players. Little is known about early events, and the images that do exist of early Australian athletic events primarily depict men. These reveal that by 1893 a style of sportswear very similar to modern athletic garments had been adopted, with competitors wearing an undershirt and knee-length close-fitting trousers. Competitive women's running in Australia did not commence until 1926, when the first state championships were held in Sydney, New South Wales. This much later start for women compared to men was in part due to medical beliefs about women's supposed athletic limitations, but also because major international competitions, such as the Olympics, did not encourage female participation in athletics or many other major sports.

The first Australian female competition uniform, issued to the only female athlete on the Australian 1928 Olympic team, Edith Robinson, consisted of a white half-sleeve pullover with green and gold bands around the neck, sleeves, and hem and a pair of knee-length black bloomers. This old-fashioned style was different from that currently worn by English and North American competitors, and so Robinson, faced with a six-week sea voyage to attend the games, borrowed a portable, hand-operated sewing machine and converted her issued garments to a short-sleeved blouse and shorts. As noted in the official history of the Australian Women's Amateur Athletic Union (Gould 1973), for many years the Australian competition uniform was a white sleeveless singlet with a map of Australia on the front and white shorts with green-and-gold stripes down each side. Despite what many thought about the style, the shorts were a reasonable mid-thigh length, not knee-length. Photos of Eileen Wearne competing at the 1932 Los Angeles Olympic Games support this. Little changed for the gold medal–winning relay team at the 1956 Melbourne Olympics. Brisbane-born runner Norma Croker Fleming, reminiscing in 2000, commented that prior to the Melbourne Games the women ran in very heavy bloomers, until athlete Shirley Strickland suggested they should get a lighter fabric and put some elastic in the legs.

All this changed in the last quarter of the twentieth century. Australia's obsession with competitive sport, although not unique, has meant that elite athletes like swimmers are beneficiaries of cutting-edge technological advances in sportswear design. Since the opening of the Australian Institute of Sport in 1981, there has been a steady move toward apparel that enhances rather than impedes performance, sometimes to the edge of controversy. Speedo's swimming bodysuit, the LZR racer, is credited with improving performance by up to 2 percent, leading some critics to call its use "technological doping." Well-funded, government-supported Australian sports teams, backed by a medal-hungry public, have had access to state-of-the-art sports technology, including special suits and uniforms. Ongoing improvements in fabric technology, coupled with intense global brand competition, have led to a range of modern-day sportswear uniforms with textile names like Techfit Powerweb, ForMotion, ClimaCool, and ClimaLite appearing in a range of sports, such as golf, athletics, and even formal Olympic team outfitting.

Major sports brands, especially global corporations like Nike and adidas, entice wearers to purchase their products through their associations with elite athletes. adidas launched the global Impossible is Nothing campaign in 2007, profiling international sports stars and everyday athletes by sharing their stories of defining moments in their lives. These included Australian athlete

Cathy Freeman of Australia celebrates with both Aboriginal and Australian flags after winning gold in the 400 meters final during the Commonwealth Games in Victoria, Canada, 23 August 1994. Tony Feder/Allsport.

(hurdles) Jana Pittman Rawlinson and swimmer Ian Thorpe. Engineered, modern clothes help keep the wearer from getting too hot and sweaty, while still allowing free movement and flexibility, for cyclists, rowers, netballers, and swimmers, but also for other fitness-oriented people like the weekend jogger.

Twenty-first-century partnerships between the Australian Olympic Committee and various large sportswear corporations have seen adidas and Nike provide dress and competition uniforms for Olympic teams. Nike, the official outfitter for the 2000 Australian Olympic team, introduced the Swift Suit, a hooded unitard, which they had been developing since 1997. Famously first worn by Cathy Freeman in her 400-meter gold medal–winning performance at the Sydney Olympics in 2000, there was much debate at the time as to whether the fabrics provided any measurable performance increase, or if the suit worked primarily on the psychology of the wearers and their opponents. The suit, and various truncated versions of it, was adopted by other track athletes, including Matt Shirvington, an Australian sprinter. According to Nike, the Swift Suit can regulate heat and reduce drag, thus maximizing the athletes' potential. It is a closely fitting, individually tailored, and highly revealing one-piece outfit, which leaves little to the spectators' imagination. The media's focus on what Shirvington's tight outfit revealed shows much about the continued power of clothing to unsettle accepted social mores. The change from restrictive, cumbersome clothing at the start of the twentieth century to the almost naked look of modern celebrity athletic sportswear, while providing templates for fashionable and comfortable clothing, has been deemed a contributing factor in the growing problems young people experience with body image.

Since the later part of the twentieth century, sport has played as prominent a part in the Australian media environment as it does globally. Via the media, Australian sporting heroes are promoted, and consequently what they wear and when they wear it takes on increased significance. Pivotal moments, such as Cathy Freeman's use of the unitard Swift Suit at the 2000 Olympics (she was the country's first Aboriginal track and field athlete to win an Olympic Gold medal), have become part of Australia's cultural mythology, particularly in relation to the ongoing process of reconciliation between Aboriginal and non-indigenous Australians. Her self-identification as both an Aboriginal and an Australian was highlighted after each victory by wearing (wrapping or carrying) as symbolic markers the flags of both cultures.

At heart, sportswear is still ruled by its utilitarianism, except function is increasingly enhanced by technological innovation, underpinned by sponsorship dollars through the global professionalization of sports. The styling of Australian sportswear tends to be international, with teams using unique combinations of color and pattern to distinguish players from their competitors. This allows fans to instantly identify with their team's performance. At both the professional and amateur level, sportswear has become a target for corporate marketing purposes and branding. The clothes the average sportsperson now wears are increasingly designed for performance and fit, to which leading designers add a fashion dimension. Sport and its participants continue to influence the types of products that sportswear brands develop, as the obsession with high-performance bodies and textiles filters through to garments that allow individuals to actively pursue a finely tuned body if not sporting prowess. Australia's place as a global sporting nation, with its individual elite athletes, such as swimmers, and highly competitive team sports players, noticeably in cricket and football, contributes to a fashion-sport fusion in the twenty-first century.

References and Further Reading

Blainey, Geoffrey. *A Game of Our Own: The Origins of Australian Football*. Melbourne: Information Australia, 1990.

Craik, Jennifer. *Uniforms Exposed: From Conformity to Transgression*. Oxford: Berg, 2005.

Daniels, Stephanie, and Anita Tedder. *A Proper Spectacle: Women Olympians 1900–1936*. Petersham, Australia: Walla Walla Press, 2000.

Egan, J. *The Story of Cricket in Australia*. Melbourne, Australia: Macmillan, 1987.

Gould, Nell. *Women's Athletics in Australia: Official History of the Australian Women's Amateur Athletic Union*. Sydney, 1973?

McKay, Jim, John Hughson, Geoffrey Lawrence, and David Rowe. "Sport and Australian Society." In *A Sociology of Australian Society*, edited by Jake M. Najman and John S. Western, 275–300. South Yarra: Macmillan Australia, 2000.

Pascoe, Robert. *The Winter Game: The Complete History of Australian Football*. Port Melbourne, Australia: The Text Pub. Co., 1995.

Quinn, Bradley. "Sportswear." In *Techno Fashion*, 185–200. Oxford: Berg, 2002.

Schreier, Barbara A. "Sporting Wear." In *Men and Women: Dressing the Part*, edited by Claudia B. Kidwell and Valerie Steele, 92–123. Washington, DC: Smithsonian Institution Press, 1989.

Stevenson, Deborah. "Women, Sport and Globalization: Competing Discourses of Sexuality and Nation." *Journal of Sport and Social Issues* 26 (2002): 209–225.

Andrea Mitchell, Christine Schmidt, and Jinna Tay

See also Swimwear, Surfwear, and the Bronzed Body in Australia; The Melbourne Cup and Racewear in Australia.

PART 6

People and Dress in Australia

Convict Dress in Australia

One hundred and sixty thousand convicts, most of them men, were transported to the Australian colonies between 1788 and 1868. The management of these convicts en route to and within the colonies was an enormous undertaking, requiring a vast bureaucracy to organize it efficiently. Clothing the convicts was a significant part of this management; it provided the opportunity to regulate convicts, distinguishing them from free colonists and classifying their position within the penal system. However, supply difficulties, parsimony, and convict resistance to authority all conspired to make a coherent system of dressing convicts at best difficult to apply. Up to the 1820s convict clothing was often indistinguishable from that of free settlers. The transportation system became more regulated from the 1820s, and after 1839 all convicts passed through barracks, penal stations, and settlements, allowing the wearing of uniforms to be more rigorously policed.

The nature of clothing worn by transported men, women, and children is complicated by the convict system in Australia itself and its operation under extremely difficult circumstances. Information about all convicts' dress comes from documentary evidence, including official records, images, and newspaper reports, and the evidence presented by surviving clothing held in Australian public collections, in particular three major Tasmanian collections: the Tasmanian Museum and Art Gallery, the Queen Victoria Museum and Art Gallery, and the Port Arthur Historic Site Management Authority. No examples of convict women's and children's clothing survive in public collections, but from other sources some information about these garments can be deduced.

CONVICT TRANSPORTATION: A BACKGROUND

Britain endured profound social upheaval during the late eighteenth and early nineteenth centuries. The Enclosure Acts (1750–1801), the Industrial Revolution (starting in the mid-eighteenth century), and the mass unemployment of soldiers following the Napoleonic Wars (1804–1815) produced a large number of displaced and disaffected poor. The growing middle class became increasingly insistent that crimes against property by what they saw as a hostile rabble should be savagely punished. Eventually, more than two hundred crimes incurred the death penalty; however, many sentences were commuted to transportation. This global system saw about 250,000 convicts shipped across the world to colonize new territories, including what is now known as Australia.

After losing the American War of Independence, Britain could no longer transport convicts to North America, so it looked elsewhere to relieve the growing prison population. At various times between 1788 and 1868 it sent convicts to the Australian colonies—New South Wales (at that time including Queensland), Victoria, and Van Diemen's Land (now Tasmania), and Western Australia. Most were young, single, working-class men convicted of petty theft. The majority had prior convictions, although today their crimes seem trivial and opportunistic. There were also small numbers of "gentleman" convicts and some political prisoners. Several thousand were juveniles, some as young as nine. Sentences ranged from seven years to life. Few returned home.

Providing clothing for this large number of convicts became a significant problem. Initially, convicts were assigned to work for private masters or in government gangs, according to their trade, length of sentence, and conduct. The Assignment system aimed to punish, to teach useful skills, and to provide a labor force to develop the fledgling settlements. Although the colonies' earliest governors sought to issue distinctive clothing to assigned convicts during this period, supply difficulties mostly prevented them. Regulation increased in the 1820s. More convicts were accommodated in barracks and sentenced to government work gangs, and they were issued distinctive uniforms. The formation of probation stations in Van Diemen's Land from 1839 made the wearing of convict uniforms easier to enforce through to the end of the transportation period. These uniforms form the basis of Australian public collections of convict clothing.

CONVICT MANAGEMENT AND CLOTHING

The philosophy of convict management gradually adopted in the colonies was derived from the ideas of prison reformers such as John Howard (1726–1790) and Jeremy Bentham (1748–1832) and included views about the clothing of prisoners. The colonies' penal authorities were convinced of the need to make convicts conspicuous and readily distinguishable from free settlers, and to make their status within the penal system apparent. In this way convicts would feel humiliation and disgrace and would be encouraged to progress toward reform and reintegration into society. Increasingly, authorities sought to achieve this by issuing garments in specific colors and applying markings, such as stamped or stenciled broad arrows (the symbol of government property), numbers, and letters, although the style of clothing remained typically working-class. Convicts in jails, gangs, and penal settlements were to be dressed in clothing that could not readily be converted into civilian wear to assist escape.

The clothing worn by Australian convicts changed frequently throughout the period of transportation. Styles, fabrics, and colors were fluid, depending upon the period, place, supply, season, employment, and modifications to the penal system. Until the 1820s convict dress often reflected social and financial, rather than penal, status. Convicts were issued with loose-fitting slops (ready-made, ill-fitting clothing) on arrival in the colony, sometimes supplemented by cast-off items from the master or mistress. These cheap, ready-made garments were, for both men and women, consistent with British working-class clothes and indistinguishable from the clothes worn by free working-class colonists. At times these convicts could be distinguished from sailors and poor colonists more by the dirty threadbare condition of their clothing than its fabric, style, and color.

Standard issue for male convicts in New South Wales in the early nineteenth century included a blue working-class-style short jacket, a shirt probably of linen, a pair of trousers of duck (durable, closely woven cotton) or gurrah (a coarse Indian muslin), a pair of stockings, a pair of breeches (knee-length pants), a pair of shoes, a hat, and a cap made of worsted (a fabric made from long wool-fiber yarn, with a firm texture and no nap). Overseers were issued gray pantaloons (tight-fitting trousers) and blue coatees (short close-fitting coats) to denote their higher status, while watchmen wore green jackets. Blue and gray were the most frequently used colors, as blue woad and logwood dyes were inexpensive. Convicts serving as boatmen, timber-getters, and other tradesmen wore clothing and footwear suited to their respective duties. These included smocks for agricultural and pastoral workers, oilskins for boatmen, and wooden clogs for charcoal burners.

At this time convicts were not forced to wear government-issued slops. Some well-to-do "gentleman" convicts had the means to acquire fashionable clothing suitable to their social class. Well-dressed convicts disturbed the colonial elite, for it was impossible to discern their status through their clothing. They contended that all convicts should be clothed in a manner reflecting their penal condition. But not everyone agreed; some wealthy colonists preferred to dress bonded servants in their own livery rather than have them serve at table in convict slops. Colonial authorities tried to use clothing to reward favored convicts. For example,

thirty "better quality" suits were sent to Sydney in 1793, to be issued to trusted convicts undertaking more important duties.

With clothing in short supply up to at least 1820, garments issued to convicts became commodities that could be profitably sold or bartered, often for alcohol. Sometimes naked, near-naked, or cloaked with kangaroo skin, these convicts were, in authorities' eyes, perilously close to the state of savagery they perceived in the continent's Aboriginal population. The colonial elite were appalled by this manifestation of extreme disorder in the colony, and authorities issued regulations forbidding the sale of government slops.

Throughout the 1810s authorities became more intent on using clothing to distinguish convicts from the rest of society and from each other. The establishment of barracks, jails, and penal settlements allowed controls to be more easily applied. In 1814 Lachlan Macquarie, the governor of New South Wales, introduced black-and-white parti-colored clothing (humiliating clothing, sewn together in panels of alternate color) for refractory convicts, men undergoing secondary punishment, and men in work gangs. Derived from medieval jesters' and fools' costumes, parti-colored clothing had been introduced in British prisons around 1791 and identified men on the lowest rung of the penal hierarchy. Macquarie intended it as a mark of humiliation and saw it as a more humane alternative to corporal punishment. After 1822 colonial parti-colored clothing was usually yellow and black. It continued to be issued to ganged convicts in penal settlements until the end of transportation to Western Australia in 1868. As a mark of humiliation, parti-colored uniforms were successful; these so-called magpie suits were loathed by convicts.

A GOVERNMENT JAIL GANG.
Sydney N.S.Wales.
London,Published,August 10.ᵗʰ 1830 by J.Cross, Holborn, opposite Furnivals Inn.

In 1830 convicts in jails and barracks continued to wear a variety of hats, shirts, trousers, and jackets despite attempts to regulate clothing, as is evident from the lithograph "A Government Jail Gang," Sydney, New South Wales (1830), by Augustus Earle (1793–1838). National Library of Australia.

Records reveal that some convicts separated the component parts and restitched them as single-colored suits. They then dyed the yellow with homemade dye to render them less conspicuous during escape.

Classification of convicts intensified in the 1820s as rates of transportation soared and the system became more closely regulated; increasing numbers of jails and convict barracks were built, and work gangs were formed. Convicts in barracks were issued uniforms. These could be coarse gray or yellow jackets, waistcoats, and trousers marked with arrows, initials identifying the barracks, and personal identifying numbers. Yellow, traditionally a European color of disgrace, had been introduced for convict clothing in 1817. Convicts wearing yellow were sometimes called canaries. When Port Arthur, the best-known convict station, opened in Van Diemen's Land in 1830, the majority of men imprisoned there wore yellow, while those in positions of trust, such as house servants and convict clerks, wore gray.

Even as clothing became more regulated, there were variations, depending on the availability of manufactured garments and fabric arriving on ships and in the Commissariat stores. Contemporary images show gangs dressed in a variety of garments, including striped clothing, parti-colored uniforms, and clothing covered in broad arrows. Gray, yellow, and blue clothing continued to be issued through the 1830s and beyond. Red waistcoats were issued in Van Diemen's Land in the 1830s to use up surplus stock in the Commissariat stores. The introduction of the probation system in Van Diemen's Land in 1839 allowed tighter regulation of clothing, as all convicts had to pass through probation stations. Almost all convicts in that colony now wore penal uniforms, classified according to their status within the system. This also occurred in Western Australia after transportation was introduced in 1850.

Clothing for convicts took account of the seasons. Summer wear in most colonies consisted of coarse linen or cotton garments, often striped. They were commonly made of gurrah and duck. In winter convicts were issued coarse woolen or flannel (twilled, loosely woven wool or worsted fabric with a slightly napped surface) clothing; like the summer wear it was of a standard and unfitted cut. Woolen and leather hats, often with brims ill-designed to protect the wearer from the intense colonial sun, completed the attire.

In Western Australia summer clothing issued to each convict consisted of a jacket and waistcoat, trousers of duck or dowlas (a coarse, plain linen), four cotton shirts, two pairs of cotton socks, two cotton neckerchiefs, a pair of boots, and a hat made of felt (nonwoven cloth made by compressing wool or fur). In winter convicts were issued a dark gray suit of fustian (a strong cotton or linen), two flannel shirts, two pairs of woolen socks, two handkerchiefs, and a second pair of boots.

FEMALE CONVICTS AND CHILDREN

In the early years women were issued a jacket, petticoat, cap, shift (a loose, unfitted dress or slip), hat (sometimes of straw), one pair of shoes, and one pair of stockings. By 1829 women were issued two sets of garments, suggesting that supplies had become more reliable. Both women and men were also issued neckerchiefs from the earliest years to the end of the transportation period. Only one of the many thousands of neckerchiefs issued, a blue-and-white checked example, survives in a public collection.

Women in assigned service wore contemporary working-class clothing and cast-off garments from their mistresses. Convicts in female houses of correction were categorized into classes from the 1820s by introducing differing dress, markings, and badges. Second- and crime-class convicts at the Hobart Female House of Correction had a yellow "C" prominently displayed on their clothing, but interestingly, female convicts were never subjected to the humiliation of parti-colored dress. Although prison authorities sought to reinforce categorization by providing different clothing for each class of convict, the lack of regularity in issuing of slops made attempts to conform to British penal standards unsustainable. Indeed, much of the clothing issued to women in the Hobart Female House of Correction in 1828 was almost indistinguishable from that issued to female convicts thirty years earlier. In accordance with the ideas of British prison reformer Elizabeth Fry (1780–1845), it was plain, drab, and coarse; this was held to be important to avoid the arousal of passions and to maintain order.

Again, following Fry, female convicts were banned from wearing jewelry, more colorful clothing, or fashionable hairstyles. Authorities saw such adornment as a reassertion of slatternly working-class culture and individuality over penal conditioning. It was also thought to provide sexual cues and invite prostitution. Groups like the "flash mob" in the Hobart Female House of Correction subverted such regulations by wearing silk scarves and earrings.

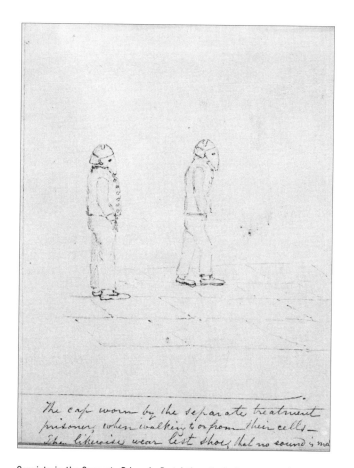

Convicts in the Separate Prison in Port Arthur, Australia, were made to wear cowls over their heads when outside their cells, as depicted in this lithograph from *Sketches Taken in the Australian Colonies* (1853) by Frederick Mackie. National Library of Australia.

Convict dress was also supplied to children, although we have no information about clothing supplied to girls. Boys at Point Puer, the boys' reformatory at Port Arthur in operation between 1834 and 1849, were issued each year two jackets, two pairs of trousers, two pairs of boots, two striped cotton shirts, one cloth waistcoat, and one cap. Sheepskin was the favored material for boys' outer clothes, as it was more durable than woolen cloth. The boys made their own sheepskin clothes in the workshops on site; as part of their rehabilitation, they were trained in many trades, including tailoring.

MANUFACTURE

Although most clothing was imported from England and India, problems with supply forced penal authorities to begin manufacturing cloth and clothing in the colonies, initially by female convicts at Parramatta in New South Wales. Later, convicts in barracks, female houses of correction, penal settlements, and probation stations manufactured clothing. Clothing was also occasionally assembled by convicts during the passage from Britain. It appears, however, that output was usually insufficient to meet colonial demand.

Tailoring was an important industry at Port Arthur. This was a large punishment station, operating between 1830 and 1877 for secondary offenders, that is, those who had reoffended while in the colonies. It was designed to be as self-sufficient as possible, and to provide goods for government consumption through intensive industrial production. It produced thousands of pairs of trousers, jackets, waistcoats, and shirts, which were issued to convicts throughout Van Diemen's Land.

As well as making clothes for local distribution, convicts were generally issued thread to repair clothing; this was essential, as clothing was of poor quality, subject to very heavy use, and not always replaced every six months as intended. The early garments were mostly hand-stitched. Later, clothing, including that issued in Western Australia, where transportation was not introduced until 1850, was more often machine-stitched; this reflected the increasing accessibility of sewing machines from the 1850s.

SURVIVING GARMENTS

Garments surviving in public collections do not adequately reflect the full range of clothing issued to convicts. The collections fail to represent the early transportation period or female dress, and they over-represent parti-colored clothing. Little lightweight summer clothing survives, and none in Tasmania.

Extant waistcoats and jackets are remarkably consistent in design, fabrics, and sewing techniques. Waistcoats are short and relatively shapeless. Most are hand-stitched with a beige-colored thread, using coarse fulled (a process of cleansing, then moistening, heating, and pressing) wool. They feature stand-up collars and six buttons, each with four holes, usually of black enameled metal. Gray, yellow, parti-colored, and red examples survive. Few waistcoats have pockets, as these were seen to be hiding places for contraband.

Stylistically, the yellow, gray, and parti-colored jackets are very similar to the waistcoats and are made from similar woolen material. Each has six buttonholes at the front as on the waistcoats, and usually a single button at each wrist. One jacket has bone instead of enameled buttons. As with the waistcoats, few

jackets have pockets, while seams are more likely to be hemmed, and some of the later jackets are partially machine-stitched. Most surviving jackets are stamped with WD (War Department). An unusual late Western Australian white duck jacket held by Fremantle Prison is a rare example of summer issue. It is a more professionally produced hand-sewn jacket with a high waist and generous rolled collar and is marked with orange broad arrows and a WD.

Yellow and parti-colored trousers survive, although some are incomplete. They are generally made from the same coarse woolen fabric as the jackets and feature drop fronts and concealed buttoning on the outside leg opening. Most are marked with broad arrows on the exterior. The outside leg openings facilitated dressing and undressing when wearing leg irons. Working-class trousers featured drop fronts, which were used in convict trousers throughout the transportation period, although in Western Australia trousers had buttoned flies.

Two pairs of brown corduroy (durable cotton pile fabric with lengthways ribs) trousers in Tasmanian collections, both without markings, cannot be confidently provenanced as convict issue. One of the corduroy pairs had buttoned side openings added later to accommodate leg irons. While government tenders for the supply of trousers gave corduroy as an option, it is not certain that it was ever issued. Two striped shirts with full sleeves, partial front opening, and stand-up collar survive, although from a later period. Shirts of this design were worn by working-class men for many decades.

The only surviving garment that might relate to female convicts is a machine-stitched black felted wool cape. Made of four panels, with a narrow collar and three buttonholes, it features several letter and number markings on the interior as well as broad arrows. Some researchers, however, believe that this garment may have been a police constable's cape.

Convicts were issued a variety of headwear. Leather hats with fold-up brims were ubiquitous; they appear in several colonial images and are well represented in public collections. When unfolded they have an inverted pleated crown and semicircular sides, which can either fold up or be let down to form a brim. They are lined with soft, tan-colored leather, and a brown ribbon or leather thong holds the flaps in place. These hats, which were marked with broad arrows on the inside, unequivocally identified wearers as convicts.

Convicts were also issued woolen hats. Many of these have a high crown and feature valley folds, curved sides, and a woolen bobble in the center of the crown. Those surviving in collections were made of felted wool, usually gray and knitted in the round, and have prominent markings. Several dark brown caps, similar to Monmouth caps, a popular style originating in the Welsh town of Monmouth, also survive. These are also knitted in the round and feature a cloche shape (soft and close fitting with a deeply rounded crown) with a flared rim. A knitted loop is attached to the rim and a toggle on the crown. Few of these are marked.

Cowls were introduced in the Separate Prison at Port Arthur to further enforce complete isolation and separation, which was thought to lead to contemplation and reform. The surviving Port Arthur cowl is made of cambric (a fine white linen or cotton fabric). This may be a lining rather than a complete cowl. Contemporary observers noted cowls of dark woolen material, and industrial returns list the manufacture of linings for Separate Prison hoods. These were worn over the head and covered the face, leaving only small eyeholes. This minimized peripheral vision and prevented the convict from seeing any of his fellow prisoners on the rare occasions he was allowed out of his cell. These cowls, which were designed to work on the mind, replaced the physical forms of coercion and intimidation of previous years. Surviving cowls provide stark and troubling evidence of the inhumanity inherent in many aspects of the penal system.

There appears to be little to distinguish convict footwear from that worn by the free working class. Although some footwear was marked with broad arrows, this may only imply that it was manufactured within the convict system. Boots and shoes were made in the colonies, both by private commercial concerns and by convict workers such as those at Maria Island in Van Diemen's Land in the late 1820s. At Port Arthur sufficient footwear was made to sell on the open market and export to Britain. Generally, however, particularly in the early transportation period, the supply of footwear suffered from the same problems as other convict clothing—supplies were inadequate to meet demand and frequently arrived in poor or damaged condition.

Markings are found on a number of surviving garments, although many remain unmarked. Convict uniforms were inscribed in a variety of ways. Numbers usually added to the inside of jackets and waistcoats and the outside of trousers are thought to indicate sizes. There are no numbers on surviving shirts. Broad arrows, used to identify government property including convict clothing, are found on many items. The Board of Ordinance oversaw the supply of clothing between 1827 and 1855, and their BO mark always appears in association with a broad arrow. The War Department assumed responsibility for issuing clothing in 1855, and their WD mark is also associated with a broad arrow and, often, a letter A. These markings have become important indicators allowing surviving garments to be roughly dated. Both the numbers and government marks are usually small and inconspicuous. In contrast, place names, such as PA (representing Port Arthur) and HM Hobart GAOL, are always found on the outside of garments and are usually large and conspicuous.

CONCLUSION

Of the vast numbers of garments issued to the 160,000 convicts transported to the colony between 1788 and 1868, only a tiny proportion of those issued to men can be found in Australian public collections. Surviving examples only reflect some of the clothing issued; they do not represent summer dress, early period issue, or children's and women's clothing, while parti-colored clothing is over-represented, although it was only issued to a minority of male secondary offenders.

Parti-colored waistcoats, jackets, and trousers have become synonymous with convicts in the popular imagination, perhaps because they represented the most titillatingly gothic aspect of the convict experience, the man in chains under heavy punishment. This bias has been reinforced in Australian public culture, particularly after the publication of Marcus Clarke's eagerly read newspaper serial and then novel, *For the Term of His Natural Life*,

in 1874, and its subsequent release as a feature film in 1927. Clarke, drawing on the already widely accepted stereotype but also on his own interviews with convicts and ex-convicts, stressed the more horrific aspects of the convict system. Most convicts in the film wore parti-colored clothing while enduring fearful privation, oppression, and punishment.

In Australia convict items carry a heavy symbolic burden. Few prison uniforms of the same period survive in Britain and other former colonies, so it is through the prism of fewer than one hundred items, together with scattered documentary and pictorial evidence, that the entire story of this aspect of British transportation to Australia can be read. These fragile garments and documents express complex and changing ideas about how prisoners should be controlled and managed, how their status was to be reflected, both to the prisoners themselves and to society at large, and how their public humiliation was to be used against them, in order to compel them to turn from criminality to social usefulness.

The history of clothing convicts in the Australian colonies reveals the authorities' deep-rooted fear of the disorder and contagion believed to emanate from convict populations, and their concerted attempt to contain them. Systemic inefficiency and parsimony worked against this ambition. Convicts managed, on occasion, to use this clothing to their own advantage on the black market and in escape attempts. In the end, like the convict system itself, convict dress is perhaps best seen as a site of tension and class conflict.

References and Further Reading

Ash, Juliet. *Dress behind Bars: Prison Clothing as Criminality*. London: I. B. Tauris, 2009.

Historical Records of Australia. Sydney: Library Committee of the Commonwealth Parliament, Canberra: Australian Government Printing Service, 1914–1925, 1997–2008.

Historical Records of New South Wales. Sydney: Government Printer, 1892–1901.

Maynard, Margaret. "A Form of Humiliation: Early Transportation Uniforms in Australia." *Costume: The Journal of the Costume Society* 21 (1988): 57–66.

Maynard, Margaret. *Fashioned from Penury: Dress as Cultural Practice in Colonial Australia*. Cambridge: Cambridge University Press, 1994.

Young, Linda. "The Experience of Convictism: Five Pieces of Convict Clothing from Western Australia." *Costume: The Journal of the Costume Society* 22 (1988): 70–84.

Julia Clark, Linda Clark, Kim Simpson, Ian Terry, and Elspeth Wishart

See also Images as a Resource for the Study of Australian Dress; Settler Dress in Australia.

Subcultural and Alternative Dress in Australia

- Nineteenth-Century Subcultures
- Bodgies, Widgies, and Beats
- Surfers, Hippies, and Ferals
- Mods
- Skinheads, Punks, and Sharpies
- Dressing Up

From the beginning of European settlement in New South Wales in 1788, Australians were using alternative forms of dress, body decoration, and modification, visibly expressing individual and collective identities, aesthetic codes, values, beliefs, and cultural experiences different from the dominant culture. Some developed personal style statements, and others have been part of collective subcultural expressions linked to interests, lifestyles, and philosophies. Most have been youth-generated, chiefly imported from Great Britain and the United States, yet showing differences of expression among the country's major cities. Australia has experienced a plethora of subcultures. A selection is reviewed here, but this coverage cannot be considered comprehensive or do full justice to the breadth of subcultural expression.

NINETEENTH-CENTURY SUBCULTURES

By the 1830s colonial society in Australia was made up of civil and military officers, private gentlemen, free settlers, ex-convicts or emancipists, the colonial-born "currency lads and lasses," laborers, and convicts. Conscious of fashion's role in signifying status and respectability, the colonial elite distanced themselves from the convict and working class through fashionable dress. The first to challenge the strict codes of appearance and behavior were British convicts. Faced with an uncertain future, men, and some women, used tattoos to record their personal identity, family history, religion, and relationships, marking themselves with their own and/or their sweetheart's or wife's names or initials, sometimes combining heart and anchor symbols. Other tattoos listed the convict's genealogy, preserving identity within a family. The date of trial or transportation was often recorded, as were crosses, crucifixes, and Masonic symbols, while other unidentifiable marks suggested membership in a gang or other subculture.

By the mid-1800s Australia's capital cities, Sydney and Melbourne, were well-established centers of commerce and entertainment. After mid-century the economy boomed, but by the late nineteenth century growing inequality between Australia's rich and poor was exacerbated by economic depression. This, plus the speed of urbanization, led to areas of the cities becoming slums. Australia's so-called larrikin subculture had uncertain origins about then, emerging in overcrowded working-class areas of Sydney and Melbourne, and later in Adelaide. *Larrikins* were young men and their female companions variously called *larrikinesses*, *donah*, or *clinah*. They divided themselves into local gangs, or "pushes," with one of the earliest described as the Cabbage-Tree Mob, after their preference for hats made of plaited fiber from the native cabbage tree palm, *Livistona Australis*.

Evoked in contemporary poetry, novels, cartoons, and newspapers by the 1880s and 1890s, larrikins were often associated with criminal activity, intimidation, and violence. However, the Australian media has had a long history of reporting youth gangs and subcultures in negative and sensationalist tones, creating an air of moral panic for the middle classes. Much of the leisure time of working-class youth then was spent on street corners and in dancing saloons, making their socializing very visible, leading to accusations of lounging around the streets and engaging in loutish and drunken behavior. Interestingly, they were frequently depicted as music-hall characters, and often "costume" ideas were interchanged between street and stage.

Dress was one of their primary defining features. Information on their distinctive appearances comes from police and media reports, descriptions from poets and writers—such as Louis Stone's book *Jonah*—and cartoons in *The Bulletin*, a national news and current affairs magazine. They were often disparaged as having an undersize physique and low brow. Larrikins wore the dominant mode of male dress, the three-piece lounge suit, but altered its proportions. This gave a more flamboyant and sexualized edge, debasing its serious intent of evoking a man's respectability, good character, and industriousness. These suits were usually dark, with the jacket cut very short and tight, revealing the fly and seat of the pants, while waistcoats were discarded or low-cut, revealing an expanse of clean white shirt front. Detachable collars were often discarded in favor of neck scarves or neckerchiefs. The trousers were tight-fitting, revealing the contours of the legs; some were tight to the ankle, while others flared in a bell shape from the knee. Hats varied from small, hard, round bowlers to soft, wide-brimmed black felt styles. Much attention was focused on highly polished, high-heeled boots with pointed toes, featuring perforated decoration or metal caps. The sartorially spectacular boots were said to be an effective weapon for kicking an opponent.

The donah's dress was based on contemporary fashions, but the colors were described as gaudy at a time when earthy muted tones were fashionable. The over-embellishment with trimmings was deemed vulgar. The bright clash of colors seemed to run from the bodice and skirt to the layers of petticoats and stockings revealed by a relatively short skirt. Outfits were finished with a feather boa, topped by a large hat decorated with an abundance of feathers.

Larrikins were accused of intimidating another group of alternative dressers, women cyclists. In the 1890s bicycle riding took off as sport and leisure activity for mainly middle- and upper-class women. The bicycle brought to women's lives freedom, independence, and speed. Bicycling clubs opened up new social and recreational opportunities outside the home, in mixed company and in environments where their behavior could not be monitored by family. Public censure followed. For most of the 1800s women had been expected to be passive and modest in dress, their primary sphere of influence and occupation being the home. But by the 1890s they were becoming involved in tennis and cycling and political activities such as the suffrage movement, and taking a greater part in Australia's economic life.

A cartoon of a larrikin and a donah dancing, from *The Bulletin*, 1894. Here the larrikin wears a tight suit jacket, a short round bowler, flared trousers, and pointed shoes. The larrikin's suit was based on a popular men's suit but with the proportions altered to highlight his difference. The donah's dress was similar to contemporary women's fashions but with gaudier colors, shorter skirts, and plenty of accessories like feather boas and big hats. Drawing by Tom Durkin.

The area of greatest concern for moralists, and a target for street harassment, was the new "rational" dress some women cyclists adopted, also worn in Britain and America. This was a bifurcated garment of voluminous, loose-fitting bloomers, knickerbockers, or pants, seen as a masculine form of clothing, revealing women's previously unseen legs—a drastic departure from accepted modes of day-wear, which was more normally a high-collared bodice and full floor-length skirt over a corset and layers of petticoats. So fierce was the condemnation of "wheelwomen" wearing the bifurcated garment that they compromised with an outfit similar to that of middle-class women entering the workforce: white shirts with a high Eton collar and tie and ankle-length skirts, less full and shorter than the norm and without petticoats. A matching jacket was worn over the shirt in colder weather and a wide-brimmed straw boater kept the sun off the face.

BODGIES, WIDGIES, AND BEATS

African American subcultural style made a brief appearance in Australia during World War II. Sydney's first zoot-suiter appeared in a newspaper report in 1943. The style, imported from

America and copied by Australian tailors, was quickly repressed due to strict clothing regulations. From June 1942 clothing had been rationed to an increasingly limited number of items. In the same year the federal government introduced regulations restricting material and trims. The zoot suit, with its oversize draped jacket reaching almost to the knees, broad padded shoulders, wide lapels, oversize bow tie, and high-waisted baggy trousers narrowing to tight cuffs at the ankle, used an extravagant amount of material, flouting government restrictions. The government quickly confiscated examples and sought to prosecute tailors making the style.

Australian youth subcultures thrived in the period of peace and prosperity following World War II. The economy boomed, and the conservative government of Robert Menzies encouraged industrial development and mass immigration from Europe to help build the economy and boost population. Near full employment meant families could buy homes and cars and gave teenagers (the new demographic) leisure time, independence, and spending power to develop their own styles and cultural interests. At this time young Australians were primarily influenced by American popular culture and consumerism, particularly music and fashion trends. These were introduced through increasingly diversified and accessible forms of mass media, including radio, movies, pulp fiction, magazines, television, records, and local and international bands, many presenting alluring stories of deviant teenage behavior. The Australian media played an important part in constructing an image of normal teenagers as well as deviant ones. The *Australian Women's Weekly* introduced its "Teenager's Weekly" lift-out in the late 1950s. Teenagers could have their problems solved, read about their favorite pop stars, and peruse articles ridiculing the extreme forms of peer behavior expressed by bodgies, widgies, and Beats. In the late 1950s rock 'n' roll appeared on Australian television in the form of the quite conservative show *Bandstand*, with family appeal, and the slightly wilder *Six O'clock Rock*, both of which presented a relatively wholesome vision of teenage culture and style. New ranges of consumer goods specifically aimed at young people assisted in differentiating them from the conservative dress styles and limited range of leisure activities enjoyed by their parents.

There was one group of teenagers of particular concern to parents and authorities because of their wholesale adoption of American dressing, dancing, foods, and argot, along with what was perceived as a troubling lack of respect for adults. Found in cities and country towns all over Australia, bodgies and their female companions, the widgies, were generally working-class youth who used clothing and rebellious attitudes to stick out from the bland conservatism of mainstream Australia. As with the earlier larrikins, bodgies and widgies were vilified by the media, with frequent sensationalist reports of criminal activity, violence and internecine street fighting, sexual promiscuity, laziness, and lack of respect for authority. The name *bodgie* is believed to come from the slang word meaning "fake," initially applied to black marketeers impersonating Americans and selling Australian cloth as American product.

Initially the bodgie wore a modified zoot suit, with single-button, mid-thigh-length draped jackets, brightly colored shirts with button-down collars, skinny ties, and loose-fitting trousers narrowing into tight cuffs. The hairstyle was a critical part of the look, a much-groomed component based around American styles. Bodgies favored that of Hollywood film star Cornel

Wilde—appearing in *A Song to Remember* (1945) with his hair combed straight back and full on the top and side. This was very different from the regular hairstyle for Australian men, short and neat, with a part, described as "short back and sides."

Bodgies and widgies' favorite meeting places were suburban dancehalls, where they gathered to jive and jitterbug and listen to bands playing swing and bebop. They also frequented American-style milk bars, where they ate American-style hamburgers, listened to records on the jukebox, and played pinball machines. They would gather on the streets, but the police dispersed groups whenever they congregated in public.

Widgies wore tight-fitting, below-the-knee pencil skirts or, for dancing, full circle ones over layers of stiffened petticoats, off-the-shoulder embroidered peasant blouses with a drawstring neckline, tight-fitting sweaters and cardigans over uplift bras, and slim fitting jeans or mid-calf-length matador pants. Shoes ranged from flat matador-style slippers to high-heeled shoes or slip-on, backless scuffs. The hair was pulled back into a ponytail or cut short, and worn with large hoop earrings. In cold weather the outfit was topped with a duffel coat, a thick, three-quarter-length outdoor coat of coarse wool, with four front fastenings and occasionally a hood. While these styles were not that different from what other teenage girls were wearing, it was the way the widgie wore them that caused outrage. Everything was worn tighter, more revealing, and full of sexual allure; thus the effect was considered more provocative than the demure styles of their peers.

By the mid-1950s the bodgie style was changing as American films like *Blackboard Jungle* (screened in 1955) introduced American rock 'n' roll to Australian audiences. The insolent brooding sensuality of Marlon Brando as a leather-clad biker rebel in *The Wild One* and the teenage angst of James Dean in *Rebel Without a Cause* inspired a more radical style of dress, in contrast to the neat suits or trouser-and-shirt combinations otherwise worn. Emulating the style and attitude of Brando and Dean, bodgies had a more aggressive and dressed-down look, adopting blue denim jeans or trousers tightly pegged into the ankle, tight-fitting T-shirts, black shirts, and black leather jackets. The hair was brushed straight back from the forehead and worn very full on top or with a quiff at the front, combed in from each side and parted down the center back, creating a hairstyle popularly known as the DA (Duck's Arse). It was a hairstyle that required constant attention and products like Brylcream to keep it in place.

Beat culture also had an impact on young adults from the late 1950s to the early 1960s, with mainly middle-class college- and university-educated youth emulating the American Beat generation. They met in coffee bars, pubs, and jazz cellars to discuss the work of Beat poets and authors, and New Wave continental films, and to express dissatisfaction with the conservatism and conformity of Australian society. They expressed their rebellion by dressing down, in contrast to the well-groomed appearance of many contemporaries. Clothing was disheveled and oversized rather than fitted. Men's clothing was worn loosely, with baggy trousers, polo neck pullovers, and desert boots. Hair was worn long, and, at a time when most men were clean-shaven, a short beard and mustache were favored. Much black clothing was worn at a time when it was considered inappropriate for daywear. Clothing for women included thick mohair and wool skirts, baggy sweaters, flat shoes, and thick black stockings, with hair piled into a purposely disheveled "birds-nest" effect, while eyes were dramatically outlined in heavy black eyeliner. Both men and

This pure wool dance costume with a checked pattern was worn by the jitterbug dance champion Barry Frawley, and made by Andy Ellis, ca. 1956. The suit exemplifies the type of clothing associated with a style of rock 'n' roll dancing that was viewed as new and daring in the 1950s. While the suit is the performance costume of a professional, the narrow trousers pegged at the cuff have that in common with bodgie streetwear. Gift of Barry Frawley. Powerhouse Museum.

women wore loose-fitting, mid-thigh-length duffel coats with toggle fastenings.

SURFERS, HIPPIES, AND FERALS

Contemporaneous with the bodgies and Beats in the late 1950s were surfers (or surfies), a male-dominated subculture that began to turn the sport of surfboard riding into a lifestyle. Although the terms are sometimes used interchangeably, surfers see themselves as the true soul surfers (people who live the total surfing lifestyle, including making a living associated with surfing), whereas surfies love surfing but otherwise follow more traditional career and lifestyle paths. During the 1960s surfing's popularity boomed against a background of surf music, some imported, like the Beachboys' "Surfin USA," but also from local bands—the Denvermen and the Atlantics. Surf music's popularity coincided with the decline of rock 'n' roll, and this, combined with the hedonistic allure of surf culture, led to resentment and reports of confrontations between surfies and rock 'n' roll aficionados, the bodgies.

The increasing affordability of cars encouraged some to drop out rather than conform to the five-day working week of mainstream Australia. Instead they traveled the extensive tracts of surf beaches located along the eastern, southern, and southwestern coasts of mainland Australia and parts of Tasmania, following the good weather and waves, living the nomadic life of the soul surfer waiting for the perfect wave.

Surfers initially wore the same swimwear as other beachgoers, based on the short-legged, close-fitting swim trunks worn in America, popularized in surf movies like *Gidget* and *Blue Hawaii*. Later the looser-fitting, Hawaiian print board shorts (often close to knee-length) were adopted. To maintain their lifestyle some surfers established businesses associated with surfing, enabling them to earn money. Among those who moved from surf products to clothing were companies Rip Curl (originally making surfboards in 1969 and expanding into surf clothing in the 1980s), Billabong (1973), and Quiksilver (1970). They started out selling surf shorts to small surf shops along the coast but have since become well-known international brands. Away from the surf, the "look"—sun-bleached disheveled hair, a golden tan, branded board shorts, and T-shirt featuring company logos and graphics—was sometimes accompanied by sheepskin boots called ugg boots. These warm ankle-length boots were worn with tanned leather on the outside and soft fleece on the inside, keeping the feet warm in colder weather.

At the end of the 1960s, like their British and American counterparts, other dropouts became known as hippies, articulating some of their ideals through dress. They were antifashion and critical of an industry that encouraged people to conform to fashion trends by continually updating their wardrobe. Hippies obtained their clothing from secondhand markets, opportunity, charity shops, and each other, styling clothing elements to create an individual look. Jeans and T-shirts were key components of men's and women's dress, customized with floral embroidery, patches, antiwar buttons, and peace symbols. Hippies adopted loose, flowing, layered garments, including a mix of homemade and homespun garments topped with chains of inexpensive tribal jewelry.

Themes of universal love and respect for all humans were reflected in the adoption of a wide array of clothing drawn particularly from exotic cultures whose lifestyles were perceived as simpler, more authentic, and closer to nature. Some visited these cultures, traveling the hippie trail through Asia and returning with Afghan jackets and Indian shawls. Neatness, appropriateness, cleanliness, and displays of wealth and status were disregarded in favor of dressing down in untidy, unironed, discordant outfits, wearing hair and facial hair long and uncombed, with jangling and tinkling sounds of ethnic jewelry and the new aromas of perfumes made from patchouli oil and sandalwood.

In the mid-1990s groups of young "feral" ecologists came together to express their concern over the environmental problems facing Australia and to fight the ongoing degradation and exploitation of the natural environment. Emerging from a confluence of the hippie and radical alternative communities of the 1970s were the confrontational environmental activists of the 1970s and 1980s, with nature-based spiritualism and rituals of the pagans. Anticapitalist and anticonsumerist, they lived a self-sufficient lifestyle reflected in their dress, layers of handmade, handcrafted, and recycled clothing, either found, swapped with friends, or purchased from local markets and charity stores, often dyed, patched, embroidered, and remade. Hair was uncombed, dreadlocked, trimmed with beads, or wrapped in colored fabric.

They favored tribal or handmade jewelry created from found items like feathers and parts of bird skeletons. Tattoos included a wide variety of motifs selected for their individual and spiritual significance. Common were face piercings like lip and eyebrow rings and barbells, nose rings, and studs, multiple ear piercings, and ear plugs.

MODS

Australia adopted a "populate or perish" approach to immigration after World War II, fueled by labor shortages, fear of invasion after the Japanese bombing of Darwin, and proximity of the war in Southeast Asia. An assisted migration program initially favored British and then more broadly European immigrants. Between 1946 and 1972 more than a million "ten pound poms" (subsidized British immigrants who paid ten pounds each) came to Australia on this scheme. Young British men brought subcultures from their homeland, which for some helped articulate their identity in a new country and provided a like-minded community through which they could maintain difference. Teenage interest shifted from America to Britain, with immigrants bringing with them Mod style, rhythm and blues, and the music of The Who, the Kinks, and the Rolling Stones.

Fastidious about appearance, Mods cultivated a neat, well-groomed, and conservative look, with males favoring slim-fitting, three-button, Italian-style suits and girls A-line mini-dresses, neat skirts, and blouses. An element of discord in the men's appearance was the collar-length hair with heavy fringe. Females held their neat shoulder-length hair back with a wide headband, or otherwise cut their hair into a short bob. The neat suits and dresses were in contrast to their somewhat wild and distinctive dance style. Youth-orientated, music-based magazines like *Go-Set* (an Australian publication) brought news of local music, fashion, and teenage concerns to the Australian teenager, including pages on Mod style.

This first wave of Mod style was quickly absorbed into mainstream fashion but was revived several times, making more of a subcultural statement in the early 1980s when the dress of this immaculate and tight-knit group became the butt of jokes, and sometimes violence from other, more overtly masculine subcultures like skinheads and sharpies. Pete Townsend's Mod-themed rock opera film *Quadrophenia* opened in Australia in 1980, fueling a Mod revival. For teenagers, tired of the anti-everything, nihilistic, punk aesthetic, the Mod focus of dressing up and looking smart was attractive. They had to obtain most of their gear through secondhand charity shops or have local tailors alter or make up 1960s-style three-button suits. They gathered at the few clubs featuring 1960s-style music and traveled to events on Italian motor scooters. To keep warm and keep their clothes pristine, both men and women wore U.S. army fishtail parkas from disposal stores. While Mod revivalists no longer had strong links with Britain, they continued the affiliation stylistically by sewing British flags to their parkas.

SKINHEADS, PUNKS, AND SHARPIES

British migration brought skinhead subculture to Australia in the 1970s. Although it attracted relatively small numbers of predominantly male members, it spread through most of Australia's capital cities from Perth to Adelaide, Melbourne, Sydney, and Brisbane and has experienced various revivals up to the twenty-first century.

Sharpies in Melbourne, 1973. The subjects show several typical traits of the subculture's dress code, including the tight-fitting, custom-knitted cardigans and jumpers and the short hair on top with "rats tails" at the back. Photograph by Rennie Ellis. © Rennie Ellis Photographic Archive.

In Perth in particular, the "skins" subculture was initially concerned with maintaining and expressing English identity and keeping the connection with "home" in the face of racial taunts from Australian-born youth. Usually drawn from working-class backgrounds, skinheads were a highly visible subculture cultivating an aggressive masculinity in their dress, matched by intimidating and violent behavior and a lifestyle revolving around drinking, fighting, and comradeship. Some members became associated with homophobic, neo-Nazi, and racist activity as well as being implicated in harassment and personal attacks on Asians and Jews.

Their hair was cut very short over the entire head (called a "no. 1 cut" after the setting on an electric razor). They preferred straight-legged American-brand jeans (Levi, Wrangler, and Lee), sometimes splatter-bleached and worn cut short or with the bottoms rolled up to mid-shin to show off heavy, laced Doc Marten boots in black or Oxblood red. In fighting, the boots and the front of the head were used to kick and butt opponents. These clothes were worn with T-shirts with the names of English football teams and favorite Oi bands (a brand of music favored by skinheads, with a fast, aggressive beat) or sports shirts by British clothing companies Ben Sherman and Fred Perry, or American Golf brand Penguin. In cooler weather close-fitting, lightweight, V-neck Fred Perry or Pringle brand pullovers and cardigans were added under denim jackets. Those in the colder southern cities of Melbourne and Adelaide wore sage green air force flight jackets. Tattoos were used to express English affiliations and racist beliefs.

This informal dress style served for daytime, whether hanging out in public spaces or in pubs and at football matches. The older skinheads with more money, who wanted to get into bars and clubs, had to adopt a smarter, less aggressive style of dress to get past doormen and dress regulations. For them hair was worn a bit longer on top, Doc Marten brogues replaced the heavy boots, with white or red socks showing at the bottom of the neater Sta Prest tapered pants or straight-legged jeans, worn with a Ben Sherman shirt with button-down collar or local Australian-brand Bonds sports shirts.

From the mid-1960s a distinctly Australian subculture, the sharpies, began to emerge, reaching its peak of popularity and style in the 1970s. Based mainly in Adelaide and Melbourne, they were predominantly working-class youth, many from low-income families, who gathered into suburban gangs and took on the skinhead mantle of street violence and intimidation, while developing a quite expensive and smart, "sharp," style of dressing. The main components of their dress were commissioned from local clothing manufacturers and shoemakers. Sharpies formed a contradictory front, with their aggressive posturing and street violence yet feminine and fastidious dress style. By the 1970s they had become strictly ranked in territorial suburban gangs that roamed the streets fighting each other for fun.

Sharpies wore a mix of Crestknit brand sports shirts, Western-style shirts, or T-shirts featuring logos or gang names such as the Blackburn Sth Sharps, worn with tight straight-legged tweed or pinstriped tailored pants or high-waisted jeans by Levi, Lee, Wrangler, or local Melbourne brand Staggers. Pants and jeans were cut short in the leg and sometimes worn with suspenders. The most important element of their outfit was a tight-fitting, custom-made, machine-knitted pullover or cardigan. One of the best-known brands was the Connie cardigan many Melbourne sharpies preferred. Sourced from a local knitwear factory run by Greek migrants, sharpies ordered the front-buttoning cardigans with personally customized designs featuring blocks of color and thin and broad stripes over the body, sleeves, and collar. The outfit was finished with leather, handmade chisel-toe shoes with a basket-weave upper. These were also acquired from migrant shoemakers such as Venus and Acropolis Footwear. They used continental barbers to cut the distinctive sharpie haircut, very short on top with longer "rats tails" of hair at the back. All the elements of dress were worn short, tight, and undersize relative to contemporary dress.

Girls were a minority in the sharpie subculture—the males' violent and sometimes misogynist behavior did not attract women. The female sharpies who did belong wore similar outfits to the men except when they dressed in short, almost undersize, A-line tent dresses or pleated tartan mini-kilt skirts with cardigans and clumpy cork-soled platform shoes.

Not only did sharpies draw on local clothing manufacturers, but they favored local bands like Lobby Loyde and the Colored Balls and Billy Thorpe & the Aztecs, who played loud, hard blues and rock music. Playing in pubs and suburban halls, the sharpies developed a distinctive dance, which involved an aggressive forward jerking of the neck and head in time to the beat. By the end of the 1970s the subculture was dying out, some disillusioned with the aggressive lifestyle and wanting to get into new disco venues. They were also seeing the emergence of another more spectacular subculture, the punks.

From the mid-1970s proto-punk rock bands like the Saints, Boys Next Door, and Radio Birdman were playing in Sydney, Melbourne, and Brisbane, but more influential on style and tastes were U.S. punk bands the Stooges and New York Dolls, until the arrival of British punk in 1976. Punks' anarchic, fast, loud music and bad-taste lyrics connected with those tired of the peace, love, back-to-nature utopian vision of the hippies, and what were seen as facile lyrics, dressed-up style, and ambivalent sexualities of disco music and glam style. Punk's nihilism was played out against a background of political conservatism, rising unemployment, and an increasingly apparent gap between rich and poor.

Punks came from a mix of backgrounds, including a significant element of middle-class, university-educated youth. Most bands dressed down in "non-image" jeans and T-shirts, shirts with sleeves torn off, singlets, and sometimes leather jackets. On the street individuals were being influenced by the first wave of British punk and the style emanating from Vivienne Westwood's shop SEX in London. Do-it-yourself outfits featured homemade trousers created from shower curtains, string vests purchased from army surplus shops, studded dog collars remade into belts, inexpensive lingerie worn as outerwear, plastic "tits" and black patent-leather pants, high-heeled shoes, fishnet stockings, and multiple studs in the ears. Intended to shock, the aggressive, overtly sexual element of dress usually associated with sex shops and transgressive practices affronted mainstream respectability.

When a second wave of hardcore punk bands emerged in the late 1980s, some band members and individuals adopted the distinctive British street punk stereotype. Brightly colored dyed hair was shaved and gelled into dramatic upstanding mohawks and spikes. T-shirts carried controversial and sometimes pornographic imagery and text, belts and cuffs were covered in metal studs, jeans were a torn and distressed patchwork of fabrics trimmed with multiple straps and zippers. On the feet were heavy, calf-length Doc Marten lace-up boots. Over this came black leather motorbike jackets customized with hand-painted band names and logos, studs, badges, and anarchic and offensive images. In addition, women wore tartan mini-skirts and torn fishnet stockings. News of the local punk scene spread through local fanzines like *Self Abuse*, *Pulp*, and Sydney punk-zine *Spurt*, while overseas news came through global music publication *NME (New Musical Express)*.

The punk revival in the 1990s and 2000s took on a more politically and socially aware role as part of do-it-yourself culture, viewed as a way of escaping capitalism's emphasis on consumption and instead finding other ways of living more broadly beneficial to the community and the planet. Communicating through the punk-zines (self-published magazines), music, and festivals, they espoused ideals of antiracism, antihomophobia, vegetarianism, and egalitarianism. Their clothing reflected the origins of punk style, comprising a mix of secondhand, homemade, remade, and modified commercial clothing. T-shirts included imagery and text from punk bands overlaid with homemade patches (pieces of fabric, screen printed or painted with images or text reflecting the owner's beliefs or favorite bands). Jeans were worn and ripped, splatter-bleached, and trimmed with zippers and patches of tartan fabric. Hanging from the waist was a "bum flap," a decorated rectangular flap of fabric at the front and back.

DRESSING UP

In contrast to punks of the 1970s and 1980s was the dressed-up glamour of the New Romantics, emerging from London's club scene and arriving in Australia in the early 1980s. Men and women began to individually experiment with dress, hair, and makeup, creating their own glamorous gender-bending fantasies. In Sydney the Recreational Arts Team (RAT) staged "RAT parties," providing a creative outlet for those who wished to dress and party creatively. They attracted a mix of heterosexual bohemians, gay men and women, and drag queens. RAT parties typically had audiovisual presentations, bizarre props, party drugs, innovative lighting, underground cabaret groups, the best DJs in town, and unusual live performances. They provided a venue for a circle of creative people to express themselves on a larger scale than previously. The RAT parties altered Sydney's night life and were forerunners of the dance parties and raves of the 1990s.

The rave consisted of gatherings of hundreds, sometimes thousands, of people in unused warehouses or out-of-the-way outdoor locations, dancing to the beat of electronic music and high-tech light shows. Rejecting alcohol in favor of bottled water and a new "love" drug called Ecstasy, ravers were able to dance all night in a friendly, loving ambience, many found a relief after the often aggressive atmosphere of other music venues. Hardcore ravers wore loose-fitting, easy-to-dance-in, oversize jeans and T-shirts printed or patched with colorful cartoon characters, reworked smiley faces, puns on well-known trademarks, and love

A male goth photographed in 1998 at La Vendor Fashion Gala, staged at the Universal Theatre in Melbourne. He has long dyed hair and wears dramatic eye make-up and lipstick. The inclusive and creative Goth subculture has been one of the most popular and enduring youth cultures in Australia from its appearance in the late 1970s. Photograph by Ilana Rose. Powerhouse Museum.

ameliorating the moods and insecurity associated with puberty and adolescence. For men it offers freedom from limitations of the macho, dressed-down style of most young Australian men. Its subcultural inclusivity and visually creative and experimental mode have given it wide appeal and longevity. While many young people discard subcultural style when they enter the workplace, conforming to the sartorial expectations of their new environment, goth Web sites offer advice on creating a wardrobe that satisfies individual creativity while fitting in with the corporate environment.

Drawing on gothic literature, horror films, dress of the medieval period, the eighteenth and nineteenth centuries, and the style of members of gothic bands of the 1980s, female goths wear flowing floor-length black velvet dresses trimmed with black lace, lace-up Edwardian-style ankle boots, fishnet stockings, and tightly laced corsets outside the dress. Men wear black trousers, T-shirts, or white shirts trimmed with dandy-inspired frills, jabot, lace collars and cuffs, frock coats, long black coats, and capes. Outfits for men and women are accessorized with silver jewelry including pendants, chokers, earrings, and rings featuring Christian and Celtic crosses, bats, spiders, Egyptian ankhs, pentagrams, and occult imagery. Hair is worn long and dyed black, the face dramatically made up with ghost-like white foundation, dark exaggerated eyeliner, and eye shadow, with dark red or black lipstick.

Since the 1990s the goth subculture has diversified and crossbred with other subcultures musically and sartorially, creating a generation of subgenres. These include traditional goths who look back to styles of the 1980s, cyber-goths, industrial goths, metal goths, psychobilly goths, and gothic Lolitas. These subgenres have introduced a plethora of new elements to the original goth style, but common to all is the elaborate and time-consuming dressing ritual required before appearing in public. With this comes an element of creative competition. The cyber-goths' playful futuristic aesthetic features elements, inspired by Japanese Manga characters, that include layers of multicolored synthetic hair extensions caught up on each side of the head in large ponytails. Industrial goths wear fetish and fetish-inspired garments and materials including PVC Victorian outfits, corsets, and waist cinches trimmed with straps and buckles, trousers trimmed with long bondage straps, D-rings and buckled straps, straightjacket-style coats, and PVC nurse role-play costumes. Heavy knee-high bondage boots featuring rows of buckled straps or laces are worn by men and women. The hair and makeup of the Japanese geisha has inspired a geisha-goth look, with hair drawn up in a chignon trimmed with chopsticks, white face makeup with red accents around the eyes, and obis (based on Japanese obi sashes) made of PVC. Punk and fetish have inspired the studded and spiked leather and PVC dog collar–style chokers and wristbands. Body piercings including eyebrow jewelry in the form of rings or barbells, and labret rings through lips, are popular, as are tattoos.

Black American hip-hop culture arrived in Australia in the early 1980s via movies like *Wild Style* and *Beat Street*, introducing the four key elements of hip-hop—break-dancing, MCing (rapping), graffiti art, and DJing (turntablism), as well as an increasingly distinctive style of dress. Hip-hop has enjoyed various waves of popularity. Initially it had an underground following with little popular recognition or support from the mainstream music industry. But by the 2000s it had gained acceptance, with the music played on commercial radio stations, and hip-hop clothing style became influential on street fashion. It has had broad appeal across middle- and working-class youth, primarily males,

and peace symbols, referencing the utopian vision of the hippies while alluding to the effects of Ecstasy.

In the late 1990s Phat pants and shorts made a spectacular appearance on the dance floor. Fitted at the waist and increasing in width to the floor, they were trimmed with light-reflecting stripes and shapes, with numerous large pockets on the outside and multiple small pockets inside to hold everything from bottled water to money and drugs. They were particularly associated with the Melbourne rave scene and a distinctive dance style, the Melbourne Shuffle. Phat pants were later given a darker edge by the goth and punk scene with the addition of bondage straps, fetish trims, chains, and zippers.

Goths are the most popular, diverse, and enduring of Australian subcultures. Emerging in the early 1980s, they inherited elements from the theatrical, sexually ambiguous New Romantics and the bleak alienation of punk. Large groups of goths exist in most Australian capital cities. Even relatively isolated and conservative country towns include a few.

Goth culture's fascination with death and decay and its mysterious, melancholy, and romantic outlook appeal to teenagers, generating many hip-hop musical subgenres trying to express a distinctive Australian hip-hop identity, rapping in Australian accents or Aboriginal dialect, using Australian slang, and speaking about Australian culture, from socially conscious left-wing rappers and ecological hip-hop to Christian rappers and misogynist bloke-style hip-hop.

Australian hip-hop evolved into a casual, comfortable, brand-conscious mix of street style and sportswear. By the 1990s it was better defined, comprising oversize loose-fitting jeans, cargo pants, or track pants, designer-label tracksuits, oversize basketball jerseys, and T-shirts. These were worn with brand-name tracksuit tops with striped detailing, hooded zip-front sports jackets and hooded sweatshirts nicknamed "hoodies," and topped with baseball caps (sometimes worn backwards). The key component of hip-hop style has been sneakers from high-end sportswear companies (Nike, Puma, or adidas), particularly rare and limited-edition styles. Accessories include showy chains, pendants, and designer-brand sunglasses. Elements of hip-hop style cross-fertilized with other subcultures' dress, including surfers and skaters, while hooded sweatshirts and baseball caps became key components of mainstream streetwear. In the 2000s hip-hop style became dressier and flashier, with T-shirts featuring graffiti throw-ups and hoodies with intricate colorful graphics and gold foil prints, trucker-style hats, and sagged, skinny-leg jeans, with low crotch and dropped waistband revealing the underwear.

Many post–World War II subcultures continued in waves of revivals into the early 2000s, with Australian youth able to choose from and move between a plethora of subcultures, including Mod, straight edge, rockabilly, psychobilly, death rockers, heavy metal, raver, skater, fetish, goth, punk, and Emo. Subcultures borrow and incorporate stylistic elements and ideas from each other, creating subgenres of subcultures like goth punks and skate punks reflecting these crossovers. While subculture members remain sartorially spectacular outsiders to mainstream society, elements of their clothing styles are often referenced or incorporated in high-end and street fashion.

References and Further Reading

Braithwaite, John, and Michelle Barker. "Bodgies and Widgies: Folk Devils of the Fifties." In *Two Faces of Deviance: Crimes of the Powerless and the Powerful*, edited by Paul Wilson and John Braithwaite, 27–45. St Lucia, Australia: University of Queensland Press, 1978.

Cockington, James. *Long Way to the Top, Stories of Australian Rock and Roll*. Sydney: ABC Books, 2001.

De La Haye, Amy, and Cathie Dingwall. *Surfers Soulies Skinheads and Skaters: Subcultural Style from the Forties to the Nineties*. London: Victoria and Albert Museum, 1996.

Jarratt, Phil. *The Mountain and the Wave: The Quiksilver Story*. Huntington Beach, California: Quiksilver Entertainment, 2006.

Kent, David. "Convicts' Tattoos: Human Reality amid Catalogues of Misery." *ozhistorybytes* no. 8. http://www.hyperhistory.org/index.php?option=displaypage&Itemid=744%0p=page (accessed 29 January 2009).

Moore, David. *The Lads in Action: Social Process in an Urban Youth Subculture*. Aldershot, UK: Arena, 1994.

Polhemus, Ted. *Streetstyle from Sidewalk to Catwalk*. London: Thames and Hudson, 1995.

St. John, Dr. Graham. "Alternative Cultural Heterotopia: ConFest as Australia's Marginal Centre." Ph.D. dissertation, La Trobe University, 1999. http://www.confest.org/thesis_confest_july_1999.pdf (accessed 29 January 2009).

Tao, Kim. *Bodgies, Westies, and Homies: Growing Up in Western Sydney*. Smithfield, Australia: Fairfield City Museum and Gallery, 2006.

White, R., ed. *Australian Youth Subcultures: On the Margins and in the Mainstream*. Hobart: Australian Clearinghouse for Youth Studies, 1999.

Glynis Jones

See also Swimwear, Surfwear, and the Bronzed Body in Australia; Popular Music and Dress in Australia.

Queer Dress in Australia

The history of queer dress in Australia resides in unpublished theses, memoirs, diaries, photographs, and the memories of gay, lesbian, and transgender people. Changing understandings of sexual practice, from situational, private, and criminalized, to open, liberationist, and commodified, have impacted upon queer dress codes, clothing styles, and bodily appearance. Male homosexual acts were decriminalized in New South Wales (NSW) as late as 1984; in Tasmania, in 1997. Australia's queer history extends back into the convict period of transportation, when the social concept of homosexuality was nonexistent, and further back in time to same-sex rituals and relationships that were a part of some indigenous cultures. Nineteenth-century Australia tended to view same-sex behavior as something that happened elsewhere, in the fleshpots of Paris or the decadence of fin-de-siècle London. Most of the surviving evidence of queer "coteries" is metropolitan twentieth-century and is strongly biased toward the city of Sydney. It includes reference to cross-dressing, prostitution, and vaudeville, as much of the historical record resides in the scandal sheet, including caricature, police photography, and newspaper crime reports and exposés.

The idea of Australian dress can be extended to a broader sense of its place as a Commonwealth country and as part of the former Empire; thus, some New Zealand examples illuminate the Australian experience in a similar Eurocentric settler society. An account of a gay Aborigine's life in Melbourne in the interwar and postwar years provides a case study of the transformation of an individual's queer style as he moved from Australia to the heart of the Empire in London in the 1960s. This idea of "crossings" and "traffic" is necessary, as Australians have frequently moved between their continent and various queer "homes"—for Australians predominantly London until the 1950s and New York from the 1970s. Class plays a large role in the history of queer dress in Australia, as it was central to both gay and lesbian horizons and possibilities, and evidence can be cited from literary and autobiographical texts as well as imagery. In the 1970s and 1980s queer liberation politics joined with the Australian craft revival and "funk" of the 1970s to create influential and adventurous modes of dress. With good weather and strict licensing laws, the role of nightclubs was less important to queer culture in Australia than in cities such as London and New York. Sydney dance party events of the 1980s and 1990s generated particular ways of dressing. The Sydney Gay and Lesbian Mardi Gras parade and party, as well as gay dance party dress, had an impact on Australian "straight" commercial fashion in the 1980s and 1990s. Even the 2000 Olympics' closing ceremony contained a queer trace of dressing, in terms of costumes and vignettes, which lies at the heart of many Australian characteristics and stereotypes.

THE BUSHMAN AND THE AESTHETE

The shortage of women and the dominance of male homosocial environments were marked in the Australian colonies. Sydney was called the "Sodom of the South Seas," in part to discredit transportation of convicts. Sodomy in the coal mines was an obsession of British government inquiries, notably the infamy of Van Diemen's Land (later Tasmania), with its mines at Port Arthur, where, according to the novelist Marcus Clarke in his book *His Natural Life* (1870–1872), the prisoners lived underground and worked half-naked. The culture of hedonism, promiscuity, heavy drinking, pub life, and mixed-class socializing that characterized life in the colonies still pervades Australian gay life today. There is evidence of what historian Robert Aldrich calls "conjoined" same-sex male couples in nineteenth-century Australia, including the famous bushranger Captain Moonlite (Andrew George Scott, 1842–1880). One of Ned Kelly's infamous criminal gang included Steve Hart (1859–1880), who rode through the bush in women's clothing, ostensibly a disguise. Aldrich describes the late-nineteenth-century wealthy Brisbane civic leader James Mayne (1861–1939) as part of a family of "homosexually inclined" brothers. Mayne dressed in formal coats with gloves, a bowler hat, diamond tie-pin, and boutonnière.

Homosexuality was often associated with foreigners and cosmopolitan affectation. Marcus Clarke described the following scene set in Hobart Town, 1838: "Clad in glossy black, of the most fashionable clerical cut, with dandy boots, and gloves of lightest lavender—a white silk overcoat hinting that its wearer was not wholly free from sensitiveness to sun and heat—the Reverend Meekin tripped daintily to the post office, and deposited his letter" (Clarke, book 4, chapter 1, 1870–1872: 352–353). George Francis Alexander Seymour (1871–1940), future Marquess of Hertford, lived in Queensland for a brief time from 1895. He shocked locals by wearing a sequined outfit to perform dances and hosting male-only parties. William Lygon (1872–1938), later Earl of Beauchamp, governor of New South Wales from 1899, lavished praise on the natural grace of naked athletes and lifesavers. He was disgraced as a homosexual in his English divorce case in 1931 and became the subject of the famous statement by King George V: "I thought men like that shot themselves."

INTERWAR AUSTRALIA: PANSIES AND EXPATRIATES

During the first few decades of the twentieth century, many creative individuals found the presence in Australia of stringent censorship and the absence of a substantial art world reason enough to force them to become expatriate. Thus, a substantial part of

Australian queer dress was conducted on foreign soil. Patrick White (1912–1990), for example, Australia's Nobel Prize winner in Literature (1973), conducted one of Australia's great same-sex love affairs with Manoly Lascaris (1912–2003), a fifty-year relationship that lasted from 1941 until White's death. White spent his youth in England, from 1936 writing from rooms in London, sitting at a modernist desk designed by the queer interior decorator Francis Bacon (1909–1992), later the famous painter, described by White as "wearing rather too much lipstick." White explored same-sex relationships and observed the London scene, but always through the eyes of someone whose background and accent marked him out as different, with a nonmetropolitan background. White's homosexual circle included the Australian expatriate painter Roy de Maistre (1894–1968), described in his youth as a prissy little boy who wore a bow tie even when playing. De Maistre's youth in Australia was one of such dandiacal and fastidious style that at art school in Sydney he was nicknamed "The Duke" and also described as passionless, a snob, and social, all ways of characterizing a distrust of fashion in Australia. Clothes feature in many of White's sharp characterizations in letters and novels. In his London youth he wore Jermyn Street shirts, expensive suits, and a cloak garnished with a gardenia to the theater. Later in life, having returned to Australia after World War II, White described his pleasure in the purchase of well-cut English jackets, which were meant to last him a decade.

Camp is a semiprivate code not visible to all. Australian art deco and genteel modernism were inseparable from fashion and fantasy and were frequently viewed as a female or effeminate style. Cultural nationalist and the director of Melbourne's National Gallery of Victoria from 1936–1941, J. S. MacDonald famously claimed that modernist art practice had been spread by women and "pansies," meaning homosexual men, and in 1934 he cited Australian men working in the fashion and appearance industries as being very much to blame: "these *beings* can trim a hat or tie a bow with any girl." Gay male artists and commercial designers in Sydney lived their queer lives discreetly on moderate incomes with a few beautiful clothes. Australian men were urged in an advertisement of 1926 in the up-market women's fashionable society magazine, *The Home*, to adopt "tone-dressing" and to cease their fear of color and pattern in male clothing. The flower painter Adrian Feint (1894–1971), who never resided outside Australia, produced a small body of work about queer fashion style. His disguised self-portrait etching of a fin-de-siècle dandy entitled *The Collector* (1925) (National Gallery of Australia) carried the suggestion of eye and lip makeup, and depicted a top hat, cane, plaid suit, and cape.

As well as suggesting difference and excess, aristocratic dress codes might also have been adopted because the suggestion of wealthy assurance could excuse eccentric behavior considered outré. Feint's bookplate for "John Gartner" (wood-cut, 1938) shows a languid young male with a nipped-in waist, straw boater, and heavily lashed eyes. His cover design for *The Home*, July 1929, featured a "Rum Corps" officer transformed into a heavy-lidded and made-up male beauty, recalling the Ballets Russes who were touring Australia at that date, as well as Rudolph Valentino and the world of Hollywood film. Feint and his male friends were described in *The Home* in 1930 as "giving a London touch to the party with their well-cut clothes and their air of having chosen their ties and socks not haphazard but with a nice deliberation." The idea of bohemianism generated the transgressive Arts Balls,

which were held in Sydney from the 1920s until 1964. A 1925 sketch by Mandi McCrae of one such ball in *The Home*, September 1925, delineates a transsexual, two men with arms akimbo, and several gender-indeterminate figures. Other notable balls included Drag and Drain in the 1930s and 1940s and Artists and Models in the 1950s and 1960s. Press stories include descriptions of cross-dressed men in enormous dresses riding in delivery vans, and of a live dove—sometimes a pigeon—worn in a cage as part of a Marie Antoinette headdress.

In the interwar years a queer urban subculture coalesced for the first time in Sydney around art deco sites and buildings: city hotels, the Archibald Fountain by night, and the new high-density housing of Kings Cross, Potts Point, Darlinghurst, and East Sydney. Boonara, a middle-class flat building in Woollahra, built by a widow and a "spinster" in 1918, was let only to women and one male artist, William Lister Lister (1859–1943). The wealthier queers conducted their lives at private dinners, where ironic cross-dressing provided entertainment. They used camp girls' names such as Connie, Simone, Zena, and Maude. Cross-dressing was a popular diversion for groups of gay friends, who hired country and beach houses for private parties. In contrast to their everyday suits in which they tried to "blend," a rare surviving photograph shows a group of seven male "Joan Crawfords" in turbans and long bias-cut dresses snapped on a New Zealand beach near Christchurch in 1947 (private collection).

A queer sensibility can tell us as much as a queer identification. Australia's first interior decorator, Margaret Jaye, was probably a lesbian, and the nation's first furniture and industrial designer, Molly Grey, was photographed in 1935 with a severely Sapphic hairstyle and equally severe dress featuring oversize mannish collar, bow tie, and cuffs. The writer Eve Langley (1904–1974) (who changed her name to Oscar Wilde in 1954) and her sister June cross-dressed in country Gippsland where they were known as the trouser women. They may have dressed this way for safety, male privilege, and pleasure. Kylie Tennant (1912–1988) wrote *The Battlers* (1941) about cross-dressed women and wore men's clothes to research her novels. An all-woman Shakespeare company existed in Melbourne in the 1930s.

Camp is perhaps the greatest contribution that Sydney has made to the visual arts in Australia, tying together practices as disparate as the queer artists Adrian Feint's genteel modernism and William Dobell's (1899–1970) expressionist realism and beyond to James Gleeson's (born 1915) surrealism. Art critic Robert Hughes recognized this in his analysis of Sydney style, the "frothy camp" and "hip-swishing sailor boys" of what he famously described as the "charm school" in *The Art of Australia* (1966). Donald Friend (1915–1989) was one of this "charm school" of artists, also frequently expatriate and living with local men in Bali. In 1946 he resided in Sydney with a group of other queer artists, dancers, and designers in Merioola, a run-down mansion in Edgecliff popularly known as Buggery Barn. Here Friend wore a wide leather belt to show off his slim waist. Others of the group included the international costume designer Loudon Sainthill (1919–1969), his partner, the theater critic and gallery director Harry Tatlock Miller (1913–1989) (later director of the Redfern Gallery, London), and artist Justin O'Brien (1917–1996). An artfully posed photograph of Sainthill shows the artist painting in an Edwardian-style dressing gown in the daytime. It is in this type of slightly raffish garment, arms akimbo, that George Lambert (1873–1930), the well-known Australian painter who

Participant wearing an elaborate costume at the 2006 Sydney Gay and Lesbian Mardi Gras parade. Getty Images.

the troops to perform for the entertainment of the forces. The Australian Armed Forces had twenty concert party groups and gave twelve thousand performances in Australia, the Middle East, and the Pacific (1940–1946). The Kiwi (New Zealand) Concert Party wore drag made from muslin, dishcloth, silver paper, and real fashions. As well as performing in the Middle East, the Kiwis continued to tour for nine years after the war. Photographs show extremely exaggerated wigs and makeup; this was not a drag of impersonation, rather exaggeration. The sylph-like figure of John Hunter, a journalist wrote, "was envied by many women."

As queer theory academic Chris Brickell has argued, the drag performers pretended that they had been co-opted for their army roles and benefited from long-held views of carnival and the theater, but in fact their drag acts "drew from, and subsequently inspired, gay civilians' own drag performances." *Smith's Weekly*, *The Bulletin*, and the *New Triad* mocked "wasp waists" and "goo goo boys" who worked in retail and enjoyed theater. Cross-dressing was also associated with street prostitution. Police crime photography documented in the recent exhibition City of Shadows: Inner City Crime & Mayhem 1912–1948 (Justice and Police Museum, Sydney, 2006) shows the arrest of female cocaine dealers in decrepit fox stoles as well as cross-dressed male sex workers from the late 1930s or 1940s wearing coats with huge rabbit-fur-trimmed sleeves, turbans, and makeup. The men still look decidedly male, suggesting that a part of their sexual charge came from precisely this lack of ambiguity; it was clear that they were not women. The images are reminiscent of the American documentary photographer Weegee (Arthur Fellig, 1899–1968), who documented the New York underworld of the 1930s and 1940s.

In the 1950s Australia saw an increasing witch hunt on queer sexuality, fueled by the churches and the demands of the police. The popular press built on the sensational reporting of the interwar years: "Degenerate Dressed up as a Doll … St Kilda Sensation—Man-Woman Masquerader" (1919); "Queer Queans" (1920); "Curious Creatures—Painted and Powdered Effeminates" (1921). Even the 1950s American muscle culture magazines were banned in Australia, and the Kinsey Reports on sexual behavior were not reported by the mainstream press. From this period there are reports of the homosexual men called "yellow socks," identified by the police force in the working-class town of Newcastle (NSW). A police raid on a Sydney Kings Cross bar in 1954 found men "resplendent in the latest fashions" who could down "their beer with a wharfie's aplomb." Lesbian butch and femme subcultures had emerged by at least this date, in which one partner was styled in a hyper-feminine way, the other donning trousers and shorter hair. Academic Gavin Harris notes that Lillian Armfield, New South Wales's first policewoman, claimed that department stores had to blacklist lesbians who tried to "recruit" from among their "innocent" customers. In the 1960s the Sussex Hotel hosted lesbian "pimp-butches" called "king dicks," who wore three-piece Italian suits and pointy shoes, and who ran "strings of prostitutes." The first Sydney lesbian bar, Ruby's, opened in 1976 with a back bar for butches and cocktail space for femmes. At Yvonnes's Place (from 1980) femmes wore a lot of makeup and knitted see-through dresses, or tight leather trousers and stilettos.

had been resident in Edwardian London, presented himself in *Self-Portrait*, 1922 (National Portrait Gallery, Canberra). "I am a luxury, a hot house rarity.… Scoffed at for preciousness. Despised for resembling a chippendale chair in a country where timber is cheap," he wrote to his wife. A detractor called him "tricked out in brocade." The artist brothers Jack (1900–1990) and Ray Lindsay (1903–1960) were attacked in the street in 1920s Brisbane for wearing black crepe-de-chine ties to the local fish-and-chip shop. These are the types of gestures that marked out a fashion of provocation for this conservative and discreetly closeted era.

CITY OF THE PLAIN

World War II was a watershed for Australian queer identity. Historians have noted how port cities such as Sydney and San Francisco threw large numbers of young men together, away from their families, in new types of housing such as bachelor flats, which permitted an escape from the boundaries of the nuclear family. These port cities, always points of "crossing," were the ones that developed large homosexual communities, often in neglected inner-city areas, in the 1960s and 1970s. World War II was also notable for the large numbers of female impersonators plucked from

"BLAK" AND QUEER

The matter of queer culture and indigenous peoples is contentious but significant. Queer indigenous people have been prominent for several decades in art forms such as dance, where they contribute to new formulations of ideas of "blak beauty," *blak* being a term consciously deployed by contemporary queer visual artists such as Brook Andrew (born 1970). Dress is a significant part of the narrative of the survival story of indigenous dancer and choreographer Noel Tovey (born 1934). His autobiography, *Little Black Bastard* (2004), charts a story from abandonment and child abuse to a life as an actor and dancer in London in the 1960s. Tovey describes life in Melbourne in the 1950s, when queer culture and cross-dressing opened up new possibilities for this gay youth. Tovey recounts the police harassment of his drag queen friends in Melbourne, which included their being fined for wearing women's clothes. In New South Wales this was a summary offense of indecency, which was still used by police in the 1970s; drag queen performers had to wear male underpants or else risk arrest. This was the fate of the Melbourne drag queen Max Price, known as Mildred Pierce, "who looked more like a truck driver than her Hollywood namesake." The Arts Ball in Melbourne is described by Tovey as "the only night of the year when the police turned a blind eye to the number of drag queens looking for a cab." Characters at the ball included Puss in Boots and Greta Garbo, who refused to talk to anyone all night. For a court appearance on a trumped-up charge, Tovey saved his money to buy a "salt and pepper tweed suit" in order to look respectable. In 1960s London Tovey wore the soft casual clothes indicative of new modes of leisure that Shaun Cole also identifies as markers of queer style. Tovey was later involved with the spectacular "Awakenings" opening sequence at the 2000 Sydney Olympic Games, directed by indigenous arts practitioners Stephen Page and Rhoda Roberts.

Other parts of the oral history or "hidden history" of Aboriginal assimilation through dress have been explored in contemporary art practice. Queer blak artist Clinton Nain (born 1971) links his queer identity with dress codes. In the exhibition White King, Blak Queen (1999), Nain stained canvases and fabric with bleach to suggest the way Aboriginal people had been forced to adopt white clothes and assimilate, a comment also on his own subject position within contemporary gay culture, predominantly a white one in Australia.

LIBERATION POLITICS AND DRESS

William Yang (born 1943) has photographed aspects of queer Brisbane and Sydney since 1969. In that year he photographed David Williams, or Beatrice (born 1935), who performed in drag at the Purple Onion Club, Sydney (opened 1962), singing to the sounds of "The Sound of Mucus" and "A Streetcar Named Beatrice." The clothes matched the crude titles: synthetic crinolines and huge feather hats. Yang's photographs of the queer art world in the early 1970s show a predominance of denim, with interesting cuts, and one subject wearing the Vivienne Westwood "Tom of Finland" pornographic T-shirt. In the late 1970s the openly gay artists Peter Tully (1947–1992) and David McDiarmid (1952–1995) emigrated to New York, where they were patrons at the first house club, Paradise Garage. Becoming interested in the idea of "urban tribes," from WASPs to punks and gays, they introduced to Australia their eclectic sets of clothes and jewelry, some made of found objects such as plastics, many referencing indigenous peoples' garments. The pair were overtly camp and queer in their use of amyl nitrate bottles and KY jelly tubes as jewelry and art

(McDiarmid, Secret Love exhibition, Hogarth Galleries, 1976). This practice coincided with an upsurge in the crafts community in Australia, and their designs found a currency beyond gay party and dance communities. Some were sold at fashion designer Katie Pye's shop Hieroglyphics. Its title indicates the interest in bricolage that characterizes the introduction of postmodern ideas into Australian craft and design. A queer element was also present in Linda Jackson (born 1950) and Jenny Kee's (born 1947) famous fashion emporium Flamingo Park, which included the jewelry, textile, and garment practice of Tully and McDiarmid. That Jackson, the famous designer of Australian-themed textiles and fashions, had a girlfriend adds a different slant to the reading of her parades, which drew on the female power exhibited by 1920s and 1930s designers such as Elsa Schiaparelli and Madeleine Vionnet.

Performance and dance parties were highly significant within Australian queer history. In the 1970s a type of radical drag or "gender-fuck" theater developed in Sydney, performed by Doris Fish (Phillip Mills, 1953–1991) (who moved between Sydney and San Francisco), Simon Reptile, and Miss Abood (Danny Abood). Abood has been wearing dresses in the street since she moved to Sydney from the country in 1972 and was a founder of drag group Sylvia and the Synthetics (established 1971). Their makeup and grotesque costumes prefigure some of the strategies of performance artist Leigh Bowery and also refer to Weimar Germany, or an approximation of it. Yang also documented drag costume parties in suburban houses in the 1970s that provide some connection with the verbal description of drag parties of the interwar years. The 1970s parties emphasized hedonism and gender-fuck—the wearing of a frilled dress with a hairy chest and beard, for example, and also featured a great deal of partial nudity, which later became an essential and politicized component of the dance party circuit.

Both gay dance parties and leather-only events were held in Sydney from 1981. The dance parties included dress drawn from the Tom of Finland iconography, while creative figures such as Peter Tully came dressed with a Native American headpiece. Dance parties were held almost weekly in the late 1980s, run by RAT (Recreational Arts Team) and Sweatbox. Performers included Grace Jones (born 1948), who famously fell off the stage during her performance. The dress at these events was extremely diverse and perverse: muscular bodies, tight striped leggings, mixtures of orientalist dress worn by men of Asian descent in an ironic taking back of their cultural background, gender-fuck drag in which hairy arms mingled with a cheap nylon wig. The Australian gay scene was multiracial from the beginning, including Asian and Arabic men, but they found it difficult to challenge conventional ideas of male beauty. The use of Malaysian-born Che Kun Wu, the first Asian male cover model photographed for the national gay magazine *Campaign* (1992)—in a bathing costume—met with surprise and racist letters of complaint.

Yang's photographic practice also includes photographs of gays who wished to "blend," whose clothes appear very ordinary, with a slight edge that can only be read through the focus on casual softness. An example from the early 1990s, featuring Sydney's most famous decorator and also one of the richest press heirs, shows men aged in their fifties, sixties, and seventies wearing soft casual clothes, leather jackets, turned-down collars, and chinos. For the upper middle class an inconspicuous appearance was necessary to maintain privacy in a time when homosexuality was little understood or accepted. The gay artist Donald Friend painted a dining-room mural based on the Four Seasons in 1964 for newspaper heir James Fairfax at his country residence Retford Park, an example of a coded and semiprivate joke.

SYDNEY GAY AND LESBIAN MARDI GRAS

The Sydney Gay and Lesbian Mardi Gras is a cultural phenomenon that developed from a political protest in the winter of 1978 to become one of the country's premier summer festivals. The month of February is devoted to sporting and cultural events that culminate in the street parade and dance party. The party was conceived initially as a solution to crowd control. From February 1982 the showgrounds on Anzac Parade, at a right angle to notable gay hot spot Oxford Street, became the venue for the celebration designed to disperse the large crowd. The party, which reached participant numbers of 19,500 in 1995, could never house the parade viewers, who numbered 230,000 in 1991. The party, which has declined in significance in recent years, was once the highlight of the festival and parade and was also a part of the culture of Sydney dance parties, which from 1989 virtually became weekly events. Entrepreneurs, often circumventing archaic licensing laws, attracted large numbers of queer men and women to parties with varied acts, DJs, and themes. The parties are associated with euphoric dancing, sometimes facilitated by drug taking. September Sleaze Ball, also run by the Sydney Gay and Lesbian Mardi Gras as a fund-raiser, is the other important night in this particular gay calendar. It is often promoted as a themed fancy-dress event. The first concept party for Sleaze Ball was held in 1985.

Revelers at dance parties in the 1980s and 1990s borrowed from older conventions of the masque, the fancy-dress ball, and the carnival, as well as mirroring the carnivalesque interest in perversity and fantasy. Venetian dress was a popular mode of dress in the mid-1980s, relating to both carnival and London "Blitz" culture at nightclubs associated with Steve Strange and the New Romantics' flirtation with the dissolution of gendered sartorial codes. Party dress used to be different from that worn at the parade, as many participants wore street clothes to watch the parade, which begins in the late afternoon, and then subsequently changed for the night into party outfits.

Mardi Gras costumes derive their energy from a range of artisanal approaches, from the amateur to the highly refined. Participants adopt different approaches toward fancy dress. One approach stems from a long tradition of elaborate fantasy, in which the wearer emulates something or someone. The best example of the latter is the work of English-born Ron Muncaster (born 1936). Drawing upon the visual tradition of Erté, the Arabian nights, and orientalism, Muncaster produced exceptional costumes for himself and his partner, Jacques Straetmans, to wear, winning Best Costume in 1992. "Queen Sequina with her Nicky in a Twist," 1992–1993, was exhibited at the National Gallery of Australia in 1994. Worn with special Ferragamo-style platform shoes, these costumes radiate and extend the body at a time when the physical body was under threat from AIDS. Muncaster and Straetmans have also appeared in costumes including the outline of a paniered eighteenth-century court dress, traced in chain metal (1991), and in 1992 "Arabesque," a glittering confection of minarets, gilded and lit from within. Such costumes are based on the orientalist fantasies of Paul Poiret and his circle, who organized elaborate fancy-dress balls in Paris in the 1910s. Another

Mardi Gras reveler dressed in 1992 as a water fountain, referring directly to a Poiret fashion print of 1913, set in the gardens of Versailles. The type can be traced back to fantastic architectonic costumes popularized in eighteenth-century prints, men dressed as capitals and columns, for example. The amplification of the scale of the body here becomes a celebratory gesture of queer empowerment.

Another type of costume is more ironic and postmodern and marks a departure from the Arts Ball camp tradition of the interwar years. Brenton Heath-Kerr (1961–1995) was the great proponent of this type of dressing. His "Gingham Woman" character (1991) was inspired by 1950s fashion style and designed to be incongruous among the seminudity of a raunchy dance party. Mauve and white fabric completely encased the wearer, and the fabric extended to a matching handbag, a cigarette holder, and the silhouette of a bouffant hairdo. With a face completely shrouded by fabric, the domestic costume acquired an eerily menacing nature, the slit-like mouth and eyes found in bondage suits here transformed to homely gingham. The character directly influenced a catwalk model in one of Jean-Paul Gaultier's parades; the designer had attended the Mardi Gras party at which Heath-Kerr "performed." Heath-Kerr's other famous creation was "Kake" (1992), the "Tom of Finland" character, astonishing for its perplexing ambiguity. The emblematic leatherman

The "Gingham Woman" was designed and made by Brenton Heath-Kerr for the 1991 Sleaze Ball, held in Sydney. The costume is made of blue-and-white checked Lycra gingham and comprises a full bodysuit (including gloves and stockings) and mask with holes for the eyes, nose, and mouth, a bra top, and a miniskirt. The cut-out bouffant hairdo is also covered in gingham. Powerhouse Museum.

was here translated to a set of cut out and articulated body parts describing front and back, worn over a black body stocking. The flat face, torso, and biceps were paired with real gloves and boots, and, reminiscent of "Superman Fantasy" (1977) by the American photographer Arthur Tress, an erect penis was raised at times throughout the night. Heath-Kerr's motivation was to produce a figure who would both question and deflate that period's focus on a certain male muscular physique, which some critics maintain is a product of anxiety about the male body in the age of AIDS.

Australians are deeply ironic, and the Mardi Gras parade frequently makes reference to fashion. "There's no other whore like Daphne Jones" was the title of one participant, who wore the black-and-white hounds-tooth check in a vulgar low-cut dress and gloves, the check being the trademark of that upper-middle-class department store, satirizing their advertising slogan "There's no other store like David Jones." The idea of the provincial, anglophile, prim matron, a feature of the writing of Patrick White, is often played out in the parade, including repeated appearances by one participant who carries the sign "New Zealand." Satirizing the uniforms and national denominations seen at the Olympics, as well as referring to the antipodean tour of Queen Elizabeth II in the 1950s, "Miss New Zealand" wore a patterned 1950s shirt-waisted frock (an old-fashioned term frequently used in Australia for a dress until the 1970s), white gloves, straw hat, handbag, strand of pearls, earrings, and court shoes. The long hair on her chest and legs and stubble under carefully applied rouge betrayed the conceit, and the joke about Australian/New Zealand rivalry and provincialism was well played. Designers Jenny Kee and Linda Jackson had already reappropriated the term *frock* with a camp inflection in the 1970s.

UNDERWEAR AS OUTERWEAR

The significance of Mardi Gras for the older participants was that it removed queer sexuality from the "secret" confines of semi-legal bar and club locations and the private parties to the space of the public street. The theme "Be You in 1992" carried with it the suggestion of throwing off the shackles of a straight appearance and imposed identity. The diversity of body types, affiliations, and dress styles, as well as the mixing of gay, lesbian, queer, and transgender people, also was not customary in the commercial gay scene. The public face of Mardi Gras in a country that had been deeply prejudiced toward gay and lesbian peoples was remarkable, including its entry via the media into Australian living rooms, being first televised live by the national broadcaster the Australian Broadcasting Commission in prime time in 1995.

Photographs of the participants at the Sydney Gay and Lesbian Mardi Gras represent a small portion of the queer community, but the pictures are nonetheless telling. In the early 1980s the "clone" look dominated the men, a type of hyper-masculine and faux working-class maleness marked out by large mustaches, checked flannelette shirts suggesting the worker, and blue jeans. Leather jackets and farmer's overalls also were common. Women are a mixture of butch and femme style with either very long or very short hair. Peter Tully was artistic director of the parade from 1982 to 1986, and under his direction it took on a festive air with more visual coherence. In 1983 $6000 of Australia Council for the Arts funding was secured for the design of the parade, which showed a strong influence from traditional and contemporary art practices: New York Greenwich Village Halloween Parade,

Keith Haring, Memphis design of the 1980s, Australian vernacular, and California funk. McDiarmid made a Mexican dance of death figure with HIV-positive volunteers, an act of reclamation and visibility. Other important Mardi Gras workshop staff and designers have included Ron Smith, Doris Fish, and Philippa Playford, all of whom were conscious of the strong vaudeville tradition of Australia. The ironic appropriation and recasting of iconic Australian clothing forms began as early as 1985, when a marching group wore torn Chesty Bond singlets (Bonds sleeveless undergarments), advertised using the slogan Chesty Bond, and were often worn as exterior garments in public chiefly by the working class.

In the 1980s and 1990s gay men on the club scene and at dance parties frequently wore undergarments such as boxer shorts and exercise Lycra as outerwear, before the straight community adopted this stance. Overdeveloped musculatures were fashion items, and steroid use was common within an easily accessible black market. All-over body waxing and shaving were widespread, creating an appearance of a pneumatic "Michelin man," which Australian gay men ironically called "muscle Marys." Anabolic steroids cause the body to retain water, creating an appearance of puffiness in the skin, which matched the appearance of North American pornographic movie stars. Several Australian sleepwear companies achieved high sales in this period, and the Bonds singlet was reinvented as a garment for middle-class consumption among both men and women. Revelers at Mardi Gras parties in 2007 made direct borrowings from the notion of masquerade as well as mirroring its interest in cross-dressing and fantasy. Many more choose to wear everyday street fashions that are comfortable and easy to dance in. Gay clubbers are more likely to go to a fashionable store where there are as many straight men purchasing fashions, although gay-themed underwear and swimwear continue to be retailed.

2000 SYDNEY OLYMPICS, QUEER SPACE, AND RECONCILIATION?

Aspects of Australian queer style and Mardi Gras pervaded even the closing ceremony of the 2000 Sydney Olympics. It resembled a slightly disjointed parade, with funny floats and marching muscle boys and drag queens. Keen eyes had already noticed that many of the beautiful "women" on Australian fashion designer Peter Morrisey's (born 1962) South Pacific "Arrivals" floats in the opening ceremony had started their lives as men and were well-known Sydney transsexual entertainers. Indeed, the "Arrivals" floats, packed with boogying dancers in extraordinary costumes, resembled scenes from many nightclubs, indicating the strength of the clubbing aesthetic in contemporary visual culture. Both ceremonies, but particularly the closing, showed a marked influence of Peter Tully as artistic director of Sydney Gay and Lesbian Mardi Gras, when an optimum level of design wit and excellence pervaded the evening. The stylized industrial rig above the rockers in the opening was McDiarmid's Mardi Gras Dance-of-Death figure meets the industrial town of Newcastle. The silver hot-panted "pit chicks" who carried the false eyelashes, lavish stiletto shoes, and giant mascara for the bewigged Priscilla bus (referring to the popular 1994 film *The Adventures of Priscilla, Queen of the Desert*) in the closing ceremony were a direct reference to legendary Mardi Gras floats such as the giant hairspray can (1987) and the Imelda

Marcos shoes (1987). The forty-two marching drags sported some of the best-looking and finest fabricated drag outfits in Australian history. Pop star Kylie Minogue (born 1968) appeared in pink feathers and surrounded by cerise-suited dancing boys to deliver her rendition of ABBA's "Dancing Queen," and a camp aesthetic was beamed into lounge rooms of the world. Whereas the opening ceremony made reference to the serious icons of Australian art—Tom Roberts, Sidney Nolan, western desert indigenous art—the closing was frothy, fluffy. The parade structure apart, a camp aesthetic pervaded the piece.

The bearded Pucci-Gucci-wearing Vanessa Wagner (Tobin Saunders), one of Sydney's cleverest drags, rode the Priscilla bus, perched in the heart of its giant wig, beneath silver-clad Cindy Pastel (Ritchie Finger), on whose life story the Priscilla movie was based. Wagner was an inspired choice for the honor; not only does she host the Annual Bondi Beach drag races in hairy torso and bikini, she has run reconciliation dance parties and fair days around the inner-city, working-class suburb of Redfern, where she is very popular with Aboriginal children. She is an exemplar of different subsets of Sydney urban life working together to create a more harmonious and tolerant society, in which queer dress and strategies have played a role.

References and Further Reading

Aldrich, Robert. *Colonialism and Homosexuality*. London and New York: Routledge, 2003.

Brickell, Chris. "Parallel Worlds?: Queered Spaces and the Art of Camouflage." Online paper. Queer Space: Centres and Peripheries conference, University of Technology, Sydney, 2007. http://www.dab.uts.edu.au/conferences/queer_space/proceedings/veils_brickell.pdf.

Clarke, Marcus. *His Natural Life*. Edited by Stephen Murray-Smith. Harmondsworth, U.K.: Penguin, 1987. (This edition reprints the original serial version published in the *Australian Journal*, 1870–1872.)

Doyle, Peter. *City of Shadows: Sydney Police Photographs 1912–1948*. Sydney: Historic Houses Trust, 2005.

Gott, Ted. *Don't Leave Me This Way: Art in the Age of AIDS*. Canberra: National Gallery of Australia; Melbourne, London, and New York: Thames & Hudson, 1994.

Gray, Anne. *George W Lambert Retrospective: Heroes and Icons*. Canberra: National Gallery of Australia, 2007.

Harris, Gavin. "Heteronormativity and Its Discontents: Towards a Cultural History of Metropolitan Gender and Sexual Dissidence." Ph.D. dissertation, University of Sydney, 1999.

Hughes, Robert. *The Art of Australia*. Harmondsworth, U.K.: Penguin, 1966.

Johnson, Heather. *Roy de Maistre: The Australian Years 1894–1930*. Melbourne, Australia: Craftsman House, 1988.

Loccisano, Elio. *A Decade of the Sydney Mardi Gras*. 2nd ed. Sydney: Stampyourself, 1998.

Marr, David. *Patrick White: A Life*. Sydney: Random Century, 1991.

McNeil, Peter. "Designing Women: Gender, Sexuality and the Interior Decorator c 1890–1940." *Art History* 17, no. 4 (December 1994): 631–657.

North, Gerry. *The Night of Your Life: Sydney Gay and Lesbian Mardi Gras*. Sydney: Rural and City Media Services, 1992.

Phillips, David, and Graham Willett. *Australia's Homosexual Histories: Gay and Lesbian Perspectives V*. Sydney: Australian Centre for Lesbian and Gay Research, 2000.

Tilgals, Kirsten, ed. *Absolutely Mardi Gras: Costume and Design of the Sydney Gay and Lesbian Mardi Gras*. Sydney: Powerhouse Publishing, 1997.

Tovey, Noel. *Little Black Bastard: A Story of Survival*. Sydney: Hodder, 2004.

Wafer, Jim, Erica Southgate, and Lyndall Coan, eds. *Out in the Valley: Hunter Gay and Lesbian Histories*. Newcastle, Australia: Newcastle Regional Library, 2000.

Yang, William. *Friends of Dorothy*. Sydney: Macmillan, 1997.

Peter McNeil

See also The Australiana Phenomenon in Australia; Urban Menswear in Australia.

Popular Music and Dress in Australia

- Music and Dress: 1950s–1980s
- Punk, Politics, and Surf
- Australian Designers and Musicians as Designers
- Music and Dress from the 1990s—Revealing and Evolving
- Snapshot: Kylie Minogue

Australian pop and rock music has been inseparable from fashion since the 1950s. Australia had a popular musical culture from the first days of European settlement, but in the 1950s rock 'n' roll and pop began to dominate other musical forms. Taking shape as an industry, they were supported by and supported the arrival of television, the growing print media, and radio, which continued to be an essential social bond and cultural disseminator. Dress was increasingly the key that proved to audiences that Australian musicians were as up to date as those overseas. Australian popular music from the 1950s, as in the United Kingdom and the United States, produced iconic garments, alternating between the personal styles of musicians but also tapping into the power of fashion trends and stylists. Some Australian musicians designed for themselves or launched fashion labels. Certain designers were favored by some musicians, while styles of dress or individual garments became synonymous with a band or solo performer, and evolutions of style were characteristic of musicians with long careers.

MUSIC AND DRESS: 1950s–1980s

Australian fashion and music in the 1950s and 1960s were both perceived as inferior to their respective industries in the United Kingdom, Europe, and the United States, and Australian talent was given less coverage by the local media. Covering hits by overseas musicians provided the repertoire of the majority of Australian musicians, but the birth of rock 'n' roll, the emergence of teenagers as a category of consumer culture, and the growth of the media developed Australian audiences ready for their own music. Early 1950s radio favored U.S. musicians, and by 1956 television brought their slick suits into lounge rooms. Australian musicians including Johnny O'Keefe, Col Joye, Lynne Randell (known as "Little Miss Mod" for her fashionable dress and haircut), and Little Pattie (Patricia Amphlett) introduced local themes to this music, as they turned to local dressmakers and tailors to replicate the styles they saw U.K. and U.S. musicians wear on tour and in films. Bands favored smart suits or sports jackets with shirts and ties, with band members often dressing identically. More extroverted performers such as O'Keefe, dubbed "The Wild One," wore suits featuring vibrant colors, lamé, or fur trim. Women musicians followed fashion trends and were featured in magazines wearing designs by popular brands.

By 1958 youth and music television included *American Bandstand*, soon replaced by an Australian version and followed in 1959 by the Australian Broadcasting Commission (since 1983 known as the Australian Broadcasting Corporation or ABC) television program *Six O'Clock Rock*, hosted by O'Keefe. Radio included Top 40 hit lists, and the transistor radio made music portable, giving teenagers more independence from their parents' musical preferences.

Migration to Australia boomed in the 1950s and 1960s, and many new arrivals became stalwarts of Australian music. Some brought with them new music from the United Kingdom, and others, like the Bee Gees, had it sent over by relatives. If they could not be part of the excitement generated by the Beatles and other bands "back home," they would start their own; the Easybeats, with English, Dutch, and Scottish members, were one example. Following the Beatles tour in 1964, local musicians were even more inspired to form their own bands. The Seekers, the Twilights, Masters Apprentices, and Billy Thorpe and the Aztecs ranged across folk, pop, and rock. Their dress mixed influences from U.K. or U.S. bands with fashion available locally. In 1967 Normie Rowe was crowned King of Pop, establishing national music awards. Queen of Pop was added in 1972, although there was a Best Female Artist award from 1969, and by 1987 these were superseded by the Australian Recording Industry Association Awards (ARIAs). Kings of Pop like Rowe and Johnny Farnham, who were good-looking and dressed in the latest fashion, set a benchmark for pop stars to look as good as they sounded. Music television included the *Go! Show*, Billy Thorpe hosting *It's All Happening*, Johnny O'Keefe's *Sing Sing Sing*, and variety shows such as *In Melbourne Tonight*. The first weekly music magazine, *Go-Set*, was launched in 1966. Style inspiration now came not just from films starring U.S. musicians or the covers of imported records, but from the streets of London itself, as bands including the Seekers, the Easybeats, and the Bee Gees traveled to record in England. This pattern of travel to England and later Europe and the United States would continue to infuse Australian musicians' dress as they bought clothes while overseas and brought ideas back to Australian designers or tailors.

By the 1970s distances between capital cities of each state (Brisbane, Sydney, Melbourne, Adelaide, and Perth) resulted in distinct music scenes in each city, but the necessity of touring to make a living in a large country with a small population made musical cross-pollination inevitable. Like the British and U.S. media, Australian media used genres or styles including pop, rock, indie (independent or "alternative" music and musicians, not signed to major recording companies), punk, and New Wave to label musicians. While some musicians fell easily into these categories, many worked across styles, in both their music and dress. The alternative or indie bands emerging in the 1980s could have Top 40 chart hits, country music could cross over into pop, a rock band could write a pop song, or a singer who recorded pop could tour with a band that rocked, and terms such as *punk* and *New Wave* could confusingly be applied to the same band. While media, especially the music press such as *RAM* (*Rock Australian Magazine*), *Juke*, and the street press (free weekly entertainment newspapers published in major cities) repeatedly drew divisions between mainstream and commercial, and alternative and independent music, and how musicians in each category were supposed to dress, there was really no clear divide.

Chrissy Amphlett of the 1980s band Divinyls performing. She favored school uniforms as her stage outfits and modified the clothes provocatively to suit her wild act. Michael Ochs Archives/Getty Images.

Venues for music ranged from small pubs to large theaters, including large football and Returned Soldiers League (RSL) clubs. Andy Partridge of U.K. band XTC stated that, due to the size of some venues, the pub circuit in Australia looked as if film director Stanley Kubrick had designed it. The term *pub rock* came from this background, where audiences demanded strong performances. For many this term became interchangeable with the spirit of Australian music, but it could also be derogatory. The impact of television and video on music fashion was immense. The ABC's weekly television program *Countdown*, broadcast nationally between 1974 and 1987, was essential viewing for music fans. It included hits by overseas musicians but featured Australian music, which host Ian "Molly" Meldrum, in later years wearing his distinctive version of the brimmed "Aussie" slouch hat, supported fanatically. Color television from 1975 encouraged performers to dress spectacularly, whether their ultimate audience would be an inebriated pub crowd or thousands of screaming young girls at Festival Hall in Melbourne. Pop bands Sherbet and Skyhooks could strut their extreme glam/sci-fi styles on the sparking stage sets of *Countdown* and play to a harder audience in pubs, still dressed extravagantly.

Musicians mostly wore what was fashionable at the time, but some had garments made specifically for them. Glam and glitter, with influences from David Bowie to the New York Dolls, produced some wild extremes. Sherbet won hearts with satin jumpsuits, jackets, platform boots, and makeup. Garments, rather than being bought "off the rack," were designed and made by independent designers, tailors, or dressmakers running small businesses, sometimes friends of the band (including girlfriends and mothers). Many of these designers' names have not been documented and do not appear on the garments. However, some, such as Richard Tyler, whose designs included satin bomber jackets for Sherbet, went on to greater mainstream fame in the United States. As Sherbet matured and its teen audience decreased, it moved from stadiums to pubs and its members dressed down to casual wear.

At the peak of their popularity Sherbet was pitted by media and their followers against Skyhooks, whose dress aimed for the outrageous and combined elements of glam, including sci-fi-style makeup; theatrical additions such as giant collars, fake breasts, and hands sewn onto garments; a jester costume; and an all-white suit. Their stage props included a giant penis that expelled Twisties (a snack food), and their dress paralleled the humor of their socially incisive lyrics. In the band Hush members' Asian heritage infused their stage design and dress, with dragons mixed into the glam. From the 1970s there was substantial Asian migration to Australia, and while many bands had more mixed ancestry, moving away from early Anglo-Celtic dominance, Hush remains one of the few to display their background in their dress.

Uniformity was favored by many bands, either uniforms connected with specific occupations or all band members dressing alike. Moving on from the matched suits of the 1950s, many bands during the 1960s and 1970s practiced color or style coordination. This produced some photographs that are amusing in retrospect, including the band Fraternity all dressed in red, featuring Bon Scott before he found tight denim and AC/DC. Pictured in pink ensembles were Zoot, whose members Beeb Birtles of Little River Band and Rick Springfield subsequently had success in the United States but toned down their style. The child stars the Bee Gees wore matching waistcoats in their early performances, and years later dressed alike in white for *Saturday Night Fever*. Peter Allen shed the tame matched outfits of early duo the Allen Brothers for flamboyant shirts and a passion for sparkle.

AC/DC guitarist Angus Young has been Australia's best-known uniform exponent in his schoolboy variations, including caps. Watching his performance inspired Chrissy Amphlett of the 1980s band Divinyls to wear school uniforms. Amphlett had no role models of what a woman rock singer could be and was initially a shy performer, but wearing uniforms transformed her. She ranged from demure to dominating, seductive to scary in a series of different uniforms, trashing or tarting them up with changing accessories including stockings (sometimes torn), shirts and ties, and bold lipstick. Amphlett gave school uniforms a wickedly powerful sexuality, more darkly erotic than Britney Spears's schoolgirl costume for the video "... Baby One More Time" twenty years later. Amphlett eventually moved out of uniforms, and her dress continued to evolve through provocative, sophisticated, and powerful styles. Bon Scott of AC/DC also appeared in a girl's school uniform with makeup and wig on *Countdown*.

Singer Jeff Duff wore many uniforms but is best known for overtly theatrical dress that included body stockings, fake breasts, and makeup. Like Australian performance artist Leigh Bowery, Duff found acceptance for his wild style in the London club scene. Dismissed by some as a Bowie clone, Duff remained one of Australia's more dapper musicians. His devotion to uniforms

Australian band the Birthday Party (earlier known as the Boys Next Door), a dark postpunk band featuring Nick Cave, ca. 1980. Some of the band's customized clothing signified the do-it-yourself ethic of punk in an antifashion mode that did not copy the typical elements of British punk style. Photograph by David Corio. Michael Ochs Archives/Getty Images.

and suits is a stark contrast to his extraterrestrial and gender-play outfits. The 1980s band Big Pig had an unusual lineup of no guitars, multiple drummers and percussionists, and female and several male singers, and their dress declared their difference. Their uniform was black butcher-style aprons over black pants, arms and backs exposed, which underlined the physicality of their performances.

PUNK, POLITICS, AND SURF

Dress considered specific to musical genres varied from city to city and was distinct from the overseas styles they drew from. Punk was not the same as in the United Kingdom or United States. While Australia did experience a recession in 1974 (and again in 1982 and the early 1990s), social conditions were not identical, and what was considered punk music and dress in Brisbane was very different from that of Melbourne, and both were different again from the inner-city Sydney scene. In Brisbane the conservative government, restrictions on public gatherings and protest, and associated police brutality motivated musicians differently from the art school/dole (unemployment benefits) aesthetics that influenced music in Melbourne and Sydney. Many punk musicians were middle class, not working class, with a different complexity to their rebellion. Compared to the United Kingdom, Australian punk generally was more focused on music than dress, though elements of revolt did cross from the musical spirit into visual style.

Coupled with limited finances, the fight to look individual resulted in a mix of disheveled and distressed or highly stylized outfits made from sparse resources. Bands often customized or made their own clothes, assisted by fledgling designer music fans. Some fan-designers such as Jenny Bannister turned their talent into successful businesses, eventually crossing several decades and styles. The dress signifiers of U.K. punk, from bondage gear to spiked hair, were adopted by some Australians, but more interesting in their antifashion stance were those punk and postpunk bands such as the Saints, the Boys Next Door/the Birthday Party featuring singer/songwriter Nick Cave, Radio Birdman, and Celibate Rifles. Some of Cave's early shirts survive and evidence the do-it-yourself punk attitude embraced by creative individuals who were part of the independent music and art scenes and who produced customized garments for the band. Black shirts and the band's distinctive symbol became synonymous with Radio Birdman. Many musicians who were labeled punk in the late 1970s, when the movement flourished, and into the 1990s, when the tag was still applied to bands like the Hard-Ons, consistently denied and defied the label. It has been argued that the Saints played punk before the Sex Pistols, the definitive punk dressers; however, the Saints were not styled as the Sex Pistols were, but as with many musicians who struggled to make a living, they performed in everyday clothes. Split Enz played in the United Kingdom before punk exploded there, and though their music and look was very different from that of the plethora of bands that eventually bloomed under punk and New Wave, their costumes, wild hairstyles, and makeup saw them labeled punk in Europe.

Rock musicians often had dress rules just as stringent as those that were dictated to pop stars by the music industry and expectations of their fans. Combinations of denim or leather pants and jackets with T-shirts, shirts, or singlets (iconic Australian sleeveless vests), chosen from mass-market fashion brands through to independent designers, were standard. These were often accessorized with studs, chains, and tattoos and finished with boots from Dr. Martens or Blundstone (hard-wearing, elastic-sided boots), or the elaborate creations of Melbourne shoemaker Rocco Bufalo, which became essentials in the wardrobe of many bands, including overseas bands visiting Australia. The working-class associations of pub rock, even though audiences were often middle class, affected dress. Hunters and Collectors (1980s) was labeled a "singlet band" (the singlet has particular iconic status within Australian working-class culture), though their singer argued he wore singlets for practical reasons, the heat and sweat of performing, rather than as working-class affiliation. Jimmy Barnes (ex–Cold Chisel) continued to reference his origins in the song "Working Class Man," though he moved from jeans and T-shirts to more expensive stage clothes. The Angels' take on the rock formula had some members almost perpetually wearing sunglasses, while singer Doc Neeson mixed in suits, vests, shirts, and ties. Rose Tattoo took the tough look to its ultimate, with countless tattoos among the members, led by shaved-headed Angry Anderson, who was not as ferocious as his name and looks implied.

Many alternative or indie bands dressed from "op shops," the Opportunity Shops now gentrified as "vintage," which sold inexpensive secondhand clothes. Musicians who did not have a record company funding their wardrobe were on tight budgets, often living on unemployment benefits. Buying instruments, travel between shows, and alcohol and drugs were often higher priorities than clothes, and op shops allowed cultivation of styles musicians could not otherwise afford. Some who appeared to cultivate the op shop style, such as snappy dresser Dave Graney, who featured in a cover shoot for *Elle Australia* magazine, actually have a deep appreciation of clothes and invest substantially in their dress. Graney's Australian style heroes are diverse: 1960s model and one-time James Bond George Lazenby, progressive 1970s South Australian premier Don Dunstan, and Nick Cave. While Graney's suits tended to be loud, members of other bands such as You Am I, the Triffids, the Jackson Code, and the Blackeyed Susans were more subtle, and their choice of suits, waistcoats, and ties lent them an air of gentility even when rocking out. Joe Camilleri has been an impressive collector of hats, loved the feel of a good shirt and Italian shoes, always liked to look as good as he could, and once claimed he dressed up to do the dishes. He believed you should wear what suits you, not what is in fashion, and that the quality of a garment is more important. Nick Cave moved from his disheveled and tattered early style to having immaculate suits made, the epitome of a bad boy musician maturing gracefully.

The Go-Betweens did not adopt the clichés of rock dress. Robert Forster was partial to midriff-baring cropped tops, makeup, and the occasional dress, but it was the less flamboyant Grant McLennan who despaired of outer suburban pub bands and their audiences in the early 1980s. He declared that Australian rock was the lowest form of entertainment, and it was not the fault of the bands, but of the public who loved black T-shirts and thongs (rubber sandals). The dress of a band's audience could say much about how the band was perceived. A band may move on in musical and dress style, while its audience lags behind. Nick Cave gigs were a prime example, with people in the audience dressed in punk or postpunk style years after Cave had moved on from early the Boys Next Door and Birthday Party to his Bad Seeds style. This was especially ironic as punk was about change and against institutionalizing anything, which included dress. The Hard-Ons, a band with punk attitude that refused to fit the cliché look, believed even punk, with its negation of previous musical styles and dress, eventually became authoritarian. Photographs of crowds in pub venues and at music festivals from Ourimbah (New South Wales central coast, 1970) and Sunbury (Victoria, 1972–1975) to The Big Day Out (originated Sydney, 1992; from 1993 gradually extending to tour other Australian capital cities and New Zealand, continuing in 2009) are evidence of the changes in fashion worn by Australian music followers. This could range from flared pants and long hair to the suburban sharpies or "sharps" subculture in the early 1970s with their confrontational style, including tight pants, tight knitted cardigans, and hair cropped short on top and long at the back.

Midnight Oil's stage wear was sometimes as heavy on sociopolitical content as its lyrics. They co-opted the Aboriginal flag and wore slogan T-shirts far more pointed than those worn by Frankie Goes to Hollywood or Wham! For the closing ceremony of the 2000 Olympic Games in Sydney, the Oils performed in black clothes printed with the word SORRY in white, showing they opposed the government's refusal to apologize to indigenous people for the persecution of past decades, particularly the trauma of the "stolen generation" of children forcibly removed from their parents and fostered into nonindigenous families. Drummer Rob Hirst also provides an example of customization; a vest he bought at a disposal store and, in his words, "bastardized" by dyeing, cutting, and stitching is now in the Powerhouse Museum collection in Sydney.

Surf culture is essential to the island continent. Surfing featured in music and lyrics from the Atlantics, Deltones, and Little Pattie, through Tamun Shud, to Midnight Oil and Mental As Anything. The Australian heat meant beachwear of singlets, T-shirts, and shorts was often the most practical stage dress, and some musicians were actually devoted surfers. Country music and dress style crossed into pop but also tinged punk in bands Sacred Cowboys and the Johnnys. The Models emerged from punk and New Wave and into mainstream pop, but on one tour became the Clampetts, acting as support band to themselves by dressing country-and-western style and using American accents. Most audiences were oblivious that the two bands were the same people.

AUSTRALIAN DESIGNERS AND MUSICIANS AS DESIGNERS

If a musician becomes successful, his or her record company may fund clothing or designers offer them items, so bands who once wore everyday clothing on stage have sometimes started to look like style leaders. INXS was a prime example, with Michael Hutchence dressed by designers such as Morrissey Edmiston (Peter Morrissey and Leona Edmiston). Other Australian designers who became linked with specific musicians for part of

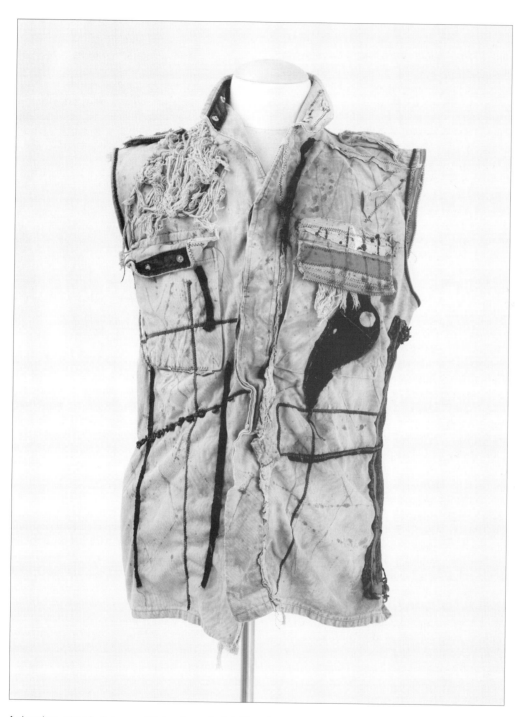

A sleeveless cotton jacket as modified and worn by Rob Hirst, drummer for Australian rock band Midnight Oil, in the late 1970s. Purchased at Chatswood disposal store, it was then dyed an irregular light blue shade from the original khaki, and the sleeves were cut off at the shoulders. The jacket is decorated with many patches of multicolored material, with loose threads and fraying all over. Gift of Rob Hirst. Powerhouse Museum.

their careers or were celebrated for designing specific outfits worn by musicians included Linda Jackson and singer Marcia Hines, Martin Grant and Kate Ceberano, and Katie Pye, who dressed Pseudo Echo and Real Life. Some designers had international success. Richard Tyler, who dressed the Masters Apprentices, Skyhooks, and Sherbet, moved to the United States and designed for Rod Stewart before establishing his own label and designing for several other brands. Fleur Thiemeyer also began designing costumes for Australian musicians and moved to the United States, where musicians she designed for included Olivia Newton-John, Ozzy Osbourne, Rod Stewart, and Pat Benatar.

Some musicians designed for themselves and their bands. Noel Crombie, percussionist and drummer of Split Enz, was largely responsible for development of their style. The Split Enz Collection in the Performing Arts Collection, Melbourne, includes sets of stage wear from 1974 to 1984. Crombie's inspirations included visual artists and fabrics. The garments feature exaggerated shapes, oversized buttons, appliqué, ultra-violet fabrics, and hand-painting, and each set has a theme and name, such as "New Clownz," "Dizrythmia," and "The UV's." The collection includes garment sketches and photographs of Split Enz, which show the process of image creation from design to realization as garments, to presentation on stage or video, album cover, or promotional photograph. Their makeup and hairstyling was as colorful and groundbreaking as the clothes, the whole ensemble designed to be viewed at a distance in large venues as part of elaborate shows. The vibrant splicing of colors show possible connections to the clothing designs of the Futurists, particularly Giacomo Balla.

One musician dressing an entire band as Crombie did is unusual, but there are many examples of musicians customizing their own clothes. The Powerhouse Museum holds a jacket elaborately modified by Reg Mombassa (real name Chris O'Doherty), a member of the band Mental As Anything and known for his art featured on clothes by the brand Mambo (aimed at the youth market, Mambo combined elements of urban and surf culture and was initially known for its use of bold graphics, often with a surreal or black humor). Mombassa created the jacket for his other band Dog Trumpet's early 1990s video "I'm So Handsome," and the garment parallels the humor of the song. A Mansworld brand jacket was painted and appliquéd items were added, from an empty shampoo bottle to a mirror, some attached with tape, others held by the paint. Large cardboard cones protruding from the jacket allude to the Jean-Paul Gaultier cone bra worn by Madonna. Many of Mombassa's outfits had a retro sensibility and intentionally tacky or brash clashes of color or shine.

Many lesser known musicians excelled at distinctive dress. Susie Beauchamp and Goose (Stephen Gray) of Box The Jesuit (1980s) mixed elements of rock, goth, glam, and children's dress-up boxes. Goose was fearless in his embrace of trashy dressing, in the band or in the Stark Raving Elvis Show, an annual tribute event featuring inner-city Sydney bands. TISM (This Is Serious Mum, 1980s on) members never reveal their identities or show their faces but create different masked guises that are as humorous as their lyrics. Mother Goose (1980s) initially dressed to resemble nursery characters, including a sailor-suited child and a bumblebee, but lost impact when they gave these up for everyday clothes.

Jimmy and the Boys (1970s–1980s) included elements of leather and bondage wear beyond standard borrowings of punk. Keyboard player "Joylene Hairmouth" preferred twisted drag with headwear inspired by Carmen Miranda and appeared in one video in a female nurse's uniform. Singer Ignatius Jones later

A wool jacket with black lining customized from a manufactured men's suit by Reg Mombassa for the 1991 video for Australian band Dog Trumpet's single "I'm So Handsome." He decorated it with enamel paints and glitter and attached items discovered at an "industrial recycling place," like the protruding cardboard cones and the small mirror. Jacket originally tailored by Samuel Edwards at Mansworld. Modifications designed in Sydney by Reg Mombassa. Gift of Reg Mombassa. Powerhouse Museum.

adopted a more elegant style for his swing-influenced band, Pardon Me Boys, in keeping with his collection of 1940s ties. Jones subsequently became a major event director, responsible for Sydney's Millennium Celebrations and the closing ceremonies of the Sydney Olympics. Traces of his time in Jimmy and the Boys and as editor of Australian *Stiletto* style magazine are evident in his inclusion of local fashion and music icons in his event work.

By the 1990s it became common internationally for musicians to model for designers in advertising campaigns, do catwalk modeling, or to have their own fashion labels. Australian musicians had a track record of advertising fashion brands, having their clothes provided by fashion businesses, and even having their own labels. A leaping Johnny O'Keefe added action to a 1961 *Vogue Australia* photograph. After 1970s band Zoot folded, two of its members were persuaded to form another band, which was named Frieze, as it was sponsored by suit manufacturer Frieze Brothers. Eurogliders (1980s) was sponsored by denim brand Fabergé, though singer Grace Knight took a sewing machine on tour with her and enthused about making her own stage clothes. Many musicians modeled. Before her musical success Deborah Conway's (1980s band Do Re Mi and subsequent solo career) modeling assignments ranged from Linda Jackson's art clothes to the cover of a knitting pattern book, and Nfamas, of 1200 Techniques (1990s), had parallel careers as a model and musician. Kate Ceberano (1980s on) advertised RayBan, and Michael Hutchence of INXS modeled for Romeo Gigli. Kylie Minogue paraded on the catwalk for Antonio Berardi early in his career, did fashion shoots with Karl Lagerfeld for *Vogue Australia*, modeled her own Love Kylie lingerie range, and starred in an Agent Provocateur advertisement astride a mechanical bull. Since 2000 Delta Goodrem has launched a signature lingerie label, and the Veronicas, singing sisters Jess and Lisa Origliasso, designed clothing for department store Target. Rose Tattoo singer Angry Anderson became the "face" of Blundstone boots (well-known Australian footwear), with a workingman's singlet showing off his tattooed arms, capturing the brand's tough aesthetic.

From the 1960s the House of Merivale boutiques imported new music to play in the store and promoted the newest styles popular overseas, and many musicians shopped there. This was the first Australian example of selling fashion with a strongly music-influenced aesthetic, later seen in labels such as Morrissey Edmiston, Wheels & Doll Baby, and Lover. In 1983 Olivia Newton-John and friend Pat Farrar opened the Koala Blue store in the United States, stocking labels such as Prue Acton, Linda Jackson, Jenny Kee, Stuart Membery, and Katie Pye. The store became a fashion chain, since closed. By the 1990s the mutual theatrics of fashion and music were demonstrated by Marcia Hines, Christine Anu, and other musicians appearing as dual entertainment and fashion exemplars in parades from designers such as Peter Morrissey and the department store David Jones.

The music-fashion crossover constantly influenced Australian magazines, with photo shoots featuring movements such as punk made palatable for the mainstream market and features on achieving the style of individual musicians. *Vogue Australia*, *Harper's Bazaar Australia*, and *Elle Australia* featured mainstream designers and musicians. *Rolling Stone Australia* ran fashion shoots featuring musicians at festivals and pages on musicians' dress. Other Australian magazines including *POL*, *Rag Times*, and *Stiletto* (Australia) presented more subculture style and alternative designers, mixed in with music and arts. The designers supported by those magazines were often the same people involved in collectives such as the Melbourne-based Fashion Design Council, which in the 1980s staged parade events that included new, edgy designers and involved stylists, makeup and hair artists, musicians, and others in ways that fed ideas back and forth between these creative areas. Many of the designers working in these events were also dressing and styling musicians, as the video clip became the predominant promotional tool, and fashion and music in the London club scene and documented in U.K. magazines such as *i-D* and *The Face* were devoured by Australian fashion followers and adapted by fashion leaders, including musicians.

While fashion magazines and overseas musicians continue to provide inspiration, some possible connections can also be traced between dress of earlier Australian entertainers and post-1950s musicians. While Kylie Minogue's "Showgirl" costumes could mimic showgirls from anywhere, they echo the elaborate, feathered costumes of dancers in Australian Tivoli musical productions. A local precursor for Minogue's skimpy gold hot pants dates to the 1920s when all-female band Lynette and Her Redheads (billed as the Seven Sirens of Syncopation) wore brief gold lamé outfits, with net skirts added for modesty, as their costumes were considered too daring by management at some venues.

Musicians' dress is often at the extreme of fashion, but some did influence the average Australian. Olivia Newton-John's

For her 1981 "Physical" music video, Olivia Newton-John poses next to a weight machine in a gym wearing a white leotard, a blue shirt tied at the waist, and a white sweatband. Unimedia/Getty Images.

transformation in *Grease* and her video "Physical" helped sell leggings and the trend of athletic clothing, and after Kylie Minogue wore a new trend such as cargo pants, designers reported substantial rises in sales.

MUSIC AND DRESS FROM THE 1990s—REVEALING AND EVOLVING

Some dress choices reflected social practices specific to a time. Many conservative or negative attitudes have changed, but some continue in Australian society and in turn influence music and dress. These include attitudes toward women musicians, from within their own bands, from the broader industry, and from audiences, and attitudes toward indigenous musicians. As recently as the mid-1980s bands such as Gondwanaland, No Fixed Address, and The Warumpi Band were seen by some journalists as introducing nonindigenous Australia to the music of what some considered foreign lands, that is, the Australian Outback, the Red Centre (Central Australia), and the Far North. The didgeridoo (an indigenous wind instrument made from tree limbs or trunks) was viewed as an instrument only familiar to most from Aboriginal corroborees (gatherings that included music and dance).

Fortunately, general knowledge of Australia's indigenous culture is slowly improving, thanks in part to musicians such as Yothu Yindi, Kev Carmody, Archie Roach, and the Pigram Brothers. Few indigenous musicians wear their own culture's dress, but many proudly wear the Aboriginal flag or its colors, red, yellow, and black, on a badge or T-shirt, or even in the paint work of a guitar (Yothu Yindi). Some sidestepped expressing any cultural affinity through dress to follow everyday fashion trends. While women not of Anglo or European descent rarely feature on Australian fashion magazine covers, despite the diversity of races in the population, Torres Strait Islander musician Christine Anu graced the cover of *Vogue Australia*, appearing as much a fashionable commodity as regular cover models Kylie Minogue or Delta Goodrem.

From the 1990s "slutwear," or revealing dress worn by female musicians, and adopted by many nonmusicians, has been a media issue. Australian women musicians have walked a fine line between confident expression of their femaleness and dealing with the reality of pub audience challenges to "show us your tits," when what they really want to display is musical talent. Musicians including Renee Geyer, Marcia Hines, Kate Ceberano, Deborah Conway, Jenny Morris, Wendy Matthews, Missy Higgins, Lisa Gerrard of Dead Can Dance, Sarah McLeod of Superjesus, and Katie Noonan have used fashion to their advantage without resorting to exploitative styling. Some have taken the flash-more-flesh way, from late 1980s singer Colette, who owned dozens of tight bike shorts and crop tops, to Holly Valance, who gave the impression of being naked in the video "Kiss Kiss." Some musicians in the 1970s had dressed as revealingly as those thirty years later, and while the media focused on women undressing, male

musicians led the way. In the 1970s Sherbet posed wearing a few bubbles, and Buffalo members were photographed cavorting in underpants, with one member pantless and full frontal. In the 1990s Ron Peno of Died Pretty stripped off for *Rolling Stone Australia* magazine, as did Angie Hart of Frente for *Juice* (Australia) magazine, and Deborah Conway wore only chocolate and cakes for her *Bitch Epic* album cover.

Musicians have been pressured by record companies, management, and the press to dress or look a certain way, including demands to have their teeth fixed or lose weight. While the music industry does not like to admit it, these pressures resulted in some musicians developing diet pill and other addictions and disordered eating. General pressures of the musician's life may add to body image problems, including touring, which is not always favorable to eating healthily and encourages drinking and use of other recreational substances. One of the few to talk openly about this was Daniel Johns of Silverchair, who in 1999 revealed his struggle with anorexia in an interview with *Rolling Stone Australia* and in the song "Ana's Song—Open Fire." The pressures to dress a certain way and to disguise aging are yet to be researched, but with many musicians now in their third decade under public scrutiny, perhaps there will be more revealed about this aspect of music fashion in the future.

Australian music fashion is not simply Michael Hutchence and Jenny Morris performing together in a Driza-Bone coat (oilskin coat iconic of Australian outback style) and Akubra hat (rabbit-fur felt slouch hat), Kylie Minogue in an Australian flag jacket, or other symbolic garments. Often it is about embracing many distinct styles and transformation throughout their careers,

"Showgirl" costume, worn by Kylie Minogue at the closing ceremony of the Sydney 2000 Olympic Games. The costume comprises an elaborate feathered headdress and a pink, beaded body corset in a showgirl style. The body corset is made in hot pink shot silk and features a halter neck and boned bodice with beaded tassels across the hip line. Imitation crystals are attached to the neckline, bodice, and pant section. The elaborate headdress consists of a tiara supporting three pink ostrich feathers above the crown. The front of the tiara includes fifteen prongs extending upward in a lyrebird design and three prongs curving downward along either side of the jawline. Designed by Michael Wilkinson. Made by Julie Bryant of the Costume Ceremonies Workshop. Part of the Sydney 2000 Games Collection. Gift of the New South Wales government. Powerhouse Museum.

with musicians evolving, like Olivia Newton-John's character in *Grease*, from naïve to show-stopping, or in reverse as they go from newly famous to established artist, or youth to maturity. Musicians with long careers are like anyone susceptible to changes in their dress style. While Ol' 55 and Dynamic Hepnotics referenced the style of previous decades throughout their careers, Hoodoo Gurus dressed with a 1960s psychedelic influence that matched only some of their music. The group the Church has continued to be labeled a psychedelic band due partly to paisley shirts they wore in their early days and featured on the *Heyday* album cover, despite their music and dress styles moving on. When first successful, Silverchair were teenagers in jeans and T-shirts and labeled grunge by some. Ten years later they were men, and their style had matured to include tailor-made garments flashy enough for stadium performances, such as Daniel John's mirrored suit.

Some musicians' styles change not through influence of fashion trends, age, or personal taste. Illness caused dramatic style changes under public scrutiny for Kylie Minogue and Delta Goodrem. Minogue favored scarves and then revealed a new short hairstyle, but she had already worn short hair and wigs previously in her career. Goodrem appeared in a fashion magazine without hair and explained she had seen long hair as an inextricable part of her but had to evolve her style dramatically due to illness. She subsequently grew her hair long again.

The Internet is expanding sources for viewing dress, as YouTube, and record company, band, and fan Web sites resurrect bands through their videos and in performances on television music shows that predate MTV, such as *GTK*, *Sounds*, *Countdown*, *Nightmoves*, *Rock Arena*, and *Rage*. They enable closer examination of what musicians wore and of Australian fashion generally. While stylists became omnipresent by the 1990s and many musicians increasingly lost their edge of individuality, in the twenty-first century the Internet's ability to inexpensively expose new musicians has seen more distinctively dressed musicians become popular, such as Jet, Wolfmother, and the Sleepy Jackson. Combined with a flourishing of fashion designers and labels that have more potential to internationally publicize and export their designs than did designers previously, the future may see Australian music dress reach a larger audience than ever before.

The bands and musicians mentioned are a small sample of Australian popular music, and it is not possible here to include all the garments, designers, and stylists that have assisted musicians in creating their dress, or detailed information on genres, such as country or hip-hop, that crossed over into popular music. Information about Australian musicians is accessible in many forms; however, specific information about their dress is scattered across books, newspapers, and magazines, including a thriving music press, archival television footage and video, albums, singles, and video covers, and archives of record companies and photographers. Many garments disappeared with the bands and musicians that wore them. Even so, Australian museums and archives have in their collections many artifacts from pop culture. The Performing Arts collection, Melbourne, is home to the extensive Kylie Minogue and Split Enz collections and artifacts from AC/DC, Nick Cave, Divinyls, Peter Allen, and other musicians, including garments, accessories, costume sketches, photographs, and publicity materials. The collection of the Powerhouse Museum, Sydney, includes costumes worn by Mental As Anything, the Divinyls, Hush, Sherbet, Midnight Oil, Jenny Morris, William Shakespeare, Olivia Newton-John, and Johnny O'Keefe, and garments made to promote a band or merchandise to its fans, such as a "Know Your Product" T-shirt from the Saints.

Snapshot: Kylie Minogue

Perhaps one of the Australian performers and musicians best known for their dress is Kylie Minogue. Though her ability as a musician has been debated by the media, especially in her early career, her skills as an entertainer have maintained her popularity since the 1980s. Minogue is Australia's outstanding example of a performer who understands how to create a perception of evolution in her music through the power of dress, using it to magnify shifts in her musical styles, such as her change from pop ingenue to sexy siren to independent artist and back to pop princess. She is also a highly successful businesswoman.

Assisted by teams of creative designers and dressers, Minogue has created some of pop's top style moments, beyond the notorious gold hot pants featured in the video "Spinning Around" (2000). William Baker, Minogue's long-time creative director, studied theology and sees parallels in religion and pop: the power of the image and icon, and the constructed ability to inspire devotion from their followers. Baker was intensely aware of the identity changes achieved through dress by Madonna, Boy George, and their predecessors such as David Bowie. Minogue has been compared to Madonna for her ability to dramatically change style and has even been accused of being a copyist, but in some instances she has been ahead of Madonna, for example, she was the first of the two to wear a kimono in a video.

Minogue similarly collaborates in the manipulation of her image, with the evolution of her looks assisted by stylists, clothing designers, makeup artists, hairdressers, video directors, photographers, and others involved in the music industry processes. Dolce & Gabbana, Julien Macdonald, and Karl Lagerfeld for Chanel have been among her favorite designers for stage and video performance, as well as red carpet appearances and on tour. Other designers Minogue has worn include the late Alexander McQueen, John Galliano, Roland Mouret, Antonio Berardi, Jean-Paul Gaultier, Viktor and Rolf, Nicolas Ghesquière for Balenciaga, Julien Macdonald, Azzedine Alaïa, Stevie Stewart and Sandy Gordon, Stella McCartney for Chloé, and Helmut Lang. Minogue also brought attention to designers such as U.K.-based Fee Doran of Mrs Jones, responsible for the revealing white hooded jumpsuit in the video "Can't Get You Out of My Head" (2001), and Owen Gaster. For shoes and accessories she has also mixed internationally established names including Manolo Blahnik, Stephen Jones, Jimmy Choo, Vivienne Westwood, Judy Blame (aka Chris Barnes), and lesser-known designers such as Johnny Rocket.

Australian designers who have dressed Minogue include mainstream designers such as Morrissey and Edmiston, Collette Dinnigan, Jenny Bannister, Ian McMaugh, Mark Burnett of Princess Highway, Stephen Galloway, Michael Wilkinson, Xen Pardoe Miles, Gursel and Jean Ali, and stylist/designer Nicole Bonython, with accessories by Dinosaur Designs, Philip Rhodes, and Kevin Murphy.

For much of her career Minogue has been based between London and Paris and has been able to draw on the cream of designers and stylists, but she has stated that while part of her craves more and more glamour, another part wants to be in Australia, in Birkenstocks, getting dirty and smelling the eucalyptus trees. She confirmed her Australian connection by donating a major collection of costumes to the Performing Arts Collection, Melbourne. The Kylie Minogue Collection includes garments, shoes, and accessories worn on stage in tours and one-off events, for videos and photo shoots, and for red carpet appearances. Signs of wear on some garments remind the viewer of the demands on dress in performance, while more elaborate garments give an appreciation of the impracticalities and discomforts of a musician's dress experience. She is one of the few performers whose dress has been the subject of a major solo exhibition, Kylie—The Exhibition, shown in 2006–2007 in Australia and at the Victoria and Albert Museum in London, Manchester Art Gallery, and Kelvingrove Art Gallery and Museum in Glasgow.

References and Further Reading

Amplett, Chrissy, and Larry Writer. *Pleasure and Pain: My Life.* Sydney: Hodder Australia, 2005.

Baker, William, Janine Barrand, Kylie Minogue, and Frank Strachan. *Kylie: An Exhibition.* Melbourne, Australia: Victorian Arts Centre Trust, 2005.

Baker, William, and Kylie Minogue. *Kylie: La La La.* London: Hodder & Stoughton, 2002.

Breen, Marcus, ed. *Missing in Action—Australian Popular Music in Perspective.* Vol. 1. Melbourne, Australia: Verbal Graphics, 1987.

Carroll, Chrystene, Bob King, Tony Mott, Wendy McDougall, and Adrienne Overall. *Crows Nest (Australia): Still Noise.* Sydney: ABC Enterprises, 1991.

Cox, Peter. *Spinning Around: The Festival Records Story.* Sydney: Powerhouse Publishing, 2001.

Dreyfus, Kay. *Sweethearts of Rhythm.* Sydney: Currency Press, 1999.

Go-Set. Various editors. Melbourne, Australia: Various publishers, 1966–1974.

Hayward, Philip, ed. *From Pop to Punk to Postmodernism: Popular Music and Australian Culture from the 1960s to the 1990s.* Sydney: Allen & Unwin, 1992.

Joel, Alexandra. *Best Dressed: 200 Years of Fashion in Australia.* Sydney: William Collins, 1984.

Juke. Various editors. Melbourne, Australia: Various publishers, 1975–1994.

McFarlane, Ian. *Encyclopedia of Australian Rock and Pop.* St. Leonards, Australia: Allen & Unwin, 1999.

McGrath, Noel. *Australian Encyclopedia of Rock.* Collingwood, Australia: Outback Press, 1978.

Nimmervoll, Ed. *Friday on My Mind: A Year-by-Year Account of Popular Music in the Australian Charts.* Rowville, Australia: The Five Mile Press, 2004.

Performing Arts Collection. The Arts Centre, Melbourne. This is an online resource listing the collection's holdings including costume and performance dress. http://www.theartscentre.com.au/discover/collections-and-research/performing-arts-collection-directory.aspx.

RAM (Rock Australia Magazine). Various editors. Sydney: Various publishers, 1975–1989.

Rolling Stone Australia. Various editors. Sydney: ACP Magazines, Ltd., 1967–.

Stafford, Andrew. *Pig City: From the Saints to Savage Garden.* St. Lucia, Australia: University of Queensland Press, 2004.

Warner, Dave. *Countdown: The Wonder Years 1974–87.* Sydney: ABC Books, 2006.

Sue Ryan

See also Independent Australian Fashion; Subcultural and Alternative Dress in Australia.

Children's Wear in Australia

- Early Twentieth Century
- Post–World War I Styles
- World War II and After
- Brands

A comprehensive account of the history of children's wear in Australia has never been published. Even so, by using Sydney department store mail-order catalogs—it is likely similar catalogs were issued by department stores in other Australian cities—and clothing advertisements from the late nineteenth to the early twenty-first century, we are able to get a sense of the kind of dress available for Australian children. These sources must be used with discretion, for they were aimed primarily at middle-class families of relatively high disposable income. Due to the lack of more precise information, it is not possible to determine how many children wore the styles advertised, or exactly who adopted the modes of fashion on offer, so the precise demographic covered by the catalogs is hard to determine. Clearly, mail-order catalogs serviced both urban and country dwellers, although it is assumed that urban customers were more likely to shop in the stores themselves than regional customers. Children might come from a wealthy "squatter" landowning background in a rural area and occasionally visit town, but their parents probably relied mainly on mail ordering. Country children were as likely to

wear urban fashions on formal occasions as city dwellers. Trucks literally took the large, distinctive red-bound catalogs of Anthony Hordern, Universal Providers, into the countryside by the ton.

Catalogs show how children's dress and fashion trends were to an extent unique to Australia, even if strongly linked to those of American or English children. The social climate of Australia differed from that of North America and Britain, for everyday life was often more informal, especially on pastoral stations. Since few families in Australia had servants, much was expected of housewives in terms of domestic chores such as laundry work, encouraging them to acquire simpler clothes. Access to the seaside and beachside living affected the clothing of children as well as adults. The Australian climate made for more practical, loose-fitting styles, and the wearing of sensible hats to guard against the sun. Yet catalogs tell us only one side of the story of children's dress. If we look at photographs, literary descriptions, and paintings, we get a broader range of information. And catalogs tell us nothing of the life of the poor, especially during the Great Depression of the late 1920s. Catalogs were primarily targeted at the socially conscious middle classes, but clothes advertised may not have been worn as illustrated, and it is unlikely the children of poorer working families could afford them. However, second-hand clothing was readily available, and many mothers were of necessity capable seamstresses. One suspects that many children wore such adjusted clothing.

Defining what is meant by a child is difficult. The following general definitions have been arrived at by using terms and sizes from catalogs of the time, international texts, the childhood

Two children at a tea party, early twentieth century. The boy wears a thick jumper and short trousers, and the girl wears a long white dress, typical of the European style of children's wear worn in Australia at this time. Photographer unknown. Tyrell Collection. Powerhouse Museum.

activities for which certain styles are generally intended (such as playing or more formal occasions), and assumptions from modern definitions of the terms. Those aged 0–2 are termed infants; those 2–6 toddlers (certainly a problematic term from the viewpoint of the twenty-first century); those 7–12 as older boys and older girls; and 12–16 as juveniles or teenagers. The term *teenager* came to have special meaning in the 1960s and needs to be defined here as one given to older juveniles, having turned 16, who broke away from emulating their parents and formed a singular social identity. Teenagers are thus socially awakening young people, being still under the guardianship of their parents as primary clothing purchasers, but asserting themselves and gravitating toward fashion trends suggested by magazines and overseas streetwear. Many, what one might consider unfamiliar, terms for children's clothing are used in the catalogs. Like modern-day advertisements, it is unclear if these terms had general currency, so they are not all defined in the glossary.

EARLY TWENTIETH CENTURY

It appears that children's wear in Australia, and indeed all over the world, at the start of the twentieth century was very much a sign of how adults viewed the place of children in society. Then, as in the previous century, adults expected children to dress in ways reflecting their own behavioral and societal values. Store catalogs from the turn of the century assumed that English tastes would appeal to Australians acquiring children's styles, and that the mother of the household was the primary purchaser of the children's clothing. Types of girls' wear for sale suggest that older girls were expected to emulate the styles worn by their mothers, other than when playing. For playtime activities children of both sexes were encouraged to wear practical outfits.

Catalogs offered older boys formal styles advertised as sac suits: boxy single-buttoned jackets with small lapels and tapered trousers in navy blue serge, a twill fabric that has diagonal lines or ridges made up with a two-up, two-down weave. The sac suit was worn high to the collar with shirt and tie, which, when accompanied by a small bowler hat and matching walking cane, gave the boy the appearance of a small adult. A coat style known as a Chesterfield, with cape and black, diagonal worsted Italian cloth lining, was suggested for older boys as well as Scarborough cloaks in tweed or cashmere, sometimes waterproof but always in dark colors. For younger and older boys there were reefers, pea coat–styled short jackets of blue serge or fancy nap cloth in gray or brown, double-breasted with gilt anchor buttons. Short, knee-length knickerbockers (baggy knee-trousers) were available, with a three-buttoned detail running down the thighs. Such clothing was intended to be worn while visiting or receiving visitors on semiformal to formal occasions, especially for the socially aware urbanite. Boys in regional areas and outback stations, particularly (but not only) the less affluent, would probably most often be seen in short pants and old shirts, probably discarded ones of their fathers cut down by their mothers.

For older boys there were garments emulating adult uniforms, such as the naval suit, which came in a variety of styles called the Maritime, the Man-o'-War, and the Commodore. Such suits were mostly accompanied with flannel or drill (coarse fabric) bib lanyards, a twisted fabric that was placed around the neck like a baby's bib, complete with a whistle, sailor collar, and cuffs to match. The suits themselves were of white drill or navy blue, sky twill or white pique (a cotton with raised parallel cords or ribbing). Alternatively, should the older boy be busily playing with his hoop and stick down the street, he might be attired in a jacket suit, a version of the sac suit with short knickerbockers and bow tie, or a similarly styled Devon suit, made from pleated tweed or blue serge (a worsted fabric). For younger boys the so-called American blouse suit had a large, squared Peter Pan collar with buttons down the front and a rope with tassels that tied around the collar. The similar Norfolk suit was pleated at the back in fancy tweed, neat checks, or stripes, with a belt and shirt collar and knickerbockers. The Harrow suit, introduced around 1910, consisted of a coat, vest, and knickerbockers, worn with underwear and long socks for summer. For older boys too, catalogs recommended an English-styled Eton or dinner suit for the evening, complete with top hat and cane to resemble their fathers, whereas smaller boys were restricted to the washing suit sailor style with a straw boater hat and fly fronts. Younger boys were "prettily" dressed in styles called Albany, Stanley, or "Little Nipper"— double-breasted, fancy jackets in dark brown or navy, featuring gilt buttons and accompanying knickerbockers. Of course such styles taken from catalogs were not necessarily worn as intended. Many children had only one "best" outfit, and the poor may have had just one outfit of any sort, often secondhand. Mothers also repaired and altered outfits to suit their own personal preferences and to add their own sense of individual style.

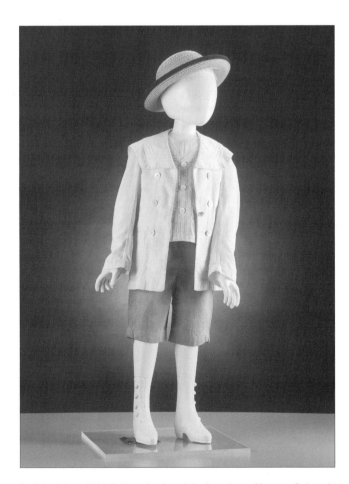

Boy's jacket, ca.1900, in the collection of the Powerhouse Museum, Sydney. At this time Australian boys were dressed in clothes that were miniature versions of adult styles. Powerhouse Museum.

In the pre–World War I years young girls wore clothes similar to their mothers, such as a cream or beige calico or muslin smock for sleeping, gathered at the neck. English and American styles appeared to dominate girls' day-wear, and the younger girl could skip rope or play with her Indian rubber dolls in a variety of colorful dresses. Button details varied from single-breasted down the front or side, twin rows, or zigzagged across the body. Pleats were also fashionable for both younger and older girls, who wore their smocks and skirts in cream or navy serge, perhaps with sateen bodices in the same colors, or even Japanese silk blouses. They also wore plain outfits featuring a lightweight striped "zephyr" fabric. Day-wear styles could be worn with a bonnet. Dainty black beaver coats and tunics in winter seem to have originated from the early 1900s American style of low-waisted fashion, and they came in brown tweed or black satin to wear with white socks and buckled shoes.

Infant girls were dressed in smocked voile frocks, which featured pin-tucked skirts and yokes, and sleeves smocked at the wrist. More so than their older brothers and sisters, who resembled little men and women, they were made to look like Victorian dolls, no doubt for more formal occasions, with crocheted outfits threaded with satin ribbon and features of bows and lace. Mark Foys Ltd. and Anthony Horden and Sons Ltd., in Sydney, boasted in their catalogs (early 1900s) of hand-knitted cream wool jackets and pilchers (cotton diapers) as well as three-quarter-length cream wool carrying coats in extra fine Shetland wool. Carrying coats were designed as going-out coats, in which mothers carried their babies. Once again, serge tunics appeared to be popular then, as well as bonnets, such as those used for christenings, made of silk and fastened by a great bow under the chin, or the hand-knitted silk bonnet style, which had two rows of ribboned cord. The carrying outfits themselves were always made longer than the infant. Nightwear included soft white flannelette gowns with collar or square neck, or a fine linen mitered collar. Lace, which featured on the most expensive babywear, included imitation Cluny-brand insertions patterned with five-petaled flowers. In addition, clothing could feature imitation or mercerized Torchon or Maltese lace, finer and more exquisitely detailed.

POST–WORLD WAR I STYLES

In the years during and immediately after World War I (known then as the Great War), children's wear continued to be largely reflective of adult styles. It was only for playing that styles were practical and child-friendly. The romper suit is an example, which for either sex came in plain and striped blue material or plain white and was gathered above or at the knee with a patterned detail on the front. Advertised for boys were striped Galatea (strong cotton) tunics in the style of the Roman tunics of the late 1800s, or suits in tussore silk, while girls had daisy-embroidered muslin frocks featuring big bows. At this stage, poplin, a ribbed fabric of silk, rayon, wool, or cotton, was widely used, commonly styled as tiny kimonos for infants and girl toddlers, and up to the early twenty-first century these have survived as part of staple Australian newborn and infant wear. Like their mothers, girls started appearing in clothing that had lace detail fronts, not as elaborate as Edelweiss, Guipure, or Parisian lace designs, but with worked details, in Swiss muslin or Japanese silk.

In the wartime summer of 1916 and 1917, styles for boys were advertised for "thrifty mothers." Pajama suits for boys came in flannelette or Japanese crepe, and undershirts were made either of strong cotton, pure wool, or a mixture of the two, "like father's." Woven underwear for both sexes of infant age included cream wool pilchers much as before, flannel or flannelette gowns, knitted cream wool or silk bootees, and infant's waterproof pilchers. In catalogs of the early 1920s romper suits looked like small boiler suits, with long sleeves, a yoked bodice, short knickerbocker legs, and an opening at the seat. On formal occasions babies could also wear muslin bibs, trimmed with lace and embroidered designs, when held tightly by their mothers on Turkish toweling squares like carrying blankets. Girls wore calico knickers, underclothing with trimmed edges, and bear suits for bedtime, fleeced at the back for breathability and comfort.

The 1920s, with a more sophisticated consumer culture in place, saw a greater variety of styles. Many garments seemed to depart from adult fashion, thus recognizing the active lifestyle of children. Yet interestingly, in the mid-1920s the low-waisted, knee-length dress of adult women echoed something of the styles of the young girl, though often made from different fabrics. Older and younger boys wore clothing of water-resistant materials such as the scout suit, buttoned to the neck, featuring twin patch pockets and belted knickerbockers, ideal for outside activity. In

A young girl and her lamb, Australia, early twentieth century. She wears a ribbon in her hair, a knee-length dress, white socks, and buckled shoes. English and American styles appeared to dominate girls' daywear at this time. Photographer and studio unknown. Powerhouse Museum.

comparison, advertisements for boys continued to depict suits and heavy coats in striped or fawn-colored cotton poplin, or suits with pleated fronts open at the neck and belted in the back, which allowed greater movement.

The late 1920s was the time of the Great Depression, and for many families life was desperately difficult and luxuries nonexistent. Some stores ceased to issue mail-order catalogs in the mid-1920s. Late in the decade, perhaps due to the opening up of textile imports from the United States, boys' wear appeared more distinct from styles worn by girls, departing from the beautiful doll look and the sailor suit of the prewar period to more practical styles. The emphasis on freedom of movement meant boys could wear gabardine double-breasted coats in fawn or sax blue finished with a belt at the back. Gabardine, a tough tightly woven fabric, was commonly used because of its ability to withstand a great deal of wear and tear. For girls there were stocking suspenders, including the sports suspender belt, or a wraparound sports girdle in fancy pink with elasticized top for expansion. More restrictive styles in girls' underwear included white woven liberty-printed bodices. Most children slept in sleep-suits that were all-wool, woven and unshrinkable, with a flap at the back for that midnight trip to the lavatory. Girls' styles of nightwear were pink, whereas boys' were blue, and some featured an embellished pocket in the shape of a butterfly, or a frill gathered at the ankle. Both boys and girls often wore cloth dressing gowns in blue, pink, or animal designs, corded at the waist.

During the daytime in the 1920s boys to the age of sixteen could wear a number of differently designed caps and hats, the most popular made of fur felt in styles with plain brims or black silk bands, or "greaseproof" leather in steel gray, slate, or fawn. Boaters were also available in fine-grade straw with medium or wide brims. Varsity caps (in more modern times known as baseball caps) in navy flannel were more fitting for younger boys and juveniles, as they fixed firmly to the head and could not fly off as easily, whereas older boys could don golf caps in a light tweed mixture or fawn gabardine. Boys wore Oxfords (low shoes) in black or tan calf, which had a circular vamp across the front and a welted sole. There were also galoshes (boots), or Derby boots, which had a slightly different wrap design across the front, more like ankle boots, with stout, serviceable soles, and made of black yearling calf. School boots, Balmoral boots, and the famous Dally M Football boots came in box hide with a holed front feature running across the toes. Such boots were worn with long golf hose with fancy or plain turnover tops to emulate the rugby player Herbert Henry "Dally" Messenger, one of Australia's memorable icons, who was relatively short, with a pot belly, yet remained firmly in the Australian public's imagination as the bright sports star whom one's opponent could never predict. Little changed in terms of children's wear in Australia during the 1930s. Photographic archives indicate that boys wore shorts and a shirt, sometimes with a tie and a jacket or knitted jumper, and girls wore short dresses, sometimes with ribbons in their hair. For more formal wear girls wore a hat and a jacket (in winter); shoes and socks were the expected attire, and older boys had to wear shoes.

WORLD WAR II AND AFTER

Australia suffered considerably during World War II and like Britain faced problems of clothes rationing. According to the Australian Bureau of Statistics, in 1942 the primary reasons for clothes rationing were due to a fall in imports, increased armed services demands, and reduced labor for local production of textiles and garment making. Supplies were unable to meet demand at normal consumption rates, and a review was made of the stock positions of materials and garments, with the likely rate of future demand based on past consumption. It was considered that men could afford to suffer a reduction on the prewar rate of slightly less than half, women one-third (except for expectant mothers), children (5–15 years) one-fifth (subject to supplementary issues for out-size children), while clothing production for infants should remain at prewar levels. Coupons for clothing expired in November 1945, although rationing for other commodities continued.

Australia was late in embracing the English and American use of overalls, made famous by Levi Strauss during the nineteenth century. By the late 1940s overalls were for sale of all-wool flannel and adjustable straps, with crossbars at the back to keep them in place on the shoulders. 1940s fashion for girls included the cotton dress called Sister Sue and twin sets (cardigan over pullover, most often in the same color), while older girls were no different from their mothers in swinging wool skirts of tartan or top coats. For boys there were "sloppy Joes" of brushed flannel cotton fabric (used in the late twentieth and twenty-first centuries for tracksuits), which often came with Disney motifs; girls could wear "sloppy Sues," sweaters made of soft cotton for sports activities, with crew neck and long sleeves, available in lemon or white. Also available for girls were smart tailored slacks in good-quality milled tweed, roomily cut with adjustable waistbands. Colors were more adventurous, in brown, bottle, aqua, royal blue, and "American beauty" gray.

After the war came the hope of a return to peacetime prosperity, and clothing became a major manufacturing industry in Australia during the 1950s. The word *teenager* was first used in the 1940s and gained popularity in the early 1950s with the advent of Hollywood films and rock music. In Australia, in the years after the war, the social climate changed to one that included more leisure. In 1948 the standard work week was reduced from forty-four to forty hours for most employees, and Friday and Saturday night "flicks" changed the way families socialized and spent time together. Teenagers could socialize in different ways, including joining groups that rejoiced at the end of the war while roller skating or ice skating.

The 1950s saw an introduction of new fabric trends, with velveteen corduroy dresses for teenage girls and reversible raincoats for teenage boys. Younger boys could wear popular Repton shirts, which boasted "nine lives" in wearability and washability for the active working boy. Jeans could be worn cuffed with checked cowboy shirts, and blazers made of flannel, and overalls. Girls could wear flared skirts in rayon or snug denim tracksuits in preshrunk, fleecy lined denim. Wind jackets and cardigans were also available for the trendier teen as well as cotton windbreakers and jacquard pullovers in a variety of adventurous patterns and colors. Children were being offered fashions that allowed them to indulge in sophisticated outdoor social activities, perhaps imitating the affluence of America. Jodhpurs, for example, were for sale as a fashion item in rainproof gabardine or corduroy. Jodhpurs were as fashionable as wind jackets, while pilot suits for younger girls between toddler and juvenile age could feature tapered slacks. Riding boots in calf or Clark Shoes' Pathfinder walking shoes could be worn during the day, and camel-hair zippered boots at night. Sleeves were capped and skirts were fuller—below the knee for had increasing choice in purchasing decisions. Cheery jackets in laminated nylon (never creasing) and frisky, bottle green, flared jersey slacks were advertised as having the ability to make children happy. Cat suits, Orlon slack suits with flared legs and sleeveless tops, and parkas or windbreakers by Exacto or Bri-Nylon were offered to style-conscious teenagers. Scarves could be worn around the head and short skirts over slacks as well. The label Bonds became synonymous with underwear, bringing out cotton interlock T-shirts for boys and men. Cottontail briefs were one of this iconic Australian company's most famous items. Hippie briefs, nylon slips, chenille singlets with raglan sleeves—an item that has since become a basic stock item—dressing gowns, and the South Australian firm Onkaparinga's pure wool dressing gowns gave teenage girls the style they needed at night. During the day male toddlers could be clothed in Beatles-styled swinging safari suits or "free 'n' easy" wool slacks.

BRANDS

The 1970s and 1980s saw the tendency of children's fashion toward sportswear and trendy casual attire increasingly label-driven; children were assumed to be as conscious about their appearance as their parents. At the same time children's clothing safety standards were reinforced in Australia, including items being fire-reductive (reducing the number of items made of synthetic nylon or rayon fabric), and parents were being made aware of the sun and its effects by campaigns to encourage use of sunscreens and hats.

While boys could wear casual jacket suits, cotton sports shirts, and boxers, the girls were in "gay shifts" and dressy young styles such as cotton gingham, "it" girl swinging A-line dresses, and Jamaican-styled parka blouses in bold floral print designs. Beachwear, important to the Australian lifestyle, included the country's famous brand, Speedo nylon racing swimsuits, terry toweling beach jackets, and trunks-and-bra (bikini suits) in Hawaiian designs. Barely a plain fabric was to be seen in catalogs and advertising, in line with adult tastes of the 1970s.

Apart from some "preppiness" (elitism associated with eastern American colleges) in youth styles that emerged, including multicolored vests and undershirts and flat Dunlop sneakers, boys' wear, girls' wear, and babywear maintained a steady course toward casualness and comfort. Boxer shorts and other cotton clothing, including Bonds singlets and T-shirts for both boys and girls, marked the Australian summers and helped define an essential Australian quality to the dress of Australian children. Babies and infants wore Bonds tank-top ribbed singlets or the enduring Wondersuit, a stretch coverall. Nappy (diaper) liners were still part of mainstream use rather than the disposable brands available in more recent times. In the twenty-first century clothing made by Bonds for children, and for babies the Wondersuit and the Grobag, are items readily available on the Internet. This form of purchasing is now offering consumers another convenient way to shop from home, much like the service of early mail-order catalogs.

With the increasing prevalence of marketing targeted at children rather than parents, magazines dedicated specifically to children arose, such as *Shop4Kids*, the European *Studio Bambini*, *Vogue Kids*, and a specific edition of *Donna Hay Magazine*, produced by the Australian chef of the same name, covering children's food and clothing. Local labels such as Fred Bare and the

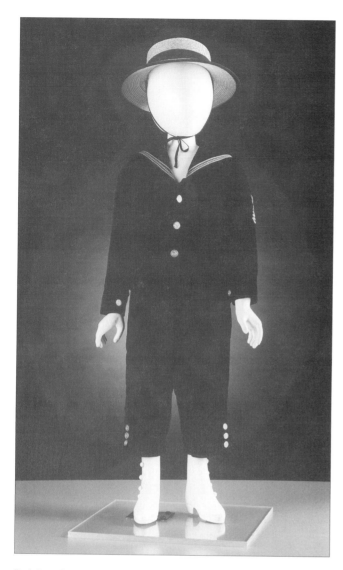

Boy's two-piece sailor suit, ca. 1915–1925, held in the Powerhouse Museum, Sydney. Later to be replaced by more practical styles, the sailor suit was a popular prewar item of dress for Australian children. Powerhouse Museum.

juveniles. Yet younger and older boys wore much the same thing as before: flannel trousers and preshrunk "buckaroos" (much like jodhpurs) and overalls. Boys' clothing surged toward functionalism and was specially styled "to grow with the boy," including features like extra fabric layers inside knickers, hems and cuffs that could be lengthened, generous cuts that allowed for growth, and reinforced pockets and inside breast pockets. Denim was an enormous presence by then, perhaps influenced by Hollywood movies, reinforcing the comfortable everyday wearability of jeans. Boys could wear navy denim; fleecy lined heavyweight denim jeans, which were four-pocketed; riveted and preshrunk jeans, often with double seat; and zip-front styles with secret money pockets.

The 1960s saw a lowering of waistlines and the widening of ankle cuffs in both boys' and girls' wear. Australian children were referred to as "tots and teens," and emphasis was placed on value and fashion before functionalism and utility. Easy care was the emphasis when thinking about the wardrobe. From a consumer perspective it was the 1960s that gave rise to the idea that children

New Zealand brand Pumpkin Patch began to make mass fashion for children less expensive. High-end labels for infant girls were introduced, such as BIG by Fiona Scanlon. One of Australia's most significant fashion designers, Collette Dinnigan, has produced gowns, dresses, and formal wear for christenings in silk, taffeta, and expensive fabrics. Global brands, including Burberry, Cacharel, and French brand Petit Bateau for infants of both sexes, have made an enormous impact on the emerging fashion of babies from three months upward, and consumer spending for children's fashion has risen. For boys the trend has been to appear as fashionable as their girl playmates in GANT, Ralph Lauren, and ESPRIT, all international brands, which can be mixed with chain-store fashion such as Big W supermarket brands, Hong Kong–based Cotton On, or Australian Target's own label, which concentrates on fulfilling boys' appetites for pirates, skulls, dinosaurs, and nonbranded motifs. Toys and branded children's entertainment have raised the awareness of fashion among children too. Examples are Bratz dolls, based solely on the desire to be fashionable among peers, and franchised brands like the Olsen Twins, who established a girls' clothing line called Mary-Kate and Ashley in 2000. The latter became controversial because it originally included g-strings and push-up bras for girls aged under twelve.

The future of children's wear is clear in Australia. It is a market gaining rapidly in profile. Where adults would once purchase fragrances and cosmetics in their favorite label, in the first decade of the twenty-first century they purchase diversified kids' accessories from Gucci and other high-fashion labels. The child is no longer a silent adult who has not quite come of age, but an independent-minded influencer of fashion purchases, their age sometimes hard to determine in their adult-like clothing. They are more than happy to be an accessory to their parent's sense of status, so long as the parent is willing to pay for fashionable dress, accessories, and makeup.

References and Further Reading

Anthony Horden and Sons Pty, Ltd, Mail Order Catalogues. 1898–1924. Australia.
Callahan, Collen, R., and Jo B. Paoletti. "Is It a Boy or a Girl? Gender Identity and Children's Clothing." In *The Fashion Reader*, edited by Linda Welters and Amy Lillethun, 125–128. London and New York: Berg, 2007.
David Jones. Mail Order Catalogues. 1946–1978. Sydney, Australia.
Ewing, Elizabeth. *History of Children's Costume.* London: B. T. Batsford, 1977.
Farmers Mail Order Catalogues. Autumn and Winter 1926–1949. Australia.
Guppy, Alison. *Children's Clothes 1939–1970.* Dorsett, Australia: Blandford Press, 1978.
Rose, Clare. *Children's Clothes since 1775.* London: A.C. Black, 1958.
Scandrett, Elizabeth. *Breeches and Bustles: An Illustrated History of Clothes Worn in Australia 1788–1914.* Lilydale, Australia: Pioneer Design Studio, 1978.

Michelle Bakar and Vicki Karaminas

See also Footwear in Australia.

PART 7

First Nation People (Māori) of New Zealand

Introduction to Māori Dress

- Dressing the Land
- Material Sources and Textile Technology
- Dressing the Skin
- States of Dress, Varieties of Garment
- Additional Body Supplements
- Agency of Dress
- Dress as Indicators of Identity and Cultural Unity

When early Eastern Polynesian navigators explored Te Moana-Nui ā-Kiwa ("The Great Sea of Kiwa," or the Pacific Ocean), they discovered the world's largest oceanic archipelago, Aotearoa—New Zealand. The temperate climate of this geographically isolated land had produced a restricted range of flora and fauna. Away from their tropical homelands, the voyaging ancestors of the Māori people discovered that survival in the colder climate required significantly warmer clothing. They experimented with new and semifamiliar resources, adapted existing fiber skills to endemic materials such as *harakeke* (*Phormium* spp., New Zealand flax), and explored the potential of available avian and mammalian species. Weft-twining techniques developed to enable the construction of waist and shoulder garments that met their altered needs.

Concepts relating to these heterogeneous forms of dress became highly specific. Elements of hairstyle, headdress, facial and body tattooing, use of ocher, oils, and perfumes, neck and ear pendants, clothing, and weapons became marks of individual identification within strong, dynamic, tribal communities. Customary Māori dress was never static: Māori had their own keen sense of fashion and style. High-status garments were sometimes decorated with dog skin, feathers or bird skin, or attachments of plant materials; at other times they resulted from skilled fiber preparation, naturally dyed colors, intricate borders, and the expertise of the weaver.

Modern knowledge of the history of this dress is derived from evidence found in oral traditions and archaeological artifacts, eighteenth- and nineteenth-century material collections, and graphic images and journals of European explorers and settlers, and supported by work of ethnologists and indigenous scholars. However, early descriptions of Māori dress and translations of stories tended to underestimate the significance of different tribal terminologies and conflate basic descriptions. In consequence, many regional variations and subtle nuances became lost; work endeavoring to recover such losses continues.

DRESSING THE LAND

Situated in the South Pacific Ocean, between 166–180 degrees longitude and 34–48 degrees latitude south, Aotearoa/New Zealand consists of two main islands with a third in close proximity and a number of offshore islands. The climate is warmer in the north, becoming progressively cooler in the south. New Zealand was formed from the land mass that was originally part of the Gondwana supercontinent; its initial isolation and diverse topography produced an unusual but limited variety of flora and fauna. With dry tussock highlands meeting forests of dense, damp bush, it lacked the cotton and linen resources of the northern hemisphere. Apart from small reptilian species, it was devoid of quadrupeds. Instead, a range of flightless birds thrived with few predators; other birds shared air space along with three small types of bat, while an assortment of marine mammal species inhabited the shoreline.

Although estimates vary, the ancestors of Māori, the indigenous people, probably discovered New Zealand sometime before 1000 C.E. Normal clothing for these eastern Polynesian navigators presumably consisted of barkcloth loincloths and occasional ponchos or shoulder wraps. Successive voyages of pioneers brought existing weaving and cordage skills with them—skills essential for sailing and surviving at sea. They also brought specific plants intended to assist in maintaining their customary lifestyle. Instead, the significantly cooler climate obliged the migrants to make considerable changes in order to survive. Not the least of these included the development of hard-wearing rain capes and warmer clothing to cope with the unfamiliar winter weather.

Little evidence exists of how the early descendents of these migrants clothed themselves. Wooden beaters found in the North Island indicate that there were widespread efforts to produce barkcloth, but the climate failed to adequately support the *aute tāranga* (paper mulberry, *Broussonetia papyrifera*), which was brought from the tropics. Attempts to utilize indigenous ribbonwood and lacebark trees (*Hoheria* spp.) may have created a local product, but the few, fragile remnants of plain barkcloth recovered appear too weak to have made functional clothing.

Originally, clothing resources may have seemed comparatively limited. Familiar species of coconut, pandanus, hibiscus, or banana used elsewhere in the Pacific were absent, and alternative fiber sources were needed. Two furred mammals arrived with them, the *kūri* (Māori dog, *Canis familiaris linnaeus*) and the *kiore* (Polynesian rat, *Rattus exulans*), both being potential food and skin resources. Settlers hunted many of the new species of birds, a number of which provided useful skins, and which initially included the large flightless *moa* species (*Dinornis novaezealandiae*).

One South Island moa-hunting community inhabited the Wairau Bar, where excavations have revealed the remains of thousands of these large birds. Dated to the latter half of the thirteenth century, this location is currently among the earliest known archaeological sites in New Zealand. Although the inhabitants may have also woven materials, evidence of bone needles and awls (tools for making holes) show that their owners were sewing, in all probability making sizable garments of moa bird skin. *Moko* (tattooing) instruments indicate that they practiced some form of personal tattooing. Necklaces of carved bone reels and whale-tooth pendants, recovered from burial sites, suggest that wearing such ornaments was significant in their lives.

Engraving after Sydney Parkinson's drawing of a New Zealand Māori warrior. Parkinson was the artist on board Captain Cook's voyage to the Pacific in 1768. The sitter's facial *moko*, smooth barrel-roll *piki* hairstyle, set with a *titireia* (tall whale-bone comb), along with the *reiputa* (whale-tooth pendant) at his neck, all indicate his high-born status. His ear pendants of human teeth and smoothly polished *pounamu* (greenstone) are attached with a strip of precious *aute* (barkcloth), and his cloak was made using the double-paired twining technique. Getty Images.

The phenomenon of the whale-tooth pendant was important throughout the country. Using Neolithic tools, some genuine whales' teeth were split and intricately carved to create delicate chevron pairs, or to produce anthropomorphic appendages showing close affinity with bone artifacts from the Cook, Society, and Marquesas Islands. Other whales' teeth were carved or etched with facial features. However, perhaps when authentic teeth were not available, large stone whale-tooth pendants were painstakingly replicated in serpentine and argillite, while smaller teeth were carved from moa or dog bone. The huge amount of time, energy, and dedication expended in these undertakings points to the high cultural and perhaps spiritual importance of the items, but their true significance to the people who made them is unlikely to ever be known.

Over time, and perhaps successive waves of migration, the newcomers adapted to their new land. The term *māori* simply described things that were normal and natural; *tangata Māori* identified ordinary people. (It was after the mid-nineteenth-century arrival of European settlers that the indigenous "New Zealanders" began to be called "Māoris.")

Gradually, these people came to call themselves *tāngata whenua* (people of the land). They lived in small, predominantly self-sufficient groups, with an *ariki* (chiefly leader) who was usually, but not exclusively, selected by right of primogeniture. Based in settled or fortified villages (*pā*), these were hunting, gathering, and horticultural communities that eventually spread throughout the land. Their lives were shaped by the ideas and practices of their forebears. Sharing a common culture and dialectic versions of the same language, and maintaining strong kinship bonds to common ancestors, they held a collective concept. At any significant gathering, the impressive attire of the ariki reflected on his people; an affront to one individual was interpreted as an insult to the group. They engaged in intertribal gifting and exchange, or intertribal warfare to achieve reparation or when ancestrally held lands were deemed to be threatened.

Connected by their tribal affiliations, Māori people still acknowledge kinship bonds to mutual ancestors and to ancestral lands. While variations exist between different tribal groups, for tāngata Māori the customary protocols and processes that have been handed down from the past continue to have relevance. For Māori the term *tuku iho* (customary, from the past) has no implication of inertia but conveys a sense of deliberate and conscious linking with ancestors, or using an ancestral rationale to guide an activity. The same sense is not adequately communicated through the use of *traditional* or *habitual*—which terms carry a sense of static, nonthinking repetition for Māori.

Concepts of *tapu*, *noa*, and *mana* influenced every aspect of customary Māori life prior to European contact and in the twenty-first century still retain authority in many situations. Within the context of appearance tapu is broadly interpreted as a form of restriction and inaccessibility, and an indication of latent danger; conversely, something made noa was rendered safe for use. Mana indicates a prestigious quality, a state of authority or power. In the tribal environment the *rangatira* (person of chiefly status) held a personal quality of great mana; this made the individual's physical being tapu and potentially hazardous to those of lesser status. It extended a person's identity, permeating clothing and belongings of the owner, to such a degree that an article could stand for the individual or be used to reserve something for the owner's exclusive use.

MATERIAL SOURCES AND TEXTILE TECHNOLOGY

Gradually, Māori developed in-depth knowledge of the indigenous flora, ascertaining cosmetic, medicinal, and manufacturing properties. Plants identified as potential weaving resources included the leafy green epiphyte, *kiekie* (*Freycinetia baueria*), the so-called cabbage tree, *tīkōuka* (*Cordyline australis*), a hardy mountain variety, *tī tōī* (*Cordyline indivisa*), the swamp-growing *kuta* (*Scirpus lacustris*), sand-loving sedge, *pīngao* (*Desmoschoenus spiralis*), and the downy-leafed mountain daisy, *tikumu* (*Celmesia spectabilis/coriacea*). Ultimately, a range of widely available harakeke species became the materials of choice.

Weavers would have begun using harakeke in similar ways to tropical pandanus and coconut leaves, splitting long strips to plait baskets, sails, or mats. But the convenient midrib of the coconut frond was absent, and new joining methods were needed. This probably accelerated learning to extract the strong *muka* or *whitau* (fiber) by scraping the epidermis from the leaf with the edge of a mussel shell. This fiber enabled the development of new twined textiles. Gradually, weavers discovered that different cultivars of harakeke had different properties. Some were better for plaited products, while others produced fibers of various qualities: strong for cordage or firm garments, softer, glossy, or whiter fibers for different uses. Fibers were sorted into similar lengths; strands were "topped-and-tailed" to ensure consistent strength of the final yarn, then plied on the worker's leg. Plied muka could be further softened by beating and washing. It could also be dyed: Earthy hues of yellows, tan, and red ocher were extracted from various sources, and herbal or ash mordents applied, while black was achieved by steeping material in iron-rich mud, as elsewhere in the Pacific.

Rāranga (the basic term for Māori weaving) involves two specific off-loom techniques. The first, in fact called rāranga, is a flat plaiting process, using prepared strips of fresh leaves from plants with long leaves. Designs were based on plain- or twill-weave patterns. The second, using fiber, evolved gradually; early textiles employed passive weft threads, anchored to the vertical warp by half-hitch looping. Eventually, *whatu* (weft-twining) developed, using *whatu aho patahi* (single-pair wefts) or *whatu aho rua* (double-pair wefts). Similar methods were utilized in fish and eel traps in many parts of Polynesia. Compacting or spacing wefts, along with introduced color via warp or weft, or as ornamental tags or tassels, allowed diversity of garment styles. The development of *tāniko*, a uniquely Māori weaving technique, enabled intricate, geometrically patterned, colored borders.

Weft-twining had numerous applications. It provided the basic construction of layered waist and shoulder garments. For these, harakeke leaves were harvested, prepared for use by removing the central rib and the outer edges, and the blade split into similar widths. These were slightly softened, being pulled over a sharp edge, then sections of the epidermis were scraped away, creating a simple pattern with areas of exposed fiber. Finally, the epidermis was stripped from the tail end of the strip, producing the warp strands. Depending on end use and weaver's preference, the leaves could be further divided by thumbnail into narrower widths.

Most garment weaving commenced at the hemline. Leaving a broad fringe of semiscraped warp ends loose, strands were joined horizontally by the twining process; additional leaves were incorporated to achieve the required garment width. A second row of leaves was placed over the first, each fibrous end adding into the previous warp, all being twined together about a finger-joint below the first row of twining. Successive rows were overlaid, each weft spaced from the previous row. When the desired length was attained, the waistband (or neck edge) was finished off, ties were added, and the completed garment was reversed to hang correctly. The outer surface had loose strands to the waist or hip, while the firmly woven interior was modest, potentially warm, with shaping rows incorporated for comfort and fit. Ultimately, the unscraped leaf sections dried, curling, forming tubes; flexibility was maintained where the epidermis was removed; exposed fibers also absorbed dyes and highlighted patterns. Resourceful inventiveness of Māori weavers ensured a great diversity within the limitations of available materials.

DRESSING THE SKIN

While the major items of clothing were essentially waist or shoulder garments, the basic elements of Māori dress can be divided into three components: body modifications of skin or hair, body supplements that constitute actual clothing, and body supplements of personal adornment or weaponry added to create a specific appearance. However, classification difficulties occur because names of items varied between different tribal groups, some tribes used identical names for entirely dissimilar objects, and some words have a variety of meanings.

The most prestigious and permanent form of Māori body modification was *tā moko*: the slow, painful practice of tattooing. The ultimate in personal appearance, marking high status or some important life event, moko is a specialized study. However, *haehae* (lines) were a second enduring form of skin marking. It was customary for mourners to lacerate their skin, producing tears of blood; an 1833 witness recorded: "they presented a shocking spectacle, so besmeared with blood we could not recognize any person." Three decades later, graphic artists showed the marks of such scarring on the arms and breasts of older females, indicating that some women still engaged in this practice.

Less permanently, skin and hair could be modified by applying red ocher mixed with oil. Captain James Cook recorded that "the clothes as well as the bodies of the natives were so bedaubed with red that one could hardly touch one of them without becoming besmeared." Some collected cloaks and combs still retain traces of color. Facial painting included *tuhi-kōhuru* (diagonal lines), *tuhi-māreikura* (horizontal lines), and *tuhi-kōnekeneke* (a dotted pattern). Sometimes the entire face was colored red; other times it might be half red and half blackened with charcoal dust; occasionally, blue clay rings were marked around the eyes. Young people enhanced their appearance by applying a specific type of pollen to their faces. Complex scented oils were blended, then gifted or traded in this precash society. They were enjoyed equally by men and women and used for both therapeutic and grooming purposes: enhancing the hair and massaged into limbs.

Hairstyles conveyed considerable information about the wearer. Social status could be indicated by whether hair was long or short and by how, or whether, it was dressed or ornamented; other styles and names were regionally specific. Most men wore their hair long, and tied up, in a *puhi* or *rahiri* (bunch), or twisted in a single *tiki* or *putiki* (knot) or multiple knots on the crown of the head. In 1769 Cook's artist Sidney Parkinson illustrated the *tikitiki* (a double-knot style from the east coast of the North Island): two small, neat rolls of hair at the crown of the head, closely wrapped with *akatea* vine. In the Bay of Islands, Parkinson depicted a *piki*, a localized, small, tight "barrel-roll" worn across the top of the head; this young man's ariki heritage was confirmed by other accoutrements he wore. With the head the most tapu part of the body, hairdressing was problematic for high-status individuals; a chief's hair could only be dressed by someone of sufficient status not to be affected by the chief's own tapu state. Hair was also modified by applying oil or ocher; however, beards were not always favored because they detracted from facial moko.

In mourning the hair was often closely cropped. Nonetheless, in some areas hair worn loose and seemingly unkempt was a sign that the wearer was mourning an unavenged death. Sometimes, these two styles combined to present a shaven head with a long dreadlock or single plait hanging at the left temple; this remained untended until vengeance was achieved. Less information exists about women's hairstyles; heroines' hair was tied up in legend, but most women seen by eighteenth-century explorers had short hair.

STATES OF DRESS, VARIETIES OF GARMENT

In certain situations the correct form of dress was no clothing. Perceptions of modesty in the Māori world varied considerably from subsequently introduced Christian norms. Near nudity could be entirely appropriate for males; Cook described men wearing little but a penis-cord fastened from the prepuce to a belt around the waist. Furthermore, despite some specific warrior garments, men usually went into battle naked, and young children did not normally wear clothing.

Concepts of female modesty during the same era differed to a lesser degree. While women's breasts were generally exposed, the genital area was not. Cook's journals record an incident when a group of women, unexpectedly surprised while harvesting seafood, hastily hid and made seaweed *maro* (aprons or loincloths) to cover themselves. Conversely, in the same period but in a different region, some old women deliberately drew aside their bird-skin maros to expose themselves, in a form of insult to the French crew of the *St Jean Baptiste*.

Nonetheless, in specific circumstances, a naked state related directly to the tapu nature of the task being undertaken. Acquiring sacred knowledge was a particularly tapu activity, but women, and certain items such as cooked food, had the capacity to remove tapu, rendering everything into a noa condition. Thus, young men entering a customary *Whare Wānanga* (House of High Learning) might first be obliged to remove their clothing to ensure that both knowledge and learning remained inviolate.

As elsewhere in Polynesia, the body supplements that constituted the major items of Māori clothing were basically rectangular shapes wrapped around the torso. Although other items were worn, the core group is divided into waist and shoulder garments. Waist garments are further divided into *tū* and *tātua* (types of belt), maro, and *rāpaki* (usually a wraparound form of kilt); shoulder garments consisted of capes and cloaks.

Belts were worn by both sexes and were many and varied in form. The tātua was a broad band worn by men, woven of muka and fastened with long strings attached at each end. *Tātua-pūpara* were plaited from strips of harakeke and folded longitudinally, with the leaf ends doubled inside; this supplied some protective

An unidentified Māori group of four, wearing similar cloaks. This is one of many studies of the Māori of the East Coast and Hawke's Bay, New Zealand, produced by the Napier-based Samuel Carnell in the 1870s and 1890s. Photograph by Samuel Carnell. Samuel Carnell Collection, Alexander Turnbull Library, Wellington, New Zealand.

padding for the wearer in battle. Simultaneously, with the folded edge worn uppermost, it provided a pocket for carrying small items. Some were woven in plain colors, with subtle twill-based patterning; others had bold patterns using yellow pingao or strips of black-dyed harakeke.

Women and girls wore *tū* (multistranded belts), which were often named from the material used in making them and sometimes incorporated sweet perfumed plants, which responded to the warmth of the human body. The *tū-whārariki* was plaited with the pliant mountain flax, *whārariki* (*Phormium cookianum*), whereas the *tū-maurea* used bright reddish-yellow sedge leaves of *maurea* (*Carex* spp.), wrapped around a muka core. Sweet scented *kōpuru* moss (*Lophocolea semiteres*) was inserted into some belts, simply tied around the waist. The *tū-karetu* had several plaited strands of sweet-scented *karetu* grass (*Hierochloe redolens*), with its brittle midrib removed. In comparison, the women's *tū-muka* was a complex belt, consisting of twelve muka cords, of which four were colored black, four were colored red, and four were white (undyed). Joined at each end, with plaited tying extensions, the intricate cordage had a central double-plied core, closely wrapped with further two-ply yarns, creating firm cords some 0.2 to 0.3 inch (6 to 8 millimeters) in diameter. Several examples of this belt exist, but the significance relating to numbers and colors of cords in its design is lost.

Similarly, diverse forms of maro were worn by men and women, made from various botanical sources, or from bird or dog skins. While *maro-aute* were presumed to be barkcloth and probably worn as elsewhere in Polynesia, most New Zealand maro were triangular shapes, suspended from a belt or ties. Often a single piece, sometimes a second part might be worn at the rear, or a cord or extension of the maro passed between the legs and fastened to the waistband at the back.

One simple form, the *maro-poroporo*, was made from sweet-smelling dry leaves of *Solanum avicluare* and worn by prestigious young women. Where the lake club-rush was available, long spongy stems of kuta (*Scirpus lacustris*) were harvested for the *maro-kuta*, worn by women and girls. *Maro-kōpua* and *maro-waiapu* were superior styles worn by ariki women; weft-twined using undyed cream- or honey-colored muka, they had taniko borders and decorative black *hukahuka* (falling attachments), or patterns in black and yellow. The styles *maro-kau* or *maro-kore* (without) were worn by unmarried women, while *maro-nui* (large) or *maro-pūrua* (abundant) signified married women.

Bird-skin maro were also varied. In the south green feathered skins of the kākāpō (*Strigops habroptilus*), a nocturnal ground parrot, became waist garments for the daughters of local chiefs; those of weka (*Gallirallus* spp.), the common wood hen, may have served the less privileged. Other bird-skin examples were noted in Northland (North Island) in 1769. Four years later a red-feathered woven maro, faced with white dog skin and decorated with pieces of iridescent paua shell (*Haliotis* spp.), was purchased at Queen Charlotte Sound. Reportedly worn by women for dancing, similar garments were recorded elsewhere on Cook's final voyage in 1778, suggesting this style was once quite widespread. Dog-skin maro were recorded in oral histories but were probably exclusive to male ariki. Two alternative maro, the *maro-huka* and the *maro-tūhou*, made roughly of leaves, were reserved for ritual use by tohunga (holders of special knowledge).

Rāpaki were just one of a variety of kilt-like, wraparound waist garments that could be worn over the maro or may have supplanted it: interpretations of this terminology vary widely. In some regions this garment was woven cloth, sometimes from old cloaks; in others it consisted of strips of partially scraped green harakeke, weft-twined as previously described. Other waist garments (skirts) of this construction included the *piupiu*, *kinikini* or *pokinikini*, *pihepihe*. These garments rustled and swung according to the motion of the wearer. This was particularly important in performance, when the sounds created by the dry culm-like harakeke pieces, slapping rhythmically against the moving bodies of entertainers, enhanced their presentation.

A multipurpose shoulder garment probably developed soon after the maro. The *tāpeka* was a large, malleable garment woven from muka; swathed around the torso, with upper corners tied at the throat or fastened on the chest, it left the arms and legs free. It could be worn around the shoulders as a cloak and possibly also served as a sleeping cover. Some were depicted during Cook's visits, but they appear to have fallen out of use during the following century.

The majority of shoulder garments were either cloaks or capes; the term kākahu is now applied to either. They were made in three basic ways: rāranga-woven with leaf strips, whatu-woven with fiber, or from skins stitched together. Very few leaf-strip cloaks remain. Usually woven in panels, they have fringe-like overlapping joins. Some were dyed black, but one example in the

British Museum has bold diagonal checks of natural and black, and a variety of attachments highlighting the joins, showing that color, design, movement, and sound were important elements for the weaver.

Pre-eighteenth-century *kahu* or *'ahu* (as Cook heard the word) included garments stitched of bird skins, in addition to pelts of rat skin, dog skin, and sealskin. Remnants of kākāpō and weka garments have been identified from South Island burial sites, the segments joined with muka thread using a form of knotted blanket stitch. South Island kuri skins were joined (and in some cases repaired) the same way. In the North Island the use of rat skins occurs in oral tradition, while a stitched kiwi-skin cloak was observed as late as 1824. However, a remnant of a *kahu-kekeno* (sealskin) and one complete *huru-kurī*, a full cloak of eight dog pelts (including tails and ears), show an entirely different stitching technique. These seams were made by folding in the furred edges, laying the two sections of folded pelt together, and sewing a double running-stitch seam through the resultant four thicknesses of skin. This "mock French" seam was embellished on the suede side with hanging strips of fur-tipped dog skin, showing that the huru-kurī was designed to be reversible.

Whatu cloaks developed alongside those of pelts or skins. They can be divided into the prestigious, finely woven, and specifically named formal styles, or the rougher, lower-grade, *mai* garments for working wear. Among the most highly esteemed whatu-based items were the *kahu-waero* and the *kākahu-kura*. White kurī were carefully tended for their valued tail hair; *waero* were attachments made of this long white hair. The *kaupapa* (woven base) of the kahu-waero was completely covered with *awe* (clusters of waero), contrasting against a dark tāniko border at the hem. Often featured in stories, only one such kahu-waero still exists; now with many of its sewn clusters missing, it was already old and worn when traded around 1770. The *mahiti* was a similar style, with scattered single tassels rather than clusters.

In comparison, *kahu-whero* or *kākahu-kura* were striking red-feathered cloaks (whereas *kahu-kura* were colored red with ocher). Feathers from rare red *kākā-kura*, mutant parrot-like birds, or red underwing feathers of the kākā subspecies (*Nestor meridionalis*) were incorporated in the twining process. Feather clusters were placed along a warp strand; the calami (hallow shaft) was secured with one twist of the twining process, then bent 180 degrees and firmly anchored with the following twist. In this way hundreds of feathers were attached, completely covering the surface of the garment. Exclusive ownership of white dogs and relative scarcity of red feathers, combined with high labor content, ensured that these garments remained the prerogative of those with substantial mana.

By the time of Cook's voyages these cloaks were rare, and a new form of *kahu-kurī* (dog-skin cloak) was in vogue. This style had a strong, closely woven kaupapa, completely overlaid with narrow, vertical strips of dog skin stitched in straight rows. The technique allowed new creativity in arranging colored furs. The *puahi* used only white dog skin; a black version with white bordering the front and neck edges was a *tōpuni*. The *awarua* (two rivers) had vertical stripes of two colors. Block or checkered patterns were achieved; possible combinations seemed almost endless, dependent only on availability of the basic materials. Dog skins were available to few and reflected status; thus even a few strips of skin attached to the corners or border of cloaks gave plain garments more prestige.

A special class of warrior cloaks included kahu-kurī of two types, the stitched *tāpahu* or the *tahiuru*, in addition to the *pauku* or *pukupuku* (thick closely woven cloak). These were sometimes soaked in water, as swollen fibers gave increased protection against certain weapons. More than one might be worn, providing greater defense. However, kurī numbers declined. They interbred with introduced dogs and the species eventually became extinct. Introduced dogs did not have the same type of hair, and dog skin lost its mana.

Other styles of cloak emerged to become indicators of chiefly status. In the late eighteenth century introduced stripes of darkly dyed warps or contrasting weft yarns produced design interest. During the early 1800s *kaitaka* and *aronui* were the most esteemed. These finely woven cloaks acquired their high value from their smooth, glossy muka, the precision of their weaving, and the beauty of their multicolored taniko borders. Variations included the *korohunga*, parawai, and *parakiri*, with ornamental borders, but when woven from edge to edge, instead of the more customary hem to neckline, the cloak became a *paepaeroa*.

The pliant white muka ground of the *korowai* (a type of cloak with fringing) was achieved by bleaching and beating the fiber before weaving. This style was distinguished by its black-dyed twisted muka cords of hukahuka and a thick black fringe forming a collar at the neck. Many variations stemmed from this type, according to the type of hukahuka and how they were arranged. Hukahuka on *whakahekeheke* fell in vertical stripes, those of the *kuiri* in squares, the *koimutu* were marked in blocks, but the *momutu* were looped. The *potopoto* had closely twisted black hukahuka, the *raho-kuia* had loosely twisted black or colored two-ply cords. Other forms included the *hihima* (entirely white with white hukahuka), the *waihinau* (black with black hukahuka), and the *tahuka* (without hukahuka). A new adaptation followed the availability of wool. Replacing hukahuka, small bobbles of red wool were studded in patterns on the surface of the *ngore*, while the *korowai-ngore* combined both black hukahuka and red bobbles. The ngore may have reflected the *pekerangi*, an earlier style that used small tufts of red feathers, but the post-European pekerangi incorporated fragments of colored material as surface decoration. The *korirangi* had two types of hukahuka, black muka strings and *pokinikini* (little tags of scraped, dyed, and dried harakeke, which rattled when the wearer moved).

Feather cloaks, *kahu-huruhuru* (furred or feathered), achieved a revival in the early twentieth century. Following the demise of the kuri, and the decimation of kākā, in consequence of settler guns and destroyed habitat, the nocturnal kiwi (*Apertyx* spp.) assumed greater significance. Numerous kiwi feathers were required to create a *kahu-kiwi*. According to preference, clusters were prepared with feathers arranged to lie smoothly, or ruffled, turning out from each other. The latter method produced a surface that quivered at the slightest breath. Other kahu-huruhuru styles were named for the indigenous species utilized, such as the colorful *kahu-kereru* (*Hemiphaga novaeseelandiae*, native wood pigeon). More vivid creations were achieved by combining feathers from different bird species in geometric patterns, or experimenting with bold new figurative designs that included card motifs and lettering. Concurrently, Māori also began using the feathers of introduced bird species, such as pheasant and even peacock.

Rain capes, such as *pake*, were always functional garments, influenced far less by whims of fashion and style, but still incorporating touches of color. They were made in similar ways to the rāpaki, with overlaying layers of partially scraped harakeke or other materials adding to the warp, then twined to create a firm cape with a thatched appearance. Along with the pake, *pekerere*, *pora*, *pukaha*, *pureke*, *tatara*, and *tuapora* were other capes that provided warmth or wet-weather protection. *Timu* tags were attached in a different manner; partially scraped strips of harakeke were inserted (like feathers) and their ends doubled over to produce multiple rain-shedding layers. A thick plait finished the neck edge. Variations of this style included the black-and-yellow checkered *mangaeka*, and the *tihetihe*, with yellow tags spaced through the black ones.

Tōī, kiekie, and tī kōuka leaves provided alternatives to harakeke. The black-dyed *kahu-toi* was a highly prestigious warrior's rain cape; labor-intensive and long-lasting, the strong leaf midrib was removed and the leaves retted to assist extraction of the harsh coir-like fiber. The *pēia* and *para* were made using retted kiekie fiber, while the *whanake* was a rain cape of tī kōuka leaves; and a South Island variation utilized tussock grass.

ADDITIONAL BODY SUPPLEMENTS

Well-dressed Māori used a range of supplementary items to enhance their appearance. Ephemeral supplements included feathers, flowers and leaves, seeds, and shells. Other personal ornaments were *heru* (bone or wooden haircombs), neck and ear pendants carved from bone or stone, and long cloak pins of bone or shell. Depending on circumstances, the addition of handheld weapons could make the final dress statement. However, other items could be worn as circumstances required. These included *pōtae-taua* (mourning caps) and a variety of footwear.

Hair could be dressed with feathers and a comb. Red feathers were part of the legendary *raukura* (feathered headdress), and Parkinson's uncolored images include some of these tall feathered chiefly headdresses, which are no longer known. Parkinson also portrayed white *tākapu* (gannet) and *toroa* (albatross) feathers that were fashionable in the eighteenth century. The white-tipped, black tail feathers of the now extinct *huia* (*Heteralocha acutirostris*) were always highly esteemed; the *marereko* was a warrior headpiece of twelve such feathers, and sometimes an entire wing or bird skin might be worn as an ear pendant. Being rare, red feathers were much prized; kākā feathers contrasted well against the black of huia, while the long tail feathers of the tropical *amokura* (*Phaethon rubricauda*) were exclusive to ariki. Feathers of the infrequently visiting *kōtuku* (*Ardea sacra*, white heron) were also prized.

Tall prestigious haircombs were the prerogative of chiefs. The smooth, one-piece, whalebone *titireia*, worn upright at the back of the head, was an immediate indicator of status. Some regional styles were ornately carved; other heru were carved from bird bone and sometimes human bone. Two styles of wooden heru were made: a smaller version of the titireia and a composite form with slivers of wooden teeth twined inside a wooden frame. Heru took on the tapu nature of the head they adorned; they could never be used by another person, and damaged combs were hidden or buried in swamps to protect all parties.

Flowers were also worn in the hair at times; Parkinson shows many indeterminate botanical circlets worn by women during 1769–1770, but when a kahu-kūri-clad chief placed a flower in his hair for his portrait in 1844, he demonstrated that this was acceptable for someone of his status. Some ariki women wore coronets of tikumu leaves; further wearing of greenery is discussed later. Aute strips were used as hair ties and for attaching ear pendants.

Ear pendants took a variety of forms. *Pōhoi* and *kōpū* were white balls of downy albatross skin; other glossy pendants of bird skin hung to the shoulder; and sometimes a small live bird was worn. However, pendants of *pounamu* (greenstone) were highly treasured. Sourced only on the west coast of the South Island, pounamu was widely traded, being valued throughout the country for its hardness, color, and multiplicity of uses. Long, smoothly polished pounamu eardrops took their names from their specific shapes. *Mako* (shark teeth) were prized ear pendants; like the ancient whale-tooth pendant, these were also replicated in bone, as well as shell and pounamu.

Neck pendants were also made of ivory, bone, tooth, or pounamu. In the 1870s the large *rei-niho* (sperm whale tooth) was paramount among pendants. Unlike the ancient forms, this was always a genuine tooth, sometimes carved or marked with eyes or some facial element. Worn by chiefs, at the base of the throat, it was suspended from a cord of eight or twelve strands plaited around a central core. The alternative heirloom pendant was the *hei-tiki*. Carved from pounamu (or sometimes whalebone) the hei-tiki bears some resemblance to a female embryonic form, but its origins are lost. Such *taonga* (treasures) were buried with their owners, but like titireia, they were recovered during the *haihunga* (exhumation ceremonies). Hei-tiki acquired great mana from the ancestors who had previously worn them and as such were acknowledged and wept over. (They held no role of talisman or religious significance as sometimes alleged.)

Other pounamu pendant forms alluded to bats or eels. Ephemeral pendants included perfumed balls of impregnated bird skin or resins, suspended from intricate multicorded strands, and worn by both men and women. *Aurei* (cloak pins) were made of ivory or bone, or a paua shell rim; these long, slim, slightly curved pins were used to fasten cloaks in place, but they were also enjoyed for their sound when wearing a cluster that rattled together. A variety of weapons could complete the formal appearance: pounamu, whalebone, and wooden clubs of diverse forms such as *mere*, *taiaha*, *tewhatewha*, and more. As such, they form an extensive class of their own.

Another broad range of body supplements consisted of mourning headwear. In 1769 men and women at Queen Charlotte Sound were depicted wearing large, dark-feathered mourning caps; but this variety is unknown from elsewhere. In other regions women wore woven muka pōtae-taua with tags of seaweed. Other designs created a visual barrier between the eyes of the wearer and her world. One regional style, made from hollowed gourds, had dog tail hair fringing to cover the eyes; women wore this type continually until it disintegrated and fell off. Another woven muka chaplet had attachments of black, dried seaweed, or the epidermis of the kuta rush hanging from it, in natural colors of white and pale yellow, or dyed black and brown. Tied at the back of the head, the attachments hung over the face and all around, concealing the wearer. Alternatively, metallic-green tail feathers of kēreru or iridescent black of *tūī* (*Prosthermadera novaeseelandiae*), still attached to the skin, were used; the feathers swayed as the wearer moved about.

Historically, wearing green leaves around the head was a customary indication of mourning. The appropriate leaf species varied regionally; in many areas large, shiny, bitter-tasting,

In this portrait Te Rangituke, chief's son of Kawakawa, Bay of Islands, New Zealand, wears a finely woven, honey-colored, glossy *paepaeroa* (high-status cloak). Spaced weft-twining runs vertically through the garment, and bands of subtle-hued, intricate *tāniko* weaving (in ocher-red, tan, and brown) border the front edges and hem. He has a full facial *moko* (tattoo) and holds a traditional *taiaha* (weapon) decorated with white *awe* and red feathers. At his foot lies a carved *waka huia* (feather box), but his ear ornament of red ribbon with gold coin shows his modernity. Rangituke traveled between Sydney and New Zealand and could dress for both worlds: immaculate in European clothing one day, impressively robed in high-status Māori dress the next. Beside him is his young son wearing a red cape, almost certainly rubbed with ocher, and holding a musket—the new prestigious weapon. His wife is depicted with a partial lip tattoo and a brown cloak with a thick plait at the neck-edge. Oil painting on canvas by Augustus Earle, 1827. Alexander Turnbull Library, Wellington, New Zealand.

heart-shaped leaves of *kawakawa* (*Macropiper excelsum*) or the widespread bracken fern *āruhe* (*Pteridium esculentum*) were customary. In northern regions the *raurenga* or kidney fern (*Trichomanes* [*Cardiomanes*] *reniforme*, Forst. f) was used. Also called *taringa hakeke* for its ear-like shape, this was one of the filmy ferns, which quickly wilted and drooped over the face of the wearer. Sitting in separate rows, men and women plaited it into the hair of the person sitting in front—thereby avoiding issues of tapu status. The tremendous variety of mourning wear indicates a major factor in the lives of old-time Māori.

Footwear was of lesser importance. For the most part Māori went barefoot, but occasionally woven sandals, or a combination of sandal and legging, were used. The muka *panaena* was described as little more than a toe cap tied at the ankle; the *parengarenga* or *kopa* and *tahau-taupa* were woven muka leggings, wrapped around the shin and laced in place. Combination leggings and footwear called *rohe*, and *tumatakura*, were used for protection against spiky groundcover; green harakeke *papari* lined with moss may also have protected against cold. Sandals, called *parewai* in the north, *pāraerae* in the south, were made of harakeke or tī kōuka, but the latter were longer-lasting, especially when made *torua* (double-layered) as opposed to *tahitahi* (single-layered). In winter paraerae were padded with tussock to insulate against the cold. However, footwear was primarily functional and never considered a formal dress item.

AGENCY OF DRESS

In the natural Māori world dressing well not only reflected the wearer's status but also the importance of an occasion. Fine garments worn for planting seed *kūmara* (sweet potato) signaled the importance of this event to ensure a bountiful harvest. The successful outcome of a battle might be influenced by the suitable appearance of the leading chief. Special attention paid to dress made particular statements. In the story of Rongomaiwāhine, when her mother prepares her to go to a new husband, combing her daughter's hair, adorning it with the finest feathers, and wrapping her in a prestigious cloak, the mother is endorsing her daughter's decision. However, when another young woman dressed in her finest, she had a very different message. Te Aohuruhuru felt so violated by the elderly husband who had exposed her beauty to his friends as she lay asleep that she made a decision. Wearing her best cloak and feathers, she climbed to a cliff top from where she could see her husband with his friends at sea. As they returned, they heard her singing a lament, then she leapt to her death before them. Te Aohuruhuru was stating what a treasure her husband's action had cost him.

Cloaks could convey other messages; one was a tacit call for assistance. Te Rangimowaho sought allies for a planned campaign. He deliberately burned holes in his cloak, then wore it to visit a potential ally, Raha. On arriving, he placed the damaged cloak on Raha's shoulders; Raha understood its message and allowed it to remain, signifying his willingness to assist. Another arrival, Tohiamanu, instantly assessed the situation and took the cloak onto his shoulders, indicating his support. In a different situation an ariki widow, Pareraututu (born ca. 1796), visited a nearby chief, Tukorehu, after a number of her local chiefs were killed. For days she sat silently, wrapped in a kahu-kūri that was also a *kahu-mamae* (garment of pain). Eventually, Tukorehu took heed of the unspoken request. When he lifted the cloak from

Pareraututu and placed it on his own shoulders, he undertook to resolve her pain. (This garment is held in the Auckland War Memorial Museum.)

These interactions took place between individuals of similar status. In other circumstances the mana of an individual precluded their personal items (a virtual extension of the self) being touched by those of lesser status: the high-born could mark or set aside an item or even a human being for themselves merely by placing their garment over it. Tribal histories record many examples. En route to his mother's people, when the young chief Tawhaki discovered a tree full of snared birds, he marked the tree for his exclusive use by hanging his cloak on it. In the 1700s the chief Te Rangiwhakaputa, arriving in a beautiful unpopulated bay, leapt ashore to claim the land for himself and his people by spreading his *rāpaki* on the beach. The full name of the beach is Te Rāpaki-o-Te-Rangiwhakaputa. In the nineteenth century the chieftainess Te Rangi Topeora claimed an enemy warrior for herself by covering him with her cloak. And in the common good a chief might place a ban on certain activities, such as local fishing during a particular season, and mark the place by hanging his garment there, a visible extension of his invisible mana.

Moreover, the possessions of such a rangitira (high status male or female) became imbued with an element of personal identity, infused with the owner's mana, and as a result were equally as tapu as the individual. For this reason such garments could not be worn or even touched by other, ordinary people, even after the original owner had died. Following the owner's death, personal items were either buried with the deceased or exposed to the elements at the tomb site. Only heritage items, buried with their owner, might be subsequently retrieved and the tapu ritually lifted to allow the taonga to be reused.

Changes occurred as European influences spread. Māori began to adopt the use of coffins, which were usually draped with a prestigious cloak. In the nineteenth century it was common for the cloak to be buried with the coffin, but as fewer cloaks came to be woven, this practice began to change. In the twentieth century it became possible to read the destination of a cloak covering a coffin. If the neck edge of the garment were placed toward the neck of the deceased, the cloak would accompany the coffin on its final journey; should the neck edge be laid toward the foot of the coffin, it remained with the living. Since the 1970s new cloaks are being woven; a family cloak is now reused at both somber and festive ceremonies, gradually accumulating additional mana from such usage.

DRESS AS INDICATORS OF IDENTITY AND CULTURAL UNITY

Despite changes over the years, cloaks, capes, and variations of piupiu continue to play a significant role in establishing both cultural identity and unity in the twenty-first century. Concurrently, some adopted colonial practices are now customary, and different personal adornment supplements have evolved.

Initially, Māori weavers enjoyed exploring the weaving potential of new resources introduced by European settlers; they experimented with corn husks in place of customary leaf materials, adopted time-saving candle wick and mop-cotton yarns in place of customary warps, and delighted in the variety of colors available in wool, cotton yarns, and other commercially dyed products. But colonial policies during the nineteenth century saw a decline in cultural arts as the Māori population struggled to survive. By the early twentieth century weaving arts were diminishing. In photographs individuals often signaled their heritage by wearing single-layered piupiu around their shoulders in place of a cloak, and sometimes pounamu jewelry set in gold, in European fashion.

Other changes occurred; wearing black was not a precontact Māori response to death. This practice developed following the death of Queen Victoria's husband in 1861. Black clothing became the mandatory expression of mourning, as with British colonial women who mirrored the English dress codes. Māori women who were financially able followed the lead of the settler hierarchy, although photographic evidence shows the practice varied considerably, occurring less in rural localities.

Adopting this colonial practice had great significance, ultimately instigating a new form of twentieth-century customary dress. Formal pōwhiri (welcoming) protocols include a call for visitors to come forward, bringing spirits of their dead with them in order that they may be greeted and mourned. Visitors advance slowly in a close group, then stop silent, momentarily, recalling the deceased, before continuing. This procedure effectively places everyone in a temporary state of mourning; accordingly, conscientious women wear long black clothing in this setting. Concurrently, women are expected to wear skirts rather than trousers; some wearing trousers will wrap a rug around their waists at such times.

Using greenery with black clothing remains the most visible expression of deep mourning for Māori women. This was particularly evident at the tangi for the Māori queen Te Arikinui Dame Te Atairangikaahu (1931–2006). Dressed in black, their black head scarves wreathed with green leaves, the hosting group of female mourners held leafy green branches fluttering in their hands. Black-clad family mourners with leafy coronets sat beside the coffin, which was dressed with a kiwi feather cloak. Behind them, the wall of the meetinghouse was draped with more cloaks. This tangihanga epitomized the elements of chiefly Māori funereal dress.

The twentieth century witnessed the revival of cultural arts and the continuing evolution of dress. The Waikato leader Princess Te Puea Herangi (1884–1952), who worked to achieve cultural regeneration combined with social progress for her people, become an iconic figure in somber clothing and white head scarf. Similarly, the figure of eighty-year-old Dame Whina Cooper (1895–1994) leading a Land March the length of the North Island in 1975 became nationally recognized with her head scarf, long skirt, and walking stick.

The Māori Women's Welfare League, formed in 1951, took a lead in reviving and maintaining the teaching of cultural arts. Tourism played a part; sightseers wanted to view concert parties; the performing groups compromised, reducing the piupiu to a single layer worn over a bright red skirt, with a faux tāniko, stitched bodice. But the basic skills survived. Dame Rangimārie Hetet (1892–1995) and daughter Diggeress Te Kanawa played important roles in revitalizing cloak making. In 1969 Emily Schuster (1927–1997) founded the weaving school at the Māori Arts and Crafts Institute in Rotorua. Part of the cultural renaissance, since 1983 Te Roopu Rāranga Whatu o Aotearoa, the national organization of Māori weavers, has continued promoting weaving arts, encouraging a return to authentic techniques and materials. In the twenty-first century courses are taught in groups and institutions around the country. But, apart from harakeke, access to customary resources can be problematic. Dispossession of Māori lands, swamp draining, land clearances, forest industries, and the legislated creation of reserves and national parks in an attempt to stem the destruction of indigenous flora and fauna have all contributed to the diminished availability of valued weaving resources.

Despite these factors, various items of dress continue to demonstrate cultural identity and unity in the twenty-first century. A customary form of functional kete (carry bag) woven in natural colors, or bright commercially dyed hues, is a new statement of identity for Māori women in European dress. No longer red, raukura have become albatross-down, worn by women of one specific regional affiliation. Bold pounamu pendants continue to be worn, often over black clothing. The rare whale-tooth pendant has returned, carved with new designs, proudly worn by men in formal European dress. Māori art has become an international commodity; artists are creating revived forms of hei-tiki using contemporary media. And contemporary forms of cloak and cape appear at every important function where Māori choose to celebrate their identity.

References and Further Reading

Angas, George French. *Savage Life and Scenes: Being an Artist's Impressions of Countries and Peoples at the Antipodes.* London: Elder & Co., 1847.

Beaglehole, J.C., ed. *The Journals of Captain James Cook on His Voyages of Discovery.* Vols. 1–4. London: Cambridge University Press, 1955–1971.

Beaglehole, J.C., ed. *The Endeavour Journal of Joseph Banks 1768–1771.* Vol. 1. Sydney: The Trustees of the Public Library of New South Wales in Association with Angus and Robertson, 1962.

Beattie, James, and Atholl Anderson. *Traditional Lifeways of the Southern Māori: The Otago University Museum Ethnological Project, 1920.* Otago, NZ: University of Otago Press, 1994.

Best, Elsdon. *The Māori As He Was; A Brief Account of Māori Life As It Was in Pre-European Days.* Wellington, NZ: Government Printer, 1974. (Originally published in 1925.)

Buck, Peter Henry (aka Te Rangi Hiroa, aka Sir Peter). "On the Māori Art of Weaving Cloaks, Capes, and Kilts." *New Zealand Dominion Museum Bulletin,* no. 3, 69–90. Wellington, NZ: Dominion Museum, 1911.

Buck, Peter Henry (aka Te Rangi Hiroa, aka Sir Peter). *The Evolution of Māori Clothing.* New Plymouth, NZ: Thomas Avery & Sons, 1926.

Duff, Roger. *The Moa-Hunter Period of Māori Culture.* 3rd ed. Wellington, NZ: Government Printer, 1977.

Earle, Augustus. *Narrative of a Residence in New Zealand. Journal of a Residence in Tristan da Cunha.* Edited by E.H. McCormick. Oxford: Clarendon Press, 1966. (Originally published in 1832.)

Hamilton, Augustus. *Māori Art.* London: The Holland Press, 1901. (Reprint, Wellington, NZ: The New Zealand Institute, 1972.)

Hopa, Ngapare. *The Art of Piupiu Making.* Wellington, NZ: A. H. & A. W. Reed, 1971.

Joppien, Rüdiger, and Bernard Smith. *The Art of Captain Cook's Voyages.* Vols. 1–3. New Haven, CT, and London: Yale University Press, 1985.

Ling, Roth H. *The Māori Mantle.* Halifax, UK,: Bankfield Museum, 1924. (Reprint, Carlton, Bedford, UK: Ruth Bean, 1979.)

Mead, Sidney M. (aka Hirini Moko Mead). *The Art of Taaniko Weaving: A Study of Its Cultural Context, Technique, and Development.* Wellington, NZ: Reed, 1968.

Mead, Sidney M. (aka Hirini Moko Mead). *Traditional Māori Clothing: A Study of Technological and Functional Change*. Wellington, NZ: A. H. & A. W. Reed, 1969.

Nicholas, John Liddiard. *Narrative of a Voyage to New Zealand, Performed in the Years 1814 and 1815, in Company with the Rev. Samuel Marsden, Principal Chaplain of New South Wales*. Vols. 1–2. London: James Black and Son, 1817.

Papakura, Makereti. *The Old-Time Māori*. London: Victor Gollancz Limited, 1938.

Parkinson, Sydney. *A Journal of a Voyage to the South Seas, in His Majesty's Ship The Endeavour: Faithfully transcribed From the Papers of the late Sydney Parkinson, Draughtsman to Sir Joseph Banks, Bart. In his Expedition with Dr. Solander round the World; and embellished With Twenty-nine Views and Designs, engraved by Capital Artists. To which is now added Remarks on the Preface, By the late John Fothergill, M. D. F. R. S. &c.* London: C. Dilly, 1784. (Reprint, London: Caliban Books, 1984.)

Pendergrast, Mick. *Te Aho Tapu: The Sacred Thread*. Auckland, NZ: Reed Methuen, 1987.

Pendergrast, Mick. *Māori Fibre Techniques: A Resource Book for Māori Fibre Arts: Ka Tahi Hei Tama Tu Tama*. Auckland, NZ: Reed, 2005.

Te Kanawa, Diggeress. *Weaving a Kakahu*. Wellington, NZ: Bridget Williams Books Limited in association with Aotearoa Moananui a Kiwa Weavers, 1992.

Patricia Te Arapo Wallace

See also Introduction to the Dress of the Pacific Islands; Dress of the Cook Islands.

Māori and European Dress: Cultural Exchanges in New Zealand

- European Dress as Gift and Barter, 1769–1830s
- Trade, Travel, and Dressing for Different Worlds
- Gender, Status, and Modified Dress
- Missionaries, Modesty, and Regulated Dress, 1815–1840s
- Spread of European Dress, 1840s–1880s
- Cultural Cross-Dressing

dress changed the way Māori signified identity, status, gender, and modesty, and it affected movement and the performance of various customary activities. The desire or pressure to acquire European dress altered the value of traditional commodities, and its adoption negatively affected Māori health. By the end of the nineteenth century European dress had completely replaced customary dress for everyday use, although women's styles developed some characteristic features. However, Māori continued a process of change in customary dress, transforming its most significant components into attire that, through its specific ritual or symbolic significance, continues to preserve and evoke pride in a distinctive cultural identity.

EUROPEAN DRESS AS GIFT AND BARTER, 1769–1830s

Māori initially experienced European dress during the sporadic visits of English and French scientific and commercial explorers in the last three decades of the eighteenth century. From the early 1790s to the late 1830s sealers, whalers, and traders increasingly frequented New Zealand coastal communities, seeking food supplies, flax, timber, curios, and women. As well as iron tools, muskets, tobacco, and new plants and animals for food, Māori were

From the late eighteenth century Māori have used dress as one of the means of negotiating and accommodating European culture, especially during the great influx of settlers in the mid- to late nineteenth century. Initially, Māori selectively combined European garments and accessories with their own dress, both as fashionable novelties and as a means of enhancing or gaining social standing. Over a much longer period of time Māori were required to wear European dress by Christian missionaries and eventually felt compelled to do so in order to live and work in an increasingly Europeanized world. The adoption of European

"The Great Ngati Maniapoto Chief Wahanui, Family and Friends at his House—Alexandra," 1885. Wahanui Huatare (seated, center) appears with family and friends, wearing predominantly European clothing, combined with cloaks. The women's dresses date from the 1850s or 1860s, while the men's and boys' are almost contemporary. The woman at center right is wearing a print dress layered over the top of another dress or longer petticoat. The woman seated on the ground (far right) appears to have a petticoat draped around her shoulders. Photograph by Alfred Henry Burton. Canterbury Museum, New Zealand.

able to acquire a growing range of *Pākehā* (European) garments, accessories, and textiles that were utilized as dress.

These included shirts, waistcoats, jackets, breeches and trousers, gowns and skirts, handkerchiefs and neckerchiefs, drawers, caps, stockings, boots, cloaks, blankets, old sheets, lengths of red print and blue-and-white calico, medals, beads, combs, razors, looking glasses, earrings, ribbons, and sundry trinkets. Most of these were trade goods that originated in England, India, New South Wales, and North America. The clothing was generally secondhand, much of it sold in bundles by traders who gathered up old-fashioned or worn-out garments and textiles for redistribution across Britain, to its colonies and plantations, and to parts of Europe. Crews on whaling and other ships usually carried a personal supply of old clothes that were used to patch their own garments but were also used for barter.

The first exchanges of dress followed the arrival of English explorer James Cook's *Endeavour* at Tūranga-nui Harbor (Poverty Bay), on the east coast of the North Island, on 9 October 1769. Cook's party left a gift of beads in a hastily abandoned village and later offered trinkets to the leader of a party of Māori warriors. Three Māori youths were taken aboard the *Endeavour*, where they were dressed up in European garments. The eldest boy, Te Haurangi, was also presented with a cloak of red serge (worsted wool or cotton fabric, diagonally twilled on both sides). This later became renowned as the battle garment named Te Makura, worn by *rangatira* (chiefs) of his *iwi* (tribe), Rongowhakāta.

In the Polynesian protocol for ceremonial welcomes, generous gifts of valuables such as prestige cloaks increased the *mana* (spiritual power or authority) of the giver, demonstrated their wealth and high status, and established a relationship of good will and protection. During subsequent first encounters with Cook and the French explorers Jean-François-Marie de Surville (1769) and Marc-Joseph Marion du Fresne (1772), rangatira in various coastal settlements presented items of dress such as personal *kākahu* (cloaks) decorated with dog skin and *tāniko* (woven geometrically patterned) borders, as well as ornaments and handheld weapons of bone or *pounamu* (New Zealand jade or "greenstone"). In addition to iron spike-nails and hatchets, the Europeans offered boat cloaks of red or green baize (coarse woolen fabric) and flannel (soft, plain or twilled woolen cloth), jackets of red broadcloth (high-grade cloth woven from finest felting wool), and lengths of calico and red print (cotton fabrics with printed decoration on one side).

Red (*kura*) was a *tapu* (sacred) color and thus had particular spiritual and social significance. Rangatira may have assumed the color had similar cultural associations for Pākehā, particularly as they first observed it in the garments and textiles presented or worn by the ships' captains, officers, and "gentlemen scientists" or military personnel. All these appeared to be people of mana, counterparts of the *kaumātua* (elders), principal and subordinate rangatira, *tohunga* (priests or experts in tradition and rituals), and warriors, who dominated the highly stratified Māori society. The cloak Te Makura might have been considered the equivalent of a *kahu-kura*, a rare and highly esteemed type of cloak that was completely covered with red feathers taken from *kākā* (*Nestor meridionalis*), a species of native parrot. Only those of highest hereditary or achieved status, and with great mana, were entitled to wear such dress, which embodied all the achievements of its previous owners as well as that of its current wearer.

TRADE, TRAVEL, AND DRESSING FOR DIFFERENT WORLDS

In these early contacts between Māori and Europeans, only some dress items were exchanged as formal gifts, most being the subject of barter. Māori already had a system of intertribal trade in various kākahu and other garments. Some kākahu had a greater economic value than others, based on their importance as indicators of status and mana. For most tribes at this period cloaks ornamented with dog skin (*kahu-kurī*) were considered too precious to be traded and would only be exchanged for other items as a token of friendship between social equals.

At first, Māori considered all or most European dress items and textiles to have very high cultural (and therefore economic) value—that is, they were perceived as rare, difficult to acquire, accessible only to those of highest status, and embodying mana. This view was quickly modified. It became obvious that even Pākehā "commoners" such as ordinary sailors had pieces of red or other colored cloth, as well as beads, ornaments, and old clothes, which they were willing to exchange with Māori of any status who had anything to barter. By the early 1800s clothing, dress-related accessories, and textiles were still eagerly sought by Māori, but iron chisels, nails, tomahawks, and muskets took precedence.

High-ranking Māori did not part indiscriminately with their most valuable ornaments, weapons, and fine cloaks. These items of dress distinguished kaumātua, tohunga, and principal rangatira from each other, from warriors of lesser status, and from commoners. The barter price rose exponentially as lower-ranking ambitious chiefs and warriors acquired Pākehā clothing and textiles through trading. It was the beginning of a trend that, up to the 1840s, saw many prominent Māori leaders seek increasingly elaborate and expensive European garments, as they tried to maintain the requisite visual distance from those of lower status. During the 1830s, for example, the South Island chief Tuhawaiki obtained not only the full dress uniform of a British aide-de-camp (complete with gold-laced trousers, cocked hat, and plume) for himself, but also a set of red-coat uniforms for his personal bodyguard. Conversely, some older rangatira rejected European dress altogether, again distancing themselves from ambitious, younger challengers.

Starting in the late eighteenth century but increasingly during the first decades of the nineteenth century, sons of rangatira and young commoners journeyed abroad, sailing to Australia, the Americas, Britain, India, and the islands of Southeast Asia and the Pacific, typically as crew on whaling ships. They were kitted out with sailors' ready-made cloth jackets and canvas trousers, striped or checked cotton shirts, and caps, which they brought back to New Zealand, together with other articles of dress and goods acquired as payment for their work. Some rangatira visited Norfolk Island and Port Jackson (Sydney) in New South Wales. There they mixed with the British officials, leading free settlers, and missionaries whom they considered social equals. Other chiefs sailed to England, where a few succeeded in their desire to meet the British monarch. In most cases these men returned to New Zealand with gifts of clothing, elaborate uniforms, and even armor. In 1814, for example, New South Wales governor Lachlan Macquarie ordered British officers' uniforms and new suits with scarlet coats for each of three rangatira visiting Port Jackson from the Bay of Islands.

Despite their keenness to acquire European clothing, Māori adventurers returning home characteristically shed the hard-won Pākehā garments in favor of their own dress, often before disembarking from the ship. Clothes and textiles were stored away for later piecemeal distribution among male and female relatives, partly as a form of largesse and partly because they were regarded as novel or prestigious to wear on some ceremonial occasions or when dealing with Europeans.

The voluntary putting aside of introduced clothing before or on rejoining their own people had been noted earlier by Cook, Surville, and others. Richard Cruise was a British officer on board the *Dromedary*, which was based in the Bay of Islands for ten months in 1820. He described how Repero, a chief's son who had returned on the ship from a stay in Parramatta, New South Wales, went ashore dressed in Pākehā clothing and carrying a large supply of other garments. Several days later the boy returned, wearing Māori dress and with his face coated in red ocher and oil. He explained that he should not have appeared in his village wearing anything but traditional dress and was now very ashamed and embarrassed by this transgression.

While it was polite and usually sensible (if not actually required) to adopt Pākehā garments and mannerisms when cohabiting, socializing, or working with Europeans, it was unacceptable to do so when reentering *Te Ao Māori* (the Māori world), at the point when rituals of welcome occurred. Through their dress, Māori had begun making clear statements about which "world" they were functioning in, at any given time—a practice that continues to the present.

GENDER, STATUS, AND MODIFIED DRESS

Pākehā garments were often worn in strange configurations and with little regard for gender differentiation, well into the 1840s. This practice started before widespread direct contact with Europeans. Māori customary dress was based on a wrapped or draped garment, rather than one that was shaped, fitting, and bifurcated, and so the correct way to wear Pākehā dress was not obvious.

Additionally, up until 1814 and the arrival of the missionary wives, only male Europeans visited New Zealand. Māori thus had no opportunity to observe that Pākehā dress signified gender mainly through differently constructed garments, rather than by different ways of wearing a universal garment. Similarly at this period, Māori and European body modifications sent different messages about gender. The Europeans were mostly clean-shaven, with relatively short hairstyles that resembled those of Māori women, while Māori men often grew beards, were tattooed on the face as well as the buttocks and thighs, and wore their long hair in topknots.

By the 1830s many Māori in northern coastal communities were well aware of how, and by whom, Pākehā clothing should be worn. Nevertheless, European dress codes were still largely irrelevant in Te Ao Māori. Pākehā clothes and textiles were used selectively and experimentally to extend the variety of garments worn in traditional manner, or were relocated to the role of innovative, fashionable accessories, to exhibit wealth and status.

Joel Polack, a trader who lived at Hokianga and Kororāreka during the 1830s, recorded the practice of men wearing female European dress. If a man possessed several gowns, he would often wear them all at the same time, arranging them in such a way as to show a section of each garment. Māori dress ignored the contours of the body, instead treating the trunk as a simplified geometric shape—either a rectangle, or one or more triangles. Thus, the men's arrangement of gowns reflected a traditional composition of overlapped cloaks, creating triangles to emphasize the vertical line and therefore the height of the wearer. Combined with increased bulk, it was an effective way of conveying the dignity and grandness of chiefly rank.

Polack also described the novel dress worn by some of those attending the *haihunga* (exhumation rites) of the deceased chief Ti Koki. One man displayed contrasting black-and-white stockings on his arms, while another had fastened a shirt in apron fashion around his otherwise naked waist. This man also sported a pair of canvas trousers wrapped around his throat like a gigantic neckerchief. Not to be outdone, one woman had donned a pair of trousers, although other women were more restrained, wearing checked shirts and gowns beneath woven flax cloaks.

Lengths of cloth and blankets were immediately useful to Māori because they could be worn in traditional cloak- or kilt-like fashion. European blankets became the most widespread and longest-lasting item of transitional or adapted Māori dress across

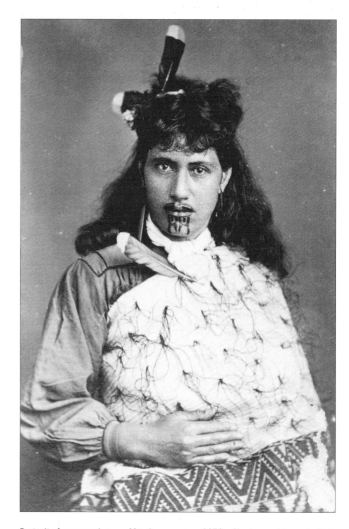

Portrait of unnamed young Māori woman, ca. 1870s. She has a chin *moko* (tattoo), *pounamu* ear pendants and *huia* feathers in her European-styled hair, and is wearing a "roundabout," or shirt, and neckerchief beneath a *korowai* cloak with wide *tāniko* border and a *huia* feather. Photograph by Foy Brothers. Canterbury Museum, New Zealand.

all classes and both sexes. They replaced some types of cloak, and their universal popularity contributed to the near loss of more complex traditional weaving skills.

The earliest blankets included among trade goods seem to be the tartan-patterned examples loaded on George Vancouver's ships *Discovery* and *Chatham*, which left England in April 1791. In April 1820 at Kororāreka (Russell), Richard Cruise noted the enthusiastic trading of vegetables for warm articles of clothing and blankets at the onset of cold weather, and by the 1830s blankets (*paraikete*) were probably the most numerically significant components of modified dress. Folded and draped in traditional arrangements, they were increasingly used as an alternative to utility capes and finer cloaks, even for formal occasions. In 1834 Edward Markham commented on the scarcity of kākahu and *kaitaka* (finely woven cloaks with a plain *kaupapa* or foundation, ornamented with colored and/or patterned borders), stating that both men and women now favored large, thick "English blankets."

For men, blankets also eventually replaced the kilt form of *pākē*, a utility garment of *harakeke* (New Zealand flax, *Phormium tenax*), originally worn by men and women as both a cape and a kilt. The blanket supplanted the latter by being folded in half and secured around the waist with a woven harakeke or leather belt. Blanket kilts were part of the otherwise conventional British infantry uniform worn by Māori who fought on the side of Europeans during the Land Wars of the 1860s, and they were even adopted by some of the British soldiers.

Blankets varied from plain to those with striped borders, large checks, and smaller-patterned tartans, all designs that related visually to the tāniko motifs found on kaitaka. Their popularity later encouraged newly established New Zealand woolen mills to manufacture blankets specifically for the Māori market. A surviving paraikete from the mid-1880s (Canterbury Museum, Christchurch, New Zealand) is of loosely woven worsted wool yarn, tartan-patterned in tan, cream, and yellow with a fine scarlet over-check.

Paraikete are commonly seen in painted and photographic images, some as late as the 1920s, when elderly women in particular were still using them as mantles over the top of European dress. Mothers continued to drape smaller rugs or blankets to form a sling or harness in which they could "back-pack" their babies or infants.

Rugs or blankets are still used on modern *marae* (meeting grounds) as additional warm wraps. However, the closest modern equivalent of a paraikete as everyday clothing may be the loose-fitting, check-patterned, and brightly colored woolen bush or work shirt known as a *swanni* (an abbreviation of the manufacturer's brand "Swanndri"), favored by many Māori as well as Pākehā.

MISSIONARIES, MODESTY, AND REGULATED DRESS, 1815–1840s

Māori children commonly went completely naked until the age of six or seven, and for adults nudity or seminudity was normal when hard work was undertaken or in battle. Most Europeans found this dress code disturbing and "uncivilized." The English Protestant Christian missionaries, in particular, also saw it as immoral and sinful. Dressing Māori in so-called suitable European garments was seen as means of "civilizing" them, a state regarded as necessary for conversion to Christianity.

Missionary ideas of suitable clothing were based on a notion that Māori were the equivalent of the working-class "deserving poor" of England. Accordingly, Church Missionary Society (CMS) school pupils in 1815 were to be clothed in homemade garments of the same cheap, brown woolen fabric or "stuff" commonly used in English charity schools. From the mid-1820s to the 1840s the color of the gowns for older girls was an equally serviceable dark blue. This was a hue traditionally found in working-class clothing, because the dyes that produced it were cheap, but it was also associated with the traits of humility, piety, and godliness that the missionaries wanted to cultivate in Māori.

The dress styles for girls and women at the mission stations were variously described in missionary journals and letters of the 1820s to the mid-1850s as English "bedgowns" and aprons, round pinafores with sleeves, loose print garments similar to nightgowns, and "roundabouts" of striped blue fabric. None of this was fashionable attire, especially the flared, T-shaped, thigh-length jacket known as a bedgown. This was originally a stylish eighteenth-century "at-home" garment, which later became part of working-class women's dress. It was worn with a "petticoat" (a skirt-like outer garment) and secured with an apron.

Although *roundabout* was a term later used to describe a boy's or sailor's waist-length jacket, the missionaries seem to have applied it to both the full-length girl's dress cut like a nightgown, and to the waist-length, blouse-like garment that remained popular with Māori girls and women right up to the early twentieth century. Both were ample forms gathered to a yoke, with long, generous sleeves gathered at the wrist or left open. The short roundabout was worn over a skirt.

All of these clothes were relatively simple to make and thus served another purpose—that of teaching Māori women to construct their garments in the European fashion and from European textiles. The provision of male garments was more complicated. The missionary men cut out trousers from white cotton duck (canvas) or moleskin (a robust twilled cotton) and taught these skills to Māori boys and young men. The trousers were sewn up by the European and Māori mission women, who also made checked or striped shirts and blue or white smock-frocks for the boys. According to American artist Augustus Earle, who lived in the Bay of Islands for nine months during 1827, the missionaries insisted that each boy's luxuriant hair be cropped short and hidden beneath a tightly fitting Scotch bonnet (a soft, round, brimless, woven hat).

By the 1830s short hair had become the sign of a Christian or "missionized" Māori male, replacing the traditional topknot, while long hair was encouraged in girls and women, thus completely reversing traditional styles. The practice of *moko* (tattoo) was being actively discouraged, as many missionaries regarded it as an "abomination" and a sign of the devil.

The missionaries ruled that the provided garments could only be worn at the mission station, because children of chiefly families were often sent to school just to get European clothing. Adult Māori living in the approved European fashion within the mission station or attempting to do so in their own villages were supplied with clothing and blankets from the CMS stores, and sometimes, by the 1840s, with secondhand garments obtained from the missionaries or their supporters.

Initially, older girls were occasionally allowed to weave themselves more familiar Māori garments, using flax provided by the mission. However, they could only wear these to do dirty work around the mission station or if they went home to visit their families. Customary modes of dress were thus associated with degrading work within the European community and (by implication) with the supposedly inferior non-Christian traditional lifestyle. In 1856 Vicesimus Lush described being taken by canoe on the Waikato River to the Taupiri Mission Station. Shortly before arrival, the men stopped paddling while they changed into Pākehā trousers, woolen shirts, neckerchiefs, and boots in order to comply with the mission station dress regulations. This practice of dressing differently in the Māori and the European worlds had been initiated by Māori but was now reinforced by the missionaries for different reasons.

SPREAD OF EUROPEAN DRESS, 1840S–1880s

Many more Europeans started to acquire land and settle in New Zealand after 1840. Māori men seeking work or living at places like the southern shore–based whaling stations were now better placed to obtain clothing and textiles. They were issued with the same clothing as the Pākehā whalers: duck and flushing (strong woolen cloth) trousers; baize and regatta (blue-and-white-striped twilled cotton) shirts; red flannel jackets, short, fitted monkey jackets (sailors' rough-weather jackets) of thick dark blue cloth, and long coats; shoes and half boots (close-fitting boots reaching just above the ankle); sou'wester (waterproof) hats and fur caps; and comforters (long scarves).

Young Māori men continued to travel abroad in search of adventure. In April 1853 Lush observed a group in Auckland who had recently returned with plenty of money from the Australian goldfields. They had spent it on the latest Pākehā fashionable clothes, gold-headed walking canes, and cigars, and they had grown long beards in the European style.

Lutheran missionary Johann Wohlers, who lived on Ruapuke Island in Foveaux Strait from 1844 to 1884, remembered the period 1850–1860 as one of widespread transition from Māori to European customs. By 1860 his older converts came to church in clean and neat (if sometimes patched) Pākehā clothes. However, he also noted that younger Māori were no longer content with plain or secondhand dress, preferring new, fashionable garments. In 1874 Alice Lees described several such young Ngai Tahu men in the coastal town of Oamaru in the middle South Island. They had adopted the type of dark blue jackets, white scarves, and white straw sailor hats worn for boating by English university students.

It was no longer just the missionaries, but also the new settlers who preferred that Māori wear European clothing. Chief Justice Sir William Martin, for example, refused to allow Māori men into his house unless they wore at least a blue shirt and white trousers. The requirement to wear European dress (as distinct from Māori adopting and adapting European garments on their own terms) had became a political act, by which not only the land but its inhabitants were being colonized.

Chiefs and higher-ranking families acquired fashionable dress and attended social functions in the larger towns, where they occasionally mixed socially with Pākehā. In January 1870 Ellen Fox referred in a letter to the Māori women she had seen at a reception given by the governor, Sir George Ferguson Bowen, and his wife. All were dressed in lace-trimmed silks and velvets and adorned with jewelry. From this period onward, formal painted and photographic portraits, a number of which began to be commissioned by higher-ranking Māori themselves, usually show both men and women in fashionable middle-class clothing and hairstyles, indistinguishable from that of the Pākehā colonists.

The transition to European dress for ordinary Māori women, however, had in general been very much slower, even in the coastal trading settlements. Initially, they acquired beads, ribbons, earrings, and other novelty objects to replace or complement traditional displays of shells, feathers, flowers, and pounamu ornaments. Missionary fashions aside, it was not until the 1850s or later that European women's dress filtered through to remoter parts of New Zealand. Even then, unfamiliar skirts and petticoats were often worn in the same manner as harakeke mats and cloaks, arranged over one shoulder, leaving the other arm free.

Posed photographs taken by Pākehā in various small rural Māori villages during the 1880s have an element of dressing up for the camera. Some outfits were obviously supplied by the photographer, appearing on different women in different villages. This suggests that European garments were still less accessible to women but were considered desirable. Most garments were outmoded and motley in style—a mixture of print, checked, and striped cotton gowns more typical of the 1850s or 1860s, or plain and patterned shirts or roundabout-styled blouses worn with full skirts of similar materials. Traditional kākahu, or pākē worn diagonally across the chest, were often added over these clothes (a convention first noted by Polack in the 1830s), as were blankets worn like shawls or cloaks.

Family portrait of Hone Wetere Te Rerenga with his wife and son, 1885. Te Rerenga is wearing conventional European shirt, tie, waistcoat with watch chain and fob, suitcoat, trousers, and boots, with a large greatcoat. His wife wears one long ear pendant (probably *pounamu*), with feathers in her long, European-styled hair. She wears a floral print "roundabout" and a plain skirt, beneath a *korowai* cloak with *tāniko* borders, and is barefoot. Their young son is wearing a European brimless cap, jacket, trousers, and boots. Photograph by Alfred Henry Burton. Canterbury Museum, New Zealand.

Many rural women retained their traditional short hairstyles, but some started to wear head scarves, a fashion that became very popular from the early 1900s onward. Occasionally, a more fashionably dressed younger woman was photographed in a reasonably up-to-the-minute hat, and some appeared in men's casual hats.

CULTURAL CROSS-DRESSING

Wearing the clothes of another society (cultural cross-dressing) often requires an adjustment of posture and movement. Māori soon found that European garments were not always compatible with customary styles of fighting and dancing, or for hunting and fishing. For many years men were reluctant to wear trousers when engaged in such activities, finding them an encumbrance to easy movement. The modified style of dress eventually adopted by rural Māori women allowed them to function comfortably in a domestic environment that for many years saw little change from the traditional. Daily food growing, gathering, and preparing, activities such as weaving, and traditional postures involving reclining or sitting on the heels would have been uncomfortable if not impossible in most full manifestations of nineteenth-century female dress.

In the mid-1880s James Inglis observed that although Māori men living near Auckland, Napier, Wanganui, and in the Taranaki region wore European dress by day, at night they reverted to their customary lighter-weight garments, with bare heads and bare feet. Inglis and many others, including Māori commentators, attributed part of the high mortality rate among Māori in the mid- to late nineteenth century to the improper use of European clothing. This included wearing wet garments and blankets, or discarding clothing when overheated and at night when it was cold. Both practices resulted in people contracting severe chills that often resulted in fatal chest infections.

The expense and initial scarcity of European clothes also led to the sharing of garments, and consequently any contagious diseases they might have harbored. Ngāti Porou chiefs complained in 1860 about unscrupulous traders who paid for produce with rotten and probably filthy clothing. European garments were too expensive to replace regularly and required frequent laundering to keep clean and kill germs. This was a new concept, and the lack of required facilities in Māori villages made it a difficult or almost impossible task for very many years.

Although Māori plaited sandals and leggings from harakeke or other plant fibers, for use in rough, slippery, or cold conditions, they normally went barefoot. There are many records of the discomfort caused by unfamiliar and poorly fitting European leather boots and shoes. In 1820 Richard Cruise commented that Māori had no difficulty running barefoot over sharp rocks and rough ground. Wearing shoes, however, made them so crippled they could hardly walk. As the pressure grew to conform to wearing full European dress, traditional skills were sometimes used to produce European-styled footwear woven from harakeke. In the late 1850s Dr. Walter Buller also recorded Māori in Canterbury (the middle region of the South Island) wearing thick stockings inside sturdy flax sandals if they could obtain no European shoes.

By the 1880s the majority of Māori chose or felt obliged to dress in some form of European clothes for everyday wear, both within Māori communities and when participating in activities in a Pākehā environment. While men's clothing styles were largely indistinguishable from those of their European counterparts, rural Māori women seemed to have consciously developed a comfortable but unfashionable style utilizing loose-fitting gowns or full blouses with skirts. They chose to ignore European dress gender conventions by adding men's hats, waistcoats, shirts, and jackets, and by smoking pipes in public. Unfashionable or unconventional color and garment combinations, such as the scarlet, crimson, and green velveteen blouses with shabby black skirts, a man's ordinary suit jacket teamed with a blue neckerchief, red apron, and a mauve skirt described in 1902 by Edith Searle Grossman, continued to strike most Pākehā as both "curious" and "picturesque."

Poverty, lack of access to good quality clothing, and the demographics of isolation played a considerable role in developing this idiosyncratic dress, but it also seems Māori women deliberately choose to maintain an alternative image or identity to Pākehā even while wearing European garments. Migration to towns and cities from the 1930s, but particularly from the 1960s onward, eventually broke down most of these style differences.

The early ways of wearing European dress to maintain a unique identity have been mirrored by a consistent retention and development of some traditional garments as costume, for use by both sexes on special occasions, or in ceremonies of considerable spiritual and social significance. Within this context Māori women have again created another distinctive costume specifically gendered to themselves. This comprises a calf-length or longer black dress (or skirt and blouse), shawl, and the traditional *pare* (headband or chaplet) with *kawakawa* or other green leaves, which is worn by those in mourning and by ceremonial mourners. A fusion of European protocol (the black garments) and the ancient headwear associated with bereavement and remembrance of *tipuna* (ancestors), the combination is a statement of Māori uniqueness.

Māori responses to European clothing and ornamentation since the eighteenth century illustrate the way dress can assist the process of acculturation, while helping retain a distinctive cultural identity. Māori initially indulged in a process of selective cultural cross-dressing, enabling them to experiment with new aspects of an increasingly dominant foreign culture on their own terms.

Māori women in particular created a distinctive style of Europeanized dress for themselves, only partly in response to restricted access to a source of quality, fashionable garments. This dress enabled them to fit in with a changing world to a reasonable degree, while at the same time retaining their own identity.

Traditional dress associated with highly significant social and spiritual situations gradually assumed the role of costume and thus survived the acculturation process when more mundane garments fell into disuse and were lost from the cultural repertoire. Some traditional dress developed new forms to answer a need in the context of ceremony and ritual. Dress has been one means by which Māori have explored alternative images of themselves and in the process retained their cultural identity.

References and Further Reading

Bell, Leonard. *The Māori in European Art: A Survey of the Representation of the Māori by European Artists from the Time of Captain Cook to the Present Day.* Wellington, NZ: Reed, 1980.

Brittan, S. J., G. F. Grace, C. W. Grace, and A. V Grace, eds. *A Pioneer Missionary among the Māoris 1850–1879. Being Letters and Journals of Thomas Samuel Grace.* Palmerston North, NZ: G. H. Bennett & Co., n. d.

Cruise, Richard A. *Journal of a Ten Months Residence in New Zealand.* London: Longman, Hurst, Rees, Orme, Brown and Green, 1823.

Drummond, Alison, ed. *The Auckland Journals of Vicesimus Lush 1850–63.* Christchurch, NZ: The Pegasus Press, 1971.

Drummond, Alison, ed. *The Waikato Journals of Vicesimus Lush, 1864–8, 1881–2.* Christchurch, NZ: The Pegasus Press, 1982.

Earle, Augustus. *Narrative of a Nine Months Residence in New Zealand.* Christchurch, NZ: Whitcombe & Tombs, 1909. (Originally published in 1832.)

Hawthorn, H. B. "The Māori: A Study in Acculturation." *American Anthropologist* 46, no. 2, part 2 (1944).

King, Michael. *Māori: A Photographic and Social History.* Auckland, NZ: Heinemann Reed, 1989.

Markham, Edward. *New Zealand or Recollections of It.* Edited by E. H. McCormick. Wellington, NZ: R. E. Owen, Government Printer, 1963.

Ollivier, I., C. Hingley, and J. Spencer, eds. *Extracts from Journals Relating to the Visit to New Zealand of the French Ship St Jean-Baptiste under the Command of J. F. M. de Surville.* Wellington, NZ: Alexander Turnbull Library Endowment Trust with Indosuez N. Z., 1987.

Polack, Joel. *Manners & Customs of the New Zealanders.* Vol. 1. London: James Madden & Co., 1840. (Reprint, Christchurch, NZ: Capper Press, 1976.)

Porter, Frances, ed. *The Turanga Journals 1840–1850—Letters and Journals of William and Jane Williams, Missionaries to Poverty Bay.* Wellington, NZ: Price Milburn for Victoria University Press, 1974.

Reed, A. H., and A. W. Reed, eds. *Captain Cook in New Zealand—Extracts from the Journals of Captain James Cook Giving a Full Account in His Own Words of His Adventures and Discoveries in New Zealand.* Wellington, NZ, Auckland, NZ, Sydney: A. H. & A. W. Reed, 1969.

Jennifer Quérée

See also Introduction to Māori Dress; Moko Māori: Skin Modification; The Māori Pari (Bodice); Hawaiian Dress Prior to 1898; Niue: Dress, Hats, and Woven Accessories; Missionary Dress in Samoa.

Moko Māori: Skin Modification

The Māori people settled Aotearoa (New Zealand) from the islands of the eastern Pacific, coming in successive waves over many centuries. They brought with them the languages, music, belief systems, and technologies of their cultures of origin. They also brought the practice of permanent skin modification. Tattoo chisels similar to those used in western Polynesia have been found in some of the earliest excavations. With the new environment came new resources: massive hardwood forests, nephrite and argillite stone, countless new fiber plants, and prolific bird life. A distinctive culture evolved in the more temperate islands of Aotearoa, demonstrated in part by a differing form of facial adornment. The name of this is *moko*; *ta moko* is the process, and moko is the outcome. For men it reinforces a particular Māori aesthetic, that of a stylish aristocrat stepping out with his hair finely dressed and oiled, secured by an elaborate bone comb, and embellished with lace-like heron or downy albatross feathers, with nephrite jade or whale ivory pendants hanging from the ears and neck. Depending on the season, he might be layered in cloaks, beneath which a beautiful folded belt encircled the hips, a looped cord holding his penis in place. These items clothed his body; the body itself was a complex composition of tattoo design—spirals, geometric lines, and other shapes swirling on his face, legs, buttocks, back, and arms.

Although not discussed here, the aesthetic also affected a tall, narrow-hipped, lean, trapezoid look, with the shoulders broadened dramatically by twisted dog-skin tags or complex braided borders that lifted the observer's eye above the gored fabric, which was shaped to the wearer's body. A *rangi paruhi*, or finely tattooed face, was the ultimate style statement, occasionally enhanced by the glistening, perfumed oils of the titoki (*Alectryon excelsum*), raukawa (*Nothopanax edgerleyi*), or other plants.

Moko had many functions. It was worn to fascinate, terrify, and seduce through the skin. It was carried to imprint, honor, immortalize, and remember in the flesh and was intended to enhance, transform, and extend through the body to the soul itself. In the old Māori world every adult had some form of inserted ink, if not on the face, definitely on the body, for even the most

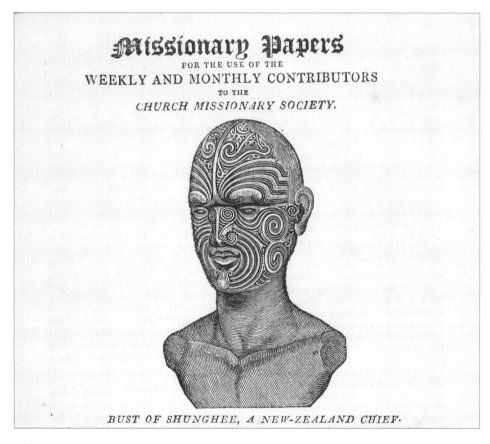

The bust of Shunghee, a New Zealand chief, as represented in *Missionary Papers*, ca. 1815. The illustration clearly shows the bold spiral forms of basic *moko* (Māori skin modification). Europeans had disdain for the tradition and sometimes condemned it, but it thrived until at least the Treaty of Waitangi in 1840. Wood engraving by Hongi Hika. Alexander Turnbull Library, Wellington, New Zealand.

humble and enslaved prisoner of war had designs, however crude or self-imposed, on the flesh.

For the first eighty years of contact the European traders, whalers, escaped convicts, sealers, travelers, and even missionaries were fascinated with tattoos. They recognized the discipline and beauty in the designs, and they admired the aesthetic, while not quite understanding it. By the mid-nineteenth century, due to the relentless efforts of Christian missionaries, and the escalating settler incursions on coastal and inland tribal territories, fascination was replaced by hostility. For a few rare Europeans the romance endured as they chose to assimilate, to live as Māori warriors, and to assume the full face and body markings of the Māori fighting chief. In the early 1800s two such famous personalities were Barnet Burns, an enterprising flax trader, and John Rutherford, an armorer and mercenary, the latter being an especially glamorous figure, with work from Hawai'i and the Marquesas embellishing his skin. They lived in the troubled, changing times of the 1820s, a period known as the Musket Wars.

MOKO: TECHNIQUES AND DESIGNS

The tattoo technique for face and forehead differed from that applied to the buttocks and thighs. Lower bodywork, as well as covering the shoulders, back, and arms, was achieved by the puncture technique, piercing the skin by tapping a miniature hoe-shaped instrument with a small wooden mallet stick. The instrument, called an *uhi*, comprised a bone chisel with a serrated comb-like edge that held and inserted the pigment. This was lashed to a wooden haft. Large blocks or stripes and swirls of color were achieved in this way.

Work on the face differed significantly, and it is this technique that continues to impress and confound even generations later. Its most enduring visual record is found in the nostalgic portraits of the Māori by Charles Frederick Goldie, made at the turn of the twentieth century. This form of moko involved traumatizing and cicatrizing the facial skin, creating channels of greenish-black colored scar tissue, which was raised in noticeable relief. The chisels used were like scalpels, whose straight cutting edge sliced into the skin. To achieve a more textured effect, the lines would be reopened over many sessions. This caused the color to intensify in the scar tissue, which was often deeply incised as it was widely stretched across the skin.

As in the Pacific islands of their origin, Māori used soot from burned organic material to make *ngarahu*, or tattoo pigment. This was mixed with oils, plant juices, and spring water. For the lighter, yet larger work on the body, the soot of the *aweto*—a vegetable caterpillar (*Cordiceps robertsii*)—was used; for the face the preferred source substance was the resin of the *kahikatea* (*Podocarpus excelsum*) or *kauri* (*Agathis australis*), both of which ensured a lustrous black. The process of manufacture was challenging, ritualized, and finely tuned, and the inky end product could last for many seasons.

Mainly men and some women worked as *tohunga ta moko*, or practitioners of this esteemed art form. Like woodcarving, architecture, and canoe construction, it was usually the domain of particular families, or clans, and many celebrated artists were actively sought after, and their work commissioned. Often they inscribed clients in groups, visiting a village to work, and staying for some time; they were an elite class, and the more famous artists commanded very high fees, in coveted weaponry, elegant garments,

and fine jewelry. They perfected an aesthetic whose impact was closely associated with Tu Matauenga, the god of war.

Serious tattooing began in adolescence, and available economic resources determined the extent. Undertaking the process of moko was usually a collective project, although every individual carried a unique design; no two patterns were ever the same, because the conformation of the face or body determined the design and the placement of the patterns. What suited a broader face with flatter planes would not work on someone with lean aquiline features; similarly, lower bodywork was consciously applied to enhance the shape and cater to the vanity of the wearer.

The basic patterns in moko Māori are flowing lines, curvilinear or geometric, often repetitive, extending into and developing from serpentine or spiral forms. Different regions have different terms for these designs.

For women the facial design field was usually confined to a central panel covering the mid-brow, the nostrils, the upper lip, then both lips, and the chin. Some extended into the throat and continued down to the genitals. Many women also had elaborate thigh and leg designs, and some female war leaders in New Zealand's North Island assumed the full rangi paruhi, or a half-pattern, with just one side enhanced. The Kai Tahu people of New Zealand's South Island were noted for the high number of full-face moko women, though this unique practice had declined by the early nineteenth century. Vulval marking also occurred, particularly in aristocratic families, whose young women often confirmed strategic political alliances through marriage. Such work was always undertaken by female practitioners.

Both cicatrisation and puncturing caused intense pain, and the process was carefully managed with a series of ritual prohibitions, or *tapu*, which involved both operator and patient. For the latter no food was allowed except a nutritious broth offered via a special feeding device or *korere*; there was to be no intimate physical contact and no peering at reflections until the wounds had healed. The operator was also restricted, forbidden to feed him- or herself or have any contact with food or common substances, and the actual site itself was regarded as off limits. This controlled the activity and reduced the risk of contamination—even though they had no knowledge of "germs," they knew about infection. Acquiring moko was fraught with risk, yet to sustain or embellish their body art, the ancient Māori went back for more, despite the intolerable pain of the process.

James Cook and the voyagers who followed him brought metal with them, a material that changed the art form, and within two generations, many artists included *rino* (iron) chisels in their tool sets. Despite missionary condemnation and European contempt, the rangi paruhi became even more detailed and impressive. For the sake of beauty and personal reputation, people endured the pain.

EIGHTEENTH TO TWENTIETH CENTURIES: DECLINE

In 1840 the Treaty of Waitangi was signed between the many (but not all) Māori chiefs and the British Crown. It is significant that a number of the signatories actually chose to inscribe the document with a small pattern from their facial moko, this subtle glyph effectively conveying their mana, or chiefly authority, to the process. Other legal instruments, particularly land deeds, were similarly authorized. Within a few years of its signing, the settlers breached the treaty, and decades of conflict, aggression, distrust, atrocity, and invasion ensued.

The tattooed face became a powerful symbol of resistance for many Māori, whereas for others it seemed in decline. Arthur S. Thomson, an Anglican missionary, reflected that as his cohort considered it the "Devil's art," the incoming settlers' plain faces were setting an effective example. By the end of the nineteenth century the scourge of foreign diseases, the extensive land confiscations after the land wars, and the sheer demographic weight of settler numbers had all reduced the Māori population to 42,113 in 1896, a fraction of its earlier size. The challenge confronting Māori was the task of adapting to a society that was becoming increasingly industrial and urbanized. The political view was that the faster Māori engaged in the detribalization project and assimilated into modern society the better. Assimilation meant an expected wholesale commitment to the new *Pākehā* (European) mainstream society.

Māori were pressured to discontinue the practice of moko. They rallied, however, and in subtle ways, they resisted. Māori women continued to have their chins inscribed late into the twentieth century, so that there has always been a tattooed Māori face seen upon the *marae*—the ceremonial courtyards—of New Zealand. By the early 1970s there were just over seventy elderly women left with the *moko kauae*, or inscribed chin tattoo. Many had work applied by a third technique, similar to the *irezumi* tattoo technique of Japan; tight needle clusters were lashed with cotton to a small firm stick and pushed into the flesh with a regular, swift rhythm. The sharps, often as many as twelve or fifteen, held the ink momentarily then released it into the top layers of skin. It was regarded as less painful and much quicker than the traditional uhi technique, which it superseded in the first decade of the twentieth century. Itinerant artists, including two women, traveled to many rural communities, but by 1945 the practice had discontinued. Many wearers of the twenty-first century grew up with such women as memorable, other-worldly matriarchs. They inspired and awed generations of young people; they were a symbol of courage, resilience, and canny transformation.

Moko is about metamorphosis, about change, about crisis, and about coping with that crisis. To many contemporary wearers, the descendants of those first illustrated chieftains encountered by Cook, painted by artists such as Sydney Parkinson, Augustus Earle, Joseph Jenner Merrett, Frederick Goldie, and Goffried Lindauer, moko remains a strategy, a means of engagement, an expression of self.

LATE TWENTIETH CENTURY: REVIVAL

Moko manifests pride, celebration, and identity for Māori people in the twenty-first century. For many decades it was regarded as outmoded, unnecessary, and regressive, certainly by the colonizing Pākehā, and to an increasing degree by urbanized and relocated Māori. Meanwhile, Māori language, culture, and lands continued to be threatened by government policy, and the inertia caused by dispossession and the colonial process. Yet these same Māori, urbanized and relocated, still marked their own arms, or thighs, or hands, or ankles, and occasionally faces. At school, in prisons, at youth camps, on rugby trips, it was something that Māori simply did: the inscribing of the skin, the pricking in of color with ballpoint pen, Indian ink, pencil lead.

In the late 1960s and early 1970s new excitement and vitality were stirring in the Māori world, the world of both city and country. Urban activist groups like Nga Tama Toa and Te Reo Māori, inspired by the civil rights movement, the anti–Vietnam War protests, and the growing ulcer of rugby contact with apartheid South Africa, Māori grievances were boldly thrust into the public arena. Land, culture, and language all became major concerns, and what some described as the "Māori renaissance" burst forth, expressed not only in political confrontation and resolution but in the arts—music, performance, fine arts, photography, film, and television. Like Māori language, Māori design was becoming more and more pronounced; it was beginning to define a New Zealand imagery.

By the late 1980s it was center stage, dramatically, inventively, upon Māori skin. *Kapa haka* (performing arts teams), as early as the 1940s, used eyebrow pencil and black marker pen moko to enhance their performance. This deepened and broadened as the decades passed, with patterning no longer two lines on the chin for females and four lines on brow and cheeks plus a spiral on either side for males, instead of the finer cicatrization of former generations. Painted-on moko became an art form; for the wearer it meant something special even for the period of performance. By 1990, with the engagement of gang-affiliated artists and their homemade rotary guns, and through the commitment and passion of one master carver who trained with Pākehā tattooists, the technique became permanent. Sophisticated electric machines were purchased and mastered, and the work moved from the forearms and the shoulders, from the wrists and the ankles, to the face. It became an assertion of being Māori, of confronting the viewer, of reminding each other that pride was beneath and upon the skin; that it could be there, forceful, indelible, and forever.

Māori customary art, through the influential Te Māori exhibition, which traveled across the United States and throughout New Zealand in the 1980s, followed by smaller but equally impressive shows in Australia and the British Isles, was going global. The films *Utu* (1983), *The Piano* (1993), and *Once Were Warriors* (1994) brought the tattooed face once again into the consumers' consciousness; moko design was mainstreamed and featured on the catwalks of Milan and Paris, in the collections of Thierry Mugler and Paco Rabanne. The modern "primitive" movement recognized the elegance inherent in what they considered an extreme form of body modification. Māori skin art and later Māori skin artists flourished in London, Amsterdam, Berlin, and Sydney, following the international convention circuit that also featured traditional Samoan chisel masters. Celebrities advertised and accessorized particular forms, and particular artists; clothing chains like adidas and Canterbury launched campaigns reflecting the new trend, which was also explored by comic books and video games. These appropriations have continued to cause considerable debate and controversy.

In the moko world there is another issue that is equally contentious and engaging. It concerns women, and women as artists and not just helpers or "stretchers" (attendants whose hands manipulate, stretch, and assess the skin being worked on). This role is a key factor in the uhi or chisel technique, and also in the machine tattoo of the larger body areas, such as the back, thighs, and buttocks of bigger recipients.

Contemporary moko practitioners, most of whom are male, constantly deal with the expectations of those that seek out their skills and knowledge. They find themselves treading

A head and shoulders portrait of Anehana, with full facial *moko* (skin modification), from the Auckland district, ca. 1900. At this point the Māori population was being pressured to assimilate into the new urban society, and the fully inscribed face became rare in the twentieth century. Alexander Turnbull Library, Wellington, New Zealand.

unfamiliar waters and being challenged by the art and its forms, application, technologies, and sense of commitment to the culture from which it stems. Much is expected of them. They are assumed to be competent designers and technicians, narrators of symbolic histories resourced from a deep familiarity of the Māori world as well as orators of wisdom and practitioners of the arcane. They are valued for bringing status to those families and communities they belong to, and to those whose skins they mark. But not all artists wish to assume such an exalted position, choosing instead the more humble label of *kai ta*—someone technically skilled in moko design and its application. How tohunga ta moko and kai ta are to be viewed and valued continues to be negotiated between themselves and those they mark, their families, communities of interest, and the broader tattoo community. Into this mix has come a small group of females; in the early twenty-first century only four Māori women are in active practice.

Reflecting the Western tattoo environment, men still considerably outnumber women artists, yet in the customary Māori context there were numerous female practitioners. Their work is still remembered. However, the notion that tattoo, and its associated acts of penetration, inflicting pain, spilling blood, and leaving a permanent reminder, must be a male-only domain continues in the twenty-first century, with women experiencing resistance in a number of ways. There are few opportunities available to a woman to train and gain competence unless she apprentices herself to her husband, her boyfriend, or her brother. The scarcity of female role models, even non-Māori, often results in isolation and loneliness. For decades tattoo was seen as a closed male fraternity worldwide, its secrets and techniques and mysteries closely guarded. Since the 1990s it has opened up through celebrity enthusiasm and patronage, and the growing assertion by some practitioners and increasing numbers of admirers that it is a significant art form. For Māori women artists the common experience is that they are rarely invited to moko workshops, exhibitions, international exchanges, arts festivals, and conventions. But this situation is slowly changing, as more women organize their own events and take up machines and especially uhi chisels, for which they are leading exponents.

Henriata Nicholas, a leading chisel artist, has reflected that one of the interesting things to challenge her were the negative attitudes from some of the moko fraternity, who suggested that *wahine* (women) should not do moko. Considering the centuries of moko history of female artists inscribing female bodies, of moko being an everyday element of the everyday Māori world, this misogynistic view is ill-informed.

WEARING MOKO: VIEWING MOKO

What of the skin and bodies that artists mark? Wearers' lives are changed by moko, for the viewer's gaze falls differently on their marked bodies. They are sometimes expected to be drug-free, clean-living, and exceptional moral and cultural role models. Like artists, wearers often face challenges from within their own Māori communities, usually related to being embellished with marks associated with authority, mana, and prestige, sometimes being queried about processes of preparation, permissions, and support. Perhaps, beneath these challenges lies an anxiety for the viewer—what do these marks mean for me? How am I to "be" with you?

In public spaces, like streets, parks, beaches, supermarkets, and cafes and community spaces, schools, workplaces, marae, Māori villages, or at *hui* (Māori gatherings), moko wearers understand that they will attract attention. In contexts where Māori are a devalued ethnic minority, moko wearers are marked as different not just by the dominant culture but by other Māori too. This creates an interesting dynamic, in which moko wearers have to reconcile the validity of their ethnicity and cultural identities and their marks of difference and meaning both to others and their own families and communities. Moving through challenging spaces becomes a mission in anticipating and reading reactions and associated meanings, determining responses that are realistic and legitimate for the context, assessing the consequences of responses taken (or not), and learning from the experience.

Central to the mission is the need to identify and understand the various and variable effects of this practice, including causing stress to others. For example, a bar owner may view a facial tattoo as offensive—something that threatens to disrupt the norms and values of and between bodies within the bar space. Represented in facial tattoo are images that challenge social relations: images of marginality (anticonformists, outcasts, gangs), criminality (antisocial, lacking moral standards, violence), and pathology (madness, impairment, evil). Moko intrudes upon and challenges "clean," "honest," and "respectable" faces, bodies, and spaces. When moko is presented as cultural survival, pride, and identity, it silently contests the assumed rights of dominant groups. It signals the continued existence and resistance of Māori and points to all the failed efforts to make Māori subservient. Moko takes on a symbolic power. It questions hegemony by presenting alternative ways of viewing and being. Moko and the embodied become acutely political; even if the wearer believes that it is merely fashionable, often the viewer perceives a political statement.

With a power to disturb and disrupt the ancient spiraling, curving lines of moko take on talismanic properties. Through moko the mystic past is brought forward. This is the nature of the gift created by artists; it is the artwork worn on the skin that endures and has meaning. Most artists who apply the ink are aware of this, as they watch their designs walk away with the wearer usually in a daze of endorphins. As a Pacific customary practice, the properties of *tatau/tau* (this is the generic term for "tattoo" in the Pacific) are believed to embody transformative magic. For Māori art makers particularly (in both the past and the contemporary worlds), this transformative magic has engaged with and often challenged others, transcending time, ethnicity, and place.

This transcendence is understood by tohunga ta moko and also by proud carriers of that art form today, so much so that the voice of an elder of nearly a century ago resonates in the hearts of moko people today. His words are achingly familiar. Netana Rakuraku, one of the very last of the warriors with an inscribed face, explained to a visiting journalist in 1921 what the art meant for him: *"Taia o moko, hai hoa matenga mou"* (Of your moko, you cannot be deprived. Except by death. It will be your friend forever).

References and Further Reading

Best, Elsdon. "The Uhi-Māori, or Native Tattooing." *Journal of Polynesian Society* 13 (1904): 165–172.

King, Michael, and Marti Friedlander. *Moko: Māori Tattooing in the 20th Century*. Wellington, NZ: Alister Taylor, 1972.

Mead, Sidney M. *Traditional Māori Clothing; a Study of Technological and Functional Change*. Wellington, NZ: Reed, 1969.

Nikora, Linda Waimarie, Mohi Robert Rua, and Ngahuia Te Awekotuku. "Wearing Moko—Māori Facial Marking in Today's World." In *Tatau/Tattoo—Bodies, Art and Exchange in the Pacific and Europe*, edited by N. Thomas, A. Cole, and B. Douglas, 191–203. London: Reaktion, 2005.

Nikora, Linda Waimarie, Mohi Robert Rua, and Ngahuia Te Awekotuku. "Renewal and Resistance: Moko in Contemporary New Zealand." *Journal of Community and Applied Social Psychology* 17 (2007): 477–489.

Rua, Mohi Robert. "Moko: Māori Facial Tattoos—the Experiences of Contemporary Wearers." Master's thesis, University of Waikato, 2003.

Te Awekotuku, Ngahuia. "Māori: People and Culture." In *Māori: Art and Culture*, edited by Dorota C. Starzecka, 26–49. Auckland, NZ: David Bateman, 1996.

Te Awekotuku, Ngahuia. "More Than Skin Deep: Ta Moko Today." In *Claiming the Stones/Naming the Bones: Cultural Property and the Negotiation of National and Ethnic Identity*, edited by Elazar Barkan and Ronald Bush, 243–258. Los Angeles: Getty Press, 2002.

Te Awekotuku, Ngahuia. "He Maimai Aroha: A Disgusting Traffic for Collectors: The Colonial Trade in Preserved Human Heads in Aotearoa, New Zealand." In *Obsession, Compulsion, Collection: On Objects, Display Culture and Interpretation*, edited by A. Kiendl, 77–91. Banff, Canada: The Banff Center Press, 2004.

Te Awekotuku, Ngahuia. "Mata Ora: Chiseling the Living Face—Dimensions of Māori Tattoo." In *Sensible Objects: Colonialism, Museums and Material Culture*, edited by Elizabeth Edwards, Chris Gosden, and Ruth B. Phillips, 121–140. Oxford and New York: Berg, 2006.

Te Awekotuku, Ngahuia, Linda Waimarie Nikora, Mohi Robert Rua, and Rolinda Karapu. *Mau Moko: The World of Māori Tattoo*. Auckland, NZ: and Honolulu: Penguin and Hawai'i University Press, 2007.

Ngahuia Te Awekotuku,
Linda Waimarie Nikora,
and Mohi Robert Rua

See also Tahitian Tattoos; Fijian Dress and Body Modifications; Dress of the Cook Islands.

The Māori Pari (Bodice)

The *pari* is a Māori bodice of the *rāranga* type, worn with a *piupiu* (a type of fibrous skirt) and Māori jewelry by women in cultural performances including competitions, concerts, and festivals. Rāranga is a generic naming for plaited (as opposed to loom) handweaving practices undertaken mostly, though not exclusively, by Māori women. Māori performances usually occur in order to promote traditional practices, but for some they include a more material reward or prize money or are part of fund-raising for various reasons such as overseas travel to other such festivals. The pari is an intriguing example of women's clothing, but in spite of its high visual profile in performances for competition and tourism, there is very little known about its origins and its evolution. Various forms of pari, along with their wearers, are frequently used as a visual representation of Māori culture, despite the fact that the garments and their role and meanings in performance are rarely acknowledged. Even up to the first decade of the twenty-first century no museum or art gallery has held an exhibition featuring this often worn, significant item of clothing. Owing, at least in part, to the limited information published on the subject, those interested must rely largely on oral history and firsthand ethnographic observation for information. For this reason a personal account of these garments, as worn in the author's own family, a reminiscence recorded in 2007, is included in the Snapshot section.

At first sight the pari might seem unimportant and incidental to Māori culture. On closer examination one can see that it provides audiences with valuable insights into contemporary cultural practices involving Māori clothing, which prevailed over an extensive period of time, despite variations resulting from introduced materials and cultural interchange. It is relevant to consider various aspects of the pari in terms of how, when, and why it was created, the usual wearers, and the broader social significance, particularly in its role as a signifier of Māori culture.

It is important to consider the translocal, transnational, and international social contexts where public displays of Māori culture occur. Therefore, as an indication of the pari's ubiquity within and beyond its origins in Aotearoa (the Māori name for New Zealand), a selective number of examples in both that country and Australia are examined. The use of the pari in Australia is important to mention because of the country's close proximity to New Zealand, and its high migrant Māori population compared with other countries. This "trans-Tasman" focus enables comparisons to be made based on design and other technical features, on functionality as related to public performances, and on the pari's role as an emblem of group belonging within and beyond Aotearoa. This situates the garment within wider social contexts (including some Australian settings) with regard to issues of cultural authenticity, representation, identity, and spirituality.

Social values assigned to pari by both individuals and groups of people vary. The pari's rāranga origins and connections are barely acknowledged, and not all parties consider them equally authentic culturally, given their links with the tourism industry and notions of "tourism kitsch." Yet despite the commercialized context in which they can be found, pari are rarely for sale other than on dressed souvenir, miniature "Māori dolls." These dolls, usually made from brown colored plastic in so-called traditional Māori costume, were a popular tourist-orientated commodity in the 1960s and 1970s. Since then they have fallen out of favor, as consumers have become more aware that the Māori people might feel the designers and manufacturers were degrading their people and their culture. Therefore, although pari are frequently associated with commercial public performance, they are no longer commonly sold as commodities.

ORIGINS AND DESIGN OF THE PARI

Christian ideals of modesty, necessitating the concealment of women's breasts under clothing, certainly had a role to play in the design of those pari that first appeared at the turn of the twentieth century, but a scarcity of recorded information makes attempts at determining exact dates and social motivations more educated surmise than established fact. Nevertheless, the pari is most certainly an early-twentieth-century example of specially constructed dress for Māori cultural performances that became increasingly popular in relation to a burgeoning tourism and public entertainment industry. The specialized role of the pari in such performances continues to be in vogue even in the twenty-first century.

Pari have been made in a number of ways, and a materially based account of pari should accept both standardized as well as varied, inconsistent, and innovative creative practices relating to its use in a number of contexts within Aotearoa and beyond. One such material-based discussion revolves around the *kuta* plant (*Eleocharis sphacelata*), which grows in lakes throughout Aotearoa. Kuta is highly prized by Māori weavers as much in the twenty-first century as it was in the past, and many pari have been made of this material, although *muka* was also widely used. Muka are processed New Zealand flax (*Phormium tenax*) fibers used for *tāniko* weaving (a form of Māori handweaving, a weft-twining technique) consisting of horizontal and vertical warp and weft. It is more durable than kuta. Probably the first pari were made with tāniko weave using muka, although there is no firm evidence for this. Kuta pari are generally braided with kuta fibers so that the warp and weft cross diagonally as they do in *kete* baskets, which is a type of rāranga weave. Both muka and kuta fibers were bleached and then dyed, using mainly natural dyes and mordants from tanekaha and other trees and black mud pools, but also commercially available synthetic dyes. Pari are not necessarily, then, constructed exclusively from tāniko weaving, as could be assumed by the small amount of published information on this subject. Pari construction has more likely been contingent upon available materials and innovative creativity.

A detail of Jo Diamond's wool needlepoint *pari* with various symbols of identity and belonging, Aotearoa (New Zealand), second half of the twentieth century. The intricate design includes references to plants and *nga hau e wha* (the four winds). Photograph by Jo Diamond.

The technical construction of the pari varies, although it is often assembled with thin shoulder straps attached to a broad, sometimes darted panel measuring from above the bust to the waist. In some cases a skirt or underskirt is attached at the waist. The designs on the main panel are the most emblematic feature. Although earliest examples of the pari were made with tāniko techniques, they have since undergone several revolutionary technical and design changes. Since British colonization, European weaving and needlework technologies, cross-hatched embroidery, needlepoint, and tapestry pieces have influenced their construction, giving rise to a variety of new designs and motifs. The latter may include Christian references such as crosses, angels, and churches. Words may also be included in the design, including school, church, or family names.

Construction of the pari has often depended on the commitment of family groups, usually women. Family or other group members, including the male leaders or tutors of *haka* (Māori dance) groups would often also create pari designs and patterns. Pari designs are often emblematic of an entire performance group, the same design being worn by all female performers, almost like a uniform. An audience can distinguish such a group from others because of the way this garment dominates visually on stage.

As a variation on this uniform role (one design for all), a group's pari collection may comprise a variety of designs contributed by individual members. Each pari, in this case, can symbolize the extended family of an individual performer as well as that family's *iwi* (tribal) affiliations. In a genealogically connected sense they can be considered as quintessential Māori cultural signifiers.

In technical terms pari range from those made from tāniko and needlepoint to diagonal *rāranga* that is similar to that of kete (baskets) and *whāriki* (mats), exemplifying syntheses of various forms of creativity. While they are often used to signify Māori belonging, they also resonate with Māori cultural adaptation to modern influences, including the introduction of new natural fibers such as wool, as well as synthetics, plus more recent techniques of making them.

In terms of materials used, pari construction is often a matter of choices made within family circles in relation to their access to material resources (natural and synthetic), and various identifications with the local school, church, or other organizations and institutions. Thus, these garments may often symbolize cultural belonging both to particular geographic and institutional locations.

THE AUSTRALIAN PARI: AN UNACKNOWLEDGED MIGRATORY EMBLEM

The pari is an important even if largely unacknowledged part of Māori culture wherever it is worn and wherever it goes. Numerous examples have either been transported from Aotearoa into Australia, or have been designed by groups of the Australian Māori migrant population in a similar way to those made in Aotearoa. In the early twenty-first century in Sydney alone, numerous examples of pari exist among various Māori performance groups. These garments are strong features of cultural events, including multicultural festivals. In mid-1999, for example, the Sydney-based Māori culture group named Te Kotuku performed at the Sydney Opera House for a program of multicultural events that took place over a year entitled "Sundays 'round the House.'" Sydney's Mitchell Library archives contain photographs of pari worn earlier in the 1950s in Sydney. A discursive silence surrounds these pari that matches other neglected aspects of migrant Māori history in Sydney and other parts of Australia. Without further study the presence of pari in Australia, along with the Māori people who have designed, made, and worn them, will remain effectively absent from Australia's multicultural history.

One Māori community in Australia that has worn the pari is worth detailed consideration. The pari is sometimes a taken-for-granted item in the regime of Canberra's resident Māori cultural performance group, Te Rere o Te Tarakakao (TROTT), which begins with practice sessions, involves fund-raising activities, and culminates in public dance displays. Female performers of this group wear a distinctive pari as part of their uniform. Other than its color, the garment appears very similar to other tapestry and tāniko ones that dominate the design of most in Aotearoa.

The garment is obviously emblematic, at the very least because of its colors. Predominantly green and gold, these colors evoke other Australian team uniforms, particularly within competitive sports, and are the TROTT pari's most Australian reference. Its design composition is geometrical, incorporating complex patterns of oblongs achieved by a series of diagonal tapestry stitches. The tapestry takes on average three to four weeks to complete.

Though this pari is an emblem for the group (including its references to Māori culture and Australian residence), its significance is not directly acknowledged within the wider Canberra community, which tends, like many other communities within and beyond Aotearoa, to venerate *kākahu* (cloaks) and weapons. The latter syndrome fits neatly into stereotypes applied by wider non-Māori society, that all Māori people are essentially warriors. This view has been cultivated by movies such as *Once Were Warriors* of 1994, which includes many references to male Māori warlike behaviors in the past, and of course the frightening form of haka that continues to be performed by the "All Blacks" football team prior to international rugby matches.

TROTT's pari also represents the group's metaphorical attachment to the Tarakakao, a species of godwit whose migratory flight path extends between Aotearoa and Australia. The design is repeated on other components of the group's performance apparel, such as the *tāpeka* (men's bandolier-like band worn diagonally across chest and back) and *tīpare* (headband). Owing to the group's popularity among various audiences in Canberra, and its involvement with the New Zealand High Commission, the pari is well known locally. Yet the actual meanings and history behind the pari and its design apparently escape the knowledge and interest of many spectators.

Often the non-Māori wives and mothers of group members make the pari and take on responsibility for their upkeep. These women also take on other supporting roles in the group meetings and performances, such as ensuring that their children (and their performance apparel) are present. A cooperative effort between Māori and non-Māori ensures that every performer wears the appropriate attire, and this objective often supersedes all other concerns, including frictions within the group.

When the group was asked if the pari was or was not a *taonga* (highly valued item), it was important not to prompt or influence a staged response. The question was posed whether the pari was important to the group and how its importance compared with that of other taonga that also made up the group's stock. Most respondents were adamant in their support of the pari's importance to the group, although no in-depth reasons for this assigned value were offered. Some of the younger members took it as an essential, though not critically assessed, part of their participation in the group, as did some of the older members. It is definitely not the case that any consciousness of, or education program about, the pari and its function as a cultural signifier is high on their list of priorities. The group, under the instructions of its haka tutor, was more interested in achieving a good, if not excellent, performance. To this end, the garment becomes part of a uniform that must look immaculate along with the rest of the performer's appearance. The pari and other parts of the performance apparel are therefore usually well kept, and participants are most careful to wear it with a minimum of non-Māori accessories. Accordingly, jewelry such as rings and watches are prohibited, while taonga such as *pounamu* (greenstone pendants) and *manaia* (bone pendants) are encouraged during the performance. The pari becomes part of a regime that seeks to promote an impression in the audience at least of an authentic Māori performance. The garment is therefore part of a value-building presentation that promotes Māori culture within an Australian social context.

For some women and girls the pari and other items of TROTT's performance apparel are definitely taonga. However, a sense of its value among the younger members has to be actively maintained by the adults. Overall, the group's primary contact with rāranga is through the pari and that small group of women who nurture plants for rāranga. A preference for *whakairo* (wood carving, exclusively undertaken by men) and other male-exclusive activities persists, though no express attempts are made to diminish the importance of the pari and other rāranga items.

THE CANBERRA PARI: SPIRITUAL REFERENCE, CULTURAL CONTINUITY

Aspects of Māori spirituality can also be applied to TROTT's green and gold pari. While issues surrounding *tapu* (sacredness or restricted nature) and *noa* (the lifting of tapu or rendering nonsacred) have not been openly discussed by TROTT, this does not mean it does not exist. At one practice session a senior female member, supported by her elders in Sydney and Aotearoa, instructed the women and girls on why it was incorrect to raise their arms above shoulder height during performances, allowing the audience to see their armpits. The reason for this precautionary advice relates to the Māori myth involving the god Tāne and his search for a mate with whom to procreate. According to this narrative, in his search Tāne tried to fertilize and therefore bring to life a female form that he fashioned from earth by sexually penetrating it, via its various orifices. One of these was the armpit, which, with its hirsute covering, is comparable with the female vulva. According to one interpretation of Māori custom (in this case by the group leader), both vulva and armpit are tapu parts of the female body. The narrative of Tāne's search for a female *uha* (essence) has thus traveled over time to Canberra and TROTT's female performers.

The ubiquitous presence of pari as cultural emblems usually (though not always) designed and made by Māori women and their significance to Māori cultural groups is offset by its notable exclusion from dominant rāranga and other Māori cultural discourses that tend to privilege other clothing items, such as cloaks. Yet notions of tapu and noa are associated with these performance garments. Thus, there are a variety of important values associated with them, extending beyond the question of whether or not they are authentically demonstrative of Māori culture, given their tourism-based origins.

The pari is a telling symbol of social issues relating to Māori values and representation, both for Māori people and *Pākehā* people (Europeans). Although now readily accessible on the Internet, the cultural significance of pari, along with the identities of their wearers, still remain undetermined. It remains clear that these garments are doubly marginalized by the dominant discourses on Māori culture that continue to deny the significance of rāranga and its weavers. Pari are pivotal examples of cultural creativity that should be taken into account when considering notions of authentic Māori culture, its cultural production, and ways in which Māori women have been visually represented since British colonization, particularly in the twentieth century.

Snapshot: The Pari as Personal Cultural Property

My mother, Te Mihinga Diamond, once told me that she had worn a *pari* made from *kuta* during her youth. She had worn it at school performances of haka and action songs. My mother's father reputedly had a hand in its design and construction technique. We were talking about the 1940s, when Māori children's cultural competitions took place in and near Kaikohe, her birthplace on the North Island. Many years later, when I became acquainted with kuta in the process of learning *rāranga* at Kohewhata Marae, a Māori equivalent to a community center near Kaikohe, I remembered my mother's kuta pari. Its significance became more established after obtaining a photograph of my mother wearing it in the 1940s. The photograph shows a diagonal rāranga technique, one more associated with making *kete* (carry bags) and *whāriki* (mats) than for an item of clothing.

At first it seemed that my mother's pari design was a "one-off," something that was made only once in connection with her school in the 1940s. However, the discovery of a photograph in the pictorial collection of the Alexander Turnbull Library, National Library of New Zealand, Wellington, altered that viewpoint. The photograph's main focal point is a young Māori woman wearing a pari. It is woven with the same diagonal rāranga technique as is my mother's pari, but incorporating a darker-colored design. This photograph features a Māori performance group that won a local competition in 1947, in Maraeroa, near Kaikohe, Maraeroa being a small settlement close to Utakura, my maternal grandfather's birthplace.

My mother recalled a similar pari design that featured in a dance performance competition between her father and his close cousin Nika Anihana. She was more inclined to associate the Maraeroa pari and competition group with the latter man, though we are all part of the same extended family. It is not possible of course to corroborate my mother's recollections with written records beyond those provided by the catalog of the Alexander Turnbull Library. Unfortunately further research efforts have been hampered by the likelihood that records of the pari have disappeared along with the people who wore and designed them. For instance, my grandfather designed a pari, but he passed away some fifty years ago. Nevertheless, given that the style of garment generated from the region of Maraeroa appears to be unlike any other, one can surely designate this particular style as one indigenous to that area. Consequently, one can attribute its introduction into Kaikohe Native School (where my mother received her education in the 1940s) to my grandfather's community-oriented effort in furthering the Maraeroa pari style. It is clear from this example that pari have been constructed at various times throughout the twentieth century using materials and techniques in highly innovative ways.

The pari has also been a ubiquitous feature of my own upbringing. In my late teenage years, while taking part in a university-based Māori performance group, we female performers were instructed to produce a pari that specifically

Te Mihinga Diamond, wearing a *kuta pari* in the 1940s, Kaikohe, North Island, Aotearoa (New Zealand). The photograph shows a diagonal *rāranga* technique, one more associated with making *kete* (carry bags) and *whāriki* (mats) than an item of clothing. Photograph courtesy of Jo Diamond.

signified our family and tribal affiliations. This pari was to be used at various times during concerts as an alternative to the gold-and-black pari that formed part of the university's standard *haka* uniform. My mother and her eldest sister designed my pari and I helped with its tapestry-based construction. It has a very intricate design bearing references to plants indigenous to the northern climes of Aotearoa. It also has a central design that denotes *nga hau e wha* (the four winds, symbolically referring to a union of people from "all four corners" of the world).

My mother was, at the time it was made, very protective of this pari, thinking its design might be stolen and used for someone else's material gain and fame. Her concern was not unfounded and resonates with many cultural property issues that continue to apply in the twenty-first century. As Māori scholar Linda Tuhiwai Smith has pointed out, Māori people are generally reluctant to divulge information and are suspicious of those investigating traditional practice, due to insensitive and exploitative research techniques experienced in the past.

Apart from this kind of concern, my mother subsequently expressed reservations about discussing pari in general. She associated them with the *tapu* (sacredness or restricted nature) of Māori women's bodies and certain items of their clothing. This association relates to the tendency among some Māori women, including my mother, not to speak openly, especially in public, about "intimate" apparel. This subject, considered as tapu, remains closed for discussion. It reminds us that empathetic research needs to be part of any public discussion of the pari, as the views of some Māori women may differ from those of others, depending on their backgrounds and sensitivities.

With encouragement from my parents at the time of its completion, a Catholic priest blessed my pari, ensuring its safety on my future travels. It has since lost its original red polyester fabric lining and has, in the interim, been converted into a shoulder bag. I now keep it as an unembellished tapestry panel and am currently considering framing it as one would a picture. It has retained its original shape and color, and I still call it my pari because of its initial purpose; this *taonga* (highly valued item) may have changed in shape over time, but not in cultural significance.

The photograph of my mother wearing a kuta pari in the 1940s links with a photograph of a pari worn by children in a cultural competition in Maraeroa, North Island of Aotearoa, in the 1950s. The latter photograph is held by the National Library of New Zealand. In describing relationships between my mother's pari and the Maraeroa example, one can only touch the surface of a history of the pari in its many different forms, a history that deserves far greater engagement in Aotearoa, Australia, and elsewhere.

In discussing the story of my own pari, which has traveled with me to Australia then back again to Aotearoa, and another green and gold example worn by a Māori cultural performance group in Canberra, my intention is to broaden the local context of my mother's pari, and the Maraeroa example, to a transnational one.

References and Further Reading

Diamond, Jo. "Revaluing Rāranga: Weaving and Women in Trans-Tasman Māori Cultural Discourses." Ph.D. dissertation, Australian National University, 2003.
Mead, Hirini S. *Te Whatu Tāniko: Tāniko Weaving Technique and Tradition.* Auckland, NZ: Raupo Publishers, 1999.
Smith, Linda Tuhiwai. *Decolonizing Methodologies: Research and Indigenous Peoples.* London: Zed Books, 1999.

Jo Diamond

See also Introduction to Māori Dress.

PART 8

European (Pākehā) Dress and Fashion in New Zealand

Resources for the Study of European Dress and Fashion in New Zealand

The historical factors of settler life inevitably influenced the reasons why clothing has been saved. Much emphasis was placed on fashionable, quality clothing of women, although there have been other kinds of dress acquired and ideas about collecting have changed substantially in the twenty-first century. Regional factors, the scattered location of museums and collections, their particularities of acquisition, and the limited state of research into the subject are discussed below. Little has been published on collections of dress in New Zealand, and therefore most of the information about clothing items either made in New Zealand or brought to New Zealand by immigrants has been gathered from personal communications and visits to the collections.

TYPES OF COLLECTIONS AND PATTERNS OF COLLECTING

The collecting of European dress by public museums in New Zealand has mirrored patterns of collecting in the Western world, in which dress was originally acquired in an ad hoc manner, often relying on individual donors and collectors. This passive mode of collecting has contributed toward the particular gaps and biases found in dress collections, where items have often been kept for their association with events or prominent people, for their sentimental value, or for inherent aesthetic qualities. Generally, collections are largely skewed toward examples of women's dress, comprising better-quality garments, evening dresses, and treasured items such as wedding dresses and christening gowns. Everyday dress and menswear is largely under-represented because it was not given the same priority and was more likely to be worn for longer periods and subsequently disposed of. As a result, such items that do survive are now given more emphasis than they originally commanded. Importantly, what has been preserved and has entered public collections influences our perceptions of the past.

A survey of New Zealand collections reveals that dress is largely collected for its historical value, either for its associations with particular people, events, or regions or for its ability to contribute to the understanding of the lives of New Zealanders. Only a few museums collect dress with an applied arts or design emphasis. Since a number of the collections are located in relatively small towns or regional centers, each museum tends to focus on collecting items that have a connection to their particular area, and local donors have played an important role in shaping these

collections. However, often very little is known about the history or provenance of these garments beyond the name of the donor. Past practice meant such information was not typically recorded at the time of acquisition, and many of the dress collections were inadequately cataloged.

Historically, collections of dress were often marginalized within museums, with the subject matter not given serious consideration. In many cases the collections in New Zealand have, and still do, rely on dedicated volunteers and honorary curators to provide the much-needed care and specialist knowledge required for such collections. Dress and textiles are particularly vulnerable to damage from exposure to light, environmental changes, and attack from insects. Since the 1990s international shifts in the museum profession have required that these institutions be more responsible in the way they collect, maintain, and document their collections. As a result, many of the dress collections in New Zealand have benefited from the instigation of more rigorous collection policies, which have provided the framework for their management. A number of museums have also initiated cataloging and storage projects, coupled with training workshops conducted by professional textile conservators. Consequently, there is a growing recognition of the value of these collections as important resources of historical and cultural value. While large parts of the collections are, for practical and conservation reasons, kept in storage, since the early twenty-first century regular exhibitions and symposia have been staged, which acknowledge dress as an important resource for object-based research to interpret New Zealand history, culture, and identity.

PUBLISHED WORKS

There is a noticeable absence of published histories on New Zealand dress. These amount to a smattering of monographs and articles in various edited books and journals. Two primary books that provide an overview of New Zealand dress are Eve Ebbett's standard text, *In True Colonial Fashion: A Lively Look at What New Zealanders Wore* (1977) and Richard Wolfe's *The Way We Wore: The Clothes New Zealanders Have Loved* (2001). Ebbett's book covers nineteenth- and early-twentieth-century European dress in New Zealand, using quotes from diaries and letters, and is well illustrated with historical photographs from public and private collections. Wolfe provides an overview of everyday dress from World War II to the turn of the twenty-first century, focusing on local manufacturers and retailers in the New Zealand clothing industry. Wolfe also looks at idiosyncratic elements of New Zealand dress, such as the origins of the jandal and the black singlet and their place in defining cultural preferences. The book is of interest for the diverse selection of local photographs and advertising graphics and for its spotlights on individuals and their dress.

Two texts published since the 1990s have given cultural insights into very specific and different aspects of New Zealand dress. *The Loving Stitch: A History of Knitting and Spinning in*

New Zealand (1998), by Heather Nicholson, details the cultural and creative aspects of universal craft practices in a country that has relied on wool as an important economic commodity. Although museums around the country stage regular and varied exhibitions on dress, few are supported by accompanying publications. One exception is *The New Zealand Gown of the Year*, by Claire Regnault, produced in conjunction with the Hawkes Bay Museum exhibition Fashion on Wheels, in 2002. The book gives an important insight into the attitudes toward fashionable dress in New Zealand during the late 1950s and early 1960s. A welcome addition to local studies on dress are two publications. The first, *Looking Flash: Clothing in Aotearoa/New Zealand*, published by Auckland University Press in 2007, provides a compilation of essays covering three centuries of dress, from pre-European Māori cloaks to late-twentieth-century fashion. The second is a series of interviews with thirty contemporary New Zealand fashion designers, written by Angela Lassig and published by Te Papa Press in 2009.

In recognition of the need for a specific forum, the New Zealand Costume and Textile Section was established in 2002 with the aim to provide an academic and supportive network for those working and researching in the field of dress. The organization holds an annual symposium and publishes *Context* three times a year, including a wide variety of articles on historical and contemporary dress, museum collections, exhibitions, and aspects of clothing conservation.

OVERVIEW OF COLLECTIONS: NORTH ISLAND

The following collections are listed in geographical regions from north to south.

The Kauri Museum (Matakohe). Located in the heart of the historic kauri timber area in the Northland, the Kauri Museum features displays that tell the story of the Kauri tree, its associated industries, and the people who worked in them. European migrants came to this remote area in 1862 to work, either cutting timber or digging gum. The collection includes examples of everyday and fashionable dress and incorporates dress into displays featuring aspects of life in the region during the nineteenth and early twentieth centuries. An important part of the collection is the photographic archive, which includes images by well-known photographers Tudor Collins and Harold Marsh. These images provide an important reference for everyday dress specific to the area and the time. In 2008 a selection of these photographs could be viewed on their Web site in the Gallery of Historic Photographs. The Web site is at http://www.kauri-museum.com/

Whangarei Museum. The collections in the Whangarei Museum focus on the histories and peoples of the Whangarei and Northland regions. Items of dress are housed both at the museum and at the Clarke Homestead, which is located in the Heritage Park.

A large proportion of the collection comprises twentieth-century women's wear, the majority being underwear, nightgowns, and accessories such as shawls, collars, and gloves. There are a couple of late-nineteenth-century dresses in fair condition and a large number of items of infants' and children's wear. Menswear is not as well represented and includes some day-wear and numerous accessories. There are also a number of men's and women's uniforms in the collection. Of interest are the early-twentieth-century fashion drawings by Whangarei artist Olive Udy. The

majority of the collection is in storage and few items are displayed in the Clarke Homestead. The Web site is at http://www.whangareimuseum.co.nz/

Warkworth Museum. Warkworth Museum north of Auckland documents European settlement and the lives of the pioneering families of the area. The museum relies on donations, and since 1990 it has built an extensive collection of dress dating from the nineteenth century to the present. Many items were worn by local residents. The collection is strong in women's wear, including wedding gowns from 1910 to 1999, evening gowns, women's outerwear and underwear, nightdresses, bathing costumes, hats, and shoes from the 1920s to the 1960s. Of note is a rare nursing gown from the 1830s in a printed cotton of brown-and-green foliage pattern. Discreetly hidden in the front gathers of the bodice are two vertical slits for nursing a baby. Another unusual item is a 1930s woman's jacket made of black Abyssinian monkey skin. Men's and children's wear are not as well represented; however, there are a number of pre-1930s girls' day dresses. Of interest is a striking small boy's cape and dress from 1886 in dark red wool and trimmed with red velvet. There is also a collection of men's, women's, and children's uniforms, which includes military, police, fire brigade, Red Cross, St John, nursing, Scouts, and Girl Guides. The current collecting policy now focuses on items prior to 1945. In 2008 there was a small selection of dress on display in the historical exhibits within the museum. The Web site is at http://www.wwmuseum.orcon.net.nz/

Auckland Museum (Auckland War Memorial Museum): Tamaki Paenga Hira. The Auckland Museum has extensive collections of fashionable and everyday dress dating from the nineteenth century to the present, as well as a large collection of military uniforms. These collections are located within the Applied Arts and History departments. The latter represents examples of both international and New Zealand–made dress within the context of a broader collection of decorative arts and design. A particular strength is the representation of local, Auckland dressmakers, manufacturers, and designers. In the last decade the museum has mounted a number of exhibitions celebrating New Zealand manufacture and design, notably Next to Nothing: A History of Lingerie (1997) and the work of independent fashion labels World (2004) and Zambesi (2005). Dress in 2008 was displayed in the two galleries dedicated to New Zealand and International Decorative Arts. Among the twentieth-century and contemporary labels represented are Zambesi, World, Marilyn Sainty, Nicholas Blanchet, Kevin Berkahn, Bruce Pappas, El Jay (who had the New Zealand license for Christian Dior), Emma Knuckey, Rosemarie Muller, Trilby Yates, and Annie Bonza.

In contrast to the Applied Arts collection, the History collection acquires items of dress that reflect the history and lives of New Zealanders, with a particular focus on the Auckland region. The stories that relate to these garments are of primary importance and often provide the rationale for acquiring many of these examples of everyday dress. Dress may also be included as part of a larger collection of items that are acquired together in order to represent a particular subject, such as the collection of knitting, which includes historical knitting patterns donated by the author of *The Loving Stitch*, Heather Nicholson.

The History collection also contains significant items of European dress that belonged to early settlers from the Auckland region and the Bay of Islands, where some of the first European settlements were established in the early nineteenth century. Of note are a printed cotton dress from about 1828 worn by Mary Ann Williams, wife of one of the early missionaries in the Bay of Islands, and a man's shirt hand-stitched by Elizabeth Beddgood in 1849, also from the same region. Throughout the museum, items of dress and occupational and military uniforms tend to be integrated into the thematic history displays, contributing to the representation of New Zealand history and the exploration of cultural identity.

The museum's pictorial collection houses an extensive photographic archive that has been indexed to include "costume." Discrete collections of particular interest are the fashion drawings by the Auckland fashion designer Bruce Pappas and images from the Belwood Studios in Auckland, which photographed weddings from the late 1940s to the 1960s. The Web site is at http://www.aucklandmuseum.com/

Museum of Transport and Technology—MOTAT (Auckland). The Museum of Transport and Technology (MOTAT) represents a diverse range of dress from nineteenth- and twentieth-century garments and accessories, which form part of the Victorian Village collection, to uniforms relating to public transportion and military aviation. Items of clothing in 2008 were integrated into a variety of the displays throughout the museum. The exhibition Stepping into the Sunshine: Victorian Women Go Public in Sport and at Work 1880–1914 (2007) included a nurse's uniform, a blouse and skirt appropriate for a teacher, day dresses from the 1890s and 1906 suitable for playing croquet and tennis, a riding habit from the late nineteenth century, and a woolen bathing costume from 1914. An extensive dress and textile collection is housed in one of the buildings that form part of the Victorian Village. The collection extends well beyond the time frame of the village (1848–1900) and includes a large representation of items from the early twentieth century, including evening dresses, christening gowns, underwear, and accessories. The majority of the pieces relate to women's and children's wear, with menswear again being less well represented. The collection has developed over the years through gifts, and a volunteer textile collection manager has worked to adequately store it. The museum's collection policy now limits collecting to the themes of transportion and technology. In the future items of dress or uniforms will only be acquired where they have direct relevance to these aspects of the collection. The Web site is at http://www.motat.org.nz/

Howick Historical Village (Auckland). Howick Historical Village was opened in 1980 as a living museum that interprets life during the early period of colonization in Auckland. Howick was one of the main sites settled by the Fencibles—retired soldiers, mainly from England and Ireland, who were encouraged to settle in the colony to defend the young capital from possible attack by Māori. The soldiers and their families arrived in the area between 1847 and 1852 under the Fencible scheme. The five-acre site in Howick consists of Fencible dwellings from the area, which were moved on site to create the village. Interiors are fitted out to reflect life during the 1850s, and, where appropriate, items of historical dress are occasionally displayed. The village has a large collection of dress that mostly dates from the 1850s to the early twentieth century. From the beginning, donations of dress that fell outside of the interpretation period of the village were accepted, but now the collection policy has narrowed collecting to the period of interpretation and, more specifically, to items that pertain to the history of Howick. Housed on site in the old homestead, the dress and textile collection largely remains in storage and numbers around two thousand items. Predominantly comprising women's outer- and underwear, the collection also includes accessories, such as paisley shawls, infant and children's wear, and a few military uniforms. Significant items in the collection are two day dresses from the 1850s, one in a fine checked wool and the other a vibrant pink silk taffeta. Also of interest is a hand-stitched frock coat from the mid-nineteenth century, an 1887 wedding dress with known provenance, and three wedding dresses dating from 1904, 1910, and 1938, which were worn by three generations of brides from a local family. The Web site is at http://www.fencible.org.nz/

Waikato Museum of Art and History, Te Whare Taonga o Waikato (Hamilton). The Waikato Museum's social history collection includes items of dress that contribute to the museum's goal of interpreting the history of Waikato and providing a focus for local identity. Objects are collected for their historical and regional connections. Items fall under subject classifications of Costume (men's, women's, infant's, and children's), Ceremonial (Masonic and Church), Societal (recreation, evening and day-wear, domestic), Lifestyles (including representations of community diversity), and Uniforms (military, school, local industry). Highlights of the collection include beaded dresses from the 1920s and 1930s, women's colonial dresses, evening dresses, and local artist Ida Carey's (1891–1982) collection of dresses that date from the 1880s. Dress was, in 2008, included in various historical displays throughout the museum. In addition, the Hamilton City Library holds a significant photographic archive of local images, which can be accessed through the library's index. The Web site is at http://www.waikatomuseum.org.nz/

The Elms (Tauranga). Beginning in 1835 the Elms was the site of the Church Missionary Society in Tauranga, and the property was occupied by Rev. A. N. Brown and his descendants from 1847 until the mid-1990s, when it was opened to the public through the Elms Foundation. The dress and textile collection is of particular significance because all the items have a known provenance. Belonging to various family members, many are labeled with the names of the owners. From the accompanying information, textiles brought out on the voyage can be dated to 1801, and garments worn by the family date from the nineteenth and early twentieth centuries. The collection has been fully cataloged and remains in storage. Some items of note are a peach-colored tulle dress from the 1890s, a mushroom-colored silk dress with military-style trimmings from 1870–1875, a gray-and-maroon silk dress with ecru lace trimming of the early 1880s, and an early-twentieth-century beaded silk cape. The Web site is at http://www.theelms.org.nz/index.html

Rotorua Museum of Art and History. Opened in 1969, the museum collects dress as part of the Social History collection and focuses on items that relate to the region since European settlement. Most of the examples of dress fall within the Norma and Bob Evans textile collection. Collected across four generations of the Evans family, this unusual collection consists of objects that relate to everyday life in the twentieth century and includes examples of utilitarian garments. The museum also houses a collection of swimwear that reflects the town's position as a premier spa. A noteworthy aspect of the collection in connection with dress is the museum's extensive archive of historical photographs relating to the region. The Web site is at http://www.rotoruamuseum.co.nz/

Hawkes Bay Museum and Art Gallery (Napier). The Hawkes Bay Museum has collected dress since the 1930s, when local

A dinner dress from 1924, made from silk voile with printed cotton bands. Gift of Mrs H. Acton-Adams. Canterbury Museum, New Zealand.

families began to donate items to the newly built museum. The dress collection numbers over three thousand items and comprises mainly women's wear, including accessories, but also contains some menswear and military uniforms. The majority of the collection dates from the late nineteenth century to the 1970s and represents both local makers and New Zealand designers. It is particularly strong in Victorian and Edwardian dress. During the 1990s garments by New Zealand designers were brought into the collection, including labels by Bobby Angus, Trilby Yates, Babs Radon, Colin Cole, and Roswitha Robertson. In 1999 the museum received the New Zealand Gown of the Year archives and a number of the dresses that date from the late 1950s to early 1960s. The museum has been active in mounting exhibitions of dress and textile design and also producing related publications, notably *Fashion on Wheels* (2002), and the textile design exhibition Avis Higgs: Joie de Vivre (2000). Higgs was a New Zealand textile designer working in Australia in the 1940s and later in New Zealand, creating designs for dress fabrics. The Web site is at http://www.hawkesbaymuseum.co.nz/

Te Manawa, Manawatu Museum and Art Gallery (Palmerston North). Located in Palmerston North, the Manawatu Museum forms part of the regional cultural center known as Te Manawa.

Dress features as one of the main collections within the Social History section of the museum. Major European settlement began in the Manawatu region in the 1860s, and items of dress in the collection date from this period. However, the strength of the collection lies in women's wear dating from 1900 to 1970. The focus for collecting is clothing made or worn in the Manawatu region, with future collecting to celebrate local innovation. The museum occasionally mounts exhibitions dedicated to dress, such as Best Dressed (2006), but otherwise dress history is integrated into the social history exhibitions. Acquisitions include garments made in the 1980s and 1990s by local fashion designer Therese Regan and a selection of wedding dresses made by local designer Rachel Johnson in the 1980s. The museum is also planning to strengthen its representation of menswear with the acquisition of works by a couple of well-established local tailors. The Web site is at http://www.temanawa.co.nz/

Whanganui Regional Museum (Wanganui). The museum has approximately twenty-five hundred items of European dress in its collection, including hats, shoes, and uniforms. These date from the mid-1880s to the present. Strengths of the collection include women's clothing from the 1880s, 1920s, and 1960s–1980s, Victorian and early-twentieth-century christening gowns, uniforms from the New Zealand Wars in the mid-nineteenth century to World War II, and ecclesiastical garments. Dress as of 2008 was exhibited within the colonial cottage display and in a six-month rotating display in the Whanganui Gallery. Current programs for acquiring dress maintain a regional focus. For example, the museum ran a project whereby people were encouraged to donate T-shirts with designs and slogans that relate to the region. Similarly, the school uniform collection has been strengthened through an oral history project, which, in addition to collecting the uniforms, gathered information about the students' school life. The museum also houses a collection of photographs from the 1870s onward, which include references to dress worn in the region. Its main strengths are a collection of small nineteenth-century photographs mounted on card called *cartes de visite*, from the 1870s and 1880s, and studio portraits from the 1880s to the 1920s. There is also an important collection of photographs by William Partington of Māori on the Whanganui River, which illustrates the crossovers between Māori and European dress. The Web site is at http://www.wanganui-museum.org.nz/

Puke Ariki (New Plymouth). Puke Ariki houses a research center and museum that document and display the heritage of the Taranaki district. Dress falls under the textile collection and includes women's wear, military and civilian uniforms, work-wear, children's wear, sportswear, hats, and shoes, most of which belonged to local settlers and residents. The collection dates from the early nineteenth century to the present. Notable items include rare examples of Armed Constabulary and Taranaki Militia uniforms from the New Zealand Wars, nineteenth-century wedding outfits that belonged to well-known Taranaki settler families, and a rare example of a 1930s "make do" child's petticoat cobbled together during the Depression. There is also a collection of the New Zealand–designed Swanndri jackets. Made from wool and invented in Taranaki in 1913 to protect farmers from the elements, these waterproof garments continued to be manufactured in the region until 1975. The Web site is at http://www.pukeariki.com/en/

The New Dowse (Lower Hutt). Opened in 1971, the Dowse Art Gallery (renamed the New Dowse in 2007) established itself in the 1980s as a leading collection of New Zealand decorative arts and design. The Dowse organizes an active program of innovative exhibitions and events that address the crossovers between art, design, and popular culture. In contrast to many of the other regional collections, the Dowse collects dress and body adornment from a design point of view, concentrating on how the artist has utilized the materials, incorporated decorative elements, and acknowledged the body. The body adornment collection, including necklaces, brooches, and rings, is one of the largest in the country. The Dowse is active in acquiring works by contemporary designers and artists. Examples are hand-dyed and -embroidered garments from the 1980s by Kerrie Hughes, an 1880s-inspired Gauguin gown (2001) by Jo Torr made in contemporary Polynesian printed floral cotton, and handcrafted bags by Vita Cochrane and Maiangi Waitai. The Web site is at http://www.dowse.org.nz/

Museum of New Zealand Te Papa Tongarewa (Wellington). Known as Te Papa, the Museum of New Zealand was created in 1992 from the existing National Art Gallery and National Museum. Invested with the task of preserving and presenting the *taonga* (treasures) of New Zealand's peoples and interpreting the country's heritage for national and international audiences, Te Papa's collecting policies and displays have introduced alternative ways of representing New Zealand history and culture, with a marked focus on reflecting the lives of ordinary people.

Historical and contemporary dress is collected within the areas of social history and design. The collection comprises over seven thousand items of dress and textiles of European and New Zealand origin. There is a small collection of eighteenth-century dress, which arrived in New Zealand with early settlers, and also some rare examples of garments that were unpicked for the voyage out during the nineteenth century in order to conserve space. Collecting as of 2008 focused on New Zealand material, and items from overseas are rarely acquired, except when there is a notable New Zealand link. The dedicated decorative arts gallery, Eyelights, regularly exhibits displays of historical and contemporary dress. Strengths of the collection are nineteenth-century women's dress and twentieth-century New Zealand ready-made labels, nineteenth-century lace, and nineteenth- and early-twentieth-century shawls. An active program of acquiring New Zealand fashion design reflects an aim to represent local creativity and innovation. Twentieth-century and current labels include Kevin Berkahn, Michael Mattar, Annie Bonza, Liz Mitchell, Doris de Pont, Kate Sylvester, Sabatini, Gubb & Mackie, Nom*D, Zambesi, Marilyn Sainty, Karen Walker, Miranda Brown, and World. In 2001 the museum instituted a five-year project to document New Zealand Fashion Week, collecting garments and related ephemera, and in 2002 mounted an exhibition that looked specifically at the first New Zealand Fashion Week.

Complementing the collection of dress in the History department, the Māori and Pacific collections have acquired outfits by the New Zealand–based group Pacific Sisters and examples from Auckland designer Doris de Pont's 2003 collection, featuring fabric incorporating the work of the artist John Pule.

Additional resources for the study of dress are the museum's photography and archives collections. The former houses collections of nineteenth-century cartes de visite and the work of twentieth-century New Zealand advertising and fashion photographers, such as Gordon Burt, who worked in Wellington from the mid-1920s to the 1950s. The latter is actively acquiring material from the fashion journalist, Carolyn Enting. The Web site is at http://www.tepapa.govt.nz/

OVERVIEW OF COLLECTIONS: SOUTH ISLAND

Canterbury Museum (Christchurch). Since its foundation in 1870, the Canterbury Museum in Christchurch has exhibited examples of dress and accessories. Collecting began sporadically, shaped by donations from local families, and now falls under the care of the senior curator of Decorative Arts. The collection focuses on items from the region or those that have links to Canterbury history and local people and now numbers around fifteen thousand items. The Canterbury Museum was the first museum in New Zealand to establish a permanent display area for dress, in 1959. Since then the museum has staged a changing program of exhibitions around dress, from chronological displays to thematic-based exhibitions, and has maintained an active acquisitions program. The collection is extensive and includes items of European dress worn by European settlers from the mid-nineteenth century through to contemporary New Zealand dress. Nineteenth-century dress is strongly represented, but in 1984 the museum acquired a large collection of New Zealand–made off-the-rack women's clothing from the 1920s through the 1980s, as well as examples of men's and children's dress from the period. Collected by Mollie Rodie Mackenzie with the intention of starting her own museum of fashion, the approximately five thousand items provide an important documentation of everyday New Zealand dress of the twentieth century.

In 2008, collecting aimed to strengthen a number of underrepresented areas, such as men's clothing, sportswear, and occupational dress. The museum is looking to add examples by early local professional dressmakers and milliners, and later well-known Canterbury designers, such as Barbara Lee, as well as dress that has cross-cultural references. It is also seeking to strengthen the collection with garments from the mid-1980s to the present. The museum houses a rare example of castaway clothing, worn by the survivors of the *Dundonald*, who were shipwrecked in the Auckland Islands for eight months in 1907 and resourcefully made clothes for themselves from sailcloth and the skins of sea lions. The Web site is at http://www.canterburymuseum.com/

South Canterbury Museum (Timaru). Located in Timaru, the South Canterbury Museum houses a collection that relates to the natural and human history of the region. It contains an extensive collection of social history artifacts and includes dress and textiles from the past 140 years. Its archival collections include local photographs, information files, and newspapers.

The collection of dress dates from the mid-nineteenth to the mid-twentieth century, with a primary focus on items either made or worn by people living in the region. There are a number of items that were transported to New Zealand by European settlers, such as two English dresses from the 1820s, brought out around the 1860s. The Hope collection contains several examples of dress, such as an eighteenth-century stomacher and fragments of European embroidery, which were in the possession of an old Canterbury settler family. Mid- to late-nineteenth-century dress includes men's, women's, and children's garments, a highlight being wedding outfits for both bride and groom, dating from 1863. There is also a trio of ball gowns dating from 1868, 1895, and 1909, which belonged to Sarah Elworthy. The museum also has a collection of garments from the 1880s with established provenance, while the early twentieth century is well represented by a group of day and evening dresses that belonged to Rosamond Teschemaker. There are good examples of 1930s day dresses, which belonged to Mrs. Phyllis Howe, and a large collection of clothing from the 1960s to the 1980s. As of 2008, a designated costume exhibit has changing displays that feature mid-nineteenth- to early-twentieth-century items from the collection. The Web site is at http://www.timaru .govt.nz/services/museum/

Otago Museum (Dunedin). The first items of European dress to enter the Otago Museum were acquired by donation in the 1940s and included dresses from early European settlement, lace, and paisley shawls. Dress now forms an important part of the collection and is acquired via donation and purchase under the care of the Curator of Humanities and the honorary Curator of Dress. The focus is on dress worn by New Zealanders, with an emphasis on Otago provenance. Collection strengths are nineteenth- and early-twentieth-century women's dress, including the Harris collection—a group of late-nineteenth- to early-twentieth-century women's designer clothes from Europe, which is on long-term loan. The museum also has a comprehensive collection of accessories. Elements of the collection are regularly displayed in short-term exhibitions, which have ranged in topic from nightwear to ties and clothing featuring rose motifs. The Web site is at http://www.otagomuseum.govt.nz/

Otago Settlers Museum (Dunedin). The Otago Settlers Museum was founded in Dunedin in 1898. Originally documenting the histories of early British settlement, it broadened its collecting to reflect the various waves of immigration to the region throughout the twentieth century. The museum houses a rich collection of memorabilia dating back to the mid-nineteenth century, including portraits, photographs, documents, and clothing. The collection of dress numbers over four thousand items, including men's, women's, and children's outer- and underwear, accessories, a collection of paisley shawls, and uniforms. The museum houses a significant collection of nineteenth-century dress with Otago provenance. In a number of cases the wearer has been identified and cross-referenced information has been found in portraits, photographs, and documents in the archive collection. This resource was utilized to great effect in the exhibition Fabulous Frocks! (2003), when photographs and brief biographies of the owners were displayed alongside their garments. Items of dress are exhibited in the Smith Gallery of Otago's Scottish pioneers and are regularly included in specially mounted exhibitions. The museum also has a collection of local newspapers and material relating to immigration, such as shipping lists and biographical and genealogical information about early European immigration to the region. The Web site is at http://www.otago.settlers .museum/

Eden Hore collection (Naseby). The Eden Hore collection in Central Otago is a private collection, which can be visited by appointment. Comprising around 230 New Zealand–designed high-fashion garments dating mainly from the 1970s, it was assembled by Eden Hore, a sheep and cattle farmer, and is displayed at "Glenshee," a property near Naseby. Hore's initial interest in fashion was driven by a desire to see local product being utilized in the world of fashion. His early collecting included hand-spun and handwoven woolen garments, as well as items made of leather, but it soon expanded to high-fashion garments, many of which were finalists in the Benson and Hedges

Awards and Australian Gown of the Year. All of the garments were created by New Zealand designers for the local market and include works by fashion houses Kevin Berkahn, Vinka Lucas, Colin Cole, Babs Radon, Pat Hewitt, and Trish Gregory. Visits are by appointment.

Southland Museum and Art Gallery, Niho o Te Taniwha (Invercargill). Housing collections of art, natural sciences, and human heritage, the Southland Museum and Art Gallery focuses on collecting material that relates to Southland and the subantarctic region of New Zealand. The collection of clothing and accessories falls under the scope of the human heritage collection and consists largely of adult dress relating to the period of European settlement from the 1860s to the early twentieth century. The majority of the collection was acquired by the museum between the 1950s and 1970s, when it was developing the pioneer displays and the Victoriana gallery, the latter opening in 1971. The clothing collection, which numbers over one thousand items, mainly consists of women's dress and undergarments, but also includes children's wear, uniforms, ecclesiastical dress, and accessories such as hats, shoes, parasols, shawls, gloves, handbags, and fans. The museum incorporates some items of dress in its permanent displays in the Victoriana Gallery, the History and Technology Gallery, and the Subantarctic Gallery. Notable pieces in the collection are a pink-red wedding dress dating from 1862, made by a relative of the donor, and a fur jacket created by a local furrier in the 1920s (remodeled in 1960s), constructed from numerous small triangular sections of fur from between the ears and nose of Otautau stream rats. There are also around forty nineteenth-century evening gowns and capes from the 1920s to the 1960s. The Web site is at http://www .southlandmuseum.com/

Archives and Online Databases

Alexander Turnbull Library, National Library of New Zealand. Part of the National Library of New Zealand in Wellington, the Alexander Turnbull Library is the major repository for New Zealand books, manuscripts, ephemera, and photographs. Its catalogs can be accessed online, and its *Timeframes* Web site provides access to an extensive pictorial online database. The Web site is at http://www .natlib.govt.nz/atl

Matapihi is an online database administered by the Turnbull Library, with links to contributing collections in New Zealand, including the Auckland Art Gallery, Auckland City Libraries, Christchurch City Libraries, and Te Ara—The Encyclopedia of New Zealand. Its Web site is at http://www.matapihi.org.nz/

Auckland City Libraries. Heritage Images Online is an extensive archive of photographic images in the Auckland City Library's Special Collections, including the Firth Collection of studio portraits and fashion photography taken by Auckland photographer Colin Firth between the late 1930s and 1970s. Its Web site is at http://www.auck landcitylibraries.com/heritage/photographs. Central libraries in the major cities also hold pictorial archives and local newspapers.

New Zealand newspapers and magazines. The following is a selection of newspapers and magazines that are relevant to fashion research. They can be found in major public libraries and research centers. The earlier publications are on microfiche.

Apparel, 1972–2003

Australian & New Zealand Apparel: The Business of Fashion, 2003–

Black, 2006–

ChaCha: Fashion and Style, May 1983–January 1988

Eve: The New Magazine for All New Zealand Women, June 1966–December 1975

Grace, June 1998–January 2001

More: For New Zealand Women, 1983–1996

New Zealand Fashion Quarterly (previously *Fashion Quarterly*), 1987–

New Zealand Illustrated Magazine, November 1899–September 1905

New Zealand Women's Weekly, January 1934–

Next, 1991–

NZ Pictorial News, 1924–1934 (name change December 1930 to *The NZ Home Pictorial*)

Pavement, 1993–2006

Pulp, 2001–

The Ladies Mirror: The Home Journal of New Zealand, July 1922–March 1963 (title change 1926 to *Ladies Mirror*)

The New Zealand Weekly News, November 1863–August 1971

The Weekly Graphic and Ladies Journal, 1890–1907

Thursday: The Magazine for Modern Women, 1968–1976

Woman's Choice, August 1954–December/January 1959

References and Further Reading

Anonymous. *Revealing Treasures of the Elms: Textiles and Associated Articles of the Nineteenth Century.* Tauranga, NZ: The Elms Foundation, n.d.

Berkahn, Kevin, and Maggie Blake. *Berkahn—Fashion Designer.* Auckland, NZ: HarperCollins, 1999.

Ebbett, Eve. *In True Colonial Fashion: A Lively Look at What New Zealanders Wore.* Wellington, NZ: A. H. & A. W. Reed, 1977.

Le Vaillant, Louis. *New Zealand Design and Decorative Arts from the Collection of the Auckland Museum.* Auckland, NZ: Reed, 2006.

Lloyd-Jenkins, Douglas. *Avis Higgs: Joie de Vivre.* Napier, NZ: Hawkes Bay Cultural Trust, 2000.

Malthus, Jane. "One Man's Fantasy: The Eden Hore Collection of High and Exotic Fashion Garments." In *Looking Flash: Clothing in Aotearoa/New Zealand,* edited by Bronwyn Labrum, Fiona McKergow, and Stephanie Gibson, 222–241. Auckland, NZ: Auckland University Press, 2007.

Maynard, Margaret. "Terrace Gowns and Shearer's Boots: Rethinking Dress and Public Collections." *Culture and Policy* 3, no. 2 (1991): 77–84.

Nicholson, Heather. *The Loving Stitch: A History of Knitting and Spinning in New Zealand.* Auckland, NZ: Auckland University Press, 1998.

Quérée, Jennifer. "The Collection and Display of Costume and Textiles at the Canterbury Museum." *Newsletter,* The Costume & Textile Section of the Auckland Museum Institute 1 (July–October 2002): 6–8.

Quérée, Jennifer. "Seabirds, Seals and Sailcloth: The Clothing of the Dundonald Castaways." *Costume* 37 (2003): 75–94.

Quérée, Jennifer, and Andrew Paul Wood. "Beyond the Black Singlet: The Mollie Rodie Mackenzie Collection of Twentieth Century New Zealand Clothing." *Records of Canterbury Museum* 17 (2003): 48–75.

Regnault, Claire. *The New Zealand Gown of the Year.* Napier, NZ: Hawkes Bay Cultural Trust, 2002.

Wolfe, Richard. *The Way We Wore: The Clothes New Zealanders Have Loved.* Auckland, NZ: Penguin, 2001.

Laura Jocic

See also Designer Fashion in New Zealand.

Dress and Fashion in New Zealand

In the twentieth century the development of women's dress and fashion in New Zealand, including hairstyling and cosmetics, was not a unique national story contained within geographical boundaries. From the late nineteenth century and throughout the next, the dress of New Zealand women closely followed overseas developments, particularly in France and later Britain and America. The fact that a major Wellington department store, Te Aro House, would advertise, in 1894, their new dressmaking department head, Madame De Verney, as a former well-known artist from Worths (sic) of Paris assumes both general public familiarity with the fashion house and its cachet, and the commercial value of making the link with France. Over the years those who could afford fashionable attire might have purchased a dressmaker's version of a French outfit or a copy of the latest Balenciaga sheath from a *British Vogue* magazine, or visited a department store, in any major New Zealand city, to buy the most recent Christian Dior model made under license in New Zealand by El Jay, or even a version of a Norman Hartnell outfit.

The country's fashion history in the twentieth century evidently shadowed international developments, without the time delay assumed of a nation geographically isolated from the major centers—Paris, London, Milan, and New York—as they shifted in relative significance over the course of the century. This acknowledges the presence of effective mechanisms by which news of the latest trends and examples of fashionable garments could be communicated to consumers and manufacturers. It is possible, then, to trace the waxing and waning influence of various international fashion centers through local marketing and publicity, though, particularly in the pre- and immediate postwar periods, emphasizing links with Paris, the world's acknowledged fashion capital of the day, was paramount. This reassured the buying public in the largest New Zealand cities, especially Auckland, Wellington, Christchurch, and Dunedin, that their styles were completely up-to-date in an international, and not just a local, sense.

Major events influencing the development of dress and fashion internationally, conflicts such as World Wars I and II, the worldwide Depression of the early 1930s, and ongoing technological and communication innovations have also impacted on New Zealand, serving to synchronize its experiences with those of the rest of the Western world. The country's larger narrative of fashion and dress in the twentieth century also mirrors that of Australia, especially so since the development of the Closer Economic

New Zealand beachwear fashion in 1966, with fabrics by immigrant Dutch designer Frank Carpay and garment designs by Robert Leek (for Frank Carpay Designs Ltd). Courtesy of the Hawke's Bay Cultural Trust—Ruawharo Ta-u-rangi Carpay collection. Hawke's Bay Museum and Art Gallery, Napier, New Zealand.

Relations Trade Agreement (ANZCERTA) between the two countries on 1 January 1983.

WOMEN'S DRESS AND FASHIONS FROM THE 1890s

In spite of being granted the right to vote on 19 September 1893 and enjoying increasing emancipation, fashion-conscious New Zealand women at the turn of the twentieth century largely followed the dictates of Paris in their dress, including the "pouter pigeon" silhouette (named after the breed of pigeon able to distend its crop and thus produce a large, puffed-up breast) and the more restrictive hobble skirt, the latter popular just prior to World War I. For a very few knowledge of the late-nineteenth-century dress reform movements of Britain and America is attested by a booklet issued in 1893 encouraging the adoption of the knickerbocker outfit (a masculinized form of dress that included full trousers fastened just below the knees) as the only suitable dress for New Zealand women. They were encouraged to form dress reform groups through the local Country Women's Associations throughout the country. Even so, there is little evidence that this mode of dress enjoyed widespread adoption.

By the turn of the twentieth century New Zealanders were able to buy locally manufactured ready-made clothing from department stores that could be found in all the major cities and larger regional towns, as well as specialty shops. Mail-order catalogs such as those of Laidlaw Leeds (later Farmers' Trading

Company) allowed rural customers to obtain the latest styles in fashionable clothing, as well as serviceable and practical garments including underclothing. Mass-produced clothing, though stylish, was generally not high fashion, and the local garment industry was much less developed and diverse than overseas equivalents, so custom tailoring, dressmaking, and home sewing remained a very significant source of garments.

The impact of World War I served to assist in the emancipation of women in New Zealand. This in turn influenced a radical change in their appearance through the widespread adoption of straighter, loosely cut clothing, which was to dominate during the 1920s. Rapidly changing variations of this theme, mainly dictated by Paris, were reflected quickly in the garments of ready-to-wear manufacturers. Like similar modern young women the world over, the New Zealand version of the so-called flapper bobbed her hair, flattened her chest, began to use a little makeup, and adjusted her hemlines upwards in step with her global sisters.

In the 1920s many local woolen manufacturing companies began diversifying from the production of yarn, fabric, and blankets to produce underwear and ready-to-wear clothing. Kaiapoi (Dunedin), Roslyn (Dunedin), and Petone (Wellington) mills were three such companies producing woolen fashions for the New Zealand public.

The worldwide economic Depression following the 1929 Wall Street crash affected the lives of many, as reflected in frank confessions about personal hardships in the "Over the Teacups" section of the *New Zealand Women's Weekly* (founded in 1932), but increasingly over the course of the 1930s women turned to Hollywood for ideas about fashion. While a focus on the movies provided an escape from the reality of everyday life, it also offered New Zealanders a fresh and compelling source of inspiration for new styles in clothes, hair, makeup, and body image. Salons offered Marcel waves as worn by the stars, with one, Auckland's Marinello Shoppe, advertising that they would soon be installing a "Vaper [sic] Marcel" permanent waving machine de luxe, to be operated by their own Marcel "Diploma Specialist," M. H. Fox. Makeup (theatrical style by Tangee), depilatories, slimming potions and devices (such as the Charnaux perforated latex corset), tanning lotions (Max Factor's Sum R Tan), and freckle removers (Mystic Freckle Cream) were locally made and imported products offered for sale that were often endorsed by, or linked to, movie stars.

The development of less expensive synthetic fibers, such as rayon and artificial silk (a popular brand in New Zealand was Celanese), enabled everyday New Zealanders to adopt what were more body-conscious American styles to achieve the fashionable look they desired. The new wonder fiber, Lastex, was widely advertised by the late 1920s. It was used for the new lightweight, better-fitting foundation garments, which were imported or made by Auckland's new, ultramodern Berlei factory, set up in 1923, a branch of the highly successful Berlei corset company in Sydney. A nation of sunbathers and surfers, New Zealanders enthusiastically embraced the new styles of figure- and flesh-revealing swimsuits from America.

Although Paris remained the international fashion capital through to the 1960s at least, American influence grew steadily. The popularity of Hollywood movies brought new fashion inspiration and began to shift the source of that inspiration from Europe to America. At least on screen, Paris continued to represent the Hollywood fashion ideal, so the change of emphasis was often more a case of an American filter being applied to European-originated fashion concepts. The growing hegemony of Hollywood's influence in the 1920s was cemented in English-speaking territories like New Zealand by the advent of sound, and the mass distribution of Hollywood movies had the power to ignite sudden worldwide trends in fashion.

One such example was *Morocco*, directed and obsessively designed by Josef von Sternberg in 1930, and starring Marlene Dietrich in her first American film. Her first onstage appearance as cabaret singer Amy Jolly incited and excited the international cinema-going audience with her assault on traditional ideals of femininity, wearing a formal man's tuxedo dinner suit including trousers and a top hat. The gender transgression extended to kissing a woman on the lips and tossing a flower to Gary Cooper. An advertisement for fashion designer Trilby Yates's Auckland clothing salon, Ladies Paradise, in 1933 offers as daring day-wear for the modern New Zealand woman a "Marlene Dietrich trouser suit" at five pounds, five shillings.

WORLD WAR II UNTIL THE 1960s

Clothing rationing, introduced on 29 May 1942, put an end to the ready availability of many of the new materials, such as elasticized fabrics, that had become indispensable to a fashionable life. Rationing and wartime shortages also limited access to many other materials associated with the construction of clothing, prompting magazines such as the *New Zealand Home Journal* (1934–1974) to offer style for all occasions with patterns for making utility garments that were coupon-light. Knitting patterns too became increasingly popular additions to most women's magazines. In the absence of nylon hosiery, which was mainly available as treasured gifts from visiting American GIs stationed in military camps around the country, most local women got by with mended stockings, or new stockings of inferior materials, or painted their legs with products such as Cyclax brand "Stockingless Cream" to provide the appearance of stockings. During wartime making-do compromises led fashion to lose much of its formality, a trend that would only be amplified in later decades.

While the dropping of the atomic bomb on Hiroshima inspired Monterey Cosmetics (Christchurch) to create its "devastating" Atomic Red lipstick in 1945, the real international fashion event of the postwar era that was to affect New Zealand was Dior's "New Look" in 1947 and the revival of the French fashion industry. This news began to dominate the women's pages of magazines, which had dropped or severely curtailed the topic of fashion during wartime. Some filled their fashion pages with images of American film stars wearing glamorous high-fashion apparel. There was debate in some magazines, immediately following the end of the war, about the future capital of global fashion—Paris, London, or New York. The impact of the New Look turned the attention of New Zealand journalists once again to Paris. The silhouette of this new style was widely adopted by local clothing manufacturers at all levels, as well as being recreated by professional dressmakers and home sewers. Many clothing manufacturers and retailers were quick to exploit the apparent necessity for new styles of underwear to help mold the New Look silhouette. In response, New Zealand's Berlei factory developed its Tru-to-type foundation, catering to five figure types and with thirteen variations, specifically to meet this demand.

Interest having turned toward Paris as the source of fashionable credibility, in the next decade London fashion came to be particularly enthusiastically profiled in New Zealand owing to the strong historical, imperial links with Britain. New Zealand has always had a strong sentimental attachment to London fashion, and in the immediate post–World War II years London was favored over Paris as the "new fashion capital." The mania that accompanied royal visits to New Zealand, such as the proposed (but canceled) tour of 1949 and that of the young Queen Elizabeth in 1953, provided much inspiration for fashion, including a broad interest in the styles worn by members of the British aristocracy. Visits by the queen's milliner Aage Thaarup in 1953 and 1955, and licenses to produce royal warrant labels, including Hardy Amies and Rayne shoes, gave an imprint of royalty to New Zealand fashion, in addition to the local popularity in the 1950s of designers associated with royalty such as Norman Hartnell.

The rebuilding and development of industry in postwar New Zealand embraced new synthetic fibers such as Orlon, which were made into clothes that particularly targeted a younger generation, who had managed for almost a decade without access to good-quality natural fabrics such as silk, linen, and wool. The new easy-care, washable, and fast-drying fibers suited the lifestyles of postwar New Zealand women, who, if not working, were leading busy lives as modern housewives. Synthetic bras and corselettes made by Hurley Bendon (later Bendon), the first corsetry manufacturer founded in New Zealand (in 1947 by Ray and Des Hurley), carried warnings not to attempt to iron them.

After the war up-to-date hairstyles, including some marketed as appropriate to Dior's New Look, were available in New Zealand from the growing number of hair salons, including Auckland's chic Kays of Auckland Continental Salon and Kays of Auckland French Salon. Claiming to be the sole New Zealand member of the Syndicat de la Haute Coiffure Française, from the late 1950s Kays offered up the new fashions of leading Parisian hairstylists within days of their being released. Any magazine aimed at women provided advertisements for the increasing number of cosmetic brands available, with many made in the country under license to major English, French, and American companies. In sync with changes in fashion, cosmetic lines began offering seasonal changes, in particular lipstick and nail colors.

Relatively unscathed by World War II and with greatly increased political and cultural dominance, America, which had risen in New Zealanders' consciousness along with the rise of Hollywood in the 1920s and 1930s, continued to be a major source of fashion ideas as well as France and Britain. New Zealanders loved the casual, colorful fashions emanating from California, which had broadened its apparel industry in response to the needs of film stars for off-screen wardrobes and was catering to California's outdoorsy, informal lifestyle, not unlike that of New Zealand. The selling power of Hollywood is evident in the large number of Californian brands selected by New Zealand garment companies to manufacture under license in the post–World War II period. Sbicca shoes and Cole of California are two prominent examples.

European fashion trends would often reach New Zealand refracted through Hollywood's lens, as did influences closer to home. When Pacific patterns and styles enjoyed a vogue in the 1950s, it was not a reflection of New Zealand's place in the Pacific. Nor was it the increasing migration of Pacific island peoples to the country, but the secondhand inspiration of an American trend driven by the popularization of Hawai'i as the ultimate leisure destination in films of the 1930s through to the 1960s. As a consequence, the fashions derived more from Hawai'i than from New Zealand's closer Pacific neighbors during these decades. When Hurley Bendon created a leisure collection comprising men's printed cotton trunks and women's printed cotton sunsuits, the prints as well as the name of the range were of Hawaiian inspiration. So too were immigrant Dutch designer Frank Carpay's fluid and colorful designs for screen-printed toweling, used from the mid-1960s for beach towels and simple beach attire like mini-dresses, shifts, hooded tops and jackets, and cover-ups.

It was only with the development of the studio craft movement in New Zealand from the 1950s that a stylistic consciousness of New Zealand's closer Pacific neighbors began to inform New Zealand design. And it would not be until the 1980s that the Pacific would become a dominant presence in New Zealand design.

With the rise of "swinging London" and Carnaby Street fashions in the mid- to late 1960s, Britain truly dominated, for a time at least, New Zealand fashion. Youthful consumers of the 1960s increasingly interested in fashion were drawn to Britain and its new designers, like Mary Quant. The fashion needs of this growing youth culture were answered by the mushrooming of boutiques selling original designs, primarily inspired by London fashions. While revolutionary styles such as the minidress (a dress that reached the knee and above) were readily available by 1965, the adoption of the shortest styles did not always meet the approval of more conservative parents, as attested by the letters from teens to youth-orientated magazines such as *Playdate*. The ready availability of "Mod" fashions and "Op-Art" and "Space Age" styles, including Courrèges-inspired plastic chain-mail dresses and helmet-style bonnets, demonstrates the immediacy of inspiration derived from magazines, television, and international travel. After the opening of Auckland International Airport in 1966, special youth fares made travel to the world's fashion centers easier than ever before.

FASHION NEWS

New Zealand women have always wanted to be kept informed about the latest trends in fashion, even in periods and situations when news from abroad was scarce or delayed. News from "home" (Great Britain) in personal correspondence often included information about changes in hem length, popular colors, or fashionable accessories—sometimes swatches of fabric or annotated illustrations cut from newspapers and women's magazines were enclosed.

International fashion news was a staple of women's magazines throughout the twentieth century. New Zealand newspapers were also filled with descriptions of fashionable attire. The authority of Paris fashion was clear in relayed descriptions of dress at society soirées in London and snippets of fashion news, which often conveyed information about the latest fads. In the fashion columns or women's pages of newspapers, fashion snippets from abroad often reported on minutiae, such as the popularity of the butterfly as a decorative motif in 1905, or on sensational styles or stylish society wardrobes. References to Paris fashion and to designers such as Worth, Doucet, and Paquin, and English designers like Lucille, were common.

A fashion show at the James Smith department store in Wellington, New Zealand, ca. 1953. Photographer unknown. Alexander Turnbull Library, Wellington, New Zealand.

A local audience could choose to enthusiastically embrace, or reject as outlandish or impractical, the latest extremes of Parisian couture, with Paul Poiret providing much fodder for newspapers in the 1910s, the information supplied by overseas correspondents or by telegraph from the Press Association. A typical example demonstrating the speed with which fashion news could reach remote New Zealand was Wellington's *Evening Post* report, a day after it occurred, of a scene at the Vienna Opera House on 6 March 1911. It was caused by two society women, dressed in Poiret's harem skirts, who were forcibly held, by women, in full view of the audience, who shouted for half an hour that "our [Viennese] women shall not wear trousers." At the other extreme of public approval, Parisian designers such as Regine and Paquin were held in the utmost esteem, with detailed descriptions of garments worn by prominent members of London society enthusiastically and regularly reported in newspapers.

The general desire for information regarding the latest overseas fashion trends was especially evident from the 1920s onward. *The Mirror* (1922–1963), a stylish publication dedicated to women that was modeled on *Harper's Bazaar*, provided photographs and idealized sketches of the latest French fashions. Such magazines aimed at the social set presented syndicated images of fashions by Patou, Lanvin, Vionnet, and Chanel, alongside locally designed garments, heavily influenced by Paris. These were modeled by young, local society women. Newspapers and popular magazines more frequently commented on the rise of the flapper, and cheaply printed periodicals such as the *New Zealand Home Journal* (1934–1974) focused on providing sketches and pattern layouts for more serviceable garments for the entire family. They also included patterns and ideas for knitwear, the fashionability of which was undeniable but not generally cutting edge.

During the Depression of the early 1930s, while popular magazines aimed at the lower to middle classes offered practical advice on economizing and making clothes last longer, for example, by turning cuffs and collars, many also continued to comment on high fashion. The *New Zealand Women's Weekly*, for instance, offered snippets during the 1930s from London-based columnists Ellie Bailey and Edith Manners, and fashion expert Crystal Lindstrom reported seasonally for them from the Paris fashion shows.

From the late 1940s and during the 1950s the absolute latest in fashion news from Paris and London arrived via airmailed articles from correspondents and wires from international news agencies. Progressive general periodical *Newsview* (1945–1954) prided itself on the speed of its fashion reports and that they were not syndicated articles, some being written by a New Zealand–born fashion journalist, Gwen Robyns. From the late 1940s she airmailed both images and words, her "London Letter" reporting styles spotted on London streets, as well as tips on new trends observed at the designer garment showings she attended. Through Robyns's reports, leading English designers such as Dorville, Digby Morton, Susan Small, Michael Sherard, and Hardy Amies became familiar names to *Newsview*'s readership. Occasionally comments were made as to the suitability of these fashions to the New Zealand climate, but more often this was not the case.

Beyond the coverage provided by general women's magazines, there was a growing demand for more detailed reports and dedicated fashion publications. The Fashion Bookery, a trade bookshop, was established in the mid-1930s in Auckland to serve the consumer need for detailed international fashion information, among both professionals and the general public, and carried a wide range of publications devoted to fashion. Through the Fashion Bookery, access to the latest fashion periodicals, such as American *Harper's Bazaar* and British *Vogue*, was also possible.

A popular source of images for many journals, providing up-to-date information about women's fashion, were leading fashion and textile trade journals of the day such as *Swiss Textiles*. Often these were images of work by little-known European designers, and they frequently bore little or no resemblance to the styles described in the accompanying articles. The New Zealand Wool Board, set up in 1944, distributed images received from similar bodies around the world, in particular the International Wool Secretariat (IWS) in London, and these were also well used in local publications.

In 1958 *New Zealand Vogue* debuted, providing extensive documentation of the latest European and American styles. Running only until 1968, it represented the country's most significant dedicated fashion publication until the emergence of *New Zealand Fashion Quarterly* (from 1982). Although this new wave of New Zealand fashion publications gave increasing attention to the work of local designers, international fashion news remained a staple.

PUBLISHED PATTERNS AND HOME DRESSMAKING

Since the nineteenth century home dressmaking has been a significant factor in the production of clothing and fashionable dress in New Zealand. To assist the home sewer, a wide range of commercially printed patterns was available since at least the turn of the twentieth century, with many imported from the United States, the source of some of the most prominent brands used throughout the century: Butterick, Simplicity, McCall, and Vogue. Vogue patterns offered the home sewer a closer link with Paris couture, particularly with the development of their Vogue Couturier patterns in the 1960s.

There were many ways women could respond to the latest fashion news, even if they could not go out and buy a Paquin gown for themselves. Adoption of a particular innovation could always be achieved by the adaptation of existing garments or the modification of a dress pattern. Alternatively, a new style could be commissioned from a professional dressmaker. A Poiret-inspired tangerine-colored silk and oriental-style brocade evening gown (Te Papa collection), made or commissioned by a student to wear to a Wellington Arts Ball about 1910, provides evidence of a clear understanding of Poiret's stylistic hand.

The introduction of German-designed Burda patterns in the 1960s provided the possibility of better-fitting clothes with their multisize patterns, which had to be traced off onto one's own paper. A number of prominent contemporary New Zealand fashion designers, including Liz Mitchell, recall that the flexibility of Burda patterns provided them with their first experience of creative pattern making. Evidence in New Zealand museums shows that during times of hardship, such as the Depression and World War II, it was common for women to share their patterns with friends and family by tracing them onto newspaper or cheap butcher's paper. Some museum collections include such patterns folded and tied with thin scraps of fabric and annotated with a brief descriptive note such as "Betty's lovely skirt." The absence of instructions assumes a high level of knowledge regarding the construction of garments.

Most New Zealand women's magazines of a more general domestic slant offered dress patterns. The *New Zealand Home Journal* published illustrations, cutting layout diagrams, and brief instructions for garments for the whole family. From 1958 *New Zealand Vogue* featured extensive coverage of fashions exclusively made from their patterns, the details of the relevant fabrics and trims provided as an adjunct to the feature.

During the first half of the twentieth century New Zealanders were able to attend an increasing number of commercially run dressmaking, tailoring, and pattern-cutting schools, some of which developed their own commercial patterns as a sideline. Some of these businesses formed relationships with popular journals such as *Newsview* by offering a mail-order pattern service.

Around 1940 Druleigh Styles, a long-established College of Dressmaking and Pattern Cutting, which advertised itself as "New Zealand's Leading Fashion Institute," offered an innovative variation on the customized pattern concept. In a well-produced booklet with stylish Hollywood-inspired letters spelling its name, and a glamorous image of Columbia film star Margaret Lindsay, Druleigh offered patterns for the garments illustrated in the booklet, cut to the customer's individual measurements, on completion of a detailed measurement sheet. Using an image of another star, the college stated that it could cut patterns "from pictures like this," while also scouting for potential students for their dressmaking course. It also advertised the availability of personal tutoring, as well as a correspondence course for country students. A canny marketing strategy was to place these "Druleigh Styles" booklets in the staff rooms of businesses throughout Auckland, Wellington, and Hamilton.

During the 1950s New Zealand publishers such as Reeds issued numerous comprehensive publications on dressmaking at home to fill a need presumably created by the decline of full-time dressmaking courses, the movement of more young women into the workforce, and a (perceived, at least) decline in dressmaking skills among young women.

INTERNATIONAL IMPORTS AND LICENSING OF FASHION

Just as information about international fashion has always freely circulated within New Zealand, so overseas fashion garments have been part of the local fashion landscape, available for purchase locally or on view in fashion shows. The speed with which they arrived in the country was often remarkable. Evidence in early-twentieth-century newspapers and women's periodicals shows that retailers all over New Zealand commonly sold unique as well as mass-produced imported garments. In March 1910 the major Auckland department store John Court advertised a shipment of exclusive model gowns (only one of each was imported) hand-selected by their buyer in Berlin and Paris for sale to discerning women. Retailers also sold garments under license to overseas designers, most notably after World War II. The predominance in New Zealand museum collections of French-labeled clothing from the 1920s over other high-quality garments suggests that certainly in the early part of the twentieth century imported fashion garments were an important component of fashionable wardrobes.

Very wealthy New Zealanders sometimes brought entire wardrobes back to New Zealand from England, Europe, or America. In this way international garments could become part of the local fashion landscape, to be passed on, emulated, or even criticized. The daughter of a New Zealand official posted to the United Nations office in New York in the late 1940s remembers being exposed on their return to criticism for their new dresses and her mother's nylons and department-store-bought designer "best dress," for the reason that in 1949 New Zealanders were still suffering postwar shortages.

During the Depression, and particularly after World War II, when protectionism of local industry was at its height, imported fashions became scarce. In the 1930s New Zealanders were encouraged to "buy New Zealand made" (a 1933 advertisement for Westcraft handbags exhorts: "Buy 'Westcraft' goods and help New Zealand industries"). After experiencing clothes rationing during the war and up to 1947, severe import restrictions had also been placed on parts of New Zealand industry at the cessation of hostilities in an effort to foster local production, making it increasingly difficult for retailers to import a range of categories of foreign-made garments, and indeed imports remained scarce until the 1980s.

Licensing of fashion, which began to increase rapidly from the late 1940s, provided a way for New Zealand manufacturers and retailers to bring coveted international styles to local customers without violating government import restrictions. One of the first major fashion licenses to be granted after the war, noted in the *New Zealand Retailer*, was to Korma Textiles of Auckland for Californian swimwear label Rose Marie Reid. Providing the bathing costumes of choice for swimming star Esther Williams and the Duchess of Windsor, the label's products included "ultra metallic suits," probably made entirely of the new Lurex fiber, invented in 1948. These were previewed to a select group of journalists and retailers at a special mannequin parade held in Auckland in June 1948.

Some manufacturers took extreme measures to ensure that their most exclusive fashion lines were as up-to-date as possible. A fashion illustrator, Kate Coolahan, working for major Wellington department store DIC, recalls being flown to Auckland in the early 1950s for a brief appointment in a bond store with a roomful of mannequins wearing the following season's couture garments from Paris. She had a limited time to sketch them carefully, recording all the special details including the texture of the fabrics and trims. This practice of bringing couture garments into the country for a very brief time, but not taking them through customs, was a way for manufacturers to avoid prohibitive import duties. Coolahan's sketches of the gowns were reproduced in attractive books sent to affluent DIC clients around the country for selection of styles, and then recreated for them by DIC's appointed manufacturer.

Dior was a couturier whose work was licensed in New Zealand. Even with New Zealand fashion retailers opposing the dissemination of information about his New Look, it was established fashion currency within a year of its launch in Paris on 12 February 1947. For instance, by 1948 New Zealand manufacturers were referring to this New Look in their advertising for women's fashionable clothing, as well as underwear and corsetry. Department stores wasted no time in devoting their premium window spaces to the display of reproduced garments illustrating the new silhouette, as admired in New Plymouth (North Island) by the members of the Federation of Garment Manufacturers and their partners at the group's annual conference there in May 1948. Particularly appreciated were the windows dressed by Mr. C. Stone for Messrs. McGruer's Ltd., which comprised one shop mannequin wearing lingerie and another a New Look evening gown in a bedroom setting, with a banner reading "The New Look means a New Foundation."

One of the first major fashion parades to celebrate the style was held in Wellington in August 1948. With well-known New Zealand personality Selwyn Toogood as master of ceremonies, the shows ran for over an hour every day for one week at the James Smith department store. Using fifteen mannequins, over one hundred garments were shown, from swimsuits to ball gowns; all displayed the most appealing trends of the new silhouette, according to the *Retailer of New Zealand* in 1948. C. H. Andrews, a Wellington designer and manufacturer of display equipment, noted in a report completed in June 1948 that special mannequins, designed and made locally for the display of New Look garments, were particularly popular with retailers.

As one of the most significant women's fashion labels to be made in New Zealand under license, Christian Dior was manufactured under strict conditions in Gus Fisher's El Jay Auckland workrooms. El Jay produced Dior from the early 1950s to the 1980s, making it the longest-established Dior license held outside Paris. Fisher embraced Dior's model fashions wholeheartedly, turning his downtown Auckland premises into a replica of Dior's Avenue Montaigne salon, and even staging formal fashion shows there for his clientele, his models wearing the same makeup and hairstyles recently sported by their Parisienne counterparts.

Another way that New Zealanders could view imported couture garments was firsthand through traveling fashion shows.

From 1948 until her retirement in 1956, Wool Board publicity officer Mary-Annette Hay assembled important collections of British, French, and Italian couture garments (all made in wool), handpicked by foreign Wool Board representatives direct from the fashion shows in which they debuted. Hay promoted the use of wool in New Zealand by traveling all around the country presenting dramatized fashion productions, which showcased these garments to a public starved for sartorial luxury. Working with the local department store in each center in which she presented her productions, Hay also promoted New Zealand fashion and clothing alongside couture by incorporating into her productions locally manufactured garments available in the host store.

With the introduction of flights to Australia and further afield from 1948, affluent New Zealanders were more easily able to travel and purchase international fashion for themselves. This also allowed clothing manufacturers to travel and select garments to copy, which, while not a new practice, could be carried out more swiftly. In line with shifts in international fashion influences, the number of English and Australian licenses increased from the 1960s, with London cult label Mary Quant and Australia's John J. Hilton and Sportscraft labels appearing locally. With the lifting of import restrictions in the 1980s, licensing of foreign brands by New Zealand garment manufacturers, as well as other companies, ceased to be necessary or economically viable.

THE RISE OF THE DESIGNER

The rise of the designer is a central narrative of twentieth-century fashion, and this is particularly true for New Zealand. The century began with an underdeveloped local fashion industry (although the manufacture of everyday clothing was strong) and an outward-looking attitude to fashion, and it ended with a strong local fashion identity, predicated on the work of several generations of "name" designers and a healthy local fashion industry, although much manufacturing in the twenty-first century takes place in China.

Despite the fact that there were professional dressmakers in New Zealand throughout the twentieth century (some of whom, such as Trilby Yates, garnered considerable personal reputations in the first half of the century), the emergence of the fashion designer as an identifiable public persona with a signature style is a post–World War II phenomenon. Before then, much of the high-fashion end of the New Zealand dress market was represented by model gowns directly copied from imported examples.

It is difficult to know when the first truly original fashions were designed in New Zealand, but certainly by the 1920s there were a number of women with their own salons advertising exclusive locally conceived fashions. One of Auckland's leading makers of clothes for society women until the early 1950s was fashion designer Flora McKenzie, described at the time as a dressmaker, who began advertising her label Ninette in fashionable New Zealand ladies' magazine *The Mirror* from the 1920s. She is reputed to have taken the lead of the major international designers and had her own house models show her garments to intending clients.

McKenzie's legacy was passed to young Aucklander Bruce Papas, reputedly New Zealand's first official, legally indentured fashion apprentice. Under McKenzie the highly talented Papas learned all aspects of the fashion business, including construction and couture techniques that he employed in his own work as head designer for Auckland department store Milnes (later Milne and

Babs Radon dress, ca. 1960, designed by Barbara Herrick. The Babs Radon label was held up as one of five pioneers of a distinct New Zealand fashion culture in *New Zealand Vogue*'s summer 1963 issue. Photograph by Bernie Hill. Courtesy of the Herrick Archive and Hawke's Bay Museum and Art Gallery, Napier, New Zealand.

Choyce) in the 1950s and early 1960s. Later he left Milnes to set up his own fashion house Papas, being one of a number of young designers at the time to emerge from high-fashion and model gown manufacturing to found their own business. Like Papas, small manufacturers of quality fashion garments, and emerging designers, such as Auckland-based Emma Knuckey, worked in high-quality fabrics, which they manipulated using couture techniques. This appealed to mature women who had previously patronized the high-end, import fashion market. They favored natural fibers with a strong reputation for quality, such as Irish Moygashel linen, Harris Tweed from Scotland, and Swiss Abraham and Alexander silk.

In its summer 1963 issue *New Zealand Vogue* profiled "five leaders of New Zealand couture"—Emma Knuckey, Babs Radon, Colin Cole, Bruce Papas, and Joan Talbot—acknowledging them as the architects of a distinct New Zealand fashion scene, which they compared with those of London, New York, and Rome. Other New Zealand fashion designers who came to prominence in the 1950s and 1960s include Michael Mattar, Rosemary Muller, and Lea Draysey. While many of these "creatives" were described during the 1950s by *Vogue* as "dress designers," by the 1960s they had become identified in the popular press as "couturiers."

The emergence of designers as public personalities with brand value was facilitated by the national publicity generated by a series of fashion competitions and awards, such as the New Zealand Gown of the Year, established by Tam Cochrane in 1958–1964, and the Gold Shears, established in 1963. From the late 1950s the New Zealand Wool Board, in an effort to promote the use of New Zealand wool in high fashion, had also offered Gold Awards for women's fashions and an annual Supreme Award, the latter won by Auckland designer Babs Radon in 1962. The Wool Board would later present its major award through the Benson and Hedges Fashion Design Awards, which began life in 1964 as the Wills Design Award. The Benson and Hedges Fashion Design Awards (so named in 1965 and renamed the Smokefree Fashion Awards in 1996) grew out of the Gown of the Year competition for high-fashion evening wear and became one of the longest-running and most prestigious New Zealand fashion competitions.

By entering such prominent fashion competitions, many of these designers were able to raise their profiles and attract new clientele. When Bruce Papas won the first Gold Shears Award in 1963, his employer Milnes put the gown in pride of place in their street-front window, from where it was purchased by a visiting European concert pianist. Prominent commissions such as gowns for society weddings or seasonal balls also served as good publicity for up-and-coming designers, both among fellow guests and the general public, through reports in newspapers' social pages.

Many of these emerging designers now provided the fashionable New Zealand woman with the opportunity to purchase original design, albeit with a nod to current international styles. At the same time, working at the cusp of the emergence of a youth culture that demanded its identity be expressed through clothing styles, Papas, Knuckey, and other designers met the needs of these new target consumers by designing separate labels, such as the Deauville line by Papas (for Milnes) and Miss Knuckey by Emma Knuckey.

From the early 1960s a second generation of designers began to emerge, some, like Auckland designer Annie Bonza, receiving their training in the workrooms of small high-fashion garment manufacturers making copies of imported couture, in her case prominent Auckland label Pour Vous. Bonza, known formerly as Ann Cole, traveled to Sydney before returning to Auckland to found her own boutique, Annie's Clothes, in the late 1960s. Another woman following Bonza's example was highly respected Auckland designer Marilyn Sainty. Sainty also traveled to Sydney, where she set up her own boutique, Starkers, in the late 1960s, before returning to New Zealand to establish her own label, Marilyn Sainty, which she sold through her Scotties boutiques until her retirement in 2005.

As part of a shift away from fashion as exclusively the preserve of the well-heeled, often mature woman, New Zealand began to show the influence of a new and younger market for clothes in the early 1960s. This included the growth of boutiques as a novel kind of retail outlet. Popular youth magazine *Playdate* regularly profiled the latest and hippest boutiques, their garments often modeled by television personalities and pop stars. References to "Swinging London" and "Mod Culture" abounded. Imported clothing had remained scarce after 1947 and was deemed luxury fare until government deregulation in the 1980s allowed clothing manufactured overseas to be easily imported for retailing. This resulted in both the growth in the availability of prêt-à-porter from major international fashion labels in selected boutiques, and the mass influx of cheaply manufactured clothing from Asia. Since the 1990s it is interesting to note that New Zealand–made designer fashion has come into its own and reversed the dependence on overseas inspiration by developing its own overseas export industry.

References and Further Reading

Daley, Caroline. *Leisure and Pleasure: Reshaping and Revealing the New Zealand Body 1900–1960*. Auckland, NZ: Auckland University Press, 2003.

Gregg, Stacy. *Undressed: New Zealand Fashion Designers Tell Their Stories*. Auckland, NZ: Penguin, 2003.

Labrum, Bronwyn, Fiona McKergow, and Stephanie Gibson, eds. *Looking Flash: Clothing in Aotearoa/New Zealand*. Auckland, NZ: Auckland University Press, 2007.

Lloyd Jenkins, Douglas. *At Home: A Century of New Zealand Design*. Auckland, NZ: Godwit Books, 2004.

Regnault, Claire. *The New Zealand Gown of the Year*. Napier, NZ: Hawkes Bay Cultural Trust, 2003.

Wolfe, Richard. *The Way We Wore: The Clothes New Zealanders Have Loved*. Auckland, NZ: Penguin, 2001.

Angela Lassig

See also Urban Fashion Culture in Australia; Resources for the Study of European Dress and Fashion in New Zealand; Designer Fashion in New Zealand.

Snapshot: Paua Shell Costume Jewelry in New Zealand

New Zealand's best-known costume jewelry is made from the iridescent shell of the *paua* (the Māori name for *Haliotis iris*), a species of abalone only found in the sea around New Zealand. Paua shell was a material used by Māori to highlight the eyes of figures in their carving. Alfred Atkinson in Wellington first introduced the use of paua shell to New Zealand jewelry in the early years of the twentieth century. He produced individually crafted pieces of shell jewelry, which sold through a fine arts network. Arts and Crafts ideals held by Atkinson influenced his choice of paua shell as a vernacular material to embellish jewelry inspired by the local environment. Before Atkinson's use of paua shell in New Zealand, it had been used in jewelry by Arts and Crafts practitioners in Britain from 1890, most notably by C.R. Ashbee in his peacock pendants, probably because the iridescent blue-green colorings of the shell mimicked the colors of the peacock, a favorite Arts and Crafts motif.

Arthur Morrison, a trained jeweler, explored the commercial potential of paua shell for souvenir jewelry in the late 1920s. Morrison's paua shell "Art Souvenirs" grew out of the democratizing of domestic tourism during the 1920s and the demand for affordable souvenirs of a specifically New Zealand character. In particular his paua shell native bird brooches developed as emblems of an emerging national identity during the 1930s. Unfortunately, Morrison's company, the New Zealand Art Souvenirs Ltd., did not survive the Depression years. His initiative, however, was taken up by G.D. Beatson in Blenheim and the Soldiers' Civil Re-establishment League in Wellington, who successfully established workshops—the latter under Morrison's guidance—for the production of paua shell jewelry. At the Centennial Exhibition in Wellington, held over the summer of 1939–1940 to commemorate the establishment of New Zealand as a British colony, locally produced paua shell jewelry was readily available as "Exhibition Mementos."

The strong association that developed between paua shell and a New Zealand identity was not just the result of the shell's uniqueness to the country's coastal waters, but also the realization by early manufacturers that paua shell costume jewelry making (that is, jewelry using semiprecious materials) could be developed, with government protection, as a unique New Zealand activity. Shells had been exported to Britain since the days of Captain James Cook's voyages in the eighteenth century, mainly for the production of buttons and as inlays for furniture. By 1939, however, imports of paua shell jewelry manufactured in Birmingham were occurring, and calls were made to the government to preserve the industry for the nation by licensing paua shell manufacturing and placing a moratorium on the export of unprocessed shells. The government, on that occasion, declined the application on the grounds that the developing industry was too insignificant to warrant protection under the Essential Industries Act of 1936.

At the start of World War II the renamed Disabled Servicemen's Re-establishment League (DSRL) was appointed as government agents for the training and rehabilitation of disabled servicemen. A paua shell jewelry training center was opened by the League in Wellington in 1942 to cater to the demand for souvenirs by many of the one hundred thousand American GIs stationed in New Zealand from 1942 to 1944. This turned paua shell manufacturing into a lucrative enterprise, not just for the DSRL but also for G.D. Beatson. When approached in 1943 by the League to provide protection for the interests of disabled soldiers engaged in paua shell jewelry making, the government was more forthcoming: The export of raw shell was prohibited in 1943, and the industry became subject to Standard Specifications when it was licensed in 1946. The specifications were written in close consultation with the League and favored the approach taken by the DSRL to produce high-quality paua shell jewelry. The specifications stipulated the box-mounting of paua shell in silver or gold and barred the use of glue and lacquer in the production process.

The close association that developed in the public's mind during the war between paua shell jewelry and disabled servicemen was based on the sale of such jewelry through the Disabled Soldiers' shops. The inherent patriotism of this association positively affected the popularity of paua shell jewelry. Lured by paua shell's profitability and the preferential treatment offered to returned servicemen in their application for paua shell manufacturing licenses, many entered the industry following demobilization. Mastercrafts and Paua Opal Products were set up by returned servicemen in Auckland in 1946; together with G.D. Beatson and the DSRL they dominated postwar production of paua shell jewelry.

New Zealand Tui Native Bird Brooch, *paua* shell and sterling silver, manufactured by Paua Opal Products Ltd. in the 1960s. 1.5 inches (40 millimeters) wide by 1.3 inches (34 millimeters) high. Photograph by Petronella J. M. van de Wijdeven.

Delicensing of the industry in 1960 and the subsequent revision of the Standard Specifications in 1964 opened the way for costume jewelry manufacturers to use paua shell in their products. Calls for a relaxation of the Standard Specifications had come from tourist operators early in the 1960s, who maintained that the high quality of paua shell jewelry put it beyond the reach of most tourists. The search for cheaper alternatives led to the development of paua chip or flake jewelry, in which paua shell particles are suspended in resin, with the first patent for such a process taken out in 1968. The use of base metals and the introduction of gold and chrome plating were further innovations in the 1970s. Some of these developments were triggered by an increase in international visitors following the opening of Auckland's new airport in 1965 and the subsequent influx of Japanese tourists beginning in the 1970s, who preferred gold-plated to silver-mounted paua shell jewelry.

The pressure on paua shell manufacturers to satisfy the demands of a fast-growing tourist industry for souvenirs led to the debasement of paua shell jewelry as tourist kitsch. It was not until the Paua Dream exhibition—organized in Auckland in 1981 by the Fingers Studio Jewelry collective—that a sense of pride was restored in the local population for paua shell as costume jewelry, with an ability to reference the special character of New Zealand as a Pacific nation.

REFERENCES AND FURTHER READING

Calhoun, Ann. *The Arts and Crafts Movement in New Zealand 1870–1940: Women Make Their Mark*. Auckland, NZ: Auckland University Press, 2000.
Shepherd, Winsome. *Gold and Silversmithing in Nineteenth and Twentieth Century New Zealand*. Wellington, NZ: The Museum of New Zealand Te Papa Tongarewa, 1995.

Petronella J. M. van de Wijdeven

See also Resources for the Study of European Dress and Fashion in New Zealand; Dress and Fashion in New Zealand.

New Zealand Textiles and Apparel Sectors

Development of the textile and apparel sectors in New Zealand can be traced from settler society to the early twenty-first century, influenced by geography, communication, trade policies and agreements, government assistance, and fashion and technical developments of Western Europe and the United States. During this period there were times of dependence, then relative self-sufficiency in the late nineteenth and much of the early twentieth century. The change to greater dependency on imports during the late twentieth century resulted from removal of quotas, tariff reductions, and consequential competition from external suppliers. New Zealand's temperate, variable climate and geographical features influenced development of specialty garments and products.

CLOTHING AND TEXTILES IN NINETEENTH-CENTURY SETTLER SOCIETY

The number of Europeans estimated to be in New Zealand prior to 1830 was fewer than one thousand (among an estimated seventy thousand Māori), but by 1881 this had increased to an estimated five hundred thousand, more than half being migrants, mostly from Britain. Settler society in New Zealand was based on land, the prospect of economically viable sheep farming, and exploration for gold. Improved economic and social position seem the likely motives for many migrants, who brought with them their own ideals of opportunity, and ideas of behavior and dress. Two features of textiles and apparel of the period were, first, that textiles and apparel required for life in New Zealand were brought to New Zealand by the settlers; and, second, that geographic isolation restricted supply of new products, stimulating development of local manufacture to meet settlers' needs.

Prospective settlers were issued with guidelines, including lists of clothing and other provisions, contents of the lists depending on the migrant's class. The laborer's wife was advised to stock up with household linen and clothes that would not go out of fashion quickly, with fabric, shoes, boots, and plenty of underclothing; the gentleman's wife was to include more extensive and elaborate items. Some migrants were themselves competent in clothing manufacture. Eleven "sempstresses" arrived in Nelson in 1842, thirty-two sewing-skilled females arrived in Auckland in 1851, and, during the 1850s and 1860s, 177 milliners, dressmakers, and needlewomen were brought to New Zealand as assisted immigrants by the Canterbury Province.

Deliveries of fabrics and clothing were intermittent, advertised in local newspapers and available for purchase from merchants selling from tents, wagons, or general stores. The origin of most of these textiles was likely to have been the United Kingdom and Australia, with cotton, silk, and woolen goods imported through the port of Nelson as early as 1864. During the mid-nineteenth century trade was essentially exchange. A writer going by the pseudonym "An Old Identity" in 1879 described "the settler's wife, when she had trudged to town from the Taieri, or Green Island, with her butter and eggs, getting in exchange some 'grey wursit' or perhaps a blue shirt, or a pair of mole trousers for the gude man, or some ribbons for the lasses." But retail and wholesale establishments were beginning.

Industries developed in New Zealand despite reported displeasure at the competition created for British equivalents. This attitude was apparently held intermittently by New Zealand governments, tending to stifle domestic industrial development. Early industrial sites and products were strictly utilitarian. Woolen mills were established by the 1880s, producing wool blankets and rugs. Boots and shoes were manufactured from leather produced locally. Gold miners, unable to secure appropriate clothing, stimulated local manufacture of apparel, textiles, and footwear. Bendix Hallenstein and brothers, having established a general store on the Victorian (Australian) goldfields, came to New Zealand in 1862 and set up stores in Queenstown, Lawrence, Cromwell, and Alexandra. Difficulty in obtaining men's clothing for those stores led them to open a factory in Dunedin (The New Zealand Clothing Company, 1873) and Invercargill in the early 1870s and a retail store in Dunedin (1876). Retailers reportedly preferred imported to locally made goods, spurring the Hallenstein brothers to establish the Drapery and General Importing Company of New Zealand Ltd. (DIC) in Dunedin (1884), Christchurch (1885), and Wellington (1890). Although the gold rush had peaked by the 1870s, industrial and commercial developments continued in Otago in particular.

Dressmakers advertised for customers from the earliest days of settlement. Clothing for women and children was made by dressmakers employed in department stores, in their homes in the larger towns, or as itinerants. Until the late 1890s dressmakers may also have been milliners. Sewing machines were used for stitching apparel from at least as early as 1850, with domestic sewing machines readily available from the 1860s. Sewing machines were likely to have been imported to Britain from either the United States or Germany and re-exported to New Zealand. Diaries, photographs, and museum collections indicate that prevailing western European fashions of fabric, design, and construction were followed.

RAW MATERIALS AND PROCESSING

New Zealand is known for production of wool fiber, with sheep farming dating to 1834, which expanded rapidly following development of the frozen sheep meat trade to Britain (from 1882). Most early flocks were merino, succeeding mainly in the high country of the South Island. Introduction of other breeds more suited to downland conditions, such as the Lincoln, followed. Changing

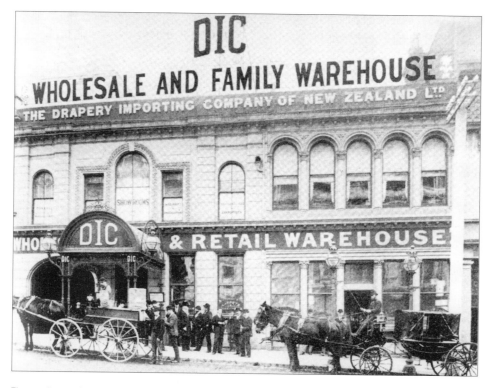

The warehouse of the Drapery and General Importing Company of New Zealand Ltd. in Dunedin on High Street, 1884. The Hallenstein brothers established DIC after indication from retailers that they preferred imported goods over locally made ones. Hocken Collections, Uare Taoka o Hakena, University of Otago.

sheep numbers were reflected in the amount of greasy wool produced (that is, wool weighed prior to scouring): 1,770,000 tons in 1950–1951, 3,807,000 tons in 1980–1981, 3,053,000 tonnes in 1990–1991, and 2,367,000 tons in 2000–2001. Most wool was exported in a greasy state to Britain during the early part of the twentieth century, but Britain's accession to the European Economic Community in 1973 (European Union, 1993) necessitated redirection of New Zealand's external trade. About the same time a greater proportion of wool was scoured in New Zealand prior to export.

Marketing of wool and wool products specifically from New Zealand (including use of the Fernmark brand) did not occur until 1995 and followed the New Zealand Wool Board (a statutory body under the Wool Industry Act, 1977) withdrawing from membership of the International Wool Secretariat. Further differentiation followed with the the establishment of the New Zealand Merino Company in 1996 and its integration of many elements of the trade from producer to manufacturer to retailer. A wool industry review by McKinsey and Co. in 2000 recommended further specialization and greater vertical integration through processing for each wool fiber sector (fine, mid-micron, strong).

New Zealand farming diversified during the late 1970s, linked partly to removal of subsidies. Other sources of protein fiber were developed, including various forms of goat fiber (cashgora, cashmere, mohair), alpaca, and opossum. Production of fiber marketable as cashmere was achieved by the Tolaga Bay Cashmere Company, but cashgora required marketing as a "new" protein fiber. Alpaca (*Lama pacos*) for fiber and progeny were imported as part of the diversification. New Zealand is infested with opossum (*Trichosurus vulpecula*), and fiber from the

opossum, blended with other fibers, has been used for knitwear and bed throws. Manufacturers of products from this group of protein fibers and blends struggled to define properties of both fibers and products, adapt to variability in fiber properties, and manage small fiber volumes.

Skins and hides provided another raw material for clothing and footwear, with processing evident in early New Zealand, for example, the Michaelis, Hallenstein, and Farquhar Tannery near Dunedin, in 1881 (renamed Glendermid Ltd. in 1918). Expansion and diversification of animal-based farming during the twentieth century led to formation of other companies, such as New Zealand Light Leathers Ltd. near Timaru in 1973, and processing of a wider range of skins and hides to finished leather (for example, that of deer and fish).

Yarn has been manufactured in New Zealand since the late 1840s, principally from wool but later from both wool and wool blends: for example, polyamide at Summit Wool Spinners in Oamaru (previously the Summit Factory, established 1881), both opossum and alpaca at WoolYarns New Zealand, and opossum or alpaca at WoolYarns New Zealand, Wellington (1940s) and Qualityarns NZ Ltd., Milton (1999). Woolen cloth was produced as early as 1848 at Nelson, although most woolen clothing was imported until the 1870s. British machinery was purchased in 1871, and Scottish personnel were hired to establish a woolen mill near Dunedin. This became the Mosgiel Woollen Company, which produced wool yarn, woven woolens, and worsted fabrics, blankets, rugs, shawls, and hosiery. Also established in Dunedin were the Kaikorai Mill (1874) and the Roslyn Woollen Mill (1879). The Roslyn Woollen Mill was part of perhaps New Zealand's first vertically integrated company, with ownership of four sheep stations, yarn and fabric processing, knitted apparel production (hosiery, underwear), and warehousing of imported and locally made goods (as Ross and Glendining Ltd.).

The Kaiapoi Woollen Manufacturing Company near Christchurch (1875) was to have been a flax processing plant, but, prior to any such activity, it became a woolen mill. Wool-based textile processors proliferated—Alliance Textiles (NZ) Ltd. (Timaru, 1871); Oamaru Woollen Factory Company (Oamaru, 1883); Onehunga Woollen Mills (1885); and Bruce Woollen Manufacturing Company Limited (Milton, 1897). The Napier Woollen Mills began in 1902, and a large wool store built by Williams and Kettle about 1904 established Ahuriri as a center of wool fiber–related activities through the twentieth century, with organizations such as the New Zealand Wool Testing Authority. Thus, processing of wool fiber to various stages of product was well developed by the early twentieth century, and New Zealand exhibited elements of self-sufficiency. International developments in knit processes during the latter part of the twentieth century led to expansion of the knitted fabric/garment sectors in New Zealand: Auckland Knitting Mills Ltd. (Auckland, until the 1980s); Manawatu Knitting Mills (Auckland, mid-twentieth century); Designer Textiles Ltd. (Auckland, early 1970s); and Levana Textiles Ltd. (Levin, early 1960s). Freeing the New Zealand market to imported goods and the steady reduction of tariffs from the late 1980s hastened rationalization of both weaving and knitting sectors; that is, business consolidation, amalgamation, closure, or expansion.

Although much of the textile industry in New Zealand has been based on wool and wool-rich blends, other fibers constitute greater volumes and percentages of world total fiber demand. Figures in 2005 show this: manmade fibers 34.29 million tons, 57.1 percent of total fiber demand; raw wool 1.23 million tons, 2.1 percent of total fiber demand. Volumes of wool fell slightly over ten to fifteen years to 2005, whereas volumes of other fibers, particularly synthetics, increased. World demand for wool accounted for 5.5 percent of total fiber demand in the early 1980s, but this had fallen to 3.0 percent by the mid-1990s. Whether the actual volume demand for wool and wool-blend products worldwide has decreased is unclear, as is whether consumption of wool and wool-blend products in Australasia, per capita, exceeds that in other comparable countries.

Processing of other fibers also occurred. New Zealand flax (*Phormium tenax*) was processed from 1843, with extraction of fiber mechanized around 1860. Production peaked in 1873, an estimated 161 mills then operating, and again when various external armed conflicts resulted in shortages of sisal and jute. Flax was processed in Southland, Canterbury (Geraldine), and the Manawatu (Shannon, Foxton), export having ceased from the 1930s, but commercial production continuing until the 1980s. A linen flax industry operated from 1936 to provide Britain with fiber during World War II, continuing until 1950; a cotton processing plant opened in Nelson (1970s), although cotton was not grown in New Zealand; nylon-6 was processed in Shannon, and both polyester and acrylic yarns in Auckland (1970s), again with the required raw materials being imported. These apparel and textile processing ventures were probably doomed from their early stages.

APPAREL MANUFACTURE AND RETAIL

Suppliers in early New Zealand combined the functions of manufacture with retail of apparel and textile goods. Drapers and clothiers established businesses in many towns; those in Dunedin in particular flourished during and following the gold rush. Suppliers were one of three general types. First, there were suppliers of a wide range of goods including garments, materials/haberdashery, household linens, and furnishings (imported goods selected by their own buyers in Britain or by the proprietor during visits there; or locally made). These often had workrooms and frequently supplied customers outside the region (Brown, Ewing and Co., Dunedin, early 1840s; Robert Brown and Co., Dunedin, 1868, and Oamaru, 1891; H. and J. Smith, Invercargill, 1900). Perhaps these suppliers were among the first to provide services for made-to-measure and mail-order clothing. Second, there were specialist suppliers principally of clothing, imported ready-made or made to order by dressmakers and/or tailors employed by the company (Herbert Haynes and Co., Dunedin, 1861; Milligan and Co., Oamaru, 1868; A. F. Cheyne and Co., near Dunedin, 1874). Third, there were manufacturers and merchants of ready-made clothing (the New Zealand Clothing Factory, of Hallenstein Brothers and Co., Dunedin, 1873, and Invercargill, early 1870s).

Important changes during the latter part of the nineteenth and the first part of the twentieth centuries included the consolidation of the wholesaler/importer role, development of labor unions, and the expansion of ready-to-wear. The businesses of merchants and warehousemen (i.e., wholesalers) who imported goods such as fabrics, trimmings, and footwear (typically from Britain) flourished with the geographic isolation of New Zealand and the need to stock supplies for three to six months. These wholesalers, Sargood Son and Ewen (Dunedin, 1861) and Ross and Glendining Ltd. (Dunedin, 1862), for example, were middlemen between manufacturers (outside New Zealand or in their own companies) and retailers, positions maintained until the 1950s. Factory production of clothing increased, but concern about work conditions for employees was expressed from the late 1880s. The Tailoresses Union (formed 1889) contributed to improvements in apparel manufacture. Ready-to-wear clothing became more accessible in both variety and cost, and standardizing the sizing was attempted by the (then) Standards Association of New Zealand. Standards were based on agreed (rather than actual) body dimensions and later converted to metric measurements (1972–1975). Compliance with sizing standards was never mandatory.

At selected dates during the twentieth century the number of clothing manufacturing establishments and average number of employees per establishment were: 1900–1901, 391 establishments, 6 employees per establishment; 1950–1951, 753 establishments, 26 employees per establishment; 1980–1981, 904 establishments, 28 employees per establishment, indicating small-scale operations by international standards, but also masking the existence of several larger organizations. Removal of restrictions to New Zealand market access from the mid-1980s (quotas and steady reduction of tariffs to one of the lowest tariff profiles in the developed world) led to major changes in industry structure. Manufacture in New Zealand was characterized by comparatively greater costs for various forms of compliance, services, and labor than those for external competitors. Several companies relocated part or all of their production for this cost advantage, while others ceased production and focused on retail. Niche companies began during the latter part of the twentieth century, typically as owner/operator (Orca as a manufacturer and retailer of a specialist clothing brand for sport; Untouched World as a wool- and leather-clothing manufacturer and retailer promoting New Zealand as environmentally sensitive).

New Zealand's apparel and textile retail sector became both fragmented and concentrated from the 1970s. Prior to this, several medium-sized regional department stores existed, considered leaders in style, such as Ballantynes, Christchurch (from 1854), Beaths, Christchurch (1860), Kirkcaldie and Staines, Wellington (1863), Smith and Caughey, Auckland (from 1880), and Arthur Barnett, Dunedin (1903), along with independent small specialist stores. From the 1980s much apparel retail was through larger companies, including discounters (such as the Warehouse, 1982) and specialist chains both New Zealand in origin (Hallensteins, Glassons, Max) and from Australia (Sussan, Country Road), with the department store having a much smaller share. Variety chain stores like Woolworths and McKenzies all but disappeared as suppliers of apparel. Emphasis on quick response and control of product quality resulted in some retailers developing their own brands. The distinction between retailers and manufacturers again became blurred.

WOMEN'S, MEN'S, AND CHILDREN'S APPAREL AND FOOTWEAR

The women's wear sector continues to be characterized by a large number of small companies, often owner-operated, often with a relatively short life, and too numerous to name. Examples from the mid-twentieth century include Cantwell Creations (Christchurch, 1946) and Emma Knuckey and Rosemary Muller (both Auckland, 1950s). Examples from the latter part of that century include Zambesi (1979), Jane Daniels (1986), and Paula Ryan (1997), all located in Auckland, and Ashley Fogel (1991), in Wellington.

The menswear sector has been characterized by a small number of companies producing principally suits, jackets, and trousers for sale in New Zealand and Australia. Hallensteins, which made men's and boys' clothing from early in New Zealand history, ceased manufacture and became retail-only during the second part of the twentieth century. Lane Walker Rudkin Ltd. (Christchurch, 1904) manufactured swimsuits, rugby jerseys, and underwear during the early twentieth century, acquiring the Jockey license in 1938 and experiencing growth with technological changes of the 1940s–1950s and the protected New Zealand market. The Cambridge Clothing Company (Auckland, 1868) and Rembrandt Suits Ltd. (Wellington, custom tailoring in 1930s and broader-scale manufacturing from 1945) have both manufactured suits, jackets, coats, and trousers, offering a small made-to-measure service, and manufacture several brands under license. Keith Matheson (1977), initially a manufacturer of jeans (Jeanmakers), refocused to suits and jackets, distributing these through his own retail outlets.

Men's shirts were manufactured in New Zealand by Lichfield (Christchurch, 1916–1917), a company contracted to supply the armed forces during World War I. Several international brands were made under license, such as Saville Row and YSL (Yves St Laurent). With the phasing out of import licensing during the 1980s, local manufacture ceased in 1989, and the company has been an importer/wholesale distributor since then. Ambler and Co. (Auckland, 1919) manufactured shirts, sleepwear, ties, robes for men, and later a few items for women. Deane Apparel in

Christchurch (late 1930s) manufactures industrial clothing, including corporate wear.

As for children's wear, attending a school in New Zealand between the ages of around eleven to seventeen years and sometimes also between the ages of 5 to 10 years typically requires wearing a uniform. Early in the twentieth century uniforms for girls consisted of skirts and blouses, and from around 1910 gym frocks, the latter becoming the norm for almost seventy years, varying only in color and accessories. Developments in the textile sector and fashion generally were reflected in the uniform, including use of crease-resistant fabrics, polyamide (nylon) hosiery, shorter skirts (1960s), and knitted outerwear (1970s). A tartan kilt replaced the gym frock in a number of schools during the latter part of the twentieth century, and less formal styles of dress were also adopted. For much of the twentieth century uniforms for boys consisted of shorts, shirt, blazers, jerseys, long socks, and caps, senior boys in many schools wearing long trousers. When knitting and sewing were typical activities in the home (early to mid-twentieth century), elements of the school uniform were made there, with necessary supplies obtained from local retailers. Home-sewn children's clothing was common during much of the first half of the twentieth century.

Manufacturers of children's wear service the uniform market for schools (Argyle Manufacturing Ltd., Argyle Schoolwear Ltd., Auckland; Bromley Clothing Ltd., Auckland; Tudor Clothing Ltd., Dunedin) or for sports teams (Canterbury Apparel, for example). A specialist children's sector also exists (for example, Trelise Cooper Kids, MerinoKids). Hallensteins and several other companies produced children's clothing for much of the twentieth century but, following quota removal and gradual reduction of tariffs, specified the product in New Zealand and contracted manufacture elsewhere. Pumpkin Patch, which began as a single retail store and mail-order catalog for children's wear (1991), later expanded in New Zealand and Australia and opened retail outlets in Britain.

Knitwear has been produced in New Zealand since the late nineteenth century. The Roslyn Woollen Mills produced underwear in wool from 1880, and much of the school uniform knitwear supply has been met by New Zealand manufacturers and retailers. Tekau Knitwear (Ashburton) Ltd. (Ashburton, 1932) focused on all-wool, machine-washable knitwear. Glengyle Knitwear (NZ) Ltd. (Auckland, 1951) produces classical knitwear in many blends; Tamahine Knitwear (Dunedin, 1970) produces wool and wool-blend knitwear; and Optimum (Auckland, 1990) produced fashion knitwear in a range of fibers. Norsewear (Norsewood, 1960) is a manufacturer of socks including the Farm Fleck (standard issue at Scott Base in Antarctica and for the New Zealand armed forces), as well as other knitwear. Socks, stockings, and various forms of hosiery have been manufactured also since the late 1880s, in wool in the early days and in other fibers sometimes blended with wool during the twentieth century (for example, Columbine Industries Ltd., Gisborne, 1951).

A key property of knitwear is softness, achieved through fiber selection, blending, and finishing treatments. Several specialty knitwear companies developed during the latter part of the twentieth century, for example, the Tolaga Bay Cashmere Company, manufacturing cashmere and cashmere/silk-blend knitwear using locally grown cashmere fiber, processing at various sites, and retailing in specialty shops. Silkbody (Dunedin) designs a range of "next-to-skin" knitwear, comprising silk, cotton, and wool (typically blended), manufactured in China and packaged and dispatched from Dunedin throughout New Zealand, and from China to Australia and Britain.

Technologies for manufacturing lingerie and swimwear are similar, hence both were produced by Expozay (Tauranga, 1970s) and Moontide International Ltd. (Auckland, 1980), manufactured offshore during the early twenty-first century. Bendon (Auckland, 1947) produced underwear for both women and men, closing the Auckland plant in 2000. Much of the design and distribution continues from New Zealand, with considerable market penetration in Australia. The company contracted Elle MacPherson, an Australian fashion model, to develop underwear lines for both females and males during the 1990s. Other lingerie companies and brands include the Underwear Club, initially Timaru-based but manufactured in China, and Liberty of Manawatu Knitting Mills (1887).

Production of footwear in New Zealand seems to have its origins in the 1860s, and by the 1870s several factories had been established to meet local demand. Christchurch was the site of a number of businesses: Michael O'Brien, which produced Premier brand boots; William Harris (1860s), later a major footwear retailer for much of the twentieth century; and Nathaniel Suckling (1871). Many other towns had boot makers focusing on custom work and repair. Robert Hannah and Company began boot making near Hokitika (1870), moving the business to Wellington and becoming another major footwear retailer of the twentieth century. Companies were also established in Auckland (the Pioneer Boot Factory, 1870; Henry Brennan, 1875; Marler Shoes, late 1880s) and Dunedin (James Mollison and Son, 1860; Otago Boot and Shoe Warehouse, approximately 1872; McKinlays Footwear Ltd., 1879; J. B. Frame and Sons, formerly Frames Bootworks, 1890). The latter company manufactured from 1917 until 2004 and thereafter became retail only.

Roman sandals, part of the uniform for many schools, have been manufactured since the mid-1950s (for example, by Douglas Sandals Ltd., Auckland, 1949). Rubber footwear (gumboots such as Red Bands, from 1956, and jandals) and canvas sports shoes were manufactured from 1939 by the Marathon Rubber Footwear Ltd. (Christchurch). The company was renamed Skellerup Industries and manufactured offshore from the late 1980s. Against this trend, however, Kumfs Shoes NZ Ltd. (Auckland, 1933), specializing in "comfortable shoes," responded to changing demographics in New Zealand (specifically an increasing number of Polynesians, including Māori, with generally broader feet) and expanded the factory during 2000 to increase production for local and export markets. C. A. Craigie and Co. Ltd. (Auckland, 2000) sells footwear incorporating fish skins, *paua* shell, and wool felt. Footwear for sport has been provided by the Ideal Shoe Co. Ltd. (Wellington, 1919), including rugby boots worn by the Invincibles (New Zealand rugby football team of 1924). Companies/ brands/retailers of the latter part of the twentieth century included David Elman, Kumfs, Andrea Biani, McKinlays, Minx, Briarwood, and Minnie Cooper.

At selected dates during the twentieth century the number of footwear manufacture establishments and average number of employees per establishment were:

- 1900–1901, 126 establishments, 21 employees per establishment
- 1950–1951, 133 establishments, 38 employees per establishment
- 1980–1981, 108 establishments, 48 employees per establishment.

This indicates small-scale production by international standards, but also masks the existence of several larger organizations.

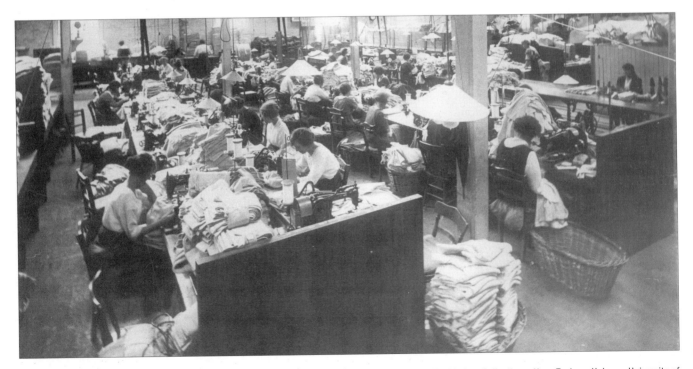

Machinists in the Roslyn Woollen Mills, Dunedin, New Zealand, 1921. Photograph by Muir and Moodie. Hocken Collections, Uare Taoka o Hakena, University of Otago.

During much of the twentieth century footwear for New Zealanders was both imported and locally made, with English products often perceived as superior to those locally made.

RECREATIONAL OUTERWEAR

The sporting, outdoor life typical of many generations of New Zealanders is reflected in clothing and outdoor goods produced. For example, Arthur Ellis and Company Ltd. (Dunedin, 1877; reformed and renamed Ellis Fibre, 1990) produced feather-down jackets used for the Trans-Antarctic Expedition of the mid-1950s. For recreational and competitive yachting/sailing, Line 7 (Auckland) produces wet-weather gear. For rugby union, Lane, Walker, Rudkin (later Canterbury International, Christchurch) produced heavy cotton knit jerseys and woven shorts. For hunting and fishing, a Swanndri or Swanny (a work shirt, woven wool, essentially unchanged from its inception in 1913) has been manufactured in Timaru. Several of these companies extended their ranges to general casual wear, recognizing that the sedentary style of city living was often accompanied by an illusion of "being active." In the latter part of the twentieth century, other companies recognized opportunities in this outdoor market (Earth, Sea, Sky, Christchurch, 1990; Icebreaker, Wellington, 1995; Macpac Wilderness Equipment Ltd., Christchurch, 1973; Kathmandu, Christchurch, 1987).

INFLUENCES ON THE DOMESTIC AND INTERNATIONAL MARKETS

New Zealand's geographic location, environmental characteristics, and outdoor style of living have influenced the domestic and international markets for apparel. The raw, angular, and geologically new land, long coastlines, and many rivers mean New Zealanders have ready access to water for sport and recreational activities such as fishing, boating, kayaking, and surfing, influencing the demand for and use of clothing and recreational products. Environmental sensitivity and sustainability, broad issues of the late twentieth and early twenty-first centuries, are relevant to production, use, and disposal of textiles and clothing, so some production practices have been altered. For example, the New Zealand Merino Company Limited introduced Zque (2006) to enable auditable tracking of wool fiber, taking into account animal welfare and environmental, social, and economic sustainability.

The small population, widely dispersed, has challenged most forms of communication and transport. By the late nineteenth century services in rail, road, and coastal shipping had developed, as had utilities, but the location of early manufacturing was determined largely by population distribution. Electronic communication of the late twentieth century facilitated domestic and international manufacture and retail, for supply and management of raw materials, for managing different locations of manufacture and distribution, and for information on fashion trends. Electronic commerce was supported by the Model Code for Consumer Protection in Electronic Commerce (2000) and the Electronic Transactions Act (2002). EziBuy, Palmerston North (1978), began with mail order, a simple catalog distributed in New Zealand, and by the early twenty-first century had extended distribution to Australia and to retail stores in several cities in New Zealand. Postie+ developed from the Dellaca Store, Westport (1946), and expanded to become a successful mail-order service during the 1980s–1990s.

Government policies and alliances have had major effects on New Zealand's clothing and textile manufacture and retail. The British Commonwealth of Nations and Commonwealth Preferences (British Preferential-Reciprocal Trade Act, 1907) resulted in the dominance in external trade of Britain, Ireland, and Commonwealth countries from early New Zealand European settlement until Britain joined the European Economic Community (1973; European Union, 1993). Formal trading arrangements between Australia and New Zealand, such as the New Zealand–Australia Free Trade Agreement (NAFTA), 1965, and Australia–New Zealand Closer Economic Relations Free Trade Agreement (ANZCERTA), 1983, continue to have important effects. Several New Zealand manufacturers became more viable with the expanded retail market of the combined New Zealand and Australian populations, and a number of New Zealand companies relocated manufacture and distribution operations to Australia. Australian retail fashion chains such as Country Road, Sussan, and Jacqui-E operate freely in New Zealand in the twenty-first century.

Management of external trade provided successive governments the opportunity to protect local manufacturers of clothing and textiles through application of quotas, tariffs, and preferences. In 1881 a tariff of around 20 percent on imports gave protection to the clothing, footwear, and other manufacturing industries, and additional tariff protection for the clothing and textiles industry was provided for many decades from 1895. Prior to 1987 any person importing clothing required a license to import and paid duty ad valorem of the tariff at 40 percent or at a fixed rate per item, being charged the higher of the two. Import licensing was phased out beginning in December 1987, and tariffs were reduced beginning in the early 1990s (apparel: from 40% in 1991 to typically 19% in 2006; textiles: from 26.4% in 1991 to typically 12.5% for woolen fabrics, with some items tariff free; footwear: from 35% in 1991 to typically 19% for adult footwear and tariff free for children's footwear in 2006). These changes in tariffs reduced protection generally and speeded change, transforming manufacture and retail, with relocation of much manufacture outside New Zealand. Tariffs were frozen from 1 July 2005, perhaps because adoption of free trade by New Zealand, however admirable, was too ambitious. For consumers, though, liberalized access and easier communication during the late twentieth and early twenty-first centuries ensured that product choice at retail increased and that high fashion from elsewhere in the world was available in New Zealand.

More direct forms of government assistance to the clothing and textile industries date back to the Otago Provincial Council's bonus for the first 5,000 yards (4,572 meters) of woolen fabric produced in the province. This offer led to the first woolen mill being established at Dunedin (1871) and, four years later, the Kaiapoi mill at Christchurch, following a similar but larger bonus offered by the Canterbury Provincial Council. Intermittently, New Zealand governments have supported the clothing, textiles, and footwear sectors and exporters in other ways; given assistance with regional development through labor during the 1960s and 1970s; and accelerated depreciation on plants and machinery.

New Zealand dress and fashion has been influenced by many events and developments in western Europe and the United States throughout its history, examples of overseas styles being readily available through the press. International trends in retailing also affected New Zealand. Compared to the United States, for example, development of shopping malls was slow, the first being Lynn Mall in Auckland (1963); mall development continued in the twenty-first century. Discount clothing retailers developed during the 1980s, generally sited in low-cost premises, offering either clothing of a lower quality with a very high stock turnover or excess retailer/manufacturer stock, or both (Dressmart, Bendon, Barkers).

New Zealand's clothing and textile sector from the mid-nineteenth to the early twenty-first centuries, thus, features a cycle from import dependency to relative self-sufficiency, and a return to import dependency. There is early evidence of vertical integration, of mail order, and of made-to-measure services for apparel and footwear, the influence of successive governments in development of both manufacture and retail, and the critical role of wholesalers during much of the twentieth century. There has been dependence on and development of local resources for niche products and market segments, and a long and close association with Australia in manufacture and retail, from early New Zealand settlement to becoming essentially one market.

References and Further Reading

An Old Identity [pseud.]. *The Old Identities: Being Sketches and Reminiscences during the First Decade of the Province of Otago, NZ.* Dunedin, NZ: Mills, Dick and Co., 1879.

Barnett, S. *Those Were the Days—Series from The Weekly News.* Auckland, NZ: MOA Publishers, 1989.

Brookes, B., A. Cooper, and R. Law. *Sites of Gender—Women, Men and Modernity in Southern Dunedin 1890–1939.* Auckland, NZ: Auckland University Press, 2003.

Brookes, B., C. Macdonald, and M. Tennant, eds. *Women in History—Essays on Women in New Zealand.* Wellington, NZ: Bridget Williams Books, 1992.

The Cyclopedia Company Limited. *The Cyclopedia of New Zealand.* Wellington and Christchurch, NZ: The Cyclopedia Company Limited, 1897–1908.

Denton, M.J., and P.N. Daniels. *Textile Terms and Definitions.* 11th ed. Manchester, UK: The Textile Institute, 2002.

Graham, J. "Settler Society." In *The Oxford History of New Zealand,* edited by G. W. Rice, 112–140. Auckland, NZ: Oxford University Press, 1992.

Hector, J. *Phormium tenax as a Fibrous Plant.* Wellington, NZ: New Zealand Government, 1892.

Laurenson, H.B. *Going Up, Going Down—The Rise and Fall of the Department Store.* AUP Studies in Cultural and Social History. Vol. 2. Auckland, NZ: Auckland University Press, 2005.

McLintock, A.H., ed. *An Encyclopaedia of New Zealand.* Wellington, NZ: R. E. Owen, Government Printer, 1966.

Meat and Wool New Zealand. "Statistics." 2007. http://www.meatand woolnz.co.nz (accessed 28 January 2009).

Simpson, P. "Global Trends in Fibre Prices, Production and Consumption." *Textile Outlook International* 125 (2006): 82–106.

Statistics of New Zealand. "Manufacturing and Trade." 1994–2007. http://www.stats.govt.nz/ (accessed 28 January 2009).

Thornton, G.G. *New Zealand's Industrial Heritage.* Wellington, NZ: A.H. and A.W. Reed, 1982.

R. M. Laing and C. A. Wilson

See also Retailing, Clothing, and Textiles Production in Australia; School Uniforms in New Zealand.

Black and New Zealand Dress

The color black features in New Zealand dress in distinctive ways that are the product of the nation's particular history and culture. It is frequently evoked as New Zealand's national color, primarily because of its lengthy association with the game of rugby union and the uniform of other key sporting codes. More recently, the supposed affinity between this hue and the work of leading fashion designers has cemented the association. The color black has connections across other groups within New Zealand society, including Māori; and, as with other Western nations, it had become a fashionable color choice for men's and women's urban everyday wear by the late twentieth century.

MĀORI AND BLACK DRESS

Wearing black clothing dates back to the Roman period; it was also the signature color of the dukes of Burgundy in fifteenth-century Europe, and it is associated with dandyism as well as formal wear for bourgeois men in the nineteenth century. As Valerie Mendes has noted, black has also long been associated with disaster, death, and mourning. In many European countries widows wore black for the rest of their lives. The introduction of chemical dyes in the 1850s did away with the necessity for fixing agents to achieve a true black with natural dyes, making it an easier process and cheaper. Coupled with Queen Victoria's lengthy period of mourning for her consort, Prince Albert, who died in 1861, the demand for black silk crepe, jet jewelry, and other requirements increased dramatically. The custom of deep mourning lapsed after World War I because of the high number of soldiers who died, which made the elaborate public funerals and associated activities seem indulgent and tasteless. New Zealanders followed English etiquette in mourning, as in other cultural rituals.

Late in the nineteenth century Māori women began to wear black clothes for *tangi* (funerals), and the practice continued in many areas, long after Europeans in New Zealand had stopped wearing full mourning clothes. At many other formal occasions on *marae* (sacred meeting places for tribal life), such as important *hui* (meetings) or welcoming visitors, black clothes are also worn. For example, at signings of land and other resource claim settlements with the Crown under the Waitangi Tribunal process, the tribes present an image of a sea of black, studded with greenstone jewelry, feathers, and other traditional ornamentation. The reasons for the continued wearing of black long after it had disappeared in the wider society are the subject of conjecture. A number of explanations have been offered: it is something that those in authority did, so it was not questioned; it is customary and therefore must be retained; it is a way of ensuring that everyone is tidy and wearing the same; and it is a reminder of *Hine-nui-o-te-po* (the great goddess of death/the woman of the night), who is the source of life for all people and who receives all into her arms.

BLACK ON THE SPORTS FIELD

New Zealanders' more general association, and obsession, with the color black appears to have begun with rugby. The black uniforms with a silver fern (the fern symbol comes from the silver underside of the leaf of the New Zealand tree fern—*Cyathea dealbata*, called *ponga* in Māori) have become national icons. The origins of this uniform are murky. During the first tour overseas to Australia in 1884, players wore a dark blue jersey with a gold fern on the left breast, dark knickerbockers, and stockings. The Natives (a team made up predominantly of Māori players) wore black uniforms for their overseas tour of 1888–1889. A uniform of black jersey (a pullover shirt that seems to have varied from three-quarter to short sleeves, although the latter may have been pushed-up full-length sleeves) with silver fern, black cap with silver monogram, white knickerbockers, and black stockings was specified when the New Zealand Rugby Union was established in 1892. However, historical photographs suggest that white shorts may have been used instead during these early years. By 1901 (but no one is sure exactly when), the white knickerbockers had been replaced with black ones, and together with a black jersey, a canvas top with no collar, and a silver fern, the all-black uniform was complete.

It was worn in 1905–1906 when the first team to be called the All Blacks toured the British Isles; they were known as the "Originals." According to one of the Originals, the name of the team was the result of a printer's error, which stuck. After the match against the Hartlepool Clubs on 11 October 1905, at West Hartlepool, which New Zealand won 63–0, the reporter accompanying the team noted that the whole team, backs and forwards alike, had played with speed and precision as if they were "all backs." This comment was repeated after the Northumberland game on 14 October (31–0) and the Gloucester City Club match on 19 October (44–0). But when the New Zealand team arrived at Taunton to play Somerset County (21 October), they found the whole town placarded with posters welcoming the "All Blacks." The reporter found that the printer had in error inserted the letter L in "Backs." Everyone liked the name, and from that time the players were known as All Blacks (and not All Backs). The All Blacks jersey is considered worldwide the most recognizable of all rugby jerseys.

As a result of the All Blacks' prowess and fame, other codes in New Zealand adopted variations on their name, and the wearing of black sportswear is widespread. The national women's rugby union team is known as the Black Ferns, and players wear a black uniform, while the men's and women's national hockey teams, who also wear black uniforms, are known as the Black Sticks. The men's national basketball team is called the Tall Blacks. In 1995 the Team New Zealand syndicate contesting the America's Cup yacht race won with their boat, nicknamed "Black Magic"

Māori wearing black as they invite guests to a *pōwhiri* (welcome ceremony) for veterans of the Vietnam War as part of Parade '98 in Wellington, New Zealand, 30 May 1998. The woman in front holding a *taiaha* (weapon) is also wearing her customary flax *piuiu* (skirt) and is garlanded with green leaves that are often worn on ceremonial occasions. Photograph by John Nicholson. Dominion Post Collection, Alexander Turnbull Library, Wellington, New Zealand.

because of its black hull and swiftness. The national men's cricket team, who wear traditional white in test cricket and black uniforms for one-day matches, became known as the Black Caps in 1998 after their sponsor held a competition to name them. Successive teams at the Olympics and Commonwealth Games have worn variations on the black uniform, and they carry a black flag with a silver fern. Internationally famous athletes such as Jack Lovelock (gold medal for the mile, 1936, Berlin Olympics), Yvette Williams (gold in the long jump, 1952, Helsinki Olympics), Peter Snell (gold in the 800 meters, 1960, Rome Olympics), Murray Halberg (gold in the 5,000 meters, 1960, Rome Olympics), and John Walker (gold in the 1,500 meters, 1976, Montreal Olympics) all wore a black singlet with silver fern. Subsequent Olympic success in rowing, windsurfing (boardsailing), canoeing, equestrianism, yachting, and cycling has seen black uniforms a familiar sight on the podium in these sports.

The wearing and promoting of black is de rigueur off the field as well. Māori fashion label Kia Kaha sells a "Black Out Supporters Range" of generic black clothing with silver fern and New Zealand map logos for any sporting occasion where individuals want to show their patriotism. Attendees at any match involving New Zealanders overseas are often energetically challenged by a sea of black-clad supporters with black flags ahoist and black-and-white painted faces.

Because of the enthusiasm of sports fans in popularizing black as a national color, New Zealanders also wear black en masse at other important national occasions when they are overseas. These include the annual Anzac Day ceremonies, which commemorate the anniversary of the landing of New Zealand and Australian soldiers—the Anzacs—on the Gallipoli Peninsula in 1915. The Gallipoli location has become a pilgrimage site for increasing numbers of New Zealanders and Australians, where New

Zealanders are clearly distinguishable by the color of their dress. The linking of black, national pride, and civic ceremony has led to periodic debates about whether the national flag should be overhauled. The notion of using more black in it is often raised. The New Zealand flag has a royal blue background with a Union Jack in the first quarter and four five-pointed red stars of the Southern Cross, with white borders on the fly. Some feel that while it reflects the nation's British heritage, it does not say anything about modern New Zealand. Critics note that many Commonwealth countries have changed their original flag prescribed by Britain when it still ruled them. Yet the prospect of a mainly black flag, because of its other connotations of death and funerals, may not, in the end, appeal.

FARMING BLACK

Alongside the All Black jersey, the next most recognizable item of black dress in New Zealand is probably the black singlet. It has also become a symbol of national identity. As Stephanie Gibson has recounted, it was first manufactured as a practical item for male farmers and shearers in the early twentieth century, but it has subsequently come to represent hard work and rural values more generally. Its origins are usually attributed to Jacky Howe, the Australian shearer, who found the sleeves of flannel undershirts restrictive and tore them out, converting them to singlets, and thereby inventing a practical work shirt. Because of the annual flow of laborers and shearers back and forth across the Tasman Sea between Australia and New Zealand at the turn of the twentieth century, the new singlet caught on and became known as the "Jacky Howe" in both countries.

These customized and homemade singlets were worn in a range of colors in the early twentieth century, as occupational dress codes relaxed. Their adoption was assisted by the establishment of local woolen mills, and by the 1920s men were wearing manufactured woolen singlets in dark blue or black as if they were a uniform. These early singlets had high collarless necklines and tight armholes to maintain respectability. By the 1940s and 1950s the color black dominated, and the singlet had a deeply scooped neck with looser armholes, allowing for more airflow and mobility. It was long—almost to the knees—and made of coarse heavy wool. The strength of the wool and its ability to keep the lower back warm and soak up sweat proved ideal for shearers, who are prone to lower back trouble as they bend over the sheep. Workers for freezing companies also donned the singlet as practical and safe, and it became the garment of choice among a range of manual workers: shearers, farmers, hunters, trampers, laborers, railway workers, truck drivers, freezing workers, forestry workers, miners, and fishermen. Some men liked them so much they wore them all the time.

From the 1970s the black singlet underwent further changes. As the slaughtering industry changed its practices with new hygiene regulations for the American and British markets, standard white singlets, shirts, trousers, aprons, and hats, laundered on site, replaced the black garments. Shearers also changed their habits. American sportswear and underwear began to shape the New Zealand market at this time, and shearers started wearing lighter wool and cotton variants, in a range of colors. In the twenty-first century a multitude of colors, styles, and decorative elements can be seen, alongside the original black woolen version. In fact, the black singlet continues to appear in art, postage stamps, advertising, comedy, and cartoons as a symbol of the exemplary "Kiwi bloke," a strong, self-sufficient, down-to-earth, industrious man. Alongside the rugby jersey the black singlet, usually adorned with a silver fern, has appeared at the Olympics from New Zealand's first appearance at Antwerp in 1920. In elite sport it has an aura of strength and power and combines function, fashion, and symbolism, as Stephanie Gibson has shown so well.

Beyond the farm and the athletics track the black singlet has appeared as a female fashion item since the 1980s. The traditional version was long enough to be worn as a dress over shirts and tights, skirts, or trousers, with a large belt at the waist, and was cheap, warm, and practical, memorably described as being like comfort food, the "macaroni and cheese" of clothing. Gay men

The All Blacks wearing their black uniform, by then well established, with a silver fern over the left breast and a white collar, in the Second Test match against the Springboks (South Africa) at Athletic Park in Wellington on 4 August 1956. Photographer unknown. Evening Post Collection, Alexander Turnbull Library, Wellington, New Zealand.

have also appropriated the modern version. Worn as a tight-fitting, short (hip-length) garment of cotton or synthetic fibers, preferably in white or black, it is also a statement about style and physicality.

DARK FASHION

Dark hues have also had an enduring alliance with late-twentieth- and twenty-first-century fashion. Two internationally successful companies in particular—Zambesi and Nom*d—have cemented a global profile for New Zealand designer fashion that is characterized as edgy, gothic, and darkly intelligent. As commentators have argued, they made black beautiful. This extended to their personal wardrobes. Nom*d designer and co-owner Margarita Robertson has been wearing only black since the 1980s. The garments of both companies share a restricted palette, heavy construction (or deconstruction), asymmetry, and an eclectic mixing of vintage and new shapes and fabrics. According to Peter Shand, the curator of a Zambesi retrospective at the Auckland Museum in 2005, Zambesi designs have a touch of melancholy, and the suggestion of disquiet or of depths never entirely revealed. Robertson's work has been compared to the look and mood of Belgian designers such as Dries Van Noten and Martin Margiela. Fellow designer Karen Walker, whose work is quite different, nevertheless acknowledges that there is a heavy, ominous, slightly restrained kind of feel to New Zealand designer fashion. She believes that it comes from the culture, the landscape, and what she describes as the personality of the country.

The English fashion media warned prospective buyers at the 2004 New Zealand Fashion Week to "mind the black." Lisa Armstrong claimed in *The Times* that New Zealand's addiction to black clothing was an attempt to differentiate itself from Australian Fashion Week. She declared memorably that Sydney is Paris Hilton and Auckland is Jean-Paul Sartre, without the life-long existential crisis. The equation of black and New Zealand fashion has been definitively captured in the fashion and lifestyle quarterly *Black Magazine*, begun in 2006. Its editorial line proclaims that black is the color of New Zealand and the color of fashion.

Robertson and her sister Elizabeth Findlay, the designer and co-owner of Zambesi, grew up in Dunedin, and both have spoken about the enduring influence of the southern New Zealand city on their designs. Dunedin is also known for its alternative music scene, particularly in the 1980s, a period described as one of feverish alternative strummings and black jerseys. Musicians of the time have noted subsequently that the black jersey is an icon of the Dunedin sound, as it came to be known. The reason that black clothes became Dunedin's "glad rags" is subject to debate and speculation, from the plausible to the more wild ideas, as with the wearing of black by Māori on important occasions. Among the factors proffered are that it is a throwback to the largely Scottish Presbyterian ancestors that settled the city; that it is flattering, practical, and hides dirt and spills; or that it is a tribute to the All Blacks. Others point to the gothic streak in the New Zealand personality, as outlined by Sam Neill's documentary on New Zealand film, *The Cinema of Unease*. Darkness is a frequently perceived distinguishing characteristic of New Zealand fiction, film, art, and design.

Specific cultural references to clothing have also been employed. Some surmise that a preference for black jerseys stems from the inner bogan speaking. *Bogan* is an Australasian term of both derision and endearment for those suburban and rural working-class people who are poorly educated, uncultured, unsophisticated, and proudly unfashionable. Bogans wear a distinctive wardrobe of black jerseys, black jeans, and T-shirts, and have mullet haircuts with short front and sides and long and straggly backs. Others employ a high-culture reference to 1950s beatnik culture, with its black sunglasses, black polo neck jerseys, and hipster cool. Dunedin has long been famous for its alternative, artistic, and rebellious cultural life in music, fashion, literature, and art and design, and this is expressed in designer and everyday fashion.

EVERYDAY BLACK

Black dress made its appearance outside mourning and religious rituals in a range of other contexts that were not unique to New Zealand. As in many other Western nations, black became the dominant shade of men's fashionable garments in the nineteenth century, epitomizing, as John Harvey has detailed in his book *Men in Black*, male authority and expertise. The dark suit remained a mainstay of men's wardrobes through the twentieth century and beyond. As women began to successfully climb the corporate ladder by the late twentieth century, work-wear for both sexes favored black suits, even when shirts, ties, and blouses might be more colorful accents in an overwhelmingly sober ensemble. As Valerie Mendes has shown, the color black dominated high fashion in the early 1980s and rapidly spread to all areas of the retail market. Internationally it remained de rigueur in the 1990s and 2000s, and in New Zealand especially so in the four main cities of Auckland, Wellington, Christchurch, and Dunedin. In the artistic world in New Zealand, as elsewhere, black has been the color of choice, almost a uniform, for curators, artists, and writers. It is particularly evident at exhibition openings, readings, and other public performances.

At the other end of the spectrum, as the black jersey in Dunedin's cultural scene reminds us, black dress has an enduring place in antifashion and antiestablishment practices. This can be seen in the dress of beatniks, punks, and goths, as well as bikers and gangs. New Zealand's Black Power, modeled after the U.S. movement, was formed by Māori youth in the eastern North Island town of Whakatane in the 1960s in response to the rival Mongrel Mob gang. It then spread throughout New Zealand over the next two decades and is particularly attractive to Māori and Polynesian people. This use of black may be jeans, denim, or leather jacket, but this is curiously counteracted by the extraordinary colorfulness of many Polynesian festive and nonfestive clothes. In the past and in the present, examples of all of these wearings of black dress can be found in New Zealand urban, rural, and domestic environments.

Although New Zealand dress shares in international practices of wearing black garments, something singular remains in the adoption of this shade as the country's national color. It has been explained as a collective psychology driven by isolation, fear, and the continuing search for an identity, and simultaneously as a demonstration of New Zealanders' attachment to darkness and the underworld, reflecting the Polynesian inheritance. Whatever the reasons and motivations, the color black remains a literal and symbolic feature of "New Zealandness," in an array of communities and in a variety of spaces, both sporting and nonsporting, within and outside the country's borders. The connection is clear whether one is wearing a black New Zealand identity T-shirt while a tourist in London or New York; waving a black flag with a silver fern at Lords cricket ground or cheering on the All Blacks in Sydney; rushing out to buy the latest gothic garment from Zambesi or Nom*d, as seen at *Fashion Week*; wearing a singlet in the shearing shed; or attending a tangi (funeral) in Northland.

References and Further Reading

Armstrong, Lisa. "Black Belies the Kiwi's Sunny Nature." *The Times* (London), 27 October 2005, 12–13.

Fitzgerald, Michael. "Southern Gothic: Karen Walker's Edgy Designs Reflect the Darker Tones of her Native New Zealand." *Time South Pacific*, 24 May 1999, 60.

Gibson, Stephanie. "Engaging in Mischief: The Black Singlet in New Zealand Culture." In *Looking Flash: Clothing in Aotearoa/New Zealand*, edited by Bronwyn Labrum, Fiona McKergow, and Stephanie Gibson, 206–221. Auckland, NZ: Auckland University Press, 2007.

Gregg, Stacy. *Undressed: New Zealand Fashion Designers Tell Their Stories*. Auckland, NZ: Penguin, 2003.

Harvey, John. *Men in Black*. London: Reaktion Books, 1995.

Kavka, Misha, Jennifer Lawn, and Mary Paul, eds. *Gothic NZ: The Darker Side of Kiwi Culture*. Dunedin, NZ: Otago University Press, 2006.

King, Michael. *Maori: A Photographic and Social History*. Auckland, NZ: Heinemann, 1983.

Mendes, Valerie. *Black in Fashion*. London: V & A Publications, 1999.

Patterson, Colin. "Black Power Shapes Our National Identity." *Dominion Post*, 30 May 2007, B6.

Shand, Peter. *Zambesi: Edge of Darkness*. Auckland, NZ: Auckland War Memorial Museum, 2005.

Tansley, Rebecca. "Dark Queen of Fashion." *North and South*, March 2008, 48–53.

Bronwyn Labrum

See also Rural Dress in Australia; Military and Civil Uniforms in Australia; Sportswear in Australia.

Designer Fashion in New Zealand

The shape and form of designer fashion in New Zealand have changed over time. In the 1940s and 1950s designer fashion referred to traditional haute couture (literally, "high sewing") and was narrowly defined in terms of custom-made garments produced to high specifications for wealthy women clients. New Zealand emulated designs from Europe and received seasonal dictates and imports from established fashion capitals, particularly London, Paris, and large cities in North America and Australia. However, as the twentieth century wore on, designer fashion activity broadened. During the 1990s the definition of designer fashion offered by Mintel, a London-based market research company and supplier of consumer intelligence, was adopted in several high-profile reports on New Zealand industry. Along with couture, designer fashion encompassed three main sectors: international designers (a label dominated by one name); diffusion lines (designers producing high street ranges for specific stores); and high fashion (up-and-coming new designers usually endorsed by celebrities). Since the 1990s New Zealand–made designer fashion has courted an overseas export profile, which might be thought of as a cultural economy. This has meant that, along with the receipt of designer fashion imports, New Zealand itself is a distributor of original designer fashion, with an aesthetic based on its locale and a rich fusion of multicultural influences.

Queen Elizabeth II was admired for her style during the royal tour of Australia and New Zealand in 1953 and 1954. She is pictured here delivering a speech of thanks on the lawns of the ancient treaty house at Waitangi on 19 January 1954. The contrast between European couture and Māori ceremonial dress is apparent. Popperfoto/Getty Images.

FROM ROMANCE TO REALISM: 1940 TO 1980

During World War II New Zealanders were subject to the rationing of clothing, footwear, and household linens. Restrictions were introduced in 1942 and continued to 1947. These austerity measures had an obvious impact on the production of luxury goods such as fashion garments and accessories, as well as the importation of such items from Britain and New Zealand's emerging trade partners the United States and Canada. New Zealand manufacturing was geared toward the mass market and the supply of practical civilian clothing and military uniforms, and this was to have a lingering effect on the nation's wardrobes well beyond wartime. Unlike its Australian neighbor, Christian Dior's fashionable postwar "New Look" was not an instant hit in New Zealand. Instead, the country's summer fashions of 1948 continued with the military, masculine feel of previous years. Designer-made fashion was a narrowly defined, elite pursuit, and in New Zealand the wearing of it tended to be confined to the wives of wealthy businessmen, diplomats, and society ladies. It was not until the early 1950s that New Zealanders more generally developed a heightened appetite for designer fashion. This was aided by the 1953 and 1954 tour of Australia and New Zealand by Queen Elizabeth II, whose extensive couture wardrobe featuring designs by Britain's Norman Hartnell was carefully detailed in press reports of the day and much admired by the general public.

By the turn of the decade this mass interest in, if not actual consumption of, high-end fashion was met with numerous national, annual fashion showcases run by both private entrepreneurs and trade associations. Examples include the Golden Shears Award (established in 1961), the New Zealand Wool Board Awards (established in 1960 but possibly a little earlier in a different form), and the New Zealand Gown of the Year contest (established in 1958). The latter event took the form of a traveling show in which ball gowns, designed and made by professionals and skilled amateurs alike, were judged by the popular vote of audiences in provincial towns and cities. Throughout the contest's history, most gowns took a romantic form based on either a modernized crinoline silhouette or a long column sheath. All had to be wholly designed, cut, and made up in New Zealand, but their evocative names show that designers were influenced by a cultural mix of references, for example, Kathleen King's "Golden Lotus" (1964), Peggie Wilson's "Vienna Bon Bon" (1963), Roswitha Robertson's "Tosca" (1962), Nigel Rodda's "Versailles" (1961), and Lea Draysey's "Ao-tu-roa" (1958). A handful of these designers used the competition to launch or bolster successful design careers. Lea Draysey, Rosalie Thomson, Roswitha Robertson, Emma Knuckey, and Jane Lang were among those to develop national profiles for themselves, while other celebrated talents of the time, such as Kevin Berkahn and Gerhard Stecker, spent periods of their professional life as designers working overseas.

With the more vibrant mood of the 1960s well under way, New Zealand turned its back on the tradition, glamour, and pure escapism of live events such as the Gown of the Year. A new youth-driven culture was in the ascendant, and younger, futuristic designs took a lead role in shaping fashion, drawing inspiration from the democracy of the street with its denim-clad teenagers, rather than the elite spaces of the ballroom and its evening gowns. The youth of New Zealand embraced teenage, subcultural fashions emerging out of Britain and the United States. However, for the most part, due to import restrictions, these looks had to be recreated domestically, thus invigorating the local, independent designer-retailing sector. From the mid-1960s New Zealand, and Auckland in particular, was home to a rash of unconventional fashion boutiques, which closely resembled those popularized by contemporary London designer Mary Quant. In Auckland a fifth of the city's 250 ladies-wear shops traded as boutique enterprises. These included Jennifer Dean, Bizarre, Nova, Annie Bonza, Countdown Boutique, Paraphernalia Boutique, C.A.T. Shop, The Way In, Hung on You, London Affair, Top Gear, and, perhaps the best known, Tigermoth, which opened in 1970. Such establishments as His Lordship's Stable and The Vault catered to fashion-conscious males.

The proliferation of another innovation of the era, the television set, meant that the profiling of design-led and highly creative fashion was not restricted to the metropolitan centers of New Zealand. Commencing in 1965, between 1967 and 1998 the Benson and Hedges Fashion Design Awards (later known as the Smokefree Awards) were televised on an annual, long-standing basis, signaling the show's popularity and a demand for current fashion information among the New Zealand public. *The Corbans Fashion Collections* (later known as *The Wella Fashion Report*) of the 1980s and 1990s took televised local fashion even further in its form as a regularly broadcast series.

New Zealand fashion of the 1970s arrived in an explosion of color. Paisley and floral motifs were popular, as were flared and bell-bottomed trousers, and new textile innovations such as flexiwul, crimpline, and tricel allowed for versatility of both design and use. In sharp contrast to these modern advancements, designers also drew on heritage styles and the fashion archive to inform their work. Vintage clothing was readily available by the late 1960s at well-known general markets at Brown's Mill and Cook Street, Wellington. Auckland's Ponsonby Road market opened in 1974. All had an eclectic mix of new and recycled goods, which included period clothing and even some Polynesian dress. Importantly, these markets also functioned as a platform for emerging New Zealand designers to experience their first, affordable, and easily accessible taste of the apparel business, with young design graduates and fashion aspirants being able to set up shop and peddle their wares.

FROM DEREGULATION TO DESIGN: 1980 ONWARD

Broader economic and political events were to have significant effects on the nature and character of the New Zealand fashion industry during the 1980s. New Zealand entered a world of free marketing and deregulation, and the country was soon accepting an increased amount of foreign imports, which included fashion and footwear items. Mass-market and middle-market apparel tended now to be sourced almost exclusively offshore from lower-wage countries such as Fiji and, later, China, specializing in the manufacture of high-volume, low-quality, cheap clothing products. Clothing imports to New Zealand of this type rose from NZ$129 million in 1985 to NZ$480 million in 1996. In 1985 imports of footwear were double those of the previous year. The implications for the broader domestic apparel and textile industry were dramatic. Mills and manufacturing plants closed down, and there were mass redundancies throughout the country.

Nationally, the number of workers in the apparel sector dropped from 31,000 in 1985 to 16,700 in 1997.

This story of deregulation and the attendant demise of domestic manufacturing was one not unique to New Zealand. As in the contexts of other developed, postindustrial economies, manufacturers were forced to reconsider their approach in order to survive. Rather than attempting to compete head-to-head with mass-market imports, they shifted focus to the smaller but potentially lucrative niche of the market that was designer fashion, investing in new technologies and encouraging innovative, directional designs that were set apart from the blandness of mass apparel. Importantly, bound up in this shift was a more outward-looking perspective in which the exploration of overseas export markets for the receipt of local, high-end, New Zealand–made designer fashion became integral. For the first time New Zealand designer fashion began to develop an overseas profile, and the small, specialized owner-operator designer-retailer was at its center. By the late 1990s it was widely accepted by government, industry, and the general public alike that New Zealand's economic future depended on the value-added products and skilled expertise characteristic of small to medium enterprises (SMEs). New Zealand fashion design was one of several local "creative industries" (definitions of the creative industries vary but the list generally includes those image-rich domains such as filmmaking, music, tourism, crafts, design, fine arts, galleries, museums, and even restaurants) championed nationally as the darlings of this emerging strategy. Designer fashion was now being viewed as a sector quite distinct from the remainder of the country's textile, clothing, and footwear (TCF) industry, which remained in decline.

The shape and form of the New Zealand designer fashion industry in the new millennium is difficult to grasp. Prior to 2001, official statistics were generated only for the all-encompassing TCF industry, and as such any growth in the more specialized designer sector is based on estimates. New Zealand government bodies such as Trade and Enterprise New Zealand have adopted a loose version of the Mintel definition of designer fashion, which is broad and has been subject to generous interpretation. The first report was published in 2001 and identified 119 companies, accounting for 1,500 employees, as meeting the designer fashion criteria. Of these, 72 percent had a turnover of less than NZ$2 million in the 2001 financial year and 69 percent employed fewer than ten full-time staff. The report confirmed the relative youth of the designer fashion industry, with 66 percent of firms established in the 1990s and 13 percent set up since the year 2000. In 2002 designer fashion domestic sales totaled NZ$120 million and designer fashion exports represented NZ$40 million out of a total of overall clothing exports of NZ$260 million. It is approximated that 70 percent of New Zealand's designer fashion exports go to Australia, and export accounts with department stores and mixed-label boutiques are usually held in Japan, the United States, and the United Kingdom.

A further way to assess the size and shape of the industry is to note that, since its inception in 2001, forty to fifty designers have exhibited in the main program at each of the annual New Zealand Fashion Weeks. Of these designers, however, only about

Zambesi, as with many other New Zealand fashion labels, has entered into design and sponsorship collaborations with the commercial and charitable sectors. Zambesi's Neville Findlay, Elisabeth Findlay, and Tulia Wilson (all seated) were appointed in 2004 to design Air New Zealand's new uniforms. Photograph by Michael Bradley/Getty Images.

half have had a range portfolio warranting a solo show. In 2002 the New Zealand government's marketing agency, Market New Zealand, listed Karen Walker, World, Kate Sylvester, Nom*d, Zambesi, and Trelise Cooper (together with outdoor garment labels Line 7 and Icebreaker and children's label Pumpkin Patch) as being key industry players. In October 2004 *Style* magazine listed the ten top designers as Karen Walker, Trelise Cooper, Kate Sylvester, Elisabeth Findlay of Zambesi, Keith Matheson, Liz Mitchell, Adrian Hailwood, Helen Cherry of Workshop, and Patrick Steel and Murray Crane of Little Brother, Little Shit.

Unlike North America and Europe, there are no major corporate design houses akin to Ralph Lauren or Donna Karan operating out of New Zealand, but luxury goods companies such as LVMH do have a minor presence as retailers or as sponsors of national lifestyle and sporting events. Louis Vuitton, for example, sponsored part of the America's Cup when it was hosted by Auckland in 1999 and 2003. For the most part, however, the New Zealand designer fashion industry consists of independent, local labels. These firms usually have a single site that doubles as both workroom and retail shop. Virtually all their manufacturing is done by local cut, make, and trim firms (CMTs) or by individual outworkers. Employees are flexibly skilled and required to take on a range of roles, from the finishing of the actual garment to administration, fit modeling, and sales. The emphasis in this niche industry is on the production and supply of distinctive, often unique garments with a high economic and symbolic value. Garments tend to be made by hand, and these individualized production methods allow customers to be involved in the selection of fabrics, trims, and tailoring preferences. Adaptable operating practices like varied opening hours and lay-by services also enable the delivery of a distinctive product and consumer experience. Even those designers who make up the top echelon of New Zealand designer fashion, some of whom are now multimillion-dollar firms with product portfolios extending to eyewear, jewelry, children's wear, and lingerie, continue to run their businesses as family concerns. They champion a hands-on approach in which their business identities and personal identities are closely linked.

With some notable exceptions the demographic of these designers is female and *Pākehā* (European). Indeed, New Zealand, perhaps not unusually, has an extended fashion industry populated overwhelmingly by women. As well as designing, women work as design studio employees, wholesale and public relations agents, industry officials, and fashion writers and editors, and, of course, women form the traditionally acknowledged cohort of prime fashion consumers. In the new millennium, however, New Zealand's expanding capacity in export education and international migration more generally has had its own effect on both the profile of designer fashion consumers and the workforce. Large numbers of relatively well-to-do, fashion-conscious youth from Asia have migrated temporarily to New Zealand for study opportunities in higher education and at English-language schools, bringing with them high spending power and a desire to consume high-end commodities such as designer fashion. So, too, a mix of highly skilled Pākehā and immigrant laborers, predominantly drawn from Southeast Asia, are employed as home workers, often engaged on a piece-rate basis and poorly regulated. In general, these workers employed in the garment production side of the designer industry (such as garment technicians, pattern cutters, and sample machinists) are part of an aging workforce, and a labor shortage coupled with talk of a skills crisis pervades.

Individual designers have sought to address this problem by getting involved with immigration policy and have lobbied to get pattern makers and sample machinists added to the list of occupations needed in New Zealand. The shortage has been exacerbated by the closure of virtually all garment construction courses in the tertiary education sector, due to an increasing demand for training programs in design rather than manufacture.

EXPORTING FASHION, EXPORTING NEW ZEALAND: THE CULTURAL ECONOMY

Three events participated in the unfolding story of the designer fashion industry during the 1990s: the success of New Zealand designers at Australian (1997), Hong Kong (1998), and London (1999) fashion weeks. Significantly, these three events are similar in nature, taking the form of high-profile spectacles in locations external to New Zealand. No one really anticipated the success of individual designers who went, seemingly against the odds, to wave the New Zealand flag for a few days during these overseas fashion showcases. New Zealand press coverage from the time used an almost pioneer rhetoric to report the success at these events, claiming that designers from New Zealand had taken on, and won over, long-established fashion centers. In proving itself overseas, the coverage goes on to suggest that New Zealand design moved beyond its parochial national boundaries to be internationally competitive on the global stage. The local fashion media has been important in identifying and championing the emerging designer fashion industry. Indeed, the growth of the New Zealand fashion press has coincided with the rising profile of designer fashion. *New Zealand Fashion Quarterly* is the prime locally produced title dedicated entirely to fashion. Further, numerous monthly lifestyle magazines include regular, substantial articles on fashion, as well as allied pursuits such as cosmetics, fine dining, the arts, and high-end consumables. In 2004 the national newspaper the *New Zealand Herald* began producing a Saturday lifestyle magazine in which fashion features heavily, and there is a trade press, led by the publication *Apparel*.

In addition to the media, New Zealand government officials picked up on this idea that designer fashion was a means of competitive advantage. Similarities with and validations by fashion institutions and fashion personalities external to New Zealand became a key way of confirming New Zealand's own designer fashion credentials, as well as promoting the country itself as a fashion—and fashionable—destination. In 1997, for example, Trade New Zealand assisted the design companies Zambesi, World, Moontide, and Wallace Rose to accept an invitation to show at Australian Fashion Week, the first New Zealand designers to be granted the honor. It was hoped that a New Zealand presence at this event would enable more New Zealand clothing exporters to break into the all-important, and larger, Australian market. Quite unexpectedly, however, the New Zealand designers were heralded as the stars of the 1997 show and received a return invitation, along with spectacular endorsements from the Australian press. Maggie Alderson of the *Sydney Morning Herald* wrote of Australian Fashion Week that "without the darker, more intellectual view of those New Zealand designers ... [it] was like eating a meal that was all dessert."

A similar scenario emerged a year later in 1998 when designer Karen Walker participated in Hong Kong Fashion Week. The

New Zealand design house Nom*d presented a Cold War aesthetic in their Autumn/Winter 2003 collection. This meeting of Pacific South and Eastern Bloc is illustrative of the fusion of different cultural influences that runs more broadly through New Zealand fashion. Photograph by Dean Purcell/Getty Images.

New Zealand Wool Board employed Walker's designs, which were made using wool fabrics from local polwarth and corriedale sheep, as a conduit through which to increase wool sales in Hong Kong, a high-value market. The wool board initiated Walker's involvement in the event and funded her participation, but the emphasis for them was on "their" traditional textiles rather than Walker's designs per se. All that, however, changed dramatically when the collection that Walker exhibited was later picked up by U.S. pop singer Madonna, who wore a pair of Walker's "Killer" trousers for a performance at the 1999 MTV music awards ceremony. Walker suddenly found herself with an international patron, and the story made headline news in the New Zealand press, promoting Walker to a household name. This external recognition of, and exposure for, New Zealand design was once more evidenced in the case of the spring edition of London Fashion Week, 1999. The NZ Four show comprised New Zealand firms Zambesi, Karen Walker, World, and Nom*d and deliberately emulated the success of a group of designers from Belgium known as the Antwerp Six. Sponsorship for the NZ Four was provided by Wools of New Zealand and by the New Zealand Way, a joint branding exercise between Trade New Zealand and Tourism New Zealand. The involvement of Wools of New Zealand was primarily, as it had been with Hong Kong Fashion Week, about selling wool products into high-value markets. However, for the other sponsors the venture had broader implications. It represented an effort to add sophisticated, creative, and metropolitan nuances to the rural, colonial, and green images traditionally used to brand export industries. The NZ Four show received extensive, complimentary reviews from the assembled international critics, and all the New Zealand design firms involved courted new export accounts. These sales, in turn, encouraged a second wave of designers to explore offshore markets.

These export activities and the national symbolism bound up in them illustrate how, in the late 1990s, the New Zealand designer fashion industry came to be employed, and thought about, as a "cultural economy." Sociocultural anthropologist Arjun Appadurai first coined this term in 1990 in a growing literature on globalization. Later uses of the term have tended to refer to the changing industrial sector and the economic imperatives underlying the production and consumption of image-rich, identity-forming products (such as designer fashion). In this permutation studies of cultural economy examine the confluence of creative and commercial worlds and also encompass the governance of these. The development of policy initiatives, for example, which recognize the cultural sector as a source of regional and national income generation, are included in this.

In the New Zealand context designer fashion was one of the creative industries harnessed by Prime Minister Helen Clark's Labor government to assist in the driving of national economic prosperity, primarily through export investment. Still further, and somewhat uniquely, Labor went on to utilize New Zealand's burgeoning overseas fashion profile in the updating of perceptions of "New-Zealand-the-nation" around the world. In this way designer fashion became an important component in a national rebranding campaign, one in which New Zealand was to be imagined globally as less rural and more urbane. The perceived glamour and sophistication of an increasingly buoyant, home-grown, and externally validated designer fashion industry was to aid the new symbolic connection along with targeted state-led policy directives. In 2001 the country's economic development agency, Industry New Zealand, named "fashion, apparel and textiles" as one of five industries to be targeted as part of its regional development strategy (the others were music and film production, tourism, light manufacturing and communications, and biotechnology). Collectively these were described as "job-rich, high-skill, high-value export industries." So, too, the case of designer fashion is touted as a blueprint for traditional manufacturing activities yet to make the transition to value-added products in this vision of a more creative, talent-led New Zealand. In 2002 the chief executive of Industry New Zealand, Neil Mackay, set out such a vision: "New Zealand must be seen as a talent heavy and talent friendly nation if it is to succeed in the global market place where the qualities exhibited by our designer fashion industry are at a premium."

A NEW ZEALAND LOOK?

New Zealand as a country of both product and design origin provides a unique selling point in a competitive, saturated fashion marketplace, yet elements of a defining New Zealand aesthetic are difficult to pin down. Fashion designers talk of the creative freedom afforded by New Zealand's geographical remoteness. So, too, these designers also identify their clothes as being products of their locale and having a distinctive New Zealand character to them. New Zealand designers borrow from their natural surroundings and make reference to the local flora and fauna in their collections. References to local Māori and Polynesian culture are also in evidence. At Australian Fashion Week, Sydney, 1998, New Zealand designer label Moontide introduced its Māori designs, with feather cloaks and temporary *moko* (real moko are tattoo-like, permanent markings, carved on skin) drawn on the chins of models. Auckland-based designer Susan Scarf (formerly Silk Road) has featured Māori patterns in her textile designs and has used prints that feature images of New Zealand flax and manuka. Kate Sylvester drew inspiration from New Zealand's native wildlife in her 2002 collection titled Birds, and Workshop Denim's T-shirts printed with traditional *tiki* (traditional ornaments created by Māori) images are typical of their Pacifika-informed design ethic.

Along with these more obvious local design cues, New Zealand designers also talk about their clothes being infused with national character traits. Karen Walker, for example, explains that her clothes are "casual, effortless, cool, and fun," and this discourse of unrehearsed, inherent stylishness is a design theme iterated by her peers. It is important to note that these same New Zealand designers simultaneously look to external influences and serve up collections that mix the country's colonial heritage and European settler history with a growing cultural presence from Asia. In 2001, for example, Liz Mitchell created a high-profile collection titled Fragments of a New World, which combined Scottish plaids with Māori and Pacific Island cues, and her Kiss of the Dragon (2003) collection drew heavily on Japanese and Chinese cultural history.

Evidence of this hybridization of cultural and national references goes beyond actual designs and fashion garments themselves to extend across the gamut of the New Zealand designer fashion sector. So, for example, French-based beauty company L'Oréal held naming rights to New Zealand Fashion Week for the first three years of the event, before Air New Zealand took on its sponsorship. This multicultural, multinational mix is also apparent in the museum sector, where local designers are exhibited alongside, or in succession to, those from overseas. The Museum of New Zealand Te Papa Tongarewa in Wellington hosted exhibitions on Italian designer Gianni Versace in 2001

and a traveling exhibition from the Kyoto Costume Institute in 2003 on Japonism in fashion. Auckland Art Gallery, too, has a record of presenting visiting fashion exhibitions: Worth to Dior (1995) and Couture to Chaos (1997) were from the collections of the National Gallery of Victoria, Melbourne. In 2003–2004 Auckland Art Gallery utilized its own holdings to present Flaunt: Art/Fashion/Culture, which juxtaposed the works of contemporary New Zealand designers with historical European offerings. These connections stretch, too, to the broader commercial and social world, with individual New Zealand fashion designers entering, increasingly, into de facto business and charitable relationships with an eclectic range of national and international partners. Designers have teamed up with European car manufacturers, paint suppliers, telephone companies, cancer and mental health charities, and property developers, suggesting that their status as celebrities is well established and that they have eclipsed their material product to become eponymous creative and entrepreneurial forces.

References and Further Reading

Appadurai, Arjun. "Disjuncture and Difference in the Global Cultural Economy." *Public Culture* 2 (1990): 1–23.

Blake, Maggie. *Berkahn: Fashion Designer*. Auckland, NZ: HarperCollins, 1999.

Blomfield, Paul. *The Designer Fashion Industry in New Zealand: Industry New Zealand Scoping Study*. Wellington, NZ: Industry New Zealand, 2002.

Goodrum, Alison. "Exhibition Review: The First New Zealand Fashion Week." *Fashion Theory* 8, no. 1 (2004): 99–104.

Goodrum, Alison. "Exhibition Review: Flaunt: Art/Fashion/Culture." *Fashion Theory* 9, no. 1 (2005): 89–94.

Goodrum, Alison, Wendy Larner, and Maureen Molloy. "Wear in the World? Auckland's Designer Fashion Industry." In *A Sociology of Auckland*, edited by Ian Carter, David Craig, and Steve Matthewman, 257–274. Palmerston North, NZ: Dunmore Press, 2004.

Gregg, Stacy. *Undressed: New Zealand Fashion Designers Tell Their Stories*. Auckland, NZ: Penguin, 2003.

Larner, Wendy, Maureen Molloy, and Alison Goodrum. "Globalization, Cultural Economy and Not-So-Global Cities: The New Zealand Designer Fashion Industry." *Environment and Planning D: Society and Space* 25 (2007): 381–400.

Molloy, Maureen. "Cutting Edge Nostalgia: New Zealand Fashion Design at the New Millennium." *Fashion Theory* 8, no. 4 (2004): 477–490.

Regnault, Claire. *The New Zealand Gown of the Year*. Napier, NZ: Brebner Print, 2003.

Wolfe, Richard. *The Way We Wore: The Clothes New Zealanders Have Loved*. Auckland, NZ: Penguin, 2001.

Alison Goodrum

See also Global Positioning of Australian Fashion; New Zealand Textiles and Apparel Sectors; Wearable Art in New Zealand; Pacific Sisters: Urban Pacific Art, Fashion, and Performance.

Snapshot: A Māori Fashion Designer

In the twenty-first century Māori fashion labels such as Kia Kaha have taken Māori fashion onto the streets and catwalks of New Zealand and around the world. But one of the pioneers of Māori fashion blazed a pathway decades before, not on the catwalk, but in the halls of Parliament. Followers of indigenous fashion owe a huge debt to Whetu Tirikātene-Sullivan, who supported the development of modern Māori fashion through the patronage of artists and designers, and who was its best advertisement.

Whetu Marama Tirikātene, born in 1932, is of Ngāi Tahu and Ngāti Kahungunu descent and is the daughter of the late Sir Eruera Tihama Tirikātene, first a member of Parliament for the Rātana movement and then a member of Parliament for Southern Māori, working with the Labour Party, and Lucy Matekino Soloman. Both parents also had non-Māori descent: English and Danish/Jewish, respectively. When her father died, Tirikātene won the by-election for his seat and was sworn in as the sixth woman member of Parliament in 1967. She became the first Māori woman cabinet minister, serving as associate minister for social welfare (1972–1974), minister of tourism (1972–1975), and minister of the environment (1974–1975). She used her position not only to advocate for the learning and teaching of the Māori language in tertiary institutions, its use in state broadcasting, and its more general retention, and for the resolution of Māori land issues, but also to champion Māori culture, specifically art and design through fashion.

From her maternal grandmother she had learned dressmaking and designing skills, which occupied her when her parents were away on electorate business. A government social worker, in 1964 Tirikātene graduated from Wellington's Victoria University School of Political Science and Public Administration with a BA. At the time she entered Parliament in 1967 she was enrolled in a PhD program at the Australian National University, where she met her husband, Denis Sullivan. Despite her dedication to learning and public service, she also found time to become a New Zealand women's champion fencer and the New Zealand ballroom and Latin American dancing champion. She put the same effort and dedication into her involvement with fashion and design, which were equally political matters for her.

In Tirikātene-Sullivan's young adult years New Zealand fashion design did not yet exist on a broad scale. Most fashion was retained under license to British designers and manufacturers. When she was at Victoria University a key group of fashion designers came to the fore, including Barbara Herrick (Babs Radon), Joan Talbot (Tarantella), Colin Cole, and Guss Fisher. They used New Zealand fibers, such as wool, but still followed international style and imagery. It was only in the 1970s, largely due to Tirikātene-Sullivan's initiatives, that another group of designers and makers, who used local materials and indigenous ornamentation, found a ready market.

This trend had its genesis in Tirikātene-Sullivan's parliamentary work. In her first year she campaigned tirelessly against a Māori Affairs amendment bill, which allowed land

Whetu Marama Tirikātene-Sullivan wearing a design with a Māori *koru* motif, ca. 1960. Photograph by Stanley Polkinghorne Andrew. S. P. Andrew Collection, Alexander Turnbull Library, Wellington, New Zealand.

to be bought from Māori owners if deemed by a government "improvement officer" not to be in productive use. In a tribute to her advocacy Māori artist Sandy Adsett sent her a length of fabric printed with his version of the *mangopare* (hammerhead shark) motif, which customarily represented survival or a fighting chief. The length was not initially intended as high fashion, but rather as furnishing fabric for cushion covers or a curtain. As a well-traveled and fashionable woman herself, Tirikātene-Sullivan saw its potential as a garment. She had it made into a sleeveless minidress (a short, close-fitting dress, usually worn above the knees). This was a bold statement about being a Māori and being contemporary in a bicultural society.

In 1971, four years after she entered the House and with a punishing schedule, her husband encouraged her to find a creative outlet for herself. With the thorough training of her grandmother, and having learned weaving from the elders at Rātana Pā, a settlement famous as a center of the Māori spiritual movement, she turned again to handcrafts. In partnership with her husband she established an Ethnic Art Studio in Wellington and Auckland and sold Māori, Pacific, and Asian crafts. She did some designing herself, having obtained permission from her elders to use traditional motifs, and was particularly pleased that most of those who were selling through her shops were married women. The Wellington shop was managed by a retired London-trained machinist and pattern maker who was able to make contemporary styles from custom-made lengths of fabric.

She commissioned a large number of garments incorporating Māori motifs by contemporary Māori artists, such as Sandy Adsett, Para Matchitt, Cliff Whiting, and Frank Davis. She wore these at her many public engagements, and they were generally regarded as her signature style. For many New Zealanders this was the first time they had seen such traditional elements in a new context. Before Tirikātene's initiative the use of Māori motifs was limited to a small number of predominantly *Pākehā* fabric designers and artists who used these as abstract or modernist decorative elements, from an aesthetic, rather than cultural, point of view. An exception was the Christchurch silk printer Pākehā Fanny Buss, with whom she codesigned woodblock prints with motifs such as *whakairo* (decoration usually associated with carving) and *kōwhaiwhai* (painted pattern on meetinghouse rafters), and then later more loosely painted Māori motifs. By inviting a number of craftspeople to contribute to the design and production of a garment, Tirikātene-Sullivan created a working style that related to traditional approaches rather than a European-style gallery or fashion house. As her public profile increased, particularly after her appointment as minister of tourism, she traveled extensively and effectively became the patron of contemporary Māori fashion and its best advertisement. She encouraged the use of New Zealand crafts and design, Māori and otherwise, in tourist hotels and established national tourist design awards.

In 1993 Tirikātene-Sullivan was made a member of the Order of New Zealand. She was the second-longest-serving member of Parliament when she left in 1996. Her interest in and advocacy of Māori fashion did not stop, and the generations following her lead remain in her debt.

REFERENCES AND FURTHER READING

Cornwall, Sue. "MP Funds Empathy with Fashion-Art." *New Zealand Women's Weekly*, 11 December 1972, 8–10.
Lloyd-Jenkins, Douglas, and Lucy Hammonds. "The Koru in New Zealand Textiles and Fashion." Unpublished paper presented to the Seventh Textile Symposium, Otago Museum, Dunedin, NZ, March 2008.
McCallum, Janet. *Women in the House: Members of Parliament in New Zealand*. Picton, NZ: Cape Catley, 1993.
Wolfe, Richard. *The Way We Wore: The Clothes New Zealanders Have Loved*. Auckland, NZ: Penguin, 2001.

Bronwyn Labrum

See also Resources for the Study of European Dress and Fashion in New Zealand.

PART 9

People and Dress in New Zealand

Liturgical Robes in New Zealand

- The Power of Liturgical Robes
- Arts and Crafts Influence
- Commercial Manufacture
- Post–World War II—Accepting Changes and Cultural Differences

Liturgical dress worn by members of the Roman Catholic Church played an important part in daily life and religious observances, and rituals from birth to death, in colonial New Zealand. In 1838 Marist Catholic missionaries landed in the north of New Zealand, where most of the twelve Catholic mission stations were established. At this time seventy thousand Māoris were dispersed throughout the country, and there was a small European settlement of approximately twenty thousand, mostly in the ports and coastal areas. Wesleyans and Anglican missionaries had arrived before the Catholics, and the Presbyterians were in Otago and Southland beginning in 1848. Interestingly, Māori showed a disposition toward Catholicism, for the elaborate robes, long rituals, and the bilingual masses engaged them.

Vestments, such as chasubles, copes, and dalmatics, played a significant role in the history of the Catholic Church in New Zealand, adding to the splendor of both religious and secular occasions. These garments survive today in collections of the Museum of New Zealand Te Papa Tongarewa (Wellington), Auckland Catholic Diocesan Archives (ACDA), Holy Cross Museum (Mosgiel), Home of Compassion (HOC) (Wellington), and St Anne's (Auckland). They reveal some of New Zealand's Māori and European Catholic ecclesiastical heritage, their functions, fabrics, shapes, religious scenes, symbols, and iconography changing over the years. Prior to the reforms initiated by the Second Vatican Council (1962–1965), design elements specific to New Zealand were absent in ecclesiastical vestments. Subsequently, decoration included foliage and religious symbols, with Māori and Pacific Island patterns and motifs.

Other rare sources include relics from wartime, such as one of the earliest surviving vestments in New Zealand, an eighteenth-century red silk dalmatic brought to the country from Monte Casino by a Polish soldier. Perhaps never worn, it was given by his descendents to the ACDA collection. Dalmatics are typically shin-length silk tunics with sleeves, often worn underneath the chasuble. This one is embellished with silver bullion (coiled silver wire), silver and gold lamaellae (thin sheets of gold or silver cut into narrow strips and spun around a silk or fine linen thread core), and tiny flat and shaped silver sequins. An angel with a painted face is part of the main shield on the front of the garment.

The Concilio di Trento (Council of Trent) of 1545–1563, a reformist council of the Roman Catholic Church concerned with discipline, strongly encouraged the use of luxury in ecclesiastical wear, reinforcing the wearing of vestments as an essential part of worship. For the celebration of mass it was considered necessary for clothes and decoration to be precious and sumptuous, as well as immediately recognizable. Initially most New Zealand vestments were brought to the country by bishops, priests, or settler families, or they were sent by missions.

THE POWER OF LITURGICAL ROBES

From the time of the arrival of Catholic missionaries, the color and motifs of ceremonial vestments had a significant social impact. The first Catholic clergy arriving in significant numbers were from Lyon, following their voyage through the South Pacific Islands aiming to convert the people of the Pacific to Catholicism. In 1838 the young French bishop Jean-Baptiste François Pompallier appeared as a striking figure, resplendent in his liturgical dress, complemented with his pectoral cross and ruby ring, carrying his crozier, as he walked ashore at Hokianga Harbour, Northland, North Island. Pompallier, the founder of the Roman Catholic Church in New Zealand, descended from a wealthy silk merchant and was one of the first of a contingency of Gallic clergy from Lyon. He arrived able to speak some Māori, was soon eloquent in the Māori language and in English, and became an influential leader. In January 1838 the bishop offered his first mass at Totara Point, Hokianga, wearing liturgical robes that introduced color and visual splendor, giving him a powerful presence. Within ten months he had converted forty-eight Māoris, mostly chiefs, and their wives and families to Catholicism.

At the signing of the Treaty of Waitangi, New Zealand's founding document, between the British Crown and the Māori, in 1840, the bishop's appearance must have seemed impressive. He wore full canonicals, a dark purple robe, buttoning close down the center, purple stockings, and an order suspended from his waist, and he carried his gold bishop's cross and wore a large ruby ring, whereas the members of the Church of England were dressed in black. Some of the Māori chiefs were clothed with dog-skin mats featuring longitudinal stripes of black-and-white hair, and others wore woolen cloaks of crimson, blue, and brown given by Bishop Pompallier. He joined the procession immediately behind Captain Hobson, the queen's representative, and sat on the governor's left in a prominent position. Bishop Pompallier considered that Catholicism best served Māori spiritual interests. Although he would have preferred French sovereignty, he effectively upstaged Anglican and Wesleyan (Methodist) representatives by securing protection for the Catholic faith and thus set a precedent for religious freedom in New Zealand.

The purple color of his soutane (a form of cassock) and sash would have been a rare sight in colonial New Zealand, as this preceded the invention of coal tar dyes by Sir William Henry Perkin in 1856. Pompallier wore his long purple soutane and sash, liturgical ring, and great tasseled hat for liturgical activities, including saying mass. These clothes were attractive to the Māori. The Catholic clergy were soon criticized by the Wesleyan missionaries for introducing a religion that was alluring to the local people because of the splendor of the Church's vestments and ceremonies. Nevertheless, Pompallier's liturgical robes clearly contributed to the influence of the Roman Catholics and thus to the establishment of mission stations and the christening of approximately one thousand Māori throughout New Zealand.

The contrast between the dress of the bishop during his day-to-day activities, his black cassock, purple buttons, and sash, and that of both the local people and non-Catholic missionaries would have been immense. The cassock was a sleeveless, open-fronted, ankle-length piece of cloth closed with a fastener over the breastbone, and roughly semicircular in shape when laid out flat. His purple stockings and broad episcopal hat were conspicuous and, it was noted, contrasted with the clothes of the elderly Māori men who welcomed him onto their *marae* (meeting place), draped in their large mats of weft-twined flax overlaid with strips of dog skins. While traveling across difficult terrain, crossing rivers on horseback, the bishop's purple stockings were often visible. Purple stockings were originally reserved for use by the pope but later became part of an episcopal wardrobe. The ACDA collection includes a pair of purple stockings, crudely darned in orange wool, perhaps by a bishop himself.

The revival of vestment wearing in the early 1800s in Europe spread to New Zealand. French influence can be identified in a straight-sided, so-called roman-style chasuble that was worn at Jerusalem, a small mission settlement on the far reaches of the Whanganui River in New Zealand's North Island. The chasuble was the principal mass vestment, worn by a priest, bishop, or archbishop, usually made of a rich material and embellished with an orphrey. Orphreys are elaborate bands, often embroidered and applied to chasubles, copes, and dalmatics. The chasuble covered and protected all the other vestments and was long regarded as the symbol of love, which crowns all other virtues. This particular vestment, in the HOC collection, features gold in the weft, a gold-braid orphrey, and satin-stitch embroidery, with the Chi Rho symbol surrounded by isolated floral motifs. The Chi Rho monogram incorporates the first two letters of the Greek word *Christos* symbolizing Jesus, and in Latin the letters can be read to mean *In Hoc Signo*—"by this sign." Foliage was an often-occurring motif in chasuble designs, differing in characteristics in different periods, and this foliage design is typically French. Real gold was woven intricately into the embroidery using a satin-stitch technique to cover leaves and petals molded in hard cement, typical of a style from Lyon.

Gold was used for many Roman Catholic Church festivals, jubilees, and celebrations, and for the embellishment of all types of vestments. In the mid-nineteenth century rare cloth-of-gold chasubles were worn on feast days. More commonly, the vestments were made of rich brocade silks or satins with elaborate gold work and floral symbolism embroidered in colored silks, typical of a style introduced by French missions. Most lacework and embroidery came from France and Belgium. Although at ease with Māori culture, the missions provided Māori with a French environment, including French lacework, embroidery, statues, bells, and altar vessels for worship. Beyond practicalities, the functioning of the church furnishings was symbolic and ritualistic. Māori and English alternated in the services, delivered by French, Māori, and Irish priests.

During Pompallier's journey to France in 1859 he recruited French sisters to work in the New Zealand missions, including Suzanne Aubert, who founded the Sisters of Compassion, Jerusalem, and maintained the French influence. The French sisters and priests were supported by women's mission group sewing circles that worked in various parishes in France to produce crates of vestments and embroidery for New Zealand missions. In Nantes, St. Etienne, St. Chamond, and Lyon women made chasubles and other embroidered items and ran lotteries. Jessie Munro's detailed research of archive documents reveals that French priests from the Jerusalem mission visited Lyon in 1860 and admired crates of vestments ready for shipment. Design inspiration for the French women possibly originated from the well-established French ecclesiastical manufacturing industry.

ARTS AND CRAFTS INFLUENCE

The influence of British pre-Raphaelite artists, and of the Arts and Crafts movement generally, on design and the ecclesiastical arts extended to New Zealand. This nineteenth-century revival of interest in religious art and changes to Anglican high church and Catholic ecclesiastical services brought about reforms in the shape, texture, and embellishment of vestments. The reuse of old patterns was novel in the mid-nineteenth century, although it was to form the basis of what has come to signify traditional ecclesiastical design. Different textile techniques introduced an entirely fresh outlook for the use of stitch, color, and fabric in religious embroidery. From the 1850s, prompted by historicism and the desire to enrich the liturgical setting and heighten the aesthetic experience of worship, the new Anglo-Catholicism of the Oxford Movement, and in particular William Morris, increased interest in ecclesiastical design. Morris was renowned for his church paintings, decorative paintings, church plate, stained glass, and embroidered altar frontals. The architect Augustus Pugin's influence on embroidery after the publication of his *Glossary of Ecclesiastical Ornament and Costume* in 1868 was considerable. This publication was used as a virtual pattern book, and by this means Pugin reintroduced sacred imagery for vestments worn in church interiors.

Other nineteenth-century ecclesiastical architects, having designed and detailed their buildings, would further design embroidery work that unified architecture, interiors, and vestments, using design symbols in the gothic revival style. Many of the early New Zealand mission churches were built in the gothic style, for example, Pukekaraka Church, Otaki, in the lower North Island. Ecclesiastical designs were promoted in exhibitions and available internationally in pattern books and magazines from the 1840s for both professionals and amateurs, written by architects, priests, and monks. Other artists devoted themselves to giving material expression to the sacramental ideas underpinning the theological Catholic revival.

An extravagantly decorated cope remains in the St. Anne's collection in Ponsonby, Auckland, said to have been worn by Bishop Pompallier. The cope was typically a semicircular-shaped processional garment that usually had an orphrey, and sometimes a hood. Originally hoods were worn as an ancient covering for the head, serving as a mark of dignity. This cope's hood features Jesus, and the alpha and omega symbols, with a circle of text serving as a design border, surrounded by a stylized floral and leaf pattern in bright synthetic colors. Alpha and omega are the first and last letters of the Greek alphabet, a reference in the Book of Revelation to the second coming of Christ: "I am the Alpha and Omega; the beginning and the end, the first and the last" (Rev. 22:13). The embroidery design bears a striking resemblance to the Dalmatic of Charlemagne, which featured a Byzantine style, later popular at the Vatican and used for dalmatics. By the end of the nineteenth century and the beginning of the twentieth century, human figures were used as pictorial illustrations, and hoods were decorated with complicated compositions. Embroidery followed the trends set by architects and designers, such as Pugin and Morris, and single figures of apostles and saints were portrayed on special-occasion vestments for the bishops and on processional and sanctuary banners.

New Zealand's rugged landscape provided challenges for the clergy. In the 1870s Bishop Redwood, from the Wellington diocese, began pastoral visits on horseback in his leather leggings, waterproof coat, and large wide-brimmed, waterproof south-wester hat. Tracks were rough, potholed, and muddy. His ecclesiastical wardrobe was crammed into his saddlebags as he enthusiastically visited Māori church openings and performed christenings. The Māoris reciprocated the enthusiasm, eagerly anticipating Bishop Redwood's appearance in his robes, golden miter, and staff for their special church services, welcoming him with a feast. Typically at religious ceremonies he wore the purple and red vestments of the episcopate, capped with a miter, and with a gold cross and chain around his neck. His coat was made of a carmine silk twill fabric with cuffs, worn with a short white fur cape. He cut a striking figure in his canonical robes. It is likely Redwood's connections with Lyon, and his successive visits to Rome, where he met five popes, facilitated his acquisition of vestments. In his day-to-day activities Redwood filled the role of a figurehead well, and his dress was the customary clerical outfit of the day: black shoes, trousers and shirt, white collar, and long black double-breasted frock coat.

In early colonial times both Bishop Pompallier's and Redwood's purple garments provided a striking contrast to the subdued colors used by the Māori people in everyday and special-occasion clothing. As Māori converted to Catholicism, the textiles played an important role, adding visual brilliance to religious celebrations, an outward display of devotion of the Catholic people. The dress accorded respect to the wearer and contributed significantly to the display of unity at religious ceremonies. Many, or even most, of the embroidered vestments appear to have been offered as gifts to churches by missions, nuns, pioneer Catholic families, or individuals on an occasion important either to the church concerned or to the donor personally.

COMMERCIAL MANUFACTURE

Commercial embroidery manufacture in New Zealand was started by the Robért family in Palmerston North in 1876. The Robérts were originally French Huguenots who fled to London and established an embroidery business there. They introduced new embroidery technology and skills at the height of embroidery popularity. In the 1920s they employed one hundred embroiderers to make highly decorative ecclesiastical and military designs using gold bullion and sterling silver thread. Robért produced vestments anonymously, simply signing them on the interior with a discreet signature. Increasingly, commercial suppliers of vestments became available. Receipts reveal the purchase of vestments by priests and bishops from various commercial suppliers, including a long black cloak from the House of Vanheems, London, worn by bishops and priests during the 1890s. Other vestments continued to be sent from France, such as a fiddle-back-shaped chasuble in the ACDA collection, made of fine gold and mauve silk brocade. It features the Chi Rho circle with crosses stitched in gold and purple on the back of the

vestment and a stylized floral repeat pattern, with gold colored lining.

The new dyestuffs of the nineteenth century and, above all, Perkin's mauve and the more strident aniline green became popular colors for vestments in the late nineteenth century. The use of color linked directly to specific days or the seasons of the Christian year, a practice unchanged since the Middle Ages, and vestments with their symbolism conformed to the appropriate liturgical color. Strict instructions governed the use of different colors. Red was worn for Whitsun or Pentecost, symbolizing the fire of the Holy Spirit, and for the feast of the apostles and martyrs who shed their blood. Black was worn for Good Friday and for mourning, purple for the days of repentance in Advent and Lent, green for Sundays and days between Trinity and Advent, and between Epiphany and Lent, being the color of new life and growth. Basic design rules were enhanced by designers' individual creativity in the choice of materials, with shimmering fabrics and brilliant colors embellished in a commercial style. Embroidered and woven brocade silks displayed a riot of color, with lavish use of gold embroidery. Purple, green, and red sandals complemented the vestments.

Vestments represented in painting were an important source for design inspiration, and work produced in the mid- to late nineteenth century was prompted by historicism. Embroideries were inspired by images like Peter Paul Rubens's 1620–1622 painting *St. Ignatius of Loyola*, in the Norton Simon Art Foundation, Pasadena (formerly in Warwick Castle), showing an elaborately baroque-style chasuble, which was a widely published design seen in embroidery pattern books. The late-nineteenth-century vestments, worn in the candlelit interiors of the early New Zealand churches, probably looked very dramatic. A striking emerald green satin cope in the collection of Te Papa Museum features the Chi Rho symbol, embroidered lavishly with gold metal thread, surrounded by rich gold fringing. An emerald green chasuble of satin-weave silk, also held by the museum, features orphreys embroidered with a floral pattern in gold and yellow thread (chain stitch, couching, and satin stitch padded with card). In the French style (one that originated in the seventeenth century), the orphreys are characterized by a "pillar" on the front of the vestment forming a vertical pattern and a cross on the back with a Chi Rho symbol in the center, edged with a red/gold/silver braid; the remaining outer edges of the vestment are embroidered. Other styles are highlighted in another Te Papa set comprising a semicircular cope, stole, veil, and burse, which is a small free-standing pocket, made of a rose-colored floral damask. The chasuble orphrey features a Lamb of God figure within circles of thorns and a floral motif, and texts are embroidered in gothic script in gold thread and colored embroidery. These vestments were worn at the Hill Street Cathedral, Wellington, until 1978.

One of the most spectacular religious occasions involving vestments was the Golden Episcopal Jubilee, Bishop Redwood's diamond jubilee, held in 1924. It included a most extravagant procession journeying from Hill Street to Buckle Street, Wellington, the route thronged with thousands of people. In the procession of the Blessed Sacrament were dalmatics, voluminous semicircular gothic-styled chasubles, and copes. Emerald green walked beside red, ivory beside violet. One hundred priests paraded in cassock and surplice (a white liturgical tunic with sleeves made of fine cotton or linen), and monsignori, bishops, and the archbishop were in robes of purple. At this time highly decorative interpretations of pre-Raphaelite and Art Nouveau designs were readily available. The dress contributed significantly to the display of unity. Yet the splendor of the vestments obscured the real economic situation for the clergy, who were reliant on contributions from people who were themselves enduring hardship following World War I.

The roman-style, straight-sided, stiffened chasuble became the norm. An unusual set of church vestments for requiem mass, including a chasuble, two dalmatics, two stoles for a priest and deacon, a veil, burse, and cope reflecting Arts and Crafts influence, is included in the Te Papa Museum collection. The chasuble, made of black satin, features lavish embroidered orphreys of a stylized floral pattern on the front and the Chi Rho symbol on the back in gray and mauve tambour work and silver thread, surrounded by small crosses. The embroidery is an Arts and Crafts–style design inspired by a medieval color pattern of a stylized vine, a symbol of the redeemer, and floral motifs, repeated vertically, surrounded by isolated small crosses. This is similar to a shaded-stitch South Kensington design promoted in Hinda Hands's 1907 book, *Church Needlework*, which was used by nuns and other amateur embroiderers. This book was so popular that it was reprinted five times up to the 1950s.

Convent workshops were important centers of vestment making and embroidery. Embroidery demanding skill and delicacy of shading, such as these Te Papa works, was frequently made by nuns. Some nuns did embroidery as a source of income, and convents were important centers for vestment embroidery. Certain authorities considered embroidery as a form of recreation for the sisters, and it was regarded a privilege to embroider a vestment for a priest. The Sisters of Mercy also raised money by selling embroidery such as Berlin wool work and commissions for military insignia. A lace surplice most probably worn at the Wellington cathedral, in the Te Papa collection, features Chinese characters crocheted on hem and sleeves, lined with red, and is likely to have been made by the Sisters of Joseph, North Sydney.

Increasing commercial manufacture of vestments occurred from the early twentieth century. From the 1920s the supply of vestments from Australia gained momentum as advertisements for Pelligrini's, Sydney, appeared in the *New Zealand Tablet*, the Catholic newspaper. The Dunedin tailors, Reddells Ltd., supplied a mauve brocade cope to Bishop Lenihan to supplement his purchases from J. P. Begg and Vanheems, London. New Zealand firms such as Robért and Reddells, women's religious orders, and the embroidery guilds were all active in introducing skills and achieving and maintaining extremely high standards in craft and vestment design.

POST–WORLD WAR II—ACCEPTING CHANGES AND CULTURAL DIFFERENCES

Vestments worn by the clergy during religious services, once rich and luxurious, became progressively drabber during and after World War II. Fabric choices and embellishment were influenced by fabric and thread shortages and became standardized and less precious due to wider use of wool and the arrival of new synthetic materials on the market. Changes occurred in other ways too. In 1944 Wiremu (Bill) Te Awitu was ordained as the first Māori priest, and he practiced first at Wairoa, then Jerusalem. He was fondly admired by the New Zealand poet James K. Baxter, a Catholic, who established a commune for alienated and dispossessed youth at Jerusalem. Although paintings by nuns depicting Māori motifs were included in Māori Bibles by the late nineteenth century, they were not used on vestments until Pa (Father) Henare Tate introduced the use of Māori iconography on his red cope and white dalmatic, worn in the Auckland Diocese and Hokianga, north of Auckland, in 1962. Perhaps sensing a relaxation in the Vatican mandates, Pa Henare Tate organized a group of women in the Hokianga to design and make vestments incorporating *kowhaiwhai* (golden-yellow flowers of a New Zealand tree) and other patterns used on Māori cloaks. His knee-length cope featured Māori designs, worn over a full-length dalmatic, with a decorative stitched Māori border at the hem. The Second Vatican Council (1962–1965) had a significant influence in underlining the "poverty" mission of the Church, allowing more freedom for local self-expression. This established a trend that corresponded to the progressive simplification of vestments, in terms of use of fabric and shape. The modernizing process resulted in some vestments finding their way into secondhand shops to raise money for church funds.

Prior to the 1960s, embroidery followed artistic and iconographical formulae linked to both the aesthetic orientation of the era and Catholic mandates. Guided by the mandates, the design of the vestment and embroidery at times followed closely the trends set by artists in other fields such as fine art and architecture. Throughout the 1970s, however, a gradual commitment was made to biculturalism in Māori and *Pākehā* (European) relations, and to multiculturalism. At the time the non-European population consisted of 400,000 Māori, 100,000 Pacific Islanders, and a growing number of Asian immigrants, including Vietnamese and Kampuchean boat people. In Apia, Samoa, Carmelite Sisters began to produce lightweight vestments featuring Samoan motifs, and this led to the development of indigenous-styled vestments in Tonga, the Cook Islands, and New Zealand. Pacific Island influence is evident in a *tapa* (barkcloth) gothic-style semicircular chasuble and stole, first worn by Peter Makalio, a Samoan priest, for his ordination in St. Patrick's Cathedral, Auckland, in 1986, held by ACDA. The front has a Chi Rho in red, while the reverse has a cross with clasped hands. Scattered Pacific Island emblems are stenciled on outer edges of the chasuble, and extra fragments of tapa cloth have been applied in several areas on the inner side where the tapa has thinned. The stole has plain colored tapa ends with a stenciled cross and a brown pattern. Different bishops and priests began to incorporate patterns from Pacific Island culture into their chasuble, stole, miter, and, sometimes, alb designs. Typically by the 1980s bishops would have a full set of Māori, Samoan, Cook Island, and Tongan vestments to appeal to multicultural congregations. At a significant service at Totara Point in 1983, commemorating Bishop Pompallier's first mass, Cardinal Williams wore a full-length vestment decorated with Pacific Island motifs.

The Sister Disciples of the Divine Master, the silent Order of Clairs Sisters, Ponsonby, Auckland, continue the vestment-making tradition and embroidering full time. In the twenty-first century the use of vestments has diminished, and the more voluminous gothic rather than roman style is in vogue. It is considered appropriate for clergy to wear colored shirts for everyday wear. There is a simplification of clothes, with a clear differentiation from the ostentation and stylistic characteristics of earlier vestments, reflecting a more casual attitude to dress and incorporating wider cultural influences.

References and Further Reading

Catholic University of America. *New Catholic Encyclopedia*. San Francisco, London, and Sydney: Catholic University of America, 1967–1979.

Colenso, William. *The Authentic and Genuine History of the Signing of the Treaty of Waitangi, New Zealand, February 5 and 6, 1840*. Wellington, NZ: Government Printer, 1890.

Hands, Hinda. *Church Needlework: A Manual of Practical Instruction*. London: G. J. Palmer, 1907.

Johnstone, Pauline. *High Fashion in the Church*. Leeds: Maney Publishing, 2002.

Keys, Lilian. *The Life and Times of Bishop Pompellier*. Christchurch, NZ: The Pegasus Press, 1957.

King, Michael. *God's Farthest Outpost: A History of Catholics in New Zealand*. Singapore: Penguin, 1997.

King, Michael. *The Penguin History of New Zealand*. Auckland, NZ: Penguin, 2003.

Munro, Jessie. *The Story of Suzanne Aubert*. Auckland, NZ: Auckland University Press, 1996.

Wilson, J. *The Church in New Zealand: Memoirs of the Early Days*. Dunedin, NZ: New Zealand Tablet Printing and Publishing, 1910.

Sandra Heffernan

See also Ceremonial and Religious Dress in Australia; Resources for the Study of European Dress and Fashion in New Zealand.

Antarctic Explorer Wear

- Early Explorations: Work Clothes
- Science, Exploration, and Clothing
- Hand- and Headwear
- Footwear
- Leisure Wear

Clothing worn in the Ross Sea region of Antarctica demonstrates important design changes developed to assist wearers with extreme weather conditions. Antarctic clothing history is split into two main eras: the heroic era from 1840 to 1917 and the scientific era from 1940 to the twenty-first century. Exploration that occurred between these eras was mainly sea-based for commercial reasons (sealing and whaling) and did not affect clothing design in any major way. At the beginning of the heroic era of Antarctic exploration, most of the clothing and equipment used was initially based on Arctic exploration.

The continent of Antarctica is situated within the Antarctic Circle below 60 degrees south and reaches to the South Pole at 90 degrees south. It is a land mass covered with ice averaging over two kilometers (about one and a quarter miles) thick and is surrounded by permanent ice shelves and seasonal sea ice. It is the coldest, highest, driest, and windiest continent on Earth. Temperatures can range from −59 degrees Celsius (−74 degrees Fahrenheit) to +8 degrees Celsius (47 degrees Fahrenheit). There

are no indigenous people. It is vital that anyone who lives in the region have protective clothing in order to survive.

The first expedition to venture into the Antarctic Circle was James Cook on the *HMS Resolution* in 1772. Between 1839 and 1843 the British Naval Expedition under James Clark Ross on the *HMS Erebus* discovered the Ross Sea, Ross Island, and Mounts Erebus and Terror. The Ross Sea region contains the remaining huts from the heroic era explorers, Carsten Borchgrevinck (1898), Robert Falcon Scott (1901 and 1910), and Ernest Shackleton (1909), as well as New Zealand's permanent research station, Scott Base, and the U.S. McMurdo Station. In this period all equipment, food, and supplies were brought by ship, and each expedition needed to plan for several years, which inevitably included decisions about clothing. There was virtually no communication with the outside world, and each expedition, once in Antarctic waters, had to survive unaided.

Over time, the development of transportion and communication technology allowed more people to travel to Antarctica for shorter periods of time and made regular resupply possible. Heroic era expeditions numbered tens of people, whereas in the twenty-first century there may be several thousand working in the Ross Sea in any summer season. Until the late twentieth century clothing was designed for men, as few women visited the sub-Antarctic and Antarctic in the earlier years. Women became more common in Antarctica beginning in the 1960s, but changes in clothing to accommodate women happened slowly.

Protective clothing is critical in the inhospitable environment of Antarctica. It must shield against wind, snow, and cold, keep the body warm, particularly the torso, head, and extremities, be

Officers and men in costume for the play *Ticket of Leave* on the *Discovery* Expedition, 1901–1903. Scott's crew performed the first play in Antarctica, as a means of boosting morale, and this involved the use of dress-up clothes, including women's attire. Canterbury Museum, New Zealand.

easy to remove, and allow free movement. The most effective cold-weather clothing uses several lightweight layers rather than one or two heavier ones. These provide greater flexibility of use, trap warm air, which acts as insulation, and allow individuals to regulate their own body temperature. In addition, layering aids ventilation, thus reducing perspiration buildup. Antarctica is dry, so most Antarctic clothing does not have to be waterproof.

As an antidote to the harsh and extreme weather conditions in Antarctica, during the heroic era those living there started the habit of planning leisure activities, especially in winter darkness, to prevent boredom and maintain morale. Scott, with his naval background, was particularly aware of the importance of morale. The men of Scott's *Discovery* Expedition wrote and performed the first play in Antarctica and took appropriate clothes to do so, including women's attire for dressing up. The officers of his second *Terra Nova* Expedition took clothing for use when they were off duty, including evening slippers, which made the men feel they still had some of the comforts of home.

EARLY EXPLORATIONS: WORKING CLOTHING

Clothing used during the early exploration period was made from natural fibers including cotton, wool, and leather. James Ross chose clothing for his explorers based on Inuit dress, which he had studied during his earlier Arctic expeditions. There was a distinction in dress between sailors and the shore parties. Sailors wore the typical clothing of the time: thick cloth trousers and woolen overcoats buttoned high up the neck. The shore parties (or exploring parties) wore clothing based more on Arctic clothing, with multiple layers of cotton, wool, and leather, often fur-lined. Wolverine or reindeer fur was used, as it does not freeze.

Clothing had not altered by 1898 when Borchgrevink completed the first intentional winter on the Antarctic continent. This expedition remained close to the coast and did not venture into the interior; therefore, there was no experience to guide Scott in the 1901–1904 British National Antarctic Expedition (BNAE) that aimed to explore the Polar Plateau toward the South Pole. While Scott discussed clothing with experienced Arctic explorer Fridtjof Nansen, he had some preconceived ideas. He valued fur only for mittens and footwear and relied on wool, heavy cottons like gabardine, and other natural fibers such as camel hair for garments.

All members of the BNAE, regardless of rank, were clothed the same way. They wore a thick suit of underclothing, one or sometimes two layers of flannel, or a woolen shirt, a knitted jersey, a pair of woolen or pilot cloth (coarse twilled blue cloth with a nap on one side) trousers, and a boxy-shaped jacket. In inclement weather the men wore thick waterproof canvas gabardine over-trousers and jacket. Necks, cuffs, and waists had drawstrings, sometimes with wooden toggles, to tighten and seal against blowing snow and wind. Burberry gabardine was extensively used for the external layers, as it was waterproof and lightweight. To reduce the amount of blowing snow getting under clothing, helmets were often joined to outer jackets, which could be tucked into the over-trousers. The gabardine over-garments were difficult to remove and did not breathe, so they trapped perspiration. This was an issue, as Scott intended to man-haul sleds but did not realize how much effort would be required or perspiration produced. While moving, the perspiration moisture remained warm, but at rest the sweat froze, making the clothing heavier and reducing its insulation quality. It was also difficult to

Dr. E. A. Wilson in October 1911, on the *Terra Nova* Expedition, 1910–1913. Explorers in the heroic era often used thick waterproof gabardine over-trousers and layers of wool for warmth. Photograph by H. Ponting. Harry Pennell Collection. Canterbury Museum, New Zealand.

dry clothing when traveling. This expedition confirmed for Scott the importance of layering for insulation from the cold. Shackleton used the experience he gained under Scott when choosing the clothing for his British Antarctic Expedition of 1907–1909.

Experience of Inuit clothing, which Roald Amundsen (*Fram* Expedition 1909–1911) gained during his childhood in Norway, gave him an advantage when planning expeditions. He adapted Inuit garments to make them more suitable for Antarctic exploration. Felted suits were made from Norwegian navy blankets with reindeer- and wolf-skin garments on top and an outer windproof layer of gabardine. These garments, modeled on the clothing worn by the Netchelli Inuit, were very light, about half that of woolen equivalents, and they kept the wearer warm in temperatures as low as –60 degrees Celsius (–76 degrees Fahrenheit). The disadvantage was that they did not breathe, became heavy with moisture, had long drying times, and would freeze if left wet. Amundsen designed the clothing to fit loosely to help reduce sweating and allow ventilation. This planning helped this expedition succeed in reaching the South Pole on 15 December 1911.

SCIENCE, EXPLORATION, AND CLOTHING

Clothing continued to be based on multiple layers until three of the largest expeditions to date began what is known as the scientific era. The United States Service Expedition (1939–1941), Operation Highjump (1946–1947), and Operation Deep Freeze (1955–1959) completed aerial surveys, planned bases, and tested equipment. American clothing test results were shared with the twelve nations participating in the scientific programs of the International Geophysical Year (IGY) of 1957–1959. New Zealand also used this information when planning the Trans Antarctic Expedition (TAE) of 1956–1959.

New Zealand kit for the IGY and TAE included short or long cotton underwear with string or woolen undershirts. Woolen underwear was only necessary in temperatures below −17 degrees Celsius (2 degrees Fahrenheit). Civilian shirts were worn for inside work. Other items included a hand-knitted, zipper-front turtleneck jersey and a quilted, down-filled, zipper-front waistcoat and jacket, with matching quilted trousers, all manufactured by Arthur Ellis & Co., New Zealand. The outer layer of clothing comprised windproof trousers and parka with fur-trimmed hood made from ventile (lightweight cotton). The fur trimming kept the face warm and out of the wind but restricted vision. The parkas were oversize to fit over other layers, which caused problems as they caught on objects and, being lightweight, tore easily. In addition, they lost their windproof quality in high (above 30 knots, 35 mph) winds and ballooned up, reducing their insulation value. The expedition members altered the outer layers by attaching drawstrings to the ankles on the trousers and around the waist and lower edge of the jacket.

A significant change in Antarctic outdoor clothing occurred beginning in the 1970s with the use of synthetic fabrics, primarily polypropylene and polytetrafluoroethylene (PTFE). PTFE is semiwaterproof and allows perspiration to be drawn away from the body through small breathable pores, preventing the fabric from freezing onto the body when activity ceases. Synthetics are also usually lighter than natural fiber equivalents and take up less space.

Since the start of the scientific era clothing has had a base thermal layer of fine wool, polypropylene, or wool/polypropylene mix. The next layer changes depending on the weather, individual body physiology, and the activity planned. In the New Zealand Antarctic Programme this layer includes a polar fleece overall (salopette, usually worn with a jacket) or trousers and polar fleece (polypropylene fleece) shirt or wool/synthetic-mix top. The outer layer still provides the main wind protection. All New Zealand Programme participants are issued with an extreme cold weather (ECW) jacket and salopettes. The jacket with attached hood, including sun visor, has a windproof, synthetic, down-proof fabric (very densely woven fabric that prevents the feathers in the down from working through) outer layer with synthetic lining. These layers are quilted together and have a batting layer comprising either down (the insulating underfeathers of water birds, used since the 1960s–1970s) or a mixture of down and synthetic Dacron-type insulation (used since the 1970s–1990s). The batting traps air and provides a warm insulating layer without adding excessive weight. In good weather (above −15 degrees Celsius, or 5 degrees Fahrenheit, with minimal wind chill), an outer layer of unlined windproof anorak and salopettes may be sufficient and allow more ease of movement.

Outer garments have features designed for the environment. Fabric flaps under and over the zipper, the outer flap attached to the garment with Velcro, reduce loss of heat through the zipper teeth. Elasticized cuffs on the jackets both prevent heat loss and allow trapped heat to circulate around the hands and fingers, an area of particular susceptibility. The jacket hood can be drawn around the face, reducing heat loss, protecting from blowing snow, and shading from sun glare. The salopettes have full-length zippers down each side, again with flaps and Velcro fastening. Some designs attach the rear braces to the outside of the side zip, enabling the back portion to drop down for easy toileting without removal of clothing.

Few companies make Arctic-weather clothing or are interested in doing so, because the market is small, unless they can also sell overseas (especially in the United States and in northern countries with Arctic regions). In 2007 the New Zealand outdoor clothing company Earth Sea Sky (previous owners of Arthur Ellis & Co.) designed a new clothing system for the New Zealand Antarctic Programme. The new system comprised seven layered garments per person, allowing the wearer to adjust to changes in temperature, wind chill, and activity. For the first time a complete range of women's sizes was created. Prior to this men and women wore the same clothing. Women would usually be allocated salopettes with a drop-down back portion, but otherwise there was no clothing designed specifically for women's body shape. Often this resulted in poorly fitting outer clothing layers, especially around chests and hips, and in women trying to find suitable commercially available underlayers. It is only since the 1990s that the number of women working in Antarctic has risen enough to impel clothing suppliers to design for their specific needs and body shape.

The thermal layers are made from lightweight Tecnopile Micro Fleece with a second and warmer Polartec Fleece layer if required. The Polartec is made in the United States and chosen for its extreme durability. The ECW jacket was lightened and made from a hard-wearing polyester/cotton windproof fabric with streamlined pocketing. A second option for the outer layer was a semitailored soft-shell (tightly knitted fabric) zipped jacket with a woven stretch nylon outer face, soft polyester inside face, and fully windproof and waterproof laminate in between. A new Primaloft jacket (a synthetic fill equivalent to down) was designed to layer underneath the ECW jacket or soft-shell jacket in very cold conditions. The Primaloft jacket is suitable as an outer jacket in warmer conditions. Waterproof breathable fabric salopettes complete the outer layer.

Some manual activities, such as heavy machinery driving, cause high wear and tear on clothing. In these cases fire-resistant Carhartt brand overalls and jackets are issued for outdoor work. The overalls are made from either cotton duck (a heavy, plain-woven cotten fabric sometimes known as canvas) or a mixture of cotton and high-tenacity nylon with a nylon quilted to polyester arctic-weight lining. They have multiple patch-type pockets and side loops for holding tools. The legs are zipped to either the knee or mid-thigh with a protective, Velcro-fastened flap to allow removal of boots. Zippers are made of brass, which withstands cold temperatures. The overalls are reinforced at the knees and have a high back and double-layer front bib, held up by elastic suspenders with nylon center-release buckles that are specially made for low temperatures. The lined, quilted Carhartt jacket has multiple patch pockets with protective over-flaps, as does the front two-way brass zipper. The sleeves have an inner rib-knit cuff to retain heat without restricting circulation.

Because bases are heated, personnel working inside wear clothing appropriate to their job. For general work this is usually casual clothing such as jeans, T-shirts, sweatshirts, or polar fleece tops. Scott Base chefs wear commercially available cotton trousers, jacket, and cap. Appropriate safety clothing is worn in the carpentry and mechanical workshops and garages. Within most bases ECW clothing may not be worn indoors, to keep snow out and reduce wear on flooring. ECW jackets and salopettes are hung on hooks with boot racks below, close to external doors for convenience.

HAND- AND HEADWEAR

Retaining warmth in the hands and head is very important to prevent hypothermia and to retain dexterity in the fingers. A variety of these articles are required to meet both the environmental and personal needs of those working or exploring in Antarctica. Hand- and headwear must retain warmth, be flexible, and work in different combinations.

Expedition members in the 1840s wore knitted woolen gloves and thick cotton caps and neck scarves, the typical seaman's clothing of the time. Scott in the early 1900s used hats that covered the head and neck, woolen mittens with long cuffs covering the forearm, and bulky felt or fur over-mitts. Apsley Cherry Garrard, on Scott's second expedition, described adding a nosepiece to his gabardine helmet to prevent sunburn, in essence creating a full-face balaclava. Garrard lined his balaclava with knitted wool.

Headwear worn in the IGY and TAE was based around an Arthur Ellis & Co. balaclava of windproof cloth filled with down and quilted. In the American testing its design was considered to be far superior to anything previously used. Other headwear did not change significantly from the heroic era and consisted of a range of woolen and gabardine hats and helmets.

Use of synthetic fabrics is the main change in head- and handwear since the TAE. For general activities thin polypropylene gloves are worn under a layer of either knitted woolen or windproof polypropylene gloves. In inclement weather nose-wiper mittens (oversize multilayer mittens) hung on a detachable webbing strap round the neck are used to rewarm hands. Nose-wiper mittens are made of leather, PTFE, or both, usually with a sheepskin outer over the back of the hands, used to wipe the nose. Detachable quilted liners made of padded synthetic fabric or felted wool are fastened to the outer with domes at the cuffs that reach halfway up the forearm. Leather gloves are used for manual work, as they are hard-wearing. Fleece-lined waterproof PVC (polyvinyl chloride) gloves with thin polypropylene gloves underneath are used when working with wildlife and in wet areas, as they are easily wiped clean on the outside yet retain warmth.

Since the 1980s headwear consists of a polypropylene or wool double-layer balaclava, or hat and a polar fleece neck gaiter (neck tube). The neck gaiter allows warm air to pass from the body to the head. In addition there may be a windproof hood with shade brim fastened under the chin. Deep field parties are also issued a natural fur or fur-lined hat with earflaps. Until the 1990s these hats were usually imported and used reindeer or wolverine fur; however, twenty-first-century hats are created in New Zealand from possum fur. They have excellent warmth and windproof qualities but are not effective in wet conditions.

Goggles protect the eyes from blowing snow, and from drying out with the wind and sun glare, both from the sky and reflected from the snow. Borchgrevink's expedition used a darkened glass rectangle set into a leather headband. This fitted into the eye gap of a balaclava-type helmet and thus reduced the risk of sunburn on exposed skin. Scott's and Shackleton's expeditions used

Ernest Shackleton aboard the *Nimrod*, after the return of the Southern Party, March 1909. He carefully chose layers of clothing for his own venture after his experiences with the standard clothing on Scott's earlier expedition, which had consisted of several lightweight layers rather than a few heavier ones. Here he wears a warm cap, knitted outer jumper and strong trousers. On a later expedition he wore Finneskoe boots made entirely of reindeer skin. Photographer unknown. Canterbury Museum, New Zealand.

wooden or metal goggles with a leather strap around the head. The goggle portion was solid with cross-shaped slits in the wood or metal that let only a fraction of light in. While these reduced the danger of snow blindness, they also diminished visibility and made it harder to distinguish changes in the surface of the ground. Amundsen used dark mesh individual eyepieces with metal edging attached to a leather strap. Their main advantage over other designs was that they retained peripheral vision.

Several types of eye protection were used in the IGY and TAE, including goggles comprising a single lens mounted in rubber with a thin felt lining, giving maximum protection to the face and good vision. A short nose guard gave additional protection and comfort. The lenses were usually green, which, in the 1950s, was thought to provide the best protection from glare. Goggles with an elastic headband, made from orange celluloid lenses and side pieces joined together with cotton bias binding edging, were also used. Bakelite separators on the sides held the lenses away from the eyes and gave excellent peripheral vision. From the 1970s huge advances in sunglass technology were made, enabling Antarctic personnel to choose from a range of commercially available goggles or sunglasses with high levels of ultraviolet (UV) protection.

FOOTWEAR

A natural body defense mechanism to the cold is to constrict blood flow to extremities, in order to keep the core of the body warm for as long as possible. This makes the feet more susceptible to cold-related injuries such as frostnip and frostbite. Footwear, therefore, is very important and needs to be adaptable for the activity being performed as well as retaining warmth in all conditions. The various materials available and the widely contrasting surfaces found across Antarctica have resulted in the evolution of a large range of footwear. Some are useful over several terrains and temperature ranges, while others are for a specific use. Some footwear is designed to be used in combinations, such as boots with crampons or skis.

Heroic era footwear shows evidence of adaptation and experimentation to better fit the terrain and activity. Boots were generally made from leather, rather than rubber, as it was warmer, did not cause as much perspiration, and could be easily repaired. The disadvantage was the drying time when wet and the difficulty of keeping the leather supple and not distorted in shape. Any distortion aggravated by perspiration and cold conditions could cause blisters or lead to frostbite and gangrene. To offset this, boots were worn a larger size than usual for the wearer, with insoles and one to two pairs of woolen socks. The size allowed space to wriggle the toes, helping to retain circulation and reducing the likelihood of foot problems.

Boots often had hobnails put into the soles for traction on icy or slippery ground. Shackleton's men made homemade hobs, in which an additional layer of leather was attached to the soles and then nails with shaped heads pushed in. One issue was the use of nails not specially intended as hobs. The shaft of the hobnail needs to be long enough to firmly hold the nail but short enough not to protrude into the inner sole layer of the boot and aggravate the wearer's foot.

Amundsen designed boots for his expedition. This was the first known attempt to adapt existing boots for use as a ski boot with a steel binding at low temperatures. He remade the boots three times before they had the correct combination of stiffness for control when skiing and flexibility to allow movement. The boot had a thick leather sole without nails and a canvas upper of ankle height. A wide band of reinforcing leather around the boot and fastened to the sole helped with skiing control. The canvas helped circulation and dried quickly but required felt insoles and multiple woolen socks for warmth. Some pairs had squared toes for attaching the ski bindings.

Finneskoe boots (Finnish footwear made entirely of fur, including the soles) were worn on Shackleton's 1914 British Imperial Transantarctic Expedition, as they, unlike leather, did not crack in the extreme cold. The boots were usually made from reindeer skin with the fur on the outside, sewn with gut and with inner linings of dried sennegrass (Norwegian hay), which absorbed the sweat from feet, reducing foot problems such as cracked skin or loosened toenails. Finneskoes were very warm but had minimal grip due to the outer fur layer.

During the TAE and IGY, New Zealand participants used rubber boots worn with multiple pairs of socks. These were satisfactory in temperatures above −17 degrees Celsius (2 degrees Fahrenheit) and were especially good when warmer temperatures caused slushy snow around the base. From the 1980s leather Sorrel boots, a type of boot with separate felted linings, were used in warmer and snow-free conditions and around bases. In higher altitudes and colder temperatures both rubber boots and Sorrels were inadequate to keep feet warm, and mukluk boots (original footwear of the Arctic Yipik peoples) were worn.

Mukluk boots in various guises have been used in Antarctica since the nineteenth century due to their suitability for use on cold, dry snow. Early mukluks had a moccasin-type foot portion with a canvas upper, fastened with a drawcord at the top of the calf. An additional cord at ankle level provided extra support. The boot had removable inner linings, helping to keep the feet dry and healthy. Mukluk design has evolved to include synthetic materials and a purpose-built inner bootie. The calf-length, quilted, insulated canvas boot with leather reinforcing provides a high level of thermal insulation. Their drawback is that they take a long time to dry out and are therefore unsuitable for wetter areas, such as the sea ice edge and marine drilling sites. Mukluks come with a quilted padded inner bootie with reinforced sole that can be worn as tent slippers. They have thick rubber soles, usually with an extra leather or rubber layer between the sole and the boot for additional insulation.

Scott Base has central heating and is kept at 18 degrees Celsius (65 degrees Fahrenheit) inside, so footwear worn indoors does not have to withstand cold conditions. During the IGY a soft suede, fleece-lined shoe with rubber sole was issued for inside work. Indoor footwear is often of slip-on type with some grip on the sole. Due to the dry conditions there is a high fire risk in Antarctica. When a fire alarm goes off all personnel vacate the base immediately, and so it is advantageous to have footwear that is quick to put on.

A range of socks are worn, and these are usually woolen or have high wool content. Socks woven with a loop stitch are most effective at moving moisture away from the skin while providing some cushioning. Multiple layers of thinner socks may also be worn, depending on personal preference.

LEISURE WEAR

Following in Scott's footsteps, and following practices started during the heroic era, leisure activities in the twenty-first century still play an important part in the life of Scott Base. The leisure clothing taken to or available in the base reflects the range of activities undertaken by all people working in Antarctica. Outdoor activities may use specialist clothing and footwear such as commercially available plastic double-insulated climbing, tramping, and ski boots—however, ECW clothing is always carried in case of sudden weather change. Indoor activities may require specialist sporting clothing suitable for the particular sport, such as basketball, netball, or indoor climbing, all of which are available at the U.S. McMurdo Station close to Scott Base. In the same way a wide range of fancy-dress clothing and costumes is kept at Scott Base for use in themed parties held throughout the year. These include traditional events such as the skirt party, toga party, and Halloween, which have been celebrated for decades.

There is generally a strong sense of camaraderie in the culture of an Antarctic base. At Scott Base this reflects itself in clothing designed and worn on the Ice (the colloquial term for Antarctica). Of note are the rugby jerseys made specifically for the annual match between Scott Base and McMurdo Station personnel. Each base designs a logo and chooses a jersey color to be made in New Zealand, sent to Scott Base, and worn for this sporting event. These jerseys are only worn for one Antarctic summer season and are redesigned by Scott Base personnel to suit the team composition and base culture each year. Another example is the T-shirts designed by and for the fire crews at Scott Base. These crews complete an intensive training program in New Zealand before deployment to Antarctica. Fire awareness and fighting is an important safety feature of all Antarctic bases. Each austral summer the fire crew at Scott Base designs, and has made and sent from New Zealand, special limited-edition Fire Crew T-shirts to be worn by Antarctic personnel.

References and Further Reading

Amundsen, Roald. *The South Pole: An Account of the Norwegian Antarctic Expedition in the Fram, 1910–1912*. London: Sir John Murray, 1912.

Mawson, Douglas. *The Home of the Blizzard*. 2 vols. London: William Heinemann, 1915.

Parsons, Mike, and Mary Rose. *Invisible on Everest; Innovation and Gear Makers*. Philadelphia: Northern Liberties Press, 2003.

Quartermain, L. B. *New Zealand and the Antarctic*. Wellington, NZ: A. R. Shearer, Government Printer, 1971.

Scott, Robert Falcon. *Scott's Last Expedition: The Personal Journals of Captain R. F. Scott*. 2 vols. London: John Murray, 1973.

Natalie Cadenhead

See also New Zealand Textiles and Apparel Sectors.

The Social Significance of Institutional Dress in New Zealand

- Institutions of Healing and Care
- Institutions for "Social Problems"
- Institutions of Control and Punishment
- Clothing as Work and Punishment

As a settler colony, New Zealand inherited its range of institutions, its modes of operation, and its day-to-day practices from Britain. This legacy included the forms of dress worn by institutional staff and residents, although they were modified to suit the distinctive economic, political, and cultural context that developed in the South Pacific nation. Generally, institutional dress was more rigid and strictly adhered to in the nineteenth century and became more casual by the end of the twentieth century, for both staff and residents. Institutional dress differed according to the type of establishment: for treatment, custody, and control, or punishment. Often it is easier to find out about the experiences of staff, whose activities appear in annual reports and institutional archives. Patients and inmates are usually invisible in the records, and even their case notes or entries in registers reflect the preoccupations of the staff rather than those being treated or disciplined. The archives are more revealing and accessible in the nineteenth rather than the twentieth century, because they are less professionalized, use less technical language, and also do not conform to privacy issues present today (more recent documents are often unavailable). The following examples show that institutional dress constructs the social, cultural, and racial identities of those wearing it. Instilling new habits of docility, obedience, discipline, and reliability, this kind of clothing actively produced distinctions and hierarchies, and fitness for purpose. Through these processes it became an indicator of status or lack of it, and of conformity with, or forced departure from, social and community norms. Dress was particularly important for female residents, because the institution was trying to instill or maintain a certain type of dependent femininity. In the process staff attempted to control bodies as well as appearances.

INSTITUTIONS OF HEALING AND CARE

Hospitals and lunatic asylums, as they were then called, were the first state institutions established in the country. New Zealand's small population meant that it lacked large reserves of private wealth or traditions of philanthropy, so that most settlers looked to the government to assist in the provision of welfare services. Immigrants hoped to escape the poverty and degradation of their homelands but found that they were confronted with them again in this unruly and unstable new world. Within a few years of settlement the governor and other officials were themselves employing the destitute, setting up relief work schemes, and handing out rations and clothing to both Māori (indigenous) and Pākehā (European/nonindigenous). Māori quickly took to selective wearing of European clothing, often combining both traditional and Victorian garb, and not surprisingly it was the European blanket that Māori first found valuable. Among other things, it saved them the time it took to make cloaks from prepared and woven flax (*Phormium tenax*), feathers, and dog hair. The distribution and use of blankets by Māori differed from other colonial outposts, where they were used to clothe slaves. In Australia, as Margaret Maynard has shown, governors, Aboriginal Protectors, and mission stations issued them to Aboriginals as charitable items, as a form of social control (by rationing them according to behavior), as a way of exerting moral influence, and to allow access to settlement areas. Māori obtained other European clothes through trade for land or sometimes by stealth or force. For example, in 1839 the New Zealand Company, which planned and populated the Wellington settlement, paid for the acreage in goods that included shoes, umbrellas, hats, shirts, jackets, trousers, red nightcaps, calico (a plain white cotton fabric that is heavier than muslin), ribbon, handkerchiefs, and two suits of superfine clothes.

In 1846, four years after the founding of the colony with the signing of the Treaty of Waitangi between *iwi* (Māori tribes) and Queen Victoria, Governor Grey established four state hospitals. These were to serve both the Māori population and indigent settlers. While the patients might not have had dress requirements—although the very few Māori who used these institutions might have been persuaded to adopt European attire—nursing staff at hospitals came to wear dresses and caps (but not uniforms as such), clothing that signified hygiene and authority. Until 1870 nursing was done informally by missionaries and other kindly women, whereas men were employed in institutions. Following the Crimean War of the mid-nineteenth century, Florence Nightingale initiated widespread nursing reforms. She prescribed a formal uniform as the key to disciplined training and performance. It consisted of a combination of dress and pinafore, plus a cap covering the hair and a cape for streetwear, and it became the standard theme of nurse uniforms for over a century. Nightingale-trained nurses were evident in New Zealand from 1870, and in the larger institutions they wore caps, aprons, and starched cuffs.

Nursing uniforms differed slightly from hospital to hospital but followed British precedent. In 1893 nurses at the first hospital in the regional township of Palmerston North wore heavy navy serge reaching to their black boots, with high stiffened collars and white aprons buttoning on to "baby bodices" and stiff turned-back white cuffs. Their white caps were high and frilled round the front. Later they wore blue-and-white striped galatea, a good-quality cotton material. White is said to signify cleanliness, purity, and authority, as well as life, but it was also a color that could be easily maintained through bleaching agents, in an era when fabric and dyeing technology was rudimentary. Nurses were not registered until 1901, and through the twentieth century the shorter white uniforms, caps, and capes remained until colored uniforms, trousers, and going without caps became the norm in the 1990s. Status is still observed between different levels and kinds of nursing, either through color or lapel stripes.

An anonymous donor provided new dresses for these girls from St. Joseph's Orphanage in Upper Hutt and arranged for the girls to be transported into Wellington to see the pantomime *The Princess and the Swineherd*, on 14 December 1968. Dominion Post Collection, Alexander Turnbull Library, Wellington, New Zealand.

The first public lunatics' building also made an early appearance in New Zealand's history. It was established at Karori in Wellington, two years after the 1852 Constitution Act. By the 1880s the main cities and major towns all had psychiatric institutions, often attached to hospitals and jails. Provincial governments were forced, through lack of public interest, to administer and fund the new institutions. The Department of Lunatic Asylums was the first state social service established after the abolition of the provinces in 1876. Again, Māori were very much in the minority in these and other institutions, as they had their own forms of healing and social practices. The institutions were situated in rural outskirts of larger centers of population that supported them, until large-scale urbanization beginning in the 1940s. As such, they became forbidding places and increasingly isolated even when surrounded by urban development.

The social significance of clothing in these gradually more isolated and overcrowded institutions is striking. According to the annual report of the Auckland Lunatic Asylum, for example, which exceeded three hundred patients in the early 1880s and had nearly a thousand patients by 1910, staff found that strong dresses (made of canvas, like straitjackets) prevented what they saw as unnecessary waste of clothing. It is clear that staff had to deal with difficult patients in an era before drug treatment and had to run an economically efficient institution with barely adequate funding. Other evidence confirms that they had less concern with issues of self-presentation, let alone respectability or dignity. The process started with committal to the asylum, a formal medico-legal examination process carried out by justices of the peace and doctors. It involved routines of humiliation and self-mortification that were more like jail. Inmates often knew full well what was happening to them. At the Auckland Lunatic Asylum Charles J. proclaimed in 1890 that he was an "inmate," not a "patient" (Labrum 1990, p. 223). Once an individual entered the asylum, his or her estate was in the hands of the public trustee, who received all their personal property, clothes, and money. After being bathed and dressed the men had their hair cut. According to staff, their clothing was serviceable and provided adequate warmth. Although there was no conscious decision to create a uniform, a standard dress became the norm. There were many comments about the tattered and drab appearance of patients and the prison-like style of the dress. In 1874 the superintendent acknowledged in his annual report that patients were aware of the differences in their dress once inside the institution, and he believed this change from civilian dress might prejudice their recovery.

For men trousers and coats of moleskin (a heavy, durable cotton fabric with a short, thick, velvety nap on one side) and blue striped or pink checked shirts were the standard issue, while women, who were a much smaller proportion of the population, donned calico combinations, cotton petticoats, and galatea cloth frocks that official visitors described as shapeless, heavy, dark, and unattractive because they were all made from an identical pattern. In colder weather staff distributed flannels and jerseys. Patients' boots leaked, however, and many did not wear enough clothes. Only in the mid-1880s did patients receive a second set of clothing. It seemed as if asylum patients were back in the English workhouse. The indignity of being bathed by an attendant, standard haircuts, and even a partial uniform reduced inmates' feeling of control over their appearance; they were always noticeably different from others.

There was no privacy in the asylum. In 1897 Alice Schoch, the official visitor to the Porirua Asylum, "respectfully" suggested that the female patients should be given dressing rooms, because they had to change their clothes in cold, open corridors. Unsurprisingly, patients protested and attempted to subvert the rhythms of asylum life, especially through destroying their clothing, which took on even greater symbolic significance than it might on "the outside." Yet this action only confirmed their unfitness for "normal life." Significantly, one of the key symptoms of madness that led to many female admissions was dressing improperly or immodestly or appearing unclothed. Once inside the institution, others purposely refused to eat or maimed themselves, and the men in particular attempted, sometimes successfully, to run away. A more profound if less spectacular form of resistance took the form of complaining, especially to official visitors on their periodic visits.

In the twentieth century psychiatric hospitals, as they were now called, remained the most underfunded sector of the public health system. Although improving the physical amenities and the standard of clothing, food, and recreational facilities were considered as important as medical treatment, conservative approaches to spending and reform, and the impact of World War II, meant that patient clothing, as well as bed linen, remained in short supply. Patient clothing continued to be regarded in uniform or corporate terms, and inmates were thus neglected as autonomous, functioning human beings. A new, female, minister of health whose term began in 1947, Mabel Howard, took a personal interest in patients and their environments. At her behest clothing became more varied. Female patients who were considered able to appreciate it received underwear, and for the first time menstruating women were able to have sanitary napkins. Shortages continued through the 1950s.

Clothing was still not routinely considered to be part of patient dignity and comfort, however. Sometimes when patients were undressed in the evening, their clothes were dropped in a heap in whatever state they were in, and then the same garments were put on again, perhaps in a different combination, in the morning. Shoes might be taken from the ward collection, rather than being individually fitted or "owned," and used for different patients depending on who was resident that day. Only with new rehabilitation measures in the 1960s and 1970s was clothing individually fitted. Ward sisters (the senior nurses in charge of the wards) could make a difference by insisting that patients had their own clothing and that they were treated more humanely.

INSTITUTIONS FOR "SOCIAL PROBLEMS"

Settlers found welfare to be as pressing a problem as health. The plight of children was often desperate and received somewhat more community interest than the sick or insane. Welfare institutions for orphans and destitute children appeared very early. By the mid-1870s there were ten institutions for orphaned, criminal, or neglected children in the main centers, of which two were industrial schools run by the Justice Department. The total number of orphanages increased markedly after the 1900s, and they were mostly run by churches, which preferred to provide institutional care. By 1929 there were at least eighty private and denominational children's homes throughout New Zealand, containing anywhere from five to several hundred children. They continued to expand until the 1960s.

The state was the least involved in this area of welfare endeavor, as from the early twentieth century it had a firm policy of boarding out or fostering state wards wherever possible. Lyttleton Orphanage in the southern city of Christchurch was the exception. It suffered a checkered history due to local politics and changing committees that held sway. In 1886 there were seventy-one boys and thirty-two girls resident. They were not necessarily actual orphans; sometimes one or both parents still were alive, but poverty or illegitimacy forced the parent's hand. The children experienced a tedious sequence of housework, schooling, meals, and more work.

Children in New Zealand orphanages do not appear to have customarily worn set clothes. British charity schools adopted uniforms in the sixteenth century, which under industrialization in the nineteenth century became the model for school uniforms. These enabled pupils to be clothed as cheaply as possible and to make them distinctive. The clothes, of poor quality, were designed to make the pupils aware of their responsibility for their situations. Yet in New Zealand children suffered from a lack of and poor-quality garments, as the institutions were forced to rely on what they could provide, or more usually on cast-offs and charity donations.

There were frequent complaints against the management and staff of the Lyttleton Orphanage, including a Commission of Inquiry in 1905. In terms of clothing the situation was dire. Children went out to school without ulsters (long, loose overcoats) and sometimes sat all day in wet clothes, a matter made worse by the cold climatic conditions of the area. In 1866 a new master reported on a severe shortage of clothing, dirty bedding, and only one comb for ninety-six children. Regular baths were only instituted just before the inquiry.

Clothing was regularly part of attempts by institutional managers to punish and shame. According to a 1905 inquiry, "crude psychological victimisation" was visited on the children in a number of ways. As well as being forbidden to talk for a month, and taunted about their backgrounds, children were dressed in "grotesque costumes" for outings.

Homes for the elderly indigent were another form of institutional response to social problems in the nineteenth century. The number of elderly increased by 50 percent between 1896 and 1901 as the settler population aged, and the majority of those institutionalized were men over sixty-five who did not have wives, children, or other family support. They were itinerant laborers, or swaggers, who walked the rural countryside looking for work, old gold miners, and others who were not entitled to the statutory old-age pension that was available from 1898, because of the moral and residency clauses and increasingly rigid means-testing. These men—and a smaller proportion of women—filled up a growing number of institutions. In the North Island there were Old Men's and Old Women's Refuges in Auckland and the Napier Refuge, while in the South Island there was the Otago Benevolent Institution at Caversham in Dunedin, the Ashburton Old Men's Home, and one in Nelson by 1885. Their number had grown to twenty by 1920. Although residing in an institution was often a far better solution than facing life alone, some homes were anything but homely. Auckland's Costley Home of the Aged Poor, with its pretentious façade, ornamental balustrades, and Corinthian columns, was in reality dirty and comfortless. Lice and bedbugs were rife, and bed linen and clothing were left

This man is posed as a sleeping *swagger*, New Zealand, about 1920. His patchwork blanket would be rolled up as swag strapped to his back, with his *billy* (kettle), cup, and pillow tucked inside. His pipe and *bowyangs* (straps to hold up trousers) lie beside him, and he sleeps in his well-worn boots. Photograph by Frank J. Denton. Alexander Turnbull Library, Wellington, New Zealand.

unwashed in bad weather because laundry work from outside the home took priority. According to a 1903 Royal Commission on the Costley Home, even fresh linen appeared half-washed, and residents' clothing was thin and dirty.

All residents were issued garments, however meager, but that does not tell us what that clothing meant and how it was used (and misused). The old men, used to being their own masters and in their own company, were not easily institutionalized. Their bad behavior and rebelliousness, and the obvious delight with which they fought with the authorities, extended to clothing. The two charges of buying illicit alcohol and pawning clothes to pay for it often appeared together in the records.

INSTITUTIONS OF CONTROL AND PUNISHMENT

Homes for the elderly and orphanages were part of an extensive institutional network that had developed by the late nineteenth century. This system extended to rescue homes for single mothers and industrial schools for rebellious children, as well as institutions for the deviant and criminal. Again clothing features as a key part of institutional life and in the avowed context of control and punishment, rather than cure or care.

From 1864 to 1903 a number of women's homes, also known as refuges or rescue homes, were opened by churches or run by committees of evangelical laywomen. Initially aimed at the reform of prostitutes, soon a variety of reasons lay behind admissions: some were pregnant, some out of work or in danger of being run in by the police if they did not "hide out." Others came from jail or were ill and had no one else to turn to. Later homes mostly provided maternity care for unmarried mothers, a high proportion of whom were domestic servants. As well as caring for ill and pregnant women, the homes attempted to train them in virtuous domesticity. Required to be resident for one or two years in the first homes, gratitude soon turned to mutiny and insubordination, and often escape. Once again clothing played a key role in institutional life. The inmates of the Dunedin Female Refuge had their clothing taken from them upon entry and were charged with larceny if found outside the home in institutional clothing. As well as domesticity, the residents were being taught how to dress, and the meaning of different kinds of clothes.

State-run industrial schools catered to juvenile delinquents from 1867 on, and the numbers within them grew dramatically in the last two decades of the nineteenth century, until the state began to close down its institutions in the early twentieth century. Only two reformatories (for the uncontrollable or those who had been sentenced to prison and were therefore too unruly for the industrial schools) opened: Te Oranga for girls and Burnham for boys, both near Christchurch. Those sent to Te Oranga from 1900 until its closure in 1918 were not just subject to the strap, the birch, or solitary confinement. A number of punishments focused on clothing and appearance. These were symbolic, as Bronwyn Dalley has argued, and relied on humiliation more than physical discomfort, but it is significant that they took this form. Offenders were made to wear a runaway or punishment dress, and their hair was cropped short, a particular chastisement reserved for women. The dress was garish and its color and "attached appendages" were meant as an insult to women, who were assumed to be usually neat and tidy in their appearance. Dalley notes that,

in practice, this goal was thwarted. Other inmates took little notice, and the wearer may even have felt like an individual, and therefore noticed for once, in an environment where everyone else wore drab clothing. Haircutting was more humiliating, and its effects lasted longer, although it was publicly condemned. At a time when women wore their hair long as a sign of their adult femininity, it was clearly meant to single out such offenders and make them appear masculine. It was used extensively in women's institutions as a means of control.

There were prisons in the major settlements by 1850. Although some were very crude, and until the Gaolers Act of 1859 run as individual institutions, they followed British models. Chronic overcrowding and a lack of basic facilities and national coordination continued through the nineteenth century as the central government and provincial councils turned their attention to more pressing problems, such as the wars of the 1860s, land sales, immigration, and public works. Considerable change was inaugurated under the first inspector of prisons, Arthur Humes, who served from 1880 to 1909, and John Findlay, the minister of justice from 1909 to 1911. Yet the use and meaning of clothing in prisons, particularly for female inmates, were marked by continuities rather than change.

There was no formal uniform as such, but a set of prescribed clothes and colors and fabrics. A list for women compiled in 1916 itemized boots/shoes, coats/cloaks, hats/bonnets, blouses, skirts, dresses, a slip bodice, corset, petticoat, chemise, nightdress, drawers (undergarments), stockings, gloves, collars, belts, handkerchief, tie, and umbrellas. It is clear from the records that many of these items were recent additions and that not all prisons made provision for them. It depended on whether the inmates themselves could make them and on the availability of fabric—calico was used for nightwear, for example. Staff complained about the difficulty of providing for older and younger women, and short- and long-term prison sentences. They felt it was desirable to classify the women and institute a progressive hierarchy of clothing with the introduction of their own style and color privileges. Individual matrons recognized that it was difficult to look tidy in old, faded dresses but felt that some prisoners would look that way regardless of what they were wearing. Specific items of clothing led to other difficulties: the lack of shawls for women sitting in draughty corridors sewing and knitting, open-style (probably gaping) drawers that afforded no protection in windy outdoors conditions, and woolen stockings that had to be worn in the heat of summer. It was only in 1914 that sanitary napkins were provided for the women for the first time.

Most female prisoners conformed to penal discipline. It was more common for women to deny specific aspects of the regime rather than to reject everything. Some particularly opposed the official oversight and organization of aspects of their personal hygiene, such as washing, changing clothing, or having a tidy cell. Refusing to conform may have been a way to assert some control over at least some aspects of their confinement. Others refused to perform any labor.

CLOTHING AS WORK AND PUNISHMENT

In institutions that contained both sexes the women and men were physically separated and had different jobs and recreation. The actual work performed derived from the financial and administrative needs of the establishment, even if it was supposed to be occupational therapy. It kept costs down. Mostly women were kept inside, especially as numbers grew, while men could work outside on prison and asylum farms and gardens, and in workshops. Work was both training and punishment in these institutions. The more work undertaken, the more staff deemed a patient to have recovered or to have redeemed themselves. This was meant to inculcate work habits, discipline, and order.

For women work revolved around (re)training in domesticity, which necessitated a further set of social meanings for institutional dress. Their labor included cleaning the institution, sewing, clothing manufacture for other institutions and for themselves, and the laundry of inmates and staff—often by hand, in primitive conditions, and on an industrial scale. Even in women's reformatories, where female residents could go outside, dressmaking and laundry work were major parts of their daily life. Women did extremely heavy laundry work, described at the time as "downright slavery." In 1899 thirty-two women did the weekly and daily wash at the Auckland Lunatic Asylum, including blankets and quilts for over four hundred people. If one was compliant, there was a path of promotion from laundry work up to needlework and knitting. At the Hokitika prison on the South Island's west coast, Sarah Sheehan blamed her illness on the fact that the jailer expected her to wash the clothing of each of the twenty male prisoners detained. Given the onerous duties expected of such women, and the existing indignities and inadequacies of institutional dress, the negative associations it held were reinforced.

In these ways dress was as fundamental to institutions of care, control, and punishment as the architecture, the interior space, the daily regime, meals, and interactions with other residents and staff. An intrinsic part of the disciplinary apparatus of these establishments, dress was a literal materialization of the power relationships and subjectivities that such institutions attempted, not always successfully, to create.

References and Further Reading

Brookes, Barbara. "Women and Madness: A Case-Study of the Seacliff Asylum, 1890–1920." In *Women in History*, vol. 2, edited by Barbara Brookes, Charlotte Macdonald, and Margaret Tennant, 129–147. Wellington, NZ: Bridget Williams Book, 1992.

Craik, Jennifer. *Uniforms Exposed: From Conformity to Transgression.* Oxford: Berg, 2005.

Dalley, Bronwyn. "Women's Imprisonment in NZ, 1880–1920." Ph.D. dissertation, University of Otago, 1991.

Dalley, Bronwyn. "From Demi-Mondes to Slaveys: Aspects of the Management of the Te Oranga Reformatory for Delinquent Young Women, 1900–1918." In *Women in History*, vol. 2, edited by Barbara Brookes, Charlotte Macdonald, and Margaret Tennant, 148–167. Wellington, NZ: Bridget Williams Book, 1992.

Ebbet, Eve. *In True Colonial Fashion: A Lively Look at What New Zealanders Wore.* Wellington, NZ: A. H. & A. W. Reed, 1977.

Labrum, Bronwyn. "Gender and Lunacy: A Study of Women Patients at the Auckland Lunatic Asylum, 1870–1910." Master's thesis, Massey University, 1990.

Labrum, Bronwyn. "Hand-Me-Downs and Respectability: Clothing and the Needy." In *Looking Flash: Clothing in Aotearoa/New Zealand*, edited by Bronwyn Labrum, Fiona McKergow, and Stephanie Gibson, 112–131. Auckland, NZ: Auckland University Press, 2007.

Maynard, Margaret. *Fashioned from Penury: Dress as Cultural Practice in Colonial Australia.* Cambridge and Melbourne: Cambridge University Press, 1994.

Maynard, Margaret. "Blankets: The Visible Politics of Indigenous Clothing in Australia." In *Fashioning the Body Politic: Dress, Gender and Citizenship*, edited by Wendy Parkins, 189–204. Oxford and New York: Berg, 2002.

Prebble, Kate. "Ordinary Men and Uncommon Women: A History of Psychiatric Nursing in New Zealand Public Mental Hospitals, 1939–1972." Ph.D. dissertation, University of Auckland, 1997.

Tennant, Margaret. *Paupers and Providers: Charitable Aid in New Zealand.* Wellington, NZ: Allen & Unwin/Historical Branch, 1989.

Tennant, Margaret. "'Magdalenes and Moral Imbeciles': Women's Homes in Nineteenth Century New Zealand." In *Women in History*, vol. 2, edited by Barbara Brookes, Charlotte Macdonald, and Margaret Tennant, 49–75. Wellington, NZ: Bridget Williams Book, 1992.

Bronwyn Labrum

See also Convict Dress in Australia.

Snapshot: The Swanndri in New Zealand

Since its invention in the early twentieth century, the Swanndri, a woolen bush shirt, has become synonymous with New Zealand's outdoor lifestyle. It started life as farmers' garb and was designed by English emigrant William Henry Broome, who in 1902 had settled in New Plymouth in the rural heartland of Taranaki North Island at the age of twenty-one. The son of a shoe manufacturer, he established himself as a clothier and tailor. His business flourished, and in 1935 he went into partnership with C. W. Lynch, establishing the menswear shop Broome and Lynch in downtown New Plymouth.

Although he wore three-piece suits and smart hats and was interested in high fashion—referring to himself as a mercer (a dealer in textiles)—Broome realized that there was a gap in the market for warm and dry outdoor clothing for men who worked on the land. His solution was a woolen work shirt, with short sleeves and a laced front. His innovation was to dip the woolen fabric in a secret formula to make it weatherproof. The New Zealand firm Bruce Woollen Manufacturing Company, in Milton, Otago, produced the fabric. The weatherproofing process involved the immersion of the sewn garments in the formula, six at a time, in a large concrete tub more than 2 meters (6.5 feet) long for two days. This was carried out in a shed in the backyard of his home on Doralto Road, where his children assisted, although they hated the smell. The shirts shrank unevenly, so they were marketed as one size fits all. After being pegged out to dry they were bundled into parcels of three, delivered to his shop, and posted out to customers.

Broome promoted his bush shirts in innovative ways and registered his own trademark. He displayed one outside his shop on a dressmaker's dummy with water from a hose running over it. Miraculously, the dummy remained absolutely dry. He regularly exhibited his garments at New Plymouth's

Two Māori men eating fish and chips before the British versus Māori rugby game at Athletic Park in Wellington, New Zealand, on 3 August 1950. They are wearing variations on the classic Swanndri, most probably the "outdoor jacket" available from that decade, demonstrating how the rural garment had become a city staple. Photographer unknown. Evening Post Collection, Alexander Turnbull Library, Wellington, New Zealand.

Winter Show, next to an extra Swanndri suspended in a water-filled crate. It could last four days before the water penetrated it completely. In 1913 he registered the distinctive and now classic trademark for this ready-made clothing: a swan in a circle with the name Swanndri below it. The name was a combination of *swan* and *dry*. There are various stories as to why the word has two *n* letters. Either it was a slip of the pen or a deliberate choice.

After Broome's death his son Brian manufactured the shirts for three and a half years. He then licensed tailor John McKendrick of John Mack Limited to use the trademark, in return for a royalty. McKendrick manufactured the garments in his Waitara factory and added a hood and long sleeves. He also introduced preshrunk fabrics, which did away with the uneven shrinkage that occurred during the chemical process. The garments could now be made in different sizes. By the 1950s the range had extended to jackets with front zips, available in khaki and a range of three tartans. They were advertised as "outdoor jackets" and were manufactured in Hunting Stewart tartan, Cameron tartan, and Hunting McPherson tartan. The fabric pattern maintained the link to the outdoors, even though they were increasingly worn in urban spaces. Subsequently, the garments were also known as Dri Coat jackets, with the added benefit of flannel lining for warmth, and were available in a wide range of checks and plain shades. McKendrick obtained the entire rights in 1964 and manufactured a wide variety of clothing under the label.

Alliance Textiles (NZ) Limited of Timaru bought the trademark in 1975 and sold the Swanndri brand in both New Zealand and international markets. By this time it had become firmly identified as "Kiwiana," a shorthand for "objects and images widely adopted and agreed upon as symbols or icons of national identity," through its appearance on a stamp issue and in an opening exhibition at the new national museum. The *New Zealand Post* described the popular 1994 stamp range as containing "items that are affectionately regarded by New Zealanders themselves as important and familiar parts of their national culture." The black singlet and gumboots, rugby football shoes, and jandals (slip-on sandals), as well as the pavlova dessert (a meringue cake topped with whipped cream and fruit), fish and chips, and the kiwifruit, all appeared alongside the Swanndri. On the Sheep's Back, an exhibition that opened at the Museum of New Zealand Te Papa Tongarewa in 1998, explored the varied role of wool in New Zealanders' lives. It contained a segment on clothing manufactured from wool, including the Swanndri. The exhibition development team launched a nationwide competition inviting people to send in their favorite Swanndri stories. The winning garments—often well-worn, stained, and faded—were displayed along with their stories. Staff were amazed at the huge response and at the number of people who referred to their bush shirts as "Old Faithful."

In 2004 Swanndri New Zealand Ltd. purchased the brand from Alliance Textiles. The new company sells more than seventy styles for men and women and has diversifed into urban and tourist markets, including a summer-weight version of the wool fabric. The most popular style remains the long bush shirt called "The Original." Around three thousand of these are sold each year, with the most popular color being olive, followed by the blue and black-and-red and black-checked versions.

By 2005, when Swanndri announced its partnership with internationally renowned New Zealand fashion designer Karen Walker, the once humble garment had traveled far from its rural roots. Karen Walker's Swanndri product line, described as "looking at Swanndri through urban eyes," spanned "modern, timeless pieces" including luggage, outdoor clothing such as trench coats and jackets, T-shirts, and scarves. As well as checked wool and a new range of colors, other fabrics such as cotton, nylon, and moleskin were featured. Now considered as iconic as the All Black rugby jersey, it is worn as a unisex garment in either the classic or designer versions, in the bush, on the land, and in the city.

REFERENCES AND FURTHER READING

Barnett, S., and R. Wolfe. *New Zealand! New Zealand! In Praise of Kiwiana*. Auckland, NZ: Hodder and Stoughton, 1989.
Gibson, Stephanie. "Engaging in Mischief: The Black Singlet and New Zealand Culture." In *Looking Flash: Clothing in Aotearoa/New Zealand*, edited by Bronwyn Labrum, Fiona McKergow, and Stephanie Gibson, 206–221. Auckland, NZ: Auckland University Press, 2007.
Wolfe, Richard. *The Way We Wore: The Clothes New Zealanders Have Loved*. Auckland, NZ: Penguin, 2001.

Bronwyn Labrum

See also Rural Dress in Australia.

School Uniforms in New Zealand

New Zealand has a strong and continuing tradition of school uniform in secondary (high) schools. Nearly everyone going to school in New Zealand since the 1940s wore a uniform for between five and thirteen of their formative years, although their experiences are likely to have been different from those of their parents and the next generation. The meanings and the functions of school uniforms are culturally and historically specific, and in New Zealand they altered considerably over the twentieth century according to changing educational and social objectives of schools and the education system. Uniforms have both reflected and influenced ideas and beliefs about class, gender, the status of children, and the idea of the person. While their earliest and most consistent function is to carry school identity, they have also been used in different ways by schools as a disciplinary technique and to prepare students for projected futures in the adult world of work.

As a form of dress, uniforms have also been used as modes of expression by the people who wear them, always linked to levels of uniformity within particular schools and also reflecting fashion trends to some extent. Unlike other countries, notably the United States, in New Zealand the practice and meanings of school uniforms have not been seen as incompatible with students' rights and freedoms, because they have arisen in conjunction with a cultural, social, and political system that has not placed the individual in opposition to the group.

EARLY DEVELOPMENT

The history of school uniforms is closely connected to the educational history of this country. Although some European schools were established in colonial New Zealand with the arrival of the first missionaries in 1814, it was not until the 1850s that education began to be formally organized, following the first waves of colonial settlement. Education remained haphazard until the Education Act of 1877, which introduced compulsory, free, secular, primary education funded by the central government. This placed education within the reach of every New Zealand child and laid the foundations of a progressive and egalitarian education system. Secondary school, however, remained the privilege of a wealthy minority until 1903, at which time the Liberal government introduced free places in secondary schools for those passing the entry examinations. Many more children were able to attend secondary school after this time, both boys and girls.

There were nearly as many Māori children enrolled in state education as in the so-called native schools in 1900. Although never segregated, state and native schools had different curricula and were administered by different government departments. A few denominational schools were established specifically for Māori at this time, and these offered a limited number of scholarship places. Private schools continued to offer an exclusive or denominational education largely independent of state funding and have remained an important minority in New Zealand secondary education. Secondary-school-age girls and boys were educated separately, a tradition imported from Britain, along with key teaching staff and much of the early curriculum.

Sports uniforms were the only uniforms in early secondary schools. Otherwise, students wore streetwear appropriate to their age and gender, often very similar to their British equivalents. Boys appearing in 1880s school records wore striped cricket blazers and elaborate caps. Girls in hockey teams wore assorted plain dark skirts to ankle length and white blouses of various styles, usually with a low collar and worn with a loose, striped tie. The tie was the critical element. When they were the same color and design, ties served to unite appearances and thus created a uniform in spite of varying dress styles within a team.

In the nineteenth century senior girls wore women's fashionable styles to school, while junior girls wore shorter skirts, often with a white pinafore. Most boys wore versions of the men's suit throughout secondary school, having abandoned the short pants of childhood by ten or eleven years of age. The age of maturity for boys and girls was thus constructed differently in dress styles, and these distinctions in age hierarchy and gender continued as a feature of school dress. The development of school uniform styles also differed according to gender throughout the twentieth century, with boys' uniforms settling into a standard configuration very early on, while girls' uniforms were subject to numerous reconfigurations in parallel with changing ideas about the status of girls in education and their place in the world.

The prototypical junior boys' uniform first appeared in the 1900s. It was a straightforward adaptation of existing boys' wear, reformulated as uniform through regulation of components, consistency in color, and sometimes a school tie. This classic style consisted of a collared shirt with a breast pocket, short trousers in the same dark color, dark socks to the knee, often with a stripe at the top, and dark shoes or boots. A prevalence of short trousers at this time reflects the changed age status for boys, concurrent with an increase in school-leaving age to fourteen and symbolizing their deferred maturity. A British-style blazer was sometimes worn, and later (after the 1930s) more commonly a V-neck pullover in a similar shade with stripes at the neck edge. This classic junior boys' uniform remained remarkably static throughout the twentieth century, undergoing only minor changes and varying only in details among different schools. Most boys' uniforms were dark in overall color, with stripes in one or more contrasting colors to indicate school identity. Senior boys wore either men's suits or a more formal version of the junior boys' uniform, but including a tie and long trousers.

The first school uniform item for girls was the hatband in school colors, worn in city schools in the 1890s, suggesting that school identification was the main function. Many girls wore fashionable dress to school, but a simpler style increased in popularity during the 1900s. This rather plain style of combined separates

Girls' hockey team, New Zealand, 1910. In many girls' secondary schools, sports uniforms predated school uniforms. Photographer unknown. Courtesy of Elaine Webster.

consisted of a dark long skirt, white blouse, and tie. Worn by girls for both school and sports, versions of this style were also worn by women working in the retail and education sectors. This combination evolved into the first school uniform for girls during the 1910s. Still worn by senior girls in some schools into the 1920s, it was never completely standardized. Answering the need for appropriate dress for girls in the relatively new social category of secondary-school girl, it would have been more comfortable and practical than fashionable dress of the early 1900s. Although corsets may still have been worn, blouses were looser in fit and could be laundered more readily. This was especially important for gym classes. These classes were part of school curriculum and promoted as necessary for female health, and although the need for suitable gym clothing was being discussed, it had not yet been developed. Physical fitness and health were new ideals in "racial improvement," while girls' secondary education in general was promoted as vital to their anticipated futures as wives and mothers.

Tie wearing was a common feature of schoolgirls' dress from the 1890s and remained an important feature until at least the 1970s. Ties invariably add formality to appearances and remain coded as an element of male dress. By incorporating them into their uniforms, girls symbolically staked a claim to an education equal to that of boys, while the content and purpose of girls' education remained controversial into the 1970s. Ties were seldom worn by junior boys, although they were the norm in private schools and worn by many senior boys.

UNIFORMS ESTABLISHED

In the 1910s the gym frock was introduced into New Zealand, also from Britain. This was a truly innovative style. Suitable for both sports and school wear, it became almost universal as girls' school uniform for over fifty years. The gym frock could accommodate the full curriculum including study, sports, and notions of hygiene and decorum. By the late 1920s gym frocks had almost completely replaced skirt and blouse combinations as the preferred school wear for girls, and they were also worn by choice in schools without uniforms. Uniformity remained low, however, since they were worn with shirts of assorted styles, with or without ties, with blazers or cardigans, and black stockings or short socks. All these variations could be seen in one school.

In 1939 Peter Fraser, minister of education in New Zealand's first Labour government, set into motion education policy and reform in New Zealand, entrenching a distinctly egalitarian and democratic ideology that persists to the present day. At its heart was the dictum that every New Zealand child, from whatever background, had the right to a free education to the best of their ability and according to their needs. This replaced the system of educating children according to their backgrounds, such as educating rural children for a life of rural labor while reserving for upper-class boys the education necessary for entry to the professions. In theory, then, a child's education would no longer be limited by background, but only by his or her own ability and aspirations. This egalitarian ideology, although never fully realized, has been interpreted variously in different decades. Beginning in the late 1930s the ideology of equality implied sameness. This manifested as a tendency to value individuals primarily as members of groups, facilitated by school uniforms, which reduce differences in personal appearance and reinforce group identity. During the 1940s school uniforms were adopted in many secondary schools, while uniforms throughout New Zealand became more standardized, contributing to a marked rise in uniformity. Uniformity (the appearance of sameness among many) is achieved through availability and consistency in uniform items,

The girls on this sports team are wearing a summer uniform style that first appeared in New Zealand during the 1940s. This style was worn in some schools into the late 1960s; the photograph is dated 1950. Photographer unknown. Courtesy of Elaine Webster.

uniforms, including home science teachers and teachers responsible for military cadets. Variations in school uniforms were limited to gender, seniority of boys, and school identity. New Zealand in the 1950s was deeply conservative, and in schools the uniform supported this conformity and compliance with authority. But the winds of change were blowing. During this decade many new schools were established for families building homes in the new suburbs, and also to cater to the great postwar surge in population (the so-called baby boomers). Many of the new schools were coeducational. Many Māori moved to the city in search of work, and by the end of the decade most Māori students were educated in the state high schools rather than rural native schools.

Urban and population expansion were accompanied by economic prosperity in the 1960s and the advent of distinctly youth fashion, when young people no longer followed adult styles but preferred the new fashions of their own generation. Education was increasingly understood as contributing to democracy and economic growth, while new progressive education theories from America were infiltrating teaching in colleges and schools, placing greater emphasis on the development of the individual. The Currie Report of 1962 called for improvements in equality of opportunity, reinterpreting equality in relation to individuals, rather than equality in educational provision. This shifted emphasis away from the appearance of sameness and uniformity associated with regimented structures, parades, rote learning, and the authoritarian approach to teaching. Something new was called for.

These changes produced a radical shift in uniform style and practices. Completely new and diverse styles of uniforms appeared. Simple tunics or separates were introduced, although uniform changes were only for girls. Some schools introduced quite radical modern styles, such as pillbox hats, but the innovations were short-lived. Many schools introduced different uniforms for senior girls and different color combinations for summer and winter, so that schools as a whole became more diverse in appearances. A decline in uniformity was inevitable.

Students were also questioning uniform controls and practices. The main challenges to school authority were through hem lengths and hairstyles, especially boys' long hair, and in this students were not alone. Young teachers wore distinctly young fashions to school. Younger men wore their hair longer and grew mustaches, beards, and sideburns, in striking contrast to the clean-shaven look and "short back and sides" haircuts of the older generation. Boys' widespread uptake of this fashion was not surprising, since it provided an important opportunity for them to participate in youth culture and at the same time repudiate the schools' control over their bodies. Almost every boy grew his hair long, generating outrage in many quarters and highlighting intergenerational conflict. The issue of boys' hair was argued in the courts in *Edwards v. Onehunga High School Board of Trustees* in 1974. The New Zealand Court of Appeal ruled on whether a school board could pass a rule governing appearance, deciding that this was reasonable if it prevented "dangerous, outrageous, rebellious or socially offensive dress or hair styles." The courts also held that *reasonable* governing of dress and appearance was within the ambit of matters to be controlled by the school board, which still stands under section 72 of the Education Act of 1989. While schools have never relinquished their right to maintain appearance rules, acceptance of long hair was unavoidable.

Women teachers of all ages showed more of their bare skin and wore much shorter skirts. Some girls wore their skirts very

wear style (how the individual wears it), and also through regulation and enforcement.

Uniformity was not evident in New Zealand schools until the late 1930s, and by the 1950s it had become the norm. This time period straddles World War II, and without doubt the war also influenced attitudes and expectations regarding uniforms in general. Other factors also contributed, including growth in New Zealand's clothing manufacturing industry, stricter import limits, and New Zealand's small population, making uniformity not only possible but in some ways inevitable. As Elisabeth Wilson has pointed out, mass production of clothing always inclines appearances toward uniformity.

Once schools had taken more formal control over students' appearances, they were then committed to a regime of regulation, inspection, and enforcement. Standard uniform items had to be sourced and supplied, and schools also had to make provision for the changing seasons. New Zealand is a temperate country, and in parts of the country summer temperatures often reach the high 20s Celsius (80s Fahrenheit) or more. Uniforms consisted of layered components, many of them woolen, and they were simply too hot. The first summer uniforms for girls appeared in the 1940s concurrent with increased uniformity. These were adaptations of fashionable summer dress styles, many of which could be made at home using patterns supplied by the school, in regulation cloth. For boys summer uniforms were made of summer-weight fabric, and some were a lighter color but continued in much the same style.

REVOLUTION

The 1950s were a pinnacle in school uniform history in New Zealand. Uniforms were worn in nearly all secondary schools, and styles were remarkably consistent throughout the country. All dental nurses visiting schools, and some staff members, wore

Girls' typing class, about 1950, New Zealand. The highly formal appearance of these uniforms results from the combination of gym frock with shirt and tie, while the consistency of styles worn creates high uniformity, which reached a pinnacle in the 1950s. Photographer unknown. Courtesy of Elaine Webster.

short. Both teachers and students were less formal in their appearances, in keeping with wider fashion trends. Comfort and self-expression replaced respectability and conformity in many, although not all, schools. Tartan skirts or kilts first appeared in this decade, in what was to become another very long-lasting style. Worn with shirts, jerseys, or blazers, this combination was widely adopted during the 1970s and 1980s and continues into the 2000s as the most common secondary-school uniform for girls. New summer styles of uniform appeared for junior girls, many based on a new style of a semifitted tunic dress. Hats and gloves were still compulsory in some schools, although efforts were made to modernize them, creating some quite striking effects, but by the end of the 1970s they had been abandoned. In schools making even small changes or introducing distinctions, the result was fragmentation of overall appearance of the school, reflecting the shift from unity to plurality.

The changes begun in the 1960s accelerated, and in the early 1970s more radical changes in the uniform practices of many schools were evident. Probably the most radical change was the introduction of mufti for senior students. Mufti is when students wear their own choice of dress to school. This was a logical extension of changing education policy in a climate of progressive liberalism. Senior students were given more opportunities for participation and decision making, making the uniform an anachronism, at least for this group. Nearly all schools allowed their students to wear mufti for the last one or two years of school, and several schools abandoned the uniforms entirely. A few schools retained their uniforms and even

increased their formality, identifying with tradition and conservatism instead.

Senior boys' uniforms underwent changes in this time. Some suits were modernized, but most were abandoned in favor of uniform-style trousers and blazers, effectively introducing an explicit school uniform style for this group. In some schools senior boys wore men's summer walking shorts with knee-length socks, replicating an acceptable men's business style. In all cases senior boys' status remained an important distinction, and their uniforms continued to reflect the formality of men's business dress, anticipating their likely futures. Future expectations for girls remained ambiguous, although generally they were expected to include active participation in fashion. Fashion concessions were the norm, as schools have always allowed a degree of fashion participation through hem lengths and volumes, position of the waistline, and hairstyles. Both girls and boys participated in fashion to some extent, although, unlike boys, girls were given regular updates in school uniform styles, especially summer styles.

UNISEX AND INFORMAL UNIFORMS

Explicitly unisex dress appeared in society, fashion, and the media during the late 1960s, and by the mid-1970s women could choose to wear trousers in most workplaces. While some women teachers wore trousers in school trousers were not common as a uniform option for girls until the 1990s. From the early days of secondary schools both boys and girls had worn ties and blazers, so that elements of unisex school wear were already commonplace on a limited basis. In the 1970s the classic V-neck boys' school jerseys began to be worn by girls, and by the 1980s they were worn as unisex uniform items in many schools. This and other unisex uniform items reduced gender distinctions, helping to unify appearances in coeducational schools (about half of New Zealand's secondary schools have been coeducational since that time). Increased use of unisex uniform items reflects education policy of the time, when sexual equality in school was actively promoted. As unisex wear became more popular with school authorities, interestingly students themselves continued to make gender claims in their dress. As more girls wore jerseys, fewer senior boys did, and in many schools girls chose not to wear the trouser option, although they gave other reasons for this.

What proved to be another major style shift began in the 1980s with the introduction of cotton knit uniform items, especially the polo shirt, spelling the end of ties and, within ten years, ousting the school jersey as well. A more casual approach to appearances characterized the 1980s, and teachers also wore more relaxed styles, such as sports shoes. Patterns of uniformity were changing, as uniform choices contracted in some schools and proliferated in others. By the 1990s most junior boys wore long trousers, if only in winter. Other distinctions based on age and gender were removed, a trend assisted by cotton knit shirts. These shirts were unisex, modern, easy to care for, low in cost, informal, comfortable, and adaptable to different sizes and shapes. In a changing economic climate many of these features were desirable yet also served to underline differences between state and private or denominational schools, where traditional and formal uniforms had been retained.

During the 1990s many schools adopted corporate-style uniforms. This followed neoliberal reforms made in the education and other social sectors in the late 1980s promoting individualism, competition, and "user pays" (a policy in which end users or consumers pay full costs for services previously funded through state revenue) and reformulating egalitarianism as parity and equity. The concept of school image emerged, distinct from reputation, as schools began to describe themselves in marketing terms and to compete for students. Efforts to generate and market school image naturally included the uniform, while success in school was crucial in a period of high unemployment. Schools linked success with the increased formality, higher uniformity, and reduced uniform options associated with more traditional, conservative schools. Mufti came to be associated with lack of discipline, and many schools reduced their mufti options. Schools were more clearly divided than previously according to class, and students were expected to conform to the school. Although democratic participation, individuality, and personal choice had been fostered through mufti in the 1970s, the ideology of success in the 1990s was not so much personal as material. Success was also interpreted as belonging to both the individual and the school. School uniforms settled into their narrowest range since the 1950s, reflecting this decline in plurality.

Although for many sectors of New Zealand society the political climate of the 1990s was harsh, during this time Māori students made some important gains in terms of cultural status and distinctions. The Education Act of 1989 embedded the principles of biculturalism into schools, interpreted by many school boards during the 1990s as (among other things) requiring them to allow Māori students to wear *taonga* (items of cultural significance to them) with the uniform. Typically these items are bone or greenstone pendants, and they are widely worn. Allowing some cultural expression has became an acceptable dimension of school uniform in New Zealand, reducing monoculturalism and indirectly benefiting students from other cultures. This may partly explain why Muslim head scarves have not posed a problem in New Zealand.

Most schools are involved in uniform sales to some extent, and many provide assistance with uniform purchase to families

Transition in uniform styles can be seen in this 1975 photograph from the records of a private boys' school in New Zealand. Senior and junior boys are wearing the new uniforms, replacing senior suits, while one junior boy is wearing the old-style jacket and short trousers, with his V-neck jersey just visible underneath his suit jacket. Photographer unknown. Courtesy of Elaine Webster.

experiencing financial hardship. Limited assistance is available through government agencies. Cost of uniforms varies greatly between schools, and nearly always girls' uniforms are more expensive than those for boys.

SCHOOL UNIFORM PRACTICE

School uniforms in New Zealand have developed as a practice with a range of functions, some of which are particular to this country, and some that are common to uniforms elsewhere. School uniforms carry multiple identification functions, they create and maintain hierarchies between students, staff, and also age groups in the student body, and through their distinctions they are used by schools to define what matters. Since their inception school uniforms in New Zealand history have become more similar as uniformity increased, assisting in the formation of school identity and the creation of the wider identity of schoolgirl and schoolboy, symbolizing the cohesion of the New Zealand education system while inscribing a variety of cultural meanings, including gender and social class. School uniforms have also been instrumental in challenging such meanings. Students identified through their uniform as belonging to a particular school are also brought into a set of expectations concerning their behavior on and off school grounds. While this was an extension of school power onto the bodies of children, it also made schools responsible for them and allowed schools to partake in student success, creating educational relationships based on school identity.

As Jennifer Craik has pointed out, enforcement is a central issue. Uniformity makes enforcement practices necessary, involving the school in regulation, based on defining and limiting uniform items and wearing styles, and consequences for noncompliance. Inspection levels in New Zealand schools range from very detailed, including measurement of hem length, use of hair ties, and even regulation underwear, to a more cursory inspection of the group to identify only what is obviously out of place. Compliance and enforcement can be seen in levels of uniformity, while school identity can be maintained at a minimal level through the use of school uniform items and colors. In New Zealand it is more usual for schools to accept a range of formality and compliance consistent with identification functions. In most schools senior students are provided with an opportunity to dress in more formal uniform, while more informal appearance at junior levels is allowed for. While discipline and control are always part of uniform practice, they are the primary function in only a minority of New Zealand schools.

STUDENTS' VIEWS

Students from a range of schools were interviewed in 2004. In general, they supported the practice of school uniform, very much depending on how this was enforced and the extent of uniformity required. School uniforms meant different things depending on students' own sense of themselves and their relationships with the school. When uniformity was not too high, students experienced uniforms as "protection" or "shelter." This was strongly linked to the capacity of school uniform to minimize differences in financial backgrounds, and to form a kind of social camouflage during the junior years. Thus development of the individual was fostered *inside* the group, not at the expense of the group, strengthening group belonging and participation in school.

Wearing the uniform reinforced the feeling of belonging in the school, while students acknowledged the need for some enforcement to maintain any kind of uniform and to allow the positive functions of uniform to operate. They understood uniforms as increasing social tolerance and allowing social interactions across social boundaries. Most students did not need major differences in dress to feel they were expressing themselves, yet some self-expression was vital for well-being. This need could be met at the level of detail. Uniform practices allowing some self-expression support both individuation and group participation, framing these processes in positive relation to each other rather than as competing goals.

These specific meanings of school uniform can only exist in social and historical contexts where these values are supported by education ideologies and school practices. School uniforms in New Zealand have supported democratic ideals through much of the twentieth century. Through multiple changes and reversals, school uniforms have maintained a breadth of possibilities consistent with the persistently fluid class system and egalitarian ideals of New Zealand society.

References and Further Reading

Brookes, B., A. Cooper, and R. Law, eds. *Sites of Gender: Women, Men and Modernity in Southern Dunedin 1890–1939*. Auckland, NZ: Auckland University Press, 2003.

Brunsma, David L. *The School Uniform Movement and What It Tells Us about American Education*. Lanham, MD: ScarecrowEducation, 2004.

Craik, J. *Uniforms Exposed: From Conformity to Transgression*. New York: Berg, 2005.

Fry, R. *It's Different for Daughters: A History of the Curriculum for Girls in New Zealand Schools, 1900–1975*. Educational Research Series. Wellington: New Zealand Council for Educational Research, 1985.

Joseph, N. *Uniforms and Non-Uniforms: Communication through Clothing*. New York: Greenwood Press, 1986.

McVeigh, B.J. *Wearing Ideology: State, Schooling, and Self-Presentation in Japan*. London: Berg, 2000.

Middleton, S., and H. May. *Teachers Talk Teaching 1915–1995: Early Childhood, Schools and Teachers' Colleges*. Palmerston North, NZ: Dunmore Press, 1997.

Openshaw, R., G. Lee, and H. Lee. *Challenging the Myths: Rethinking New Zealand's Educational History*. Palmerston North, NZ: Dunmore Press, 1993.

Webster, E. "History in Photographs: A Century of School Uniforms in New Zealand." In *Proceedings of the Fifth Annual Symposium of the New Zealand Costume and Textile Section: Unleashing Collections: Cloth, Costume and Culture*, 82–88. Wellington: New Zealand Costume and Textile Section, 2006.

Webster, E.I. "New Zealand School Uniforms in the Era of Democracy: 1965 to 1975." *Costume: Journal of the Costume Society* 42 (2008): 169–186.

Wilson, E. *Adorned in Dreams: Fashion and Modernity*. London: Virago, 1985.

Elaine Webster

See also The Social Significance of Institutional Dress in New Zealand.

Wearable Art in New Zealand

- Wearable Art: An Overview
- Entries in the Wearable Art Awards
- Film and Television
- Cultural Tourism
- Pasifika Design
- New Zealand Designer Fashion

The term *wearable art* frequently summons images of tie-dyed, knitted, or crocheted dress that often quirkily references the personal iconography of the individual wearing it but that is not original in conceptualization and design. The New Zealand Wearable Art Awards, begun in 1987, challenge this perception. With a design goal to take art "off the wall and out of static display," this annual competition, which attracts international entries, and which is also a theatrical event in its own right, lays down the gauntlet for innovative design that redefines and challenges what it is physically possible for the human body to support. As a consequence, the Wearable Art Awards have energized New Zealand's film, television, and tourism industries, the broader visual arts community, and designer fashion, as well as a number of established design competitions.

WEARABLE ART: AN OVERVIEW

Historically, wearable art, or art-to-wear as it is known in North America, emerged out of the counterculture aesthetics of the 1960s. The term loosely referred to the customized surface design of dress using a variety of techniques, such as embroidery, beadwork, painting, dyeing, and patchwork, as a statement against the generic look of mass-produced dress, especially jeans. JoAnn Stabb has identified the West Coast of North America, specifically the San Francisco area, as the home of wearable art, where customizing one's dress was a popular do-it-yourself activity that resulted in dress with a strongly autobiographical content. For example, scraps of lace from an elderly relative's dress, or memorabilia from an individual's involvement in an organization or event, would be patched, embroidered, or beaded onto dress. In addition to this personal imagery, signs and symbols appropriated from Eastern religions provided a popular visual resource and reflected a growing interest in Eastern belief systems. Alexandra Jacopetti has stated that many, herself included, found the doctrines of Eastern religions difficult to understand in literary form but could relate to the principles of the religion when expressed visually.

Unlike wearable art, which has in the past been created with a personal intent, New Zealand Wearable Art is the outcome of a design competition held annually in September. New Zealand Wearable Art is not necessarily wearable in the sense understood in North America. In New Zealand, Wearable Art is a design created to be worn and performed in by a model, not worn by the individual who makes it, and not made to be sold in art and craft

clothing boutiques for other individuals to purchase and wear. For the awards show the design is worn and performed by a model, not the designer. It is a criterion of acceptance that an entry represents a cohesive design concept and thought process. For example, "Binding Thoughts," the 2003 supreme award-winning design by Greta Tapper, was created in response to her experience of depression when she felt that her "hands were bound" and she was unable to express her thoughts. The design consisted of a dress that had been scrawled with words. Attached to the front and back of the skirt of the dress were two large open books with blank pages. The words on the body of the dress represent the thoughts that a person who suffers depression is often unable to articulate—hence the blank pages of the open books. The female model who exhibited this design at the Wearable Art Awards had her mouth bound and her hands chained to her sides, further emphasizing Tapper's own experience of depression. "Binding Thoughts" represented depression as an entity. The cohesiveness of Tapper's design translated a personal experience into a form that made a poignantly universal statement.

The Wearable Art Awards initially began as a one-off promotion for the William Higgins Gallery, a small rural art cooperative situated in the Nelson region, located at the top of New Zealand's South Island. Such was the success of the first awards that Suzie Moncrieff, the awards organizer, decided to hold them again the following year. The competition has grown phenomenally since. Part of the awards show's early success is due to the community support it received from the region in which it was launched. Nelson, one of New Zealand's smaller cities, is home to a vibrant arts community, which rallied behind Moncrieff, volunteering hours working behind the scenes of the awards show to ensure the survival of the competition. This community spirit had a large payoff in terms of annually boosting incomes in the region through tourist promotion of the event. In 2003 the final awards show was held in Nelson. Since 2004 the awards have been held in New Zealand's capital city, Wellington. The success of the awards meant that it had outgrown the resources of the Nelson region and needed a larger venue and city infrastructure to continue to grow.

In 2001 the New Zealand Wearable Art Awards were rebranded the World of WearableArt. The rebranding project included the adoption of the acronym WOW—a play on the name World of WearableArt, as well as "wow" as the hoped-for audience response to the extravaganza that is the awards. Rebranding the awards coincided with the opening, in Nelson, of the World of WearableArt and Collectable Cars museum. The museum includes information on the history of the awards as well as a display of past entries, including the award-winning designs. The car collection is housed separately from the Wearable Art exhibition, but props and scenery from Wearable Art shows are creatively displayed alongside the cars to situate them within a historical context. Although the awards show has moved to Wellington, the Wearable Art office remains in Nelson, as does the museum.

The design aesthetic of wearable art in the New Zealand context reflects Moncrieff's fine arts background in sculpture. Moncrieff set the awards' design goal, and through her ongoing involvement with the competition she continues to monitor the standard of entries, thus ensuring that her design instruction is constantly

Entries are judged blind and exhibited in an onstage extravaganza of music, choreographed dance routines, and small performances. In 1999, for example, a trapeze artist performed an introduction piece to announce the section titled The Ties That Bind. In line with that year's millennial theme this particular section sought creative interpretations on marriage through the ages, the trapeze act symbolizing enduring ideas embodied in wedlock—trust, partnership, and support.

ENTRIES IN THE WEARABLE ART AWARDS

In spite of Moncrieff's sculpture-oriented vision, initial entries in the Wearables, as they are affectionately known, reflected former types of interpretation in wearable art and included creative hand-knits and tie-dyed and felted garments, some of which had a New Zealand twist; one jersey, for instance, featured the tui, a New Zealand native bird.

The inaugural supreme award winner was Niki Jiménez, a sculptor from the Nelson region. Her winning entry, "Wild Walker," however, did not reflect her usual kinetic sculptural aesthetic. At that time Jiménez was experimenting with movement in sculpture using ball bearings, springs, and other devices to set her work in motion by touch or wind. Her entry in the Wearables was quite different; it was static, and there was nothing in her entry that moved in the way her sculptures did. "Wild Walker" consisted of an animal-print skirt, a breastplate featuring a big foot, and a decorated staff and cap. The entry was constructed from textiles and cardboard. The following year another resident from the Nelson area, Deborah Quaife-Macfarlane, took away the supreme award. Quaife-Macfarlane's entry, "Self-Defence," was a papier mâché dress with conical-shaped breasts and a tulip-style skirt. The boldly colored dress was painted with images representative of the Nelson region, including flowers, fish, and sunshine—the region has one of the highest recorded number of sunshine hours in New Zealand. Although "Self-Defence" retained the dress form, it was an advance from "Wild Walker," as it exaggerated and extended from the body and could have worked as a sculpture off the body.

The supreme award–winning design acts as a visual signifier, propelling the competition forward, with entrants trying to outdo the innovative interpretation of wearable art offered up by the preceding year's winner. In the beginning there were few of these trailblazer works. It was not until 1991 that an entry appeared that took the interpretation of wearable art to another level, one beyond references to the earlier meaning of wearable art, to the sort of work Moncrieff had in mind when she set her design instructions.

The entry "Pallas Athene" was designed by Donna Demente, a multimedia artist who paints, holds mask-making workshops, and is involved in community performance and installation work. Originally from Auckland, since 1995 Demente has lived in the lower South Island city of Oamaru, where she is actively involved in the preservation of Oamaru's Victorian heritage. In 2007 she worked from the Grainstore Gallery, an art cooperative of which she is a member, the gallery being based in the city's heritage precinct. Demente is well known in Oamaru, both for her art practice and for her unique style of dressing, which is Victorian-inspired with a contemporary twist.

"Pallas Athene," which won the supreme award, consisted of a papier mâché torso of the female figure. The torso incorporated

"Binding Thoughts" by Greta Tapper, the winner of the supreme award at New Zealand's World of WearableArt Awards in 2003. The dress is scrawled with words, and two giant open books with blank pages are attached to the front and back. The model has her mouth covered and her hands chained to her sides. Photograph courtesy of WOW® Ltd: "Binding Thoughts," Greta Tapper, Nelson, New Zealand.

challenged. The instruction is to take art off the wall and out of static display, to adorn the body in wildly wonderful ways, and to celebrate this creativity in a lavish and unique onstage spectacular that will inspire all.

The awards are structured around a number of themed sections. These vary annually, and there are also a number of special prizes. Popular sections include the Bizarre Bra category, Illuminated Illusion (for this section entrants are required to use materials that will glow in the dark), Pacific (later renamed Oceania), Avant-Garde, and Weddings. In some years one-off categories are introduced to reflect current events; for instance, for the 1999 awards the entire show was themed around the Millennium. The winning design from each section, and those that receive a special award, go forward for consideration for the supreme award. The supreme award is presented to the design that takes the interpretation of wearable art to a new level and thus lays down a challenge for the succeeding year's entrants to go one better in their interpretation of Moncrieff's design goal.

three casts of female faces and included symbolic references to Athena, the Greek goddess of wisdom, craft skills, and prudent warfare. Athena is also known as Pallas Athene or Athene. Reviewing the 1991 awards, Helen Schamroth has noted that "Pallas Athene" had a "mobile sculptural quality" that made it significantly different from entries that had gone before. Schamroth has noted the way in which in Demente's entry the body became the "vehicle for transporting the idea, the image having a strong identity of its own" (1999, p. 32). "Pallas Athene" was a reinterpretation of a protest piece created by Demente to express her objection to a Miss New Zealand pageant. Demente was protesting at what she saw as the dehumanization of models by the fashion industry. As Naomi O'Connor has noted, the idea was to put the body itself on parade, by attaching faces to the body. Demente was working with the idea of giving the body a face and a sense of identity. She felt that this sense of identity was denied to the contestants in the Miss New Zealand competition, where there is a strong emphasis on the body itself, its measurements, and how the women look in certain items of dress.

After her 1991 win Demente became a regular entrant in the awards. In 1996 she entered her medieval-themed wedding entourage. Titled "Conjunctio," and accompanied by a large cast of fringe characters, the work had its first outing at the artist's own nuptials, a public performance piece in the Oamaru Public Gardens in June 1996. Demente was one of a number of entrants in 1991 to use materials that did not have a fiber basis. Hiro Ejima, a Nelson painter and sculptor, entered a cape titled "Miracle Travel," which was made from recycled compact discs and old recording tape. Ejima, an awards judge in 1990, had noticed that most of the entrants in that year were still working in fiber. This prompted him to design "Miracle Travel." As the model paraded Ejima's entry down the awards stage, structured as a runway, the discs caught the light, entrancing the audience with a kaleidoscope of color.

In 1994 Moncrieff was forced to assess the viability of the Wearables. Audience numbers had remained static for three years, and the awards were struggling financially—Moncrieff had mortgaged her home in 1993 to ensure the show's continuation. In efforts to revamp the competition the wool and knit/weave sections were retired, both sections that dictated a fiber medium, a medium preconstrained by its association with the older meaning of wearable art. Likewise in 1996 the silk section was retired, and in 1998 special awards for the most creative work in silk and wool were established. The demise of the fiber-dictated sections further encouraged entrants to experiment with materials like metal, wood, electronics, plastic, and engineering technologies. The supreme winner in 1994 was Mandi Kingsbury for her entry "Magpie." "Magpie" was constructed from pieces of aluminum, party whistles, chains, and bottle tops, and it made a cacophonous sound as the model walked down the stage. Adding to the noise were "chirping" shoes made from bellows. Kingsbury has a background in textile design and, some time after her win, moved to Dubai to work as a freelance stylist and fashion and jewelry designer.

The materials entrants now use for the design of their wearable art entries are numerous and often surprising. Past entries have included designs made from fish skins, old telephones, cutlery, vehicle license plates, and strips of bacon sealed inside plastic. Not all Wearable entries are serious in statement and intent. The popularity of the Bizarre Bra section is due largely to the number

"Pallas Athene" by Donna Demente was the winner of the supreme award at New Zealand's World of WearableArt Awards in 1991, and it was noted for its innovation at the time. It consisted of a papier mâché female torso with several faces sculpted on it, interpreted as a symbolic protest at what the artist saw as the dehumanization of models by the fashion industry. Photograph courtesy of WOW® Ltd: "Pallas Athene", Donna Demente, Oamaru, New Zealand.

of witty interpretations on the brassiere. Design educator Sue Prescott's 1996 Bizarre Bra entry, "A Lick and a Promise," epitomizes this wit. The design consists of two cups held in place by gold-gloved hands. The cups overflow with large swirls of vanilla ice cream, each topped with a "nipple" of pink ice cream. Prescott's brassiere design is completed by the model's red sequined hat, which is festooned with pink tulle and brimming and with an abundance of ice creams in the cone.

FILM AND TELEVISION

In 1999 the supreme award went to "Superminx," designed by Simon Hames. This was a significant design, because it tested the limits of what is possible for the models, who wear the Wearable Art entries, to exhibit. "Superminx," comprising two imposing feline-themed thrones, required each model to swagger across the stage on the palms of their hands and the soles of their feet, the models' backs becoming the "seat" for each throne. The title of the work referred to car parts Hames had used in the construction of the design, parts from his Hillman Hunter Superminx. Constructed primarily of velvet, Lycra, plywood, and possum fur, the two thrones had high backs and feline faces.

Hames is a freelance prop maker who works in New Zealand's burgeoning film industry. His association with the Wearables has given his curriculum vitae a distinct edge. As well as being a supreme award winner, he was also a member of the awards art department, creating props for the annual shows. So Hames is one of a number of entrants whose career in the New Zealand film and television industry has a synergetic association with the Wearables.

Susan Holmes, an awards stalwart who has variously worked as a clothing designer and a teacher (running textile-dyeing and wearable art workshops), also has a background in costume design. She designed the costumes for the television series *Greenstone*, *Hercules*, and *Xena*. Holmes has been quoted as saying that the Wearable Art awards have given her the opportunity to design without the commercial and characterization constraints that are an inevitable aspect of her clothing design and television work. Holmes first entered the awards in 1990. In 1996 she won the supreme award for "Dragon Fish," a fantastical creature made from hand-painted silk, basket weave, and cane. "Dragon Fish" features a large wingspan and a long silk tail. The model ran in this entry to give flight to the silk wings and the tail. In motion the weightlessness of the silk conveyed the ethereality of a creature in flight.

A newer, regular entrant in the awards is Carly "Tree" Harris, a costume technician at Weta Workshop in Wellington. Weta Workshop is a visual effects company, which notably won a number of Academy Awards for the visual effects in the New Zealand film director Peter Jackson's *Lord of the Rings* trilogy. Harris was involved in this project, along with Jackson's next venture, *King Kong* (2005), and the Andrew Adamson–directed *The Chronicles of Narnia: The Lion, the Witch, and the Wardrobe* (2005). She has also created "texture" in animation, through the creation of prototype costumes for the film version of the Microsoft game Halo.

When not working for Weta, Harris spends her time creating entries for the Wearables, for which she has had considerable success, as well as working as a stage costumer and dresser for Wellington-based theater productions. Harris sees a unique creative partnership between her work at Weta and her work as a wearable artist and for the theater. The work she enters in the Wearables helps her to understand how a design can be performed. She has had a number of successes. In 2006 she won the Avant-Garde section for a work titled "She Looks Good in a Sack," a design that played with the idea of creating a glamorous dress using unconventionally glamorous materials such as sacking.

In recognition of the creative contribution of the Wearables to the New Zealand film and television industry, Weta established a special award in 2005. This award is annually presented to the design that pushes the boundaries between wearable art and design for film and television. The award is blind-judged by Richard Taylor, the founder of Weta. The inaugural winner was Harris for an entry titled "Caged Bird."

CULTURAL TOURISM

Moncrieff's dream is to have the Wearables exhibited on a worldwide stage, possibly through regional competitions. The Wearables has subsequently formed a close relationship with Tourism New Zealand, which has used condensed versions of the Wearables shows abroad to promote New Zealand. In 1995 the Wearables won the Best Cultural Tourism category of the New Zealand Tourism Awards. The following year, 1996, the Wearables won the Outstanding Achievement in the Arts section at the Fifth New Zealand Event Management and Event Marketing Conference. In the same year Tourism New Zealand invited the Wearables to Singapore to perform a thirty-five-minute Taste of New Zealand Wearable Art show at Kia Ora New Zealand, the board's main trade event in Southeast Asia. Moncrieff has since returned to Singapore and has also shown mini-versions of the Wearables in Japan and Dubai. These snapshot shows assist in promoting the awards and encouraging entries from the Middle East and Asia. The Wearables also receive entries from Australian designers, with the Australian experimental *shibori* (a Japanese-inspired fabric-dyeing technique) artist Patricia Black being a notable and regular entrant.

Helen Clark, when New Zealand Prime Minister and minister for culture, was a long-term supporter of the Wearables

"Superminx" by Simon Hames, which won the supreme award at New Zealand's World of WearableArt Awards in 1999. The costumes were constructed of velvet, Lycra, plywood, possum fur, and parts of Hames's Hilman Hunter Superminx. Dressed as feline-themed thrones, the models had to move on their palms and soles with their backs forming the "seat," which set a new precedent of physical difficulty in the competition. Photograph courtesy of WOW® Ltd: "Superminx," Simon Hames, Wellington, New Zealand.

and its partnership with cultural tourism. In 2002 Moncrieff enlisted Clark as a model for the awards show. Clark modeled a Pacific-themed design made by Holmes and titled "The Crest of the Wave." The image fused a national identity, in the form of Ms. Clark, with a garment that embodied an aspect of the New Zealand environment. This union revealed the burgeoning relationship of New Zealand Wearable Art with cultural tourism. Indeed, Wearable Art has come to be perceived as a New Zealand cultural icon.

PASIFIKA DESIGN

Since 1993 the number of Pacific-inspired designs in the Wearables has increased. This was due to the establishment of a Pacific section, later renamed the Oceania, and the parallel development of Pasifika fashion shows. These latter shows fuse traditional Pacific themes with a unique urban Pacific identity. The Pasifika fashion shows are not wearable art in the original sense, or in the New Zealand Wearable Art sense. But they are an important design competition on the New Zealand calendar, and there is an obvious cross-flow of ideas between Wearable Art and Pasifika fashion. In both competitions the designers utilize the competition to make statements on Pacific issues, ideas, and identities. A regular entrant in the Wearable Art awards in the 1990s was Niwhai Tupaea of the Pacific Sisters, a collective of urban Pacific multimedia artists who work together on fashion-related projects and have a significant involvement in the Pasifika fashion shows.

The Pasifika fashion shows began in 1993 under the direction of Rosanna Raymond, an Auckland model and member of the Pacific Sisters. The shows were initially held as part of a larger community project, called Pasifika. Pasifika, an annual festival that takes place in March, celebrates the diversity of Pacific peoples through static displays, performance, and food stalls. The fashion shows were only an aspect of the Pasifika festival. The first Pasifika fashion shows were held in association with the Auckland City Council and SPINDA (South Pacific Island Nations Development Association). Day shows were held at the Pasifika Festival at Western Springs, an outdoor events venue in Auckland. Evening shows were held at the City Finance Plaza (1993, 1994) and Auckland Town Hall (1995).

Raymond had been asked to help organize the fashion show because of her involvement in Pacific Island fashion activism. In the early 1990s Raymond was exploring the European construction of the "exotic dusky maiden look" in Polynesian tourist brochures. She wanted to reclaim the dusky maiden image and promote an urban Pacific vision through fashion, a vision that contradicted ideas of modesty inherited from missionaries. Raymond was dismayed at the lack of involvement Pacific Islanders had in fashion. For example, Pacific Islanders were never featured in fashion advertisements. She noticed a renaissance in Pacific Island and Māori culture generally, particularly in music and the contemporary arts, but she felt that Pacific Island street styles and fashion were being overlooked.

The original Pasifika fashion categories were: traditionally inspired, three-piece collection, wearable arts, urban Pasifika streetwear, Pasifika evening wear, menswear, and bridal wear. Early on, two distinctive categories of design began to emerge, urban Pacific street- and work-wear and modifications of traditional designs based around the *mu'umu'u* and *puletasi*. The mu'umu'u was introduced to Pacific women by missionaries and is a loose-fitting dress made of lightweight material. The puletasi is a figure-hugging version of the mu'umu'u, often worn by young women.

In 1996 the Auckland City Council took over the running of the event, holding it at the St. James Theatre in central Auckland, which separated it from the main Pasifika Festival at Western Springs. The council, however, wanted to focus on the larger Pasifika festival, rather than just the fashion show. At this point Stan Wolfgramm, a Pacific Island male model, producer, and businessman of Tongan/Cook Island descent, stepped up and took over the idea. The show was rebranded Style Pasifika, and the competition expanded to include ten categories: Painted Body Art, Traditionally Inspired, Asia Pasifika, Pasifika Hero, Pasifika 3-Piece Collection, Urban Pasifika Streetwear, Pasifika Menswear, Pasifika Evening Wear, Pasifika Bridal, and Parent and Child. The introduction of the Pasifika Hero category in 2003 celebrates and acknowledges *fa'afafine* and New Zealand's gay community. The fa'afafine are boys who are raised as girls in Samoan culture, where they have traditionally shared women's work; however, they are becoming more Westernized, and as a result comparisons have been made with the drag queen. The Pasifika Hero category is to date the only section in New Zealand design competitions to exclusively celebrate the gay community. Entries in Pasifika are not restricted to Pacific Islanders, although the Pacific Island people run the show and set the parameters and boundaries.

NEW ZEALAND DESIGNER FASHION

The impact of the Wearables on New Zealand designer fashion was officially recognized in 1993 by the country's premier fashion design award, the Benson and Hedges Fashion Design Awards, with the establishment of an Avant-Garde section. The Benson and Hedges ran from 1964 to 1998. Government legislation banning tobacco sponsorship resulted in rebranding of the awards as the Smokefree Fashion Design Awards in 1996. The competition folded in 1998 because of an inability to find another suitable sponsor. When the Benson and Hedges/Smokefree awards collapsed, the Wearables picked up the Avant-Garde section, thus allowing room for fashion designers to create designs without commercial constraints.

The Avant-Garde section of the Benson and Hedges Awards was designed to cater to the steady flow of what were idiomatically described as "whacky" creations, inspired by the Wearables. Sian Robyns notes that organizers of the Benson and Hedges Awards described the inclusion of a fashion avant-garde section as a move to "separate the 'weird' and wonderful from the mainstream." This move placated critics of the Benson and Hedges Awards, who believed the event had lost touch with the commercial reality of fashion. Inaugural entries in the Benson and Hedges Avant-Garde section included a hand-dyed toga decorated with inflated condoms, a gown embellished with surrealism-inspired lips, a vinyl corset and hooped skirt, and a dress made of papier mâché and feathers.

Entries gradually became more sophisticated. Entrants in the 1997 Avant-Garde section were asked to create a garment themed around what they believed the world would be like in 2005. The award was taken by design educators Deborah Crowe and Kim Fraser for "Dual Outlook" (1997). The garment consisted of a visor and body shield made of woven copper and a Lycra sheath made of copper-coated polyester. The women had envisioned the "future" to be a world in which people would need protection and healing from a technologically saturated environment. This prompted them to use copper, known for its healing and energizing properties, as their primary material.

Annah Stretton, the name behind the New Zealand fashion design label Annah S., visually acknowledged the impact of the Wearables on her design practice when she launched her winter 2005 collection, titled Feral Beauty, at New Zealand Fashion Week 2004. The finale design for the Feral Beauty collection was "Beauty and the Beast," a beaded wedding dress worn with a boar's-head mask. "Beauty and the Beast" was designed for the Avant-Garde section of the 2004 Wearable Art Awards, where it was highly commended. Stretton's incorporation of her Wearable Art entry into her New Zealand Fashion Week show is an acknowledgement of the way that the Wearables energize New Zealand designer fashion. It is also a reminder that prior to the establishment of New Zealand Fashion Week in 2001, the Wearables were one of few avenues for New Zealand designers to showcase their talent nationally, or even internationally, if their design was one of the ones selected to tour in the minishows held abroad to promote cultural tourism.

There are a number of other significant and well-established events on the design competition calendar in New Zealand that have a wearable art component. Three long-standing competitions include the Hokonui Fashion Design Awards, Trash for Fashion, and Ag Art Wear. Although each was established with a different agenda, there is a flow of ideas between the competitions in terms of design and the multimedia nature of the shows.

The Hokonui Fashion Design Awards began in 1988, a year after the Wearables started. Initially the competition was a "make and model" event for design talent in the rural township of Gore, at the bottom of the South Island, New Zealand. It has since grown to a design competition of international standing, with entrants from overseas. In addition to the typical fashion design categories of Menswear, Three-piece, and Evening, it includes an Art Couture section to allow designers freedom to express their creativity. Like the Wearables, the Hokonui Fashion Design Awards are open to anyone and attract a mix of students from fashion design institutions and individuals with a flair for design.

Trash for Fashion was established by the Waitakere City Council (Auckland) in 1996 as an after-party for those involved in Keep Waitakere Beautiful's Operation Spring Clean. Trash for Fashion aims to encourage the design of dress out of recycled, inorganic, and organic materials. All entries must adhere to the recycle and reuse philosophy to the extent that no staples or other introduced materials are allowed, forcing entrants to become creative in working out how their designs will hold together on the body. Like the Wearable Art Awards, Trash for Fashion is now a registered event.

A smaller and unique wearable art competition is Ag Art Wear. Ag Art Wear is associated with the Mystery Creek Agricultural Fieldays, which are held annually in the Waikato region of the central North Island. The competition was started in 1995 to make the fieldays appeal to a wider audience. Entrants are required to apply innovative thinking to translate farm materials into wearable art.

Complementing these professional design competitions are a raft of grassroots wearable art competitions that take place throughout New Zealand, either connected to festivals such as winter carnivals, as fund-raising events, or as therapeutic creative activities in communities, schools, and homes for the elderly. There are also a number of commercial events with a wearable arts twist, which owe their origins to the New Zealand Wearable Art Awards. Speights Brewery annually hosts a "beerable" art award. Targeted largely at the postsecondary student population, entrants are required to construct wearable art using only Speights products; this could be bottle tops, posters, and advertising material. Primary and secondary schools also frequently hold their own little wearable art awards, while the Wearables organizers actively seek entries from design institutions within the postsecondary school sector. The Wearable Art Awards organizers encourage these grassroots competitions, which they view as essential for igniting the imagination of a new generation of New Zealand wearable artists.

Wearable art in New Zealand has come to simultaneously refer to the trademarked event, WearableArt, launched by Moncrieff in 1987, and an innovative attitude toward designing for the body. This attitude lends a unique vibrancy to the country's tourism, film and television, visual art, and designer fashion communities.

References and Further Reading

Colchester, Chloë, ed. Clothing the Pacific. Oxford and New York: Berg, 2003.

Dale, Julie Schafler. Art to Wear. New York: Abbeville Press, 1986.

Jacopetti, Alexandra. Native Funk and Flash: An Emerging Folk Art. San Francisco: Scrimshaw Press, 1974.

Leilua, Iulia. "Super Style." Spasifik (July/August 2004): 20–25.

Mallon, Sean, and Pandora Fulimalo Pereira. Pacific Art Niu Sila: The Pacific Dimension of Contemporary New Zealand Arts. Wellington, NZ: Te Papa Press, 2002.

O'Connor, Naomi. Wearable Art: Design for the Body. Nelson, NZ: Craig Potton Publishing, 1996.

Potton, Craig. Angels and Bacon: Wearable Art. Nelson, NZ: Craig Potton Publishing, 1993.

Robyns, Sian. "At the Cutting Edge." The Dominion (Wellington), 27 March 1993, 9.

Schamroth, Helen. "Wearable Art." Craft New Zealand 38 (Summer 1999): 31–32.

Smith, Natalie. "The Wearables and the Montana World of Wearable Art™ Awards: What It Is and What It Means." Journal of New Zealand Art History 25 (2005): 33–44.

Stabb, JoAnn C. "The Wearable Art Movement: A Critical Look at the State of the Art." Surface Design Journal 13 (Fall 1988): 29–35.

Taouma, Lisa. "'Doubleness of Meaning': Pasifika Clothing, Camp and Couture." In The Art of Clothing: A Pacific Experience, edited by Susanne Küchler and Graeme Were, 111–120. London: UCL Press, 2005.

Tuffery, Gena. "Rising Star, Cathy Harris." Next (January 2007): 36–37.

Natalie Smith

See also Pacific Sisters: Urban Pacific Art, Fashion, and Performance; Pacific Street Styles in Auckland.

Pacific Sisters: Urban Pacific Art, Fashion, and Performance

- Origins
- Forging Kaupapa
- Design Work
- Art and Performance

Under the banner "Pacific Sisters," a group of fashion designers, artists, performers, and musicians based in Aotearoa (New Zealand) began working together in the early 1990s. Of predominantly mixed Polynesian (a subgroup of Pacific peoples, including Māori, the first nation peoples of Aotearoa) and European heritage, their work has responded to the unique multicultural urban environment of Tamaki Makaurau (Auckland), home to the world's largest urban population of Pacific peoples. The group's dress design, art practice, and fashion and storytelling performances juxtapose different Pacific identities in an urban environment in order to inform and inspire. Their "fashion activism" is driven by desires to confront many assumptions about Pacific culture, renegotiating common Western stereotypes, as well as internal expectations of Pacific beauty, sexuality, and cultural behaviors. Their blend of Western and Pacific craft techniques and materials in their designs incorporates environmental considerations.

Initially at the fringes of arts practice, Pacific Sisters' emergence coincided with a new wave of urban Pacific arts and cultural expression. Their work, in which dress plays a central part, helped to forge a pathway into mainstream New Zealand popular culture. It later gained widespread recognition in Europe and the Pacific through participation in arts festivals and other events. Their art, linked to the body and performance, continues to recontextualize the wisdom and knowledge of the Pacific in a diverse urban domain. Coming together periodically around their collective work as designers, artists, and educators, their projects aim to improve the profile and network of creative peoples of the Pacific, symbolizing through dress and art their inherent values.

The following artists' statement accompanies the group's "21st Sentry Cyber Sister—An Urban Excessification Personification," a costume commissioned in 1998 for the permanent Pacific Collection of Te Papa, the Museum of New Zealand. It fully encapsulates their strong concerns and intentions: "She guards the door to our *whare* (house). She is the 'determinator' of all who enter. There is no room here for racism, trials and tribulations. Dedicated to the preservation of our tribal culture and our struggle towards self-determination. We recycle resources from our urban environment, traditional and contemporary fibers, to produce distressed deconstructed wearable art pieces that express our uniqueness as an urban tribe. While still following the paths created by our Ancestors, we are united in the cycle where our past meets our futures."

ORIGINS

The name Pacific Sisters was arrived at collectively after members of the group worked together on local theater productions doing wardrobe and styling. The name recognizes the common Pacific heritage among members, inclusive of Māori, and acknowledges the significant roles of women within Pacific cultures. The group's first fashion show (their own initiative) was held at the Powerstation, Auckland, in 1991 and called Te Hau Wairua Wahine (The Spirit of Women, or Breathing Spirit). During this period in New Zealand a contemporary indigenous perspective on culture, including dress, was still relatively unknown. This show included bright green *tapa* (barkcloth) print fabric made into tailored suits for men and red tapa print *puletasi* (two-piece outfits with a long skirt and short- or long-sleeved blouse) with coconut shell "dog collars" for women. Selina Forsythe, Suzanne Tamaki, and Niwhai Tupaea are the founding members, later introducing other women and a network of supporters who at different times have been central in contributing to the areas of dress design, art, music, performance, and production. Among these are Favaux Valepo, Rosanna Raymond, Ani O'Neill, Jeanine Clarkin, Feeonaa Wall, Ema Lyon, Bethany Edmunds, Sofia Tekela-Smith, and others. Key collaborators include Karlos Quartez, Greg Semu, Lisa Reihana, Darryl Thompson (DLT), Jean Clarkson, Henry Ah-Foo Taripo, Te Miringa Hohaia, Maaka Pepene, and others.

Pacific Sisters' exploration of identity in their work relates closely to Māori struggles for cultural sovereignty and common efforts to assert a unique Pacific heritage for New Zealand, as opposed to early Eurocentric viewpoints. While Pacific Islanders share ancestral ties with Māori, and a common Pacific geographical location, this historical relationship in New Zealand is made more complex by ongoing debates around bicultural identity and increasing multiculturalism.

The country's development as a bicultural nation came after the establishment of an English settler government in the midnineteenth century. The subsequent colonization of Māori, who descend directly from eastern Polynesians who arrived approximately a thousand years earlier, caused a rapid loss of population, resources, and *mana* (power, authority, or prestige) by the early twentieth century. But in the 1950s and 1960s rules about non-European immigration into New Zealand were relaxed to fill a steady demand for labor. Pacific Islanders began arriving in a series of large-scale migrations. Most went to live and work in Auckland, which was to become a multicultural, vibrant center for arts and dress practices. Others traveled further south to centers like Wellington and Christchurch. In the 1970s an uprising of Māori protest, inspired by the earlier civil rights movement in America, intensified a renaissance of interest in traditional arts and language by the mid-1990s. A new generation of urban Pacific Islanders (many identifying as "New Zealand–born") began to participate in the arts and culture scene, and out of this, the dress design and performance work of the Pacific Sisters emerged.

During this time the colonial past still dominated mainstream *Pākehā* (white settler) cultural attitudes. For instance, popular music, theater, art, fashion, and the media were focused largely on imported material from Europe and America. Commercial infrastructures supporting the local creative industries were limited, and this made it even more difficult for minority Pacific people (including Māori) to achieve their own creative expression. Yet in reality much of New Zealand's local creativity was happening underground, mixing ethnicities and influences, but not reflected in the wider consumer market, including dress.

In the mainstream fashion industry of New Zealand, design ideas and beauty ideals originated from the northern hemisphere. The distinctive faces of Polynesians were largely missing in the fashion press and on the books of casting agencies, with media interests typically portraying them in the context of social problems or lighthearted stories. As evolving identities began to be tentatively defined through new music, record labels, a variety of arts practices, theater, dance, magazines, festivals, and highly innovative fashion shows, a pioneering mood around New Zealand identity swept through into mainstream popular culture. In this context the dress and the work of the Pacific Sisters was significant.

FORGING KAUPAPA

A Pacific Sisters' *kaupapa* (philosophy) developed from a desire to represent their indigenous backgrounds with integrity in a popular cultural environment. This kaupapa guides decisions for creating work and collaborating with artists who have similar objectives, and it encapsulates the following ideals and concepts. The concept of identity is central. To stay connected to their Pacific ancestry within a Western environment is considered important. This involves addressing outdated colonial viewpoints, while maintaining the visibility of contemporary developments in Pacific Sisters fashion shows or editorials. Models are a range of sizes, shapes, skin tones, and gender orientations, conveying the increased diversity of Pacific identities, who also defy conventional Western modes of beauty within commercial fashion. Regularly staging projects that engage homeland and other urban-Pacific audiences and artists is important to the group for cultivating links and sharing ideas. Utilizing local talent for fashion shows or participating in weaving workshops with community groups are some activities that help raise awareness and aid collective participation in handling issues affecting the long-term global future of Pacific culture.

Many Pacific peoples share a common set of societal values, and this is interwoven into the group's dress design, artwork, and performances. The significance of family is recognized, as are the values of respect, care, service to the community, and *kaitiakitanga* (guardianship of the land). Enabling these values in the way they work and in their relationships with all people encourages a foundation of Pacific consciousness. For example, this can directly affect the structure of the group's performances, which often acknowledge ideas about dress, ceremonial protocols, and established social relationships within Pacific culture and the audience. This perspective is a natural extension of firsthand experiences of other contexts when dress and performance come together and where the entire community is represented. Within celebrations, rituals of encounter such as welcoming visitors, school "Pacific-themed" concerts, or sports like *kilikiti* (Samoan cricket), dress is viewed as a direct means of enhancing the mana of the wearer and/or supporting the kaupapa of the occasion, by

being constructed or brought out to aid communication of the event's purpose. Overall, this approach suggests a counterweight to the pervasive model of Western popular culture, which generally puts commercial interests first. Balancing Western and Pacific ideologies in their work is ongoing; however, celebrating the unique qualities within both is a focus of this process.

Learning is also important to the group. Gathering knowledge from within contemporary art, popular culture, and the indigenous world provides opportunities to investigate distinctions between Pacific and Western societies. Different lifestyles, languages, art forms, techniques of making clothing for the body, and traditional material culture, as well as historical change, and social, political, or religious order inform and inspire their art. This process is then developed through practical application, oral transmission, and scholarship.

The group aims to create work that facilitates a transfer of knowledge to the viewer as they observe or are being entertained by it. An example is the Pacific Sisters' enactments of the Mangaian legend, "Ina and Tuna," which recounts the origins of the coconut palm and its many different uses. Found in variant form throughout the Pacific, it discusses the universal themes of desire, love, sacrifice, and renewal. Using coconut shell for the costume of Tuna, the Eelgod highlights the long-held value associated with the coconut's versatility as a material. Significantly, the story is observed as an example of local "normal" sexual behavior by providing an insight into Pacific attitudes toward sexuality before missionary influence.

Politics is of significant value to the group. Priority is given to addressing consequences of European hegemonic rule over the Pacific during the late nineteenth and the twentieth centuries. Locally the redress of Māori issues is supported, with the peoples' right to *tino rangatiratanga* (absolute sovereignty). In 1998 an opportunity to reflect this belief was taken during a "handing over" ceremony of the work "21st Sentry Cyber Sister" to the Te Papa Museum of New Zealand (Wellington). A tino rangatiratanga flag with the colors red, white, and black was wrapped around one member's body, and others wore T-shirts highlighting the Māori cause. The movement's colors have also been the basis of other items of dress, such as an early shell "waistcoat" made by Ani O'Neill.

Another important aspect considers the roles of Pacific women in society, including perceptions of beauty, sexuality, and their participation in the political system. Women in the past were the main creators of dress, conveying power, prestige, and status in society. The group's use of traditional Pacific materials is a direct reference to the value of this role and upholds the strong binding force of women throughout all societies. Other themes explore gender roles and identities, health, racial tolerance, and regional environmental concerns such as natural resource management, global warming, and nuclear testing.

The issue of language and terminology is crucial. Pacific Sisters' fluency in their Pacific heritage language(s) varies; however, its use is promoted in order to deepen understanding of Pacific cultures. The influence of Māori and, increasingly, other Polynesian languages on New Zealand English has stimulated a reflective and often playful use of language. Many Polynesian loanwords are used, particularly in the text of narratives, situations requiring use of protocols, or when delineating dress, materials, cultural concepts, and people. Examples are *maro* (apron), *'ei katu* (flower headdress), *pule* (cowrie shell), *pu'a* (carob seed),

"21st Sentry Cyber Sister," 1998. This was a collaborative Pacific Sisters work by Niwhai Tupaea, Suzanne Tamaki, Rosanna Raymond, and Ani O'Neill, given to the Te Papa Museum of New Zealand in a ceremony at the Te Papa *marae* (meeting place). Each dress component was gently removed from the wearer and given to Te Papa amid prayer, speech, and song, revealing finally a red-and-black layered slashed body stocking. The components are: a *huruhuru* (feather) headpiece; a black woven PVC backpack with *koorari* (flax flower stem) and feather spears; *tapa* (barkcloth), ink, and pheasant-feather disc earrings; a red, white, and black plastic cord choker; a beef-bone neckpiece; a *huruhuru*, *harakeke* (flax phormium tenax), and shell *korowai* (cloak); a *tupe* (seed), *pule* (cowrie shell), and *pu'a* (bead) waistcoat; coconut shell bra; *tapa* and ink armbands; red, white, and black plastic cord bracelets; a recycled videotape hula skirt; and a natural fiber *maro* (apron) with button detail. Te Papa Museum of New Zealand, Wellington.

mauri (life force), *meaalofa* (gift of thanks), *suga*, pronounced "su-nga" (girl), and *fa'afafine* (transgender). Other words and phrases are slang hybrids of Pacific or Pacific and English. Examples are *salagi* (a Samoan/European person), *samaori* (a Samoan/Māori person), or *fula fuga suga*, pronounced "fuller fu-nga su-nga" (a larger Pacific woman in a floral dress).

Dress terminology used by Pacific Sisters is sometimes applied as a counter to past ethnographical classifications of Pacific dress, in which much of the context for their creation was left out, consequently causing potential loss of meaning for the viewer. Depending on the context, the group may initiate terminology to clarify the intention of their work, preferring, for example, *taonga* (treasures) over *jewelry*, or *body adornment* over *costume*, despite debates against the attachment of value (or not) to particular dress terminologies. For instance, use of the term *frock* for everyday wear is about a playful ribbing of conservatism in the fashion establishment.

Their reasoning is that the communication of cultural meaning is the underlying basis of their dress; the pieces, including streetwear, are imbued with the expectation of an ensuing performance, ritual of encounter, or sometimes just a walk down the street. All acts are potential markers of identity, intentional or otherwise, and all begin with the creative act of getting dressed.

DESIGN WORK

Pacific Sisters' approach to design was initially motivated by a lack of Pacific (including Māori) representation in mainstream New Zealand. The late 1970s saw P.A.C.I.F.I.C.A. Incorporated founder Eleitino Paddy Walker introduce Pacific music and dance to the New Zealand catwalk, but it wasn't until the inclusion of an "Oceanic" category within the premier mainstream fashion show, the Benson and Hedges Awards (and later others), that marked a change of attitude. Even so, contemporary Pacific clothing continued to exist on the periphery, mainly limited to souvenirs produced for overseas buyers. Overall, the mainstream market was dominated by a Western aesthetic; however, an increased demand for local goods reflecting a New Zealand Pacific identity developed into populist Pacific-branded items, so-called Kiwiana (iconic Pākehā cultural kitsch). Although Pacific Sisters often have an ironic view of this, they also embrace Kiwiana as part of growing up in New Zealand.

The group term their design approach "kaupapa-driven frock," which over time extended beyond casual streetwear into a more concentrated form of fashion activism filtered through art installation, exhibitions, and storytelling performances. Reworking established narratives of the Pacific and highlighting contemporary indigenous concerns is a strong point of focus connected to attitudes around art making found in early Pacific societies. In these early societies dress was intrinsically linked to people's desire to communicate values and beliefs of their culture, as a means of reinforcing cultural identity and ultimately survival. Generally expressed in language first, this sense of purpose expanded outward into the song, the dance, and the occasion, in turn supported by the material culture. After Western colonization and Pacific peoples' systematic conversion to Christianity beginning in the nineteenth century, many past cultural practices, including dress, were banned or drastically altered. The erosion of a traditional context for dress left much of its expression in the control of outsiders, and traditional dress was relegated to appearances at special occasions

or formalized performances. This shift has undermined deeper layers of meaning and subtlety and increased the likelihood of an interpretation as "spectacle" by the uninformed observer.

Underpinning these circumstances was an aversion to Pacific peoples' apparent lack of dress, which was considered shameful by missionaries and other outsiders. The media and tourist industries' excessive attention to these stereotypes has compounded them by appealing to the curiosity and whimsy of the spectator. Terms like *primitive, heathen, erotic, exotic, passive*, even *savage* have endured as common Western perceptions of Pacific culture. For example, in the twenty-first century the image of the "dusky maiden" with her smooth brown skin, fine features, and petite form swaying in a grass skirt is still marketed as the welcoming face of a Western escape into Pacific paradise. The notion of traditional Pacific dress has undergone noticeable change in the minds of the region's peoples. Their dress was largely replaced with styles that emphasized modesty and a broad covering of the body, deriving from the point of first missionary encounter. In a paradox European needlecraft technologies like sewing, crochet, and embroidery have been adopted and readily adapted. The imported forms now reach beyond their colonial origins to form an integral part of many Pacific peoples' sense of dress, older ones having been afforded similar qualities, as material indicators of indigenous spirituality.

In a climate of postcolonial indigenous reclamation, Pacific Sisters offer their reinterpretation of these outdated images, especially around the dusky maiden. Her stereotypical vulnerability is replaced with a refreshingly honest portrayal of female expression, emphasizing instead strength, grace, wisdom, or raw sexuality. The cultural values and practices of the ancestral Pacific are present, but so too is the reminder that innovation and interpretation have long existed and continue to develop within the region.

The group's design and styling as it has evolved covers three main aspects. There is a juxtaposition of urban streetwear with contemporary iconic Pacific dress, which includes the Aloha shirt (bright Polynesian-themed shirt), *lavalava* (sarong), puletasi, *mu'umu'u* ("mother hubbard"–style dress), or *'ie fai taga* (a men's formal wrap with pockets). This juxtaposition can work in the reverse, with items of Western-style dress referencing the shape or textural qualities of Pacific dress of the past, such as a crocheted shawl or poncho suggesting a traditional Māori cloak. Next there is the customizing of streetwear with materials that accentuate an individual identity, and finally, making dress that transforms a person into a character from history or imagination, in a literal layering of dress components masking the persona and increasing the overall dramatic effect.

Accessification is a term the group uses to describe this process, indicating the mass of accessories and the means of applying them. Individual layers can be items of Western dress deconstructed and customized, acting as a substitution for the physical parts of the body such as skin. Further items of dress are then made to clothe the body of the character. Face and body painting, together with the oiling of the performer's own body and specific parts of the dress, such as coconut shell "nipple shields," completes the creation of the character. As well as the effect of adding shine and inducing a pleasant aroma, this final layer is akin to the entry of mauri (life force) into the being.

The group uses and recycles what material is available from their environment, an approach informed by habits of resource gathering in the Pacific that continue today. The value of materials used in making attire was related in the past to how they were acquired. Materials that were scarce, difficult to extract, human in origin, or foreign were generally of higher value, and that value then transferred to people who carried the necessary mana or status to receive them. For Pacific Sisters, recycling of materials is also a way to practice environmental sustainability and make significant cost savings. Opting to find modern alternatives for organic materials counters often time-consuming preparation or nonavailability of the original materials.

They are attracted to combinations of (organic) traditional Pacific materials and synthetic ones. Fusing these materials with Western and Pacific craft techniques allows for greater experimentation; however, particular use of Pacific techniques helps maintain cultural links in their work. For example, use of an eight-plait braiding technique directly relates to the Māori legend of demi-god Maui and his snaring of the sun. It is said the ropes Maui used were plaited to that specification. Research into older techniques is learned from people like *mamas* (grandmothers) or from educational resources.

Common organic materials, mostly found in the bush and sea, are processed and then used. Sometimes they are found as "rubbish," donated, traded, bought from secondhand "opshops," or obtained from specialist sources. Organic materials include seeds, beads, seashell, coconut shell, pearlshell, paua shell, tapa (barkcloth), feathers, cow bone, bird bone, eel skins, boars' tusks, shark teeth, fish vertebrae, driftwood, *kiri'au* (native hibiscus raffia), leather, wool, leaves, flowers, sennet (plaited coconut fiber), flax, and various fabrics such as hemp, hessian, silk, jute, and cotton.

Common synthetic materials are sourced from opshops, as surplus from industrial manufacturers, or bought. They include cord, raffia, videotape, recycled clothing, ribbon, fishing line and lures, videotape, hessian, string, ink, plastics, florist ribbon, silk flowers, safety pins, plastic beads, buttons, zippers, various body stockings, scrap metal, elastic, paint/dye, and various fabrics such as polyester, nylon, Lycra, and PVC (polyvinyl chloride, a hardwearing synthetic resin). Customized urban streetwear created by the Pacific Sisters for an individual might incorporate a denim jacket and jeans embellished with tapa, beads, seeds, shells, and different accessories such as a feather necklace, bracelet, earrings, or a tapa skullcap.

A key dress component of the Pacific Sisters style is the "waistcoat," the first designed by Niwhai Tupaea as part of the costume "Haere O te Tupuna" (Welcome to the Ancestors) for the World of Wearable Arts show (1994). This idea developed out of the crossing of shells and beads across the torso, an established style of dress in the Pacific. The original waistcoat was made of small cowrie shells using a simple *lei-* (garland-) making technique. Other waistcoats have used different pattern designs and combinations of mostly organic materials. The materials required for assembly are extensive and as such considered of great value. Hence they are worn for performance or special occasions only. Each waistcoat expresses the unique identity of the Sister who makes it. According to Tupaea in correspondence with the author in 2007,

> The "waistcoat" is the signature to the Pacific Sisters. It is a symbol of protection and identity. When it was in the process of making I kept thinking of an invisible cloak, an extension of skin and spirit…. Who ever wears the waist-

coat [feels] a sense of grounding, whether they [know] it or not. That was the purpose of the coat. Metaphorically it is your *tupuna* (ancestors) protecting you from harms way. A coat of great mystical power not only given to me but to whom ever has the mana to wear it. Each Sister who has created their coat has given great power to it. It's our connection to each other, a reminder of our history together.

ART AND PERFORMANCE

Pacific Sisters' work has occupied many public and commercial spaces locally and internationally and has been recognized by winning awards in various New Zealand fashion design competitions: Pasifika (1994, 1995), World of Wearable Art (1997), Style Pasifika (1997), and Trash to Fashion (1998, 1999). Selected highlights in their development include the Pasifika fashion day and evening shows (1993–1995), held in association with the Auckland City Council. Group members were among the many designers and cast, with Rosanna Raymond as director and Feeonaa Wall as production coordinator. These shows created the first mainstream platform in New Zealand for an "Urban Pacific" fashion aesthetic, and they promoted the diversity of Pacific culture. New designer categories reflected this, such as Traditional Costume, Traditionally Inspired, Mu'umu'u, Lavalava, and Urban Pacific Streetwear, placed alongside more familiar sections like Beachwear, Evening Wear, Bridal, and others.

Bottled Ocean (1994), at Auckland City Art Gallery, was an early exhibition of major New Zealand contemporary Pacific art, in which their "living installation performance" combined dress with performance and oratory, highlighting these indigenous forms in new contexts. This idea developed in their storytelling endeavors. In Ina and Tuna (1994–1996) hula skirts made from black videotape, together with a multimedia presentation, brought a modern edge to an ancient tale. Two notable performances were the video-wall adaptation with Lisa Reihana for the Interdigitate Festival at the Aotea Centre, Auckland (1995), and the Pageant of Costumes, Tala Measina, 7th Pacific Festival of Arts, Samoa (1996). Festival organizers' resistance to the inclusion of a contemporary Pacific element eventually marred the group's full participation. However, festival-goers and many Samoan locals welcomed another work staged nearby called Motu Tagata (Island People) (1996), a fashion show with twelve other contemporary Pacific designers from New Zealand.

The "Agents of Change" (2000) performances with Lisa Reihana for the prestigious twelfth Biennale of Sydney brought their urban Pacific identities to a new audience. In a similar vein Pasifika Styles (2006–2008) marked the first major exhibition in the northern hemisphere of contemporary Pacific works. Rosanna Raymond was co-curator, and other Pacific Sisters were within the wide selection of artists.

Enhancing the cultural basis of the group's dress and narratives within a contemporary platform means deliberately ensuring that their presentations situate the viewer within a localized urban Pacific sensibility. Approached holistically, the kaupapa is infused within the structure of performances, the design of the physical space, the choice of music and images crafted for video and publicity, and the involvement of other performers or designers. Models may accentuate meanings through movements influenced by Pacific dance or ceremony, urban street dance, the gay nightclubs, and fa'afafine culture.

A typical Pacific Sisters fashion show enlists the viewer on a journey through all five senses. On arrival, fresh plaited greenery, flowers, and giant plastic lei are generously dispersed throughout the venue, the catwalk a canvas for patterns created with moody lighting and the projection of images. Plant and oil fragrances saturate the air. To begin, the sounding of *pū* (conch shell) affirms the activation of Pacific ritual. *Karakia* (prayer) and *waiata* (song) are exchanged, acknowledging the connections between artists, audience, and the work. The presence of children and elders is welcome and promotes the community *wairua* (spirit).

Intimate vignettes of spoken word, dance, song, and comedy are next, as *taonga puoro* (traditional Māori instruments) signal the start of the headlined fashion. Feather, bone shell, tapa, leather, plastic, and raffia are intensively layered and combine as body adornment amid an eclectic mix of deconstructed island- and streetwear. Texture, color, and pattern are strongest, emanating a vivid "tribal tone." Modeling is antiformulaic, capturing the essence of the dress in a flurry of model strut, *kapa haka* (Māori performance arts), hip-hop, *taualuga* (Samoan or Tongan ceremonial dance), and larger-than-life drag, inspiring shouts of support from the audience. To end, an "open section" invites the audience to showcase their own styles and talent on the catwalk. It is a village atmosphere onstage and off, shocking to some, sensual and strong to others, bringing out a feeling of the *po'ula* (festive nights) back from the time before missionaries outlawed them. Later, food is offered, a traditional way of diffusing the *tapu* (sacred) nature of the proceedings and demonstrating *manaakitanga* (hospitality) toward those attending. Titles like Tribe Vibe and the Extended Family Mix (1998), Nga Kura (The Sacred Red Feather) (1997), SubURBAN Islands (2001), and many others extend the importance of the kaupapa in the work of the Pacific Sisters. They continue to use fashion as a form of activism and to express evolving Pacific identities within an urban environment.

References and Further Reading

Küchler, Susanne, Graeme Were, and Glenn Jowitt. *Pacific Pattern*. London: Thames and Hudson, 2005.

Lay, Graham. *Pacific New Zealand*. Auckland, NZ: David Ling Publishing, 1996.

Leota-Ete, Jakki, Rosanna Raymond, and Shigeyuki Kihara. "Body Beautiful. New Zealand Fashion—Pacific Style." In *Pacific Art Niu Sila: The Pacific Dimension of Contemporary New Zealand Arts*, edited by Sean Mallon and Pandora Fulimalo Pereira, 91–101. Wellington, NZ: Te Papa Press, 2002.

Mallon, Sean. *Samoan Art and Artists, O Measina a Samoa*. Nelson, NZ: Craig Potton Publishing, 2002.

McIntosh, Tracey. "Hibiscus in the Flax Bush: The Maori-Pacific Island Interface." In *Tangata O Te Moana Nui: The Evolving Identities of Pacific Peoples in Aotearoa/New Zealand*, edited by Cluny Macpherson, Paul Spoonley, and Melani Anae, 141–154. Palmerston North, NZ: Dunmore Press, 2001.

Neich, Roger, and Fulimalo Pereira. *Pacific Jewelery and Adornment*. Auckland, NZ: Albany David Bateman, 2004.

Raymond, Rosanna. "Getting Specific: Fashion Activism in Auckland during the 1990s: A Visual Essay." In *Clothing the Pacific*, edited by Chloe Colchester, 193–208. Oxford: Berg, 2003.

Stevenson, Karen. "Refashioning the Label, Reconstructing the Cliché: A Decade of Contemporary Pacific Art 1990–2000." In exhibition catalog *Paradise Now? Contemporary Art from the Pacific*. Auckland, NZ: David Bateman in association with the Asia Society, 2004.

Vercoe, Caroline, and Robert Leonard. "Sisters Are Doing It. Fashion, Dance, Art: New Zealand's Pacific Sisters." In *Art Asia Pacific* 14 (1997): 42–45.

Wendt, Albert. "Tatauing the Post-Colonial Body." http://www.nzepc.auckland.ac.nz/authors/wendt/tatauing.asp (December 2007). (Originally published in *Span* 42–43 (April–October 1996): 15–29.

Feeonaa Wall

See also Wearable Art in New Zealand; Pacific Street Styles in Auckland; Photographic Representations of Pacific Peoples; Missionary Dress in Samoa.

Pacific Street Styles in Auckland

- Early 1990s: Pacific Fashion Activism
- 1995: Contemporary Pacific Tattoo Goes Mainstream
- Late 1990s: The "Polynisation" of the Street
- 2000 to 2005: Political Positioning
- 2005 to 2008: Represent

A *moko* with a kilt…a *"Kalo* and Fried Corned-Beef" (KFC) T-shirt…*tapa*-printed hoodies worn with *lavalavas* … a *tupenu* with clogs … the hint of a *pe'a* above jeans … urban Pacific street style brings a distinctly Aotearoa (New Zealand)–Pacific flavor to international trends and labels, fusing together elements of the local and the global, the high-tech and the handcrafted, Pacific motifs and multinational branding, haute couture and factory standard issue. Particularly associated with Auckland, known as the "First City of the Pacific," this marriage of the island and the urban is fresh, exciting, and dynamic. It cannot be divorced from its wider links to the creativity of New Zealand fashion activists like the Pacific Sisters, Pasifika fashion shows and associated events, wearable art more generally, and more recently institutional endorsement.

Media and popular representations of Pacific peoples have long adhered to well-established stereotypes such as the "dusky maiden" and the "noble savage," the alluring women of the "velvet" paintings, and Hollywood ukulele-strummers in Hawaiian shirts and grass skirts, images that relied heavily on clothing—or its absence—to connote the children of "Paradise" to a Western market. In reality many of the first generation of Pacific migrants to New Zealand in the 1950s spent their working week in school uniforms or the blue-collar attire of the working classes. On weekends Saturday's sportswear gave way to Sunday's church clothing: women in white *mu'umu'u* dresses and finely woven hats, men in shirts and wrap skirts known variously as *lavalava* (Samoa), *tupenu* (Tonga), *sulu* (Fiji), *pareo* (Hawai'i), and *pareau* (Cook Islands), children in their Sunday best. Later generations have added to these modes of dress, subverting Western stereotypes in the process, to create the contemporary fashion sensibility we characterize as urban Pacific street style.

This street style can be categorized into five periods spanning the early 1990s to 2008, each with clear themes and innovations. Prior to 1990 urban Pacific street style was a largely unacknowledged phenomenon, due to the general lack of visibility of Pacific peoples in the popular media at the time. Though the 1980s saw the emergence of John Pule and Fatu Feu'u, the first Pacific painters to enter New Zealand's art canon, contemporary Pacific fashion and distinctive street clothing remained quite literally on the suburban fringes of Auckland for another decade.

EARLY 1990s: PACIFIC FASHION ACTIVISM

Influential fashion activist Rosanna Raymond, one of the Pacific Sisters collective, known for its fashion designs, performances, and music, recalls watching young Pacific Islanders from Otara, in South Auckland, coming into the central city on Friday and Saturday nights in the late 1980s and early 1990s, incorporating their fathers' work boots into their urban outfits. Raymond, a model and artist, was working as a freelance stylist and talent scout for local magazines and designers; she drew her early inspiration from these indigenous style innovators. In collaboration with photographer Greg Semu she brought brown faces and edgy Pacific fashion into mainstream media and put Pacific street fashion onto the map, maintaining ideological commitments and the sense of irony and humor that characterizes the group.

The fashion activists of the early 1990s represented and reached out to a hungry Polynesian youth audience, who were inventive, brown, and talented. Raymond customized a pair of denim jeans and matching jacket with Tongan barkcloth (*ngatu*) and wore the resulting Pacific suit out nightclubbing. The outfit would later be exhibited as an artwork and is immortalized in a photograph taken by Greg Semu called "G'nang G'near" (1993) as a seminal image of this era. While the title of the photographic work was drawn from slang spreading in the new Pacific gay scene, Raymond's reworked denim also referenced prison gang culture. The recycled *tapa* (barkcloth) motifs mirrored the tattoos associated with Polynesian gangs, and the earning of a gang "patch." More generally this ensemble signified a new "patch-worked" Polynesian community undergoing great change as the second generation of New Zealand–born Pacific Islanders negotiated being urban New Zealanders while sustaining their sense of cultural belonging.

Raymond obtained patches of ngatu from roadside rubbish collections, hand-stitching them over the denim suit to give it a fresh identity as Pacific street fashion. Ngatu and other forms of barkcloth (known generically as *tapa*) are highly valued in Pacific cultures as exchange items. The juxtaposition of ngatu with denim highlighted the significance of work gear as a new form of currency for Pacific peoples in urban Auckland. In Semu's photograph "G'nang G'near," Raymond's barkcloth-covered suit is worn by a model posed against a backdrop of *fala* mats, directly acknowledging the skills of mat and tapa makers in the Pacific and its diaspora, while the hand-stitching and appliquéd techniques on the garments pay homage to other textile traditions, such as Hawaiian and Cook Islands' quilts. The denim symbolizes Pacific women employed as machinists in garment factories and Pacific men employed in manual labor. Raymond overlaid this urban reality with ngatu as a way of making these people visible—literally layering a Pacific skin onto a working-class uniform of jeans jacket and pants.

The "G'nang G'near" image shows the back of the denim jacket and jeans, in direct reference to Polynesian constructions of time that place the known past in front of ego and the unknown future behind. Facing the past with back to the future, the model in barkcloth and denim suit embodied, metaphorically, the present; a young person dressed in multilayered reality, and approaching the future with identity proudly displayed. Worn to nightclubs by Raymond and displayed in the window of Paris Texas, arguably in the early 1990s the "coolest" street clothing shop in central Auckland, the barkcloth-covered denim exemplified the movement of Pacific textiles and fashion concepts from the Islands to an urban diaspora.

The late *tufuga ta tatau* (Samoan tattoo master) Suluape Paulo II, with Samoan sportsman Steve Fonoti in Suluape's studio in Velvet Crescent, Otara, South Auckland, in 1995. Fonoti displays his *pe'a*, a Samoan tattoo that expresses Polynesian ancestry and identity on the skin between the waist and the knees. A *pe'a* is applied in a very painful process that takes weeks and is considered to be a Samoan male rite of passage. Photograph by Greg Semu. Auckland Art Gallery Toi o Tamaki.

Pasifika fashion shows began in 1993, directed by Raymond, initially part of a broader Pasifika annual community festival, which celebrated the diversity of contemporary Pacific people. From the start of the Pasifika fashion event, categories such as Sunday Best Whitewear, Contemporary Wearable Art, and Lavalava highlighted many of the central influences on urban Pacific wear and emphasized timeless *style* over more fleeting *fashion*. In 1994, fellow Pacific Sister Ani O'Neill won Style Pasifika with an ensemble of deconstructed cardigans, old woolen shirts, nighties, and underwear worn as outerwear; the collection was called Mama Grunge. Modeled by young women, the clothing recycled garments worn by elder Pacific women, known in O'Neill's Cook Islands community as "Mamas." Mama Grunge referenced Sunday church clothing, Pacific bridal styles, and the ubiquitous "mother hubbard" dress or mu'umu'u, introduced to the Pacific by missionaries and their wives.

In O'Neill's hands these garments were given a contemporary street sensibility with an obvious nod to the grunge aesthetic so popular among young people at the time. The appropriation of modest garments associated with Pacific elders as raw materials for sexy youth fashion was subversive yet respectful, acknowledging the Mamas as the backbone of Pacific Island community and life. The layered garments, so typical of grunge styling, mimicked the layering of waist wraps found in traditional Pacific Island ceremonial clothing, and O'Neill's own Mamas' way of layering clothing for comfort. This custom is referenced directly by the wrapping of printed fabric over trousers, the layering of shorts over jeans or tracksuit pants, or by the wearing of dresses and skirts over trousers, a look that dominated New Zealand fashion in the 1990s. O'Neill further acknowledged Pacific textile practices by referencing the *tivaevae*, or appliquéd quilts and crochet work made by Cook Island women, and accessorizing her otherwise urbane garments with shell necklaces and floral garlands (*lei* or *ei*). Her styling referenced beauty pageants and the importance these have in Polynesian contemporary culture as celebrations of community identity and pride.

"G'nang G'near" and Mama Grunge epitomized the 1990s blending of Western clothing styles with recognizably Pacific aesthetics and styling and introduced urban Pacific street style to New Zealand's mainstream fashion media.

1995: CONTEMPORARY PACIFIC TATTOO GOES MAINSTREAM

By the mid-1990s Pacific designers, models, and artists had become an influential part of New Zealand's fashion scene, and annual events such as Pasifika had raised the visibility and accessibility of Pacific art forms. *Pasifika* is a term originally used by New Zealand–born Pacific Islanders as a framework for valuing and assigning meaning to contemporary Pacific culture and expression in all its manifestations. It was coined to reflect lived urban realities and to generate cultural pride, but its appropriation as a mainstream marketing phrase threatened to subvert this intention. The successful infiltration of mainstream media by the urban Pacific innovators of the early 1990s became a double-edged sword.

A group of Pacific artists, and the motifs with which they would become associated, were also becoming familiar to art collectors and aficionados in New Zealand: Fatu Feu'u's frangipani paintings; Michel Tuffery's bull sculptures; Ani O'Neill's handicraft techniques including Cook Islands quilting (*tivaevae*), crochet, and plaiting; John Pule's *hiapo*-derived paintings; John Ioane's carved cowrie shells; and Jim Vivieaere's innovative and uncompromising approach to art curation and installation. Somewhat ironically, contemporary Pacific artists and designers continued to struggle against many of the same stereotypes and clichés of the 1980s, except now they had been repackaged as the aesthetic called Pasifika.

At street level the thrust of the Pasifika aesthetic was moving from clothing to bodies, specifically those adorned with Pacific tattoo. In 1995 Greg Semu took a series of photographs of Samoan tattoo (*tatau*), called "O le Tatua Samoa," one of which shows the late *tufuga ta tatau* (Samoan tattoo master) Suluape Paulo II with Samoan sportsman Steve Fonoti in Suluape's studio in Otara, South Auckland. Fonoti displays his *pe'a*, a Samoan tattoo worn by men from their waist to their knees. Obtaining the *pe'a* is a very painful process that can take several weeks to complete and is a rite of passage for Samoan males. Its design is unique, like a portrait, but also expresses the recipient's Polynesian ancestry, identity, and pride.

Semu's unstyled snapshot of South Auckland life shows Suluape and Fonoti in casual clothes. Suluape wears a hooded sweatshirt with an American football print, a lavalava (waist wrap) over jeans, and sports sandals with socks. The lavalava is standard wear for men in the Pacific Islands and is often layered over trousers in Auckland's more temperate climate. Fonoti is clad only in a lavalava and *ula fala* (a necklace made from the seeds of the pandanus tree). The everyday clothing and comfortable stance of both men allowed Semu to illustrate the growing acceptance of, and appreciation for, Samoan tatau in mainstream Auckland's art and design communities. Fonoti's pe'a is not the sole focus of the image, but rather just one part of a greater narrative about life in the Samoan diaspora. The "O le Tatua Samoa" series also included a set of three photographs of Semu receiving the pe'a and extended versions of the *taulima* (tattoo armband) from Suluape Paulo II. Though the pe'a and *malu* (the female counterpart to the pe'a) are easily covered by Western clothing, the taulima is harder to conceal. Worn around the bicep or the wrist, it is a highly visible marker of cultural identity.

Concurrently, Māori *ta moko* (facial and body tattooing) was experiencing unprecedented global visibility due to the

Siliga and Luisa Setoga, running the Popohardwear T-shirt stall at Otara Markets, in 2007. Many popular T-shirts designed and sold by the local vendors in Auckland critique aspects of urban Pacific culture with reference to the migrant Polynesian experience in New Zealand. Photograph by Giles Peterson.

international success of the New Zealand film *Once Were Warriors* (1994). A snapshot of the pressures facing predominantly Māori families in urban Auckland, the film's visual impact owed much to *tohunga ta moko* (Māori tattoo master) Inia Taylor; Taylor himself has a pe'a from Suluape, with whom he worked.

Once Were Warriors catapulted its stars and creative team to international stardom and introduced Māori tattoo tradition and practices to a global mainstream audience, and onto the skins of international celebrities; Michael Franti (from Spearhead and Disposable Heroes of Hiphoprisy), Robbie Williams, and Ben Harper all wear moko, designed and applied by, respectively, Inia Taylor, Te Rangitu Netana, and Gordon Hatfield. Other notable contemporary proponents of ta moko include Derek Lardelli, Rangi and Julie Kipa, and Riki Manuel. Their new clients included young people off the street, Pacific rugby players and sportspeople, and media personalities, as well as international celebrities and musicians. Moko even made it onto the cover of fashion bible British *Vogue* in October 2000, when a naked Robbie Williams bared his arm moko alongside model-of-the-moment Giselle Bundchen (clad only in a sequined Union Jack bikini). Moko imagery made further forays into the fashion arena via printed clothing. Tohunga ta moko Gordon Hatfield and Māori fashion designer Jeanine Clarkin collaborated to produce garments and fabrics featuring *kauae* (Māori women's facial tattoo), while designers such as Jean-Paul Gaultier, Gianni Versace, and Thierry Mugler readily appropriated ta moko motifs for their own collections.

The heightened international visibility of Pacific tattoos, and the migration of their motifs onto clothing, gave an urban perspective to a traditional practice, and promoted acceptance and dissemination among a wider audience in New Zealand and the world.

LATE 1990s: THE "POLYNISATION" OF THE STREET

The resurgent popularity of tatau and ta moko, and its appearance on international celebrities, helped to usher in a new phase of street styling, which unashamedly, yet "Pasifikally," drew upon American music culture. Jim Vivieaere coined the term *Polynisation* to describe the reappropriation of Polynesian ideas and values by Polynesians, the ways in which Polynesian and American popular culture melded, and also the possibilities presented by these transactions.

During the late 1990s hip-hop culture came to the fore in Auckland, and its key elements were rapidly adopted and adapted. At this time the Pacific Sisters were preparing for Motu Tagata (meaning Island People in pidgin Polynesian), their fashion event at Tala Measina—The Seventh Polynesian Festival of the Arts in Samoa (1996). It was the first time a contemporary multicultural group from New Zealand had been invited, as the festivals until then typically promoted a platform for celebrating the traditional arts.

The Pacific Sisters prepared a body of clothing that has become known as Tamatoa (literally "strong man"). It contained obvious references to hip-hop clothing, but the garments were indigenized and customized to reflect Pacific aesthetics and sensibilities. What appeared to be hoodies were actually more formal jackets, their plackets lined with tapa-printed fabric, the tapa detailing being like patches of urban Pacific pride. Tamatoa was photographed for the cover of a local street magazine: Shot against a backdrop of graffiti, the cover was an image of boys "in the neighborhood." Where one might expect to see jeans, the young men wore lavalavas; around their necks hung strings of shells and seeds. The accessories purchased from opportunity shops (secondhand stores) included shell necklaces from Niue, cowrie shells from Tonga, boar tusks from Papua New Guinea, shark teeth and seed necklaces from Samoa, and *pu'a*, carob seeds from New Zealand—a celebration of Pacific diversity. All of the jewelry was reworked by the Pacific Sisters, utilizing traditional plaiting techniques.

Jewelry was becoming the medium of choice for many Pacific artists and designers in the late 1990s. *Pākehā* (the Māori name for European New Zealanders) jewelers Warwick Freeman and Alan Preston were among the first to make high-end contemporary Pacific jewelry from locally sourced organic materials. They were quickly joined by Pacific jewelers and artists such as Niki Hastings-McFall, Sofia Tekela Smith, Chris Charteris, Gina Mattchitt, Areta Wilkinson, George Nuku, and Rangi Kipa; their work is represented in collections around the world and used in fashion shoots in New Zealand and overseas.

"Stuck in Traffic I" (1999) is a necklace by Hastings-McFall based on a Solomon Islands breastplate form called the *kapkap*, which is traditionally associated with chiefly status. The kapkap is an object of adornment, a form of currency, and a signifier of rank and value. "Stuck in Traffic I" references car culture, in

The South Auckland designers Letufa Taniela (left) and Ofa Mafi (right) at Otara's Fresh Gallery, in 2007. Mafi is wearing a screen-printed dress she designed, which incorporates Tongan tattoo patterns and repetition of the word OTARA. Taniela wears a large decorative brooch made from a "found" fabric remnant, which she has screen-printed. The design is typical of her pop art sensibility, which favors kitsch custom embellishment and transformation through decoration. Photograph by Giles Peterson.

particular the significance of mag-wheels in urban hip-hop communities. Cars are symbols of wealth, status, power, and achievement; of making it in the Western world. The low-rider styling favored by aficionados of American hip-hop culture has been Polynised in Auckland, where dashboards are adorned with fake-flower lei (flower garlands) and sign-written rear windows commemorate young friends and family members who have died on the roads. "Stuck in Traffic I" used a traditional sign of wealth, with a strong visual reference to current obsessions, to create a reflection of Hastings-McFall's neighborhood, and a composite of past and contemporary values. "Stuck in Traffic I" is Pacific "bling," rooted firmly in historical ways of reckoning value and status.

2000 TO 2005: POLITICAL POSITIONING

By 2000 staples of street fashion and urban accoutrements had been reworked and co-opted into service as new icons of Pacific style and signifiers of status and identity. At the dawn of the new millennium urban Pacific street style had become viable as high-end clothing and jewelry, but the accompanying price tags often precluded their purchase by a Pacific audience. After decades of marginalization as tourist items it was time for the more egalitarian T-shirt to bask in the spotlight, as a site for political commentary. Street style had also been recognized by institutions like the Museum of New Zealand, giving a permanent home to this Pacific creativity.

In 2000 Shigeyuki Kihara's controversial installation, Teuanoa 'i—Adorn to Excess (1999), was purchased by the Museum of New Zealand, Te Papa Tongarewa. It included logo-jamming T-shirts such as "Fobie" instead of "Barbie"; "KKK" instead of "KFC"; and "Fuk N Save" instead of supermarket chain Pak 'n' Save, targeting the corporate identities Kihara perceived to be exploiting Pacific peoples. The Museum of New Zealand's purchase acknowledged the wider creative industry in South Auckland, using T-shirts for parody and subversion. Tackling even highly negative stereotypes such as "FOB (Fresh off the Boat)," "Bunga," and "Coconut," T-shirt designers helped to reclaim these terms, which have become a source of pride and are used with affection by contemporary Pacific peoples. Suddenly it was "cool" to be "Fobbielicious."

New Zealand's high-end fashion designers and stylists responded with fashion spreads shot in Auckland's Pacific suburbs. In April 2004 Staple magazine shot on location in Otara Mall, just around the corner from the T-shirt vendors in Otara market, featuring a male model in a "Bro" T-shirt from up-market label Huffer and a girl in a hoodie designed by internationally renowned fashion designer Karen Walker. The irony is that these elite fashions are out of reach for many in the Pacific Island community—statistics reveal that despite some progress over the last decade, Māori and Polynesians remain at the bottom of the economic scale in New Zealand.

T-shirts designed and sold by local vendors critique aspects of urban Pacific culture, both local and global, including the socioeconomic reality of being Polynesian in New Zealand. A design by Siliga Setoga (in the collection of the Museum of New Zealand) references the boat on which his father traveled from Samoa to New Zealand in 1966. The text reads: "SS Matua 1966. Shipping the finest produce from the Pacific to New Zealand 1950s–1970s. Bananas, cocoa beans, copra, taro, factory workers, cleaners, labourers, taxi drivers, hospital kitchen staff, fruit pickers and dream builders."

"SS Matua" charts and shares Setoga's personal narrative, making it accessible to other young Samoans and Pacific Islanders and representing a shared history. Other T-shirts utilize in-house satire, like the rebranding of Coca-Cola as "Coconuts—Better than the real thing," to speak directly to the Pacific Island migrant experience, emphasizing the links between Pacific Islands rather than the differences. Thus, they promote a pan-Pacific identity within a diasporic and sometimes disadvantaged community.

The affordability and portability of T-shirts sold at Auckland's street markets (a locus for diverse Pacific communities) has ensured their popularity on the street. The publicity that followed their purchase by major institutions such as the Museum of New Zealand further spread their messages, even affording certain images and designers cult status in New Zealand.

2005 TO 2008: REPRESENT

T-shirts continue to dominate the urban Pacific fashion scene, but young art and fashion graduates are also working their own brands in the face of dominant global icons such as Nike and adidas, in spite of the constant presence of cheaply produced knock-offs. While New Zealand's top designers capitalize on being "down with the brown," Auckland's young Pacific designers instead choose to "represent": to make a statement with their presence, words, and actions. Represent has become a political catch-cry used by a new wave of fashion activists, who have unprecedented access to media exposure via the global phenomenon of social networking over the Internet, providing extraordinary opportunities to promote, sell, and "represent." This Internet-savvy generation, now fresh out of art school instead of just off the boat, tend to think global and act local.

Many later designers have grown up in South Auckland, the birthplace of urban Pacific street style, and they now design and manufacture their labels there. Unlike their parents, for whom the pressure to provide for family (both in Auckland and "at home") entailed an early entry into secure professions, they have had the privilege of choosing to follow careers in design. Their clothing, fabric, and body adornment designs do not depend upon stylized Pacific motifs for significance but rather reflect their lives lived in (sub)urban Auckland.

Their designs employ many of the key elements described earlier, such as layering, recycling, and customization, and subversion of culturally damaging stereotypes. Designer Ofa Mafi often wears a screen-printed dress of her own design over trousers, a signature Pacific style. Her printed fabrics incorporate Tongan tattoo patterns, and urban graffiti that read "OTARA": a succinct expression of pride in both her island and urban homes. Designer Letufa Taniela makes large brooches from "found" fabric remnants she screen-prints with her own image. Their bright colors and kitsch embellishments, which include sequins, feathers, and lace, reflect a pop art sensibility also found in contemporary graphic design pop culture globally. They are used in this case to satisfy Taniela's desire for decoration, transformation, beauty, and adornment. A recurring theme in her designs, Taniela's positioning of herself as a "dusky maiden" subverts the power of this stereotype's traditional objectification. It demonstrates an awareness of art history and Western stereotypical representations of Pacific women.

Taniela and Mafi have designed a T-shirt to be worn with baggy shorts, a contemporary take on the Christian requirement to dress modestly. The T-shirt combines contemporary urban tapa designs and graffiti "tagging" to create a medallion of pride, which echoes the shape of a mag-wheel. Figuratively it can also be read as an urban peace symbol, a reflection of current social problems. South Auckland has an active gang culture identified by the colors they wear in the form of bandanas. While some T-shirt designers protest against American gang influences in incendiary terms, others express their politics in more subtle and nuanced ways; for others this involves literally wearing one's heart on one's sleeve. Just as rear windshield texts commemorate loved ones killed on the roads, clothing too is customized to respect the deceased. Following the death of a teenager in a car accident in Otara, young people applied his image to T-shirts, caps, and bags. By wearing his image on their bodies they expressed their grief, making a personal and political statement about violence in the community.

This is an example of veiled knowledge: Everyone in Otara knew to whom the clothing was referring, but outsiders did not. A young boy wore his grief with the T-shirt printed to be read from the back, his cap slung backwards and a printed bag worn on his back hip; in true Pacific style the wearer enters the future backwards, equipped with a bold lesson from the past. Thus, to "represent" is to express pride in one's community and neighborhood, but also to expose—with brutal realism—the things that threaten it in its hope for a better future.

Pacific artists, body artists, and designers face major challenges in the twenty-first century, navigating the worlds of their ancestors and their global urban reality. In Auckland the fluidity and diversity of urban Pacific street style is reflective of the energy of this, the largest South Pacific city. It is a contemporary fashion sensibility grown in the communities of Auckland's "Pacific" suburbs and refined by designers and artists to appeal to mainstream fashion media.

The five periods discussed here detail the island connections and urban manifestations of clothing and body adornment in Auckland, identifying key aspects of urban Pacific street style and its evolution. Drawing upon the customs of diverse Pacific cultures, and marrying them with global trends and Western archetypes to create something fresh, urban Pacific street style is not elitist fashion, nor is it a neo-tribal style. Rather, it conveys the multilayered experiences of Polynesian urban communities in Auckland; it is a personal signature, born out of multifaceted relationships to the islands and urban environments that are now called home.

References and Further Reading

Colchester, C., ed. *Clothing the Pacific*. Oxford: Berg, 2003.

Pereira, P. F. "Identities Adorned: Jewellery and Adornments." In *Pacific Art Niu Sila: The Pacific Dimension of Contemporary New Zealand Arts*, edited by S. Mallon and P. F. Pereira, 39–52. Wellington, NZ: Te Papa Press, 2002.

Stevenson, K. "The Island in the Urban: Contemporary Pacific Art in New Zealand." In *Pacific Art: Persistence, Change and Meaning*, edited by A. Herle, N. Stanley, K. Stevenson, and R. L. Welsch, 404–414. Adelaide, Australia: Crawford House Publishing, 2002.

Te Awekotuku, N., and L. W. Nikora. *Mau Moko: The World of Māori Tattoo*. North Shore, NZ: Penguin Viking, 2007.

Velvet Dreams. DVD. Directed by Sima Urale. Aukland, NZ:: Vincent Burke and Clifton, May 2005.

Vercoe, C. "The Many Faces of Paradise." In exhibition catalog *Paradise Now? Contemporary Art from the Pacific*, 34–47. Auckland, NZ: David Bateman in association with the Asia Society, 2004.

Zemke-White, K. "Reverse Resistance: Pacific Engagement with Popular Music in New Zealand." In *Pacific Art Niu Sila: The Pacific Dimension of Contemporary New Zealand Arts*, edited by S. Mallon and P. F. Pereira, 117–133. Wellington, NZ: Te Papa Press, 2002.

Giles Peterson and Billie Lythberg

See also Moko Māori: Skin Modification; Wearable Art in New Zealand; Pacific Sisters: Urban Pacific Art, Fashion and Performance.

PART 10

Peoples of the Pacific: Overview

Introduction to the Dress of the Pacific Islands

- Melanesia/New Guinea
- Micronesia
- Polynesia
- Post-European Clothing

The Pacific Ocean covers one-third of the earth's surface and is inhabited by hundreds of cultural groups. Some twenty-five thousand islands, ranging from tiny specks of coral to the large island of New Guinea, are occupied by physically diverse peoples, many of whom have mixed and intermixed. Environments range from snowy mountains to raging volcanoes, from steaming rain forests to parched deserts, from coral atolls to volcanic outcrops. These Pacific Islands are usually divided into three historic cultural complexes known as Melanesia ("black islands"—which includes closely related New Guinea), Micronesia ("small islands"), and Polynesia ("many islands"). For their clothing indigenous people exploited what was available from the land and the sea that surrounded them, and different cultural dress practices evolved in all areas.

More than twenty-five million people inhabit the Pacific Islands in the twenty-first century. Some have lived in small separate groups of only a few hundred, and others are part of island-wide chiefdoms, but over the years large port towns and cosmopolitan cities have developed. The people speak a vast number of languages and dialects of the Austronesian and Papuan language families—some mutually intelligible over wide expanses of ocean, and others unintelligible to the residents of the next village. Most island people tended to use what was available locally for their clothing, with some trade with nearby islands; long-distance trade with the continents was virtually nonexistent. As the islands are in tropical and subtropical zones, warm clothing was unnecessary in most regions, except at high altitudes in New Guinea, the interior of a few large islands, the southern extremities of Polynesia in Easter Island (Rapa Nui), and the South Island of New Zealand (Aotearoa).

Clothing was primarily constructed of plant leaves and the inner bark of certain trees. In general, there was no tradition of tailoring or sewing, but clothing was based on loincloths for men and wraparound skirts and shoulder coverings for women. Body attachments were made from flowers, seeds, and other plant materials; shells and other jewels from the sea; and local materials such as greenstone. Skin was oiled and usually shiny, perfumed, and painted, and often permanently altered with tattoo and scarification. Feathers from land and sea birds furnished finishing touches, and in New Guinea skin from mammals was used. Color was important, especially red and in some areas yellow, along with black and white. The absence and removal of clothing made statements about aesthetics and protocol; for example, in some parts of Polynesia it was necessary to strip to the waist in the presence of a high-ranking chief. Most of the islands were not blessed with metal, and, except for New Guinea, mammals consisted only of pigs, dogs, rats, and bats. Mammal skin was not tanned or made into leather, but dog hair and human hair were used.

Dress in the Pacific Islands is grammatically structured and is part of the larger activity for which it is worn, which varies from everyday clothing to ritual and ceremonial finery. This grammar involves structure, style, and meaning; one must learn about the various pieces of dress, the materials from which they are made, how they can be stylistically varied, their syntax (rules about how they can and cannot be put together and for what occasions), designs with which they are embellished, who can wear them, and what meanings are ascribed to them. For example, in Hawai'i pieces of clothing that were worn above the waist could not be worn below the waist, and in Tonga designs on barkcloth skirts encode information about the village in which they were made. Certain pieces of dress may have derived from gods, ancestors, or historical figures, but are retained and perpetuated in contemporary life as cultural and aesthetic artifacts. Dress and its history are important, even if their meanings have been changed or forgotten as reference points for cultural identity. Meanings are not inherent in dress but are ascribed to pieces of clothing and their stylistic presentation by groups of people at specific points in time, and they need to be culturally decoded in order to be understood.

MELANESIA/NEW GUINEA

The large land mass of New Guinea, along with the islands of Melanesia, is a complex maze of sociocultural groups, having a checkered history of outside influences and colonization. Global politics of the nineteenth and twentieth centuries resulted in political boundaries that are not the same as cultural or social ones. The western half of the island, Irian Jaya or West Papua, has become politically a part of Indonesia, while the modern political entity of Papua New Guinea is an independent member of the British Commonwealth and includes not only the eastern half of the island of New Guinea but several large and small islands—New Britain, New Ireland, Manus, the Trobriand Islands, and Bougainville (part of the Solomon Island chain), many of which are only distantly related culturally. The Torres Straits Islands are culturally related to New Guinea but are politically part of Australia. Island Melanesia includes the independent archipelagos of the Solomon Islands, New Caledonia, and Vanuatu (formerly New Hebrides). When dealing with dress it is more appropriate to use cultural rather than political boundaries, yet politics influences the way in which social groups construct themselves and their history. Remnants of colonial attachments to Britain, France, or Germany continue to influence clothing style.

In general, owing to the warm and humid climate, before colonization everyday clothing was minimal. Often men went almost completely naked, except for penis coverings and netted bags they carried hung from their shoulders or from their foreheads. They frequently wore ornaments that went through the septum of the nose and had bracelets on their upper arms to hold necessities such as knives. Adult women traditionally wore a skirt of leaves that hung from a plaited waistband and also carried netted bags.

Men and women dancers from the village of Kanokupolu, Tonga, wear wraparound barkcloth skirts with designs that indicate in which village the barkcloth was fabricated. The central dancer, Princess Pilolevu, wears a special skirt made of scallops cut from a fine pandanus mat decorated with shell beads. 1975. Photograph by Adrienne L. Kaeppler.

Many social groups on both sides of the political divide of New Guinea have a number of general features in common, such as social organizations centered around "bigmen," who become leaders based primarily on individual or family achievement, rather than chiefs, who are born to ascribed leadership positions (as in Polynesia). Each tribal grouping, and in some cases each individual village, differs in significant ways from the others. This diversity is manifested in hundreds of languages and dialects, as well as underlying concepts of political structures and social relationships, the fabrication and use of material culture by men and women, exploitation of the natural environment, religion and ritual, clothing, folklore, music, and dance.

In New Guinea large political units were rare; the effective sociopolitical grouping was often only a single village—sometimes with as few as a hundred people. Larger groupings, referred to by Europeans as clans and tribes, cooperated among themselves during wars and ceremonies as well as for exchanges of pigs, valued shells, localized craft productions, and spouses, but were not viable politically. In many areas elaborate rituals and dramatic ceremonies were presented—often connected with the building of a men's house (large structures in which ceremonial objects were kept and that served as the meeting place for adult men), initiation and puberty rites, warfare, and funeral ceremonies. These were occasions for spectacular displays of the visual and performing arts; carved and painted figures and ceremonial boards were often used, and elaborate costumes and body painting were characteristic. Huge masks for men representing spirits, totems, and ancestors made their appearance to the accompaniment of singing, drumming, and dancing. Each area, tribe, and even village differed from others in details and style of clothing, as well as the underlying concepts associated with clothing, body paint, ornaments, and hairstyles.

The inhabitants of island Melanesia have some elements in common with New Guinea but differ significantly from island to island and from group to group. Before European contact in Vanuatu women often wore only narrow plaited waistbands, and many were tattooed. Men frequently wore barkcloth belts, penis wrappers, face painting, hair combs, and belts and armbands decorated with shell beads. Certain garments, such as barkcloth belts painted with black and red triangular motifs, symbolized political power, while other vest-like garments marked grades in secret societies. A series of mask forms and styles also indicated a man's achievement in these graded societies. On the island of Pentecost in Vanuatu men wore long, narrow mats plaited from pandanus leaves as loincloths, while women wrapped wider mats around their hips. Both often had purple or red designs, which indicated the social status of the maker and/or the wearer. In Ambae, Vanuatu, pandanus textiles worn by men hanging from their belts indicated their status in a graded pig-killing system.

Ritual clothing in New Caledonia included wooden masks, which were surmounted by human hair wigs and feather overgarments, while in other areas performers were enveloped in shredded leaves. In modern times male New Caledonian dancers wear dramatic face paint of half black and half white along with their traditional fiber skirts, while women usually wear versions of the introduced "mother hubbard" dresses. For their important rituals and dances Solomon Islanders traditionally wore a variety of valued shells and conical headdresses attached to huge leaf costumes that enveloped the whole body.

Most studies carried out on dress in Melanesia and New Guinea have focused on dance costume, masks, and body paint. This ritual clothing is worn as part of ceremonies, with an emphasis on rhythm, created by hourglass drums, slit drums, and rattles, and made visual by the massed human bodies as they move together in an elaboration of rhythm. Some costumes are composed primarily of attachments that move and emphasize this visual rhythm. In New Guinea bird of paradise plumes and other feathers extend from headdresses, back, bustle, or arms. Hanging rattles of seeds or shells are attached to legs or costumes, or held in the hand. Cuscus skin ripples like vertical waves, and shredded leaves and fibers cascade and bounce. Penis coverings of gourd, shell, or bark are curved forward and upward to emphasize the up-down movement of this part of the body. The outfit emphasizes rhythm, while at the same time the rhythm shows off the outfit—together they create a mass rhythmic statement.

Many traditional rituals have been supplemented by Christian ceremonies, especially weddings, which have added a whole new occasion for elaborate dress. As Lissant Bolton has shown for Vanuatu, wedding dresses vary from "island dresses" to Western bridal attire, and they vary from village to village, in color, fabric, and decorations that mark the brides' new status. But while wedding clothes have markedly changed, old ideas and concepts are invested in new styles and materials. At other ceremonial events, such as annual shows at Goroko and Hagen in Papua New Guinea, male and female participants continue to wear traditional self-decoration but made of modern materials and paint, sometimes with washable tattoos.

MICRONESIA

The cultural and geographic area known as Micronesia, located west of the international dateline and north of the equator, includes several archipelagos whose environments vary from steep mountains, as in Pohnpei, to coral atolls, like Ulithi, with its forty-one fringing islets, to the dramatic underwater Marianas Trench. The more than twenty-five hundred islands, with a land area of less than three thousand square kilometers (eleven thousand square miles), are encompassed in a typhoon-spawning area of the Pacific Ocean about the size of the continental United States. The several island groupings—Caroline Islands, Mariana Islands, Marshall Islands, Kiribati, and the Micronesian outliers—have cultural affiliations within and beyond their geographic locations. By the nineteenth century relationships went even further. The indigenous people of the Mariana Islands, the Chamorro, for example, intermixed with Mexicans, Filipinos, and Spaniards, adding complexities of imported style to regional dress.

On small islands surrounded by a vast ocean, Micronesians were intimately dependent on the sea, and survival depended on knowledge of it and continual rapport with it. Although each inhabited island with the waters around it produced the basic essentials for living, overseas trading was a feature of Micronesian life. Nearly every island had its own specialty—fine mats, unique dyes, particular shell ornaments—and exchanged it for something unusual from another area. In the "Yap Empire," including the high island of Yap and numerous low coral islands to the east, people were enmeshed hierarchically in a political and economic grouping through which tribute, gift exchanges, and religious offerings traveled in various directions. Included were finely woven loincloths, pandanus mats, and coconut oil.

It is for their loom-weaving that Micronesian textiles and clothing are best known. Found in many islands in the Carolines, the horizontal-tension backstrap loom is closely related to Indonesian looms, from which they probably derived. Simple forms of backstrap looms were used in Kosrae and Pohnpei. The looms were strung with a continuous spiral warp that encircled a warp beam attached to a frame and a second unattached warp beam (or breast beam); these were separated from each other by a distance of half the desired finished length of the fabric. The breast beam was tied to a strap that encircled the waist of the weaver, whose body tension held the warp taut. The weaving proceeded by passing the weft yarn through an open shed with fixed heddles that separated threads of the upper plane of the circular warp and moved the circular fabric around the warp beams. In other areas, such as the Marshall Islands, the continuous spiral warp was wrapped around a series of wooden pegs set into a bench-like loom.

Though the loom was relatively simple, the resulting cloth was varied in design, color, and decoration. Fibers used were primarily those from banana stalks and the inner bark of the hibiscus tree. Traditional colors were black, red, and yellow, but European dyes

Wearing colorful wraparound cotton skirts, or *lavalava*, at a chief's installation in the Solomon Islands in 1976, Baelelea men carry flat, painted carvings of hornbills and other birds. Photograph by Adrienne L. Kaeppler.

in blue, purple, green, and a brighter red were introduced early. Embellishment consisted of shell and glass beads and European yarn, or thread unraveled from European cloth.

There are descriptions of a nine-strand band pattern on women's skirts in Fais Island, and the design organization is replicated in traditional tattoo patterns, architecture, canoes, and village plans, based on dual opposition and the separation of villages into chiefly and commoner sides. These designs are also found in the elaborate borders of Fais Islands shrouds. Although they were woven in the style of women's wraparound skirts, rather than being worn they were presented to the chief, who imbued them with sanctity by placing them on his spirit-shelf for four days as an offering to his ancestral spirits. According to Donald Rubinstein, they were then used for investiture, initiation, and burial of men of rank.

Although Yapese men loom-wove a special cloth that was a form of currency, the textile arts are primarily associated with women. One type of cloth woven by women on Pohnpei was so valuable that it could be exchanged for a canoe. Pohnpei and Kosrae women made fine loom-woven textiles, especially narrow belts with woven patterns incorporating shell and glass beads. These banana-fiber belts were about six inches (fifteen centimeters) wide, so fine that they sometimes numbered eighty warps per inch. In Kosrae the design was strung into the warp by tying in different colored threads, while the weft primarily bound the warps together into a fabric. In Pohnpei extra wefts added designs with a brocading technique. Women in the Marshall Islands plaited pandanus dress mats with motifs worked in with darker-colored hibiscus fiber. They were worn in pairs by women; one mat was worn like an apron in front and the second mat overlapped it back to front. About a meter (three feet) square, they were held in place by a cord belt. During important ceremonies male chiefs wore one of these mats like an apron over his wraparound skirt.

In Nauru men and women wore girdles and small square or rectangular mats plaited from pandanus leaves and decorated with hibiscus fiber. "Maternity mats," with additions of shells, seeds, and feathers, were worn by pregnant women and are said to indicate clan affiliation. Dancers from Kiribati wore mats, and the principal female dancers wore huge dance skirts that were swung side to side and over their heads.

In addition to covering their bodies from the waist to the knees with the finely woven wraparound skirts and belts, Micronesians carried plaited fans and wore decorated combs carved from wood, ornaments of coconut shell, and temporary jewels of fresh leaves and flowers. Fine baskets were used to hold personal items, such as the leaves, betel nuts, and lime used in betel chewing (which turned teeth and saliva red). Shell ornaments (also a form of currency) included belts, necklaces, bracelets, and earrings featuring orange *Spondylus*, white *Conus*, white *Trochus*, and other shells, along with colored coral and turtle shell. Skin was elaborated with tattoos and made shiny with scented coconut oil.

A traditional currency, known as "men's money," is thought to be derived from a type of Asian porcelain that found its way to Belau through the Philippines, and from glass beads and bracelets from Chinese sources. It consists of a limited number of named pieces of opaque glass and other materials, not found in the Pacific Islands, formed into beads and bars. The pieces are used as necklaces by women to exhibit the family's wealth or during pregnancy and after the birth of a first child. Although worn by women, these currency pieces are owned by men and are exchanged between men. In the twenty-first century replicas are used by Belaun women as jewelry and are purchased by tourists as mementos of their visit to Belau.

Warfare resulted from political rivalry, revenge for murder, and disputes over land and women. Warriors from Kiribati and Nauru wielded shark-tooth-edged spears and hand weapons and shielded themselves by wearing helmets made of the skin of porcupine fish with quill-like spines, knotted coconut fiber leggings/pants, and body armor that covered the torso and had an additional head-and-neck protective shield that rose from the back of the armor. The body armor was made of coconut fiber and decorated with human hair in designs often based on diamonds. The back shield was especially important for protection from flying stones. Although the armor had a protective function, it must have also functioned as a psychological and visual deterrent.

POLYNESIA

The islands of Polynesia form a roughly triangular shape in the eastern Pacific Ocean, lying primarily to the east of the international dateline. Hawai'i, New Zealand, and Easter Island are

A gourd penis covering embellishes a Telefolmin musician at the Pacific Festival of Arts in Papua New Guinea, 1980. A nose ornament pierces the septum of his nose. Photograph by Mary Jo Freshley.

the points of the triangle, and many of the islands are hundreds and even thousands of kilometers from their nearest neighbor. Polynesians interpreted their world and organized their lives according to an underlying set of principles based on descent from the ancestral gods. A generative power, *mana*, was linked with genealogical rank, fertility, and protocol and was protected by various restrictions and concepts known as *tapu*. Through mana and tapu, chiefs were able to control access to important food resources and to sacred materials used for religious rites and chiefly status, and to control labor for work on sacred sites and the fabrication of status objects. The wearing of special clothing and body attachments, as well as tattooed skin, indicated status and rank, and certain embellishments were visual symbols of prestige, power, authority, and status.

Clothing and jewelry worn by chiefs retained a residual sacredness after they were worn; fine mats were worn and presented generation after generation, and occasions on which they were used became part of them. Contact among Polynesian islands brought trade and imported objects, and designs were borrowed from island to island. Shells and pearls from the Austral Islands, Tuamotu Islands, and Cook Islands were imported into the Society Islands. Fiji, Tonga, and Samoa exchanged feathers, mats, barkcloth, ideas, and spouses.

The Polynesian body aesthetic is linked with the hierarchical scheme of society. In general, the Polynesian view was that high rank or wealth was associated with lighter skin and an abundance of flesh. This was taken to its logical extreme in Mangareva where the children of high-status parents were secluded in houses to keep their skin light and fed to make them as corpulent as possible. The parts of the body that required coverings varied with gender and rank. Women were usually covered from the waist to the knees, and men usually covered the genital area—that is, the procreative parts of the body were normally hidden. Women's calves were expected to be heavy and those of men muscular.

Clothing in Polynesia was made chiefly of plant leaves and barkcloth—structured primarily as loincloths for men and wraparound skirts and shoulder coverings or leaves attached to fiber waistbands for women. In some areas ponchos made of barkcloth or plaited pandanus were used by men and women. Polynesia is well known for the making of barkcloth by beating the inner bark of certain trees, especially that of the paper mulberry (*Broussonetia papyrifera*), cultivated specifically for the purpose. The outer bark is removed and the inner bark soaked in water to soften it. It is then beaten, usually with a wooden beater on a wooden anvil, to make it wide and soft. The pieces may be felted, pasted, and/or sewn together to form larger pieces. The East Polynesian process is based on felting. In Hawai'i felting was achieved by two separate beatings. After soaking in water the first beating produced long strips that could be dried and stored until needed. For the second beating the dried strips were soaked, lightly beaten, placed in layers between banana leaves, and left for about ten days to mature by "retting." The partially rotted and layered strips were felted, by beating, into a finished rectangular piece. In West Polynesia each piece of inner bark was beaten separately and then several were pasted together with vegetable paste.

At this stage the cloth became a medium for artistic expression. Decoration varied from island to island and required another series of tools, as well as dyes and perfumes. Barkcloth wraparound skirts and *malo* (loin coverings) were decorated with complex designs. In a few instances barkcloth was sewn,

for example, in Hawai'i sheets were stitched together along their long side to make wraparound skirts of several layers for ranking female chiefs, and in Easter Island small pieces of barkcloth were sewn together to make cloaks. It also served as ties for wraparound skirts, and a unique Easter Island belt has two pieces of turtle shell encased in barkcloth. In addition to clothing and bed coverings, barkcloth served for wrapping the dead and wrapping images of gods and ancestors, and huge pieces of it were used in ceremonial presentations, weddings, and funerals.

Barkcloth was often presented to a person of rank in a dramatic flourish. For example, in Fiji a chief presented himself to a higher chief clothed in hundreds of feet of the material, and he disrobed either by spinning to unravel wrapped barkcloth or by dropping a huge looped barkcloth dress as an aesthetic gesture in honor of the receiving chief. In Tahiti it was presented wrapped around a high-ranking individual; it was unwound from the giver and rewound onto the receiver. In Samoa a large piece of barkcloth might be worn with one end wrapped around the wearer and the other end trailing as a train. In Samoa an orator wore a barkcloth wraparound skirt, held a staff, and placed a flywhisk over one shoulder while presenting his speech. Since the mid-nineteenth century a headdress (*tuiga*) has been worn by the *taupou* (young chiefly female) or *manaia* (young chiefly male) for *kava* mixing and dancing. It classically consists of a barkcloth cap surmounted by human hair, feathers, a headband of nautilus shells, decorated sticks, and other elements.

People of status wore finer clothing, especially ornaments and combs. In addition, they carried fans, flywhisks, and staves of authority. The missionary John Williams described the marriage ceremony of a woman of status in Samoa. She wore a fine mat that extended from her waist to her ankles, and a headdress of leaves and flowers, a necklace of large blue beads, and her skin was anointed with scented coconut oil and colored with turmeric rouge.

Funerals were important occasions for self-presentation. Self-mutilation, such as cutting off finger joints in Tonga, or cutting oneself with a shark-tooth implement and tattooing the tongue in Hawai'i, were common. Hair was cut, and ragged mats were worn in Tonga. Most elaborate was the ritualized performance of the chief mourner in the Society Islands, where in a spectacular display of grief at the death of a chief or other important person, a priest or close relative of the high-ranking deceased brandished a shark-tooth-edged stave. He was dressed in an elaborately constructed costume and accompanied himself with a pair of pearl-shell clappers. The most important parts of the dress were two complementary crescents—one above the head and one in front of the chest. On the large wood chest-crescent were mounted several large pearlshells. Attached to the bottom of the crescent was a sparkling chest apron made of rows of thousands of tiny slips of pearlshell, sewn together with fine coconut-fiber sennit. The face of the wearer was covered with a mask of a few large pearlshells or pieces of turtle shell with only a small peephole through which to see. The top pearlshell of this group was the base for the upper crescent, consisting of the tail feathers of the tropic bird. The mask was attached to a barkcloth head covering that held it in place. Other long pieces of barkcloth formed a skirt and ties, and a long apron of the same material was covered with carved pieces of coconut shell. The costume was completed with a barkcloth cape and sometimes a feathered cape and tassels.

Clothing worn during warfare illustrated rank and wealth. In Tahiti the highest chiefs wore a huge war bonnet fronted with

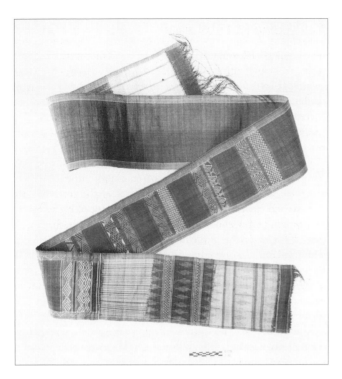

A loom-woven belt from the Caroline Islands, about 1840. The horizontal-tension backstrap loom used in such areas most likely has its roots in Indonesian textiles. Department of Anthropology, National Museum of Natural History, Smithsonian Institution, Washington, D.C.

a feathered construction that formed an overarching forward crescent above the wearer's head. Complementing this crescent were two crescent-shaped chest and back protectors called *taumi*, which protected the vital parts from sling stones and other missiles. They had a sacred protective quality as well. They were made of a base of sennit, covered with feathers. An outer fringe of dog-tail hair repeated a series of inner crescents of shark teeth, and they were finished with round pieces of pearlshell and rosettes of feathers.

Elaborate feathered headdresses were characteristic of the Austral islands, Tuamotus, the Marquesas, and Tonga. High-status Māori wore tail feathers of the *huia* bird (*Heteralocha acutirostris*), singularly or in multiples. The head of the female huia had a curved tapered bill and was worn as an ornament of the neck and ears.

Feathers were particularly important in Hawai'i, where cloaks and capes were made of a fiber network and entirely covered with tiny red and yellow feathers from honeycreepers and honeyeaters. They were worn, along with feathered helmets, during sacred and dangerous situations such as warfare and religious ceremonies. A similarly decorated sash carried with it the right to rule, and plumed standards called *kāhili* were carried to herald the presence of individuals of rank. Cloaks and capes were worn by male chiefs and embedded the social metaphor that one's genealogy is one's sacred protection. Designs were incorporated as the feathers were being tied to the backing of knotted fiber, for instance, by adding yellow feathers or occasionally black or green ones from other honeycreepers or honeyeaters. Yellow feathers came from birds that were primarily black—the yellow tufts were removed and the birds released—making the yellow ones rare and valuable.

Feathered helmets, *mahiole*, were sometimes worn with the cloaks. Made of a basketry foundation, they were of two main styles—one with a wide low crest, the whole of the helmet being covered with long, round, stiffened fiber strips to which feathers were attached; the second with a high narrow crest covered with netting for similar attachments. Feathers were red, black, green, and yellow, and women made and wore head and neck ornaments (*lei*) in a variety of colors and designs. Red was the sacred color in Hawai'i, as elsewhere in Polynesia, and red feathers were considered among the most sacred natural products. In Hawai'i it was also important that a son could not wear the clothing of his father; nor could a daughter wear the clothing of her mother. A father could wear the clothing of his son, but apparently only if the child were not of higher rank through the female line. It was best not to wear clothing that had belonged to someone else if one did not want to make one's body vulnerable.

The skin was often tattooed, in different parts and degrees for men and women, and scented with perfumed coconut oil. In the Marquesas yellow and reddish paint was used to enhance the color of the skin, and in Easter Island elaborate painting adorned the skin of men during rituals. The Polynesian term *tatu* (or some variation of this gloss) is the origin of the English word *tattoo*. It was carried to its high points in the Marquesas and among the New Zealand Māori, although considerable portions of the body were also tattooed in Samoa, Tahiti, Hawai'i, Easter Island, and elsewhere. Tattoo was done by dipping into a black dye a prepared tattooing implement—made of bone, turtle shell, or seashell hafted to a stick somewhat like an adze—placing it on the skin, and striking the implement with a mallet or other striking tool. This broke the skin and implanted the dye. It also caused the blood to flow and gave considerable pain.

Clothing and embellishments demonstrated the sanctity, rank, and wealth of the people who wore them and the skill and patience of the specialists who made them. Materials used in Polynesian ornaments were those of high value, either because of their sacred qualities—such as red feathers or hair—or because of their rarity—such as greenstone, whale ivory, turtle shell, pearls, and pearlshell. Māori greenstone and whaletooth ivory were used for earrings and pendants. Whalebone was used for combs and breastplates, *civavonovono*, which combines Fijian-style whalebone breastplates and Tongan shell necklaces into a form distinctively Fijian. Turtle shell was used on headdresses and bracelets. In Tahiti pearls were used as earrings, and pearlshells were used in necklaces and on mourning dresses. Rare shells were used as pendants, on headdresses, and to decorate dance costumes. Characteristic of West Polynesia were necklaces of carved ivory pieces shaped to curved points and strung. Decorative combs were made from coconut midribs bound together with fine sennit and enhanced with beads or carved of wood in delicate openwork. In addition, ephemeral items were made of flowers—often sewn in elaborate, painstaking constructions—as well as seeds and other parts of plants.

Human hair probably had a sacred quality because it came from the tapu part of the body, either from ancestors or defeated enemies, thus capturing their mana. Human hair was used in wigs, headdresses, necklaces, fans, and belts; and the white beard-hair of old men was a decoration used in the Marquesas. Feathers, especially tail feathers of tropicbirds and red feathers of various kinds, were used in headdresses, flywhisks, waist girdles,

Body armor from the island group of Kiribati, collected on the U.S. Exploring Expedition between 1838 and 1842. It is made of twisted and knotted coconut-fiber sennit. The armor has a shield that rises from the back to protect the neck. Department of Anthropology, National Museum of Natural History, Smithsonian Institution, Washington, D.C.

and rings. Human and animal teeth (including shark, dog, and pig) were formed into necklaces, bracelets, head ornaments, and gorgets (chest ornaments). Coconut fiber was used in flywhisks, combs, and belts.

Clothing was plaited from the inner bark of the hibiscus tree or prepared pandanus leaves, and for special occasions it might be made of intricately intertwined coconut fiber overlaid with red feathers. The most important valuables, especially in West Polynesia, were fine mats, usually plaited from specially prepared pandanus strips—sometimes as many as thirty to the inch—which were named and imbued with their owner's mana. These were worn and presented during important rituals such as funerals and weddings and were inherited from generation to generation. The criteria by which they were evaluated included fineness, color, type of leaf from which they were made, how old they were, and most importantly on what occasions they had been used in the past and by whom.

POST-EUROPEAN CLOTHING

The coming of Europeans changed the Oceanic world in many ways. The introduction of European cloth and clothing augmented, but did not replace, indigenous cloth or clothing until well into the nineteenth century. For example, in Hawai'i in the 1820s the wearing of a naval officer's jacket with a barkcloth malo was not an incongruous combination (as Europeans viewed it), but a replacement of one high-status shoulder covering with another. Female chiefs wore long-sleeved silk dresses, and male chiefs took pride in military uniforms. Red trade cloth was highly valued because of the sacred color and continued to be used in the same way as indigenous barkcloth. In Hawai'i red cloth was taken apart into fibers and pounded into barkcloth, thereby enhancing color but not changing technique. In New Ireland printed European cloth was integrated into *tatanua*, dance masks.

After first European contact Pacific clothing was not really changed; but dramatic changes came with the secondary influx of missionaries, who were focused on covering the body—especially on women covering their breasts. Although Pacific Islanders were accustomed to the importation of new gods from their neighbors or other islands or from inspiration of priests, they were not accustomed to a new god outlawing the old gods, and especially the missionaries' condemnation of ritual organization and its associated concepts of mana and tapu, disregard of sacred sites, and interdiction of dancing. Much of traditional society centered on these activities and sacred places, and chiefs and religious practitioners were not anxious to have their authority undermined. In some cases those with authority forbade attendance at Christian services, and unless the chief or headman was converted, there was little hope that Christianity would succeed. When Christianity finally took hold, the devotion to the new god was similar to the devotion to the old gods—only ritual occasions occurred more frequently, every Sunday rather than seasonally. Missionary wives introduced cloth, sewing, and the arts of embroidery and quilt making. Pacific women were quick to take up these new pastimes, adapting them to their own forms and designs. In Polynesia many of the functions and tapus associated with barkcloth were transferred to quilts—which in some areas, such as the Cook Islands, have replaced barkcloth for presentation at weddings, funerals, and other ceremonies. With the aid of missionaries ponchos made of barkcloth moved from Tahiti to Samoa and Niue, and probably elsewhere.

There is no doubt that Europeans had an important impact on Pacific dress, but the changes accommodated Pacific ideas about clothing, not just copying, for instance, wearing a military jacket with a loincloth. In the twenty-first century clothing has become part of cultural and ethnic identity. Local arts festivals are held regularly, and every four years a grand Pacific Arts Festival is held in one of the areas of the Pacific. Here, twenty or so Pacific nations gather to present old and new artistic practices, to share their arts, and to learn from each other. Performers often wear traditional dress made of indigenous materials. Clothing based on the so-called mother hubbard dress has reappeared as the fashionable *mu'umu'u* (loose informal dresses), and the Hawaiian *holokū* (a comfortable, long gown with a high neck and sleeves to the wrist) has undergone stylish alterations over time. In some areas cloths used for wraparound skirts have been transformed into loose versatile *pāreus*, wrapped and styled, even stitched, into attire worn over the whole body, and the Aloha shirt and locally made and designed T-shirts can be found everywhere in the Pacific. The wraparound skirts of men, though still worn on national and ceremonial occasions, have been almost universally replaced with trousers. Since the last decades of the twentieth century, even women have worn trousers, although in many areas they are still considered "not quite right." Elizabeth Cory-Pearce has noted that on public occasions Māori women wearing trousers will wrap a piece of cloth, or even a jacket, over their pants if they rise to speak or perform. The indigenous lack of footwear has been replaced by rubber slippers, sneakers, boots, and fashionable shoes with platforms and high heels. Ceremonial occasions or dancing, however, still require bare feet.

Pieces of indigenous clothing were acquired by European explorers and Christian missionaries during the late eighteenth and nineteenth centuries and taken to various European countries, especially Britain, France, and Germany, where they became part of private collections and museums. Although some pieces are now in Pacific metropolitan centers, such as Pape'ete, Honolulu, Suva, Auckland, Port Moresby, and Noumea, a large proportion are in overseas collections. These museum collections are regularly consulted by indigenous researchers for historical information about their cultural identity, and by designers as the basis for twentieth- and twenty-first-century fashion.

In the twenty-first century high fashion in the Pacific takes us back to materials used in former times combined with globalized style. Elaborate wedding dresses are made of white barkcloth, and clothing is cut to reveal small or large tattoos. Pacific designers of clothing and jewelry are featured in shops in Auckland, Honolulu, Pago Pago, Guam, Port Moresby, and elsewhere. Pacific models parade on fashion catwalks, at local and regional "Miss" contests, and at transvestite extravaganzas such as the annual "Miss Galaxy" contest in Tonga. In 1995 an antinuclear fashion show in Suva protested French nuclear testing and included a Tahitian-inspired presentation, "No More Bikinis," to remind the audience that the bikini bathing suit was named for nuclear testing on Bikini Atoll, in the Marshall Islands. An annual event that attracts a wide number of performers from across the Pacific is the Pasifika festival, held in Auckland. Beginning in 1993 this cultural event initially included a fashion show. In 1996 the fashion show was moved from the suburbs into central Auckland and separated from the main Pasifika cultural festival. It was also rebranded as Style Pasifika. Here, Pacific-inspired clothing designs and body art are showcased within a range of categories, including streetwear and evening wear. Although Style Pasifika is organized by Pacific Island people, entry is not restricted to those of Pacific Island descent.

With social changes and increased contact with the East and West, clothing styles throughout the Pacific continue to evolve. While some traditional concepts have persisted, others have been reconstructed, and modern adaptations have been created. In Samoa, Tonga, and Fiji women continue to wear wraparound skirts beneath their dresses to cover their legs to the ankles. In Tonga men and women still wear *ta'ovala* and *kiekie* waist garments and decorations over their clothing, whether they wear traditional or modern dress. Tattoo has become fashionable, not only for indigenous men and women, but for those of European descent as well. Baskets in new forms take the place of women's purses and handbags. These use colors from imported dye and are also made for the tourist market. Artistic creativity continues to flourish, sparked by cultural and ethnic identity and tourism in response to an ever-changing world.

References and Further Reading

Bolton, Lissant. "Dressing for Transition: Weddings, Clothing and Change in Vanuatu." In *The Art of Clothing. A Pacific Experience*, edited by Susanne Küchler and Graeme Were, 19–31. London: UCL Press, 2005.

Bonnemaison, Joel, Kirk Huffman, Christian Kaufmann, and Darrell Tryon. *Arts of Vanuatu*. Honolulu: University of Hawai'i Press, 1996.

Colchester, Chloe, ed. *Clothing the Pacific*. Oxford: Berg, 2003.

Cory-Pearce, Elizabeth. "Surface Attraction: Clothing and the Mediation of Maori/European Relationships." In *The Art of Clothing. A Pacific Experience*, edited by Susanne Küchler and Graeme Were, 73–87. London: UCL Press, 2005.

Kaeppler, Adrienne L. "Poetics and Politics of Tongan Barkcloth." In *Pacific Material Culture*, edited by Dirk A. M. Smidt, Pieter ter Keurs, and Albert Trouwborst, 101–121. Leiden, Netherlands: Rijksmuseum voor Volkenkunde, 1995.

Kaeppler, Adrienne L. "The Accouterments of Musical Performance." In *Garland Encyclopedia of World Music*. Vol. 1, *Australia and the Pacific Islands*, edited by Adrienne L. Kaeppler and J. W. Love, 345–352. New York: Garland Publishing Company, 1998.

Kaeppler, Adrienne L. "Kie Hingoa: Mats of Power, Rank, Prestige and History." *Journal of the Polynesian Society* 108, no. 2 (1999): 168–232.

Kaeppler, Adrienne L. *The Pacific Arts of Polynesia and Micronesia*. Oxford: Oxford University Press, 2008.

Kooijman, Simon. *Tapa in Polynesia*. Honolulu: Bishop Museum Press, 1972.

Küchler, Susanne, and Graeme Were, eds. *The Art of Clothing. A Pacific Experience*. London: UCL Press, 2005.

Rubinstein, Donald. "The Social Fabric: Micronesian Textile Patterns as an Embodiment of Social Order." In *Mirror and Metaphor: Material and Social Constructions of Reality*, edited by D. W. Ingersoll Jr. and G. Bronitsky, 63–82. Lanham, MD: University Press of America, 1986.

Thomas, Nicholas, Anna Cole, and Bronwen Douglas, eds. *Tattoo. Bodies, Art and Exchange in the Pacific and the West*. London: Reaktion Books, 2005.

Treide, Barbara. *In den Weiten des Pazifik Mikronesien. Ausgewählte Objekte aus den Sammlungen der Museen für Völkerkunde zu Leipzig und Dresden*. Wiesbaden, Germany: Dr. Ludwig Reichert Verlag, 1997.

Adrienne L. Kaeppler

See also The Social World of Cloth in the Pacific Islands; Hawaiian Dress Prior to 1898.

Photographic Representations of Pacific Peoples

The first camera arrived in the Pacific shortly after it was invented in France in 1839, and photographs of Pacific Islanders were taken during several European voyages in the 1840s. Most of these photographs have not survived. Permanent European traders, settlers, and regular visitors increased after the founding of Botany Bay (Sydney) in 1788 and the growth of port towns at Honolulu, Papeete, Levuka, and Apia; and an accessible collection of photographs, many recording the dress and accoutrements of Islanders, dates from after the 1870s. By this time there were Europeans with cameras either living in Fiji, Papua New Guinea, Tahiti, New Caledonia, and elsewhere, or visiting briefly on trading, scientific, and naval expeditions that crossed the Pacific, through Melanesia, Micronesia, and Polynesia.

Typical photographers were German Carl Meyer, who arrived in Fiji in 1922 and by 1930 had taken seven thousand photographs, and Australian Thomas McMahon, who had thousands of his photographs of the colonial world in Melanesia and Micronesia published in illustrated magazines, newspapers, and encyclopedias between 1917 and 1923. Meyer traveled widely in Fiji, McMahon across most of the southwest Pacific, always on the lookout for compositions well away from the usual photography locations. They took many portraits using a natural backdrop. Like other photographers, they did not deliberately focus on dress, fashion, or body decoration, but their many village scenes, picturesque views, and group and individual portraits offered intimate detail of what Pacific Islanders outside the European-dominated port towns were wearing. Their photographs appeared as postcards under their names but were also often wrongly attributed to a studio or publisher. The colorful and unusual customary dress of Pacific Islanders became a favorite subject for tourist photographers in the late twentieth century.

The early photographers copied the composition and subject matter of voyage artists of the preceding three centuries. These depicted a particular European fascination with indigenous dress, decorative arts, body art, tattoo, ceremonial or political symbols incorporated into dress, and costumes that accompanied the Pacific Islander's highly ceremonial and ritualized life cycle, celebrations, and sociopolitical events. The partially clothed bodies of Pacific Island females, as well as males, also attracted photographers' attention. By the late nineteenth and early twentieth century photographic depictions highlighted fully dressed females in "mother hubbard" dresses and men in cotton pants and calico shirts, reflecting the Pacific Islander's widespread adoption of European clothing, mostly due to Christian mission influence.

Photography tells us much about how Europeans regarded Pacific Islanders and what they felt was important to record. Photographs, mostly black and white until the mid-twentieth century, were taken with specific audiences in mind, as European photographers framed the image they believed readers back home wanted to see. We can learn much about dress practices and intercultural relations in the postcontact period by careful examination of these images. If we look beyond the superficial, they also show that Islanders were not passive subjects. Photographers of the Colonial period approached their subjects with deliberate ethnographic interest, but also other interests, when dress, body modifications, and records of physical ways of wearing were merely incidental to depictions of housing, weapons, canoes, and village scenes. For example, in 1950 the ornithologist E. T. Gilliard visited the middle Sepik region in Papua New Guinea and took 1,150 slides and 300 black-and-white photographs. Although there are important images of Iatmul women included, with headbands made of *cuscus* (possum) and bird of paradise headdresses, and men with white painted faces carrying parrot feather tassels, these aspects of dress were not the focus of his research.

On the other hand, some early photographers showed a Euro-American ethnographic fascination with indigenous bodies, scarification, hair styles, jewelry, and costume. Typically the resident or visiting photographer saw something unusual, or staged a mise-en-scène (a carefully staged tableau or setting), and this singular message was sent off to be published as a cover, frontispiece, or illustration for a book, magazine, newspaper, or encyclopedia, or turned into a postcard, lantern slide, or studio print. Readers far away then read into the same image many other messages. In the twenty-first century photographers continue to be fascinated with Pacific Island cultures but tend to ignore modern dress, focusing instead on ethnic clothing and *bilas* (a Pidgin English word for self-adornment in Papua New Guinea) worn temporarily for a wedding, funeral, staged tourist shows, cultural festivals, or school graduations.

Published photographs acquired multiple meanings. The same image could be taken by a professional photographer, appear in an official colonial report or a university lantern-slide lecture, be made into a tourist postcard, or appear as a full-page sepia plate in a serial encyclopedia like *Countries of the World*, *The New World of Today*, or *People of All Nations* (ca. 1920s), as an advertisement for a shipping line, or in a cropped version as a frontispiece for a book such as Herman Norden's *Byways of the Tropic Seas* in 1926. Photographs like these might capture several intersecting elements of Pacific Islander fashion and dress. A photograph of a north Malaitan "bigman" or leader in the Solomon Islands might show a spear, a dress accessory for indigenous people who lived by hunting and fishing and who needed to be wary of enemies at all times. It might also show a shoulder bag, a bone nose piercing or earlobe piercing, a forehead ornament, a bandolier of strung shells, a money-bead arm strap, or the special shell necklace worn by unmarried young men. Although this was normal attire for a young Malaitan leader, it was unusual, exotic, and fascinating for readers in Europe and America. Despite never being likely to see an actual Pacific Islander, from repeated sightings in illustrated publications the reader might have felt familiar with and been able to identify a Malaitan male subject and his dress as coming from the Pacific.

Dancing in a large moving group, sitting, squatting, or sometimes standing were popular poses for photographers' subjects. These were posed in the studio, staged outdoors, or snapped during a Fijian *meke* (dance performed by a large group), usually in the village *rara* (open village square or meeting ground). A variety of fans, headdresses, flowers, jewelry, and clubs accompanied each meke. There were customary meke, but also district specialties and choreographed dance-dramas to depict recent events. *The Cyclopedia of Fiji* noted in 1907 that there were a variety of mekes performed on grand occasions, and that dance was the most popular of all pastimes. Often depicting two hundred elaborately costumed performers and supported by twenty or more musicians, these photographs of authentic meke, as well as staged tourist versions, serve an important historical purpose today as costumes, body art, decorative arts, and weapons were depicted that have become obsolete or forgotten over the last 150 years.

The life of indigenous people in faraway locations was fascinating to Euro-Americans. The distant "native" was seen as having desirable characteristics compared to the Western world where the rapid pace of modernity had overrun old ways. Photography allowed viewers to enjoy an anthropology lecture or museum exhibition in their own home. The photography of the Pacific peoples, as well as in Africa, Asia, and Central and South America, was responding to a popular Euro-American interest in indigenous culture, tradition, technology, art, craft, and physical appearance. It allowed Euro-Americans to peek from their armchairs at the clothed and partially unclothed frontier and colonial world.

BELLES AND DANDIES

Photographs of Islanders were accompanied by intriguing captions, often using terms like *belle* and *dandy*. The use of the term *belle* was ambiguous. Religious organizations such as the London Missionary Society (LMS) used this phrase regularly in captions, lantern-slide lectures, postcards, and illustrated magazines. Both partially and fully clothed Pacific Island women could be referred to as belles. For example, in an early-twentieth-century New Zealand illustrated periodical, a photograph of a Cook Island woman in a full-length dress was captioned, "A South Sea belle dressed to kill." In 1906 the Papuan Administration included a "village belle" in a semiofficial, annual report on Papua that appeared in *Australia Today*, a popular illustrated magazine. The young woman's breasts were discreetly obscured. In the 1920s, for a lineup of four partially clothed young girls, an overly prudish LMS cataloger in London used the village location and "boys" for the caption when the only boys visible were in the very distant background. The "Orangerie boys" captioning was presumably to divert Christian eyes from the breasts of the four young female dancers in the foreground. The early-twentieth-century pictorial supplements in New Zealand newspapers such as the *Otago Witness* and the *Auckland Weekly News* also included belles, but by 1915–1925 these had disappeared, and Pacific Island women were uniformly depicted in mother hubbard dresses and local variations of the latest European fashions.

A clear opposite to the belle was the so-called dandy, a Papuan man thought to be deliberately over-dressed, overtly fashionable, often wearing flowers in his hair, or dressed elaborately in ethnic style for a dance-drama performance. In photographs of the dandy the intention and meaning differed in several respects from images of belles. The dandy image had complex meanings, but at the simplest forensic level revealed the elaborate efforts

made by indigenous men in Papua New Guinea and elsewhere in Melanesia to use hairstyles, wigs, masks, rings, feathers, and local or imported odds and ends to declare their position in society. Although photographs of male bodies adorned with flowers might seem to mock and satirize drab and staid European male dress, the photograph of the decorated dancer was also ethnographic, capturing elements of performance and ritual, and it was a record of the amazing, often huge decorations worn in ceremonial performances. The propensity of Roro, Mekeo, Hula, Marshall Lagoon, Highlands, and other New Guinea males for self-ornamentation, as part of their daily attire, meant that indigenous men did not need to be dressed up by the photographer.

In publications in 1900 and 1913 the missionary photographer H. M. Dauncey included male dandy images, and a hagiography of the missionary W. G. Lawes in 1909 also included a photograph of a Kabadi male said to be "ready for an afternoon promenade." Photographs of Papuan men with a crown of fuzzy hair decorated with flower petals continued to be published for many decades. The soft, aesthetic image of a Papuan with flowers in his hair suggested, for missionary fund-raising purposes, that Christian conversion could change the alleged hard savagery of the cannibal. Dandy images continued beyond World War I, and one appeared as a photographic study in the journal *Australian Photo-Review* as late as 1925, but at no time did they match the popularity of partially clothed Papuan belles in books and magazines or in private albums. The elaborately dressed female belle and male dandy were rarely photographed together. The dandy, occasionally captioned "a real swell," was a comic, stereotyped figure, denied actual identity when depicted away from his language group. Removed from his Papuan cultural setting and normal customary behavior, he was theatrically constructed to conform to the humor and curiosity conventions of Europe.

The access provided to professional and amateur photographers at modern festivals such as the Heiva in Tahiti, the Mt. Hagen Show in the Papua New Guinea highlands, and the regional Festival of Pacific Arts means that colored photographs of males with gaudily painted male faces, feather headdresses, and shell necklaces, and historical links to earlier dandy imaging, continue to appear on airline posters, travel brochures, and television lifestyle programs.

STUDIO DRESS AND PORTRAITS

Portraiture, both of single sitters and of groups taken in the studio or outdoors, became an established genre for photographers in the Pacific. Pacific Islanders liked to have their portraits taken. These photographs also recorded, as a memory device, their dress, hairstyles, facial tattoos, nose and ear piercings, necklaces, weapons, and headdresses. Westerners meanwhile valued portraits as ethnographic records, but also as romantic visualizations, offering access to allegedly authentic, pre-European contact costumes and daily wear. In studio portraits the partially clothed male and female models' imported cotton clothes were discarded. As the elaborate costumes were usually from a supply kept by the photographer, the truth value or cultural veracity of necklaces, armbands, clubs, fans, spears, and costuming was unreliable. For distant audiences during the Colonial era these individual and group portraits appeared to offer intimate, visual connection and answered to a widespread curiosity about the diversity of world cultures and peoples.

Partially clothed males and females, dressed in materials made from local flora, fauna, and decorative art, or in European clothing, or a mixture of both, and accompanied by nets, clubs, or palm fronds, were popular studio compositions. The lithe bodies of young females were preferred to those of older women. Beyond the studio, in posed village settings or snapped by wandering photographers, females by the late nineteenth and early twentieth centuries were normally covered by Western-introduced cotton dresses, *sulu*, and capes. Looking to another market, by 1900, in those parts of the Pacific visited by photographers wanting pictures for the voyeur market, women were asked to undress for the photograph.

The compromise between photographer and subject, and between postcard proprietors and the prurient public, was evident when the partially naked bodies in studio portraits were captioned as customary representations, thus masking their voyeuristic intent. On the other hand, book and magazine editors and postcard publishers often used airbrushing or hand shading to obscure exposed breasts. The multiple interpretations of postcard photographs depicting semiclothed females include elements of overt and disguised voyeurism, defiance, reluctant participation, opportunism, and matter-of-fact ordinariness.

In a fascinating series of four carefully posed studio shots, also used later for postcards, a notable Fijian woman, Adi Cakobau, the granddaughter of Ratu Seru Cakobau, high chief and so-called king of Fiji, was depicted at the turn of the century in various fashions over a thirty-year period, as new styles of European clothing were adopted by chiefly families. This series of photographs revealed her changing attire as she moved from being a teenager to middle age. Although unable to escape the anonymity of captioning as a princess or belle, her fine clothes, posture, and countenance suggest that Adi Cakobau (who personally insisted on wearing European dress) retained her integrity and individuality. This rare visual biography is important historically, as it provides evidence of aging and the adoption of European fashion. It also shows how, by resisting a photographer's call to undress, some Fijian women managed to avoid voyeuristic imaging, contrived poses, and imposed costuming.

In many group portraits a political agenda can be detected in the sitter's adoption of dress. In a photograph in 1900, during the New Zealand governor's visit to several islands recently annexed by Great Britain or by New Zealand, the so-called king and queen of Niue were lined up with members of their family and wore suits and dresses typical of portraits in Australia, New Zealand, Europe, or America. For distant readers dress in this manner symbolized Niueans' modernity as well as the hegemonic ambitions of New Zealand. We are unsure of the meaning for the Niuean elite (if they ever happened to see the photograph), but wearing these clothes probably served the same modernist purpose at a personal level.

Dress also was used as a form of protest. In a group portrait taken in 1908, when the Māori leader Rua's delegation had traveled to Wellington, New Zealand, to negotiate with the colonial government, seven of the men in the delegation were dressed in *Pākehā* (European) style, with waistcoats, starched collars, ties, and suits, and displayed fob-watches. One unnamed Rua follower wore a worker's blue serge jacket without a tie or buttoned collar and wore his hair long to declare his membership in the "Israelites," a Māori group. His choice of dress seemed to be a deliberate political statement to show he was a more radical or nonconformist follower, and different from the others who had

perhaps adopted a conventional European dress code to appease the Pākehā.

Group portraits included the formal lineup, randomly seated or standing exterior groups, and the crowded ranks of native police, World War I servicemen, and labor battalions that went to Europe, or indigenous colonial militia who served in the Home Defence Force. An array of indigenous men in European uniforms, or in the case of Fiji a wraparound cloth skirt and imported shirt, suggested to readers in Europe the existence of a successful colonial administration, the bringing of order, a subservient indigenous population, and loyalty to empire. The uniforms symbolized how the Pacific had become part of a global system. The propaganda use of photographs of uniformed indigenous police and soldiers to symbolize authority, law and order, good government, and the benefits of colonial administrations was found in all colonial photography. The uniformed lineup was a signifier of colonial authority in the Pacific as it was in Africa and Asia. Fiji's indigenous police officers had an additional photogenic quality— their unique wraparound skirt, the *isulutavatava*. The policeman wearing this fringed sulu continues today as a tourist icon for Fiji and a compulsory fashion shot for tourists.

Studio wedding and family group portraits were popular worldwide among the expatriate colonial population, and traveling photographers often staged these portraits in external settings. Pacific Islanders also paid for similar photographs. The normalcy of the indigenous wedding and family group photographs posed in European dress disguised the marginalized status of Pacific Islanders, who suffered racial discrimination on the fringe of expatriate, port town enclaves. These photographs of suit-wearing men and Pacific Island women in the latest Paris fashions may have misled readers in Europe to believe that Fijians, Kanaks, Samoans, and Tongans were acculturated and assimilated and had moved fully away from past social practices and protocols. What the photography does reveal is that Christian, hard-working, and relatively affluent Pacific Islanders were aware enough of the medium to use portraiture to claim a space in the new colonial order. This was using photographic portraiture to show aspirations and modern lifestyle in a disposable, collectible, and exchangeable format. The portraits suggest that Pacific Islanders, as Europeans, Africans, and South Asians, had a good sense of what constituted appropriate pose, gesture, and appearance, no doubt with guidance from the photographer and from witnessing portraits previously taken of their friends.

In a Pacific Islander's desire to possess a studio portrait in European-style clothing, we can see accommodation to colonial society, or what historians have termed a strategy for survival. The dress, pose, and format suggest that Pacific Islanders were borrowing a European emphasis on proper conduct, identity, and social position. However, as proper conduct, customary conventions, and status were also highly valued in the Pacific Islands, an alternative reading might suggest agency rather than borrowing.

Portraits that incidentally depicted industrial clothing and the hybrid practice of adding custom (*kastom*) decorations were sometimes taken in the field with natural backgrounds and occasionally with a portable, painted backdrop. Most individual, husband and wife, wedding, or small group portraits were taken in a studio. For example, in Townsville, Australia (where Islanders were used as indentured labor), Noumea, Apia, or Tahiti, portraits of Pacific Islanders dressed in fine clothes, with a hand resting on an empty chair to hold the subject stationary, utilized

Irobaoa of Suaba, To'abaita, North Malaita, Solomon Islands, ca. 1900–1915. This young Malaitan man holds a spear and has a shoulder bag, a bone nose piercing, earlobe piercings, a forehead ornament, a bandolier of strung shells, a money-bead arm strap, and a special shell necklace, as worn by unmarried young men. Photographer unknown.

a common, worldwide, studio portrait pose. A studio portrait in 1902 of three Pacific Islander laborers, John Mann, Peter Knowles, and Jix Thinee, for example, depicted them well dressed in the male fashions of the day and was typical of studio photography taken of indigenous people in the colonies. The Queensland laborer portraits, exaggerating the glamour of the well-dressed individual, were in the style of swagger portraits and relied on the same poses and similar props. This was not evidence of colonial domination or oppressive commodification. As Hudita Mustafa has shown of Dakar, Africa, the choice of dress was central to indigenous portrait making. When Pacific Islander field laborers could dress themselves up in the studio, as well as the teachers, bank clerks, and shop owners in town, they actively distanced themselves from the actualities of their daily lives.

POSTCARDS

Many Pacific Islanders were photographed for the highly popular postcard trade. Overlapping ethnography, voyeurism, and profit

making, these photographs carried captions about villages, chiefs, canoes, fishing, weaving, or dancing. For the postcard market and later for tourists, Pacific Islanders dressed up for dances and rituals, often in costumes of unreliable authenticity. But postcards also recorded vibrant, proud dancers publicly affirming, for example, their Samoan, Tongan, Kiribati, or Fijian way of life. The large number of postcards of dances and dance costumes enabled distant audiences to visually gain access to what visiting author Beatrice Grimshaw, in books like *In the Strange South Seas* (1907), called Fiji's secrets and charms. The costumes and performances photographed in situ and subsequently made into postcards were real enough, and travelers might come across such dancers while wandering down a path to a village rara. Color tinting was sometimes added later to highlight the folds and layers of *tapa* or leaf material in the dancer's costumes. Readers in Brisbane in 1909 and Argentina in 1912, who we know received postcards like these from Suva, Fiji, would not have known the colors were false.

A long-standing juxtaposition popular in postcards—past practices against modern, native against Western, before against after—relied on stage-managed scenes in which an alleged cannibal or villager in attire and body modifications made from local materials was posed alongside a convert, laborer, or policeman in imported long pants, leather belt, buttoned shirt, and hat, and often carrying a cane. In one example, the Australian photographer Thomas McMahon posed four men on the phosphate mining island of Ocean Island (Banaba) in successive stages of dress from the "picturesque native" stage through to the "dude" stage. This sequence was published in illustrated newspapers and serial encyclopedias, and McMahon noted the men earned good wages, spent money freely on clothes and at church, and were seen as great "swells." Clothing symbolized, for European audiences and the Pacific Islanders themselves, the transition from traditional to Westernized lifestyles. This type of imaging continues today in the worldwide visual juxtaposition of Papua New Guinea Highlanders with a painted face and feather headdress alongside mining trucks and mobile-phone towers.

INDUSTRIAL PHOTOGRAPHY

Pacific Islanders worked in mines and trade stores, on wharves, ships, and plantations, and they served as policemen, teachers, and mission pastors. Industrial photography reveals there was not a common workplace fashion or style. Other photography reveals that indigenous working men and women often wore the rough clothes typical of workers in Europe, were alert to dressing up on Sundays for church, and regularly strolled about in town in the latest fashions—bowler hats, fly collars, bow ties, wide-brimmed hats, waistcoats, and as crinoline dresses of brocade.

Portrait photographers may have humanized workers in the nineteenth century by dressing them up or by asking them to hold clocks, books, canes, musical instruments, and hats, but indentured workers also preferred, for their own cultural reasons, to dress up in Western clothes. In New Zealand's thermal regions photographers asked Māori working as guides to pose for head-and-shoulder portraits with their traditional woven cloaks turned upside down to reveal the intricate design along the bottom. Photographs of Pacific Islanders at work therefore raise several questions relating to photographs as objects, and the function of portraits in individual and community biographies. Gen Doy has noted that portraits can show us the subject as another person, but the depictive function of portraits in representing the clothing choices, imposed and borrowed fashions, and blending of ethnic and Western preferences of an individual member of a class (in this case, of indigenous indentured workers) also acknowledges that photographs are historically and socially constructed. Looking through the image, beyond the depictive function, raises questions about meaning and brings to the foreground issues otherwise relegated to the margins.

Of equal concern is the photographer's and sitter's motivation in choosing what was the traditional formal portrait format of Europe and America. There are further complications. Deborah Poole has suggested that visual images like photographs reveal a comprehensive organization of people, ideas, and objects revealing social relationships, inequality, power, class structures, and the production and exchange of material goods and commodities. In the case of Pacific photographs they reveal workplace attire, fashions, and cross-cultural synergies in choosing how to present oneself in the public domain, often beyond the subject's own community. To understand the kind of organization Poole has in mind means drawing on art history, economic history, imperial and Pacific histories, the history of photography, anthropology, and the life histories of the two million or more Pacific Islanders who were workers or signed contracts as indentured laborers.

The archive of group portraits of indentured Pacific Island workers at plantations and mines includes many lineups, often of several hundred workers, and these provide evidence of industrial clothing, and particularly the cross-cultural fashion that developed when wearing imported European clothes along with local body decoration such as necklaces, armbands, and shell ornaments. By adding some indigenous items from their own cultural practices to European dress, workers blended European and Pacific accessories and made statements about their redefined bodies and their status within their own social hierarchies and cultural values, but perhaps they also did so to parody, mimic, or caricature their bosses and European overseers.

In the late nineteenth century, as a mark of their success, sugarcane plantation owners, mill operators, and small farmers commissioned photographs of Pacific Islander laborers imported into Queensland, Australia. Portraits were also commissioned by workers to record an event, a presence, a change of status, or a departure. Other scenes or individual and group portraits were taken by traveling photographers for human-interest stories and pictorial features they might later sell to capital city and provincial weekend newspapers and magazines. For example, portraits of well-dressed (in European style) Pacific Islander weddings, church groups, and families appeared in the illustrated weekend newspaper *The Queenslander* in 1901, 1906, and 1909, but these were exceptional rather than regular appearances. Because the Pacific Island Labour Trade in Queensland was politicized, some photographs of laborers in loincloths, or in field laborer's clothing, were used prior to the deportations in 1906–1908 as propaganda in political campaigns for and against the labor traffic. The dress codes, at the insistence of the photographer, sitter, or those commissioning the photograph, varied considerably from rough fieldwork clothes to the best and latest fashions that provincial shops could provide.

PHOTOGRAPHY AND DRESS: THE PROBLEMS

Photographs of Pacific Islanders need to be used with extreme caution. A warning here is that when searching the archive of

photographs for evidence of dress and fashion, researchers must avoid the error of creating a generic Pacific category, or attributing deep, symbolic meanings to what was primarily a memory device. For instance, the veracity of some early tattoo photographs is questionable, because not only did photographers add extra flourishes to tattoos, but also blackening to highlight them, complaining that tattoos along the Papuan coast were too blue to be captured on film. On the other hand, Pacific Islanders had an anthropomorphic, figurative art tradition, for example, similar to the Yoruba in Africa, and this may have motivated Islanders toward accepting photographic portraiture as a visual record of people and events.

Pacific images fall into popular categories, for instance the widow in mourning in a net headdress or fully covered by a bark or leaf cape. The cradle, or string bag, worn by or, more properly, hung from the head by Papua New Guinea women primarily to carry babies, but also pigs, firewood, and food gathered outside the village was another popular image. Yet another was the depiction of hairstyles, particularly in Melanesia where large mops of curly hair could be shaped or bound, or could become the base for elaborate headwear creations, usually for dance-dramas and major rituals, like the towering Buka Island headdress worn by young men not yet of marriageable age. In an illustrated magazine article on "New Guinea Hairstyles" in 1945, ex–patrol officer G. M. Read reported that because New Guineans were normally seminaked and therefore had less opportunity to demonstrate their individuality, so hairstyles were accentuated rivaling modern Western fashions in the ingenuity of their design.

Yet photographers and commentators ignored the cultural meaning of the hairstyles depicted. Captions did not note rites of passage, performance, or seasonal festivals. They usually provided brief, comical, and racist commentary. Some photographs show the variety of regional hairstyles in Papua New Guinea, but elsewhere in the Pacific the short, straight hairstyles of Micronesians and the long, wavy hair of Polynesians were not photographed so enthusiastically. Thus, interpretative caution needs to be observed not only because of diverse motives of the photographers and their subject stereotypes, but because of what we now know are the complex political, spiritual, and cultural meanings attached to the dress and fashion depicted.

An opportunity shot taken of a group of Pitcairn Islanders visiting a passing ship shows how researchers today forensically examine old photographs originally taken for different purposes. This group portrait was taken because Pitcairn Islanders, the descendents of Polynesians and the British *HMS Bounty* mutineers, had a compelling and mysterious history and were rarely sighted outside of Pitcairn, itself only occasionally visited by outsiders. Researchers in the twenty-first century may now detect in the Pitcairn photograph the influence of hybrid British fashions, missionary dress codes, and Polynesian weaving and basket ware in their hats and dresses.

Photographers, often being preoccupied in an ethnographic sense with the concept of "native"—bodies, nature, and savagery—rarely set out to depict dress, fashion, or decoration as a topic of interest in itself. Looking past the initial message in the massive archive of the generalized, iconographic, imagined Pacific, researchers are now going back to trawl the visual archive for evidence of specific clothing, decorative and artistic practices, and cultural changes. Europeans carrying cameras photographed studio and exterior group portraits, elaborately dressed dancers, widows, and powerful chiefs (all popular photographs), but it was nearly always racial difference—the ethnographic other—that motivated them. We now have these depictions of dress and fashion only because the photographer's main purpose was to frame a good shot of a newly discovered villager, a seminaked female, a likely labor recruit, a recent mission convert, a muscular wharf laborer, or a uniformed, obedient, and loyal member of the native police.

Pacific Islanders sitting or standing informally in the foreground or background of random village views do provide evidence of dress codes, fashion, style, and design, and through this window an insight into colonial relationships, as well as kin and clan motivations and personal aspirations. But the photography archive with its proliferation of accoutrement, artifacts, and adornment in individual photographs, mise-en-scène, and staged exterior images is also important in revealing both the character and interests of the sitters, and contextually the wider history of dress and fashion. As historical evidence of Pacific Islander dress and fashion, photography is important in a documentary sense, because each image tells us about a person, their individual response to new situations, and the place they spatially occupied in their own world, albeit the superficial, imposed colonial world. But as Gen Doy notes, the true nature of the sitter is ultimately inaccessible. In photography the dress, body decoration, bilas, external appearance, rhetorical gesture, and figure of the subject are revealed, but the interior or soul is not.

References and Further Reading

Batchen, Geoffrey. "Ere the Substance Fade: Photography and Hair Jewellery." In *Photographs, Objects, Histories*, edited by Elizabeth Edwards and Janice Hart, 34–46. London: Routledge, 2004.

Doy, Gen. *Picturing the Self: Changing Views of the Subject in Visual Culture*. London: I. B. Tauris, 2005.

Edwards, Elizabeth. *Raw Histories: Photography, Anthropology and Museums*. London: Berg, 2001.

Geary, Christraud. *In and Out of Focus: Images from Central Africa 1885–1960.* Washington, DC: Smithsonian Institution Press, 2002.

Jones, Lynette. "The Pareu: Persistence and Revival in a French Polynesian Folk Art." In *Artistic Heritage in a Changing Pacific*, edited by J. C. Dark and R. G. Rose, 84–90. Bathurst, Australia: Crawford House, 1993.

Landau, Paul. "An Amazing Distance: Pictures and People in Africa." In *Images and Empires: Visuality in Colonial and Postcolonial Africa*, edited by P. Landau and D. Kaspin, 1–40. Berkeley: University of California Press, 2002.

Maynard, Margaret. "Staging Masculinity: Late Nineteenth Century Photographs of Indigenous Men." *Journal of Australian Studies* 66 (2001): 129–137.

McMahon, Thomas. "Evolution of Dress among the South Sea Islanders." *Sydney Mail*, 8 January 1919, 15.

Mustafa, Hudita. "Portraits of Modernity: Fashioning Selves in Dakarois Popular Photography." In *Images and Empires: Visuality in Colonial and Postcolonial Africa*, edited by P. Landau and D. Kaspin, 172–191. Berkeley: University of California Press, 2002.

Poole, Deborah. *Vision, Race and Modernity: A Visual Economy of the Andean Image World*. Princeton, NJ: Princeton University Press, 1997.

Read, G. M. "New Guinea Hairstyles." *Walkabout Magazine*, April 1945, 30–32.

Sprague, Stephen. "Yoruba Photography: How the Yoruba See Themselves." In *Photography's Other Histories*, edited by C. Pinney and N. Petersen, 240–260. Durham, NC: Duke University Press, 2003.

Max Quanchi

See also Missionary Dress in Samoa.

The Social World of Cloth in the Pacific Islands

- Properties of Cloth
- Material Transformations

Portable, malleable, absorbent, and textured, often with colored patterns that attract or repel the mind, cloth the world over is essential for all manner of fastenings and constructions that give form to the social relations that are conceived as dependent upon the actions of the body. Pacific societies are unique in expressing, perhaps more fervently than observed elsewhere, the centrality of cloth to identities of kinship and political authority, as cloth is harnessed and transformed into surfaces that allow for the binding and dissolving of connections in the social world. Whether cloth comes in the form of mats woven from the leaves of the pandanus plant, of quilts stitched from cotton, or of printed sheets of finely beaten bark, Pacific cultures use the symbolic potentialities of cloth, present in its material capacity to be bound and wrapped, to transform the common into the unknown and unknowable, to make visible spiritual processes and the power conferred onto initiates or ritual specialists. This transformative function of cloth and the processes it evokes are not only applied to objects such as plants or statues, which are consecrated through the act of wrapping in cloth, but to human beings in general, especially to human manifestations of gods and ancestors, as well as to ritual specialists.

What we can thus learn from the use made of cloth in Pacific cultures is what cloth does, not what it means. Cloth is the vital agent through which kinship identities are translated into political authority, for holdings and exchanges of cloth underwrite the political hierarchies of lineages, titles, and chiefs that are found across the Pacific. Cloth casts light on the nature and the complexity of the social and cosmological order by virtue of a visual analogy that is drawn between the material potentialities of cloth and forms of social relations. This agentive capacity of cloth in the Pacific was first described by the anthropologist Annette Weiner (1989). Although cloth is relegated as "fibre arts" to the closets of museums and overlooked by curators and theoretically minded anthropologists alike, Weiner has helped to throw light on the overarching significance of a single category of textile or cloth, as she called it, including all objects made from threads and fibers, such as Australian Aboriginal hair strings; Māori flax cloaks; leaves such as Trobriand banana leaf bundles; and bark, such as Polynesian barkcloth. Thanks to her inspiring research, we readily acknowledge that such cloth-like things form a category of wealth that has remained of unrivaled significance to the political economy of the Pacific.

Much research has taken place into the social world of cloth in the Pacific in the wake of Weiner's path-breaking work. Such ethnographic studies, however, showed that not all cultures in the Pacific share the same expectations of what cloth is, or what it does. Lissant Bolton, for example, has reported from Vanuatu that there is no single word meaning *textile*, and that each of the twenty-five recorded artifacts made of pandanus is considered to be a distinctive type of object, although made from the same

material. On the mainland of Papua New Guinea research has shown that the art of wrapping and unwrapping by means of a long web of soft, pliant cloth, which so profoundly supports ritual in Polynesia, is almost absent, whereas the line, the string, and the frond form the composite design elements of fiber arts and dress. There thus appear to exist two different cultural traditions, with a specific positive versus negative attitude toward cloth, broadly corresponding to the geographical distribution of Austronesian- and non-Austronesian-speaking language groups. The ideas evoked by the materiality of cloth and the impact on dress in the Pacific are important to trace.

PROPERTIES OF CLOTH

Cloth throughout the Pacific presents an apt analogy for the regenerative and degenerative processes of life. This may not be apparent when looking at cotton, which is imported into the Pacific from China and the United States in large quantities, but it impresses itself upon us as an important feature of cloth when realizing that cotton has come to coexist with, and in some places to substitute for, a range of locally available materials. Such local materials, as well as imported cotton cloth, in turn are now being replaced by new synthetic materials. Cheap, tough, and formable, such new materials are the stuff of everyday life, found in the form of polyethylene, in flexible and rigid varieties, used in packaging film, insulation, and domestic items, often the by-products of consumer goods shipped in from abroad. The selection of new materials, such as plastic bread-bags transformed through plaiting into brightly colored hats, shows that what people are concerned with is the form-giving potential inherent in the material.

Materials are of such preeminent importance across the Pacific because of the premise that they come already imbued with socially potent ideas; this assumption of the inherent relation between the material and the conceptual appears quite foreign from a Western perspective, which takes ideas to reside in the immaterial realm of abstraction, impressing itself on the material as form, but never infusing it. In the Pacific acts of concrete material expression involving dress, such as apron-like wraps crocheted from the stem of a hibiscus plant, together with the making and donning of accessories, such as looped net bags worn with the daily outfit, are held responsible to deliver an idealized understanding of age and social status. Symbolic significance is assigned thereby both to the materials from which dress and accessories are made and to the techniques used in manufacture. The materials chosen for dressing the body speak volumes about different kinds of social relations by virtue of the place-making capacity they invoke. Coconuts, for example, washed up ashore to sprout into new palms or planted in newly weeded gardens as convenient temporal markers of the fallow periods practiced in shifting agriculture, provide the fiber for the Cook Island's finely plaited *rito* hats. These are a distinguishing feature of contemporary Cook Island Christian attire and use the unopened shoots of the top of the coconut palm woven together. They provide a metaphor of migration and of growing offshoots of one family in many locations all over the world.

Pandanus leaves, on the other hand, which are the treasured possessions of families that remain resident in the homelands of Tonga or Samoa, are taken from palms grown in sites that usually have been cultivated for decades by one and the same resident family. Its leaves, which come in varying colors, sizes, and shapes, have, when dry, distinctive colors, textures, and material properties that are especially useful for weaving fine mats. In Tonga mats woven from bleached, dyed, or softened pandanus leaves have historically been used as bedding, clothing, and burial wrappings. They are often presented as gifts or are displayed as potential gifts in life-cycle ceremonies. Called *taonga*, or treasures, the value of these mats is defined according to distinct categories, which correspond to the structures of hierarchy pervading social life. Dressing in Tonga aspires to a Tongan way called *faka*-Tonga, which involves the wrapping of special stitched and tailored clothing by unstitched cloth, usually mats woven of pandanus leaves or girdles crocheted from the threaded inner stem of the hibiscus plant or other thread-like materials. Such coarse waist-to-hip wrappings, known as *ta'ovala*, were worn layered over barkcloth or leaf skirts as part of formal dress prior to missionization; in the twenty-first century short mats that are worn wrapped about the midriff and fastened with a braided cord at the waist are a standard aspect of Tongan Christian dress, even among diaspora communities overseas.

It is easy to see how pandanus serves in the self-fashioning of powerful ideas of property and descent, since the wearing of mats as part of daily dress makes visible one's status in relation to others. In Vanuatu, for instance, a special group of textiles woven from pandanus, called *singo*, is significant to status alteration ceremonies and is worn as a display of achievement by both men and women. There are two types of singo. The smaller one, called *singo tuvegi*, is worn by men hanging from a belt at the front, and by women wrapped around their hips. There are in turn several different named types of this smaller variation of singo, distinguished from one another by the design plaited on the body of the cloth, and subsequently highlighted through a dyeing process. Each subtype is attached to a grade or series of grades in the men's status alteration system, called *huqe*, and is part of a set of dress elements specific to that grade. The second main type of singo, called *singo maraha*, is a cloth that is essential to the women's status alteration system, *hururu*. This cloth is not worn but is an essential attachment to another cloth valuable known as *maraha*, crucial to the exchanges that mark the ceremonies of grade acquisition. Singo maraha are finely plaited, long and narrow strips of cloth, each distinguished by the designs that are plaited into and stenciled onto them. This cloth can be made only by some women who have paid for the right to learn how to make them, and to learn the special stenciling technique used in dyeing them, which is sometimes used on women's clothing. The right to plait singo is generally passed from a woman to her son's wife and remains a well-guarded privilege.

The potency that is attributed to singo explains the restrictions on its production, handling, and use. A woman who is making, or even has been merely touching, a singo would wash her hands prior to touching food or holding a child, fearing that it could damage the eyes and skin through contamination. Most dangerous of all is the debris from the making of singo, the bits and pieces of leftover pandanus and the rubbish from the stenciling process, which must be carefully gathered together and buried at the foot of a fruit-bearing tree, whose fruits are in turn restricted

The *Tivaivai Taorei* ceremonial quilt is a meticulous cloth tradition unique to the Cook Islands. This example was produced by Akaiti Ama, ca. 1998, and belongs to the Rarotongan Hotel. Photograph by Susanne Küchler.

to those who have rights to the cloth. It is this association with food, both raw and cooked, that is significant in Vanuatu in distinguishing types of cloth that are all made of the same material using the same technique of manufacture, that share the same basic form and are all dyed red, but that are not considered to be the same kind of object at all.

Pandanus leaves, unlike the leaves of the coconut palm, may be dyed through an elaborate process or decorated through interweaving of wool or the attachment of parrot feathers, as is done in Samoa to distinguish fine mats, the most valued of all mats. Nowhere else is the staining of pandanus leaves in multiple colors of brown, black, red, and yellows as important as in the Cook Islands, where colorful sleeping mats are still the treasure of a household and have inspired the stitching of patchwork quilts, which have supplemented sleeping mats in most exchanges. Quilts are never used as dress, except at a boy's first haircut ceremony when a quilt is draped around his shoulders and at funerals when quilts are wrapped around the body of the deceased person and are placed into the grave.

The manner of construction of quilt patterns through the enumeration of geometrically repeated and thus symmetrical forms is also found in the patterns on Cook Island dress. It can be sharply distinguished from the cloth quilts and cloth patterns made in Tahiti and Hawai'i, where patterns are inspired by the production of barkcloth. When a young man's hair is ceremonially cut while sitting on a quilt stitched from imported cotton, or when the dead are wrapped in the same quilts as they are placed into their graves, powerful ideas are evoked that assign significance to the foreign and the beyond in the sustenance of prosperity and of the regeneration of life. Whereas outsiders may be drawn to Pacific dress as an impressive display of cultural diversity, a Pacific perspective would focus on the multiple social connections and allowances that are provoked by cloth materials and the patterns and forms wrought from them.

Arguably, the most famous and distinctive medium for Pacific cloth is barkcloth, a type of fibrous material deriving from

New Ireland women scrape taro in preparation for feasting. The women are dressed in *meri bilaus*, a missionary-inspired smock worn by women throughout Papua New Guinea. 2000. Photograph by Graeme Were.

the bark of the paper mulberry tree. Barkcloth, more commonly known as *tapa*, is found across the breadth of Polynesia as well as in some parts of Melanesia, including Papua New Guinea, though its production has largely ceased there with the influx of European cloth. To make barkcloth, women strip the bark from the tree trunk, clean it, and leave it to dry before soaking it overnight. The soaked bark is beaten on a wooden anvil with a special implement resembling a mallet until it forms a thinly fibrous material. This process results in a series of small, thin strips, which are joined together, either through gluing or through beating to create a rigid and thick cloth. The final process in the completion of barkcloth is the application of patterns across its planar surface. In Tonga patterns are rubbed onto the cloth, while in Fiji fragile stencils are used to paint on geometric patterns. In Niue decorative motifs are applied freehand.

In contrast to Polynesia, where long lengths of barkcloth form pathways at life-cycle ceremonies, Melanesian cultures place special value on barkcloth that appears in the form of strips to create openwork compositions instead. If barkcloth is used as clothing in everyday life or in ritual in Papua New Guinea, the material is mostly stiff and covers the body like a hull or a shell. When barkcloth is used in the context of men's ritual life, it is spread and tied to frames and fixed in such a manner as to turn the soft material into something that appears stiff. In some places, such as Goroka or Collingwood Bay in Papua New Guinea, barkcloth is tied to a frame and carried like a shield or a board. By stretching it over frames spectacular masks are produced among the Baining of central New Britain and among the Elema in the Papuan Gulf. In the Highlands of New Guinea masks are made of bark, with barkcloth often forming just one component of many in the fabrication of elaborate wigs. Brigitta Hauser-Schäublin has pointed to the prevalence of multiple and prolific combinations of decorative

elements as a kind of assemblage including leaves, fronds, flowers, fruits, nuts, and feathers, as well as necklaces, belts, plaited bands, and meshwork cloth, which in Papua New Guinea tends to outweigh the significance of planar sheets of cloth.

MATERIAL TRANSFORMATIONS

There is no doubt that Pacific dress in the twenty-first century is shaped by attitudes to cloth that indicate a great deal about the history of its peoples, reflected in the growing body of literature on the introduction of European clothing into the Pacific. Missionaries saw the adoption of European clothing as a sign of conversion, yet how clothing was imposed and received varied greatly from place to place, reflecting distinct histories of colonization and missionization across the Pacific, but also ideas invested in cloth and its transformative potential from a local perspective. Richard Eves, for example, has argued in his discussion of Methodist missions in New Britain, Papua New Guinea, that the introduction of clothing was only "skin deep," resulting in merely superficial changes that could outwardly be observed in the transformation of the imported clothing itself, such as the unraveling of knitwear and its reworking into openwork designs, yet that did not lead to lasting transformations at the societal level. Graeme Were has expressed similarly the need to trace preconceptions of clothing, which informed the manner in which cloth was taken up and accommodated. In his account of the trade in printed cotton into this part of the Pacific in the nineteenth century, he shows how calico was not simply worn around the waist or tied around the neck like an apron but was transformed by tearing it into strips, which adorned heads rather than bodies. By contrast, Nicholas Thomas has argued that clothing that had been introduced into Polynesia constituted a kind of technology toward a new being in the world, through its impact on deportment and attitudes to cleanliness and domesticity, including timekeeping.

Up to the twenty-first century, dress, and in particular women's dress, is marked by the diverse histories of clothing in the region. The Anglicans introduced blouses and skirts for women, a style that remained characteristic of women's dress in north Vanuatu and the parts of Papua New Guinea where the influence of the Anglican Church was strong. The Presbyterians, on the other hand, especially in southern Vanuatu, introduced dresses that were a simplified version of European dress at the time, known as "mother hubbard" dresses. The long sleeves and long skirts of the dresses made it difficult for women to maintain physical labor, giving rise to gender differences and to new sentiments of domesticity in a more pronounced manner, compared to regions where cloth was radically altered to suit preexisting expectations. The mother hubbard dress has been adapted to numerous local styles, as dresses are commonly decorated with binding, ribbons, and lace, or at the very least with pleats folded into the fabric—features of dress that have become a symbol of rural and island-based conservatism.

In Hawai'i the *holokū*, which originated in 1820 as an adaptation of an American day gown, shows how cloth facilitated the translation of preexisting ideas of status into material forms that have outlived their colonial past. First adopted by Hawaiian queens as a means of achieving a layered look in dressing the body, one that previously could only be arduously achieved using barkcloth then worn by Hawaiian women as day-wear, the holokū is now formal wear for ritual and festive events celebrating local identity. As in Hawai'i, other island nations of eastern Polynesia had long associated the wearing of upper body garments with status. Museum collections document the importance of a *tiputa*, a poncho made of barkcloth, which was worn widely across Tahiti and the Cook Islands. The donning of layered upper body garments by leading figures aboard ship and by high-ranking Polynesians themselves persuaded other less keen Polynesians of the power of stitched

clothing and of ways of harnessing this power by adopting Christianity. Another example of the way European-introduced cotton cloth and ways of dressing were transformed into visual icons of Pacific modernity is the Samoan two-piece outfit (*puletasi*), modeled on the Western skirt and top.

It was not just clothing, however, that was inspired by the arrival of cloth and of new technologies of sewing and cutting that allowed for innovative transformations of the new material. Home furnishings—such as pillow covers, throws, and bedspreads, as well as wall hangings—have been produced by women all over the Pacific, but nowhere as notably as in eastern Polynesia, where women have been sewing elaborate and huge quilts for over a century. Measured in units of time devoted to stitching and valued accordingly, quilts are a gift of highest value and are rarely on display, but are commonly stored in treasure trunks until returned to the maker, often at death when they are wrapped around the deceased person and layered in the grave. The association of cloth with binding the dead and the living is reflected in the visual imagery of these quilts, which is strikingly abstract in the use of symmetry and yet concrete with the reference to flowers and plants whose acquisition punctuates the biography of their makers.

Visual and verbal associations link cloth to domains of everyday life in ways that account for local preferences for cloth and ways of transforming materials. There are, for example, in Vanuatu and in Tonga, a number of associations between local cloth production using pandanus leaves and cooking. In Vanuatu the name *singo* is thought to refer specifically to designs for which there is a special or restricted food. Cloth is "cooked" over the fire and is transformed and made complete in the same way as root vegetables that are baked in a fire and transformed into edible food. Women literally ingest the power of singo, on account of its affinity with the cooking of food. In Tonga the term *ta'ovala* is derived from *tata'o*, which refers to the practice of covering freshly slaughtered pigs or taro in order to bake them in an earth oven.

An assortment of brightly colored printed cloth displaying hibiscus motifs in a fabric shop in Nuku'alofa, Tonga, 2004. Photograph by Graeme Were.

So a ta'ovala is also worn as a covering that overlays one's other clothes or that is worn as the outermost layer, wrapping the offering that it contains. Ping-Ann Addo points out that the ta'ovala are indeed "baked," as they are customarily soaked in seawater and then buried in the ashes of burned lime coral to give a yellowish tint to the light brown fibers, which become soft to the touch and have acquired a smoky smell.

The world of cloth in the Pacific is not a uniform one but demonstrates a complex picture of the history of the Pacific. This is because the new moral economy of mind and body, which missionaries aimed to extend to Pacific Islanders by virtue of the introduction of clothing, met with preexisting ideas and concerns surrounding cloth-like materials. This in turn led in certain places to the fervent use of the new clothing and in others to its radical transformation into openwork and composite designs and into layered assemblages such as quilts. Imported needlecraft technologies such as sewing, embroidery, and crocheting enabled across the Pacific the modification of traditional fiber arts using either locally available materials or a combination of both. Cutting, sewing, and folding cloth enables Pacific Islanders to this day to harness and control the power contained within its textured surface.

References and Further Reading

Addo, P. A. "God's Kingdom in Auckland: Tongan Christian Dress and the Expression of Duty." In *Clothing the Pacific*, edited by C. Colchester, 141–167. Oxford: Berg, 2003.

Bolton, L. "Classifying the Material: Food, Textiles and Status in North Vanuatu." *Journal of Material Culture* 6 (2002): 251–268.

Eves, R. "Colonialism, Corporeality and Character: Methodist Missions and the Refashioning of Bodies in the Pacific." *History and Anthropology* 10, no. 1 (1996): 85–138.

Hammond, J. *Tifaifai and Quilts of Polynesia*. Honolulu: Hawai'i University Press, 1986.

Hauser-Schäublin, Brigitta. *Leben in Linie, Muster und Farbe*. Basel, Boston, and Berlin: Birkhauser, 1989.

Hauser-Schäublin, Brigitta. "The Thrill of the Line, the String and the Frond, or Why the Abelam Are a Non-Cloth Culture." *Oceania* 67, no. 2 (1996): 81–106.

Jolly, M. "European Perceptions of the Arts of Vanuatu: Engendering Colonial Interests." In *Arts of Vanuatu*, edited by J. Bonnemaison, 267–277. Bathurst, Australia: Crawford House, 1996.

Küchler, S., and G. Were, with photographer Glenn Jowitt. *Pacific Pattern*. London: Thames & Hudson, 2005.

MacKenzie, Maureen A. *Androgynous Objects: String Bags and Gender in Central New Guinea*. Chur, Switzerland, and Philadelphia: Harwood Academic Press, 1991.

Rongokea, L. *Tivaevae: Portraits of Cook Island Quilting*. Wellington, NZ: Daphne Brasell Associates, 1992.

Thomas, Nicholas. "The Case of the Misplaced Ponchos: Speculations Concerning the History of Cloth in Polynesia." *Journal of Material Culture* 4, no. 1 (1999): 5–20.

Weiner, A. *Inalienable Possessions: The Paradox of Keeping-While-Giving*. Berkeley: University of California Press, 1992.

Weiner, A. B. "Why Cloth? Wealth, Gender and Power in Oceania." In *Cloth and Human Experience*, edited by A. B. Weiner and J. Schneider, 37–72. Washington, DC: Smithsonian Institution Press, 1989.

Were, G. "Pattern, Efficacy and Enterprise: On the Fabrication of Connections in Melanesia." In *Clothing as Material Culture*, edited by S. Küchler and D. Miller, 159–175. Oxford: Berg, 2005.

Susanne Küchler and Graeme Were

See also Introduction to the Dress of the Pacific Islands; Hawaiian Dress Prior to 1898; Barkcloth Body Wrapping in Tonga; Fijian Dress and Body Modifications.

PART 11

Polynesia

Hawaiian Dress Prior to 1898

Hawai'i is an archipelago in the Pacific Ocean, a chain referred to simply as Hawai'i or the Hawaiian Islands. The six major islands are Oahu, Kauai, Maui, Molokai, Lanai, and the Big Island, that is, Hawai'i. The latter name is rarely used, in order to reduce confusion, since Hawai'i (the archipelago) became an American state in 1959. Until the late eighteenth century the peoples who inhabited these islands shared a common culture, although they were somewhat divided politically in that each had its own ruler. Following customary beliefs, clothing and body aesthetics, including tattoos, were hierarchical and status indicators. Although people were spread across the island chain, they moved easily back and forth by canoe, as distances were not great. This ease of movement of people led to commonalities in their material culture of dress. Kings and queens had homes on various islands and enjoyed the different climates each had to offer. In the 1780s King Kamehameha I started unifying the islands, and in 1810 political unification was complete with the establishment of the Kingdom of Hawai'i. The geographical location, its flora and fauna, and its hierarchical social structure were instrumental in shaping the kinds of dress worn by indigenous people.

Until Western contact began when American and European sailors visited the Hawaiian Islands in the late eighteenth century, there are no written records, and it is only possible to account for the history of Hawaiian dress from this point on. For the present purposes the period up to 1898 is considered, which is when Hawai'i was annexed as an American territory. Captain James Cook first visited the Islands in 1778, and in the late eighteenth century sailors, during brief visits, made thorough observations of dress. From the early nineteenth century on, we see the influence of the American missionaries who settled in Hawai'i, and they began the process of Western acculturation. In doing so they had an enormous impact on local dress. In the late nineteenth century acculturation continued, becoming evident in the dress of Hawai'i's residents, particularly the *paniolos* (cowboys) and plantation workers.

CUSTOMARY DRESS IN HAWAI'I

In order to understand dress in Hawai'i prior to the late nineteenth century, it is important to grasp the general role of dress as a form of material culture in the Islands before Western contact. Textiles, clothing, and other forms of material culture were used to both signify and sustain social inequality. The society was a stratified one in which the common people, their royal class (*ali'i*), kings, queens, and the gods were intimately connected. Social status was based on genealogy: Kings, queens, and the royal class were considered to have been descended from the gods, and these nobles had power (*mana*) as a result of that divine lineage. Textiles and clothing that were worn by the ali'i also had mana due to that association. Consequently, these items were symbolically connected to power and authority.

The major features of Hawaiian dress in the eighteenth and early nineteenth centuries included feathers worked into capes and helmets, barkcloth, tattooing, and ornaments worn on the body. Status was made visible through all of these forms but was literally embodied through tattooing. The body itself was an object of art that indicated the social importance of individuals in society. Descriptions of Hawaiians written by the first sailors to visit the archipelago noted that both men and women had tattoos, and these were applied to the body in an asymmetrical manner. The front of the body, one side of the face, and legs and hands were tattooed. Not solely a form of body modification, tattooing was sanctioned by the gods and controlled by numerous rules based on social status. Tattooing was an important rite of passage that represented the transition from childhood to adulthood; it showed the wearer's strength and the ability to bear pain. Throughout the nineteenth century kings and queens had the finest tattoos, and the wives had their fingers and the back of their hands tattooed. Perceived as providing for spiritual and magical protection, tattoo motifs were symbolic of an individual's genealogy. Designs for tattoos were similar to those used in barkcloth. Motifs used were generally linear and included rows of geometric shapes such as triangles, chevrons, lines, and others, including turtles, crescent arches, and lizards.

Other forms of body modification included *lei* (a garland) worn around the neck and head. In the eighteenth century lei were generally made of feathers and other materials such as ivory and shells. A particularly important necklace was the *lei niho palaoa*, as it was the primary symbol of the ali'i rank. This necklace featured a pendant that was made of ivory in the shape of a hook. It was strung on strands of braided human hair. Women also wore bracelets and anklets made of natural materials including ivory, seeds, shells, and dog teeth.

Garments made of feather work were highly treasured throughout Polynesia, but those made in Hawai'i were considered the most detailed in their execution. These elaborate garments covered in feathers were capes (*'ahu'ula*; meaning red shoulder coverings). They were worn by male chiefs in dangerous situations, such as war. The cape symbolized that the wearer's genealogy was his sacred protection and that his high status came from his genealogical descent from the gods. Rare feathers were used in these cloaks and were attached to a backing of knotted fiber. The red feathers of the *'i'iwi* bird and yellow feathers that came from birds that were primarily black were most preferred for cloaks and helmets. The feathered helmets (*mahiole*) were designed with a crescent-shaped crest on top. These helmets were generally made of basketry and covered with the same red and yellow feathers that were used on the feather-work capes.

Throughout the Polynesian islands, barkcloth was used for textiles in the eighteenth and nineteenth centuries. In Polynesia it was called *tapa*, but in Hawai'i it was called *kapa* and was used for bed coverings and garments. Hawaiian kapa has been considered the finest form of barkcloth throughout Polynesia, due to its fine texture and the quality of the applied design motifs. Barkcloth was made by women, who first stripped the inner bark of the paper mulberry tree. The fibers were subjected to two sets of beating in a process referred to as felting. After the first beating the resulting strips of stiff material were dried and stored for later use. When ready to continue the process, women took the dried strips and rehydrated them by soaking the strips in water. Next they were beaten again, then laid between layers of banana leaves and left to mature by retting (a process in manufacturing fibers whereby the bast is separated from the woody core by soaking). The strips were then joined to each other through beating them together into a felted sheet. To make a large sheet of kapa, smaller pieces were sewn together with an awl (or in the nineteenth century, a needle) and a fine, thin strip of kapa used for thread.

Clothing was made of kapa from the eighteenth to the mid-nineteenth centuries. The sheets were quite thick, but in the nineteenth century Hawaiian women beat the kapa into much thinner sheets. Design motifs changed as well, from large angular designs seen in the eighteenth century to smaller designs in the nineteenth century. These often incorporated circular motifs and watermarks in the kapa. With the introduction of metal tools that began at the end of the eighteenth century, the designs in nineteenth-century barkcloth became much more intricate. Prior to the gradual adoption of Western-styled dress in the nineteenth century, standard Hawaiian clothing consisted of only a brief lower body covering for both sexes. Men wore a loincloth called the *malo*. It was made of long narrow strips of kapa with two designs, and when it was folded lengthwise the designs showed. In addition, if men were from the ali'i class, they might also be covered by a cape called a *kihei*.

All Hawaiian women wore the *pa'u*, a wrapped garment of kapa that was worn in several layers, the number of which was determined by rank. Generally the top layer had stamped geometric designs applied to it, and the design motifs used were similar to those used in tattoo. The pa'u passed several times around the waist and was three to four feet (or about one meter) long. The amount of barkcloth, its quality, and the extent of decoration on it all indicated social class and rank. Women also wore the kihei, tied over one shoulder, if they were ali'i.

The arrival of Western trade goods began with Captain James Cook's visit to the Hawaiian Islands in 1778. Other ships stopped by in the next forty years, and barter between the sailors and Hawaiians began. The demand for men's Western clothing began when some of the more enterprising Hawaiian men, both commoners and ali'i alike, began trading with sailors for their shirts, hats, and pants. The Hawaiians traded a variety of items of their material culture, such as feather capes, for the clothing. Soon thereafter, the ali'i took over trading, because by 1810 they controlled the sandalwood forests and used the wood in trade with sailors and merchants for Western textiles and apparel. The ali'i amassed quantities of Western consumer goods, including clothing, regarding it as a means of symbolic display of their high social rank. First worn by them as a novel means of status display, Western-styled clothing became firmly associated with upper-class status in the nineteenth-century.

The transition from the kapa malo for men of the commoner class to Western clothing was slower than for the male chiefs, who obtained Western clothing earlier as they had more goods to barter. The transition to Western dress for women was also slow, because dresses and other items of clothing for women did not enter the Hawaiian Islands until the arrival of American missionaries in 1820. Until then, Hawaiian women acquired woven cloth from their men or as gifts from sea captains, but since they did not know how to sew, they continued to wear the kapa pa'u. For queens, as many as ten layers of kapa were worn, while for commoners the number of layers was few. Lengths varied according to status as well. On very special occasions the queens would wear over seventy yards of kapa at a time; when wound around the body the thickness of the cloth held the arms out in a horizontal position. Although kapa was customary fabric for the pa'u, it could not be cleaned, did not wear well, and even just one layer was stiff to wear. As noted in early-nineteenth-century diaries and journals, Hawaiian women substituted fabrics such as calico for kapa in the pa'u.

HAWAIIAN DRESS IN THE EARLY NINETEENTH CENTURY

Many changes in Hawaiian society occurred after the overthrow of the religious *kapu* system in 1819. Until then, numerous rules enforced the separation of the chiefly class from commoners; one such example was that the colors red and yellow were reserved for use only by ali'i. In 1820 American Christian missionaries arrived to create permanent homes and missions among the indigenous Hawaiians. In doing so, the missionaries set the process of Westernization into motion. Although some Western goods had arrived in the prior forty years, these items did not significantly change the culture. It was not until people from America settled there permanently that the process of acculturation began in earnest. The missionary men and women had two goals: to Christianize the islanders and to simultaneously "civilize" them, and toward that end the missionary ladies' first goal was to clothe them. In spite of the changes that occurred during this period, the Hawaiian monarchy was still strong, and the class system kept providing the social structure that continued to focus on clear status differences between the chiefly class and commoners. While the type of textiles and garment styles in Hawaiian dress changed, as kapa was replaced by woven fabrics, the function of dress as a marker of social differences continued.

Liholiho (the son of Kamehameha the Great) was king when American missionaries arrived in 1820. Since he was on another island at the time, his queen and other ali'i met the missionaries' ship, dressed in their finest kapa. The American gowns (in the style of 1819, with their high waists, narrow skirts, and long, tight sleeves) enchanted all the Hawaiian queens. In order to stay in the islands the missionaries needed the permission of King Liholiho. Queen Dowager Kalakaua was to accompany them and (not knowing how to sew) demanded a new dress to wear for the meeting with the king. She presented the missionary wives with white cambric for the construction of her new gown. In order to fit her large size and to adapt to the hot, humid environment, the missionary wives adapted their high-waisted style for a loose, comfortable, fitted garment, replacing the high waistline with an above-the-bust yoke. The end result was a basic dress that was simply a full, straight skirt attached to a yoke with a high neck and tight sleeves. This dress was called the *holokū*, and the missionaries also gave Queen Kalakaua a chemise to wear underneath. The chemise was called *mu'umu'u* but was not worn often, since the Hawaiians did not see the logic in wearing two layers of clothing. Mu'umu'u were used as house dresses and swim dresses in the nineteenth century.

One of the most rapid and visually noticeable changes was that after the arrival of missionaries, the Hawaiians began to shed their traditional barkcloth garments and eventually adopt Western-styled clothing. Because the missionary wives felt that converting the ali'i would lead the commoners to accept Christianity, they wanted to get in the good graces of the ali'i, and to do so, these women gladly made clothing for Hawaiian royalty, who wanted Western-style clothing as an expression of status. It was the main hope of missionary wives that the ali'i could be persuaded to adopt Western notions of modesty and propriety; however, the two groups had different motives for covering the body. Hawaiians came to use actual European fashions to display status, but also to indicate that their ruling classes were modernizing. While covering the body was essential to the missionaries, Hawaiians considered that dress depended on rank and social occasion, and the ready acceptance of European fashions was in contrast to some other Pacific islands. Nevertheless, there was a covert reason that the missionaries insisted on the wearing of holokū, for in this instance it visually identified and separated the Hawaiians from Westerners.

The diaries of missionary women report that those women who had been Christianized adopted the holokū as daily dress by 1822. However, it took a great deal longer for this style to become uniformly associated with Hawaiian women, due to status differences among the indigenous population. The early converts were ali'i, who had already acquired Western textiles through trade. When missionary wives required "modest" dresses to be worn by all women at the missions, the wives immediately became seamstresses for the ali'i. The queens brought out their stores of brocades, silks, and chintzes, and missionary wives were pressed into service. The wives soon found the constant demands for sewing to be an overwhelming job. On the other hand, the ali'i were glad to have holokū made for them by the missionaries, because it reinforced their higher social status. Showing the complex ethnic transformation associated with the holokū in the 1820s and 1830s, Hawaiian women often wore the pa'u, made of kapa, over the holokū.

In the 1830s the missionary women taught Hawaiians to sew, and soon commoners began to make the holokū of kapa, which connected indigenous textiles to the Western design of the holokū. Due to the high value of Western textiles, kapa was used by commoners until the late 1830s, when they were able to barter for fabric. At this time men of the commoner class became skilled carpenters and built Western-style houses for missionaries. Hawaiians traded labor and koa wood planking for fabric for their women, who were often involved with the mission and needed dresses. Due to the missionaries' need for housing, and the Hawaiians' desire to Westernize, by the 1840s the holokū, made in either kapa or calico, replaced the pa'u and became the standard dress for Hawaiian women, who worked in it, were married in it, and were buried in it. The holokū was the universal dress of all Hawaiian women by the time photographers arrived there in 1860.

HAWAIIAN DRESS IN THE LATE NINETEENTH CENTURY

Hawaiian men were particularly fond of the sailor's loose-fitting shirts called "frocks", transliterating the word frock into palaka. Frock shirts were made of heavy cotton fabric. One form of the fabric was a plaid that is now known as palaka; it became a favorite fabric for men's jackets and was worn with trousers as typical male attire by the end of the nineteenth century.

By mid-century cattle had become a problem on the Big Island. The problem started in the late eighteenth century, when five longhorn cattle were given to King Kamehameha the Great by the English sea captain George Vancouver. Kamehameha protected the cattle from slaughter, so that by the mid-nineteenth century, wild herds needed to be tamed. King Kamehameha III found a solution in that he brought Spanish-Mexican cowboys into Hawai'i in the 1830s to teach Hawaiians to ride horses, to round up cattle, and, ultimately, to develop working ranches. These cowboys were referred to as paniolos (derived from the word español); they were highly skilled artisans in leatherwork and braiding and brought with them cow ponies and Spanish saddles. Paniolo dress developed as a result of strong Spanish and Mexican influences. The clothing was functional work dress. Heavy trousers were tucked into high laced boots. Long-sleeved light-colored shirts had two breast pockets. Leather chaps and vests were worn, as well as a large neckerchief.

Paniolos wove hats from long leaves from the hala tree. These were called lauhala hats and were accompanied by elaborate hatbands made of flowers, shells, and feathers. These bands derived from the earlier Hawaiian tradition of lei making. The hatbands were functional in that they helped secure the hat to the head, but equally important was their use as a form of embellishment. Paniolos made flower leis on a daily basis. They were worn around the neck, and leis made for the hat, referred to as haku leis, helped communicate where on the island the paniolo was working, because different flowers grew in the wide variety of ecosystems on the island. The lei hatbands were said to attract women and became a key feature of paniolo style.

During the early nineteenth century the indigenous Hawaiian population began to suffer from a lack of resistance to Western diseases, and by 1872 about two-thirds of the population had died. Original land ownership was being replaced by expatriate owners, and by the middle of the nineteenth century sugar plantations were a rapidly growing part of the economy. However, due to the decimation of the local population, laborers had to be imported into Hawai'i to work on the plantations. These immigrant workers came with distinct customs, languages, and practices. The plantations provided rudimentary housing for the migrants and their families, who came from China, Japan, Okinawa, Korea, the Philippines, and Portugal, with housing sections for each of the ethnic groups. The immigrants lived and worked together in close proximity on the plantations and had to adapt rapidly to each other. Assimilation occurred quickly, and a creole form of language, called pidgin, and a hybrid form of dress, called plantation dress, developed in this multicultural context. The first to arrive on the plantations were the Chinese; the men wore their hair in queues (braids of hair hanging down at the back of the head) together with the pounded indigo jackets and loose trousers typical in their homeland. Chinese women also wore simple jackets over pants for work, and silk jackets with embroidered accents over double layered silk skirts called "paired aprons" for social occasions.

Japanese immigrants began arriving in the 1860s and came with a wealth of fabrics that would become important to Hawai'i over the years. Cottons, silks, and even linens were used, often in striped patterns. A favorite fabric was kasuri, whose design came from the yarns being tied and dyed prior to weaving. Japanese workers on the plantations brought work clothing from home, but it did not take long for them to adopt the heavy fabrics and rugged styles of work clothing brought to the Islands by other migrant workers. Japanese women made work clothing for both themselves and their husbands, primarily from heavyweight blue cloth. Men wore these heavy jackets to provide protection from the cane. They were cut straight and worn just below the waist; they had long sleeves and a pointed collar, and often the yoke was padded with rice-bag material to facilitate carrying the heavy cane on their shoulders. By the end of the century a softer plaid fabric was used, and the *palaka* jacket became the preferred style. Protection from the sun was critical. For both men and women hats were varied. Workers wore coolie hats, lauhala hats, and straw hats of various types. The women in the plantation communities wove lauhala hats and sold them to plantation workers.

By the 1890s there were many different ethnic groups working on the plantations. Creolization, both in language and dress, occurred rapidly as a result. Women adapted design ideas from various ethnic groups in Hawai'i, and a unique form of plantation work dress was created that was protective and functional, quite similar across the ethnic groups. For most workers in the nineteenth century the basic garments were a jacket, a dirndl skirt, a wide sash of black fabric, and a straw hat. The Japanese women redesigned and shortened their kimono to include the closer fit of Chinese jackets. The end result was a *kasuri* jacket that had elements of both cultures' dress styles. Breeches were worn under the skirts, with aprons on top, straw or sunbonnet hats, leggings of denim, and protective footwear.

For the majority of women in Hawai'i who did not work on the plantations, by the late nineteenth century the transition from indigenous dress of kapa pa'u to Western-styled clothing was complete. Following its adoption by royalty, who were the first to become Christianized, the holokū and its undergarment, the mu'umu'u, were then adopted by commoners, who wore simply styled holokū for everyday wear and dressier holokū for special events such as church and social gatherings. In the 1870s trains were added; the length varied with the formality of the occasion, and the holokū became a formal gown for commoners. While the long sleeves and high necklines persisted for day dresses, lower necklines and short sleeves became acceptable for formal occasions. Trains became standard, and ruffles and pleating became common decorative elements on late-nineteenth-century holokū.

Female ali'i, however, had a larger wardrobe and a wider variety of options. The ali'i lived and interacted with both Westerners and the indigenous Hawaiians; not surprisingly, they dressed according to the occasion. The ali'i occasionally wore traditional pa'u of kapa, most frequently for rituals; they wore holokū at home for informal occasions; but in public they wore Western dress. In the latter half of the nineteenth century the ali'i became closely involved in European court life, visited Europe regularly, and patronized European couturiers, keeping up with society events, and they generally wore European fashions in public, especially for formal and state occasions, such as the coronation of King Kalakaua in 1883. However, they spent most of their time at home in the very comfortable holokū. A visitor who had been to a ball with the queen and her attendants noted that "the ordinary native women [the queen's attendants] had *holok* on, many of expensive and rich materials," and was surprised to see that, at the ball later on, the queen and her retinue changed out of European dress into holokū.

Through the 1870s the holokū was simply styled, but due to the increased influence of European styles, it began to lose some of its fullness. At the same time, Hawaiian women had become more slender as they had begun to adopt the Western body ideal; they no longer associated large body size with high social status. By 1873 the holokū was worn by nearly all Hawaiian women and was considered the official dress of the Islands, whereas Westerners exclusively wore American and European fashion. The relatively loose holokū, both plain and with assorted trimmings and trains, continued to be the dominant style for Hawaiian women through the 1880s. Lace, eyelets, ruffles, and trims became popular in the 1890s, along with leg-of-mutton sleeves. These Edwardian design details would become extremely popular at the turn of the century. The styles of the late-nineteenth-century holokū dominated twentieth-century holokū design and continue to do so.

Toward the end of the nineteenth century the black holokū was popularized by two famous Queens. Queen Ka'ahumanu wore black holokū exclusively throughout her lifetime. In her name a women's organization devoted to the care of Hawaiian people and preservation of their culture was instituted. Black holokū, hats, and gloves have been worn by members of the Ka'ahumanu society since that time, and this practice continues. After the overthrow of the Hawaiian monarchy in 1893, Queen Liliuokalani wore only black holokū. Although she had always preferred pastels such as lilac, Queen Liliuokalani wore black until her death, as a symbolic protest for what was considered an illegal overthrow. The holokū came to represent Hawaiian ethnicity without the connotations of class difference between ali'i and commoners. Indeed the holokū and mu'umu'u became entrenched as Hawaiian women's dress. Class and ethnic distinctions blurred by the turn of the century, due to the influx of various ethnic groups into Hawai'i, and a new chapter of dress emerged once the United States annexed it as a territory. Today the definitive symbol of Hawai'i is the Aloha shirt, which was developed in the early twentieth century.

It should be noted that the large College of Tropical Agriculture and Human Resources Historic Costume Collection exists at the University of Hawai'i at Manoa with items dating from the eighteenth century. The Bishop Museum and the Mission Houses Museum in Honolulu also have clothing and textile collections, primarily dating from the eighteenth century.

References and Further Reading

Arthur, Linda. "Cultural Authentication Refined: The Case of the Hawaiian Holoku." *Clothing and Textiles Research Journal* 15 (1997): 129–139.

Arthur, Linda. *Aloha Attire: Hawaiian Dress in the Twentieth Century.* Atglen, PA: Schiffer Publications, 2000.

Bird, Isabella. *Six Months in the Sandwich Islands.* New York: G. P. Putnam, 1882.

Bishop, Serano. "Jubilee Celebration 1837–1887." *The Forbes Notes.* Unpublished manuscripts. Mission Houses Museum, Honolulu.

Chamberlain, Maria. Letter to James Patton. Unpublished manuscripts. Mission Houses Museum, Honolulu.

Kaeppler, Adrienne. *Artificial Curiosities: Being an Exposition of Native Manufactures Collected on the Three Pacific Voyages of Captain James Cook.* Honolulu: Bishop Museum Press, 1978.

Kawakami, Barbara. *Japanese Immigrant Clothing in Hawaii 1885–1941.* Honolulu: University of Hawai'i Press, 1993.

Paniolo O Hawai'i. Videotape (VHS). Directed by E. Lee. Honolulu: FilmWorks, 1997.

Thurston, Lucy. *Life and Times of Mrs. Lucy G. Thurston, Wife of Rev. Asa Thurston, Pioneer Missionary to the Sandwich Islands.* Ann Arbor, MI: S. C. Andrews, 1882.

Linda Boynton Arthur

See also Tahitian Tattoos; Dress of the Cook Islands; Dress of the Chamorro; volume 3, The United States and Canada: Dress in Hawai'i since 1898.

Niue: Dress, Hats, and Woven Accessories

- Historical Context
- Weaving Techniques and Materials
- Hat Weaving in the Twenty-first Century
- Bags and Baskets
- Fans
- Festive Accessories and Dance Costumes

The small Polynesian island of Niue is one of the highest coral islands in the world. Only its plateau, rising with steep cliffs above a jagged coastline, can be inhabited. Throughout Niue's history droughts and famines have been experienced with regularity. There are no rivers on the island, and, although soil is fertile, vast stretches of land have been exhausted by shifting cultivation and ill-advised agricultural programs of the past. The soil is easily blown off by frequent and often devastating tropical cyclones, which hit the island every five to ten years. Visits by outsiders were so rare in Niue that there is hardly any written knowledge of their dress until the arrival of European missionaries in 1861. A decade prior to that, Samoan missionaries had a major impact on the culture by introducing European and Samoan clothing styles for men and women that coincided with their beliefs about modesty. In the twenty-first century, for the most part Niueans wear modern Westernized clothing, but for young people's dance performances fiber material costumes are specially created. As a large majority of Niueans live in New Zealand, they have adopted pan-Pacific everyday clothing like T-shirts, blouses, shirts, and women's dresses. It is the Niueans' skills as weavers of intricate hats and accessories, however, that has brought them renown.

HISTORICAL CONTEXT

Archaeological, linguistic, and oral history evidence suggest that the island was settled from Tonga and Samoa in prehistoric times. Contrary to other Polynesian archipelagos, characterized by hierarchical social systems, Niuean society has always been an egalitarian one, without hereditary nobility, or bearers of inheritable high-ranking titles. This inevitably impacted on types of dress. Accordingly, with the exception of feather girdles, which seem to have been reserved for powerful warriors, there were apparently no differences in the kind or elaborateness of clothes.

Early European explorers and missionaries were deterred by the Niueans from entering the island's inhabited plateau, so Samoan missionaries were sent to Niue by the London Missionary Society (LMS) in 1849. Before the first European missionary—and that means chronicler—settled on Niue in 1861, the Samoans dramatically changed the island's culture. They concentrated the population in villages around churches and established the Ekalesia Niue (Church of Niue) as a center of power, something that has persisted parallel to other political forces until the twenty-first century. Furthermore, Niueans were encouraged to

dress completely in European attire, and most evidence of pre-Christian clothing and weaving has not been documented. The missionaries imposed their ideas of modest dress and apparently introduced Samoan-style mat and basket weaving. This is why there is hardly any information on pre-Christian Niuean dress. Early European sources mention that the men coming alongside or on board their vessels were unclothed or dressed only in a *hiapo* loincloth, their long hair and beards decorated with seashells and fish bones. As Europeans seafarers did not set foot on the inhabited island plateau, and as canoes were taboo for Niuean women, no evidence exists of women's clothing at that time. Since the 1850s *tiputa* (hiapo ponchos) were worn and Samoan-style barkcloth, probably imported from Samoa. In the 1880s large stiff barkcloths with distinctive, intricate designs were documented and collected, but their production ended before 1900. It is doubtful whether they ever served as dress; instead, they might have been made for purposes of donation or means of fundraising for the church.

Since the 1860s, due to the scarce living conditions on the island, but also due to the rigid regime of the church, with its law enforcement systems of fines and hard labor, many young men left the island to work as plantation hands or sailors in other parts of the Pacific, though usually returning after a couple of years. Furthermore, beginning with the 1870s Niueans themselves served limited terms as missionaries on a number of other South Sea Islands. Work migration, which is a prominent trait of today's Niuean society, thus has a continuity since the mid-nineteenth century and, together with the missionaries' influence, exposed Niueans to a variety of Pacific, Australian, European, Latino, and North American clothing types and accessories, such as hats, sashes, fans, jewelry, clothing mats, and "mother hubbard" dresses. Many of today's Niueans consider Western dress with Niuean accessories as part of their heritage and identity.

Having been a British protectorate and annexed by New Zealand shortly after in 1901, Niue gained its independence as a self-governing state in free association with New Zealand in 1974. As this includes the option for New Zealand citizenship, most Niueans have chosen New Zealand to be their country of settlement. Starting after World War II and gathering extreme momentum in the 1970s and 1980s, by 2005 there were only twelve hundred inhabitants left on the island, and about twenty thousand living in New Zealand. As contacts, visits, money, and gift remittances between both groups are frequent, Niueans form a truly transnational community, adopting new materials in weaving and styles of clothing that are typical for New Zealand cities with their own cosmopolitan setting with immigrants from different parts of the Pacific, Asia, and Europe.

Pan-Polynesian fashion is seen in women's semiformal and formal attire worn to functions, to church, or for visits. It consists of a long skirt with a colorful blouse, accompanied by a woven hat, and often a smart woven fan and basket. Cotton fabric with Pacific designs, for example, frangipani or *tapa* motifs, mass-produced in Asia for the Pacific customer, is made into blouses, shirts, or loose mother hubbard–style dresses for occasions like this. Mirroring village groups in Niue, Niueans in New Zealand form weaving, choir, church, or city district groups; each group appears at functions in its own distinctive uniform clothing, comprising blouses

Social dancing at a Mother's Day party, Avatele village, Niue, 2005. The "mother hubbard"–style dresses and men's shirts are made from tie-dyed and printed cotton, and the garlands are made from fragrant leaves and flowers. Photograph by Hilke Thode-Arora.

and shirts of the same fabric, sometimes screen-printed with the name and location of the group. These group clothes are found in Niue as well. It is a characteristic of many contemporary Pacific cultures, for those with interests in common, to wear clothes for special occasions that show their distinct affiliation.

The overwhelming majority of Niuean migrants live in New Zealand's cities, most of them in Auckland. A modern approach to fashion worn by younger urban women is the use of pan-Pacific accessories like seashell and coconut jewelry, and of woven items like bags, backpacks, and hats. Informal clothing in Niue and New Zealand for men and women usually consists of loose trousers or Capri pants, jandals, and T-shirts. While some T-shirts are part of group uniforms, screen-printed T-shirts with specifically Pacific designs and catch-phrases have become an established part of individual fashion statements in New Zealand and the Pacific. The late hip-hop legend Phil Fuemana (of part-Niuean ancestry) coined the term *urban Pacific* for the sub-culture of first generation New Zealand–born Pacific Islanders who often grew up in South Auckland. They embraced impulses from American hip-hop as well as British punk and creatively integrated them into their own youth culture. This has become a thriving design industry of T-shirts whose taglines and images pick up Palagis's (Caucasian's) racial stereotypes of Pacific Islanders and give them an ironic twist. Niue-specific T-shirts of this kind are rare; they usually use wordplay with Captain James Cook's infamous labeling of Niue as "Savage Island." Beyond urban Pacific youth culture, and without its wry subtexts, several Niueans on the island and in the diaspora are producing T-shirts with Niue-specific motifs and lettering, for example, remembering sports or historic events, or depicting exclusively Niuean tapa designs, or those of canoe or other clubs.

Owing to Niue's contact history, there are hardly any records of the modes of dressing and the female work of weaving in the pre-European era. Although myths and historical sources mention a goddess skilled in weaving, and hair girdles (*kafa*), as well as valuable feather girdles (*hega*) for warriors, not a single piece of factual woven evidence exists in early museum collections prior

to the 1880s. As touching and entering a canoe was—and to some degree still is—taboo for women, the early European visitors only met men coming alongside their vessels, and they did not set foot on the inhabited plateau before the mid-1850s. By this time the mode of dressing had already been completely adjusted to Christian ideas of modesty. From the 1870s onward woven accessories such as mats, hats, and baskets are mentioned by the chroniclers. Niuean traditions state that it was the wife of Tion-epaea, a Niuean missionary to Tokelau returning home with his family in the 1870s, who introduced hat weaving to the island. As in other parts of the Pacific under LMS jurisdiction, adolescent girls and married women were expected to cover their hair with a European-style hat in church services, leading to an enthusiasm for and a large production of hats over wide parts of the Pacific around 1900. Some scholars and modern-day Niueans claim that fine mat, fan, and basket weaving was introduced by the Samoan missionaries and their wives.

When straw hats were fashionable for European summer and recreational fashion between the 1880s and 1920s, tens of thousands of woven hats, including imitation panama hats, left Niue as trade goods, mainly destined for New Zealand, and rivaled copra and edible fungus sent to China as the island's most important export articles. Since then, there has been continuous weaving activity by women (and some men), partly as commodities whose sale would buy them necessities and little luxuries, partly for personal use as mats, hats, fans, and baskets. Arguably, the fluctuations in copra and cash crop prices were counterbalanced by an increased or decreased production in exportable weavings. By the 1950s the island's weavers' association had organized large-scale production for export, coordinating demands from overseas traders for distinctive woven items with the supply by the weavers from the different villages. This financially successful system gradually collapsed with increasing emigration, resulting in loss of production capacity.

Apart from its economic aspect, weaving has since the early twentieth century provided the women with the possibility of following international fashion styles by copying up-to-date accessories like handbags or hats in woven—and that means affordable—form. Triggered by modern means of travel and communication, as well as by the presence of Pacific Islanders from many different regions in Auckland, pan-Polynesian and inner-Niuean fashions are developing, changing, and being discarded with breathtaking rapidity.

In each Niuean village a women's group also functions as a weaving group. Once a week, women come together for handicraft and discussion of village affairs, deciding on issues and lines of action to be taken up with the village council or church as the voice of the women. All but the very sparsely populated villages organize an annual Show Day, where, besides vegetables, specified types of woven objects, handicrafts, sewn clothes, and bed sheets with matching pillow covers, as well as Cook Islands–style quilts, or *tivaevae*, are put on display and judged by jurors from a different village, as well as appraised by Niueans from all over the island.

In Auckland as well, there are more than twenty Niuean weaving groups spread over the city, predominantly recruiting their members along Niuean village lines. At the same time Niuean-language preschools and self-help groups provide meaningful cultural meeting places for women in the New Zealand diaspora. Good weavers have prestige and are economically successful. As in Niue, there are annual Show Days drawing large numbers of the community. Niueans agree that today their best weavers are found in New Zealand.

WEAVING TECHNIQUES AND MATERIALS

Niueans use four basic weaving techniques: right-angled interlacing, oblique interlacing, twill weaves, and half-hitch coiling. In a strict methodological classification of textile techniques, all these are actually plaiting and not weaving (as in loom-weaving or the Melanesian/Micronesian "half-weaving"). Weaving, however, is the term considered appropriate by the Niueans, and the term used in a number of English-language publications.

The weavers refer to interlacing and twill weaves as *lalaga*; to half-hitch coiling as *tia*. While lalaga is done with several materials, tia usually implies building up open-work of pandanus or synthetic materials over bent coconut midribs, which are completely covered after the process. In spite of its artfulness, tia is considered a minor technique by Niueans.

Coconut and pandanus leaves have been the most frequent raw materials for weaving. Especially in the southwest, Niuean arrowroot (*pia*) has been used for hats and fans but is on the decline. The inner bark of hibiscus provides soft handles for baskets and trimmings for hats, fans, and dance costumes.

There are many varieties of pandanus in Niue, each resulting in a distinctive texture and color of the weaving strand when properly processed. Expert weavers have their special tricks and secrets in caring for their plants; cutting the right leaves; preparing them by curling, boiling, smoothening, storing, and sometimes dyeing them with natural or chemical colors. Natural colors usually are brown and black.

With the emigration to New Zealand many women found themselves in a situation that did not enable them to weave any longer. Coconut and pandanus, which do not grow in New Zealand's moderate climate, were rarely available and did not offer the standards or quality that Niueans required of their weaving material. Besides, the double bind of having to care for very large families and at the same time make a living in a cash economy,

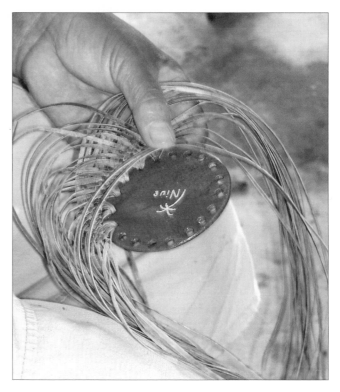

The weaving of a hat (*pulou lapa*) is begun by inserting strands in a wooden centerpiece. Makefu Village, Niue, November 2003. Photograph by Hilke Thode-Arora.

often working in three jobs per day, did not leave the women any leisure time to weave before retirement age. Dearly missed as a significant cultural activity over decades, the turning point came in the 1980s. In a common workshop of Māori and Pacific Islanders, Māori weavers instructed and authorized the immigrant women in the technological and ritual preparation and use of flax, their centuries-old and traditional weaving material. This resulted in a boom of flax-weaving among elder Niuean women, as among other Pacific immigrants. Niuean weaving has a reputation of being especially fine, and it therefore managed to establish itself successfully in the handicraft scene. Some women do styles similar to Māori weaving, like *kete* or decorative flowers, while others are creatively experimenting with new forms and models. Nontraditional materials like raffia and plastic are included in these experiments. Apart from that, many women have mastered what were originally Western skills like crocheting, knitting, and embroidering and are excellent seamstresses. As in Niue, weaving and needlework are partly meant to be sold, partly to be used for personal and social requirements.

HAT WEAVING IN THE TWENTY-FIRST CENTURY

Except for a simple sun hat from coconut leaves with midribs (*pulou lau niu mata*) used by both sexes, Niueans differentiate between men's and women's hats. While men's hats always serve as work, sun, or leisure-time hats, women's hats are predominantly used for festive or official occasions. While weaving, hats are built up around wooden blocks, with different shapes for men's and women's hats, to ensure an even form. Men's hats usually have a high crown and an oval outline and are woven in such a way that the top of the crown looks—or can be—indented, thus looking like a Western fedora hat. Baseball caps have largely replaced men's hats in Niue and New Zealand. However, after tropical cyclone Heta, which left Niue nearly treeless in 2004, woven hats, probably more airy than fabric in the hot sun, were again increasingly used.

Women's hats sport a flatter crown with a roundish outline. Their most important function still remains covering the head during frequent church services, although they can be used to complete the outfit of a well-dressed lady in calf-length skirt and brightly colored blouse, going to town, to a function, or to pay a visit. An unusual hat draws attention to its wearer, singling her out from other churchgoers. Accordingly, extravagant new trimmings are constantly devised for what are bodies of relatively uniform shapes of hat. Hats are made from rare materials like pia or stripped coconut leaves, or they are woven from fine pandanus strands not broader than one or two millimeters (0.039 to 0.078 inches), thus making the hats special. Being different, but at the same time easy to obtain, Western women's hats from fabric are increasingly used, especially on those Sundays that require white attire.

Apart from the single-color white (pulou tea) and brown (pulou kaki) pandanus hat worn by both sexes, Niueans differentiate a number of (not necessarily mutually exclusive) categories, identified by design, material, or technique. The pulou fiofio or kilakila ("mixed" or "spotted" hat) is made from ecru and brown (or black) pandanus strands, forming a regular design. When featuring a zigzag pattern called fitipiu or vekaveka (referring to a specific blossom or bird's plumage), weavers consider it the most traditional variant for men and women.

The most difficult part of hat weaving is the beginning, which is situated at the center of a completed hat's top. Niueans do not share expert knowledge easily, be it boat building, planting, fishing, animal luring, traditional medicine, or weaving, as they consider it part of their mana (power), and of their competitive edge in an otherwise egalitarian society. Accordingly, weaving skills, as other proficiencies, are rarely acquired by formal teaching, but rather by observing and trial and error, as well as by secretly unraveling other weavers' pieces. Women who marry into another village are often not included in the local weavers' secrets, especially in the complex art of hat weaving, involving eighty strands or more. Introduced from the Cook Islands in the mid-1990s, mother-of-pearl center pieces with drilled holes to insert the first strands and thus substitute the complicated woven beginning of a hat have spread quickly in Niue, and are now made of more stable polished wood, often incised with a palm tree and the word Niue. The borrowing of this technique has enabled more women to make hats, and pulou lapa (hats with wood piece) have become a frequent sight in church services both in Niue and New Zealand ever since. They are women's hats, usually made from pandanus, but sometimes from stripped coconut leaves.

Probably another innovation from the Cook Islands is the pulou pupu (hat with holes), made in open-work. Its special challenge lies in achieving a regular pattern, which is somewhat eased by increasing the hole sizes from the top center toward the edge of the rim. Young coconut pinnae (leaflets or single leaves of a coconut frond) are stripped, removing the yellowish-green outer layer, to achieve the material for the pulou lau niu fole (hat from peeled coconut leaves). Boiled and left to dry in the sun for many days, the very fine strands turn white. Only some palms have leaves

suitable for stripping, and the Niueans use this material rarely, as the removal of young leaves is seen as unhealthy and growth-inhibiting for the tree. Accordingly, but also due to the white color and special shine of the strands, the hats are considered precious. Peeled coconut leaves have been used in Samoa as well, so this might be a technique introduced by Samoan missionaries.

The hollow arrowroot stalk is cut in halves lengthwise to obtain its fibers, which then have to be dried in the sun to receive their distinctive shine. As the delicate pia strands tend to coil extensively during weaving, only small pieces can be made from them. More than eighty strands for the usual kind of hats would be too troublesome to handle; consequently, arrowroot hats (pulou pia) are formed from long woven bands sewn together, thus being at the same time pulou tui or pelupelu (sewn or hemmed hat). The southwestern neighboring villages of Avatele and Tamakautoga are the centers of pia growth and processing, and their technique has been carried forward to pandanus as well, resulting in hats sewn from long bands laid spirally over a hat block in such a way that a regular ecru-black design evolves. While the delicate and shimmering pia hats are generally valued, sewn pandanus hats are not considered very artistic by weavers from other villages and immediately identify a wearer as being from the southwest.

While all these hats are woven in lalaga, there are pulou tia (hats made in half-hitch coiling) from pandanus as well. Bright colors have a distinct aesthetic appeal to Niueans as to other Polynesian people. Vivid blossoms in hair and garlands are eye-catchers and show a festive mood. Not surprisingly, weavers in New Zealand accepted colored raffia or plastic bands easily, especially as these materials do not require time-consuming preparation of strands. Many pulou tia therefore are at the same time pulou lefia or palagi (hats from raffia and other Western materials).

Around 1990 a hat type made from bread-bags appeared among Niuean weavings. The idea of using plastic bags in which sliced bread is sold in supermarkets seems to have been borrowed from Māori women. But while the Māori women crocheted the strips cut from the bags into hats, Niuean weavers sort them by colors, twine each strip, and interweave them. Due to their originality, bread-bag hats (pulou palesitiki—plastic hats) sell easily with Pākehā (people of European descent) customers in New Zealand, so that a number of Niueans produce them as a specialized commodity. Furthermore, as these hats are light, rainproof, and crushable compared to hats from natural materials, they have established themselves as workday and sun hats among Niuean women.

BAGS AND BASKETS

As with hats, Niueans classify bags and baskets (kato) according to material, form, and function. While coconut baskets mostly serve as containers for food donations, harvesting, fishing, and seafood collecting, or ritual functions, it is pandanus baskets that have developed into women's fashion accessories. One of the most widespread types is the cuboid, double-walled kato pakafa (four-sided basket), woven in lalaga technique. Bottom and inner sides are usually made in right-angled interlacing of broad strands, while the outer sides are done in a multicolored design of very fine strands interlaced or twill-woven. Baskets like this can be found all over Central Polynesia, and there are hints that this type was introduced to Niue by a Tongan woman married to a Niuean in the 1950s. Kato pakafa come in many sizes and versions—with or without lids; divided into several woven interior compartments;

as small, pendant-like bags worn around the neck; or the size of and used as briefcases. Apart from being sold to tourists and in New Zealand, they are predominantly used as formal handbags by Niuean women.

A more casual kind of accessory is the *kato paipa* (pipe bag), a flat lalaga bag whose sides are joined by a seam instead of a woven bottom. Said to have originally come into existence in the 1940s as a small pipe bag for smokers of both sexes, it is now found in all sizes. Modeled on Western handbag fashions are the *kato peti* (purse), a small, often handleless clutch; as well as the *kato gege* (purse formed like a clamshell), a bellied, stiff, pompadour-shaped pouch with a narrow opening on top; and the *kato palau* (drum-formed basket), a pillbox-type handbag. Half-hitch coiled baskets (*kato tia*) are primarily used as shopping baskets. There are round and oval ones, and an oval variant tapering toward the bottom known as *kato poti* (boat-formed basket). Since the early 2000s a weaver of Makefu village has specialized in polygonal kato tia.

Niueans often classify baskets according to their handle form. Baskets with two opposed, unconnected, and usually soft loops are referred to as *kato lapiti* ("rabbit" baskets), as the oval outline of the handles suggests the shape of rabbit ears. A handle form frequent in kato tia consists of a stiff grip running high above the basket, forking on both sides into two angled parts near the brim. As the angle reminds the weavers of the two outer toes of a bird claw, these baskets are called *kato huimoa* ("chicken-feet" baskets). Occasionally, ladies' bags and baskets are made from coconut strands, but they have not developed into distinct types like the pandanus baskets.

In New Zealand flax bags (*kato halakiekie*—bags from cut flax) often copy the form of the Māori *kete* (flat, bottomless bag from New Zealand flax) and come in all sizes and many colors. Flax is predominantly woven in the lalaga technique. Backpacks from flax (*kato fafa*) have become another stylish accessory adapted from Māori weavers.

Around 2000 Niuean women in Auckland started making bags called *kato hala palesitiki*—bags from the colored plastic straps that are used to tie bulk goods together, claiming this to be the result of experimenting with waste material that their husbands had brought home from work. These bags often have a serrated rim, resembling Niuean bags from the early 1900s. Recycling the bulk goods bands into bags and other articles seems to be an idea that originated in Indonesia in the 1990s and spread by a few globally operating companies. Plastic strap bags made from different colors were a fashion accessory all over the Western world in the early 2000s. Many Pacific weavers in New Zealand make and use these bags. Like the bread-bag hats, they are bendable and robust as compared to their counterparts from natural materials, and they need no preparation or dyeing. Due to the high demand by Pacific weavers, large New Zealand home improvement stores now sell color-assorted coils of these plastic straps.

FANS

An exclusively Niuean type of fan is the *iliili tuai* (old fan), which must have come into existence in the 1880s or earlier. Finely woven from split white coconut leaf, its handle, in older specimens often carved from the hard black *kieto* wood, is adorned with delicate black designs made from human hair or horse tail, sometimes interwoven with brown coconut fiber. Said to have been reserved for people of eminence, like pastors or their wives in the past, it still is a precious and elegant fan, all the more so as only two or three Niuean women were able to weave it in the early 2000s.

Simple fans made from interweaving the coconut frond pinnae provide the best airflow, and the material is widely used by Niueans for that purpose. Fans from pandanus, however, though not as functional, are considered much more stylish and come in round, oval, diamond, circle, and half-circle forms. They can be made in lalaga or tia technique and sport different colors, fringes from feathers or wool, or appliqués of colored hibiscus bark strips. Most worshippers take a fan to church, and a formal lady's outfit is completed by a smart fan.

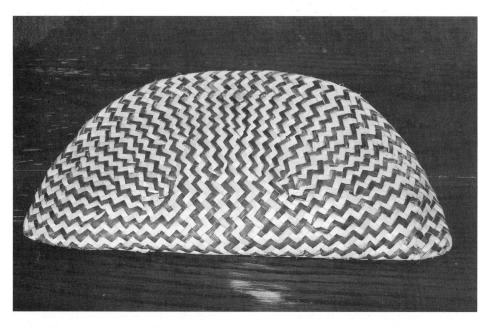

A half-circle-shaped clutch purse (*kato peti*), of ecru and black pandanus, woven by Tapu Vaha using the *lalaga* technique (interlacing and twill weaves). Auckland, New Zealand, ca. 2003. Photograph by Hilke Thode-Arora.

FESTIVE ACCESSORIES AND DANCE COSTUMES

On market days in Niue's capital Alofi, or for festive occasions, Niueans wear lei, garlands from blossoms, fragrant flowers, seeds, fibers, or seashells. In New Zealand these are often replaced by lei woven from flax or brightly colored synthetic ribbons beaded with artificial flowers or little woven balls. In Niue women, and sometimes men, adorn themselves by putting a fresh, fragrant flower behind their ear or in their hair. As the puritanic rules of the Ekalesia Niue do not encourage wearing fresh flowers in church, a thriving fashion of artificial flowers has come into existence. While some of these are made from a coarse barkcloth variety, an innovation borrowed from the Cook Islands in the early 2000s, others are woven from pandanus, flax, hibiscus bark, or synthetic strands. Garlands, woven bands, ribbons, balls, and flowers are, among factory-made items, also used as hat trimmings, which provide the body of a hat with individuality and originality. Unusual, extravagant hats are the pride of Niuean women, and the creativity and fantasy in fashioning them are limitless. Often, hats get redecorated completely after some time.

Woven headdresses, skirts, and costumes plaited from different fibers are in vogue for young people's dance performances. At certain life-cycle events, especially hair-cutting and ear-piercing ceremonies (Niuean rites of passage for boys and girls), children and teenagers entertain the guests with solo or group presentations. Similarly, village groups of minors show singing and dancing for touristic "cultural evenings." Once a year a beauty pageant is held in Niue for sending a contestant to the Miss South Pacific contest. In New Zealand most of the secondary schools have cultural performance groups of Māori and Pacific Islanders, who compete in one of the world's largest Polynesian performing arts events, the annual Polyfest. All these occasions require specially made dance costumes, which are supposed to have traditional as well as innovative elements. The design and manufacture of these outfits, which consist to a large part of natural fibers, and coconut and shell accessories, as well as of smartly entwined or redecorated *pareos* (sarongs), usually fall to the creative and experienced female elder relatives of the young people, and considerable pride is taken in the sophisticated results.

It is mostly boys who wear pareos or grass skirts, sometimes with shirts or fiber capes to cover the upper body. The dancing costumes for soloist girls or pageant contestants are often modeled in Samoan, Tongan, or Tahitian style, using clothing mats, knotted strands, or sometimes coconut bras, thus demonstrating pan-Pacific developments in dress. Girls' dress for school or family functions is less sexy and does not show so much skin; fiber or cotton skirts and blouses are used. Weavers earn esteem in designing and making these innovative and time-consuming outfits, and long after use, they are sometimes put on display in the family home.

Contemporary Niuean dress is a blend of missionary, Western, Pacific, and pan-Polynesian fashion influences as well as Niuean creativity in molding, recreating, and independent invention. Similarly, for quite a number of Niuean weaving styles, their origins as Niuean, or adopted from elsewhere, cannot be established without doubt. It is predominantly fine workmanship and quality-mindedness, and a distinct focus on incessant observing, experimenting, and improving, even when working with forms and materials adopted from somewhere else, that seem to have been the essence of Niuean clothing and of weaving since the mid-nineteenth century. Niuean dress and weaving of hats and accessories is a hybrid, pragmatic, and authentic part of Pacific textile production.

References and Further Reading

Colchester, Chloë. "T-Shirts, Translation and Humour: On the Nature of Wearer-Perceiver Relationships in South Auckland." In *Clothing the Pacific*, edited by Chloë Colchester, 167–191. Oxford and New York: Berg, 2003.

Cole, Shari, and Vitolia Kulatea. *Cultural Crafts of Niue: Pandanus Weaving*. Suva, Fiji: Institute of Pacific Studies, University of the South Pacific, 1996.

Leota-Ete, Jakki, Shigeyuki Kihara, and Rosanna Raymond. "Body Beautiful: New Zealand Fashion—Pacific Style." In *Pacific Art Niu Sila: The Pacific Dimension of Contemporary New Zealand Arts*, edited by Sean Mallon and Pandora Fulimalo Pereira, 90–191. Wellington, NZ: Te Papa Press, 2002.

Loeb, Edwin M. *History and Traditions of Niue*. Honolulu: B. P. Bishop Museum, 1926.

Moyle, Richard. "Sounds Pacific. Pacific Music and Dance in New Zealand." In *Pacific Art Niu Sila: The Pacific Dimension of Contemporary New Zealand Arts*, edited by Sean Mallon and Pandora Fulimalo Pereira, 102–115. Wellington, NZ: Te Papa Press, 2002.

Neich, Roger, and Mick Pendergrast. *Pacific Tapa*. Auckland, NZ: David Bateman and Auckland Museum, 2004.

Pereira, Pandora Fulimalo. "Lalaga: Weaving Connections in Pacific Fibre." In *Pacific Art Niu Sila: The Pacific Dimension of Contemporary New Zealand Arts*, edited by Sean Mallon and Pandora Fulimalo Pereira, 77–89. Wellington, NZ: Te Papa Press, 2002.

Ryan, Thomas F. "Prehistoric Niue: An Egalitarian Polynesian Society." Master's thesis, University of Auckland, 1977.

Seiler-Baldinger, Annemarie. *Textiles: A Classification of Techniques*. Washington, DC: Smithsonian Institution Press, 1994.

Smith, Percy. *Niue: The Island and Its People*. Suva, Fiji: Institute of Pacific Studies, University of the South Pacific, 1993. (Reprint from the *Journal of the Polynesian Society*, 1902 and 1903.)

Sperlich, Wolfgang B. *Tohi Vagahau Niue: Niue Language Dictionary*. Alofi and Honolulu: Government of Niue and University of Hawaii Press, 1997.

Thode-Arora, Hilke. "'Eine gute Frau sitzt niemals müßig.' Rezente Hüte und Körbe niueanischer Flechterinnen." *Baessler-Archiv* 53 (2005): 159–179.

Thode-Arora, Hilke. "'How Can We Weave in a Strange Land?' Niuean Weavers in Auckland." *Pacific Arts* 3–5 (2007): 46–59.

Thode-Arora, Hilke. "Verflochten in Beziehungen. Über das heutige Sammeln neuerer polynesischer Flechtkunst." In *Expeditionen in die Südsee. Begleitbuch zur Ausstellung und Geschichte der Südsee-Sammlung des Ethnologischen Museums*, edited by Markus Schindlbeck, 165–186. Berlin: Dietrich Reimer Verlag and Ethnologisches Museum, Staatliche Museen zu Berlin, 2007.

Hilke Thode-Arora

See also Pacific Sisters: Urban Pacific Art, Fashion, and Performance; Pacific Street Styles in Auckland; Missionary Dress in Samoa.

Missionary Dress in Samoa

The first European Christian missionaries to establish a station in the South Pacific were members of the London Missionary Society (LMS) who arrived in Tahiti in 1797. Over the next one hundred years a number of European Christian denominations established missions there. For example, mission stations were established in Tonga by Wesleyans (1826) and Marists (1832), and in the Gilberts and Ellice Islands (now Kiribati and Tuvalu) by the LMS (1877) and the Catholic Sacred Heart Mission (1881). In Samoa alone, stations were established by Tongan preachers of the Wesleyan Mission (1828), the LMS (1830), and the Roman Catholic Mission (1845). Missionary teaching in the South Pacific resulted in considerable changes to the customary dress of indigenous people. The effects of these changes are still evident in dress worn across the Pacific in the twenty-first century, particularly in the clothing of women.

Much of our understanding of the changes Christian missionaries brought to South Pacific dress and adornment appears in their propaganda. They sent home a mass of material: letters, reports, photographs, and drawings, with the express intention of persuading European congregations, who funded the mission, that converting indigenous people to Christianity was both possible and worthwhile. Of course, this literature is biased. The missionary enterprise was primarily dedicated to the dissemination of Christianity, and the depiction of constant progress toward this goal was at the heart of missionary writing and image production. It is also a Western perspective on indigenous cultures and often censors indigenous rejection, selection, or adaptation of missionary teachings. Moreover, the propaganda generated by the range of Christian denominations working in the Pacific Islands is rarely concordant. Mission societies did not always agree on methods of conversion or cultural policies, including matters related to indigenous dress. Missionary attitudes toward clothing also changed over time. For example, the first missionaries to the South Pacific proselytized about covering the naked bodies of Islanders; however, views were to alter toward the last quarter of the nineteenth century, with many missionaries regarding partial nudity appropriate for both the climate and occupations of the South Pacific Islanders.

To gain some purchase on the complex process of cultural encounter between missionaries and indigenous societies, scholarship since the 1990s has argued that historical analyses must focus on specific activities in singular contexts. An important case in mission history is Reverend George Brown's Wesleyan Methodist teaching in Samoa from 1860 to 1903. As general secretary for the Executive Committee of the Board of Missions, Brown played a crucial role in shaping the broad lines of mission policy in the South Pacific. At the time Brown worked in Samoa, missionary societies of various denominations were debating the benefits of Europeanizing Pacific people. These debates had an important influence on Brown's attitudes to how Samoan men, women, and children should be dressed, and they can be seen played out in a collection of photographs Brown produced of his mission. These photographs reveal an ambivalent approach to the clothing of Samoans and, to some extent, indicate the selective way they responded to his attempts to change their dress.

REVEREND GEORGE BROWN'S PHOTOGRAPHS OF THE SAMOAN MISSION

Photography was an attractive escape for European missionaries like Brown, who were working in foreign cultures. It offered a diversion from work and alleviated the extreme isolation they felt. Photographing indigenous people was also part of a learning process for them. Photographs documented the customs, the beliefs, and the daily life in a culture that was new and often bewildering. In the collection of Brown's photographs at the Australian Museum, Sydney, there are 175 images of Samoa, from a total of 921 photographs he produced in the Pacific. Often Brown would display his photographs to European congregations in magic lantern presentations, and he selected a series of photographs to illustrate his books, *Pioneer Missionary and Explorer* (1908) and *Melanesians and Polynesians* (1910). Though Brown did not document the other uses of his photographs, one can assume that they were also viewed as curiosities and collected by interested Europeans. This assumption is based on the evidence of prints in the George Brown Collection at the Mitchell Library, State Library of New South Wales in Sydney. These prints are in formats popular at the turn of the twentieth century, and, significantly, many are postcard size, suggesting their collectability. Another avenue for the distribution of Brown's photographs was the contemporary popular press. Brown often had letters and photographs documenting his mission's progress published in the *Sydney Morning Herald*.

Brown lived and taught in Samoa continuously from 1860 to 1874, and sporadically until 1903. His ordination as a Methodist minister took place in Sydney on 10 September 1860, shortly after his marriage to Miss Lydia Wallis, the daughter of a New Zealand Wesleyan missionary. After his ordination Brown arrived in Samoa, where his official job with the Wesleyan Methodist mission was to supervise fellow missionaries in the field, local ministers, catechists, and teachers, and to gain new converts as prospective mission teachers in the large school at Satupaitea. Overall, his photographs reflect his ideological position as a Methodist missionary and relate to singular aspects of his life in the Pacific during his stay there. A subject that caught his particular interest was the Samoan *tulafale* (orator), who is often shown in his photographs holding a *to'oto'o* (staff) or *fue* (whisk). Brown's interest in oratory makes sense, given his task to deliver regular sermons to indigenous congregations.

Brown's photographs suggest that missionary attitudes toward Pacific dress were not static; rather, there were changing responses to dress and body modifications of local men, women, and children. Many images reveal ambivalence toward the development of Western ideas of identity and "civilization" in Samoa, gender and racial distinction, and the exercise of power. For example, his photographs of partially naked Samoan men and women conform to missionary policies in the late nineteenth century, when cultural assumptions about the "dignity of clothes" were being discarded. This contrasts with attitudes toward nudity in the early nineteenth century, when the LMS introduced Samoans to a sense of shame about bare skin.

CONVERSION AND THE SIGNIFICANCE OF EUROPEAN DRESS

For missionaries working in the Pacific, European dress was a sign of Christian conversion. But from the point of view of indigenous people, this was not always the case, and European dress did not necessarily mean the same thing to them. Missionary photographs of Islanders converted to Christianity and wearing European dress were captivating to a loyal audience of supporters in Europe. Missionaries often sent "before" and "after" photographs of Islanders to congregations in Europe. In most of these the "before" photograph would present an indigenous person in a "heathen," that is, a nonconverted state, usually seminaked and dirty, clutching *aitu*, or spiritual objects, and weapons. The "after" photographs portrayed indigenous subjects converted to Christianity. They would be dressed in European clothes, the men in white shirts, pants, and hats, the women in full cotton dresses and straw bonnets. Often the "after" photograph presented Islanders engaged in some form of work, for example, the building of a new church, or garment making. Congregations in Europe were led to believe that with the adoption of European clothes, Island converts had also acquired European manners and mores, like morality, charity, cleanliness, frugality, and self-sacrifice. Albert Pearce, a missionary at Kerepunu in the early 1800s, underscored the signifying value of dress by noting his pleasure at seeing his congregation clothed in European garments as a marker of their progress toward "civilization."

Brown photographed many conversion portraits while working in Samoa. Before he arrived in Samoa the LMS had introduced the *tiputa*, a barkcloth poncho, a sign demonstrating a Samoan was a Christian. By the time Brown arrived in Samoa the tiputa had been replaced by white cloth as a marker of Christian conversion. A small number of Brown's conversion portraits feature men dressed in dark blazers; however, the more common image is that of Samoan Christian men wearing white shirts, wraparounds of calico cloth, and hats. The Samoan Christian women wear white "mother hubbard" dresses, long, wide, loose-fitting gowns with long sleeves and high necklines, introduced probably by LMS missionaries from about 1838 and worn with variations across the Pacific Islands. Significantly, the loose cotton dresses completely cover up the bodies of women. This is an important point for postcolonial authors who argue that Christian missions were intent upon covering up the bodies of women as evidence of a cultural progression toward a Western, civilized way of life.

The missionary imposition of European dress also implied that indigenous women were engaged in activities of sewing or garment making in the Islands. These activities were directly linked to conversion, because those who attended church were required to wear fabric skirts and blouses, rather than their former attire. Though Samoan women had a long history of weaving and craft work, for missionaries like Brown, sewing and garment making was explicitly linked to European "civilization." These activities were associated with European morality, which held that women should not be frivolous or idle, but actively engaged in a profitable use of their leisure time. Embroidery and ornamental accomplishments were considered appropriate pastimes, for they signified gentility. The act of embroidery for the purpose of providing comfort was visible proof of a woman's love and devotion for her husband, family, and friends. Through their practice of sewing and garment making, Samoan women were thus urged to become the moral equivalent of their European counterparts.

Sewing and garment making were also regularized activities, performed by groups of women working around the mission station during stipulated hours. Brown, and other missionaries in the Pacific, sought to impose this kind of domestic and institutional order. The missionary agenda was for Christianity to become part of the social fabric, not a marginalized part of Samoan life. Missionaries sought to change gender roles and the division of labor in the Islands. Brown discouraged Samoan women from working the land, which he considered derogatory to women and inimical to an improvement in morals. He sought to impose a division of tasks between the sexes in which the men should work the land, dig, plant, and grow the food, and women should make clothes and bonnets and attend to household work. For Brown the dress of Samoan Christian women was to reflect their roles as household managers, and their activities in cloth making and domestic work. His approach is typical of missionaries in the Pacific, who sought to impose a new temporal regime of work, leisure, celebration, and worship. He aimed to create a mission more like a macrofamilial structure that reorganized work and social life in Samoa.

In Brown's conversion portraits aitu, or spiritual objects, weaponry, and wooden sculptures are rarely shown. Instead, Samoan Christians are frequently photographed holding umbrellas. Missionaries in the Pacific often ceremoniously burned weapons and held public bonfires for the desecration of aitu. Such events signaled the overthrow of savage customs. Weaponry and "heathen" idols belonged to a former order, an order associated with a lifestyle rapidly being replaced by a new set of values. The umbrellas carried by Samoan Christians not only marked their conversion, but the progress of "civilization" in Samoa.

MISSIONARY AMBIVALENCE TOWARD "HEATHEN" SUBJECTS

In contrast to his conversion portraits, Brown photographed many Samoan men, women, and children in their supposedly heathen state. For Brown these photographs were just as important as conversion portraits. They functioned as evidence of what Samoans were like before converting to Christianity. The important point was that Samoan men, women, and children must appear redeemable. If heathens were represented as pure evil, or objects of loathing, there was no reason for the Christian congregations, who funded the mission, to pity them or consider the mission worthwhile. Postcolonial authors recognize this dilemma as the ambivalence of missionary rhetoric, that is, the desire to create identities for Pacific people as almost the same as Europeans, but not quite.

Brown's approach to "heathen" dress in Samoa reflects this ambivalence. A number of his photographs show nonconverted men dressed as they would be for battle. In his book *Melanesians and Polynesians* Brown explains that Samoan warfare posed the greatest threat to the spread of Christianity and was thus discouraged by missionaries. His photographs show Samoan warriors wearing the *malo*, a small strip of fabric passing between the legs with a girdle of leaves, and anklets of shredded leaf. The warriors are often pictured holding clubs. Typically the club was about three feet (one meter) in length and was made of a red, close-grained hard wood. The handle had a sennit, a cord of plaited coconut fibers, wound tightly round it, so that it would not slip in the hand. Some photographs show *manaia*, the chief's son, dressed for battle, where his status is indicated by a *tuiga*, an elaborate headdress of human hair. Interestingly, Brown did not photograph any Samoan warriors marked with *tatau* (tattoo). This is a conspicuous absence on a warrior's body, given that *tatatau*, the process of tattooing, was recognized as a necessary rite of passage for young Samoan men and was designed to seal or defend the body. Christian missionaries associated tatatau with aitu, or spirit worship, and where possible had it banned from Samoan society. Accordingly, Brown's warriors lack any body markings.

In most of Brown's photographs of nonconverted subjects, the usual dress of Samoan men and women is what he calls a wrapper, a skirt of print or calico, and no special distinction is made in the clothing of the sexes. The photographs reveal no tribal peculiarities of dress. In *Melanesians and Polynesians* Brown notes that on special occasions men wore a skirt of native cloth overlaid with a woven mat, and women an *ie sina*, a white, shaggy flax mat, which was worn so as to show part of one thigh. He notes that many of the patterns used to embellish native cloth were made by rubbing dye over a print block made of raised fibers sewn on to dry leaves of the pandanus (a tropical tree, the leaves of which are used for weaving). This method of printing produced what Brown describes as very beautiful and regular patterns. Interestingly, in *Melanesians and Polynesians* he claims that his subjects are particular about fashion; however, he does not explain what a fashion system might mean in Samoa. In his photographs of "heathens" neither Samoan men nor women cover their feet. Some are pictured with a piece of cloth bound around the head or a banana leaf tied around the head so as to keep their hair dry. One of Brown's photographs pictures a Samoan subject wearing sunshade visors made of a piece of plaited coconut leaf. Often Brown photographed men wearing boar tusks as a pendant on the breast, and finger rings made from tortoise shell.

What is striking about Brown's "heathen" subjects is the absence of moralizing. This restraint is noteworthy. Tribal wars, for example, posed a very real threat to the spread of Christianity. In Brown's photographs Samoan people, while not Christian, are not so loathsome as to render mission efforts hopeless and worthless. They are not so different from Europeans that they are beyond salvation. Brown has photographed Samoans as different, but redeemable.

In his photographs of "heathen" women Brown specifically creates an identity that is different from that of European women but also capable of being saved. He produced a number of photographs of the Samoan *taupo*, a ceremonial maiden. In his photographs the taupo strikes a defiant pose, with one arm raised across her body, the other brandishing an intricately carved club. She is always bare-breasted and wears an *'ie toga*, a fine mat wrapped around the bottom half of her body. Many Samoan women wore the *'ie toga*, featured in a number of Brown's photographs. When worn by the taupo, however, the addition of feathers and open-weave edges enhanced the skirt's value and thus announce the taupo's higher social status. Perhaps the most striking of the taupo's garments is her headdress, the *tuiga*. Brown pictures an elaborate tuiga, of many decorative parts, which are built up around a *pou*, a postlike foundation made from wrapping cloth around the head. On this foundation rests a mass of light brown–colored human hair and a *lave*, which is a decorated framework of wooden sticks worn at the front of the headdress. The lave that the taupo wears in Brown's photographs is decorated with flowers, or at other times it might be decorated with small glass mirrors. A *fuiono*, a forehead band, is tied across the front and base of the lave, helping to hold it in place, and is itself decorated with nautilus shells. In *Melanesians and Polynesians* Brown describes a particular mode of dressing the hair that was used as a symbol of virginity, irrespective of the Samoan woman's rank, in which the head was shaved down the middle and the hair left long on either side. This was sometimes plaited, or on other occasions wound around the forehead, and it hung loosely over the shoulders. Brown's taupo wears an *ula fala*, a necklace of pandanus fruit, and another shorter row of pearl-like beads. Each of the striking articles worn by the taupo is clearly defined, and he makes no attempt to obscure them from view.

In other photographs of nonconverted female Samoans, Brown focuses on jewelry and headdress, armlets and bracelets of small shells, and necklaces of flowers. In many he includes domestic objects like woven mats and baskets. In *Melanesians and Polynesians* Brown praises the work of the women, describing what he calls attractively ornamented baskets, plaited from a fine kind of pandanus leaf. Unlike his missionary predecessors, he photographed a number of bare-breasted women. In his publication of 1910 Brown notes that no idea of indecency was attached to a very small girdle of leaves worn by a man, or to women who have their breasts uncovered, and he adds that children went naked for the first few years of life. In his photographs of bare-breasted women he draws attention to adornments that clearly require the skillful weaving of plant fibers. Many Samoan women are pictured wearing *ula*, necklaces made from fresh leaves or scented flowers, or an *'ula fala*, a necklace that signaled social status by its bright red paint. They are photographed wearing *taulima*, armlets, and *tauvae*, anklets, made from leaves or shells. In their hair they wear decorative combs made from coconut midribs, and they are often shown seated closely to woven pandanus baskets. For Samoan women these functioned as markers of status or office, or alternatively could simply be items of decoration.

On the other hand, for the European viewer of Brown's photographs, the adornments signified the morality of Samoan women. In the context of nineteenth-century Europe, craft and design were testament to a woman's profitable use of her leisure time and her efforts to provide comfort for her husband, family, and friends. In Brown's photographs he explicitly associates Samoan women with craft and design, considered by nineteenth-century Europeans as useful accomplishments. His focus on the embellishments, headdress, and articles of craft helps to create a "lifestyle narrative" around Samoan women. In *Melanesians and Polynesians* he points out that every Samoan woman made girdles of leaves for herself, her husband, and her children, and most women spent many months weaving a single fine mat. By directing attention to the extraordinary weaving of adornments, mats, and baskets, Brown shows the use of the Samoan women's leisure time and their domestic work. The associated sexuality and implied immorality that comes with uncovered bodies of the Samoan women is offset, or at least softened, by Brown's strong claim for their moral characters, evidenced by their craft.

The LMS records that one of the jobs of the Christian missionary in indigenous cultures was to cultivate an appreciation of what is tasteful and beautiful. In many of Brown's photographs, including those of bare-breasted women, there is a softness and appeal that is unlike the sexual assertiveness of eroticized images of Samoan women found in commercial photography. The photographs have a narrow depth of field and a hazy focus. Many of his female subjects are seated and lean in toward one another. Light is diffused from above and to the side of the subjects, which creates a softened aesthetic. In their formal treatment Brown's photographs are very similar to pictorial photography produced in Europe. His photographs exhibit the same aesthetic as their European counterparts, and it might be argued that he has represented Samoan women as sharing in what is tasteful and beautiful in Europe.

MISSIONARY DEBATES ON EUROPEANIZING INDIGENOUS DRESS

Brown's lack of moralizing in his photographs of Samoan "heathens" might be interpreted as part of the period's debates on the benefits of Europeanizing indigenous cultures. His lack of harsh judgment on the matter of female nudity, for example, can be understood as a reflection of changes in missionary policies on Pacific dress. By the third quarter of the nineteenth century, LMS missionaries were being instructed not to Europeanize indigenous converts. They were advised to remember that indigenous people were foreigners and to let them continue as such. The new policy directed missionaries to Christianize indigenous cultures, without needlessly changing them. LMS missionaries were strongly discouraged from making indigenous people "Englishmen."

The new LMS policy was part of a broader movement in which missionaries themselves were hostile to numerous developments occurring in their own cultures. Industrialization and urbanization in Europe were perceived by many as the cause of religious and moral decline. The market economy with its emphasis on self-interest and material success was seen as in some sense inconsistent with the Christian message. Late-nineteenth-century missionary thinking was focused on the destructive impact of Westernization on indigenous societies. There was concern that the weakening of tradition in "civilized" societies would lead to the erosion of communal bonds and result in moral disintegration. The break-up of community, the decline of tradition, and the erosion of moral values during the Industrial Revolution in Europe were factors regarded to be the precursors of a destructive process in Africa, Asia, and the Pacific. For this reason, missionary societies insisted it was imperative that potential converts in the colonial world should not identify Christianity as Western.

Missionary doubts about the benefits of Europeanizing extended to dress. Samuel McFarlane, a missionary working in the Pacific toward the end of the century, believed that a simple girdle of leaves was more suitable than European clothing for indigenous people of the Pacific. In 1894 C. Sylvester Horne from the LMS described the ideal dress in the Pacific as suitable to the climate and the occupations of the wearers. Whereas in the early nineteenth century the LMS introduced a sense of shame among Samoan people toward bare skin, Horne described the necessity for dress based on the grounds of health and questioned the "dignity of clothes." Brown's photographs of bare-breasted Samoan women also indicate that by the end of the nineteenth century, Methodist missionaries had shed their cultural assumptions about nudity and the necessity to cover up. Similarly, Anglican missionaries in New Guinea were not convinced of the superiority of the Europeans and did not want a parody of European "civilization" by dressing indigenous people in Victorian garments.

In the context of these debates Brown's approach to Samoan dress was not straightforward. Many of his photographs reveal inconsistencies. For example, in a good number of his photographs Samoan women are dressed as Europeans, but Samoan men are not. This inconsistency is very interesting, as in most indigenous cultures in the twenty-first century, it is men who wear European clothing and women continue to wear dress based on indigenous customs. The ways in which men are dressed in Brown's photographs might be attributed to nineteenth-century missionary beliefs about the importance of preserving indigenous culture. They represent Samoan life with visible signs of differences from European culture. Given Brown's position as a Methodist missionary, perhaps it is unsurprising that he often photographed Samoan women in "mother hubbard" dresses and straw bonnets. The feminine ideal of nineteenth-century Europe was in marked contrast to often erotic and overtly sexual representations of Pacific women in popular literature. Brown distances Samoan women from the sexualized female stereotype of popular literature, and by depicting women in Europeanized clothing he in turn signals the importance of Western manners, mores, and, in particular, morality.

Perhaps Brown's photographs of Samoan children describe the ambivalence of his position most clearly. Photographs of children were very popular among nineteenth-century missionary societies. Unlike adults, children are perceived as naturally innocent. For the Christian missionary, children were not perpetrators of heathenism, but rather its innocent victims, and photographs of children persuaded European congregations that funding missions was worthwhile. Like children in Victorian England, Samoan children were clothed as miniature adults. This holds true in missionary photography, whether they are clothed in European or indigenous dress. Brown photographed children variously dressed in Victorian blazers or 'ie toga, a fine mat wrapped around the body. One of Brown's photographs, titled "Native Minister's Family," shows a young Samoan boy dressed in a white shirt with a thick silk ribbon tied around his neck and holding a miniature to'oto'o, an orator's staff. It is as if the boy is mimicking a biblical character, like a shepherd guiding his flock. Alongside him sits another boy, dressed in a blazer and white cloth wraparound, and two girls wrapped in 'ie toga. One girl holds a delicately patterned wooden ili pau, or fan. The ili pau was made from a single thin wafer of timber with a thick handle, and shapes were cut through the body of the fan, forming an ornamental open-work body. Brown's photograph shows the girl holding the fan so that the intricate patterning on the body is fully displayed. In other photographs children, including girls, are barefoot and bare-chested, holding whisks.

The inconsistent mix of European and indigenous dress in Brown's photographs is perhaps a reflection of the dualism that runs through missionary thinking. To be sustainable, the missionary project could not escape a commitment to assimilation and the fundamental unity of humanity. Brown's aim was to incorporate the Samoan into a familial relation with the civilized European. However, missionaries, like other colonizers in the Pacific, still defined the indigenous subject in terms of his or her difference from Europeans. The missionary agenda, therefore, is centered on competing desires: to represent both the sameness and difference of indigenous people compared to Europeans. Brown's Samoan children dressed in European attire contribute to a sense of sameness with the European Christian audience for whom the photographs were intended. On the other hand, the children dressed in woven Samoan skirts, and holding indigenous objects, signify difference from that audience. This complexity reflects the competing aims of the Christian mission and results in a collection of multivalent images.

MISSIONARY DRESS AND SAMOAN AGENCY

Inconsistencies in dress might also reflect the selectivity of Samoan responses to missionary contact. While Brown introduced changes to dress, Samoans were active agents in how these changes and transformations were managed. The important point is that regardless of missionary intentions, new styles and materials could not so much be imposed, as offered for reinterpretation and revision by Samoans to suit their own situations and purposes, tastes, and aesthetics. For example, it is now widely recognized that when the LMS introduced barkcloth ponchos into Samoa, they were not part of a repressive missionary law, but sought out by Samoan people as a garment that contributed to a sense of identity and collectivity. Another case in mission history reveals that in the absence of straw bonnets supplied by missionaries, Samoan women made their own from turtle shell. Many mission histories record that new items were quickly taken up by recent converts and were much coveted. One case records that the English Union Jack, the flag of Great Britain, was for a short time highly sought after and used as a garment. The popularity of new items was not so much a reflection of the mission's strength, but indicative of a culture in Samoa that was organic and innovative, accustomed to change irrespective of European contact. Materials introduced by missionaries were often selectively absorbed; for example, the taupo's tuiga, or headdress, remained composed of human hair, but it was decorated with glass or mirrors, materials that were introduced to the islands by missionaries. At times missionary teaching was rejected outright, as in the case of Samoan tatatau, the process of tattooing, which persisted despite being condemned by European missionaries.

The inconsistencies in Samoan dress seen in Brown's photographs could be as much a result of Samoan agency as the ambivalence in his approach to Samoan culture. Many of Brown's photographs reveal local adaptations of European dress, not unusual across the Pacific. In photographs of Samoan men imported cloth was incorporated into the local wraparound style. Some women are pictured wearing printed cloth, and the new patterns often reappeared in *siapo*, barkcloth, designs. In some of Brown's photographs women are clothed in mother hubbard dresses, but the neckline is at times decorated with textured *ula* (necklaces) of leaves, flowers, fruit, or seeds. One photograph of a Samoan taupo shows her wearing a *titi*, a waist garment, of plaited plant fibers alternating with strips of striped cotton fabric.

Whether they were driven by forces external or internal to Samoan culture, changes in Samoan dress were neither uniform nor static. The scenario is further complicated by the fact that most of our understanding of changes in this clothing comes through missionary propaganda. Brown's collection of photographs was produced with a specific audience in mind: European Christian congregations. The photographs are biased, and European audiences brought a whole set of values and assumptions to their viewing of this imagery. The complexity of Brown's view of Samoan dress and body modification needs to be understood in terms of the nature of missionary literature and the missionary agenda, its inherent ambivalences, the wider context of mission policy on indigenous dress, and the agency of Samoan people themselves.

References and Further Reading

Ashcroft, Bill, Gareth Griffiths, and Helen Tiffen, eds. *The Post-Colonial Studies Reader*. London: Routledge, 1995.

Bolton, Lissant. *Oceanic Cultural Property in Australia. A Pilot Study of Major Public Collections*. Canberra: Australian National Commission for UNESCO, 1980.

Brown, George. *Pioneer Missionary and Explorer: An Autobiography, A Narrative of Forty Years Residences and Travel in Samoa, New Britain New Ireland and Neighbouring Islands*. London: Clowes and Sons, 1908.

Brown, George. *Melanesians and Polynesians: Their Life Histories Described and Compared*. New York: Benjamin Blom, 1910.

Horne, C. Sylvester. *The Story of the LMS 1795–1895*. London: London Missionary Society, 1894.

Langmore, Diane. *Pacific Islands Monograph Series*. Honolulu: University of Hawai'i Press, 1989.

Mallon, Sean. *Samoan Art and Artists*. Honolulu: University of Hawai'i Press, 2002.

Parker, Rozsika. *The Subversive Stitch: Embroidery and the Making of the Feminine*. London: Women's Press, 1984.

Robert, Dana. "From Missions to Mission to Beyond Missions: The Historiography of American Protestant Foreign Mission since World War II." *International Bulletin of Missionary Research* 18 (1994): 146–162.

Thomas, Nicholas. "Colonial Conversions: Difference, Hierarchy and History in Early Twentieth Century Evangelical Propaganda." *Comparative Studies in Society and History* 34 (1992): 366–389.

Webb, Virginia-Lee. "Missionary Photographers in the Pacific Islands: Divine Light." *History of Photography* 21 (1997): 12–22.

Prue Ahrens

See also Dressing the Body in Samoa; Fijian Dress and Body Modifications; Dress of the Cook Islands.

Dressing the Body in Samoa

- Tattooing
- Waist Garments
- Body Embellishments and Headdresses
- Colonial Encounters and Samoan Style

Samoa consists of two large tropical islands and six smaller ones in the Pacific Ocean, northeast of Fiji. Its people are of Polynesian descent, and the islands have had a complex history of regional interaction. The tropical environment furnished flora and fauna utilized by the people of these islands for the construction of clothing and body modifications. During the nineteenth century dressing the body involved not only covering with garments but also marking or coloring the skin, wrapping it in images, or coating it in oil. Descriptions of Samoan clothing and dress dating from the early nineteenth century tended to focus on the simple leaf skirt and a small selection of textiles made from various plant fibers and other material. However, Samoan clothing and dress has ranged from the simple to the elaborate, in combination with personal embellishments, headdresses, and other forms of textiles. Up to the twenty-first century clothing and garments have been reinterpreted and re-presented, as new styles, tastes, and cultures have come into contact with Samoa with increasing frequency. Samoan body modifications, in particular tattoos, have also spread beyond the country with the diasporic movement of its people.

TATTOOING

Tattooing or *tatau* was and still is an important form of dressing the body for many Samoan people. Despite missionary censure in some cases, tattooing persists in Samoa. There are two main forms of tatau. Men wear *pe'a*, a densely rendered set of markings that begins on the lower back. It completely covers the lower body down to the knee and is finished off with a small group of motifs at the navel. The women wear *malu*, a set of markings less dense than the pe'a, starting at the upper thigh and extending down the legs and finishing behind the knee. There are other smaller and popular forms of tatau such as arm and wristbands, but the pe'a and malu are most important in Samoan ceremonial contexts.

A distinctive feature of Samoan tattooing is how the markings are made. In the twenty-first century, despite the availability of electric tattooing machines, many Samoan tattooists prefer to do their work with a set of handmade tools called *'au ta*. In the nineteenth century the *'au* were made of three small parts consisting of a small bone comb with very fine teeth, carefully sharpened to perforate the skin and deliver the pigment. The comb was fixed with strands of coconut fiber to a turtle-shell plate, which in turn was fastened to a thin stick forming the handle. The *'au* were each made differently and designed to render a different quality or thickness of line. Tools with a wide comb were used for filling in large dark areas of the tatau, while narrow combs were used to make very fine lines, small motifs, and dots.

There are structural elements in the design of the tatau that most *tufuga* (tattooing experts) would follow, but they filled in the structure in a variety of ways using a widely shared set of symbols and motifs. A number of factors influenced the standard of work. These ranged from the skill of the tufuga to the tattooed person's social status, how much they paid for the work, the availability of time, the tufuga's schedule, the condition and color of the subject's skin, and how the subject handled the pain.

The importance of Samoan tattooing in the nineteenth and early twentieth century has been the subject of much close study. In brief, pe'a was worn by *soga 'imiti* (untitled young men). Men of this status were like special attendants, responsible for performing duties for *matai* (village chiefs) in ceremonial contexts such as title bestowals. Women of rank known as *taupou* wore the malu and had similar responsibilities, representing their families and villages on ceremonial occasions. These roles still exist, although people who perform them are not always tattooed. Tattooing is normally paid for with Samoan valuables such as *'ie toga* (fine mats). As imported goods and cash economies have become important, other items, including printed fabric, clothing, and cash, have been accepted for payment.

WAIST GARMENTS

In Samoa the making of clothing after European contact, and the skills of embroidery, sewing, and weaving, were fostered and nurtured among the women of the villages. As well as covering and embellishing the body, garments worn in Samoa communicated social messages. They signified people's social status, their wealth, the occasion they were attending, or place they were traveling to. Garments could indicate membership in a certain group or organization, and even a person's occupation. Some of these uses and purposes have changed over time, and some of the textiles and garments documented in the nineteenth century have disappeared. But Samoan dress and its design remain laden with innovation, significance, and value.

Probably one of the oldest and perhaps the most simply made of Samoan waist garments was the *titi* (skirt). Worn by men as well as women, either on its own or as an overskirt, its style and appearance have persisted through many influences and changes. Its simple but functional form is still worn in the twenty-first century on important occasions, at dances and festivals, but also on fashion catwalks.

Anthropologist Te Rangi Hiroa provides the most complete description of Samoan waist garments, as they were in the late 1920s. He identified two types of titi. In one, strips are attached to a braid or cord that forms the waist attachment, some types of which may be plaited afterwards. The other commences with a weaving technique, finishing with the waist attachment. Titi were made from a variety of plants and were worn as an overskirt on top of longer garments. They were temporary, made for the occasion, and lasting only a day or two. *Titi lauti* were usually made from the leaves of the *ti* (*Cordyline terminalis*), a shrub that grows two to three meters (6.5 to 9.8 feet) high with lance-shaped leaves. The leaves of various varieties of this plant produce different colors, widths, and lengths that were taken advantage of usually dyed red or green, although sometimes purples, yellows, and white are used.

The *'ie tutu pu'upu'u* was a short woven waist garment with braided tails and hanging fringes. When the garment was worn, it was doubled over, with the braids and fringes forming what is essentially a one-piece skirt and overskirt. Te Rangi Hiroa recorded three varieties of this type of garment. They varied in their technique of manufacture, the color they were dyed, and the material. Examples he described were bleached white, but they could also be dyed black in a mixture of black candlenut dye and brown *o'o* dye.

An important garment and symbol of status is the *'ie toga* or fine mat. Although often presented as a mat in important ceremonials, the *'ie toga* can also be worn as a skirt, held in place around the waist with a belt of barkcloth, called *fusi*. Two fringes of feathers—one on the front and one on the back—were often incorporated into the design of these mats, so that when they were folded over one could see two rows of feathers at the same time. Some *'ie toga* made especially to be worn featured openweave edges as a further enhancement. The *'ie toga* would be worn in this way only by taupou, *manaia* (untitled son of a high-ranking chief), or high-ranking *matai*.

Similarly, in the nineteenth and early twentieth centuries the *'ie fau* and *'ie sina* were shaggy mat-like waist garments worn on important occasions by women of status. The term *shaggy mat* is an appropriate description of the garments, as the entire outer surface of the mat is covered in thin strings or tags attached to the main body of the mat by a special technique. This made them very clumsy and heavy to handle compared to other similar-sized textiles. The *'ie fau* was a brown shaggy garment made of the bast of the *fau tu* (*Hibiscus tiliaceus*), a variety of hibiscus. Its natural coloring was a yellowish brown, and its characteristic thick shaggy covering was achieved by attaching the long fiber tags very close together during the weaving process. In general, the *'ie fau* were coarse in texture.

By contrast, the *'ie sina* was finely made and softer in texture. Its distinguishing quality was its white color, from which it also derives its name. It was made from the bast of the *fau pata* (*Cypholophus heterophyllus*). The fine and delicate appearance of the *'ie sina* was achieved by splitting the fiber into very narrow wefts with a shell. Again fiber tags attached during weaving created the shaggy appearance of the *'ie sina*. On completion, the whole garment was bleached by soaking it in seawater and drying it in the sun. Later it would be repeatedly washed in freshwater and treated with the leaf of the fisoa plant, which assisted the development of the garment's white color. Shaggy garments were also stained a dark red using a mixture of earth in a wooden bowl, or black by submerging the garment in the mud of a swamp. The dark red garment was called *'ie ta'ele* after the soil used to color it, the black garment *'ie fuipani* after the *pani* bark stain used to ensure that the swamp mud adhered.

John Williams, a missionary in Samoa writing in the early 1830s, gives a description of how an *'ie ta'ele* was worn and what accessories could be worn with it. He said that the dress of the chief female was a shaggy red mat that hung around her loins about halfway to the knee, a corner lifted up to expose most of the left thigh. In the twenty-first century the *'ie sina* and *'ie fau* are no longer made and seem to have almost disappeared from memory. Very few Samoans are familiar with the names of these garments or recall ever seeing one in their lifetime. However, good examples still survive in museum collections.

Three Samoan women wearing long, loose, European-influenced dresses made from various patterned fabrics. These are typical of the modest female clothes introduced by missionaries, often called "mother hubbard" dresses. 1890s. Photograph by Thomas Andrew. Te Papa Museum of New Zealand, Wellington.

by the garment makers. Once the leaves were stripped from the shrub, the maker would braid them together or attach them to a separate braid made from *fau*, the bark bast of the hibiscus tree.

In a similar way, titi were also made from bast of the fau (*titi fau*) and fagai'o (*titi fagai'o*) as well as pandanus (*titi fala*) plants and feathers (*titi'ula*), but in these examples the leaf and feather elements were hung from cords. The fau and fagai'o were used to make a woven form of waist garment, characterized by a wide waistband woven in a check pattern with individual fibers hanging down, forming the length of the skirt. A variation on this style saw the waistband woven in a twill pattern with rosettes and other details attached. Titi fala were made from stripped pandanus leaf undersides discarded in the weaving of certain types of mat. They were sometimes dyed with turmeric or imported dyes, and the hanging elements were decorated with pieces of pandanus sewn on, giving an appliquéd effect.

The titi'ula were made from the red feathers of the Fijian parakeet. They were scarce and much sought after, making the feathers extremely valuable. For this reason the titi'ula signified rank or status and was usually worn by taupou (daughters of high-ranking chiefs). In 1927 Te Rangi Hiroa noted that in the absence of the preferred red feathers, titi'ula were often made from the green feathers of the Samoan parakeet. In the twentieth and early twenty-first centuries titi'ula were made from chicken feathers

BODY EMBELLISHMENTS AND HEADDRESSES

Additional items were also used to dress the body in nineteenth-century Samoa, including flower wreaths and necklaces of whale tooth, flowers, and seeds. Strings of blue beads acquired from Europeans were treasured and worn as bracelets or necklaces. John Williams mentions women wearing one or two beads on the ear. Coconut oil and turmeric were other elements that completed a woman's attire. Williams, when describing the woman wearing the red shaggy mat, says that her body was covered in scented oil. She was then tinged with an orange-colored powder made of turmeric. Around her neck there was a row of large blue beads. A pair of bracelets of beads of the same color were strung around her arms.

Headdresses for men and women were an important accessory for dressing the body in nineteenth-century Samoa. They consisted of a leaf or flower worn in the hair, a piece of *siapo* (barkcloth) wrapped around the head, or an elaborate and constructed assemblage of feathers, shells, and dyed hair, called a *tuiga*. The ad hoc and often one-use nature of headdresses and personal embellishment in general has allowed for a great deal of innovation and invention.

The most elaborate and certainly the most important headdress is the *tuiga*. As one of the most recognizable symbols of Samoan status, it was worn by manaia and taupou. The tuiga still retains an important place in Samoan communities, although aspects of its appearance and design have been greatly modified and changed.

The tuiga as it was at the turn of the century is described in detail by Augustin Kramer and Te Rangi Hiroa. It was typically a composite headdress made of several parts that were put together when required for wear. These parts were built up around a post-like foundation or *pou* made from wrapping cloth around the head. The ends of this cloth were tied and twisted into position, so a post-like form projected from the top of the head. This became the foundation and support for the other headdress elements that were tied onto it.

The first elements tied to the pou were the *lau ulu*, consisting of several strings to which were attached many long tassels of hair. Some of these strings were made long enough to hold up to thirty tassels of preferably thick frizzy hair. The more tassels and strings of hair, the thicker the tuiga would appear. The preferred color of the hair was a very light brown. So the very dark hair of most Samoans was lightened by one of two bleaching processes. The first was achieved by rubbing the hair with coral lime and then exposing it to the sun and rain for up to several months. The second method involved soaking the hair daily in salt water and exposing it to the sun until the hair bleached to satisfaction. The juice of wild oranges is also said to have assisted in developing the preferred light brown hair color. In the twenty-first century, in the absence of suitably processed hair, light brown–colored synthetic wigs are known to be used, although in most cases the human hair component is replaced with feathers.

The *lave* was a decorated framework of wooden sticks worn at the front of the headdress. This framework was either tied together or fixed to a plate of a material such as turtle shell. The individual sticks of the lave had strips of barkcloth tightly wrapped around them. Te Rangi Hiroa suggests that the lave formerly comprised the *selu tuiga*, a decorated comb made from coconut midrib. This, he says, was superseded by the wider open framework or lave that

is used in the twenty-first century, its greater surface area allowing for small glass mirrors to be incorporated into the design.

The *pale fuiono*, or forehead band, was tied across the front and base of the lave, helping to hold it in place. The forehead band was once made of a braided strip of coconut fiber decorated with two rows of cut nautilus-shell pieces. Imported especially from Tonga, these nautilus shells were very rare and valuable. Occasionally two pale fuiono were worn at the same time to create a more prominent band of decoration. The use of the pale in this way can be seen in many turn-of-the-century photographs. In the early nineteenth century John Williams mentions people wearing them on several occasions. In the twenty-first century pale fuiono are made from all kinds of applied decorations, especially beads and sequins. But the nautilus shells are especially rare.

Once all these pieces were fitted together on the head, the tuiga was complete. The finishing touch was often a set of red parakeet feathers attached on top as added decoration. In the absence of a lau ulu these red feathers alone could be worn on the head. Depending on which material dominated the tuiga, the headdress was called a *tuiga 'ula* (red feathers) or a *tuiga lau ulu* (human hair).

When Te Rangi Hiroa wrote his description of the tuiga in the 1920s, he said that the drawback of the tuiga was that it was not put together in a structurally permanent combination. In the twenty-first century the most common type of tuiga is exactly that, with tuiga in Samoa and New Zealand being made as one-piece hat-like structures with all the appendages and decorations attached to the outside. It is a very rare thing to see the old style of composite-type tuiga. But despite these material and cosmetic changes, the tuiga still holds its place as the headpiece of the chiefly family and is still used in much the same way for the same dances and ceremonial occasions.

COLONIAL ENCOUNTERS AND SAMOAN STYLE

Accounts from the nineteenth century demonstrate that Samoans were very adaptable in their attitudes to dress and made the most of any new materials or creative opportunities that came their way. Because of this, the missionaries had a major influence on the dress of Samoans, as they did on many Pacific Island cultures. The arrival of the missionaries in the early nineteenth century, and the traders and merchants who followed, saw the introduction of new materials and styles, as well as new ideas of modesty and appropriate attire. Among the first garments the missionaries introduced were hoodless barkcloth ponchos, or *tiputa*. The tiputa had significance as a type of uniform of those people who had converted to the Christian faith. They signified the wearer's association with the new religion and their membership in a new group in the community. John Williams mentions that converts distinguished themselves by wearing a piece of white cloth over their heads or shoulders, or sometimes the cloth was tied around the head or neck. But the missionaries also introduced other unsuitable items of clothing that were more a hindrance than an asset in the tropical climate. These new items included straw bonnets and the long, all-covering "mother hubbard" dress, as well as white shirts and trousers.

Significantly, these new items were quickly taken up by new converts and were much coveted and sought after. The skills of a few creative individuals soon provided local substitutes made in place of the real thing. Writing in 1861, missionary George Turner

A portrait of Talolo wearing a *tuiga* (headdress), Samoa, ca. 1890. The headdress is made from feathers, human hair, a mirror, and rows of nautilus shells. His neck is adorned with an *ula lei* made from cut-down whale teeth. He also wears a sash and waist garment of European cloth. Photograph by Thomas Andrew. Te Papa Museum of New Zealand, Wellington.

said that Samoan women were rarely seen without a tiputa and that straw bonnets and shawls were in great demand. He said that women showed great ingenuity in making a novel and durable substitute for the bonnet. A fascinating example of local craftsmanship is in the British Museum, made from pieces of turtle shell carefully stitched together, creating a very robust and solid version of a bonnet. The edges of the bonnet have been covered and finished in what appears to be a patterned cotton cloth, thus preventing cuts or abrasions from the sharp shell.

Tiputa were elaborated upon with siapo-inspired designs and patterns, and two examples exist made from finely woven pandanus. One of them, held in the Museum of New Zealand, has red cloth sewn around the edges, with tufts of red wool thread forming small feather-like decorations. Pieces of siapo were also worn as turbans for fishing or as protection against club blows during war. However, in times of peace only chiefs were permitted to wear such turbans. Turbans were also the distinctive marker of the Fitafita guards in American Samoa. Finished decorated pieces of siapo were made into full-length garments and bodices. Late-nineteenth-century photographs show long dresses for women made from what appear to be pieces of siapo sewn together. In recent times the undecorated barkcloth itself is becoming a sought-after material by Pacific Island dressmakers and designers. Its raw qualities capture an understated natural fiber look that is appealing and finds a place on catwalk garments and in the dress of brides and bridesmaids.

For men the white shirt and a wraparound of calico cloth became very popular and widely used in the late nineteenth century. There are many old photographs from Samoa of chiefs and others wearing various combinations of local and introduced dress including hats, blazers, and naval jackets. Turner said that "clothing in the climate of Samoa was a burden," but the demand for these types of cotton goods increased with every year that he was in the islands. The calico wraparound lavalava could be very plain, for example, in a straight blue color, or patterned in a wide range and variety of designs. For a short time in the mid-1880s an interesting and popular choice in the town of Apia were the colors of "old England" itself. British consul at the time, William Churchward wrote that recently a favorite pattern was that of the Union Jack, which suddenly made an appearance as big handkerchiefs, used either as lavalavas or as shawls. According to Churchward, one British patriot, outraged at the use of the British colors in this way, tried to seize upon and confiscate every Union Jack he saw worn by a Samoan, either paying for it or exchanging it for something less conspicuous. This did nothing but increase the trade in the fashionable article, so by the time this man had given up his cause he had become the happy owner of hundreds of yards of Union Jacks, and a good number of Royal Standards.

As more imported cloth became available, other styles and types of garment were made and incorporated with local dress. It is possible that at this time printed patterned cloth influenced siapo patterns and compositions, as it did with similar textiles in other Pacific islands such as Tahiti. Certainly the conventions of siapo mamanu (freehand-decorated barkcloth) provided ample scope for this to occur. Other garments became part of the Samoan wardrobe from the late nineteenth to early twentieth centuries, including the 'ie faitaga and the puletasi. The 'ie faitaga is a specially cut lavalava for men that has been machine-stitched along its waist edge and fitted with pockets and in some cases a belt fitting. It is believed that this style was introduced by native medical practitioners returning from Fiji, where the form of the lavalava had in some instances acquired a distinctive cut and appearance. The puletasi is the most popular of Samoan women's formal garments. It is a two-piece outfit consisting of a long skirt and a short- or long-sleeved blouse. Seen almost everywhere Samoans are found, it is cut and decorated to suit different occasions. The tidy appearance of the puletasi makes it a popular choice of uniform with choirs and school dance groups, and it is often decorated with printed bands of siapo motifs and patterns.

In the twenty-first century Samoans are still inspired by nineteenth-century style. Clothing effectively represents ethnic identity and culture, both in Samoa and across the contemporary diaspora. Samoans draw on the past for inspiration and as a reference point for authenticity. There has been persistence and change in Samoan dress, but oils and turmeric are still used on certain occasions, necklaces and wreaths are made instantly and as needed for a performance, tattooing still marks the skin, and 'ie toga are still treasured exchange valuables and garments.

Dressing the body remains a creative and innovative process. It still relates to participation in the social and cultural life of Samoan communities, but also the circumstances of where they live, whether it is in Los Angeles, Honolulu, Auckland, or Apia. Contemporary Samoan dress and fashion is influenced by international style and taste, and it draws on popular culture and high fashion.

References and Further Reading

Churchward, William. *My Consulate in Samoa: A Record of Four Years Sojourn in the Navigators Islands, with Personal Experiences of King Malietoa Laupepa, His Country, and His and His Men.* London: Richard Bentley and Son, 1887.

Hiroa, Te Rangi (Peter Buck). *Samoan Material Culture.* Bulletin 75. Honolulu: Bernice P. Bishop Museum, 1930.

Kramer, Augustin. *The Samoan Islands.* Vols. 1 and 2. Auckland, NZ: Polynesian Press, 1994 and 1995.

Turner, George. *Nineteen Years in Polynesia: Missionary Life, Travels, and Researches in the Islands of the Pacific.* London: John Snow, 1861.

Williams, John. *The Samoan Journals of John Williams 1830 and 1832.* Edited by Richard M. Moyle. Canberra: Australian National University Press, 1984.

Sean Mallon

See also Pacific Sisters: Urban Pacific Art, Fashion, and Performance; Pacific Street Styles in Auckland; Missionary Dress in Samoa; Tahitian Tattoos.

Snapshot: *Ta'ovala* and *Kiekie* of Tonga

The wearing of waist wrappings such as *t'ovala* and *kiekie* in modern daily life distinguishes Tongan dress from that of its neighboring Pacific archipelagos. Indeed, the basic working dress of civil servants and the school uniforms of students consist of tailored clothing termed *vala faka-palangi* (foreigners-style clothing), complemented for both sexes by a ta'ovala or for women by a kiekie. Compared to barkcloth production, both ta'ovala and kiekie can be made by a woman on her own, as the materials are easily accessible and the tools for the manufacture process, if needed, can be handled by a single woman.

The ta'ovala, worn by both men and women, is a rectangular waist mat, which varies in size from ten inches to three feet (about 25 to 91 centimeters). Tied around the waist with a piece of *kafa*, or plaited coconut sennit rope, a ta'ovala can cover the area between midriff and ankles. Usually different varieties of pandanus (*Pandanus* spp., a tropical tree, the leaves of which are used for weaving) are used to plait these garments. Wool or cotton may be added as trimmings. They may sometimes be created from innovative materials and techniques, including black and gold threads, plastic lacing, gift-wrapping ribbon, or burlap sacking to plait and dark green yarn to knit. According to Heather Young Leslie, a specialist in Polynesian studies, certain aesthetic principles such as smooth surfaces, flat straight edges, square corners, and parallel-running fibers are much admired. Moreover, age, use, and social experience are decisive elements in the ranking of ta'ovala.

The kiekie, which translates as a decorative waist garment worn by women, covers the hip area, sometimes extending to mid-calf-length. It allows for more freedom of movement than the ta'ovala, which may account for the kiekie's popularity. Made of pandanus, hibiscus bark, videotape, plastic baubles, fishing line, cloth tinsel, imported peacock feathers, shells, lacquered coconut shell, horsehair, or any other material that gives an aesthetically pleasing effect, kiekie take the shape of belts with several vertically dangling rows. The materials are almost as varied as the techniques utilized: macramé techniques, crocheting, machine sewing, or drilling. While kiekie are typically removable waist garments, cultural anthropologist Ping-Ann Addo noted a woman wearing a *kofu kiekie* or "kiekie dress" in Auckland in 2003. It consisted of a long-sleeved, brown-and-white shirt over a skirt, and, starting at the shirt's waistline, dangling strips of matching fabric gave the impression of braided strips attached to a kiekie. Addo has seen similar garments worn among Tongans in California.

ORIGINS OF WAIST GARMENTS

The ta'ovala originated out of practical considerations: It covered the barkcloth skirt, thus preventing it from tearing and the wearer from inadvertently exposing his or her private parts. Some Tongans believe the kiekie is a modernization of the ta'ovala. However, certain scholars point to possible eighteenth-century precursors of the kiekie collected during Captain James Cook's voyages to Tonga (1773, 1774, 1777),

Boys from Tonga High School wearing *ta'ovala* with red cotton trimming and girls in macraméd hibiscus fiber *kiekie* during the yearly school parade in Nuku'alofa, Tongatapu, Tonga, 27 May 2003. Photograph by Fanny Wonu Veys.

which show analogous shapes and techniques. They argue that kiekie are as historical and traditional as are ta'ovala.

With the arrival of the missionaries in the 1830s, new, mainly white garments were introduced. These were considered comfortable in a tropical climate and were believed to convey proof of cleanliness. Moreover, the missionaries thought that the effort needed to keep clothes white would give Tongans a good lesson in industriousness. However, Addo conjectures that Tongans associated plain white clothing with white barkcloth worn by commoners, and that therefore Tongan Christian converts continued to layer woven waist garments—being signs of rank, respect, and duty—on top of their Western-style clothes. Historical evidence shows that in the late nineteenth century, woven waist garments were hardly affected by the imposition of sumptuary laws that banned the making and wearing of indigenous cloth.

The continuation of the female art of making waist garments was also supported by the 1875 Declaration of Rights, guaranteeing the personal freedom of chiefs ('*eiki*) and commoners (*tu'a*) alike. The fact that commoner women no longer lived on the chief's ground resulted in chiefly women turning their attention away from organizing commoner women's labor and instead becoming more active in church and educational organizations. In so doing, commoner women were empowered with new incentives of their own. All sources agree that the late Queen Sālote (1900–1965) was instrumental in encouraging the ordinary daily wearing of waist garments as markers of Tongan custom and identity. She hoped to balance out the advantages of post–World War II modernization and certain changes she felt were too rapid.

SIGNIFICANCE

Waist garments have become a standard feature of Tongan formal dress and are worn to events of religious, state, and

A woman making a *kiekie* with pandanus, shells, and nylon fishing line in Pahu, Tongatapu, Tonga, 4 June 2003. Photograph by Fanny Wonu Veys.

community significance. They have become a symbol of Tongan identity. Tongans see themselves as respectably dressed if they wear a ta'ovala or kiekie. The wearing of these garments signifies respectability to such a degree that they can be worn with any type of dress, including long trousers instead of the usual *tupenu* (mid-calf-length cotton wraparound skirt). The waist garment provides the Tongans with a means to make a visual statement about their position in society. In this the ta'ovala takes precedence over the kiekie, as very fine ta'ovala, suggests Adrienne Kaeppler, are inherited and form indications of wealth and status. This is even clearer among the noble classes, where ta'ovala are used during weddings or funerals to flaunt and legitimize genealogical claims to chiefly lines. In short, age, use, social experience, and *faiva* (skill) are important principles that affect the system of ranking. On certain ceremonial occasions, such as church services, the kiekie is acceptable dress and is even encouraged among women who have attained the status of *akonaki* (instructor) in the Methodist Chiefly Church.

While in the twenty-first century barkcloth clothing is used exclusively for ceremonial and festive dress, waist garments are far more a part of daily clothing. Jehanne Teilhet-Fisk originally suggested that Tongans see the wearing of the ta'ovala as a way of binding their country around them. Through the deployment of new and contemporary materials and techniques, contemporary Tongan women materialize and reimagine key practices, significances, and ideologies in their ta'ovala and kiekie. Waist garments, in addition to being an item of identity, embody rapidly changing economic and political realities experienced by the Tongan people over the last two hundred years.

REFERENCES AND FURTHER READING

Addo, Ping-Ann. "God's Kingdom in Auckland: Tongan Christian Dress and the Expression of Duty." In *Clothing the Pacific*, edited by Chloë Colchester, 141–163. Oxford and New York: Berg, 2003.

Kaeppler, Adrienne L. "Kie Hingoa: Mats of Power, Rank, Prestige and History." *Journal of the Polynesian Society* 108, no. 2 (1999): 168–232.

Teilhet-Fisk, Jehanne. "Clothes in Tradition: The Ta'ovala and Kiekie as Social Text and Aesthetic Markers of Custom and Identity in Contemporary Tongan Society." *Pacific Arts* 5 (1992): 44–52; *Pacific Arts* 6 (1992): 40–65.

Young Leslie, Heather E. "'…Like a Mat Being Woven'." In *Hybrid Textiles: Pragmatic Creativity and Authentic Innovations in Pacific Cloth*, edited by Ping-Ann Addo, Heather Young Leslie, and Phyllis Herda. Special issue in honor of Jehanne Teilhet-Fisk. *Pacific Arts. The Journal of the Pacific Arts Association* 3–5 (2007): 115–127.

Fanny Wonu Veys

See also Barkcloth Body Wrapping in Tonga.

Barkcloth Body Wrapping in Tonga

Barkcloth, or *ngatu*, made by women from the paper mulberry tree, occupies a prominent position in the life of the twenty-first-century inhabitants of the Western Polynesian kingdom of Tonga. It is presented, worn, and displayed during first birthdays, weddings, investitures of chiefs, and funerals. Barkcloth as wrapped clothing evolved from a small piece of barkcloth in front of the pubic area to clothing that covers the lower part of the body, a style that initially characterized chiefly dress. In the mid-nineteenth century barkcloth eventually became limited to the specialized realm of ceremonial clothing, and its everyday aspects were taken over by imported Western dress. From the late twentieth century changes in barkcloth materials occurred. Funerary wrapping has remained similar from the eighteenth century up to the present. Ngatu, the material and its motifs, continues to occupy a prominent position in everyday objects, artwork, and catwalk clothing in the Pacific. It is clear that even when used as a means of enveloping the body, barkcloth conjures up ideas that extend beyond clothing: Barkcloth wrapping includes notions of protecting and controlling, a form of cultural skin, communication of status and identity, female power, and the enmeshment of past and present.

WHAT IS BARKCLOTH?

In Tonga ngatu is usually made from the inner bark of the paper mulberry tree (*Broussonetia papyrifera*), which is cultivated specially for barkcloth making. Since, in the tropical Pacific, the paper mulberry tree does not flower or set seed, the plant has to be propagated from cuttings or suckers. Once the tree has reached its required thickness and height (the stem is about three to five centimeters, or 1.18 to 1.9 inches, in diameter, and two to three meters, or 6.5 to 9.8 feet, in height)—usually after about two years, when the brown bark turns silvery white—the tree is cut and the bark is stripped off. The thin outer bark is removed, and only the inner bark is used. This is soaked in water and beaten with a grooved wooden beater (*ike*) on a wooden anvil (*tutua*). In order to obtain a barkcloth of an even thickness, the piece of bark is folded continuously while being beaten. The strips of barkcloth are then glued together with half-boiled tapioca root or baking flour boiled in water to form larger pieces.

In Tonga barkcloths have traditionally been decorated by means of rubbing boards, which are made of coconut leaf sheaths, pandanus leaves (*Pandanus tectorius*, a large tropical shrub or small tree), and coconut leaf ribs that are sewn together with hibiscus fiber and coconut fiber. Those rubbing boards, or *kupesi*, are then fixed onto the barkcloth-making bench (*papa koka'anga*). Two layers of long runners of white barkcloth are placed horizontally

and vertically over the papa koka'anga, and reddish brown dye is rubbed on them. When the piece is finished, it is laid out in the sun to dry, and at a later time the designs are overpainted and accentuated with black dye. As Adrienne Kaeppler has noted in her studies of barkcloth designs, some record a visual history of important events, places, and people of Tonga, a fact that makes Tongan barkcloth decoration unique in the Pacific. In the eighteenth and nineteenth centuries the designs were exclusively geometric, whereas from the late nineteenth century onward naturalistic motifs and rubbed writing specifying the subject matter of the ngatu coexisted with geometric designs. These more representational motifs range from animal depictions such as lions, pigeons, and flying foxes to trees, plants, and floral designs to objects including water tanks, churches, houses, airplanes, bicycles, musical instruments, and tennis rackets. The edges of a piece of barkcloth are usually left undecorated, but numerals indicate from the late nineteenth century onward the length of the ngatu.

Pre-nineteenth-century accounts by Europeans never refer to Tongan barkcloth in the vernacular language but instead prefer to call it "(their) cloth," "Indian cloth," or "paper-cloth." It is only from the nineteenth century onward in the account of William Mariner, who was adopted by Tongans after most of the crew of the *Port-au-Prince* had been killed in 1806, that the local name *ngatu* appears along with variations on the word *cloth*. Jules Dumont d'Urville, a French voyager, clarified in 1827 to a European audience the distinction between ngatu, meaning barkcloth, and *tapa*, referring to the undecorated edge of a piece of barkcloth.

A woman removing the outer bark from the paper mulberry tree stem, Pahu, Tongatapu, Tonga, April 2003. To make barkcloth, the outer bark is discarded, and the inner bark is soaked in water and beaten flat. Photograph by Fanny Wonu Veys.

However, from the late nineteenth century onward *tapa* has been used as an Anglicized synonym for barkcloth.

BARKCLOTH BODY WRAPPING: A HISTORICAL OVERVIEW

The enveloping of people in barkcloth has a long history that can be traced using linguistics, archaeology, written documents, visual representations, museum collections, and fieldwork. One has to be aware that historical sources for Tonga and for the Pacific in general are European and American and therefore give us a Western historical perspective on Pacific history. Linguistic and archaeological research in Western Polynesia suggests that the paper mulberry tree was introduced from Southeast Asia by the earliest settlers, the so-called Lapita people, in the first millennium B.C.E. This does not mean the plant was used for barkcloth making, but it does imply that the tree was considered important enough to be brought into the newly settled areas.

The earliest documentation for Tonga dates back to descriptions and drawings made during the Dutch voyage of Jacob Le Maire and Willem Corneliszoon Schouten, who in 1616 were the first Europeans to reach the Tongan islands of Niuatoputapu, Tafahi, and Niuafo'ou. On sailing toward Niuatoputapu (the most northerly island in Tonga) on 8 May 1616, Le Maire reported that people in Tonga were dressed in barkcloth, covering only the lower parts of their bodies. That same day Schouten described a dress that might be a skirt or a loincloth, but he was less clear about the material of which the clothing was made. He, however, observed that their clothing had a strange color. Schouten's account includes an illustration of this encounter with a *tongiaki*, a Tongan double canoe. It is the earliest depiction of Tongans by Europeans. A close examination of the people on the canoe reveals that all the Tongans are unclothed. This is in stark contrast to the fully clothed Europeans on the small boat. The lack of clothes in the drawing does not correspond to the accounts of both Schouten and Le Maire, but it shows the artist's focus on contrasting Europeans and Tongans. Later, Abel Tasman was sent by Batavia's Dutch governor-general Anthony Van Diemen, the company's resident administrator, to explore the Pacific. Of the Tongan places Tasman visited in 1643, he, like his Dutch predecessors, talks about men wearing a small piece of cloth in front of their pubic area.

During James Cook's visits to Tonga in 1773 and 1774 (second voyage) and in 1777 (third voyage), numerous observations were made of the use of barkcloth as wrapping. Cook and William Wales, the surgeon on the second voyage, stressed the fact that men and women were dressed the same in a piece of barkcloth wrapped around the waist, extending to the knees, but leaving the shoulders uncovered. The naturalist Johann Reinhold Forster confirmed these accounts but added a physical description of the pieces, describing them as shiny, oiled, glazed, and dark brown. His son Georg Forster pointed to gender differences: Most of the men were unclothed, while the women and some of the men wore an ankle-length barkcloth skirt. David Samwell, the surgeon's mate on Cook's third voyage, distinguished between the clothes of the common people and the chiefs, who wore a larger quantity of barkcloth to signal their rank. Ngatu as ceremonial clothing was also noted by Charles Clerke, an officer on Cook's third voyage.

George Vason, a member of the London Missionary Society, in an account of his four-year stay in Tonga (1797–1801), mentions the clothing of a chief. He distinguishes between the clothing of *hou'eiki* (high-ranking Tongans) wearing large pieces of colored and patterned barkcloth, often combined with a mat wrapped around their loins, and *tu'a* people (low-ranking Tongans) wearing less elaborate wrappings. Women in particular wore barkcloth in a similar way to chiefs, but of the uncolored variety, with a waist mat or a girdle made of leaves.

Examples of eighteenth-century barkcloth from Tonga can be found in museums in Göttingen, Wörlitz, Oxford, Stockholm, Newcastle-upon-Tyne, Berne, Neuchâtel, Florence, St. Petersburg, and Madrid. These pieces were not solely acquired through barter or active collecting but were also given or presented by Tongans to European sailors. This begs the question whether the collected pieces of barkcloth are the same as the pieces that enveloped people's bodies. Pictorial material gives an insight. The artists William Hodges and John Webber worked on Cook's second and third voyages, respectively, but they only depict people wearing draped white clothing. However, a drawing by Juan Ravenet, one of the three artists accompanying Alessandro Malaspina, who visited Vava'u in 1793, shows a chiefly woman with a distinctively patterned dark barkcloth or *ngatu 'uli*. These motifs can be found on barkcloths collected during Cook's second and third voyages.

Clothing in the nineteenth century remained quite similar to that described in the late eighteenth century. Indeed, John Williams, of the London Missionary Society, visiting Tonga, noted the barkcloth and mat clothing of the king and his children during the baptism of the king on Sunday, 7 August 1831. William Waldegrave's 1830 descriptions as commander of the *Seringapatam* include both men and women wrapped up in barkcloth and mats, so that they seemed almost invisible.

By the 1850s a considerable change in everyday dress was occurring: Barkcloth was being complemented by imported cotton. Oswald Brierly, a British artist who crossed the Pacific on HMS *Meander*, noticed in 1850 that indigenous female teachers also wore cotton blouses. Wrapped barkcloth and mats remained appropriate only for ceremonial occasions. Significant is the fact that cotton tailored garments appear first on the upper body, which had been left uncovered by both men and women up till this time. Cotton cloth did not initially replace the sometimes enormous lengths of wrapped barkcloth but found a niche that was figuratively and literally not covered by barkcloth.

While these changes were occurring, barkcloth remained an important item of everyday clothing. Lieutenant Herbert Swire, who sailed on the *Challenger* in 1874, points to the fact that barkcloth wraparound clothes were commonly worn inside the house and when performing everyday tasks, while it was considered proper to wear European-style clothes for Sunday church service. Aylic Marin, who visited Tonga in the 1880s, described the son of Tungi, a chief on Tongatapu, as wearing a large piece of barkcloth draped in the Roman way, but he stressed that this was only to go out. At home he wore a barkcloth belt or even crepe paper in different colors.

In 1875 the Law on Tapa was issued. It was drawn up by Shirley Baker, a Wesleyan missionary, and it stipulated that from 1876 to 1878, the manufacture and wearing of indigenous cloth were to be progressively eliminated. (The fact that Tonga is the largest barkcloth producer in the early twenty-first century proves

A woman beating the inner bark of the paper mulberry tree as part of the barkcloth-making process, Pahu, Tongatapu, Tonga, February 2003. Photograph by Fanny Wonu Veys.

that the law did not work; after 1878, when the law was no longer active, barkcloth production clearly started again.) Baker passed this law to the advantage of a particular textile firm that sought a market for cotton cloth. Wearing painted barkcloth was outlawed and its production restricted to one day a week. Conversely, mat weaving remained relatively unrestricted; one of the main reasons was that mat weaving was silent and did not involve noisy activities such as beating fibers for hours as for barkcloth. Importantly, Methodist missionaries considered it a "work of patience" and a first step toward training the women in sewing, which hopefully would provide them and their families with further (cotton) clothing. By the end of the nineteenth century Victorian-style dress was encouraged. Thus, Tongan everyday clothing consisted of bonnets, sewn gowns, trousers, and swallow-tailed coats. Barkcloth, however, continued to be used for ceremonial dress. Tongan barkcloth was still made extensively, using naturalistic designs to commemorate and celebrate historical events and the monarchy.

By the twentieth century Tonga had become the largest producer of barkcloth in the Pacific, providing not only their neighboring areas such as Samoa and Fiji with ngatu, but also overseas Tongan communities in New Zealand, Australia, and the west coast of the United States, where the pieces were worn during life-cycle events and exchanged as part of ceremonies. It is precisely in this Tongan diaspora, and more specifically in New

Zealand, that Tongan barkcloth designs started to feature in interior decoration schemes. This so-called Pacific accent became more entrenched as barkcloth-derived motifs spread from contemporary art, to use on T-shirts, in murals, in signage, and even in corporate art, where they served as a cliché for Pacific presence. The use of barkcloth in modern dress is perhaps epitomized in artist Rosanna Raymond's early 1990s creation of a pair of jeans completely covered with patches of barkcloth (in the collection of the National Gallery of Victoria, Australia).

From the 1990s onward New Zealand fashion designers, supported by the media, began to encourage the development of a more typically Pacific fashion industry. Although key designers were still talking about being influenced by Europe—specifically Italy, France, and Belgium—they were also looking to their Asian Pacific roots for inspiration. The new cultural and national references include the use of barkcloth.

In the twenty-first century changes in barkcloth materials occurred. In 2003 a royal wedding took place between the granddaughter of King Tupou IV, 'Eiki Sālote Lupepau'u Salamasina Purea Vahine Arii 'o e Hau Tuita, and the son of a chief, Matai'ulua-'i-Fonuamotu Fusitu'a. Besides some large-scale barkcloth presentations, on the occasion of the signing of the wedding register on 6 June 2003, the family members of Lupepau'u made a dramatic appearance. From the front of the palace, which faces the sea, they walked slowly toward the west side of the palace, weighed down by the enormous volume of barkcloth wrapped around their waists. The barkcloth wrappings were removed and piled up under the tent where this particular part of the ceremony took place. Some of these barkcloths were only partially made of beaten paper mulberry bark, or not at all. This so-called ngatu pepa (paper barkcloth) has been studied by Ping-Ann Addo. It consists of a lower layer of vylene, a synthetic fabric, normally used as interfacing, covered with an upper layer of beaten inner bark. It is often mockingly called ngatu pālangi (European or Western barkcloth), ngatu haafekasi (half-cast barkcloth), or ngatu loi (fake barkcloth). Sometimes both barkcloth layers are replaced by vylene, but customary geometric and naturalistic motifs continue to be reproduced in Tonga and in diasporic communities.

TONGAN BARKCLOTH: A PERSISTENT PRACTICE

Despite the emergence of Western-style cotton clothing and the nineteenth-century restrictions imposed on barkcloth manufacture, its production and use have continued uninterrupted in Tonga. This is in contrast to other parts of Polynesia, where barkcloth was abandoned soon after European contact, by the 1840s in Tahiti and by the later nineteenth century in Hawai'i. The reason for the persistence of Tongan barkcloth is due to a number of factors ranging from technical to social and functional.

The fact that Tongan barkcloth is not as finely beaten as in other parts of Polynesia and is characterized by a mass decorating technique by means of rubbing blocks could account for its continued use. However, this argument fails to explain why—if the rapid production of large quantities matters so much—women actively choose not to increase production by using the barkcloth-making machine designed by Geoffrey Houghland, a Peace Corps member in the 1980s, a topic studied by anthropologist Jehanne Teilhet-Fisk. It is clear that the pleasing sound of the beater hitting the anvil, the fact that the machine needs to be

Women assembling and rubbing barkcloth (*koka'anga*), Tofoa, Tongatapu, Tonga, February 2003. Photograph by Fanny Wonu Veys.

maintained and repaired by men, and the importance of the communal effort play a role in preferring to beat ngatu by hand.

While in many other Polynesian societies the importation of textile garments contributed to the disappearance of barkcloth clothing in everyday life, in Tonga it continued to play a role in ceremonial clothing and in presentations. In eastern Polynesia the traditional gods and their images wrapped in barkcloth were the focus of attack by missionaries, because they were associated with non-Christian magico-religious rituals and practices. The symbols of the ancient belief systems disappeared together with the need for barkcloth production in central and marginal Polynesia. The transmission of the great skill and experience needed to beat and felt the inner bark to a fine paper-thin cloth became irrelevant when barkcloth was no longer in demand. The number of women able to produce the best-quality barkcloth finally became so small that even the reduced needs could not be met.

In contrast, Tongan use of barkcloth in ceremonies and as a high-status exchange product was viewed positively by the missionaries, as is evident from missionary James Watkin's praise for the pleasing dress of a chiefly bride during her wedding on 9 April 1833. For many of the Christian missionaries the fact that converts were covered from top to toe with barkcloth, instead of walking around bare-chested, meant the newly converted Christians manifested an inner redemption. Since the demand for barkcloth persisted, the technical know-how and its transmission were continued.

As Steven Hooper has explained, missionaries failed to understand that in Western Polynesia and more specifically in Tonga, where god images were less common than in other parts of Polynesia, living people would act as vessels for the god and would be treated as a kind of god image by being wrapped in barkcloth. Wrapping with barkcloth and mats as a way to contain *mana*—a Polynesian term that in its widest sense means divinity-sanctioned efficacy, or generative potency—was also not understood. Because the missionaries in Western Polynesia attributed a decorative function to barkcloth and did not comprehend its linking and protecting significance, they did not oppose,

but rather encouraged barkcloth production and use, in contrast to what their colleague missionaries did in other areas of Polynesia. Missionary attitudes thus contributed to the continuation of barkcloth as a custom in Western Polynesia. Even in the twenty-first century the Wesleyan Methodist Church acts as a driving force in the perpetuation of barkcloth production and use, both in the kingdom of Tonga and in its diaspora communities.

Another complementary explanation for the persistence of barkcloth in Tonga is that ngatu plays an important role in the social organization of the kingdom. It is generally accepted that the various artistic and social domains in Tonga share similar conceptual structures, which can be explained in musical terms: drone (*laulalo*), melody (*fasi*), and decoration (*teuteu*). The overall design of Tongan twentieth- and twenty-first-century barkcloth also encodes this conceptual framework made up of three elements. According to Adrienne Kaeppler, the straight lines that define the overall space and layout can be considered the drone of the piece. The element that characterizes a ngatu, or the so-called melody, is the named motif, the essential feature. The final overpainted designs, which elaborate on the central motif, are the decoration. These three stages are also present in barkcloth manufacture. The first stage is the beating, or *tutu*, the second process is the *koka'anga*, the assemblage of the beaten pieces into a large full barkcloth, and finally the last process is the *tohi ngatu*, or painting of the barkcloth. These three stages are similarly present in Tongan music, dance, and social organization.

The production and use of barkcloth demonstrate how past and present are enmeshed. During the preparations for the royal wedding of Princess Lupepau'u and the son of a chief, Fusitu'a, one of the ngatu the women were folding at the parental house of the groom had designs derived from eighteenth-century Cook voyage barkcloths. For this wedding bed barkcloth the ngatu-making women had been inspired by photographs of historical cloths that had been circulating among them. The way in which Tongan women see a direct connection between historical and contemporary barkcloth reveals that its purpose is being kept alive. Indeed, through its use as dress and thus its display in ceremonies and its function in exchange, the product was and remains essential in forging kinship relationships. Drawing on these rich cultural resources, barkcloth not only brings the past to the present in an adapted form but contributes to the enmeshment of past and present. It moreover highlights the attitudes of Tongans toward history and the past, which is a living rather than a printed custom, and is present in objects that are constantly being renewed.

THE SIGNIFICANCE OF TONGAN BARKCLOTH

How can barkcloth wrapping be understood? What does it tell us about its indigenous significance in Tonga? Evidence from late-eighteenth-century accounts suggests that barkcloth was highly valued. David Samwell observed in 1777 that of all of Tonga's manufactures, cloth was the principal one. The importance of barkcloth is confirmed by Francisco Antonio Maurelle, a French explorer, who remarked on 5 March 1781 in Vava'u that barkcloth was valued higher than mats. William Mariner explained that in early-nineteenth-century Tonga there was a difference between objects produced by women and those produced by men. Barkcloth belongs to that category of objects made exclusively by women and is referred to as *koloa*, or "prestigious objects." Both in the twentieth and twenty-first century commoners as well as chiefly families have their own circulation of koloa. These objects are considered treasures. Koloa can be redistributed, but the most precious ones will be conserved and can be inherited.

According to Phyllis Herda, in the past a piece of barkcloth did not become koloa until a chiefly woman acted upon it in a chiefly manner. Thus, labor of commoners did not make the piece of barkcloth automatically koloa. Following the Tongan notion of chiefliness, it was the mana of the chiefly woman, her presence and skill, that was imbued in the cloth. It can therefore be argued that the word *koloa* does not simply refer to the type of object— barkcloth, mats, and so on—but also to a specific object in which the mana of a chiefly person is incorporated. Kaeppler has noted that koloa is the complementary domain to *ngāue*, products derived from men's agricultural work and animal husbandry. The contrast between ngāue and koloa reflects the high status of women in Tongan society. While ngāue are, like men, powerful, koloa are, like the women themselves, valuable: Women control life through birth-giving, introducing the life of people, and they also initiate the "life" of barkcloth.

Barkcloth as clothing shows that there is a close relationship between clothing and the ecological and climatic environment. Historical sources stressed the same idea. Indeed, when in the eighteenth century Johann Reinhold Forster described the wearing of upper garments (in a period when these were not commonly worn), one could interpret this as hinting at the protective side of barkcloth.

A number of scholars offer particular interpretations of Tongan barkcloth wrapping. Barkcloth envelops people's bodies as protection from supernatural forces. The anthropologist Bradd Shore explains that Polynesians live in a dangerous world, because breach of etiquette or chiefly protocol can bring about disturbances in potency that do not merely have social repercussions, but cosmic consequences as well. Every potency or mana, when uncontained and disorganized, could diminish rather than enhance human life. It is therefore important to have a means to control these forces or to be protected from them.

Both Valerio Valeri and Alain Babadzan have offered the view that wrapping with barkcloth is a way of redirecting and binding potency. Wrapping of people going through life events such as weddings, investitures, and funerals reproduces the process by which the mind reaches the idea of god. In Polynesia wrapping removes the person from sight and creates the experience of a

Relatives wrapped in barkcloth and mats at a royal wedding, Nuku'alofa, Tongatapu, Tonga, June 2003. Photograph by Fanny Wonu Veys.

passage from a concrete reality to an invisible one. Therefore, it is collectively accepted as a sign of godly presence and represents the person's control of divine potency. Wrapping is more than sacralization. The inward person is restrained by its envelope, yet what is inside reveals itself indirectly through what is outside. Wrapping can thus symbolize human control of the divine, the "taming" of it at the very moment it attains full divinity.

As anthropologist Annette Weiner has argued, billows of cloth can have a double meaning: They mask the person's vulnerability but add volume to his or her presence. It is generally accepted that people at the center of rituals (chiefs, newborns, newlyweds, or corpses) are in a liminal position and are therefore particularly vulnerable to being affected by the mana of others or of contaminating their surroundings with their mana. Barkcloth separates, protects, and encloses those people. Mariner's nineteenth-century account of the Tongan marriage of the eldest daughter of Fīnau to the Tu'i Tonga describes the use of wrapping in a wedding ceremony but does not speculate on its symbolic value. The wrapping on that occasion was carried out with Samoan fine mats, which has a similar meaning in Tonga when done with barkcloth. Mariner described an early-nineteenth-century burial where the corpse was wrapped in koloa (mats, barkcloth, scented coconut oil). These descriptions demonstrate that the ritually appropriate intervention by means of wrapping with barkcloth, oil, and mats acts as a controlling device of the potentially disruptive influences of the recently departed. According to Steven Hooper, wrapping and binding are thus conceptually linked in the notion of protection.

Mourners are only allowed to wear mats. Historical accounts and contemporary events, however, confirm barkcloth did/does play an important protecting role in wrapping the corpse. The surgeon on James Cook's third voyage (1776–1780), William Anderson, described in 1777 how people who were buried were first wrapped in barkcloth, and William Mariner noticed the same for the funerals he witnessed during his four-year stay in Tonga in the early nineteenth century. John Thomas, a Wesleyan missionary, witnessed on 24 May 1830 the wrapping of a child in barkcloth. The Wesleyan missionary David Cargill also reported corpses being wrapped in barkcloth on 19 March 1834. Missionary Matthew Wilson observed that for the burial of Chief Vaea of Houma, held in September 1844, barkcloth was used to wrap both the body and the house. The funerary ceremonies for King Tupou IV in September 2006 similarly involved the wrapping of the king's body in several layers of barkcloth. This was not, however, visible to the large audience. The funeral on 9 March 2003 of a woman in the village of Lifuka in Ha'apai was more explicit: The whole village witnessed how her body was carefully wrapped in barkcloths and mats and then carried to the concrete grave, which was lined with barkcloth.

According to ethnohistorian and anthropologist Serge Tcherkézoff, wrapping and binding people in barkcloth provides them with a cultural skin—next to the natural skin—which protects and contains them at the same time. The layering of clothes/skins is important. In 1793 Juan Ravenet, an artist on Malaspina's Spanish exploring voyage, visited Tonga and depicted a young woman, Fatafehi, and a young man called Latu. This drawing offers a good opportunity for illustrating the layered skin concept. Latu is tattooed from his waist to his knees (women in Tonga were never tattooed). It is notable that the young woman is wearing a mat or a piece of barkcloth exactly on the place where Latu

A woman's body, wrapped in barkcloth and mats, is carried out of church, Hihifo village, Lifuka island (part of the Ha'apai central group of islands), Tonga, March 2003. Photograph by Fanny Wonu Veys.

has his tattoos, that is, from waist to knee. Tattooing is like an extra skin, much like barkcloth when wrapped around the body. The difference is that tattoos form an integral part of the body, whereas barkcloth is a removable "skin." It seems that people in liminal positions, which include life-changing events such as births, weddings, installations of a chief, and funerals, are accumulating skin upon skin. For example, a person can have a tattoo, be shining with coconut oil, and be wearing a piece of barkcloth with a mat and leaf girdle on top. Indeed, the characteristics of the material used—barkcloth—are remarkable. One might suggest that the bast from which it is made protects in its natural situation the vulnerable central part of the tree in the same way as the processed material forms a skin for people in a vulnerable situation.

Barkcloth clothing in Tonga plays a nonverbal role in communicating status and identity, and it aids in human interaction. Types of barkcloth, as well as songs and poetry, are used in cultural exchanges between villagers, church groups, and families as part of presentations during weddings, funerals, and installations of chiefs. Looking to a cultural example beyond Tonga, an interesting phenomenon can be noted. From about the middle of the nineteenth century Fijians who wanted to communicate high status would not only wear Tongan-style clothing—the wraparound skirt covering the body from the waist downwards—instead of the Fijian loincloths for men and short grass skirts for women. They also wore Tongan-style barkcloths decorated with rubbed designs instead of the more typically Fijian stenciled type. Tongan objects were incorporated into Fijian chiefly regalia, and the Tongan way of doing things was associated with high status and power. Indeed, Chief Seru Cakobau (around 1815–1883), also called king of Fiji, appears in photographs dressed in the Tongan-style wraparound cloth instead of the loincloth depicted in earlier drawings of Fijians, thereby making a statement of chiefliness through his affiliations with his important Tongan neighbor. As Wesleyan missionaries converted Fijians to Christianity with the help of Tongan teachers, the Tongan-style wraparound bark-cloths came to be associated with Christian identity, supplanting local native dress.

The way in which barkcloth reinforces the stratified sociopolitical system based on social status and societal rank might explain why in Tonga barkcloth is still omnipresent in the twenty-first century. Barkcloth in Tonga and in the Tongan diaspora communities is associated with the cultural reproduction of the kin group and the wider society through the part it plays in birth, marriage, rituals of death, and investiture.

References and Further Reading

Addo, Ping-Ann. "Commoner Tongan Women Authenticate Ngatu Pepa in Auckland." In *Hybrid Textiles: Pragmatic Creativity and Authentic Innovations in Pacific Cloth*, edited by Ping-Ann Addo, Heather Young Leslie, and Phyllis Herda. Special issue in honor of Jehanne Teilhet-Fisk. *Pacific Arts. The Journal of the Pacific Arts Association* 3–5 (2007): 60–73.

Babadzan, Alain. "The Gods Stripped Bare." In *Clothing the Pacific*, edited by Chloë Colchester, 51–75. Oxford and New York: Berg, 2003.

Beaglehole, J.C., ed. *The Journals of Captain Cook on His Voyages of Discovery*. Vol. 3, *The Voyages of the Resolution and Discovery 1776–1780*. Cambridge: Published for the Hakluyt Society at the University Press, 1967.

Beaglehole, J.C., ed. *The Journals of Captain Cook on His Voyages of Discovery*. Vol. 2, *The Voyages of the Resolution and Adventure 1772–1775*. Cambridge: Published for the Hakluyt Society at the University Press, 1969.

Campbell, I.C. *Island Kingdom. Tonga Ancient and Modern*. Christchurch, NZ: Canterbury University Press, 2001.

Forster, George. *George Forster 1754–1794. A Voyage Round the World*. 2 vols. Edited by Nicholas Thomas and Oliver Berghof. Honolulu: University of Hawai'i Press, 1999.

Herda, Phyllis. "The Changing Texture of Textiles in Tonga." *Journal of the Polynesian Society* 108, no. 2 (1999): 149–167.

Hooper, Steven. *Pacific Encounters. Art and Divinity in Polynesia 1760–1860*. London: British Museum Press, 2006.

Kaeppler, Adrienne L. "Melody, Drone, and Decoration: Underlying Structures and Surface Manifestations in Tongan Art and Society." In *Art in Society: Studies in Styles, Culture and Aesthetics*, edited by Michael Greenhalgh and Vincent Megaw, 261–274. London: Duckworth, 1978.

Kaeppler, Adrienne L. "Art and Aesthetics." In *Developments in Polynesian Ethnology*, edited by Alan Howard and Robert Borofsky, 211–240. Honolulu: University of Hawai'i Press, 1989.

Kaeppler, Adrienne L. "Art, Aesthetics, and Social Structure." In *Tongan Culture and History*, edited by Phyllis Herda, Jennifer Terrell, and Niel Gunson, 59–71. Canberra: Department of Pacific and Southeast Asian History, Australian National University, 1990.

Kaeppler, Adrienne L. "Poetics and Politics of Tongan Barkcloth." In *Pacific Material Culture. Mededelingen van het Rijksmuseum voor Volkenkunde*, edited by Dirk A. M. Smidt, Pieter ter Keurs, and Albert Trouwborst, 101–121. Leiden, Netherlands: Rijksmuseum voor Volkenkunde, 1995.

Kaeppler, Adrienne L. "Kie Hingoa: Mats of Power, Rank, Prestige and History." *Journal of the Polynesian Society* 108, no. 2 (1999): 168–231.

Kaeppler, Adrienne L. "The Structure of Tongan Barkcloth Design: Imagery, Metaphor and Allusion." In *Pacific Art. Persistence, Change and Meaning*, edited by Anita Herle, Nick Stanley, Karen Stevenson, and Robert L. Welsch, 291–308. Adelaide, Australia, and Honolulu: Crawford House Publishing and University of Hawai'i Press, 2002.

Kooijman, Simon. *Tapa in Polynesia. Bernice P. Bishop Museum Bulletin* 234. Honolulu: Bishop Museum Press, 1972.

Küchler, Susanne, and Graeme Were, eds. *The Art of Clothing: A Pacific Experience*. London: UCL Press, 2005.

Mariner, William. *An Account of the Natives of the Tonga Islands, in the South Pacific Ocean: With an Original Grammar and Vocabulary of Their Language*. 3rd ed. Edinburgh and London: Constable, 1827.

Neich, Roger, and Mick Pendergrast. *Traditional Tapa Textiles of the Pacific*. London: Thames and Hudson, 1997.

Raymond, Rosanna. "Getting Specific: Fashion Activism in Auckland during the 1990s: A Visual Essay." In *Clothing the Pacific*, edited by Chloë Colchester, 193–208. Oxford: Berg, 2003.

Shore, Bradd. "Mana and Tapu." In *Developments in Polynesian Ethnology*, edited by Alan Howard and Robert Borofsky, 137–173. Honolulu: University of Hawai'i Press, 1989.

Tcherkézoff, Serge. "On Cloth, Gifts and Nudity: Regarding Some European Misunderstandings during Early Encounters in Polynesia." In *Clothing the Pacific*, edited by Chloë Colchester, 51–75. Oxford and New York: Berg, 2003.

Teilhet-Fisk, Jehanne H. "To Beat or Not to Beat. That Is the Question: A Study on Acculturation and Change in Art-Making Process and Its Relation to Gender Structures." In *Pacific Material Culture. Mededelingen van het Rijksmuseum voor Volkenkunde Leiden*, edited by Dirk A. M. Smidt, Pieter ter Keurs, and Albert Trouwborst, 122–148. Leiden, Netherlands: Rijksmuseum voor Volkenkunde, 1995.

Valeri, Valerio. *Kingship and Sacrifice: Ritual and Society in Ancient Hawaii*. Chicago and London: University of Chicago Press, 1985.

Weiner, A.B. "Why Cloth? Wealth, Gender, and Power in Oceania." In *Cloth and Human Experience*, edited by A.B. Weiner and J. Schneider, 33–72. Washington and London: Smithsonian Institution Press, 1989.

Fanny Wonu Veys

See also Tahitian Tattoos; Fijian Dress and Body Modifications.

Dance Costumes in French Polynesia

Among the customs French Polynesians perpetuate in the twenty-first century, the public performance of choreographed group dances is one of the most popular and highly enjoyed by local audiences. These may be as a school celebration, a way to acknowledge and greet important visitors, an accompaniment to the large buffets that local residents and visitors enjoy at the tourist hotels, or as part of the yearly music and dance competitions known as *Heiva*. Viewed as a locus of artistic creativity in the culture, costumes, often using natural resources, are an integral part of performance, and audiences place high value on the originality and skilled craftsmanship displayed in costuming the dancers. Dance dress worn by amateur and professional troupes on the island of Tahiti, taken as a particular example, is both representative of larger practice throughout French Polynesia and capable of being modified over time and space by local island aesthetics and preferences.

A BRIEF HISTORY OF DANCE COSTUMES

The earliest reports of voyagers Samuel Wallis (1767), Louis Antoine de Bougainville (1768), and James Cook (1769) document a history of elaborate dress for dancers in presentational dances that entertained both the chiefs and the general population. A famous drawing by John Webber, artist on Captain James Cook's third voyage to the Pacific (1776–1780), depicts female dancers in yards of finely beaten white *tapa* (barkcloth), gathered around the waist with long pleats extending to the upper back and shoulders of the performers. Feathers cover the breasts and hang in tassels from the waist, while a crown of finely braided human hair that Cook described as "near a mile long...[and] without a single knott" (Cook 1968, 126) adorns the head, the most sacred part of the body. Admired makers were those who skillfully incorporated fresh flowers in this elegant headwear. In a remarkable contrast, the male dancers have no head adornment at all and wear an undecorated barkcloth wrap tied at the waist.

The Protestant missionaries who introduced Christianity in 1797 found certain aspects of traditional culture incompatible

Costumes of the dance troupe Tamari'i Teahupo'o, winners of the *Heiva* prize for Best Traditional Costume, with contrastive but complementary designs for men and women, Tahiti, 2006. Photograph by Jane Freeman Moulin.

with church ideology. Dance—connected in their eyes to pre-Christian practices, drunkenness, debauchery, and prostitution—was prohibited by law in 1845. Special attire disappeared as performances moved from the public eye to hidden practice, and Christian assemblies took prominence over chiefly entertainment. Then, in the late 1800s, colonial politics reconfigured "tradition" as national celebration, prompting activities tied to the commemoration of the July French Fête Nationale, or "Bastille Day," which added competitions in music (1878), "ancient costumes" (1892), and dance (1894). Competitions between island districts had been a feature of precontact Tahitian life; in this new context they became a way for Tahitians to transform French political markers into expressions of Islander identity and values. Turn-of-the-century photographs document the splendid costumes at these fêtes, including tapa (barkcloth) skirts made from the bark of paper mulberry, *aute* (*Broussonetia papyrifera*), and breadfruit, *'uru* (*Artocarpus altilis*), trees; *tiputa* (ponchos) of woven pandanus leaves (pandanus is a tropical shrub-like tree) or decorated tapa; and *revareva* streamers made from the thin white sheath that covers a newly emerging coconut frond. As fine and delicate as a strip of tissue paper, revareva waves delightfully in the breeze and is still a highly prized addition to head garlands and the most special dance costumes. Other period photos show female dancers in long "mother hubbard" dresses with hip sashes or fiber strips tied over them; men wear long-sleeved, white dress shirts with "grass skirts" over their long, dark, tailored pants.

By the 1930s costuming changed substantially. Shirts and mother hubbards disappeared as dancers became comfortable revealing the body once again. Women in some troupes bared their midriffs, and long trousers for men were no longer requisite. Also, during this time the skirt of thin strips of hibiscus bark (*Hibiscus tiliaceus*) became the standard for Tahitian dance, and certain features of costuming appeared, namely dance shawls, headdresses, and tassels around the waist.

Throughout the latter half of the twentieth century, two distinct costume categories prevailed: an ensemble of natural materials, *le grand costume*, for dances accompanied by slit-drums and membranophones; and, for dances performed to guitar and ukulele-accompanied songs, a fabric *costume en tissu* based on the *pāreu* wraparound cloth just under two meters (two yards) in length. The annual July celebrations, renamed Heiva i Tahiti in 1986, constituted the highlight of the dance year, and Tahitian audiences eagerly awaited the stunning display of costume design and handicraft that was presented. Toward the end of the century organizers initiated subsidies to help artists fund the extraordinary creations for the large troupes of forty to a hundred dancers that Tahitians prefer. In the 1990s the addition of a third category, *le costume végétal*, designated costumes incorporating a primary use of fresh or dried local plant materials and reflected artistic trends using these materials in new and different ways. With the turn of the century Heiva officials deemed the grand costume and costume végétal obligatory for competition; the costume en tissu became optional. This development aligns with Pacific-wide attempts to reclaim Islander identities in a postcolonial world, and the Tahitian move to autonomy and independentist politics; it also underscores changing notions of the tie between costume and dance genre.

The growth of dance schools throughout the 1990s and early twenty-first century also influenced dance attire by necessitating age-appropriate wear and prompting new approaches to costuming.

Whereas dance had previously been the realm of the youthful, fit teenager and young adult segment of the population, the newly initiated dance school competition in 2006 featured overwhelmingly female participants ranging from three to sixty years of age. Children's costumes appeared; dance schools became sensitive to mature performers' desire for modest attire (sometimes harkening back to the mother hubbard dress with the new addition of a thick vegetal belt); and, in the absence of subsidies, most teachers opted for simplified dress—all departures from former ways of presenting dancers at grand events. Moreover, several schools replaced the pāreu with long dresses and flowing cloth skirts, reflecting the influence of international Tahitian dance competitions abroad and expanding the possibilities for fabric costumes.

As with variations in costume over time, there are also variations between locales. French Polynesia includes 128 islands within five archipelagos—the Society, Tuamotu, Austral, Mangareva, and Marquesas Islands—each of which has music, dance, and attire specific to the place. Islanders view these variations as an important aspect of community identity, with costume uniqueness often dependent on the resources of the specific island. For example, festival dress on the Marquesan island of Fatu Hiva incorporates the fine handmade tapa for which the island is famous; dance skirts from Rapa, the southernmost island in the Austral archipelago, employ the *'ä'eho* reed (*Erianthus floridulus*) particular to the mountains of Rapa and its cool climate; costumes on the Tuamotu Islands feature shell and mother-of-pearl decorations reflecting the atoll environment. Because Tahiti is the country's economic and administrative center, however, performing artists tend to emulate Tahitian dance forms, choreographic ideals, and dance attire even as they strive to place a unique, localized stamp on them. Because of this central position in the cultural life of the country, the focus here is on Tahitian dance dress—recognizing this as only one of many variations of costume existing in French Polynesia

COSTUMING THE DANCER

For Tahitians the moment of performance brings to life the valued arts of poetry, music, and dance. All of these gain increased importance by wearing festive dress that Tahitians view as beautifying the performers, displaying the artistry of local designers and craftspeople, and adding cultural importance to the event. Dance also brings together the skill and wisdom of well-versed adults who share their knowledge with the youthful performers, instilling, among other ideals, appreciation for the beautiful handcrafted items worn—and often made—by the dancers. Whether calling for simple garlands, or an entire costume, performances offer dancers repeated opportunities to learn and refine the art of making costumes.

Unlike the wide range of ages found in dance schools, participants in amateur and professional troupes fall within normative ages of about fifteen to twenty-eight. Amateur groups exhibit a range of body types; however, professional troupes carefully select dancers with desired physical attributes, including slender (but not skinny) bodies, average to tall height, developed musculature for men, and scar-free, tanned skin. Competition score sheets from the 1970s offer a window on Tahitian aesthetics of the ideal dancer, spelling out desired skin color (brown; not too light or dark) and including points for women's hair, with a preference for long, dark, thick, waist-length tresses. Although frowned upon

Male costumes of the dance troupe Tamari'i Teahupo'o, Tahiti, 2006. Varnished pieces of coconut shell and yellow *more* fibers on a background of white *tapa* with white *more* fibers form the main design elements. Photograph by Jane Freeman Moulin.

before the mid-1980s, tasteful Polynesian tattoos are admired for both sexes, with women's tattoos tending to be smaller and on the ankles, waist, and lower torso while men's large tattoos appear on legs, arms, chest, back, and buttocks.

The annual Heiva competition prompts months of rehearsal, careful gathering and preparation of plants and flowers, and long hours of costume construction. The judges' score sheets assign points for apparel, allocating 14 percent of the total score to group attire and reserving a special award for the best costume. Evaluation criteria include respect for traditional colors, coordination with the dance theme, beauty of the costume, how the costume carries on stage, originality and quality of materials, originality in conception, and research into the chosen materials. In 2006 each participating group received 1,500,000 CFP (Pacific francs used in French areas of the Pacific), roughly US$16,225, to help satisfy regulations that allow only newly created costumes. The following discusses the art of costume preparation and examines in detail exemplary attire in each of the three main categories.

LE GRAND COSTUME

Dance costumes in the twenty-first century reveal Tahitian desires to connect with the past and yet to incorporate fresh ideas reflecting the originality of Tahitian artists and current aesthetic values. The grand costume includes several items: *more* (dance skirt),

tāupo'o (headdress), hātua (belt), a chest covering that includes a tāpea tītī (bra) for the women and tāhei (shawl) for the men, and occasional items carried in the hands, such as 'i'i (dance whisks) of hibiscus fiber or fresh greensand tāhiri (fans) of plaited pandanus or coconut leaves. A neck adornment—strands of shells or seeds, an ornate necklace, or a gorget (collar) incorporating feathers, barkcloth, and other local materials—may complete the ensemble. In an example of intra-Polynesian exchange, some Tahitian male dancers have borrowed the Samoan practice of tying strips of fresh or dried fibers around their upper arms and calves. All costume parts coordinate in terms of chosen materials, design motifs, and color. For competition, judges also evaluate how well the costume relates to the overall theme of the performance and, through their scoring, reinforce the ethno-aesthetic system of what constitutes acceptable and exceptional dance attire.

The more skirt is the basic element of the grand costume; the term *more* also refers to the fibers themselves. Often called a "grass skirt" by outsiders, the more is made from the bark of the *pūrau* (*Hibiscus tiliaceus*) tree. Historically, Tahitians tied strips of leaves around their waists, but a thick skirt of fiber strips starts to appear in photographs around 1900. Manufacturing the skirt is a time-intensive process of cutting straight horizontal branches, making a longitudinal cut to remove the bark in one piece, soaking this in water for several days, scraping off the dark outer bark, and hitting the light inner bark to flatten and thin the fibers. After drying the fibers thoroughly the bark is split into fine strips and knotted onto a cord to form a skirt. A second row of interlacing cordage, about six centimeters (2.3 inches) below, holds the top edge flat and secures the strips evenly.

More fibers are naturally off-white but may be whitened with lemon juice or dyed to a desired shade. Since at least the 1970s makers have used convenient commercial dyes; however, traditionalists prefer the bright yellow of re'a (turmeric) juice and the red obtained from 'aute (*Hibiscus rosasinensis*). In addition to the natural tone Tahitians call "white" and the favored colors of yellow and red, which for Tahitians are the colors of royalty, some troupes employ secondary colors like brown, black, or even orange if these tie into the theme of the dance. For example, the district of Puna'auia is well known for the wild oranges that grow deep in the Punaru'u valley; not surprisingly, their dancers appeared at the 2006 Heiva in orange-colored more to present the songs and dances of the district. Because of the strong preference for traditional colors, those produced by natural dyes, Tahitians avoid pink, blue, green, purple, or fluorescent shades, except for highly commercialized productions intended for tours abroad. Occasional creative attempts have meant dyeing the bottom edge a different color, layering skirts of varied colors and lengths, or making more of multicolored strips, but the overwhelming preference is for solid-colored skirts. Women wear the skirt knee-length or ankle-length, while men usually cut it at the knees. With fewer Tahitians willing to invest the time required to produce more, costs have risen accordingly. Also, small producers have problems assuring reliable delivery of the one hundred skirts required by large dance troupes. In an example of globalization and new purchasing patterns, many directors order more from Micronesia through a supplier in Honolulu who can guarantee large quantities and consistent coloring for dyed skirts.

Island resources serve as inspiration for the costume designer, a role increasingly assigned to a costume specialist rather than assumed by the dance director, as in earlier years. The designer carefully selects motifs and materials for various costume parts, considering the chosen theme as well as the color, texture, and light-reflective qualities of the materials. He or she may use matching costumes for male and female groups or incorporate complementary but slightly modified ideas. Sometimes the designer prefers bold contrast between gender groups and opts for separate costumes of differing colors or designs, while still maintaining visual links that unite the two sets. Innovation and creativity are key in designing the various costume components. Tahitians produce such a variety in size, shape, and design elements that it is difficult to designate a general style.

The costumes of the troupe Tamari'i Teahupo'o, directed by Adolphe Raveino and winners of the first prize for Best Traditional Costume in 2006, are a useful example to consider. The striking costumes of this amateur troupe emphasize contrast between the male and female dancers. The two sets of costumes are unique, although united in color (yellow and white with brown accents), materials (more, tapa, and varnished coconut shell), and motif (flat rounds of fiber strips that resemble starbursts, often with a round piece of coconut shell at the center). Both use the basic more skirt, tāupo'o headdress, and hātua belt; in addition, men wear a tāhei shoulder covering and women wear a bra and large necklace. Dance whisks complete the women's costume.

White more and white headdresses establish the fundamental colors and materials for the men's attire. Recalling the sixty- to ninety-centimeter- (23.6- to 35.4-inch-) high feathered headdresses worn by Tahitian chiefs, the tāupo'o amplifies the height and presence of the dancer. This headdress, of moderate size by Tahitian standards (approximately forty centimeters, or 15.7 inches, high overall), frames the upper part of the head with a vertical semicircular shape, a feature that anchors this creation well within costume styles that developed during the second half of the twentieth century. A sturdy, wide band encircles the head, and a stiff backing holds the vertical front portion upright; both are covered with white tapa. A slight elongation of the central high point provides an interesting modification of the basic semicircular shape, and white more fibers (approximately fifteen to eighteen centimeters, or 5.9 to 7 inches, long) line the entire outer edge to extend the overall size of the headdress. Five small yellow starbursts along the edge alternate with diamond-shaped pieces of varnished dark-brown coconut shell to establish the primary visual motif, the latter providing a contrast in color and mild reflective quality. Transposed to a large white starburst with coconut shell center set over four leaf-shaped pieces, this motif becomes the headdress's centerpiece.

The hātua belt echoes the same materials and visual elements. Worn over the top edge of the skirt, belts require a sturdy backing material, such as dried pandanus leaves of the fara pae'ore variety. This belt, covered with white tapa, features the alternation of yellow starbursts with coconut-shell centers and white starbursts affixed over four diamond-shaped coconut-shell pieces.

The tāhei for this costume is a bandolier worn over the left shoulder and fastened at right hip level. Duplicating the patterns of the hātua, and with white more sewn to the lower edge, the tāhei, with its fringe, replicates the look of the belt, overlapping the top edge of the skirt. The overall costume, therefore, presents unified elements on the torso and unique, but closely related, designs for the head.

The women's costume reverses the color scheme. Whereas men wear white with yellow accents, women have yellow skirts

The female costumes of the dance troupe Tamari'i Teahupo'o feature the ornamental use of white *more*, *nī'au*, and *tapa* against yellow *more* skirts and dyed yellow *tapa* belts and hats with the brown accents of varnished coconut shell pieces, Tahiti, 2006. Photograph by Jane Freeman Moulin.

and headdresses with a secondary use of white for the bra and ornaments. The yellow tapa headdress, more pointed than the male version, incorporates starbursts and coconut-shell pieces but treats them differently. A seven-pointed, star-shaped cutout of white tapa with a large coconut-shell center fills the vertical middle section of the headdress. Thin braids of more loop around the edge and outline five round pieces of varnished coconut shell; three white starbursts mark points at the top. Five small bundles of stiff white nī'au fibers, made from the young, unopened parts of the coconut flower, are spaced along the central upper edge. Each of the middle three bundles also contains a six- to seven-centimeter- (2.3- to 2.7-inch-) wide strip of curled white tapa and long white more fibers that flow down over the dancer's hair to create a spectacular effect from all sides. The necklaces have two rows of yellow starbursts with coconut-shell centers affixed to a base of braided white more, from which loose fibers hang along the bottom. The dancers wear strapless bras of plain white tapa and carry 'i'i whisks of yellow more; when not needed, whisks hang by loops from the lower arms.

The hātua is covered with yellow tapa and, in a visual link to the headdress, uses design motifs based on the same shapes, materials, and braided loops. Certain features place this belt in the twenty-first century, notably the thick bustle of yellow more about sixteen to eighteen centimeters (6.2 to 7 inches) in length at the rear of the belt and the five protruding bunches of long white more that hang down almost to knee length. Each bunch also contains two long curled strips of white tapa and several white nī 'au fibers, thereby linking the belt to the headdress and providing additional freely moving material to accentuate and amplify the women's hip movements.

The total effect of the two sets of costumes is magnificent. Drawing on complementary but different designs and colors and incorporating highly valued, natural fibers, the final product is a tasteful blending of historical elements with innovative twists that lend a new look to older ideas of performance dress.

LE COSTUME VÉGÉTAL

In contrast to the durable fibers of le grand costume, the vegetal costume utilizes primarily fresh flowers and greenery. Dancers may also incorporate dried leaves and plant parts, and women wear bras covered with fabric or natural materials. There are many variations of the basic costume parts—dance skirt, *hei* (neck garland), and *hei 'upo'o* (head garland)—each creation a burst of color and texture that provides a veritable peek into Tahiti's verdant gardens.

In 2006 the first-prize winner in this category was the troupe Hei Tahiti, directed by Tiare Trompette, whose stunning women's costume prompted admiration among judges and audience. Applying fresh plant parts to fabric, Trompette successfully brought to the Tahitian stage for the first time a technique favored by Western Polynesians. In this creation petals of the red ginger flower (*'ōpuhi*) are layered individually like fish scales onto a base of red fabric. The slightly curved shape of the petals and their waxy shine create a richly textured, light-reflective surface. The mid-calf-length skirt, worn low on the hips like all Tahitian dance skirts, avoids a solid block of color with vertical slits that allow for free movement; a strapless bra, covered with the same petal-layering technique, completes the ensemble. *T'iati'a mou'a* (*Davalia solida*) ferns decorate the skirt's lower edge and cover the left breast, and complementary touches of ferns add green to the right side of the bra and the dancers' hair. The overall appearance is one of elegance and beauty, in which the simplicity of the cut and reduced number of costume parts allow viewers to focus on the magnificent color and texture of the ensemble. Importantly, Tahitians do not read these costumes as sexualized.

While the women's attire conveys elegance, the men's costume does communicate virile masculinity. Men begin the dance wearing a shawl and a belt of large oiled green *'autī* (*Cordylnie frutcosa*) leaves sewn onto a red fabric backing. Shredded red *'autī* leaves, secured on strips of dried pandanus, are tied around upper arms and calves. As the dance progresses, the men shed the shawl and belt to dance in a simple red *maro* (loincloth) that reveals their fit bodies and displays their tattoos. Dance director Coco Hotahota is credited with "undressing" male dancers in the 1990s, and the subsequent use of maro reflects this influence.

LE COSTUME EN TISSU

The fabric costume generally uses the pāreu wraparound cloth, a coordinated bra for females, and adornments of shells, fresh flowers, or greens for the neck and head of all dancers. Male dancers typically wrap the pāreu in a style known as *tihere*, adopted from the apparel of copra workers who needed to protect one thigh

while husking coconuts. This style of wrap offers dancers a tight-fitting garb that shows off the body while providing freedom to perform the scissor-like leg movements integral to Tahitian male dancing. Some dance directors, however, prefer a simple fabric loincloth or—replicating an idea borrowed from Hawai'i in the late 1980s—a maro with rectangular pieces covering the front and rear of the dancer while leaving the sides exposed.

Women tie the pāreu into a skirt at either ankle length or above the knee. A simple knot on the side now replaces the *viri*, a style of rolling the top edge of the pāreu, favored by dancers during the 1990s. Matching or color-coordinated strapless bras have largely replaced those made from two coconut-shell halves. Pāreu come in a variety of colors and patterns. Competition favors traditional colors (white, yellow, and red), allows blue and green for fabric costumes if related to the theme of the dance, and prohibits fluorescent colors (noted in the Heiva 2006 regulations). Elaborating the basic pāreu with creative touches (e.g., shells, appliqués, fishnet, etc.) may contribute to the theme of the dance and the costume's visual appeal. Because the fabric costume is optional for competition, no award is given in this category.

The addition of hei—and, for women, often a dance belt of leaves, ferns, or flowers—adds to the overall effect of the costume and foregrounds the art of garland making that is such an essential part of being a performer. While men may help in gathering and preparing materials or making leaf or fiber cordage, many leave the making of hei to females, who perfect the techniques of working with flowers and greens to create finely crafted garlands for the head, neck, and women's hips. An experienced person skillfully uses fragrance and color to create hei that demonstrate the dexterity and artistic eye of the maker as well as knowledge of the local environment. Directors are sensitive to the linking of song text and costume, so that dance songs highlighting specific flowers will call for hei made of those flowers. The hei allows dancers to beautify themselves; it also is a way to admire and embrace the beauty of nature invoked in the songs and dances.

French Polynesians realize how much time and expertise is invested in making costumes and hold them in high esteem, appreciating their often-ephemeral nature as a special part of an event. The Tahitian preference for novelty and the emphasis on original creations for the Heiva suggest a continued evolution in dance costumes over the coming years. As long as large-scale performances remain important for the community, dancers will respond with new and unusual ways to turn everyday plants into magnificent hei, and costume designers will amaze and delight audiences with their innovative uses of local and imported materials.

References and Further Reading

Beslu, Christian. *Cartes postales anciennes de Tahiti*. Papeete, Tahiti: Times Editions/Les Éditions du Pacifique, 1987.

Cook, Capt. James. *The Voyage of the Endeavor 1768–1771*. Edited by J.C. Beaglehole. Sydney: Boydell Press, 1968.

Moulin, Jane Freeman. *The Dance of Tahiti*. Papeete, Tahiti: Les Éditions du Pacifique, 1979.

O'Reilly, Patrick O. *Dancing Tahiti*. Dossier 22. Paris: Nouvelles Éditions Latines, 1978.

Jane Freeman Moulin

See also Introduction to the Dress of the Pacific Islands.

Tahitian Tattoos

- Tapu and Arioi
- Wrapping and Tatau
- European Contacts and Christianization
- Cultural Identity and Festivals
- Youth Culture and Tatau/Tattooing
- Globalization of Tatau/Tattooing

Tatau is permanent tattoo marking on the body, a term used here to describe Tahitian tattoo motifs. The term *tattoo* refers to Euro-American tattoos and the process of making these designs. As it is significant for Tahitians to differentiate their motifs from others, the terms *tatau* and *tattoo* are both used, and the term *tatau/tattoo* will indicate traditional motifs made with Western methods. Once a person puts ink on the skin, he or she will live with the motifs, designs, or words that the ink depicts. For this permanency, tatau was and is a strong way for people in Tahiti to form and express their identities on the surface of the body as man or woman; Tahitian, Ma'ohi (indigenous people and culture in the Society Islands), or Polynesian; tattooist, artisan, or dancer. This definition of identities through tatau has been taking various forms in the different periods of Tahitian history.

The history of tatau is discontinuous. Tahitian contact with European people began in the late eighteenth century. In the pre- and early contact period with Westerners, tatau was related to the system of *tapu* (sacred interdiction). It was considered as one of the wrapping practices, which controlled the influence of tapu. Tatau was abandoned due to the suppression of Christian missionaries in the 1830s, but it was revived in the 1980s as part of a cultural revitalization movement. Tatau of the pre- and early contact period was, however, lost. After a long absence it was reinstated as a practice that is extensively implicated in youth culture, gender relationships, cultural revitalization, modernity, and prison culture. While developing their tatau motifs, tattooists in Tahiti have also introduced Euro-American, Japanese, and other Polynesian tattooing techniques and designs into their work.

TAPU AND ARIOI

Prior to the eighteenth century tatau was embedded in the social system and cosmology, which were closely related to the concept of tapu. The world consists of *po* and *ao* in Tahitian cosmology. Po was the domain of the gods and signified dark and night. It was the place where the dynamic transformation of birth and death took place. In po, Ta'aroa, the supreme god, digested the bodies of the dead and reproduced the new human bodies. Ao was the domain of human beings and signified light and day. The relationship between po and ao was not a simple dichotomy, but rather complementary in ordering the natural and social world.

In this dual-structured world people who had *mana* (divine power) were considered tapu, and dangerous to those who were not tapu. People who were close to gods, such as chiefs, infants,

Tahitian *tatau* (tattoo) depicting shaded Marquesan *tiki* (god figures), twenty-first century. Photograph by Makiko Kuwahara.

children, and women who were in menstruation or before and after childbirth, were tapu and were secluded from the other members of the society, because tapu was contagious by touch and by being in the same place. Tapu system made differences in class, gender, and age and controlled social interaction among these different people.

The institution of Arioi also illustrated social differences in the notion of tapu and mana and was highly relevant to tatau. Arioi was a religious cult, originating in Raiatea, an island of the Society Islands and a religious center of eastern Polynesia. It consisted of both male and female members from all ranks, and it worshipped the god 'Oro. Cult members traveled from one island to another and gave drama, dance, speech, and athletic performances.

Arioi was regarded as an ideal that represented and dealt with mana to set the best living condition for human beings, because the symbolism and activities of Arioi implied their connection with significant domains of society: war, land, harvest, and population. The members were given a special house to stay in during their visits to other islands and many gifts, such as hogs, breadfruits, and *tapa* (barkcloth for clothing). Their decorated bodies and performances were offerings to 'Oro. Although people offered gifts to the Arioi, indirectly they were worshipping 'Oro in return for bountiful harvests. Arioi played a mediating role between 'Oro and human beings in this religious exchange system.

Arioi had unique tatau of eight grades. The higher they were graded, the more heavily they were tattooed. The highest grade of Arioi were *avae parai* or *arioi maro 'ura*, who were tattooed completely black from the feet up to the groin. *Harotea* were the second grade, who were tattooed crosswise on both sides of the body from the armpits downward toward the front. *Taputu* or *haaputu* had diversified curves and lines radiating upward toward the sides from the lower end of the dorsal column to the middle of the back. *Otiore* had light prints on their knuckles and wrists and heavier ones on their arms and shoulders. *Hua* had two or three small points upon each shoulder. *Atoro* had one small stripe down the left side. *Ohe-mara* had a circle around the ankle. The new members of Arioi were *tara-tutu*, who had small marks in the hollow of the knees.

WRAPPING AND TATAU

Tatau was intrinsically linked with the tapu system, and Arioi was based on wrapping practices. Wrapping and uncovering occurred in both conceptual and empirical domains. According to the chant collected in the nineteenth century, the supreme god Ta'aroa came out of an egg-like shell, which transformed into all living and nonliving creatures. The universe was created out of shell from a state of nothing. Shell was the origin of all materials and living creatures, including human beings. Women were also considered the shell, because human beings come into the world by women.

Another instance of wrapping was found in the ritual called *pa'iatua*. In the ritual god figures were taken out to the sun from a depository in the *marae* (temples for Tahitian religion), and the braid that wrapped the god figures and feathers inside them were removed. The god figures were anointed with perfumed coconut oil, stuffed with new feathers inside, wrapped with new braid, and placed back in the depository.

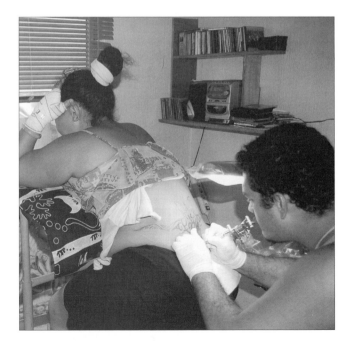

A woman's *tatau* (tattoo), Tahiti, ca. 2000. While men are often heavily tattooed on the shoulders, arms, and legs, women are usually tattooed only around the navel or ankle, or on the back. Photograph by Makiko Kuwahara.

The significance of the ceremony was in the accumulation of mana and transferring it into the feathers stuffed inside the god figures. The braid that wrapped the god figures created a boundary between ao and po. People transferred mana from po to ao by uncovering and rewrapping the god figures. The observers came to understand the nature of po by finding the god figures as merely wooden sticks. The god figures and the rituals of pa'iatua embodied the creation of the world by the gods.

Human bodies were another object to wrap and uncover. As a general fashion, both men and women wrapped their bodies with cloth made of tapa. In addition to this, there were a number of wrapping practices observed in special and ceremonial occasions. For instance, newborn infants and their cords, as well as dead bodies, were wrapped. The adolescents, who were tattooed or bleached, were also wrapped. Warriors were wrapped with cloth around their bodies for protection from the attack of enemies. Dance costume consisted of enormous lengths of cloth, which was wrapped around the waist and legs. Wrapping was also a significant part of the ceremony of *taio* (friendship contract).

The skin was analogous to cloth, and another significant material for wrapping. According to the cosmological meaning of wrapping, tatau rewrapped the body by creating a second layer of the skin. After the operation of tatau the inscribed parts, covered with blood and serum, were peeled off in a few days, showing the new skin with pictures. Tatau was the physical experience of wrapping and uncovering of the skin.

Tahitians controlled the tapu restrictions by wrapping themselves with tapa, in the case of tapu people to prevent their mana from flowing away, and in the case of non- or less-tapu people to protect themselves from the influence of others' tapu. Tatau, which covered the surface of the body with pictures, was another way of wrapping the body. Particularly, tatau made under the armpits, which consisted of a few dots, and on the buttocks, which consisted of blackening part with geometric motifs during initiation ceremonies, transformed infants' strong tapu bodies into adults' less-tapu bodies by wrapping them, making them available for marriage and childbearing.

Except for Arioi's tatau, those on high-ranking people, and those on buttocks and armpits indicating maturity, the choice of tatau motif and design depended upon each individual's taste. Motifs and designs were often geometric, such as angular motifs (straight lines, squares, crescents, lozenges, the figure Z, zigzags, and stars) and curvilinear motifs (wavy lines and circles). They were also figurative, such as plant forms (convolvulus wreaths, coconut trees, and breadfruit trees), animal forms (fishes, dogs, birds, and quadrupeds), inanimate objects (clubs and spears), and human figures (boys gathering fruit, men posed in battle, fleeing from or pursuing the enemy, triumphing over a fallen foe, and carrying a human sacrifice to the marae).

The method of tatau was to dip a needle made with bird or pig bone or shark's teeth into the ink, which was soot of burned candlenut (nuts of kukui, *Aleurites moluccana*) diluted with water, and tap it with a mallet into the skin.

EUROPEAN CONTACTS AND CHRISTIANIZATION

Tahitian contact and interaction with European people began in 1767 with the arrival of the English ship *Dolphin*, led by Samuel Wallis, followed soon afterwards by Louis Antoine de

Bougainville in 1768. Captain James Cook visited Tahiti in all his three explorations in the South Pacific from 1769 to 1779. Although troubles such as minor skirmishes and thieving by the islanders were reported, Tahitians and European explorers, seamen, and merchants established a relatively friendly rapport and exchanged Tahitian products (fruits, woods, meats, etc.) and European commodities (weapons, iron implements, clothes, etc.).

The exchange also took place on the body in the form of tatau/ tattooing. The seamen inscribed the date that they first saw Tahiti, a star, a *taumi* (Tahitian breastplate), and so forth, using the Tahitian tatau method. Some people were even tattooed on their buttocks in the Tahitian way. Tahitians tattooed their bodies with the designs of European objects such as muskets, swords, pistols, goats, fleurs-de-lis, compasses, and mathematical instruments.

In 1797 missionaries associated with the London Missionary Society arrived aboard the *Duff* in Tahiti. The islanders, who had already been accustomed to European explorers and merchants, showed a friendly attitude toward the missionaries. The missionaries, however, found it difficult to teach Christian doctrines and convert local people at the beginning because the 'Oro cult was powerful in Tahiti, and the missionaries had not acquired the local language in the early stage of their mission. In the late eighteenth century the island of Tahiti was divided into districts, which were ruled by chiefs. Pomare I, supported by European explorers and merchants, achieved control over the whole island with the effective use of European weapons and commodities. After the death of Pomare I, his son Pomare II inherited the throne and converted to Christianity. The islanders, who endured wars and falling population due to epidemics, gradually started to doubt their own religious beliefs.

The missionaries combined with the local chiefs to establish legal codes that punished those committing theft and adultery, and they suppressed traditional customs, including tatau motifs. Those who broke the legal codes and got tattooed were punished with physical labor. Men were assigned to work on construction of roads and women to make mats and cloth. Another punishment for those who continued tatau was tattooing intended to erase the design by blackening, but which resulted in intensifying it. Those who tattooed someone were daubed, probably with mud and ash, and exposed publicly. In one documented case a criminal had the word *MURDERER* tattooed on her front. Tattooing tatau motifs was not only the object of prohibition, but tattooing was also a way of punishment.

Tahitians did not simply let the legal codes control their bodies but reacted against this political pressure by using their bodies. Many people were infuriated by the burning of the god figures and the destruction of maraes by Pomare II and those who had been already converted. They took up arms in revenge and to restore the god figures.

The second reaction occurred later among those who had been already converted to Christianity. Those people, who knew enough of both religions to be able to compare the two, well understood the inefficacy of traditional religion. However, they were discontented with strict Christian discipline and legal codes. They were tattooed, went to the mountains, and returned to the way of life before Christianization. Tatau continued sometimes as an expression of protest against the missionaries and later secretly for a while, but it was rarely practiced when most Tahitians had converted to Christianity.

Twenty-first century Tahitian *tatau* (tattoo) with a dolphin design in the center. Figurative designs depicting animals such as dolphins, sharks, rays, turtles, and lizards have become popular among tourists and French people living in Tahiti. These designs often have Marquesan motifs filled inside. Photograph by Makiko Kuwahara.

CULTURAL IDENTITY AND FESTIVALS

After tatau was suppressed by the missionaries in the 1830s and the practice was abandoned, it took 150 years until Tahitians began decorating their bodies with ink again. Influenced by independence movements in the 1970s and cultural revitalization movements throughout the South Pacific, Tahitians recognized the significance of their own culture and the importance of passing it on to the next generation. Maco Tevane founded l'Académie Tahitienne in 1972 and published dictionaries and a grammar text of Tahitian language, promoting its teaching at schools. Office Territorial d'Action Culturelle (OTAC) was founded in 1980 for supporting cultural activities that were not only those considered traditional in the strict sense, but also contemporary dances, theater, and painting. At Centre des Métiers d'Art, founded in 1981, many young people learned carving and painting and became artisans and artists. Some tattooists learned carving at the Centre before they became professionals.

Before the revival of tatau Euro-American styles of tattooing had already been introduced to Tahiti since the 1970s, particularly on the streets and in prison. This tattooing was considered an antisocial practice for criminals or prostitutes by the majority of people in Tahiti. Differentiated from Euro-American tattooing, tatau was inspired by the Tahitian recognition of the significance of their own culture and formation of cultural identity and was used to decorate the body of artisans, dancers, and musicians.

It was not easy to revive tatau that had not been practiced for over 150 years. The motifs were reproduced by referring to the illustrations and photos made by Karl von den Steinen and Handy W. Chatterson, who conducted ethnographical fieldwork in the Marquesas in the early twentieth century. Contemporary tatau thus consists of mostly Marquesan motifs, arranged with creativity by each tattooist. Traditional tools and methods were reintroduced by a practitioner from Samoa, where tattooing had continued even under Christianization.

Since then tatau has played a significant role in representing cultural and ethnic identity, especially at art festivals taking place in and outside of Tahiti. *Heiva* is an annual festival where dancing and singing performances and contests, artisan exhibitions, and sports and beauty contests are held over four weeks in July. Many dancers and musicians who perform at Heiva are tattooed. While men are often heavily tattooed on the shoulders, arms, and legs, women are usually tattooed only around the navel, ankle, or on the back. There are always five to ten tatau stands in the artisan village at Heiva. At Festivals of Pacific Arts, which take place every four years in one of islands in the South Pacific, many members of French Polynesian delegations, such as dancers, musicians, and artisans, are also tattooed. Tatau has been considered a significant Tahitian or Polynesian cultural emblem in terms of ethnic identity formation within the territory and in the South Pacific.

YOUTH CULTURE AND TATAU/TATTOOING

While tatau has been revived as a "traditional culture" in the context of cultural revitalization and recognition, its development also strongly links to youth culture. Through tatau/tattooing, adolescents define their gender and ethnic identities and establish their bond with those of the same age. Youths aged from the late teens to their early twenties, and this period of life, are called *taure'are'a* in Tahitian. Male taure'are'a help their fathers or uncles work and in their spare time enjoy music, play sports, drink beer, and smoke cigarettes or marijuana with friends of their age. Female taure'are'a help with domestic work and child care and also spend time with female friends of their age. Taure'are'a, especially males, often quit school, leave their own village and island, and wander about in other districts or islands, relying on their friends and relatives. Taure'are'a is a significant period for learning gender roles and establishing social relationships, which is necessary in order to become a member of the society, rather than a transitional period during which children become adults.

For male taure'are'a tatau/tattooing is a significant way of marking gender and ethnic differences on the body. One of the significant aspects about male taure'are'a is that they alienate themselves from females by bonding with other males. Male taure'are'a frequently use sexist language and tease or refer to women in their male-centric conversation. They call each other *brad*, which is derived from *brother* in English, and try hard to establish a friendly rapport. This enforces a bond among men as well as prevents male taure'are'a from directing their competitiveness toward male rivals, by having women as "the other" who intervene among men. This alienation also occurs in ethnic relationships when "the other" is French people. There are many mixed-blood French and Tahitian people, and Tahitians get on well with French relatives, community members, or work colleagues. Tahitians, however, often argue about independence from France and sometimes use contemptuous expressions referring to French men, such as *taioro* (a derogatory term that means "uncircumcised penis"), in everyday conversation.

These differences in ethnicity and gender are often expressed on the body. The ideal body of male taure'are'a is the "warrior's body" of "traditional society," which is muscular, well tanned, and heavily tattooed. The "warrior masculinity" is reflected in the representation of cultural and ethnic identity expressed, for example, in the Tane Tahiti contest (the male beauty contest) at Heiva. Unlike the Miss Tahiti contest, competitors are assessed not only on physical beauty but also on their knowledge and skills in traditional culture: dance, stone lifting, coconut preparation, and so on. Most title holders are heavily tattooed. While representing tradition, this "warrior masculinity" also emphasizes the physical differences of male Tahitians from women and French men.

Many taure'are'a tattoo or are tattooed. Those who are dexterous and good at drawing, tattoo their friends on streets or at houses. Tatau/tattooing is a way of killing time as well as having fun with friends. Since the problem of the transmission of HIV through blood transfusion was recognized, tatau using traditional tools was prohibited by the Department of Health in 1986. As a substitute for traditional tools, the tattooists started

A dragon design *tatau* (tattoo), Tahiti, ca. 2000. Photograph by Makiko Kuwahara.

using remodeled electronic traveling shavers, which are easy to purchase at a reasonable price at local shops. A disposable needle is attached to the device. Remodeled traveling shavers, which operate on batteries, are also suitable for taure'are'a tatau/tattooing, which often occurs outside, where electricity is out of reach. Consequently, these tools have been widely spread among young people.

Tattooed people are usually proud of the tatau/tattoo they have acquired and of their friend who made it. Solidarity among peers in the district is enhanced by having the same style of tatau/tattoo. Taure'are'a are embedded in their local, gender, same-age, and ethnic relationships, but at the same time relate themselves to global youth culture through tattooing. It has been accepted and enthusiastically developed by taure'are'a who not only consider tatau an emblem of ethnic identity, but also link it to Euro-American antisocial youth culture.

GLOBALIZATION OF TATAU/TATTOOING

Besides ethnic identity formation and taurea'are'a culture within Tahiti, global tattoo culture also contributes to the increasing popularity and development of tatau/tattooing. Which no longer remains only a pastime among taure'are'a. Some tattooists, who had been tattooing their family, relatives, and friends of taure'are'a relationship, have become professionals with the increasing number of tourists and French people who want to be tattooed. They are required to maintain hygiene, improve technique, and import tattoo machines, ultrasonic and sterilization equipment, and inks from Europe and the United States.

The tatau designs have also been changed. Figurative designs that form animals such as dolphin, shark, ray, turtle, and lizard have become popular among tourists and French people living in Tahiti, because they prefer to have a small tatau rather than those covering whole shoulders and loins as do Tahitian dancers, musicians, artisans, and taure'are'a. These figurative designs have Marquesan motifs filled inside.

Tahitian tattooists can easily access foreign designs and techniques of tattooing through magazines, the Internet, and interaction with other tattooists. They have started tattooing styles and designs of other places in the world, such as Europe, the United States, Japan, and other Polynesian islands, such as Samoa, Hawai'i, New Zealand (Māori), and Marquesas. They also combine tatau with these styles and designs. Some shade and color their tatau, which originally consisted of only black filling.

The location of tatau in the global tattoo world also affects the development of tatau. Polynesian tattooing, including Tahitian tatau, is considered "tribal" or "black" in the wider world. Tribal style has various patterns but is basically only black in color, and curvilinear with pointed ends. "Tribal" and "black" refer to those that are and were practices of non-Western origin. These categories of style are a lingua franca among the members of the global tattoo world, which use the categories to indicate the style they want, and practitioners compete with each other under these categories at tattoo convention contests. Tatau is considered one form of "tribal" tattooing and is located as such in the global tattoo world.

For Tahitians "tribal" style is generally a different style from "Tahitian" and "Polynesian" style, although Tahitian tattooists sometimes consider the black spiral style both "tribal" and "Polynesian." They do not regard both categories as mutually exclusive but maintain the differences of each style and incorporate one into the other. The tattooists who prefer Euro-American, Japanese, tribal, and other Polynesian designs and styles understand the origin of each element. Through globalization, Tahitian practitioners receive copious information on other tattooing and economic advantages that enable them to access new technology.

In addition to the global tattoo world, the popularity of tatau has also been enhanced by Western exoticism of Tahiti. Tahiti has been portrayed as a paradise to Western countries since early European contact, and this image has also been developed by European writers, musicians, and artists, and later spread worldwide. Polynesian people, especially women, have been ascribed the image of being sexually extravagant.

While these exotic images have previously been derived only from female Tahitian sexuality, recently male sexuality has begun to contribute to the paradisiacal images of Tahiti in books, postcards, and tourist posters. It does not necessarily mean that all tourists visiting Tahiti want to copy the Tahitian male body, but some get a tatau/tattoo with a design such as a dolphin or turtle as a souvenir of their stay in the islands. These tatau/tattoos are often based on and support the representation of paradisiacal sexuality.

The globalization of tatau/tattooing was well demonstrated in events that took place in French Polynesia. The first tatau/tattoo festival, Tatau i Taputapuatea, occurred in the marae Taputapuatea at Raiatea in April 2000. Tattoonesia took place over four days in Moorea in November 2005, and in Tahiti in November 2006. Heavily tattooed people from Tahiti, Marquesas, Europe, the United States, Japan, Australia, New Zealand, Samoa, Hawaii, Rapa Nui, and the Cook Islands assembled there for the tatau/tattoo festival and conventions. Many journalists from tattoo magazines, photographers, and filmmakers from everywhere in the world also came there to document these picturesque events. While watching tatau/tattooing and talking to the practitioners, the visitors enjoyed not only tattoo-related events such as tatau/tattoo contests, workshops, photography exhibitions, and film screening, but also the events familiar to Tahitian festivals such as dance performances, a fashion show, shopping for artisan-made products, and tasting traditional Tahitian food. Tahitian tattooists established friendships with the international practitioners and have learned different styles and techniques during the festivals and conventions.

Besides these tatau/tattoo events in French Polynesia, with increasing international recognition of tatau, more Tahitian tattooists participate in conventions in Europe and the United States. Some even perform Tahitian/Marquesan dance there. Some of them wander about in Europe and the United States while working as guest artists at tattoo studios. They are often interested in tattooing in Euro-American or Japanese styles, but clients usually expect them to tattoo in Polynesian styles in the visiting studios. These guest artists learn the Euro-American style and technique of tattooing and establish a network with fellow artists. Once back in Tahiti, those who have experienced the global tattoo world can offer young people and tourists new styles and techniques. Young tattooists situate themselves in the global tattoo world by representing ethnic identity as "Tahitian" or "Polynesian," and by partially responding to Western interests and desires.

References and Further Reading

Coirault, Claude, and Marie-Hélene Villierme. *Tatau: Maohi Tattoo.* Auckland, NZ: Tupuna, 1993.

D'Alleva, Anne. "Christian Skins: Tatau and Evangelization of the Society Islands and Samoa." In *Tattoo: Bodies, Art and Exchange in the Pacific and the West*, edited by Nicholas Thomas, Anna Cole, and Bronwen Douglas, 70–90. London: Reaction Books, 2005.

Gell, Alfred. *Wrapping in Images: Tattooing in Polynesia.* Oxford: Clarendon Press, 1993.

Handy, W. Chatterson. *Tattooing in the Marquesas. Bulletin 1.* Honolulu: Bernice P. Bishop Museum, 1922.

Kuwahara, Makiko. "Tahitian Tattooing in the Christianization Process: Ideological and Political Shifts Expressed on the Body." *Man and Culture in Oceania* 15 (1999): 23–43.

Kuwahara, Makiko. *Tattoo: An Anthropology.* Oxford: Berg, 2005.

Lavondes, Anne. "Un modèle d'identité: le tatouage aux îles de la Société." *Cahiers des Sciences Humains* 26, no. 4 (1990): 605–621.

Ottino-Garanger, Pierre, and Marie-Noëlle Ottino-Garanger. *Le Tatouage: L'Art du Tatouage en Polynésie, Te Patu Tiki.* Teavaro, French Polynesia: Didier Millet, 1990.

Thomas, Nicholas. *Oceanic Art.* London: Thames and Hudson, 1995.

Thomas, Nicholas, Anna Cole, and Bronwen Douglas, eds. *Tattoo: Bodies, Art and Exchange in the Pacific and the West.* London: Reaction Books, 2005.

von den Steinen, Karl. *Die Marquesaner und ihre Kunst. Studien über die Entwicklung primitiver Südseeornamentik nach eigenen Reiseergebnissen und dem Material der Museen.* Vol. 1. Berlin: Hacher Art Books, 1925.

Makiko Kuwahara

See also Dress and Appearance in Tahiti; Moko Māori: Skin Modification.

Dress and Appearance in Tahiti

Tahiti is one of the Society Islands and the largest island of French Polynesia. It has a tropical climate, and its flora and fauna have been fundamental to the attire made by indigenous Tahitians. Body modification in early Tahiti was used as a visual marker of status within a highly ranked society. The Tahitian social system was founded in a system of primogeniture, in which one's rank was determined by birth, a system that necessitated a wealth and complexity of embellishment and regalia to denote the power and status of each individual. Articles of attire were also used as a sign of elite generosity, given to reward allegiance and good deeds, and to honor visiting dignitaries.

Status and identity are ideas that have often been marked visually. Status could also be acquired through ability. A chief is born, not created; but good warriors were acknowledged, as were artists. As such, nobility was established and supported by the chief. The use of objects of bodily embellishment as gifts was an essential means of marking achievement and recognizing status. The best example of this is the use of barkcloth (*tapa*) as a presentation. The Tahitians believed that all gifts must be accompanied by something produced by hand—tapa. The amount given signaled the status of the recipient.

In 1797 the first British missionaries settled at Papeete (designated the capital after French annexation in 1842). The British immediately became aware of the diverse ways in which tapa was worn, the design patterns used in tattoo, and the Tahitian fondness for earrings. It is from early European journals, as well as the collections acquired by explorers, that any knowledge of customary Tahitian dress can be had. It is also due to the British importation of cloth, missionization, and colonization that the dress of Tahiti evolved in the nineteenth century. Attire continued to assert status, but it also demonstrated newfound relationships and economic well-being.

CUSTOMARY DRESS AND APPEARANCE

The most important material for clothing produced in Tahiti before European contact was barkcloth (tapa), which was manufactured in a variety of textures, colors, and sizes. Tapa was made primarily from the inner bark of the paper mulberry tree and initially was undecorated. An essential element of daily dress, its variety allowed the Tahitians great diversity in what and how tapa was worn. The creation of tapa was a long and labor-intensive process, which added greatly to its value. This process included collecting the stalks and limbs, stripping the outer bark, soaking the inner bark, scraping this softened bark, resoaking it, and then beating these softened fibers. After this process was complete the fibers were left in the sun to dry and bleach. They were then beaten and felted into larger pieces of cloth, dyed, and decorated.

At the time of the explorer James Cook's first visit in 1769, tapa was either undecorated or decorated simply using a small length of bamboo as a stencil. Prior to Cook's last visit in 1777, however, Tahitian women began to experiment (perhaps after viewing the floral prints on imported cloth) and created cloth using ferns,

"A dance in Otaheite," plate number 28 in James Cook's *A Voyage to the Pacific Ocean* (1784), showing two female dancers wearing elaborate costumes in Tahiti. Engraving by John Keyes Sherwin. National Library of Australia.

leaves, and pods as stencils. The designs of these materials included a free flow of color as well as a bold graphic character from the flora and fauna of the islands. This aesthetic is unique within the Pacific in relation to tapa production.

Tapa, the basis for all clothing, was worn in a variety of styles. Men wore a *maro* (loincloth) and women an *ahu-pu* (a length of cloth wrapped and gathered either above or below their breasts). A *tiputa* (poncho) would offer extra protection, covering their shoulders. The Tahitians also wore tapa dyed with a water-resistant pigment in wet weather. Turbans were created from tapa and were frequently seen worn especially by high-ranking males. In addition to this, turbans were also used as military regalia.

Tapa was a marker of status. The quality of tapa varied from a rough burlap to something like a soft cotton flannel. Thus, texture was one means of distinguishing status. Color was also a factor, as was design. Bright yellow (turmeric) and red (a sacred color) were only worn by the elite. Chiefly women would compete for artistic recognition. The majority of people wore little tapa, and what was worn was of rougher quality and often brownish in color. Thus, a chief was immediately recognized by the color and quantity of his garments. George Robertson, ship's master on Cook's first voyage, noted that a chiefly woman had clothing different from the rest but worn in a similar manner. What he called her skirt was white, her petticoat white and yellow, and her gown red.

Tapa was used to reinforce chiefly authority due to the restrictions placed upon the materials of which it was made. Some materials were only used by the elite and some were for religious use. The color and amount of clothing worn distinguished rank and signaled an affluent lifestyle. Tapa also played an important function as tribute and chiefly prerogative in the form of reciprocity. Hence, the storing and giving of tapa became another visual signal of chiefly status.

EMBELLISHMENTS

The Tahitians utilized a variety of embellishments, which enhanced their dress and appearance. These ranged from flowers to pearls, shells to plaited hair. Each of these accoutrements reinforced a personal aesthetic as well as the person's status within Tahitian society. *Tapea taria* (earrings) in particular were worn to enhance an individual's daily appearance. These were made from a variety of materials, the most valued by the Tahitians being pearls. Again, the British were quick to notice these, suspended with human hair, in the ears of elite women. The British interest in these pearls quickly led the Tahitians to hide them during European visits. Typically, pearl earrings were worn in clusters of two or three and signaled the status of the wearer. As with many aspects of Tahitian life, value was often given to objects that were either labor-intensive (tapa) or had a high cost to acquire (necessitating long-distance trade or danger), and pearls fit this latter category.

In addition to pearls, shells, seeds, and flowers were worn in the ears of Tahitians. Shells and seeds, like pearls, were drilled and tied with human hair. These earrings offered an opportunity to the Tahitians to assert a personal aesthetic. Earrings coupled with flowers, worn either behind the ear or placed through the ear, as well as garlands and wreaths, added color and scent to the appearances of both men and women. Floral garlands as well as whale-tooth and pearlshell pendants further embellished the neck.

Hair was used to decorate and complement appearances. As noted, earrings were suspended from the ears with human hair, but hanks of braided human hair were also either utilized to embellish the neck (from which a pendant was suspended) or worn upon the head (usually as part of a dance costume), somewhat like a hat. When worn to decorate the head, these braids were observed with both flowers and pearls added to them, and as such they enhanced the dancer's beauty.

Tahitians wore headgear, typically of two kinds: *taumi-upo'o* (turbans) and *taumata* (sunshades). Turbans were worn either as protection in warfare or as a signal of status among elite males—the amount of cloth wrapped around the head denoted status. The taumata, on the other hand, were as popular an accoutrement as sunglasses are today and would have served the same purpose. Shielding one's eyes from the sun would have been a necessary part of one's dress. There are examples of these that are finely plaited from pandanus or palm, but there are also descriptions of impromptu sunshades of coconut leaves, produced quickly when needed.

COSTUME

The Tahitians created a number of costumes worn for entertainment (dance performances, musical interludes, dramas), for warfare, and for elite persons. The distinction made here between costume and dress was that dress was worn on a daily basis, whereas costumes were worn for special performative occasions. The Tahitians were fond of "entertainments," and these were a part of any exchange, celebration, or visit. Typically they were hosted by a chief and performed by the *arioi*, an institutionalized group of traveling performers. *Heiva* (entertainments), as well as impromptu dances and dramatic interludes, were frequently seen and commented upon by the British. Spectacles hosted by chiefs, particularly those in honor of the visiting British, often included elaborate dance costumes, gifts, and plays. James Wilson, captain of the *Duff*, described such a costume in 1799. He noted the dress of women as long white petticoats of fine cloth with a red stripe about ten inches (roughly twenty-five centimeters) from the hem. Women also wore a kind of vest or corset of white or colored cloth, which came right up under the arms and covered the breasts. They attached two bunches of black feathers onto this at the tip of each breast. Several tassels of the same feathers hung around the waist and reached as far as the knees. Frequently the costume of the dancer became a gift to a visiting dignitary, the amount of cloth signaling status, especially in the case of men.

Cook, as a dignitary, was himself given a *taumi*. This wearable object, worn suspended from the shoulders, front and back, was primarily associated with war and warrior status but was also a part of this gifting tradition. Taumi were status objects, as they were comprised of valuable goods. They were constructed of a cane backing onto which were tied feathers and sharks' teeth. Feathers, sharks' teeth, and dog hair were sumptuary goods and the prerogative of the elite. Feathers made reference to the gods, sharks' teeth were symbols of power and strength, and dog hair necessitated long-distance trading networks.

Taumi were also important in complex warrior costuming, as they were both a functional and protective warrior device. They signaled both prowess and gratitude: prowess on the part of the warrior and gratitude on the part of the chief who presented taumi to the best warriors and/or men that had proved their allegiance. Warrior costuming, however, varied greatly depending upon the role of the wearer. Some wore turbans to protect their heads from blows; others wore little more than their maro. The most elaborate costuming was reserved for the *ari'i* (chief), priests, and high-ranking *toa* (warriors), whose attire included not only the taumi, but also *fau*.

Fau were headwear four to six feet (1.2 to 1.8 meters) in height. Made with a cane foundation, these were frequently both covered and trimmed with feathers, creating an imposing figure ten to twelve feet tall. The front "lip," decorated with iridescent feathers, would shimmer in the sunlight creating a "halo" or "aura" effect. Fau added significantly to the grandeur of both the wearer and the scene. Cook thought the dress of the fighting chiefs grand but extremely cumbersome and "ill calculated for the day of Battle" for they seemed to be designed "to Shew themselves to the best advantage" rather than to be functional (Cook, quoted in Beaglehole 1961, 385) Even though both the taumi and fau served as protective gear, their function was to denote the wearer's relationship with the gods. By dressing in feathers the chiefs and warriors presented themselves as representations of the gods and therefore symbolized the gods' presence.

Typically, ari'i wore the same type of clothing as their constituents, but the quality, color, design, and amount would be different. Elite costume, like warrior costume, was worn sporadically. Two costumes in particular deserve mention, the *maro 'ura* and the mourner's costume. Unfortunately, there are no extant maro'ura, yet an excellent description was offered by Lieutenant King on Cook's third voyage in 1777. He noted that it was a broad cloth ten or twelve feet long (about three to three and a half meters) wrapped like a girdle, with a kind of flouncing of seven rounded pieces at one end. From the names given it seemed to King the garment was worn like a common maro or piece of cloth that hid a man's genitals, although he only saw it presented and not worn by the chief. It was made of bright yellow feathers taken from a dove native to the island and had some red and a few green feathers interspersed with the yellow. The maro'ura was very bulky (a sign of status), but more than this, to have the right to wear it was as important as wearing it, for it denoted the divine right of its wearer to rule. Each chiefly family used the maro'ura as a means of reiterating their rights over land and people, and their genealogical links with the gods.

Another important item of status was the mourner's costume, worn after the death of an elite person. A close relative of the deceased would don the costume, and, with the aid of assistants, the chief mourner would appear in the village, scurrying about to chase all bad spirits out of the area. The idea was to give the spirit of the dead a clear path to the other world. This costume covered the entire body, and again it was made of valuable items. The basis of the costume was tapa. Attached to the front in an apron-like fashion were pieces of coconut, strung in such a way as to dangle and clatter with movement. The headdress was made of feathers with a face mask of mother of pearl. The chest area consisted of a breastplate of mother of pearl in a crescent shape. Suspended from this were thin pieces of mother-of-pearl shell strung together. The back was a cape of black feathers. Besides the fact that this object/person only appeared at the death of a high chief, the costume was seen as valuable, as its parts were highly esteemed. Such a costume was observed on Cook's first visit, but try as hard as he could, Cook was unable to acquire one. This emphasizes the outfit's value at the time.

TATTOO

Tattoo played a significant role as a marker of status, wealth, and pride in Tahiti among both men and women. In customary society tattoo functioned as a means of creating and marking social differentials and establishing social identities. Body modification was used to make strong political and cultural statements concerning an individual, the group, and the elite. The placement of a tattoo readily marked status within a complex social hierarchy. The notion of embellishment as a visual code denoting status, power, and economic and political clout, as well as satisfying an aesthetic, is not new, nor is it specific to Tahiti. It is, however, interesting that the assumptions concerning body modification in Tahitian society after European contact have been revived to make strong political and cultural statements at various times in the island's history.

The "operation," as many explorers called it, was described by the naturalist Joseph Banks, who traveled with Cook on his first voyage. The color the Tahitians use is lamp black, "which they prepare from the smoak of a kind of oily nutts usd by them instead of candles" (Banks, quoted in Beaglehole 1962, 1:336) They kept this in coconut shells and mixed it with water occasionally. Their instruments for pricking this under the skin were made of flat bone or shell, the lower part cut into three to twenty sharp

A YOUNG WOMAN of OTAHEITE, bringing a PRESENT.

"A young woman of Otaheite bringing a present," plate number 27 in James Cook's *A Voyage to the Pacific Ocean* (1784). In Tahiti the costume of a dancer was frequently presented as a gift to a visiting dignitary, the amount of cloth signaling status, especially in the case of men. Engraving by Francesco Bartolozzi. National Library of Australia.

teeth, according to the purpose. The upper part was fastened to a handle. The teeth were dipped into the black liquor and then driven by quick sharp blows struck on the handle with a special stick. This penetrated the skin so deeply that every stroke was followed by a small quantity of blood, or serum at least, and the marked part remained sore for many days before it healed.

Having a tattoo was deemed essential to the Tahitians, particularly the *taomaro* (buttocks tattoo). The significance of the taomaro is not completely understood, but its role as an indispensable element of Tahitian body modification did not go unnoticed. Explorer journals have frequent passages describing the operation as well as the designs, and Cook's artists used these motifs in their depictions of Tahitians. The taomaro were not only considered to be honorable and esteemed designs, but, according to Cook, they also seemed to be their great pride, and both men and women showed them off with great pleasure. There appears to have been a direct association between the taomaro and the social maturation of the individual, and his or her changing status from child to adult. The coming of age, the desire to be sensually attractive, the wish to participate in adult society, one's aesthetic sensibility, and one's ability to endure pain have all been signified by tattoos.

The arioi also had extensive tattoos placed upon their bodies. These were added to over time and distinguished the different ranks within this dramatically hierarchical society. Clearly, tattoo was a permanent mark of social status and position and one readily visible.

There were other marks that distinguished the elite from the commoners. However, it appears that more than denoting a specific status, tattoo enabled the Tahitians to suit their own fancy. The explorers frequently commented on the lace-like appearance of the marks worn by women on their hands and feet, and they also suggested that some men wore tattoo as if they were breeches. This apparent ad hoc nature of Tahitian tattoo escalated after the arrival of the Europeans and interaction with explorers and whalers in the late eighteenth century. Later in the nineteenth century tattoos began to include foreign objects and words, signaling both a personal aesthetic and a relationship with the outside world.

ADAPTED DRESS AND APPEARANCE IN TAHITI

The exchange of goods between the Europeans and Tahitians was not a one-way system. Many sailors left Tahiti with tattoos; many Tahitians acquired cloth. The importance of these relationships cannot be over-emphasized. A naval ship was as stratified as Tahitian society, so it was easy to establish trading relations with appropriate partners. Of course "the old trade" was rampant; but so was the desire for iron. As Cook was offered cloth, so he offered it. Military regalia was exchanged for military regalia. As such, British goods became a part of the Tahitian status system. As a canoe signaled control/power/trade, so did a red British jacket.

The eventual importation of British cloth in 1810 was to change the Tahitian system of attire forever. During the Cook period (1767–1780) it was only the ari'i who possessed British cloth. They quickly recognized the advantage of acquiring it instead of continuing the arduous process of producing it, and as such it rapidly replaced tapa as a signal of status. By the turn of the nineteenth century British clothes were being worn, as well as British styles fabricated of tapa. The style and the cloth both signaled a relationship with the British. At end of the nineteenth century

Tahiti's elite, as did those in Hawai'i, often appeared in the latest European fashions. However, most Tahitians still continued to wear customary dress.

The London Missionary Society, whose first missionary arrived in Tahiti in 1797, introduced the "mother hubbard" dress, and this, along with the introduction of *pareu* (printed cotton cloth), signaled the end of the traditional system of dress. There became a direct correlation between being Christian and dressing "properly." However, Tahitian women quickly asserted a Tahitian identity as they began wearing pareu over their dresses. Men as well combined the British cotton shirt with the pareu worn over their maro. By the mid-nineteenth century Tahitians had combined the ease and comfort of tapa with the utility of cotton cloth.

Pareu, a lightweight fabric, mostly English-made, began to be imported into Tahiti by 1820. Even though tapa was worn infrequently at this time, pareu replaced tapa production in Tahiti. Printed in solid blue, deep red, or green backgrounds with large white hibiscus, breadfruit, and other floral designs, pareu became synonymous with Tahiti. The emergence of bright colors, bold patterns, and highly contrasting color combinations marked the emergence of a unique aesthetic that persists into the twenty-first century.

In the early to mid-nineteenth century missionary influence was key. Missionaries' notions of propriety encouraged changes in the Tahitian system of dress and embellishment. The wearing of hats to church was one such change. It is interesting how quickly the Tahitians adapted the English bowler. Woven from pandanus or hibiscus fibers (using the same technologies as the customary taumata), the Tahitian hat epitomized a willingness to incorporate and adapt outside designs and influences into their system of attire.

In the late nineteenth century Tahiti became a shipping crossroads in the southern Pacific. The economic prosperity this provided created the opportunities for an emergent class of wealthy (frequently *demi*, or of mixed Tahitian/European heritage) Tahitians who dressed in the latest European fashions. Fashion again signaled status. European and military dress was worn on formal occasions (when Tahitians asserted an equality with their British and French counterparts). For example, the Pomares (the royal family) were frequently photographed in either French or British military uniform, which not only asserted their position as kings, but also placed them on an equal footing to the European business sector and colonial officials. The wearing of pareu offered a less formal Tahitian identity. The variety of dress, from the customary to the modern, afforded both a personal and Tahitian aesthetic.

As the Colonial era progressed and Tahiti became a French colony, the importation and utilization of European cloth signaled this new economy. Cloth had also been a marker of status, and it continued to play this role into the twentieth century. The Tahitian willingness to incorporate and adapt new items into their system of bodily attire underlies this process of change. As dress, and especially the incorporation and adaptation of European dress, visually demonstrated a Tahitian identity, it continues to do so. During times of strong colonial intervention in particular, the Tahitians would use dress (in performances, daily attire, and within tourist venues) to assert their identity. Dance performances, particularly those seen during the Heiva (an annual celebration of Tahitian art and culture), continue to draw upon the customary dance and warrior costuming of the Cook period. Taumi, fau, and even the mourner's costume are utilized, both as a means of asserting Tahitian identity and as authenticating the historical nature of the performance. The mother hubbard has transformed; using pareu material (bright floral prints) and tapering around the bust and waist, it has now become as prevalent as the Hawaiian *mu'umu'u* and is frequently worn as a uniform within the tourist industry. Just as tapa was at the center of their traditional system of clothing, pareu has taken on that role in the twenty-first century. Pareu is seen everywhere and ranges in function from a beach wraparound, to sleeping attire, to car seat and bed covers—it is ubiquitous to Tahiti. Even though French and globalized world fashion, and as part of that new materials and styles, predominate to create a Tahitian appearance in the twenty-first century, the Tahitian system of attire and embellishment, and its key function in the signaling of status and identity, remains.

References and Further Reading

Beaglehole, J.C., ed. *The Journals of Captain James Cook.* Vol. 2, *The Voyage of the Resolution and Adventure, 1772–1775.* London: Hakluyt Society, 1961.

Beaglehole, J.C., ed. *The Endeavour Journal of Joseph Banks 1768–1771.* 2 vols. Sydney: Angus & Robertson, 1962.

D'Alleva, Anne. "Representing the Body Politic: Status, Gender, and Anatomy in Eighteenth-Century Society Islands Art." *Pacific Arts* 13–14 (1996): 27–34.

D'Alleva, Anne. "Representing the Body Politic: Status, Gender, and Anatomy in Eighteenth-Century Society Islands Art." Ph.D. dissertation, Columbia University, 1997.

Henry, Teuira. *Ancient Tahiti. Bernice P. Bishop Museum Bulletin 48.* Honolulu: Bernice P. Bishop Museum, 1928.

Jones, Laura. "The Pareu: Persistence and Revival in a French Polynesian Folk Art." In *Artistic Heritage in a Changing Pacific*, edited by Philip J. C. Dark and Roger G. Rose, 84–90. Honolulu: University of Hawai'i Press, 1993.

Kaeppler, Adrienne L., Christian Kaufmann, and Douglas Newton. *Oceanic Art.* New York: Harry N. Abrams, 1997.

Kooijman, Simon. *Tapa in Polynesia. Bernice P. Bishop Museum Bulletin 234.* Honolulu: Bernice P. Bishop Museum, 1972.

Oliver, Douglas. *Ancient Tahitian Society.* 3 vols. Honolulu: University Press of Hawai'i, 1974.

Rose, Roger. "The Material Culture of Ancient Tahiti." Ph.D. dissertation, Harvard University, 1971.

Stevenson, Karen. "Dispelling the Myth: Tahitian Adornment and the Maintenance of a Traditional Culture, 1767–1819." Ph.D. dissertation, University of California, Los Angeles, 1988.

Stevenson, Karen, and Steve Hooper. "Tahitian Fau—Unveiling an Enigma." *Journal of the Polynesian Society* 116, no. 2 (2007): 181–212.

Karen Stevenson

See also Dance Costumes in French Polynesia; Hawaiian Dress Prior to 1898; Tahitian Tattoos.

Fijian Dress and Body Modifications

- Body Alteration
- Face and Body Painting
- Hair (*Drau ni ulu*) and Grooming (*Qaravi ulu*)
- Personal Ornament (*luku-uku*)
- Masks
- Female Clothing
- Male Clothing
- Dyed and Figured Barkcloth
- Missionary Intervention
- Fijian Clothing in the Early Twenty-first Century

"Modes of painting the face," drawing by Thomas Williams, published in *Fiji and the Fijians: The Islands and Their Inhabitants* (London: Alexander Heylin, 1858). This drawing shows the many styles that Fijians use from a combination of colors, techniques, and patterns. Drawing by Thomas Williams. Courtesy of Roderick Ewins.

Geographically, Fiji sits where the arbitrarily defined three triangles of Melanesia, Micronesia, and Polynesia intersect, and it shares many cultural elements with its neighbors on all sides, though Polynesian elements predominate. Bodywear has always been strongly differentiated in terms of age, gender, and social status. Nineteenth-century Christian missionary and colonial government intervention altered every aspect of custom, including bodywear. Items with any symbolic connection with the old religion and warfare were abolished, while age and gender differences were modified, sometimes reversed, to fit acceptable European values. What was customary bodywear up to the mid-nineteenth century and what is considered "typically Fijian" in the twenty-first century are as dramatically different as bodywear in medieval Britain compared with modern styles, but even many of the changed forms are distinctive and recognizably Fijian.

From first contact in the eighteenth century many Westerners described Fijians as being "naked" or "near naked." Actually, both men and women used an extensive array of bodywear. Early Wesleyan missionary Thomas Williams (in Fiji 1845–1873) noted that in Fiji's climate, dress was unnecessary for utility, and he credited Fijians' modesty for such covering as they did adopt. He opposed the imposition of European mores, but his church *did* make it a condition of conversion that Fijians transform most of their customary wear. Prudery and conservatism played their part, but even more critical was the fact that the old religion underpinned almost all cultural and social matters, including bodywear. Eliminating people's ancestor-based religious beliefs included removing the potent visible symbols of these that they carried on their bodies. The incoming British colonial government supported many such bans, since warfare and cannibalism were also both integral to Fijian religion, but unacceptable in the new civil order.

BODY ALTERATION

Commencing in early childhood, both males and females practiced many body alterations, dictated by their religion and occasioned as mourning sacrifices for chiefs or relatives. Any who shirked these obligations could anticipate such savage retribution at the hands of the guardians of the path to the afterworld (*bulu*) that everyone submitted to them. The most basic was the amputation of successive joints of little fingers. Even in the twenty-first century one name for the little finger is *ilolokunimate*, or "sacrifice for the deceased." After them, little toes could be amputated. The arms, back, and breast could be burned with firebrands to raise rows of cicatrices or scars (*imacamaca*). Perhaps most immediately noticeable was the vertical slitting of one or both earlobes to insert ornaments (*isaunidaliga*), first a plant stalk or leaf, then a "spring" of rolled leaves or barkcloth to distend the hole, through a variety of objects up to purpose-made disks over two hundred millimeters (7.9 inches) in diameter. Most prized were plugs carved of whale-tooth ivory, an attractive material with surpassing spiritual significance for Fijians. Curiously, ubiquitous as they were, only a handful of ear ornaments have survived in museums. Totally absent from collections are the bones or carved wooden dowels reportedly worn through the nasal septum by some Vitilevu highlanders, who exhibited more Melanesian traits than their lowland and small-islander neighbors.

Finally came genital alteration, by which boys and girls were initiated into adulthood on the occasion of the death of a senior relative or important chief. Boys about the age of puberty were circumcised (*teve*) as a group, their foreskins cut off by a priest and buried with the deceased, along with amputated fingers of both sexes and, in the case of important males, with wives who were strangled to accompany them into the afterworld. Circumcision, "validated" by Judeo-Christian practice, was the only form of body alteration not suppressed by either Christian or government edict.

On the same occasions girls who had reached or were approaching menarche began a lengthy process of tattooing (*veiqia*), by at least one account accompanied by clitoral mutilation. Female tattooing is common in Melanesia, whereas in Polynesia male tattooing is the rule, but not in Fiji. Paradoxically, Samoa and Tonga credit the origin of their male tattooing to Fiji, with curious legends to explain the gender reversal. Female elder experts presided. Their instruments were little adze-like tools (*iqia*) with bound-on citrus thorns or twin-toothed picks of tortoise shell or bone. A stick or tiny paddle tapped the heel of the adze to drive the pick into the skin, blood was mopped off with a barkcloth swab, and soot obtained by burning candlenuts of the *lauci* tree (*Aleurites triloba*) was rubbed into the wounds. This apparently had antiseptic properties and remained ingrained as a permanent tattoo.

There were regional variations in tattoo detail, but the essentials were universal. The primary target was the pudendum and extended outward from there. It might extend to the upper thighs, hips, and buttocks, up as far as the waist, giving the external appearance of blue-black shorts visible above and below their fiber hip-girdles (*liku*). Frequently it was less extensive, largely concealed by the liku. Designs comprised patterns of straight, diagonal, circular, and spiral lines and dot patterns. Choice was reportedly dictated solely by the initiate's fancy, and no symbolic meaning was ever recorded for the motifs themselves. It seems probable that it was the totality of the tattoo that carried meaning, which is consistent with the figuration on barkcloth.

Also tattooed were the backs of the hands and knuckles, lines up the arms and across the chest above the breasts, and lines from the small of the back to the top of the shoulders. Some groups had bands encircling the mouth and/or small clan insignia such as stars on the cheeks. Clitoral mutilation may also have taken place. When the whole process had been completed, small semicircles would often be tattooed at the corner of a girl's mouth to signify that she was now complete and eligible for marriage.

By the second half of the twentieth century, virtually no one, even in remote areas, still bore bodily evidence of the old ways. While some young people today have their ears pierced or affect very small tattoos, these relate to world fashions and not at all to Fijian custom, unlike the resurgence of tattooing in Samoa, New Zealand, and elsewhere.

FACE AND BODY PAINTING

Fijians have always rubbed scented coconut oil (*waiwai saluaki*) on their skin to keep it soft, supple, and sweet-smelling. On special occasions people of all ages glisten with oil. Formerly, however, men and women also had what numerous observers noted as a "passion for daubing the face (*veiqisa*) with colored powder"—particularly but not only for festivals, rituals, or war. Their palette was limited to red earths (*qeledamu*) and the golden yellows and oranges of turmeric (*rerega*), carbon black (*loaloa*) from soot or fungus spores (*qumu*), and kaolin clay or burnt-coral-lime white (*vulavula*), all mixed into a binder of oil.

Brilliant vermilion (*kulakulā*) in particular was keenly sought in trade with Europeans, and once the lipstick plant (*Bixa orellana*) was introduced, its brilliant seed coating was preferred to muted red clays. Women frequently painted their faces uniformly red, sometimes with a fine black line around each eye reminiscent of the kohl eye-lining of Asia, while men painted their faces using combinations of colors in individualistic and endlessly creative patterns of waves and stripes, circles, spots, and stars, as well as simple vertical and/or lateral subdivisions of the face. Descriptions and illustrations call to mind the face and body painting still practiced in parts of New Guinea. For war, black predominated, also rubbed on arms and torsos. Where it occurred naturally, antimony (*Vatu resse resse*) could be rubbed on the skin, imparting a metallic sheen, and the washing-blue introduced by Europeans proved irresistible, as it did to other Pacific Islanders.

This painting was more than mere "daubing," however. Colors had symbolic denotations, and by painting themselves Fijians assumed the splendor and protective aura of their cosmology. The auratic power of golden turmeric was also invoked in childbirth;

A Fijian man with an ornate hairdo and *wasekaseka*, a sawn whale-tooth gorget, Levuka, Fiji, ca. 1890. Photograph by John Waters. Courtesy Rod Ewins Collection.

mother, baby, and their clothing were smeared from head to foot with it, and in death the deceased was often liberally coated in turmeric. The faces and torsos of great warrior chiefs were also painted black, ready for battle, and with favorite weapons at hand they were deemed ready to confront the terrors of their afterworld.

Missionaries and colonial administrators had the same problems with face and body painting as they did with body alteration, and it survived only in vestigial form. Modern dance performers often wear black spots on their cheeks, foreheads, and chins, and less often smeared on arms and chests. But these are mere tokens of the wonderful multicolored body artistry of their ancestors. In the twenty-first century, however, such cosmetics as are worn by Fijian women are those developed for African Americans.

HAIR (*DRAU NI ULU*) AND GROOMING (*QARAVI ULU*)

Reflecting their genetic history, Fijians' hair ranges from frizzed like their Melanesian neighbors to the northwest, to curly or wavy like their Polynesian neighbors to the east. The head throughout Polynesia is regarded as sacred, particularly in the case of chiefs and priests, and taboos include the hair and anything placed in it or used to dress it. Men and women frequently bleached their hair with lime and/or colored it wholly or in sections. Young girls have always worn their hair no more than two centimeters (about three-quarters of an inch) long. During their teens it is allowed to grow. Formerly they grew long locks (*tobe*) to hang down on one side, but by the mid-1980s only a very few girls in the southern islands of the Lau group followed the custom, and it may since have vanished altogether.

These "virgin plaits" were cut off by the husband on the nuptial night. In the nineteenth century his womenfolk would crop the bride's hair close the following day, and she thenceforth wore it fairly short. Drawings and descriptions reveal that most commonly, it resembled the top of a barrister's wig, cropped over the top but slightly turned up around the edges. However, while their menfolk were abandoning their elaborate hairstyles, Christianized women increasingly wore their hair long, and by the twentieth century "Afro-style" hair was the female norm. Some men also followed this fashion, particularly policemen (who actually had to get permission to cut it), but by the 1980s very few men still wore long hair. By then some young urban women started wearing their hair short, but following modern Western, not historical Fijian, styles.

With women's access to extravagant headdress circumscribed, Fijian men had the field to themselves. Described repeatedly by outside observers as dandies, they were normally full-bearded and very meticulous about their coiffures, with all classes spending much time and trouble on it. Even small boys had their hair cut in fanciful forms, and as they grew into manhood they became increasingly particular about its length and styling. To tease it out they (or in the case of chiefs and priests, sanctified attendants) used objects like long knitting needles, made of wood and called *balabala* after the black tree fern used (*Cyathea lunulata*), or of tortoise shell or human fibulae and called *iqeu*. These were "parked" in the hair and beard, where they served as scratchers (*imilamila*) of resident vermin.

Hair could reach a meter and a half (about five feet) in circumference and be sculpted into elaborate shapes. A chief's complex hairdo might take two full days to dress, so he took great care to preserve it for days. This was assisted by Fijians' use (like their neighbors on all sides) of quite tall headrests (*kali*) made principally of timber or bamboo, which kept the head off the ground during sleep. In addition, chiefs alone were permitted to wrap their hair in a fine gauzy barkcloth hair scarf (*isala*). They are often called turbans. This is misleading since they were not thick and coiled like a turban, their large size due solely to the great mop of hair they enclosed.

Delicate combs (*iseru*), with teeth of coconut leaflet midribs (*sāsā*) or wood, were for fashion, not function. These and other ornaments, generically called *itekiteki* and often decorated with shells, beads, or feathers, were also stuck in the hair or beards. Once they started wearing their hair longer, women also appropriated these ornaments for dance and ceremony. A visitor even described seeing young women impaling fireflies on sāsā to stick in their hair for a nighttime dance performance, where they continued to flash for hours.

Some chiefs wore frontlets (ornaments or bands on the forehead) made of the prized scarlet feathers of the *kula* parrot (collared lory—*Phigys solitarius*), and there is one illustration of a splendid chief's woven feather headdress with a corona of flight

Tobe virgin plaits worn by Lefila Takayawa, Fipe Jeni (both seventeen years old), and Korovou Neimani (twenty years old) on the way to a friend's birthday party, Namuka Island, 1985. Short jackets and matching skirts are popular formal dress among young Fijian women. Photograph by Roderick Ewins.

or tail feathers, reminiscent of those of eastern Polynesia, though sadly none appears to have survived. In some places chiefs alone might stick in their hair the paired trailing tail feathers of the *lawedua*, or white-tailed tropic bird (*Phaethon lepturus*). Other warriors would use the graceful red and black tail feathers of the *toaniveikau tagane*, or jungle fowl cock (*Gallus gallus*).

Male dandies affected wigs, much as their European counterparts had in the eighteenth century. Large ones were particularly in vogue in the Colo Highlands of Vitilevu, and they earned the men there the European sobriquet of "Big-heads." Made of human hair, often colored in whole or in part, sometimes with ringlets (*qaliqali*) cascading from them, wigs were ingeniously fashioned on frames of basketry or coconut-coir sennit cord. They could also serve to partially redress the temporary disfigurement caused by the mourning custom of cropping the hair and shaving beards. (In the twenty-first century most men lack long hair or beards, so in yet another reversal they neither shave nor cut their hair for about three months as a sign of respect, until a lifting of mourning ceremony normalizes matters.) The hair for wigs was cut from slain enemies, hence their common name *ulumate*, or "dead-head." The sacrilegious violation of one's head and hair was a final and particularly extreme insult to inflict on the victim. As warfare and cannibalism ceased, and the ready supply of human hair with it, horsehair was sometimes used, and large imposing wigs could even be made of tightly packed leaves, fastened to the frame and singed on the outside to quite convincingly resemble tightly curled hair.

PERSONAL ORNAMENT (*IUKU-UKU*)

Both sexes have always frequently worn vines, green or colored leaves, and perfumed flowers on their heads and bodies for dances and ceremonies. Flowers (*seni*) are worn either singly or as woven garlands. Simple daisy-chains (called *sinucodo*) of several flower species may be worn in the hair and around the neck, arms, or wrists. As well, armlets, wristlets, and leg ornaments (*vesa*) may be made of specially woven vine, black sennit, or pandanus, sometimes ornamented with beads or shells. There are also barkcloth versions, cut into strips and lacy fringes. Male leg ornaments are worn just below the knee, female ones around the ankles. Larger flower constructions called *salusalu* are similar to the lei of Hawaii and like them are particularly a token of welcome and farewell.

Formerly, on arms and/or wrists, both sexes wore bangles (*qato*) made by cutting rings from large trochus or cone shells, and finger rings (*mama*) made by heating and curling strips of tortoise shell (*taku*). Necklaces (*itaube*) were and still remain popular. They are made by threading a great diversity of things onto string made from the inner bark of several plants. Most common are many hard seeds of different colors and a variety of small shells. Particular favorites here as elsewhere are the shiny red seeds of the red bead tree (*diridamu*—*Adenanthera pavonina*) and small white to yellow necklace shells (*vocovoco*—*Melampus luteus*). Most valued were the small *bulileka* white cowries (*Cypraea luponia*), a full necklace of which (*tababuli*) was considered equal in value to two or three muskets.

Pieces of shell used to be ground into small donut shapes that were threaded together—work so painstaking that it explains the eager uptake of European colored beads. Teeth were also favored, from small whale teeth to those of dolphins, sharks, dogs, even rats, and finally humans, which, like the hair in wigs, had the added zest of deriving from enemies' heads. A number of particularly valued shells were worn singly as pendants (*itaubebuli*), such as the white egg-cowrie *buli qaqau* (*Ovula ovum*). Considered potent charms like other white cowries, they were also used to decorate temple finials, canoes, and the cords on kava bowls (*tanoa*). The rare golden cowries *bulikula* (*Cypraea aurantium*), being gold to orange, were reserved for chiefs' pendants, as were *isōvui* (*Gloripallium* sp.), also in the red-orange spectrum. A prized warrior's chest pendant was a boar's tusk that had grown into a circle or spiral (*itaube batinivuaka*).

An object of unique symbolic power in Fiji is the *tabua*, the tooth of the sperm whale (*Macrocepohalus physeter*). Teeth were originally obtained from beached migratory whales, but the advent of Yankee and other whalers improved access enormously. Large teeth have holes drilled in the ends and a thick sennit cord attached, but contrary to popular belief they are seldom worn and almost certainly never were. Tabua are the most valued object for ritual presentation, and the thick square plaited cord, so unsuitable as a neck strap, actually plays a symbolic role in presentation rituals.

However, tabua could be fashioned into a variety of objects intended to be worn. Small teeth were either threaded as full necklaces (*sisi*) or tightly bound to a woven sennit band to make choker-style necklets (*vuasagale*). The most prized form was made of tabua carefully sawn lengthwise into strips, which were ground to a fine taper and bound together. Called *wasekaseka*, these were worn with the points outward. Linguistic archaeology indicates that these were developed in Fiji but later adopted by Tongans, Samoans, and other neighbors. Before the nineteenth century Tongans of the Ha'apai group had become specialist workers of whale-tooth ivory and effectively cornered the trade in these and a variety of other ivory articles exported to the virtually insatiable Fiji market.

Most exotic and prized of these were discoid breastplates (*civavonovono*), generally around fifteen to twenty centimeters (5.9 to 7.8 inches) in diameter (the size of a bread-and-butter plate), made either completely of cut ivory pieces impeccably jointed and bound together, or more commonly of pieces of ivory attached to and/or inlaid into large black-lipped pearlshells (*civa*—*Meleagrina margaritifera*). They probably evolved from the huge whalebone breast-shield discs Tongans had earlier developed, perhaps as protection against Fijian war-arrows. The spiritual weight of the tabua version made them highly prized chiefly objects in Fiji, and importation was so voracious that few if any remained in Tonga, so they have been widely accepted as Fijian artifacts. There can never have been more than a few dozen made, each so distinctive in design that individual museum specimens can often be identified in early field photographs, worn by chiefs.

MASKS

While tourists eagerly buy the carved wooden masks on offer in shops and stalls, these are purely tourist articles dating from the 1950s. Fijians never carved or wove masks like those of New Guinea or Africa. However, they did formerly make masks to be worn by special (male) performers in certain dances associated with first-fruits ceremonies. Very few survive in museums, and descriptions are sparse.

The main type was named *matavulo*, from *mata*, or face, and *vulo*, the fibrous gauze wrapping the leaf bases of coconut palms

Matavulo helmet mask, collected in Fiji, 1840. The mask is usually worn by "gremlin" dancers in first-fruits ceremonies. National Museum of Natural History, Smithsonian Institution, Washington, D.C.

from which they were fashioned. The simplest were flat sheets of vulo, cut to size and with holes for eyes, nostrils, and mouths, and frequently warrior face paint, tied to the face and worn in conjunction with a wig. An elaborate helmet version was fashioned over a basketry frame. It roughly resembled a human face, with an integral human hair wig running into a mustache and beard. Armed with clubs or spears, the performers wore leaves from neck to foot, recalling the Green Man of Celtic lore, with whom they shared other qualities, since they were held to embody the mischievous and often malevolent jungle gremlins called *veli*, *qica*, or *driai*. The masks and clowning antics of these *velinimeke* (gremlins of the dance) enhanced the illusion of possession and tinged audience amusement with fear. As with all Fijian spirits, veli were ancestral beings, zealous guardians of crops, and their compliance was necessary to free the first fruits for use.

FEMALE CLOTHING

Clothing, like body alteration and decoration, was sharply gender-differentiated. Female clothing was the ultimate in simplicity and brevity, while full ceremonial male clothing was extensive. The only thing males and females shared was that both went naked in childhood. Broadly, this persisted until they underwent the genital alterations described previously, initiating them into adulthood. However, at between eight and ten years of age girls were given an interim garment consisting of two short fringed panels with ties at each end. The two minimal components were worn back and front, tied together at each end and leaving both hips bare.

Their tattooing complete, girls could at last don the liku. It was still very brief, both shorter and stiffer than those they would later wear as married women. Girls' liku had a waistband about fifty millimeters (two inches) in depth with a fringe about ten centimeters or so (four inches) in length on the lower edge. The waistband on a mature woman's liku was about 125 millimeters

(4.9 inches) in depth with a longer fringe that increased in length with their age but seldom exceeded twenty centimeters (7.8 inches), giving a total length of only about thirty centimeters (11.8 inches) for matrons.

Manufacture was fairly standard. They were intricately woven from any combination of the processed inner bark or bast of the wild hibiscus (*vau*—*Hibiscus tiliaceus*) and/or sennit, sedge (*kuta*—*Eleocharis dulcis*), and other fibers, even strips of barkcloth. Thirty or forty centimeters (11.8 to 15.7 inches) of loose fibers at either end served as ties. The waistband was robust, often multi-colored and patterned, and its weave was somewhat elastic. Only this allowed them to stay in place, since they were worn slung low as hip-girdles, appearing to both restrict the legs and stay in place precariously. Observers were unanimous, however, in saying that women contrived by their actions to maintain total modesty. On special occasions several liku might be worn tiered, their colors and patterns carefully chosen. Such carefully woven items were valuable, and when engaged in rough work such as gardening or fishing, females instead wore work girdles (*isuai*) made of banana leaves.

MALE CLOTHING

Male clothing proclaimed manhood, incorporated cosmology and group identity, and defined social status. Boys had no intermediate garment, going from nudity to the *malo* loincloth only following circumcision, an event that prompted rituals, gift exchanges, and feasts. The malo (its name throughout Polynesia) was the primary garment. It was a strip of barkcloth or *masi*, a fabric beaten out from the white inner bark (bast) of saplings of the paper mulberry (*Broussonetia papyrifera*). Manufactured solely by women, who were forbidden its use as clothing, it was critical to male rites of passage. It has always been recognized as the most important women's valuable, and they had charge of masi when first dressing boys following initiation, or men in new malo in the renaming ritual after killing their first enemy. Women still retain this ownership in ritual presentations and exchanges.

A single beaten-out bast constitutes the delicate gauzy fabric used for isala or vesa, but for robust cloth such as that required for malo, two or more basts are felted together during beating. The height and girth of saplings used dictates that one piece of felted cloth is normally about two meters long (six and a half feet) and half a meter (twenty inches) wide. Typically, for commoners' malo, two of these were end-joined, producing a cloth about four meters (thirteen feet) by half a meter (twenty inches), and there are numerous pieces of masi of roughly that size in museum collections. It was worn like a T-bandage, wrapped around the waist and brought up between the legs. The free ends hung down in front and behind, and in the case of chiefs (and *only* chiefs), much longer malo were made, so that the rear free end formed long trains (*malo yara* or *itini yara*) to drag along the ground. One or two throwing-clubs, without which no adult male felt fully dressed, would be thrust into the waistband.

Essentially the same type of cloth could be wrapped around the waist as a cummerbund (*ioro*). When going into battle this was tied high around the ribs as a sign of challenge. But when ceremonial gift presentations were being made, enormously long masi might be wrapped around the torso, sometimes looped downward and caught up again, the whole affair so cumbersome that the bearer's arms stuck out akimbo. Yet so cunningly

A drawing of *likus* (women's hip-girdles) by Thomas Williams, published in *Fiji and the Fijians: The Islands and Their Inhabitants* (London: Alexander Heylin, 1858). The *liku* on the left is worn after completion of tattooing, and the one on the right is a mature woman's girdle. Courtesy of Roderick Ewins.

was it arranged that a single tug could release the whole thing to the ground, the wearer stepping out to leave their gift. There was a term for a 100-fathom- (185-meter-) long cloth of this sort, *katudrau*. No one could wear that without buckling under the weight, and others would assist.

A surviving chiefly prerogative is to wear a sash (*iwābale*), a single two-meter (6.5-foot) length of masi worn over one shoulder. In some places, if the wearer's highest rank came from his father, it is worn over the right shoulder, if from his mother, over the left shoulder. In the rare event that they have equal status, he might wear two sashes, bandolier-fashion. In the twenty-first century noble women may also wear sashes.

Finally, warriors had their own form of liku, which they wore over their malo into battle, ritual, and dance. This was a knee-length fiber skirt, more sparsely and simply plaited than women's liku. The most valued material for these was the rhizomorphs ("roots") of a plant fungus called *wāloa* (*Armillaria* sp). With a hard outer skin these resembled long black bootlaces, and the resulting skirt was called *liku wāloa*.

DYED AND FIGURED BARKCLOTH

The symbolism of masi was carried in its coloration and/or figuration. The vast majority was left white (*masi vulavula* or *seāvu*). However, that intended for chiefs might be either rubbed with coconut oil and turmeric to dye it golden (*masi vakarerega*), or then smoked over a slow-burning fire to a rich golden-brown color (*masi kuvui*). Red through gold, the colors of gods and chiefs, may be applied to any or all chiefs' garments, including the hair scarf, sash, cummerbund, loincloth, and arm and leg ornaments.

In addition to dyeing it, there were several technologies employed for figuring cloth, of which two are still commonly used. The generic term is *masi kesa* (painted barkcloth), the act of

figuring *kesata*. The method most common here, but quite unique in the Pacific, is stenciling. Designs are cut into leaves (or, in the twenty-first century, other stiff materials—light cardboard or even X-ray film), and color is daubed through these holes onto the cloth. As with face painting, the colors used embody Fijian cosmology: The sacred red-browns and black (the color of the temporal world, night, and death) are both applied to cloth, the natural white color of which signifies day, light, life, and the spirit world. In addition, black is the female signifier, white the male.

The small motifs are exclusively geometric, mostly triangle-based with some rectangles, chevrons, and zigzag forms. Though nicknamed for various things they are imagined to resemble, there is no evidence that they ever depicted anything in that literal way. They actually comprise that far rarer thing, a highly sophisticated abstract design system, the totality of which carries meaning. The regional and clan identity of the users was conveyed by which particular motifs were used and by the overall design arrangement on the cloth. Much of this group specificity is progressively being lost, submerged in a sort of pan-Fijian masi design system in which makers freely borrow motifs from one another and employ new motifs derived from playing-card suits and lace-paper-doily patterns. However, it is still possible to identify several broad regions by the figuration of their cloth.

A related form of printing, in which the large motifs are plotted by folding and lining the cloth and painted on using a coconut leaflet as an edge-mask rather than a cutout stencil, is almost obsolete, practiced only occasionally and only in northeastern Fiji. It is called *bolabola*. The second still-common system of figuration came from Tonga and is found particularly in the areas of strong Tongan influence. It uses a sewn plate (*kuveti*) of pandanus leaves (*voivoi*) with pieces of string (*wāvau*), sāsā, or pandanus sewn to the surface to create complex and relatively organic patterns. The barkcloth is placed over these and rubbed over with a swab

Curu Malaka of Moce Island, Fiji, stenciling a *gatu vakaviti* ceremonial cloth in 1985. She wears a work shirt over her *sulu* (skirt) and is sitting on the *tasina* section of the cloth, which has been rubbed in the Tongan manner. The stencil is made of X-ray film, with several motifs cut into it, and it is being used to stencil one of the groups of three spots called *tusea* that are scattered across the *tasina*. Photograph by Roderick Ewins.

carrying rather watery red-brown paint, quite like doing brass-rubbings in the West. This method of printing is used in particular for large cloths called *gatu vakatoga* (Tongan-style cloth), or, in hybrid form, half-rubbed and half-stenciled, *gatu vakaviti* (Fiji-style Tongan cloth), the Tongan word for barkcloth, *ngatu*, being spelt *gatu* in Fijian. Being a reddish-brown color overall, the former are still adopted for spiritually significant rites of passage and, for the same reason, in the late nineteenth century became very popular among high chiefs as wraparound "togas." The large *gatu vakaviti* were formerly used as mosquito nets (*taunamu*—an alternative name for them in some places) and were and still are important ceremonial curtains, especially indispensable in marriages.

While both the manufacture and figuring of the cloth in these two technologies is exclusively women's work, a quite unique type of figuration was formerly produced by Vitilevu Highlands men, though women still made the cloth. "Rollers" or "liners" were made from single sections of bamboo or wooden cylinders, with raised encircling lines created either by binding with string or by carving. The form called *lewasaga* had fine lines and grooves with solid and groove about equally wide. Another form called *noa* had most lines spaced that way, but periodically a number of much wider raised bands. The band count was said to indicate the number of *itokatoka* or extended families in the geopolitical entity (*vanua*) of the maker group. As in the Tongan style, figuring was by rubbing, but here the lewasaga was rolled along progressively beneath the cloth, first totally in one direction, then in another,

and so on, the rubbing creating a dark-toned cross-hatch. Finally the noa was used, rolled in one direction only and with intervals between, creating a series of broad bands. This very dark cloth was made for malo and also for mosquito curtains and screens. It was called *liti*, and it could have areas left plain and then either painted with solid red, figured with short lines using special wooden combs dipped in red or black paint, or even stamped with simple wooden blocks with carved patterns, reminiscent of potato cuts. Very few of either of these tools survive, and this highland men's printing has been obsolete for half a century.

MISSIONARY INTERVENTION

From just before the middle of the nineteenth century, the missionary project (primarily Wesleyan Methodist, with some Roman Catholic) became well established. Above all intent on stamping out "heathen" practices, they imposed a number of drastic changes on converts, despite the greater understanding and empathy of a few missionaries. Ear ornaments, the docking of digits, cicatrisation, and tattooing were all abolished. Face and body painting (construed as war-related) were permitted only for dance. The long and ornate hairstyles of men were discouraged, along with the wearing of wigs. Finally, men were required to abandon the malo, the essential symbol of their manhood, in favor of a Tongan *vala*, a wraparound garment. The generic term for clothing in Fijian is *isulu*, and they called this alien new garment *isulu vakatoga* (Tonga-style garment), usually abbreviated to *sulu*. Contrary to what some have suggested, Fijians did not meekly adopt this change. In fact, having to dress "like women" was an enormous impediment to conversion for many men.

While their old religion forbade women the use of masi, the new one required that they wear skirts instead of skimpy liku, and as masi was the only cloth readily available to them, they too started wearing masi sulu. Malo cloth was too narrow for this and longer than necessary, so instead of end-joining masi to make it double-length they started edge-joining it during manufacture to make it double-width, for both male and female skirts. The only reminder of the liku of women and of warriors was the colored pandanus dance skirts.

While many men and women continued to frequently wear nothing above the waist for decades, this too was discouraged. Men wore handed-down singlets (*siqileti*, a name now also applied to T-shirts) or shirts (*sote*), while women added to these handed-down dresses dubbed *vinivō*, from *pinafore*. These were typically not ankle-length and were simply pulled over their sulu, which became a *sulu-i-rā*, or underskirt, the resulting layered effect perhaps reminiscent of their previous layered liku. This layering has persisted ever since in women's formal attire.

For ceremonial dress a further masi overskirt was often added, and sometimes a cummerbund as well. Alternately, they might wear a blouse and shift (*tatara*), with layers of masi over that. In the twenty-first century masi makers sell sets of three masi as *mataisulu tolu*—three-layered skirts. What is most curious is that this has become unisex. Men's exclusive use of masi and their proud malo have vanished, and their ceremonial masi is virtually indistinguishable from the evolved female form.

FIJIAN CLOTHING IN THE TWENTY-FIRST CENTURY

For casual wear around the home both rural and urban women commonly wear a short-sleeved cotton frock (sometimes with puffed shoulders) or a blouse or T-shirt outside or tucked into a sulu, and in cooler weather a sweatshirt. They go barefoot or wear plastic flip-flops (*sabisabi*), eminently practical when protocol is to remove shoes before entering a house. For more formal occasions they favor the layered dress and underskirt, commonly called *sulu jiaba* (from the word *jumper*). The underskirt is frequently a fabric with a sheen and is invariably worn long. The overdress ranges from plain to brightly patterned and may be of various lengths, from thigh to knee to calf. Some urban women now affect a garment remarkably like a Chinese cheongsam, with slit skirt. Also popular is a jacket that comes down to the hips, worn with a matching long skirt. For formal or office wear urban women use a full range of modern female footwear, with either the formal styles just described or a range of Western dresses, even these often modified to local taste. Pantsuits are rare. Recreationally,

Ceremonial barkcloth worn by William and Louisa Nanovo, Vatulele Island, 1993, at the ceremony of recognition by their chiefly clan. Note the virtually identical "unisex" barkcloth *mataisulu tolu* (three-layered skirts). William also wears an *iwābale* sash and an *itini yara* train of red-brown barkcloth, *masi kuvui*, held by an aunt. Photograph by Roderick Ewins.

urbanites may wear T-shirts and jeans, though skirts remain common, more so perhaps than in Western countries.

Trousers (*tarausese*) gradually replaced isulu vakatoga for men, and in the twenty-first century the latter are mainly worn casually in the home or village, in the evening after work, or when sitting and idly talking with friends around the kava bowl. In the village khaki shorts or long trousers and T-shirts are the usual daytime dress, and like women they either go barefoot or wear flip-flops. Where the terrain is harsh, some wear sneakers.

For formal wear the sulu went up-market in the form of a very smart kilt of heavier cloth and with pockets (*sulu vakataga*), buttoned at the waist. For soldiers and policemen the lower edge is cut into a row of triangles to make a very distinctive garment, *isulutavatava*. Worn over underpants (*sapota*) or shorts (in this application called *koniveredi*), with a business shirt and tie, together with a smart (often matching) coat or blazer (*kote*), the sulu vakataga has become for Fijian men a source of as much pride as is a Scotsman's tartan kilt, another "invented tradition." The sandals developed for Fijian policemen to wear (*ivāvā ni ovisa*), with a solid upper and sling back, have become ubiquitous formal men's footwear, particularly with sulu and bare legs. Western suits (*sutu*) and shoes are of course worn by many businessmen. Casual wear for urban youths is generally the same as it is worldwide, T-shirts and jeans, or shirts with trousers or shorts made by local Indian tailors.

Fijian customary bodywear has traveled a long path. There has been profound change and much loss, and there have been unexpected reversals. But change has also thrown up proud new symbols that identify Fijian men and women anywhere they go in the world. While they have accommodated their customs to a global era, their bodywear still proclaims them a proudly unique people, as it always did.

References and Further Reading

Clunie, Fergus. *Yalo i Viti*. Suva: Fiji Museum, 1986.

Clunie, Fergus, and Walesi Ligairi. "Fijian Mutilatory Practices I: Earlobe Slitting and Distortion." *Domodomo: Fiji Museum Quarterly* 1, no. 1 (1983): 22–44.

Clunie, Fergus, and Walesi Ligairi. "Traditional Fijian Spirit Masks and Spirit Masquers." *Domodomo: Fiji Museum Quarterly* 1, no. 2 (1983): 46–71.

Colchester, Chloë. "Objects of Conversion: Concerning the Transfer of Sulu to Fiji." In *The Art of Clothing: A Pacific Experience*, edited by Susanne Küchler and Graeme Were, 33–47. London: UCL Press, 2005.

d'Urville, Dumont, and Jules Sebastien César. *Voyage au Pole Sud et dans l'Oceanie sur l'Astrolabe et La Zélée*. Vol. 1, *Atlas Pittoresque*. Paris: Gide, 1841–1846.

Eagleston, J. H., and J. W. Osborne. "Journal of the Ship 'Emerald' in Fiji. 1834–5." 1833–1836. Pacific Manuscripts Bureau Microfilm #225. Original held in Essex Institute, Salem, MA, The James Duncan Phillips Library.

Ewins, Rod. *Fijian Artefacts: The Tasmanian Museum and Art Gallery Collection*. Hobart, Australia: Tasmanian Museum & Art Gallery, 1982.

Ewins, Rod. *Staying Fijian: Vatulele Island Barkcloth and Social Identity*. Adelaide, Australia, and Honolulu: Crawford House Publishing and University of Hawai'i Press, 2007.

Ewins, Rod. "Fiji Historical Photographs from Rod Ewins's Personal Collection." 2000–2007. http://www.justpacific.com/fiji/fijiphotos/ (accessed 30 July 2008).

Roth, Jane, and Steven Hooper, eds. *The Fiji Journals of Baron Anatole von Hügel*. Suva: Fiji Museum, 1990.

Tischner, Herbert. "Theodor Kleinschmidt's Notes on the Hill Tribes of Viti Levu." *Domodomo: Fiji Museum Quarterly* 2, no. 4 (1984): 145–191.

Wilkes, Captain Charles. *Narrative of the United States Exploring Expedition during the Years 1838–1842*. Vol. 3, *Fiji*. Philadelphia: Lea & Blanchard, 1845.

Williams, Thomas. *Fiji and the Fijians*. Vol. 1, *The Islands and Their Inhabitants*. Suva: Fiji Museum, 1982. (Reprint of original: London: Alexander Heylin, 1858).

Roderick Ewins

See also Missionary Dress in Samoa; Dressing the Body in Samoa; Barkcloth Body Wrapping in Tonga; Bilas: Dressing the Body in Papua New Guinea; Dress in New Caledonia; Body Ornaments of Solomon Islands.

Dress of the Cook Islands

- Dress before European Contact
- European Clothing—Innovation and Incorporation
- Dress and Modernity in the Cook Islands
- Dress and "The Politics of Tradition"
- Snapshot: The Mu'umu'u

Cook Islands dress of the twenty-first century is a vibrant mixture of local, Western, and regional influences. Traces of the islands' missionary and colonial history are also evident and reflect an ongoing incorporation of external styles and aesthetics. Since the Cook Islands gained independence in 1965, the revival of local dress practices of the past has been viewed as an important way of forging an independent nation-state. Traditional dress, primarily worn in performance contexts in the early twenty-first century, has become a key vehicle for debates about the nature of Cook Islands identity, and the islands' authentic national culture and traditions. The social history of Cook Islands dress shows that the concept of tradition, rather than reflecting a timeless, fixed heritage, is a complex term; what constitutes tradition changes along with social and political concerns of specific periods of history and is also shaped by forms of social differentiation such as gender and age.

The Cook Islands are a group of fifteen islands spread over 770,000 square miles. They are named after Captain James Cook, who charted the southern islands in his expeditions of 1773 and 1777 (Aitutaki, Atiu, Mangaia, Manuae, Ma'uke, Mitiaro, Rarotonga, and Takutea make up this group). The southern group primarily consists of volcanic formations with fertile soils and tropical vegetation. The northern group (Manihiki, Nassau, Penrhyn, Pukapuka, Rakahanga, Palmerston, and Suwarrow) are predominantly low-lying coral atolls with lagoons and sparse vegetation. The marked difference in the geography of these two groups has had a large impact on the materials used in the production of clothing.

DRESS BEFORE EUROPEAN CONTACT

While there were noticeable differences in the language and culture of the north and south groups of the Cook Islands, dress played a central role in exhibiting gender difference and status distinctions throughout the islands. As in Polynesia generally, social status was largely ascribed by position in a hereditary, stratified system of paramount chiefs (ariki), lesser chiefs, and titled positions, such as priests and commoners. There is evidence of trade between the two groups and the neighboring Society Islands; pearlshells from the northern islands, for instance, were highly valued in the south and used as ornamentation for significantly ranked individuals.

In the southern group the use of barkcloth as clothing was widespread (it is now commonly known as tapa in the Cook Islands, although the term is nonindigenous). Tapa was principally made by women from paper mulberry bark (Broussonetia papyrifera). It was produced in an extended process of soaking fiber

in seawater, beating it into sheets, and sun-drying it before decoration. Some were partially waterproofed with coconut oil. Men wore tapa as a loincloth (maro) and women wrapped it around their torsos. William Wyatt Gill, an early London Missionary Society (LMS) minister, described this latter garment as a petticoat that an unmarried girl wore above the knee and when married it was brought down below the knee. Cloaks (tikoru) and ponchos (tiputa) were worn by both sexes. The everyday garments of commoners were largely undecorated. By contrast the cloth of chiefs and their families was colored yellow, red, and black through the application of dyes made from various roots and berries.

Chiefly garments commonly had fringed edges and were decorated with stencils of leaves and flowers and geometric designs, either drawn freehand or made by perforating the cloth using the "snowflake" technique of folding and cutting. These designs, and their accompanying status distinctions, were also reproduced in tattooing practice (and in various other material cultural forms such as carving). Male chiefs were the most heavily and elaborately tattooed, from neck to toe. Women were tattooed but more sparsely than men. The designs encompassed geometric and curvilinear shapes and figurative representations of plants, animals, and occasionally humans. Some designs used for tattoos and clothing were also a means of marking tribe membership onto the body; each tribe owned specific motifs, and replication of these was forbidden by outsiders. At the same time, however, innovation and elaboration of particular motifs occurred as new influences were introduced from neighboring tribes and islands.

Further ornamentation included finely plaited lengths of human hair woven around the ankles, wrists, and neck, quantity again indicating rank. As protection from the sun, everyday wear included pare (hats) made from coconut fronds and other leafy plants. These hats were often enhanced with scented flowers and ferns. Single blooms worn behind the ear or through pierced earlobes completed this aesthetic. Coconut oil, scented with flower essences, was applied to the body and the long hair of both men and women, producing a shimmering quality that was much admired.

On festive and ceremonial occasions a wider range of material was employed. Fresh green leaves from the ti plant (Cordyline terminalis) were plaited into skirts (titi). Plaited ti leaves were also used as arm and leg bands and headdresses and were draped across the torso. More permanent skirts and capes were made from treated hibiscus fiber (Hibiscus tiliaceus), pandanus, and dried banana leaves. These were finely decorated with colored seeds and shells. Chiefs' ceremonial garb included precious materials such as large pearlshells fashioned into polished breast ornaments and conical hats made from coiled sennit (cord made from coconut fiber) with colorful bird feathers attached. Red feathers and red dyes were particularly significant additions to chiefly garments.

Barkcloth was not produced in the northern group of islands, as its vegetation lacked the variety of the southern group. The coconut tree was the main source of material for clothing and ornaments. The outer green leaves of the coconut were stripped and plaited into skirts, loincloths, ponchos, and capes, and the young inside leaves soaked, processed, and dried into fine strands of white "straw" (rito) and then assembled into garments. Women

A male dance costume comprised of *maro* (loincloth), pearlshell necklace, *ti* leaf headdress, and plaited pandanus fishing basket, Cook Islands, early twenty-first century. Photograph by Dean Treml.

did not cover their torsos, wearing a short titi as everyday wear and cloaks and capes for festivities. Chiefly status was signified by decoratively woven pandanus waistbands, cloaks, and headdresses made from sennit and feathers. In common with the southern islands, people of the north used shells, flowers, and hair for ornamentation; however, tattooing was not practiced.

Unlike Fiji, Tonga, and Samoa, barkcloth is no longer widely made in the Cook Islands. By the early twentieth century it was only made sporadically throughout the islands, and there is only small-scale barkcloth production on the island of Atiu, principally for the local tourist market. Similarly, garments made from ti leaves and pandanus and coconut fiber were replaced as everyday wear by cotton cloth introduced by travelers and missionaries in the nineteenth century.

EUROPEAN CLOTHING—INNOVATION AND INCORPORATION

European cloth and clothing was not introduced in any sustained manner until members of the LMS began proselytizing in the Cook Islands. In 1821 John Williams landed on Aitutaki, leaving two Society Islander converts to begin teaching Christianity; various other Society Islanders and European pastors followed,

and by 1864 each island of the Cooks group was considered by the LMS to be under Christian influence.

From this time on, concerted effort was made to repress aspects of Cook Islands culture that were considered "heathen." The LMS introduced what they called the blue laws: laws that aimed to transform Cook Islanders' social organization. This included transforming ideas about bodily display and dress. Cook Islanders' clothing was deemed to be inappropriately revealing, and the adoption of European clothing was viewed as visible evidence of interior conversion to more pious and civilized beliefs. Until missionaries had enough cloth to make European-style clothes, they encouraged islanders to clothe themselves "decently" in tiputa (ponchos) at all times. Wearing flowers as adornment, oil on the skin, and tattooing were prohibited as they were seen to be overly sensual forms of adornment. Similarly, dance and ceremonial occasions, for which the most elaborate clothing forms were produced, were repressed by missionaries, as these events were considered either forms of idolatry or debauchery.

As imported cloth became more widely available, it was fashioned into European garments. Women's traditional dress was replaced by "mother hubbards" (now called *mu'umu'u*), long gowns reaching from neck to ankle. Trousers, shirts, and coats were introduced for men. As well as being introduced to European clothes, men's hair (previously worn long) was cut short in European style, and women's long hair was required to be tied back in buns. The LMS also aimed at establishing what they considered to be productive activity among locals and making missions economically self-sufficient. To this end, John Williams in 1833 brought spinning wheels, a warping machine, and a loom, in order that Rarotongan women could begin production of their own cloth and clothes.

The LMS's aim of producing devout and somber individuals was countered somewhat by the uses to which locals put their new European clothing. Pastors complained that some chiefly women attended church in luxurious ball gowns with lace and satin detailing, parasols, and decorative bonnets. Ranked men also adopted European clothing, particularly naval and military uniforms, as new ways of expressing their political power. These images suggest that in the absence of traditional clothing, titled individuals sought to utilize European clothing to express their authority.

It was not until the British made the Cook Islands a protectorate in 1888 that the islands of the north and south were grouped together as the Cook Islands. They were then annexed to New Zealand in 1901. During the New Zealand Colonial period (1901–1965) efforts to Europeanize Cook Islanders continued, although the bans on some local practices were relaxed to some extent. Officially sanctioned displays of Cook Islands culture took place for occasions such as the visits of New Zealand dignitaries, Commonwealth events, and Christmas celebrations. Certain costumes thought to be traditional were made for dancing. These were now not worn against bare skin as in the past, but over European clothing, to conform to prevailing Christian norms of modesty. These costumes and other locally made items such as mats and fans were presented as gifts to official visitors.

The introduction of European clothing affected practices of both localization and accommodation to the foreign ideological influences introduced by the LMS and British and New Zealand colonizers. European materials were incorporated into Cook

Islanders' wardrobes to express traditional status hierarchies and new identities that became available through the acquisition of European skills and education.

DRESS AND MODERNITY IN THE COOK ISLANDS

Cook Islands dress and performance costume of the twenty-first century is modern clothing but retains aspects of its pre-European forms. It bears the influences of both the missionary and Colonial periods. Cook Islanders wear a variety of clothing—now generically called *kāka'u*, the Cook Islands Māori word (the language of the Cook Islands) for clothing—that is classified as traditional, island-style (influenced by other nations of the Pacific region, particularly Samoa and Tahiti) and *papa'a* (European clothes). The style of clothing worn is largely determined by age, gender, and status, and also by type of occasion.

In 2007 around twelve thousand of the fifteen thousand resident Cook Islanders were living on the island of Rarotonga, the islands' administrative capital. Due to limited employment opportunities, the majority of Cook Islanders, an estimated seventy thousand, were living abroad, primarily in New Zealand, Australia, and North America. Cook Islanders are highly mobile, frequently traveling to and from the Cook Islands for business, education, and family matters. This mobility and the large tourist industry (concentrated in the southern group) means there is a flow of ideas, images, and materials from the West, other Pacific nations, and diasporic Cook Islander communities. Twenty-first-century Cook Islands dress is a dynamic composite of these various influences.

The tourist industry and the public service employ the majority of Cook Islanders, and it is commonplace for employees of both to wear island-style garments. Island print material (called *pareu*) is cotton fabric covered with brightly colored flower, leaves, and geometric patterns. These designs have formal similarities with designs found on early barkcloth and tattooing, and other material culture forms such as carving and *tivaevae* (embroidered quilts). Women wear island print dresses or skirts and tops and men wear island print shirts with shorts or trousers. Many workplaces, banks, restaurants, hotels, and supermarkets have pareu material uniforms. Both women and men will often wear a fragrant flower (*poi*) behind their ear.

On formal occasions, ranging from government functions to school presentation nights, island-style clothing is also the most common clothing choice. Many women wear long mu'umu'u dresses made from pareu material, and men wear island shirts from the same fabric and dark trousers. Those who can afford it purchase these outfits from local fashion designers, who screen print and design them. Sweet-smelling floral headdresses ('ei katu) or floral necklaces ('ei kaki) complete this formal attire. They are made primarily from gardenia, frangipani, and green foliage. Black pearl necklaces, rings, and earrings, cultivated in the northern group and in the Society Islands, are also popular among Cook Islands women.

Clothing is still used to signify chiefly or titled status. This is most obvious in ceremonial situations such as chiefly investitures. However, in everyday contexts high-ranked individuals may wear all-white clothing to signify their status, shirts and trousers for men and long white dresses for women.

Church attendance and related religious events are undertaken by the majority of Cook Islanders. At the Cook Islands Christian Church (the descendant of LMS Protestantism), island print dresses and shirts are worn to church services (although more subdued colors and patterns than everyday garments are chosen). European clothes, long skirts and loose shirts for women, are also acceptable. A distinctive aspect of church dress is the hats women wear. These are often handwoven from rito, the young shoots of coconut palms, with polished pearlshell insets. Rito hats, fans, and purses are made primarily by women from the islands of Manihiki and Penrhyn in the northern group.

It is primarily teenagers that choose to wear European-style clothing such as jeans, shorts, singlet tops, and T-shirts. T-shirts are a clear amalgamation of local and European aesthetics. The T-shirt, as a global clothing form, is overlaid with images and text that engage with issues of Cook Islands identity, issues of place, kinship, and belonging. A number of retail outfits print lettering and designs on T-shirts for the local and tourist markets. The locally brewed beer, Cooks Lager, has an image of Captain Cook as its logo, and it is found on the bottle labels and on a T-shirt that is a popular purchase for tourists and locals alike.

Many T-shirts feature place names, such as "Aitutaki 07" and "Ma'uke Island Girl," and Polynesian design motifs; others depict the heroic deeds of Polynesian warriors and gods (these are particularly popular with young Cook Islands men). T-shirts are also used to depict local events and issues. Groups traveling for sports and dance events have T-shirts made up as a collective uniform to advertise the purpose of the trip and the groups' island or village of origin. As Cook Islands' extended families are spread across the diaspora, family reunions are commonly held as a way to reunite members and for important family events. Large numbers of family members who travel abroad or to the family's island of origin have T-shirts with lettering proclaiming their purpose, such as "Tunui Family Reunion 07." This text is

Woman dancers wearing *pareu* skirts, coconut bras, and shell necklaces, Cook Islands, early twenty-first century. Photograph by Dean Treml.

accompanied by images of coconuts, local flowers, and Polynesian designs.

At home Cook Islands men and women wear light cotton sarongs (also called pareu) tied at the waist by men and around the chest for women. At the beach women may wear a pareu tied around her torso over her bikini. This is because to display the upper thigh is considered immodest. Long shorts fulfill a similar function.

DRESS AND "THE POLITICS OF TRADITION"

In 1965 the Cook Islands became self-governing in "free association" with New Zealand. The associated state relationship means that Cook Islanders have local political autonomy, but automatic entry to and citizenship status in New Zealand. New Zealand provides aid and handles foreign affairs and defense in consultation with the Cook Islands government. Since independence there has been a renaissance in the production of indigenous garments, particularly for ceremonial, performance, and festive contexts.

Clothing designated as "traditional" is worn primarily in ceremonial contexts, such as chiefly investitures, and as part of dance performances, which take place for tourists and at local festivities. Tapa is still central to the investiture of chiefs. It is imported from Tonga and Samoa and then fashioned into three ceremonially significant garments: a *marokura* (waistband), *pā'oa* (tapa dress), and tiputa (poncho). The chief is carried on a platform to the *marae* (sacred site) in a garment of plaited ti leaves. There he or she is undressed and during a series of chants invested with each item of tapa clothing and, finally, a sennit hat (*pare ariki*). Tapa is also used in a performance genre called *pe'e* (chant), performed during significant national occasions, to welcome important guests, and in historical plays.

The costumes worn in performance contexts share much in common with pre-European dress. For fast drum dances (*ura pa'u*) both men and women wear *pareu kiri'au* (grass skirts). These are dyed various colors and decorated with shells, tassels, and decorative waistbands. Women's skirts reach to the knee, or most commonly the ankle, with a decorative titi over the top, which serves to emphasize hip movements, a distinctive component of the female dance style. Men's grass skirts are knee-length, as the feature of their dance is scissor-like leg actions. This movement is further accentuated by leg bands of the same material tied mid-calf. Plaited headbands, often with pearlshell features, are also common. While men's chests are bare, women mainly wear a coconut bra, a neo-traditional item that was probably introduced from Tahiti, the Cook Islands' closest neighbor. For slower, action songs (*kaparima*), performed by women, their costumes are usually a long pareu, titi, and headdress made from ti leaves adorned with fresh flowers. Both male and female dancers oil their skin to make it gleam while they perform, and the combination of fragrant oil, fresh scented flowers, and leaves adds to the aesthetics of the performance. Within these broad costume types there is considerable experimentation with new materials, colors, and designs. Innovation is highly valued, and popular new styles are readily copied by others. Inspiration for new costume designs come from studying early European missionaries and researchers' texts, dance costume fashions from Tahiti, and trends from other Cook Islands.

It is around dance costumes that ideas about tradition and cultural authenticity are passionately debated. In the Cook Islands, as throughout much of the Pacific, the revival of cultural practices viewed as traditional accompanied decolonization. One early initiative was a national festival of dance, which brought teams from all of the islands to compete as part of annual independence celebrations. Since its inception in 1966 this dance festival (now called *Te Maeva Nui*, the Big Festival) has been surrounded by public contestation about the nature of Cook Islands customs. The conflict tends to crystallize around dance costumes, particularly female ones, demonstrating how dress is often a potent vehicle for contesting values about the past, cultural identities in the present, gender, and morality. For example, while the coconut bra is, in the early twenty-first century, considered a traditional item on most of the islands, dance teams from the northern islands have queried the traditional nature of this item. They prefer their female dancers to perform in tops made from cloth or fiber, as they view the coconut bra as too revealing and hence compromising of the social standing of their female dancers.

What constitutes traditional Cook Islands costuming is also contested along generational lines. Older Cook Islanders always insist that it is traditional for female grass skirts to sit high on the waist, and that dancers who wear them below the navel are ignoring the past and are overtly sexualizing their dance practice. In contrast, younger performers argue that the older generation still has a missionary mindset with their concerns about covering up female bodies. Members of this younger generation suggest they are returning to the original spirit of Cook Islands dance customs, a dance practice free from the moral restrictions imposed throughout the islands' missionary and colonial history.

While the line between traditional and nontraditional is malleable and contested, there has been a process of traditionalization that began in the Cook Islands after independence in 1965. Particularly in the last twenty years there has been a move toward using natural materials and objects to create both ceremonial and performance costumes. Raffia grass skirts and plastic flowers that were popular in the 1950s and 1960s have been replaced with natural fibers, seeds, shells, and fresh flowers. This trend toward traditionalization is also evident in everyday dress. Increasingly, young fashion is not based on European clothing but on local and pan-Polynesian styles. Pareu material dresses, island shirts, and sarongs are becoming more popular as everyday wear. Handbags and purses woven from pandanus were, until recently, only purchased as souvenirs by tourists. Today, fashionable young women would not be seen without one.

The shifts in Cook Islands clothing styles both reflect the influence of historical forces and attest to the ongoing creative and novel approach Cook Islanders take to their dress. While missionary and colonial administrators sought to impose European clothing as a mark of civilization and modernity respectively, Cook Islanders took up these foreign forms in unpredictable ways. They were both incorporated into existing forms of social distinction and used to display new forms of wealth and status. Contemporary Cook Islands society is similarly reassembling cloth, design, and adornment in ways that move beyond the simple categorization of traditional or modern, European or Cook Islands dress. Clothing remains a vital and vibrant local practice of identity construction and expression.

Snapshot: The Mu'umu'u

From the mid-nineteenth century missionaries introduced dresses to Pacific communities worn by European women at the time. These have been called "mother hubbards," a name that most probably derives from the illustrations from the poem "Old Mother Hubbard" (by Sarah Catherine Martin, published in 1805). They were long, loose-fitting, with full sleeves and a high, yoked neckline and were made from dark materials for weekdays and white for Sunday church. The mother hubbard reflected the Victorian sensibilities of missionaries and their belief that the adoption of modest clothing by indigenous groups was a sign of civilized Christian behavior. In the twenty-first century variations of mother hubbards are worn throughout the Pacific. In Papua New Guinea they are called *meri blouse*, in Vanuatu *islan dress*, and *mu'umu'u* in Hawai'i and the Society and Cook Islands. Everyday mu'umu'u have shorter hemlines and sleeve lengths to suit the tropical climate. Dour colors of the past have now been replaced with bright floral and decorative Polynesian motif prints. Bell-shaped mu'umu'u with puff sleeves, frilled hems, and lace trimmings are particularly worn by *mama*—women over the age of fifty; however, younger women are increasingly wearing more fitted versions of mu'umu'u to work instead of European-style sundresses.

Rather than viewing the mu'umu'u as an antiquated leftover from the missionary era, this item of clothing is a clear example of innovation and incorporation of European fashion into local fashion and aesthetics. The mu'umu'u now has the status of national dress in the Cook Islands and elsewhere in the Pacific. As part of the annual *Tiare* (flower) Festival, a Mama's Mu'umu'u Competition is held, where older women parade their new hand-sewn mu'umu'u to a large and appreciative audience. For official formal occasions young women wear dressy mu'umu'u. These are often purchased from Cook Islands designers and are usually floor-length, fitted to the body, and with detailed ruffles. Design details follow both Western and regional Polynesian fashion, particularly trends in Tahiti. Young women also perform solo dances in these dresses at formal occasions such as government events, or important birthdays of family members. These contemporary mu'umu'u comply with Cook Islands conventions of modesty by covering thighs but are nevertheless striking and sensual—a far remove from the versions promoted by missionaries.

References and Further Reading

Alexeyeff, Kalissa. *Dancing from the Heart: Movement, Gender and Cook Islands Globalization*. Honolulu: University of Hawai'i Press, 2009.

Bolton, Lissant. "Gender, Status and Introduced Clothing in Vanuatu." In *Clothing the Pacific*, edited by Chloë Colchester, 119–139. Oxford and New York: Berg, 2003.

Gill, William Wyatt. *The South Pacific and New Guinea Past and Present: With Notes on the Hervey Group, and Illustrative Song and Various Myths*. Sydney: Government Printer, 1892.

Gilson, Richard. *The Cook Islands 1820–1950*. Edited by R. Crocombe. Wellington, NZ, and Suva, Fiji: Victoria University Press in association with the Institute of Pacific Studies, University of the South Pacific, 1980.

Hiroa, Te Rangi (Sir Peter Buck). *The Material Culture of the Cook Islands (Aitutaki)*. Memoirs of the Board of Ethnological Research. Vol. 1. New Plymouth: Thomas Avery and Sons, 1927.

Hiroa, Te Rangi (Sir Peter Buck). *Arts and Crafts of the Cook Islands*. Bulletin 179. Honolulu: Bernice Pauahi Bishop Museum, 1944.

Küchler, Susanne. "The Poncho and the Quilt: Material Christianity in the Cook Islands." In *Clothing the Pacific*, edited by Chloë Colchester, 97–116. Oxford and New York: Berg, 2003.

Küchler, Susanne, and Graeme Were, eds. *The Art of Clothing: A Pacific Experience*. London: UCL Press, 2005.

Lamont, E. H. *Wild Life among the Pacific Islanders*. London: Hurst and Blackett Publishers, 1867.

Thomas, Nicholas. "The Case of the Misplaced Ponchos: Speculations Concerning the History of Cloth in Polynesia." *Journal of Material Culture* 4, no. 1 (1999): 5–21.

Kalissa Alexeyeff

See also Hawaiian Dress Prior to 1898; Dance Costumes in French Polynesia; Dress and Appearance in Tahiti; Dress in Kiribati.

PART 12

Melanesia

Bilas: Dressing the Body in Papua New Guinea

- Codes and Contexts of Bilas
- Headdresses and Wigs for Bilas
- Masks
- Colonial Influences on Bilas
- The Emergence of New Bilas
- Bilumwear

Papua New Guinea is a nation of some six million people in the twenty-first century and lies at the western end of the Pacific Ocean, north of Australia. It is the eastern half of the whole island of New Guinea, which is the second-largest island in the world after Greenland. It gained political independence from Australia in 1975. The nation has always both intrigued and fascinated people with one unusual factor: There are over eight hundred distinct languages spoken. This is an indication of the many different and unique cultural groups, each with their own forms of dress, who laid claim to the various parts of the country and called it home for thousands of years. Each cultural group had its own language, history, knowledge, and art practices. Artists within these cultures—both men and women—were responsible for distinctive designs, patterns, songs, dances, and stories.

The various communities embellished their bodies as part of normal everyday life, and for their many elaborate ceremonies and rituals. Influenced by the environment, its resources, and their worldview, attaching objects, tattoos, and cicatrices on various portions of the body, swathing it with oil and ocher colors, plus wearing of spectacular headdresses and masks were ways through which people of these different cultures expressed themselves. This self-adornment, or *bilas* as it is termed in Pidgin (New Guinea Creole, a mixture of English, German, and local dialect words first used during the Colonial era), is both widespread and varied over the area. Some broad areas of bilas will be discussed and specific examples drawn from various parts of the country. These include: *bilasim sikin* (the body as a site for embellishment); headdresses and masks for bilas; colonial influences on bilas; and, *bilumwear*—the emergence of new bilas.

The abundance of plant and animal life in the tropics meant that the natural environment provided a rich source for communities to use a variety of plants and animals to make their bilas. Bark from selected trees, leaves from coconut and sago palms and banana plants, selected bamboo plants, fiber from the pith of plants including sago palm, seedpods from plants, and flowers of many different plants all provided a multitude of different bilas for communities. Birds offered the most opportunities. Feathers and bones were gathered from egrets, parrots, lorikeets, eagles, owls, cassowaries, and the different types of birds of paradise. The plumes of the birds of paradise were considered highly valuable and were most widespread for bilas. In the twenty-first century this bird is stylized in the national crest. Teeth from dogs, curved boar tasks, fur from marsupials, skins from lizards and marsupials, and pig tails were also considered valuable and made into some of the most stunning bilas. From the sea, different types of coral and shells were gathered. Carefully cut and shaped by craftspersons, these were transformed into fine articles to wear and to decorate the body.

Changes in self-embellishment have always been a part of communities. New visions and ideas emerged among the makers of bilas through dreams, revelations, and other encounters, leading to a readjustment of the old and familiar ways or the emergence of completely new designs and types of dress. The arrival of Europeans in Papua New Guinea from the early 1800s was one most notable encounter that affected the various cultures and their bilas, both for everyday wear and special occasions. Some of the old ways were lost and then forgotten. Others, quite remarkably, have survived. People have also taken up new and different bilas without hesitation. In bilas loss, continuity and the emergence of the new provide interesting and challenging horizons on the cultural landscape. It is very clear that discussion under the rubric "bilas" is a complex field, so several themes will be identified, but to account for all the cultures and their ways of self-embellishment is not possible.

The multitude of ways in which the different cultures in the country accessed bilas from the environment was a significant point in how the different communities viewed the world and lived within it. In each there were specific values, beliefs, and histories that underpinned peoples' ways of accessing materials for bilas. Stories and myths informed views about plants and animals, and because of these the colors, designs and patterns, and objects created from them had specific meanings and values. The relationship between communities and the environment stressed cooperation and coexistence. There was an intricate and interconnected cosmos of people and nature as a rich source of bilas, which gave people an important sense of being meaningful and productive members of their world.

CODES AND CONTEXTS OF BILAS

All the many different cultures in Papua New Guinea, in a variety of ways and for different occasions, decorated the body. Distinctive designs and patterns from a diverse range of material were used to adorn men, women, and children. In everyday life the bilas that was worn by members of communities was quite different from those types used for ceremonies and festivities. The special occasions included situations where new life was welcomed to the community, coming of age, marriage, peacemaking, and mortuary ceremonies. The preparation and use of material from the local environment—animal skin, fur, teeth, feathers, and bones—for the various items that were designed and put together showed remarkable attention to detail and deftness. Some bilas were made by men, some were the exclusive zone of women. For certain occasions with some cultural groups dress for women was prepared by women only, as was the case for men. With other groups such practices did not matter greatly: Some bilas, while they might have been made by men or women, were worn by both. Often the separation of making of bilas was determined by the community's intentions and plans for the ceremony.

Simbu women of Papua New Guinea waiting for *singsing*, in full regalia for a celebration. The Princess Stephanie bird of paradise feathers and shells are considered very valuable. Different communities get together to present their festive dress at annual events like the Hagen, Goroka, Lae, and Port Moresby Shows, which have been running regularly since the 1960s. Photograph by Mark Eby.

Fine and intricate in construction, bilas were worn by men and women of all ages on various parts of the body. Children were given little trinkets like beads and rings to wear. As they grew into young men and women, the head, nose, ears, hair, neck, arms, fingers, ankles, and toes were sites for embellishment. There were different kinds of bilas: those that were for everyday wear, and others for elaborate ceremonial occasions. Bilas as an everyday affair referred to modifications of the body that were permanent. Physical changes to the skin and parts of the body were significant aspects of bilas bestowed upon young men and women when initiated into the communities, and for mortuary ceremonies. Then there was bilas for other ceremonies, including birth, marriage, and peacemaking. The latter was often made by specialists with specific skills and knowledge and required time both to gather and prepare materials and to construct. These included elaborate masks, feathers, oils, tapa cloth, and net bags (*bilums*) made from bark. For safekeeping they were kept in homes or specially constructed places. There were also beads, wristbands, ankle-bands, armlets, and headbands made from shells, seed pods, insects, animal teeth, and bones. Often parents and relatives would pass the bilas to their children to wear and keep. Complementary to bilas that were made, used, and kept were other types usually gathered and created for the occasion and discarded soon after the event. Intense and striking, and displayed for very brief time, these included ocher and ash-based colors for face and body painting, oils and fragrances, and an assortment of plant material. Some of these processes of bilas were very intricate and elaborate.

A common approach for people to identify where a person or group of people belongs is often their bilas; what they wear may represent (for the viewer as well for the wearer) where they come from and set them apart from others. This is often a simple and convenient way to use bilas and is a cultural practice used to identify and categorize people. However, culture here is also defined as the way the world is made sense of and given meaning by people. Individuals belong to and associate with others in a group; what each member sees and makes sense of within the self and with others is through a shared system of meaning. With this concept of culture bilas is a window into a myriad world, a code system of meanings and a physical indication of what lies deep within people. Since bilas is an activity engaged in by people, a particular people's bilas cannot be treated as mere objects. Objects do not possess meaning; meaning is given by people, and meaning is certain to change as people come into contact with others and their ways of making sense of things. In sum, any talk about bilas needs to be closely linked to an understanding of how a people makes meaningful the world around them.

One method of doing this is through bilasim sikin, or embellishment of the body. Tattooing is the most recognized method of decorating the body for the lifetime of an individual in Papua New Guinea, as well as within the Pacific. The process of creating tattoos was long and often painful. Sharp, delicately prepared needles were used to pinprick skin surfaces with clan designs, either from head to toe or on parts of the body, and locally prepared charcoal-like dyes were allowed to permeate the perforated skin surface. These, when cured, formed darkened patterns on the body. The provinces of Oro and Central have been notable for decorating entire bodies of young females with designs that belonged to their communities to form very elaborate, fine tattoos. In other parts tattoos were discreetly put on the forehead or at the corners of the eyes and along the arms. In areas of the Central Highlands young women had their entire faces decorated with tattoos. In communities along the Sepik River young men had incisions made to form neat rows on the upper part of the body trunk on the front and the back. The incisions were cured using locally prepared substances that left raised skin surfaces to form patterns on the body. Other cultures perforated, enlarged, and elongated parts of the body, including ear lobes, nasal septums, toes, and fingers.

In the Morobe Province the earlobe was perforated and then elongated in order to wind it around the ear. Sometimes it was allowed to hang to reach as far as the shoulders. Other times decorated bones, animal fur or feathers, and treated parts of plants were inserted into the prepared earlobes. In the inland and mountainous regions of the highlands of Western and West Sepik Provinces, the nostril cones were incised and cured to insert black pin-like feathers from the cassowary bird. The nasal septum was also pierced, and small decorated bamboo pipes were inserted and worn. In fact, modifying the earlobes and the nasal septum was common in and around the mainland of New Guinea. These processes of shaping or reshaping the body and parts of it were often marked as rites of passage, a point of transition from childhood to adulthood. Once endured successfully, the individual felt connected to and was accepted by others as a member of the group. All cultures in Papua New Guinea recognized the body to be a site for embellishment. They also believed that a body so finely decorated and attuned for a person in the community elevated and celebrated the human qualities of endurance, stamina, and beauty.

HEADDRESSES AND WIGS FOR BILAS

A striking feature of bilas has been the range and variety of elaborate headdresses, masks, and physical structures constructed and worn by performers during special occasions. The wigs and structures of Highlanders, including the *peng koiim* of the mid-Wahgi and the *kanggar* of the Bena, the male headdresses of Morobe and Siassi Island, the head and body masks of the Ramu and Sepik regions, the Tubuan, Dukduk, and Baining head and body masks of East New Britain, the Malangan masks of New Ireland, the Upe hats of Bougainville, the spectacular platforms of bird of paradise plumage for headdresses of the Mekeo in Central Province, the body masks of the Papuan Gulf, and the physical structures worn by dancers in Gogodala and Kiwai cultures of the Western Province all indicate the sweeping variety of these

The Asaro Mudmen of Papua New Guinea. Their masks are constructed with mud layered on a framework that covers the face. The rest of the body is covered in mud, and the dancers (all male) move around gently waving their fingers, as if they were brushing away flies. There is no singing or music accompaniment. Performances sometimes take place at events like the Hagen, Goroka, Lae, and Port Moresby Shows, first convened in the 1960s. Photograph by Augustine Dominic.

customs in the country. Makers of these masks and headdresses were artists of renown in each community. Prior to a major event the artists were commissioned to prepare the masks and headdresses. A selection of plant, animal, and human-derived material was collected, and construction often involved specific knowledge and skills and followed set rituals. The artists deftly transformed the collection into some of the most spectacular and sublime bilas for the grand occasions that were part of the rich patchwork of cultures in the country.

The Highlands region has been noted for the wigs that have been worn by men in everyday wear and during special ceremonies by both men and women. As boys grew into men, the transition was usually marked by the wearing of a wig. For special ceremonies the Southern Highlands, Enga, and Western Highlands Provinces were home to three distinctive yet related styles of wigs. The base of the wig was usually made to conform to the size of a dancer's head, and specially selected dried flowers, which were easy to ply together, provided a round and slightly elongated "ball." Upon this ball of dried flowers, human hair was knitted in to form a circular platform. Another type of platform was more elongated, into an oblong shape with a flat top of some sixty to seventy centimeters (twenty-four to twenty-eight inches) in length. The rest tapered onto the head in the shape of the upper end of a funnel. Both types of wigs of dried flowers and human hair were kept intact with small woven net bags inserted on the wig from the top with its neck to reach around the back and front of the head. Some good length of woven twine was used to fasten the wig onto the head by tying the open ends of the net bag round the head. Once completed, the wigs became platforms for some of the most elaborate headdresses, made up of bird feathers, marsupial fur, leaves, flowers, insects, and assorted shells, beads, and bones. Toward the easterly part of the Highlands, including the mid-Wahgi area of the Western Highlands, and the Simbu and Eastern Highlands provinces, the wigs were not so pronounced. However, the selection and arrangement of feathers, predominantly parrot, lorikeet, and Princess Stephanie bird of paradise feathers for the smaller wigs, provided for an elaborate affair for both male and female dancers.

MASKS

Masks were also an elemental part of bilas in Papua New Guinea. In the Highlands the unique mask was from the Asaro area in the Eastern Highlands. The headpiece was constructed predominantly of special clay pasted on a structure. A face was created with rather large eye sockets and holes for the ears, an exaggerated nose, and a deformed mouth. Around the mouth were planted pigs' teeth and tusks, while shell shaped like a thumbnail was hung through the nose, creating a rather menacing and at the same time petrified look on the mask. Once the masks were donned, the rest of the bodies were washed with the same clay, and the male dancers moved silently and deliberately, with arm actions that looked as if they were brushing away flies. Sometimes sharpened bamboo ends were inserted on the fingers to elongate them. The first-ever mud masks, according to legendary tales recounted by the elders of the clan that owned them, were created to reclaim their land back from an enemy tribe that had once chased them off it. Masks from other cultures, including the middle Sepik, the Dukduk, and the Tubuan, were usually carved and shaped out of soft wood, or woven using cured material,

including cane and bamboo. Upon the foundation holes for eyes were made or woven balls, and elongated proboscises were attached. Palm fronds and leaves from specific plants were also attached. Ocher colors were used to paint the masks, which were decorated with feathers, shells, and other ornaments attached around the edges.

The Mekeo and other cultures of the Central Province have been noted, among other cultures, including Goroka in the Highlands, the Gogodala in the Gulf, Bainings in East New Britain, Malangan in New Ireland, and the East Sepik regions, for their intricate headdresses for male dancers. In the Central Province, for the Mekeo and other cultures, while the female headdress was small yet very intricate, the male structure worn on the head was quite striking. The headpiece was shaped in a half circle with a diameter of about 1.5 meters (about 4.9 feet) and with pliable and sturdy material like cane. The central portion of the structure had on it a blazon of patterns plaited with bark and twine and hand-drawn ocher designs. A large collection of the Raggiana bird of paradise plumes bordered the fringes of the half-moon structure. Emerging from the center and through the middle of the half-moon structure, past the plumes for another meter (3.2 feet) above the dancer, would be a small stick richly decorated and a lone plume or feather that would bob back and forth as the dancer moved. The entire structure was attached to the head and around the shoulders of the male dancer. A female dancer sometimes danced behind the male, holding onto a small cord attached to the highest part of the main headdress. The dance movements were slow and deliberate, with light steps and a slight movement of the head and shoulders back and forth. Because of the immensity of the headdress, any slight movement of the body would send the lone feather quivering back and forth. A sea of male dancers would take small steps forward and back, accompanied by rhythms obtained by striking a taut reptile skin that covered one end of a hollowed wooden drum. Female dancers with small headdresses behind the male dancers would sing and sway to songs, making the performances real spectacles.

Painted faces were also notable in many cultures in Papua New Guinea. Decorating the body with color ranged from a general smearing of the body with clay, ocher, or seed-based colors to meticulous designs painted on the body. The face was the most prominent site, and the painting was very intricate and elaborate, because of the range and variety of delicate patterns and colors used. Special oils and fragrances derived from plants were also rubbed on the bodies in order to transform them into an intoxicating site of rich patterns, dazzling colors, and enthralling aromas for both performer and onlooker. The Highlands region from as far south as the Southern Highlands and east toward the Simbu was most noted for facial designs. Here customary colors of white, black, red, and yellow were used, obtained mostly from ochers. During special ceremonies both male and female dancers had their faces painted with customary patterns. Among the Mekeo in the Central Province the immense headdresses were accompanied by some of the most intricate and elaborate facial decorations for both men and women. Dominant colors were yellow and red. Lines of yellow followed the contours of the face, starting just below the eyes and running down to the jaw. Red was placed between the lines of yellow and circled areas around the eyes and the tip of the nose. In the Highlands, especially the Southern Highlands, in parts of the Huli, the face was graced with yellow, and red dots and circles were placed under the eyes

Hagen Dancers putting the final touches on their faces. The three men are preparing to go to a celebration requiring informal attendance attire, as shown by the pompom feathers on the wig platforms made of cassowary and parrot feathers. The formal decorations are much more elaborate affairs. Papua New Guinea, late twentieth century. Photograph by Mark Eby.

and on the bridge of the nose. The Melpa in the Hagen area of the Western Highlands used a combination of red, yellow, black, and white color. In the Enga area of the Highlands black was very prominent, especially for the face, with white interspersed in a single line that went below the eyes, over the bridge of the nose, and one line down the nose. It was the custom to obtain the black from pulverized charcoal mixed with oil or fat, and the white, red, and yellow from clay.

Many of the cultures described constructed platforms for a range of feathers worn on wigs and structures, and faces were meticulously decorated, transforming the dancers into stunning creatures with movements that were quite elegant and graceful—like the male birds of paradise in full courting ritual.

COLONIAL INFLUENCES ON BILAS

Early European explorers and missionaries who arrived on the shores of Papua New Guinea were both amused and appalled at the way the people were dressed. Women were scantily clad with grass skirts, men with penis gourds or thin barkcloths to cover their private parts, while children ran around naked. In the eyes of the Europeans these people were primitives and savages. Pierced earlobes and nasal septums with bones and various odd

objects put through them and an assortment of necklaces, armbands, and anklets made from beads and bones further convinced the Europeans that the people possessed very little of what they viewed as sensible dress, and that they therefore had virtually no idea of personal dignity and social civility.

Members of the indigenous communities were filled with fear, curiosity, and wonder in those early encounters with the Europeans. Drawn by these feelings, they hung around from a distance and gradually moved closer to look at the new arrivals in their strange-looking dress and paraphernalia. In order to make contact with the local people, the explorers and missionaries began to offer them various kinds of trinkets, salt, tobacco, tools, and fashion items including cloth, parasols, hats, mirrors, and trinkets of shells and beads. Initially the new and different shapes, colors, and tastes were viewed with suspicion, but as the locals realized these were harmless they hastily grabbed the new things and tried them for themselves. Demonstrations, tastings, and modeling between the two groups made for rather novel and amusing encounters. During this time the explorers set up camps and outposts and claimed everything that lived and moved in the new lands for their kingdoms and duchies back home. Filled with the agenda of pacification, the "primitives and savages" were forced to discard their ways and take on the new.

Plantation workers in Papua New Guinea in the 1950s were forced to discard their traditional dress and made to wear *laplap*, a simple knee-length cotton cloth garment. Men from various parts of the country were rounded up and brought to plantations; because of their different cultures and dress, the *laplap* was given out to them to wear for purposes, it was said, of human dignity, hygiene, control, and identification. Unknown photographer. Collection of Michael Mel.

The *laplap* was one of the earliest forms of colonial bilas that was imposed on the local people (especially men). It comprised a knee-length cloth made of cotton (often white and plain) a little over a meter (3.2 feet) long and was worn by wrapping it around the waist. Sometimes leather belts were handed out, and these helped to fasten and hold the laplap in place. After claiming land and making an outpost the colonial masters recruited young men to work as tea-boys, cleaners, and gardeners (*hausboi*), and the laplap was the most common apparel worn by them. Carriers (*kagoboi*) went on patrol with colonial administrators, often tracking great distances into new areas, to establish further outposts and recruit itinerant workers (*wokboi*) to work on coconut, tea, coffee, and rubber plantations set up by colonial entrepreneurs. The workers termed kagobois, wokbois, and *bushkanaka* (*kanaka* was a derogatory colonial term for local people), and their group leaders, known as *bosboi*, were easily recognizable by the laplaps they wore. The early native policemen (*polisboi*) recruited by the colonial administrators were given a dark blue laplap with a red strip on one edge and a large leather belt as their uniform. Later some of the policemen were also given a V-neck shirt and a beret to wear as part of the uniform. Local interpreters (*tanimtok*), who served as vital links for communication between the indigenous people and colonial masters, were fitted out in similar attire. Some men in the villages who became leaders of communities, then known as *luluais* and *tultuls*, were also given laplaps and caps, which they wore in and around the villages to instill the new rules and regulations.

Missionaries persuaded local people to turn from their old ways to the new. Some of the locals were recruited as evangelists to work with the missionaries, and these early church workers were given white laplaps to wear. They helped to teach the early missionaries the local language, and gradually Bible stories, prayers, and hymns were translated into the local language. A visible mark of conversion to Christianity was the wearing of new bilas as a mark of the change. After baptism the early converts were given rosaries, crucifixes, and small silver medals with images of saints to be worn around the neck. A piece of white material was worn as laplap. The women, along with the laplap, were told to cover themselves with a waist-length top that had a round neck, and usually long sleeves, but their garments were sometimes short-sleeved or even sleeveless.

THE EMERGENCE OF NEW BILAS

Arising from colonial influences, what has become a "national" bilas is worn in the twenty-first century, which includes the laplap and the *meriblaus* (a short-sleeved, round-neck blouse for women derived from European dress). In the context of its diverse cultures and communities, the laplap and meriblaus have a unique place as a Papua New Guinean mode of everyday bilas. They are made by mothers in their homes with readily available manual sewing machines from different kinds of imported fabric (plain colored or printed and mostly polyester and cotton). They are sold in shops and on street corners. In rural and semiurban areas women wear the meriblaus and laplap, while the men have moved to shorts, trousers, and shirts as conventional bilas. For Papua New Guineans in urban areas more and more styles of fashion have become options, through various media and travel overseas. The question of what to wear has become a matter of choice: jeans, skirts, shorts, and trousers, and a range of shirts, jackets, and other tops provide a plethora of introduced clothing. In this context emerging secondhand clothing companies (importing secondhand stock from Australia) have turned into thriving businesses. In the face of this fashion evolution the meriblaus and laplap continue to be worn. Men, and women especially, wear these garments on special occasions. In so doing, the laplap and meriblaus, which had their birth in the days of the luluai, tultul, tanimtok, bosboi, polisboi, kagoboi, hausboi, and bushkanka, have found a niche as the national bilas for Papua New Guinea.

The bilas of the past is no longer visible except in pictures and books. Sometimes, on special celebratory occasions, members of a community get together to present their bilas at annual events like the Hagen, Goroka, Lae, and Port Moresby Shows. What is interesting during these events is that with cultural change, many customary items of bilas have been replaced with modern materials. For example, the face paints are made up of an array of water-based colors. Blue and green, among other colors, have begun to appear alongside the customary colors of yellow, red, black, and white, with the major difference being that the colors are more intense in their brilliance. Tattoos on the bodies of young girls being prepared for performance, once achieved through delicate and painful processes, no longer seem necessary. Instead, within an hour or less tattoo patterns of the past are outlined on the bodies of these performers using washable black markers and ink. Armbands, necklaces, and beads once made from objects often obtained from the natural environment that involved a lot of preparatory work are now made from polystyrene and other cheaper material, readily available as discarded stuff, transformed and sold on the streets and in craft markets.

Many of the makers of the bilas have moved into the towns, and so access to material from the natural environment is not so convenient. People have resorted to more readily available plastic-based material in a great range of colors, easily pliable and more durable. The availability of modern tools like axes, knives, metal needles, and so forth has added to the ease and dexterity with which the makers of bilas have been able bring about new and interesting creations. A major concern, though, is whether the newer and more attractive-looking bilas is not as good as the old and therefore less valuable. Faced with the rising tide of modernization, the loss of customs and heritage makes the local people look with nostalgia into the past, denying or not readily accepting change. Conversely, the abilities of bilas makers and those that wear the newer bilas to take on and transform the new and different into their own bilas must be noted.

BILUMWEAR

The transformative processes are particularly evident in the emergence and popularity of the *bilum*, in the way it has been made and popularized as a fashion item. The string or net bag, otherwise known as the bilum in Pidgin, has been ubiquitous in the social and cultural lives of Papua New Guinea communities. As a practical object, the bilum has served a range of purposes: as a carry-bag for firewood, food, knick-knacks, and personal items, and as a hammock for babies to sleep in, either hung or carried. Within the social and symbolic landscapes in the various cultures, the bilum is both practical and a conceptual idea for carrying and bringing forth. The notion that one has always been carried in a bilum and that motherhood is about the bilum of life is significant. Then there is the intricate balance between people in relationships. The bilum serves as an important metaphor for

understanding and appreciating birth, motherhood, maintenance of maternal relationships, exchange of food and valuables, maternal ties, and death.

Construction of the bilum is unique. Fiber from an indigenous plant in some cultural groups (especially in coastal areas) and bark in most other communities was obtained and prepared to make small shreds of fiber. Women then twisted these into a long continuous twine or string on their thighs. By running the twine around a small strip of dried pandanus leaf, tiny loops were formed and linked with each other to form a net. The net was then folded over and joined together on the sides to form an enclosure or pouch, with an open mouth and two arms extended out. The two arms would serve as handles, or one handle when tied together. The bilum pouch, once laden with cargo, would be carried on the back with the joined arms forming a handle held by a woman on her head. For men the handle was usually thrown over the head and onto the shoulder to have the handles across the body and the bilum pouch hanging on the side. Usually shapes and sizes of bilums were largely determined by the purposes for which the net bags were used; carrying harvest from a garden to the home; a hammock for infants and children to sleep in; an object to carry that was strung over the shoulders to be worn on the side by men or over the head and thrown on the back to be worn by women. The bilum was extremely versatile in its use, and at the same time greatly admired.

Over the years patterns and designs for the bilums were varied. Some were kept plain, while others were richly decorated with patterns and designs. Along with the patterns some bilums had various curious items attached to them, including bones, feathers, and dried seeds. The patterns of the bilums were achieved in a couple of ways. Very fine twine would have marsupial fur of gray or white inserted into the fibers as they were twisted on the thigh. Other twine was sometimes painted red or purple by rubbing the leaves of plants that had the rich pigment in them. All the prepared fine twine was then woven by making strips of small linked loops to make the net-like apron. Once completed, the net-like apron was folded to form a net bag with handles. Those bilums that were finely made were usually reserved for young brides, for carrying newborn children, and for gifts. Those that were coarse and large in loop were for carrying firewood, food, and a variety of objects. Smaller versions were also worn by men as hats.

In the twenty-first century, with the influx of a variety of fibers and colors, women have shown remarkable resilience in maintaining customary knowledge and also demonstrating creativity in adapting to new media, as they continue to make the bilum as an add-on for bilas. Hats made in the bilum style have also grown in popularity for both men and women and can be regarded as a popular fashion accessory. Moving beyond the bilum of natural fiber, the multitude of polyester or synthetic fiber in an array of colors has provided opportunities for new styles of bilums to emerge. Some of the other interesting bilums have had chicken and cassowary feathers inserted into the twisted twine. Others have had plastic wrappers from chewing gum, trimmed plastic, and Christmas tinsel inserted in the twine. As the bilum makes its way to Western contexts via travelers like tourists, collectors of "primitive" art, and anthropologists (often identified as experts on local art), they broker meaning and authenticity for the bilum as artifact, craft, or even tourist art. The makers of the bilum provide an opportunity to demonstrate the capacity of Papua New Guinean women to articulate a voice of continuity and difference.

A woman from the Wahgi Valley, Papua New Guinea, wearing garments typical of everyday wear in the early twenty-first century, as opposed to traditional dress. Photograph by Mark Eby.

Some Papua New Guinea women, who continue to draw on customary skills and at the same time are open to creative innovation, transform the bilum into fine bilumwear. They have challenged the conventional labeling of the bilum as merely mundane. Indeed, according to these women, it can be and is an object of fine art and fashion. Full-length dresses, skirts, tops, ties, and ponchos in bilum style have been made by women and have been bought in the towns to be worn on special occasions. Slowly the idea of having to wear an original fashion item like a dress or top made in the bilum style has gained momentum for numbers of young men and women.

Bilas and the way it was understood and practiced in Papua New Guinea has undergone many changes. Men and women in the communities have taken to wearing the introduced bilas and have discarded the traditional. As less and less of the old bilas is worn and displayed, the knowledge and skills to make it will be forgotten and lost to memory. These changes then bring to the forefront important questions for Papua New Guineans: Are the ways of their heritage to be lost and forgotten, and who are Papua New Guineans without them? In the face of these important questions the people have made concerted efforts to celebrate and reassert age-old skills and knowledge passed on from mother to daughter and father to son. One of the objects for bilas that has emerged in this way is bilumwear—an example of how the old and the new have combined to provide a way for Papua New Guineans to find a name through their bilas.

References and Further Reading

Cochrane, Susan. *Contemporary Art in Papua New Guinea*. Sydney: Craftsman House, 1997.

Corbin, George. "Salvage Art History among the Sulka of Wide Bay, East New Britain, Papua New Guinea." In *Art and Identity in Oceania*, edited by Alan Hanson and Louise Hanson, 67–83. Honolulu: University of Hawai'i Press, 1990.

Crawford, Anthony. *Aida: Life and Ceremony of the Gogodala*. Bathurst, Australia: Robert Browne and Associates, 1981.

Hanson, Alan, and Louise Hanson. "Introduction: Art, Identity, and Self-Consciousness in Oceania." In *Art and Identity in Oceania*, edited by Alan Hanson and Louise Hanson, 1–14. Honolulu: University of Hawai'i Press, 1990.

Lewis, Phillip. "Tourist Art, Traditional Art and the Museum in Papua New Guinea." In *Art and Identity in Oceania*, edited by Alan Hanson and Louise Hanson, 149–163. Honolulu: University of Hawai'i Press, 1990.

MacKenzie, Maureen. *Androgynous Objects: String Bags and Gender in Central New Guinea*. Philadelphia: Harwood Academic, 1991.

May, Patricia, and Margaret Tuckson. *The Traditional Pottery of Papua New Guinea*. Kensington, Australia: Bay Books, 1982.

Mel, Michael. "Pasin Bilong Bilas." In *Contemporary Art in Papua New Guinea*, edited by Susan Cochrane, 127–156. Sydney: Craftsman House, 1997.

Newton, Douglas. *Massim: Art of the Massim Area, New Guinea*. New York: Museum of Primitive Art, 1961.

Serra, Eudald, and Alberto Folch. *The Art of Papua New Guinea*. New York: Rizzoli International Publications, 1977.

Strathern, Andrew, and Marilyn Strathern. *Self-Decoration in Mount Hagen*. London: Gerald Duckworth, 1971.

Strathern, Andrew, and Pamela Stewart. "Netbags Revisited: Cultural Narrative from Papua New Guinea." *Pacific Studies* 20, no. 2 (1997): 1–29.

Michael Mel

See also Torres Strait Islander Dress, Australia; Textiles and Dress of the Motu Koita People.

Textiles and Dress of the Motu Koita People

- Early Regional Influences on Dress
- Men's Ceremonial Dress
- Women's Ceremonial Dress
- Colonial Impact and the Development of Modern Textiles

P apua New Guinea, the eastern half of the island New Guinea (the second-largest island in the world), lies just north of Australia and has several hundred outer islands. Annexed and subdivided by the Germans and British in 1884, Papua New Guinea became an independent nation in 1975. The country has a vast variety of cultures and at least eight hundred languages. The Motu and Koita people inhabited the southern coastal and immediate inland areas of Papua New Guinea, living between the western coastal village of Galley Reach, the national capital Port Moresby, and Hood Point along the southeast coast. Even though the Motu and Koita are distinct peoples, a great deal of cross-cultural exchange has occurred over the centuries, and they have become generally known as the Motu Koita people. This racial mixture, in combination with their location, has contributed to a unique textile and dress style that distinguishes these people from the rest of Papua New Guinea and the Pacific Islands region.

Motu Koita textile construction was strongly influenced by the environment, a harsh, semiarid microclimate in the rain shadow of the Owen Stanley Mountain Range. Unlike most of New Guinea, the area receives less than 1,270 millimeters (fifty inches) of rain per year, primarily during the months of January to May, with an average daytime temperature of 25 to 30 degrees Celsius (77 to 86 degrees Fahrenheit), all of which contributes to scarcity of raw materials for textile construction in the dry season. So trade provided additional materials for textiles, including those for spectacular dance attire. These dance costumes are complex and extravagant, some featuring six-foot- (1.8-meter-) high headdresses for the men. The women's clothing of finely constructed dance skirts and feather tiaras was made to complement their full-body tattoos.

The Koita (also known as the Koitabu) have inhabited the Sogeri Plateau adjacent to the costal city of Port Moresby and immediate inland areas for some three thousand years. The Motu were the last to migrate into the central south coast area, with an archaeological record dating between twelve hundred and seventeen hundred years. They arrived in three waves, the first settling near the present site of the capital city, Port Moresby, and subsequently at coastal sites both south and north of there. The Motu brought new technology, superior sea craft, ceramics, and an extensive trade system. They were outstanding long-distance navigators and, most importantly with regard to acquisition of textiles, conductors of ocean trade, commanding large areas of the coastal economy. They came to be the dominant cultural core of the Papua New Guinean central southern coast, quickly becoming the reigning cultural group by aligning with the Koita, developing long-standing interrelationships through the sharing of marriage partners, trade routes, and coastal village sites, as well

as clothing components and techniques. By the middle of the sixteenth century the Koita often lived with the Motu on the islands of Bootless Inlet, just south of Port Moresby. By the late twentieth century the Koita were inhabiting the coastal area around Port Moresby between Galley Reach and Bootless Bay, mostly in maritime villages, either separately or as minority sections of larger Motu villages.

EARLY REGIONAL INFLUENCES ON DRESS

Although the overall design of Motu Koita dress and dance costume was unique to the group, portions of their attire were strongly influenced by their trade activities and personal interactions with their trade partners. Their harsh environment limited types of materials available for textile construction, and they completed their attire through trade. The Motu Koita had access to several types of bark for *tapa* (barkcloth), banana leaves for clothing decoration, and pandanus, palm leaves, and various grasses for skirts. The ocean supplied them with several types of shells for their jewelry, and indigenous birds contributed feathers for both men and women's headdresses. The headdresses and their designs were distinctive to the Motu Koita; components might be traded, but not the overall design.

As long-distance conductors of the *Hiri* (a six-month return voyage from the Motu homelands to their trade partners in the Papuan Gulf), the Motu exerted a strong cultural and economic influence upon the peoples of the south coast, from the Orokolo and Kerema in the Papuan Gulf area, and the inhabitants of Yule Island to the west, to the groups south of the Port Moresby area along the central southern coast in the east. Using *lakatoi* (large two- and three-hulled outrigger sailing canoes), the Hiri voyages began before European contact and continued until World War II. Sago palm flour, strands of shell money, shell armband currency, and Motu ceramics were the basis for the six-month return voyage from the Port Moresby area to various villages in the Papuan Gulf. The dry coastal climate of the Motu Koita homelands was not supportive of reliable agriculture, with erratic rains and frequent famine; thus, they often had to supplement their diet with sago palm flour obtained from the Papuan Gulf. These trade activities also provided opportunities through which to collect raw materials such as plant fibers, dyes, and feathers for textiles and body attachments. Motu textile designs, choreography, jewelry, dance-wear components, and elaborate feather headdresses were obtained through their Hiri trade partners, the Koita, Mekeo, Doura, Nara, Solien Besena (an influential subclan of the Motu Koita), and the Roro. In addition, more casual trading partners along the coast exchanged *ageva* (trade beads made from shells, unique to south coast Papua New Guinea), shell armbands, *toea* (shell jewelry and money used in dance attire and for trade), *doa* (spiral pig tusks), and *mairi* or *kina* (crescent-shaped necklaces made from golden lip clamshell) for sago leaf women's skirts, plumage, and men's headdresses, thus making the Hiri one of the primary sources of cultural transmission from the Papuan Gulf to Point Hood, east of Port Moresby.

The effect of intergroup trade on Motu Koita dress is illustrated through their activities with the Roro and Mekeo peoples.

The *oaoa* (individual motifs, designs, and headdress compositions) was an essential commodity obtained from the Roro people and had a strong influence on Motu Koita textile and dance-wear design. Oaoa patterns were carved in low relief on boards, and their motifs were then repeated in textiles and feather-work used in headdress designs and painted men's dance costumes. They were recognized as hereditary property of the chiefs, who had the sole right to construct, use, and trade them. According to Charles Seligman, the eminent twentieth-century ethnologist, the older out-of-fashion oaoa were often sold to their trading partners, as were the *kangakanga* (feather headdresses) of the Mekeo people. In these instances the right to use the oaoa or kangakanga was extended to the trading partner on a limited basis that allowed only for conventional representations or derivatives of the designs. As early as 1873, ethnologists noted that the oaoa designs and figurative patterns were often translated to Motu Koita textiles, belts, and pouches.

MEN'S CEREMONIAL DRESS

The most elaborate use of materials, both indigenous and imported, is to be found in men's ceremonial attire. Before colonial governmental intervention men's customary everyday wear consisted of a *sihi* (plant-fiber breechcloth or perineal band) held in place by a woven or stiff bark belt and accompanied by woven arm and ankle bands. Men's clothing was strictly functional, constructed from common plant materials like banana fiber, processed pandanus leaves, and various inner tree-bark fibers.

Customary ceremonial dress for men was a combination of elegant jewelry, fiber decoration, elaborate headdresses, and stylish coiffure. Men would add ageva and dog-teeth necklaces accented with decorative *kapkap* (shell jewelry featuring a filigreed turtle-shell design attached to a circular bailer shell base) and kinas or mairi. All of the shell and dog-tooth jewelry items featured textile mounts made of twined, woven spun bark cordage obtained from ficus, tulip, or hibiscus tree bark. In addition to their jewelry, the men wore numerous woven and shell armbands, woven garters, and barkcloth belts, decorated with painted and clipped pandanus leaf streamers. Customary textile paints were obtained through mixing powdered charcoal, lime derived from burned shells, shredded tree bark, or other plant fibers with a fixative made of a latex-type sap obtained from certain trees and vines. Barkcloth, used for special men's wear, was made from beating and felting the inner bark of the ficus tree, hibiscus, or paper mulberry tree. Ficus fiber produced a dark brown coarse fabric, while tree hibiscus and mulberry produced a finer, tan to light tan fabric. Freshly made barkcloth was dried and painted to make belts, *sihi* (breechcloths), streamers, and a unique knee-length barkcloth cape decorated with geometric clan designs. The ceremonial dance sihi featured ankle-length front and rear decorative panels that covered the majority of the man's thigh and leg. The capes were designed to cover the back of a high-status man in ceremonial dance and to display the clan's design on a large surface. The parading of this cape was akin to displaying a clan's heraldry banner. As with oaoa, specific color combinations in dance wear, tattoo patterns, and choreography were all graphic symbols used to individualize a Motu Koita clan's identity.

Particular interest was paid to the man's face and head. A tiara of fine feathers, usually in a monochrome color scheme, framed the upper face and hairline, along with a decorative shell septum decoration and complementing woven headband. *Tubuka* (tall elaborate headdresses made of feathers and cane woven onto a large frame) were worn by a select group of village leaders and dancers for special occasions and reciprocity feast ceremonies. These beautiful feather sculptures can be seen in numerous early-twentieth-century archival photographs of the Motu, Solien Besena, and Roro people. The designs in the headdresses used by twenty-first-century Motu Koita and Solien Besena men mirror those illustrated in Seligman's 1910 research and field photos. The best-dressed, and most important, male dancers and drummers wore the tubuka as they led the dance, setting the pace with their characteristic slow rhythm, which mimicked the human heartbeat. In their costume finery the men represented the collective power and wealth of the clan through their attire and dance posture, portraying a strong vertical visual element in the use of their elaborate and animated, three- to four-foot-high (about one meter) tubuka. The tubuka featured two basic shapes: arched and vertical ladder. The forms incorporate red and greater bird of paradise, cockatoo, parrot, and other colorful feathers on a feather-covered lattice. Portions of the headdress were deliberately hinged to the main framework, along with feather-covered wand-like extensions, to provide several animated sections of the headdress. The hinged portions usually feature an entirely preserved and flattened bird that is attached to sway backward and forward in time to the drumbeat, thus adding an extra theatrical element to the dance performance. Solien Besena artist Wendi Choulai has noted at the end of the twentieth century that the overall choreography was designed to present the audience with a vision of clan unity. Through their grouping and similar costumes, the dancers portrayed an impressive unified block, displaying the collective supremacy and strength of the clan.

WOMEN'S CEREMONIAL DRESS

Inherent in the show of clan accord was the acknowledgment of duality based upon gendered roles and contrasting costumes. While the men wore large vertical, multicolored, animated headdresses and elaborate jewelry, the women had small *ubi* (women's feather tiara), shin-length, multilayered *rami* (a skirt commonly constructed from palm leaf fiber), simple jewelry, and tattoos. The women embodied the horizontal, grounded element of the performance, as they danced close to the earth with their skirts often dusting the dance ground. Seligman has described the dance characteristics in detail, observing that their rhythm was exemplified through the women's consistent, slow rocking of the pelvis while shifting from leg to leg. This motion in turn caused the muscles of their backs to produce a rotary movement of the hips and animate the skirt's inherent fluidity. Choulai has described the women's skirt movement as imitating the movements of the "willy wag tail" or the white-breasted thicket fantail (*Rhipidura leucothoraxa*). This particular bird sports a long, black-and-white tail that fans out and sways vigorously from side to side when it is agitated or performing a mating dance.

There were occasions when the young women incorporated a fierce, high swing that exposed the tattoos on their buttocks and thighs; they often competed to see who could produce the highest swing. Before missionary intervention young newly tattooed girls would incorporate these high swings during special ceremonial

A Motu Koitabu girl from the Gulf of Papua swings a layered dance skirt as she performs a Hiri Hanenamo dance on Ela Beach, during the Hiri Moale festival in Port Moresby, on 15 September 2005. The Hiri Moale festival, invented to celebrate Motu Koita Hiri trade history, has become an event where the variety of customary dance attire of different villages is demonstrated, which has, in turn, led to a revival in the use of older kinds of materials and textile work. Torsten Blackwood/AFP/Getty Images.

dances performed on *dubu* (two-story decorated platforms supported by richly carved posts with crab-claw-shaped finials). The performance of such dances, with the spectators standing below the dubu, shocked the missionaries, but a survey of early colonial photo albums will show that it was a favorite photo subject for colonial men.

The majority of the rami used by the Motu Koita originated in the Central Province villages immediately west and east of Port Moresby. The primary skirt material was obtained from the leaves of the sago and other local palms, which grew in abundance along the coastal areas. Banana stem, hibiscus, and coconut leaf were also used occasionally, but they were not as supple as sago palm fiber. To obtain the soft, pliable, one-half-millimeter-wide (0.019-inch-wide) strands needed to produce full, animated rami, women often engaged in a five-to-seven-day process. Each palm leaf section was removed from the main petiole, or middle stem of the large mature palm frond. The leaves were then soaked in fresh- or seawater to obtain a light tan color, or dried in the sun to produce a rich orange brown or deep gold color. The leaves were shredded from the tip to the base of the leaf, leaving a small portion intact at the base. Fibers were occasionally colored with

various mineral- and plant-based dyes that were complementary to the natural fiber colors.

The fibers were bundled into small workable segments for dyeing; some segments were dyed completely, while others were tied so they would produce horizontal stripes, a color block, or a checkerboard pattern. Plain panels of fiber were interspersed with dyed and tie-dyed segments to provide a series of decorative motifs. Skirts with color panels were often worn over plain skirts to provide a fuller profile and a more animated swing. The common method of dyeing consisted of soaking or rinsing the fibers in freshwater, cooking small batches in dye, and finally rinsing and drying the dyed fibers. The primary colors used in Motu Koita and south coast skirt decoration were red, yellow, green, and black. Red and green were the common colors used in customary dance skirts, while black was primarily used with lighter tan fibers for funerary ceremonies. Permanent black dyes were difficult to produce, as most plants produced a dark brown or gray, not a true black. According to Roslaie Christensen, an educator and ethnologist in the 1970s who collected information for the Madang Teacher's College in Papua New Guinea, turmeric produced yellow, red dye was obtained from the fruit of the pandanus and *Bixa Orellana* plants, green from the *buge* and *Panicum sarmentosum* plants, and black from the *Adenostema hirsutum* plant, mangrove tree leaves, or wild banana sap.

The skirts were constructed on a foundation of twisted bark fiber cord, which also served as an adjustable skirt tie. Small segments of 105 to 110 skirt-length shredded leaf fibers were secured by a square knot before being attached to the waist cord. The segments were attached to the foundation cord by a combination of knotting and tying the fibers over and into the cordage, making sure that smooth, equal-length segments of fiber were evenly attached. After each segment was secured on one end by a square knot, a small remnant (about five centimeters, two inches) remained; this material was then used to create a decorative ruff that accented the skirt waistband. The ruff was often colored to highlight the skirt design and jewelry, such as the decorative *kapkap* or *roro* (a filigreed turtle-shell medallion attached to a circular bailer shell base). As a finishing touch, skirt-length pandanus and banana leaf streamers were also attached to the top of the skirt ruff.

Before World War II jewelry, full-body tattoos, and an ubi completed the women's dance costumes. While the women displayed less jewelry than the men, they did wear a combination of different types of necklaces made from kina shells, dog teeth, toea, doa, or decorative seeds. They also wore shell or woven cane bracelets on their upper arms, to which they added decorative pandanus and banana-leaf streamers as well as flowers. Ankle bands made from matching streamer materials completed their ensemble. The ubi was usually worn low on the forehead, forming a feathered halo that framed the woman's face. A combination of different-length, colorful feathers from birds such as the parrot and cockatoo was carefully woven into a semicircular cane framework. Ubi were commonly two or three layers, with the shorter, brighter feathers immediately on the forehead, and contrasting those of medium-length feathers sandwiched between the lower and top layer of longer ones. The longest feathers were usually white and clipped into decorative designs to enhance the halo effect. Women often added flowers, dots of facial pigment, and feathered earrings of complementary colors to embellish the ubi and complete the overall profile.

A heavily overloaded *lakatoi* (a huge Papuan trading canoe) carries Motu Koitabu from Manubada Island to Port Moresby for the Hiri Moale festival on 15 September 2005. Tribes from all over Papua New Guinea descend on the capital to participate in this annual festival, which was devised as a celebration of Motu Koita Hiri trade history, coinciding with the anniversary of Papua New Guinea gaining independence from Australia in 1975. Torsten Blackwood/AFP/Getty Images.

COLONIAL IMPACT AND THE DEVELOPMENT OF MODERN TEXTILES

Colonial laws had a profound impact upon the construction of dance costumes and daily dress. With little exception the Motu Koita were unable to wear European-style shirts, blouses, and dresses, as the 1919 Native Regulation made it an offense. When the ban was lifted around 1940, women were allowed to wear *meri* blouses (a loose-fitting, hip-length top featuring a large simple yolk and puffed, short sleeves, introduced by missionaries) or a long gathered skirt that could double as a strapless top if pulled up to the underarms. In ceremonial performances women began to wear sleeveless tops or meri blouses with their traditional rami. Men's breech cloths or sihi were replaced with embroidered or appliquéd *laplaps* (a textile skirt-like wrap) or an occasional work-issued pair of shorts. Both men's and women's clothing would have been constructed of cheap imported cotton, such as calico or broadcloth. Another influential factor in dance costume development was the loss of individual dance styles and the depletion of many cultural activities due to vigorous London Missionary Society activities. The Society was encouraged by the colonial government to begin the deculturalization process of the Motu Koita people through religious conversion and the establishment of schools.

Ceremonies and dances that were deemed immoral or licentious were discouraged, which in turn curtailed most ritual activities, including clothing construction. By the 1950s numerous Motu Koita dance styles were merged into more general dances that preserved portions of the funerary-related Guma Roho (a dance ceremony to complete the mourning process), Hiri trade, birth and initiation celebrations, and a few secular dances. Many conglomerate dance ceremonies were affiliated with cultural

retention movements and were performed on European holidays such as Easter and Christmas.

The declaration of Papua New Guinea's independence from Australia in 1975 was the catalyst for a Motu Koita customary dance costume revival. The Hiri Moale festival was instigated to celebrate Motu Koita Hiri trade history, and was held in conjunction with the annual Papua New Guinea independence holiday. The festival became an event where specific versions of dance attire from several different villages could be highlighted. Some clothing still combined a mixture of imported and customary textiles. For example, in certain costumes, strips of imported material replaced natural fiber streamers as adornment on men's and women's costumes, or sago fiber was replaced by a synthetic fiber, but in the twenty-first century groups seem to be competing for the most use of customary material in their attire. The highlight of the festival is the selection of the Hiri Queen, *Hiri Hanenamo*, who represents the ideal of customary values. The young women who compete for this position wear the most time-honored clothing, tattoos, and jewelry. The Hiri Queen competition has been very influential, as many of these young leaders of style have eliminated synthetic materials and given new relevance to the adaptation of "old" styles and textiles.

Outside of the clothing revival in the realm of the Hiri Moale Festival, other Motu Koita were exploring new expressions of dress. In the 1980s Motu Koita daily, urban dress reflected the average department and trade store clothing found in most Western cities. It was in the area of customary and special-occasion textiles that innovation and refinement were to be found. In 1986 Wendi Choulai became the first Motu Koita member and Papua New Guinean woman to receive a degree in textile design from the National Arts School in Papua New Guinea. Through her studies she introduced a new line of printed textiles, fashions, and rami inspired by Papua New Guinea, Solien Besena, and Motu Koita designs. Her textile pieces could be described as contemporary wear, as they dealt with modernity and change in Solien Besena and Motu Koita culture, incorporating nontraditional textiles in a customary format.

While still at the Art School, Choulai opened PNG (Papua New Guinea) Textiles, a workshop and studio in Port Moresby through which she could train and employ squatter settlement-based artists. Choulai, with the assistance of her family and two National Art School students, Ostin Harupa and Demitrius Lakore, ran one of the first textile production businesses in Port Moresby. In 1987 their textiles were commissioned by the national airlines, Air Nuigini, for uniforms, and by the International Travel Lodge Hotel for interior decoration. Politicians and wealthy Papua New Guineans began to adopt their textiles and fashions as status wear, which in turn influenced others to adopt and view Motu Koita and Solien Besena art in a new light. In 1987 Choulai and her partners organized their first textile and painting exhibit, at the Mila Mala Market gallery in Port Moresby; this launched both their clothing and textiles lines. She became a major spokesperson for Motu Koita and Solien Besena textile art and, when overseas, a representative of Papua New Guinea.

From 1984 to 1993 Choulai represented Papua New Guinea in several overseas art venues. For these events she developed performance-based exhibits as a way to promote Motu Koita and Solien Besena textile heritage, blending her textiles, fashions, and paintings into an educational presentation. One of Choulai's first rami prototypes was the "Tru Kai" (true food) dance skirt, made from shredded one-hundred-kilo (220.5-pound) nylon rice sacks, which when worn displayed the "Tru Kai Rice" logo. Other pieces included the "Sportsgirl Skirt" made from shredded Sportsgirl (an Australian women's-wear clothing store) plastic shopping bags, sago fibers, and silk panels. Both of these works were created as a commentary on Motu Koita women's preference for foreign products over customary items.

Choulai moved to Melbourne, Australia, in 1994 to pursue her master's degree in fashion and textile design from the Royal Melbourne Institute of Technology. By the time she completed her degree in 1997, her artistic activities in Australia had become a catalyst for new Motu Koita textiles in Papua New Guinea as well as in Australia. In 1996 she was invited to exhibit her work in the Second Asia-Pacific Triennial of Contemporary Art in Brisbane, Australia. As the first Motu Koita artist to be invited to the Triennial, she decided to present the Guma Roho, a funerary ceremonial dance dedicated to her grandmother. After lengthy negotiations with her elders and their Koiari trade partners, Choulai began making rami for the ceremony. "Wearable Grass Skirt 1" was constructed of batik and hand-dyed silk, interspersed with sago fiber panels from a customary rami. The other rami, "Wearable Grass Skirt 2" and "Wearable Grass Skirt 3" and the "105 Skirt," incorporated various combinations of raffia, sago palm, plastic, and hand-painted and seriographed silk and cotton textiles.

Her modern version of the "Guma Rami" (a dark skirt that in the past was used in the Guma Roho ceremonies) featured sago fiber bleached and dyed with commercial dyes to obtain true black-and-white fibers, representing the Solien Besena's colors

for the sky and sea. For the elder dancers she designed the "Grass Skirt Design" and "Roro Shell" laplap series in silk, linen, and cotton. Using silk-screening techniques to apply reactive dyes, opaque pigments, and transparent pigments in horizontal repeats, the "Grass Skirt Design" pieces featured patterns that emulated the flash of colors produced by the sway of the customary dance skirts, while the "Roro Shell" piece featured a repeat design of the filigreed turtle-shell design. Choulai noted that the "Grass Skirt Design" pieces represented the merger of the present with the past, reuniting the Australian-based Solien Besena and Motu Koita, diasporic New Guinea people who now live in Australia, with the Papua New Guinean clan. By incorporating noncustomary materials into customary skirt design, Choulai was addressing the impact of the urban milieu, twentieth-century aesthetics, and recycling on the continuation of Motu Koita dance ceremonies and costume construction. Choulai's fame as a textile artist, producing new ideas in her work, has inspired other Motu Koita and Solien Besena dancers to reexamine the role of textiles in ceremonial and daily wear.

References and Further Reading

Choulai, Wendi. "Art and Ritual: Aina Asi A Mavaru Kavamu." *Artlink* 16, no. 4 (1996): 49.

Choulai, Wendi, and Jacquelyn Lewis-Harris. "Women and the Fibre Arts in Papua New Guinea." In *Art and Performance in Oceania*, edited by Barry Craig, Bernard Kernot, and Christopher Anderson, 211–217. Bathurst, Auatralia: Crawford House Press, 1999.

Christensen, Roslaie. *The Collection and Preparation of Local Materials: A Handbook on Materials Available in Papua New Guinea Which Are Suitable for Use in Primary Schools*. Madang: Madang Teachers College, 1974.

Dutton, Thomas, and H. Brown. "Hiri Motu." In *Language, Culture, Society and the Modern World, Fascicie 1*, edited by S. E. Wurm. Pacific Linguistics Series C-No. 40. Canberra: Australian National University, 1977.

Knauft, Bruce. *South Coast New Guinea Cultures*. Cambridge: Cambridge University Press, 1993.

Lewis-Harris, Jacquelyn. "'Anina Asi A Mavaru Kavamu': We Don't Dance for Nothing. Solien Besena Cultural Retention in Urban Australia." Ph.D. dissertation, Washington University, 2004.

Lewis-Harris, Jacquelyn. "Not Without a Cost: PNG Contemporary Artists." *Visual Anthropology* 17, nos. 3 and 4 (2004): 273–292.

Moore, Clive. *New Guinea, Crossing Boundaries and History*. Honolulu: University of Hawai'i Press, 2003.

Seligman, Charles. *The Melanesians of British New Guinea*. Cambridge: Cambridge University Press, 1910.

Tau, Olive. "Wendi Choulai." In *The Second Asia-Pacific Triennial of Contemporary Art*, edited by Caroline Turner and Rhana Devenport, 111. Brisbane, Australia: Queensland Art Gallery, 1996.

Jacquelyn A. Lewis-Harris

See also Dance Costumes in French Polynesia; Bilas: Dressing the Body in Papua New Guinea.

Dressing the Body in Bariai

- Colonial and Later Dress of West New Britain
- Concepts of the Body
- Firstborn Ceremonies
- Minor Ceremonies
- Major Ceremonies
- Mortuary Dress, Spirit Beings, and Firstborns

The name Bariai defines a linguistic and cultural group of about three thousand people (in 2005) who live in a dozen villages along a part of the north coast of West New Britain Province, Papua New Guinea. Concepts of the body and ceremonial body wear, in particular interrelated ceremonies for the firstborn child and for mourning, are crucial to understanding how Bariai communicate culturally meaningful messages about self, status, and the cycle of life and death that describes their worldview. The messages are accomplished by altering the body and skin through body reshaping, filing or knocking out teeth, nakedness, clothing, paint, powder, perfumes, tattooing, scarification, cicatrisation, hairstyle, jewelry, and other ornamentation, augmentation, or deformation. Significant too is the appreciation for beauty and a pleasing appearance through nonverbal messages that are culturally and historically specific. This is the first ethnographic account of Bariai dress.

A firstborn Bariai boy being decorated by parental helpers (*baolo*), Papua New Guinea, 2003. Photograph by Naomi M. McPherson.

COLONIAL AND LATER DRESS OF WEST NEW BRITAIN

The Bariai were and still are subsistence horticulturalists growing taro, sweet potatoes, cassava, and sago as their staple crops, augmented by fish and seafood. Pigs, raised by women and transacted by men, are both items of exchange and consumption. Even in 2007 the Bariai have no serviced roads, electricity, piped water, or reliable sea transport, and few sources of steady cash income. In 1913 the Bariai experienced their first contact with foreign colonizers. The first official census in 1914 noted 829 people. The Roman Catholic mission arrived in 1937.

Colonial officers who infrequently patrolled the Bariai area tell us relatively little about indigenous clothing in their reports. The 1915 *Government Gazette* notes that where there were no European settlements, children went naked, men wore simple waistbands, perhaps loincloths (*malo* in the Bariai language) of painted bast, a palm tree fiber, and women wore *odoa* (Bariai for short fiber or leaf skirts). Where villages were close to European settlements or men had served as indentured labor elsewhere, men wore a cotton *laplap* (sarong in the Tok Pisin language), while women continued to wear odoa. (Tok Pisin is one of three official languages in Papua New Guinea, with English and Motu. All Bariai speak Tok Pisin, and children learn it simultaneously with their local vernacular, Bariai. With the exception of the grammatical structure the two languages are very different.)

Over the years the Bariai were exposed to, and had imposed on them, Western dress codes. A patrol report dated 1969 describes men's daily wear as shorts or a laplap, perhaps a shirt or singlet.

Women's wear was a cotton laplap. They went bare breasted except in the company of Europeans or missionaries, when they covered their breasts with a loose knee-length blouse. Older women in villages continued to wear the traditional fiber skirt. This was still the case in 1981. By 2005 traditional daily apparel had disappeared, replaced with jeans, shorts, and cargo pants, T-shirts, dresses, and plastic purses. Only the body wear associated with Bariai firstborn children and mortuary ceremonies is still worn. Bariai ceremonial body wear exposes and communicates the inner true beauty and strength of the self, social identity, and achieved status differentials in what is an ostensibly egalitarian society. Since competence, renown, prestige, and power are personal qualities conditional upon the response and admiration of relevant others, these qualities can only be validated through public display. Indeed, the Bariai create and build their self-identity, communicating intangible personal qualities during displays of ceremonial dress that accompany distributions of wealth in the name of their firstborn child. Relevant others who witness and receive food and wealth validate achievement according to cultural values and aesthetics, depending on whether or not the food and wealth are suitably abundant, properly displayed, cooked, and distributed, and the firstborn's decorations are fresh, carefully applied, and beautiful.

CONCEPTS OF THE BODY

The Bariai concept of *sulu* encompasses essential or vital essences that are contained in body fluids such as semen, blood, and sweat. Humans are created from parental vital essences at conception and during gestation and, once born, acquire more vital essence

A firstborn Bariai girl dressed in fiber skirt (*odoa*), Papua New Guinea, 2005. Photograph by Naomi M. McPherson.

through the food and learning they absorb. From infancy to adolescence the child's body becomes strong, straight, and well-rounded, eyes bright and skin glowing with health. Rubbing coconut oil on the body enhances the natural beauty of youthful skin. Colorful, scented flowers and leaves tucked into carved trochus-shell or sea-turtle-shell armlets, worn on the upper arm, attract admiring eyes. A line of red paint from the side of the nose to the edge of the mouth or on the temple is sexually attractive, as is wearing anything (plant or cloth) that is red or yellow. Hair is both beautiful and seductive, and the Bariai traditionally styled their hair by shaving it off around the head and forehead, leaving hair only on top of the head. This hairstyle is no longer worn except when the child (or a corpse) is shaved so clan decorations can be painted on the head. Men are usually clean-shaven and hair is normally cropped short except while in mourning, when hair and beards grow long and unkempt.

In the premissionary past both girls and boys had their earlobes cut and stretched to near shoulder length, the stretched lobe covered with turtle-shell rings being considered a sign of beauty. By age sixteen to nineteen young people are considered marriageable. They are sexually mature, at the height of their beauty, their vital essences at their peak potential. A couple's firstborn child (*lautave* in the Bariai language) is the inheritor of this most powerful parental and ancestral vitality.

FIRSTBORN CEREMONIES

Bariai society is based on an ideology of egalitarianism, a belief that everyone has equal access to resources. But this does not

guarantee equal ability to maximize them. While everyone has the same opportunity to have a firstborn child in whose name they can accomplish valued ceremonial work, some excel at this while others do not. Bariai society is characterized by a creative and dynamic tension between egalitarianism and the high value placed on competition for the achievement of personal renown. In order to deal with this seeming paradox, parents invest all their resources in their firstborn, who stands as exemplar of who and what they have shown themselves to be.

The relationship between body wear and communication of self is evident immediately upon the birth of a couple's first child. The parents now lose any identity as individuals, including their names. They are referred to as *lautave itna/itama* (the mother/ father of their firstborn). They are forbidden to wear cloth, fiber, paint, flowers, or leaves that are red or yellow; scent; or scented leaves and flowers. They cannot cut or dress their hair, or wear attractive clothing or ornamentation. They must earn back the right to wear various items of dress and adornment by accomplishing firstborn ceremonial work.

Firstborn ceremonies are individual accomplishments by the parents, who do the work together. These ceremonies focus only on the firstborn child, not the second and subsequent children. Thus, all boys are superincised and all girls get their ears cut/ pierced, but younger siblings are not dressed in finery or celebrated. There are seventeen firstborn ceremonies, taking up to twenty years to complete. The ceremonies are not necessarily performed in any particular order, although those that require large amounts of wealth or pigs or taro gardens are usually the last to occur, as the parents build up their trade networks and pig herds and become master gardeners. The firstborn is an exemplar only and does not inherit its parents' achieved status. Both the firstborn and his or her younger siblings will have their opportunity to excel when they become parents and embark on firstborn ceremonial work.

All Bariai households are involved in one or another ceremony at any time. As parents are ready to distribute food and wealth in the name of their firstborn, they will do so without special timing or in any particular sequence. The couple thus gradually creates their social identities as competent, participatory members of society, along with their self-identities as individuals of strength, power, and prestige. All firstborn ceremonies are contingent upon parental resources to provide and distribute food and wealth and to compensate their *baolo* (reciprocal helpers), who are responsible for gathering the finery and dressing and displaying the firstborn. As parents accomplish the ceremonies, their reputation is enhanced and they are gradually released from the taboos on dress and behavior they have been observing since the birth of their child. Any parent who wears or permits their firstborn to wear any item of finery associated with firstborn work without having accomplished that work will suffer the opprobrium of others.

MINOR CEREMONIES

Firstborn ceremonies can be either minor or major. Minor ceremonies are usually accomplished by the time the child is four to six years of age; they primarily acknowledge the child's early activities, development, and appearance. There are ceremonies for the child's first fish, first trip to the reef, or first visit to the home of its mother's sisters. Others focus on body wear and finery and

Bariai women and girls in full dance regalia, Papua New Guinea, 2003. Photograph by Naomi M. McPherson.

on resources the parents are too young to have produced them-selves (coconut, betel nut, and sago palms) but have inherited from their parents and ancestors. Thus, the firstborn is perceived to be a conduit of wealth from the ancestors to those who receive that wealth in the name of the firstborn.

To acknowledge the child's first tooth, parents are required to distribute large quantities of betel nut, sprouted coconuts, and taro stalks for distribution to those who share "blood" with the child. Taro is food par excellence, the staff of life. The sprouted coconut symbolizes the sprouting tooth breaking through the in-flamed gums, causing them to bleed, a condition associated with the red spittle produced while chewing betel nut (*Areca catechu*). With few exceptions everyone chews betel nut mixed with betel pepper (*Piper betle*) and powdered lime, which, over time, blackens the teeth. Black teeth were considered attractive and white teeth embarrassing. In the past Bariai blackened their teeth by wear-ing a *keto* (stem of a particular plant) like a tooth guard on their teeth for weeks. Colors—red (blood, vitality), white (death, new growth/sprouts), and black (transition, change, emptiness)—are key symbolic values in all firstborn ceremonies. The distribution of sprouted coconuts and taro stalks promises future food and wealth for the recipients.

Another minor ceremony focuses on the child's first haircut. Parents and firstborn are not permitted to cut their hair until the child is able to walk. By this time, with their long, untidy hair and their lack of fine colorful clothing, parents are bedraggled. Shiny black and luxuriously thick hair is a mark of beauty that the Bariai enhance with plant dye from the *bonbone* plant (*Impatiens hostii*) to make their hair blacker and shinier, thus attractive to the opposite sex. The bonbone has small, dark, reddish-black leaves, which, when crushed and cooked with shredded coconut, pro-duce a very black, oily dye. More recently people use purchased hair dyes or the carbon in flashlight batteries.

Around the age of three to five years, the ceremony to mark the first wearing of clothes occurs. Clothing is gender-specific, and firstborn boys were dressed in a malo (decorated barkcloth loin covering) made from the mulberry plant. Nowadays firstborn

boys wear a cotton laplap, and firstborn girls acquire their first brightly dyed odoa.

Regardless of gender, the firstborn is then painted with facial clan designs and dressed in colorful, scented flowers and leaves, especially the *dalme*, a long yellow scented leaf. These fragrances on the body are attractive and beautify the child. Fragrance is also the medium for love magic to attract a potential sexual partner. The child is carried through the village by its baolo and back to its parents. Until this ceremony has been accomplished, mother and child are taboo from wearing the scented dalme leaf as an item of personal finery.

MAJOR CEREMONIES

Major ceremonies entail enormous amounts of labor to grow food, raise pigs, and collect wealth items. Each occasion is accom-panied by large distributions of cooked food, especially taro and pork (or live pigs). In addition, parents must also present food and pigs to their ceremonial partners or baolo (a married couple from the same clan but of different lineage to the firstborn and the parents). Their job is to collect all the finery and to dress the firstborn and the mother (but not the father) before parading them through the village. There are several major ceremonies that focus on decorative finery and personal appearance. The items of finery are culturally valued objects acquired through trade with other non-Bariai groups, thus demonstrating parental ability to sustain long-distance trade networks. Red ocher, used for body paint, was one such item received in trade and celebrated by deco-rating the firstborn in *pulo budisiŋa* (watery red paint). (Note that the ŋ in Bariai is a linguistic symbol for a particular sound, some-thing like the "ng" sound at the end of "sing" in English.) Covered in paint, the firstborn is elaborately decorated (which can take hours) in flowers, leaves, a dog-tooth headdress, shell wealth neck-laces, boars' tusks, armlets, and anklets, before being paraded once through the village for all to admire. The finery is then removed.

For the *dildilŋa* ceremony the child's body is painted red on one side and black on the other. Color symbolism is multivocal, and red is associated with blood, energy, vitality, and beauty; black is associated with transitions, loss, and regeneration. The hair is shaved back several centimeters (an inch or more) to highlight a line of white paint traced around the hairline. This white paint is associated with protective *namir*, clan designs of spirit entities that empower and protect the child. The back of the child's waistband (a barkcloth or cotton band) carries a cascade of red, green, and yellow crotons (*Codiaeum variegatum*), which form a bustle. Crotons range in color from yellow and orange to red and purple, sometimes on the same plant, and have variegated edges, stripes, and spots. Crotons, dracenas, and especially red cordylines have large glossy variegated leaves and are key decorations. Whole branches are inserted in the firstborn's waistband in the midst of the bustle. In her or his hair the child wears a large white feather, similar to that adorning the topknot on the head of the *aulu* (masked spirit dancer). Draped around the child's neck are boar's tusks (heirlooms) and strings of *vula misi*, the most highly valued shell money. This is very similar to the regalia women wear when dancing; the sexually seductive bustle and the colorful plants wave up and down, wafting perfume laden with love magic. Body paints can be purchased in towns, and red ocher is no longer an important item of exchange; however, the dildiŋa body-paint ceremony continues.

The ceremony of *poipoi sara* (woven black armband) celebrates successful parental trade relations by displaying the child wearing valued trade goods. The finery in this instance is an armband woven by the Lolo people from a vine that grows only in the

mountains on the northwest tip of West New Britain. The vine is like a thin string of licorice, very fine and shiny black. The armband, worn on the upper arm, is an intricate and delicate weave with long fringes, made wide for men and narrower for women. Once the poipoi sara ceremony is performed, complete with a large pig, cooked taro, and the firstborn decorated and wearing the armbands, both the parents and the child are permitted to wear the armbands anytime as an item of personal finery.

Sago fringe is a highly symbolic item that parents and child are prohibited from wearing until they have performed the ceremony *tianŋa buru* (they eat [the pig of] sago fringe). The sago palm, *mama* (*Metroxylon sagu*), is a dietary staple. The palm matures in fifteen to twenty years and must be cut down and processed for its starch before it sends out its efflorescence. Because the trees take so long to mature, ceremonies around sago flour connect the firstborn with previous generations who planted the palms. The unfurled spathe of a new sago frond, a pale yellowy-green, is shredded into lengthwise strips. This fringe creates the full-length skirts worn by the aulu masked spirit dancers and decorates anything new, such as a house or canoe. For the sago frond ceremony, which also marks the first time the child is permitted to participate in sago processing, the firstborn is elaborately decorated with shell wealth, boars' tusks, and the sago spathe fringe.

Upon the birth of their firstborn, parents and child are forbidden to wear the color yellow, a color of vitality. They must earn back the right to wear yellow by channeling their vitality into production. Cooking grated turmeric with grated coconut produces oily yellow body paint. An older source of yellow used for body paint and to dye women's fiber skirts was obtained from the wild sugar cane grass *pitpit* (*Saccharium edule*). This wild grass also produces an edible seed head, hence the association between the color yellow and the distribution of pitpit. For this *liliu daŋa* (bathed in this thing), both mother and firstborn are covered from head to toe in a wash of yellow body paint. Clan designs are painted in white on their faces, and they are elaborately dressed in predominantly yellow and red foliage. The child is more splendidly arrayed, with yellow dalme leaves (a type of dracena) and red feathery flowers (*Salvia spenders*) in the armbands. She or he has a ruff-like collar of red, yellow, and green crotons around the neck, similar to the *ŋagarekŋa* (ceremonial ruff) worn by the aulu masked spirit dancers. The child also wears large quantities of wealth, such as a boar's-tusk necklace, and strands of shell money. Once this ceremony is completed, parents and child may wear yellow whenever they wish.

The *otŋa dadaŋa*, an extravagant ceremonial presentation of taro, requires simultaneous planting of at least four very large taro gardens. When the gardens are ready to harvest, both mother and firstborn (but not father) are covered in yellow body oil, leaves, and flowers. The finery is extremely heavy to wear, and support by others is needed for the mother and child to walk through the village. The finery is then removed and the two walk to their gardens to oversee the harvesting of the taro. The ceremonial exchange partners and their workers harvest three gardens. When they return to the village, the baolo carries decorated taro for display at the firstborn's house.

A few days later, women from all Bariai villages congregate in the firstborn's village and are taken to the fourth garden, grown specifically for the purpose. Here they harvest the entire yield of taro, they otŋa dadaŋa, that is, they clear out/harvest the garden. Each woman is entitled to keep all the taro she reaps. The successful accomplishment of this horticultural feat removes the

Katrin Bogana, a Bariai woman, showing facial clan designs called *leleki*, Papua New Guinea, 2005. Photograph by Naomi M. McPherson.

taboo on wearing the color red. Some parents never accomplish this, therefore never earning the right to wear red. Their firstborn can do this if and when she or he performs oŋa dadaŋa for her or his own firstborn.

MORTUARY DRESS, SPIRIT BEINGS, AND FIRSTBORNS

Even in death the body is beautified. Prior to burial close kin wash the deceased's body, dress it in finery, shave the hair about ten centimeters (3.9 inches) all round the head, and paint red and white clan designs on the deceased's face. The corpse is removed from the place of death to an area large enough to accommodate mourners. The body is laid out on a new pandanus mat in the center of the room and covered up to the chin with a new brightly colored cotton sarong. The corpse is mourned and buried within twenty-four hours, although villagers mourn for the next two days. On the third day the *arilu* feast, to send away the ghost of the deceased, is distributed and people resume normal activities. Over the next seven to ten years there follow a number of mortuary ceremonies culminating in the *ololo kapei* (big feast/dance) that brings together the firstborns, the aulu spirit beings, and the recent dead (those deceased since the last ololo kapei) for weeks of dancing, eating, and socializing, culminating in an extravagant pig exchange. During this ceremony firstborn girls have their earlobes cut for the elongation process (now merely pierced), and firstborn boys undergo superincision.

The Bariai maintain that all deaths impoverish the survivors. Mortuary wear outwardly expresses their inner sense of impoverishment. Men in mourning do not shave, and both male and female kin of the deceased do not cut their hair until certain ceremonies are accomplished to release the mourners from their observances. Bushy unkempt hair and beards and dull, usually black clothes represent loss and mourning. Some kin might choose to taboo certain favorite foods or activities the deceased enjoyed. Close kin display their grief and loss in ways that mirror the impoverishment of parents of a firstborn. The deceased's spouse, in particular, is subjected to elaborate mourning practices. For a number of years both *asape* (widow) and *beget* (widower) are restricted in their activities and dress. During the three days of mourning prior to sending the ghost away, he or she remains locked in the house. The widow(er) cannot expand activities or remove any aspect of mourning dress until the deceased's kin perform various mortuary ceremonies that release the widow(er) from a specific mourning observance.

Widows are subjected to more extreme forms of mourning dress than widowers. Similar to parents of a firstborn, a widow is reduced to nothingness, even losing her name; she is simply known as asape. For several months after her husband's death a widow remains near her house. After a year or more the circle of her activities gradually widens. Black, a color symbolic of transitions, death, and nothingness, communicates the grievous loss of her spouse and helpmate. Her body is covered in *diŋa itae*, black soot from wood fires (literally "fire excrement"). Her hair is covered in black soot mixed with rendered pig fat then twisted into globules of greasy tendrils. Her dirty, blackened skin, unkempt hair, and dreary clothing are unattractive.

The pig fat on her skin and hair quickly turns rancid, as she is forbidden to bathe. Her day-to-day wear is restricted to widow's clothes called *aimaramara*, an undyed, somewhat ragged fiber

A Bariai widow in contemporary mourning dress consisting of a black sarong and meri-blouse, Papua New Guinea, 2005. Photograph by Naomi M. McPherson.

skirt of shredded pandanus or coconut leaves. Daily it gets dirtier and more ragged. Asape wears a necklace (ŋagolŋanai in Bariai) braided from her husband's laplap, with his favorite spoon, pipe or comb attached. More strips of the deceased's clothing are braided by her *affines* (relations by marriage) into two long strings worn criss-crossed over her chest (reminiscent of the firstborn wearing shell money wealth).

Eventually, all mourning dress and restrictions on movement are removed, one at a time, at the behest of her deceased husband's kin, so the widow gradually resumes a normal existence. As the very last item marking her widowhood, her affines (in-laws) cut off the braided strings and necklace and present her with new brightly colored clothing. The traditional dress for widows was discontinued in the early 1990s, and asapes no longer wear pig grease in their hair or blacken their bodies. In the twenty-first century they wear a black cotton sarong and black *meri*-blouse (meri means woman, women, or girl in the Tok Pisin language). They are still restricted in their movements and continue to wear the braided cloth strips that can only be removed by their husband's kin.

The most important firstborn and mortuary ceremony, the ololo kapei (big feast), requires the presence of the aulu, autochthonous spirit beings discovered by Akono, a mythic culture hero.

Akono climbed an areca palm after a cluster of red betel nuts that surrounded a large central nut. Akono picked them and dropped them to the ground. When he climbed down he was surrounded by magnificent aulu. The central aulu is called Asape, and the smaller, paired aulu are Aulu Iriau, her youthful sons. The widow spirit-being dances alone in her skirt of widow's weeds made of dried and faded coconut fronds. Her head is square and has no colorful decorations. The Aulu Iriau dance in pairs. Like all youth, they are at the apex of their beauty.

Their tall conical masks are made of bast, painted white and stretched over a rattan frame. The facial features and clan designs on the back of the mask are painted in red and black (or blue). The face has big eyes, depicting shedding tears for the dead, elongated and decorated ear lobes, and a long, elegant nose. The *namaria* is a plant burr that is the foundation of the topknot that supports cassowary plumes and brilliantly colored parrot, rooster, and eagle feathers. The aulu skirt is made from the shredded pale yellow-green sago palm spathe. Its ŋagarekŋa, made of colorful crotons, cordylines and dracenas, is the same item of finery worn by the firstborn and her or his mother in the otŋa dadaŋa. The back of the ruff has branches of crotons and scented leaves, steamed to make them more pungent. The aesthetics of the presentation are judged according to the beauty of the decorations and how the dancers make the skirt and the bustle of leaves sway seductively and rhythmically during the dance. During the dances sound becomes part of the aesthetic experience with drumming and singing, but also with the swishing of the aulu skirts and the women's odoa as they dance.

The aulu owned by a clan are summoned forth to witness the clan's firstborn bloodletting rite during which blood, a vital essence passed through ancestors to the firstborn, is spilled on clan land. The aulu represent the spirit realm of the original generative ancestors, the recently deceased represent the process of degeneration consequent on production and reproduction, and the firstborn represents the concept of regeneration and the future. At the ololo kapei the many ceremonies in the name of the firstborn and the deceased converge to describe a cycle of generation, degeneration, and regeneration. Bariai mortuary and firstborn ceremonies and the traditional finery associated with them encompass a cycle of life and death that together describes their worldview.

A concept of beauty or aesthetic is the most culturally relative yet universal of all human concepts. While the firstborn is the exemplar of parental attributes and achievements, the firstborn is also an exemplar of Bariai aesthetics and values communicated via the body. Beauty is an expression of the self, and of culturally valued characteristics and attributes, such as the ability to work hard in production and reproduction, to forge and maintain kin and trade friendship networks of exchange, and to accomplish ceremonies in the name of their firstborn. Intangible attributes and evidence of accomplishment are displayed via firstborn ceremonial dress. Textures, colors, scent, paint, shells, tusk heirlooms, the manner in which skirts, leaves, and flowers sway and wave during walking or dancing, all signify the inner beauty of the self. As parents develop beyond sexual maturity, they become productive and socially competent. They also inexorably age as they use up finite vital essences in the process. Having transferred all of themselves and their beauty in the name of their firstborn, parents eventually die, and their deaths strip the survivors of their beauty and presence. Survivors communicate that loss with the drab, black, and debeautified body wear of mourning. Traditional body wear does not conceal, it reveals the self and what it means to be Bariai.

References and Further Reading

McPherson, Naomi, ed. *In Colonial New Guinea: Anthropological Perspectives*. Pittsburgh, PA: University of Pittsburgh Press, 2001.

McPherson, Naomi. "Gender and Cosmos Emplaced: Women's Houses and Men's Houses in Northwest New Britain." *Pacific Studies* 27, nos. 1 and 2 (2004): 68–96.

Scaletta, Naomi M. "Primogeniture and Primogenitor: Firstborn Child and Mortuary Ceremonies among the Kabana (Bariai), West New Britain, Papua New Guinea." Ph.D. dissertation, McMaster University, 1985.

Naomi M. McPherson

See also Asmat Dress; Bilas: Dressing the Body in Papua New Guinea.

Asmat Dress

T he Asmat people live along the southwest coast of New
Guinea. In this extremely damp, swampy climate, being
unclothed is more practical than wearing garments. Besides, in
a society where experiencing danger is common, clothes can be
troublesome because they may easily catch on rough undergrowth
and thorny plants. Until the 1960s Asmat men left their genitals
uncovered and children and women went partly naked. Westerners thus reported that they wore nothing, but the Asmat themselves believed their bags, bracelets, and girdles to be clothing.
Particular attire was indeed worn daily and on festal occasions
by men and women, or for battle dress, often reflecting specific
meaning that related to headhunting. As a consequence of their
own worldview, the Asmat classified dress according to gender,

although there were also androgynous aspects. A connection was
made between finery and the world of men and between skirts
and the world of women, who wore skirts every day, although
men did wear dancing skirts on special occasions. Myths and
symbols also affected their dress. Later, between 1953 and 1963,
when the Dutch colonized the area, the Asmat considered own-
ing an article of Western clothing a status symbol. When Dutch
New Guinea became part of Indonesia in 1963, the goal was to
integrate the Asmat as one of the many peoples of this country.
They were encouraged to put on modern secondhand clothes including T-shirts, which they sometimes tore deliberately for symbolic reasons. This creation of a cross-cultural style of dress still
underlines their identity.

DRESS AND FIRST EUROPEAN ENCOUNTERS

Information about dress before the seventeenth century is scarce.
The Dutch explorer Jan Carstensz was one of the first Westerners to see Asmat people, in 1623, but only from afar. The first
description comes from Captain James Cook. He disembarked
in September 1770 in present-day Cook's Bay, in the neighborhood of the village of Pirimapun. This encounter was unpleasant
because the Asmat attacked his sailors. After firing upon them
the seamen returned to the ship, followed by between sixty and
one hundred natives. While Cook and his crew had no time to

Warriors in southwest New Guinea, 1955. One man (far left) has a bracelet on his upper arm with a bone dagger attached. Other items of dress are armlets plaited
with thin strips of rattan; one armband of interwoven strips of rattan with crocheted human hair strands attached to it and others made of twisted rattan; cuscus-fur
headbands; white feathers; a nose piece of bone and another of shell; a breast ornament of shell; and girdles. Tropenmuseum, Amsterdam.

study their appearance attentively, he mentioned whitish pigment on the bodies of Asmat men. In precontact times and even during the period of first contact with Europeans, warriors applied body painting as a form of protective battle dress.

During Dutch military explorations between 1907 and 1913 the Asmat coast and rivers were mapped and attention was paid to sketching, note taking, and collecting objects of material culture, because it was expected that these would soon disappear. When early explorers collected bags, they often also obtained their contents and were thus able to make an inventory of men's requisites. Small bags, used as amulets, contained magical substances, and other bags held items such as a tuft of tobacco, lumps of sago, utensils like a bamboo knife or a mussel shell, a piece of bark string, and various ornaments. But they also came across signs of earlier contacts with the Western world, like pieces of coke (coal) and a broken bottle; the last item could be traced back to a government patrol undertaken in 1906. The officials collected the very first Asmat objects, by using sign language and offering knives, empty tins, and bottles for barter.

The Asmat were called Manoewe, which means "people who are eaten by people," and they were feared by neighboring peoples who did not practice ritual headhunting. Because of their aggressive character, visits from Europeans were scarce and only possible under police protection. Western travelers spent little time in this remote and harsh environment. Their information is only fragmentary, and communication was impossible. It is occasionally found in travel logs, for instance *Walkabout* (1936) by the British Walter Moyne, who sailed a few rivers in the Asmat area and collected during these expeditions two mask costumes, a bag, and some ornaments.

Although initially research was hampered, the situation changed when a Dutch missionary, Gerard Zegwaard, settled in the area in 1953. The Dutch government appointed Zegwaard as an ethnologic reporter on Asmat culture, of which he later became a specialist. Permanent contact with the Western world was consolidated when the Dutch government founded Agats, the county town of the Asmat area. Until then the Asmat lived pretty much untouched. This means contact with Europeans was limited before 1904, and sporadic even until 1954. Interference of the government in this period was mainly restricted to pacification. From 1954 the goal was slow and cautious acculturation, to prevent a sudden disrupture of the culture. This meant that the mission did not introduce a dress code for church attendance, and those civil servants, many trained in ethnology, or others who traveled through the area were urged to write about their experiences with the local people and collect material culture, including ornaments, where they could. The partial opening of the area after 1954, however, made it possible to start on more or less systematic collecting and research activities. Because stress was put on acquiring art objects, not much attention was paid to Asmat dress. Michael Rockefeller (son of an American governor at the time), prior to his well-publicized disappearance in 1961, was a collector, but he obtained only a few skirts, dancing belts, nose ornaments, bone daggers, and a variety of ceremonial mask costumes. His collection is housed in the Metropolitan Museum, New York. Photographs by post–European contact travelers show that clothing hardly differed between what we know of precontact attire and that which they saw. In fact, the only difference was that some men wore shorts and undershirts, and occasionally shirts, trousers, or a cap, probably obtained from the travelers themselves.

Large-scale headhunting was discouraged by the government, and these practices remained small-scale. Before pacification the Asmat could only achieve prestige via warfare, for headhunting stratified their sociopolitical organization. Leadership was based on merit but above all depended on courage, power, and capability shown on headhunting raids. In this society big warriors and successful headhunters were favored. Moreover, they distinguished themselves by specific insignia and had the liberty to put on finery every day, in contrast with others who were only permitted to do this during festivities.

Since headhunting was admired, successful warriors were allowed to have white cockatoo feathers attached to their ornamental bags. To signal prestige only high-ranked men were permitted to wear their bags on the chest, and others had to place them on the back. In normal circumstances every man was permitted to wear an *ese* (bag). As no clothes were worn with pockets, daily requisites were carried in these bags. Otherwise the strap was placed on the forehead. Armbands were also practical for stowing indispensable items. Asmat men often had a bracelet on their upper arm, so that they could put a bone dagger or other utensils behind it. These armlets were worn with pride. Wristlets protected and possibly also strengthened a person's wrist when practicing archery and were used for that reason. There were also armbands made of bow string to be used as a reserve string. Mostly armbands were simply plaited with thin strips of rattan.

A notable woman of the village Sjuru, southwest New Guinea, ca. 1955, with a cuscus-fur headdress, feathers, a nose piece, body painting, necklaces of teeth, armlets, a girdle, and a skirt. Tropenmuseum, Amsterdam.

Others of twisted rattan were fire-making equipment. Sometimes men wore a number of these armlets. The ring of rattan was used with two pieces of wood tied together, to make fire. The pieces of wood were firmly held on the ground with the toes. The bracelet was unrolled, looped under the wood, and then swiftly pulled back and forth in order to cause friction to generate heat. Within ten seconds the tinder of scraped rattan would begin to smoke. Occasionally Asmat men wore waist girdles, which could stow away an axe, for example.

In contrast with men, married women covered their private parts by wearing fiber skirts in everyday life. When girls married they received an *awer* (skirt) made by the bridegroom. Putting on this skirt was a sign of her acceptance as a female. Thus a skirt was regarded as a symbol of womanliness. These daily-wear skirts were made of a narrow plaited girdle to which smooth and glossy fibers of young sago leaves were attached. The fringes were bunched together between the legs and caught up at the back. On special occasions women would wear a loose dancing belt with beautiful patterns around their waist above the awer.

Next to these waist girdles, Asmat wore various kinds of festal accessories. Wearing finery was not restricted to men. In certain circumstances wives of important men were allowed to wear finery as a symbol of their status. For instance, the *bipané* (nose piece of shell), consisting of two spirals made out of cymbium shell to imitate the tusks of a wild pig, were worn through the septum by men and sometimes by women. Both leading men and women put on headbands made of pelts of spotted cuscus fur, or plaited headgear in dark and light patterns to which decorative cassowary feathers and quills or sago-fiber tassels could be attached. Like men, notable women could also have tufts in their hair called *tsjinimjiwi* (small bundles of feathers on a pointed stick). Headdresses with loops of sago leaf fibers tied to them functioned as wigs. Boys during their initiation wore special hair extensions made of fine plaited loops of sago-palm leaf in pre-European and early contact times. The job of hairdressing was done by their uncles, and with this hairstyle the initiate was attired as an adult headhunter. The Asmat considered finery, and the organic materials from which it was made, to be important.

MATERIALS FOR DRESS

The Asmat live in one of the wettest places in the world, where tropical temperatures and humidity sometimes rise above ninety percent, so they developed rainwear that covered the head and shoulders. These rain capes were made from long dried flexible slips of pandanus leaves. They were folded in two and the short sides were sewn, with a needle made of the quill of a ray and a thread made of bark fiber. As this kind of rainproof clothing is so practical, it is still used in the twenty-first century. These capes protect people and their bags, and perhaps a child on the back of its mother. At the same time they offer freedom of movement for arms and hands.

However, the most important function beyond practicalities is that dress was, and still is, a spiritual matter. Significance of dress lies particularly with festal occasions and war. For these special occasions the environment provides an abundance of vegetable materials, for example, rattan; bamboo; several seeds like those of rattan, abrus, and coix (also known as Job's tears); grass; various other fibers; and a large diversity of materials of animal origin. All of these organic materials reflect the impact of the region on

An Asmat headhunter with hair extensions made of fine plaited loops of sago palm leaf, southwest New Guinea, 1955. Tropenmuseum, Amsterdam.

dress, as well as reflecting the significance of hunting-gathering activities. Such connection can, for instance, be observed with sago, their staple food. Fibers of sago leaves are plaited and used as fringes in daily and ceremonial apparel. Materials from the fish and small game that supply the diet were also commonly applied to dress.

Sea fishing and hunting is men's work, and symbolic meaning is attached to materials related to fishing and linked with hunting and headhunting practices. Warriors until the middle of the twentieth century put on ornaments as part of battle dress. Since success in hunting offers esteem, some objects of finery refer to hunting. Tusks of hunted boars are regarded as important chase trophies, and, because the Asmat identify a pig as a human being, these teeth are also associated with headhunting. Every pair of tusks on an armband showed the number of heads taken by the wearer. The tusks of these armlets had holes through which a rattan string was pulled to bind them together. Tusks might also be worked into necklaces, sometimes together with coix seeds and cassowary quills. Teeth of pigs, of cuscuses, and of dogs (indispensable companions on hunting expeditions) were threaded with bark string to make necklaces, now and then combined with human teeth. As well as ivory, bone was a material that shows the success of the hunter. Pig bone, but also cassowary bone and even human bone, was worked into *biotsj* (nose pieces). Flying fox feet, cassowary and eagle claws, hornbill beaks, and parts of breast shields or heads of capricorn beetles were also applied to prestigious attire in various ways. People of the Brazza River in the interior wore fish bones through their pierced nostrils. Fish bones and various seashells were also strung into necklaces.

Women's work yielded materials related to headhunting, such as pigments made of mussel shells, commonly used for body painting. For this purpose mussel shells were dried in the sun to fade, then burned and pulverized to make white pigment. The powder was mixed with water into a smooth paste, which was applied as body paint with a little sponge of sago leaves. There were various secret recipes to make the pigment whiter, by mixing it with back shields of a specific crab, or with white cockatoo feathers. Asmat associated both this crustacean and this bird species with headhunters. The pigment was probably the kind of body paint observed by Captain Cook. Body paint was, and is, used on festive occasions. For example, Michael Rockefeller photographed Asmat with a white line above their eyebrows, on their cheeks, and around their mouths. These pictures also show white bands around upper arms, and stripes or bows on chests, as well as zigzag or waving lines on their legs.

Cosmetics for daily use were made of pulverized charcoal mixed with lizard grease, a reptile that is also on the menu of the Asmat. It is likely these cosmetics continue to be used. The paste was put on the forehead and around the eyes and nose. Sago flour was also applied as a pigment in body decoration. To put sago paint on someone's forehead was a sign of friendship. This gesture was therefore related to taste. But on the other hand, people could wear sago paint as a protection on their forehead in order to avert mischief. Sago flour was sometimes mixed with pigment of mussel shells, to be used as body paint. The reason may not be only technical. For example, mingling stinging nettle in pigment had to do with the tactile sense and was related to warfare.

Warriors rubbed their skin with nettles to prepare themselves mentally for a fight, for the prickling effect is assumed to have excited them for battle.

The Asmat attached meaning to analogies between people, animals, plants, and other natural phenomena. Red pigment was formerly applied when men went to war. They put dye-stuff, made of burned ocher mixed with water, in a circle around the eyes to look like a black cockatoo, which gets red around the eyes when it is angry. The warrior or hunter with red-rimmed eyes wanted to resemble a black cockatoo and frighten his supposed future victims.

In relation to nature the Asmat, like animals, continue to be trained to trust their senses. They are very attentive to sounds and scents when they wander through the jungle. They are aware of movements of people in the vicinity by listening to rustling noises. In this way materials used for paraphernalia may also refer to the senses. The auditory aspect of perception is, for instance, stimulated by the swish of the dried sago-palm leaves of double-layered Asmat dancing skirts. The olfactory sense is either stimulated by embellishment or scent is masked. On festive occasions people may stick fresh flowers and leaves in their hair or in their armbands, so that their fragrance may be smelled. On the other hand, when men go out hunting they mask their scent by rubbing clay on their bodies. Materials of contrasting tactility were often used together in finery. Dour shell and kneadable beeswax were combined in bipané (nose ornaments), and plain Job's tears seeds were attached to the pliable soft cuscus fur of headbands. A comparable contrast can be seen when a tight plaited band of bark string was combined with flexible cassowary feathers. It is not clear whether or not this contrast had meaning for the Asmat, but they classified the things they wore according to certain

Two boys in the men's house of the village Warkai, southwest New Guinea, ca. 1955. They wear ear ornaments with coix seeds and cassowary quills, a bone nose piece, armlets on the upper arms, a necklace, and a breast ornament of bamboo associated with headhunting. Tropenmuseum, Amsterdam.

principles. The structure was based on their own worldview, which was connected with the way they related to the surrounding environment.

MYTHS AND SYMBOLS

According to the anthropologist Adrian Gerbrands, symbolism of the Asmat was dominated by headhunting and by the links between people and trees. The two themes were related and often hard to distinguish. Human and tree were interchangeable: human heads and fruit were the same; the human torso was similar to a trunk, and arms and branches, feet and roots were alike. Because their system of identities and color symbolism was so important, the Asmat considered a dark-colored animal like a pig as a human being, because its color is similar to the complexion of the Asmat. That is why the hornbill, the black king cockatoo, the flying fox, and also animals that eat fruit, like the cuscus, were associated with headhunters. Asmat warriors believed they were transformed into these fruit-eating animals by wearing embellishments made of materials from them. Attired in this way, they considered themselves as these other beings, which they called their "younger brothers."

In terms of their mythology the Asmat defined their environment by a strict dichotomy between men and women, which according to them reflects the cosmic contrast of upper world and underworld. On this their philosophy was grounded. The basic principle for men was that life emerged out of death. This offers an explanation for headhunting and cannibalism, which was meant to supply new life force to the community. Life force was supposed to reside in the brain, so brains of enemies were eaten by elders; however, consuming human flesh was of lesser importance. The themes of food, sexuality, and headhunting were interlaced in Asmat culture. A central belief (one secret among men) was that one had to kill to create life, and therefore headhunting as a fertility rite was considered to belong to the male sphere. Life force was considered a spiritual matter, in contrast with female fertility, which implied actual reproduction. As fertility was vital to the Asmat, both male and female strategies were needed for the survival of the group. For women this was linked to expansion and protection of the group as well as maintenance of territory. It is not known whether this symbolism is current for the Asmat in the twenty-first century.

This complementary structured view of the world is also recognizable in a gender division of feasts and objects. Skirts were associated with the female sphere, but they were not exclusively worn by women; sometimes during festivities men might also wear dancing skirts, and even men's houses were decorated with a skirt, before use. As human beings have androgynous aspects, a female skirt also had a masculine dimension as it was decorated with leaves of the tree commonly used for dugouts. This soft wood tree (*Octomeles Sumatra Datiscaceae*) was regarded as typically masculine.

Myths are told about dress and role patterns. For example, there are stories about female war leaders who did not wear skirts as long as they stood at the head of a number of fighting men. After they had fallen in love with a man, they finally agreed to put on a skirt.

The word *ew pitsjin* (crocodile hide) occurs on a few inventory cards of the Tropenmuseum in Amsterdam, which holds a number of Asmat items of dress. It appears to be a name of a

A Papua man of the village Warkai, southwest New Guinea, ca. 1955. He wears sago paint on his forehead as a protection and to avert mischief. Tropenmuseum, Amsterdam.

particular plaited motif on a skirt's waistband. Some other names appear on these cards as well, for example, *fotsj pitsjin* (cuscus hide), *amber pitsjin* (snake hide), and bat hide. These patterns were formed by a combination of light and dark fibers. There are references in myth to different motifs of plaited waistbands of skirts, demonstrating the relationship between myth and material art. There are links to food as well, for the fauna mentioned are considered by the Asmat to be appetizing. Moreover, another waistband pattern, consisting of small black spots, refers to the eyes of sago larvae, considered as *iram pok* (magic food) and a delicacy because of the association with headhunting.

Finery like headbands, white feathers, nose pieces, breast decorations, girdles, shells, bracelets, and armbands was associated with the accomplishments of the male sphere, bestowing power and energy on the wearer, and was regarded as armament. In Asmat myths attire is used as a declaration of war to threaten an enemy, for it represents male qualities like courage and readiness to fight. Only initiated successful headhunters were allowed to put on these ornaments. A man who had never killed anyone was classified with women and children and had no right to wear them. Some finery was also regarded as a kind of women's magic, because it was supposed to make them irresistible to men. But again, direct interpretation is difficult. In fact, the dichotomy between men and women is complex, for male objects have female aspects and vice versa. This equivocation leads to a kind of paradox. The status of a decorated man was associated with a blooming sago palm, and the sago palm was a symbol for the female. Gerbrands never took this paradoxical aspect into account, but it was mentioned by the Dutch missionary Gerard Zegwaard.

Sometimes necklaces made of teeth of a wild boar or of dog's teeth and also heads and claws of cassowaries were attached to bags as an ostentatious sign. In early times bags decorated with white cockatoo feathers indicated that the wearer of the bag was a good headhunter. These white plumes covered the red-and-white painted motifs on the bag or were attached along the sides. Yet ese could be ambiguously gendered.

Formerly women were allowed to wear decorated ese at feasts if their husbands were good headhunters, but in modern times women use these bags more often and no longer only for special occasions. They are still made by the women and belong to the female sphere, according to Asmat philosophy. Narrators of myths mention that women actually originate in a kind of bag called *jirikésé* (women's bag). These jirikésé have a strap at the upper edge and two straps at the back, so that they can be carried in different ways: over the head or over the shoulders to carry heavy loads such as sago. Before 1953 the production of jirikésé was probably restricted to a few villages, where only certain women were allowed to plait them.

CEREMONIAL DRESS

For certain occasions and during certain periods there were rules for dressing, some related to specific events of the life cycle. For instance, there was the special skirt given to the bride for her wedding, or a girdle worn by a man as a sign of mourning, as well as that worn by widows during the mourning period. This latter consisted of a hood of plaited sago frond and a combination of bands and strings tied around the body, or a sleeveless jacket and a skirt put together with upper armbands. Armlets into which human hair was worked could be worn as a sign of grief, when the hair came from a man who was in mourning and whose head was shaven. This type of armband might also have been braided with the hair of a groom and then used during his wedding.

In major societal rituals special outfits were used, for instance *jipae* (spirit masquerade costumes), which were used to commemorate the recently deceased of the village. In the twenty-first century these feasts are still held, albeit in a shortened version. Masquerade costumes in postcontact times may provide income for the Asmat, as the artifacts are afterwards sold as works of art.

The jipae feast originally comes from northwest Asmat and has spread to central Asmat. The mask wearers represent recently deceased persons, and the wearer is put on par with the man or woman he represents. The masquerade costume itself is considered to be so sacred that nobody ever says its real name, *fum* (string of bark tissue). This refers to the material used and may not be mentioned in public. So people describe it as a mat, because at the end of the ceremony the costume is rolled in a mat and stored in a secret place in the man's house. However, the accompanying skirt of sago-palm leaves is removed and is burned. Some of these outfits were collected when Europeans first made contact with the Asmat.

Although women do most of the plaiting, the activity is not entirely restricted to them; the exception that proves the rule is that skilled men plait masquerade costumes. The fabrication of spirit costumes, materials as well as technique, is secret and takes several weeks or even months. First, men collect bark, which is

Warsekomen, a prestigious man of the village Sjuru, southwest New Guinea, ca. 1955, with a cuscus-fur headdress, necklace of teeth, breast ornament, bracelets, and a bag with white feathers. Tropenmuseum, Amsterdam.

dried to make string cords used for the masks. Only men are allowed to work in this sacred linking technique. It resembles knitting because of its appearance and its elasticity, and both the producers of the cords and of the masquerade costumes work in the men's house of the main host.

The jipae outfit consists of different parts: head, a broad neck, and a body, all made separately and later joined. White and red painted stripes stress the ribbed surface of the costume. Wooden panels placed on cylinders represent the eyes of the masks, and the nose is decorated with a nose piece of wood or pigs' bone. The ears are embellished with sago-leaf fibers, rattan fibers, or cassowary quills. These ornaments are connected to male ostentation. Gerbrands noticed that the most important decoration of the mask is a *piniw* (stick with white cockatoo feathers), which was stuck on the back of the mask. This was definitely a headhunting symbol. Sometimes a plaited penis can be recognized at the bottom of the costume. All masks have a skirt of sago-leaf fibers. This has primarily a practical function; the skirt conceals the wearer—who also smears his legs with mud in order not to be recognized—and the movements of sago fringes underline the movements of the masks. Possibly, though, this has a symbolic connotation; the upper part of the jipae masquerade costume is clearly considered as masculine while the skirt is associated with the feminine aspect.

In a few settlements in northwest Asmat jipae is called *je-ti* (spirit mask). Here *jiwawoka* (female mask) and *doroe* (male mask) are anthropomorphic spirit masks that engage in a struggle. For the jipae festival two distinct types of masquerade costumes are also made. These are called "elder brother" and "younger brother." The elder brother is a spirit mask figure, the most important, while the younger brother is a profane, entertaining mask figure. The name *ifi* refers to the leaf from which the costume is made. The cylindrical frame of it is made of strong and flexible rattan. When there is a wood carving of a turtle on top, it is also known as *mbanembar* or *manawas* (fun mask). A turtle is a symbol of fertility because it lays so many eggs. The fun mask clearly has a fertility function. According to Gerbrands, small children were ceremoniously presented to the mask wearer, who carefully touched the nipples of the girls and testicles of the boys and told them to grow up fast. The mask feast articulates fertility, and more specifically social reproduction.

At dawn on the day of the jipae (spirit masks) feast, the rattan basket mask figure is noticed across the river. He is picked up by a canoe, and when he arrives in the village he is chased by children. Children love these ifi, manawas, or mbanembar, because of their amusing walks and unexpected movements. They pelt the mask wearers with fruits and seed boxes, and boys in particular play with the mask. In the late afternoon the climax of the jipae feast is announced by the fun mask. The wearer of the basket specimen accompanies the spirit costumes on their way from the woods into the settlement. Their coming is considered the return to the village of the recently deceased (in jipae-mask appearance) for one evening and night.

The narrative connected with the fun masks is about a small orphan boy who was left unprovided for and lived all on his own. He was called Mbanma, which means "the cunning thief," because hunger forced him to steal food. Having invented a spirit mask, he tricked women by scaring them with it, so that in panic they always left their loads of sago. Village men discovered his trick but were impressed with its cleverness. They kept it secret from the women, but orphans never again were left alone. This story ensures that spirit masks receive plenty of food when they visit villagers.

The festivities end with an adoption ritual in which the names of the deceased pass on to other persons, who will take over their engagements and obligations, so that their spirits are urged to leave the village forever. This is called the feast of the armbands, and these *kon* (armlets) are regarded as sacred as the spirit mask costumes and are likewise named after the deceased represented by the ceremonial spirit mask costumes. Kon are made of rattan and decorated with a plume of cassowary feathers, and they seal the adoption of the family members of the deceased. In the final phase of the ritual of the jipae, people who are not related to the honored deceased chase the masks away to retreat in the woods, albeit not forever, for they return again when a similar feast is held.

DRESS AFTER EUROPEAN CONTACT

A new era emerged in 1963, with the devolution of sovereignty to Indonesia. In the 1970s it became clear that coastal Asmat had entered the modern world, for they were wearing modern secondhand clothing. Even so, during festivities people combined modern garments with their traditional prestigious attire like dancing skirts, aprons, girdles, and necklaces of dog teeth and armlets. Age-old customs are elastic and dynamic, constantly revised and adjusted to circumstances. At feasts customs are

A young man in a *jipae* (spirit) mask, southwest New Guinea, 1955. *Jipae* masks are used to commemorate the recently deceased of the village. Tropenmuseum, Amsterdam.

practiced more or less in the old ways as a form of replication of the ancestral way of doing things. For instance, the use of body painting remains prevalent in ceremonies, and during initiation bodies of the young boys are covered with diluted pigments of red ocher.

New materials have been introduced, such as glass beads, plastic, and nylon, which may be used in necklaces. Since the 1980s plastic has been used as a substitute for shell. Another interesting example appeared in the village of Sawa-Erma. At first sight this remarkable aesthetic headgear seemed to be decorated with little white feathers, but a closer look showed these were pieces of foil from throwaway plastic bags. Introduction of Western materials is important to note, but a shortage of indigenous material is a factor. In the future headbands made of fur of spotted cuscus will probably disappear, because in the twenty-first century there are scarcely specimens left to hunt. Asmat already plait headbands with a dotted pattern as a substitute for cuscus fur.

Secondhand clothing, which arrives in big bags in the county town Agats by boat, was new at the end of twentieth century. These leftovers of Western consumer society are worn here, even if ragged, for the wet climate makes clothes damp, and they easily get torn and frayed. People often cannot afford washing soap, so textiles become the color of muddy rivers. This shabbiness is regarded as one of the consequences of globalization, but it is a

Western preconception. The Asmat take pride in wearing mass consumer goods.

When in 1992 the Dutch artist Roy Villevoye went to the Asmat area, he noticed that tears as signs of wear were regarded by local people as elements that gave them their own character. Wear and tear is a way to make clothes special, and the Asmat sometimes make tears deliberately in articles like T-shirts, mostly those worn by men. Women also wear these torn T-shirts, but as a sleeveless one-piece garment over a blouse or other underwear. During successive visits Villevoye observed that there was a trend for tears to become more and more apparent. The tearing was made at regular intervals, occasionally linked with plaiting techniques; the resulting flounces were interwoven with other strips of textile. This meant that the Asmat had developed their own unique cross-cultural, even up-to-date style for their T-shirts, although it seemed to the Western eye like a sign of poverty. In fact, this Asmat preference for torn clothing is not unique; Pacific Islanders generally have fervent beliefs in the animacy of cloth and clothing, and in this case, by cutting, ripping, and tearing fabric, it is felt that its power can be harnessed.

Photographs by Roy Villevoye are not romanticized but make clear what the West seems to misunderstand. Asmat who live a subsistence life according to their traditions are not the "unspoiled" people Westerners would like them to be. In his series entitled "Erma Catwalk" inhabitants of the village of Erma are seen wearing these deliberately torn T-shirts. The T-shirts, accompanied with photographs, are exhibited semipermanently as the Installation Refashion (1999) in the National Museum of Ethnology in Leiden. Here, the catwalk is a tree trunk that lies in the mud of the swamp. The photography shows another reality than a European fashion catwalk, so the title is ironic, although according to Asmat criteria the torn clothes are stylish.

These items raise many issues. For instance, should these objects belong in an ethnographic museum collection? The Asmat esteem Western T-shirts they have adapted to their own requirements as much as their traditional dress. But the adaptation conflicts with Western clothing norms, so these shirts confront us with problematical issues relating to effects of globalization. By 2001 these T-shirts were less in evidence. Television has been introduced in the county town Agats, and American-style haircuts are copied and adapted to frizzy hair. Asmat men have their own aesthetics, and for a period they wore Band-Aids all over their bodies, not to cover wounds but as a sign of toughness. In fact, these plasters are used like ornaments as a kind of "love magic" to impress women. This shows that the Asmat create their own styles, sometimes inspired by international trends, demonstrating that clothing still remains very important to them.

References and Further Reading

Gerbrands, Adrian A., ed. The Asmat of New Guinea. The Journal of Michael Clark Rockefeller. New York: The Museum of Primitive Art, 1967.

Konrad, Ursula, Alphonse Sowada, and Gunter Konrad. Asmat, Perception of Life in Art. Mönchengladbach, Germany: B. Kühlen, 2002.

Küchler, Susanne, and Graeme Were, eds. The Art of Clothing: A Pacific Experience. London: UCL Press, 2005.

Moyne, Walter. Walkabout: A Journey in Lands between the Pacific and Indian Ocean. London: William Heineman, 1936.

Schneebaum, Tobias. Embodied Spirits. Ritual Carvings of the Asmat. Salem, MA: Peabody Museum of Salem, 1990.

Smidt, Dirk, ed. Asmat Art. Woodcarvings of Southwest New Guinea. Singapore, Leiden, and Amsterdam: Periplus Editions and the Rijksmuseum voor Volkenkunde, Leiden, 1993.

van der Zee, Pauline. "Kunst als contact met de voorouders. De plastische kunst van de Kamoro en de Asmat van West Papua." Ph.D. dissertation, Universiteit Gent, 2005.

Zegwaard, Gerard. "Headhunting Practices of Netherlands New Guinea." American Anthropologist 61 (1959): 1020–1042.

Pauline van der Zee

See also Bilas: Dressing the Body in Papua New Guinea; Dressing the Body in Bariai.

Dress of Vanuatu

Vanuatu is an archipelago of about eighty small islands in the southwestern Pacific. It is one of the most linguistically complex regions of the world: More than 113 languages are spoken in these islands by a population (at the start of the twenty-first century) of about 200,000. This linguistic diversity is matched by cultural diversity: Not just every island, but every district has had its own distinctive knowledge and practice, and often, its own distinctive dress styles. This diversity from place to place has also been matched by changes over time. New ways of dressing and new materials (acquired on trading expeditions to other areas) resulted in modifications to local dress over the more than three thousand years since the islands were first inhabited. European settlement in the archipelago, which began in earnest about 1840, had significant consequences for this diversity. Europeans brought loom-woven cloth with them and introduced their own styles of clothing. Over time people in Vanuatu adapted these clothes to suit their own context, creating, for women especially, a new "national" dress. These introductions also affected the evolving transformations in local dress styles.

INDIGENOUS CLOTHING

The climate of Vanuatu varies from subtropical in the south to tropical in the northern islands. Across the archipelago the days are hot. Clothing is rarely needed to keep the body warm, and before the colonial incursion the basic items of dress were fairly minimal. Clothing was worn to suit locally specific notions of modesty and to indicate the wearer's position and status. Some items of clothing or body modification were also worn to protect the individual spiritually, both in this life and the next. This survey of traditional dress draws in part on earlier work by F. Speiser and by A. Mabonlala, as well as on research undertaken by Vanuatu Cultural Centre fieldworkers.

A distinctive aspect of Vanuatu material culture in general, but especially of clothing, is the extensive knowledge about and use of leaves. Leaves for clothing include large ones that were used like a piece of cloth, for example as a wrapper; unprocessed smaller leaves suspended from a belt or bound into a waistband; or processed leaves used to make fiber skirts or plaited textiles. Certain leaves were worn to add color and/or perfume to the body. Across all the Vanuatu islands dress was appropriate to context. What people wore to work in their food gardens, or to hang out in their own home yard, was less elaborate and more practical than what they wore to meetings and ceremonies and to travel. Thus, on Laman Island near Epi in central Vanuatu, women remember that in the past they made work skirts from untreated cordyline leaves quickly bound into a waistband. These skirts were disposable: They wore them until the leaves wilted and became too thin—and then they made another.

This ink-and-wash drawing by Philip Doyne Vigors (ca. 1850) depicts a woman from Aneityum, in the southern part of the Vanuatu archipelago, wearing a fiber skirt and carrying a plaited basket. Such skirts were always tailor-made: cut to the appropriate length for the owner's height but also to reflect her age and status. Alexander Turnbull Library, Wellington, New Zealand.

The tremendous diversity of clothing styles across the archipelago can be grouped into a number of basic styles of dress for both men and for women. In the northernmost islands, the Banks and Torres, men were unclothed, while women were the same or wore a slim waist strap, sometimes plaited and sometimes stenciled, using a red vegetable dye. On the large island of Santo most women wore a narrow string belt from which a single leaf was suspended in the front (and caught and held between the thighs). Sometimes a bunch of leaves was suspended at the back. Men wore narrow plaited mats suspended from a waist belt, or sometimes leaves suspended in the same manner.

In parts of the central islands of Malekula and Ambrym, and in all the southern islands from Erromango to Aneityum, women wore skirts made of strips of fiber (known, misleadingly, as grass skirts). The materials and form of these skirts varied greatly from place to place. They could be made of a variety of leaves, of shredded bark, such as hibiscus, of banana fibers, of pandanus, or, on the southern islands, of ferns, of moss, or of other leaves. The fibers were bound or plaited into a waistband. Such skirts were always tailored—the length of the waistband and the length of the skirt were specific to the particular woman for whom the skirt was made. In the same general region men wore a penis wrapper—that is, a covering of some kind of material wrapped around the penis and attached to a belt. There are a great number of distinctive types of penis wrappers, so much so that, for example, people in the different districts of the island of Malakula have been distinguished by this clothing, known as "big *nambas*" (an area where the penis wrapper is intentionally bulky) and "small *nambas*" (where the penis is wrapped neatly in a leaf). In some places the wrapper has been tied to the belt so that the penis is held erect, while in other places it hangs down, sometimes lengthened by the wrapper.

From the north to the center of the archipelago, from the Banks Islands to Efate, women made plaited pandanus textiles. These textiles, sometimes known as mats, were woven from the long thin leaves of the pandanus palm, dried and softened, and slit into long ribbons. The leaves were plaited together in a technique that can be described as oblique interlacing or diagonal or oblique plaiting. Plaited pandanus textiles, made for wearing, were sometimes subjected to further treatments to ensure the resulting fabric would be soft and comfortable to wear. Textiles to be worn were designed for specific purposes. The Banks Islands' narrow plaited strap for use by women was made to be tied at the front with tassels hanging down. Elsewhere in this region women wore pandanus textiles wrapped around their waists and held in place by a waist strap, or by ties extending from the body of the textile at the corners. In Ambae, Pentecost, and parts of Maewo, and in the central islands from Epi to Efate, men wore narrower textiles suspended from a belt at the front, passed through the legs and secured by passing over the belt at the back. In some cases these textiles were plain, in others they were dyed a solid block of color, and in yet others they were stenciled with designs. The stenciling technique, log-wrap stenciling, is unique to this region. The textile is bound to a log. A stencil cut from banana palm spathe or built up with pieces of leaf stem is bound over it and the whole then plunged into a bath of boiling vegetable dye.

In the past many aspects of dress were symbolic: They provided information about the person wearing that item. Warfare and fear of sorcery restricted people to living in their own districts; they did not move freely from place to place. Men did make extensive trading expeditions, especially from island to island, although the opening of a new trading relationship—travel to a new place—often involved moments of danger and risk. Women did not travel casually, but, unlike men, they sometimes made radical moves at marriage, occasionally marrying right outside their group or even their island. What restrictions on movement meant was that on occasions, such as major rituals when many people came together, people did not necessarily know each other, nor know what had happened in each other's lives. Clothing that signaled social location was important on such occasions. People could figure out the rank and status of another person by what they were wearing, and sometimes also know what place they came from.

From the center of the archipelago to the northernmost island, one of the main foci of social life was status alteration rituals (sometimes known as graded or secret societies). These varied in form and content from place to place, but in all, individuals progressed through a series of grades or levels, gaining political, economic, or spiritual power and capacity as a result. Status alteration systems were gender-specific; in most places men

and women progressed through different though often interdependent ones. Men's systems were often focused on the killing of pigs; women might achieve a grade through pig killing or, for example, in Ambae or Pentecost, by producing and presenting a large number of pandanus textiles.

Achieved status was often marked by the right to wear certain decorations—head, arm, and leg embellishments, necklaces, belts, tattoos, and scarifications—or certain designs. On Ambae special textiles were made to signal achieved rank. A plaiting technique, which laid out the design in a raised weave, like bas-relief, overlaid with color through log-wrap stenciling, created these designs. The same designs were woven into shell-bead armbands, which men earned the right to wear. Feathered sticks were also worn in the hair to mark achieved status. Other items were placed elsewhere in the hair. Pigs' tails, for example, were worn as status markers in Santo, Malo, and northern Malakula. Pigs' tusks, carefully grown in a curving circle (by knocking out the pigs' opposing lower incisors), were a particularly important sign of achieved status. The length of the incisor, and hence the growth of the curve, was identified in named stages. In many places the stages were associated with different status levels. A full-circle tusk might be worn as an armband or as a neck pendant. In some cases a pendant was made of a pair of tusks bound side by side as opposing spirals. In the Banks Islands both plaited waist straps and straps made from a single pandanus leaf could be stenciled with powerful female status designs. Status achievements also carried with them the right to wear specific leaves and flowers. People could be and were punished for wearing, for example, red hibiscus flowers or a croton leaf species if they had not acquired the right to do so.

Across the archipelago dress for ceremonies and especially for dancing emphasized movement. Headdresses, leaves, and flowers worn in armbands and in the back of the belt, and in some places long fiber skirts, could all move with and against the movements of the wearer. Oiled bodies added to that effect by reflecting light in movement.

In central Vanuatu, in the area now known as Shefa, where social status was inherited, chiefly families possessed the right to wear certain textile designs that belonged simultaneously to their family line and to the place they came from (since family and place were completely interconnected). Here the textile designs were not created through stencils, but rather plaited using pre-colored pandanus. Whereas textiles in the northern region were always dyed red, sometimes with the addition of yellow dye on the fringes, these central Vanuatu textiles used a variety of red, yellow, and black colors. The wearing of such a textile not only indicated that the wearer belonged to a high-ranking family, but also suggested the place from which they came. These designs were applied to both men's and women's clothing textiles and, for example, to the textiles made to carry a baby of chiefly rank. It seems that ordinary people may have worn undyed plaited textiles in the same style.

In Erromango, southern Vanuatu, women wore twenty to thirty layers of fiber skirts, partly in response to the island's cooler climate and the location of most villages high in the hills. The outer skirts were generally made of widths of pandanus leaf, which were decorated by incising them with designs before the leaf dried. A child wore her skirts short, but as soon as she was engaged, she wore them to her ankles. Married women wore very long skirts, cut at the front to just touch the ground, but sweeping like a train behind them. Women married to or descended from chiefs also had the right to wear painted barkcloths draped around their shoulders at feasts and other rituals. These barkcloths were decorated with a combination of freehand drawing and dyeing, using local black, red, yellow, and brown dyes.

In parts of the archipelago widowhood was also marked in clothing. In Santo widows wore a long black cord, with shell beads attached, coiled around their bodies from their hips to their breasts, like a bodice. This was worn for about a year until the last mortuary ceremonies were completed for a woman's husband, after which the widow was free to remarry.

Tattooing and scarification were practiced variously across the region. In most areas women were tattooed more extensively than men, in some cases over their whole body from neck to knee, in some cases just on the face. Tattoos commonly indicated high social rank, although in some places, including Ambae, all women were tattooed, the number of tattoos increasing through their lives according to their rank and also that of their husband or father. Body markings were not always aimed at the living so much as at the next life. Tattoo designs were sometimes directed at life after death; on Maewo, for example, it was necessary to have a small tattoo on the wrist in order to be able to use fire in the afterworld. The piercing of the nasal septum was widespread, and in many places nose ornaments were placed in the hole. In several areas it is reported that nose piercing had a specific purpose related to the body after death—on Tanna it was thought necessary in order that the soul be able to leave the body after death.

EUROPEAN INTRODUCTIONS

European cloth began to be available in the islands from the 1820s as a trade good. European clothing was introduced primarily by missionaries, who saw its adoption as an outward and visible sign of conversion to Christianity. Missionaries perceived this as the adoption of modesty in dress, but in fact many islanders found the new clothes lacking in modesty and continued to wear local clothing underneath them—some men continued to wear penis wrappers under their trousers or sarongs, while women wore grass skirts under the voluminous loose dresses provided for them.

The very significant impact of the wearing of European clothing was that it erased or obscured the signs of personal identity and status worn on the body. Body modifications such as tattooing and scarification were no longer visible, and textiles and other items of dress declaring status were laid aside. Instead the wearers adopted a new singular identity as a Christian convert. European clothing also introduced new class distinctions, especially for women. The dresses that women were given to wear were not the same as those for European women for the period, being in fact more similar to nightdresses than to day dresses. These dresses were often called "mother hubbards," a designation that marked them specifically as "native" dresses. Clothing also revealed denomination affiliation. Mother hubbard dresses were primarily Presbyterian (the dominant denomination in the archipelago). Anglican converts wore blouses and long skirts.

European clothing was not adopted immediately and completely. In many areas people continued to use local clothing for daily work, donning cloth for church on Sundays. In the southern islands women continued to wear fiber skirts on weekdays until about 1970, sometimes with a cloth blouse to cover their breasts. Men wore lengths of cloth as sarongs from about the turn of the twentieth century, adopting trousers by the 1980s. However, lengths of cloth, purchased from trade stores, have continued to be widely used. When new they are often presented in exchanges where plaited pandanus textiles would previously have been used. They are used to make dresses and shirts, to carry babies and objects. Many women carry a length of fabric with them habitually, wrapping it around their dress to protect it from dirt, tying it as

As part of the traditionalist revival, people again wear traditional dress for ceremonies and other special occasions. These young girls asked to dress in pandanus textiles like their elders during a women's status alteration ceremony, Central Maewo, Vanuatu, 1997. Photograph by Lissant Bolton.

Noella Dick, from Tongoa Island, wearing a "flag dress," an island dress made in the colors of the Vanuatu flag. Port Vila, Vanuatu, 2005. Photograph by Lissant Bolton.

a belt to raise an island dress hem when working in a garden or on a reef, or using it as a shawl if the air is cool. Locally specific privileges of rank and status had a longer tenure than other forms of clothing. The right to wear certain items, such as leaves, flowers, or feathers, are in the early twenty-first century still observed, as are the rights to wear grade textiles (textiles that incorporate grade- or rank-specific designs (rather like the hoods on academic gowns), armbands, and head attire. However, as status alteration and other rituals are less and less practiced, these textiles and embellishments are less common.

The Presbyterian mother hubbard dresses were gradually modified. The original design required the use of a paper pattern to cut the fabric, especially for the neck of the dress. Some time before World War II an innovation that simplified the construction of the dress was introduced, probably at the Presbyterian Training Centre on Nguna island off north Efate. This allowed the fabric to be cut without reference to a pattern and also made very economical use of the fabric. A length of cloth is gathered to a simple bodice with an open neck, without a collar, and a second longer length gathered to the first, so that the dress billows out at the hem. Sleeves are gathered to the bodice on either side. This style of dress was introduced through the Presbyterian region of the country, by people trained on Nguna, or from Efate more generally. It was then passed along to other places by those who learned how to make it. Using hand-operated sewing machines, women throughout the country make this dress style. Although initially every place had a different name for the dress—often naming it for the place from which it had come—Lissant Bolton

shows that in the national lingua franca, Bislama, the dress came to be known as *aelan dres*—island dress.

In early decades island dresses were decorated on the bodice, sleeves, and hem with ribbons and lace purchased from local trade stores. In some areas it became popular to add a square of fabric, known as a wing, to the side of a dress at hip height. The origin of this introduction is not known. Wings, ribbons, and lace reflect the aesthetic of movement associated with different indigenous dress styles. With the introduction of valued added tax in the mid-1990s, the cost of these additions became prohibitive, and at the turn of the twenty-first century a new dress style developed, embellished with pleats and cuts in the fabric, and ribbons made from it.

Despite the range of other dress styles available to women, island dresses have had an enduring popularity among ni-Vanuatu women. (*ni-Vanuatu* is the correct way to describe a citizen of Vanuatu.) Although Anglican women continue to wear T-shirts and skirts, there would be very few ni-Vanuatu women who do not own at least one island dress. Upon independence in 1980 island dresses were adopted as national dress for women. No suitable male equivalent has been found, and men do not have a nominated national dress. In the late twentieth century some women from the island of Tongoa developed the "flag dress," that is, an island dress made using plain fabric in the colors of the national or provincial flag. On public days and especially for parades women from central Vanuatu commonly wear flag dresses. The popularity of this dress style has increased steadily since it was first introduced.

CONTEMPORARY TRADITIONAL DRESS

By 1980 European clothing conventions were accepted broadly across the archipelago. A traditionalist enclave on the island of Tanna, where people decided to reject incoming cultural innovations and to live as much as possible in the ways of their ancestors, is one of the few areas where people continue to use local dress—penis wrappers for men and fiber skirts for women. The valorization of indigenous knowledge and practice as *kastom*, especially through the work of the Vanuatu Cultural Centre, has led to the conscious use of indigenous clothing styles for ceremonies such as status alteration rituals, exchanges, and feasts, and for performances at local arts festivals or for tourists. Most men do not hesitate to don textiles or penis wrappers for such occasions. In the Banks Islands, where men were previously unclothed, they now commonly wear a piece of cloth wrapped around their hips. The use of local clothing styles poses difficulties for those women who have come to feel uncomfortable about leaving their breasts exposed. Not all women find this a problem, but where they do, a number of innovations in local dress have developed. In areas where women wore textiles wrapped around their hips, in the early twenty-first century they make and wear a similar textile to wrap around their chests. On southern islands women continue to wear fiber skirts and drape a piece of store-bought cloth around their upper body and tie it on their shoulders.

Local textiles have also been affected by the introduction of commercial dyes. These dyes were introduced to mark bags of dried coconut (copra) produced for export, and they are sold in local trade stores throughout the archipelago. While in the northern region plaited pandanus textiles continue to be dyed

Men from Malakula, dressed and decorated to perform a powerful dance at the opening of the new Vanuatu Cultural Centre building in November 1995. Photograph by Lissant Bolton.

red—but the red of the commercial dyes, not the red of vegetable dyes—in the south women have taken to dyeing their fiber skirts in brightly colored patterns. Such patterns include, for example, a checkerboard effect of colored squares alternating with squares of undyed fiber. On Tanna the bright colors of the skirts match the brightly colored cloth with which they drape their chests. Instead of or in addition to leaves and flowers, Tannese women add brightly colored tinsel as a further decoration, and dye the feathers they wear in their hair.

In the Shefa area of central Vanuatu the plaiting customs that produced the chiefly textiles have now been almost entirely forgotten. Here women refer to island dresses as their "traditional" clothing, and the dresses and men's shirts have replaced textiles in the exchanges of goods that occur on occasions such as marriage. However, these clothes are not deemed suitable for dance performances at arts festivals, both locally and overseas, and as a result other styles have developed. In some places like Nguna women use dried banana-leaf skirts. In Tongoa they have developed a style of plaited textile, which men wear over a belt, but which women now wear wrapped around their hips, and with a second textile to cover their breasts.

Since 1990 more and more ni-Vanuatu have moved to live in urban contexts, in the capital, Port Vila, or in Luganville, on Espirtu Santo. Here, often in shantytown settlements, people have been exposed to global fashion trends through television and DVDs, through watching tourists, and through the secondhand clothing market. As a Vanuatu Young People's Project report describes, bales of secondhand clothes brought into the country and sold both in shops and in informal market contexts grant people the opportunity to look smart more inexpensively. Young people who can afford to do so have adopted some international fashion markers, such as the wearing of sneakers. Most controversially young women have also adopted the wearing of trousers, both loose culottes and more fitted styles, including jeans. This move has been the subject of sustained opposition from men, especially from chiefs and other leaders who argue that to wear trousers, and hence to wear men's clothes, is to be disrespectful toward both *kastom* and the community. Although trousers are becoming widely accepted as clothes women wear for manual work and inside the home, there is still opposition to them. This reflects, especially for central Vanuatu, so widespread an acceptance of European dress conventions that indigenous dress codes have been forgotten; it also seems to reflect a tension in Vanuatu with the pace of change in the last several decades, of which changing dress has become symbolic.

References and Further Reading

Bolton, Lissant. *Unfolding the Moon: Enacting Women's Kastom in Vanuatu*. Honolulu: University of Hawai'i Press, 2003.

Bolton, Lissant. "'Island Dress That Belongs to Us All': Mission Dresses and the Innovation of Tradition in Vanuatu." In *Body Arts and Modernity*, edited by E. Ewart and M. O'Hanlon, 165–182. Wantage, UK: Sean Kingston, 2007.

Cummings, Maggie. *Young Women Speak: A Report on the Young Women, Beauty, and Self-Image Video Training Project*. Port Vila: Vanuatu Young People's Project, Vanuatu Cultural Centre, 2002.

Mabonlala, A. "Le vêtement feminine a Vanuatu". Unpublished manuscript in Vanuatu Cultural Centre archives, n.d.

Speiser, F. *Ethnology of Vanuatu: An Early Twentieth Century Study*. Bathurst, Australia: Crawford House Publishing, 1990. (Originally published in 1923.)

Lissant Bolton and Jean Tarisesei

See also Dress in New Caledonia.

Dress in New Caledonia

New Caledonia, situated in the southwest Pacific Ocean, comprises a number of islands including the Loyalty Islands, Isle des Pins, and Isle Bélep. The warm climate and tropical vegetation have had a substantial influence on what the inhabitants have worn and do wear. In the past the indigenous people of New Caledonia, the Melanesian Kanaks, embellished their bodies in various ways. Subsequently, evangelical missionaries urged these people to hide their bodies. In the twenty-first century consumerist society once again has encouraged people to dress up the body, each generation following its own particular fashion. In 1953 author Jean Mariotti noted the gradual integration of the Kanaks into the global economy, suggesting that by this time whatever part of the country a person was from, that person used a mixture of imported products for tools, clothes, and food. These could include the sarong, a desirable item that might be made in Manchester, UK, or Mulhouse or Lyon in France, a knife and an axe from Langres (also in France), matches that replaced former wood striking could come from a Norwegian pine, and a pipe perhaps from Saint-Claude, France.

Despite their long history of using local flora and fauna for their dress, younger generations in the twenty-first century have participated wholeheartedly in global fashion. Military jackets, T-shirts, and long skirts have, with some exceptions, almost entirely superseded sarongs and "mother hubbard" dresses (capacious garments introduced by missionaries). An exception is that female cricket teams continue to wear multicolored "robes mission."

TRADITIONAL CLOTHING

Pre-European morality in New Caledonia differed greatly from that in modern Western society; the body was practically unclothed, except for symbolic protection of intimate parts. It was not really about hiding these from view, since bagayous (penis coverings), which left the testicles visible, were not exactly g-strings, and the women's skirts were extremely short, with nothing underneath. In fact, it was about emphasizing the natural qualities of the body, either through clothing or through various modifications.

In the nineteenth century the clothing customs of the original Kanaks were also very different from those of Europeans, when men wore suits and women wore long gowns that hid their ankles. Certain authors considered that these customs and clothes were a product of "savagery." In fact, Kanak modesty and eroticism coexisted, both being marks of the universality of human sentiment, not that different from ideas of dignity and the sexual connotations of dress experienced in the modern world. The absence of actual clothing can also be explained by New Caledonia's relatively mild climate and by the poor technical quality of the plant materials on hand.

Men wore the bagayou, of threshed bark or bamboo, to which a free-hanging piece of fabric was attached. This covering was held up by a belt of flying fox hair, a matted cord made by rolling the hairs of the largest specimens of the species. These belts were often embellished with white porcelain, called ovule, which was a gendered symbol reserved for men. Their heads were often covered by a hat of balassor, a material made of banyan. This piece of clothing/finery hugged the head of the notable Kanak tightly, being a turban of varying lengths, depending on one's place in society. It was often fashioned into original shapes, sometimes imitating the shape of a mushroom, sometimes resembling a bulging beret. At times, during cold snaps of the cool season, important men would throw a sort of covering of fibers or tapa (barkcloth)—called a raincoat in the village of Hienghene—over their shoulders. These ceremonial garments or items of comfort for the elders were seemingly worn infrequently and disappeared with the introduction of materials made of Western wool.

Women wore short, pale red skirts of spun fibers or tapa, like those still preserved in the Musée Le Havre. Such skirts of bourao (a form of hibiscus) and banyan fibers, or narrow strips of tapa, were fixed on a length of a rope of coconut hair. This tapa skirt could be about six and a half feet (several meters) long when unwrapped, as it enfolded several times the waist of the wearer, eventually hanging at the back. Possessing feminine resonance, these cone-shaped skirts could be passed around in exchanges between groups. With an uncovered bust the Kanak woman never connected her body shape with seduction, rather with the items with which she dressed herself. Indeed, jewelry among the Kanak women of the past was an extremely important form of embellishment. In fact, Father Georges-Henri Luquet noted in 1926 that the Melanesians displayed items on all possible parts of their bodies.

Jewelry consisted primarily of necklaces and was adopted mainly by women. The most common was made of a string of flying fox hair, generally trimmed with seeds or shells. The more beautiful ones were made of jade green "pearls" of serpentine, polished and pierced in the center. Only the wives of the chiefs had these, and they could be composed of more than two hundred items—the result of a technique of meticulous feminine labor that had evolved over several generations. Bracelets were worn by both men and women indiscriminately. They sometimes consisted of cylinders, which narrowed to a point, like a cone, and were sometimes made of multiple threads of flying fox hair mixed together and embellished with pearls or shells. Generally worn on the arms, they were also used to decorate the ankles or calves. They were woven by the women, who later dyed them a dark brown.

Weaponry can form part of both martial and ceremonial dress, as it did in New Caledonia. No warrior would leave home without his club (kare) or spear. Likewise, men often wore a small string bag full of rocks for their slingshots, hanging from a headband, and a few throwing sticks fastened to their belts as other forms of body attachment. As for the chiefs, during displays of weaponry they would flaunt an ostentatious serpentine battle-axe. For special occasions Kanaks also practiced body painting.

Paint was essentially limited to the face and chest: kaolin for white, candlenut or mushroom pollen for black, and the leaves of a desmodium (a tropical plant), whitewashed with coral lime paste, to make blue. The ethnologist Maurice Leenhardt noted early in the twentieth century that body coating was undertaken to signify varying mental states, such as depression or exaltation. In sorrow, it was ash and white earth. Endeavoring to encourage rain, the priests would paint themselves in black as if to wrap themselves in "the impenetrability of the clouds."

Apart from embellishments worn or painted, the Kanaks also embraced permanent styles, that is to say modifications imposed on the body itself. One such alteration consisted of transforming the earlobe into an earring by making a piercing, and gradually enlarging it by introducing progressively wider cylindrical objects. One observer noted that during an important period of mourning, the lower part of the earlobe, reduced simply to a string, was shredded as a sign of grief. Similarly, the practice of aesthetically shaping the face or skull of newborns was observed. In Touho, in the northern part of New Caledonia, the head was flattened on the sides, making it as narrow as the neck. In the Balade area it was flattened obliquely, and the forehead was pressed down. On Bélep Island boys' faces were stretched to give them a soldier-like appearance, and girls' chins were raised in such a way as to round off the face.

Tattooing, less frequent among the Kanaks than body painting due to the color of their skin pigmentation, was practiced by diverse methods. Relief tattooing was achieved by the scarring of voluntary wounds, produced either by applying a vegetable-based blistering agent or by burning the skin. Tattooing, strictly speaking, consisted of making blue-colored figures by injecting under the skin several substances, such as charcoal made from candlenut or the soot of vegetable juices mixed in a cooking pot. Masculine body art evoked the warlike and was primarily restricted to sorcerers and chieftains. On the other hand, it was more popular as a sign of beauty with the women, who mainly tattooed the lips, the bottom of the face, the chest, and the arms. In the late nineteenth century these designs were made up of continuous parallel straight or curved lines or alternatively cruciform or circular tattoos. In 1911 the ethnologist Fritz Sarasin considered that 4 percent of men were tattooed, and double that for women. In the twenty-first century the fashion of tattooing has reappeared with the immigration of Tahitians and Wallisians, consisting almost exclusively of the inscription of the names of loved ones or contemporary motifs: the cross, anchors, and mermaids.

CLOTHING OF THE PAST: A SYMBOL OF RELIGIOUS DEVOTION

Since the 1860s the inhabitants of the Loyalty Islands who were baptized as Christians were known as "those who are clothed." The arrival of missionaries with their gospel teachings was, among other things, given concrete expression by profound modifications in dress, strongly influenced by the canons of Christian morality, both Protestant and Catholic. Missionaries therefore induced the men to replace their bagayous with fabric (*mwânöö* or *manous*), modeled on Polynesian and Fijian sarongs and *lavalava* (cloths tied around the waist). Since manous were impractical for work the colonists encouraged the Kanaks to wear shorts, and government officials obliged them to wear polo or other shirts during their visits to colonial centers.

A family in New Caledonia, late nineteenth century, showing the influence of Christian dress. The woman wears a "mother hubbard" style of dress, the man wears trousers of European type, and even the children are well covered, one apparently in a European shirt and indigenous wraparound cloth. Photographer unknown. Collection of Frédéric Angleviel.

As far as women were concerned, the process took place in two stages. First, the missionaries deemed that the customary short skirts did not sufficiently cover the bodies of believers. As such, they made the women either lengthen their skirts or attach a petticoat. Subsequently, they introduced the "mother hubbard" dress, which was initially simply a cylinder of material of one pleasant color with two armholes and a collar. This body covering was soon replaced by styled dresses, made from more delicate material, and in a wider variety of colors and prints (flowers, shells, butterflies, geometric shapes)—the addition of petticoats and lace was, for a long time, an inescapable element of the artistry of Kanak fashion. Mother hubbard dresses therefore combined quality with modesty. They were garments adaptable to all the activities of daily life: worn for fieldwork, handmade for tribal events, a uniform dress for cricket, and a dress made with the latest materials and collar for special occasions. They could have well-made buttonholes or collar trimmings, sturdy fabrics, sober patterns and prints, Mao collars, or even long sleeves (unsuitable for the climate).

Kanaks rarely wore shoes. Rather they were accustomed from a young age to walk barefoot both on the grass of the central streets and the flat areas of coral. But when they "came down" from their habitation to the closest village, they put on Japanese sandals or thongs (slip-on sandals), and those who worked in the mines or who traveled far from a county town made a practice of wearing solid walking shoes.

KANAK FABRIC AND TRIMMINGS

Plant-based fabrics, cords made from flying fox hair, and the bark of trees and bushes are at the root of customary clothing. Kanaks married these materials in multiple ways in order to dress and embellish their bodies. Fabric, or balassor, is made from plant fibers worked patiently with the help of wooden hammers, better known under their generic name, tapa beaters. Made from the phloem of broussonetia for a white tint or the Pacific banyan (*Ficus prolixa*) for a red tint, every dialect gives this fabric a different name: *tillit* in Ajië and *tili* in Cemhui. In the Canala area (in the North Province), like everywhere else, balassor became part of the composition of a multitude of everyday objects: *kwiöö-mwâmwâ* (ceremonial clothing), *jùù-xata* (skirts), *puunêmûû* (belts), *nii* (penis coverings), *mwâxata* (turbans), *jingâ* (raincoats), *jô mê jia* (ornamental spears), and *xata* (plaited cord).

Banyan, cloudberry, paper mulberry, and the Ficus species are planted and maintained everywhere, but manufacture and wear of the bark fabric are reserved for men. This is different from Tonga, for instance, where barkcloth is made by women. In the cool season, early in the morning, the bark of the shrub is removed all in one piece from the base and then placed on a flat surface. The bark is regularly beaten from the inside out, using the *chëixata* (a kind of mallet of *âbiwa*, or ironwood of the *casuarina* species). Once it has been beaten, the bark of a shoot the length of a short bamboo stick produces a strip about eleven inches (thirty centimeters) long. The beating technique differs depending on whether one wants simply to obtain flattened fibers (for a penis covering, for example), or large sheets of material. In the twenty-first century the cloth *manou* has taken the place of bark fabric.

Kanaks used fibrous cords, plaited flying fox hairs, and rope made of coconut fibers as trimmings. The cords made an appearance in all of their clothing: belts, bagayous, skirts, the ties of raincoats, and the fastenings of embellishments. Men could use them unaccompanied to encircle their bodies as many times as the total length of the cord allowed. These plaits of flying fox hair, called *ngolo* in the south of the main island, could also provide the base material for the composition of Kanak money. Furthermore, at the time of their marriage women were offered a large skein of plaited hairs of several strands, true wealth that indeed followed them, sometimes into the grave. They used these same cords as ligatures (for throwing *assegai*, or slender spears, and for the handles of clubs) or as ornaments including the decoration of gourds. The necks of axes were woven in sparterie (a species of grass) and decorated with shells.

In the Loyalty Islands, because the flying foxes were smaller and the coconut tree ubiquitous, the Polynesian technique of making string from coconut fibers was widely used. And once soaked in seawater, these ropes became practically rot-proof, making them indispensable for everything related to the production of canoes and fishing tools. Customary soft furnishings were made from a collection of all the threads (plaited, twisted, and fringed) and trimmings (cords, lace, shoulder straps, ribbons) that were destined for the decoration of clothes, weaponry, or tools distinctive to the Kanaks. Often, sparterie and other basketwork were decorated with flowers. In the twenty-first century the latter are often replaced by cords in vibrant colors.

In the Loyalty Islands the fiber of coconut trees and plaited bulrush often replaced cords made of flying fox hair. In the same archipelago various dance accessories were made from vegetable fibers. The most common consisted of a bundle of cords, whose bottom, attached tightly, tapered to a loop. Sometimes the long and narrow tail feathers of the *phaëton rubricauda Bodd* (red-tailed tropic bird), from Ile Surprise, the island of the birds, jutted out of the bundle. In the early twenty-first century these accessories, simplified and embellished with wool or seersucker, still constitute an appreciated component of customary dance dress.

HAIRSTYLES AND HEADDRESSES OVER THE YEARS

Headdresses were not simply worn as pieces of clothing or embellishment. They also allowed for the creative expression of individuals, and their complexity was the pride of the wearer or their clan. Everyday hairstyles, austere hairstyles of mourning, and celebration hairdos differed a great deal, and if the Kanaks never favored the heaped headgear of the Papuans, neither were they reduced to embellishing their hair as in the eastern Pacific.

Only men had set headgear: cylinder or turban. The former, called a *tidi*, real stovepipe shapes without edges or a base, and decorated with yellow fringes, was composed of closely woven and trellised plaits, and shaded black. This basketry was blackened with the help of grilled candlenut fruit. Thus, the hair came out and down again from the top. Ornaments were fixed to its stiff side: huge white ovules, plumes of all sizes, or crescent-shaped motifs of mother-of-pearl. These headbands, which held up pendants of mother-of-pearl and shell beads, hugged the temples of chiefs and other people of note. The two circular facings situated at the level of the ears could make one think, when found isolated in a museum, that they were female finery. These fake bra cups consisted of pieces of decoration or magical objects, and feathers were attached to them.

The mourner's turban, which continued to be in use until World War II, was worn continuously from the day on which the corpse was carried until the lifting of the period of bereavement. As they could neither take the turbans off in public nor let them touch the ground, mourners had a post close to their solitary hut where they could hang them up. These tall headdresses, which looked like huge mushrooms, were sometimes twice as tall as the head on which they were mounted. In fact, Jules Patouillet noted in his book *Trois Ans en Nouvelle Calédonie*, published in 1873, that mourners handmade these extraordinary hats, which constituted a mortuary taboo. The hat was like a melon, one meter (about one foot) in diameter (just over three feet), often more, and woven with small branches of sarsaparilla intertwined with tree ferns.

As for the hair itself, Georges-Henri Luquet noted in 1926 that one of the rarest hairstyles was one where both sides of the head were shaved, with a large crest in the middle. In the north and the Loyalty Islands the chiefs wore a sort of helmet as a war headdress, formed by a large seashell tied beneath the chin with laces of bat hair, which passed through four holes. In the same period young people, who previously colored their hair with ash, now used lime slurry or hydrogen peroxide. The dark pigments being removed, the hair took on a brownish-red tint.

In 1911 Fritz Sarasin remarked upon the gradual changes in the hair of the Kanaks. It appears the hair was quite fine in youth, wavy or in ringlets of a more-or-less clear brown hue, which then gave way to the coarser, curly (or spiral, to be precise) adult growth of a brownish-black color. When left uncut, this hair became an imposing and bushy mass. The New Caledonians treated their hair as works of art, styling it in different ways. Many indigenous people cut their hair very short, more so the women than the men. The fashion was to trim the back and the sides of the head, so that the top was left adorned with hair of a certain length. Sometimes the head was entirely shorn, save for a strand that hung down over the forehead. In the Loyalty Islands there was a great variety of hair types: wavy, spiral, or ringlets.

To complement these hairstyles, men enjoyed adding white plumes of large cock feathers. The most beautiful of these, sometimes termed *aigrettes* (feather tufts), featured kingfisher feathers at the base—or those of any other magically endowed bird—against the support rod. For festive celebrations men also fixed small tufts of white feathers to their hair, by attaching them to thin sticks or finely cut fern leaves. Combs, carved from wood or bamboo, had uses both practical and decorative.

In the past women styled their hair using sticks arranged in a ridge behind their heads. A legendary father rebuffed a suitor, pretending that his young daughter refused him by saying: "Your message has struck the sticks on her neck, it hasn't reached this woman." The practice fell out of usage in the last century; women were content to use a tortoise-shell or carved wood comb in their hair, which served as both a brush and a scraper. After the introduction of bamboo to imitate the shape of the old combs, they added chiseled geometric motifs. Every part of the main island favored its own particular style of comb: flat-backed; semicircle-backed; long stem-backed; carved geometric-motif-backed.

Similarly, Melanesian women, abandoning the postnuptial practice of wearing their hair very short, took up the habit of covering their heads with a piece of cloth, or holding their hair back with hair bands or ribbons. The elderly preferred to keep their hair short, wrapping it in dark-colored woolen caps. In the Loyalty Islands it has been the custom for a long time to comb the hair at length after having carefully massaged it with coconut oil.

In some places aged men often still wear hats, reminiscent of the imposing vegetable fabric head coverings of their chiefs of old. As for women, after having followed the example of Europeans during the interwar period, a time when for settlers wearing a hat was regarded as a vital barrier against the tropical sun, they have come to appreciate the protection given by hats or bonnets.

THE EMERGENCE OF AN OCEANIC FASHION

Kanak fashion has changed rapidly under the pressure of youth, who covet the latest modern trends. In view of the abundance of cheap, mass-produced, and up-to-date clothing available since the later twentieth century, the clans have been won over by globalization. Sparkling colors and light materials are in circulation, in the colorful and leisurely so-called Oceanic style. New clothing customs have had a significant impact on both the interior and the islands, investing the Kanaks with a sense of being part of the wider metropolitan area of Nouméa, at once the main place of work and the scene of new life.

Young people and urbanites were the first to diversify their wardrobes, leaving behind the manou and mother hubbard dresses of the past in favor of fresh combinations: shirts and pants, blouses and skirts, T-shirts and shorts. The last combination has won the favor of all New Caledonian communities. The Kanaks care less for metropolitan fashion; three-piece suits, ties, evening dresses, or high heels are worn only for official gatherings or formal festivities. Men perpetuate Oceanic fashion, matching "Polynesian" print shirts with light pants, whereas women like full and colorful dresses. Young women may have corn-row tresses, and older women short shaped hair. Rasta bonnets with Bob Marley T-shirts and manous are popular with youth culture. In the twenty-first century, and probably into the future, the younger generations are at the forefront of change, as much in the suburbs as in the villages. Just as world music has become established, new clothing styles are taking over the body, little by little. It is remarkable that the bare bodies of yesteryear became the cramped bodies of yesterday and the free bodies of today.

References and Further Reading

Angleviel, Frédéric. "Vêtements et parures du temps passé" and "Etoffes et passementeries kanak." In *Chroniques du pays kanak*, 2:40–47, 48–53. Nouméa, New Caledonia: Planète Mémo, 1999.

Brouzeng, Cécile. "Jupes de fibres: richesses des femmes." In *De jade et de nacre. Patrimoine artistique kanak*, 92–94. Paris: Réunion des musées nationaux, 1990.

Colchester, C., ed. *Clothing the Pacific.* Oxford: Berg, 2003.

Kakou, Serge. *Découverte photographique de la Nouvelle-Calédonie, 1848–1900.* Arles, France: Éditions Actes Sud, 1998.

Leenhardt, Maurice. *Notes d'ethnologie néo-calédonienne.* Vol. 8. Paris: Institut d'Ethnologie, 1930.

Luquet, Georges-Henri, and Marius Archambault. *Art Neo-Caledonien.* Paris: Institute d'Ethnologie, 1926.

Marchal, Henri. *De jade et de nacre. Patrimoine artistique kanak.* Paris: Réunion des musées nationaux, 1990.

Mariotti, Jean. *Nouvelle Caledonie: Le Livre du Centenaire 1853–1953.* Paris: Horizons de France, 1953.

Paini, Anna. "Rhabiller les symboles: les femmes kanak et la robe mission à Lifou." *Journal de la Société des Océanistes* 117 (2004): 233–254.

Sarasin, Fritz. *Ethnologie der Neu-Caledonier und Loyalty-Insulaner.* Munich: Kreidel's Verlag, 1929.

Frédéric Angleviel
Translated by Marissa Dooris and Vikram Iyer

See also Bilas: Dressing the Body in Papua New Guinea; Body Ornaments of Solomon Islands.

Body Ornaments of Solomon Islands

- Wearing "Money"
- Shell Ornaments
- Wood, Fiber, and Leaf
- Changing Styles

Samuel Alasa'a, a Kwara'ae elder from Malaita island (Solomon Islands) in 1984. He is dressed to show the ornaments he wore in his youth, including a shell nose pin, woven ear-sticks, a pearlshell crescent, and a rattan girdle. Photograph by Ben Burt.

The country of Solomon Islands was formed in the 1890s by British colonization of a chain of islands in the southwest Pacific region of Melanesia. From west to east these include the major islands of Choiseul, New Georgia, Santa Isabel, Guadalcanal, Malaita, and Makira, with many smaller groups from Shortland Islands in the west to Santa Cruz far to the east. Like other island Melanesians in Papua New Guinea to the west and Vanuatu to the east, Solomon Islanders live by farming, foraging, and fishing in the forests, lagoons, and oceans of the hot, moist tropics. Until the British gained military and political control during the 1900s and 1910s, local communities were self-governing and in a constant state of tension or conflict with their neighbors. This maintained differences in local language and culture between districts and, even more, between islands. There are about eighty local ethnic groups in Solomon Islands, formerly with a wide variation in styles of dress, despite a constant sharing of ideas and artifacts through exchange and intermarriage. However, people everywhere wore very little, except when they wished to ornament or decorate themselves. Then they donned a variety of fine objects, beautiful and often valuable too. A century of colonialism and globalization has produced a new Western-style uniformity, but some of these ornament traditions are still remembered.

Formerly, while working day to day, people wore only as much as they considered decent and convenient. Children wore nothing, nor did adult men in most of southeast Solomons, but in western Solomons men wore a loincloth of leaf, barkcloth, or imported cotton calico, a fashion taken up elsewhere during the Colonial period. At puberty girls in many areas would put on no more than a waistband, but when married, women everywhere wore some kind of loin covering. This was an apron or skirt of shredded bark in Makira and Guadalcanal, leaves or a barkcloth apron in Malaita, a barkcloth loincloth padded behind in New Georgia, or a barkcloth skirt in Santa Isabel. Minimal clothing allowed tattooing to enhance the body, at least where people were light-skinned enough for the designs to show, especially in southeast Solomons. In Malaita and Makira coastal people had elaborate geometric patterns tattooed or incised, especially on the face and often on the chest, sometimes made as part of coming-of-age ceremonies. Women generally cut their hair short, while men usually wore it longer, sometimes bleached with lime in New Georgia and Guadalcanal, where white wigs of plant fiber were also worn. Men usually plucked out their whiskers with shell tweezers, sometimes leaving trimmed beards or moustaches. Many people blackened their teeth with a leaf and mineral paste, both for good looks and to strengthen the teeth.

It was the way people dressed on special occasions, including when greeting foreign visitors, that most impressed early European travelers to Solomon Islands. They remarked upon ornaments of gleaming shell, beads, and teeth, carved turtle shell, and colorful plaited fiber. Pendants, ear and nose ornaments, rings, bands, straps, and girdles, fashioned from the products of the forests and the sea, were designed to show out against the dark body. As skillfully crafted and attractive artifacts, Europeans purchased them in great quantities as mementos and collectors' items. During the twentieth century they were mostly replaced by imported clothes, with some still kept as family heirlooms. In the twenty-first century few people still make and wear body ornaments, in old or new local styles, but their former richness and diversity is preserved mainly in metropolitan countries far away. There are Solomon Islands ornaments in most major museums with ethnography or world culture collections in Britain (especially the British Museum), some European countries, Australia and New Zealand, the United States, and Japan. Missionaries of the Anglican Melanesian Mission in particular collected and sold quantities of Solomon Islands artifacts to support the costs of their work. Even so, very little has been researched or published about these ornaments, apart from pictures of particular objects in art books and incidental accounts and photographs in books by travelers and anthropologists. *Body Ornaments of Kwara'ae and Malaita* by Ben Burt is the first detailed study of how Solomon Islanders used a wealth of fine artifacts to make themselves "look good" and "look important," as they say, but for other islands such work has still to be done.

Some things were worn only by men or by women. On Malaita men's rattan girdles were associated with warfare, while red fiber waistbands were worn by girls, and black-and-white beaded belts by married women. But in Solomon Islands generally, men wore the most elaborate ornaments, mainly because women took less prominent parts in the public events at which they were displayed, including the warlike raids and celebrations that played an important part in local politics. Men staged the most elaborate dance performances, wearing leaves and sometimes white lime paint with their body ornaments. The most important body ornaments were valuable and worn as best dress for visiting and for gatherings like markets, feasts, and festivals. As the heads of families and as community leaders and chiefs, men would proclaim their status through valuable ornaments, including heirlooms from ancestral ghosts, who also made them *tabu* for women to wear. It was when women were on public display, particularly when a girl was to be married in return for a big bridewealth of shell valuables, that they wore the kind of valuable ornaments more usually reserved for men.

WEARING "MONEY"

Some of the most prestigious ornaments were those that are described in the twenty-first century, in European terms, as local "moneys." Small denominations of money could be used for everyday buying and selling, although ornaments were generally less acceptable than the cash that has now replaced them for this purpose. Larger ones are still given in exchange for goods, services, and contracts, from food and artifacts to marriages and reconciliations, and formerly for killings.

In the New Georgia group in western Solomon Islands, the main form of money was rings of white shell, often worn as ornaments. For the larger rings chunks of giant clamshell were sawed with vine and abrasive sand, pierced with flint-tipped pump-drills (driven by a cord winding and unwinding around a drill-shaft with a flywheel), ground smooth with stone files and grindstones, and polished with abrasive leaves. Cone shells of all sizes were burned away by being partly buried under a fire, forming a ring from the cross-section of a shell, which was then ground smooth with stone. Even when steel tools were obtained from colonial traders, the working of shell was slow and tedious, and the rings were correspondingly valuable. Lower-value rings of clamshell and cone shell were worn on the upper arms, sometimes in numbers enough to reach from elbow to armpit. Higher-value rings of fossilized clamshell could be worn as neck pendants, the most prestigious being mounted with a carved turtle-shell plaque fringed with beads and small animal teeth. Smaller cone-shell rings were bound in rows into necklaces, and the smallest were strung as beads into valuable girdles ornamented with clusters of small teeth, larger rings, and seeds. In the late nineteenth century some communities in New Georgia, enriched by colonial trade and by raiding for captives to serve as slaves, produced great quantities of shell money-rings, which were sold and exchanged far and wide as ornaments, by European traders as well as Islanders. Shell rings were not usually exchanged as "money" beyond the western islands, but they were made and valued throughout Solomon Islands. Large rings of clam, cone, and trochus shell were worn on the arm, and smaller cone-shell rings were worn as

ornaments for the ears and nose and strung or bound many at a time into neck and leg ornaments.

In the southeast Solomons the valuables usually exchanged as money were shell beads and teeth, also drilled to be strung, which were made into ornaments throughout Solomon Islands. Since at least the nineteenth century the main source of the beads has been the Langalanga lagoon on the west coast of Malaita, where they are made from white, red, and black shell and certain black seeds, according to styles in demand among people of other districts. Shells, often purchased from far away, are broken and chipped into rough disks, ground flat on stone, and drilled, formerly with a pump-drill. They are then threaded on vine to be smoothed by rubbing with a grooved grindstone into beads of regular size and shape. The multistring denominations used for important exchanges, like the fathom-long "ten-string," which is a standard in much of Malaita, can be worn draped around the body. However, for ornaments the beads were more usually worn strung as belts and bandoliers, woven into patterned straps for the arms and waist, and strung in a net design for headbands and sashes. Dolphin teeth are also exchanged as part of the money-bead system, as a more widespread standard of value than the various kinds of beads. They were strung on necklaces, woven into bristling straps for the head and neck, and added as fringes to money-bead ornaments. Styles varied between districts and islands, with woven money-bead and dolphin-teeth straps most favored in Malaita and strings of money-beads with dog teeth as well as dolphin teeth more usual in Makira. Bat and cuscus teeth, although not used as money, were also used for certain ornaments, and so were human teeth, commemorating both venerated ancestors and defeated enemies.

Money-beads and dolphin teeth were also traded far and wide, to be reworked into ornaments according to local tastes. Like shell rings, they once traveled along inter-island networks linking people from Solomon Islands all the way to mainland New Guinea. Local ornament fashions probably changed according to the economic and political influence of the communities that exchanged the preferred moneys for goods and strategic relationships. Hence Guadalcanal and Isabel islands, trading with both the main producers of money-rings in New Georgia and of money-beads in Malaita, seem to have adopted ornament styles from both areas in early colonial times, replacing older local types of ornaments used as money.

SHELL ORNAMENTS

Shell rings, beads, and teeth, as valuables exchanged as money, or for money, were worn to proclaim the prestige of community leaders and their families. Other shell ornaments, which also had high money values because of the scarce materials and skilled labor required to make them, contributed to the glamour that wealth conveyed when worn on the body. Pearlshell pendants for the neck, cut as a crescent from the lip of the shell, were made with local variations throughout Solomon Islands. Large crescents of goldlip shell, as well as disks of the whole shell, became popular in the southeast Solomons after Europeans began trading the shell from its local sources in the mid-nineteenth century. Shell-disk pendants of white clamshell, incised with a design of frigate-birds or a cross-shaped "star," were a specialty of Malaita and Makira, worn at the neck or on the head. Open-work pendants of pearlshell and white shell, with designs of frigate-birds and fish and circles representing money-rings, were worn at the neck in New Georgia and Santa Isabel. Large shell disks with an overlay of turtle shell carved in fine open-work designs in various styles were particularly valuable and widely traded, from the northern half of Malaita to the islands of Papua New Guinea eastward. Particularly elaborate ones were developed in certain parts of west and central Solomon Islands, with the turtle shell cut so fine that it is hardly wider than a pencil line. An enormous variety of shell ornaments was made for the nose, most common being a clamshell pin worn through the septum, but also open-work pendants and shell rings. In southeast Solomons shell studs and pins or small dolphin teeth were stuck in holes in the tip and sides of the nose. White cowrie shells were common ornaments for the hair, tied individually or strung as a brow band.

Ingava, a warrior chief of Roviana in the New Georgia islands (Solomon Islands), and his wife, photographed by a Methodist missionary in the 1900s. He wears a high-value shell money-ring pendant mounted on turtle shell, as befits a chief, and a girdle of shell beads and teeth. Both have lower-value money-rings on their arms. Photograph by George Brown.

Shell ornaments, being durable as well as valuable, often became family heirlooms, sanctified as the tabu belongings of the dead ancestors whose ghosts watched over the affairs of the living. As such they could represent the political seniority inherited from these ancestors and might even be kept as relics in shrines rather than being worn. However, political leadership actually required building personal influence by supporting relatives and neighbors in family and community affairs. Valuable ornaments, like money, added substance and prestige to the public appearance of those who gave their wealth to help others, rather than serving as symbols of their authority. They were but the most prestigious of a wider range of ornaments worn to make people look good and important on public occasions.

WOOD, FIBER, AND LEAF

Ornaments of forest materials, less laborious to make and less durable than those of shell, were also less valuable. Many were plaited from shreds of vine, bark, and leaf, mostly of black, red, and yellow, often in geometric patterns. The black was from certain tough vines, sometimes stained to darken them, the red from coconut-frond cuticle or pandanus leaf stained with dye from the root of trees such as *Morinda*, and the yellow was the natural color of an orchid stem. The black and red were plaited into bands and straps, for the arms and waist and sometimes for the head, often with patterns embroidered in yellow and red on black. Malaita in particular was well known for such ornaments, and for similar red and yellow patterning on bamboo sticks and pegs worn through holes in the ears. Malaitans also made fine combs of black palm-wood sticks bound with red and yellow patterning to be worn in the hair. In south Malaita and Makira similar combs were often inlaid with pearlshell set in black putty instead. Combs, normally only worn by men, could be further ornamented with feathers or tassels of red-stained palm-leaf strips. In New Georgia and Santa Isabel red-stained shreds of pandanus leaf were braided and plaited into bands and bindings for various shell-ring and carved shell ornaments. Although local styles and tastes varied between districts and islands, all these ornaments were also traded far and wide. Western Solomon Islanders wore patterned armbands made in Bougainville, Papua New Guinea, some of which resembled those worn in Malaita, and in the twenty-first century it is often difficult to tell which of the styles now seen only in museum collections were local to which islands.

Other items of dress included eyeshades of plaited coconut leaf, worn by stylish young men, particularly in the New Georgia group. Then there were the bags to carry personal possessions, plaited from shreds of bark, which people wore hanging from the shoulder or the neck, depending on the local fashion. The finest, worn with body ornaments for special occasions, were plaited in geometric patterns, sometimes with the loose ends of the bark shreds hanging as fringes, or ornamented with shell rings or shiny dark seeds. Leaves were often added to bags or stuck in belts and armbands, particularly crotons and cordylines, which were planted for ritual purposes around villages and shrines. Scented leaves were part of the magic used to make an ornamented person even more attractive, particularly by young people when courting. There were also leaves with magic to protect people from the sorcery of enemies or jealous onlookers on public occasions.

Before the Colonial period, from the mid-nineteenth century, some islands were too remote from the rest to share much in the common traditions of what is now Solomon Islands. The Santa Cruz islands far to the east had their own distinctive styles of ornaments, with men wearing large shell-disk neck pendants, fretted pearlshell nose ornaments, and shell-money beads and earrings, all quite different from their nearest neighbors in Makira or the Banks and Torres islands of Vanuatu. Teams of young men wore such things as part of a spectacular costume for festival dances, with fringed and patterned loincloths, woven of shredded banana leaf on a backstrap loom, and hair plumes of small red feathers used for the local money. Even more isolated were the small atolls settled by people from Polynesian islands far to the east, including Rennell-Bellona, Ontong Java, Sikaiana, Anuta, and Tikopia. These people were culturally quite distinct from the Melanesians of Solomon Islands, and each was virtually isolated from contact with other islands until the Colonial period. Their styles of dress were based on loincloths and skirts of barkcloth or woven cloth, with elaborate tattooing but none of the carved shell and patterned plaiting of the Melanesian Solomons.

CHANGING STYLES

The arrival of Europeans, making regular visits beginning in the mid-nineteenth century, then shipping Islanders to work in their Pacific colonies, settling as traders, and eventually taking political control in the early twentieth century, introduced new imported materials for ornaments. Glass beads made in Europe were popular, especially the small seed beads used throughout the colonial world for patterned body ornaments and clothing, from south and east Africa to North and South America. Malaitans in particular wove these beads into larger, cheaper, and more colorful versions of the money-bead straps they already made for the arms and waist. They also experimented with novel styles such as interpretations of the British Union Jack flag and the designs on playing cards. New Georgians used glass beads to trim their money-ring pendants and shell-bead girdles, and Shortland Islanders made them into large woven bead panels to be worn on the back as dance ornaments. Glass beads came with new bead-weaving techniques, learned perhaps from the traders who supplied them and shared with other parts of the world, quite different from those used for ornaments of money-beads. A completely new kind of armband became popular throughout the Solomons, adopted perhaps from Vanuatu, with the beads threaded on bindings around a coil of twine to form geometric designs. Just as glass beads were worn in place of money-beads, so ceramic rings made in Europe for the Solomon Islands market were purchased as arm rings. These came to replace shell rings, which were being sold to foreigners from the early twentieth century. Neither beads nor rings had the money value and prestige of the local products, but they added a superficial glamour to the ornamented body, enabling people to imitate their more wealthy leaders.

Solomon Islanders first became involved in the colonial economy by selling local products, then as plantation laborers in Fiji and Queensland from the late nineteenth century and in Solomon Islands from the early twentieth century. This introduced them to new styles of dress that were both exotic and prestigious, identified with the wealth and power of new lands far away. More frequent contact with outsiders, both Europeans and Islanders, made people increasingly shy about appearing naked on public occasions and encouraged more of them to adopt loin coverings. Even so, clothes were first adopted more as ornaments, often in

ways Europeans found incongruous. They would remark upon a senior chief dressing in a jacket without trousers, and on popular items such as hats, kerchiefs, and leather belts with pouches being worn without other clothes. It was only when Solomon Islanders took up Christianity, as an alternative to the ancestral ghosts who had failed to withstand the advance of British colonial control, that they really began to adopt clothing on European terms. At first this was usually a wraparound *lavalava* for men and a skirt for women, with trousers and shirts, blouses and dresses, as these became increasingly available over the years. As a condition of spiritual support from the new religion, missionaries were able to insist on colonial standards of dress more effectively than either plantation employers or government officials. Some denominations also condemned old-style body ornaments as "heathen," and, in any case, local ornaments became increasingly more old-fashioned and less prestigious under the new colonial order. Europeans tried to discourage Solomon Islanders from competing with them in matching their own styles of best dress, but nonetheless ornaments were put away, destroyed, or sold to colonial visitors as attractive curios of disappearing exotic cultures.

This process was gradual and uneven. In Santa Isabel, Gela, and New Georgia, where strong chiefs had capitulated to demonstrations of colonial power and led whole communities into the Church in the late nineteenth and early twentieth centuries, people adopted colonial clothing generations before many of the small independent clans of Malaita and Guadalcanal. In the

A woman of Makira island (Solomon Islands), photographed by the traveler Martin Johnson in 1917. She wears a valuable combination of arm rings and ear pendants of shell, straps of dog and dolphin teeth, and strings and woven straps of money-beads. Martin and Osa Johnson Safari Museum.

inland of these islands some people have held to their ancestral religion and the ornaments associated with it into the twenty-first century, and a few still make these ornaments, for foreign export as well as local use. Elsewhere people make cheap substitutes when they need to dress in what they regard as traditional style, particularly for dance performances at public occasions such as church festivals and provincial or national celebrations. Shell ornaments inspire card or plywood crescents and plaques for the head and neck, painted white with black designs, and plastic may substitute for shell rings. New styles of loincloth sometimes replace the man's lavalava, too old-fashioned for everyday wear but too new for twenty-first-century ideas of dress of the past, while women wear bras with their fiber or calico skirts. The only ornaments of value still made and worn in any quantity are composed of Malaita money-beads, strung into necklaces and bandoliers, bands for arms and legs, and brow bands with fringes of dolphin teeth or, more usually, of seeds. These have become almost a national costume, worn by sports teams and beauty queens in the capital and featured in photographs for postcards and magazines.

For everyday wear Solomon Islanders have long preferred the best Western clothes they can afford, including long trousers and shirts for men, skirts and tops or dresses for women, and for townspeople often shoes as well. Solomon Islands identity is sometimes promoted in printed T-shirts bearing slogans or motifs adapted from local designs and in the uniform shirts of prestigious employers such as banks and hotels, but overseas fashions are equally popular. The fashion-conscious young quickly pick up new global styles, from dreadlocks to torn jeans, although they wear them in their own way, often in combination with local ornaments such as money-bead necklaces and plaited fiber rings. The clothes may look much the same, but the style often remains Solomon Islands, if not local.

Since the mid-twentieth century many Solomon Islanders have also been campaigning to reinstate the values they regard as most important in the legacy inherited from their ancestors, focusing on self-determination in the governance of local communities and resources. Some recognize their distinctive local traditions of body ornaments as a valuable part of this cultural heritage, and in the twenty-first century people are taking an increasing interest in such things as they fade into the past with each succeeding generation. The colonial museum collections and archives where evidence for Solomon Islanders' ancestral culture is preserved are a valuable resource of cultural information that may yet inspire them to recover something from their ancestral traditions in order to shape new local styles of dress and ornaments suited to the changing times.

References and Further Reading

Bernatzik, H. *Owaraha*. Wein-Leipzig-Olten, Germany: Bernina-Verlag, 1936.

Burt, B. *Body Ornaments of Kwara'ae and Malaita*. London and Honolulu: British Museum Press and University of Hawai'i Press, 2008.

Cooper, M. "Economic Context of Shell Money Production in Malaita." *Oceania* 41 (1971): 266–276.

Koch, G. *Materielle Kultur der Santa Cruz-Inseln*. Berlin: Museum für Volkerkunde, 1971.

Ross, K. "Shell Ornaments of Malaita: Currency and Ritual Valuables in the Central Solomons." *Expedition* 23 (1981): 20–26.

Waite, D. *Art of the Solomon Islands*. Geneva: Musée Barbier-Mueller, 1983.

Ben Burt

See also Introduction to the Dress of the Pacific Islands; Photographic Representations of Pacific Peoples; Textiles and Dress of the Motu Koita People; Asmat Dress; Dress in New Caledonia; Dress of Vanuatu.

PART 13

Micronesia

Dress in Kiribati

The Republic of Kiribati is a central Pacific state, which consists of thirty-three tiny atolls and reef islands scattered over a vast ocean area corresponding to one-third the size of the United States. It includes three island groups—the Gilbert, Phoenix, and Line Islands—and the island of Banaba. Apart from the Banabans, who have their own, though related, history, the Gilbert Islands chain straddling the equator is where people originally settled, and where the majority (90%) of the population continues to live. Before independence in 1979 the islands were under British colonial rule. Dress among the *I-Kiribati* (Kiribati people), whose number is approaching 100,000 in the early twenty-first century, has been influenced by ecological conditions: limited though distinct flora and fauna, numerous bird and marine species, vegetation such as coconut palms and pandanus trees, and an equable climate. Thus, clothing has not been needed to protect from the cold. Instead, the blazing sun has been more of a consideration. Thus, climate and available materials influenced customary clothing in terms of need (or lack thereof) but also had an effect on aesthetic ideals, such as dance dress. Importantly, environmental and other outside influences have always been filtered through, or sometimes countered by, cultural values, themselves subject to adaptation, particularly in the nineteenth and twentieth centuries.

Christian missionaries were the initiators of major changes in the nineteenth century, by introducing covering garments to islanders, who previously wore little or no clothing. In twenty-first-century Kiribati there are two ubiquitous local items of dress: *te be*, a rectangular cloth wrapped around the waist, worn by both men and women, and *te tibuta*, a smocked blouse for women. Simple T-shirts, shorts, and skirts are also popular everyday wear, though on the island of South Tarawa, the administrative and commercial center where the capital Bairiki is located, people may dress more formally to work. The distinction between festive occasions and everyday dress is carefully maintained; a festive outfit does not necessarily have frills and decorations, but it is presentable, neat, and well kept. One common way in which various groups mark significant occasions is by the use of uniforms, reflecting a key societal and aesthetic Kiribati value of unity and equity (*te booraoi*). Most modern clothing is either imported or sewn from imported cloth, but customary materials and techniques continue to be actively used in the context of dance (*te mwaie*), an art form that remains socially highly significant.

Market vendors in Bairiki village, South Tarawa, September 2000. The woman in the front is wearing a *tibuta* (smocked blouse) and a *be* (a cloth wrapped around the waist), and the third woman from the right also wears a *tibuta*. In the background *be* are being displayed for sale, and further behind the trees there are secondhand clothes stalls. Photograph by Petra M. Autio.

Compared to other Pacific countries, Kiribati is often viewed as rather traditional, though this should not be understood as something immutable. Life in Kiribati has long been influenced by Western and prior to that other cultures, and global socioeconomics. But customary values, the so-called Kiribati way (*te katei ni Kiribati*), are upheld by most islanders, something reflected in dress. Christianity is a major factor in the lives of most I-Kiribati. The term *custom* (*te katei*) occasionally refers to pre-Christian customs, but generally te katei refers to a way of life, including proper dress, which combines indigenous and Christian values and customs.

There has always been some cultural variation between the islands; the most notable in the early twenty-first century is between the island district of South Tarawa and the rest of Kiribati. South Tarawa, the governmental and commercial capital, has attracted large numbers of migrants from the outer islands and is generally the most Westernized. To some extent, dress reflects differences in socioeconomic status, but in Kiribati there is a strong ethos of egalitarianism, not so much among individuals as among social groups (families, households, and communities), and the ideal that wealth should be equally distributed. Kinship and community obligations tend to prevent the concentration of wealth, although there are perceivable economic differences among island people. Nevertheless, strong cultural mores value self-effacement to a greater degree than self-aggrandizement. Therefore, if affluence is reflected in someone's Western clothes, it is unlikely to be excessively flaunted. Conversely, it is equally important not to be dressed more poorly than others if an occasion calls for it.

KIRIBATI DRESS BEFORE EUROPEAN CONTACT

Information about dress before European contact is partly conjectural and should be treated with caution. It is based both on local knowledge about the past and early travelers' descriptions, the latter mostly after some interaction with Europeans had occurred. Both are potential sources of error. Christian views of a "pagan" past color descriptions of the Kiribati people when describing them as "being without clothing" or "naked." In actuality some decorative and other garments were in use but could later be ignored as they did not cover the genital area or women's breasts.

Before contact with European Christians men could go naked, whereas women in all likelihood did not. Adult women usually wore short leaf skirts (*te riri*), made of coconut palm leaves or a type of reed (*maunei, Cyperus laevigatus L.*). Men wore no clothing for everyday tasks, except for a cone-shaped hat (*te bara*), plaited from coconut or pandanus leaves, which could be worn to protect from the sun when at sea. Nevertheless, early European explorers saw some men wearing items like sashes, belts, or poncho-like garments, which also shielded from the sun. In ritual contexts and dancing men wore "dress mats" (*te be*; in contemporary dancing generally called *te kabae*) wrapped around the waist, woven from thin strips of pandanus leaves, and tied with a belt (*te nuota*) made from women's hair.

An outfit for which the Gilbert Islands were to become well known in Europe was the customary armor, which men wore in warfare. This was made of tightly knitted, plaited, or woven coir sennit and twine, sometimes embellished with designs of human hair. The armor consisted of a long-sleeved top, vest, or coat with a high back piece to protect the head, trousers, and a skullcap. A protective belt was made of coir twine or ray skin, and in addition to the cap there could be a helmet made from the spiky skin of a porcupine fish.

Children wore little clothing; girls began to wear te riri after puberty or at marriage. When traveling, a baby could be protected from the sun with its own "child's mat" (*te kie n ataei*), a fine pandanus sleeping mat, individually woven for the baby.

While to an extent true for modern Kiribati, in traditional society in particular women's sexuality was strictly controlled. A girl was supposed, under severe penalty, to remain a virgin until marriage; a married woman, on the other hand, was not to appear in public alone and sometimes wore a hood of plaited pandanus leaves so as not to tempt or be tempted by men. The processes of female reproduction were surrounded by prohibitions (*tabus*) but were also symbolically powerful. Despite some literary sources

Groups of school children wearing *kabooraoi* uniforms for the Kiribati Independence Day parade, Tabiteuea North Island, Utiroa village, July 2000. The different schools of the island will have marching competitions and give choreographed greetings to island dignitaries. Photograph by Petra M. Autio.

that imply this, it appears highly unlikely that adult women went without clothing. On the other hand, some riris that women wore in the past could be very short, a mere fringe to the Western eye. So in Kiribati modesty was not only a matter of covering but was also conveyed by proper behavior, for example sitting properly (cross-legged). That breasts were exposed was of no consequence, since they were not considered to have particular sexual connotations.

HISTORICAL DEVELOPMENTS IN DRESS PRACTICES

The Gilbert Islands had been sighted by Europeans in the seventeenth century, but regular and long-term contacts with Westerners were not established until the nineteenth century, the first being with whalers and beachcombers, then traders and missionaries. The British colonial government was the last to establish its presence in 1892. While traders made cloth available, the missionaries had the greatest effect on dressing practices. Christian missionaries included Protestants sent by the American Board of Commissioners for Foreign Missions (ABCFM) from the 1850s and the London Missionary Society (LMS), initially sending mostly Samoan teachers. The LMS established itself on the islands in the 1870s and the representatives of the Catholic Church in the 1880s.

Missionaries insisted on clothing to cover indigenous bodies, at least to church and on the mission, and with their growing influence dressing practices changed. In addition, once traders made cloth and Western clothes available, these became much-sought-after goods. Men commonly began wearing a length of cloth tied around the waist (te be) or trousers. For some activities men also wore a riri. Women could wear the *be* too, but they continued the use of riris. The latter became longer than in premissionary times. Missionaries, however, preferred women to wear more clothes. As on many other Pacific islands, Protestant missionaries introduced "mother hubbard" dresses for women: loose gowns or frocks with long sleeves and high collars.

Missionaries instilled a link between clothing and morality, the concept of nakedness being linked to shame, affecting women more than men. For example, the Kiribati word for *naked* (*beekan*) derives from the English term *pagan*. Gilbertese women, who had always been modest about their pelvic area/genitals, now encountered the idea that exposing breasts was shameful. For men, covering at least the loins was a novelty. While the original mother hubbard garment eventually fell into disuse, its influence remains in contemporary dress.

The change from short riris to mother hubbards was radical, but for the whole population transition to using clothing in the first place and secondly to wearing Western clothing was uneven and took decades. Mother hubbards were apparently not universally worn, and the use of imported and indigenous garments continued side by side in the twentieth century. Photographs and reminiscences tell us that for everyday work, women continued to wear customary grass and leaf skirts and no shirt or top well into the 1960s. Cloth dresses and blouses were highly valued and carefully saved for Sunday church and special occasions.

There have been riris of various kinds and for different purposes: for work and everyday wear, for festive occasions as well as dancing. Manufactured from coconut palm leaves or maunei reed, the leaves are attached by knotting to a coconut fiber string, which is then used to tighten the skirt at the waist. There are several manufacturing and processing techniques for riris, and they vary creatively between different types of skirts. The leaves and rushes can be boiled, dried in the sun, dyed, and smoked. Besides the color the smell is important, as well as the way the riri sounds, rustling as the wearer moves. The finished skirt can be cut to different lengths or in layers. In the twenty-first century customary riris are mostly for dancing.

DRESS IN THE TWENTY-FIRST CENTURY

In twenty-first-century Kiribati both local and Western garments are worn on weekdays. A typical Kiribati man is likely to wear either shorts or te be and optionally a T-shirt or tank top. A woman probably wears a locally made smocked blouse, te tibuta, or else a T-shirt and a be over a skirt, or over shorts in the case of younger women. Similarly, children's everyday dress consists of T-shirts, shorts, and skirts. Schools often have uniforms, though wearing them every day might not be compulsory.

Important occasions are marked with clothing. When the I-Kiribati are engaged in subsistence or household work—gardening, fishing, cooking, weaving, washing clothes—they are not much concerned with clothes. By contrast, when going to important events such as attending church, attending a party as a guest, or seeing someone off at the airport, people usually dress themselves and their children neatly; it would be shameful otherwise.

For men, more formal attire might consist of a collared dress shirt, long trousers, or a be similar to the Fijian *sulu vakataga*, a tailored wraparound garment. Women might wear more formal or festive Western dresses, but there is also a popular local dress, similar to garments worn by women in many Pacific countries. This frock is a modification of the mother hubbard dress: similarly long and loose with no waistline, but with short sleeves and no collar. The frock typically has a square or triangular neckline and slightly gathered sleeves.

Over time nineteenth-century Christian ideas of how a decent woman should dress blended with and perhaps even strengthened older, indigenous conceptions of modesty. The key issue is to conceal the area of crotch and thighs. In practice an adult woman generally wears two layers of clothing: a be over a skirt or shorts, or, if she wears a skirt, she will have a slip, shorts, or another skirt under it. The hem should reach below the knees, and even more crucially, the garment should be loose enough not to reveal the shape of the body and to enable sitting cross-legged without exposing the thighs. There have been some changes, and younger women sometimes wear loose shorts, about knee-length. In South Tarawa generally, female dressing is freer, but attitudes to clothing also vary between families and individuals.

For practical and cultural reasons the way people dress in South Tarawa tends to include more Western items. There are more manufactured clothes available for purchase, and office workers tend to dress in more formal Western clothes. Tarawa is where Western cultural influences tend to be more noticeable due to the presence of international travelers and global media access. There is no television broadcasting in Kiribati, but about one-fifth of Tarawan households have a TV and video equipment, four times as many as in rural areas. Internet access is limited mostly to South Tarawa. This does not mean that cultural influences stop in Tarawa. Outer islands may have less equipment, but films and projectors are extensively borrowed and used at feasts, where the whole village can watch. Films include standard Hollywood ones, but also Bollywood films and those from Hong Kong, so Western wear is not the only clothing seen, and fashions are selectively adopted.

These examples are some ways in which the cultural and economic effects of globalization are evident at the grassroots level. Another example is the trade in secondhand clothes, imported from Australia, for instance, and sold in Tarawa. Secondhand clothing prices, being lower than prices for new ones, mean a great variety and amount of clothing is accessible to a wide number of people.

UNIFORMS

One eye-catching feature in Kiribati is the prominent use of uniforms (*te kabooraoi*). They are worn by members of many kinds of organizations, not only schools but women's associations, island magistrates, and performance groups. The uniform in Kiribati has no particular military connotations but simply refers to prescribed clothes worn by members of a group. The Kiribati kabooraoi is not used to express rank, being the same for each member of a group, or for each member of the same sex. Examples of kabooraois could be a school uniform of a white collared shirt and blue shorts for boys and a blue skirt for girls; an orange tibuta and a violet be for the girls of a performance group; and a green frock for members of a women's club. These outfits are usually simple and cheap, often homemade, but can be made to order. A simple kabooraoi consists of a top (men in a performance group might also be bare-chested) and a be of particular prescribed colors, but there are variations.

For important occasions like the Independence Day parade or a performance competition, the kabooraoi dress can be made from indigenous raw materials. This is more demanding given the laborious manufacturing techniques, but it is valued. The requirements can include a riri of a specific kind and a pandanus dress mat or a headdress.

Although not unique to Kiribati, uniforms are a way of expressing and reproducing a particularly Kiribati value, booraoi, to which the word *kabooraoi* (to make or cause to be booraoi) directly refers. Booraoi can be glossed literally as "to meet well" and has various translations in English: even, equal, uniform, equity, harmony, agreement, conformity. Booraoi describes how a Kiribati community or a group should be and how it should function: unanimous and harmonious, dividing both burden and benefit evenly, and acting in concert. Being booraoi unifies the community. In Kiribati this communal unity is a primary value, and the kabooraoi aims to make the group even and harmonious.

Booraoi is furthermore an aesthetic value, particularly evident in dancing. When dancers perform in front of an audience, they must execute the movements in exactly the same way and in unison. The booraoiness of a row of dancers and their conduct is a paramount criterion in assessing a dance performance. In anticipation of a competition a group performing dance will pay careful attention to the dress of the dancers, as well as the kabooraoi of the accompanying singers.

DANCE DRESS

Dance dress is an area in which customary materials and manufacturing techniques are extensively used, though alongside imported materials. Kiribati dance (te mwaie, alternatively called *te bwatere* or *te ruoia*) is a highly competitive art, where groups perform in front of an audience, competing for prestige. The dancer, or dancers lined up in a row, is accompanied by a singing and clapping choir. There are several types of dancing understood as distinctly Kiribati, which can be called traditional, despite historical changes and borrowed features.

Dances are performed in a standing or a sitting position; in one dance style a kneeling position is possible as well. Shared characteristics of Kiribati dances include controlled and precise execution of the choreography and emphasis on the movements of the head, hands, and upper torso. Rather than continuous, dance is often movement from one pose to another, and there is

Dance adornments being attached to two boys for a dress rehearsal, Tabiteuea North Island, Buota village, December 1999. The *kamari* collars and single *tiebaba* straps across the chest are made of plastic beads, and the *karuru* on the arms and forefingers are made of pandanus leaves. The red-and-black fitted necklace is called *te nta*. The women with their backs to the camera are wearing *tibuta* (smocked blouses). Photograph by Petra M. Autio.

an air of extreme restraint, as the dancer balances between gracefulness and the demonstration of force. Men and women perform similar dance movements and even the same dances, though men tend to display more strength.

With the exception of the sitting dance (*te bino*), the basic dance dress is different for men and women, but many of the decorations are common to both. Women wear a riri and men a dress mat of woven pandanus (*te kabae*). On their upper body women wear a white singlet or T-shirt, or a top of woven pandanus resembling a sports bra. Men dance bare-chested. Embellishments on the neck, chest, arms, and fingers can be used by both sexes.

There are two principal kinds of dancing riri, though there are also others. *Te karoro* is a black skirt made of coconut leaves. The manufacturing process takes several days. After the leaves are woven to the coconut-fiber waistband, the skirt is dyed using a mixture of substances such as fermented coconut palm sap, certain roots, and rusty pieces of metal. Finally, the karoro is fragranced in an earth oven, treated with coconut cream or molasses and smoked by burning sweet-smelling wood. Te karoro can also be made from used videotape. Such a skirt does not need dyeing, and it is black and shiny but lacks the scent and feel of the leaf karoro. With the karoro the dancer often wears two belts: *te katau*, made of rounded pieces of black coconut shell, and *te tumara*, made of whole white seashells, whose color shines against the black skirt. There may also be a girdle made of strips of dried pandanus leaves (*te kamakorokoro*).

Te riri ni buki is only worn for dances with hip movements (*te buki*). Riri ni buki are larger, longer, and heavier than other riris, the hem reaching almost to the dancer's ankles. The garment is made of young coconut leaves, boiled and dried, leaving them a very light brown. The purpose of the voluminous riri is to emphasize the movements of the hips. Part of the beauty is the way the riri moves. As the dancer performs the various kinds of motifs with her pelvis, dipping to one side, rotating, moving from side to side or back and forth, the riri ni buki rustles, tosses, and turns, a skillful dancer swinging it as high as the level of her head.

When men do standing dances, they wear te kabae, which is woven in the traditional way from very thin pandanus leaf strips. Before the stiff and spiky pandanus leaves can be used, they have to be dried, their stalks, spiky edges, and butt removed, and either bleached in the sun or dyed with plant extracts. The leaves are then softened by pounding them with a heavy wooden mallet, and finally cut into 0.1- to 0.15-inch- (3- to 4-millimeter-) wide strips. The techniques for processing leaves and weaving a dress mat are the same as for other mats, but the kabae or be is especially valued, since the thinner the strips, the more demanding the weaving and the finer the finished item. Weaving is done by painstakingly folding and interlocking the strips to form a checkered surface and, if desired, using the colored, darker leaves to create decorative patterns against the light background. The male dancer wraps the kabae around him so that its upper brim is well above the waist and fastens it with a nuota belt made from women's hair—ideally that of a wife, sister, or other close relative.

In sitting dances (bino) both men and women use te kabae. As the dancer sits cross-legged on the floor, the mat is placed lengthwise on his or her legs. The decorations for the upper body are the same as in standing dances.

If a group is performing together in a formal competition, they will take care that every dancer is wearing the same kind of embellishments. While dancers in a village event might appear more miscellaneous, the dancing is no less competitive, and dancers

A green and a multi-colored *tibuta* and a yellow blouse, the latter combining the *tibuta* with a typical frock, placed on green and black *be*, or waist cloths, 1999–2000. The *be* to the left depicts the Gilbert Islands; the *be* to the right, Millennium Island in the Line group, with the caption "Kiribati is the first to see the Millennium Sunlight." Photograph by Petra M. Autio.

want to wear their finest decorations. Some of the possible adornments include a headdress (*te mae* or *te bau*), a wide collar (*te kamari*), and ribbons or straps worn over the shoulder and diagonally across the chest (*te tiebaba*). The arm and finger embellishments, *te karuru*, are important. They are two or three pairs of armlets tied at even intervals to the arms; a ring of a similar design is often worn on the forefinger. Attached to the strap is a decoration resembling a flower or a bundle of feathers. The name *karuru* (to make or cause to tremble) refers to the way they tremble, as the dancer moves in an utterly controlled manner, pausing transiently in the prescribed positions, sometimes trembling with exertion or emotion. The symbolic significance of the karuru comes from the fact that the tremble attests to power: Like the wind tosses the leaves of a tree, or makes a bird's wings tremble, so does the spirit of dancing (*angin te mwaie*) move the dancer.

The decorations can be made from either natural or synthetic materials. The headdress, for example, can be composed of either fresh or processed coconut palm fronds, or it can be a crown with plastic flowers. Similarly, the te kamari collar can be of fresh flowers and leaves, or plastic beads, and te tiebaba can be made from fabric, plastic beads, or woven pandanus. People's preferences vary. Modern materials, cloth and plastic, are considered to have advantages, being colorful and enabling the design of variable patterns. They also keep well. Pandanus garments have to be renewed every now and then, and leaves and flowers last only a day. Yet it is recognized that customary dance regalia demands more work and is thus valued. There seems to be a trend to return to using natural materials, also encouraged in official competitions. In the twenty-first century the use of "Kiribati things" (*bwaai ni Kiribati*), as opposed to plastic and other imported material (*bwaai ni I-Matang*), also signifies the pride that the I-Kiribati feel about their cultural heritage. In the end, however, it is the Kiribati dancing, mwaie, that gives significance to both garments and embellishments, regardless of their material.

Snapshot: *Te Be and Te Tibuta*

Te be and *te tibuta* are important items of Kiribati dress. Te be is a garment with counterparts around the Pacific. Unless referring to the customary dress mat of woven pandanus, te be is the most common Kiribati item of clothing, worn by both men and women. A modern *be* is usually 2 yards (1.8 meters) of cotton cloth about 1 yard (0.9 meter) in width; the length of the be can be adjusted by the way it is tied. The cotton cloth be is a versatile, all-round garment, suitable for work and leisure or as a nightgown; an old, well-worn be is quickly tied over one's better clothes to protect them if some manual work needs to be done; new and clean, it can be worn without embarrassment to a feast.

The cloth be is a unisex garment, but there are differences in how men and women wear it and tie it—women fold a knot on their left or right hip, whereas men fold it in the front. Men generally wear it shorter, sometimes above the knee. For women the appropriate length is below the knee. In Kiribati society the assigned sexual roles of men and women are quite traditional. There is, however, a small category of men who are biologically male but live the social role of a female, performing women's work and assuming their manners, including tying be on the side as they do. Conversely, there are very occasionally women who tie their be in the front and otherwise act as men. The customary Kiribati pandanus-leaf be (or *kabae*) is worn by men on ceremonial occasions or during dance performances.

There is a difference in the way the be is combined with other clothing. Men frequently do not cover their torsos, so they might just wear a be, or a be over a pair of shorts. Adult women cover their upper bodies with a tibuta or a shirt and generally wear the be over a skirt, dress, or sometimes shorts. In domestic settings a woman might wear just the be, wrapped around her body at the armpits and reaching down to the knees, but she would be unlikely to venture far from the house dressed in this way.

The cloth be is usually brightly colored. Decorative patterns and prints, particularly flowers, are common. National sentiments are often expressed on the be. It may have all the Gilbert Islands depicted, the name of the country, or a slogan like "*Mauri*" (health, well-being), a Kiribati greeting. Sometimes a man wears a be with his name embroidered on it, made by a woman for her husband or sweetheart. Typically the man would wear his special be to church. These embroidery designs, like those on tibuta tops, are one area where women exercise personal creativity. Some women collect designs and models in an exercise book and do not readily reveal them to people outside the family.

Te tibuta is a sleeveless smocked blouse worn by women. It has historical connections with garments elsewhere in the Pacific, but in the twenty-first century its design and style are considered typical of Kiribati. Virtually every Kiribati woman knows how to make a tibuta and owns them for both everyday and festive use. It is a loose-fitting top with a square neckline and wide shoulder straps but no sleeves, made from two pieces of cotton cloth joined together by a smocked shoulder part. The smocking is done by pleating the cloth of the upper front, shoulder, and upper back parts, fixing the small pleats with decorative stitches; the smocked part is fitted, and the rest drapes loosely.

The history of the tibuta is unknown but probably originated from two sources. In precolonial Tahiti people wore a poncho-like garment called *tiputa*, made of bark cloth (*tapa*). Encouraged by missionaries, their use spread to other islands like Samoa, where no upper-body garments had previously been worn. Since Christianity was introduced to the Gilbert Islands via Samoa as well as Tahiti, it is likely these tiputa-like articles of clothing came into use at that point. The similarity between the terms *tiputa* and *tibuta* is no proof in itself, but there is a photograph reproduced in two published works, likely to date from the 1930s, that shows a poncho-like item of woven pandanus as part of an outfit captioned "married women's dress." On the other hand, the Kiribati women's tibuta may have evolved from the mother hubbard dress. The cut of the tibuta and the typical frock resemble one another, and there are also blouses that combine the two kinds of garments.

Modern tibutas are variously embellished. The edges of the neck and armholes are decorated with crochet and cotton threads. The front is embroidered, and the sophisticated designs include flowers, ornamental shapes, and letters. Tibuta are often given as gifts, in which case the recipient's name can be cross-stitched in the front. While the basic cut of the tibuta has remained similar, women try out new styles and decorative designs, applying their aesthetic skills using embroidery, lace, and crocheting in both customary and innovative ways.

References and Further Reading

Colchester, Chloë, ed. *Clothing the Pacific*. Oxford: Berg, 2003.

Grimble, Arthur Francis. *Tungaru Traditions: Writings on the Atoll Culture of the Gilbert Islands*. Edited by H. E. Maude. Honolulu: University of Hawai'i Press, 1989.

Koch, Gerd. *Materielle Kultur der Gilbert Inseln. Nonouti, Tabiteuea, Onotoa*. Berlin: Museum für Völkerkunde, 1965. Translated by Guy Slatter as *The Material Culture of Kiribati* (Suva, Fiji: Institute of Pacific Studies of the University of the South Pacific, 1986).

Murdoch, G. M. "Gilbert Islands Weapons and Armour." *The Journal of the Polynesian Society* 32, no. 127 (1923): 174–175.

Talu, Sister Alaima, et al. *Kiribati: Aspects of History*. Suva, Fiji: Institute of Pacific Studies of the University of the South Pacific and Tarawa, Kiribati: Ministry of Education, Training and Culture, 1979.

Whincup, Tony, and Joan Whincup. *Akekeia! Traditional Dance in Kiribati*. Wellington, NZ: Susan Barrie, 2001.

Petra M. Autio

See also Missionary Dress in Samoa; Dress in the Marshall Islands.

Lavalava (Cloth) of the Rei Metau

The Rei Metau (People of the Open Sea) live on the Outer Islands of Yap in the Federated States of Micronesia, and they are therefore known as Outer Islanders. About four thousand people inhabit nine small atolls, which together make up no more than about seven square miles (about eighteen square kilometers). They understand themselves as one ethnic group, speak the same language, and live under the authority of their island's chiefs and of one paramount chief. *Lavalava* are their national dress and part of their identity. Woven by women, lavalava accompany people from birth to death, serve as a female value system within the society, and thus also reflect the high status of their makers. The Rei Metau are skilled seafarers and in the past traded with islands near and far. Among their trade items, lavalava were the most important. With the island of Yap the Rei Metau have a very elaborate tribute relationship, in which lavalava, especially the *machiye* (special lavalava woven on Fais and formerly Ulithi islands), plays a prominent role. Since the discovery by European ships and the first mention of lavalava in literature, its changes in material, color schemes, and design reflect the history of the Rei Metau.

According to their affiliations, dialects, and traditions, these islands are divided into three clusters: the Ulithi sphere of influence (Ulithi Atoll and Fais Island); the Woleai *Mechalchal* (the cluster of Woleai Islands: Eauripik, Woleai, Ifalik, Faraulep, Elato, and Lamotrek Atolls); and finally Satawal Island. The communities are based on a strictly dual system, in which both parts complement each other: women and men, the land and the sea, and the Outer Islands and Yap Island. They are the least modernized society in Micronesia, with matrilineal inheritance, a subsistence economy, strict gender segregation (especially between brothers and sisters), and an absolute chiefly power. The Rei Metau preserved their culture during the Spanish, German, and Japanese Colonial eras (1889–1941), as well as after World War II when the area was administered by the United States as a trusteeship of the United Nations, until it gained independence in 1986 as the Federated States of Micronesia. Since the 1950s changes occurred in the Outer Islands of Yap with the introduction of a Catholic mission and an American school system, both of which affected the Rei Metau's traditional dress.

DESIGN OF TRADITIONAL LAVALAVA

Males and females wear woven textiles approximately 55 to 59 inches (140 to 150 centimeters) long and 16 to 22 inches (40 to 55 centimeters) wide, with the strings of the warp as fringed ends. This dress covers the lower body of both men and women. From island to island and atoll to atoll, these textiles have a myriad of names, according to the materials they are made of, their designs, the weaving technique and pattern applied, if they are old or new, who is wearing them, who is speaking to whom about them, and in which social context they are referred to or used. For ease of use the general term *lavalava* will be used, a name the Rei Metau use only when talking to foreigners about their textiles.

Lavalava are woven of banana and/or hibiscus plant fibers. Banana fibers are produced from the stem of any musa plant that has not yet produced any fruits. After the pulp has been scraped off the layers of the stem, the fibers are left under the sun to dry and bleach. Hibiscus fibers are produced from the bark of *Hibiscus tiliaceus*, which, when soaked in the ocean for several days, falls apart into several fiber layers. These fibers are used on simple backstrap looms, consisting of two beams and a belt to regulate the tension of the warp. The color scheme consists of shiny, white, sun-dried banana fibers, while the more porous hibiscus fibers can easily be dyed. The cherished black color could traditionally only be dyed with mineral-rich soil originating in the swamps of neighboring high islands. Therefore, the patterns of the Ulithi sphere of influence and of Satawal Island contain more or bigger black designs than the lavalava of the Woleai Mechalchal, because both of them had easy access to the neighboring high islands of Yap in the east and Chuuk in the West. Here the necessary dye could be obtained from the soil. Within the dominant black stripes the textiles are embellished by minute yellow and red accents. The overall impression of a lavalava is of a wraparound, with a striking contrast of dark patterns on a light surface.

Apart from plain light (if not to say white) fiber textiles, which are produced on all islands, there are lavalava with seven horizontal wide stripes, created by the warp. They are typical of the Ulithi sphere of influence. Textiles with three dark horizontal stripes created by the warp on a wide white background, and two or three thin *tab* (brocaded weft design strips) at each end, are typical among the Woleai Mechalchal. Since German colonial rule these tab include names, or indications of when and for what occasion the lavalava have been created. Typical of Satawal Island, and yet not very popular, are textiles with many irregular horizontal stripes. Another textile that does not fit into the normal pattern of dark stripes on a white background is the *machiye* (a special lavalava made on Fais Island and formerly on Ulithi). It has an intricately brocaded dark design on each end and a wide white field in the middle. This is the only lavalava that cannot be worn on a daily basis, as it is reserved for special occasions. All these lavalava were traditionally woven from plant fibers.

LAVALAVA: THE DRESS OF THE REI METAU

Every Rei Metau woman wears her lavalava as a wrapped garment. Draped around the hips, its ends are held together to one side. Pressing the lavalava with one hand against the belly, both ends are folded to the other side (creating the impression of a Scottish kilt). The folded section, as well as the fringes, provides comfort for movement, and a belt, made of white shell and dark coconut shell discs, holds the lavalava in place. The color design

Dancing women wearing color-coordinated *lavalava*, matching belts, and decoration. Their upper bodies are decorated with turmeric. Eauripik Atoll, Yap State, Federated States of Micronesia, 2003. Photograph by Carmen C.H. Petrosian-Husa.

of these belts complements the overall dark/light pattern of the textiles. At the back the belt is worn at the waistline, and at the front it is pulled over the belly. In this way women are covered from the abdomen to the knees. The belt leaves only the portion of the lavalava at the back uncovered, thus creating a gap that can expose a view of the haunches, which the Rei Metau regard as "décolletage" and which sometimes reveal female tattoos. These tattoos support the overall pattern of dark designs on a light surface in a subtle way. Dark tattoos cover the pubic area, the upper thighs, and the buttocks, the most sexually sensitive areas of a woman's body, usually hidden by her lavalava. Therefore, her light skin enhances the delicate designs of the tattoos.

Women wear all these lavalava designs, while men, on the contrary, wear only seven-striped lavalava in the fashion of a loincloth (tied as a g-string), just covering their genitalia and leaving the buttocks bare. Habitually, the fringes of the male dress are plaited in small braids. Men's tattoos are displayed on the upper body, the buttocks, and the legs. A man's appearance can also be described as dominated by a light/dark contrast. Men and women carry their few truly personal belongings, such as a comb, medicine, charms, and tools, in a rectangular bag under their arm. One or two flower wreaths or a flower in the ear give the finishing touch to the perfect Rei Metau outfit for both sexes. The flower garlands are created to blend fragrances as well as colors. On special occasions, such as feasts and dances, women and men bind a split coconut branch, like a see-through skirt, over their lavalava and decorate themselves with young, nearly white coconut leaves, flowers, and turmeric powder.

In all accounts of early European seafarers the islanders' fascination with iron is mentioned. One of the reasons was the feasibility of dyeing their fibers pitch black with rusty iron. As a result, completely black lavalava were woven on all the islands of the Rei Metau after Western contact. In the middle of the twentieth century modernization in the form of schools reached the Outer Islands. With modern school supplies mimeograph paper was introduced to the islands. Its dark blue color and easy availability soon won over the Rei Metau, and shortly after, all black patterns of fiber lavalava were colored dark blue.

After World War II a Jesuit missionary brought European yarn to the Outer Islands and revolutionized both the weaving practices and the appearance of the Rei Metau—making them look colorful, and the garments more comfortable to wear and quicker to make. In the twenty-first century the entire color palette is used in traditional lavalava designs. During the American administration of the Outer Islands that occurred between 1945 and 1986, one new lavalava motif was invented. It is the most colorful one, called *flag* (maybe in reference to the American flag), and became one of the most popular designs. Since one high school for all Outer Island students was founded in 1963 in the Ulithi Atoll, where people from all the atolls gather, the former location-specific lavalava patterns (with the exception of the machiye) have been woven everywhere. It is, therefore, no longer possible to distinguish where a woman comes from by the lavalava she is wearing.

Rei Metau women prefer to wear polyester yarn lavalava, because it is not coarse, and the lavalava are durable, colorful, and their production is less labor-intensive. The only disadvantage is that money, which is scarce in the subsistence economies of the Outer Islands, is needed to buy the yarn. Therefore, fiber lavalava, which are considered more labor-intensive, are still woven.

A man dancing, wearing a traditional men's *lavalava* as a belt. Eauripik Atoll, Yap State, Federated States of Micronesia, 2003. Photograph by Carmen C.H. Petrosian-Husa.

LAVALAVA IN DAILY LIFE

The report of the German Südsee Expedition (South Seas Expedition) in 1908–1910 mentions that lavalava were first created by the ancestral spirit Eluelap to prevent incest. Custom requires that all men and women wear them from puberty to their deathbeds. In the female context they are sexually charged to a significant degree. This sexual connotation is indicated by a small red strip on each edge of a female's lavalava. *Cha* is the name for red, as well as for blood; thus this small red strip represents menstrual blood and motherhood, both prime female symbols. At the same time lavalava are simultaneously undergarments and outer dress and thus signify all that they conceal. Consequently, certain etiquette has to be observed when handling them in daily life, especially in the presence of men. Once the textile is cut from the loom, it is not publicly displayed but kept folded and out of the sight of men. When lavalava are transported they always have to be covered by a piece of cloth, making them effectively invisible, before they are handed over in a clandestine way. The islands of the Rei Metau are divided into male and female domains. Women can only hang and dry their outfits in the female zone, where men would never venture, while men have to dry theirs in the vicinity of a canoe or meeting house, the male domain.

When a baby is born it is first placed in a soft old lavalava. While small children run around naked, girls at the age of four to five years receive either a skirt made of young coconut leaves or two aprons made of dried ferns smelling like marzipan, worn with a belt, and covering the front and the back.

A girl's menarche, or first menstrual cycle, is one of the most joyful events in Outer Island life, celebrated over four days by the entire village. It is the moment she is considered a young woman, and as a sign of her new status she starts wearing lavalava, which she receives in abundance from family and friends. During this time the young menstruating woman is covered with turmeric and wears many layers of lavalava. These yellow-stained textiles are considered a symbol of luck and fertility. For some weeks following, the young woman lives in the menstruation hut, where she learns all necessary female skills: preparing fibers, warping, and weaving. From now on she has to take care of her own garments and has to replenish the lavalava reserve for her family. When she leaves the menstruation hut she is accomplished in all female tasks and considered a woman, and she has to behave accordingly. In the many weeks of seclusion she has put on weight and has become a plump Rei Metau beauty. Wearing a lavalava signifies that her carefree childhood has ended and that she has chores and household obligations like any adult. From now on she leads a life distant from all related male clan members. If next to a male clan member, she has to be physically lower than he, even to the extent of crawling on the floor, because wearing a lavalava is the visual proof of her status as a sexually active woman. In order to facilitate women's lives their brothers have to leave the family's house and compound when they reach puberty. This reflects the origin of the lavalava in the previously mentioned incest taboo.

Just as the first menstruation is a rite of passage marked with lavish gifts of lavalava, so is the first pregnancy. Rei Metau know that a first birth means risks for mother and baby. Hence an expectant young mother frequently receives gifts of lavalava, and her upper body and budding belly are covered with turmeric. Should the young mother die in the course of giving birth, her family will use these lavalava for her funeral. If she survives, she

Since the beginning of the twentieth century industrial fabrics, simple white, blue, or red cloths, have been imported. They replace the traditional dress for men. Young men, especially, like to wear long pieces of cloth draped in such a fashion that their buttocks are covered, while women supplement their lavalava with it by wrapping cloth over it to keep the main garment clean. In the society of the Rei Metau it is of great importance not to assert individuality. This is mirrored in lavalava production. For special occasions, such as dances, all participating women wear clothes with exactly the same colors, patterns, and designs. In the case of a three-striped textile with a brocade pattern, the occasion on which the garment was first worn and the year of its production are often woven into the garment itself.

Without exception all Rei Metau, even the chiefs whose regalia is in no way different from that of a common citizen, conform to this dress code. On many atolls toplessness is a cultural requirement (also for visitors), and Western clothes, such as caps, T-shirts, and sunglasses, are not permitted, because "our ancestors did not have them either." The decision about whether an island requires people to go without tops or not is usually made in a meeting where chiefs and elder women discuss matters of importance, and where the female voice is usually more pervasive.

will spend the next three years in close contact with the baby and will have no time to weave. She will wear these lavalava for this period. During this time she should abstain from sexual activity. As a visible sign of her sexual status, she wears an old lavalava, which is sewn together and tucked under her belt at the back. It is a symbol of her fertility but at the same time covers the alluring view of her décolletage and hides spots of postpartum vaginal discharge on her dress. This tradition is declining, as women prefer to wear mass-produced fabrics over their lavalava.

As an insurance against social obligations and family and personal needs, each family has an ample supply of new fiber and yarn lavalava. Next to these they also have a *shimw*, a stash of very special lavalava, which contains memorabilia of former family members. In the past these were mainly locks of hair (the basic meaning of *shimw*), while in the twenty-first century photographs, called *ngeol* (which can be translated as spirit), are placed into the shimw. To protect the shimw from omnipresent rodents, insects, other pests, and misfortunes, it is hung from the rafters of the house. In each family only one woman is in charge of and can access the shimw. She has to do so in the morning before she has eaten anything; otherwise, the bundle of lavalava would be spoiled. When gifts from the shimw are given it has to be made clear where they come from. The reason is that when a shimw lavalava has been worn and is old, it cannot be discarded, but has to be burned because it has a direct connection to the ancestors.

Funerals are occasions of excessive lavalava donations. A body prepared for burial is placed on a sleeping mat and several layers of lavalava. Ancestral memorabilia from the shimw are placed on the pelvis of dead women, or next to the armpit of a man, creating a bond with relatives all the way back to the clan's first woman. Members of all families bring gifts, lavalava, modern textiles, belts, and turmeric, which are heaped on top of the corpse. Lavalava from the shimw have to be declared as such and will be buried with the dead, while others, which do not fit into the coffin, are distributed among members of the family who help with the funeral, dig the grave, and handle the body. Those who have direct contact with a corpse have to observe taboos associated with the dead, and they are compensated for it. Family members who miss funerals place lavalava on the grave of deceased relatives when they arrive on an island.

On the islands of the Rei Metau lavalava accompany women through all stages of life: when they are feted as pubescent women, pregnant women, and again as young mothers. Young men, though, are only initiated on the islands in the Ulithian sphere of influence. This rite of passage utilizes machiye, which serves for the inauguration of a high chief, too. Donald H. Rubinstein calls it a "sacred burial shroud." This name suggests the machiye's most common use in the twenty-first century, when male initiation rites are no longer practiced and machiye are placed on the corpses of male relatives.

Formerly, machiye were woven on all islands in the Ulithian sphere of influence. In the early twenty-first century only women on Fais Island know how to produce these special textiles, the design of which looks different from any other lavalava. A machiye is always woven from white banana fibers. Both its ends are decorated with wide brocaded patterns made from darkly dyed fibers. Comparing machiye of the twenty-first century with old museum pieces, it is evident that over the last two hundred years design and patterns have not changed.

LAVALAVA AS A VALUE SYSTEM WITHIN REI METAU SOCIETY

Within the society of the Rei Metau lavalava are textiles whose value exceeds that of a garment. In the traditional value system they are considered female values, which are complemented by bundles of rope, the male equivalent. Both of them are used to pay for goods and services; thus, they have practical and exchange values.

Traditional education and knowledge such as of navigation, canoe building, massage, and medicine have to be bought with lavalava. The initiation rite of the navigators is the moment when the teacher officially receives his last payment, which consists of

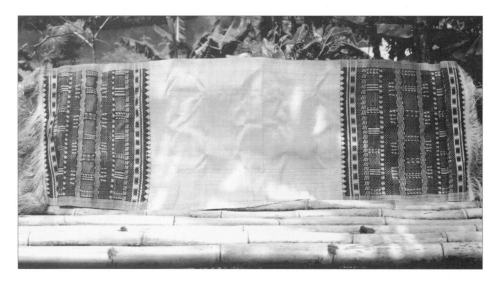

A *machiye* from Fais Island, Yap State, Federated States of Micronesia, 1982, clearly showing the intricately brocaded dark design at each end and a wide white field in the middle. This special kind of *lavalava* (cloth) is woven only on Ulithi Atoll and Fais Island. Photograph by Carmen C.H. Petrosian-Husa.

hundreds of lavalava. This is one of the few occasions that textiles are publicly displayed in a purely male domain, the canoe house.

When a taboo is broken and accordingly the spirit world upset, the consequences for the culprit, his family, and the entire population of the island could be dire, and all lives are endangered. The only way to avoid terrible punishment is compensation with lavalava and/or bundles of rope that have to be handed over to the chiefs. Hanging them in the canoe house is a public announcement of appeasement for all inhabitants of the island, as well as for their ancestors.

Another occasion for public display of lavalava is one of desperate fear. All Rei Metau men produce sweet and fermented coconut sap. In order to do so they frequently have to climb tall coconut trees. Accidents involving "fallen men" are numerous and require highly specialized treatment. In such a case a woman rushes to a traditional medical practitioner, displaying an unfolded lavalava in front of her, asking for his help. Many lavalava are displayed over the sickbed of "fallen men" and all of these function as reward for the medical treatment. On all other occasions the lavalava payment for medical remedies is handed over without any public fanfare.

Marriage is a low-key affair for Rei Metau. It is much more complicated to deal with a troubled marriage, a divorce, or a couple's reconciliation. On each of these occasions the entire lavalava resources of the family of the person found to be at fault will be given away; otherwise, all their belongings will be destroyed or carried off.

Six *lavalava* given as payment for breaking a fishing taboo (from the top: *dorri* Satawal, *flag, peich engang, normal, kar, marup*). Falalap Island, Woleai Atoll, Yap State, Federated States of Micronesia, 1991. Photograph by Carmen C.H. Petrosian-Husa.

Lavalava are a commodity exchanged at nearly every significant life event. At a birth the midwife and any woman who comes into contact with blood is compensated with a lavalava. The same applies for helpers at funerals. When arriving on an island a woman receives a new lavalava from her relatives, so that she can change into it. Official guests are greeted with lavalava. On departure once again a lavalava is handed over as a token of farewell. The Rei Metau are well acquainted with the ocean and know how dangerous a maritime journey can be. Therefore, lavalava called *tiugiutiug*, the same name given to textiles placed on a corpse, are presented to those embarking upon sea journeys.

While all lavalava can be used as clothing or be freely distributed as payment for services or gifts, this is not the case with the machiye. On the contrary, machiye can only be delivered to Yap.

LAVALAVA IN THE YAPESE EMPIRE

Yap Island, situated in the west of the Rei Metau atolls, is a high island with many resources. Its inhabitants have a different culture, speak a different language, wear different clothes, and are believed to be in the possession of powerful magic. With this they have for centuries held power over the Rei Metau and many islands to the east, by supposedly sending destructive typhoons. These islands and their inhabitants are considered the personal property of certain families in Yap's Gatchpar province. In anthropological literature this is called the Yap Empire. The Rei Metau call it a *sawey* relationship, based on the ancient belief that all the Outer Islands of Yap (which, together with Yap Island, make up with Province of Yap) and their inhabitants are owned by certain families. This means they have to deliver sawey-tribute in the form of lavalava and belts to the *saweylap* (the highest sawey), to their individual sawey, and for safety reasons, as a sort of insurance, to their hidden sawey. In short, the sawey relationship with Yap Island consists of several aspects, an official one, a religious one, an individual one, and even a secret one. The goods are later redistributed in Yap, because Yapese men wear lavalava as traditional clothing, though in a different fashion than the Rei Metau men. The Germans forbade inter-island traffic by local canoe. From then on traditional tribute trips ceased, and the Rei Metau started using the German government boat, or boats of copra traders, whenever they were available. From World War II onward Outer Islanders traveling to Yap for work or medical reasons have used irregular and expensive air services, but transportion is mainly by field-trip ship or the occasional patrol or fishing boat.

Within the sawey trade machiye textiles are specifically ordered and have to be delivered to Yap, where they are held in high esteem. Contrary to Outer Island custom, Yapese men also wear them, but according to the Rei Metau belief, the Yapese can obtain the right to kill somebody without fearing retribution by presenting a machiye to the family of the victim. In the past Rei Metau only visited Yap with the sawey fleet, stayed a few months, and returned to their home islands with gifts. Since the beginning of the twentieth century the Rei Metau started to stay on Yap longer and even to take up residence there. Due to their inferior status, they have to follow a code of behavior as well as a strict dress code. They are not allowed to wear Western clothes, their lavalava may not have bright colors, their hair must be short, and they are not allowed to wear any flowers.

CHANGES IN THE EARLY TWENTY-FIRST CENTURY

Weaving was once practiced in many parts of Micronesia, such as in Chuuk, Pohnpei, and Kosrae. However, since the beginning of the twentieth century the women of the Rei Metau are the only ones who weave and wear traditional dress on a daily basis, and not simply for cultural events. Lavalava are part of a woman's identity. Therefore many women continue to wear them even when they live abroad, under no chiefly control and following no specific island dress code. Outside of their islands and of Yap, they wear T-shirts together with their lavalava, whereas men usually wear pants and shirts. In this fashion they both feel at home in modern times. The traditional tattoos have been given up altogether.

Lavalava are not only exported to Yap but also to the neighboring islands of Chuuk, where women no longer weave and have to import lavalava from the Outer Islands of Yap. They no longer wear them on a daily basis, but only for traditional dances. Lavalava and the high esteem in which they are held on the Outer Islands have withstood modernization and cultural changes. They are a symbol of Rei Metau identity and all of the social values that are mirrored in them.

References and Further Reading

Petrosian-Husa, Carmen. "Changes in Colouring: Observations on the Islands of the Rei Metau in Micronesia." *Dyes in History and Archaeology* 14 (1996): 14–18.

Petrosian-Husa, Carmen. "Les Lavalava—Objets de valeur feminins aux iles Rei metau." *Journal de la Societe des Oceanistes* 112 (2001): 20–30.

Riesenberg, Saul, and A. H. Gayton. "Caroline Island Belt Weaving." *Southwestern Journal of Anthropology* 8, no. 3 (1952): 342–375.

Rubinstein, Donald H. "The Social Fabric: Micronesian Textile Patterns as an Embodiment of Social Order." In *Mirror and Metaphor: Material and Social Constructions of Reality*, edited by Daniel Ingersoll and Gordon Bronitsky, 63–82. Landham, MD: University Press of America, 1987.

Rubinstein, Donald H. "The Social Fabric: Micronesian Textile Patterns and Social Order." In *Art in Small-Scale Societies: Contemporary Readings*, edited by Richard Anderson and Karen Field, 70–83. Englewood Cliffs, NJ: Prentice Hall, 1993.

Carmen C. H. Petrosian-Husa

See also Dressing the Body in Bariai; Dress of the Chamorro.

Dress of the Chamorro

The Chamorro are the indigenous people of the Mariana Islands in the Western Pacific area of Micronesia. At the time of first European contact in 1521, and in subsequent visitor descriptions throughout the sixteenth century, Chamorros were described as being unclothed, or in the case of some women covered only in their pubic areas. Missionaries arrived in 1668, and the islands were subjugated by Spain from that time until American takeover in 1899. The Chamorro population was so reduced from disease and battles that the Spanish moved the remaining islanders to live in Guam in the early eighteenth century. In the nineteenth century *mestiza* dress was introduced from the Spanish Pacific Islands government in Manila, Philippines, showing that the history of clothing has been of considerable complexity. American rule since 1899 influenced the Chamorro, and increasingly everyday clothing and fashion trends have conformed to Western attire, subsequently becoming part of the global network of style. In the twenty-first century a revival of specific items made and worn as so-called national dress by a large segment of the Chamorro population has been in part based on pre-European contact artifacts. In the case of Saipan in the Northern Marianas, descriptions of dress of the Refalawash (Carolinian) people are of significance since these people are also indigenous to the islands, and certain items of "national dress" are used by both.

HISTORICAL AND GEOGRAPHICAL BACKGROUND

The Mariana Islands form a chain of fifteen islands, with the largest and southernmost island being that of Guam. Besides the other three inhabited islands of Rota, Tinian, and Saipan, there are smaller, volcanic islands, which form a five-hundred-mile crescent northward toward Japan. It is believed these people migrated from Southeast Asia as part of the Austronesian language groups that originated out of present-day Taiwan over four thousand years ago. Mariana Islands' history is shaped by their strategic location, originally as a stopover on the Spanish galleon trade routes between Acapulco and Manila, and in recent history as a U.S. military forward staging area to points in Asia.

Various piecemeal observations were made about the appearance of the Chamorro from the time of European explorer Ferdinand Magellan's encounter in 1521, for instance by his historiographer Antonio Pigafetta, who described men and women with black hair wearing it very long. Later navigator Thomas Cavendish noted men tying their long hair into one or two buns on top of their heads. In 1596 Frey Antonio de Los Angeles, whose ship stopped by the Marianas, saw some women wearing matting from the waist down, but

men seem to have been unclothed. Most observers noted women wearing at minimum a leaf (*tifi'*) attached to a cord around their waists, or a piece of paper-thin bark (*gunot*), which covered their private parts. The use of turtle-shell plates as an apron suggests status determined some forms of body modification. (Anyone who caught a turtle had to present it to the chief for distribution; therefore those wearing turtle-shell body ornamentation had been given that right by the chief.) Fragrant flower garlands for women and the use of coconut oil for both sexes indicate that smell as well as visual enhancement of the body was valued. Jesuit reports of 1669–1670 described how the women wore, according to their status, turtle shell and disks of orange *Spondylus* (a spiney oyster) shells strung together on fiber cords to form belts. Turtle and Spondylus shells were highly prized exchange valuables and status symbols. In the twenty-first century the use of the latter has been revived.

Contact with missionaries had an important effect. The first missionary, Father Luis de San Vitores, for instance, introduced clothing as a prerequisite for baptism. For a time he dressed the people in materials he had brought from Mexico, a gift that probably encouraged the conversion of many. At the start of the eighteenth century the indigenous people were subjugated by the Spanish military. Decimated from war with the Spaniards and foreign diseases, the remaining 3,500 people were concentrated on the island of Guam. Here, resettled into villages, regulations against "barbaric" practices molded the population into a semblance of the rest of the Spanish Empire. The old *chamorri* (high-status Chamorro) families evolved into a small elite class of Chamorro and Spanish mixture called *manákhilo*, or "high class." These fair-skinned mestizos (of mixed blood) became the model of beauty for Chamorros.

The influence of the Hispanic lifestyle on daily life, especially in the capital of Hagåtña, where the Spanish officials, soldiers, and mestizo population resided, was evident, for instance, in the garments of the schoolboys who attended and lived at the Colegio de San Juan de Letran in 1727. They wore a kind of vest of blue material, a white linen kerchief, and pants of white or blue linen, all ordered from Mexico. Boarders wore sombreros (woven, large-brim hats) when they left the school or went to church. Outside of the capitol city, where contact with religious authority was limited, indigenous attire was still worn. For women it consisted of a cloth wrapped from the waist to the ankle, pulled up to cover their breasts when going to town. This was sometimes modified by pinning the material over one shoulder, called a *dudus* (flirt). Attire for men consisted of a *sådi'*, or loincloth.

NINETEENTH-CENTURY COLONIAL INFLUENCES

The weakening of the Spanish Empire over the course of the eighteenth and nineteenth centuries directly influenced its colonies in the Pacific, including the Marianas. The Chamorro population was by then a mixture of Chamorro, Mexican, Filipino, and Spanish, with minimal trade or contact with the outside world. The annual Spanish galleon from Acapulco to Manila ceased in 1815, after Mexico won independence and Spain no longer had control of gold and silver mines there. Occasionally years passed before a ship arrived from Manila.

Scientific expeditions and whaling ships provided the main source of information about the Marianas during the nineteenth century, and it is not always consistent. Englishman William Haswell, first officer of the barque *Lydia*, put into Guam in 1801 for supplies. He said the inland indigenous people only put on clothing when they saw Europeans. He noted the poverty and lack of money to purchase clothing, since the Spanish governor controlled all trade, most of which came from the whaling ships. Tobacco was grown in Guam in large quantities, a great deal of which was made into cigars, and men, women, and children all smoked long, hand-rolled cigars. Haswell also remarked on the wide habit of chewing betel-nut, saying that women prided themselves on their teeth stained bright red from its juice.

Official reports by various Spanish governors to their superiors in the Philippines, along with journals and reports kept by the clergy and explorer accounts, provide a look at life in the Marianas. French explorer Louis de Freycinet in 1819 noted that at that time men's clothing consisted of long pants made of bleached cotton with a shirt of *abaca* (Manila hemp, from the inner fiber of the *Musa textilis* plant). Women wore skirts of Indian cotton, with a short shirt of any material, blue or white. Footwear was relatively rare. Leather sandals or woven *dogga* (native woven sandals) were probably used for traversing rough ground when walking from one village to another or to the family garden. In 1821 clothing was scarce, and many people were unable to cover their unclothed bodies. They resorted to collecting and manufacturing cotton and other fibers. One governor reported that they made looms and wove cloth, such as *liencecillo* (from banana fibers) for shirts and mantas (bleached cotton) for shirts and pants; and for skirts *listadillos* (striped fabric in various colors), *cambayas de corta* (lightweight Indian cotton)—although they were not able to make fast colors—and some *terlingas* (striped or checkered strong cloth). In 1822 the Ministry of Finance in Manila established an Office of Administration and stocked it with consumer goods. This ended the need for textile manufacturing in Guam, and the looms fell into disrepair. Cotton, which grew quite well on Guam, ceased to be collected.

The style that developed during the nineteenth century became known as the mestiza (sometimes spelled *mestisa*). It developed under Spanish rule in the Philippines, which also administered the affairs of the Marianas. Men's attire consisted of knee-length, loose pants, tied at the waist with a drawstring, made of bleached cotton (mantas). Long pants of mantas were used for church or formal occasions. A shirt of the same material or liencecillo (for more dressy occasions) was loose and collarless and reached to the thighs with button-down front and long sleeves. A dressier shirt had a stand-up, band collar. Men wore straw hats or sometimes sombrero-style hats whenever they went out. They tanned cowhide to make leather sandals, but these were usually reserved for special occasions. Women wore a calf-length slip (*kamisola*) of mantas with a low-cut round neck either gathered and finished with bias banding or finished with cutwork embroidery at the neckline and the hem. Over the kamisola a woman would put on an ankle-length skirt of listadillos, cambayas de corta, or terlingas. She tied it at the waist with a drawstring. When working in the home, the kamisola served as a covering for her upper body, leaving her neck and arms bare. For social occasions or church she donned a loosely woven, transparent top with a scoop neck. The front opening was usually pinned together. The sleeves developed from a bell-shaped, three-quarter-length style, gathered at the shoulders, that paralleled the hambone sleeve style of the

Victorian era. Sleeve styles around the end of the nineteenth century began to change from the soft bell-shape that draped over the arm to the starched "butterfly" look of the formal mestiza today.

Following European influence, women began to make the back of their skirts longer so that they trailed behind the wearer. When walking outside, a woman would pick up the train and tuck it into the side of her waistband. This created graceful folds in the back of the skirt and allowed the bottom of the embroidered kamisola hem to show at the side where the train was tucked. This developed into a signature feature of the mestiza skirt of the Mariana Islands.

Women covered their heads upon entering the church. Head coverings ranged from simple, white handkerchiefs, sometimes with lace trim, to large satin or lace shawls, which were folded into a triangle. The shawl fully covered her head, and the triangle fold draped down her back. Formal tops were woven of banana fiber or other stiff thread in an open-weave, transparent fabric, imported from the Philippines. The lace-embroidered kamisola showed through this top. Often for very formal wear a triangle-shaped piece of the same stiff fabric was folded over the shoulders and pinned in front with the triangle tip covering her back. This created a stiff, kimono-type collar that fitted between the tops of the butterfly sleeves. The stiffness of the fabric was often enhanced with starch made from corn or tapioca flour.

The making of gold and silver jewelry was introduced during the Spanish Colonial period. Silver- and goldsmiths, called *platerus*, likely came in with artisans imported from Mexico and the Philippines. The diary of Rose de Freycinet, who visited Guam with her husband in 1819, noted that one of the few distinguishing marks of status was that the more well-to-do women of Guam wore gold bracelets, earrings, and pendants. An illustration from this expedition shows a Chamorro woman with earrings, which may represent a stylized fleur-de-lis, and a cameo pendant on a heavy gold or silver chain. Louis de Freycinet in his account added that both men and women loved to wear a scapular or a rosary on which was usually suspended a cross or silver medallion. Bracelets and rings of bamboo design, rosette and *kamachili* (a tree whose fruit pods resemble large pea pods) patterns for pendants and earrings, were the mark of fine-quality Chamorro jewelry. Such pieces became a sign of pride and prestige when given by a groom to the bride.

Dances introduced by the Spanish authorities reflected items of dress that carried over into the twentieth century. Jacques Arago described in 1819 a dance by children he observed to entertain the visitors from the French scientific Freycinet expedition, of which he was a part. He noted a coquettish dance whereby a boy and girl flirted with each other around a sombrero placed on the ground. Adaptations of Spanish dances that carried over into the next century include a "handkerchief dance" described by elders who practiced this on social occasions in the 1920s. The man and woman clutched the ends of a handkerchief between them, rather than holding hands, preserving a modest distance. The sound created by carved wooden soles of slippers worn by women as they danced made a pleasing rhythmic accompaniment to Spanish-influenced dances.

The Carolinians (Caroline Islanders from south of the Mariana Islands) were another indigenous community who migrated to Saipan in the Northern Marianas beginning in 1815, after their islands had been destroyed by a tropical cyclone. The Refalawash, as they call themselves, brought over and carried on wearing the original indigenous dress and embellishments of their home islands. They continued to wear their customary dress into the twentieth century and only conformed to Western dress after World War II. Both men and women went topless in daily life. Women wove their wraps (*lavalava*), measuring about twenty-four inches (sixty-one centimeters) wide by four to six feet (1.2 to 1.8 meters) long, of banana and other native fibers (later of cotton threads), using backstrap looms and simple shuttles. The lavalava were wrapped around the lower body and secured at the waist. Special lavalava were also worn on some occasions by men. Fibers were dyed with natural plants and later imported dyes. Usually of alternating stripes, some patterns were more intricate and reserved for particular rituals or chiefly classes.

Throughout the nineteenth century small colonies of these people in Guam and a flourishing settlement in Saipan perpetuated their heritage. Men continued to wear loincloths consisting of a six-foot (1.8-meter) length of cotton yardage, usually red, dark blue, or yellow, intricately wrapped between the legs and around the waist. Especially for dances, the ends of the loincloth were draped artfully over their pelvis or buttocks. Both men and women wore *mwar*, head garlands of palm leaf with intricate designs created by incorporating various flower petals. Practitioners continued to create elaborately threaded necklaces made of tiny glass beads, originally brought by early traders to their home islands. These passed down through generations as heirlooms and dance adornment, and they were given for burials upon the death of a respected family member.

The art of tattoo was practiced by the Refalawash. Early photographs show intricate patterns that covered areas of the chest, back, and thighs of men and women. This practice was discouraged by religious and colonial leaders and fell out of use by the end of the nineteenth century. Chamorro and Refalawash communities on Saipan (by the early twentieth century all Refalawash had moved from Guam and resettled in Saipan and other Northern Mariana Islands) kept to themselves with relatively little cultural exchange between them throughout the nineteenth and early twentieth centuries.

THE AMERICAN PERIOD

Spanish administration of the Marianas ended abruptly in 1898 when the United States seized Guam during the Spanish-American War. Administration of the Northern Marianas was taken over by Germany, Japan, and the United States before becoming the Commonwealth of the Northern Marianas (CNMI) in 1976 and being given a commonwealth relationship with the United States. Dress styles throughout the Mariana Islands were consistent despite political changes between the Northern Mariana Islands and Guam.

An excerpt from the journal of American Lieutenant William Safford in 1900 describes women's dress in Guam as a short jacket of thin muslin, with low-cut neck and flowing sleeves, often with lace edging. In addition, women wore a trailing skirt usually of bright-colored gingham of large checked pattern, a fine white handkerchief over the head and often across the breast, and a necklace, usually of coral with gold beads at intervals, around the neck, from which a cross or medal was suspended. A few ladies dressed in the European fashion, but most of them could not endure the discomfort of stays and lacing. Shoes were made on the island, but usually with no heels. Stockings were regarded by most women as a useless luxury.

Lieutenant Safford described a unique custom he observed in 1900. When women attended daily mass at the Agana Cathedral, they dressed in this finery, wearing heelless slippers with a covered toe. There were no benches on which to kneel in the church, so the first woman would take off her slippers, place them on the bare floor, and kneel on them, leaving her bare feet slightly exposed. The next woman would likewise kneel on her slippers and cover the feet of the woman in front of her with the folds of her skirt. Each woman subsequently knelt on her slippers and covered the feet of the woman in front of her with her skirt, thus maintaining the decorum necessary to the occasion.

During the U.S. Naval administration of Guam in the first half of the twentieth century, women began to copy clothing styles in the mail-order catalogs from the mainland United States. The Singer sewing machine became a coveted household appliance, whereby women made clothing for family members. Early sewing machines were also described in a report by Governor Georg Fritz during the German administration of the Northern Mariana Islands (1900–1914). This tabletop model was operated by placing it on the floor, with the seamstress kneeling in front of it. It was operated by means of a hand crank attached to the flywheel. Later models were table-height with cast-iron supports and a foot treadle that was attached to the flywheel with a circular belt. Juan Flores of Guam talked about the sewing skills exhibited by his grandmother, who sewed a professionally tailored suit for his first Holy Communion ceremony in 1940.

Following a dark period of Japanese occupation during World War II, Americanization of Chamorros increased even more rapidly during the second half of the twentieth century. Mestizas continue to be worn as official Chamorro attire in the twenty-first century, but on most occasions American dress styles dominate the scene. Youths imitate California street trends, as observed on television and sold in local shops, and they are influenced by Chamorro relatives who live in the mainland United States and who frequently travel to their home islands in the Marianas.

CHAMORRO IDENTITY REINSTATED

A renaissance of Chamorro language and culture began in the 1970s, as U.S. federal policy responded to national minority rights issues. As more Chamorros availed themselves of higher education, they began to research their early past and to create public awareness through teaching, publishing, and nationalistic activity. The economic boom of the 1980s brought prosperity to the island in the form of jobs that provided service for the large number of tourists visiting from Japan. Huge hotel construction projects began to unearth artifacts and burial sites. Chamorro indigenous rights groups began to protest this desecration of early graves. They influenced artists in their creation of neo-Chamorro body modifications, based on artifacts discovered in burial sites prior to the period of first European contact and considered to be of ancient origin. This resulted in an interest in redefining Chamorro identity via the use of these "heritage" items.

Beginning in the 1980s a significant number of men who were members of a Chamorro rights group called *Nasion Chamoru* (Chamorro Nation) shaved their heads, except for a topknot, in imitation of the warriors described in historical accounts. Chamorro jewelry of stone, bone, and shell became an identity symbol for those who were sympathetic to the cause. Many activists wore a *Tridacna* (giant clamshell) neckpiece they called *sinahi* (quarter moon)—the thick, crescent-shaped rare artifact found in ancient burials. In the twenty-first century Chamorro jewelry makers have incorporated the use of Spondylus shell into their designs. A rare item in the past, twenty-first-century artists value this orange spiny oyster shell both for its color and for its association with what is felt to be a noble past.

The renaissance of Chamorro dance began in the 1980s and developed along similar lines. Dance group members wore replicas of ancient artifacts created by indigenous artists and made further creative uses of indigenous materials in their dress. Creators of dances that depicted their distant past borrowed ideas from other Pacific islands, in order to cover bodies historically described as unclothed. This history was represented by dance skirts of coconut leaves, breadfruit leaves, or wild hibiscus tree fibers for women; loincloths for men were often covered with shorter coconut-leaf skirts. The mestiza dress of the Spanish period was also recreated in more colorful, bolder print fabrics for women's skirts, while men's shirts replicated the white, collarless, long or three-quarter-length sleeves and loose styles of that period. Dance groups have created group identity by designing and wearing T-shirts with ancient symbols such as copies of cave drawings, sling stones, fish hooks, *latte* (very old stone house pillars), pictures of ancient warriors, and other designs along with their dance group name.

OFFICIAL CHAMORRO ATTIRE

The Department of Chamorro Affairs published a Chamorro authentication manual in 2003 that describes the official formal dress style for Guam, based on variations of the mestiza dress of the nineteenth century for men and women. This national dress is recommended wear for formal government functions and other celebrations of Chamorro culture. Variations on the nineteenth-century mestiza include an alternate style of top worn by women originally used for daily wear. Called a kimono top, it consists of a flat, oblong piece of fabric with a hole cut for the neckline, slipped over the head and tied with short strings under the arms. This style is elaborated by adding a ruffle around the edge, sometimes in a print material that matches the skirt. Modern interpretations of the mestiza train tucked into the waistband have been reduced to an elongated attachment of material along one side of the skirt, ending at a point with a finger loop to hold it off the ground. This gives the appearance of the signature folds in the mestiza skirt without the added bulk of a train. Variations of the mestiza style include one-piece, fitted long dresses with butterfly sleeves, or with the skirt fitted from waist to thighs and then flared or gathered to ankle length. The official men's formal shirt style is based on the Philippine men's *barong* shirt, with a mandarin-style collar, and long or three-quarter sleeves, worn loosely over long trousers. A more casual style incorporates various island print patterns.

The replication of ancient embellishment has produced signature pieces of great value, based on the amount of work involved to carve it and on the skill of the artist. Both Spondylus disks and the sinahi made from giant clamshell are worn as symbols of Chamorro identity and prestige. While it was historically worn by women, both sexes now wear pendants of polished Spondylus or necklaces strung into closely packed disks. There is no documentation to confirm that sinahi was actually worn in the distant past (as opposed to being a clan exchange valuable), but this has become a prestigious neck ornament for men. The thick, highly polished crescent of clamshell is drilled through each end and tied with a cord to create a choker,

ranging in size from two to five inches (5.1 to 12.7 centimeters) long. Contemporary artists have created a variety of styles from natural materials, such as stone, wood, and bone, with inlays of Spondylus.

The CNMI officially recognizes both Refalawash (Carolinian) and Chamorro groups as natives. Therefore, elements of Refalawash body modification have come into official use for social and government protocol. The mwar (head garland) is regularly used as embellishment by both Refalawash and Chamorro people and given to visiting guests of the Northern Marianas, and to a lesser extent in Guam. Children sell colorful mwar along the roadsides in the Northern Marianas, made by family members. Customary bead necklaces continue to be made by new generations of practitioners, which are valued for their past uses and used for dance group identity and purchased by collectors. Chamorro and Refalawash freely exchange cultural practices while retaining distinct identities. Chamorros of CNMI and Guam as well as Refalawash accept and use customary and contemporary tattoo designs as heritage ornamentation.

The twenty-first-century Chamorro has grown up in a dual society that acknowledges and accepts ancient heritage symbols along with contemporary American dress as part of the Chamorro identity. Family and community events reveal a variety of modern dress styles. Some wear Chamorro stone, bone, or shell jewelry; others wear gold bracelets, necklaces, and earrings based on classic Spanish-Chamorro designs. Many wear international name-brand clothing and jewelry. Chamorro dress reflects the multiple histories and ethnic mix that makes up their society.

References and Further Reading

Aguon, Katherine B., ed. *A Sense of Place: The Chamorro Authentication Manual*. Hagatna, Guam: Department of Chamorro Affairs, Division of Research and Writing, 2003.

Driver, Marjorie. *Fray Juan Pobre in the Marianas, 1602*. Mangilao: Micronesian Area Research Center, University of Guam, 1989.

Forster, Honore. *The Cruise of the "Gipsy": The Journal of John Wilson, Surgeon on a Whaling Voyage to the Pacific Ocean*. Fairfield, WA: The Galleon Press, 1991.

Freycinet, Louis Claude de. *An Account of the Corvette L'Uraine's Sojourn at the Mariana Islands, 1819*. Supplemented with the *Journal of Rose de Freycinet*. Translated and prefaced by Glynn Barratt. Occasional Historical Papers No. 13. Saipan: CNMI Division of Historic Preservation, 2003.

Garcia, Francisco. *The Life and Martyrdom of Diego Luis De San Vitores of the Society of Jesus First Apostle of the Mariana Islands*. Translated by Margaret M. Higgins, Felicia Plaza, and Juan M. H. Ledesma. Edited by James A. McDonough. Hagatna: Richard Flores Taitano Micronesian Area Research Center, University of Guam, 2004.

Haswell, William. "The Roving Printer: Remarks on a Voyage in 1801 to the Island of Guam." Reprinted in the *Guam Newsletter* 11 (1919): 1–2.

Levesque, Rodrigue, ed. *History of Micronesia: A Collection of Documents*. Vols. 1–6. Gatineau, Canada: Levesque Publications, 1992.

Rogers, Robert F. *Destiny's Landfall: A History of Guam*. Honolulu: University of Hawai'i Press, 1995.

Safford, William. *A Year on the Island of Guam*. RFT—Micronesian Area Research Center typescript copy. *Guam Recorder* (Vols. 10–13). University of Guam, 1901.

Judith S. Flores

See also Lavalava (Cloth) of the Rei Metau.

Dress in the Marshall Islands

The people of the two chains of atolls that make up the Marshall Islands have adopted styles of dress and adornment over the years to fit their cultural and social parameters. This attire reflects their aesthetics, modified by many outside influences from the times of early voyagers to the present. Dress materials and other items of embellishment were originally made from the islands' resources, such as processed leaves and dyes, while latterly cotton materials have been used, along with local materials for headdresses and jewelry.

The Marshall Islands lie in the central Pacific, ten to fifteen degrees north of the equator. They mark the easternmost settlement of the northern Pacific string of atolls and islands known as Micronesia. The twenty-nine atolls and islands consist of calcareous soils on which limited vegetation will grow, thus restricting the range of local materials for food, dress, building materials, and other social necessities. Pandanus trees provided the leaves that were processed and woven into early dress mats, and they and coconut-leaf fibers are still used to make headdresses and jewelry.

After a hundred years of control by a succession of foreign powers, these islands are now in Free Association with the United States, formal independence being achieved in 1986. The population quadrupled after the 1960s, reaching sixty thousand people in 2008. Half live on the high-density urbanized islets of Djarrit, Uliga, and Delap on Majuro atoll, and Ebeye on Kwajalein atoll, while the other half continues their traditional tenure of the other twenty-four inhabited atolls and islands. Those who live on the outer islands visit the urban centers as frequently as transportation by ship or by air allows. The United States has used Kwajalein atoll in the northern Marshalls as a nuclear testing base, and Bikini and Enewetak became the sites of a series of hydrogen bomb explosions. Bikini has become a household name for a popular type of beachwear. Cotton cloth for dress materials is an important import carried by the field-trip ships that service the outer islands or is brought by relatives returning home from overseas. Gifts of lengths of cloth are an integral part of any funeral, when they are displayed over the grave for six days. They are then redistributed to family and friends.

The economy of the Marshall Islands has relied on subsistence root and tree crops and fishing, until copra (dried coconut meat) became a source of cash income in the late nineteenth century. In the modern world that income must be stretched to buy additional foodstuffs to feed the growing population as well as other household necessities including cloth. Women sew their family cloth into shirts for men and the Hawaiian mu'umu'u (or mumu in the Marshall Islands) style for women, the latter a loose-fitting dress with a yoke and sleeves, stretching from neck to ankle. Missionaries arriving in the nineteenth century had insisted that bodies should be covered and thus introduced calico for women to construct into family clothing, in particular the mu'umu'u. Handicraft items using local fibers are constructed for local wear, as well as providing a small source of income from sales to visitors.

HISTORICAL DRESS AND THE INFLUENCE OF MISSIONARIES

The woven dress mats (jaki-ed) that Marshallese men and women were wearing at the time of first European contact in the seventeenth century were replaced in the nineteenth century by the calico mu'umu'u for women and shirts and trousers for men. ABCFM missionaries (American Board of Commissioners for Foreign Missions), from a Congregational mission out of Hawai'i, introduced a new body-covering dress code, which they expected all Marshallese to adopt, at least in public. These mu'umu'u and shirts became more colorful over the years but have remained the major style of dress, especially for church-going and formal occasions.

The first descriptions of early forms of attire were recorded both in Congregationalist mission reports to their Hawai'i office, and later by German ethnographers with the Südsee Expedition in the 1890s. Thus, there are both photographic and written accounts of dress and bodily adornment at the time of first contact. But it must be remembered that these representations were drawn from the newcomers' own cultural and gendered values. Their disapproval of what they considered "bare" bodies was an important factor that led to changes such as the introduction of the mu'umu'u for women and the shirt for men.

Before missionary times German ethnographic records show tattooing was a strongly developed form for displaying the beauty of Marshallese bodies for both men and women. Elaborate patterns were developed, and the personal strengths of those enduring the process were noted. But these designs were covered over and the practice of tattooing relegated to history when missionaries introduced cloth garments that covered the body. Thus, styles and motifs of tattooing disappeared about 1880.

Before European contact Marshall Islands people used mats woven from pandanus leaf fibers. Women wore two dress mats that covered their hips and thighs, while men wore one mat that covered the genitals; both tied these around the waist with coconut sennet. They were decorated around the outer edges, using fibers steeped in local dyes. High-status individuals (Iroij) wore mats that were more highly decorated than those of commoners (rijerbal). This dress code represented the peoples' moral values as to how bodies should be displayed or covered, including those parts that should not be exposed to public view.

In 2006 an exhibition of these customary woven mats, jaki-ed, was held in Majuro to remind people of their history and traditions. The exhibition was run under the auspices of the Marshall Islands Visitors Authority, in conjunction with local businesses. Just as the very successful reconstructions of old canoes has awakened interest in the material and aesthetics of their past, so this exhibition of old-style dress has restored a positive image of former dress styles.

The introduction of the mu'umu'u-style dress replicated missionary views of how bodies should be presented and their view of appropriate materials. They expected that women's bodies should be completely covered from neck to ankle, and that men should cover their chests. These introduced views of "decency" or acceptable body cover extended the Marshall Islands peoples' own codes of decency by continuing to cover the inner thigh, but also included covering the shoulders and breasts. Modern-day women on outer islands are not so concerned with exposing their breasts, while they find the full skirt of the mu'umu'u (even in its shorter modern version) an acceptable way to cover the inner thigh by wrapping the extra skirt material between their legs when hunkering/squatting, or sitting down. The shift style of dress worn by air hostesses in the 1960s, considered very up-to-date by young Marshallese women, was not accepted by older women because it did not allow them to squat decently. And dresses that did not have sleeves were also considered inappropriate, and labeled *teenaj* (teenager style).

Introduction of cloth garments strained the economy in several ways. The household budget had to include purchase of a bolt of material to make up the required dresses, shirts, and pants for all members of the family, both children and adults. The acquisition of a sewing machine for making these garments has also been a major budget item. Hand-driven sewing machines have become harder to find as most manufacturers in the twenty-first century produce only electric machines. On outer islands where few generators are available, access to new hand machines is a challenge. The new cloth garments also require washing, so that soap is a vital household expense. With only brackish water from wells on outer islands, or limited access to any water on the urban atolls, washing clothes requires careful planning. Social mores require that clothes be frequently laundered, ironed, and carefully stored with the family's possessions. Saturday nights are busy for the women of the household as they prepare everyone's clothes for Sunday church.

MARSHALLESE CUSTOMS AND THE BODY

Marshall Islands people hold strong standards for the care and presentation of their bodies. Beauty and modesty are matters of constant concern and have been adapted to new sets of values over time. A large body is considered the epitome of female beauty and social well-being. The mu'umu'u is thus an appropriate dress style as it covers a woman's body in accordance with standards of decency as well as being appropriate for various figure sizes and activities. The garment extends the beauty of women's bodies to their coverings.

Appearance is a matter of social approval rather than one of individual choice, though this is under challenge from outside sources in the modern world. The community drives and monitors decisions about appropriate attire. Fieldwork in the Marshall Islands since the 1960s has provided an overview of these changes and their sources of influence. Women debate the appropriateness of innovative forms of dress and ways of displaying the body, whether in the urban centers or as seen in magazines. Lipstick, for example, was formerly considered to be garish and not in accordance with *manit in Majol* (Marshallese custom), but it is accepted for women in particular forms of employment, or when relatives return from overseas. Length of skirts, whether mu'umu'us or dresses, has been as strongly criticized as in other cultures. Both moral and practical concerns are at issue.

The case of the see-through mu'umu'u introduced to Ebeye from Guam in 2002 illustrates the many dimensions of moral and material concerns held by both women and men. This mu'umu'u, made of transparent material, has been worn by several young women on Ebeye, thereby evoking comment on the pros and cons of such an innovation. The critics, or traditionalists, argue that this transparent garment reveals parts of the female body that should not be exposed to public gaze. They say that it "*kakure manit in Majol*," violates Marshallese custom, or "*ejab manit*" (is not acceptable according to custom). Supporters of this new style suggest that people should be allowed to wear what is comfortable, whatever is modern, and that such a sheer garment is a matter of personal choice. The right of an individual to wear a garment like this is also at issue here; it is considered to flout the social code, thereby sanctioning individual choice. The reaction of a female Iroij who chastised one young woman physically for wearing this new transparent garment in public raised further debate among Marshallese over the Internet in 2006–2007.

Customary values are being challenged by this new dress style. Those parts of the body that have been considered inappropriate for public exposure, thus violating rules of modesty, are part of a wider debate about the appropriateness of interpretations of Marshallese custom on a broad scale in the modern world, and about who should uphold rules of modesty and decorum. Formerly chiefs, church leaders' wives, and others prominent in public affairs were regarded as bearing that responsibility. But whether they still hold that power over the people is questionable. Resistance or objection to the limitations of custom, particularly by young people, is being voiced and implemented. The growing numbers of Marshallese communities relocated across the United States, and the influences of TV, DVDs, and other media, will heighten this debate on matters of dress codes, modesty, and whether sanctions should be applied.

DRESS IN THE EARLY TWENTY-FIRST CENTURY

Modern-day dress is typified by four modes of clothing in the islands. Everyday wear, office wear, school wear, and Sunday "best" each comprise different forms. These indicate differences both in status (rural versus urban), age, and formality.

Clothing, both on outer islands and in those urban households with limited income, is largely homemade, sewn from *nuknuk* (lengths of material). Bought in bulk at one of the urban stores, nuknuk is shipped to relatives on outer islands, or received as a gift. Every Marshallese woman is an accomplished seamstress, an art she learns at a young age. The sound of the sewing machine whizzing up a new dress or shirt is very distinctive on a Saturday night in most outer island households. It is important that a child or adult have respectable attire to wear to church on Sunday, as the budget allows.

Many women on outer islands may have five or six mu'umu'u in various conditions and are thus considered well-to-do. These garments are recycled several times from their new state; a woman may wear two at a time to cover large holes, and that same one will be cut down to make a dress for a young girl, or to make panties for girls or boys. Finally, it is likely to end up as rags used at the time of menstruation and then carefully destroyed.

The important criterion of women's day-wear is that the skirt must be full enough to wrap across the knees and between the legs when crouching on their heels, or hunkering, or sitting cross-legged on a mat. It is culturally offensive for reasons of modesty for a woman to show her thighs. Cultural rules also dictate that mature (married) women should wear dresses with sleeves. If an adult woman wears a sleeveless dress, she may be labeled a "teenager." Teenagers in the twenty-first century wear spaghetti strap tops, but these are not suitable once they have children.

Status is acknowledged by means of a woman's overall presentation of dress or mu'umu'u, her hair, and the general cleanliness of herself and her family. New embellishments, such as lace on a mu'umu'u or a necklace, indicate that the family has received a gift parcel, probably from family on the U.S. mainland. These are increasing as young people return from overseas education wearing an earring or other jewelry. Their families share pride in such new attributes.

Women's groups within the local church wear uniforms for the frequent competitions at which they display their largesse in the forms of gifts, and they dance and sing to emphasize their distinction from other such groups. Much enjoyment and laughter is generated in the planning for such occasions, for which the color of the main mu'umu'u with contrasting hem and neck frills is widely debated. Such dress is the most flamboyant form of display. For everyday wear, when working on their coconut plantations or around the house, women wear a mu'umu'u (no longer full-length), normally with a half-petticoat cut down from an old mu'umu'u underneath. The material, usually cotton, is brightly colored, with patterns similar in design to those found in Hawai'i.

In urban areas women may wear slacks/pants or *lavalava* (a length of cloth wound around the waist), both worn with a blouse. Very young children are expected to wear panties, particularly young girls, but if they wet them, they just take them off and run around naked until an older sister finds a dry pair. Young girls wear dresses to school, while young boys wear shirts and pants. Underwear, including bras and panties, are more commonly worn by the younger set, in urbanized Majuro and Ebeye, while older women insist on wearing a white cotton half-petticoat under their mu'umu'u. Women rarely wear pantyhose, unless they have lived abroad and wish to make a fashion statement.

Women's hats have become an important part of formal attire for public events. For church mature women wear a white hat purchased from Hawai'i or the U.S. mainland. For other occasions, when dressing up, a woman is likely to wear either a hat made of local materials or a headband of coconut sennit with flowers inserted. Jeans have become accepted casual wear for young urban women. For those working in paid employment, mainly in government jobs in urban areas, or teachers, more formal day attire has become the accepted style. Most women wear fitted dresses or skirts and blouses. Men's and women's clothes are purchased from the few shops or supermarkets on Majuro or Ebeye, are brought home from visits to Hawai'i or Guam, or are sent back by relatives living on the U.S. mainland. Whatever the case, those who do travel beyond the Marshall Islands are expected to bring back clothing for the family in as great a quantity as they can afford.

Missionaries had expected men to wear shirts with trousers or short pants in public. This has changed. While men may have two "good" shirts for Sundays or visiting urban centers, when working on their copra plantations or fishing, many do not wear one. Yet if being photographed, men insist on donning a shirt to be considered "decent." They frequently wear only shorts or pants when working around the village or going fishing. If they wear a shirt,

these may be worn open and just cover the back from the sun. T-shirts have become casual attire for young and old. Those that bear an inscription that reflects an American football team number and color, or a popular character such as Rambo, are considered up to date. Jeans are common for men, while style-conscious youths choose baggy shorts and trousers worn with a reversed cap. Men's shirts in the twenty-first century follow the Hawaiian style, with bright colors and designs. Government officials are as likely to wear a Hawaiian-style shirt with slacks as a full suit, which is uncomfortable in the humid climate.

Sunday church dress is markedly different from everyday wear for both women and men. Older women wear their best outfit, whether an elaborate (colored or plain) long mu'umu'u decorated with lace around the yoke or a smart purchased dress. Hats are mandatory for older women, whether a white purchased hat or one carefully made from woven pandanus fibers. Women may also wear a collar of flowers woven into a fiber band or other jewelry. Men wear their best Hawaiian shirt or a suit if a member of the lay clergy. The pastor and deacons wear black suits with white shirts and shoes—no socks or ties.

The wedding dress for an urban bride is likely to have been purchased in Hawai'i, as neither the material nor the sewing expertise is available locally. A bride's white, fitted dress with low neckline complete with train, headdress, and veil, together with some six bridesmaids and a young page boy all suitably dressed, marks a high-status wedding in an urban church. Outfitting the whole wedding party is thus very expensive and requires much forward planning to ensure all the garments arrive from overseas in time to make whatever adjustments are necessary. Outer island weddings are less Westernized, with the whole wedding party wearing new garments only as elaborate as access to the lace and other embellishments will allow.

Dressing the hair is an important part of daily life. Micronesians' hair is typically black and straight. Most women wear their hair twisted and pinned to the back of the head with a comb or other device. They wash their hair daily and add coconut oil (*piniep*), plus local flowers for their aroma. Cutting the hair is a recent custom, and a mark of urban influences. Women with short hair once were considered "teenage," but in the early twenty-first century this style is widely accepted. A few women have their hair permed at one of the few beauty salons in Majuro and Ebeye, while some women seek out black hair dye to cover any graying. Men cut each other's hair and shave each other outside the house. Men with long hair are considered to be harking back to old days, or else considered "hippies." Some sailors alight from their yachts with long hair, thus influencing some to follow such trends.

Shoes are worn by those working in urban areas, or as formal church attire. The majority of the population wears *zoris*, or thongs, to protect their feet, or else go barefoot. Zoris are expensive to maintain on the coral of the outer islands, so they may be repaired using a car inner tube, which gives them much longer life. Cuts to those with bare feet do not seem to be a problem. Young fashion-conscious women may wear heels or pointed-toe shoes on formal occasions. Men's shoes also represent a considerable investment and must be wide enough to accommodate feet that have spread over the years, when not wearing shoes. Men rarely wear socks, unless playing sports.

The dress code in the Marshalls is changing, as young people follow examples from their cousins living on the U.S. mainland or fashions they see on DVDs, in films, and in magazines.

Western-style skirts and dresses for women and suits for men are worn by those working in urban environments, and by those who bring new styles back from the U.S. mainland. Ebeye residents are influenced by the Americans of all ages living on the Kwajalein U.S. military nuclear testing base. Custom is closely confronted by comfort and conformity. Keepers of the dress code are still the older women of the community, whether Iroij family members or pastors' wives. Keeping up with the outside world is thus balanced against those interpreting modern versions of custom. Dress is one manifestation of identity, chosen by individuals, but governed by whether or not it is socially acceptable. Bodies should be covered, but to what degree is under constant revision. The bikini definitely remains unacceptable wear for the Marshallese. To live in the Marshall Islands is to participate in local custom, but at the same time to be adjusting to U.S. and worldwide standards of value and practice.

Snapshot: The Bikini

The form of beachwear known as the *bikini* is a European design for which the name of a Marshallese atoll has been appropriated. This two-piece garment has become very popular in the Western world among those women who frequent beaches and bare their bodies to obtain a suntan. But it is antithetical to the dress code of the Marshall Islands people. They had no say in its naming or adoption.

The bikini exploded onto the European fashion stage in Paris on 5 July 1946, when the designer Louis Réard, a former Parisian engineer and inventor and son of a lingerie shop owner, persuaded a model to wear it. He named the beachwear after the atoll where the United States exploded a nuclear bomb. He expected, rightly, that it would be as sensational on the world fashion stage as that nuclear explosion has been in world military history. About the same time, another French designer, Jacques Heim, introduced the "Atome," which he referred to as "the smallest bathing suit in the world." Both names were about acquiring optimal publicity opportunities through the sensational nature of this brief new style of clothing.

The bikini as designed by Louis Réard and first worn on 5 July 1946 by nineteen-year-old Micheline Bernardini, a nude dancer from the Casino de Paris. The fabric is newsprint-patterned, perhaps in anticipation of the sensation that the outfit would cause. The headline-grabbing garment is deliberately named after the atoll where the United States had exploded an atomic bomb, but its association with the island is offensive to Marshallese people. The bikini is very much at odds with the Marshallese attitude toward near-nudity. AFP/Getty Images.

The bikini so shocked the public that some models refused to wear it in the 1950s, and it was banned on beaches in Spain, Italy, and for a time in Australia. The pope denounced it as immoral. Not until Brigitte Bardot wore a bikini in Roger Vadim's film *And God Created Woman* in 1956 did American movie stars follow her boldness. Further promotion in the 1960s in Brian Hyland's song "Itsy Bitsy, Teeny Weeny, Yellow Polka Dot Bikini" secured the future of this garment in the history of Western leisurewear. At various times even more scanty versions have been available, including the monokini invented in 1964 by U.S. designer Rudi Gernreich, which omits the bra part. A further garment for men appeared much later, called the mankini. But it is the bikini that has remained popular among sun seekers since the mid-twentieth century.

The bikini swimsuit, Réard claimed, was designed for women as a symbol of freedom from the trials and restrictions of World War II, while the atomic bomb exploded over Bikini atoll represented U.S. military endeavors to prepare for the Cold War against Russia. The symbolism of the bikini as release from oppression for women is the direct antithesis of Marshallese dress principles. Baring the body except those parts covered by only two meager strips of cloth is very offensive to island custom. Marshallese women do not publicly display their bodies between the waist and the knees; the inner thigh must be covered at all times. When they enter the water they do so fully covered in a *mu'umu'u* or *lavalava*. Foreign women who try to wear a bikini while visiting Marshall Islands beaches are asked to cover up.

The association between this beachwear and the name of the Marshall Islands atoll, Bikini, has been misunderstood. A common mistake in English is to break that Marshallese name into "bi," meaning two parts, and "kini," to refer to small pieces of material. Bikini people did not give their consent for this usage, and its association with near-nudity is insulting to Bikini people's heritage.

References and Further Reading

Bryan, Edwin H., Jr. *Life in the Marshall Islands*. Honolulu: Pacific Science Information Center, Bernice P. Bishop Museum, 1972.

Pollock, Nancy J. "Social Fattening Patterns in the Pacific." In *Social Aspects of Obesity*, edited by Igor de Garine and Nancy J. Pollock, 87–110. New York: Gordon and Breach, 1995.

Pollock, Nancy J. "Fat Is Beautiful." In *Art and Performance in Oceania*, edited by Barry Craig and Bernie Kernot, 58–63. Bathurst, Australia, and Honolulu: Crawford House Publishing and University of Hawai'i Press, 1999.

Spennemann, Dirk. *Marshallese Tattoos*. Majuro Atoll: Republic of Marshall Islands, Ministry of Internal Affairs, Historic Preservation Office, 1992.

Spennemann, Dirk. "Tattooing in the Marshall Islands". http://marshall.csu.edu.au/Marshalls/html/tattoo/tattoo.html (accessed 19 January 2009).

Spoehr, Alexander. *Majuro: A Village in the Marshall Islands*. Chicago: Chicago Natural History Museum, 1949.

Nancy J. Pollock

See also Dress in Kiribati; Hawaiian Dress Prior to 1898.

Index

Italic numbers denote reference to illustrations.

Australia, dress in (*continued*)
cosmetics and beauty culture in (*continued*)
racial superiority and, 144
Rubinstein as influence on, 144, 145, 150
technological advancements in, 149
World War II and, 147
youth as influence on, 149
cotton production for, 6
couture, 132
in department stores, 132
international influences on, 132
in Melbourne, 133
in 1960s, 136
promotion of, 134
in shops, 132, 133
in Sydney, 132
trends influenced by, 132
typical patrons for, 132
demographics for, 4, 5
in department stores, 79
early development of, 84
for early settlers, 81
Australian Girl, as archetype, 83
climate as influence on, 81
clothing production, 83
during colonialism, 81
convicts and, influence on, 81
cultural identity and, 83
economic prosperity and, 81
gender as factor in, 83
gold rushes and, as influence on, 83
Great Britain as influence on, 83
home dressmaking and, 85
home tailoring and, 85
imported clothing, 81, 84, 85
larrikins, 82, 82
in literature, 77
for males, 83
organized collections of, 76
pastoral industry as influence on, 82
popular materials in, 76–77
ready-made clothing and, 85
in rural areas, 82
slop clothes, 83
as social control, 83
social status and, 83
supply availability and, 83
in urban areas, 82
for women, 83
economic history of, 9
economic prosperity and, 9–10
fashion journalism for, 74
fashion photography and, 163
in fashion journalism, 163, *164*, 166
in lifestyle magazines, 167
in modern era, 164
after 1970s, 166
origins of, 163
post-World War II, 165
footwear, 183
for Aboriginal cultures, in Western Australia, 38

for beach and swimwear, 186
Blundstones, 185
boots, 185
clogs, *187*
company certificates for, *184*
for costumes, 188
early production of, 84
for high fashion, 187
history of, 183
immigrant cobblers, 185
imports for, 183
increased demand for, *184*
mail order for, 184
mechanization of manufacturing industries for, 183
mules, *187*
raw materials for, 184
RMW, *183*, 185
in rural areas, 185
shoes, 185
for skateboarders, 188
for sports and leisure, 186
stilettos, 187
thongs, 186–187, *186*
trade schools for, 184
World Wars as influence on, 184–185
within gay and lesbian culture, 224
among Aborigines, 226
aristocratic dress as part of, 225
convict colonies and, 224
as cosmopolitan affectation, 224
cultural backlash against, 226
drag balls, 226, 227
history of, 224
liberation politics and, 227
Mardi Gras, 228–229
Olympic Games and, 229
social class and, 224
in Sydney, 225, 227, 228–229
underwear as outerwear in, 229
before World War II, 224
during World War II, 226
image resources for, 69
in fashion journalism, 74
in motion pictures, 71
in paintings and drawn images, 69
in photographs, 71
in print, 73
immigration as influence on, 81
imported clothing, for early settlers, 81, 84, 85
independent fashion and, 168
in AFW, 171
as art, 168
Art Clothes exhibition and, 153, 168
Bannister role in, 169, *169*
boutiques for, 169
clothing production for, 171
corporate financing for, 171
FDC and, 169
Jackson, L., role in, 168
Kawakubo as influence on, 172
Kee role in, 168

local designer support as part of, 172
MBP and, 172
McQueen as influence on, 172
new design models for, 171
retail for, 171
RWB, 172
S!X design cooperative, 172
"The 3Rs—Recycle, Reconstruct, Ready to Wear" and, 172
in twenty-first century, 172
in *Vogue Australia*, 168
international influences on, 7
in Kimberley region, 53
archeological evidence of, 54
armbands, 57
belts, 56–57
body modification and, 55
body painting, 55, 58
cicatrisation and, 55, 56
contemporary styles in, 58
dance costumes, 59
face masks, 58
facial hair and, 58
hairstyles, 55
headbands, 56
headdresses, 56
Historic period of, 53, 54
necklaces, 56, 57
nosebones, 54, 57
post-settlement, 58
Prehistoric period of, 53, 54
in rock art, 53
sandals, 57, 58
for women, 58
in Melbourne
couture, 133
from department stores, 84
for early settlers, 82
garment industry and, 95
garment industry in, 95
MFF and, 171
multicultural tolerance as policy and, 9
"New Look" as influence on, 132, 133, 134, 135
in North Queensland, 49
armbands, 52
bark blankets, 49
"borrowed" clothing and, 52
for burials, 52
for ceremonies, 51
climate as influence on, 49
for daily use, 50
after European contact, 49
hairstyles, 52
headbands, 50
headdresses, 51–52
for initiation rites, 52
necklaces, 50
nose pins, 50
for women, 50–51
woven baskets and, 51